## Praise for *The Wiley-Blackwell Handbook of Individual Differences*

Fresh and comprehensive, this meaty volume provides an unusually deep discussion of individual differences. With the recent explosion of research, the time is right for this wonderful update. Don't look for this handbook on my bookshelves—it will be on my desk and in use.

*Robert B. Kaiser, Partner, Kaplan DeVries Inc., USA*

Some of the world's top researchers give us authoritative and engaging overviews of the central topics in individual differences, such as personality, creativity, intelligence, genetics and evolution, work, motivation, special abilities and happiness, making this a comprehensive guide for understanding how and why people differ.

*Robert Plomin, Research Professor, Institute of Psychiatry,*
*King's College London, UK*

This handbook provides a diverse multidisciplinary collection of chapters by leading researchers. Domains covered range from intelligence to personality, interests, and motivation—and from basic research on brain functions to real-world implications in the workplace and beyond.

*Phillip L. Ackerman, Professor of Psychology, Georgia Institute of*
*Technology, Atlanta, USA*

There is much in this handbook that does not simply summarize present knowledge but foreshadows the future state of differential psychology. Of use to the beginning student as well as the seasoned psychologist, any serious psychology library should possess this handbook.

*Philip J. Corr, Professor of Psychology, University of East Anglia, UK*

This impressive collection of antecedents, contemporary theory, and the latest empirical research does not shy away from controversial stances or highlighting consensual elements of the field, making this a must-read for students, practitioners, and researchers alike.

*Richard D. Roberts, Principal Research Scientist, Research and*
*Development, Educational Testing Service, USA*

With contributions from many leading researchers in differential psychology, *The Wiley-Blackwell Handbook of Individual Differences* provides an up-to-date and comprehensive overview of individual differences research. This book will be a valuable resource for anyone interested in the field.

*Tony Vernon, Professor of Psychology, University of Western Ontario, USA*

With thoughtful and well-written chapters—ranging from the genetics of individual differences, to the relation between intelligence and personality, to the traces that different individuals leave behind in their physical environments—this handbook manages to be both highly readable and thoroughly informative.

*Colin G. DeYoung, Assistant Professor of Psychology,*
*University of Minnesota, USA*

**Wiley-Blackwell Handbooks in Personality and Individual Differences**

This important series of handbooks provides a cutting-edge overview of classic, contemporary and future trends in research across Personality and Individual Differences. Each handbook draws together a collection of newly commissioned chapters to provide a comprehensive examination of a sub-discipline in the area.

The international teams of editors and contributors to the handbooks have been specifically chosen for their expertise and knowledge of each particular subject.

The *Wiley-Blackwell Handbooks in Personality and Individual Differences* will provide an invaluable resource for advanced students and researchers as an authoritative definition of their chosen field.

# The Wiley-Blackwell Handbook of Individual Differences

Edited by Tomas Chamorro-Premuzic,
Sophie von Stumm, and Adrian Furnham

A John Wiley & Sons, Ltd., Publication

This edition first published 2011
© 2011 Blackwell Publishing Ltd

Blackwell Publishing was acquired by John Wiley & Sons in February 2007. Blackwell's
publishing program has been merged with Wiley's global Scientific, Technical, and Medical
business to form Wiley-Blackwell.

*Registered Office*
John Wiley & Sons Ltd, The Atrium, Southern Gate, Chichester, West Sussex, PO19 8SQ,
United Kingdom

*Editorial Offices*
350 Main Street, Malden, MA 02148-5020, USA
9600 Garsington Road, Oxford, OX4 2DQ, UK
The Atrium, Southern Gate, Chichester, West Sussex, PO19 8SQ, UK

For details of our global editorial offices, for customer services, and for information about
how to apply for permission to reuse the copyright material in this book please see our
website at www.wiley.com/wiley-blackwell.

The right of Tomas Chamorro-Premuzic, Sophie von Stumm, and Adrian Furnham to be
identified as the authors of the editorial material in this work has been asserted in
accordance with the UK Copyright, Designs and Patents Act 1988.

Wiley also publishes its books in a variety of electronic formats. Some content that appears
in print may not be available in electronic books.

Designations used by companies to distinguish their products are often claimed as
trademarks. All brand names and product names used in this book are trade names, service
marks, trademarks or registered trademarks of their respective owners. The publisher is not
associated with any product or vendor mentioned in this book. This publication is designed
to provide accurate and authoritative information in regard to the subject matter covered. It
is sold on the understanding that the publisher is not engaged in rendering professional
services. If professional advice or other expert assistance is required, the services of a
competent professional should be sought.

*Library of Congress Cataloging-in-Publication Data*
The Wiley-Blackwell handbook of individual differences / [edited by] Dr Tomas
Chamorro-Premuzic, Sophie von Stumm, Adrian Furnham.
     p. cm. -- (Wiley-Blackwell handbooks in personality and individual differences; 1)
   Includes bibliographical references and index.
   ISBN 978-1-4443-3438-8 (hardback)
  1. Individual differences--Handbooks, manuals, etc.   2. Personality--Handbooks,
manuals, etc.   3. Intelligence--Handbooks, manuals, etc.   I. Chamorro-Premuzic, Tomas.
II. Von Stumm, Sophie.   III. Furnham, Adrian.
   BF697.W4933 2011
   155.2'2--dc22

                              2010047214

A catalogue record for this book is available from the British Library.

Set in 10/12.5 pt Galliard by Toppan Best-set Premedia Limited
Printed and bound in Singapore by Fabulous Printers Pte Ltd

1  2011

# Contents

# List of Plates

# List of Figures

# List of Tables

# List of Contributors

Phillip L. Ackerman, School of Psychology, Georgia Institute of Technology

Ghufran Ahmad, IAE-Aix (Graduate School of Management)/INSEAD (The Business School of the World)

Marcel A. G. van Aken, Utrecht University

Patrick Ian Armstrong, Iowa State University

Rachel E. Avery, Goldsmiths, University of London

G. David Batty, University of Edinburgh

Silvia Bonaccio, University of Ottawa

Burkhard Brocke, Department of Psychology, Dresden

Catherine M. Calvin, University of Edinburgh

Tomas Chamorro-Premuzic, Goldsmiths, University of London

Roberto Colom, Universidad Autónoma de Madrid

David M. Condon, Northwestern University

Ian J. Deary, University of Edinburgh

Jaap J. A. Denissen, Humboldt-University Berlin

Ed Diener, University of Illinois at Urbana-Champain

M. Brent Donnellan, Michigan State University

Vincent Egan, University of Leicester

Eamonn Ferguson, University of Nottingham

Howard S. Friedman, University of California

Adrian Furnham, University College London

Deshani B. Ganegoda, University of Central Florida

Samuel D. Gosling, University of Texas at Austin

Linda S. Gottfredson, University of Delaware

Lindsay T. Graham, University of Texas at Austin

Robert Hogan, Hogan Assessment Systems

Paul Irwing, University of Manchester

Wendy Johnson, University of Edinburgh

Satoshi Kanazawa, London School of Economics and Political Science

James C. Kaufman, California State University at San Bernardino

Margaret L. Kern, University of California

Gary P. Latham, University of Toronto

Edwin A. Locke, University of Maryland

Natalie J. Loxton, University of Queensland

Deniz S. Ones, University of Minnesota-Twin Cities

William Pavot, Southwest Minnesota State University

K. V. Petrides, University College London

Alan Pickering, Goldsmiths, University of London

Charlie L. Reeve, University of North Carolina

William Revelle, Northwestern University

Brent W. Roberts, University of Illinois at Urbana-Champaign

Richard W. Robins, University of California

James Rounds, University of Illinois at Urbana-Champaign

J. Philippe Rushton, University of Western Ontario

Timothy A. Salthouse, University of Virginia

Carson J. Sandy, University of Texas at Austin

Dean Keith Simonton, University of California

Luke D. Smillie, Goldsmiths, University of London

Frank M. Spinath, Saarland University

Alexander Strobel, Department of Psychology, Dresden

Sophie von Stumm, University of Chichester

Rong Su, University of Illinois at Urbana-Champaign

Viren Swami, University of Westminster

Paul M. Thompson, Laboratory of Neuroimaging, Los Angeles

Kali H. Trzesniewski, University of Western Ontario

Elliot M. Tucker-Drob, University of Texas at Austin

Chockalingam Viswesvaran, Florida International University

Alexander Weiss, University of Edinburgh

Joshua Wilt, Northwestern University

# Preface

In essence, individual differences research aims to understand how and why individuals vary in their affect, behavior, cognition, and motivation. To this end, researchers in this field seek to accurately describe, explain, and measure dimensions of individual differences, to evaluate the long-term consequences of such differences, and to discover their etiologies, including their biological, environmental, and genetic bases. They employ a wide range of research tools and theoretical approaches, spanning psychometrics, brain imaging, and behavior and molecular genetics amongst many others. As a result, an overwhelming body of multifaceted evidence demonstrates that individuals differ along continua of affect, behavior, cognition, and motivation, most of which can be understood and operationalized in terms of quantifiable trait dimensions, such as intelligence and personality.

Even though individual differences are evident beyond psychological research papers, to anyone who has ever interacted with another human being, questions concerning their assessment, consequences, and etiologies remain sensitive and controversial. The idea that individuals may differ naturally and meaningfully—particularly in abilities—challenges eighteenth-century American and European ideologies of equal creation, which continue to shape Western societies, their governments, and policies (not to mention the tragic case of communist regimes). Indeed, individual differences research proclaims that there are robust, inevitable, and salient differences *between* and *within* people that are partly heritable and have long-term consequences. Admittedly, this knowledge was and is easily (ab)used to justify selection and discrimination, thereby confirming the *status quo* as irremediable and legitimate.[1] However, the possibility of malpractice and a clash with prevailing ideals do not suffice to discard a scientific discipline as thriving, exciting, and fruitful as individual differences, even if it has not, to date, gained comparable recognition inside or outside academic circles.

Therefore this handbook was developed with two closely related goals in mind. For one, we sought to compile *an up-to-date* volume that *comprehensively* spanned the diversity of individual differences research, its methods, and most recent findings as a strong, global foundation for understanding and studying individual differences. Secondly, we also hoped to demonstrate the potential and importance of individual differences as a research discipline, highlighting the *knowns* as much (or more) as the *unknowns*, so as to encourage future analyses of how and why individuals differ.

The book comprises six main sections. In the first section, William Revelle and colleagues review the historical development of individual differences and introduce the fundamental methodological tools and advances of the research discipline. The second section is dedicated to the structure and development of personality and intelligence, focusing particularly on the diverse theoretical and psychometric conceptualizations of personality, as well as on the interplay of ability and non-ability factors. In the third section, biological causes of individual differences are investigated from four specific but related perspectives: behavior genetics, molecular genetics, brain imaging, and evolutionary approaches. The fourth section puts individual differences in the context of the "real world," evaluating their role and function for work and leadership; for health, longevity, and death; as well as for society, considered from historical and present-day perspectives. The fifth section addresses the often overlooked theme of the importance of individual differences in motivation and vocational interests for academic, occupational, and personal goal achievement. The final section involves competencies beyond intelligence, such as exceptional talent, emotional intelligence, and creativity (an area of research that was almost imposed on academics by the "real-world" audience, including practitioners and decision-makers in the fields of education and human resources). This section also evaluates the importance of individual differences in love, happiness, confidence, and environmental manifestations.

With contributions from almost 60 seminal individual differences experts, this book was written for scholars and students with an interest of any kind in the psychology of individual differences. This volume may also be of interest to audiences in education and business. The chapters are written at a level comprehensible for advanced undergraduate students and the "intelligent layman" (this phrase does not intend to imply that most laymen are unintelligent).

We are grateful to Wiley-Blackwell for encouraging us to work on this project (and for always taking us out to nice restaurants—may this tradition continue for many years, regardless of the success of our Handbook and of any other projects we work on); in particular, we would like to thank "the two As" (Andy McAleer and Andy Peart, at Wiley-Blackwell). We also thank our contributors for their speedy delivery of chapters and their friendly cooperation even when they had to respond to our rather bullish and repetitive requests—editing a book is not easy, and we have learned a lot from this project (so much that we will probably edit more books in the future).

Finally, we would like to thank and dedicate this book to the following people (and here is where the editors split, for one time only):

Tomas Chamorro-Premuzic dedicates this book to Don Roberto de Baja Georgia, for his continued support, guidance, and friendship throughout this entire project—and hopefully beyond.

Sophie von Stumm dedicates this book to her grandparents, for what they were, are, and always will be to her.

Adrian Furnham dedicates this book to Benedict, his beloved son.

The editors, London, August 1, 2010

## Note

1   Such reasoning also constitutes a logical short-circuit: heritability does neither imply specific genetic effects, nor does it undercut the importance of environmental factors or the malleability of traits throughout development.

# List of Abbreviations

| | |
|---|---|
| ACE | additive genetic influences model, common shared environment model, and unique individual environment model |
| ACE | Angiotensin I Converting Enzyme |
| ACTIVE | Advanced Cognitive Training for Independent and Vital Elderly Study Group |
| AD | Alzheimer disease |
| Add Health | Adolescent Health |
| ADHD | attention deficit hyperactivity disorder |
| ANPS | Affective Neuroscience Personality Scales |
| AP | Advanced Placement |
| APOE | Apolipoprotein E |
| ARP | *Annual Review of Psychology* |
| ASI | Approaches to Studying Inventory |
| ASRM | affective startle reflex modulation |
| ASVAB | Armed Services Vocational Aptitude Battery |
| ATL | approaches to learning |
| BA | Brodmann area |
| BAS | behavioral activation system |
| BFI | Big-Five Inventory |
| BFQ–C | Big Five Questionnaire—Children |
| BiLSAT | Bielefeld Longitudinal Study of Adult Twins |
| BIS | behavioral inhibition system |
| BMI | body mass index |
| BNST | bed nucleus of the stria terminalis |
| BOLD | blood–oxygen-level dependent |
| bp | base pair |
| BPAQ | Buss–Perry Aggression Questionnaire |
| CEO | chief executive officer |
| CFA | confirmatory factor analysis |
| CHC | Carroll–Horn–Cattell |
| CHD | coronary heart disease |

| | |
|---|---|
| CI | confidence interval |
| CMC | computer-mediated communication |
| COMT | Catechol-O-Methyltransferase |
| COPS | criterion-focused occupational personality scales |
| CPI | California Psychological Inventory |
| CPS | Comrey Personality Scales |
| CSF | cerebrospinal fluid |
| CTA | cues–tendency–action |
| CV | confounding variable |
| CVD | cardiovascular disease |
| CWB | counterproductive work behavior |
| DAPP–BQ | Dimensional Assessment of Personality Pathology–Basic Questionnaire |
| DC | dichorionic |
| DIF | differential item functioning |
| DNA | deoxyribonucleic acid |
| DRD4 | dopamine D4 receptor |
| DRM | Day Reconstruction Method |
| DSM | *Diagnostic and statistical manual of psychiatric disorders* |
| DTI | diffusion tensor imaging |
| DZ | dizygotic |
| EAR | electronically activated recorder |
| EAS | EAS Temperament Scales |
| EDS | Environment Description Scale |
| EEA | equal environments assumption |
| EEG | electroencephalography |
| EFA | exploratory factor analysis |
| EI | emotional intelligence |
| EPI | Eysenck Personality Inventory |
| EQi | Emotional Quotient Inventory |
| ERP | event-related potential |
| ESM | experience-sampling method |
| ESS | evolutionary stable strategy |
| F1, F2, F3, F4 | each of the four first-order factors |
| FA | factor analysis |
| FA | fractional anisotropy |
| FACS | facial action coding system |
| FFFS | fight–flight–freeze system |
| FFM | five-factor model |
| FFS | fight–flight system |
| fMRI | functional magnetic resonance imaging |
| g–e | gene–environment |
| $G \times E$ | genome–environment |
| *Gc* | crystallized intelligence |
| *Gf* | fluid intelligence |
| GFP | general factor of personality |

| | |
|---|---|
| *Glr* | long-term storage and retrieval intelligence |
| GM | gray matter |
| GMA | general mental ability |
| GOSAT | the German Observational Study of Adult Twins |
| *Gq* | quantitative intelligence |
| GR | glucocorticoid receptor |
| GRE | Graduate Record Examinations |
| *Grw* | reading and writing intelligence |
| *Gs* | processing speed intelligence |
| *Gsm* | short-term memory intelligence |
| GSOEP | the German Socio-Economic Panel |
| GSS | general social survey |
| *Gt* | decision speed/reaction time intelligence |
| *Gv* | visual processing intelligence |
| GWAS | genome-wide association studies |
| GZTS | Guilford–Zimmerman Temperament Survey |
| HA | harm avoidance |
| HDL | high-density lipoprotein |
| HEXACO | HEXACO Personality Inventory |
| HOME | Home Observation for Measurement of the Environment |
| HPI | Hogan Personality Inventory |
| HR | hazard ratio |
| IAT | implicit association test |
| ICBM | International Consortium for Brain Mapping |
| ICC1.1 | intra-class correlation |
| ICD | International Classification of Diseases |
| Ins/Del | insertion/deletion |
| IPA | intelligence–personality association |
| IPAR | Institute for Personality Assessment and Research |
| IPDE | international personality disorder examination |
| IPIP | International Personality Item Pool |
| IRT | item response theory |
| IV | independent variable |
| JPI | Jackson Personality Inventory |
| KMO | Kaiser–Meyer–Olkin |
| L | long |
| LOD | logarithm [base 10] of odds |
| LONI, UCLA | Laboratory of Neuroimaging |
| MAO–A | monoamine oxidase A |
| MBTI | Myers–Briggs Type Indicator |
| MC | monochorionic |
| MCMI–III | Millon Clinical Multiaxial Inventory |
| MCQ | multiple-choice question |
| MD | mean diffusivity |
| MDS | multidimensional scaling |
| MIDUS | midlife development in the US |

| | |
|---|---|
| MMPI | Minnesota Multiphasic Personality Inventory |
| MPQ | Multidimensional Personality Questionnaire |
| MRI | magnetic resonance imaging |
| mRNA | messenger RNA |
| MSCEIT | Mayer–Salovey–Caruso Emotional Intelligence Test |
| MTMM | multi-trait–multi-method |
| MTR | Methionine Synthase |
| MZ | monozygotic |
| NA | negative affect |
| NEAD | Nonshared Environment Adolescent Development Project |
| NFC | need for cognition |
| NLSY | National Longitudinal Survey of Youth |
| NPI | Narcissistic Personality Inventory |
| NS | novelty-seeking |
| NSHD | National Survey of Health and Development |
| OCB | organizational citizenship behavior |
| OECD | Organization for Economic Cooperation and Development |
| OR | odds ratio |
| OSN | on-line social networking site |
| OSS | Office of Strategic Services |
| P–FIT | parieto-frontal integration theory of intelligence |
| PA | positive affect |
| PAI | Personality Assessment Inventory |
| PANAS | Positive and Negative Affect Schedule |
| PCA | principal components analysis |
| PCL–R | revised Psychopathy Checklist |
| PCR | polymerase chain reaction |
| PD | personality disorder |
| PDE4D | phosphodiesterase-4D |
| PEN | psychoticism—extraversion—neuroticism model |
| PET | positron emission tomography |
| PIQ | non-verbal IQ score |
| PISA | Programme for International Student Assessment |
| PLS | personal living space |
| PLSCI | Personal Living Space Cue Inventory |
| PMA | primary mental abilities |
| PPIK | (intelligence as) process, personality, interests, and (intelligence as) knowledge |
| PRF | Personality Research Form |
| PV | person variable |
| PWB | psychological well-being |
| RAPM | Raven Advanced Progressive Matrices Test |
| RASI | Revised Approaches to Studying Inventory |
| RD | reward dependence |
| rGE | gene–environment correlation |
| RFT | regulatory focus theory |

| | |
|---|---|
| RIASEC | realistic, investigative, artistic, social, enterprising, and conventional type |
| RNA | ribonucleic acid |
| ROI | return on investment |
| RSE | Rosenberg Self-Esteem Scale |
| RST | reinforcement sensitivity theory |
| S | short |
| SAPA | synthetic aperture personality assessment |
| SAT | Scholastic Assessment/Ability Test |
| SB5 | Stanford–Binet 5 Test |
| SCN | the suprachiasmatic nuclei |
| SD | standard deviation |
| SDS | Self-Directed Search |
| SEM | structural equation modeling |
| SES | socioeconomic status |
| SISE | single-item self-esteem measure |
| SLODR | Spearman's law of diminishing returns |
| SLS | Seattle Longitudinal Study |
| SMPY | Study of Mathematically Precocious Youth |
| SMS | Scottish Mental Survey |
| SNAP25 | synaptosomal-associated protein 25 |
| SNP | single-nucleotide polymorphism |
| SOI | Sociosexual Orientation Inventory |
| SOI | structure of intellect |
| SPANE | Scale of Positive and Negative Experience |
| SPQ | Study Process Questionnaire |
| SPT | set-point theory |
| SSREI | the schutte self-report emotional intelligence scale |
| SSRI | selective serotonin reuptake inhibitor |
| STARTS | Stable Trait–Autoregressive Trait State |
| STAT | Sternberg Triarchic Abilities Test |
| STEM | science, technology, engineering, and mathematics |
| SWB | subjective well-being |
| TAI | temperament, ability, and interests |
| TCI | Temperament and Character Inventory |
| TEDS | Twins' Early Development Study |
| TEIQue | Trait Emotional Intelligence Questionnaire |
| TIE | typical intellectual engagement |
| TMS | transcranial magnetic stimulation |
| TPH2 | tryptophan hydroxylase 2 |
| TPQ | Tridimensional Personality Questionnaire |
| TTCT | Torrance Tests of Creative Thinking |
| TWH | Trivers–Willard hypothesis |
| UCB | University of California, Berkeley |
| VBM | voxel-based morphometry |
| VES | Vietnam Experience Study |

| VIQ | verbal IQ score |
| VNTR | variable number of tandem repeats |
| VPR | visual–perceptual–rotational |
| WAIS | Wechsler Adult Intelligence Scale |
| WJ–III | Woodcock–Johnson Revised Test |
| WM | white matter |
| WMC | working-memory capacity |
| 5–HT | serotonin |
| 5–HTT | serotonin transporter |
| 5–HTTLPR | serotonin transporter-linked promotor regions |
| 16PF | the Sixteen Personality Factors Inventory |

# Part I

# Individual Differences
*An Up-to-Date Historical and
Methodological Overview*

# 1

# Individual Differences and Differential Psychology

*A Brief History and Prospect*

William Revelle, Joshua Wilt,
and David M. Condon

This handbook is devoted to the study of individual differences and differential psychology. To write a chapter giving an overview of the field is challenging, for the study of individual differences includes the study of affect, behavior, cognition, and motivation as they are affected by biological causes and environmental events. That is, it includes all of psychology. But it is also the study of individual differences that are not normally taught in psychology departments. Human factors, differences in physical abilities as diverse as taste, smell, or strength are also part of the study of differential psychology. Differential psychology requires a general knowledge of all of psychology; for people (as well as chimpanzees, dogs, rats, and fishes) differ in many ways. Thus differential psychologists do not say that they are cognitive psychologists, social psychologists, neuro-psychologists, behavior geneticists, psychometricians, or methodologists; for, although we do those various hyphenated parts of psychology, by saying that we study differential psychology we have said we do all of those things. And that is true for everyone reading this handbook. We study differential psychology: individual differences in how we think, individual differences in how we feel, individual differences in what we want and what we need, individual differences in what we do. We study how people differ, and we also study why people differ. We study individual differences.

There has been a long recognized division in psychology between differential psychologists and experimental psychologists (Cronbach, 1957; H. J. Eysenck, 1966), however, the past 30 years have seen progress in the integration of these two approaches (Cronbach, 1975; Eysenck, 1997; Revelle & Oehlberg, 2008). Indeed, one of the best known experimental psychologists of the 1960s and 1970s argued that "individual differences ought to be considered central in theory construction, not peripheral" (Underwood, 1975, p. 129). However, Underwood went on to argue (p. 134) that these individual differences are not the normal variables of age, sex, IQ,

---

*The Wiley-Blackwell Handbook of Individual Differences,* First Edition.
Edited by Tomas Chamorro-Premuzic, Sophie von Stumm, and Adrian Furnham.

or social status, but rather the process variables that are essential to our theories. Including these process variables remains a challenge to differential psychology.

The principles of differential psychology are seen outside psychology in computer science simulations and games, in medical assessments of disease symptomatology, in college and university admissions, in high school and career counseling centers, as well as in applied decision-making.

## Early Differential Psychology and Its Application

Differential psychology is not new; for an understanding of research methodology and individual differences in ability and affect was described as early as the Hebrew Bible, in the story of Gideon (Judges 6: 37–40, 7: 2–6). Gideon was something of a skeptic, who had impressive methodological sophistication. In perhaps the first published example of a repeated-measures crossover design, he applied several behavioral tests to God before agreeing to go off to fight the Midians, as he was instructed. Gideon put out a wool fleece on his threshing floor and first asked that by the next morning just the fleece should be wet with dew, but the floor should be left dry. Then, the next morning, after this happened, as a crossover control, he asked for the fleece to be dry and the floor wet. Observing this double dissociation, Gideon decided to follow God's commands. We believe that this is the first published example of the convincing power of a crossover interaction. (See Figure 1.1, which has been reconstructed from the published data.)

In addition to being an early methodologist, Gideon also pioneered the use of a sequential assessment battery. Leading a troop of 32,000 men to attack the Midians, Gideon was instructed to reduce the set to a more manageable number (for greater effect upon achieving victory). To select 300 men from 32,000, Gideon (again under instructions from God) used a two-part test. One part measured motivation and affect by selecting those 10,000 who were not afraid. The other measured crystallized intelligence, or at least battlefield experience, by selecting those 300 who did not lie down to drink water but rather lapped it with their hands (McPherson, 1901).

Gideon thus combined many of the skills of a differential psychologist. He was a methodologist versed in within-subject designs, a student of affect and behavior, and someone familiar with basic principles of assessment. Other early applications of psychological principles to warfare did not emphasize individual differences as much as the benefits of training troops in a phalanx (Thucydides, as cited by Driskell & Olmstead, 1989).

### Personality taxonomies

That people differ is obvious. How and why they differ is the subject of taxonomies of personality and other individual differences. An early and continuing application of these taxonomies is most clearly seen in the study of leadership effectiveness. Plato's (429–347 BC) discussion of the personality and ability characteristics required of the hypothetical figure of the philosopher–king emphasized the multivariate problem of the rare co-occurrence of appropriate traits:

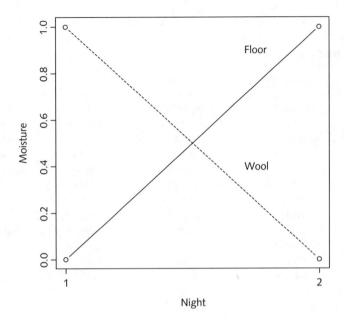

**Figure 1.1** Gideon's double dissociation test. Gideon's testing of God is an early example of a double dissociation test, and probably the first published example of a crossover interaction. On the first night, the wool was wet with dew but the floor was dry. On the second night, the floor was wet but the wool was dry (Judges 6: 36–40)

... quick intelligence, memory, sagacity, cleverness, and similar qualities, do not often grow together, and that persons who possess them and are at the same time high-spirited and magnanimous are not so constituted by nature as to live orderly and in a peaceful and settled manner; they are driven any way by their impulses, and all solid principle goes out of them. [...] On the other hand, those steadfast natures which can better be depended upon, which in a battle are impregnable to fear and immovable, are equally immovable when there is anything to be learned; they are always in a torpid state, and are apt to yawn and go to sleep over any intellectual toil. [...] And yet we were saying that both qualities were necessary in those to whom the higher education is to be imparted, and who are to share in any office or command. (Plato, 1892: *The republic*, VI, 503c–e)

Similar work is now done by Robert Hogan and his colleagues as they study the determinants of leadership effectiveness in management settings (Hogan, 1994, 2007; R. Hogan, Raskin, & Fazzini, 1990; Padilla, Hogan, & Kaiser, 2007) as well as by one of the editors of this volume, Adrian Furnham (Furnham, 2005). The dark-side qualities discussed by Hogan could have been taken directly from *The Republic*.

A typological rather than dimensional model of individual differences was developed by Theophrastus—or rather Tyrtamus of Eresos, in Lesbos (372–287 BC), a student of Aristotle who, according to his teacher, acquired the nickname "Theophrastus" ("the one who speaks like a god") for his oratorical skills.

**Table 1.1** Theophrastus's character types and the traits of the "Big Five" show remarkable similarity. "Big Five" adjectives taken from John, 1990; Theophrastus's *Characters* presented in Jebb's translation of 1870

| Extraversion | Agreeableness | Conscientious | Neuroticism | Openness |
|---|---|---|---|---|
| talkative | sympathetic | organized | tense | wide interests |
| assertive | kind | thorough | anxious | imaginative |
| active | appreciative | planful | nervous | intelligent |
| energetic | affectionate | efficient | moody | original |
| -quiet | -cold | -careless | -stable | -commonplace |
| -reserved | -unfriendly | -disorderly | -calm | -simple |
| -shy | -quarrelsome | -frivolous | -contented | -shallow |
| -silent | -hard-headed | -irresponsible | -unemotional | -unintelligent |
| talker | anxious to please | hostile | coward | stupid |
| chatty | flatterer | shameless | grumbler | superstitious |
| boastful | unpleasant | distrustful | mean | boor |
| ironical | feckless | slanderer | unseasonable | offensive |
| petty ambition | tiresome | penurious | | gross |
| arrogant | outcast | avaricious | | |
| garrulous | complaisant | reckless | | |
| gossipy | surly | officious | | |
| oligarch | evil speaker | patron of rascals | | |

Theophrastus is famous today as a botanical taxonomist. But he is also known to differential psychologists as a personality taxonomist, who organized the individual differences he observed into a descriptive taxonomy of "characters." The *Characters* of Theophrastus is a work often used to illustrate and epitomize the lack of coherence of early personality trait description; however, it is possible to organize his "characters" into a table that looks remarkably similar to equivalent tables of the late twentieth century (John, 1990; John & Srivastava, 1999; see Table 1.1).

One thousand and six hundred years after Theophrastus, Chaucer added to the use of character description in his *Canterbury Tales*, which are certainly the first and probably the "best sequence of 'Characters' in English Literature" (Morley, 1891, p. 2). This tradition continued into the seventeenth century: the character writings of that period are a fascinating demonstration of the broad appeal of personality description and categorization (Morley, 1891).

## Causal theories

Theophrastus asked a fundamental question of personality theory, which is still of central concern to us in personality theory today:

> Often before now have I applied my thoughts to the puzzling question—one, probably, which will puzzle me for ever—why it is that, while all Greece lies under the same sky and all the Greeks are educated alike, it has befallen us to have characters so variously constituted. (Theophrastus, 1870: *Characters*, p. 77)

**Table 1.2** Greek and Roman causal theory of personality

| *Physiological basis* | *Temperament* |
| --- | --- |
| Yellow bile | Choleric |
| Phlegm | Phlegmatic |
| Blood | Sanguine |
| Black bile | Melancholic |

This is, of course, the fundamental question asked today by differential psychologists who study behavior genetics (e.g. Bouchard, 1994, 2004) when they address the relative contribution of genes and of shared family environment as causes of behavior.

Biological personality models have also been with us for more than two millennia, through the work of Plato, Hippocrates, and, later on, Galen, all of which had a strong influence. Plato's placement of the tripartite soul into the head, the heart, and the liver and his organization of it into reason, emotion, and desire remain a classic organization of the study of individual differences (Hilgard, 1980; Mayer, 2001; Revelle, 2007). Indeed, with the addition of behavior, the study of psychology may be said to be the study of affect (emotion), behavior, cognition (reason), and motivation (desire), as organized by Plato (but without the physical localization).

About 500 years later, the great doctor, pharmacologist, and physiologist Galen (AD 129–*ca*216) unified and systematized the earlier literature of the classical period, particularly the work of Plato and of the medical authors of the Hippocratic Corpus, when he described the causal basis of the four temperaments. His empirical work, based upon comparative neuroanatomy, aimed to provide support for Plato's tripartite organization of soul into affect, cognition, and desire. Although current work does not use the same biological concepts, the search for a biological basis of individual differences continues to this day.

Eighteen centuries later, Wilhelm Wundt (1874, 1904) reorganized the Hippocratic–Galenic four temperaments into the two dimensional model later discussed by Hans Eysenck (1965, 1967) and Jan Strelau (1998).

## Early methodology

In addition to Gideon's introduction of the crossover experiment, Plato introduced two important concepts, which would later find an important role in psychometrics and in the measurement of individual differences. Something similar to the modern concept of *true score* and to that of a distinction between *observed* and *latent* variables may be found in the celebrated "allegory of the cave" at the opening of Book VII of Plato's *Republic* (VII, 514a ff.). For, just as the poor prisoners chained to the cave wall must interpret the world through the shadows cast on the wall, so must psychometricians interpret individual differences in *observed* score as reflecting *latent* differences in *true* score. Although shadow length can reflect differences in height,

**Table 1.3**  Wundt's two-dimensional organization of the four temperaments

|                | *Changeability*            |                     |
| -------------- | -------------------------- | ------------------- |
| Excitability   | Melancholic                | Choleric            |
|                | Phlegmatic                 | Sanguine            |

it can also reflect differences in distance from the light. For the individual differences specialist, making inferences about true score changes on the basis of observed score differences can be problematic. Consider the increases in observed IQ scores over time, reported by Flynn (1984, 1987, 2000), which are known as the "Flynn effect." It may be asked, is the Flynn effect a real effect, and are people getting smarter, or are the IQ scores going up in a process equivalent to the change in shadow length in the cave, say, because of a change in position, but not one of height in the real world? This inferential problem is also seen in interpretations of *fan-fold* interactions as reflecting interactions at the latent level rather than merely at the observed level (Revelle, 2007).

## Differential Psychology in the Late Nineteenth and Early Twentieth Centuries

Any discussion of differential psychology must include the amazing contributions of Sir Francis Galton. Apart from considering the hereditary basis of ability (Galton, 1865, 1892), describing the results of an introspective analysis of the complexity of his own thoughts (Galton, 1879), or introducing the *lexical hypothesis*, later made popular by Goldberg (1990), by searching the thesaurus for multiple examples of character (Galton, 1884), Galton also developed an index of *correlation* in terms of the product of deviations from the median and of the probable error of the estimate (Galton, 1888; see Stigler, 1989). His measure of "reversion to the mean" was later modified to the form we now know as "the Pearson product moment correlation coefficient" (Pearson, 1896).

Galton believed in the power of data analysis, whether it was developing meteorological maps of Europe, the use of fingerprints for identification, or the dimensions of character:

> ... character ought to be measured by carefully recorded acts, representative of the usual conduct. An ordinary generalization is nothing more than a muddle of vague memories of inexact observations. It is an easy vice to generalize. We want lists of facts, every one of which may be separably verified, valued and revalued, and the whole accurately summed. It is the statistics of each man's conduct in small every-day affairs that will probably be found to give the simplest and most precise measure of his character. [...] [A] practice of deliberately and methodically testing the character of others and of ourselves is not wholly fanciful, but deserves consideration and experiment. (Galton, 1884, p. 185)

Expanding upon the work of Galton, Charles Spearman, in a remarkable pair of papers in 1904, introduced to psychologists the correlation coefficient as well as the concept of reliability and corrections for attenuation:

Psychologists, with scarcely an exception, never seem to have become acquainted with the brilliant work being carried on since 1886 by the Galton–Pearson school. The consequence has been that they do not even attain to the first fundamental requisite of correlation, namely a precise quantitative expression. (Spearman, 1904a, p. 96)

In the next issue of the same journal, Spearman then introduced factor analysis and suggested a general factor of ability (1904b). More than a century after these papers, much of differential psychology may be seen as a footnote to the work of Galton and Spearman.

The research of Gerard Heymans (1908) in the Netherlands unfortunately has not received the attention it deserves among American psychologists; for it is a classic set of studies on the structure of individual differences, one based on observer ratings. Eysenck has presented a very thorough review of Heymans's work (Eysenck, 1992), as has Strelau (1998). Van der Werff and Verster (1987) reanalyzed the data using principal components analysis. In the original studies, over 3,000 physicians were asked to rate the members of one family on six types of items. About 400 physicians responded. Strelau summarizes the results, classifying them according to temperamental dimensions of activity, emotionality, and "primary vs. secondary functioning." This latter dimension may be taken as related to Introversion–Extraversion or to the temporal aspects of behavior and to the speed of switching between activities (see Atkinson & Birch, 1970 and Fua, Revelle, & Ortony, 2010 for a consideration of the temporal component). The original data reanalyzed in this way included 90 questions referring to 2,309 members of 437 families. A five-component and a three-component solution were obtained. The components represented: (1) impulsivity versus thoughtfulness; (2) activity (with two sub-components, one of continuous activity and one of "not easily daunted" activity); and (3) "bad temper" versus "good temper," which encompassed items like trusting and unselfish versus imperious and irritable. Strelau (1998) pays these important studies the respect they deserve.

The early twentieth century also saw the introduction of the IQ test (Binet & Simon, 1905; Goddard, 1908; Terman, 1916); the introduction of the hypothesis of a general factor of ability (Spearman, 1904b); and the introduction of ability (the Army Alpha test) and emotional testing for military selection (Driskell & Olmstead, 1989; Jones & Thissen, 2007; Yerkes, 1918). Differential psychologists involved in the Army Alpha/Beta project included Terman, Otis, Thorndike, Thurstone, and Whipple (Jones & Thissen, 2007). Otis went on to develop a group intelligence scale, as did Terman. The subsequent years were active times for differential psychology, seeing as they did the beginnings of the landmark longitudinal study of high-ability children (Terman, 1925; Terman & Oden, 1947). It was also a time in which IQ tests were used to screen (non-English-speaking) immigrants at Ellis Island in the United States and to argue for forced sterilization (Zenderland, 2001) for those with low scores.

Another researcher whose work has not been as appreciated by Americans as much as it should is William Stern (1910, 1914). Not only laying out a theory of differences between individuals, Stern also emphasized the study of individuality, which he wanted to reclaim from historical biographers (Stern, 1910). It is interesting to note that he was well aware of the problem of errors of memory that bias self-reports of any kind. His lectures should be of interest to all those interested in narrative approaches to the study of individuals. Stern is best known for his work on intelligence (Stern, 1914), where he developed the measure of intelligence as the ratio of mental age to chronological age. This ratio, when multiplied by 100, of course became the IQ score used in differential psychology before the change to the use of standard scores. To Stern,

> Intelligence is a general capacity of an individual consciously to adjust his thinking to new requirements: it is a general mental adaptability to new problems and conditions of life.

> Finally, the fact that the capacity is a *general capacity* distinguishes intelligence from *talent* the characteristic of which is precisely the limitation of efficiency to one kind of content. He is intelligent, on the contrary, who is able easily to effect mental adaptation to new requirements under the most varied conditions and in the most varied fields. If talent is material efficiency, intelligence is a formal efficiency. (Stern, 1914, pp. 3–4)

Subsequent work on the structure of ability followed the introduction of matrix algebra to Thurstone (Thurstone, 1935, 1947), and thus into psychology (Bock, 2007). With the ability to work with matrices, the process of applying the factor analysis of correlational "tables" became much simpler and the subsequent extraction of multiple factors of intellect more reasonable. Debates between theories of general intelligence ("$g$" theories) (Spearman, 1946), multi-factor models (Thurstone, 1933, 1935, 1947), and sampling theories of intelligence (Bartholomew, Deary, & Lawn, 2009; G. H. Thomson, 1935; S. Thomson, 1951) filled the pages of journals and the shelves of libraries.

Outside of the ability domain, empirically driven test construction in the personality and interests domains proceeded with little regard for theories of underlying individual differences. This work led to the development and validation of items that could discriminate known occupational groups from people in general. The basic principle was—and is—that, if one shares interests with people of a particular occupation, one is more likely to do well in that occupation (Strong, 1927). Interests show strong consistencies over the lifetime (Kelly, 1955) and have moderate predictive validities. More recently, two- and three-dimensional structural models have been applied to interest, as the latter were measured by the Strong Interest Inventory (Armstrong, Smith, Donnay, & Rounds, 2004; Donnay, 1997). Interests shared with those in an occupation do not imply that one has an ability for that occupation (one may share interests with opera singers, but, if one is a second monotone—that is, unable to carry a note—one is unlikely to succeed in what opera singers do).

## Mid-Twentieth Century: The High Point of Differential Psychology?

The 1930s saw the creation of the journal *Psychometrika*, the pages of which were soon filled with detailed discussions on reliability theory, factor analysis, and scale construction. Most of the work was on measuring ability, and the primary debates were between methods of factor extraction, validity estimation, and a general theory of tests.

With the publication of Gordon Allport's text on personality (Allport, 1937), Henry Murray's integration of multiple approaches to the study of personality (Murray, 1938), and Clyde Kluckhohn and Murray's integration of personality with society and culture (Kluckhohn & Murray, 1948), empirical personality research had finally reached the United States.

Following the onset of the Second World War, differential psychologists were soon involved in problems of selection and training. About 1,500 psychologists were associated with the Army Air Force selection and training program. The list of differential psychologists involved includes many future presidents of the Psychometric Society (Jones & Thissen, 2007) and leaders in differential psychology. The detailed final report of the project (Dubois, 1947) is a primer on how to do validity studies. The point biserial validities for cognitive and psychomotor tests for predicting training success, for example for pilots, navigators, and bombardiers, were roughly .45 across various samples and could be presented graphically in a manner that showed the powers of selection (Figure 1.2).

Differential psychologists primarily associated with personality and social psychology were also involved in selection, but in selection for more difficult criteria. Differential psychologists assisted with the selection of agents for the Office of Strategic Services (OSS), which later became the Central Intelligence Agency. Whereas

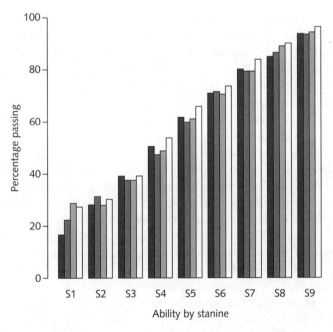

**Figure 1.2** Success rate in Army Air Force elementary pilot classes as a function of the ability scored in stanines. Cohorts 43 H–K. Figure adapted from tables in Dubuis, 1947, p. 119. While only about 20% of candidates with the lowest stanine succeeded, almost 95% of the top stanines did. Sample sizes in each cohort range from 9, 617 to 11,010

the criteria for air force pilots were clear, the criteria for success as a spy proved to be more difficult to ascertain. The predictive validities actually diminished the longer the assessment procedure lasted (OSS Assessment Staff, 1948; Wiggins, 1973).

Three more "milestones" in assessment and prediction involving differential psychology (Wiggins, 1973) were the American Veterans Administration selection of clinical psychology graduate students in the late 1940s (Kelly & Fiske, 1951), the selection of the first American astronauts, and the selection of Peace Corps Volunteers (Wiggins, 1973).

The conclusions from the VA selection study (Kelly & Fiske, 1950) are remarkably consistent with findings reported 50 years later about predicting graduate student success (Kuncel, Hezlett, & Ones, 2001): a mixture of ability and objectively assessed interests and personality variables predicts graduate student success with roughly equal ($\approx$ .25–.30) validities, which, when combined, form a multiple correlation, R, of about .4. More importantly, and in tune with the OSS findings, complex assessments based upon the interactions of assessors with applicants have no incremental validity. That is, people who are more able, interested in psychology, and lack nervous tension and irritability are more likely to succeed in clinical training than the less able, less interested, and more nervous. Having long interactions with an assessment board does not add information to this combination of temperament, ability, and interests (TAI).

## Theories of individual differences

The late 1940s through to the mid-1960s were a major time for theorizing about individual differences. In terms of theories of intellect, Joy P. Guilford's attempt to cross three *modes* of thinking—operations, products, and content—led to an ambitious attempt to measure 120 narrow factors of mental ability (Guilford, 1956, 1959). Each mode of thought had sub-components, such that operations could be divided into five: cognition, memory, divergent thinking, convergent thinking, and evaluation (Guilford, 1956); products could be divided into six: units, classes, relations, systems, transformations, and implications; and contents could be split into four: figural, symbolic, semantic, and behavioral.

An alternative model, suggesting a hierarchy of abilities, was the *fluid, crystallized, g* model of ability (the *Gf–Gc* model: Horn & Cattell, 1966), which made a distinction between processing factors (fluid) and knowledge factors (crystallized).

Raymond Cattell integrated cognitive and non-cognitive personality variables when he laid out an ambitious plan to apply factor analytic methods from ability to the personality domain and commenced a long series of studies on the structure of personality (Cattell, 1943, 1946a, 1946c, 1946b, 1957, 1966b, 1978). To Cattell (1946c), *surface traits* were clusters of observations such as self-reports of anxiety, crying, or depression; they needed to be explained by *source traits*, which could be derived from factor analysis. He elaborated the source/trait distinction in terms of those that reflect ability, those that are dynamic, and those that are stable temperaments (Cattell, 1946b). Cattell (1946c) introduced the *data box*, which emphasized that correlations can be taken over people, tests, or occasions. Although most research at the time emphasized the correlations of tests across people (R analysis), Cattell proposed to consider how people varied across tests (Q analysis), how tests varied across time (P analysis), and so on. Subsequently, Cattell (1966a) elaborated the data box into a five-dimensional analysis by adding observers and background conditions. In a series of studies using peer ratings of personality as well as self-reports, Cattell (1957) emphasized many correlated factors of personality, in what would eventually become his Sixteen Personality Factors Inventory (16PF). As a reflection of his belief in the power of differential psychology and in the need to integrate it with experimental psychology, Cattell was a founding member and first president of the Society for Multivariate Experimental Psychology in 1960.

The other grand theorist of individual differences was Hans Eysenck. He searched for consistency in individual differences by starting to use behavioral measures (Eysenck & Himmelweit, 1947); then he attempted to explain individual differences by using learning theory (Eysenck, 1952) and subsequently arousal theory (Eysenck, 1967). By blending experimental and correlational data with the best available theory, he inspired others to study the hard question of mechanism. He was never one to avoid controversy, and his popular books (Eysenck, 1953, 1964, 1965) introduced the possibility of doing rigorous research in personality and individual differences to several generations of psychologists. Eysenck was a founder and first president of the International Society for the Study of Individual Differences in 1983. His contributions to the field are discussed elsewhere in this handbook and do not need to be reviewed here.

Unlike later theorists, both Cattell and Eysenck emphasized individual differences broadly conceived. They both made contributions to the study of ability, to personality trait structure, and to psychometric methods. They attempted to integrate genetic, physiological, emotional, cognitive, and societal influences on human behavior. They both wrote prodigiously, popular trade books as well as serious monographs and articles.

Less known to most differential psychologists were the contributions of John W. Atkinson, who emphasized the interactive effects of situational challenges and individual differences to *achievement motivation*. From a formal theory of risk preference (Atkinson, 1957) to a review of the effects of situational stressors on performance (Atkinson & Raynor, 1974) to a dynamic model of motivation (Atkinson & Birch, 1970), the theory of achievement motivation integrated approach and avoidance motivational tendencies. The study of achievement motivation has now been reinvigorated through the recent studies of Elliot and Church (1997) and Elliot and Thrash (2002), who fit achievement motivation and anxiety into an approach and avoidance temperament system similar to those of Carver and White (1994) and of Gray (1970). Taking the expectancy–value framework even further forward is the work of Eccles and Wigfield (2002), who integrate achievement motivation with theories of goal-setting and interest motivation.

Perhaps unfortunately, the same period was also characterized by an explosion of personality inventories. These were developed by many different research groups. Inventories were constructed by using empirical (Dahlstrom, 1992; Hathaway & McKinley, 1951: MMPI), rational (Gough, 1957: CPI; Heist & Williams, 1957; and Warren & Heist, 1960: OPI), and factorial (Eysenck & Eysenck, 1964, EPI; Cattell & Stice, 1957: 16PF; Comrey, 1995: CPS; Guilford & Zimmerman, 1949: GZTZ;

Hogan & Hogan, 1995: HPI) methodologies—some without any organizing principle other than alphabetical (London & Exner, 1978).

Less noticed at the time but more recently seen as bearing some very rich fruit was a series of longitudinal studies started in the late 1920s, which continued through to the 1950s, for example Block (1971), Elder (1998), Kelly (1955), and Schaie (2005). As is true of many longitudinal studies, these were not for the faint of heart or for the non-sophisticated methodologist. The Oakland Growth Study and subsequent Berkeley Guidance and Berkeley Growth Study have been the source of data for developmentally oriented differential psychologists for more than 70 years (Block, 1971; Elder, 1998). The Schaie (2005) studies, for example, involved multiple cohorts sampled every 5–7 years for what is now more than 50 years. The early findings from these studies have matched later results: ability, interests, and temperament are very stable over decades. Although there is some change and character is not locked in cement, the latter is much more stable than had been thought (Roberts & DelVecchio, 2000).

# The Late Twentieth Century

Unfortunately, in the mid-1960s, after the proven successes of differential psychologists in predicting important criteria, there was a turn away from the study of individual differences, particularly in the United States. Personality trait theory came under attack as a study of small, non-replicable effects, undertaken with no agreement about the proper structural representation of personality. The research emphasis in American psychology switched to situational explanations of behavior. Studies of ability were attacked as being elitist, racist, or exclusionary. Personality researchers no longer routinely included ability measures in their studies and were not trained in the measurement of ability. Studies of occupational interests and job performance were seen as applied problems, of no interest to the readers of the top journals. Exceptions to this trend were of course the superb integrative text by Eysenck & Eysenck (1985) and a text on individual differences by Willerman (1979). Research emphasis came to be placed on "personality *x* situation interactions," which had, of course, been well studied by Atkinson (1957), Cattell (1957), and Eysenck (1967) for many years.

## Consensual descriptive taxonomies of personality

Eventually, after what some of us in the United States refer to as the "dark ages" (1968–1990), personality and differential psychology became an active area of research again. This happened partly because the European emphasis upon the biological bases of personality (e.g. Eysenck, 1967; Strelau & Eysenck, 1987) answered the situational attack, partly because there was growing evidence for genetic bases of most individual differences (Bouchard, 1994; Plomin, Owen, & McGuffin, 1994), and partly because there was growing consensus about the descriptive dimensions of personality. For, in the intervening years, a limited number of personality traits were consistently identified in peer ratings and self-reports (Fiske, 1949; Norman, 1963,

1969; Tupes & Christal, 1961), and this steadily accumulated body of evidence indicated that most self-report inventories included some—even if not necessarily all—of these so-called "Big-Five" dimensions (Digman, 1990; Goldberg, 1990). Two of these dimensions, *extraversion* and *neuroticism*, clearly matched the biologically based taxonomies of Eysenck (1967); two, *agreeableness* and *conscientiousness*, seemed to represent a splitting of what he had labeled *psychoticism* or *tough mindedness* (Eysenck, 1990); and an additional dimension of intellectual interests and *openness* to new experiences blended ability with approach motivation. Following a number of influential meta-analyses showing that personality and ability variables did indeed have predictive validity in occupational settings (Barrick & Mount, 1991; Mount, Barrick, Scullen, & Rounds, 2005) and that characteristics of bad leadership (which were a threat to organizational effectiveness) could be identified by self-report (R. Hogan, 1994; R. Hogan et al., 1990), individual differences research became respectable again.

Subsequent work discussing blends of the Big Five (Hofstee, Raad, & Goldberg, 1992; Johnson & Ostendorf, 1993) continued the atheoretic tradition of the descriptive taxonomies, but they did show how three biological dimensions (the "Giant Three") could be related to five descriptive dimensions. The development of a standard instrument (the "Neuroticism–Extraversion–Openness Personality Inventory" or NEO–PI: Costa & McCrae, 1985) to measure the Big-Five trait dimensions certainly helped, as did the forceful reviews by Costa and McCrae (1992a) and by McCrae and Costa (1997, 1999).

### The consensual structure of intelligence

On the abilities front, the review by Carroll (1993) of more than 70 years of intelligence testing integrated most of the prior studies, such as the *Gf–Gc* model of Horn and Cattell (1966), or a hierarchical model of *g* with second-order factors—verbal and educational (*v:ed*) versus spatial, practical, and numerical (*k:m*) ones (Vernon, 1965)—into a three-stratum model of *g* (Deary, Penke, & Johnson, 2010), which, in some versions (*g–Gf–Gc*), is known as the Carroll–Horn–Cattell (GHC) model (McGrew, 2009). An alternative three-level model (VPR) pitted the *v:ed* and *k:m* model against the *Gf–Gc* and suggests the importance of verbal, perceptual/memory, and rotational abilities (Johnson & Bouchard, 2005) as second-level strata in a three-level model. (Presentations with few tests tend to discuss three-level models, where the lowest level is a test, but, as the number of tests increases, the lowest level becomes the factor representing these tests.) An important concept in relating cognitive variables to criteria is the correct level of analysis (Wittmann, 1991), which helps provide an agreed upon structure to the studies of ability.

## 2000–2010

### A revival of interest

The last few years have seen a revival of interest in individual differences: not only this handbook, but also the texts by Cooper (1997), Chamorro-Premuzic (2007), and Eysenck (1994); handbooks on methods (Robins, Fraley, & Krueger, 2007) and on individual differences in social (Leary & Hoyle, 2009) or cognitive (Gruszka, Matthews, & Szymura, 2010) correlates; and edited volumes on biological bases (Canli, 2006) and on reinforcement sensitivity theory (Corr, 2008). The journal *Personality and Individual Differences* has seen its page count expand dramatically as the output of differential psychologists continues to grow. In organizational psychology, meta-analyses show the importance of cognitive (Kuncel et al., 2001; Kuncel, Cred, & Thomas, 2007) and non-cognitive (Barrick & Mount, 1991; Mount et al., 2005) predictors for real-world outcomes that include occupational attainment, marital stability, and early mortality (Roberts, Kuncel, Shiner, Caspi, & Goldberg, 2007).

## Individual differences theories applied to psychopathology

Clinical psychology has always been concerned with individual differences, and was the motivation behind developing such tests as the Minnesota Multiphasic Personality Inventory (MMPI, Hathaway & McKinley, 1943) and, later, the schedule for non-adaptive and adaptive personality (SNAP: Clark, 1993) but until recently there has been surprisingly little interchange between the personality and abilities communities on the one hand and those who study psychopathology on the other. It would seem that the emphasis on neuroticism and trait anxiety of many trait theorists would have had direct applications in theories of psychopathology, but the emphasis upon diagnostic categories rather than continuous traits has led to a lack of interaction. Exceptions to this general rule include work relating personality traits to Axis I disorders (Krueger, Caspi, Moffitt, Silva, & McGee, 1996; Trull & Sher, 1994), work on positive and negative affectivity in models of depression and anxiety (Clark, Watson, & Mineka, 1994; Watson, Gamez, & Simms, 2005) as well as applications of the five-factor model to predict personality disorders (Bagby, Costa, Widiger, Ryder, & Marshall, 2005; Costa & Widiger, 2002; Widiger & Costa, 1994). The taxonomic work of Krueger (2002), Krueger and Markon (2006), Markon, Krueger, and Watson (2005), and Tackett, Silberschmidt, Krueger, and Sponheim (2008) integrating the dimensions of normal personality with a dimensional rather than categorical organization of psychopathology (Watson, 2005) should lead to better theory development—in both of these aspects of differential psychology.

## Biological models

*Reinforcement Sensitivity Theory (RST)*   The rat-inspired reinforcement sensitivity theory (Gray, 1981, 1982; Gray & McNaughton, 2000) was developed primarily as a theory of anxiety, but has had an enormous impact upon biologically inspired personality theorists in general (Corr, 2002, 2008). As Smillie, Loxton, and Avery discuss in the present volume, RST was developed from the bottom up (from the physiology of the rat up to the behavior of the human) rather than the conventional top-down description and theorizing of most personality research. To some, RST is a projective test (Revelle, 2008), in that the way it is interpreted depends a great deal upon the investigator. This is perhaps why there is an ongoing debate about the range of the RST (Smillie, Pickering, & Jackson, 2006; Smillie, 2008, and the discussions following). It seems clear that, for at least the next decade, this will be an active research endeavor.

*Other biological models*   Contemporary biological models have benefited from technological advances in assessing neurophysiology. Magnetic resonance imaging (MRI) studies have investigated structural correlates of individual differences (Omura, Constable, & Canli, 2005; Rauch et al., 2005) from the perspective of learning theory. Depue (1995) and his colleagues (Depue & Collins, 1999) claim that individual differences in the strength of a neurobehavioral system tied to dopaminergic functioning form the causal basis for extraversion. Although research on this theory is still in its nascent stages, electroencephalography (EEG) studies generally supporting the dopaminergic hypothesis (Wacker, Chavanon, & Stemmler, 2006). Perhaps the most important methodological advance has been the use of functional MRI (fMRI) to study how patterns of brain activation relate to individual differences. In particular, Herrington, Koven, Miller, and Heller (2006) reviewed evidence suggesting that left hemisphere lateralization is associated with approach temperament. There is mixed evidence that approach temperament, consisting of extraversion, positive affect, and behavioral approach (Elliot & Thrash, 2002), predicts high performance on a variety of neuropsychological tasks that require cognitive functions specialized to the left prefrontal lobe. fMRI has also been used to study how individual differences correlate with specific brain regions (Canli, 2004; Canli et al., 2001). New technologies offer exciting opportunities for uncovering the biological bases of individual differences; however, there is also an increased likelihood that data generated by novel approaches may be analyzed inappropriately (Vul, Harris, Winkielman, & Pashler, 2009). As researching this domain moves forward, it will be important to balance enthusiasm with careful analysis and interpretation.

An important biologically based variable that affects social behavior, affect, and cognition is the diurnal arousal rhythm in animals as diverse as humans, hamsters, and fruit flies. Not only do people vary in their arousal over the day, but the time of peak arousal varies systematically between individuals. Diurnal rhythms and individual differences in phase have been used for testing theories of personality. The interactive effect on cognitive performance of impulsivity, caffeine, and time of day (Revelle, Humphreys, Simon, & Gilliland, 1980) was used to argue against the arousal theory of extraversion (Eysenck, 1967). Individual differences in diurnal rhythms as assessed by core body temperature were correlated with various measures of morningness–eveningness, as well as with voluntary sleep and awakening times (Baehr, Revelle, & Eastman, 2000). The minimum body temperature of self-described morning types was roughly two hours ahead of that observed for self-described evening types, although the behavioral response to social cues diminished the difference in voluntary sleeping and rising times between the two groups. The combination of body temperature rhythm and sleep and waking times suggests why evening people are more alert than morning ones before going to sleep, and also why they are so sluggish after awakening. Individual differences in diurnal rhythms are particularly important for sleep researchers (Taillard, Philip, Coste, Sagaspe, & Bioulac, 2003), especially those interested in sleep problems associated with adolescence versus adulthood (Crowley, Acebo, & Carskadon, 2007). The combination of social cues with an endogenous clock rhythm has important implications for other species as well—for instance in the fruit fly, where the mating habits of different species depend upon their arousal cycle (Rosato & Kyriacou, 2008).

## Genetics

Perhaps one of the clearest findings in differential psychology in the past 30 years is that almost all differences are under moderate to strong genetic control (Bouchard, 1994, 2004; Bouchard & Loehlin, 2001; McGue & Bouchard, 1998; Pedersen, Plomin, McClearn, & Friberg, 1988; see also Spinath & Johnson in this volume). Equally clear, and much more surprising, is the fact that, when doing an ACE analysis (that is, when analyzing for additive, common environmental, and unique environmental effects), there is generally little to no evidence for shared family environments. These effects are not just for the standard measures of ability, or for the Big-Five dimensions of personality. They are true for various psychopathologies, for interests, for sexual orientation, and even for religiosity. Indeed, it is now noteworthy when a differential trait does *not* show a substantial genetic component.

That something is heritable does not imply a simple genetic architecture. Heritability is just a ratio of variance which can be associated with the genetic causes of the total observed variance. Genetic effects can interact with (Caspi et al., 2002) and/or correlate with environmental variation in complex manners (W. Johnson, 2010). One of the major disappointments of the switch from quantitative behavioral genetics to molecular genetics and of the search for particular genes is how few genes have been shown to have replicable effects, and, even among those, how small the effects are. The simple "one gene–one disease" (OGOD) hypothesis (Plomin et al., 1994), which is derived from medical genetics, or its somewhat more complicated alternative, the "one gene–one system" hypothesis (OGOSH), do not seem to be supported. Even for clearly genetic traits such as height (with a heritability greater than .8), it is hard to find any single gene that is strongly associated with height. Basic concepts to remember when reading the genetic literature on behavior are that:

1   additive heritability is a hodge-podge ratio of genetic variance to total variance;
2   the less the environmental variance, the greater the heritability;
3   heritability within groups does not imply genetic causes of between-groups differences.

*Between-group versus within-group differences*   A recurring problem in inferences about genetics is whether genetic variability within groups has anything to do with genetic differences between groups. Consider the example of height (Johnson, 2010). It is well established that the heritability of height is roughly .8 within cultures. That is, about 80 percent of the variability in height is associated with genes. But it is equally well established that height changes in response to nutrition. Two groups that are genetically equivalent (North and South Koreans) differ by about 6 inches in height. How can this be? The answer is that heritability estimates, which are based upon within-group environmental variance, do not consider environmental variability between groups, nor do they say anything about how the trait will respond to environmental changes that do not vary within the group.

Related to this is the so-called "Spearman hypothesis," which claims that, if factor loadings on a variable are correlated with heritability and also with between-group differences, then the between-group differences must be genetic. A simple thought experiment shows why this is not true. Consider variables measuring overall height. Of these, some will be better measures of height than others, perhaps because of reliability issues, perhaps because the others are less valid. In this case the factor loadings on the general factor of height will be correlated with their heritability values. In addition, those measures that represent the better measure of height will show the biggest between-group differences in height. Indeed factor loadings, heritabilities, and between-group differences will be highly correlated, even though the between-group difference is due to nutrition.

## Sex differences

Are men and women different? Yes. But how and why continues to be an important question for differential psychologists. Schmitt, Realo, Voracek, and Allik (2008) examined sex differences on a short form of the Big Five (Benet-Martinez & John, 1998) across 55 different countries. The mean $z$ score of sex differences showed that women are more neurotic ($\bar{z} = .40$), agreeable ($\bar{z} = .15$), conscientious ($\bar{z} = .12$), and extraverted ($\bar{z} = .10$), and also less open ($\bar{z} = -.05$) than men. Schmitt et al. (2008) found that sex differences vary across cultures as a function of equality. That is, higher levels of health, access to education, and well-being were related to greater sex differences. These results differ somewhat from an international (but English-speaking), web-based self-selected sample of more than 50,000 participants who took a Big-Five Inventory (BFI) and reported their SAT (Scholastic Assessment/Ability Test) verbal and SAT quantitative scores (Revelle et al., 2010). In that sample, women were more agreeable ($d = .56$), less stable emotionally (d $= -.54$), less open ($d = -.30$), more conscientious (d $= .24$), and more extraverted ($d = .14$). Men and women reported practically identical SAT verbal scores, although women reported lower SAT quantitative scores ($d = -.29$). Gender differences have been reported for the facets of the NEO Personality Inventory, and are greater in Europe and America than in other cultures (Costa, Terracciano, & McCrae, 2001).

Although the stereotype is that women talk more than men, an observational study which sampled talking behavior for 30 seconds every 12.5 minutes for several days did not find a reliable difference in talking behavior between men and women (Mehl, Vazire, Ramirez-Esparza, Slatcher, & Pennebaker, 2007).

Even among amazingly talented women and men, there are reliable sex differences in interests and values (Ferriman, Lubinski, & Benbow, 2009). More importantly, these differences grow through people's career. Men were more career focused and willing to take greater risks in order to receive greater recognition. Women, on the other hand, emphasized community, family, and friendships. It seemed as if the men were emphasizing goals that differentiated them from others (inter-individual), while the women were emphasizing family and friends.

Although men and women do not differ in overall ability, the importance of mean differences in the lower-order factors of ability tests is masked when looking at overall $g$ scores. Women out-perform men in verbal and perceptual speed tasks, but do less well on visuospatial problems (Johnson & Bouchard, 2007). These sex differences, although strong, partly depend upon the method of analysis (Steinmayr, Beauducel, & Spinath, 2010). Sex differences in the variance of ability, although small, occur early in life (Arden & Plomin, 2006) and have important implications for the frequency of men and women with extreme scores.

## Integrating abilities, values, and interests

Individuals differ not only in their abilities and temperaments. They also differ in their values (Feather, 1995; Rohan, 2000) and interests (Holland, 1959, 1996). Unfortunately, although there are exceptions (Ackerman, 1997; Ackerman & Heggestad, 1997; Ferriman et al., 2009; Lubinski & Benbow, 2000), there have been few attempts to integrate research on interests with research on ability or temperament. Promising attempts are being made as part of the longitudinal study of mathematically precocious youth (Lubinski & Benbow, 2000, 2006). Ackerman and Heggestad have proposed "trait complexes" of mixes of abilities and interests and suggest that

> abilities, interests, and personality develop in tandem, such that ability level and personality dispositions determine the probability of success in a particular task domain, and interests determine the motivation to attempt the task. Thus, subsequent to successful attempts at task performance, interest in the task domain may increase. Conversely, unsuccessful attempts at task performance may result in a decrement in interest for that domain. (Ackerman & Heggestad, 1997, p. 239)

The theory of work adjustment (Lofquist & Dawis, 1969), as modified by Lubinski and Benbow (2000), is an excellent example of how to blend individual differences in abilities, interests, and values into a theory of long-term job satisfaction. Applications of this model to the long-term career choices of especially talented men and women (Ferriman et al., 2009) show the power of the model. This work, although very important, has not yet been integrated into a general theory of individual differences.

## Applications

It is important to recognize that differential psychology is not just an academic exercise in measurement and theory building. The use of inventories of ability as well as of psychomotor and personality inventories in predicting real-world criteria is an important application of our work. In a way which is reminiscent of the personality characteristics discussed in Plato's *Republic*, Musson, Sandal, and Helmreich (2004, p. 342), when predicting aviator or astronaut success, found that

> [s]uperior performance has consistently been linked to a personality profile characterized by a combination of high levels of instrumentality and expressivity along with lower

levels of interpersonal aggressiveness. This personality profile has sometimes been referred to as the "Right Stuff" [...] Inferior performance has been linked to personality profiles typified by a hostile and competitive interpersonal orientation (the "Wrong Stuff," suggesting that these individuals may not have the best characteristics for teamwork in complex settings) or to low achievement motivation combined with passive–aggressive characteristics (the "No Stuff" cluster, referring to individuals who score uniformly low on key traits).

In the context of graduate school, a combination of ability and conscientiousness predicts success across programs (Kuncel et al., 2001). Long-term follow-up studies of especially talented 12-year-olds have shown the power of ability, as well as that of interests, in predicting careers in the STEM (science, technology, engineering, and mathematics) fields (Ferriman et al., 2009; Lubinski & Benbow, 2000, 2006). It is not just raw talent that is important in determining who succeeds in a STEM career, but the mixture of verbal, spatial, and quantitative abilities, together with their interest in family and friends (Ferriman et al., 2009).

## Personality, ability and values across nations

People as well as nations differ in wealth, education, mental health, nutrition, and values (Bardi & Schwartz, 2003; Schwartz & Bilsky, 1987). Attempts at integrating between-nation and within-nation individual differences are fraught with methodological complications (Hunt & Wittmann, 2008) but also suggest interesting hypotheses about the effects of culture upon behavior (Chiao & Blizinsky, 2010). There is some work attempting to integrate values with abilities and temperament, both within and between nations (Stankov, 2009).

## Current Status and Future Directions

It is clear that differential psychology has a storied and illustrious past. It is also apparent, from the number and diversity of areas reviewed, that differential psychology currently has a firm foothold in the field of psychology and has made broad contributions to science more generally. As with any science, however, the task of theorists and researchers is not to relive the years of glory or to dwell on the misguided ventures of the "dark ages." Rather, the task is to continue to make progress and push the boundaries of knowledge by attempting to answer difficult and important questions. Differential psychology is facing such questions on all fronts, and across many levels of analysis. Questions at the forefront of contemporary differential psychology range from those about the way in which basic genetic and neurobiological characteristics contribute to individual differences (Canli, 2006) to those about the way in which high-level social and cultural systems interact to influence individual differences (Van de Vijver & Leung, 2008).

Differential psychology, at its heart, seeks to understand variation in how people feel, act, think, and want (Allport, 1937; Emmons, 1989; J. A. Johnson, 1997; Winter, John, Stewart, Klohnen, & Duncan, 1998). As such, researchers studying differential psychology tend to consider questions falling into one of four domains of effective functioning: affect, behavior, cognition, and motivation (desire)—the "ABCDs of personality" (Revelle, 2008). Briefly, affect comprises feelings, emotions, and moods; behavior comprises motor actions such as walking and talking, as well as physiological processes such as heart beat; cognition comprises thoughts and beliefs, including how one creates meaning out of the world and out of one's life; desires comprise motivational tendencies, drives, and one's short- and long-term goals. Researchers typically focus on just one of these ABCD domains of functioning, neglecting to consider connections across levels and domains.

In the domain of *affect*, there has been considerable debate over how many and what dimensions best characterize affective space, with various competing models garnering empirical support. The circumplex model of affect (Barrett & Russell, 1998; Russell, 1980) arranges affective space around the dimensions of "valence" and "arousal." In this model, positive and negative emotions are considered bipolar opposites. In contrast, other two-dimensional models of affect propose that positive and negative affects reside on two independent unipolar dimensions (Cacioppo & Berntson, 1994; Thayer, 1989; Watson, Clark, & Tellegen, 1988). A three-dimensional model has also been proposed, which incorporates a valence dimension with two independent arousal dimensions: energetic arousal and tense arousal (Schimmack & Grob, 2000; Schimmack & Reisenzein, 2002). Not only do average levels of the aforementioned affective dimensions differ between people (Watson, 2000), but recent research has also shown that the structure of affective space itself may be considered an individual differences variable (Feldman, 1995; Rafaeli, Rogers, & Revelle, 2007).

A long-standing goal of individual differences research is to predict *behavior* (Allport, 1937; Fleeson, 2001; Pervin, 1994). Indeed, predicting ongoing behavior in naturally occurring environments is extolled as a gold standard in individual differences research (Craik, 2000). With some notable exceptions, including Eysenck and Himmelweit's (1947) work on the factor structure of behavioral observations, this goal has too seldom been realized. Historically, it has been relatively difficult and expensive to collect large slices of naturally occurring behavior (Eaton & Funder, 2003; Funder, 2001); however, recent advances in methods of data collecting behavior, including electronic diaries (Green, Rafaeli, Bolger, Shrout, & Reis, 2006), portable recorders (Mehl & Pennebaker, 2003), and cell-phone methods of data collection (Collins, Kashdan, & Gollnisch, 2003; Reid et al., 2008), have made it easier to obtain data on behavior as it occurs. Such advances, combined with instruments tailored to assess behavior (Funder, Furr, & Colvin, 2000), have resulted in a growth of studies looking at how Big-Five trait dispositions are reflected in behavior across time (Fleeson & Gallagher, 2009; Mehl, Gosling, & Pennebaker, 2006; Paunonen, 2003).

The research on intelligence constitutes the most influential and well-established study of any *cognitive* individual difference variable. Real-world criteria range from job performance to mortality (Deary, Whiteman, Starr, Whalley, & Fox, 2004; Deary et al., 2010). Researchers have begun studying how personality dispositions relate to cognitive differences, most of this research focusing on the trait of openness/intellect (Costa & McCrae, 1992b; Hofstee, Raad, & Goldberg, 1992). Individuals higher in openness generally score higher on measures of cognitive ability (DeYoung, Peterson,

& Higgins, 2005; Revelle, Wilt, & Rosenthal, 2010), are seen as displaying more creative thinking, and have a greater capacity for divergent thinking (McCrae, 1987). Developing in parallel to the research on trait dispositions is the social–cognitive approach to personality (Bandura & Press, 1999; Dweck & Leggett, 1988). Researchers in the social–cognitive tradition emphasize variations in cognitive tasks, strategies, and schemata. Some of the best known research from this approach has examined differences between people who perceive ability as stable, who are labeled "entity theorists," and those who see ability as malleable, who are labeled "incremental theorists" (Hong, Chiu, Dweck, Lin, & Wan, 1999). Cognition also includes the life-narrative approach to individual differences (McAdams, 2008), which focuses on variations in how people integrate their remembered past, experienced present, and imagined future into a coherent life-story.

Research on individual differences in motivation or *desire* has made some impressive findings in recent years. A hierarchical model of independent approach and avoidance motivational dimensions has been specified (Elliot & Church, 1997), elaborated upon (Elliot & McGregor, 2001), and correlated with individual differences in academic performance (Cury, Elliot, Da Fonseca, & Moller, 2006). Higgins's (1998) regulatory focus theory (RFT), which posits that people are guided by two distinct motivational systems—promotion focus and prevention focus—has gained solid footing in the literature on motivation. Promotion focus is manifested in attempts to bring one's actual self into alignment with one's ideal selves, which reflect one's wishes and aspirations. Prevention focus leads one to bring one's actual selves into alignment with one's ought selves, that is, with the standards reflecting duties and obligations. Research on broad life goals, which had long been neglected, has recently picked up in the context of relating goals to Big-Five variables (Roberts & Robins, 2000; Roberts, O'Donnell, & Robins, 2004). In addition to nomothetic approaches to motivations and goals, idiographic assessments of what people strive for in their lives (Emmons, 1986) as well as in their personal projects (Little, Lecci, & Watkinson, 1992) have also gained popularity.

The fact that domains of functioning are studied in isolation from each other is not a criticism of the researchers involved; for indeed each level and each domain deserves careful attention. However, failure to pursue integration may leave gaps or holes (Rozin, 2007) in theories of individual differences. Therefore the state of research on individual differences is in need of frameworks in which integration across levels may be achieved. The question of integration boils down to one of organization. That is, how can theories of individual differences be organized such that the domains of functioning (ABCDs) may be connected to each other in meaningful ways?

We believe that such an integration may be forged by adopting an information-processing perspective. Specifically, individual differences in the coherent patterning of affect, behavior, cognition, and desire may be understood at three levels of information processing—*reactive, routine, and reflective* (Ortony, Norman, & Revelle, 2005). It is important to note that the reactive level, routine level, and reflective level are not separated by sharp boundaries, but lie on a continuum of complexity, ranging from more basic and immediate processes (reactive) to well-learned and rehearsed processes (routine) to complex and abstract processes (reflective).

The *reactive* level of information processing comprises rapid and efficient responses to stimuli. Responses at this level consist of a unified combination of affective and behavioral and motivational processes. For example, after touching a stove burner, the motivation to avoid pain (desire), the fear (affect), and the removal of one's hand (behavior) are likely to occur simultaneously and do not require elaborated cognition. The *routine* level comprises well-learned, everyday activities. At this level, affect, behavior, and motivation may be distinguished from each other due to the emergence of low-level cognitive processes. At the routine level of processing, an individual noticing his or her hand approaching a hot stove would be able to discriminate cognitively between the present state of not being in pain and fear (affect) and an unwanted future state of pain (desire). The individual may thus act (behavior) so as to increase the likelihood that pain does not ensue. The *reflective* level describes higher-level cognitive functioning such as self-awareness and meta-processing. At this level affect becomes enriched with cognitive content, such that conscious plans may guide behavior toward or away from well-elaborated and nuanced goals. One may safeguard the stove so that young children are unlikely to come into contact with the burners.

The above examples lead to the realization that the ABCDs constantly interact in dynamic ways across multiple levels of information processing. As such, those dynamic interactions should be a focal point of differential psychology theories, and failure to consider such dynamics may limit the generation of comprehensive theories of individual differences. By adopting an information-processing approach, the study of differential psychology becomes the study of the coherent patterning of ABCDs across time and space (Wilt & Revelle, 2009). The task of differential psychology thus becomes the task of explaining why people have different ABCD patterns across the different levels of information processing, and determining how those differences relate to important outcomes.

The ABCD approach has the potential to serve as an overarching conceptual framework for individual differences research. It is important for future research not only to integrate across levels of analysis and domains of functioning, but also to resolve some of the specific and pressing issues facing differential psychology today. As would be expected of such a broad and fast-expanding field, questions facing differential psychology involve tackling the influence of variables, from genes to virtual environments, and many questions revolve around the use of new technologies.

Although it is too early to render judgment on the usefulness of genome-wide association studies (GWAS), the high cost and limited benefits of current GWAS of disease (Kraft & Hunter, 2009) raise the question of whether individual differences research would benefit from employing such methods. Some great discoveries have been made (Amos, 2007), but the infrequency with which these findings occur suggests that the traditional GWAS method of exploring common gene variants is in need of some rethinking before it is adopted by differential psychology. Remaining in the realm of biology, serious thought should also be given to the use and interpretation of fMRI data, given the recent debate about whether current findings using fMRI inflate the relationships between brain and personality processes (Vul et al., 2009).

Developmental research on individual differences must go beyond studying genes and neurophysiological processes in isolation, to focus on interactions between biological and environmental variables by using longitudinal studies. When such interactions are found, they generate a tremendous amount of excitement (Caspi et al., 2003); however, interactions are difficult to replicate (Os & Rutten, 2009), which calls into question their validity. Further attention may be warranted due to the importance of interactions in establishing boundary conditions for theories on the etiology of disorders, as well as for identifying particular populations that might be at most risk for developing disorders.

Longitudinal studies have been instrumental in showing how differences in the Big-Five traits relate to myriad important outcomes such as mental health, mental disorders, job success, marriage satisfaction, and even mortality (Ozer & Benet-Martinez, 2006; Roberts et al., 2007). Indeed, trait psychology has been one of the most successful enterprises of personality theory in predicting and understanding healthy psychological functioning. Future research should focus on the mechanisms through which traits achieve their effects. Finding mechanistic relationships may be instrumental in developing effective interventions. Research predicting practical outcomes on the basis of traits should be balanced with basic research aimed at uncovering the etiology of individual difference dimensions. Non-intuitive but exciting ways to study basic individual differences in humans that are not confined to human beings may be explored by studying animal personality (Vazire & Gosling, 2003; Vazire, Gosling, Dickey, & Schapiro, 2007). There has been a long history of studying biological mechanisms thought to relate to personality by using animal models in drug or lesion studies (Gray, 1982; Gray & McNaughton, 2000) as well as in selective breeding studies (Broadhurst, 1975). But now observational studies of non-human animals may allow individual differences researchers opportunities to examine questions that are difficult or impossible to explore in humans.

The already vast data base on individual differences is sure to continue to grow at an increasingly fast rate, given the ease of public-domain personality assessment which specifically uses resources such as the IPIP (Goldberg, 1999; Goldberg et al., 2006). The possibility for such data to be stored in large data bases available for public use heeds the call to make differential psychology accessible to everyone. Additionally, the ability to make inferences about individual differences on the basis of the content of personal websites (Gosling, Vazire, Srivastava, & John, 2004) should only augment the richness of individual differences data that are readily available.

## Conclusion

In what ways do people differ from each other? Why do people differ from each other? To study individual differences is to ask these fundamental questions. Although the scope and importance of these questions are almost impossible to overestimate, the field of differential psychology must not be content to tackle description and theory building alone. In order for the field to realize its potential, it must also be concerned with using individual differences to predict important outcomes. What characteristics make someone a successful graduate student, military officer, or business executive? Generating knowledge about how and why people differ and applying that knowledge to improve society are the daunting tasks charged to our field; but we are well prepared. Differential psychologists are making advances in understanding characteristic patterns of affect, behavior, cognition, and motivation; these patterns may be conceptualized as individual differences in temperament, abilities and interests. There may be relatively weak correlations across TAI domains, but it is important that differential psychologist not get discouraged over these results. Indeed, loose associations among these constructs are *encouraging*, because their existence means that variables from each domain may serve as important predictors in their own right. Thus temperaments, abilities and interests may have additive and interactive relationships with practically important outcomes. The field may thus benefit from shifting its focus from correlational structure to prediction. By doing so, we may achieve another high point, similar to the one we realized in the mid-twentieth century. Indeed the future of differential psychology is more promising than it has been for decades.

# References

Ackerman, P. L. (1997). Personality, self-concept, interests, and intelligence: Which construct doesn't fit? *Journal of Personality, 65*(2), 171–204.

Ackerman, P. L., & Heggestad, E. D. (1997). Intelligence, personality, and interests: Evidence for overlapping traits. *Psychological Bulletin, 121*(2), 219–245.

Allport, G. W. (1937). *Personality: A psychological interpretation*. New York: H. Holt and Company.

Amos, C. I. (2007). Successful design and conduct of genome-wide association studies. *Human Molecular Genetics, 16*(R2), R220–R225.

Arden, R., & Plomin, R. (2006). Sex differences in variance of intelligence across childhood. *Personality and Individual Differences, 41*(1), 39–48.

Armstrong, P. I., Smith, T. J., Donnay, D. A., & Rounds, J. (2004). The Strong ring: A basic interest model of occupational structure. *Journal of Counseling Psychology, 51*(3), 299–313.

Atkinson, J. W. (1957). Motivational determinants of risk-taking behavior. *Psychological Review, 64*, 359–372.

Atkinson, J. W., & Birch, D. (1970). *The dynamics of action*. New York: John Wiley.

Atkinson, J. W., & Raynor, J. O. (Eds.) (1974). *Motivation and achievement*. New York: Winston (Halsted Press/Wiley).

Baehr, E. K., Revelle, W., & Eastman, C. I. (2000). Individual differences in the phase and amplitude of the human circadian temperature rhythm: With an emphasis on morningness–eveningness. *Journal of Sleep Research, 9*(2), 117–127.

Bagby, R., Costa, Jr., P. T., Widiger, T. A., Ryder, A. G., & Marshall, M. (2005). DSM–IV personality disorders and the five-factor model of personality: A multi-method examination of domain- and facet-level predictions. *European Journal of Personality, 19*(4), 307–324.

Bandura, A., & Press, G. (1999). Asocial cognitive theory of personality. In L. A. Pervin & O. P. John (Eds.), *Handbook of personality* (2nd ed., pp. 154–196). New York: Guilford Press.

Bardi, A., & Schwartz, S. H. (2003). Values and behavior: Strength and structure of relations. *Personality and Social Psychology Bulletin, 29*(10), 1207–1220.

Barrett, L., & Russell, J. A. (1998). Independence and bipolarity in the structure of current affect. *Journal of Personality and Social Psychology, 74*(4), 967–984.

Barrick, M. R., & Mount, M. K. (1991). The Big Five personality dimensions and job performance: A meta-analysis. *Personnel Psychology, 44*(1), 1–26.

Bartholomew, D., Deary, I., & Lawn, M. (2009). A new lease of life for Thomson's bonds model of intelligence. *Psychological Review, 116*(3), 567–579.

Benet-Martinez, V., & John, O. P. (1998). Los Cinco Grandes across cultures and ethnic groups: Multitrait–multimethod analyses of the Big Five in Spanish and English. *Journal of Personality and Social Psychology, 75*(3), 729–750.

Binet, A., & Simon, T. (1905). New methods for the diagnosis of the intellectual level of subnormals. *L'Année Psychologique, 12*, 191–244. [Translated in 1916 by E. S. Kite in *The development of intelligence in children*. Vineland, NJ: Publications of the Training School at Vineland.]

Block, J. (1971). *Lives through time*. Berkeley, CA: Bancroft Books.

Bock, R. D. (2007). Rethinking Thurstone. In R. Cudeck & R. C. MacCallum (Eds.), *Factor analysis at 100: Historical developments and future directions* (pp. 35–45). Mahwah, NJ: Lawrence Erlbaum Associates.

Bouchard, T. J. (1994). Genes, environment, and personality. *Science, 264*(5166), 1700–1701.

Bouchard, T. J. (2004). Genetic influence on human psychological traits: A survey. *Current Directions in Psychological Science, 13*(4), 148–151.

Bouchard, T. J., & Loehlin, J. C. (2001). Genes, evolution, and personality. *Behavior Genetics, 31*(3), 243–273.

Broadhurst, P. (1975). The Maudsley reactive and nonreactive strains of rats: A survey. *Behavior Genetics, 5*(4), 299–319.

Cacioppo, J. T., & Berntson, G. G. (1994). Relationship between attitudes and evaluative space: A critical review, with emphasis on the separability of positive and negative substrates. *Psychological Bulletin, 115*(3), 401–423.

Canli, T. (2004). Functional brain mapping of extraversion and neuroticism: Learning from individual differences in emotion processing. *Journal of Personality, 72*(6), 1105–1132.

Canli, T. (2006). *Biology of personality and individual differences*. New York: Guilford Press.

Canli, T., Zhao, Z., Desmond, J. E., Kang, E., Gross, J., & Gabrieli, J. D. (2001). An fMRI study of personality influences on brain reactivity to emotional stimuli. *Behavioral Neuroscience, 115*(1), 33–42.

Carroll, J. B. (1993). *Human cognitive abilities: A survey of factor-analytic studies*. New York: Cambridge University Press.

Carver, C. S., & White, T. L. (1994). Behavioral inhibition, behavioral activation, and affective responses to impending reward and punishment: The BIS/BAS scales. *Journal of Personality and Social Psychology, 67*, 319–333.

Caspi, A., McClay, J., Moffitt, T., Mill, J., Martin, J., Craig, I. W., Taylor, A., & Poulton, R. (2002). Role of genotype in the cycle of violence in maltreated children. *Science, 297*(5582), 851–854.

Caspi, A., Sugden, K., Moffitt, T. E., Taylor, A., Craig, I. W., Harrington, H., McClay, J., Mill, J. et al. (2003). Influence of life stress on depression: Moderation by a polymorphism in the 5–HTT gene. *Science, 301*(5631), 386–389.

Cattell, R. B. (1943). The description of personality. I. Foundations of trait measurement. *Psychological Review, 50*(6), 559–594.

Cattell, R. B. (1946a). *Description and measurement of personality*. Oxford: World Book Co.

Cattell, R. B. (1946b). Personality structure and measurement. II. The determination and utility of trait modality. *British Journal of Psychology, 36*, 159–174.

Cattell, R. B. (1946c). Personality structure and measurement. I. The operational determination of trait unities. *British Journal of Psychology, 36*, 88–102.

Cattell, R. B. (1957). *Personality and motivation structure and measurement.* Oxford: World Book Co.

Cattell, R. B. (1966a). The data box: Its ordering of total resources in terms of possible relational systems. In R. B. Cattell (Ed.), *Handbook of multivariate experimental psychology* (pp. 67–128). Chicago: Rand-McNally.

Cattell, R. B. (1966b). *The scientific analysis of personality.* Chicago: Aldine.

Cattell, R. B. (1978). *The scientific use of factor analysis.* New York: Plenum Press.

Cattell, R. B., & Stice, G. (1957). *Handbook for the sixteen personality factor questionnaire.* Champaign, IL: Institute for Ability and Personality Testing.

Chamorro-Premuzic, T. (2007). *Personality and individual differences.* Oxford: Blackwell.

Chiao, J. Y., & Blizinsky, K. D. (2010). Culture–gene coevolution of individualism–collectivism and the serotonin transporter gene (5–HTTLPR). *Proceedings of the Royal Society B: Biological Sciences, 277*(1681), 529–537.

Clark, L. A. (1993). *Schedule for nonadaptive and adaptive personality (SNAP): Manual for administration and scoring* [Computer software manual]. Minneapolis, MN: University of Minnesota Press.

Clark, L. A., Watson, D., & Mineka, S. (1994). Temperament, personality, and the mood and anxiety disorders. *Journal of Abnormal Psychology, 103*, 103–116.

Collins, R. L., Kashdan, T. B., & Gollnisch, G. (2003). The feasibility of using cellular phones to collect ecological momentary assessment data: Application to alcohol consumption. *Experimental and Clinical Psychopharmacology, 11*(1), 73–78.

Comrey, A. L. (1995). *Revised manual and handbook of interpretations for the Comrey Personality Scales.* San Diego, CA: Educational and Industrial Testing Service.

Cooper, C. (1997). *Individual differences.* Oxford: Oxford University Press.

Corr, P. J. (2002). J. A. Gray's reinforcement sensitivity theory and frustrative nonreward: A theoretical note on expectancies in reactions to rewarding stimuli. *Personality and Individual Differences, 32*(7), 1247–1253.

Corr, P. J. (Ed.) (2008). *The reinforcement sensitivity theory of personality.* Cambridge: Cambridge University Press.

Costa, P. T., & McCrae, R. R. (1985). *NEO PI professional manual.* Odessa, FL: Psychological Assessment Resources, Inc.

Costa, P. T., & McCrae, R. R. (1992a). Four ways five factors are basic. *Personality and Individual Differences, 13*(6), 653–665.

Costa, P. T., & McCrae, R. R. (1992b). *NEO PI–R professional manual.* Odessa, FL: Psychological Assessment Resources, Inc.

Costa, P. T., & Widiger, T. A. (2002). *Personality disorders and the five-factor model of personality* (2nd ed.). Washington, DC: American Psychological Association.

Costa, P. T., Terracciano, A., & McCrae, R. R. (2001). Gender differences in personality traits across cultures: Robust and surprising findings. *Journal of Personality and Social Psychology, 81*(2), 322–331.

Craik, K. H. (2000). The lived day of an individual: A person–environment perspective. In W. B. Walsh, K. H. Craik, & R. H. Price (Eds.), *Person–environment psychology: New directions and perspectives* (2nd ed., pp. 233–266). Mahwah, NJ: Lawrence Erlbaum Associates.

Cronbach, L. J. (1957). The two disciplines of scientific psychology. *American Psychologist, 12*, 671–684.

Cronbach, L. J. (1975). Beyond the two disciplines of scientific psychology. *American Psychologist, 30*, 116–127.

Crowley, S., Acebo, C., & Carskadon, M. (2007). Sleep, circadian rhythms, and delayed phase in adolescence. *Sleep Medicine, 8*(6), 602–612.

Cury, F., Elliot, A. J., Da Fonseca, D., & Moller, A. C. (2006). The social–cognitive model of achievement motivation and the 2 × 2 achievement goal framework. *Journal of Personality and Social Psychology, 90* (4), 666–679.

Dahlstrom, W. G. (1992). The growth in acceptance of the MMPI. *Professional Psychology: Research and Practice, 23*(5), 345–348.

Deary, I. J., Penke, L., & Johnson, W. (2010). The neuroscience of human intelligence differences. *Nature Reviews Neuroscience, 11*(3), 201–211.

Deary, I. J., Whiteman, M., Starr, J., Whalley, L., & Fox, H. (2004). The impact of childhood intelligence on later life: Following up the Scottish mental surveys of 1932 and 1947. *Journal of Personality and Social Psychology, 86*(1), 130–147.

Depue, R. A. (1995). Neurobiological factors in personality and depression. *European Journal of Personality, 9*(5), 413–439.

Depue, R. A., & Collins, P. F. (1999). Neurobiology of the structure of personality: Dopamine, facilitation of incentive motivation, and extraversion. *Behavioral and Brain Sciences, 22*(3), 491–569.

DeYoung, C. G., Peterson, J. B., & Higgins, D. M. (2005). Sources of openness/intellect: Cognitive and neuropsychological correlates of the fifth factor of personality. *Journal of Personality, 73*(4), 825–858.

Digman, J. M. (1990). Personality structure: Emergence of the five-factor model. *Annual Review of Psychology, 41,* 417–440.

Donnay, D. A. (1997). E. K. Strong's legacy and beyond: 70 years of the Strong interest inventory. *Career Development Quarterly, 46*(1), 2–22.

Driskell, J., & Olmstead, B. (1989). Psychology and the military: Research applications and trends. *American Psychologist, 44*(1), 43–54.

Dubois, P. H. (1947). *The classification program report no. 2* (Army Air Forces Aviation Psychology Program Research Reports). Defense Documentation Center Defense Supply Agency: Army Air Forces.

Dweck, C. S., & Leggett, E. L. (1988). A social–cognitive approach to motivation and personality. *Psychological Review, 95*(2), 256–273.

Eaton, L. G., & Funder, D. C. (2003). The creation and consequences of the social world: An interactional analysis of extraversion. *European Journal of Personality, 17*(5), 375–395.

Eccles, J. S., & Wigfield, A. (2002). Motivational beliefs, values, and goals. *Annual Review of Psychology, 53*(1), 109–132.

Elder, G. H. (1998). The life course as developmental theory. *Child Development, 69*(1), 1–12.

Elliot, A. J., & Church, M. A. (1997). A hierarchical model of approach and avoidance achievement motivation. *Journal of Personality and Social Psychology, 72*(1), 218–232.

Elliot, A. J., & McGregor, H. A. (2001). A 2 × 2 achievement goal framework. *Journal of Personality and Social Psychology, 80*(3), 501–519.

Elliot, A. J., & Thrash, T. M. (2002). Approach–avoidance motivation in personality: Approach–avoidance temperaments and goals. *Journal of Personality and Social Psychology, 82,* 804–818.

Emmons, R. A. (1986). Personal strivings: An approach to personality and subjective well-being. *Journal of Personality and Social Psychology, 51*(5), 1058–1068.

Emmons, R. A. (1989). Exploring the relations between motives and traits: The case of narcissism. In D. M. Buss & N. Cantor (Eds.), *Personality psychology: Recent trends and emerging directions* (pp. 32–44). New York: Springer-Verlag.

Eysenck, H. J. (1952). *The scientific study of personality.* London: Routledge & Kegan Paul.

Eysenck, H. J. (1953). *Uses and abuses of psychology.* London, Baltimore, MD: Penguin Books.

Eysenck, H. J. (1964). *Sense and nonsense in psychology.* Baltimore, MD: Penguin Books.

Eysenck, H. J. (1965). *Fact and fiction in psychology.* Baltimore, MD: Penguin Books.

Eysenck, H. J. (1966). Personality and experimental psychology. *Bulletin of the British Psychological Society, 19,* 1–28.

Eysenck, H. J. (1967). *The biological basis of personality.* Springfield, IL: Thomas.

Eysenck, H. J. (1990). Biological dimensions of personality. In L. A. Pervin (Ed.), *Handbook of personality: Theory and research* (pp. 244–276). New York: Guilford Press.

Eysenck, H. J. (1992). *A hundred years of personality research, from Heymans to modern times.* Houten: Bohn, Stafleu Van Loghum.

Eysenck, H. J. (1997). Personality and experimental psychology: The unification of psychology and the possibility of a paradigm. *Journal of Personality and Social Psychology, 73*(6), 1224–1237.

Eysenck, H. J., & Eysenck, M. W. (1985). *Personality and individual differences: A natural science approach.* New York: Plenum Press.

Eysenck, H. J., & Eysenck, S. B. G. (1964). *Eysenck personality inventory.* San Diego, CA: Educational and Industrial Testing Service.

Eysenck, H. J., & Himmelweit, H. T. (1947). *Dimensions of personality: A record of research carried out in collaboration with H. T. Himmelweit [and others].* London: Kegan Paul, Trench.

Eysenck, M. W. (1994). *Individual differences: Normal and abnormal.* Hove: Lawrence Erlbaum Associates.

Feather, N. T. (1995). Values, valences, and choice: The influences of values on the perceived attractiveness and choice of alternatives. *Journal of Personality and Social Psychology, 68*(6), 1135–1151.

Feldman, L. A. (1995). Valence focus and arousal focus: Individual differences in the structure of affective experience. *Journal of Personality and Social Psychology, 69,* 153–166.

Ferriman, K., Lubinski, D., & Benbow, C. (2009). Work preferences, life values, and personal views of top math/science graduate students and the profoundly gifted: Developmental changes and gender differences during emerging adulthood and parenthood. *Journal of Personality and Social Psychology, 97*(3), 517–532.

Fiske, D. W. (1949). Consistency of the factorial structures of personality ratings from different sources. *Journal of Abnormal and Social Psychology, 44,* 329–344.

Fleeson, W. (2001). Toward a structure- and process-integrated view of personality: Traits as density distributions of states. *Journal of Personality and Social Psychology, 80*(6), 1011–1027.

Fleeson, W., & Gallagher, P. (2009). The implications of Big Five standing for the distribution of trait manifestation in behavior: Fifteen experience-sampling studies and a meta-analysis. *Journal of Personality and Social Psychology, 97*(6), 1097–1114.

Flynn, J. R. (1984). The mean IQ of Americans: Massive gains 1932 to 1978. *Psychological Bulletin, 95*(1), 29–51.

Flynn, J. R. (1987). Massive IQ gains in 14 nations: What IQ tests really measure. *Psychological Bulletin, 101*(2), 171–191.

Flynn, J. R. (2000). IQ gains and fluid *g*. *American Psychologist, 55*(5), 543.

Fua, K., Revelle, W., & Ortony, A. (2010). *Modeling personality and individual differences: The approach–avoid–conflict triad.* Paper presented at the Annual Meeting of the Cognitive Science Society (CogSci 2010).

Funder, D. C. (2001). Personality. *Annual Review of Psychology, 52*, 197–221.

Funder, D. C., Furr, R., & Colvin, C. (2000). The Riverside behavioral Q-sort: A tool for the description of social behavior. *Journal of Personality, 68*(3), 451–489.

Furnham, A. (2005). *The psychology of behaviour at work: The individual in the organization* (2nd ed.). New York: Psychology Press.

Galton, F. (1865). Hereditary talent and character. *Macmillan's Magazine, 12*, 157–166.

Galton, F. (1879). Psychometric experiments. *Brain, 2*, 149–162.

Galton, F. (1884). Measurement of character. *Fortnightly Review, 36*, 179–185.

Galton, F. (1888). Co-relations and their measurement. *Proceedings of the Royal Society. London Series, 45*, 135–145.

Galton, F. (1892). *Hereditary genius: An inquiry into its laws and consequences* (2nd ed.). London: Macmillan and Co.

Goddard, H. H. (1908). The Binet and Simon tests of intellectual capacity. *The Training School Bulletin, 5*(10), 3–9.

Goldberg, L. R. (1990). An alternative "description of personality": The Big-Five factor structure. *Journal of Personality and Social Psychology, 59*(6), 1216–1229.

Goldberg, L. R. (1999). A broad-bandwidth, public domain, personality inventory measuring the lower-level facets of several five-factor models. In I. Mervielde, I. Deary, F. De Fruyt, & F. Ostendorf (Eds.), *Personality psychology in Europe* (Vol. 7, pp. 7–28). Tilburg, The Netherlands: Tilburg University Press.

Goldberg, L. R., Johnson, J. A., Eber, H. W., Hogan, R., Ashton, M. C., Cloninger, C. R., & Gough., H. G. (2006). The international personality item pool and the future of public-domain personality measures. *Journal of Research in Personality, 40*(1), 84–96.

Gosling, S. D., Vazire, S., Srivastava, S., & John, O. P. (2004). Should we trust web-based studies? A comparative analysis of six preconceptions about Internet questionnaires. *American Psychologist, 59*(2), 93–104.

Gough, H. G. (1957). *Manual for the California psychological inventory.* Palo Alto, CA: Consulting Psychologists Press.

Gray, J. A. (1970). The psychophysiological basis of introversion–extraversion. *Behaviour Research and Therapy, 8*(3), 249–266.

Gray, J. A. (1981). A critique of Eysenck's theory of personality. In H. J. Eysenck (Ed.), *A model for personality* (pp. 246–277). Berlin: Springer.

Gray, J. A. (1982). *Neuropsychological theory of anxiety: An investigation of the septal–hippocampal system.* Cambridge: Cambridge University Press.

Gray, J. A., & McNaughton, N. (2000). *The neuropsychology of anxiety: An enquiry into the functions of the septo-hippocampal system* (2nd ed.). Oxford: Oxford University Press.

Green, A. S., Rafaeli, E., Bolger, N., Shrout, P. E., & Reis, H. T. (2006). Paper or plastic? Data equivalence in paper and electronic diaries. *Psychological Methods, 11*(1), 87–105.

Gruszka, A., Matthews, G., & Szymura, B. (Eds.) (2010). *Handbook of individual differences in cognition: Attention, memory and executive control.* New York: Springer.

Guilford, J. P. (1956). The structure of intellect. *Psychological Bulletin, 53*(4), 267–293.

Guilford, J. P. (1959). Three faces of intellect. *American Psychologist, 14*(8), 469–479.

Guilford, J. P., & Zimmerman, W. S. (1949). *The Guilford–Zimmerman temperament survey.* Oxford: Sheridan Supply Co.

Hathaway, S., & McKinley, J. (1943). *Manual for administering and scoring the MMPI.* Minneapolis, MN: University of Minnesota Press.

Hathaway, S., & McKinley, J. (1951). *Minnesota multiphasic personality inventory: Manual.* New York: The Psychological Corporation.

Heist, P. A., & Williams, P. A. (1957). *Manual for the omnibus personality inventory.* Berkeley, CA: Center for the study of higher education, University of California.

Herrington, J. D., Koven, N. S., Miller, G. A., & Heller, W. (2006). Mapping the neural correlates of dimensions of personality, emotion, and motivation. In T. Canli (Ed.), *Biology of personality and individual differences* (pp. 133–156). New York: Guilford Press.

Heymans, G. (1908). Über einege psychische Korrelationen. *Zeitschrift für Angewandte Psychologie, 1,* 313–381.

Higgins, E. T. (1998). Promotion and prevention: Regulatory focus as a motivational principle. In Mark P. Zanna (Ed.), *Advances in experimental social psychology* (Vol. 30, pp. 1–46). N.p.: Academic Press.

Hilgard, E. R. (1980). The trilogy of mind: Cognition, affection, and conation. *Journal of the History of the Behavioral Sciences, 16,* 107–117.

Hofstee, W. K., Raad, B. de, & Goldberg, L. R. (1992). Integration of the Big Five and circumplex approaches to trait structure. *Journal of Personality and Social Psychology, 63*(1), 146–163.

Hogan, R. (1994). Trouble at the top: Causes and consequences of managerial incompetence. *Consulting Psychology Journal: Practice and Research, 46*(1), 9–15.

Hogan, R. (2007). *Personality and the fate of organizations.* Mahwah, NJ: Lawrence Erlbaum Associates.

Hogan, R., & Hogan, J. (1995). *The Hogan personality inventory manual* (2nd ed.). Tulsa, OK: Hogan Assessment Systems.

Hogan, R., Raskin, R., & Fazzini, D. (1990). *The dark side of charisma.* In K. E. Clark & M. B. Clark (Eds.), *Measures of leadership* (pp. 343–354). West Orange, NJ: Leadership Library of America, Inc.

Holland, J. L. (1959). A theory of vocational choice. *Journal of Counseling Psychology, 6*(1), 35–45.

Holland, J. L. (1996). Exploring careers with a typology: What we have learned and some new directions. *American Psychologist, 51*(4), 397–406.

*The Holy Bible: Authorized King James Version of 1611.*

Hong, Y., Chiu, C., Dweck, C. S., Lin, D. M. S., & Wan, W. (1999). Implicit theories, attributions, and coping: A meaning system approach. *Journal of Personality and Social Psychology, 77*(3), 588–599.

Horn, J. L., & Cattell, R. B. (1966). Refinement and test of the theory of fluid and crystallized general intelligence. *Journal of Educational Psychology, 57*(5), 253–270.

Hunt, E., & Wittmann, W. (2008). National intelligence and national prosperity. *Intelligence, 36*(1), 1–9.

John, O. P. (1990). The "Big Five" factor taxonomy: Dimensions of personality in the natural language and in questionnaires. In L. A. Pervin (Ed.), *Handbook of personality: Theory and research* (pp. 66–100). New York: Guilford Press.

John, O. P., & Srivastava, S. (1999). The Big Five trait taxonomy: History, measurement, and theoretical perspectives. In L. A. Pervin & O. P. John (Eds.), *Handbook of personality: Theory and research* (2nd ed., pp. 102–138). New York: Guilford Press.

Johnson, J. A. (1997). Units of analysis for the description and explanation of personality. In R. Hogan, J. A. Johnson, & S. R. Briggs (Eds.), *Handbook of personality psychology* (pp. 73–93). San Diego, CA: Academic Press.

Johnson, J. A., & Ostendorf, F. (1993). Clarification of the five-factor model with the abridged big five dimensional circumplex. *Journal of Personality and Social Psychology, 65*(3), 563–576.

Johnson, W. (2010). Understanding the genetics of intelligence: Can height help? Can corn oil? *Current Directions in Psychological Science, 19* (3), 177–182.

Johnson, W., & Bouchard Jr., T. J. (2005). The structure of human intelligence: It is verbal, perceptual, and image rotation (VPR), not fluid and crystallized. *Intelligence, 33*(4), 393–416.

Johnson, W., & Bouchard Jr., T. J. (2007). Sex differences in mental abilities: *g* masks the dimensions on which they lie. *Intelligence, 35*(1), 23–39.

Jones, L., & Thissen, D. (2007). A history and overview of psychometrics. *Handbook of Statistics, 26*, 1–28.

Kelly, E. L. (1955). Consistency of the adult personality. *American Psychologist, 10*(11), 659–681.

Kelly, E. L., & Fiske, D. W. (1950). The prediction of success in the VA training program in clinical psychology. *American Psychologist, 5*(8), 395–406.

Kelly, E. L., & Fiske, D. W. (1951). *The prediction of performance in clinical psychology.* Ann Arbor, MI: University of Michigan Press.

Kluckhohn, C., & Murray, H. A. (1948). *Personality in nature, society, and culture.* New York: A. A. Knopf.

Kraft, P., & Hunter, D. J. (2009). Genetic risk prediction—Are we there yet? *The New England Journal of Medicine, 360*(17), 1701–1703.

Krueger, R. F. (2002). Psychometric perspectives on comorbidity. In J. E. Helzer & J. J. Hudziak (Eds.), *Defining psychopathology in the 21st century: DSM–V and beyond* (pp. 41–54). Washington, DC: American Psychiatric Publishing, Inc.

Krueger, R. F., & Markon, K. E. (2006). Understanding psychopathology: Melding behavior genetics, personality, and quantitative psychology to develop an empirically based model. *Current Directions in Psychological Science, 15*(3), 113–117.

Krueger, R. F., Caspi, A., Moffitt, T. E., Silva, P. A., & McGee, R. (1996). Personality traits are differentially linked to mental disorders: A multitrait–multidiagnosis study of an adolescent birth cohort. *Journal of Abnormal Psychology, 105*(3), 299–312.

Kuncel, N. R., Hezlett, S. A., & Ones, D. S. (2001). A comprehensive meta-analysis of the predictive validity of the graduate record examinations: Implications for graduate student selection and performance. *Psychological Bulletin, 127*(1), 162–181.

Kuncel, N. R., Cred, M., & Thomas, L. L. (2007). A meta-analysis of the predictive validity of the graduate management admission test (GMAT) and undergraduate grade point average (UGPA) for graduate student academic performance. *The Academy of Management Learning and Education, 6*(1), 51–68.

Leary, M., & Hoyle, R. H. (Eds.) (2009). *Handbook of individual differences in social behavior.* New York: Guilford Press.

Little, B. R., Lecci, L., & Watkinson, B. (1992). Personality and personal projects: Linking Big Five and PAC units of analysis. *Journal of Personality, 60*(2), 501–525.

Lofquist, L. H., & Dawis, R. V. (1969). *Adjustment to work.* New York: Appleton-Century-Crofts.

London, H., & Exner, J. E. (1978). *Dimensions of personality.* New York: Wiley.

Lubinski, D., & Benbow, C. P. (2000). States of excellence. *American Psychologist, 55*(1), 137–150.

Lubinski, D., & Benbow, C. P. (2006). Study of mathematically precocious youth after 35 years: Uncovering antecedents for the development of math-science expertise. *Perspectives on Psychological Science, 1*(4), 316–345.

Markon, K. E., Krueger, R. F., & Watson, D. (2005). Delineating the structure of normal and abnormal personality: An integrative hierarchical approach. *Journal of Personality and Social Psychology, 88*(1), 139–157.

Mayer, J. D. (2001). Primary divisions of personality and their scientific contributions: From the trilogy-of-mind to the systems set. *Journal for the Theory of Social Behaviour, 31*(4), 449–477.

McAdams, D. P. (2008). Personal narratives and the life story. In O. P. John, R. Robins, & L. A. Pervin (Eds.), *Handbook of personality: Theory and research* (3rd ed., pp. 242–262). New York: Guilford Press.

McCrae, R. R. (1987). Creativity, divergent thinking, and openness to experience. *Journal of Personality and Social Psychology, 52*(6), 1258–1265.

McCrae, R. R., & Costa, J., P. T. (1997). Personality trait structure as a human universal. *American Psychologist, 52*(5), 509–516.

McCrae, R. R., & Costa, P. T. (1999). A five-factor theory of personality. In L. A. Pervin & O. P. John (Eds.), *Handbook of personality: Theory and research* (2nd ed., pp. 139–153). New York: Guilford Press.

McGrew, K. (2009). CHC theory and the human cognitive abilities project: Standing on the shoulders of the giants of psychometric intelligence research. *Intelligence, 37*(1), 1–10.

McGue, M., & Bouchard, T. J. (1998). Genetic and environmental influences on human behavioral differences. *Annual Review of Neuroscience, 21,* 1–24.

McPherson, W. B. (1901). Gideon's water-lappers. *Journal of the American Oriental Society, 22,* 70–75.

Mehl, M. R., & Pennebaker, J. W. (2003). The sounds of social life: A psychometric analysis of students' daily social environments and natural conversations. *Journal of Personality and Social Psychology, 84*(4), 857–870.

Mehl, M. R., Gosling, S. D., & Pennebaker, J. W. (2006). Personality in its natural habitat: Manifestations and implicit folk theories of personality in daily life. *Journal of Personality and Social Psychology, 90*(5), 862–877.

Mehl, M. R., Vazire, S., Ramirez-Esparza, N., Slatcher, R. B., & Pennebaker, J. W. (2007). Are women really more talkative than men? *Science, 317*(5834), 82.

Morley, H. (1891). *Character writings of the seventeenth century.* London: Kessinger.

Mount, M. K., Barrick, M. R., Scullen, S. M., & Rounds, J. (2005). Higher-order dimensions of the big five personality traits and the big six vocational interest types. *Personnel Psychology, 58*(2), 447–478.

Murray, H. A. (1938). *Explorations in personality: A clinical and experimental study of fifty men of college age.* New York: Oxford University Press.

Musson, D. M., Sandal, G. M., & Helmreich, R. L. (2004). Personality characteristics and trait clusters in final stage astronaut selection. *Aviation, Space, and Environmental Medicine, 75*(4), 342–349.

Norman, W. T. (1963). Toward an adequate taxonomy of personality attributes: Replicated factors structure in peer nomination personality ratings. *Journal of Abnormal and Social Psychology, 66*(6), 574–583.

Norman, W. T. (1969). "To see ourseles as ithers see us": Relations among self-perceptions, peer-perceptions, and expected peer-perceptions of personality attributes. *Multivariate Behavioral Research, 4*(4), 417–443.

Omura, K., Constable, R., & Canli, T. (2005). Amygdala gray matter concentration is associated with extraversion and neuroticism. *Neuroreport: For Rapid Communication of Neuroscience Research, 16*(17), 1905–1908.

Ortony, A., Norman, D. A., & Revelle, W. (2005). Affect and proto-affect in effective functioning. In J. Fellous & M. Arbib (Eds.), *Who needs emotions? The brain meets the machine* (pp. 173–202). New York: Oxford University Press.

Os, J. van, & Rutten, B. P. F. (2009). Gene–environment-wide interaction studies in psychiatry. *American Journal of Psychiatry, 166*(9), 964–966.

OSS Assessment Staff (1948). *Assessment of men: Selection of personnel for the office of strategic services*. New York: Rinehart.

Ozer, D. J., & Benet-Martinez, V. (2006). Personality and the prediction of consequential outcomes. *Annual Review of Psychology, 57*, 401–421.

Padilla, A., Hogan, R., & Kaiser, R. B. (2007). The toxic triangle: Destructive leaders, susceptible followers, and conducive environments. *Leadership Quarterly, 18*(3), 176–194.

Paunonen, S. V. (2003). Big Five factors of personality and replicated predictions of behavior. *Journal of Personality and Social Psychology, 84*(2), 411–422.

Pearson, K. P. (1896). Mathematical contributions to the theory of evolution. iii. Regression, heredity, and panmixia. *Philosophical Transactions of the Royal Society of London, Series A, 187*, 254–318.

Pedersen, N. L., Plomin, R., McClearn, G. E., & Friberg, L. (1988). Neuroticism, extraversion, and related traits in adult twins reared apart and reared together. *Journal of Personality and Social Psychology, 55*(6), 950–957.

Pervin, L. A. (1994). A critical analysis of current trait theory. *Psychological Inquiry, 5*(2), 103–113.

Plato (1892). *The republic: The complete and unabridged Jowett translation* (3rd ed.). Oxford: Oxford University Press.

Plomin, R., Owen, M., & McGuffin, P. (1994). The genetic basis of complex human behaviors. *Science, 264*(5166), 1733–1739.

Rafaeli, E., Rogers, G. M., & Revelle, W. (2007). Affective synchrony: Individual differences in mixed emotions. *Personality and Social Psychology Bulletin, 33*(7), 915–932.

Rauch, S. L., Milad, M. R., Orr, S. P., Quinn, B. T., Fischl, B., & Pitman, R. K. (2005). Orbitofrontal thickness, retention of fear extinction, and extraversion. *Neuroreport: For Rapid Communication of Neuroscience Research, 16*(17), 1909–1912.

Reid, S. C., Kauer, S. D., Dudgeon, P., Sanci, L. A., Shrier, L. A., & Patton, G. C. (2008). A mobile phone program to track young people's experiences of mood, stress and coping: Development and testing of the mobile type program. *Social Psychiatary and Psychiatric Epidemiology, 44*, 501–507.

Revelle, W. (2007). Experimental approaches to the study of personality. In R. Robins, R. C. Fraley, & R. F. Krueger (Eds.), *Handbook of research methods in personality psychology* (pp. 37–61). New York: Guilford Press.

Revelle, W. (2008). The contribution of reinforcement sensitivity theory to personality theory. In P. J. Corr (Ed.), *The reinforcement sensitivity theory of personality* (pp. 508–527). Cambridge: Cambridge University Press.

Revelle, W., & Oehlberg, K. (2008). Integrating experimental and observational personality research—The contributions of Hans Eysenck. *Journal of Personality, 76*(6), 1387–1414.

Revelle, W., Wilt, J., & Rosenthal, A. (2010). Personality and cognition: The personality–cognition link. In A. Gruszka, G. Matthews, & B. Szymura (Eds.), *Handbook of individual differences in cognition: Attention, memory and executive control* (pp. 27–49). New York: Springer.

Revelle, W., Humphreys, M. S., Simon, L., & Gilliland, K. (1980). Interactive effect of personality, time of day, and caffeine—Test of the arousal model. *Journal of Experimental Psychology General, 109*(1), 1–31.

Roberts, B. W., & Del Vecchio, W. F. (2000). The rank-order consistency of personality traits from childhood to old age: A quantitative review of longitudinal studies. *Psychological Bulletin, 126*(1), 3–25.

Roberts, B. W., & Robins, R. W. (2000). Broad dispositions, broad aspirations: The intersection of personality traits and major life goals. *Personality and Social Psychology Bulletin*, 26(10), 1284–1296.

Roberts, B. W., O'Donnell, M., & Robins, R. W. (2004). Goal and personality trait development in emerging adulthood. *Journal of Personality and Social Psychology*, 87(4), 541–550.

Roberts, B. W., Kuncel, N. R., Shiner, R., Caspi, A., & Goldberg, L. R. (2007). The power of personality: The comparative validity of personality traits, socioeconomic status, and cognitive ability for predicting important life outcomes. *Perspectives on Psychological Science*, 2(4), 313–345.

Robins, R. W., Fraley, R. C., & Krueger, R. F. (Eds.) (2007). *Handbook of research methods in personality psychology*. New York: Guilford Press.

Rohan, M. J. (2000). A rose by any name? The values construct. *Personality and Social Psychology Review*, 4(3), 255–277.

Rosato, E., & Kyriacou, C. P. (2008). Sleep, arousal, and rhythms in flies. *Proceedings of the National Academy of Sciences*, 105(50), 19567–19568.

Rozin, P. (2007). Exploring the landscape of modern academic psychology: Finding and filling the holes. *American Psychologist*, 62(8), 754–766.

Russell, J. A. (1980). A circumplex model of affect. *Journal of Personality and Social Psychology*, 39(6), 1161–1178.

Schaie, K. W. (2005). *Developmental influences on adult intelligence: The Seattle longitudinal study*. New York: Oxford University Press.

Schimmack, U., & Grob, A. (2000). Dimensional models of core affect: A quantitative comparison by means of structural equation modeling. *European Journal of Personality*, 14(4), 325–345.

Schimmack, U., & Reisenzein, R. (2002). Experiencing activation: Energetic arousal and tense arousal are not mixtures of valence and activation. *Emotion*, 2(4), 412–417.

Schmitt, D. P., Realo, A., Voracek, M., & Allik, J. (2008). Why can't a man be more like a woman? Sex differences in Big Five personality traits across 55 cultures. *Journal of Personality and Social Psychology*, 94(1), 168–182.

Schwartz, S. H., & Bilsky, W. (1987). Toward a universal psychological structure of human values. *Journal of Personality and Social Psychology*, 53(3), 550–562.

Smillie, L. D. (2008). What is reinforcement sensitivity theory? Neuroscience paradigms for approach–avoidance processes in personality *European Journal of Personality*, 22(5), 359–384.

Smillie, L. D., Loxton, N. J., & Avery, R. E. (2011: this volume). Reinforcement sensitivity theory, research, applications, and future. In T. Chamorro-Premuzic, S. von Stumm, & A. Furnham (Eds.), *The Wiley-Blackwell handbook of individual differences*. Oxford: Wiley-Blackwell.

Smillie, L. D., Pickering, A. D., & Jackson, C. J. (2006). The new reinforcement sensitivity theory: Implications for personality measurement. *Personality and Social Psychology Review*, 10(4), 320–335.

Spearman, C. (1904a). The proof and measurement of association between two things. *The American Journal of Psychology*, 15(1), 72–101.

Spearman, C. (1904b). "General intelligence," objectively determined and measured. *American Journal of Psychology*, 15(2), 201–292.

Spearman, C. (1946). Theory of general factor. *British Journal of Psychology*, 36(3), 117–131.

Spinath, F. M., & Johnson, W. (2011: this volume). Behavior genetics. In T. Chamorro-Premuzic, S. von Stumm, & A. Furnham (Eds.), *The Wiley-Blackwell handbook of individual differences*. Oxford: Wiley-Blackwell.

Stankov, L. (2009). Conservatism and cognitive ability. *Intelligence, 37*(3), 294–304.

Steinmayr, R., Beauducel, A., & Spinath, B. (2010). Do sex differences in a faceted model of fluid and crystallized intelligence depend on the method applied? *Intelligence, 38*(1), 101–110.

Stern, W. (1910). Abstracts of lectures on the psychology of testimony and on the study of individuality. *The American Journal of Psychology, 21*(2), 270–282.

Stern, W. (1914). *The psychological methods of testing intelligence.* Edited and translated by Guy Monrose Whipple. Baltimore, MD: Warwick and York, Inc.

Stigler, S. M. (1989). Francis Galton's account of the invention of correlation. *Statistical Science, 4,* 73–79.

Strelau, J. (1998). *Temperament: A psychological perspective.* New York: Plenum Press.

Strelau, J., & Eysenck, H. J. (1987). *Personality dimensions and arousal.* New York: Plenum Press.

Strong, E. K. (1927). Vocational interest test. *Educational Record, 8*(2), 107–121.

Tackett, J. L., Silber Schmidt, A. L., Krueger, R. F., & Sponheim, S. R. (2008). Dimensional model of personality disorder: Incorporating DSM cluster A characteristics. *Journal of Abnormal Psychology, 117*(2), 454–459.

Taillard, J., Philip, P., Coste, O., Sagaspe, P., & Bioulac, B. (2003). The circadian and homeostatic modulation of sleep pressure during wakefulness differs between morning and evening chronotypes. *Journal of Sleep Research, 12*(4), 275–282.

Terman, L. M. (1916). *The Measurement of intelligence.* Boston, MA: Houghton Mifflin.

Terman, L. M. (1925). *Genetic studies of genius.* Palo Alto, CA: Stanford University Press.

Terman, L. M., & Oden, M. (1947). *Genetic studies of genius.* Palo Alto, CA: Stanford University Press/Oxford University Press.

Thayer, R. E. (1989). *The biopsychology of mood and arousal.* New York: Oxford University Press.

Theophrastus (1870).*The characters of Theophrastus.* An English translation with introduction and notes by R. C. Jebb. London: Macmillan.

Thomson, G. H. (1935). The definition and measurement of "*g*" (general intelligence). *Journal of Educational Psychology, 26*(4), 241–262.

Thomson, S. (1951). *The factorial analysis of human ability* (5th ed.). London: University of London Press.

Thurstone, L. L. (1933). *The theory of multiple factors.* Ann Arbor, MI: Edwards Brothers.

Thurstone, L. L. (1935). *The vectors of mind: Multiple-factor analysis for the isolation of primary traits.* Chicago: University of Chicago Press.

Thurstone, L. L. (1947). *Multiple-factor analysis: A development and expansion of the vectors of the mind.* Chicago: University of Chicago Press.

Trull, T. J., & Sher, K. J. (1994). Relationship between the five-factor model of personality and Axis disorders in a nonclinical sample. *Journal of Abnormal Psychology, 103*(2), 350–360.

Tupes, E. C., & Christal, R. E. (1961). *Recurrent personality factors based on trait ratings* (Technical Report No. 61–97). Lackland Air Force Base: USAF ASD Technical Report.

Underwood, B. J. (1975). Individual differences as a crucible in theory construction. *American Psychologist, 30,* 128–134.

Van de Vijver, F., & Leung, K. (2008). Personality in cultural context: Methodological issues. *Journal of Personality, 69*(6), 1007–1031.

Van der Werff, J. J., & Verster, J. (1987). Heymans' temperamental dimensions recomputed. *Personality and Individual Differences, 8*(2), 271–276.

Vazire, S., & Gosling, S. D. (2003). Bridging psychology and biology with animal research. *American Psychologist, 58*(5), 407–408.

Vazire, S., Gosling, S. D., Dickey, A. S., & Schapiro, S. J. (2007). Measuring personality in nonhuman animals. In R. W. Robins, R. C. Fraley, & R. F. Krueger (Eds.), *Handbook of research methods in personality psychology* (pp. 190–206). New York: Guilford Press.

Vernon, P. E. (1965). Ability factors and environmental influences. *American Psychologist, 20*(9), 723–733.

Vul, E., Harris, C., Winkielman, P., & Pashler, H. (2009). Puzzlingly high correlations in fMRI studies of emotion, personality, and social cognition. *Perspectives on Psychological Science, 4*(3), 274–290.

Wacker, J., Chavanon, M.-L., & Stemmler, G. (2006). Investigating the dopaminergic basis of extraversion in humans: A multilevel approach. *Journal of Personality and Social Psychology, 91*(1), 171–187.

Warren, J. R., & Heist, P. A. (1960). Personality attributes of gifted college students. *Science, 132*(3423), 330–337. Available at www.jstor.org/stable/1706065.

Watson, D. (2000). *Mood and temperament.* New York: Guilford Press.

Watson, D. (2005). Rethinking the mood and anxiety disorders: A quantitative hierarchical model for DSM–V. *Journal of Abnormal Psychology, 114*(4), 522.

Watson, D., Clark, L. A., & Tellegen, A. (1988). Development and validation of brief measures of positive and negative affect: The PANAS scales. *Journal of Personality and Social Psychology, 54*(6), 1063–1070.

Watson, D., Gamez, W., & Simms, L. (2005). Basic dimensions of temperament and their relation to anxiety and depression: A symptom-based perspective. *Journal of Research in Personality, 39*(1), 46–66.

Widiger, T. A., & Costa, P. T. (1994). Personality and personality disorders. *Journal of Abnormal Psychology, 103*(1), 78–91.

Wiggins, J. S. (1973). *Personality and prediction: Principles of personality assessment.* Reading, MA: Addison-Wesley.

Willerman, L. (1979). *The psychology of individual and group differences.* San Francisco: W. H. Freeman.

Wilt, J., & Revelle, W. (2009). Extraversion. In M. Leary & R. H. Hoyle (Eds.), *Handbook of individual differences in social behavior* (pp. 27–45). New York: Guilford Press.

Winter, D. G., John, O. P., Stewart, A. J., Klohnen, E. C., & Duncan, L. E. (1998). Traits and motives: Toward an integration of two traditions in personality research. *Psychological Review, 105*(2), 230–250.

Wittmann, W. W. (1991). Meta-analysis and Brunswik symmetry. In G. Albrecht and H. U. Otto (Eds.), *Social prevention and the social sciences: Theoretical controversies, research problems, and evaluation strategies* (pp. 381–393). Oxford: Walter De Gruyter.

Wundt, W. (1874). *Grundzge der physiologischen Psychologie.* Leipzig/Bristol: Wilhelm Engelmann/Thoemmes Press.

Wundt, W. (1904). *Principles of physiological psychology.* Translated by E. B. Titchener (from the 5th German ed., 1902). London: Swan Sonnenschein.

Yerkes, R. M. (1918). Psychology in relation to the war. *Psychological Review, 25*(2), 85–115.

Zenderland, L. (2001). *Measuring minds: Henry Herbert Goddard and the origins of American intelligence testing.* Cambridge: Cambridge University Press.

# 2

# Methodological Advances in Differential Psychology

## William Revelle, David M. Condon, and Joshua Wilt

The goal of methods in differential psychology is no different from that of methods in any other science: descriptive and testable explanations of phenomena. Methods thus involve the collection and analysis of data. What distinguishes scientific fields from each other, and the field of differential psychology in particular, is what constitutes the data, the theories about these data, and the analytical techniques used to describe and model them. This chapter is divided into two main sections, which deal with the kinds and sources of data we collect and with the ways in which we model (analyze) the data. In view of the fact that entire textbooks are devoted to data collection, to design (Shadish, Cook, & Campbell, 2001), to inference (Pearl, 2000), and to each of many ways to model data (Judd, McClelland, & Ryan, 2009; Loehlin, 2004; McArdle, 2009; McDonald, 1999; Mulaik, 2010; Rasch, 1980), this review will necessarily concern the basic concepts rather than the specifics of individual methods. For a thorough discussion of research methods devoted to individual differences and limited to a narrow definition of personality (which do not include, for instance, intelligence, interests, or values), one should consult the handbook edited by Robins, Fraley, and Krueger (2007).

$$Data = Model + Error \tag{1}$$

A revolution in data analysis has occurred over the past 30 years: the recognition that we model data and compare alternative models to each other (Rodgers, 2010). This approach is summarized in equation 1—which, if we recognize that our error is someone else's signal, is better expressed as equation 2:

$$Data = Model + Residual \tag{2}$$

The process of research, then, is one of finding models that fit the data with acceptably small residual values. "Models, of course, are never true, but fortunately it is

*The Wiley-Blackwell Handbook of Individual Differences*, First Edition.
Edited by Tomas Chamorro-Premuzic, Sophie von Stumm, and Adrian Furnham.

only necessary that they be useful. For this it is usually needful that they not be grossly wrong" (Box, 1979, p. 2). The current approach goes beyond just asking for usefulness; it asks if the specified model is better than alternative models (Rodgers, 2010).

## Coomb's Theory of Data and Cattell's Data Box

The left-hand sides of equations 1 and 2 are data. What are the data that we collect? At an abstract level, data can be organized along three different dimensions: type of comparison (order vs. proximity), the elements being compared (people, objects, people × objects) and the number of comparisons (one or more; Coombs, 1964). Within this framework, a person can be said to be more than an object (e.g. when one is passing an ability test item) or to be near an object (when one is endorsing an attitude item); and one person can prefer one object to another object (be closer to one attitude than to another) or have a stronger preference than someone else. People can also differ in the way they group objects. The Coombs (1964) model continues to be used within psychometrics by virtue of the distinction between ability and preference items in item response theory (Chernyshenko, Stark, Drasgow, & Roberts, 2007) and in terms of individual differences in multidimensional scaling of situational stress.

Cattell's *data box* (Cattell, 1946) emphasized three sources of data—people, tests, and occasions—and considered how correlations can be made between tests and across people at one occasion (R analysis), just as correlations can be found between people across tests (Q analysis), or tests can be correlated within people across occasions (P analysis), and so on. Subsequently, Cattell (1966) expanded the data box to include background or preceding variables as well as observers. The data box concept has been used throughout differential psychology to demonstrate the many ways of analyzing data, but the primary influence has probably been on those who study personality, cognitive development, and change over the life span (McArdle & Bell, 2000; Mroczek, 2007; Nesselroade, 1984).

## Methods of Data Collection

Individual differences can be assessed by asking people about themselves (their identity) and about other people (their reputation) or by observing behavior (what people or other animals do), physiology, and behavioral residues. Of these, the predominant method is probably that of self-report through the use of questionnaires, projective instruments, or narratives.

### Self-report

"Do you get angry easily?" "Do you find it difficult to approach others?" "Do you make people feel at ease?" "Do you do things according to a plan?" "Do you carry the conversation to a higher level?" These are typical self-report items taken from the International Personality Item Pool (IPIP: Goldberg, 1999). They follow the basic principle that, if you want to know something about someone, you ask them. With the instruction to answer the way you normally behave, the obtained measures of traits like neuroticism, extraversion, agreeableness, conscientiousness, and openness show stability over long periods of time and correlate with suitable behavioral observations and other reports (Roberts, Kuncel, Shiner, Caspi, & Goldberg, 2007). In contrast to measures of ability, these items are thought to measure typical performance. In other words, they measure how one usually thinks, feels, and behaves rather than how *well* one *can* think.

A similar example would include self-report items that allow inference about the internal states of energetic arousal or tense arousal (Schimmack & Reisenzein, 2002; Thayer, 2000). When subjects are asked about energetic arousal (how alert, active, or vigorous one feels in contrast to sleepy, tired, or drowsy) or about tense arousal (anxious, worried, or tense vs. calm or relaxed), their scores will change over the day and in response to factors such as caffeine, exciting or depressing movies, and exercise (Revelle, 1993).

These items are direct and obvious. They may be formed into scales using factorially homogeneous keying (Goldberg, 1972), also known as an inductive strategy (Burisch, 1984). Classic examples of such inventories are the Eysenck Personality Inventory (EPI, Eysenck & Eysenck, 1968), the NEO–PI (Costa & McCrae, 1985), and the Sixteen Personality Factors (16PF, Cattell & Stice, 1957). Some inventories, however, are developed by using the empirical or external strategy of finding items that distinguish known groups from people in general, for instance the Minnesota Multiphasic Personality Inventory (MMPI; Hathaway & McKinley, 1943), or the Strong Vocational Interest Inventory (Strong, 1927). They also differ from rational or deductively constructed tests, such as the California Psychological Inventory (CPI: Gough, 1957) or the Personality Research Form (PRF: Jackson, 1967).

The advantages and disadvantages of empirical, rational, and homogeneous keying techniques were well reviewed by Goldberg (1972), by Hase and Goldberg (1967), and by Burisch (1984). In general, rational and factorial techniques work better for making predictions according to more predictable criteria, but empirical/external techniques are better able to predict very unpredictable events (e.g. dropping out of college). Tests assessing interests (Holland, 1959, 1996; Strong, 1927) have traditionally used empirical scale-construction methods and have incremental validity when predicting according to diverse criteria, such as success in graduate school (Kelly & Fiske, 1950).

Some ask how self-reports can be valid, given the tendency to dissimulate or to enhance one's self-image. Hogan and Nicholson (1988), Hogan and Kaiser (2005), and Hogan (2007) address this issue for predicting criteria related to real life (for instance for predicting leadership effectiveness in organizations). Self-report measures are quite successful at predicting this important category of criteria. Hogan, Barrett, and Hogan (2007) directly address the problem of faking and report that it did not pose real difficulties in selecting job applicants for security positions.

*Constructing self-report inventories*     Practical advice for constructing self-report inventories for the differential psychologist (e.g. Clark & Watson, 1995; Simms & Watson, 2007; Watson, 2005) emphasizes starting with a good theoretical understanding of the constructs to be measured and of the population of interest; then writing items that are clear and readable, examining the internal structure of the items, purifying the scales developed, checking for external validity in terms of correlations with criterion groups; and, finally, further refinement of items and extensive documentation. Issues to consider include breadth of the items, definition of the facets of the construct, clarity in the wording of items, response analysis using item response theory (IRT) techniques, suitability for the target population, and evidence for convergent validity, discriminant validity, and construct validity. Types of item selection techniques include: empirical items based upon known groups; homogeneous items based upon the factor/cluster structure of the domain of items; and just rational choice based upon theory.

## Narratives

Narrative approaches to individual differences have grown in popularity in recent years. Researchers collecting narrative data typically do so as a means to assess how people make sense of their lives (Pasupathi & Hoyt, 2009): Therefore the preferred units of analysis are life-stories or discrete scenes from one's life-story. Many narrative researchers work from the perspective of *narrative identity* (McAdams, 2008): from this perspective, the psychological construction and telling of a life-story brings together one's remembered past and imagined future into a narrative identity that potentially provides life with some degree of unity, meaning, and purpose (Singer, 2004). Life-stories feature particular scenes occurring at different times in one's life and, like all good stories, they convey a variety of themes through their structure, characters, and plot (McAdams, 1993).

Due to the massive number of scenes, events, and memories a person accumulates throughout a lifetime, quantitative analysis of narrative identity seems at first a daunting undertaking. Indeed, the cumbersome methods of the case study and the study of single lives are more amenable to qualitative analysis. However, modern narrative researchers have been up to the task, as the past two decades have seen steady growth in creative quantitative methodologies employed to analyze narratives.

One fruitful approach to dealing with the problem of scene selection is the introduction of the standardized life-story interview (McAdams, Diamond, St. Aubin, & Mansfield, 1997), in which people narrate a set of important scenes from their lives (high points, low points, turning points, vivid memories from childhood, adolescence, adulthood, and an imagined future scene) and trained human coders assess these scenes for structural and thematic elements. Studies employing this approach aggregate scores for such themes as emotional tone, complexity, and coherence (McAdams, 1993). Another approach for analyzing narratives, which focuses on the importance of individual scenes rather than on the entire story, is to have people narrate a self-defining memory (Singer & Blagov, 2004). Self-defining memories are especially emotional and vivid scenes that communicate how people came to be who they are today, and they may be coded similarly to the scenes in the life-story interview. An innovative method of assessing narrative data is to code the way people think about their own narratives, which is termed "autobiographical reasoning" (Habermas & Bluck, 2000). The process of autobiographical reasoning is analogous to telling a meta-narrative, as people reflect and comment on the meaning of different scenes in their own narratives and on what implications those scenes may have (McLean, 2005). Still others obviate the need for human coders by taking advantage of the ability of computerized text analysis programs to count words relevant to various thematic categories (Pennebaker, Mayne, & Francis, 1997). For example, researchers interested in how much positive emotional content is conveyed in a narrative have the ability to count how many positive emotional words—such as "happy," "joy," or "elated"—appear in their participants' narratives.

## Ability tests

The typical self-report inventory measures what people normally do. Ability tests measure how well they can do. Originally developed as predictors of poor school performance, ability tests such as the SAT (formerly known as the Scholastic Aptitude Test) and GRE (Graduate Record Exam) have become standard predictors of college and graduate student performance (Kuncel, Hezlett, & Ones, 2001; Kuncel, Cred, & Thomas, 2007). Commercial IQ tests are given in most clinical assessments. Within the field of cognitive abilities there have been two broad traditions: the psychometric measurement oriented approach and the cognitive process approach. With a better understanding of the cognitive processes involved in ability tests, it is thought to be possible to combine cognitive theory with advanced psychometric principles (e.g. item response theory) in order to create more efficient testing instruments (Embretson, 1998). Unlike the case of the open-source IPIP (Goldberg, 1999), there does not seem to be a public domain set of ability items that different labs can use. Rather there are sets of commercial tests, both in individualized and in group form, which need to be purchased, or "home brew" tests that are unique to particular lab groups.

Two fundamental assumptions of ability tests are that performance is not affected by motivational state and that all participants are performing to the best of their ability. This is, however, not true. Revelle (1993) brings compelling evidence that motivational states associated with caffeine or with diurnally variable energetic arousal affect ability test performance by up to one standard deviation. Individual differences in anxiety and stereotype threat (being at risk of confirming, as self-characteristic, a negative stereotype about one's ethnic or cultural group) have also been shown to affect cognitive performance, even on high-stakes testing.

## Other-report

The ratings of professional psychologists (Fiske, 1949), of teachers (Digman, 1963), of peers (Norman, 1963, 1969; Tupes & Christal, 1961), or of oneself show a remarkable degree of consistency in identifying five broad factors of behavior (Digman, 1990). These factors have become known as the "Big Five" dimensions of personality (Digman, 1990; Goldberg, 1990). However, not all find such a simple five-dimensional solution. Walker (1967), when comparing teacher, peer, and self-ratings among elementary school children, identified a two-dimensional circumplex structure, with primary axes that could be interpreted as activity and neuroticism.

With the use of appropriate Internet techniques, it is relatively easy is to get useful informant reports (Vazire, 2006).

## Behavioral observation

Self-report and, to a lesser extent, other-report have been the most prominent ways of assessing personality; however, perhaps the most intuitive way to do so is to observe how people actually behave. This sound reasoning underlies the use of behavioral observation. Although intuitive, behavioral observation has rarely been employed, which is due in part to the relatively high costs associated with devising a viable behavioral observation scheme (Funder, 2001). Indeed, it is much more difficult to develop a system for coding behavior, train coders, and actually conduct observations than it is to have individuals or informants fill out global personality ratings (Furr & Funder, 2007). Notwithstanding these costs, behavioral observation is worth pursuing, for the simple reason that actual behavior is what psychologists really care about (Baumeister, Vohs, & Funder, 2007). Thus behavioral observation may be held as a gold standard in differential psychology.

Behavioral observation may occur in natural settings or in laboratory settings. A long-standing goal of differential psychology has been to predict what people do in naturally occurring environments; however, it is obviously difficult to collect such data in a non-intrusive way. A new methodology, called EAR (electronically activated recorder: Mehl & Pennebaker, 2003), relies on a small recording device programmed to turn on and off throughout the day, recording for a few minutes at a time, and thus producing objective data from natural environments. Laboratory-based methods of behavioral observation by definition lack some of the external validity of naturalistic studies, but they offer controlled environments in which to examine behavior. The German Observational Study of Adult Twins (GOSAT) project of Borkenau, Riemann, Angleitner, and Spinath (2001) has had participants take part individually in structured laboratory activities designed to elicit behaviors relevant to the Big Five. Extending these researchers' methods, Noftle and Fleeson (2010) have recently reported the first results of a large-scale observational study of people interacting in group activities; these studies observed not only content of behavior, but also the degree to which behavior varies as a function of age across adulthood. Behavioral observation in the lab is not limited to adults: exemplary studies conducted by Emily Durbin and colleagues (Durbin, Hayden, Klein, & Olino, 2007; Durbin & Klein, 2006; Durbin, Klein, Hayden, Buckley, & Moerk, 2005) have used standard laboratory tasks designed specifically to elicit behavior related to the temperamental characteristics of childhood.

In each of the aforementioned studies, researchers had to make difficult decisions about what to observe. Indeed, no one study is large enough to catalogue all possible behaviors; thus it is important to consider very carefully one's theoretical reasons for choosing certain variables. Observational studies may assess discrete behaviors (e.g. smiles) by counting the frequencies of their occurrence, or by having observers make a single rating of a target on behavioral dimensions (Borkenau, Mauer, Riemann, Spinath, & Angleitner, 2004). Coding systems for behavior/emotion are available; the Riverside behavioral Q-sort (Funder, Furr, & Colvin, 2000) and the facial action coding system (FACS) developed by Ekman, Friesen, & Hager (1978) are perhaps the best known and well-validated measures. Choices also have to be made about how many observers to employ, who should observe the target behavior, and whether observation should be done live or from video recordings (Furr & Funder, 2007). These choices should be guided by the theoretical questions each study is attempting to answer. It is also important to assess the quality of coded data; indices of inter-rater agreement are typically computed as intra-class correlations (Shrout & Fleiss, 1979), which in turn may be computed in various ways in order to suit best the structure of one's coding system. The recent increase in commitment to behavioral observation and the advances in technology that make this method more feasible are moving differential psychology toward becoming a more mature science of actual behavior.

## Physiological measures

The utilization of physiological measures is typically done with the purpose of discovering the biological basis or the etiology of individual differences (Harmon-Jones & Beer, 2009). Neuroimaging techniques are among the most popular physiological measures employed; the specific neuroimaging technique used in a particular study depends on the theoretical question the study is designed to investigate. Researchers interested in how brain *structure* relates to individual differences rely on magnetic resonance imaging (MRI) in order to generate detailed images of the brain (DeYoung et al., 2010). Studies concerned with brain activity may use functional MRI (fMRI) (Canli, 2004). Functional MRI relies on the blood–oxygen-level dependent (BOLD) contrast effect in order to measure blood flow as an indicator of brain activity. Another way in which differential psychologists measure brain *activity* (Johnson et al., 1999) is by positron emission tomography (PET), which detects gamma rays emitted from a tracer introduced to the body to generate images. Functional MRI and PET have good spatial resolution but poor temporal resolution; therefore researchers interested in measuring brain processes as they occur (Wacker, Chavanon, & Stemmler, 2006) may prefer to use electroencephalography (EEG). EEG records the electrical activity along the scalp generated by neurons firing in the brain; it has good temporal resolution, but poor spatial resolution. A popular physiological measure outside of the brain is salivary cortisol (Chida & Steptoe, 2009), which relates to the hypothalamic-pituitary axis of stress-response. Other physiological measures showing reliable individual differences include body temperature (Baehr, Revelle, & Eastman, 2000), blood pressure, heart rate, skin conductance, and eye-blink startle response (Diamond & Otter-Henderson, 2007).

## Remote data collection

Perhaps the most challenging methodological question for personality researchers springs from the desire to assess individual differences in a manner that holistically reflects all the relevant aspects of personality, and to do so through the use of assessment tools with fine-grain accuracy. In fact this is generally not possible, on account of limitations regarding the number of items that individual participants are willing to take. The historical solution to this challenge has been the pursuit of accurate data which are limited to a unique domain. Today it is possible to meet the challenge through the use of remote data collection procedures and the combination of responses from vastly greater sample sizes. The technique of *synthetic aperture personality assessment* (SAPA: Revelle, Wilt, & Rosenthal, 2010) gives each participant a small subset of items from a larger item pool, and then combines the responses across subjects to synthetically form very large covariance matrices.

The main source of remote data collection comes from survey-oriented, web-based studies. Although the use of Internet samples is appealing in terms of ease of collection and diversity of the samples (Gosling, Vazire, Srivastava, & John, 2004), this relatively new method does present some unique challenges. Of considerable importance is the implementation of safeguards against the incidence of repeated participation by the same subject. The incidence of more insidious damaging phenomena (such as misrepresentation or item-skipping) is more difficult to avoid and must therefore be taken into account during data analysis (J. A. Johnson, 2005). In addition, traditional paper-and-pencil measures do not always transfer to electronic formats without distortion and, even when such migrations are possible, care must be taken to maintain validity (Buchanan, Johnson, & Goldberg, 2005). To this end, a large number of scales have been made accessible and placed in the public domain through the central IPIP repository (Goldberg et al., 2006).

While the web-based studies are the primary source of growth where the use of remote data collection is concerned, several other technologies contribute to this methodology. Some of these measures are presented below, in the context of longitudinal studies. Notably, recent advances in "self-tracking" technologies provide more reliable replacements to diary-based studies of behavioral and affective measures. One example of this technology is the EAR employed by Mehl, Vazire, Ramirez-Esparza, Slatcher, and Pennebaker (2007). Research based on the use of this device to date has explored differences in conversational habits across gender and well-being.

## National and international surveys

One consideration for researchers who are interested in exploring individual differences in longitudinal research is that data from some studies are openly accessible. For instance, the US Bureau of Labor Statistics allows free access to the results of several longitudinal surveys (though some data sets may require application). Examples of these studies include the National Longitudinal Survey of Youth (NLSY79), which has tracked about 13,000 young men and women since 1979 and their biological children since 1988 (Harvey, 1999). Many other countries (including Britain, Australia, Korea, Switzerland, Canada, and Germany) offer comparable data sets, which are openly available or can be accessed through the Cross-National Equivalent File (Burkhauser & Lillard, 2007). Of course, many research topics are not amenable to the use of pre-existing data sets. When appropriate, however, these resources can be a practical and invaluable means of conducting longitudinal or cross-sectional analyses in a fraction of the time that is typically required.

In addition to these longitudinal data sets, large-scale assessments often make use of multiple data collection methods. The Programme for International Student Assessment (PISA), for example, employs both survey methods (for collecting information about participants' backgrounds and opinions) and behavioral methods (for testing participants' aptitude in mathematics, reading, science, and problem-solving skills). The data from PISA assessments, which are conducted with 15-year-old participants every three years in as many as 65 countries, are disseminated by the Organization for Economic Cooperation and Development (OECD) and are freely available for analysis (Anderson, Lin, Treagust, Ross, & Yore, 2007; see e.g. Hunt & Wittmann, 2008, in an examination of the relationships between national intelligence, levels of educational attainment, and national prosperity). A variety of other topics are covered through similar assessments by national and international agencies, including the International Monetary Fund, the World Health Organization and the United Nations. Despite lacking the flexibility of customized designs, use of such data allows for insightful comparative analyses across countries and large groups.

## Animal research

As it has done in other fields, the study of animal behavior offers individual difference researchers the opportunity to design experiments which would be impractical or unethical to conduct with human subjects (Vazire, Gosling, Dickey, & Schapiro, 2007). Until recently, the use of animal research to study differential psychology was primarily in lesion and drug studies (e.g. Gray, 1982; Gray & McNaughton, 2000) or in multi-generation selection studies for reactivity in the rat (Broadhurst, 1975). Observational studies of ongoing behavior in non-human animals in unrestricted environments has been relatively limited, having been constrained by measurement challenges (Gosling & Vazire, 2002) and by the "specter of anthropomorphism" (Gosling & John, 1999). Research to date has included such obvious subjects as dogs and chimpanzees—in addition to more surprising choices, such as snakes and octopuses (Gosling, 2001), or the pumpkinseed sunfish (Coleman & Wilson, 1998). Such animal research is currently limited to the use of observational reports on behavior and include a number of unique challenges (Vazire et al., 2007). It is likely, however, that the ability of animal research to contribute to the study of human personality will increase over time, as best practices are identified and further developed.

## Types of Design

As has been ruefully commented upon many times (Cronbach, 1957; Eysenck, 1966; Vale & Vale, 1969), the broad field of psychology has adopted two seemingly antithetical approaches: the *experimental* and the *observational*. Reconciliations and unifications of these approaches have been repeatedly called for (Cronbach, 1957, 1975; Eysenck, 1997), but with limited success (Revelle & Oehlberg, 2008). Both approaches have the same goal: to identify (causal) sources of variance, unconfounded by other variables.

The classic difference between these two approaches has been one of emphasis: an emphasis upon central tendencies versus variation, or upon statistics emphasizing group differences ($t$ and $F$), versus those emphasizing variation and covariation ($s^2$ and $r$). But, with the realization that these statistics are all special cases of the *general linear model*, it became clear that the difference was not one of analysis, but rather of theory testing.

# Experimental Approaches

The essence of an experimental approach is *random assignment* to condition. Randomization serves to break the correlation between experimentally manipulated *independent variables* (IVs) and non-observed but potentially *confounding variables* (CVs). The set of potentially confounding variables is infinite, but includes individual differences in age, sex, social status, education, prior experience, and motivation, as well as situational variables such as time of day, immediate past experience, interactions between subject variables and experimenter characteristics (e.g. sex of subject interacting with sex of experimenter). By randomly assigning participants to experimental conditions, the expected value of the correlation of the IVs with the CVs is zero. Although never actually zero, as sample size increases, the unobserved confounding correlations will tend toward zero.

## Person by condition interactions

Experimental approaches to the study of individual differences would seem oxymoronic, for how can we randomly assign individual differences? We cannot. But we can investigate the relationship between individual differences and experimentally manipulated conditions to test theories of individual differences. The power of interactions between individual differences (sometimes called *person variables* or PVs) and our experimental IVs is that the PV × IV interaction allows for a clearer understanding of the limits of the effects of both. Interactions show the limit of an effect. By having an interaction, we can rule out many extraneous explanations. That introversion is associated with better performance in exams could be due to the fact that introverts are smarter than their more extraverted colleagues. But, with a stress manipulation that reverses the rank orders of introversion and performance, we can rule out an explanation due to ability (Revelle, Amaral, & Turriff, 1976).

*Between-person vs. within-person*   Individual differences researchers study factors that vary across individuals (between-person variability) and factors that vary across time and situation within the same individual (within-person variability).[1] It is important to realize that, although the between-person relationship for two variables will mirror the within-person relationship for those variables in some instances, this is not necessarily the case (Fleeson, Malanos, & Achille, 2002). Thus, for the same reason why questions pertaining to between-group and within-group relationships must be analyzed separately, so must investigations of between-person and within-person relationships.

## Lab-based

The power of interaction of an experimental variable with an individual difference variable was shown in a series of experimental studies examining the effect of caffeine-induced arousal on cognitive performance. Rather than finding any main effects of individual differences or of caffeine, the studies made it clear that caffeine enhanced performance for some of the people, some of the time. The first study in this series showed that caffeine and time pressure hindered the performance on a complex test similar to the Graduate Record Exam by about .6 standard deviations for the most introverted participants, while simultaneously enhancing performance to about the same degree for the more extraverted participants (Revelle et al., 1976). This was initially taken as evidence in favor of the arousal model of extraversion (H. J. Eysenck, 1967). But, with further examination, this effect proved to be true only in the morning, and only for the impulsivity sub-component of extraversion (Revelle, Humphreys, Simon, & Gilliland, 1980). This led to a rethinking of the arousal model as well as to a reconceptualization of the measurement of extraversion (Rocklin & Revelle, 1981). Indeed, further experiments involving the interactions of anxiety with feedback manipulations, and the demonstration of the independence of these effects from the caffeine effects, led to a theory which integrates trait and state individual differences with situational stressors and cognitive processes (Humphreys & Revelle, 1984).

Lab-based studies have long been a staple of the research investigating reinforcement sensitivity theory (RST: Corr, 2008). Recent studies attempting to integrate theories of functional impulsivity with RST (Smillie & Jackson, 2006) and to test whether fear and anxiety originate from separable neurobehavioral systems described by RST (Perkins, Kemp, & Corr, 2007) continue in this tradition. Additionally, research on individual differences in anxiety (Wilt, Oehlberg, & Revelle, 2010) exemplify the wide range of experimental methods available (Armstrong, Olatunji, Simmons, & Sarawgi, 2010); Fox, Russo, Bowles, & Dutton, 2001) to differential psychologists.

## Randomized field studies

Although typically associated with lab-based studies, experimental design also enhances field studies (Cook, Campbell, & Day, 1979). Consider the effect of anxiety on student performance in a gateway science course (in this case, a year-long course in biology is a requirement for a major in biological sciences: Born, Revelle, & Pinto, 2002). Prior work had suggested that performance is enhanced for women and minority students when they are assigned to study groups. To avoid confounding with a "volunteer effect," Born et al. (2002) examined how study groups interacted with anxiety and gender by randomly assigning volunteers to study groups or a control condition. At the end of the year they were able to disentangle the study group effect (by comparing those randomly assigned to study groups and their randomly matched controls) from the volunteer effect (by comparing volunteers not assigned to study groups with non-volunteers).

Many long-term health studies have randomly assigned participants to conditions. When analyzing these data, it is tempting just to include those who follow the research protocol. Unfortunately, this is where individual differences become very important, for it has been found that conscientious placebo takers have reduced mortality rates by comparison with their non-adherent counterparts (Gallagher,

Viscoli, & Horwitz, 1993; Horwitz et al., 1990; Irvine et al., 1999) That is, the behavioral correlates of personality can swamp any effects due to an experimental manipulation.

## Observational Approaches

In contrast to experimental studies, which can examine the causal relationship between environmental manipulations and individual performance, observational studies try to infer latent states on the basis of the covariance of various measures at one time or of the patterning of results across time.

### Cross-sectional studies

Far more than any other type of design, cross-sectional studies represent the predominant approach in researching individual differences. When employed to its full potential, a single cross-sectional design has the power to capture a wide variety of correlations across multiple domains and to emphasize the relevance of individual differences in the process. Most of the published literature reflects this approach and does not need to be discussed here.

### Longitudinal studies

Though substantially outnumbered by cross-sectional designs, longitudinal studies have played a crucial role in the evolution of differential psychology as a field. The primary reason why relatively few researchers have employed longitudinal designs historically is that such designs require a greater commitment of resources and are therefore thought to introduce incremental risk, especially in academic environments, where funding is uncertain and career development is often tied to publication. However, it is also the case that carefully constructed longitudinal studies can be considerably more powerful than cross-sectional designs and that this incremental power should be taken into account when comparing the merits of the two approaches (Costa & McCrae, 1992). While longitudinal studies may introduce new confounding variables, they typically reduce the variance of cross-sectional measures of a given construct by virtue of repeated measures. More importantly, they allow researchers to gather data on many topics (e.g. the stability of traits over the life span) which cannot be adequately addressed through cross-sectional approaches.

Longitudinal methods represent "the long way" of studying personality (Block, 1993), and in some cases those lengths have extended well beyond 50 years. Though these long-term studies are able to clarify a number of important issues, their explicit—and perhaps most important—goal is to identify the factors that lead to longer and healthier lives. For instance, several prominent examples of longitudinal research have explored the relationship between intelligence, morbidity, and mortality, a field recently referred to as cognitive epidemiology (Deary, 2009).

Based on the Scottish mental health surveys of 1932 and 1947 and on subsequent follow-ups, findings from Deary, Whiteman, Starr, Whalley, and Fox (2004) demonstrate that higher intelligence levels in youth are predictive both of survival and of functional independence in old age. An earlier example is Terman's Life-Cycle Study, which began in 1921 and tracked high IQ school children until their deaths (Friedman et al., 1995; Terman & Oden, 1947). Though the measures used by Terman were less developed than those in use today, they were progressive for their time and sufficient for correlating life expectancy outcomes with subsequently developed personality constructs such as the Big Five. Most notably, the findings include correlations between longevity, conscientiousness, and a lack of impulsivity.

Within the field of cognitive epidemiology, many researchers are using longitudinal methods to further specify the factors which mediate life outcomes. In terms of the differential effects of maturational and generational changes, Elder (1998) has performed comparative analyses across longitudinal cohorts within the Terman's Life-Cycle Study and with studies of the Berkeley Institute, which tracked children born approximately 10 and 20 years after the "Termites" (Block, 1971; Elder, 1998). On the basis of the age differences across these samples, Elder has focused his analysis on the differential developmental impacts of the Great Depression and of the Second World War (Elder, 1998; Elder, Shanahan, & Clipp, 1994). In the case of the Second World War, sample participants who were older when entering military service paid a higher price in terms of health outcomes and career interruption than those who entered at younger ages (Elder et al., 1994). His findings suggest that even global, historical events of this nature can have non-uniform effects across populations, effects which are largely dependent on age.

While comparison across different longitudinal designs is one method of examining cohort effects, the Seattle Longitudinal Study (SLS) achieved similar comparisons in a single study through the use of sampling with replacement (Schaie, 1994). In addition to the repeated assessment of the initial sample, findings from the SLS have been meaningfully informed by the addition of new participants at each seven-year assessment. In all cases, participants have been drawn from the membership of a health maintenance organization (HMO) group in the Seattle, Washington area and include a wide variety of professionals from white- and blue-collar jobs and their family members. Despite this limited commonality, each assessment group has included participants reflecting a wide range of ages.

Chief among the findings of the SLS is the presence of substantial generational differences across the six latent constructs according to participants' birth year. In other words, it is not only the case that participants' intellectual abilities vary by age, but they also vary differentially, from one generational cohort to the next. While several factors have been proposed to explain this effect (Flynn, 1987, 1999, 2000), correlational data from the SLS suggest that improvements and exposure to formal education are explanatory factors. In any case, the SLS highlights the unique power of longitudinal studies by suggesting that prior cross-sectional studies which explored age-related declines in cognitive ability may inaccurately estimate the degree of decline due to cohort differences (Schaie, 1994).

Among more recent longitudinal research, the Study of Mathematically Precocious Youth (SMPY) was begun by Stanley in 1971 and continued by Benbow, Lubinski, and their collaborators (Benbow, Lubinski, & Stanley, 1996) with the intent of identifying and addressing the educational needs of mathematically gifted children.

Though the scope of the study was later broadened slightly so as to include the needs of children who are gifted in other domains (Lubinski & Benbow, 2006), SMPY remains distinguished by the depth to which it has explored the relationship between the ability, the temperament, and the interests of uniquely gifted children. Assessment is ongoing, but findings from SMPY will undoubtedly inform recent efforts to encourage greater interest among students in science, technology, engineering, and mathematics (the "STEM" areas).

*Brief within-subject studies* The process of tracking subjects over long periods is both the primary advantage of longitudinal studies and the primary reason why they are not more widely implemented. Not only is it more costly and arduous to maintain contact with participants after the initial phase of data collection, but longitudinal designs seldom produce meaningful findings over a short time horizon (Costa & McCrae, 1992). One means of mitigating this aspect of longitudinal design is to limit the duration of the study and/or to increase the frequency of data collection.

When the duration of study and the frequency of data collection are drastically changed, as occurs in brief within-subject studies, the resulting design may no longer appear longitudinal in nature (though it is still clearly distinct from a cross-sectional one). Studies of this type assess participants at very short intervals, for a period of days or weeks, and are used to explore the ways in which behavior is affected by transient affective states, motivational pressures, and diurnal rhythms. Of course, these designs cannot assess the long-term stability of attributes, as typical longitudinal studies do, but this trade-off is acceptable when studying fine-grained behavioral patterns, which are often lost between the infrequent measurement intervals of long-range studies.

Historically, experiments of this nature were restricted to the use of diary formats and, as a result, they suffered from shortcomings related to data quality. Fortunately the introduction of several new technologies in recent years has helped to increase the ease of using this methodology. While cell phones are the most ubiquitous form adopted in this technology, the list includes a broad array of self-tracking tools capable of measuring an increasing number of behavioral and interpersonal activities.

Of course the use of these technologies with longitudinal designs of longer durations is possible as well, but there are limits to the participants' willingness to devote their free time to academic research. While some existing technologies are able to collect and upload data via the Internet with minimal human involvement, the most germane data typically require a degree of self-reflection on behalf of the participant. In this respect, long-term studies with high frequencies of data collection are not likely to employ current personality measures.

Nevertheless, the implementation of new data collection technologies will almost certainly influence the evolution of data collection *techniques*, and there is reason to believe that this will be especially true in relation to brief within-subject designs. One hopes that further innovative development of these technologies will lead to exciting advances in personality research.

# Methods of Analysis

If Data = Model + Residual, the fundamental question of analysis is how to estimate the model. This depends, of course, on what the model is, but in general the method is to use the appropriate computational tool, whether this is a graphical description of the data or multi-wave, multi-level latent class analysis. For almost all the problems facing the individual differences researcher, the appropriate computations can be done in the open-source statistical system, R (R Development Core Team, 2010). Developed by a dedicated group of excellent statisticians, R has become the *lingua franca* of statistics and is becoming more used within psychology. In addition to the basic core R program, which is freely available for download from the web, there are more than 2,400 specialized packages developed for different applications. A growing number of these packages are devoted to the problems of data analysis faced by the individual differences researcher (such as the *psych* package by Revelle, 2010). R is not only free, but also very powerful; it is the statistics system of choice for individual differences research.

## Summary statistics and the problem of scaling

The most simple model of data is just the central tendency. But, depending upon distributional properties such as skew, the two most common estimates (mean and median) can give drastically different values. Consider the case of family income in the United States according to the US Census from 2008. Although the mean family income was $66,570, the median income was just $48,060. Any analysis using income as a covariate needs to take into account its log-normal characteristics. Beside offering graphical tools to detect such skewness, R has many ways to transform the data so as to produce "better behaved" versions of them.

Non-linearities in the relationship between the latent variable of interest and the observed variable can lead to "fan-fold" interactions between ability and experimental manipulations (or just time), which suggest that individuals with higher initial scores change more or less than individuals with initially lower scores. Consider the hypothetical effect of one year of college upon writing and mathematics performance. Writing scores at one university go from 31 to 70, for an increase of 39 points, but at another the scores go from 1 to 7, for an increase of 6 points. Most people would interpret this interaction (a gain of 39 vs. a gain of 6 points) as reflecting either the quality of instruction or the quality and motivation of the students. But, when the same schools show that math scores at the first university improve by just 6 points, from 93 to 99, while going up 39 points (from 30 to 69) at the other school, they interpret this change as representing a ceiling effect for the math test. But this interaction is exactly the same (although reversed) as the previous one. Such interactions due to the properties of the scale are also called *floor* and *ceiling* effects, which can be eliminated with the appropriate monotone transformation. Unfortunately, these transformations tend to be applied only if the interaction goes against expectation (Revelle, 2007).

## The correlation coefficient and its nearest relatives

Sir Francis Galton may be credited with developing the theory of the correlation coefficient in his paper on "co-relations and their measurement" (Galton, 1888), which followed his paper (Galton, 1886) discussing the "the coefficient of reversion." Although the correlation was originally found by graphically fitting slopes to the medians for different values of the predictor (Galton, 1888), Pearson (1896) introduced the correlation coefficient bearing his name as the average cross product (the covariance) of standard scores:

$$r_{xy} = Cov_{z_x z_y} = Cov_{\frac{x}{\sigma_x} \frac{y}{\sigma_y}} = \frac{Cov_{xy}}{\sigma_x \sigma_y} \tag{3}$$

And then Spearman (1904b) introduced the formula to psychologists, in terms of deviation scores:

$$r = \frac{\sum x_i y_i}{\sqrt{\sum x_i^2 \sum y_i^2}} \tag{4}$$

It is equation 4 that is most useful for seeing the relationship between the *Pearson product moment correlation coefficient* and a number of other measures of correlation (Table 2.1). When the data are continuous, $r$ is known as a Pearson $r$. If the data are expressed in ranks, then this is just the Spearman rho ($\rho$). If $x$ is dichotomous and $y$ continuous, the resulting correlation is known as a point bi-serial. If both $x$ and $y$ are dichotomous, the correlation is known as $\phi$. All of these use the same formula, although there are shortcuts that used to be used. Three additional correlation coefficients are listed which, with the assumption of bivariate normality, are equivalent to a Pearson $r$.

Researchers with an experimental bent tend to report seemingly different statistical estimates of the effect of one variable upon another. These are, however, merely

**Table 2.1**  A number of correlations are Pearson $r$ in different forms, or with particular assumptions. If $r = \dfrac{\sum x_i y_i}{\sqrt{\sum x_i^2 \sum y_i^2}}$, then depending upon the type of data being analyzed, a variety of correlations are found

| Coefficient | symbol | X | Y | Assumptions |
|---|---|---|---|---|
| Pearson | r | continuous | continuous | |
| Spearman | rho ($\rho$) | ranks | ranks | |
| Point bi-serial | $r_{pb}$ | dichotomous | continuous | |
| Phi | $\phi$ | dichotomous | dichotomous | |
| Bi-serial | $r_{bis}$ | dichotomous | continuous | normality |
| Tetrachoric | $r_{tet}$ | dichotomous | dichotomous | bivariate normality |
| Polychoric | $r_{pc}$ | categorical | categorical | bivariate normality |

**Table 2.2** Alternative estimates of effect size. Using the correlation as a scale-free estimate of effect size allows for combining experimental and correlational data in a metric that is directly interpretable, as the effect of a standardized unit change in $x$ leads to $r$ change in standardized $y$

| Statistic | Estimate | $r$ equivalent | as a function of $r$ |
|---|---|---|---|
| Pearson correlation | $r_{xy} = \dfrac{C_{xy}}{\sigma_x \sigma_y}$ | $r_{xy}$ | |
| Regression | $b_{y \cdot x} = \dfrac{C_{xy}}{\sigma^2}$ | $r = b_{y \cdot x} \dfrac{\sigma_y}{\sigma_x}$ | $b_{y \cdot x} = r \dfrac{\sigma_x}{\sigma_y}$ |
| Cohen's $d$ | $d = \dfrac{X_1 - X_2}{\sigma_x}$ | $r = \dfrac{d}{\sqrt{d^2 + 4}}$ | $d = \dfrac{2r}{\sqrt{1 - r^2}}$ |
| Hedge's $g$ | $g = \dfrac{X_1 - X_2}{s_x}$ | $r = \dfrac{g}{\sqrt{g^2 + 4(df/N)}}$ | $g = \dfrac{2r\sqrt{df/N}}{\sqrt{1 - r^2}}$ |
| t-test | $t = \dfrac{d\sqrt{df}}{2}$ | $t = \sqrt{t^2/(t^2 + df)}$ | $t = \sqrt{\dfrac{r^2 df}{1 - r^2}}$ |
| F-test | $F = \dfrac{d^2 df}{4}$ | $r = \sqrt{F/(F + df)}$ | $F = \dfrac{r^2 df}{1 - r^2}$ |
| Chi square | | $r = \sqrt{\chi^2/n}$ | $\chi^2 = r^2 n$ |
| Odds ratio | $d = \dfrac{\ln(OR)}{1.81}$ | $r = \dfrac{\ln(OR)}{1.81\sqrt{(\ln(OR)/1.81)^2 + 4}}$ | $\ln(OR) = \dfrac{3.62r}{\sqrt{1 - r^2}}$ |
| $r_{equivalent}$ | $r$ with probability $p$ | $r = r_{equivalent}$ | |

transformations of the Pearson $r$ (Table 2.2). Useful reviews of the use of these and other ways of estimating *effect sizes* for meta-analysis include Rosnow, Rosenthal, and Rubin (2000) and the special issue of *Psychological Methods* devoted to effect sizes (Becker, 2003).

With an appreciation of the different forms of the correlation it is possible to analyze traditional data sets more appropriately and to reach important conclusions. In medicine and clinical psychology for example, diagnoses tend to be categorical (someone is depressed or not, someone has an anxiety disorder or not). Co-occurrence of both of these symptoms is called *co-morbidity*. Diagnostic categories vary in their degree of co-morbidity with other diagnostic categories. From the point of view of correlation, co-morbidity is just a name applied to one cell in a four-fold table. It is possible to analyze co-morbidity rates by considering the probability of the separate diagnoses and the probability of the joint diagnosis. This gives the 2 × 2 table needed for a *phi* or a $r_{tet}$ correlation. For instance, given the base rates (proportions) of two diagnostic categories (e.g. anxiety = .2 and depression = .15) and their co-occurrence (co-morbidity, e.g. .1), it is straightforward to find the tetrachoric correlation between the two diagnoses (.75). By using this basic fact, Krueger (2002) converted the co-morbidities of various mental disorders to a matrix of tetrachoric correlations suitable for factor analysis, and he was able to argue for a two-dimensional structure (internalizing and externalizing disorders) for a broad set of personality disorders.

## Multiple $R$ and the general linear model

A straightforward generalization of bivariate correlation and regression is the problem of multiple predictor variables and multiple correlation (Pearson, 1901). The problem is one of distinguishing between the *direct effect* of a predictor and its *total effect*. The total effect is the observed correlation, but the direct effect removes the effect of the other, correlated predictors. For a data matrix $_NX_n$ of N observations and $n$ predictor variables and one criterion variable, $y$, if each of the predictor variables ($x_1$ ... $x_n$) relates to $y$ with correlations $r_{xy} = r_{x1y}$ ... $r_{xny}$ and the $x$ variables are themselves intercorrelated with the correlation matrix $R$, then the predicted values of $y$ ( $\hat{y}$ ) are:

$$\hat{y} = \beta X = r_{xy} R^{-1} X \tag{5}$$

If the members of the predictor set $x_i$ ... $x_n$ are uncorrelated, then each separate variable makes a unique contribution to the dependent variable $y$, and $R^2$, the amount of variance accounted for in $y$, is the sum of the individual $r_{iy}^2$. Unfortunately, most predictors are correlated, and the $\beta$s found in equation 5 are less than the original correlations; and, since

$$R^2 = \sum \beta_i r_{xiy} = \beta' r_{xy},$$

the $R^2$ will be less as the predictors become more correlated. An interesting, but unusual, case is that of *suppression*, where a predictor $x_s$ does not relate to the criterion $y$, but does relate to the other predictors. In this case $x_s$ is still useful, because it removes the variance in the other predictors not associated with the criterion. This leads to an interesting research problem; for not only do we need to look for predictors of our criterion variable, we also need to look for non-predictors that predict the predictors!

The predictor set can be made up of any combination of variables, including the products or powers of the original variables. The products (especially when mean centered) represent the *interactions* of predictors (Cohen, Cohen, West, & Aiken, 2003; Judd et al., 2009). Basic regression, multiple regression, and graphic displays of residuals are all available in R using the *lm* or *glm* functions (which apply the linear model and generalized linear model, respectively). The latter consider cases where the dependent (criterion) variable is dichotomous, as in success or failure (logistic regression), or consists of discrete count data, such as number of days missing school or number of times married (Poisson, quasi-Poisson, and negative binomial regression).

## Spurious correlations

Although he viewed the correlation coefficient as perhaps his greatest accomplishment, Pearson (1910) listed a number of sources of *spurious correlations* (Aldrich,

1995). These are challenges to all kinds of correlation, simple as well as multiple. Among them are the problems of ratios and of sums, and that of correlations induced by mixing different groups. For the first problem, if two variables are expressed as ratios of a third variable, they will necessarily be correlated with each other. A related problem occurs when scores are forced to add up to a constant (i.e. they are *ipsatized*). In this case, even $k$ uncorrelated variables will have a correlation of $-1/(k-1)$ if they are ipsatized. As shown by Romer and Revelle (1984), the forced ipsatization of behavior ratings done by Shweder and D'Andrade (1980) led to the false claim of systematic distortion in interpersonal perception.

If data are pooled across groups, the overall correlation can be very different from the pooled within-group correlation. Recognized as a problem since Yule (1912), *Simpson's paradox* (Simpson, 1951) was seen when sex discrimination in admissions was reported at the University of California, Berkeley. In 1973, UCB admitted about 44 percent of male applicants, but only about 35 percent of female applicants. What seems to be obvious sex discrimination in admissions became a paper in *Science*, when it was discovered that the individual departments, if discriminating at all, discriminated in favor of women (Bickel, Hammel, & O'Connell, 1975). The women were applying to departments which admitted a smaller percentage of applicants.

The human eye and brain are superb pattern detectors. Using graphical displays rather than numeric tables helps detect strange relationships in one's data, which are due to various artifacts (Anscombe, 1973; Wainer, 1976; Wainer & Thissen, 1981). In a comparison between many statistical procedures, undertaken in order to detect the underlying correlation in the presence of noise, the most robust estimator (least sensitive to noise and most sensitive to the underlying correlation) was the pooled estimates of a set of students trained to look at scatter plots (Wainer & Thissen, 1979).

## Data quality: reliability

The correlation between two variables is an index of the degree to which variability in one is associated with variability in the other. It is not an index of causality, nor does it consider the quality of measurement of either variable. For $x$ may directly cause $y$, $y$ may directly cause $x$, or both may be caused by an unobserved third variable $z$. In addition, observed scores $x$ and $y$ are probably not perfect representations of the constructs that both are thought to measure. Thinking back to equation 1, the measure of $x$ reflects a model of $x$ as well as an error in measurement. This realization led Spearman (1904b) to develop the basic concepts of reliability theory. He was the first psychologist to recognize that observed correlations are attenuated (or reduced) from the true correlation if the observations contain error.

> Now, suppose that we wish to ascertain the correspondence between a series of values, $p$, and another series, $q$. By practical observation we evidently do not obtain the true objective values, $p$ and $q$, but only approximations which we will call $p'$ and $q'$. Obviously, $p'$ is less closely connected with $q'$, than is $p$ with $q$, for the first pair only correspond at all by the intermediation of the second pair; the real correspondence between $p$ and $q$, shortly $r_{pq}$ has been "attenuated" into $r_{p'q'}$. (Spearman, 1904b, p. 90)

To Spearman, the reliability of a test $p'$ was the correlation with one just like it, $p''$ (a parallel test). The problem of how to find test reliability has bedeviled psychometricians for more than 100 years (Spearman, 1904b; Spearman, 1910; Brown, 1910; Guttman, 1945; Cronbach, 1951), and we can only hope that we are coming to a solution (McDonald, 1999; Revelle & Zinbarg, 2009; Sijtsma, 2009).

*Classical test theory*   The solutions to the reliability question in classical test theory (Lord & Novick, 1968; McDonald, 1999) were extensions of the original suggestion made by Spearman (1904b) for parallel tests. If estimated with two or more tests, the reliability of the composite is a function of the number of tests going into the composite (Brown, 1910; Spearman, 1910). Guttman (1945), although arguing that reliability was only meaningful over time, proposed six different ways of estimating it. One of these six ($\lambda_3$) was discussed later by Cronbach (1951) as *coefficient* $\alpha$. Although routinely dismissed as an inappropriate estimate of reliability (Cronbach & Shavelson, 2004; McDonald, 1999; Revelle, 1979; Sijtsma, 2009; Zinbarg, Revelle, Yovel, & Li, 2005), remains the most reported estimate of reliability. But $\alpha\alpha$ is always less than, or equal to, the true reliability (Guttman, 1945; Sijtsma, 2009) and is a poor way of assessing the homogeneity of a test. A test can have a substantial $\alpha$ even though it measures two unrelated concepts (McDonald, 1999; Revelle, 1979; Revelle & Zinbarg, 2009). With the use of the omega function in the psych package, the two estimates developed by McDonald (1999), $\omega_h$ and $\omega_t$, are now easily calculated. $\omega_h$ (omega hierarchical) is the amount of variance that a general factor accounts for in a test, and $\omega_t$ is the total amount of reliable variance in a test (McDonald, 1999; Revelle & Zinbarg, 2009). $\omega_h \leq \alpha \leq \omega_t$ and only in the case of a purely one-factor test with equal item correlations will they be equal.

In addition to measures of reliability being assessed by using measures of a test's homogeneity, reliability is also of concern in measuring the same trait twice over an extended period of time. Such test–retest reliability, or stability, is not necessarily good for all measures. When one is assessing ability or a personality trait such as extraversion, test–retest reliability over extended periods of time is a sign of a stable trait. The fact that IQ scores at age 11 correlate .66 with IQ scores at age 80 is remarkable and shows the stability of IQ (Deary et al., 2004). It is important to recognize that reliability is a rank-order concept and that, even with a perfect test–retest correlation, all the scores could have increased or decreased drastically. High test–retest reliability is not necessarily a good thing: to find a high test–retest of a measure of mood over a few days would imply that it is a construct other than mood, perhaps trait affectivity. That raters give similar ratings as other panel members on a selection board (Goldberg, 1966) is a sign of inter-rater reliability, a global measure of which can be found by using the intra-class correlation (Shrout & Fleiss, 1979).

The intra-class correlation expresses the reliability of ratings in terms of components of variance associated with raters, targets, and their interactions; and it can be extended to other domains. That is, the analysis-of-variance approach to the measurement of reliability focuses on the relevant facets in an experimental design. If ratings are nested within teachers, who are nested within schools, and if ratings are given at different times, then all of these variables and their interactions are sources of variance in the ratings. First do an analysis of variance in a *generalizability study*, to identify the variance components. Then determine which variance components are relevant for the application in the *decision study* in which one is trying to use the measure (Cronbach, Gleser, Nanda, & Rajaratnam, 1972). Similarly, the components of variance associated with parts of a test can be analyzed in terms of the generalizability of the entire test.

*Item response theory: the new psychometrics* Classic psychometrics treats items as random replicates and model the total score. As such, reliability of measurement is a between-person concept that does not allow a unique specification of the amount of error for each individual. Reliability is enhanced if the true score variance goes up, and is meaningless for a single individual. The "new psychometrics" (Embretson & Hershberger, 1999), on the other hand, considers the information in each item and thus is able to talk about the precision of estimate for a score for a single person. Primary advantages of IRT procedures are that they can identify items that have *differential item functioning* (DIF) in different groups, test items can be formed into tests *tailored* for specific ability groups, and tests can be made *adaptive*. This ability to tailor a test to a particular difficulty level and, even more importantly, adaptively to give items to reflect prior response patterns is one of the great strengths of IRT. For, with a suitable item bank of many items, this allows researchers to give fewer items to any particular subject to obtain the same level of precision possible when using classical test methods. Examples of using IRT in clinical assessments include everything, from measuring ease of breathing in cardiac patients to assessing psychopathology in the clinic (Reise & Waller, 2009). There has been an explosion of handbooks (Van der Linden & Hambleton, 1997) and textbooks (Bond & Fox, 2007; Embretson, 1996; Embretson & Reise, 2000) on IRT, and now, with R it is easy to do IRT analyses. However, to counter some of the enthusiasm for IRT, McDonald (1999), then Zickar and Broadfoot (2009), suggest that classical test theory is still alive and well and worth using for many applications. In most cases, the correlations of IRT and classical estimates are very high, and perhaps the primary advantage of IRT modeling is the realization that observed responses are not linearly related to the latent trait being assessed.

## Data usefulness: validity

That a test or a judge gives the same value for a person over time is nice, but what is more important is: Do they give the right answer? Unfortunately, this is a much harder question to answer than: Is the test reliable? For what is the right answer? (Shooting an arrow into the same part of a target is reliability, hitting the bull's eye is validity, but this requires having a target.) Assessing validity requires having a criterion. This was the chief problem with selecting spies for the Office of Strategic Services (OSS Assessment Staff, 1948) as well as with selecting Peace Corps Volunteers (Wiggins, 1973)—both classics in assessment, and both suffering from an unclear criterion. If the criterion is fuzzy, validity will necessarily be low.

With the focus on data as model plus residual, validity can be said to be measured by how well the model fits, compared to other models, and compared to what we would expect by chance. We prefer to have models using fewer parameters and not to be "multiplying entities beyond necessity."[2] This implies there is not one validity, but rather a process of validation. Is a model useful? Is a model more useful than others? Is there a simpler model, which does almost as well? This has become the domain of latent variable modeling.

## Latent variable modeling

Spearman (1904b) recognized that the observed variable is befuddled with error (equation 2) and that the underlying latent (or unobserved) score should be modeled when correcting correlations for unreliability. By *disattenuating* correlations, he hoped to study the underlying mechanisms. This switch from observed to latent variables was the basis for factor analysis and for the search for a general factor of intelligence (Spearman, 1904a).

## Factor analysis, components analysis, cluster analysis, multidimensional scaling

Classical test theory is a model of how multiple items all measure a single latent trait. By knowing the latent variable and the resulting correlations of items with that latent variable, it is possible to predict the covariances between the items perfectly, by taking the product of the respective correlations with the latent variable. This is the model known as a single factor. If all the items in a correlation matrix $R$ are measures of a latent variable $F$, then the correlations can be modeled as

$$R = FF' + U^2 \tag{6}$$

where $F$ is a vector (a one-dimension matrix) of correlations of the variables with the latent factor, and $U^2$ is a diagonal matrix of residuals.

Even when generalizing this to more than one factor, equation 6 remains the same matrix equation. Equation 6, when expressed in terms of single correlations—the elements of $R$—becomes, for $i \neq j$,

$$r_{ij} = \sum_{k=1}^{c} f_{ik} f_{jk} \tag{7}$$

—that is, the correlation between any two variables is the sum of the products of their respective factor loadings on $c$ factors.

Equation 6 is expressed in matrix algebra and is (with modern computational techniques) a very simple problem. As originally developed in terms of operations on tables of correlations (e.g. equation 7), this was a difficult problem with one factor and an extremely difficult problem with more than one factor. However, with the introduction of matrix algebra to psychologists in the 1930s, Thurstone (1935) and others were able to exploit the power of matrix algebra (Bock, 2007). Recognizing that factor analysis (FA) was just a statistical model-fitting problem and that goodness of fit statistics could be applied to the resulting solutions (Lawley & Maxwell, 1963) made factor analysis somewhat more respectable. The advent of powerful and readily available computers and of computer algorithms to do factor analysis has led to much more frequent use of this powerful modeling technique.

Factor analysis models the observed patterns of correlations between the variables as the sum of the products of factors. At the structural level, this is just a problem of solving a set of simultaneous equations and (roughly speaking), if there are more correlations than unobserved factor loadings, the model is defined. Models with more or fewer factors can be compared in terms of how well they capture the original covariance or correlation matrix. However, because the factors are themselves unobservable, they can only be estimated. Thus, although completely defined at the structural level, factors are undefined at the level of the data.

This indeterminacy has led some to argue against factor analysis and in favor of principal components analysis (PCA). PCA forms linear sums of the observed variables to maximize the variance accounted for by successive components. These components, since they are linear sums of the observed variables, are completely determined. But the components, by summing the observed data, are no more parsimonious than the original data. If, however, just the first $c$ components are extracted, then they are the best set of $c$ independent linear sums to describe the data. Both factors and components have the same goal: to describe the original data and the original correlation matrix. Factor analysis models the off-diagonal elements (the common part) of the correlation matrix, while components model the entire correlation matrix. Although the two models are conceptually very different and will produce very different results when one examines the structure of a few (<20–30) variables, they are unfortunately frequently confused, particularly by some of the major commercial statistical packages. The models are different and should not be seen as interchangeable.

Exploratory factor analysis (EFA) is used to find the structure of correlation matrices where items/tests are allowed to correlate with all factors freely. Rotations toward *simple structure* attempt to reduce the complexity of the solution and to make for more easily interpretable results. The factors as extracted from an EFA and the components as extracted from a PCA are independent. But if they are transformed to a simple structure, where each item has a high correlation on one or only a few factors or components, then the factors/components probably will become correlated (oblique). What is the best transformation and how best to determine the optimal number of factors remains a point of debate, although there is almost uniform agreement among psychometricians that the number of factors with eigenvalues greater than one is the worst rule for determining the number of factors. This is, unfortunately, the default for many commercial programs.

A model which uses some of the logic of factor analysis but differs from EFA is cluster analysis. Hierarchical clustering algorithms (e.g. ICLUST: Revelle, 1979) combine similar pairs of items into clusters and hierarchically combine clusters until some criteria (for instance $\beta$, or the worst split half reliability) fail to increase. ICLUST, as implement in $R$, has proved useful in forming reliable and independent scales in an easily understood manner (Cooksey & Soutar, 2006; Markon, 2010).

An alternative data reduction and description technique that can produce drastically different solutions from FA or PCA is multidimensional scaling (MDS). MDS is also a fitting procedure, but, when working with a correlation matrix, rather than treat the correlations as deviating from zero, MDS tries to minimize the deviations of the correlations from each other. That is to say, it fits the correlation matrix after removing the average correlation. The resulting solutions, particularly when the data have a general factor (e.g. ability tests), represent how different the tests are from the average test, rather than how different the correlations are from zero. This can be particularly useful when examining the micro-structure of a battery of highly correlated tests.

## Structural equation modeling

Structural equation modeling (SEM) combines basic regression techniques with factor analysis modeling of the measurement of variables (Loehlin, 2004). Essentially, it is regression analysis applied to the disattenuated covariance matrix. In the modeling tradition, it forces one to specify a model and then provides statistical estimates of fit that can be compared to alternative models. The power of SEM is that complex developmental growth models (McArdle, 2009) or hierarchical models of ability (Horn & McArdle, 2007) can be tested against alternative models. Examples applied to personality measurement include a multi-trait–multi-method analysis of the Big Five (Biesanz & West, 2004). Perhaps a disadvantage of the ease of running SEM programs is that some users are misled about the strength of their results. Because of the tendency to draw SEM path models with directional arrows, some users of SEM techniques mistakenly believe that they are testing causal models, but they are disabused of this belief when they realize that the models fit equally well if the "causal" direction is reversed. Other users fail to realize that a good model fit does not confirm a model and that it is necessary to consider fits of the multiplicity of alternative models.

## Multi-level modeling

The correlation within groups or individuals is not the same as the correlation between groups or individuals. What appears to be a strong relationship across groups can vanish when considering the individual within groups (Robinson, 1950; Yule, 1912). What had been seen as a challenge is now treated using the techniques of multi-level modeling. The use of multi-level modeling techniques (also known as hierarchical linear models or multi-level random coefficient models) disentangle the effects of individuals from group level effects in everything, from developmental growth curve studies to studies of organizational effectiveness (Bliese, Chan, & Ployhart, 2007). The clear two–three-dimensional structure of affect, as assessed between individuals (Rafaeli & Revelle, 2006), differs from individual to individual in terms of the patterning of affect experience over time within individuals (Rafaeli, Rogers, & Revelle, 2007). What appears to be systematic effects of birth order on intelligence disappears when the effects are modeled within families (Wichman, Rodgers, & MacCallum, 2006).

## Computer modeling

Although hard to tell from reading most of the literature in differential psychology, not all theories are tested by data analyzed using the general linear model. Some theories make predictions that are best tested using computer simulations. The theories are tested for reasonableness of results rather than for fits to observations of the behavior of living subjects. The *dynamics of action* (Atkinson & Birch, 1970) and its reparameterization as the *cues–tendency–action* (CTA) model (Fua, Revelle, & Ortony, 2010; Revelle, 1986) predict a dynamic patterning of behavior that is a non-linear consequence of the initial parameters. Connectionist models of personality (Read et al., 2010) or computational models of individual differences in reinforcement sensitivity (Pickering, 2008) make similar non-linear predictions, which show the power of a few basic parameters to produce wide-ranging variability in a predicted outcome. Modeling is a method of research that has proven very powerful in fields ranging from climate research to evolutionary biology to cognitive psychology. With the ease of use of modeling software, we can expect modeling to become a more common research method in differential psychology.

## Conclusion

Differential psychology is an extremely broad area of study. We have reviewed the major themes of data collection and methods of data analysis, with the recognition that each section is worthy of a chapter in its own right. The basic theme is the equivalence Data = Model + Residual, together with the principle that the researcher needs to decide what constitutes data, what is an appropriate model, and what is reasonable to leave as a residual for someone else to model. In terms of data collection we are limited only by our imagination. Although great progress has been made since Galton and Spearman, the problems of data analysis remain the same.

## Notes

1   Sometimes between-person variability is referred to as inter-individual variability, whereas within-person variability is referred to as intra-individual variability.
2   Although this dictum is probably neither original with William of Ockham nor directly stated by him (Thorburn, 1918), Ockham's razor remains a fundamental principle of science.

## References

Aldrich, J. (1995). Correlations genuine and spurious in Pearson and Yule. *Statistical Science, 10*(4), 364–376.
Anderson, J., Lin, H., Treagust, D., Ross, S., & Yore, L. (2007). Using large-scale assessment datasets for research in science and mathematics education: Programme for International

Student Assessment (PISA). *International Journal of Science and Mathematics Education*, 5(4), 591–614.

Anscombe, F. J. (1973). Graphs in statistical analysis. *The American Statistician*, 27(1), 17–21.

Armstrong, T., Olatunji, B. O., Simmons, C., & Sarawgi, S. (2010). Orientation and maintenance of gaze in contamination-based OCD: Biases for disgust and fear cues. *Behaviour Research and Therapy*, 48, 402–408.

Atkinson, J. W., & Birch, D. (1970). *The dynamics of action*. New York: John Wiley.

Baehr, E. K., Revelle, W., & Eastman, C. I. (2000). Individual differences in the phase and amplitude of the human circadian temperature rhythm: With an emphasis on morningness–eveningness. *Journal of Sleep Research*, 9(2), 117–127.

Baumeister, R. F., Vohs, K. D., & Funder, D. C. (2007). Psychology as the science of self-reports and finger movements: Whatever happened to actual behavior? *Perspectives on Psychological Science*, 2(4), 396–403.

Becker, B. J. (2003). Introduction to the special section on metric in meta-analysis. *Psychological Methods*, 8(4), 403–405.

Benbow, C. P., Lubinski, D. J., & Stanley, J. C. (1996). *Intellectual talent: Psychometric and social issues*. Baltimore, MD: Johns Hopkins University Press.

Bickel, P. J., Hammel, E. A., & O'Connell, J. W. (1975). Sex bias in graduate admissions: Data from Berkeley. *Science*, 187(4175), 398–404.

Biesanz, J. C., & West, S. G. (2004). Towards understanding assessments of the Big Five: Multitrait–multimethod analyses of convergent and discriminant validity across measurement occasion and type of observer. *Journal of Personality*, 72(4), 845–876.

Bliese, P. D., Chan, D., & Ployhart, R. E. (2007). Multilevel methods: Future directions in measurement, longitudinal analyses, and nonnormal outcomes. *Organizational Research Methods*, 10(4), 551–563.

Block, J. (1971). *Lives through time*. Berkeley, CA: Bancroft Books.

Block, J. (1993). Studying personality the long way. In D. C. Funder, R. Parke, C. Tomlinson-Keasey, & K. Widaman (Eds.), *Studying lives through time: Personality and development* (pp. 9–41). Washington, DC: American Psychological Association.

Bock, R. D. (2007). Rethinking Thurstone. In R. Cudeck & R. C. MacCallum (Eds.), *Factor analysis at 100: Historical developments and future directions* (pp. 35–45). Mahwah, NJ: Lawrence Erlbaum Associates.

Bond, T., & Fox, C. (2007). *Applying the Rasch model: Fundamental measurement in the human sciences* (2nd ed.). Mahwah, NJ: Lawrence Erlbaum Associates.

Borkenau, P., Riemann, R., Angleitner, A., & Spinath, F. M. (2001). Genetic and environmental influences on observed personality: Evidence from the German observational study of adult twins. *Journal of Personality and Social Psychology*, 80(4), 655–668.

Borkenau, P., Mauer, N., Riemann, R., Spinath, F. M., & Angleitner, A. (2004). Thin slices of behavior as cues of personality and intelligence. *Journal of Personality and Social Psychology*, 86(4), 599–614.

Born, W. K., Revelle, W., & Pinto, L. H. (2002). Improving biology performance with workshop groups. *Journal of Science Education and Technology*, 11(4), 347–365.

Box, G. E. P. (1979). Some problems of statistics and everyday life. *Journal of the American Statistical Association*, 74(365), 1–4.

Broadhurst, P. (1975). The Maudsley reactive and nonreactive strains of rats: A survey. *Behavior Genetics*, 5(4), 299–319.

Brown, W. (1910). Some experimental results in the correlation of mental abilities. *British Journal of Psychology*, 3(3), 296–322.

Buchanan, T., Johnson, J. A., & Goldberg, L. R. (2005). Implementing a five-factor personality inventory for use on the Internet. *European Journal of Psychological Assessment, 21*(2), 115–127.

Burisch, M. (1984). Approaches to personality inventory construction. *American Psychologist, 39*(3), 214–227.

Burkhauser, R. V., & Lillard, D. R. (2007). The expanded Cross-National Equivalent File: HILDA joins its international peers. *Australian Economic Review, 40*(2), 208–215.

Canli, T. (2004). Functional brain mapping of extraversion and neuroticism: Learning from individual differences in emotion processing. *Journal of Personality, 72*(6), 1105–1132.

Cattell, R. B. (1946). Personality structure and measurement. I. The operational determination of trait unities. *British Journal of Psychology, 36*, 88–102.

Cattell, R. B. (1966). The data box: Its ordering of total resources in terms of possible relational systems. In R. B. Cattell (Ed.), *Handbook of multivariate experimental psychology* (pp. 67–128). Chicago: Rand-McNally.

Cattell, R. B., & Stice, G. (1957). *Handbook for the sixteen personality factor questionnaire.* Champaign, IL: Institute for Ability and Personality Testing.

Chernyshenko, O. S., Stark, S., Drasgow, F., & Roberts, B. W. (2007). Constructing personality scales under the assumptions of an ideal point response process: Toward increasing the flexibility of personality measures. *Psychological Assessment, 19*(1), 88–106.

Chida, Y., & Steptoe, A. (2009). Cortisol awakening response and psychosocial factors: A systematic review and meta-analysis. *Biological Psychology, 80*(3), 265–278.

Clark, L. A., & Watson, D. (1995). Constructing validity: Basic issues in objective scale development. *Psychological Assessment, 7*(3), 309–319.

Cohen, J., Cohen, P., West, S. G., & Aiken, L. S. (2003). *Applied multiple regression/ correlation analysis for the behavioral sciences* (3rd ed.). Mahwah, NJ: Lawrence Erlbaum Associates.

Coleman, K., & Wilson, D. S. (1998). Shyness and boldness in pumpkinseed sunfish: Individual differences are context-specific. *Animal Behaviour, 56*(4), 927–936.

Cook, T., Campbell, D., & Day, A. (1979). *Quasi-experimentation: Design and analysis issues for field settings.* Boston, MA: Houghton Mifflin.

Cooksey, R., & Soutar, G. (2006). Coefficient beta and hierarchical item clustering – An analytical procedure for establishing and displaying the dimensionality and homogeneity of summated scales. *Organizational Research Methods, 9*, 78–98.

Coombs, C. (1964). *A theory of data.* New York: John Wiley.

Corr, P. J. (Ed.) (2008). *The reinforcement sensitivity theory of personality.* Cambridge: Cambridge University Press.

Costa, P. T., & McCrae, R. R. (1985). *NEO PI professional manual.* Odessa, FL: Psychological Assessment Resources, Inc.

Costa, P. T., & McCrae, R. R. (1992). Multiple uses for longitudinal personality data. *European Journal of Personality, 6*(2), 85–102.

Cronbach, L. J. (1951). Coefficient alpha and the internal structure of tests. *Psychometrika, 16*, 297–334.

Cronbach, L. J. (1957). The two disciplines of scientific psychology. *American Psychologist, 12*, 671–684.

Cronbach, L. J. (1975). Beyond the two disciplines of scientific psychology. *American Psychologist, 30*, 116–127.

Cronbach, L. J., & Shavelson, R. J. (2004). My current thoughts on coefficient alpha and successor procedures. *Educational and Psychological Measurement, 64*(3), 391–418.

Cronbach, L. J., Gleser, G. C., Nanda, H., & Rajaratnam, N. (1972). *The dependability of behavioral measurements: Theory of generalizability for scores and profiles.* New York: Wiley.

Deary, I. J. (2009). Introduction to the special issue on cognitive epidemiology. *Intelligence*, *37*, 517–519.

Deary, I. J., Whiteman, M., Starr, J., Whalley, L., & Fox, H. (2004). The impact of childhood intelligence on later life: Following up the Scottish mental surveys of 1932 and 1947. *Journal of Personality and Social Psychology, 86*(1), 130–147.

DeYoung, C. G., Hirsh, J. B., Shane, M. S., Papademetris, X., Rajeevan, N., & Gray, J. R. (2010). Testing predictions from personality neuroscience. *Psychological Science, 21*, 820–828.

Diamond, L., & Otter-Henderson, K. D. (2007). Physiological measures. In R. Robins, C. R. Fraley, & R. F. Krueger (Eds.), *Handbook of research methods in personality psychology* (pp. 370–388). New York: Guilford Press.

Digman, J. M. (1963). Principal dimensions of child personality as inferred from teachers' judgments. *Child Development, 34*(1), 43–60.

Digman, J. M. (1990). Personality structure: Emergence of the five-factor model. *Annual Review of Psychology, 41*, 417–440.

Durbin, C. E., & Klein, D. N. (2006). 10-year stability of personality disorders among out-patients with mood disorders. *Journal of Abnormal Psychology, 115*(1), 75–84.

Durbin, C. E., Hayden, E., Klein, D., & Olino, T. (2007). Stability of laboratory-assessed temperamental emotionality traits from ages 3 to 7. *Emotion, 7*(2), 388–399.

Durbin, C. E., Klein, D. N., Hayden, E. P., Buckley, M. E., & Moerk, K. C. (2005). Temperamental emotionality in preschoolers and parental mood disorders. *Journal of Abnormal Psychology, 114*(1), 28–37.

Ekman, P., Friesen, W. V., & Hager, J. C. (1978). *Facial action coding system*. Palo Alto, CA: Consulting Psychologists Press.

Elder, G. H. (1998). The life course as developmental theory. *Child Development, 69*(1), 1–12.

Elder, G. H., Shanahan, M., & Clipp, E. (1994). When war comes to men's lives: Life-course patterns in family, work, and health. *Psychology and Aging, 9*(1), 5–16.

Embretson, S. E. (1996). The new rules of measurement. *Psychological Assessment, 8*(4), 341–349.

Embretson, S. E. (1998). A cognitive design system approach to generating valid tests: Application to abstract reasoning. *Psychological Methods, 3*(3), 380–396.

Embretson, S. E., & Hershberger, S. L. (1999). *The new rules of measurement: What every psychologist and educator should know*. Mahwah, NJ: Lawrence Erlbaum Associates.

Embretson, S. E., & Reise, S. P. (2000). *Item response theory for psychologists*. Mahwah, NJ: Lawrence Erlbaum Associates.

Eysenck, H. J. (1966). Personality and experimental psychology. *Bulletin of the British Psychological Society, 19*, 1–28.

Eysenck, H. J. (1967). *The biological basis of personality*. Springfield, IL: Thomas.

Eysenck, H. J. (1997). Personality and experimental psychology: The unification of psychology and the possibility of a paradigm. *Journal of Personality and Social Psychology, 73*(6), 1224–1237.

Eysenck, H. J., & Eysenck, S. B. G. (1968). *Manual for the Eysenck personality inventory*. San Diego, CA: Educational and Industrial Testing Service.

Fiske, D. W. (1949). Consistency of the factorial structures of personality ratings from different sources. *Journal of Abnormal and Social Psychology, 44*, 329–344.

Fleeson, W., Malanos, A. B., & Achille, N. M. (2002). An intraindividual process approach to the relationship between extraversion and positive affect: Is acting extraverted as "good" as being extraverted? *Journal of Personality and Social Psychology, 83*(6), 1409–1422.

Flynn, J. R. (1987). Massive IQ gains in 14 nations: What IQ tests really measure. *Psychological Bulletin, 101*(2), 171–191.

Flynn, J. R. (1999). Searching for justice: The discovery of IQ gains over time. *American Psychologist, 54*(1), 5–20.

Flynn, J. R. (2000). IQ gains and fluid *g*. *American Psychologist, 55*(5), 543.

Fox, E., Russo, R., Bowles, R., & Dutton, K. (2001). Do threatening stimuli draw or hold visual attention in subclinical anxiety? *Journal of Experimental Psychology: General, 130*(4), 681–700.

Friedman, H. S., Tucker, J. S., Schwartz, J. E., Tomlinson-Keasey, C., Martin, L. R., Wingard, D. L., & Criqui, M. H. (1995). Psychosocial and behavioral predictors of longevity: The aging and death of the "termites." *American Psychologist, 50*(2), 69–78.

Fua, K., Revelle, W., & Ortony, A. (2010). *Modeling personality and individual differences: The approach–avoid–conflict triad.* Paper presented at the Annual Meeting of the Cognitive Science Society (CogSci 2010).

Funder, D. C. (2001). Personality. *Annual Review of Psychology, 52*, 197–221.

Funder, D. C., Furr, R., & Colvin, C. (2000). The Riverside Behavioral Q-sort: A tool for the description of social behavior. *Journal of Personality, 68*(3), 451–489.

Furr, R., & Funder, D. (2007). Behavioral observation. In R. W. Robins, R. Fraley, & Robert F. Krueger (Eds.), *Handbook of research methods in personality psychology* (pp. 273–291). New York: Guilford Press.

Gallagher, E. J., Viscoli, C. M., & Horwitz, R. I. (1993). The relationship of treatment adherence to the risk of death after myocardial infarction in women. *Journal of the American Medical Association, 270*(6), 742–744.

Galton, F. (1886). Regression towards mediocrity in hereditary stature. *Journal of the Anthropological Institute of Great Britain and Ireland, 15*, 246–263.

Galton, F. (1888). Co-relations and their measurement. *Proceedings of the Royal Society. London Series, 45*, 135–145.

Goldberg, L. R. (1966). Reliability of Peace Corps selection boards: A study of interjudge agreement before and after board discussions. *Journal of Applied Psychology, 50*(5), 400–408.

Goldberg, L. R. (1972). Parameters of personality inventory construction and utilization: A comparison of prediction strategies and tactics. *Multivariate Behavioral Research Monograph, 7*, No. 72–2.

Goldberg, L. R. (1990). An alternative "description of personality": The Big-Five factor structure. *Journal of Personality and Social Psychology, 59*(6), 1216–1229.

Goldberg, L. R. (1999). A broad-bandwidth, public domain, personality inventory measuring the lower-level facets of several five-factor models. In I. Mervielde, I. Deary, F. De Fruyt, & F. Ostendorf (Eds.), *Personality psychology in Europe* (Vol. 7, pp. 7–28). Tilburg, The Netherlands: Tilburg University Press.

Goldberg, L. R., Johnson, J. A., Eber, H. W., Hogan, R., Ashton, M. C., Cloninger, C. R., & Gough, H. G. (2006). The international personality item pool and the future of public-domain personality measures. *Journal of Research in Personality, 40*(1), 84–96.

Gosling, S. D. (2001). From mice to men: What can we learn about personality from animal research? *Psychological Bulletin, 127*(1), 45–86.

Gosling, S. D., & John, O. P. (1999). Personality dimensions in nonhuman animals: A cross-species review. *Current Directions in Psychological Science, 8*(3), 69–75.

Gosling, S. D., & Vazire, S. (2002). Are we barking up the right tree? Evaluating a comparative approach to personality. *Journal of Research in Personality, 36*(6), 607–614.

Gosling, S. D., Vazire, S., Srivastava, S., & John, O. P. (2004). Should we trust web-based studies? A comparative analysis of six preconceptions about Internet questionnaires. *American Psychologist, 59*(2), 93–104.

Gough, H. G. (1957). *Manual for the California psychological inventory.* Palo Alto, CA: Consulting Psychologists Press.

Gray, J. A. (1982). *Neuropsychological theory of anxiety: An investigation of the septal–hippocampal system.* Cambridge: Cambridge University Press.

Gray, J. A., & McNaughton, N. (2000). *The neuropsychology of anxiety: An enquiry into the functions of the septo-hippocampal system* (2nd ed.). Oxford: Oxford University Press.

Guttman, L. (1945). A basis for analyzing test–retest reliability. *Psychometrika, 10*(4), 255–282.

Habermas, T., & Bluck, S. (2000). Getting a life: The emergence of the life story in adolescence. *Psychological Bulletin* (126), 248–269.

Harmon-Jones, E., & Beer, J. S. (2009). *Methods in social neuroscience.* New York: Guilford Press.

Harvey, E. (1999). Short-term and long-term effects of early parental employment on children of the National Longitudinal Survey of Youth. *Developmental Psychology, 35*(2), 445–459.

Hase, H. D., & Goldberg, L. R. (1967). Comparative validity of different strategies of constructing personality inventory scales. *Psychological Bulletin, 67*(4), 231–248.

Hathaway, S., & McKinley, J. (1943). *Manual for administering and scoring the MMPI.* Minneapolis, MN: University of Minnesota Press.

Hogan, J., Barrett, P., & Hogan, R. (2007). Personality measurement, faking, and employment selection. *Journal of Applied Psychology, 92*(5), 1270–1285.

Hogan, R. (2007). *Personality and the fate of organizations.* Mahwah, NJ: Lawrence Erlbaum Associates.

Hogan, R., & Kaiser, R. B. (2005). What we know about leadership. *Review of General Psychology, 9*(2), 169–180.

Hogan, R., & Nicholson, R. A. (1988). The meaning of personality test scores. *American Psychologist, 43*(8), 621–626.

Holland, J. L. (1959). A theory of vocational choice. *Journal of Counseling Psychology, 6*(1), 35–45.

Holland, J. L. (1996). Exploring careers with a typology: What we have learned and some new directions. *American Psychologist, 51*(4), 397–406.

Horn, J. L., & McArdle, J. J. (2007). Understanding human intelligence since Spearman. In R. Cudeck & R. C. MacCallum (Eds.), *Factor analysis at 100: Historical developments and future directions* (pp. 205–247). Mahwah, NJ: Lawrence Erlbaum Associates.

Horwitz, R. I., Viscoli, C. M., Donaldson, R. M., Murray, C. J., Ransohoff, D. F., Berkman, L., Berkman, L. et al. (1990). Treatment adherence and risk of death after a myocardial infarction. *Lancet, 336*(8714), 542–545.

Humphreys, M. S., & Revelle, W. (1984). Personality, motivation, and performance: A theory of the relationship between individual differences and information processing. *Psychological Review, 91*(2), 153–184.

Hunt, E., & Wittmann, W. (2008). National intelligence and national prosperity. *Intelligence, 36*(1), 1–9.

Irvine, J., Baker, B., Smith, J., Jandciu, S., Paquette, M., Cairns, J., Connolly, S., Roberts, R., Gent, M., & Dorian, P. (1999). Poor adherence to placebo or amiodarone therapy predicts mortality: Results from the CAMIAT study. *Psychosomatic Medicine, 61*(4), 566–575.

Jackson, D. N. (1967). *Personality research form manual.* Port Huron, MI: Research Psychologists Press.

Johnson, D. L., Wiebe, J. S., Gold, S. M., Andreasen, N. C., Hichwa, R. D., Watkins, G., & Ponto, L. L. (1999). Cerebral blood flow and personality: A positron emission tomography study. *American Journal of Psychiatry, 156*(2), 252–257.

Johnson, J. A. (2005). Ascertaining the validity of individual protocols from web-based personality inventories. *Journal of Research in Personality, 39*(1), 103–129.

Judd, C. M., McClelland, G. H., & Ryan, C. S. (2009). *Data analysis: A model comparison approach* (2nd ed.). New York: Routledge.

Kelly, E. L., & Fiske, D. W. (1950). The prediction of success in the VA training program in clinical psychology. *American Psychologist, 5*(8), 395–406.

Krueger, R. F. (2002). Psychometric perspectives on comorbidity. In J. E. Helzer & J. J. Hudziak (Eds.), *Defining psychopathology in the 21st century: DSM–V and beyond* (pp. 41–54). Washington, DC: American Psychiatric Publishing.

Kuncel, N. R., Hezlett, S. A., & Ones, D. S. (2001). A comprehensive meta-analysis of the predictive validity of the graduate record examinations: Implications for graduate student selection and performance. *Psychological Bulletin, 127*(1), 162–181.

Kuncel, N. R., Cred, M., & Thomas, L. L. (2007). A meta-analysis of the predictive validity of the graduate management admission test (GMAT) and undergraduate grade point average (UGPA) for graduate student academic performance. *The Academy of Management Learning and Education, 6*(1), 51–68.

Lawley, D. N., & Maxwell, A. E. (1963). *Factor analysis as a statistical method.* London: Butterworths.

Loehlin, J. C. (2004). *Latent variable models: An introduction to factor, path, and structural equation analysis* (4th ed.). Mahwah, NJ: Lawrence Erlbaum Associates.

Lord, F. M., & Novick, M. R. (1968). *Statistical theories of mental test scores.* Reading, MA: Addison-Wesley.

Lubinski, D., & Benbow, C. P. (2006). Study of mathematically precocious youth after 35 years: Uncovering antecedents for the development of math-science expertise. *Perspectives on Psychological Science, 1*(4), 316–345.

Markon, K. E. (2010). Modeling psychopathology structure: A symptom-level analysis of Axis I and II disorders. *Psychological Medicine, 40,* 273–288.

McAdams, D. P. (1993). *The stories we live by: Personal myths and the making of the self.* New York: William Morrow & Co.

McAdams, D. P. (2008). Personal narratives and the life story. In O. P. John, R. W. Robins, & L. A. Pervin (Eds.), *Handbook of personality: Theory and research* (3rd ed.). New York: Guilford Press.

McAdams, D. P., Diamond, A., St. Aubin, E. de, & Mansfield, E. (1997). Stories of commitment: The psychosocial construction of generative lives. *Journal of Personality and Social Psychology, 72*(3), 678–694.

McArdle, J. J. (2009). Latent variable modeling of differences and changes with longitudinal data. *Annual Review of Psychology, 60,* 577–605.

McArdle, J. J., & Bell, R. Q. (2000). Recent trends in modeling longitudinal data by latent growth curve methods. In T. D. Little, K. U. Schnabel, & J. Baumert (Eds.), *Modeling longitudinal and multiple-group data: Practical issues, applied approaches, and scientific examples* (pp. 69–107). Mahwah, NJ: Lawrence Erlbaum Associates.

McDonald, R. P. (1999). *Test theory: A unified treatment.* Mahwah, NJ: Lawrence Erlbaum Associates.

McLean, K. C. (2005). Late adolescent identity development: Narrative meaning making and memory telling. *Developmental Psychology, 41*(4), 683–691.

Mehl, M. R., & Pennebaker, J. W. (2003). The sounds of social life: A psychometric analysis of students' daily social environments and natural conversations. *Journal of Personality and Social Psychology, 84*(4), 857–870.

Mehl, M. R., Vazire, S., Ramirez-Esparza, N., Slatcher, R. B., & Pennebaker, J. W. (2007). Are women really more talkative than men? *Science, 317*(5834), 82.

Mroczek, D. K. (2007). The analysis of longitudinal data in personality research. In R. W. Robins, R. C. Fraley, & R. F. Krueger (Eds.), *Handbook of research methods in personality psychology* (pp. 543–556). New York: Guilford Press.

Mulaik, S. A. (2010). *Foundations of factor analysis* (2nd ed.). Boca Raton, FL: CRC Press.

Nesselroade, J. R. (1984). Concepts of intraindividual variabiilty and change: Impressions of Cattell's influence on lifespan developmental psycholgy. *Multivariate Behavioral Research, 19*(2), 269–286.

Noftle, E. E., & Fleeson, W. (2010). Age differences in big five behavior averages and variabilities across the adult life span: Moving beyond retrospective, global summary accounts of personality. *Psychology and Aging, 25*(1), 95–107.

Norman, W. T. (1963). Toward an adequate taxonomy of personality attributes: Replicated factors structure in peer nomination personality ratings. *Journal of Abnormal and Social Psychology, 66*(6), 574–583.

Norman, W. T. (1969). "To see oursels as ithers see us!": Relations among self-perceptions, peer-perceptions, and expected peer-perceptions of personality attributes. *Multivariate Behavioral Research, 4*(4), 417–443.

OSS Assessment Staff (1948). *Assessment of men: Selection of personnel for the office of strategic services.* New York: Rinehart.

Pasupathi, M., & Hoyt, T. (2009). The development of narrative identity in late adolescence and emergent adulthood: The continued importance of listeners. *Developmental Psychology, 45*(2), 558–574.

Pearl, J. (2000). *Causality: Models, reasoning, and inference.* New York: Cambridge University Press.

Pearson, K. P. (1896). Mathematical contributions to the theory of evolution. III. Regression, heredity, and panmixia. *Philosopical Transactions of the Royal Society of London, Series A, 187*, 254–318.

Pearson, K. P. (1901). On lines and planes of closest fit to systems of points in space. *The London, Edinburgh and Dublin Philosophical Magazine and Journal, 6*(2), 559–572.

Pearson, K. P. (1910). *The grammar of science* (3rd ed.). London: Adam & Charles Black.

Pennebaker, J. W., Mayne, T. J., & Francis, M. E. (1997). Linguistic predictors of adaptive bereavement. *Journal of Personality and Social Psychology, 72*(4), 863–871.

Perkins, A. M., Kemp, S. E., & Corr, P. J. (2007). Fear and anxiety as separable emotions: An investigation of the revised reinforcement sensitivity theory of personality. *Emotion, 7*(2), 252–261.

Pickering, A. D. (2008). Formal and computational models of reinforcement sensitivity theory. In P. J. Corr (Ed.), *The reinforcement sensivity theory* (pp. 453–481). Cambridge: Cambridge University Press.

R Development Core Team (2010). *R: A language and environment for statistical computing.* R Foundation for Statistical Computing, Vienna, Austria: Paedagogike Institut. Also available at www.R-project.org

Rafaeli, E., & Revelle, W. (2006). A premature consensus: Are happiness and sadness truly opposite affects? *Motivation and Emotion, 30*(1), 1–12.

Rafaeli, E., Rogers, G. M., & Revelle, W. (2007). Affective synchrony: Individual differences in mixed emotions. *Personality and Social Psychology Bulletin, 33*(7), 915–932.

Rasch, G. (1980). *Probabilistic models for some intelligence and attainment tests* [1960]. Chicago: University of Chicago Press/Copenhagen: Paedagogike Institut.

Read, S. J., Monroe, B. M., Brownstein, A. L., Yang, Y., Chopra, G., & Miller, L. C. (2010). A neural network model of the structure and dynamics of human personality. *Psychological Review, 117*(1), 61–92.

Reise, S., & Waller, N. (2009). Item response theory and clinical measurement. *Annual Review of Clinical Psychology, 5*, 27–48.

Revelle, W. (1979). Hierarchical cluster-analysis and the internal structure of tests. *Multivariate Behavioral Research, 14*(1), 57–74.

Revelle, W. (1986). Motivation and efficiency of cognitive performance. In D. R. Brown & J. Veroff (Eds.), *Frontiers of motivational psychology: Essays in honor of J. W. Atkinson* (pp. 105–131). New York: Springer.

Revelle, W. (1993). Individual differences in personality and motivation: "Non-cognitive" determinants of cognitive performance. In A. Baddeley & L. Weiskrantz (Eds.), *Attention: Selection, awareness, and control: A tribute to Donald Broadbent* (pp. 346–373). New York: Clarendon Press/Oxford University Press.

Revelle, W. (2007). Experimental approaches to the study of personality. In R. Robins, R. C. Fraley, & R. F. Krueger (Eds.), *Handbook of research methods in personality psychology* (pp. 37–61). New York: Guilford Press.

Revelle, W. (2010). *Psych: Procedures for personality and psychological research* [Computer software manual]. Available at http://personality-project.org/r (R package version 1.0-92).

Revelle, W., & Oehlberg, K. (2008). Integrating experimental and observational personality research—The contributions of Hans Eysenck. *Journal of Personality, 76*(6), 1387–1414.

Revelle, W., & Zinbarg, R. E. (2009). Coefficients alpha, beta, omega and the GLB: Comments on Sijtsma. *Psychometrika, 74*(1), 145–154.

Revelle, W., Amaral, P., & Turriff, S. (1976). Introversion–extraversion, time stress, and caffeine: The effect on verbal performance. *Science, 192*, 149–150.

Revelle, W., Wilt, J., & Rosenthal, A. (2010). Personality and cognition: The personality–cognition link. In A. Gruszka, G. Matthews, & B. Szymura (Eds.), *Handbook of individual differences in cognition: Attention, memory and executive control* (pp. 27–49). New York: Springer.

Revelle, W., Humphreys, M. S., Simon, L., & Gilliland, K. (1980). Interactive effect of personality, time of day, and caffeine—Test of the arousal model. *Journal of Experimental Psychology General, 109*(1), 1–31.

Roberts, B. W., Kuncel, N. R., Shiner, R., Caspi, A., & Goldberg, L. R. (2007). The power of personality: The comparative validity of personality traits, socioeconomic status, and cognitive ability for predicting important life outcomes. *Perspectives on Psychological Science, 2*(4), 313–345.

Robins, R. W., Fraley, R. C., & Krueger, R. F. (2007). *Handbook of research methods in personality psychology*. New York: Guilford Press.

Robinson, W. S. (1950). Ecological correlations and the behavior of individuals. *American Sociological Review, 15*(3), 351–357.

Rocklin, T., & Revelle, W. (1981). The measurement of extraversion: A comparison of the Eysenck personality inventory and the Eysenck personality questionnaire. *British Journal of Social Psychology, 20*(4), 279–284.

Rodgers, J. L. (2010). The epistemology of mathematical and statistical modeling: A quiet methodological revolution. *American Psychologist, 65*(1), 1–12.

Romer, D., & Revelle, W. (1984). Personality traits: Fact or fiction? A critique of the Shweder and D'Andrade systematic distortion hypothesis. *Journal of Personality and Social Psychology, 47*(5), 1028–1042.

Rosnow, R. L., Rosenthal, R., & Rubin, D. B. (2000). Contrasts and correlations in effect-size estimation. *Psychological Science, 11*(6), 446–453.

Schaie, K. W. (1994). The course of adult intellectual development. *American Psychologist*, 49(4), 304–313.

Schimmack, U., & Reisenzein, R. (2002). Experiencing activation: Energetic arousal and tense arousal are not mixtures of valence and activation. *Emotion*, 2(4), 412–417.

Shadish, W. R., Cook, T. D., & Campbell, D. T. (2001). *Experimental and quasi-experimental designs for generalized causal inference*. Boston, MA: Houghton Mifflin.

Shrout, P. E., & Fleiss, J. L. (1979). Intraclass correlations: Uses in assessing rater reliability. *Psychological Bulletin*, 86(2), 420–428.

Shweder, R. A., & D'Andrade, R. G. (1980). The systematic distortion hypothesis. In R. A. Shweder (Ed.), *New directions for methodology of social and behavior science* (pp. 37–58). San Francisco, CA: Jossey-Bass.

Sijtsma, K. (2009). On the use, the misuse, and the very limited usefulness of Cronbach's alpha. *Psychometrika*, 74(1), 107–120.

Simms, L. J., & Watson, D. (2007). The construct validation approach to personality scale construction. In R. W. Robins, R. C. Fraley, & R. F. Krueger (Eds.), *Handbook of research methods in personality psychology* (pp. 240–258). New York: Guilford Press.

Simpson, E. H. (1951). The interpretation of interaction in contingency tables. *Journal of the Royal Statistical Society, Series B (Methodological)*, 13(2), 238–241.

Singer, J. A. (2004). Narrative identity and meaning making across the adult lifespan: An introduction. *Journal of Personality*, 72(3), 437–459.

Singer, J. A., & Blagov, P. (2004). The integrative function of narrative processing: Autobiographical memory, self-defining memories, and the life story of identity. In D. Beike, D. Behrend, & J. Lampinen (Eds.), *Memory and the self* (pp. 117–138). New York: Psychology Press.

Smillie, L., & Jackson, C. (2006). Functional impulsivity and reinforcement sensitivity theory. *Journal of Personality*, 74(1), 47.

Spearman, C. (1904a). "General intelligence," objectively determined and measured. *American Journal of Psychology*, 15(2), 201–292.

Spearman, C. (1904b). The proof and measurement of association between two things. *The American Journal of Psychology*, 15(1), 72–101.

Spearman, C. (1910). Correlation calculated from faulty data. *British Journal of Psychology*, 3(3), 271–295.

Strong, E. K. (1927). Vocational interest test. *Educational Record*, 8(2), 107–121.

Terman, L. M., & Oden, M. (1947). *Genetic studies of genius*. Palo Alto, CA: Stanford University Press/London: Oxford University Press.

Thayer, R. E. (2000). Mood. In A. E. Kazdin (Ed.), *Encyclopedia of psychology* (Vol. 5, pp. 294–295). Washington, DC: American Psychological Association/New York: Oxford University Press.

Thorburn, W. M. (1918). The myth of Occam's razor. *Mind*, 27, 345–353.

Thurstone, L. L. (1935). *The vectors of mind: Multiple-factor analysis for the isolation of primary traits*. Chicago: University of Chicago Press.

Tupes, E. C., & Christal, R. E. (1961). Recurrent personality factors based on trait ratings (Technical Report No. 61–97). Lackland Air Force Base: USAF ASD Technical Report.

Vale, J., & Vale, C. (1969). Individual differences and general laws in psychology: A reconciliation. *American Psychologist*, 24(12), 1093–1108.

Van der Linden, W., & Hambleton, R. (1997). *Handbook of modern item response theory*. New York: Springer-Verlag.

Vazire, S. (2006). Informant reports: A cheap, fast, and easy method for personality assessment. *Journal of Research in Personality*, 40(5), 472–481.

Vazire, S., Gosling, S. D., Dickey, A. S., & Schapiro, S. J. (2007). Measuring personality in nonhuman animals. In R. W. Robins, R. C. Fraley, & R. F. Krueger (Eds.), *Handbook of research methods in personality psychology* (pp. 190–206). New York: Guilford Press.

Wacker, J., Chavanon, M.-L., & Stemmler, G. (2006). Investigating the dopaminergic basis of extraversion in humans: A multilevel approach. *Journal of Personality and Social Psychology, 91*(1), 171–187.

Wainer, H. (1976). Estimating coefficients in linear models: It don't make no never mind. *Psychological Bulletin, 83*(2), 213–217.

Wainer, H., & Thissen, D. (1979). On the robustness of a class of naive estimators. *Applied Psychological Measurement, 3*(4), 543–551.

Wainer, H., & Thissen, D. (1981). Graphical data analysis. *Annual Review of Psychology, 32,* 191–241.

Walker, R. N. (1967). Some temperament traits in children as viewed by their peers, their teachers, and themselves. *Monographs of the Society for Research in Child Development, 32*(6), iii–iv, 1–36.

Watson, D. (2005). Rethinking the mood and anxiety disorders: A quantitative hierarchical model for DSM–V. *Journal of Abnormal Psychology, 114*(4), 522.

Wichman, A., Rodgers, J., & MacCallum, R. (2006). A multilevel approach to the relationship between birth order and intelligence. *Personality and Social Psychology Bulletin, 32*(1), 117.

Wiggins, J. S. (1973). *Personality and prediction: Principles of personality assessment.* Malabar, FL: R. E. Krieger Publishing Company.

Wilt, J., Oehlberg, K., & Revelle, W. (2010). Anxiety in personality. *Personality and Individual Differences.* http://dx.doi.org/10.1016/j.paid.2010.11.014

Yule, G. U. (1912). On the methods of measuring association between two attributes. *Journal of the Royal Statistical Society, 75,* 579–652.

Zickar, M. J., & Broadfoot, A. A. (2009). The partial revival of a dead horse? Comparing classical test theory and item response theory. In C. E. Lance & R. J. Vandenberg (Eds.), *Statistical and methodological myths and urban legends: Doctrine, verity and fable in the organizational and social sciences* (pp. 37–59). New York: Routledge/Taylor & Francis Group.

Zinbarg, R. E., Revelle, W., Yovel, I., & Li, W. (2005). Cronbach's $\alpha$, Revelle's $\beta$, and McDonald's $\Omega_h$): Their relations with each other and two alternative conceptualizations of reliability. *Psychometrika, 70*(1), 123–133.

# Part II

# Intelligence and Personality
*Structure and Development*

# Section 1    Personality

# 3

# Personality Development across the Life Span

## Jaap J. A. Denissen, Marcel A. G. van Aken, and Brent W. Roberts

The field of personality development is rapidly developing. In the early 1970s few would have predicted that research on the sources of individual differences would be so vibrant today (McCrae, 2000). Following Mischel's (1968) influential critique of personality traits, many researchers came to believe that personality traits only existed in the mind of the beholder and were not worth studying. Fortunately not all researchers gave up. Through demonstrations to the effect that traits are not merely subjective constructs, but converge across observers (Funder & Colvin, 1988) and can be aggregated across situations to improve predictive validity (Epstein, 1983), a consensus was reached that personality traits not only exist, but also affect real-life outcomes (Caspi, 1998; Ozer & Benet-Martínez, 2006; Roberts, Kuncel, Shiner, Caspi, & Goldberg, 2007).

Before we begin with our review of the literature on personality development, some definitional clarifications are in order. First of all, in the current review we shall focus on the development of personality *traits*, which can be defined as relatively enduring individual differences in the tendency to behave, think, and feel in certain ways (Caspi, 1998). Although this definition could technically include mental abilities, ability and temperamental traits have historically been covered in relatively separate literatures. In addition, there are some indications that abilities and temperamental traits should be treated as distinct from an evolutionary genetic point of view (Penke, Denissen, & Miller, 2007). Accordingly, the current review shall concentrate on the development of temperamental personality traits (for a review of the life-span development of intelligence, see Baltes, Staudinger, & Lindenberger, 1999).

During the past two decades, the five-factor model of personality (FFM: John & Srivastava, 1999) has been accepted as an adequate working taxonomy of the

*The Wiley-Blackwell Handbook of Individual Differences*, First Edition.
Edited by Tomas Chamorro-Premuzic, Sophie von Stumm, and Adrian Furnham.
© 2011 Blackwell Publishing Ltd. Published 2011 by Blackwell Publishing Ltd.

major trait domains (see Saucier, 2003). The FFM consists of five broad dimensions: extraversion, emotional stability, conscientiousness, agreeableness, and openness to experience. Although the FFM was discovered in research on adult personality, the Big Five can also be used to describe the personality of adolescent children (Kohnstamm, Halverson, Mervielde, & Havill, 1998), and developmental precursors of extraversion, emotional stability, and conscientiousness can be identified in even younger children (Shiner, 1998). Following Roberts and his colleagues (Roberts & DelVecchio, 2000; Roberts, Walton, & Viechtbauer, 2006), we will therefore use the FFM to review and organize existing research on personality development.

Most developmental psychologists are also familiar with the construct of *temperament*, which can be defined as "individual differences in behavior that appear early in life" (Shiner, 1998, p. 309). Researchers habitually use the term "temperament" when they talk about personality differences in young children (<3 years), and they have developed age-specific measurement scales to assess them (we will come back to this issue in our section on future research). Some researchers supplement this definition with the notion that temperamental factors (also in adulthood) are somehow more "biological" or "genetic" in origin (Goldsmith et al., 1987). However, behavior genetic studies have obtained similar heritability estimates for temperament and personality traits (Spinath & Angleitner, 1998). On purely conceptual grounds, we therefore see no reason to differentiate between the two constructs (see McCrae et al., 2000). Indeed, recent theorizing on the link between temperament and personality has focused on the similarities between temperamental traits and the five-factor model of personality. For example, in Rothbart's model (see Rothbart & Bates, 1998), traits are proposed that have large similarity to the Big Five, such as surgency (extraversion), negative affectivity (neuroticism), effortful control (conscientiousness), and affiliativeness (agreeableness; see also Caspi & Shiner, 2006).

The current review is organized according to two ways of studying personality development.[1] First, studies on *mean-level change* of personality trait expression look at how groups of individuals change in their average trait levels. For example, all children between ages 10 and 16 may show a normative mean-level increase in height. Second, studies on *rank-order consistency and change* compare the continuity of individuals' *relative* trait score (e.g. their relative height in comparison with that of their peers).

# Mean-Level Change

## Methodological issues

Mean-level change in personality trait expression focuses on the average level of a trait within a sample, irrespective of individual differences. For example, if all individuals in a cohort demonstrate identical increases in physical height, *individual differences* between them are retained (e.g. Peter is the 4th tallest person in his class both at age 10 and at age 16). It is, however, interesting to study such changes, because mean levels of personality trait expression within a given population constitute the background against which individual differences manifest themselves. For example, for estimating whether a person has become relatively more antisocial between age 12 and age 16, one needs to know about the typical trajectory of aggressiveness during that period. During adolescence, an increase in antisocial behavior is normative (Moffitt, 1993). Therefore an increase in delinquent activities in adolescence may not indicate that a teenager is developing an antisocial personality, but rather that he/she is following a normative trajectory.

## Description of mean-level changes

Roberts, Walton, and Viechtbauer (2006) conducted the first meta-analysis on mean-level changes in personality trait expression. Only longitudinal samples ($N = 92$) were included in their analysis, representing a broad range of birth cohorts. Roberts, Walton, and Viechtbauer grouped their results according to two dimensions. First of all, they classified traits according their position in the FFM, with an additional distinction between two facets of extraversion: social dominance and social vitality. In addition, they compared results for eight different age categories: adolescence (10–18), college years (18–22), and the subsequent decades through to age 100 (because of a relative lack of subjects between 70 and 100, they were combined into a single 70+ category).

Three results especially stood out (see Figure 3.1). First of all, mean-level changes in trait expression occurred well into old age, disconfirming notions that personality traits stop developing after age 30 (Costa & McCrae, 1994). Second, mean-level changes in trait expression were most prominent in young adulthood, even surpassing the degree of mean-level change found in adolescence, a period which is stereotypically linked with social-emotional turmoil and accompanying personality change.

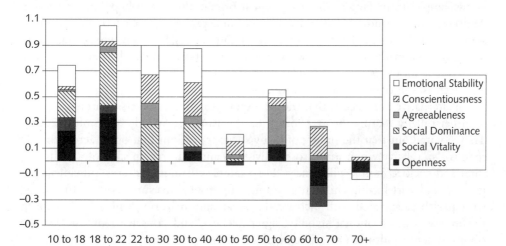

**Figure 3.1** Patterns of mean-level personality change in the Big Five (for extraversion, the facets of social dominance and social vitality are distinguished) across eight different age periods. Results are displayed as stacked standardized effect size coefficients (Cohen's *d*) indicating the difference between two time points. Figure reproduced from Roberts, Walton, & Viechtbauer, 2006, p. 14. Reprinted with permission from the American Psychological Association

Finally, changes were most prominent for social dominance, conscientiousness, and emotional stability. In contrast, openness displayed a more complex pattern, steadily increasing from adolescence to adulthood but decreasing again in old age. In addition, extraversion showed a mixed pattern of changes, with social dominance increasing well into middle adulthood, whereas social vitality did not show much change.

## Explanations for mean-level changes

The observed pattern of mean-level changes suggests that people's social–emotional trait expression matures over time (Donnellan, Conger, & Burzette, 2007). This suggestion is informed by a socio-analytic perspective according to which personality maturity is linked to the attainment of evolutionary relevant goals, such as the formation of lasting relationships and the achievement of career goals (Hogan & Roberts, 2004), two areas that have been linked to Freud's notion of love and work and to Bakan's (1966) notion of agency and communion. Consistent with this, high levels of emotional stability, agreeableness, and conscientiousness have been linked to favorable occupational and romantic outcomes (Caspi, 1998; Lodi-Smith & Roberts, 2007; Ozer & Benet-Martínez, 2006).

Two schools of thought have sought to explain mean-level changes in personality in general and the apparent increase in social–emotional maturity in particular. First of all, McCrae et al. (2000) have argued that mean-level changes are intrinsic in nature, stemming from endogenous, genetic factors that reside within every individual. Such a genetically fixed program of personality change could be seen as an evolutionary adaptation to facilitate important life-history transitions (e.g. having children). Testing this perspective, the researchers compared mean-level age changes across samples from Turkey, Germany, Great Britain, the Czech Republic, and Spain. Although these countries differ in their cultural practices, socioeconomic circumstances, and historical heritage, mean-level differences between age groups were found to be remarkably similar, with increases in emotional stability, agreeableness, and conscientiousness (in agreement with Roberts, Walton, & Viechtbauer, 2006) and decreases in openness and extraversion.

An alternative perspective that tries to explain the quasi-universal nature of mean-level personality maturation was forwarded by Roberts, Wood, and Smith (2005). They pointed out that the timing of many social transitions that occur across the life span is also relatively uniform across individuals and cultures, in spite of various cultural and socioeconomic differences. For example, in most cultures individuals get married and start having children in young adulthood. Investments in mature social roles may be associated with increases in personality maturity, which could explain the increases in emotional stability, agreeableness, and conscientiousness that are observed across cultures (we will come back to this point later).

It needs to be kept in mind, however, that McCrae et al. (2000) studied relatively modern countries in Europe, which may explain some of the similarities in their findings. This is especially problematic as the samples were not nationally representative, the Czech and the Spanish samples consisting of university students, which tend to come from more affluent, cosmopolitan backgrounds that may differ less between countries. A more convincing case for endogenous mean-level changes would involve comparing members of more disparate cultures, preferably from different continents and from different economic and cultural backgrounds (e.g. comparing Amazonian Yanomami with Australian Aborigines).

# Rank-Order Consistency and Change

The second main approach to study personality development is by focusing on the rank order of an individual within a certain population regarding a specific trait. This approach focuses on individual differences between individuals at a specific time point, irrespective of mean-level trends occurring in the general population. In the current chapter we will review both rank-order consistency and change, which represent somewhat distinct phenomena and may be influenced by different causal mechanisms. First, some degree of rank-order consistency is a definitional feature of personality traits; if individual differences are not stable, they are not referred to as traits but as states (although see Fleeson, 2001). In the following pages we will start by reviewing general patterns of personality continuity, using meta-analytic findings from Roberts and DelVecchio (2000). Second, we will discuss sources of rank-order personality change, as well as possible explanations for this phenomenon.

## Patterns and Explanations of Rank-Order Consistency

### Stability decreases with time interval

Roberts and DelVecchio (2000) conducted a meta-analysis of test–retest correlations from 152 longitudinal studies. Three major findings stand out from this work (see Figure 3.2). First of all, results indicated that personality traits become less consistent with increasing retest interval (see also Olweus, 1979). Specifically, the correlation between time interval and consistency was significantly negative ($r = -.20$, $p < .05$). Using regression weights, the authors estimated that the average consistency is .55 across a 1-year period, whereas it would be .25 across a 40-year period.

Conley (1984) proposed a formula specifying the relation between retest interval and stability: $r_{21} = R \cdot s^n$, where $r_{21}$ is the test–retest correlation between two time points, $R$ is the reliability of the measure, $s$ is the one-year stability correlation, and $n$ is the number of years between the first and the second time point. Even under favorable circumstances (yearly stability correlation and reliability of .80), however, this formula predicts that personality consistency decreases to zero after 20 years. This is not what is typically found in empirical studies. For example, Morizot and Le Blanc (2003) followed a representative sample of Canadian males between 17 and 40 years (i.e. a 23-year retest interval) and found an average retest correlation of .32 (see also Hampson & Goldberg, 2006, for a study across an even longer retest interval, of 40 years).

To account for the non-zero asymptote of personality stability, Fraley and Roberts (2005) recently devised a model of personality development that includes a stable "developmental constancy" factor that influences personality equally across the entire

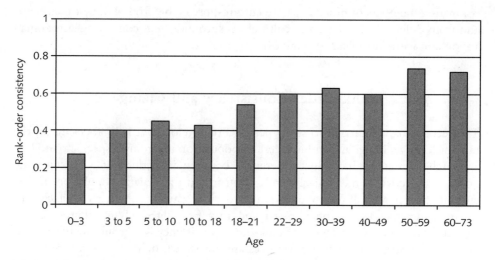

**Figure 3.2**   Rank-order test–retest correlations of personality across 10 different age periods. Figure reproduced from Roberts & DelVecchio, 2000, p. 15. Reprinted with permission from the American Psychological Association

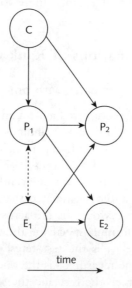

time

**Figure 3.3**   General model of personality continuity, created by Fraley and Roberts. C indicates a developmental constancy factor that exerts a continuous influence throughout the entire life span. P and E indicate personality and environmental factors at two different time points respectively. Figure adapted from Fraley & Roberts, 2005. Reprinted with permission from the American Psychological Association

life span (see Figure 3.3). Personality factors are hypothesized to be continuously and directly influenced by this factor. As a result, personality traits are more stable than would be assumed, given the typical levels of reliability of personality trait measures.

It is tempting to equate the developmental constancy factor in Fraley and Roberts's (2005) model with genetic influences. After all, it has been established that about

50 percent of the cross-sectional variance in personality traits is caused by genetic factors (Loehlin, 1992). As a person's genetic code remains invariant across the life span, it is able to exert a continuing influence. Indeed, using a longitudinal behavior genetic design, McGue, Bacon, and Lykken (1993) presented evidence that 70–90 percent of personality stability is caused by genetic factors, whereas 70 percent of personality change is caused by environmental factors (also see Bartels, Rietveld, Van Baal, & Boomsma, 2002). Accordingly, it can safely be assumed that part of the developmental constancy factor is of genetic origin.

Finally, it should be kept in mind that some forces promoting the long-term continuity of personality may be of non-genetic origin (Kandler et al., in press). For example, early experiences during a formative "sensitive" period may act as a source of continuity. Such experiences leave a lasting mark on personality development and are very difficult to reverse. For example, attachment theory (Bowlby, 1969) posits that early experiences with primary caretakers lay the foundation for a person's life-long attachment system as secure, anxious, or avoidant. In addition, once individuals achieve a stable sense of identity (Marcia, 1966), this mode of attachment may act as a stabilizing force in personality development by influencing self-presentation and niche selection.

## Stability increases with age

A second finding that emerged from the meta-analysis of Roberts and DelVecchio (2000) is that personality stability increases with age. Specifically, across 152 longitudinal studies, test–retest correlations increased from .31 in childhood to .54 during the college years, to .64 at age 40, after which they reached a plateau around .74 between ages 50 and 70 (holding constant the retest interval at 6–7 years). This means that, in childhood, 10 percent of the variance is stable between two measurement points, whereas in old age no less than 55 percent of the variance is stable across time.

In the model of Fraley and Roberts (2005), personality can become more stable because of the cumulative effect of the developmental constancy factor. Assuming that this factor taps into genetic influences, this stabilization can happen when genes assume partial control over the situation an individual encounters. Especially when children leave the parental home, opportunities for selecting environmental niches that are consistent with their genetically mediated personality should increase (Scarr & McCartney, 1983). Consistently with this, Bartels et al. (2002) found that influences on personality that are shared within families (such as family climate) decrease across time, whereas the influence of genetic factors increases. On the other hand, some authors have found a decreasing heritability; so more research is needed to draw firmer conclusions (Kandler et al., in press). It may also be that early formative experiences and a stable sense of identity contribute to the increasing stability of individual differences. For example, there is evidence that people's identity becomes increasingly stable as they grow older (Meeus, Iedema, Helsen, & Volleberg, 1999). This increasingly stable identity may act as a force promoting personality continuity.

Theoretically, three transactional mechanisms have been proposed to explain the cumulative continuity of personality across the life span (Caspi, 1998). This list has recently been expanded to six mechanisms (Roberts, Wood, & Caspi, 2008), which can be seen as more specific instances of the three original mechanisms. It should be noted that these mechanisms are represented by the cross-lagged arrows in Figure 3.3, which represents the general model of continuity proposed by Fraley and Roberts (2005).

First, reactive person–environment transactions occur when people interpret their environment in a manner that is consistent with their personality makeup (this mechanism is called reactance by Roberts et al., 2008). For example, individuals with low self-esteem are more likely to perceive criticism as threatening to their close relationships than people with high self-esteem (Murray, Rose, Bellavia, Holmes, & Kusche, 2002).

Second, evocative person–environment transactions occur when people elicit different reactions from their social environment, depending on their personality. For example, peers may react in a more hostile manner to individuals who have a reputation for high levels of aggressiveness, which further reinforces these indi-viduals' initial aggressive patterns (Dodge, 1980). A more specific application of this principle is instantiated if people are selected into environmental niches that are consistent with their personalities (Roberts et al., 2008). For example, employers use personality tests in order to hire candidates whose personalities match the require-ments of the vacancy.

Third, proactive transactions occur when people actively create environmental niches that are consistent with their personality (Scarr & McCartney, 1983). This can be achieved by at least three mechanisms (Roberts et al., 2008). First, people are attracted to environments that are consistent with their personality. For example, more intelligent individuals are more likely to seek admission to a university; this ensures that they will be exposed to an enriched environment, which further pro-motes intellectual growth. Second, the principle of attrition states that people leave environments that call for too much personality change. For example, less conscien-tious individuals may drop out of college because being a student requires too much self-discipline. Third, people may directly manipulate their environment to make it fit their personality better. For example, people who are extraverted may talk their friends into attending more parties together.

It has also been hypothesized that personality stability is dependent on the level of psychological resources that the individual brings to the situation. For example, Asendorpf and van Aken (1991) found that resilient children had more stable per-sonalities, perhaps because non-resilient children are under more pressure to change. In a study of young adults, Roberts, Caspi, and Moffitt (2001) found that personality change was more likely if individuals had lower scores of emotional stability, consci-entiousness, and extraversion (in other words were less mature), a pattern that was recently replicated (Donnellan et al., 2007).

Interestingly, the latter finding points to an interesting connection between mean-level changes in maturity and rank-order consistency. Because both increase with age, it could be hypothesized that the increase in rank-order consistency with age is a side-effect of the fact that people become more mature as they grow older (Roberts, Walton, and Viechtbauer, 2006). However, more research is needed to back up this conclusion.

## Stability never approaches unity

A final conclusion from the meta-analysis of Roberts and DelVecchio (2000) is that personality stability never approaches unity. If personality would stop developing at a certain age, retest correlations should approximate the internal consistency of the scales that are used (usually ranging between .70 and .80). As stated above, such high estimates are only found between ages 50 and 70. This pattern is inconsistent with the so-called "plaster hypothesis," which was first advanced by William James (1890). In spite of initial claims supporting this hypothesis (see Costa & McCrae, 1997; Costa, Herbst, McCrae, & Siegler, 2000), a general consensus has now been reached that personality does not stop developing after age 30 (Costa & McCrae, 2006).

The absence of perfect stability well into old age is consistent with notions of personality as a dynamic system, open to outside influences. Such a system receives its input from stable endogenous factors (e.g. the developmental constancy factor in the model of Fraley & Roberts, 2005). In addition, the system is also open to stochastic (chance) processes, which have been called the "third source" of developmental differences, besides genetic and environmental constancy factors (Molenaar, Boomsma, & Dolan, 1993). Indeed, chance processes are among the most neglected psychological mechanisms in development (see Kagan, 1998; Lewis, 1997). For example, Bandura (1982) noted the prominent role of chance encounters in the determination of people's life paths.

## Sources of Rank-Order Change

As stated by Caspi and Roberts (2001), personality change is not necessarily the flip side of personality continuity: although a close inverse relation exists between personality continuity and change, some factors may be uniquely associated with differential personality change, but not with personality continuity, and vice versa. It should also be noted that changes in rank order may occur even in the absence of changes in an individual's absolute score. For example, because Peter failed to follow the normative increase in height typical of people at his age, he has become relatively less tall than his peers.

In the following pages we will discuss possible sources of rank-order personality change. By definition, such influences can only be non-normative in nature, as normative influences are universal within a certain population and can thus only affect mean-level changes in trait expression (as we will see, however, variation in people's timing and success at mastering these normative developmental transitions can trigger personality change). In the following, we will review four sources of differential change (see Terracciano, McCrae, Brant, & Costa, 2005).

*Genetic factors*   Perhaps surprisingly given the prominent role of genes in personality stability, genes can also promote personality change. Indeed, in the previously cited study of McGue et al. (1993), genetic factors accounted for up to 30 percent of individual differences in personality change (for a more recent study consistent with these findings, see Bleidorn, Kandler, Riemann, Angleitner, & Spinath, 2009). This can occur because gene expression is a dynamic phenomenon: genes are turned on and off during various stages of development, with resulting changes in associated personality traits. For example, Huntington's disease is a neurological disorder caused by a rare allele of the Huntington gene that is passed from parents to offspring at birth. Physical symptoms in the person suffering from this disease commonly become noticeable only in a person's forties, causing profound personality changes.

*Social relationships*   Social relationships constitute a key influence in shaping human development (Reis, Collins, & Berscheid, 2000). Indeed, according to the so-called social looking-glass self, people essentially become how others perceive them to be. Conceptually, the perceptions of other people of a given individual's personality constitute his/her trait reputation (Hogan, 1996). It is highly plausible that such perceptions exert pressure on people to conform the self-ratings of their own personality traits (although, in experimental studies, the reverse has also been shown to be the case; Swann, 1987). Because most studies have relied on self-ratings in assessing personality traits, however, there is little empirical evidence to back up this prediction.

Because mating and reproducing are highly salient evolutionary tasks confronting humans, it is not surprising that romantic relationships have been shown to exert an important influence on personality trait development. Specifically, Neyer and his colleagues (Neyer & Asendorpf, 2001; Neyer & Lehnart, 2007) found that individuals who started a first romantic relationship decreased in neuroticism and increased in conscientiousness. Importantly, these changes persisted even in people who later discontinued their romantic relationships, a phenomenon suggesting that the first romantic relationship represents a formative experience toward personality maturation.

Finally, the relationship between children and their parents is often regarded as an important influence on shaping individual differences in behavior. Attachment theory (Bowlby, 1969) starts from the assumption that characteristics of the early parent–child relationship shape the subsequent formation of internal working models of the self and others. Whereas individuals with a secure attachment system have been shown to be able to form reciprocal, satisfying relationships with others, people with insecure attachment systems respond to interpersonal closeness either in an anxious–ambivalent or in an avoidant way.

In spite of the theoretical importance of early family experiences, behavior genetic studies have generally found that the effect of shared parenting influences on personality is limited (Krueger, Markon, & Bouchard, 2003; Loehlin, 1992). This is not to say that parents do not matter; rather, the effect of their parenting behaviors is likely to differ among children, because (1) siblings may react differently to the same behaviors of their parents; and (2) parents probably adjust their parenting behaviors to match the personality of the child (Lowe Vandell, 2000).

*Work experiences*   As stated above, Freud regarded the domain of work as an important venue to express psychological maturity. Being a successful worker in most professions requires that people act in a socially responsible matter. Accordingly, it can be expected that success in the work domain is related to increases in personality maturity, especially in conscientiousness. In turn, this trait has been found to be consistently associated with work-related success (Barrick, Mount, & Strauss, 1993).

A growing body of evidence is consistent with the notion that work experiences can shape personality development. For example, Roberts and his colleagues (Roberts, 1997; Roberts, Helson, & Klohnen, 2002) showed that women who increased their participation in the labor force became more agentic and more norm-adhering as they grew older. In another study (Roberts, Caspi, & Moffitt, 2003), positive work experiences were associated with increases in emotional stability, extraversion, and conscientiousness in sample of young adults. In addition, increases in work satisfaction are associated with changes toward personality maturation (Scollon & Diener, 2006; van Aken, Denissen, Branje, Dubas, & Goossens, 2006), whereas engaging in counterproductive work behaviors is associated with decreases in emotional stability and conscientiousness (Roberts, Walton, Bogg, & Caspi, 2006). Finally, Denissen, Asendorpf, and van Aken (2008) found that investment in part-time work experiences in emerging adulthood are associated with decreases in aggressiveness.

*Life events* Life experiences are often assessed by asking people how often certain major, relatively rare events happened in their lives (e.g. marriage or job loss). In a widely cited study, however, Brickman, Coates, and Janoff-Bulman (1978) found that such extreme events as winning the lottery or being paralyzed as a result of spinal cord injury were not associated with changes in subjective well-being, as people eventually adjust back to their "set-point" levels of happiness. More recently, however, Lucas (2007) criticized these results on methodological grounds and used a large and representative prospective study to demonstrate that different degrees of physical disability are associated with lasting changes in well-being. Also consistent with the notion that personality change is more likely to result from long-term exposure to an environment, Lehnart and Neyer (2006) found that relationship quality has a stronger effect on personality change in ongoing (vs. changing) relationships. Change is also more probable when there is a clear pressure to behave in the new situation and when previous responses are actively discouraged, while clear information is provided about how to behave adaptively (Caspi & Moffitt, 1993). Finally, very recent evidence points to the possibility that the amount of personality change after life events may be dependent on whether the latter occur for the first time or happened before. For example, Luhmann and Eid (2009) found that the negative effect of becoming unemployed is aggravated when this occurs repeatedly, whereas the negative effect of divorce seems to lessen after people have been divorced once.

# Future Research

Although tremendous progress has been made in understanding the principles of personality development, much work remains to be done. In the following, we will list four themes we regard as important areas of future research. Of course, this list is not meant to be exhaustive; new theoretical and methodological innovations will undoubtedly give birth to new research paradigms, which we cannot foresee in the present review.

## Alternative measurement of traits

Most studies of human personality use self-ratings to measure personality traits (Hofstee, 1994). Longitudinal research is no exception: in the meta-analysis of Roberts, Walton, and Viechtbauer (2006), there were so few observer rating studies that it wasn't possible to compare differences from self-report measures. We do not wish to argue that self-ratings have no value in personality assessment. However, they are limited to the perspective of the actor, ignoring how people are seen by others around them (in other words ignoring the perspective of the observer: Hogan & Roberts, 2004). In addition, observer ratings (but not self-ratings) can be aggregated in order to reduce subjective biases. Hofstee (1994) recommends this procedure as the best possible operationalization of personality; it is not possible to apply it in the case of self-ratings.

This is not merely an abstract methodological issue, as differences in rating source can give rise to dramatically different conclusions about the strength and direction of personality change. For example, a study of Watson and Humrichouse (2006) found that agreeableness, conscientiousness, and emotional stability increased when emerging adults' self-ratings were investigated, whereas conscientiousness and agreeableness (as well as extraversion and openness) decreased when spousal ratings were studied. The authors suggested that this effect occurred because newlyweds' overly favorable impression of their partners (the "honeymoon effect") wears off with time. Of course, this points to the fact that observer ratings may be affected by bias as well (as in the case of a relationship enhancing effect; see Morry, 2007). It should be noted that sophisticated methods have been developed to separate effects of rating bias (actor effect) and relationship quality (relationship effect) from the effect of personality (target effect), namely by using a round robin assessment procedure (i.e. a design in which various persons rate each other as well as their own personality: Kenny & La Voie, 1984).

Many personality questionnaires explicitly instruct participants to compare the target person to people of the same age and gender. Even if the instruction doesn't mention this, people often use an implicit reference group of comparable age and gender to assess personality traits. This fact potentially attenuates mean-level changes in measurements of personality trait expression (Biesanz, West, & Kwok, 2003). Because of this effect, Fiske (1972) argued for the use of behavior measures to assess personality. Indeed, the use of act-frequencies (tallies of trait-relevant behaviors across time) has been proposed to constitute a viable alternative to the measurement of traits (Buss & Craik, 1981). Rather than an alternative to the typical measurement of personality traits, act-frequencies could be used as supplementary information in order to test whether age and sex norming washes out developmental changes in personality. For example, in order to assess people's level of extraversion, one could ask how many hours per day these people spend in social situations. If this percentage decreases when people grow older, it is reasonable to assume that they have become less extraverted over time.

In order to carry out longitudinal studies that span an age period from childhood to adulthood, it is also important that researchers make sure that they assess identical constructs across time, even when the corresponding behavioral indicators change. This can be done by demonstrating the nomological and rank-order continuity between personality and temperament. Ideally, such evidence would be based on studies that (1) follow the same individuals from infancy through to young adulthood; (2) simultaneously assess both personality and temperament (taking into account possible age differences in the expression of the underlying dimensions); (3) include a broad array of validation criteria (e.g. social relationship quality, adjustment); and (4) are genetically informative. There is an urgent need for such studies in the future.

## Timing of measurement

Although recent decades have witnessed impressive improvements in statistical designs for longitudinal data analysis, only about 25 percent of studies published in the *Journal of Personality* and in *Social Psychology: Personality Processes and Individual Differences* between 2000 and 2001 used longitudinal designs (Biesanz et al., 2003). Because cross-sectional studies suffer from a variety of methodological problems, longitudinal studies are essential to understanding the principles of personality development. However, it is not enough simply to collect data over multiple points in time; in order to further our understanding of personality development, it is important to use statistical designs that are appropriate for the research question under consideration. In the following pages we will discuss two alternative approaches.

First, cross-lagged longitudinal designs can be used to study transactions between personality (P) and the environment (E). When carried out in a structural equation modeling (SEM) framework (see Figure 3.4), cross-lagged designs control for the concurrent association between personality and environment at Time 1 (Path a), as

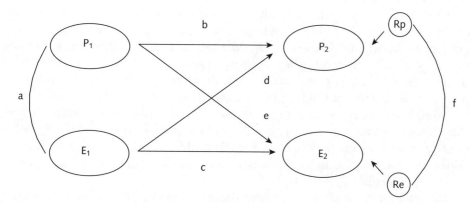

**Figure 3.4** Cross-lagged paths between personality (P1, P2) and social relationship (SR1, SR2), and correlated change of personality and environment at time 2 (Rp, Rsr), controlling for both variables' long-term stability. Figure reproduced from Sturaro et al., 2008, p. 3

well as for the longitudinal stability of both variables (Paths b and c). As a result, it can be determined whether initial levels of a variable affect the level of change in the other variable (Paths d and e). This high level of statistical control allows for tentative conclusions about the relative causal primacy of one variable (e.g. core traits) over another (e.g. surface traits: Asendorpf & van Aken, 2003). Cross-lagged analyses using SEM also allow for the analysis of correlated change (see Scollon & Diener, 2006), which is represented by the structural path between the residual variance of two variables after taking into account stability and cross-lagged paths (Path f). It should be noted, however, that correlated change is confounded by time-specific measurement error (e.g. state variance) and stays silent about the direction of effects; so this technique may be less suited to study the mechanisms underlying personality development. It should also be noted that these cross-lagged analyses are usually carried out on a full sample, which implicitly assumes the dimensional identity of a set of variables (i.e. it assumes that the interrelations among the variables in that set remain unchanged across the levels or categories of other variables, an assumption that is often not warranted; von Eye & Bergman, 2003).

Second, growth modeling of personality trajectories estimates the shape of intra-individual trajectories, which can be either linear or non-linear, and either fixed or freely estimated (McArdle & Epstein, 1987). We would argue, however, that studies need to go beyond a mere description of the shape of mean-level personality trajectories, of which meta-analytic summaries already exist (Roberts, Walton, and Viechtbauer, 2006). Moreover, studies should also include predictors of individual differences in intra-individual change, in order to uncover the mechanisms underlying these unfolding trajectories (Denissen et al., 2008; Kasen, Chen, Sneed, Crawford, & Cohen, 2006; Mroczek & Spiro, 2003). In addition, there is a need for research using growth mixture modeling with latent trajectory classes (Muthén & Muthén, 2000), so that classes of individuals may be identified that differ with regard to the shape of their intra-individual personality trajectories.

It is sometimes claimed that growth curve modeling represents an inherently more reliable way to assess personality change by comparison to cross-lagged designs. We believe the issue is more nuanced. The cross-lagged analysis essentially tries to predict (residual) change scores, the reliability of which is inversely related to the stability between two time points.[2] Using more than two data points in growth curve analysis may capitalize on the principle of aggregation, but this does not automatically increase reliability. After all, when most participants cannot be characterized by a specified growth pattern (e.g. a linear one), the within-person variance around the corresponding parameter will be relatively large and its reliability low. In both cases, we strongly call for researchers to start reporting the reliability of difference scores when they use two-wave data (using a formula by Burr & Nesselroade, 1990) or slopes when they use growth curve modeling (this is reported by the reliability of slopes program, HLM; using SEM, slopes can be calculated using a formula reported by Karney & Bradbury, 1995, p. 1101).

Importantly, it is possible to combine the quasi-causal nature of the cross-lagged design with the descriptive precision of growth curve modeling. Using growth curve modeling, one could separate initial levels (intercepts) from longitudinal growth (slopes). If the growth curves of two variables (e.g. personality and social relationships) are estimated in such a manner, the intercept of one variable can be used to predict the slope of the other one. This is akin to the logic of the cross-lagged analysis, in that initial levels of one variable predict change in the other; but in this way one predicts the *amount* of change (in other words, a negative coefficient indicates that high initial levels in one variable predict lower levels of change in the other), whereas in a cross-lagged design one predicts the *direction* of change (i.e. a negative coefficient indicates that high initial levels in one variable predict decreases in the other variable). Which design is to be preferred depends on the nature of the research question (e.g. a series of cross-lagged paths across multiple waves can highlight interesting changes in the association between two variables, whereas a latent growth curve analysis paints a more overall picture).

## Social roles and developmental tasks

Another fruitful venue for research on personality development is the integration of personality and social roles. As has long been pointed out by various scholars, human nature is inherently social, individuals depending in part on the social roles they take on (Mead, 1934). In a recent meta-analysis, the assumption of mature social roles in the domains of work and love has been associated with increasing personality maturity (Lodi-Smith & Roberts, 2007). Roberts and his colleagues (2005) have proposed a social investment theory that hypothesizes that investing in social institutions, such as age-graded social roles, outside of the self is one of the driving mechanisms of personality development in general and of greater maturity in particular. More research is needed that explicitly takes into account the quality and timing of investment in important social roles (e.g. Denissen et al., 2008), for example by using instruments that assess the latency of various life history transitions (Caspi et al., 1996).

Personality maturation has also been linked to the mastering of important developmental tasks (Cicchetti & Rogosch, 2002). A developmental task can be defined as a "task which arises about a certain period in the life of the individual successful achievement of which leads to his happiness and to success with later tasks" (Havighurst, 1972, p. 2). Developmental tasks arise from three sources: physical maturation, personal values, and societal pressures (Havighurst, 1956). Especially in the latter sense, connected to sources, a developmental task partly represents a specific culture's definition of "normal" development at different points in the life span (for example, learning to walk can be considered as a developmental task in toddlerhood; see Table 3.1). In addition to Havighurst, researchers of social–emotional development have formulated developmental issues that are relevant in their particular domain. Sroufe (1979), for example, provides a taxonomy of developmental issues in early development, in which "establishing an effective attachment relationship" next to "exploration and mastery," and then "individuation" are mentioned as salient for that domain and age. Future research should investigate the effects of mastering developmental tasks/issues on personality development by concentrating longitudinal measurements around such important transition moments.

From a theoretical perspective, it may be possible to integrate the notion of social investment with the notion of developmental tasks in explaining personality

**Table 3.1**   Developmental tasks according to Havighurst. Source: Havighurst, 1972

| *Age period* | *Developmental tasks* |
| --- | --- |
| Ages 0–6 | Learning to walk. Learning to crawl. Learning to take solid food. Learning to talk. Learning to control the elimination of body wastes. Learning sex differences and sexual modesty. Getting ready to read. Forming concepts and learning language to describe social and physical reality. |
| Ages 6–12 | Learning physical skills necessary for ordinary games. Learning to get along with age mates. Building wholesome attitudes toward oneself as a growing organism. Learning on appropriate masculine or feminine social role. Developing concepts necessary for everyday living. Developing concepts necessary for everyday living. Developing conscience, morality and a scale of values. Achieving personal independence. Developing attitudes toward social groups and institutions. |
| Ages 12–18 | Achieving new and more mature relations with age mates of both sexes. Achieving a masculine or feminine social role. Accepting one's physique and using the body effectively. Achieving emotional independence of parents and other adults. Preparing for marriage and family life. Acquiring a set of values and an ethical system as a guide to behaviour. Desiring and achieving socially responsible behaviour. |
| Ages 18–30 | Selecting a mate. Learning to live with a partner. Starting family. Rearing children. Managing home. Getting started in occupation. Taking on civic responsibility. Finding a congenial social group. |
| Ages 30–60 | Assisting teenage children to become responsible and happy adults. Achieving adult social and civic responsibility. Reaching and maintaining satisfactory performance in one's occupational career. Developing adult leisure time activities. Relating oneself to one's spouse as a person. Accepting and adjusting to the physiological changes of middle age. Adjusting to aging parents. |
| 60 and over | Adjusting to decreasing physical strength and health. Adjusting to retirement and reduced income. Adjusting to the death of a spouse. Establishing an explicit affiliation with one's age group. Adopting and adapting social roles in a flexible way. Establishing satisfactory physical living arrangements. |

development. For example, the social investments that go into establishing a career and a stable romantic relationship, which have been the focus of much (though not all) of Roberts's and his colleagues's research (e.g. Roberts et al., 2005), are listed in Table 3.1 as developmental tasks that belong to the age period 18–30. Accordingly, in other phases of the life span, personality maturity may be the result of social investments related to adjustment to a different set of developmental tasks (e.g. adjustment to aging parents between ages 30–60). This would be consistent with an argument offered by life-span theorists, who have claimed that successful aging is dependent upon adjustment to age-graded factors (Baltes, 1987) such as a changing physiology, social opportunities, and social expectations of age-appropriate behavior (Heckhausen, 1999). A more comprehensive theoretical framework is needed, which would incorporate both social investments and developmental tasks into personality development across the life span.

## Genetic underpinnings of personality development

One topic that will undoubtedly receive a lot of attention in future research concerns the genetic underpinnings of personality. Thus far, personality has been operationalized by means of consistent patterns of manifest behavior, cognition, and emotion. It is also possible, however, to operationalize "personality" by means of individual differences in genotype (i.e. by means of alleles). This level of analysis has the advantage that personality differences can be assessed without using self- or other-reports. It should be noted, however, that single-gene polymorphisms are unlikely to emerge as substitutes for broad-level traits like the Big Five. Rather, such broad traits are presumably the result of a number of interacting, pleiotropic polymorphisms associated with domain-general psychological mechanisms (Penke et al., 2007). Future studies linking specific personality traits to allelic variations are needed if one is to establish whether a limited set of polymorphisms can indeed account for the variance found in broad personality traits.

Some of the genetic influence on personality continuity may actually be mediated through the environment. Technically, such a situation is referred to as a genome–environment ($G \times E$) correlation (Plomin, DeFries, & Loehlin, 1977). For example, children of more intelligent parents share a substantial part of their parents' genes, but they may also inherit an enriched intelligence-promoting climate as they grow up. This constitutes a so-called passive $G \times E$ correlation. $G \times E$ correlations can also be reactive (environmental reactions that are contingent on one's genetic makeup) and active (resulting from the selection of an environment that matches one's genes). These latter types correspond, respectively, to the evocative and to the proactive person–environment transactions (which were discussed previously).

Because individual differences in DNA sequencing (though not necessarily in gene expression) are relatively independent of environmental variations, it is possible to study their influence in interaction with the environment. If broad personality domains exist because of shared underlying mechanisms, then personality development is likely to develop top-down, flowing from higher-order personality domains (e.g. neuroticism) to lower-order personality facets (e.g. anxiousness, depressiveness). Over the life span, these mechanisms might modulate the cognitive and affective experiences that individuals acquire by interacting with their environments. This notion is reminiscent of the distinction between highly stable "core traits," which are to a large extent under direct genetic control, and more peripheral "surface traits," which are also dependent on fluctuating environmental factors and are therefore less stable (Asendorpf & van Aken, 2003).

Caspi and his colleagues recently provided the first empirical demonstration of the notion that genes in interaction with environmental factors affect human personality change. In one study, Caspi et al. (2002) demonstrated that genetic differences in the activity of the MAOA enzyme moderate the effect of maltreatment: maltreated children who have a genotype encoding for high-MAOA expression are less likely to develop antisocial problems. In a second study (Caspi et al., 2003) it was shown that a functional polymorphism in the promoter region of the serotonin transporter (5–HTT) gene moderated the influence of stressful life events on depression, individuals with one or two copies of the short allele of the polymorphism exhibiting more depressive symptoms in relation to stressful life events than individuals who were homozygous for the long allele. These results, which have already been replicated multiple times (see Kendler, Kuhn, Vittum, Prescott, & Riley, 2005; Kim-Cohen et al., 2006), constitute promising evidence that interactions between genes and the environment can be an important agent in promoting personality change (for contrary meta-analytic evidence, however, see Risch et al., 2009).

## Conclusion

In the current chapter we have reviewed the state of the art in research on personality development. Recent empirical and meta-analytic evidence suggests that personality becomes more mature and more stable when people grow older. However, there remains much to be learned about the origins of individual differences in intra-individual change. Although "simple" longitudinal designs involving self-reports across two time points have been useful in the past, we believe that researchers should increasingly use designs that make use of multiple informants and take into account the transaction between environmental factors (such as social roles or developmental tasks) and genetic factors as influences on personality development. Although such research may be more costly in terms of funding, data collection efforts, and statistical modeling, we believe it is needed in order to propel our field toward formulating theories that highlight the processes and mechanisms underlying individual differences.

## Notes

1   We will not focus on structural continuity, individual-level change, or ipsative stability: three alternative but less studied types of stability (De Fruyt et al., 2006).
2   With the formula of Burr and Nesselroade (1990), the reliability of change scores across a 6–7-year time-interval using standardized variables with a uniform reliability level of .80 would range between .72 in childhood and .23 in old age, due to the increasing stability of personality.

# References

Asendorpf, J. B., & van Aken, M. A. G. (2003). Personality–relationship transaction in adolescence: Core versus surface personality characteristics. *Journal of Personality, 71,* 629–666.

Asendorpf, J. B., & Van Aken, M. A. G. (1991). Correlates of the temporal consistency of personality patterns in childhood. *Journal of Personality, 59,* 689–703.

Bakan, D. (1966). *The duality of human existence: Isolation and communion in Western man.* Boston, MA: Beacon Press.

Baltes, P. B. (1987). Theoretical propositions of life-span developmental psychology: On the dynamics between growth and decline. *Developmental Psychology, 23,* 611–626.

Baltes, P. B., Staudinger, U. M., & Lindenberger, U. (1999). Lifespan psychology: Theory and application to intellectual functioning. *Annual Review of Psychology, 50,* 471–507.

Bandura, A. (1982). Self-efficacy mechanism in human agency. *American Psychologist, 37,* 122–147.

Barrick, M. R., Mount, M. K., & Strauss, J. P. (1993). Conscientiousness and performance of sales representatives: Test of the mediating effects of goal setting. *Journal of Applied Psychology, 78,* 715–722.

Bartels, M., Rietveld, M., Van Baal, G., & Boomsma, D. (2002). Genetic and environmental influences on the development of intelligence. *Behavior Genetics, 32,* 237–249.

Biesanz, J. C., West, S. G., & Kwok, O.-M. (2003). Personality over time: Methodological approaches to the study of short-term and long-term development and change. *Journal of Personality, 71,* 905–941.

Bleidorn, W., Kandler, C., Riemann, R., Angleitner, A., & Spinath, F. (2009). Patterns and sources of adult personality development: Growth curve analyses of the NEO–PI–R scales in a longitudinal twin study. *Journal of Personality and Social Psychology, 97,* 142–155.

Bowlby, J. (1969). *Attachment and loss: Vol. 1. Attachment.* London: Hogarth Press.

Brickman, P., Coates, D., & Janoff-Bulman, R. J. (1978). Lottery winners and accident victims: Is happiness relative? *Journal of Personality and Social Psychology, 36,* 917–927.

Burr, J. A., & Nesselroade, J. R. (1990). Change measurement. In A. von Eye (Ed.), *Statistical methods in longitudinal research.* (pp. 3–34). Boston, MA: Academic Press.

Buss, D. M., & Craik, K. H. (1981). The act frequency analysis of interpersonal dispositions: Aloofness, gregariousness, dominance and submissiveness. *Journal of Personality, 49,* 175–192.

Caspi, A. (1998). Personality development across the life course. In W. Damon & N. Eisenberg (Eds.), *Handbook of child psychology: Social, emotional, and personality development* (pp. 311–388). New York: Wiley.

Caspi, A., & Moffitt, T. E. (1993). When do individual differences matter? A paradoxical theory of personality coherence. *Psychological Inquiry, 4,* 247–271.

Caspi, A., & Roberts, B. W. (2001). Personality development across the life course: The argument for change and continuity. *Psychological Inquiry, 12,* 49–66.

Caspi, A., & Shiner, R. L. (2006). Personality development. In W. Damon, R. Lerner & N. Eisenberg (Eds.), *Handbook of child psychology: Vol. 3. Social, emotional, and personality development* (6th ed., pp. 300–365). New York: Wiley.

Caspi, A., McClay, J., Moffitt, T. E., Mill, J., Martin, J., Craig, I. W. et al. (2002). Role of genotype in the cycle of violence in maltreated children. *Science, 297,* 851–854.

Caspi, A., Moffitt, T. E., Arland, T., Deborah, F., Amell, J. W., Harrington, H. et al. (1996). The life history calendar: A research and clinical assessment method for collecting retrospective event-history data. *International Journal of Methods in Psychiatric Research, 6,* 101–114.

Caspi, A., Sugden, K., Moffitt, T. E., Taylor, A., Craig, I. W., Harrington, H. et al. (2003). Influence of life stress on depression: Moderation by a polymorphism in the 5–HTT gene. *Science, 301,* 386–389.

Cicchetti, D., & Rogosch, F. A. (2002). A developmental psychopathology perspective on adolescence. *Journal of Consulting and Clinical Psychology, 70,* 6–20.

Conley, J. J. (1984). The hierarchy of consistency: A review and model of longitudinal findings on adult individual differences in intelligence, personality and self-opinion. *Personality and Individual Differences, 5,* 11–25.

Costa, P. T., & McCrae, R. R. (1994). Set like plaster? Evidence for the stability of adult personality. In T. F. Heatherton & J. L. Weinberger (Eds.), *Can personality change?* (pp. 21–40). Washington, DC: American Psychological Association.

Costa, P. T., & McCrae, R. R. (1997). Longitudinal stability of adult personality. In R. Hogan, J. A. Johnson, & S. R. Briggs (Eds.), *Handbook of personality psychology* (pp. 269–292). San Diego, CA: Academic Press.

Costa, P. T., & McCrae, R. R. (2006). Age changes in personality and their origins: Comment on Roberts, Walton, and Viechtbauer (2006). *Psychological Bulletin, 132,* 26–28.

Costa, P. T., Herbst, J. H., McCrae, R. R., & Siegler, I. C. (2000). Personality at midlife: Stability, intrinsic maturation, and response to life events. *Assessment, 7,* 365–378.

De Fruyt, F., Bartels, M., Van Leeuwen, K. G., De Clercq, B., Decuyper, M., & Mervielde, I. (2006). Five types of personality continuity in childhood and adolescence. *Journal of Personality and Social Psychology, 91,* 538–552.

Denissen, J. J. A., Asendorpf, J. B., & van Aken, M. A. G. (2008). Childhood personality predicts long-term trajectories of shyness and aggressiveness in the context of demographic transitions in emerging adulthood. *Journal of Personality, 76,* 67–99.

Dodge, K. A. (1980). Social cognition and children's aggressive behavior. *Child Development, 51,* 162–170.

Donnellan, B. M., Conger, R. D., & Burzette, R. G. (2007). Personality development from late adolescence to young adulthood: Differential stability, normative maturity, and evidence for the maturity–stability hypothesis. *Journal of Personality, 75,* 237–263.

Epstein, S. (1983). Aggregation and beyond: Some basic issues on the prediction of behavior. *Journal of Personality, 51,* 360–392.

Fiske, D. W. (1972). *Measuring the concepts of personality.* Chicago: Aldine.

Fleeson, W. (2001). Toward a structure- and process-integrated view of personality: Traits as density distributions of states. *Journal of Personality and Social Psychology, 80,* 1011–1027.

Fraley, C. R., & Roberts, B. W. (2005). Patterns of continuity: A dynamic model for conceptualizing the stability of individual differences in psychological constructs across the life course. *Psychological Review, 112,* 60–74.

Funder, D. C., & Colvin, C. R. (1988). Friends and strangers: Acquaintanceship, agreement, and the accuracy of personality judgment. *Journal of Personality and Social Psychology, 55,* 149–158.

Goldsmith, H. H., Buss, A. H., Plomin, R., Rothbart, M. K., Thomas, A., Chess, S. et al. (1987). Roundtable: What is temperament? Four approaches. *Child Development, 58,* 505–529.

Hampson, S. E., & Goldberg, L. R. (2006). A first large cohort study of personality trait stability over the 40 years between elementary school and midlife. *Journal of Personality and Social Psychology, 91,* 763–779.

Havighurst, R. J. (1956). Research on the developmental-task concept. *The School Review, 64,* 215–223.

Havighurst, R. J. (1972). *Developmental tasks and education.* New York: MacKay Company.

Heckhausen, J. (1999). *Developmental regulation in adulthood: Age-normative and sociostructural constraints as adaptive challenges.* New York: Cambridge University Press.

Hofstee, W. K. B. (1994). Who should own the definition of personality? *European Journal of Personality, 8,* 149–162.

Hogan, R. (1996). A socioanalytic perspective on the five-factor model. In J. S. Wiggins (Ed.), *The five factor model of personality: Theoretical perspectives* (pp. 163–179). New York: Guilford Press.

Hogan, R., & Roberts, B. W. (2004). A socioanalytic model of maturity. *Journal of Career Assessment, 12,* 207–217.

James, W. (1890). *Principles of psychology.* New York: Henry Holt.

John, O. P., & Srivastava, S. (1999). The Big Five trait taxonomy: History, measurement and theoretical perspectives. In L. A. Pervin & O. P. John (Eds.), *Handbook of personality: Theory and research* (pp. 102–138). New York: Guilford Press.

Kagan, J. (1998). Biology and the child. In W. Damon & N. Eisenberg (Eds.), *Handbook of child psychology: Vol. 3. Social, emotional and personality development* (5th ed., pp. 177–235). New York: Wiley.

Kandler, C., Bleidorn, W., Riemann, R., Spinath, F. M., Thiel, W., & Angleitner, A. (in press). Sources of cumulative continuity in personality: A longitudinal multiple-rater twin study. *Journal of Personality and Social Psychology.*

Karney, B. R., & Bradbury, T. N. (1995). Assessing longitudinal change in marriage: An introduction to the analysis of growth curves. *Journal of Marriage and the Family, 57,* 1091–1108.

Kasen, S., Chen, H., Sneed, J., Crawford, T., & Cohen, P. (2006). Social role and birth cohort influences on gender-linked personality traits in women: A 20-year longitudinal analysis. *Journal of Personality and Social Psychology, 91,* 944–958.

Kendler, K. S., Kuhn, J. W., Vittum, J., Prescott, C. A., & Riley, B. (2005). The interaction of stressful life events and a serotonin transporter polymorphism in the prediction of episodes of major depression: A replication. *Archives of General Psychiatry, 62,* 529–535.

Kenny, D. A., & La Voie, L. (1984). The social relations model. In L. Berkowitz (Ed.), *Advances in experimental social psychology* (pp. 142–182). Orlando, FL: Academic Press.

Kim-Cohen, J., Caspi, A., Taylor, A., Williams, B., Newcombe, R., Craig, I. W. et al. (2006). MAOA, maltreatment, and gene–environment interaction predicting children's mental health: New evidence and a meta-analysis. *Molecular Psychiatry, 11,* 903–913.

Kohnstamm, G. A., Halverson, C. F. J., Mervielde, I., & Havill, V. (1998). *Parental descriptions of child psychology: Developmental antecedents of the big five?* Mahwah, NJ: Lawrence Erlbaum Associates.

Krueger, R. F., Markon, K. E., & Bouchard, T. J. (2003). The extended genotype: The heritability of personality accounts for the heritability of recalled family environments in twins reared apart. *Journal of Personality, 71,* 809–833.

Lehnart, J., & Neyer, F. J. (2006). Should I stay or should I go? Attachment and personality in stable and instable romantic relationships. *European Journal of Personality, 20,* 475–495.

Lewis, D. A. (1997). Development of the prefrontal cortex during adolescence: Insights into vulnerable neural circuits in schizophrenia. *Neuropsychopharmacology, 16,* 385–398.

Lodi-Smith, J., & Roberts, B. W. (2007). Social investment and personality: A meta-analysis of the relationship of personality traits to investment in work, family, religion, and volunteerism. *Personality and Social Psychology Review, 11,* 68–86.

Loehlin, J. C. (1992). *Genes and environment in personality development.* Newbury Park, CA: Sage.

Lowe Vandell, D. (2000). Parents, peer groups, and other sozializing influences. *Developmental Psychology, 36,* 699–710.

Lucas, R. E. (2007). Long-term disability is associated with lasting changes in subjective well-being. *Journal of Social and Personality Psychology, 92,* 717–730.

Luhmann, M., & Eid, M. (2009). Does it really feel the same? Changes in life satisfaction following repeated life events. *Journal of Personality and Social Psychology, 97,* 363–381.

Marcia, J. E. (1966). Development and validation of ego identity status. *Journal of Personality and Social Psychology, 3,* 551–558.

McArdle, J. J., & Epstein, D. (1987). Latent growth curves within developmental structural equation models. *Child Development, 58,* 110–133.

McCrae, R. R. (2000). Trait psychology and the revival of personality-and-culture studies. *American Behavioral Scientist, 44,* 10–31.

McCrae, R. R., Costa, P. T., Ostendorf, F., Angleitner, A., Hrebickova, M., Avia, M. D. et al. (2000). Nature over nurture: Temperament, personality, and life span development. *Journal of Personality and Social Psychology, 78,* 173–186.

McGue, M., Bacon, S., & Lykken, D. T. (1993). Personality stability and change in early adulthood: A behavioral genetic analysis. *Developmental Psychology, 29,* 96–109.

Mead, G. H. (1934). *Mind, self, and society.* Chicago: University of Chicago Press.

Meeus, W., Iedema, J., Helsen, M., & Volleberg, W. (1999). Patterns of adolescent identity development: Review of literature and longitudinal analysis. *Developmental Review, 19,* 419–461.

Mischel, W. (1968). *Personality and assessment.* New York: Wiley.

Moffitt, T. E. (1993). Adolescence-limited and life-course-persistent antisocial behavior: A developmental taxonomy. *Psychological Review, 100,* 674–701.

Molenaar, P. C. M., Boomsma, D., & Dolan, C. V. (1993). A third source of developmental differences. *Behavior Genetics, 6,* 519–524.

Morizot, J., & Le Blanc, M. (2003). Continuity and change in personality traits from adolescence to midlife: A 25-year longitudinal study comparing representative and adjudicated men. *Journal of Personality, 71,* 705–755.

Morry, M. M. (2007). The attraction–similarity hypothesis among cross-sex friends: Relationship satisfaction, perceived similarities, and self-serving perceptions. *Journal of Social and Personal Relationships, 24,* 117–138.

Mroczek, D. K., & Spiro, A., III. (2003). Modeling intraindividual change in personality traits: Findings from the normative aging study. *Journals of Gerontology Series B—Psychological Sciences and Social Sciences, 58B,* P153–P165.

Murray, S. L., Rose, P., Bellavia, G. M., Holmes, J. G., & Kusche, A. G. (2002). When rejection stings: How self-esteem constrains relationship-enhancement processes. *Journal of Personality and Social Psychology, 83,* 556–573.

Muthén, B., & Muthén, L. (2000). Integrating person-centered and variable-centered analyses: Growth mixture modeling with latent trajectory classes. *Alcoholism: Clinical and Experimental Research, 24,* 882–891.

Neyer, F. J., & Asendorpf, J. B. (2001). Personality–relationship transaction in young adulthood. *Journal of Personality and Social Psychology, 81,* 1190–1204.

Neyer, F. J., & Lehnart, J. (2007). Relationships matter in personality development: Evidence from an 8-year longitudinal study across young adulthood. *Journal of Personality, 75,* 535–568.

Olweus, D. (1979). Stability of aggressive reaction patterns in males: A review. *Psychological Bulletin, 86,* 852–875.

Ozer, D. J., & Benet-Martínez, V. (2006). Personality and the prediction of consequential outcomes. *Annual Review of Psychology, 57,* 401–421.

Penke, L., Denissen, J. J. A., & Miller, G. F. (2007). The evolutionary genetics of personality. *European Journal of Personality, 21,* 549–587.

Plomin, R., DeFries, J. C., & Loehlin, J. C. (1977). Genotype–environment interaction and correlation in the analysis of human behavior. *Psychological Bulletin, 84*, 309–322.

Reis, H. T., Collins, W., & Berscheid, E. (2000). The relationship context of human behavior and development. *Psychological Bulletin, 126*, 844–872.

Risch, N., Herrell, R., Lehner, T., Liang, K. Y., Eaves, L., Hoh, J., Griem, A., Kovacs, M., Ott, J., & Merikangas, K. R. (2009). Interaction between the serotonin transporter gene (5–HTTLPR), stressful life events, and risk of depression: A meta-analysis. *Journal of the American Medical Association, 301*, 2462–2471.

Roberts, B. W. (1997). Plaster or plasticity: Are adult work experiences associated with personality change in women? *Journal of Personality, 65*, 205–232.

Roberts, B. W., & DelVecchio, W. F. (2000). The rank-order consistency of personality traits from childhood to old age: A quantitative review of longitudinal studies. *Psychological Bulletin, 126*, 3–25.

Roberts, B. W., Caspi, A., & Moffitt, T. E. (2001). The kids are alright: Growth and stability in personality development from adolescence to adulthood. *Journal of Personality and Social Psychology, 81*, 670–683.

Roberts, B. W., Caspi, A., & Moffitt, T. E. (2003). Work experiences and personality development in young adulthood. *Journal of Personality and Social Psychology, 84*, 582–593.

Roberts, B. W., Helson, R., & Klohnen, E. C. (2002). Personality development and growth in women across 30 years: Three perspectives. *Journal of Personality, 70*, 79–102.

Roberts, B. W., Walton, K. E., & Viechtbauer, W. (2006). Patterns of mean-level change in personality traits across the life course: A meta-analysis of longitudinal studies. *Psychological Bulletin, 132*, 1–25.

Roberts, B. W., Wood, D., & Caspi, A. (2008). The development of personality traits in adulthood. In O. P. John, R. W. Robins, & L. A. Pervin (Eds.), *Handbook of personality theory and research* (pp. 375–398). New York: Guilford Press.

Roberts, B. W., Wood, D., & Smith, J. L. (2005). Evaluating five factor theory and social investment perspectives on personality trait development. *Journal of Research in Personality, 39*, 166–184.

Roberts, B. W., Walton, K. E., Bogg, T., & Caspi, A. (2006). De-investment in work and non-normative personality trait change in young adulthood. *European Journal of Personality, 20*, 461–474.

Roberts, B. W., Kuncel, N. R., Shiner, R. L., Caspi, A., & Goldberg, L. R. (2007). The power of personality: The comparative validity of personality traits, socio-economic status, and cognitive ability for predicting important life outcomes. *Perspectives on Psychological Science, 2*, 313–345.

Rothbart, M. K., & Bates, J. E. (1998). Temperament. In W. Damon & N. Eisenberg (Eds.), *Handbook of child psychology: Vol. 3. Social, emotional and personality development* (5th ed., pp. 105–176). New York: Wiley.

Saucier, G. (2003). An alternative multi-language structure for personality attributes. *European Journal of Personality, 17*, 179–205.

Scarr, S., & McCartney, K. (1983). How people make their own environments: A theory of genotype environment effects. *Child Development, 54*, 424–435.

Scollon, C. N., & Diener, E. (2006). Love, work, and changes in extraversion and neuroticism over time. *Journal of Personality and Social Psychology, 91*, 1152–1165.

Shiner, R. L. (1998). How shall we speak of children's personalities in middle childhood? A preliminary taxonomy. *Psychological Bulletin, 124*, 308–332.

Spinath, F. M., & Angleitner, A. (1998). Contrast effects in Buss and Plomin's EAS questionnaire: A behavioral–genetic study on early developing personality traits assessed through parental ratings. *Personality & Individual Differences, 25*, 947–963.

Sroufe, L. A. (1979). The coherence of individual development: Early care, attachment, and subsequent developmental issues. *American Psychologist, 34,* 834–841.

Sturaro, C., Denissen, J. J. A., van Aken, M. A. G., & Asendorpf, J. B. (2008). Person–environment transactions during emerging adulthood: The interplay between personality characteristics and social relationships. *European Psychologist, 13,* 1–11.

Swann, W. B. (1987). Identity negotiation: Where two roads meet. *Journal of Personality and Social Psychology, 53,* 1038–1051.

Terracciano, A., McCrae, R. R., Brant, L. J., & Costa, P. T., Jr. (2005). Hierarchical linear modeling analyses of the NEO–PI–R scales in the Baltimore longitudinal study of aging. *Psychology and Aging, 20,* 493–506.

van Aken, M. A. G., Denissen, J. J. A., Branje, S. J. T., Dubas, J. S., & Goossens, L. (2006). Midlife concerns and short-term personality change in middle adulthood. *European Journal of Personality, 20,* 497–513.

von Eye, A., & Bergman, L. R. (2003). Research strategies in developmental psychopathology: Dimensional identity and the person-oriented approach. *Development and Psychopathology, 15,* 553–580.

Watson, D., & Humrichouse, J. (2006). Personality development in emerging adulthood: Integrating evidence from self-ratings and spouse ratings. *Journal of Personality and Social Psychology, 91,* 959–974.

# 4

# Reinforcement Sensitivity Theory, Research, Applications, and Future

## Luke D. Smillie, Natalie J. Loxton, and Rachel E. Avery

In this chapter we review the approach–avoidance process theory of personality proposed by Jeffrey Alan Gray (1970, 1973), now widely known as reinforcement sensitivity theory (RST). We begin by placing RST in the broader context of theory and research concerning approach and avoidance motivation. We then provide a snapshot of the animal research upon which the brain–behavior systems of RST were based. Next we discuss the vexed issue of how these systems might manifest themselves in personality space, and we review the latest empirical tests of RST as an explanation of personality variation. Finally, we consider applications of RST beyond personality: specifically, we review current opinion on the relevance of RST to psychopathology and clinical dysfunction and the potential for RST to underlie achievement motivation in learning and performance contexts. We conclude by looking to the future and highlighting a major challenge that we believe RST now faces.

## 1 Foundations of RST

### 1.1 Approach and avoidance motivation

Psychology can be defined as the study of affect, behavior, cognition, and desire, whilst personality psychology concerns the *long-term pattern* of our affect, behavior, cognition, and desire (Revelle, 2007). Psychological theories tend to emphasize some processes over others, as can be plainly said both of early behaviorism and of the cognitive theories that decelerated its radical application (Segal & Lachman, 1972). Such historical shifts of emphasis bring balance to our explanations of psychological phenomena—including individual differences, the focus of this volume—none of which is plausibly reducible to a single process. One recent shift has been to emphasize affective processes, long neglected but now increasingly recognized as

*The Wiley-Blackwell Handbook of Individual Differences*, First Edition.
Edited by Tomas Chamorro-Premuzic, Sophie von Stumm, and Adrian Furnham.
© 2011 Blackwell Publishing Ltd. Published 2011 by Blackwell Publishing Ltd.

fundamental to various domains in psychology (Damasio, 1994; Kringelbach & Berridge, 2010; Panksepp, 1998). A related area, which is enjoying its scientific renaissance after a sharp decline during the cognitive revolution, is the study of motivational processes: our desires and our distresses. The potency of motivational factors has been demonstrated from within various niches in social and personality psychology, animal behavior, and organizational psychology (Elliot, 2008).

A ubiquitous principle in motivation theory, which grew prominent in both achievement motivation and animal-learning research (see Atkinson, 1957; Hull, 1943; Lewin, 1935; Schneirla, 1959; Spence, 1956), is that of approach and avoidance (Elliot, 2008). Approach and avoidance are basic motivational orientations toward appetitive and away from aversive outcomes; we want to approach pleasure and to avoid pain. This "hedonic principle" has been recognized since the Cyrenaics (fifth–fourth century BC), and was viewed by Freud (1924) as quintessential to human nature (if not to all of nature). In the mid-twentieth century, approach and avoidance provided an organizing framework for the behaviorists, as reinforcing stimuli were functionally distinguished by the motivational orientation they elicited. Specifically, approach motivation is elicited by the opportunity for reward or termination of punishment, while avoidance motivation is elicited by the threat of punishment or termination of reward (Gray, 1973, pp. 420–424). Neuroscience research has identified various cortical and subcortical brain networks that appear to regulate approach and avoidance processes (Davidson, 1995; Depue & Collins, 1999; Spielberg, Stewart, Levin, Miller, & Heller, 2008; Sutton & Davidson, 1997; Wacker, Chavanon, Leue, & Stemmler, 2008). The consequences of these opposing motivational states are varied and striking, as continues to be revealed in a variety of domains, from social-personality psychology (Cury, Elliot, Da Fonseca, & Moller, 2006; Thrash & Hurst, 2008) to cognitive science (Markman, Baldwin, & Maddox, 2005).

It is upon the foundations of approach and avoidance motivation that Jeffrey Gray suggested that a model for personality might be built (Gray, 1973, 1991). The logic, as our colleagues and we have come to summarize it colloquially, is that between-person variation in any basic component of psychological functioning must have important implications for personality and individual differences. Gray proposed that two brain–behavior systems motivated approach of appetitive stimuli and avoidance of aversive stimuli, and emerge as stable personality traits. In his own words: "Let us suppose that there are two basic drive-and-reinforcement mechanisms […] a reward mechanism and a punishment mechanism […] Level of activity in the reward and punishment systems, then, would underlie the approach and avoidance functions, respectively" (Gray & Smith, 1969, p. 247). Further, we might "expect to observe dimensions of personality that correspond to the functioning of [these systems]" (Gray, 1991, p. 123). This deceptively simple proposal, the central tenet of RST, was novel and striking for at least two reasons. First, the bottom-up nature of RST was unconventional, as Gray frequently noted: "Analyses of personality [typically] start from human individual differences measured directly […] Suppose, instead, that we start the other way round and use our current understanding of these systems to predict the likely structure of human personality" (ibid.). Second, although motivational bases for personality had been suggested before (e.g. Lewin, 1935), RST appeared at a time when arousal-based theories of personality dominated the field (Eysenck, 1967) and the cognitive revolution was well underway.

RST has evolved considerably over the last 40 years—this openness to change and revision has been cited as one of its most commendable features (Revelle, 2008, p. 509). Recent reviews have traced these developments in detail (see e.g. Corr, 2008; Smillie, Pickering, & Jackson, 2006), and in consequence our own description will be succinct. The brain–behavior systems described by Gray and Smith (1969) were later termed "the behavioral activation system" (BAS) and "the fight–flight–freeze system" (FFFS). The BAS mediates the approach of all appetitive stimuli (Gray, 1987). Although often termed a "reward system," the BAS is understood to bring the organism into contact with reward, but not to mediate the effects of an obtained reward. As such, the BAS is really a *desire* system, motivating approach of things that we want (for a recent review, see Pickering & Smillie, 2008). The FFFS mediates avoidance of all aversive stimuli. The outputs of the FFFS are complex, in that proximal threats elicit defensive attack (i.e. the "fight" response), whilst distal threats elicit "flight" or "freezing" depending upon the availability of escape. Despite its range of outputs, the FFFS is essentially a *fear* system, motivating avoidance of perceived threat (for recent work, see Perkins, Cooper, Abdelall, Smillie & Corr, in press). A third system, also involved in the regulation of avoidance motivation, is the behavioral inhibition system (BIS). The BIS resolves conflict between the FFFS and BAS, for instance when feared stimuli must be approached (this is an approach/avoidance conflict). BIS outputs include increased arousal, risk assessment, and, of course, behavioral inhibition. In addition, at an information processing level, the BIS is thought to amplify inputs to the FFFS, and thus bias conflict resolution, in favor of avoidance. The BIS is the most thoroughly delineated component of RST (for extensive detail, see Gray & McNaughton, 2000), and it is thought of as an *anxiety* system, motivating cautious approach and preparation for avoidance.

It is worth noting that, while we prefer to emphasize the *motivational* function of the RST systems, Gray referred chiefly to their *emotional* functions, especially in the case of BIS-mediated anxiety. Of course, motivation and emotion are greatly intertwined: as Gray and McNaughton (1996, p. 63) note: "Given the role played by reinforcing events in both motivation and emotion, it is difficult to develop a theory of one that is not, explicitly or implicitly, a theory also of the other." It is nevertheless useful to draw a distinction between emotional processes characterized by motivational direction (e.g. desire, fear) and others characterized (merely) by affective valence (e.g. pleasure, sadness; Spielberg et al., 2008). Indeed, mounting evidence argues for a decoupling of affective and motivational processes, such as the finding that some negative affective states co-occur with approach motivation (Carver, 2004; Harmon-Jones & Sigelman, 2001; see also Berridge, Robinson, & Aldridge, 2008; Carrol, Yik, Russell, & Barrett, 1999; Gable & Harmon-Jones, 2008). Furthermore, the emotion-laden terms used by Gray, such as "hope" and "fear" (e.g. Gray, 1987, pp. 246–256), are firmly attached to—and, moreover, *inferred from*—motivational tendencies of approach and avoidance. For these reasons, we feel it is most appropriate (and perhaps most broadly inclusive of current opinion in this area) to refer to RST as a theory of motivation. This is in no way intended to minimize the central relevance of affective (yet motivationally directed) processes in RST, which is equally a theory of *desire* and *distress* (Deary & Johnson, 2009).

## 1.2    Animal models: the bedrock of RST

Personality theories usually attempt to explain personality data, such as its structure (e.g. Peabody & Goldberg, 1989), its constituent information processing (e.g. Humphreys & Revelle, 1984), or its very existence (e.g. Penke, Denissen, & Miller, 2007). In comparison, RST is a strange beast to encounter, as it is, in some respects, "not at all concerned with personality" (Smillie et al., 2006, p. 320). RST was developed with the aim of explaining effects of anxiolytic ("anti-anxiety") drugs in animal models of anxiety. From a wide review of the literature, Gray (1977) concluded that anxiolytics (benzodiazepines, barbituates, and alcohol) antagonized the effects of aversive stimuli (signals of punishment or non-reward, but also novel stimuli) on specific behaviors in the rat: inhibition of ongoing behavior, attention to the environment, and behavioral arousal (i.e. vigor of subsequent responding). The BIS was proposed as a conceptual mediator of these effects that also corresponded to some physiological network in the brain. That network was identified as the septo-hippocampal system, a proposal supported by converging evidence regarding the action of anxiolytics on monoamines which projected to this region and on lesions which mimicked the behavioral effects of the drugs (Gray, 1977; Gray & McNaughton, 1983). On this basis, Gray (1982) proposed that anxiety could be explained in terms of the functions of the BIS, which mediates responses to aversive stimuli.

It is important to realize that this proposal concerned *state* rather than *trait* anxiety. However, it was suggested that long-term patterns of BIS functioning manifest themselves as a stable disposition (Corr & McNaughton, 2008, p. 162), this being a core assumption in personality science, namely state–trait isomorphism (Fleeson, 2001; Revelle & Scherer, 2009). Furthermore, it was possible to consider the BIS in the context of an influential animal *trait* model that preceded RST: The "Maudsley strains" (see Broadhurst, 1975; Gray, 1987, ch. 4) were engineered, through selective breeding, as a model of emotional reactivity (and were later considered a model of susceptibility to anxiety). Wistar rats were artificially selected for on the basis of high or low defecation in the open field test (see Hall, 1934), on the principle that, in humans, loss of bowel/bladder control occurs with strong fear. After eight generations, low-reactive subjects ("low-anxious" rats) could be differentiated from high-reactive subjects ("high-anxious" rats) in terms of the behavioral profile described above. Further, the behavior exhibited by low-reactive subjects could be produced by administering anxiolytics to unselected rats (see Commissaris, Verbanac, Markovska, Altman, & Hill, 1996; Gray, 1982), which lent credence to the BIS as an explanation both for trait and for state anxiety. On the other hand, as RST evolved, the distinction between *fear* and *anxiety*, which the Maudsley strains appear to conflate, became sharper. Perhaps for this reason, differentiation of the strains using anxiety batteries has not been wholly consistent (Paterson, Whiting, Gray, Flint & Dawson, 2001). This animal model is nevertheless a seminal chapter in the RST narrative.

As RST was refined and eventually revised (Gray & McNaughton, 1996, 2000), the BIS was reconceptualized as a *conflict* mechanism (as described earlier), which better reflected the complex stimulus inputs blocked by anxiolytics. This was greatly influenced by the ethoexperimental studies conducted by Robert and Caroline Blanchard (e.g. Blanchard & Blanchard, 1990; Blanchard, Griebel, Henrie, & Blanchard, 1997). Their work evidenced a sharp distinction in rodent responses to actual versus potential threat (e.g. cat vs. cat odor). Actual threat produced the repertoire of avoidance behaviors attributable to a fight–flight–freeze system (FFFS), as described earlier (Gray, 1982, 1987). Potential threat resulted in a repertoire of "risk assessment" behaviors, including the behavioral inhibition that the Blanchards considered analogous to human anxiety. Critically, the Blanchards and their colleagues demonstrated that responses to actual threat were resistant to anxiolytic drugs, whereas responses to potential threat were blocked. Given these findings, Gray and McNaughton (2000) included "potential threat" as an example of the motivationally conflicting information that activates the BIS. At a broader level of abstraction it is still sensible to view the BIS as an avoidance system, in that its outputs (e.g. risk assessment) serve the function of *preparing* for avoidance.

The remaining system, the BAS, received relatively little attention in the primary RST literature. Gray apparently included it on logical grounds and for the sake of symmetry: "It was natural to suggest that, if anxiety reflects sensitivity to signals of punishment and non-reward, [a] second dimension might correspond to sensitivity to signals of reward and non-punishment ..." (Gray, Owen, Davis, & Tsaltas, 1983, pp. 184–185). Pickering, a colleague of Gray's (who, incidentally, gave RST its name), made the more detailed theoretical contributions to this speculative idea (e.g. Pickering & Gray, 1999; Pickering & Smillie, 2008), also drawing upon animal research. For instance, single cell recordings from dopamine neurons in monkeys reveal phasic increases in firing in response to primary rewards and, after training, in response to conditioned signals of reward (Schultz, 1998). Such research has helped establish mid-brain dopaminergic neurotransmission as a central pathway in approach motivation (Robins & Everitt, 1996; cf. Panksepp & Moskal, 2008). More recent research confirms this idea: for instance, genetically engineered dopamine-deficient mice show reduced learning from and approach of rewards (Robinson, Sandstrom, Denenberg, & Palmiter, 2005), whilst rat strains that have been outbred for behavioral reward responsivity show substantial differences in mid-brain dopamine receptor availability (Dalley et al., 2007). Perhaps complementing the Maudsley strain as a model of *distress* (fear/anxiety), this latter research may provide an animal model of *desire*.

## 1.3  Related perspectives

Just as a common currency has emerged among descriptive models of personality in the form of the various "five-factor" inventories, many theories of personality processes have converged upon approach and avoidance as central explanatory mechanisms. As noted by Revelle (2008, p. 509), the approach and avoidance processes postulated in RST have provided "the foundation of biologically driven theories [of personality]." One notable example is Cloninger's (1987) personality theory, which drew strongly upon concepts derived from RST, but focused specifically on providing a neurotransmitter account of personality. More recently, Elliot and Thrash (2002) proposed the constructs of "approach and avoidance temperament," which, they suggest, represents a common core to many major personality traits. The authors consider these constructs to be more broadly abstracted than, but nevertheless closely linked with, the biobehavioral systems of RST. Carver, Sutton, and Scheier (2000), Davidson (1995), Depue and Collins (1999), Fowles (1980), Tellegen (1985), and Zuckerman (1979) have incorporated elements of RST in their models and frameworks for personality. Some prefer to view such models as importantly distinct from RST and from each other; indeed, they are not wholly consistent in their formulations and predictions. Nevertheless, insofar as each one identifies approach and avoidance processes as providing a partial explanation for personality variation, collectively they create a broad and relatively coherent framework that can be traced to the work of Jeffrey Gray.

## 2   RST and Personality

### 2.1   From systems to traits ... which traits?

So far we have deliberatively avoided references to particular personality traits, because we do not regard RST as a theory *of* particular personality traits. As noted earlier, RST might be better thought of as a theory applied *to* the study of personality. A bottom-up extrapolation from basic approach–avoidance systems observed in animal models to major personality traits might bring to mind Jacob's Ladder (and perhaps inspire a degree of skepticism): How exactly does one get from the systems to the traits? Although the answer to this question has proved elusive, if not downright frustrating, current opinion is not dramatically different from the suggestions which Gray (1970, 1973) made some 40 years ago. The dominant personality taxonomy at that time was the two-factor model of Hans Eysenck (1967), consisting of extraversion (E) and neuroticism (N). Not surprisingly, therefore, this was the factor space in which Gray attempted to locate trait manifestations of his approach and avoidance processes. As he repeatedly noted (e.g. 1973, 1981), factor analysis, the method relied upon in part by Eysenck for his descriptive model, can determine the minimum number of dimensions in a data set, but not the appropriate rotation that would align them with their causal influences. Gray's initial application of RST to personality was in essence a critique and revision of Eysenck's model, suggesting how E and N (or similar orthogonal dimensions) might be mapped onto approach and avoidance processes.

The first argument in Gray's critique concerned the success of experimental tests of the causal processes hypothesized (top-down) by Eysenck. These tests could not robustly confirm the prediction that introverts would condition better than extraverts, which was based upon Eysenck's proposal that introverts are chronically over-aroused (Eysenck & Levey, 1972). Furthermore, work by Revelle, Humphreys, Simon, and Gilliland (1980) suggested that introverts are not *chronically* over-aroused, but rather over-aroused in the *morning* only. A better fit to the data, Gray argued, might be achieved by supposing that introverts (relative to extraverts) show superior condition-ing only to *aversive* stimuli, as data appeared to indicate. Such a prediction would follow if one replaced Eysenck's general arousal mechanism with Gray's BIS (con-ceptualized as a "sensitivity to punishment" system at that point in time). The BIS, of course, was developed as an explanation of anxiety, which clinical and personality research located in factor space between introversion and neuroticism (Eysenck, 1967; Spence, 1956). Therefore a rotation of Eysenck's factors by approximately 45° was proposed; this resulted in one dimension comprising low E and high N (*trait anxiety*) and reflecting avoidance motivation (BIS), while another, more speculatively, comprised high E and high N (*trait impulsivity*) and reflected approach motivation (BAS).

## 2.2   Challenges to trait conceptualization

Gray's (1970, 1981) critique exposed several cracks in the foundation of Eysenck's model (later acknowledged to be no longer viable; Eysenck, 1998, p. 248), and Gray put forward a highly plausible alternative. However, two decades later it was remarked: "in several crucial respects, RST has yet to be adequately tested [as a personality theory]" (Corr, 2001, p. 348). This was partly attributed to interpretive ambiguities surrounding Gray's so-called "anxiety" and "impulsivity" traits. First, although anxiety was originally depicted as a 45° rotation of Eysenck's factors, a footnote (Gray, 1970, p. 263) suggested that it was probably more closely aligned with the N factor, which implied a 30° rotation. Thus the use of introversion as a proxy for BIS sensitivity in early tests of RST (e.g. Gupta, 1976) was perhaps less than ideal. Second, the suggestion that anxiety and impulsivity reflected combinations of E and N was sometimes interpreted as a E × N interaction (e.g. Rusting & Larsen, 1997). In a detailed clarification, Pickering, Corr, and Gray (1999) stated that *additive* effects of E and N, not interactions, are expected. This paper formalized the relation-ship between Eysenck's and Gray's traits as impulsivity = 2E + N and anxiety as 2N − E. However, revisions to Eysenck's scales had produced a third personality factor, psychoticism (P), absorbing most of the impulsivity items that formerly had loaded on E (see Rocklin & Revelle, 1981). As this seemed likely to have implications for deriving Gray's traits from Eysenck's measures, further reformulation was offered by Corr (2001), in which anxiety was calculated as $n$ (E items) − E + 2N − P and impulsivity as 2E + N + P.

Unsurprisingly, many have found it simpler to test RST by measuring anxiety and impulsivity directly rather than by deriving them second hand. Sensible though this may seem, there are many conceptualizations of anxiety and impulsivity that are theoretically inconsistent with RST (as noted elsewhere; see Torrubia, Avila, & Caseras, 2008). For instance Carver and White (1994) suggested that, whilst some anxiety concepts reflect the *typical experience* of anxiety, the concept of BIS-mediated anxiety is one of *vulnerability* to anxiety. To illustrate the sharp distinction that might be made between these forms of anxiety, these authors speculated that someone who was vulnerable to anxiety states might avoid anxiety-provoking situa-tions and thereby keep his or her typical experience of anxiety to a minimum. Such issues were further multiplied by Gray and McNaughton's (2000) revision of RST, as the divorce of anxiety (BIS) from fear (FFFS) is not reflected in mainstream anxiety scales (Heym, Ferguson, & Lawrence, 2008).

Ambiguity in the interpretation of Gray's "impulsivity" trait was greater still. Gray et al. (1983) emphasize the speculative nature of the BAS = impulsivity hypothesis and acknowledge that impulsivity can be conceptualized in various ways, not all of which are consistent with the functions of the BAS (pp. 184–189). Despite this, measures of impulsivity have been used somewhat indiscriminately to test RST, yielding considerably mixed results (see Pickering, 2004). Over the last decade, the issue has been vigorously addressed in psychometric (Leone, 2009; Quilty & Oakman, 2004), behavioral (Pickering, 2004; Smillie, Dalgleish, & Jackson, 2007), neuroscientific (Krebs, Schott, & Düzel, 2009; Smillie, Cooper, Proitsi, Powell, & Pickering, 2010), and clinical or psychiatric (Dawe & Loxton, 2004; Loxton, Nguyen, Casey, & Dawe, 2008) research. This research has converged upon a distinction between *reward reactivity*, concerning approach motivation, and *rash impulsivity*, concerning poor impulse control. Evidence suggests that personality measures reflecting reward reactivity (typically associated with Eysenck's E) might be more directly related to BAS functioning than are measures that reflect rash impulsivity (which are typically associated with Eysenck's P). Further, as most measures of trait impulsivity appear to reflect the latter construct, it has been suggested that impulsivity may have been a misnomer in RST (Smillie et al., 2006).

Given the uncertainty with which pre-existing measures could be adopted in tests of RST, several researchers developed purpose-built questionnaires for assessing trait manifestations of Gray's motivational systems (e.g. Carver & White, 1994; Cooper, Smillie, & Jackson, 2008; Jackson, 2009; Torrubia, Avila, Molto, & Caseras, 2001). Although these questionnaires have proven useful for the field (Torrubia et al., 2008), they suffer from the same ambiguities as mainstream anxiety/impulsivity questionnaires. For instance, Carver and White's (1994) three-factor conceptualization of the BAS appears to combine reward reactivity and rash impulsivity (Leone, 2009), as does Torrubia et al.'s (2001) sensitivity to reward scale (Cooper et al., 2008). Similarly, as Carver and White's (1994) BIS scale predated the revised RST, it potentially conflates fear and anxiety. It has therefore been suggested that such measures should be divided into two factors to represent BIS and FFFS respectively (Heym et al., 2008). As has been remarked in previous reviews of this area (e.g. Pickering, 2004), decisive evidence that *any* of these measures successfully locates RST systems in personality space is yet to appear. Further, it has been suggested that the distance between personality (i.e. what we assess with personality questionnaires) and reinforcement sensitivity (i.e. biobehavioral processes regulating approach and avoidance) is too great for us to hope for any isomorphic convergence (Smillie, 2008). Nevertheless, the construction of RST-related questionnaires has helped conceptualize approach and avoidance processes at a personality-trait level.

## 2.3   Recent evidence linking personality traits with RST system processes

A wealth of research now exists in which candidate traits have been used to test RST as a partial explanation for personality variation. Here we will discuss just a few pertinent examples from the recent literature, as extensive reviews covering earlier literature are available elsewhere (e.g. Corr, 2008; Matthews & Gilliland, 1999; Pickering, Corr, Powell, Kumari, Thornton, & Gray, 1997). It is significant to note that, whilst these qualitative reviews have often reached fairly gloomy conclusions, a recent quantitative review (i.e. a meta-analysis) suggests otherwise: Leue and Beauducel (2008) examined findings from 38 experimental and quasi-experimental behavioral tests of RST (whittled down by strict inclusion criteria from an initial pool of nearly 4,000 relevant papers). Although the authors distinguished only impulsivity-related and anxiety-related traits (as studies examined had predated the fear/anxiety distinction in the revised RST), they were able to examine the role of "conflict," the putative input to the BIS, by distinguishing experiments which presented "incompatible concurrent goals" or "uncertainty of reinforcement" from those which did not (p. 356). The key findings of the meta-analysis were:

1   After correcting for scale unreliability and range enhancement/restriction, modest but reliable effect sizes were observed (mean true score correlations; anx = .164; imp = .211).
2   For anxiety-related traits, effect sizes were stronger and more reliable in paradigms characterized by conflict.

These are important findings, as they indicate that tests of RST have yielded positive results overall and that variation in findings probably reflects power constraints and measurement error.

Many recent tests of RST have zeroed in on the role of conflict sensitivity in BIS-related personality traits. For instance, Hirsh and Inzlicht (2008) report an event-related potential (ERP) study in which neural responses to uncertain feedback (i.e. to the presentation of a question mark rather than to accurate information) were predicted by trait N (neuroticism). In another ERP study, Leue, Chavanon, Wacker, and Stemmler (2009) varied reward expectancy from low conflict (dissimilar probabilities of reward across choices) to high conflict (equal probabilities of reward across choices). Target ERPs varied predictably with conflict, as did response time and self-reports of decision uncertainty. Furthermore, ERPs were modulated by scores on a German analogue of the BIS/BAS scales, although in quite complex ways. Somewhat clearer findings were obtained by Berkman, Lieberman, and Gable (2009), who operationalized conflict by crossing stimulus valence (appetitive/aversive) with response direction (approach/avoid). Carver's and White's BIS scores did not predict behavioral responses to aversive trials, but they did predict faster responding to conflict trials (approach-aversive and avoid-appetitive). Smillie (2009) also found that high-BIS scorers respond faster to conflict (but not to punishment) when conflict is manipulated by presenting simultaneous, incompatible approach goals. Overall, it is encouraging for RST to observe that BIS-related traits predict responses to varied operations of goal conflict.

A salient feature in the recent literature is an increased use of neuroscience methods. For instance, Simon et al. (2010) used functional magnetic resonance imaging (fMRI) to assess neural responses to monetary rewards in relation to personality scores. The Carver and White BAS scale was positively predictive of activity in the ventral striatum and medial orbital cortex (both of which are key components of ascending dopaminergic pathways) during the receipt of reward. Similar findings were obtained by Barrós-Loscertales et al. (2010) using different rewards (erotic pictures) and a different personality measure (the sensitivity to reward scale proposed by Torrubia and colleagues). The last decade has also witnessed an explosion in gene–trait association studies. For instance, a well-known polymorphism of the DRD2/ANKK1 gene was found in two studies to predict variation—in the Carver and White BAS scale (Lee, Ham, Cho, Lee, & Shim, 2007) and, from Eysenk's model, in E (extraversion; Smillie et al., 2010). In both of these studies, trait scores were higher for individuals carrying at least one copy of an allele associated with decreased D2 receptor availability, which, as discussed earlier, was found to character-ize a recent animal model of BAS-like temperament (Dalley et al., 2007). More sophisticated studies combining multiple methods have shown convergence among, for instance, psychometric markers (e.g. trait anxiety), behavioral markers (e.g. acous-tic affective startle reflex modulation, ASRM), and genetic markers of RST system function (e.g. COMT Val158Met polymorphism; Montag et al., 2008).

Some other relevant studies in the recent literature did not set out to test RST specifically, but are nonetheless highly interpretable from this standpoint. Hirsh, DeYoung, and Peterson (2009) examined "metatraits" of the Big Five in relation to 400 everyday behaviors (assessed retrospectively through self-report). One of these higher-order trait clusters, which reflect a combination of extraversion and openness (termed "beta" or "plasticity"), has been linked conceptually with the BAS, and is also thought to reflect dopamine function (p. 1096). This was found to predict a variety of specific appetitive behaviors that could be argued to reflect dispositional approach motivation (e.g. sex, dating, and parties). At a more detailed level of analy-sis, Read et al. (2010) constructed a neural network model of personality in which approach and avoidance motivation systems were included as mediators of a range of specific motives (e.g. exploration and play, avoiding harm). One broad aim of this model was to simulate dynamic responses to specific events and situations as a func-tion of traits, which were formalized in terms of RST-like system sensitivities. In broad terms, results from these simulations fit well with Hirsh et al.'s (2009) empiri-cal findings. For instance, when social or partying situations were fed into the model, a relatively greater approach system reactivity (which is the authors' formalization of Eysenck's trait E) resulted in behaviors such as "drink alcohol" and "dance," while a relatively greater avoidance system reactivity (the authors' formalization of trait N) resulted in behaviors such as "leave" and "stay in periphery." This model (too rich in details to be adequately described here) demonstrates the plausibility of the central tenet of RST: that sensitivities of basic motivation systems manifest themselves as personality patterns.

These studies represent a small fraction of the RST and related literature, which, as previous reviews have demonstrated, is more complicated than the picture we have briefly sketched here would allow one to see. Nevertheless, they do suggest a conclusion at which even the more pessimistic reviews of RST have arrived (see Pickering et al., 1997)—namely that personality is frequently predicted by various operations of RST system functions, at multiple levels of analysis. At the very least, the broad proposal that RST and related theories make with regard to personality explanation—that major personality dispositions are related to underlying approach and avoidance motivation processes—has been supported.

## 3  RST and Psychopathology

Just as Gray's theory has been applied to the explanation of personality, clinical psychologists have found in RST a useful lens through which to view a range of psychopathologies (see Bijttebier, Beck, Claes, & Vandereycken, 2009; Claridge & Davis, 2003). As noted in Gray's (1994) "Framework for a taxonomy of psychiatric disorder," many psychological disorders can be conceptualized as disorders of excessive approach and/or excessive avoidance—or of desire and distress (Deary & Johnson, 2009). In clinical settings, RST has been fruitfully applied to the study of anxiety or panic disorders (Zinbarg & Lira Yoon, 2008), of mood disorders (Alloy, Bender, Wagner, Abramson, & Urosević, 2009; Hundt, Nelson-Gray, Kimbrel, Mitchell, & Kwapil, 2007), of substance use disorders (Dawe et al., 2007; Franken, Muris, & Georgieva, 2006), of eating disorders (Loxton & Dawe, 2009), and of impulse control disorders, such as problematic gambling (Loxton, Nguyen, et al., 2008). In the following section we consider the extent to which RST may facilitate our understanding of affective disorders, addictive behavior, and eating disorders such as binge-eating.

### 3.1  Anxiety and affective disorders: disorders of extreme distress?

The application of RST to the explanation of affective disorders, and especially of anxiety disorders, flows naturally from the fact that, as noted above, RST developed from animal models of human anxiety. Gray and McNaughton consider implications of RST for a range of anxiety and affective disorders, with a particular focus on dissociating anxiety (BIS) and panic (FFFS) disorders (Gray & McNaughton, 2000, pp. 285–327; and see also McNaughton & Corr, 2008). Unfortunately, however, many of the studies examining these ideas have drawn mainly upon earlier articulations of RST (e.g. Gray, 1982). A lot of research (including longitudinal studies with prospective personality assessment, e.g. Lönnqvist, Verkasalo, Mäkinen, & Henriksson, 2009) confirms that individuals diagnosed with anxiety disorders have elevated scores on purpose-built BIS questionnaires and on related measures, such as neuroticism (see Bijttebier et al., 2009 for a recent review). As neither clinical diagnosis (Gray & McNaughton, 2000, p. 286) nor personality assessment (Heym et al., 2008) tends to clearly distinguish fear from anxiety, much of this research might be viewed as targeting the RST avoidance system at its broadest conception (i.e. BIS and FFFS). Similarly, as serotonin neurons are thought to permeate the whole defensive system (Gray & McNaughton, 2000, pp. 110–113), the same might be said of the substantial literature that has supported a role for serotonin function (Katzman, 2009) and gene polymorphisms (You, Hu, Chen, & Zhang, 2005) in anxiety disorders.

Interestingly, proposed changes to the forthcoming edition of the *Diagnostic and statistical manual of mental disorders* (*DSM*; American Psychiatric Association, 2000) converge closely with the revised RST. This will see a shift away from the grouping of disorders into diagnostic classes on *rational* grounds (similarity of symptoms), toward grouping of disorders on *empirical* grounds (on the basis of known co-morbidities and shared genetic or etiological bases: Watson, 2005). From this per-spective, Watson has proposed three *DSM* categories under the rubric "internalizing disorders": (1) a bipolar disorder category; (2) a "distress" category (which includes general anxiety disorder, dysthymia, and major depression); and (3) a "fear" category (phobic disorders). The last two of these categories map reasonably well onto the revised RST, with "distress" disorders characterized by anxiety (i.e. BIS) and by low reward motivation (i.e. low BAS; see McFarland, Shankman, Tenke, Bruder, & Klein, 2006), and with "fear" disorders characterized by avoidance (i.e. FFFS; see Urosević, Abramson, Harmon-Jones, & Alloy, 2008 for a review of the potential link between bipolar disorders and RST). This organization also fits with Zinbarg and Lira Yoon's (2008) proposal that anxiety or mood disorders can be organized in terms of fear versus anxiety or misery disorders. Such developments may allow future research into affective disorders to be more readily evaluated from the perspective of RST (see Deary & Johnson, 2009).

### 3.2   Addictive behaviors: disorders of extreme desire?

Although the neuropsychology of addiction seems to be of peripheral importance within the primary RST literature, recent theory and research in this field (e.g. Robinson & Berridge, 2003) suggests a central role for it in relation to the BAS. Motivated approach to rewarding stimuli appears to drive the use and abuse of sub-stances, suggesting that addictions can be conceptualized as disorders of extreme desire. Questionnaire measures of RST constructs are reliably correlated with drug and alcohol use, and heavy drinkers (adolescents and adults, men and women) report higher scores on BAS-related measures than lighter drinkers or non-drinkers (Franken & Muris, 2006; Knyazev, Slobodskaya, Kharchenko, & Wilson, 2004; Loxton & Dawe, 2006, 2007; O'Connor & Colder, 2005). BAS scores are also associated with a greater likelihood of meeting a diagnosis of alcohol abuse/dependence and with the use of illicit drugs (Egan, Kambouropoulos, & Staiger, 2010; Johnson, Turner, & Iwata, 2003; Loxton, Wan, et al., 2008). Support for a predispositional (in other words causal rather than correlational) role of reward/approach processes in sub-stance use includes data from the animal model described earlier, in which a drug-naïve, "reward-sensitive" rodent strain self-administered more cocaine than their non-reward-sensitive counterparts (Dalley et al., 2007).

As discussed earlier, the BAS is thought to mediate behavioral approach of reward and motivational "wanting," rather than affective "liking," of the obtained reward. Thus, in relation to substance use, the BAS seems likely to influence processes and behaviors reflecting the desire for a substance (e.g. cravings, urge to drink/use, for-mation of positive beliefs regarding substance use). Support for this view includes the findings that measures of trait reward sensitivity are positively related to alcohol craving and that reward-sensitive drinkers show a greater tendency to notice and attend to alcohol-related cues (Colder & O'Connor, 2002; Franken, 2002; Kambouropoulos & Staiger, 2009). Research in this area has also reflected the aforementioned distinction between reward responsiveness and rash impulsivity

(Dawe & Loxton, 2004). For instance, Voigt et al. (2009) found that, whilst rash impulsivity predicted more hazardous drinking, reward responsiveness was associated with less hazardous drinking. Voigt et al. suggested that this might be interpreted in terms of temporal distance from reward; hence it would appear that BAS mediates approach of long-term reward, whereas rash impulsivity brings one into contact with more immediate reward. Heym et al. (2008) have offered similar temporal distance accounts in suggesting that BAS-related measures may be distinguished in terms of sensitivity to future rewards versus immediate rewards. Along similar lines, Corr (2008) has suggested that, in an adaptive approach system, the behavioral output might be expected to vary along a temporo-spatial gradient, such that goal-focused behavior is produced at the commencement of approach (when impulsive responses should be inhibited), while more impulsive, "grab now" behavior is produced when reward is imminent. From this perspective, substance abuse may partly arise from an excessive focus on immediate rewards at the expense of long-term goals.

There is also some evidence suggesting links between BIS-related traits and substance misuse, although this has been considerably mixed. Many studies find a negative relationship between BIS and hazardous drinking or substance use (see e.g., Franken & Muris, 2006; Simons, Dvorak, & Bastien, 2008). Others find no relationship (Franken, et al., 2006; Kambouropoulos & Staiger, 2007; Loxton & Dawe, 2006, 2007). A positive association has been found with substance use in certain sub-populations (e.g. adolescent boys: Knyazev, 2004; Knyazev et al., 2004) and with the desire to drink in non-rewarded or in aversive situations (Kambouropoulos & Staiger, 2004). In part, these conflicting findings might, again, reflect temporal processes. For instance, several models of addiction highlight separable processes in the maintenance of substance abuse, one candidate being the self-medication of co-morbid distress disorders and/or the alleviation of withdrawal symptoms, which develop only after sustained substance use (e.g. Heinz et al., 2003). Thus FFFS and BIS-related processes may perpetuate drug use and relapse in later stages of addiction, while BAS-related processes may drive the initial experimentation and development of substance-related cue–response associations.

## 3.3   Binge-eating disorders: disorders of desire and distress?

Food is a primary reward, and the consumption of palatable food has long been known to increase mesolimbic dopamine availability (Hernandez & Hoebel, 1988). Not surprisingly, therefore, research using BAS-relevant trait measures has found heightened BAS in women who binge-eat (binge-eating being a defining criterion for bulimia nervosa and for the binge–purge sub-type of anorexia nervosa) and in women who score highly on self-report measures of dysfunctional eating (Kane, Loxton, Staiger, & Dawe, 2004; Loxton & Dawe, 2006, 2007). In the substance use literature, BAS-related traits have been associated with food cravings, a preference for foods high in fat and sugar, sensitivity to external food cues, and the tendency to overeat when depressed (Davis, Strachan, & Berkson, 2004; Franken & Muris, 2005). From such findings, Davis & Carter (2009) have argued that compulsive over-eating is an addictive behavior. As we suggested for drug abuse, it is additionally plausible that over-eating and binge-eating reflect temporally inappropriate appetitive responses to the wide availability of food in today's environment.

A notable characteristic of the eating disorders (especially those characterized by binge-eating/over-eating) is that cycles of approach behavior (binge) are often interspersed with periods of clearly avoidant behavior (e.g. highly restrictive eating, purging or abuse of laxatives to compensate for episodes of binge-eating). Unlike those who misuse drugs and alcohol, dysfunctional eaters consistently score higher than controls on measures of BIS (Loxton & Dawe, 2006, 2007). With the revision of RST and the separation of BIS from FFFS, the question arises as to which of the RST systems drives which dysfunctional eating behavior. For example, women who binge-eat may be overly sensitive to the availability of palatable food (perhaps due to a responsive BAS), which occasions in them overly strong cravings and desire to eat. Those who also restrict their food intake or use other compensatory strategies (e.g. purge, use laxatives) may also be over-sensitive to potential threats such as socially endorsed sanctions against weight gain (perhaps due to a responsive FFFS). In turn, the BIS may detect such conflicts (appealing food vs. threatening weight gain) and resolve them either in favor of approach behavior or in favor of avoidant behavior. Thus we can speculate that RST systems potentially impose specific eating/fasting patterns, which are observable in binge-eating disorders, anorexia nervosa, and bulimia nervosa: BAS-driven binge-eating, FFFS-driven restrictive eating, and BIS-driven binge/compensatory behaviors. Further research is required to determine if this is a useful model for dysfunctional health behaviors.

## 3.4   Conclusion

In summary, a wealth of evidence supports links between various psychopathologies and RST system functions (albeit mostly operationalized in terms of earlier concepts and measures). Furthermore, Gray and McNaughton's (2000) revision of RST coincides with, and complements, the planned changes to the *DSM*. As Bijttebier et al. (2009) state, "the RST framework has the potential to map distinct pathways to apparently similar psychopathology symptoms and, as such, play a role in identifying important subtypes of psychiatric disorders" (p. 427). Nevertheless, much work remains to be done in order to model the relationships between the components of RST and the processes by which, and conditions in which, extreme approach and avoidance traits translate into specific pathology.

## 4   RST and Achievement Motivation

Whilst the potential of RST to guide theory and research in psychopathology has been widely recognized, other promising extensions seem scarcely to have been noticed. An example we find particularly striking is an application in the area of achievement motivation. According to key theorists in this domain, "achievement motivation may be defined as the energization and direction of competence-based affect, cognition and behavior" (Elliot, 1999, p. 169). Achievement motivation concerns *competence-specific* motivated behavior—more precisely, behavior directed toward competence or away from incompetence. In this way, approach and avoidance motivation has played a crucial role in this literature, and captures what is thought to be a fundamental distinction in how achievement motivation is directed. Despite being clearly concerned with these processes, at least conceptually, RST has rarely been examined within learning and achievement contexts such as the classroom and the workplace (with some important exceptions: Bjornebekk, 2007; Farrell, 1997; Furnham & Jackson, 2008; Stewart, 1996).

Major theories of achievement motivation have followed a different developmental trajectory from that of RST, and both have tended to ignore each other. In recent years, however, an interest in specific brain–behavior processes within competence-specific contexts has emerged. Research which has considered the links between achievement-specific motives and the biobehavioral networks that process appetitive and aversive stimuli (e.g. Elliot, 1999; Elliot & Thrash, 2001) encourages the view that RST can inform a neuroscience of achievement motivation. Here we focus specifically on one of the most influential of achievement motivation traditions, that concerning achievement goals (Dweck, 1986; Nicholls, 1984). First we provide a brief overview of this literature, and then we ask to what extent RST may account for the adoption and pursuit of achievement goals within learning and performance settings.

## 4.1 Achievement goals: approaching success and avoiding failure

The achievement motivation literature has flourished over the past 70 years, much of it stemming from Lewin and colleagues' "level of aspiration" model (Lewin, 1935; Lewin, Dembo, Festinger, & Sears, 1944). This literature has introduced key achievement motivation concepts, including the notion of achievement *motives* (McClelland, Atkinson, Clark & Lowell, 1953) and, of present interest, that of achievement *goals* (Dweck 1986; Nicholls, 1984). Although not always termed as such, approach and avoidance processes have always been a central feature in the literature concerning achievement goals, most of which concern either approach of success and competence or avoidance of failure and incompetence (see Atkinson, 1957; Lewin et al., 1944; McClelland, 1951; Murray, 1938). However, it was the work of Elliot (1994) that explicated the approach/avoidance dichotomy within the achievement goal domain. Elliot recognized the inconsistent relationship between achievement goal constructs and various achievement outcomes, both positive (e.g. academic performance, effort, persistence, intrinsic motivation) and negative (e.g. surface processing, disengagement, withdrawal, anxiety; Elliot & Harackiewicz, 1996; Harackiewicz, Barron, Carter, Lehto, & Elliot, 1997; Nolen, 1988). A series of reviews (Elliot, 1994; Rawsthorne & Elliot, 1999) then suggested that achievement goal paradigms highlighting the opportunity for gain (eliciting approach) tended to produce more positive outcomes, whereas others, highlighting the opportunity for loss (eliciting avoidance), tended to produce more negative outcomes.

Elliot (1997) hypothesized that approach and avoidance motives (e.g. need for achievement, fear of failure) elicit affective states in which a valenced potentiality is anticipated—namely the possibility of success or failure—and which in turn promote the selection and pursuit of achievement goals (approach or avoid), culminating in various achievement-relevant behaviors and outcomes (such as persistence or with-drawal). A causal chain was thus proposed in which cognitive–affective states regarding the anticipation of success or failure indirectly relate to achievement outcomes via approach or avoidance processes. This motive–goal relationship received robust research support, and the need for achievement demonstrated predictive associations with approach goals, whereas fear of failure, with avoidance goals (Conroy & Elliot, 2004; Elliot & Church, 1997; Thrash & Elliot, 2002). Fear of failure also predicted the pursuit of approach goals when striving for success was identified as a means to avoid failure. Thus the pursuit of goals may relate to basic approach and avoidance motivation tendencies that, as was noted in the previous section for some psycho-pathologies, may interact in complex ways (Elliot, 1999).

In the context of a theory that has been primarily applied to personality and psychopathology, it is noteworthy that early theories of achievement motivation have always had an explicit focus on individual differences (Atkinson, 1957; McClelland, 1951; Murray 1938). This view persists today, albeit within a broader person × situation perspective: achievement motivation states are thought to be influenced by situational or experimental factors (such as cues, instructions, or incentives), but also by dispositional characteristics (that is, relatively stable trait-like tendencies either to seek success or to avoid failure), which persist across different achievement situations and over time (Hustinx, Kuyper, van de Werf & Dijkstra, 2009; Muis & Edwards, 2009). As for personality constructs, achievement motivation traits and states are believed to be isomorphic (Ward, Rogers, Byrne, & Masterson, 2004). In general, psychometric research reveals good support for the structure and validity of achievement motivation traits, demonstrating the existence, among individuals, of distinct patterns of high or low predisposed preferences for the attainment of goals of the approach type and avoidance type (Cury et al., 2006, Heggestad & Kanfer, 2000; Kanfer & Ackerman, 2000). Unless otherwise indicated, the research discussed below concerns individual differences in dispositional achievement motivation or goal pursuit, rather than situationally determined or experimentally induced achievement goals.

## 4.2   RST as a guiding framework for a neuroscience of achievement?

Questions regarding the processes underlying approach and avoidance of achievement goals suggest an obvious role for the systems of RST. Indeed, it has been suggested that BAS sensitivity underlies achievement *desire* (heightened motivation to approach success) while BIS sensitivity underlies achievement *distress* (heightened motivation to avoid failure) (Bjornebekk, 2007). As Elliot notes,

> BIS and BAS represent a neurophysiological predisposition to orient toward negative or positive stimuli [...] and individuals predisposed to orient toward positive stimuli would seem more likely to adopt [approach] goals, whereas those predisposed to orient toward negative stimuli would seem more likely to adopt [avoidance] goals. (Elliot, 1999, p. 175)

There is parsimony in this proposal; but is it plausible that phylogenetically old brain motivation systems initiate our responses to highly contextualized achievement goals?

In the past, considerable attention was directed toward establishing precise lists of "basic" BIS- and BAS-activating stimuli (e.g. conditioned vs. unconditioned stimuli; feedback vs. monetary reinforcers: see Corr, 2001; Matthews & Gilliland, 1999), and many might still draw firm boundaries between the desire for food or sex and the desire for promotion or grades. On the other hand, recent studies suggest that basic motivation systems are much more generalized than we might expect them to be (Daniel & Pollmann, 2010; Ritters, 2010; Tabibnia, Satpute, & Lieberman, 2008), and that there may be no reason to invent a new wheel for each new context in which approach and avoidance motivation processes are observed.

In support of these speculations, research shows that BAS-related questionnaires most strongly predict measures of success approach, while BIS-related question-naires most strongly predict measures of failure avoidance (Bjornebekk, 2007; Elliot & Thrash, 2002). Similar findings are obtained when assessing personality traits that have been closely linked with RST processes. For instance, extraversion and neuroti-cism tend to be most strongly related, respectively, to approach and avoidance achievement constructs (Bipp, Steinmayr & Spinath, 2008; Heimpel, Elliot, & Wood, 2006; Wang & Erdheim, 2007; Zweig & Webster, 2004). Importantly, although personality trait and achievement motivation constructs converge in this way, struc-tural equation models demonstrate their separability (e.g. Zweig & Webster, 2004). In addition, there is evidence that within-person fluctuations in personality *states* (see Fleeson, 2001) co-occur with pursuit of approach and avoidance goals. Specifically, Heller, Komar, and Lee (2007) found that state extraversion was highest during the pursuit of approach goals, whilst state neuroticism was highest during the pursuit of avoidance goals. Potentially, therefore, BAS and BIS activity (or, to use Bjornebekk's terminology, incentive and threat responsiveness) may differentially drive achieve-ment motivation. One recent study also supports Elliot and Thrash's (2001) specific suggestion that approach and avoidance motives mediate the BIS/BAS tempera-ment–goal relationship: Izadikhah, Jackson, and Loxton (2010) found that a measure of approach goal orientation mediated the relationship between BAS scores and job performance. (See O'Connor & Jackson, 2008, for highly similar findings.) Furthermore, this effect was strongest when the organizational climate was perceived to be rewarding. These results encourage the view that RST processes influence achievement behavior via motive-elicited achievement-specific states of desire for success and distress about failure (Elliot & Thrash, 2001).

A clear caveat to this research is that it has not yet considered the implications of revised RST for achievement motivation. This seems unlikely to affect the putative role of BAS functioning in the approach of competence and success, but rather, as in other domains (e.g. personality and psychopathology), it raises questions concern-ing the BIS and the FFFS. Associations between competence-specific avoidance goals and BIS measures (generally conceptualized in terms of "sensitivity to punishment") may in fact reflect the functioning of the FFFS (cf. Heym et al., 2008). Specifically, it is possible that high FFFS sensitivity in achievement situations contributes to an increased tendency to adopt avoidance goals, due to the anticipation of aversive stimuli and fear of failure. Conversely, the revised role of the BIS is suggestive of a probable role it plays in resolving any approach/avoidance conflict that an achieve-ment situation might present. This offers a possible insight into the association of approach goals with both need for achievement and fear of failure motives. Given that pursuit of approach goals can take the form of a proxy self-regulatory strategy (Elliot & Church, 1997), in which there is a conflict between the desire to approach success and the fear of failure, the BIS might play a potential role in resolving such conflict, and could perhaps explain why in some instances approach goals are associated with the experience of anxiety (Linnenbrink, 2005; Middleton & Midgley, 1997).

Much more research is required for us to progress toward a direct examination of RST system processes in relation to achievement motivation. However, research into the neural substrates of goal-directed action has implicated the same brain structures and functions connected with RST (e.g. Marsh et al., in press; Miller & Cohen, 2001). Furthermore, in possibly the first neuroimaging study of achievement, individual differences in achievement motivation predicted bilateral activity in the putamen (part of the dorsal striatum, a key structure within the reward system) during a working memory task (Mizuno et al., 2008). These findings arguably give some initial indication that achievement motivation is mediated by the RST-relevant systems, heightened desire for success being associated with greater activity in the reward system. Unfortunately, to our knowledge, there have so far been no complementary imaging studies concerning avoidance motivation within an achievement context.

## 4.3   Conclusions and further questions

Although presently at an embryonic stage, a neuroscience of achievement motivation that draws upon both RST and the achievement goal literature is encouraged by the above research. This would not be the first time that RST has been extended toward the explanation of broadly abstracted or highly contextualized phenomena. For instance, MacDonald and Leary (2005) reviewed evidence to suggest that RST systems are plausible mediators of social exclusion and separation; that "threats to one's social connections are processed at a basic level as a severe threat to one's safety" (p. 202). Similarly, opportunities for success and failure in an achievement context seem likely to be processed by the systems that evolved to bring us toward food and away from danger. This is not to say that achievement motivation can be entirely reduced to BIS, BAS, and FFFS; indeed there are many key constructs in the achievement goal literature that do not map easily to RST. For instance, a fundamental principle here is that the type of approach or avoidance goal an individual adopts, known as one's "goal orientation," is associated with different patterns of cognition and action when that individual is in an achievement situation (DeShon & Gillespie, 2005). A *mastery orientation* is concerned with the goal of developing self-referential competence, whereas a *performance orientation* is concerned with the goal of demonstrating normative competence (Elliot, 2005). While RST may guide the identification of processes that *direct* motivation in an achievement context (toward success or away from failure), it is not clear that it elucidates the *reasons* people have for adopting those achievement goals (namely the goal of developing versus demonstrating competence).

## 5   A Long Way to the Top: A Challenge for Future RST Research

The aim of this chapter has been to provide an up-to-date review of RST and its relevance to personality, psychopathology, and achievement motivation. What may appear as an optimistic, *carte blanche* application of RST to the far reaches of psychology reflects the fact that RST is concerned with processes that are fundamental to many aspects of psychological functioning. As noted by Elliot (2008, p. 6), "all animate life, from the single-cell amoeba upward, is equipped with at least some basic form of approach–avoidance mechanism that produces or regulates movement toward potentially beneficial stimuli and away from potentially harmful stimuli." Approach and avoidance processes have been recognized as fundamental to modern psychology for almost as long as modern psychology has existed (see Freud, 1924; Lewin, 1935). To this tradition, RST has made at least two important contributions. First, it has described the neuropsychology of approach and avoidance processes in rich detail (e.g. Gray & McNaughton, 2000; Pickering & Gray, 1999). Second, it has drawn the inference that individual differences may be profoundly shaped by these "bottom-up" processes (Gray, 1973, 1981). Although there is much evidence to support this inference, one should not slip from optimism to delusions of grandeur: To repeat one of our opening statements, psychological phenomena cannot plausibly be reduced to any single process. RST is entirely *unlikely* to offer a sufficient and complete explanation for *any* of the phenomena discussed—from neuroticism to alcoholism to workaholism—each of which is shaped by multiple processes at "higher" levels of analysis. A challenge for future research in RST and related areas is, therefore, to determine the way in which biobehavioral approach and avoidance motivation interfaces with these higher processes.

This challenge is not new; it has been recognized at least since Cloninger extended his RST-like "temperament" model by adding a higher "character" level to account for processes reflecting development and maturation (Cloninger, Svrakic, & Przybeck, 1993). Similarly, in Ortony, Norman, and Revelle's (2005) multi-level model of psychological functioning, RST-like systems lie at the lower "reactive" level of analysis, initiating only generic approach and avoidance responses. According to the authors, one must look to higher levels of functioning (what Ortony and colleagues call the "routine" and "reflective" levels) to understand fully how these responses are selected, executed, and interpreted (see also Revelle, 1993). Such a view seems necessary if we are to explain the diffuse outcomes (e.g. extraversion, drug addiction, achievement motivation) that putatively arise, *ex uno plures*, from these lower-level processes (e.g. BAS reactivity). Carver and colleagues reach a similar view concerning the role of effortful control, which may constrain or direct the outputs of basic approach and avoidance systems (Carver, Johnson, & Joormann, 2008). Indeed, RST system outputs that are not effortfully or consciously regulated might appear to be quite different from those that are. For instance, "[e]ffortful control constrains behavior so that gratification can be delayed, and long-term goals can be attained. It also helps people to do things they do not really feel like doing" (Carver, 2008, p. 389).

Some research has empirically examined the influence that processes at so-called higher levels of analysis may have on RST system outputs. For instance, Jackson and Francis (2004) suggested that approach and avoidance motivations are distal predictors of behavior, mediated by more "proximal," contextually specific attitudes. Their hypotheses were well supported by path analysis in a study of religious behavior. Interestingly, had they only considered simpler, direct associations between RST-related traits and religious behavior, they would have observed only weak or null effects (all bivariate $rs < \pm.14$). Similarly, Dennis (2007) showed that low scores on trait measures of BAS reactivity (a potential risk factor for depression) predicted depressed mood only for those who reported lower use of regulatory strategies such as cognitive reappraisal. It is again interesting to note that neither BAS scores nor reappraisal alone emerged as significant predictors of depressed mood in the author's regression model (all $Fs < 1$). From a review of such findings, Bijttebier et al. (2009) concluded that risk for psychopathology might be highest in those who have extreme (high or low) RST system reactivity in conjunction with low use of, or capacity for, effortful control. All of this work suggests that cognitive mechanisms and other higher processes may fundamentally shape the influence of RST system outputs on behavior.

In closing, we reflect on one of the most widely cited reviews of RST, which is also a devastating critique: Matthews and Gilliland (1999) concluded that RST's biological approach to personality explanation had not, so far, been successful. However, they also identified three ways in which RST might prevail. First, they suggested that, through the growing sophistication and availability of neuroscience methodologies, RST might reap stronger empirical support through more powerful paradigms and more precise measurement. To a certain extent, methodological advances have indeed begun to open many new doors for theories such as RST, and we believe they will continue to do so (see DeYoung & Gray, 2009; Smillie, 2008). Second, they suggested that RST be delineated at greater levels of detail and complexity—which is arguably what Gray and McNaughton (2000) achieved in their revision of RST. As discussed above, some of these revisions (e.g. the distinction between fear and anxiety) may have strengthened the explanatory power of RST. Third, they suggested that RST be extended upward, to incorporate the cognitive (and perhaps social and situational) processes through which approach and avoidance motivation is likely to percolate. This, we believe, is the next challenge to which RST must rise. It will always be a long way to the top for a "bottom-up" theory, yet proceeding in this direction may prove fruitful, if not essential, for the future of RST.

# Acknowledgments

The authors would like to thank Andrew Cooper, Sharon Dawe, Andrew Elliot, and the editors of this volume for their helpful comments on an earlier draft of this chapter.

# References

Alloy, L. B., Bender, R. E., Wagner, C. A., Abramson, L. Y., & Urosević, S. (2009). Longitudinal predictors of bipolar spectrum disorders: A behavioral approach system perspective. *Clinical Psychology: Science and Practice, 16*, 206–226.

American Psychiatric Association (2000). *Diagnostic and statistical manual of mental disorders* (4th rev. ed.). Washington, DC: American Psychiatric Association.

Atkinson, J. W. (1957). Motivational determinants of risk-taking behavior. *Psychological Review, 64*, 359–372.

Barrós-Loscertales, A., Ventura-Campos, N., Sanjuán-Tomás, A., Belloch, V., Parcet, M. A., & Avila, C. (2010). Behavioural activation system modulation on brain activation during appetitive and aversive stimulus processing. *Social Cognitive and Affective Neuroscience, 5*, 18–28.

Berkman, E. T., Lieberman, M. D., & Gable, S. L. (2009). BIS, BAS, and response conflict: Testing predictions of the revised reinforcement sensitivity theory. *Personality and Individual Differences, 46*, 586–591.

Berridge, K. C., Robinson, T. E., & Aldridge, J.W. (2009). Dissecting components of reward: "Liking," "wanting," and learning. *Current Opinion in Pharmacology, 9*, 65–73.

Bijttebier, P., Beck, I., Claes, L., & Vandereycken, W. (2009). Gray's reinforcement sensitivity theory as a framework for research on personality–psychopathology associations. *Clinical Psychology Review, 29*, 421–430.

Bipp, T., Steinmayr, R.; & Spinath, B. (2008). Personality and achievement motivation: Relationship among Big Five domain and facet scales, achievement goals, and intelligence. *Personality and Individual Differences, 44*, 1454–1464.

Bjornebekk, G. (2007). Reinforcement sensitivity theory and major motivational and self-regulatory processes in children. *Personality and Individual Differences, 43*, 1980–1990.

Blanchard, D. C., & Blanchard, R. J. (1990). Anti-predator defence as models of animal fear and anxiety. In P. F. Brain, S. Parmigiani, R. J. Blanchard, & D. Blanchard (Eds.), *Fear and defence* (pp. 89–108). New York: Harwood Academic, Church and Harwood Academic Publishers.

Blanchard, R. J., Griebel, G., Henrie, J. A., & Blanchard, D. C. (1997). Differentiation of anxiolytic and panicolytic drugs by effects on rat and mouse defense test bateries. *Neuroscience and Biobehavioral Reviews, 21*, 783–789.

Broadhurst, P. L. (1975). The Maudsley reactive and nonreactive strains of rats: A survey. *Behavioral Genetics, 5*, 299–319.

Carrol, J. M., Yik, M. S. M., Russell, J. A., & Barrett, L. F. (1999). On the psychometric principles of affect. *Review of General Psychology, 3*, 14–22.

Carver, C. S. (2004). Negative affects deriving from the behavioral approach system. *Emotion, 4*, 3–22.

Carver, C. S. (2008). Two distinct bases of inhibition of behavior: Viewing biological phenomena through the lens of psychological theory. *European Journal of Personality, 22*, 388–390.

Carver, C. S., Johnson, S. L., & Joormann, J. (2008). Serotonergic function, two-mode models of self-regulation, and vulnerability to depression: What depression has in common with impulsive aggression. *Psychological Bulletin, 134*, 912–943.

Carver, C. S., & White, T. L. (1994). Behavioral inhibition, behavioral activation, and affective responses to impending reward and punishment: The BIS/BAS scales. *Journal of Personality and Social Psychology, 67*, 319–333.

Carver, C. S., Sutton, S. K., & Scheier, M. F. (2000). Action, emotion, and personality: Emerging conceptual integration. *Personality and Social Psychology Bulletin, 26,* 741–751.

Claridge, G., & Davis, C. (2003). *Personality and psychological disorders.* London: Arnold.

Cloninger, C. R. (1987). A systematic method for clinical description and classification of personality variants. *Archives of General Psychiatry, 44,* 573–588.

Cloninger, C. R., Svrakic, D. M., & Przybeck, T. R. (1993). A psychobiological model of temperament and character. *Archives of General Psychiatry, 50,* 975–990.

Colder, C. R., & O'Connor, R. (2002). Attention biases and disinhibited behavior as predictors of alcohol use and enhancement reasons for drinking. *Psychology of Addictive Behaviors, 16,* 325–332.

Commissaris, R. L., Verbanac, J. S., Markovska, V. L., Altman, H. J., & Hill, T. J. (1996). Anxiety-like and depression-like behavior in Maudsley reactive (MR) and non-reactive (NMRA) rats. *Progress in Neuropsychopharmacology and Biological Psychiatry, 20,* 491–501.

Conroy, D. E., & Elliot, A. J. (2004). Fear of failure and achievement goals in sport: Addressing the issue of the chicken and the egg. *Anxiety Stress and Coping, 17,* 271–285.

Cooper, A. J., Smillie, L. D., & Jackson, C. J. (2008). A trait conceptualisation of reward-reactivity: Psychometric properties of the appetitive motivation scale (AMS). *Journal of Individual Differences, 29,* 168–180.

Corr, P. J. (2001). Testing problems in J. A. Gray's personality theory: A commentary on Matthews and Gilliland (1999). *Personality and Individual Differences, 30,* 333–352.

Corr, P. J. (Ed.) (2008). *The reinforcement sensitivity theory of personality.* Cambridge: Cambridge University Press.

Corr, P. J., & McNaughton, N. (2008). Reinforcement sensitivity theory and personality. In P. J. Corr (Ed.), *The reinforcement sensitivity theory of personality* (pp. 155–187). Cambridge: Cambridge University Press.

Cury, F., Elliot, A. J., Da Fonseca, D., & Moller, A. (2006). The social–cognitive model of achievement motivation and the 2 × 2 achievement goal framework. *Journal of Personality and Social Psychology, 90,* 666–679.

Dalley, J. W., Fryer, T. D., Brichard, L., Robinson, E. S. J., Theobald, D. E. H., Laane, K., Peña, Y., Murphy, E. R., & Robbins, T. W. (2007). Nucleus accumbens D2/3 receptors predict trait impulsivity and cocaine reinforcement. *Science, 315,* 1267–1270.

Damasio, A. (1994). *Descartes' error: Emotion, reason and the human brain.* New York: Penguin.

Daniel, R., & Pollmann, S. (2010). Comparing the neural basis of monetary reward and cognitive feedback during information–integration category learning. *Journal of Neuroscience, 6,* 47–55.

Davidson, R. J. (1995). Cerebral asymmetry, emotion, and affective style. In R. J. Davidson & K. Hugdahl (Eds.), *Brain asymmetry* (pp. 361–387). Cambridge, MA: MIT Press.

Davis, C., & Carter, J. C. (2009). Compulsive overeating as an addiction disorder. A review of theory and evidence. *Appetite, 53,* 1–8.

Davis, C., Strachan, S., & Berkson, M. (2004). Sensitivity to reward: Implications for overeating and overweight. *Appetite, 42,* 131–138.

Dawe, S., & Loxton, N. J. (2004). The role of impulsivity in the development of substance use and eating disorders. *Neuroscience and Biobehavioral Reviews, 28,* 343–351.

Dawe, S., Loxton, N. J., Gullo, M. J., Staiger, P. K., Kambouropoulos, N., Perdon, L. & Wood, A. (2007). The role of impulsive personality traits in the initiation, development and treatment of substance misuse problems. In P. M. Miller & D. J. Kavanagh (Eds.), *Translation of addictions science into practice* (pp. 319–337). Amsterdam: Pergamon.

Deary, V., & Johnson, W. (2009). Looking for the fundamentals of human nature. *Journal of Mental Health, 18,* 459–466.

Dennis, T. A. (2007). Interactions between emotion regulation strategies and affective style: Implications for trait anxiety versus depressed mood. *Motivation and Emotion, 31,* 200–207.

Depue, R. A., & Collins, P. F. (1999). Neurobiology of the structure of personality: Dopamine, facilitation of incentive motivation, and extraversion. *Behavioural and Brain Sciences, 22,* 491–569.

DeShon, R. P., & Gillespie, J. Z. (2005). A motivated action theory account of goal orientation. *Journal of Applied Psychology, 90,* 1096–1127.

DeYoung, C. G., & Gray, J. R. (2009). Personality neuroscience: explaining individual differences in affect, behavior, and cognition. In P. J. Corr & G. Matthews (Eds.), *Cambridge handbook of personality* (pp. 323–346). New York: Cambridge University Press.

Dweck, C. S. (1986). Motivational processes affecting learning. *American Psychologist, 41,* 1040–1048.

Egan, S. T., Kambouropoulos, N., & Staiger, P. K. (2010). Rash-impulsivity, reward-drive and motivations to use ecstasy. *Personality and Individual Differences, 48,* 670–675.

Elliot, A.J. (1994). *Approach and avoidance achievement goals: An intrinsic motivation analysis.* Unpublished doctoral dissertation, University of Wisconsin, Madison, WI.

Elliot, A. J. (1997). Integrating the "classic" and "contemporary" approaches to achievement motivation: A hierarchical model of approach and avoidance achievement motivation. In M. L. Maehr & P. R. Pintrich (Eds.), *Advances in motivation and achievement* (Vol. 10, pp. 143–179). Greenwich, CT: JAI Press.

Elliot, A. J. (1999). Approach and avoidance motivation and achievement goals. *Educational Psychologist, 34,* 169–189.

Elliot, A. J. (2005). A conceptual history of the achievement goal construct. In A. J. Elliot & C. S. Dweck (Eds.), *Handbook of competence and motivation* (pp. 52–72). New York: Guilford Press.

Elliot, A. J. (Ed.) (2008). *Handbook of approach and avoidance motivation.* New York: Taylor and Francis.

Elliot, A. J., & Church, M. A. (1997). A hierarchical model of approach and avoidance achievement motivation. *Journal of Personality and Social Psychology, 72,* 218–232.

Elliot, A. J., & Harackiewicz, J. (1996). Approach and avoidance achievement goals and intrinsic motivation: A mediational analysis. *Journal of Personality and Social Psychology, 70,* 461–475.

Elliot, A. J., & Thrash, T. M. (2001). Achievement goals and the hierarchical model of achievement motivation. *Educational Psychology Review, 13,* 139–156.

Elliot, A. J., & Thrash, T. M. (2002). Approach–avoidance motivation in personality: Approach and avoidance temperaments and goals. *Journal of Personality and Social Psychology, 82,* 804–818.

Eysenck, H. J. (1967). *The biological basis of personality.* Springfield, IL: Charles C. Thomas.

Eysenck, H. J. (1998). *Dimensions of personality.* New Brunswick, NJ: Transaction Publishers.

Eysenck. H. J., & Levey, A. (1972). Conditioning, introversion–extraversion and the strength of the nervous system. In V. D. Nebylitsn & J. A. Gray (Eds.), *Biological bases of individual behaviour* (pp. 206–220). London: Academic Press.

Farrell, M. (1997). The influence of reward/punishment and personality on pupil attainment. *Personality and Individual Differences, 22,* 825–834.

Fleeson, W. (2001). Toward a structure- and process-integrated view of personality: Traits as density distributions of states. *Journal of Personality and Social Psychology, 80,* 1011–1027.

Fowles, D. C. (1980). The three arousal model: Implications of Gray's two-factor learning theory for heart rate, electrodermal activity, and psychopathy. *Psychophysiology, 17*, 87–104.

Franken, I. H. A. (2002). Behavioral approach system (BAS) sensitivity predicts alcohol craving. *Personality and Individual Differences, 32*, 349–355.

Franken, I. H. A., & Muris, P. (2005). Individual differences in reward sensitivity are related to food craving and relative body weight in healthy women. *Appetite, 45*, 198–201.

Franken, I. H. A., & Muris, P. (2006). BIS/BAS personality characteristics and college students' substance use. *Personality and Individual Differences, 40*, 1497–1503.

Franken, I. H. A., Muris, P., & Georgieva, I. (2006). Gray's model of personality and addiction. *Addictive Behaviors, 31*, 399–403.

Freud, S. (1924). *Beyond the pleasure principle*. New York: Boni and Liveright.

Furnham, A., & Jackson, C. J. (2008). Reinforcement sensitivity in the workplace: BAS/BIS in business. In P. J. Corr (Ed.), *The reinforcement sensitivity theory of personality* (pp. 43–452). Cambridge: Cambridge University Press.

Gable, P. A., & Harmon-Jones, E. (2008). Approach-motivated positive affect reduces breadth of attention. *Psychological Science, 19*, 476–482.

Gray, J. A. (1970). The psychophysiological basis of introversion–extraversion. *Behaviour Research and Therapy, 8*, 249–266.

Gray, J. A. (1973). Causal models of personality and how to test them. In J. R. Royce (Ed.), *Multivariate analysis and psychological theory* (pp. 409–463). London: Academic Press.

Gray, J. A. (1977). Drug effects on fear and frustration: A possible substrate for anxiety. In L. L. Iversen, S. D. Iversen, & S. H. Snyder (Eds.), *Handbook of psychopharmacology: Vol. 8. Drugs, neurotransmitters and behavior* (pp. 433–529). New York: Plenum Press.

Gray, J. A. (1981). A critique of Eysenck's theory of personality. In H. J. Eysenck (Ed.), *A model for personality* (246–276). Berlin: Springer.

Gray, J. A. (1982). *The neuropsychology of anxiety: An inquiry into the functions of the septohippocampal system*. New York: Oxford University Press.

Gray, J. A. (1987). *The psychology of fear and stress*. Cambridge: Cambridge University Press.

Gray, J. A. (1991). The neuropsychology of temperament. In J. Strelau & A. Angleitner (Eds.), *Explorations in temperament: International perspectives on theory and measurement. Perspectives on individual differences* (pp. 105–128). New York: Plenum Press.

Gray, J. A. (1994). Framework for a taxonomy of psychiatric disorder. In S. H. M. van Goozen & N. E. Van de Poll (Eds.), *Emotions: Essays on emotion theory* (pp. 29–59). Mahwah, NJ: Lawrence Erlbaum Associates.

Gray, J. A., & McNaughton, N. (1983). Comparison between the behavioral effects of septal and hippocampal lesions: An annotated bibliography. *Neuroscience and Biobehavioral Reviews, 7*, 119–188.

Gray, J. A., & McNaughton, N. (1996). The neuropsychology of anxiety: Reprise. In R. A. Dienstbier & D. A. Hope (Eds.), *Nebraska symposium on motivation, 1995: Perspectives on anxiety, panic, and fear. Current theory and research in motivation* (Vol. 43, pp. 61–134). Lincoln, NE: University of Nebraska Press.

Gray, J. A., & McNaughton, N. (2000). *The neuropsychology of anxiety*. Oxford: Oxford University Press.

Gray, J. A., & Smith, P. T. (1969). An arousal–decision model for partial reinforcement and discrimination learning. In R. M. Gilbert & N. S. Sutherland (Eds.), *Animal discrimination learning* (pp. 243–272). London: Academic Press.

Gray, J. A., Owen, S., Davis, N., & Tsaltas, E. (1983). Psychological and physiological relations between anxiety and impulsivity. In M. Zuckerman (Ed.), *The biological basis of sensation seeking, impulsivity and anxiety* (pp. 181–217). Hillsdale, NJ: Lawrence Erlbaum Associates.

Gupta, B. S. (1976). Extraversion and reinforcement in verbal operant conditioning. *British Journal of Psychology, 67*, 47–52.

Hall, C. S. (1934). Drive and emotionality: Factors associated with adjustment in the rat. *Journal of Comparative Psychology, 17*, 89–108.

Harackiewicz, J. M., Barron, K. E., Carter, S. M., Lehto, A. T., & Elliot, A. J. (1997). Predictors and consequences of achievement goals in the college classroom: Maintaining interest and making the grade. *Journal of Personality and Social Psychology, 73*, 1284–1295.

Harmon-Jones, E., & Sigelman, J. (2001). State anger and prefrontal brain activity: Evidence that insult-related relative left-prefrontal activation is associated with experienced anger and aggression. *Journal of Personality and Social Psychology, 80*, 797–803.

Heggestad, E. D., & Kanfer, R. (2000). Individual differences in trait motivation: Development of the Motivational Trait Questionnaire. *International Journal of Educational Research, 33*, 751–766.

Heimpel, S. A., Elliot, A. J., & Wood, J. V. (2006). Basic personality dispositions, self-esteem, and personal goals: An approach–avoidance analysis. *Journal of Personality, 74*, 1293–1319.

Heinz, A., Lober, S., Georgi, A., Wrase, J., Hermann, D., Rey, E.R., Wellek, S. & Mann, K. (2003). Reward craving and withdrawal relief craving: Assessment of different motivational pathways to alcohol intake. *Alcohol and Alcoholism, 38*, 35–39.

Heller, D., Komar, J., & Lee, W. B. (2007). The dynamics of personality states, goals, and well-being. *Personality and Social Psychology Bulletin, 33*, 898–910.

Hernandez, L., & Hoebel, B. G. (1988). Food reward and cocaine increase extracellular dopamine in the nucleus accumbens as measured by microdialysis. *Life Sciences, 42*, 1705–1712.

Heym, N., Ferguson, E., & Lawrence, C. (2008). An evaluation of the relationship between Gray's revised RST and Eysenck's PEN: Distinguishing BIS and FFFS in Carver and White's BIS/BAS scales. *Personality and Individual Differences, 45*, 709–715.

Hirsh, J. B., DeYoung, C. G., & Peterson, J. B. (2009). Metatraits of the Big Five differentially predict engagement and restraint of behavior. *Journal of Personality, 77*, 1085–1102.

Hirsh, J. B., & Inzlicht, M. (2008). The devil you know: Neuroticism predicts neural response to uncertainty. *Psychological Science, 19*, 962–967.

Hull, C. L. (1943). *Principles of behavior.* New York: Appleton–Century–Crofts.

Humphreys, M. S., & Revelle, W. (1984). Personality, motivation and performance: A theory of the relationship between individual differences and information processing. *Psychological Review, 91*, 153–184.

Hundt, N. E., Nelson-Gray, R. O., Kimbrel, N. A., Mitchell, J. T., & Kwapil, T. R. (2007). The interaction of reinforcement sensitivity and life events in the prediction of anhedonic depression and mixed anxiety–depression symptoms. *Personality and Individual Differences, 43*, 1001–1012.

Hustinx, P. W. J., Kuyper, H., van der Werf, M. P. C., & Dijkstra, P. (2009). Achievement motivation revisited: New longitudinal data to demonstrate its predictive power. *Educational Psychology, 29*, 561–582.

Izadikhah, Z., Jackson, C. J., & Loxton, N. J. (2010). An integrative approach to personality: Behavioural approach system, mastery approach orientation and environmental cues in the prediction of work performance. *Personality and Individual Differences, 48*, 590–595.

Jackson, C. J. (2009). Jackson-5 scales of revised reinforcement sensitivity theory (r-RST) and their application to dysfunctional real world outcomes. *Journal of Research in Personality, 43*, 556–569.

Jackson, C. J., & Francis, L. (2004). Are interactions in Gray's reinforcement sensitivity theory proximal or distal in the prediction of religiosity? A test of the joint subsystems hypothesis. *Personality and Individual Differences, 36*, 1197–1209.

Johnson, S., Turner, R. J., & Iwata, N. (2003). BIS/BAS levels and psychiatric disorder: An epidemiological study. *Journal of Psychopathology and Behavioral Assessment, 25*, 25–36.

Kambouropoulos, N., & Staiger, P. K. (2004). Reactivity to alcohol-related cues: Relationship among cue type, motivational processes, and personality. *Psychology of Addictive Behaviors, 18*, 275–283.

Kambouropoulos, N., & Staiger, P. K. (2007). Personality, behavioural and affective characteristics of hazardous drinkers. *Personality and Individual Differences, 42*, 213–224.

Kambouropoulos, N., & Staiger, P. K. (2009). "Cue reward salience" predicts craving in response to alcohol cues. *Personality and Individual Differences, 46*, 78–82.

Kane, T. A., Loxton, N. J., Staiger, P. K., & Dawe, S. (2004). Does the tendency to act impulsively underlie binge eating and alcohol use problems? An empirical investigation. *Personality and Individual Differences, 36*, 83–94.

Kanfer, R., & Ackerman, P. L. (2000). Individual differences in work motivation: Further explorations of a trait framework. *Applied Psychology: An International Review, 49*, 469–481.

Katzman, M. A. (2009). Current considerations in the treatment of generalized anxiety disorder. *CNS Drugs, 23*, 103–120.

Knyazev, G. G. (2004). Behavioral activation as predictor of substance use: Mediating and moderating role of attitudes and social relationships. *Drug and Alcohol Dependence, 75*, 309–321.

Knyazev, G. G., Slobodskaya, H. R., Kharchenko, I. I., & Wilson, G. D. (2004). Personality and substance use in Russian youths: The predictive and moderating role of behavioural activation and gender. *Personality and Individual Differences, 37*, 815–843.

Krebs, R. M., Schott, B. H., & Düzel, E. (2009). Personality traits are differentially associated with patterns of reward and novelty processing in the human substantia nigra/ventral tegmental area. *Biological psychiatry 65*, 103–110.

Kringelbach, M. L., & Berridge, K. C. (Eds.) (2010). *Pleasures of the brain.* Oxford: Oxford University Press.

Lee, S. H., Ham, B. J., Cho, Y. H., Lee, S. M., & Shim, S. H. (2007). Association study of dopamine receptor D2 TaqI A polymorphism and reward-related personality traits in healthy Korean young females, *Neuropsychobiology, 56*, 146–151.

Leone, L. (2009). Testing conceptual distinctions among Carver and White's (1994) BAS scales: A comment and extension on Smillie, Jackson, and Dalgleish (2006). *Personality and Individual Differences, 46*, 54–59.

Leue, A. & Beauducel, A. (2008). A meta-analysis of reinforcement sensitivity theory: On performance parameters in reinforcement tasks. *Personality and Social Psychology Review, 12*, 353–369.

Leue, A., Chavanon, M. L, Wacker, J., & Stemmler, G. (2009). On the differentiation of N2 components in an appetitive choice task: Evidence for the revised reinforcement sensitivity theory. *Psychophysiology, 46*, 1244–1257.

Lewin, K. (Ed.) (1935). *A dynamic theory of personality.* New York: McGraw-Hill.

Lewin, K., Dembo, T., Festinger, L., & Sears, P. S. (1944). Level of aspiration. In J. M. Hunt (Ed.), *Personality and the behavior disorders* (Vol. 1, 333–378). New York: Ronald Press.

Linnenbrink, E.A. (2005). The dilemma of performance approach goals: The use of multiple goal contexts to promote students' motivation and learning. *Journal of Educational Psychology, 97*, 197–213.

Lönnqvist, J., Verkasalo, M., Mäkinen, S., & Henriksson, M. (2009). High neuroticism at age 20 predicts history of mental disorders and low self-esteem at age 35. *Journal of Clinical Psychology, 65,* 781–790.

Loxton, N. J., & Dawe, S. (2006). Reward and punishment sensitivity in dysfunctional eating and hazardous drinking women: Associations with family risk. *Appetite, 47,* 361–371.

Loxton, N. J., & Dawe, S. (2007). How do dysfunctional eating and hazardous drinking women perform on behavioural measures of reward and punishment sensitivity? *Personality and Individual Differences, 42,* 1163–1172.

Loxton, N. J., & Dawe, S. (2009). Personality and eating disorders. In P. J. Corr & G. Matthews (Eds.), *Cambridge handbook of personality psychology* (pp. 687–703). Cambridge: Cambridge University Press.

Loxton, N. J., Nguyen, D., Casey, L., & Dawe, S. (2008). Reward drive, rash impulsivity and punishment sensitivity in problem gamblers. *Personality and Individual Differences, 45,* 167–173.

Loxton, N. J., Wan, V. L. N., Ho, A. M. C., Cheung, B. K. L., Tam, N., Leung, F. Y. K., & Stadlin, A. (2008). Impulsivity in Hong Kong-Chinese club-drug users. *Drug and Alcohol Dependence, 95,* 81–89.

MacDonald, G., & Leary, M. (2005). Why does social exclusion hurt? The relationship between social and physical pain. *Psychological Bulletin, 131,* 202–233.

Markman, A. B., Baldwin, G. C., and Maddox, W. T. (2005), The interaction of payoff structure and regulatory focus in classification, *Psychological Science, 16,* 852–855.

Marsh, A. A., Kozak, M. N., Wegner, D. M., Reid, M. E., Yu, H. H., & Blair, R. J. (in press). The neural substrates of action identification. *Social Cognitive and Affective Neuroscience.*

Matthews, G., & Gilliland, K. (1999). The personality theories of H. J. Eysenck and J. A. Gray: A comparative review. *Personality and Individual Differences, 26,* 583–626.

McClelland, C. D. (1951). *Personality.* New York: Sloane.

McClelland, D., Atkinson, J., Clark, R., & Lowell, E. (1953). *The achievement motive.* New York: Appleton–Century–Crofts.

McNaughton, N., & Corr, P. J. (2008). The neuropsychology of fear and anxiety. In P. J. Corr (Ed.), *The reinforcement sensitivity theory of personality* (pp. 44–94). Cambridge: Cambridge University Press.

McFarland, B. R., Shankman, S. A., Tenke, C. E., Bruder, G. E., & Klein, D. N. (2006). Behavioral activation system deficits predict the six-month course of depression. *Journal of Affective Disorders, 91,* 229–234.

Middleton, M., & Midgley, C. (1997). Avoiding the demonstration of lack of ability: An under-explored aspect of goal theory. *Journal of Educational Psychology, 89,* 710–718.

Miller, E. K., & Cohen, J. D. (2001). An integrative theory of prefrontal cortex function. *Annual Review of Neuroscience, 24,* 167–202.

Mizuno, K., Tanaka, M., Ishii, A., Tanabe, H. C., Onoe, H., Sadato, N., & Watanabe, Y. (2008). The neural basis of academic achievement motivation. *NeuroImage, 42,* 369–378.

Montag, C., Buckholtz, J. W., Hartmann, P., Merz, M., Burk, C., Hennig, J., & Reuter, M. (2008). COMT genetic variation affects fear processing: Psychophysiological evidence. *Behavioral Neuroscience, 122,* 901–909.

Muis, K. R., & Edwards, O. (2009). Examining the stability of achievement goal orientation. *Contemporary Educational Psychology, 34,* 265–277.

Murray, H. A. (1938). *Explorations in personality.* New York: Oxford University Press.

Nicholls, J. G. (1984). Achievement motivation: Conceptions of ability, subjective experience, task choice, and performance. *Psychological Review, 91,* 328–346.

Nolen, S. B. (1988). Reasons for studying: Motivation orientations and study strategies. *Cognition and Instruction, 5,* 269–287.

O'Connor, P. J., & Jackson, C. J. (2008). Learning to be saints or sinners: The indirect pathway from sensation seeking to behavior through mastery orientation. *Journal of Personality, 76,* 733–752.

O'Connor, R. M., & Colder, C. R. (2005). Predicting alcohol patterns in first-year college students through motivational systems and reasons for drinking. *Psychology of Addictive Behaviors, 19,* 10–20.

Ortony, A., Norman, D. A., & Revelle, W. (2005). Affect and proto-affect in effective functioning. In J. M. Fellous & M. A. Arbib (Eds.), *Who needs emotions? The brain meets the machine* (pp. 173–202). New York: Oxford University Press.

Panksepp, J. (1998). *Affective neuroscience: The foundations of human and animal emotions.* Oxford: Oxford University Press.

Panksepp, J., & Moskal, J. (2008). Dopamine and SEEKING: Subcortical "Reward" systems and appetitive urges. In A. J. Elliot (Ed.), *Handbook of approach and avoidance motivation* (pp. 67–87) New York: Taylor and Francis.

Paterson, A., Whiting, P. J., Gray, J. A., Flint, J., & Dawson, G. R. (2001). Lack of consistent behavioral effects of Maudsley reactive and non-reactive rats in a number of animal tests of anxiety and activity. *Psychopharmacology, 154,* 336–342.

Peabody, D., & Goldberg, L. R. (1989). Some determinants of factor structures from personality-trait descriptors. *Journal of Personality and Social Psychology, 57,* 552–567.

Perkins, A., Cooper, A., Abdelall, M., Smillie, L. D., & Corr, P. J. (in press). Personality and defensive reactions: Fear, trait anxiety and threat magnification. *Journal of Personality.*

Penke, L., Denissen, J. J. A., & Miller, G. F. (2007). The evolutionary genetics of personality. *European Journal of Personality, 21,* 549–587.

Pickering, A. D. (2004). The neuropsychology of impulsive antisocial sensation seeking personality traits: From dopamine to hippocampal function? In R. M. Stelmack (Ed.), *On the psychobiology of personality: Essays in honour of Marvin Zuckerman* (pp. 453–476). Oxford: Elsevier.

Pickering, A. D., & Gray, J. A. (1999). The neuroscience of personality. In L. Pervin & O. John (Eds.), *Handbook of personality* (2nd ed., pp. 277–299). New York: Guilford Press.

Pickering, A. D., & Smillie, L. D. (2008). The behavioural activation system: Challenges and opportunities. In P. J. Corr (Ed.), *The reinforcement sensitivity theory of personality* (pp. 120–154). Cambridge: Cambridge University Press.

Pickering, A. D., Corr, P. J., & Gray, J. A. (1999). Interactions and reinforcement sensitivity theory: A theoretical analysis of Rusting and Larsen (1997). *Personality and Individual Differences, 26,* 357–365.

Pickering, A. D., Corr, P. J., Powell, J. H., Kumari, V., Thornton, J. C., & Gray, J. A. (1997). Individual differences in reactions to reinforcing stimuli are neither black nor white: To what extent are they gray? In H. Nyborg (Ed.), *The scientific study of human nature* (pp. 36–67). Amsterdam: Pergamon/Elsevier Science Inc.

Quilty, L. C., & Oakman, J. M. (2004). The assessment of behavioural activation—The relationship between impulsivity and behaviour activation. *Personality and Individual Differences, 37,* 429–442.

Rawsthorne, L. J., & Elliot, A. J. (1999). Achievement goals and intrinsic motivation: A meta-analytic review. *Personality and Social Psychology Review, 3,* 326–344.

Read, S. J., Monroe, B. M., Brownstein, A. L., Yang, Y., Chopra, G., & Miller, L. C. (2010). A neural network model of the structure and dynamics of human personality. *Psychological Review, 117,* 61–92.

Revelle, W. (1993). Individual differences in personality and motivation: "Non-cognitive" determinants of cognitive performance. In A. Baddeley & L. Weiskrantz (Eds.), *Attention: Selection, awareness and control* (pp. 346–373). Oxford: Oxford University Press.

Revelle, W. (2007). Experimental approaches to the study of personality. In B. Robins, C. Fraley, and R. Krueger (Eds.), *Handbook of research methods in personality psychology* (pp. 37–61). London: Guilford Press.

Revelle, W. (2008). The contribution of reinforcement sensitivity theory to personality theory. In P. J. Corr (Ed.), *Reinforcement sensitivity theory of personality* (pp. 508–527). Cambridge: Cambridge University Press.

Revelle, W., & Scherer, K. R. (2009). Personality and emotion. In D. Sander & K. Scherer (Eds.), *Oxford companion to emotion and the affective sciences.* Oxford: Oxford University Press.

Revelle, W., Humphreys, M.S., Simon, L., and Gilliland, K. (1980). The interactive effect of personality, time of day, and caffeine: A test of the arousal model. *Journal of Experimental Psycholology: General, 109,* 1–31.

Ritters, L. V. (2010). Evidence for opioid involvement in the motivation to sing. *Journal of Chemical Neuroanatomy, 39,* 141–150.

Robbins, T. W., & Everitt, B. J. (1996). Neurobehavioral mechanisms of reward and motivation. *Current Opinion in Neurobiology, 6,* 228–236.

Robinson, S., Sandstrom, S. M., Denenberg, V. H., & Palmiter, R. D. (2005). Distinguishing whether dopamine regulates liking, wanting and/or learning about rewards. *Behavioral Neuroscience, 1,* 5–15.

Robinson, T. E., & Berridge, K. C. (2003). Addiction. *Annual Review of Psychology, 54,* 25–53.

Rocklin, T., &, Revelle, W. (1981). The measurement of extraversion: A comparison of the Eysenck Personality Inventory and the Eysenck Personality Questionnaire. *British Journal of Social Psychology, 20,* 279–284.

Rusting, C. L., & Larsen, R. J. (1997). Extraversion, neuroticism, and susceptibility to positive and negative affect: A test of two theoretical models. *Personality and Individual Differences, 22,* 607–612.

Schneirla, T. C. (1959). An evolutionary and developmental theory of biphasic processes underlying approach and withdrawal. In M. R. Jones (Ed.), *Nebraska symposium on motivation, 1959: Perspectives on anxiety, panic, and fear. Current theory and research in motivation* (Vol. 43, pp. 27–58). Lincoln, NE: University of Nebraska Press.

Schultz, W. (1998). Predictive reward signal of dopamine neurons, *Journal of Neurophysiology, 80,* 1–27.

Segal, E. M., & Lachman, R. (1972). Complex behavior or higher mental process: Is there a paradigm shift? *American Psychologist, 27,* 46–55.

Simon, J. J., Walther, S., Fiebach, C. J., Friederich, H., Stippich, C., Weisbrod, M., & Kaiser, S. (2010). Neural reward processing is modulated by approach- and avoidance-related personality traits. *NeuroImage, 49,* 1868–1874.

Simons, J. S., Dvorak, R. D., & Bastien, B. D. (2008). Methamphetamine use in a rural college population: Associations with marijuana use, sensitivity to punishment, and sensitivity to reward. *Psychology of Addictive Behaviors, 22,* 444–449.

Smillie, L. D. (2008). What is reinforcement sensitivity? Neuroscience paradigms for approach–avoidance process theories of personality. *European Journal of Personality, 22,* 359–384.

Smillie, L. D. (2009). (Trait) *Anxiety: Sensitivity to goal conflict or pure punishment?* Paper presented at the 14th Biennial Conference of the International Society for the Study of Individual Differences, July, Evanston, IL.

Smillie, L. D., Dalgleish, L. I., & Jackson, C. J. (2007). Distinguishing between learning and motivation in behavioral tests of the reinforcement sensitivity theory of personality. *Personality and Social Psychology Bulletin, 33*, 476–489.

Smillie, L. D., Pickering, A. D., & Jackson, C. J. (2006). The new reinforcement sensitivity theory: Implications for psychometric measurement. *Personality and Social Psychology Review, 10*, 320–335.

Smillie, L. D., Cooper, A., Proitsi, P., Powell, J., & Pickering, A. D. (2010). Variation in DRD2 dopamine gene predicts extraverted personality. *Neuroscience Letters, 468*, 234–237.

Spence, K. W. (1956). *Behavior theory and conditioning.* New Haven, CT: Yale University Press.

Spielberg, J. M., Stewart, J. L., Levin, R. L., Miller, G. A., & Heller, W. (2008). Prefrontal cortex, emotion, and approach/withdrawal motivation. *Social and Personality Psychology Compass, 2*, 135–153.

Stewart, G. L. (1996). Reward structure as a moderator of the relationship between extraversion and sales performance. *Journal of Applied Psychology, 81*, 619–627.

Sutton, S. K., & Davidson, R. J. (1997). Prefrontal brain asymmetry: A biological substrate of the behavioral approach and inhibition systems. *Psychological Science, 8*, 204–210.

Tabibnia, G., Satpute, A. B., & Lieberman, M. D. (2008). The sunny side of fairness: Preference for fairness activates reward circuitry (and disregarding unfairness activates self-control circuitry). *Psychological Science, 19*, 339–347.

Tellegen, A. (1985). Structure of mood and personality and their relevance to assessing anxiety, with an emphasis on self-report. In A. H. Tuma & J. D. Maser (Eds.), *Anxiety and the anxiety disorders* (pp. 681–706). Hillsdale, NJ: Lawrence Erlbaum Associates.

Thrash, T. M., & Elliot, A. J. (2002). Implicit and self-attributed achievement motives: Concordance and predictive validity. *Journal of Personality, 70*, 729–755.

Thrash, T. M., & Hurst, A. L. (2008). Approach and avoidance motivation in the achievement domain: Integrating the achievement motive and achievement goal traditions. In A. J. Elliot (Ed.), *Handbook of approach and avoidance motivation* (pp. 217–233). New York: Taylor and Francis.

Torrubia, R., Avila, C., & Caseras, X. (2008). Reinforcement sensitivity scales. In P. J. Corr (Ed.), *The reinforcement sensitivity theory of personality* (pp. 188–227). Cambridge: Cambridge University Press.

Torrubia, R., Avila, C., Molto, J., & Caseras, X. (2001). The Sensitivity to Punishment and Sensitivity to Reward Questionnaire as a measure of Gray's anxiety and impulsivity dimensions. *Personality and Individual Differences, 31*, 837–862.

Urosević, S., Abramson, L. Y., Harmon-Jones, E., & Alloy, L. B. (2008). Dysregulation of the behavioral approach system (BAS) in bipolar spectrum disorders: Review of theory and evidence. *Clinical Psychology Review, 28*, 1188–1205.

Voigt, D. C., Dillard, J. P., Braddock, K. H., Anderson, J. W., Sopory, P., & Stephenson, M. T. (2009). BIS/BAS scales and their relationship to risky health behaviours. *Personality and Individual Differences, 47*, 89–93.

Wacker, J., Chavanon, M. L., Leue, A., & Stemmler, G. (2008). Is running away right? The behavioral activation—behavioral inhibition model of anterior asymmetry. *Emotion, 8*, 232–249.

Wang, M., & Erdheim, J. (2007). Does the five-factor model of personality relate to goal orientation? *Personality and Individual Differences, 43*, 1493–1505.

Ward, R., Rogers, D. A., Byrne, Z. S., & Masterson, S. S. (2004). State versus trait goal orientation: Is there truly a difference? Presented as a poster at the 19th annual conference of the Society of Industrial and Organizational Psychology in Chicago, IL.

Watson, D. (2005). Rethinking the mood and anxiety disorders: A quantitative hierarchical model for DSM–V. *Journal of Abnormal Psychology, 114*, 522–536.

You, J. S., Hu, S. Y., Chen, B., & Zhang, H. G. (2005). Serotonin transporter and tryptophan hydroxylase gene polymorphisms in Chinese patients with generalized anxiety disorder. *Psychiatric Genetics, 15*, 7–11.

Zinbarg, R., & Lira Yoon, K. (2008). RST and clinical disorders: Anxiety and depression. In P. J. Corr (Ed.), *The reinforcement senstivity theory of personality* (pp. 360–398). Cambridge: Cambridge University Press.

Zuckerman, M. (1979). *Sensation seeking: Beyond the optimal level of arousal.* Hillsdale, NJ: Lawrence Erlbaum Associates.

Zweig, D., & Webster, J. (2004). What are we measuring? An examination of the relationships between the Big-Five personality traits, goal orientation and performance intentions. *Personality and Individual Differences, 36*, 1693–1708.

# 5

# The General Factor
# of Personality
## *Normal and Abnormal*

## J. Philippe Rushton and Paul Irwing

## 1  Introduction

A recent hypothesis is that a general factor of personality (GFP) occupies the apex of the hierarchy of personality as well as the apex of the personality disorders in the same way in which $g$, the general factor of mental ability, occupies the apex in the organization of cognitive abilities (Rushton, Bons, & Hur, 2008). High scores on the GFP indicate what is meant by someone having a "good" personality; low scores indicate what is meant by a "difficult" personality, in other words someone who is hard to get along with. Individuals high on the GFP are altruistic, agreeable, relaxed, conscientious, sociable, and open, with high levels of well-being and self-esteem. Because the GFP defines clear positive and negative poles, it provides potential for understanding the socially "advantaged" (those with high levels of emotional intelligence) as well as the socially "challenged" (those more likely to suffer a personality disorder). The GFP can be viewed as a dimension of social effectiveness.

The explanation we favor for the GFP is that it arose through evolutionary selection for socially desirable traits that facilitate performance across a wide range of contexts (Rushton et al., 2008). This follows a proposal by Darwin (1871) that natural selection acted directionally, to endow people with more cooperative and less contentious personalities than their archaic ancestors or nearest living relatives, the chimpanzees. Rushton et al. (2008) conjectured that individuals high on the GFP left more progeny, since people prefer as mates, fellow workers, and leaders those who are altruistic, conscientious, and emotionally stable. People able to cooperate in groups were also more likely to win competitions and wars. The alternative to the GFP being substantive is that it results from artifacts of scale construction and from evaluative bias such as responding in a socially desirable manner.

The main empirical impetus for identifying a GFP comes from the observation that the Big-Five factors typically intercorrelate, despite claims that they are

*The Wiley-Blackwell Handbook of Individual Differences*, First Edition.
Edited by Tomas Chamorro-Premuzic, Sophie von Stumm, and Adrian Furnham.
© 2011 Blackwell Publishing Ltd. Published 2011 by Blackwell Publishing Ltd.

orthogonal. For example, Digman (1997) found a mean correlation of .26 in 14 sets of Big-Five correlations, from which he extracted two uncorrelated higher-order factors: Alpha (agreeableness, conscientiousness, emotional stability) and Beta (extraversion, openness), which he associated with socialization and personal growth, respectively. Carroll (2002) confirmed Digman's (1997) two-factor solution, but he did not report whether Alpha and Beta were correlated. DeYoung, Peterson, and Higgins (2002) also replicated Digman's solution, re-labeled Alpha as "stability" and Beta as "plasticity," found they *were* correlated (about .24), but did not test for a GFP.

Rushton and Irwing (2008) found remarkable evidence for a GFP in two meta-analyses of Big-Five inter-scale correlations, which included the 14 sets that Digman (1997) had used to establish the Big Two ($N$ = 4,496; see Table 5.1).[1] Rushton and Irwing's (2008) model explained 45 percent of the variance in stability and plasticity and 14 percent of the total reliable variance in the Big Five (Figure 5.1). Rushton and Irwing's (2008) second meta-analysis cross-validated the model by using four alternative Big-Five measures ($N$ = 4,000) compiled by Mount, Barrick, Scullen, and Rounds (2005). To provide unequivocal evidence for the GFP, they also examined a model specifying that the Big Two were uncorrelated. Since this provided a very poor fit, there was no plausible alternative to a model with a GFP.

Rushton and Irwing (2009b) further cross-validated the model in Figure 5.1 with a meta-analysis of 16 sets of inter-scale correlations (including six fully independent samples) compiled by DeYoung and colleagues ($N$ = 6,412). The largest cross-validation of the model came from 628,640 Internet respondents (Erdle, Irwing, Rushton, & Park, 2010). Together, these four analyses approximate the ideal strategy outlined by Jöreskog (1993). Designated "strictly confirmatory," prior theory and research point to the correctness of a single model, which is then tested in a representative sample and, if confirmed, shows the model is generalizable. Subsequently, a meta-analysis of 212 published sets of Big-Five inter-scale correlations ($N$ = 144,117), carried out completely independently of ourselves, further corroborated the model (Van der Linden, te Nijenhuis, & Bakker, 2010). In a review of the Big-Five literature, Block (2010) favorably cited the model, suggesting that a "solitary, apical general factor signifying only something like *fitness for collective living*" sat above both the Big Two and the Big Five (p. 17, footnote 18).

**Table 5.1**  Mean inter-scale correlations from Digman's (1997) 14 studies of Big Five factors. $N$ = 4,496; decimal points omitted. Source: Rushton & Irwing, 2008, Table 1

|  | Openness | Conscientiousness | Extraversion | Agreeableness | Emotional Stability |
|---|---|---|---|---|---|
| Openness | — |  |  |  |  |
| Conscientiousness | 20 | — |  |  |  |
| Extraversion | 43 | 12 | — |  |  |
| Agreeableness | 10 | 39 | 05 | — |  |
| Emotional Stability | 18 | 43 | 23 | 44 | — |

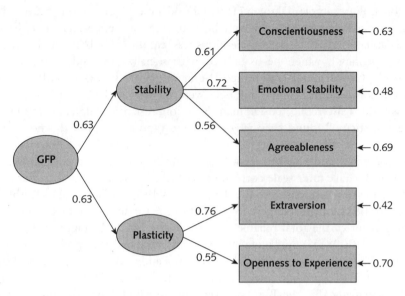

**Figure 5.1** The GFP going to the Big Two to the Big Five using the medians from Digman's (1997) 14 samples. From Rushton & Irwing, 2008, Figure 1B

## 2 Historical Background, Including Charles Darwin and Francis Galton

Charles Darwin (1809–1882) was at first extremely reticent about extending his evolutionary theory to humankind. In the fourth last paragraph of *The Origin of Species* (1859), he wrote only this: "Light will be thrown on the origin of man and his history" (p. 458). Within 13 years, however, it had become crucial for Darwin to generalize his theory to people in order to save it from alternatives that had arisen. For example, fellow evolutionist Alfred Russel Wallace (1823–1913) argued that evolution had stopped for people because their large brains freed them from the lower instincts. Philosopher John Stuart Mill (1806–1873) proposed that human morality should be based on making informed choices about the greatest good for the greatest number. Darwin took exception to these alternatives because they emphasized rationality to the exclusion of instinct and applied only to people.

Darwin (1871, 1872) maintained that evolution worked through natural selection by small gradations that required continuity between humans and other animals, even for moral and intellectual qualities. Darwin wrote, "the difference in mind between man and the higher animals, great as it is, is certainly one of degree, and not of kind" (1871, p. 105). He pointed out how all animals are altruistic in some circumstances and fight in others, and that the human expression of emotion is similar to that in cats, dogs, and chimpanzees. In regard to personality, Darwin viewed people as being more cooperative and less contentious than "primeval man and his ape-like progenitors" (1871, p. 159). He described human qualities such as "courage, sympathy, and faithfulness," and the "need for approval by others," as well as the concomitant decrease in the number of "selfish and contentious people." The latter, he wrote, "will not cohere, and without coherence nothing can be effected" (1871, p. 159).

Darwin's cousin, Francis Galton (1822–1911), was so inspired by the theory of evolution that he dedicated the remainder of his life to applying it to human differences. Galton (1869) was the first to extend the normal distribution to psychological characteristics and the first to use questionnaires to systematically assess individual differences. He devised correlations, regressions, and percentiles to measure trait relationships and he pioneered twin, family, and adoption methods to examine heritable and social transmission. It was Galton (1884) who formulated the "lexical hypothesis," that the most important differences in human transactions come to be encoded as single terms in some or all of the world's languages. He counted 1,000 words to express character in Roget's *Thesaurus* and noted the overlap in meaning.

Galton (1887) was also the first to describe a general factor of personality, just as he had earlier (1869) been the first to identify a general factor of cognitive ability. In his paper "Good and bad temper in English families," Galton used ratings from 1,981 family members across four generations to group 15 desirable adjectives and 46 undesirable ones along a single dimension. He described "temper" as a strongly marked characteristic of all animals and suggested its human meaning be inferred from the adjectives used by his respondents, adjectives which, he thought, expressed one or other of its qualities or degrees.[2]

Galton (1887) identified three times as many adjectives denoting bad temper by comparison with good temper and noted their arrangement in a bell-shaped distribution, with neutral scores in the middle, in the ratio of $2:1$ to both extremes. He reported that females averaged a milder personality than males and that temperament ran in families. When both parents were good-tempered, 30 percent of the children were good-tempered and 10 percent bad-tempered, the remaining 60 percent being neutral. When both parents were bad-tempered, 52 percent of the children were bad-tempered and 4 percent good-tempered, the remainder being neutral. Conversely, good-tempered brothers and sisters had 26 percent of their parents, uncles, and aunts as good-tempered (8 percent bad-tempered), whereas bad-tempered brothers and sisters had 29 percent of their parents, uncles, and aunts as bad-tempered (18 percent good-tempered). From these results Galton postulated that desirable traits went together because of mate preferences and assortative mating.

Follow-up studies were conducted by statistician Karl Pearson (1857–1936) at the University of London, in a laboratory that Galton endowed in 1904, and by Harvard zoologist Charles B. Davenport (1866–1944) at the Cold Spring Harbor Laboratory in New York. Davenport (1911) collated data from hundreds of families on normal traits, criminality, insanity, pauperism, and feeble-mindedness and explained them by using a version of Wilhelm Griesinger's (1817–1868) unitary concept of *insanity* (*Einheitpsychose*) and J. C. Pritchard's (1786–1848) concept of *moral insanity*, which included traits such as excessive shyness, gloominess, alcoholism, sexual promiscuity, theft, hostility, and violent temper.

The common denominator to moral insanity, which Pritchard (1835) described as "eccentricity of conduct [...] observed in connection with a wayward and intractable temper, with a decay of social affections, an aversion to the nearest relatives and friends formerly beloved" (p. 23), was self-control ("will-power"), a lack of which could cause harm to others or self. Davenport (1911) proposed that, while personality pathology could be exaggerated by stress, injury, or disease, it ultimately rested on an inherited "general nervous weakness—a neuropathic taint—showing itself now in one form of psychosis and now in another" (p. 93). "Thus in the same family may be found cases of manic depressive insanity, of senile dementia, of alcoholism and of feeble-mindedness" (p. 77).[3]

Edward Webb (1915) extended the will-power concept into the normal range with the help of a general factor of personality, which he designated $w$ (for will-power). His monograph *Character and intelligence* made the first use of factor analysis in the non-intellectual field (Spearman, 1927). College teachers and peers rated 200 21-year-old students they knew well on 39 7-point scales. The heterogeneous set of traits included: "steadiness," "perseverance," "kindness on principle," "trustworthiness," "conscientiousness," and (on the negative side) "quickness to anger," "eagerness for admiration," and "bodily activity in pursuit of pleasure such as games." Tests of intelligence correlated with components of $w$ (e.g. .34 with steadiness, .28 with perseverance, .23 with kindness on principle, .28 with trustworthiness, and .22 with conscientiousness). Subsequently, when calculating $w$, Webb (1915) partialed $g$ out.[4]

By the 1930s, a proliferation of disease categories and traits had moved the field far away from a unitary dimension. The diversification began with Emil Kraepelin's (1856–1926) separation of *manic-depression* from *dementia praecox* (schizophrenia). Some, including Sigmund Freud (1856–1939), continued to argue for a single continuum, running from normality through the neurotic disorders and out to the psychoses. Others, however, disagreed; and these included Aaron Rosanoff (1878–1943), who by the 1930s had a seven-dimensional model of normal and abnormal personality, and Hans Eysenck (1916–1997), who proposed two sharply separate continua: one from normality to psychosis; the other from normality to neurosis (Eysenck, 1970).

Thus the debate over the structure of personality and its disorders went in a very different direction from the one over cognitive ability. While the $g$ factor of intelligence rose to be of central importance, a single factor was virtually non-existent in the personality domain, where debates were mainly over two-, three-, and five-factor models. Eysenck (1970) long championed his three super-factors of extraversion, neuroticism, and psychoticism, while Costa and McCrae (1992) proposed the OCEAN Big Five, to which Eysenck (1992) countered that conscientiousness and agreeableness were sub-factors of psychoticism, while openness was too poorly defined to be of equal importance. Others proposed a Big Six and a Big Seven, as well as omnibus inventories of 16 or more factors. As in the case of cognitive ability, an integration of broad and narrow traits can be achieved by combining them hierarchically, with behavioral acts at the item level, multidimensional inventories covering the first-order factors, the Big Three and Big Five comprising second- or third-order factors, and the GFP occupying the apex.

At the 1997 Spearman Symposium on Intelligence and Personality, Willem Hofstee introduced a general "$p$-factor" (personality factor) analogous to $g$ (Hofstee, 2001). He speculated on the heritability and evolutionary significance of $p$, suggesting it had arisen as a result of natural selection, for individuals with more socially desirable traits such as competence, emotional steadiness, and reality orientation. In his analysis, social desirability was much more than a mere artifact of social perception. Hofstee (2003) even dubbed $p$ "the Primordial One" (p. 249).

It was Janek Musek (2007) who brought what he dubbed "the Big One" to theoretical center stage. He identified a GFP in three differently aged samples by using Slovenian language translations of extant tests such as the Big-Five Inventory, Big-Five Observer, Positive and Negative Affect Schedule, Satisfaction with Life Scale, and the International Personality Item Pool. Musek's analyses yielded Digman's (1997) Big Two; these were followed by a higher-order GFP, which explained 60 percent of the source variance in the Big Two and from 18 percent to 45 percent of the total reliable variance. Musek described the Big One as an optimum blend of all socially valued personality dimensions of personality. Like Hofstee, Musek conjectured that the general factor would be "deeply embedded in our evolutionary, genetic and neurological endowment" (p. 1228).

## 3 Life History Theory

Although Hofstee (2001) and Musek (2007) suggested that the GFP originated in the natural selection for desirable traits, they did not cite work on life history theory, which provides a theoretical base for understanding the GFP. Unlike conventional personality psychology, life history theory predicts hierarchically organized traits, culminating in a single, heritable, super-factor. Traits need to be harmonized, not to work independently of each other.

Rushton (1985, 1990) conjectured that "one basic dimension—$K$—underlies much of the field of personality" (1985, p. 445). Rushton (1985) proposed that human differences could be understood as part of a life history, a suite of traits genetically organized to meet the trials of life—survival, growth, and reproduction. This built on Wilson's (1975) analysis of "fast–slow" $r$–$K$ reproductive strategies, which explains how animals reach population equilibrium through birth rate, developmental speed, and mortality. Animals adopt a strategy between two extremes: they produce a large number of fast-maturing offspring, but they devote little parental care to ensure their survival (the $r$-strategy); or they invest in a few higher-quality, slower-maturing offspring and devote much care to ensuring that a larger proportion survive (the $K$-strategy). Rushton (1985) postulated that personality traits co-evolved with altruism, intelligence, attachment styles, growth, longevity, sexuality, and fecundity to form a coherent whole. Research has confirmed many of these hypotheses (Bogaert & Rushton, 1989; Figueredo, Vásquez, Brumbach, & Schneider, 2004, 2007; Figueredo et al., 2005; Templer, 2008).

Among university students, Bogaert and Rushton (1989) found correlations between intelligence, altruism, delinquency, sexual restraint, mating effort (e.g. number of sex partners), and an aggregate of items assessing family size, maturational speed, and longevity. Although the average correlation between single indices of $K$ was low, aggregate measures were predictive of a general factor, on which single items loaded an average of .31. These results held true when three separate measures of family background were statistically controlled.

In a study of 642 pairs of 25- to 74-year-old twins from the National Survey of Midlife Development in the US (MIDUS), a representative sample of 50,000 households that included twins, Figueredo et al. (2004) found a substantially heritable dimension, which they termed "Super-$K$" and which comprised three lower-order (also heritable) factors (a general personality factor, a "co-vitality" health factor, and a lower-order $K$ factor). Subsequently, Figueredo et al. (2007) used a different subset of the MIDUS sample and replicated these results with 2,095 non-twin parents who by middle-age had chosen their life niches to marry (or not), to bear and raise offspring (or not), and to create social networks. In both samples, "social privilege" was controlled by regressing out the level of education, race, and family income, which accounted for less than 10 percent of the variance and did not change the pattern of factor loadings.

In a study of 222 university students, a latent $K$ factor was found to load positively on retrospective self-reports of childhood attachment to the biological father and of adult attachment to romantic partners, and negatively with mating effort, Machiavellianism, and risk-taking propensity (Figueredo et al., 2005). Moreover, the $K$ factor correlated with several traditional higher-order personality composites derived from three different personality inventories measuring "big neuroticism" (– .24), "big psychoticism" (– .67), and (marginally) "big extraversion" (.12).

## 4    The GFP in the EAS Temperament Survey

The EAS Temperament Survey for Children (Parental Ratings) was developed by Arnold Buss and Robert Plomin (1984) to assess emotionality, activity, and sociability. Rushton et al. (2008) examined data on 575 pairs of 2- to 9-year-old South Korean twins, in which mothers rated their children on the EAS scales along with a prosocial dimension measuring sharing, helping, and kindness. The GFP accounted for 30 percent of the source variance in the four scales (42 percent of the reliable variance) and was observable by 2 years of age.

## 5    The GFP in the Guilford–Zimmerman Temperament Survey

The Guilford–Zimmerman Temperament Survey (GZTS; Guilford & Zimmerman, 1949) was the culmination of work begun in the 1930s by Joy Paul Guilford (1897– 1987), who may be regarded as the first to systematically apply factor-analytic techniques to personality structure and to arrive at an omnibus inventory. Rushton and Irwing (2009b) aggregated across the correlations for the 10 GZTS factors of personality and temperament for the 2,465 men and the 452 women in Guilford, Zimmerman, and Guilford (1976). The GFP accounted for 36 percent of the variance in three first-order factors and for 21 percent of the total reliable variance (Figure 5.2).

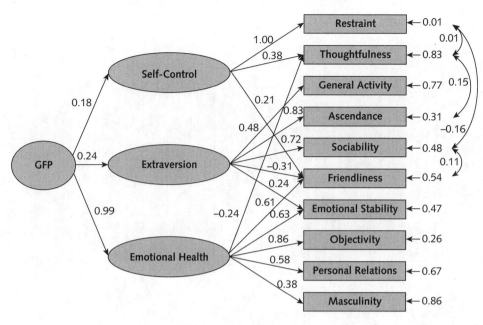

**Figure 5.2** The GFP in the Guilford–Zimmerman Temperament Survey going from the GFP to three higher-order factors to the 10 primary traits. From Rushton & Irwing, 2009b, Figure 2

## 6  The GFP in the California Psychological Inventory

The California Psychological Inventory was originated by Harrison Gough (1957), another early personality researcher who produced an omnibus inventory for use with normal people, providing scores on 20 "folk concept scales." The third edition was standardized on 6,000 people from different socioeconomic backgrounds including college students, blue-collar workers, and prisoners (Gough & Bradley, 1996, p. 62). Rushton and Irwing (2009b) extracted a GFP from the inter-scale correlations given in the manual. The GFP accounted for 35 percent of the variance in two second-order factors, 17 percent of the variance in six first-order factors, and 20 percent of the total reliable variance (Figure 5.3).

## 7  The GFP in the Temperament and Character Inventory

The Temperament and Character Inventory (TCI) was developed by Robert Cloninger to assess the seven factors in his psychobiological model of personality (Cloninger, Przybeck, Svrakic, & Wetzel, 1994). The four dimensions of temperament and three dimensions of character were standardized on 803 undergraduates. A full psychometric analysis was done on a French version of the revised TCI (TCI–R), with a 482-subject sample (54 percent male; mean age = 41 years) including clinical and

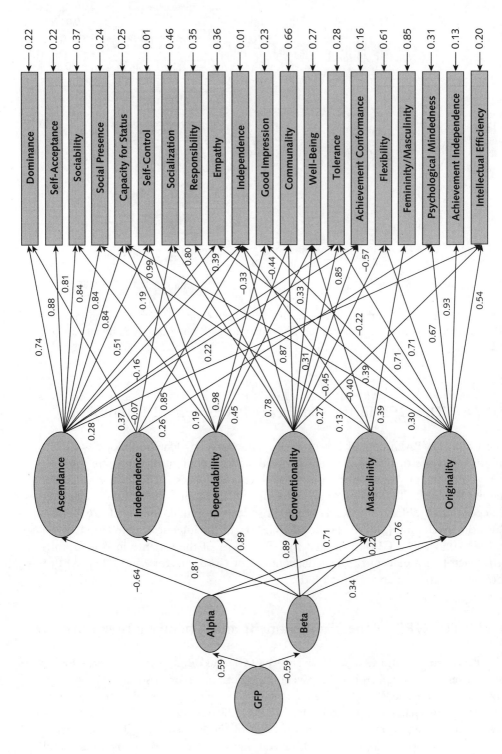

**Figure 5.3** The GFP in the California Psychological Inventory going from the GFP to the Big Two to six higher-order factors to the 20 primary traits. From Rushton & Irwing, 2009b, Figure 3

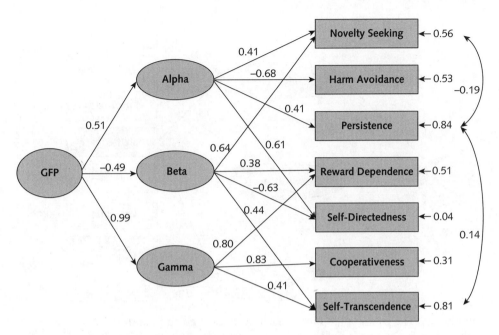

**Figure 5.4** The GFP in the Temperament and Character Inventory going from the GFP to three higher-order factors to the seven primary traits. From Rushton & Irwing, 2009b, Figure 4

non-clinical subjects (Pelissolo et al., 2005). Rushton and Irwing (2009b) combined the two validation samples by using weighted means ($N = 1,285$) and found that the GFP explained 49 percent of the variance in three first-order factors and 24 percent of the total reliable variance in a model that went from the GFP to three higher-order traits to the seven primary traits (Figure 5.4). Furthermore, a GFP was extracted from the Japanese version of the TCI in 651 pairs of 14- to 30-year-old twins, who also completed the NEO–PI–R (Rushton et al., 2009). A principal components analysis found that the GFP–TCI explained 22 percent of the variance and correlated .76 with the GFP extracted from the NEO–PI–R.

## 8 The GFP in the Comrey Personality Scales

The Comrey Personality Scales (CPS), developed by Andrew L. Comrey and now in its third edition (Comrey, 1995), has eight major dimensions, each containing several facets. Rushton and Irwing (2009c) carried out a cross-validation study of the CPS using the original validation sample of 746 mostly university students from 1970, and the updated validation sample of 2,097 mostly university students, which also included police officers and outpatients. The GFP explained 41 percent of the variance in three first-order factors, extraversion demonstrating an exceptionally high loading (Figure 5.5).

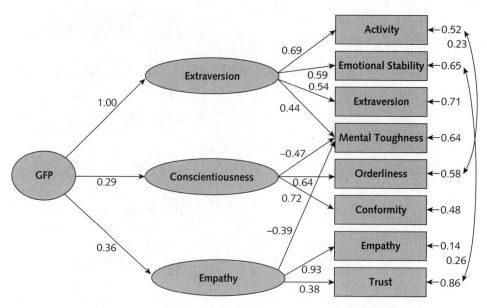

**Figure 5.5** The GFP in the Comrey Personality Scales going from the GFP to three higher-order factors to the eight primary traits. From Rushton & Irwing, 2009c, Figure 1

## 9  The GFP in the Multidimensional Personality Questionnaire

The Multidimensional Personality Questionnaire (MPQ) is a factor-analytically developed self-report instrument that measures 11 primary factors (Tellegen, 1982; Tellegen & Waller, 2008). Three, four, and five alternative higher-order solutions have been specified, especially including positive emotionality; negative emotionality; and constraint. Rushton and Irwing (2009a) tested the three- and four-factor models on the correlations among the 11 primary traits given in the test manual for the validation sample of 500 college females and 300 college males (Tellegen, 1982), but they found a very poor fit. The best-fitting GFP explained 25 percent of the variance in two second-order factors in a model that went from the GFP to a Big Two to Big Five higher-order traits to the 11 primary traits (Figure 5.6).

## 10  The GFP in the Minnesota Multiphasic Personality Inventory–2

The Minnesota Multiphasic Personality Inventory–2 (MMPI–2) is an extensively updated and re-standardized version of one of the earliest self-report questionnaires designed to help clinical diagnosis (Hathaway & McKinley, 1943). The revision contains 10 clinical and three validity scales (Butcher, Dahlstrom, Graham, Tellegen,

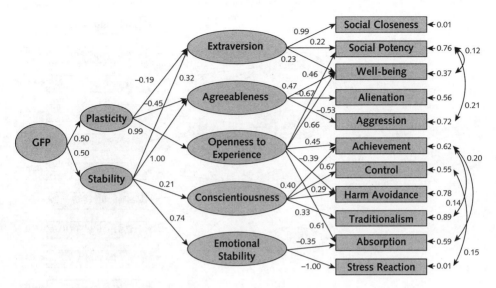

**Figure 5.6** The GFP in the Multidimensional Personality Questionnaire going from the GFP to the Big Two to five higher-order factors to the 11 primary traits. From Rushton & Irwing, 2009a, Figure 1

& Kaemmer, 1989). A nationwide sampling yielded norms based on 2,600 18- to 80-year-olds matched to the 1980 US Census. Rushton and Irwing (2009c) averaged the values given in the test manual for the 1,056+ males and 1,342+ females. The GFP accounted for 49 percent of the variance in two second-order factors and for 20 percent of the total reliable variance (Figure 5.7). Alpha was loosely interpreted as social introversion, Beta as anxiety, Gamma as asocial, and Delta as antisocial, with Alpha and Gamma giving rise to a higher-order factor that could be (negative) plasticity or externalizing behavior, and Beta and Delta giving rise to a higher-order factor that could be (negative) stability or internalizing behavior; and both of these then gave rise to the GFP. However, the high levels of co-morbidity make it prudent not to overinterpret these results.

## 11 The GFP in the Millon Clinical Multiaxial Inventory

The third edition of the Millon Clinical Multiaxial Inventory (MCMI–III) is designed to aid in the assessment of both DSM–IV Axis II personality disorders and Axis I clinical syndromes (Millon, 2006). The 175 questions directly reflect the DSM's diagnostic criteria. The MCMI–III consists of 24 clinical scales comprising 14 personality disorder scales and 10 clinical syndrome scales. Rushton and Irwing (2009d) extracted a GFP from the 24 scales for the 998 individuals of the normative sample, including males and females with a wide variety of diagnoses. The GFP accounted for 41 percent of the variance in two second-order factors, 31 percent of the variance

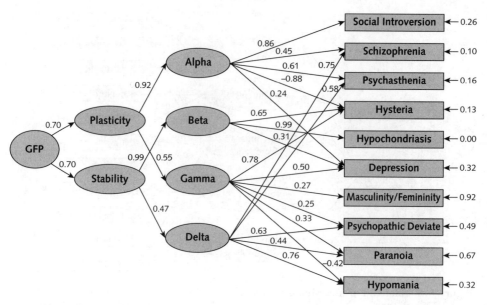

**Figure 5.7**  The GFP in the Minnesota Multiphasic Personality Inventory–2 going from the GFP to the Big Two to four higher-order factors to the 10 primary traits. From Rushton & Irwing, 2009c, Figure 2

in five first-order factors, and 26 percent of the total reliable variance in all 24 scales (Figure 5.8).

## 12  The GFP in the Personality Assessment Inventory

The Personality Assessment Inventory (PAI) is a self-administered test of the person-ality disorders designed for the clinical assessment of adults aged 18 years and older. The PAI has 22 scales comprising 4 validity scales, 11 clinical scales, 5 treatment consideration scales, and 2 interpersonal scales (Morey, 2007). Individuals respond to 344 items by using a four-point range from *false* to *very true*. The 11 clinical scales cover the neurotic, psychotic, and behavior disorders; the five treatment scales indi-cate the respondent's environmental circumstances, motivation for treatment, and potential to harm others and self; and the two interpersonal dimensions are affiliative versus rejecting and dominating versus submissive. Rushton and Irwing (2009d) carried out a quasi-cross-validation study of the PAI for two samples: a clinical sample of 1,246 patients and a normative sample of 1,000 adults matched to the US Census. A five-factor solution was the best alternative for the normative sample, which was then validated on the clinical sample. The GFP accounted for 65 percent of the vari-ance in two second-order factors, 47 percent of the variance in five first-order factors, and 27 percent of the total reliable variance in all 18 scales (Figure 5.9).

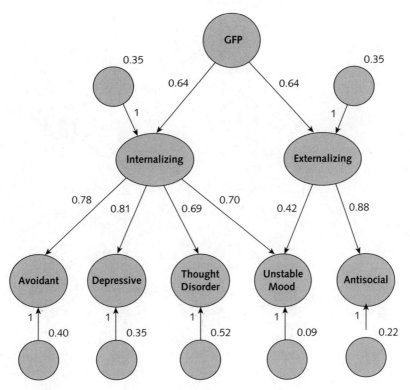

**Figure 5.8** The GFP in the Millon Clinical Multiaxial Inventory going from the GFP to five higher-order factors to the Big Two, of internalizing and externalizing, to the 24 primary traits (not shown). From Rushton & Irwing, 2009d, Figure 1

## 13 The GFP in the Dimensional Assessment of Personality Pathology

The Dimensional Assessment of Personality Pathology–Basic Questionnaire (DAPP–BQ) has 290 items with five response categories ranging from 1 ("strongly disagree") to 5 ("strongly agree"). It measures 18 factors, estimated to capture between 29 percent and 63 percent of the variance in the DSM personality disorders (Livesley & Jackson, 2009; Livesley & Larstone, 2008). In a first study, Rushton and Irwing (2009d) analyzed data from the combined clinical and general population sample (*N* = 455) of the Spanish validation of the DAPP–BQ (Gutiérrez-Zotes et al., 2008). The GFP accounted for 61 percent of the variance in six first-order factors and for 36 percent of the total reliable variance in all 18 scales.

With the publication of the DAPP–BQ manual (Livesley & Jackson, 2009), a more thorough examination was undertaken in a "strictly confirmatory" test of three validation samples. Rushton, Irwing, and Booth (2010) took for calibration the inter-scale correlations (*N* = 942) provided for the general population sample and,

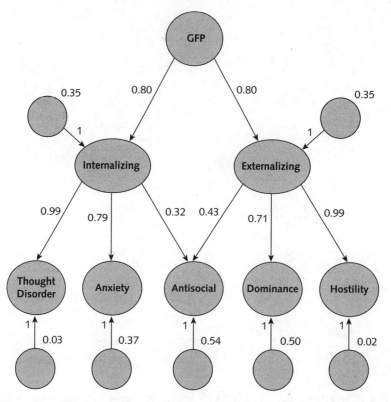

**Figure 5.9** The GFP in the Personality Assessment Inventory going from the GFP to five higher-order factors to the 18 primary scales (not shown). From Rushton & Irwing, 2009d, Figure 3

for validation, those from twin and clinical samples ($N = 1,346$ and 656). The six-factor solution from the Spanish version did not fit the US data, where four factors worked best (Figure 5.10). For the general population sample, the GFP explained 34 percent of the variance in four first-order factors and 33 percent of the variance in all 18 scales. The model fits were very similar for the twin and the clinical samples, with the GFP explaining 35 percent and 34 percent of the variance in four first-order factors and 34 percent and 30 percent of the variance in all 18 scales, respectively.

## 14   The GFP in Emotional Intelligence (and HEXACO)

The high end of the GFP is emotional intelligence (EI), which pertains to the perception and control of emotions in the self (intra-personal focus) and in others (interpersonal focus). The Trait Emotional Intelligence Questionnaire (TEIQue; Petrides, 2009) assesses 15 facets of EI, such as emotional regulation, social

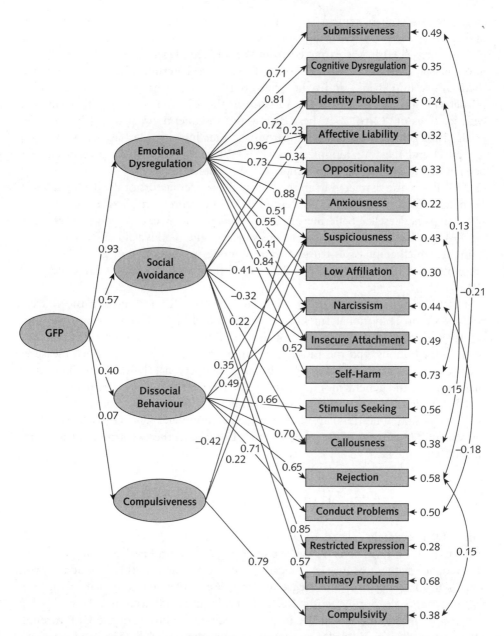

**Figure 5.10** The GFP in the Dimensional Assessment of Personality Pathology going from the GFP to four higher-order factors to the 18 primary scales. After Rushton, Irwing, & Booth, 2010, Figure 1

awareness, stress management, self-esteem, and optimism, which combine into four higher-order factors (well-being, self-control, emotionality, and sociability) and a global score. A GFP was extracted from the TEIQue facets and NEO Big Five in 316 pairs of twins by Veselka, Shermer, Petrides, and Vernon (2009), who divided their sample into twin-1 and twin-2 halves. They found that a GFP accounted for 39 percent and 35 percent of the variance in the 20 variables in the two samples, with loadings of .32 to .77. These data were subsequently re-analyzed by Rushton et al. (2009), who extracted a GFP from the four higher-order factors, along with the NEO and the four humor styles. The GFP accounted for 33 percent and 31 percent of the variance in each sample of 13 variables.

A GFP was also extracted from the four higher-order factors of the TEIQue Short Form in combination with the 60-item HEXACO Inventory in 1,192 19- to 86-year-old twin pairs (Veselka, Schermer, Petrides, Cherkas, Spence, & Vernon, 2009). The HEXACO–60 consists of five dimensions similar to the Big Five plus a sixth, honesty–humility, which emphasizes trustworthiness, modesty, and a lack of greed. The GFP accounted for 33 percent of the variance in both sets of 10 scales, with loadings of .19 to .79.

The GFP has also been extracted from two other EI inventories: the Mayer–Salovey–Caruso Emotional Intelligence Test (MSCEIT), which measures the four domains of identifying emotions, utilizing emotions, understanding emotions, and managing emotions; and the Emotional Quotient Inventory (EQi), which measures the five domains of intra-personal functioning, interpersonal skills, adaptability, stress management, and general mood. McIntyre (2010) gave these measures to 215 female and 205 male college students in combination with the Big Five from the Adjective Self-Description Questionnaire and a verbal ability scale. The GFP explained 40 percent and 38 percent of the variance in all 15 scales in the two samples, with loadings of .14 to .84.

## 15   The GFP and Subjective Well-Being

The GFP is strongly related to dispositional affect and happiness. Musek (2007) extracted a GFP from several Big-Five indicators and found it shared 60 percent of the variance with measures of subjective well-being such as the Satisfaction with Life Scale, the Positive and Negative Affect Schedule, and the Self-Liking and Competence Scale. Subsequently, Rushton and Irwing (2009a) found the well-being scale of the Multidimensional Personality Questionnaire linked to the GFP through loadings on the second-order factors of extraversion, agreeableness, and openness and on the third-order factors of stability and plasticity (see Figure 5.6). Erdle et al. (2010) found that a GFP from the Big Five shared 67 percent common variance with self-esteem in a study of 628,640 Internet respondents. Those high on the GFP experience positive affect and have expectations of future reward, while those low on the GFP experience negative affect and have expectations of future punishment. Subsequently, Rushton and Erdle (2010) found that those who score high on the GFP were not only high in self-esteem and positive affect, but low in depression as measured by the Beck Depression Inventory.

# 16   Evolutionary Genetics

Several cross-national twin studies have found that 50 percent of the GFP variance is due to genetic influence and 50 percent to non-shared environmental influence. These include studies of 322 pairs of adult twins from the UK, 575 pairs of 2- to 9-year-old twins from South Korea, 651 pairs of 14- to 30-year-old twins from Japan, and 316 pairs of 18- to 74-year-old twins from Canada and the US (Figueredo et al., 2004; Rushton et al., 2008, 2009; Veselka, Schermer, Petrides, Cherkas et al., 2009). The 50 percent GFP variance that is environmental is of the non-shared variety (e.g. due to an illness or chance friendship that happens to one sibling and not to the other). This genetic and environmental architecture is similar to that derived from numerous other studies of personality (Bouchard & McGue, 2003).

The GFP is largely a *genetic* factor, that is, individuals who are *genetically* disposed to have high scores on agreeableness, conscientiousness, and emotional stability are *genetically* disposed to have high scores on openness, sociability, self-esteem, and so on. This conclusion derives from the observation that cross-twin–cross-trait correlations for monozygotic (MZ) twins are considerably higher than those for dizygotic (DZ) twins. For example, in 642 pairs of 25- to 74-year-old twins, Figueredo et al. (2004) found that the *genetic* loadings on the GFP from the Big Five were: openness, .67; conscientiousness, .70; extraversion, .91; agreeableness, .83; and neuroticism, –.38. In a study of 575 pairs of South Korean twins, Rushton et al. (2008) extracted a higher-order GFP from a *genetic* matrix calculated from the bivariate heritabilities between the prosocial and EAS scales and found it explained 32 percent of the source variance from the four lower-order scales (47 percent of the reliable variance).

Of theoretical interest is that some of the genetic variance in the GFP is of the *non-additive* variety (dominance and epistasis). Non-additive genetic (D) variance is inferred when the correlations for MZ twins are more than twice those for DZ twins. In Rushton et al.'s (2008) study of 575 pairs of 2- to 9-year-old South Korean twins, after a GFP was extracted from a Prosocial Questionnaire and from the EAS Temperament Scales, 53 percent of the variance was found to be of the non-additive variety (Figure 5.11).

Other studies have also indicated D effects. A study by Rushton et al. (2008) extracted the GFP from 29 self-ratings in 322 pairs of British twins and found that the correlation for MZ pairs (.55) was more than twice that for DZ pairs (.14). Model-fitting gave the DE model the best fit, with D = 55 percent and E = 45 percent. A study by Rushton et al. (2009) extracted the GFP from 13 scales comprising the Big Five, four factors of emotional intelligence, and four factors of humor style in 316 Canadian and US twin pairs. The correlation for MZ twins (.41) was more than twice that for DZ twins (.05). Model-fitting gave the DE model the best fit, with D = 42 percent and E = 58 percent. A twin study by Figueredo and Rushton (2009) found that D effects could not be ruled out as a contributor to the shared variance between the GFP, a general health factor, and a lower-order life history factor, implying the GFP and good health co-evolved as mutually adapted traits through directional selection for a slow (*K*-selected) life history strategy.

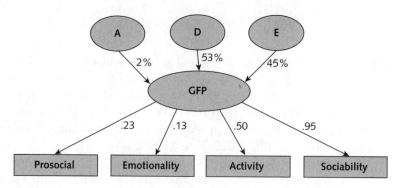

**Figure 5.11**  The genetic and environmental architecture of the GFP in the prosocial and EAS temperament scales from South Korean 2- to 9-year-olds. Note: A = additive genetic variance; D = dominance genetic variance; E = non-shared environmental variance. From data in Rushton et al., 2008

Non-additive genetic variance implies the GFP has been under recent directional selection, as expected for a Darwinian fitness character—that is, one that leads to greater reproductive success (Falconer, 1989; Fisher, 1954). The well-defined positive and negative poles of the GFP (the positive pole being cooperative and prosocial) suggest how and why unidirectional selection for personality might have occurred from "primeval man and his ape-like progenitors," as Darwin (1871, p. 159) phrased it. Those at the high end of the GFP—prosocial, open, conscientious, outgoing, agreeable, and emotionally stable—can be expected to enjoy better social relationships, and hence greater reproductive success, since people prefer as mates, fellow workers, and leaders those who are agreeable, cooperative, and emotionally stable (Figueredo, Sefcek, & Jones, 2006; Miller, 2007). Moreover, people able to cooperate in groups are more likely to win competitions and wars (Darwin, 1871).

Genetic dominance is also suggested by evidence of inbreeding depression on components of the GFP (just as there is inbreeding depression on the *g* factor of mental ability: Jensen, 1998). Inbreeding depression occurs on a trait when deleterious recessive alleles combine to lower the scores of offspring relative to parents. An Italian study found evidence that inbred families were lower on extraversion and openness (Camperio Ciani, Capiluppi, Veronese, & Sartori, 2007). A Dutch study revealed that the offspring of parents who came from the same region in the Netherlands (and so were more likely to be inbred) scored lower on sensation-seeking than those whose parents came from different regions (Rebello & Boomsma, 2007).

## 17  Neurobiology

The strategy of searching for the conceptual (and real) nervous system underlying personality will differ depending on whether the apex is viewed as consisting of a

GFP, a Big Two, a Big Three, or a Big Five. The Pavlovian concept of strength of the nervous system has often been proposed for theories of temperament, including the ancient Hippocratic–Galenic model of the four humors (Strelau, 2008). A strong nervous system (high GFP) is one that is slower to arouse and more tolerant of intense stimulation for a longer time period. A weak nervous system (low GFP) is quicker to arouse, but tires sooner.

Gray (1970) linked a strong nervous system to stable extraversion and a weak nervous system to neurotic introversion following his 45-degree rotation of Eysenck's two orthogonal dimensions. Consequently, Rushton et al. (2009) suggested that Gray and McNaughton's (2000) reinforcement sensitivity theory might constitute the core of the GFP, because it integrates the fundamental process of approach–avoidance, starting at the genes, working up through brain anatomy and physiology, and culminating in learning and experiential outcomes, including positive and negative emotionality and motivation. Three independent biological systems are postulated: a behavioral inhibition system (BIS), a behavioral activation system (BAS), and a fight–flight–freezing system (FFFS). BIS is the aversive system that controls anxiety and negative feelings such as fear, frustration, and sadness, and it is sensitive to signals of punishment, non-reward, and novelty. BAS is the approach system that results in feelings of hope, elation, and happiness and is sensitive to signals of reward. FFFS is related to extremes of negative emotion, such as panic and rage, and responds to unconditioned punishment.

The relation between the GFP and BIS–BAS was examined by Erdle and Rushton (2010) in two studies of university students ($N = 128$ and 88). The GFP was measured by summing over the scales of the Big-Five Inventory (BFI) after reverse keying neuroticism to reflect emotional stability. The GFP correlated significantly and positively with the behavioral activation system (.42, .34), generalized expectancy of reward (.57, .56), self-esteem (.45, .33), and positive affect (.62, .49), and negatively with the behavioral inhibition system (−.27, −.30), generalized expectancy of punishment (−.31, −.14 *ns*), and negative affect (−.50, −.63). In both studies, a principal components analysis found that all measures loaded on a single factor, the GFP explaining 42 percent of the variance.

The temperamental basis of the GFP was also examined by Zawadzki and Strelau (2010) by using self- and peer ratings from 32 Polish-language scales measuring the Big Five and strength of the nervous system. Zawadzki and Strelau extracted a GFP from two separate samples of 2,000+ 16- to 77-year-olds, using both self-ratings and peer ratings ($r = .89$). Since the highest loadings on the GFP were consistently from neuroticism and extraversion, they proposed that nervous system *arousal* was the core mechanism. However, since neuroticism and extraversion had different arousal systems, Zawadzki and Strelau argued that temperament should not be reduced to a single factor.

A full neurobiological system also has to include the neurotransmitters of serotonin and dopamine, which act broadly in the brain and are widely implicated in the regulation of mood. High levels of dopamine are often said to activate approach behavior and the reward system, while high levels of serotonin inhibit signals of pain and the punishment system. People at the high end of the GFP can be expected to have higher levels of serotonin and dopamine; people at the low end, lower levels.

## 18   Construct Validity

A first step regarding construct validity is to demonstrate that different procedures give rise to the same GFP. If the GFP exists, it should do so regardless of the particular inventory, extraction method, or sample. In Section 7, a GFP extracted from the Temperament and Character Inventory correlated .72 with a GFP extracted from the NEO–PI–R in 651 pairs of Japanese twins (Rushton et al., 2009). In Section 17, a GFP extracted from 32 scales using 1,000+ self-ratings showed Tucker factor similarity coefficients of .89 and .99, derived from different estimates of the factor structure, with a GFP extracted from 2,000+ peer ratings (Zawadzki & Strelau, 2010).

Irwing and Rushton (2010) carried out a large confirmatory factor model (Figure 5.12) and found separate GFPs correlated with a mean of .87 across the Jackson Personality Inventory (JPI), the Hogan Personality Inventory (HPI), the Big-Five Inventory (BFI), and the Mini-Markers, all administered to the same individuals ($N = 725$) from the Eugene-Springfield Community Sample in Oregon. Irwing and Rushton (2010) confirmed their results using pair-wise factor models, principal components analyses, principal axis factoring, and unit-weighting (mean $r = .80$). Although the inventories emphasize different aspects of personality and different philosophies of scale construction, the GFP was extracted from the HPI and the JPI just as readily as it was from the BFI and the Mini-Markers.

The main alternative explanation for the GFP is that it arises from artifacts of evaluative bias and scale construction (Anusic, Schimmack, Pinkus, & Lockwood, 2009; Ashton, Lee, Goldberg, & de Vries, 2009; Bäckström, Björklund, & Larsson, 2009). However, the GFP is extracted just as robustly from other-reports as it is from self-reports, thereby suggesting that evaluative biases are of limited importance (Rushton et al., 2008; Van der Linden, te Nijenhuis, et al., 2010; Zawadzki & Strelau, 2010). Furthermore, Rushton et al. (2009) carried out a multi-trait–multi-method (MTMM) study that found a GFP in self-, teacher-, and parent-ratings in 391 13- to 14-year-olds using the Big-Five Questionnaire—Children (BFQ–C; Barbaranelli, Fida, Paciello, Di Giunta, & Caprara, 2008). As shown in Figure 5.13, the GFP sits atop the Big Two and the Big Five, with a substantial fit to the empirical data that accounted for 22 to 54 percent of the variance in the lower-order traits.

Although measures of evaluative bias do correlate with the higher-order personality factors similar to the way they do with lower-order dimensions, they have not been found to undermine the robustness of the GFP. For example, while Bäckström et al. (2009) found that social desirability contributed to higher-order factors above the Big Five, they also found that the higher-order factors were recovered after rewriting the items to control for social desirability. Other research has found that, while social desirability scales correlated with components of the GFP, the GFP remained intact after partialing out their effects (Erdle & Rushton, 2010; Rushton & Erdle, 2010; Schermer & Vernon, 2010). Although Anusic et al. (2009) reported that self-esteem could constitute a "halo effect," and Erdle, Gosling, and Potter (2009) confirmed that higher-order factors above the Big Five were related to self-esteem, Erdle et al. (2010) also found that controlling for self-esteem left the GFP intact.

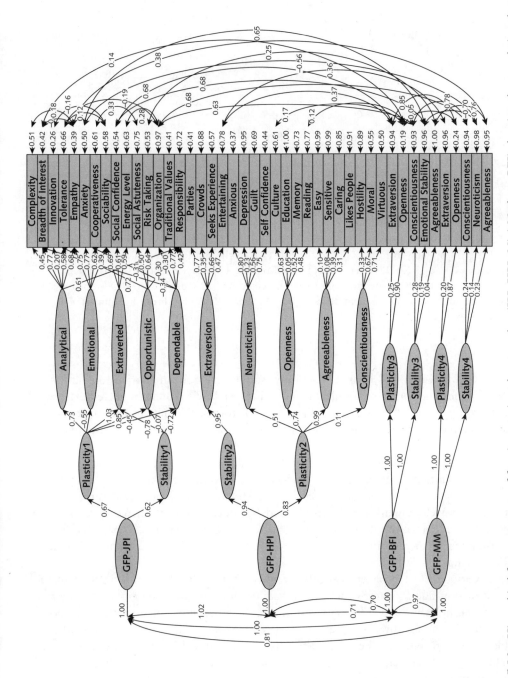

**Figure 5.12** Hierarchical factor structure of four inventories taken together (JPI, HPI, Mini-Markers, BFI) showing the correlations between the GFPs. From Irwing & Rushton, 2010, Figure 5

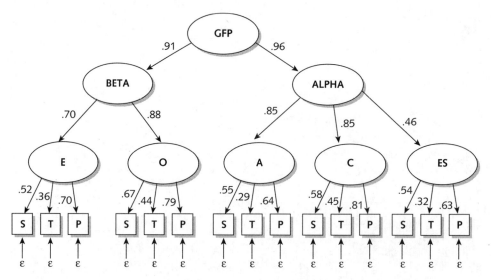

**Figure 5.13** A multi-trait–multi-method model of the GFP from self-, teacher-, and parent-ratings going from the GFP to the Big Two to the Big Five from a re-analysis of Barbaranelli et al.'s (2008) data. Note: S = self-report, T = teacher report, P = parent report. Uniquenesses of the same informant are correlated. E = extraversion, O = openness, A = agreeableness, C = conscientiousness, ES = emotional stability. From Rushton et al., 2009, Figure 2

Four multi-method construct validity studies have been carried out in the Netherlands and found that a GFP measured through self-reports predicted external criteria. One study found that a GFP extracted from self-ratings in employees with an average job experience of nine years predicted job performance rated by supervisors (Van der Linden, te Nijenhuis, et al., 2010). Another found that a GFP extracted from self-reports in adolescents predicted likeability rated by peers (Van der Linden, Scholte, Cillessen, te Nijenhuis, & Segers, 2010). A third found that a GFP extracted from personality questionnaires used by the Dutch military predicted turnover in training as well as work performance rated by supervisors (te Nijenhuis, Cremers, Van der Linden, & van de Ven, 2010). The fourth found that a GFP extracted from self-ratings predicted suitability for jobs rated by professional assessors (Van der Linden, Bakker, & Serlie, 2010).

A critique by Ashton et al. (2009) argued that the GFP is an artifact of scale construction due to lower-order facets loading on more than one factor (e.g. originality, enthusiasm, and leadership resulting in a same-signed blend on extraversion and openness). In three samples, Ashton et al. reported that models taking these blends into account fit the data better than models based on higher-order factors. They argued that, since blended models were more parsimonious, higher-order factors were not required. However, in the studies we have reported here, we could find no distinction between the GFPs extracted from the "blended" Big-Five factors (e.g. Figure 5.1) and those extracted from latent variables computed from univocal primary factors (e.g. Figure 5.6 on the MPQ; Figure 5.12 on the JPI). Moreover, Ashton et al. (2009) inadvertently biased their outcomes by (1) constructing models with only two indicators per factor, a practice that likely increased the parsimony of blended models; and (2) fitting the blended models to data before comparing them to a pre-existing hierarchical model. In any case, their model fit indices were so poor that no sensible conclusion could be drawn. More generally, advocating blended models goes against the whole history of factor analysis, which favors one-dimensional scales and factors approximating simple structure. Without univocal variables, factors tend to be indeterminate.

# 19  Discussion

The results presented here show that a higher-order general factor of personality (GFP) reliably occupies the apex of the hierarchy of personality and its disorders, and it does so regardless of whether self- or other-reports are used. A GFP has now been extracted from over 24 different personality inventories, including several sets of the Big Five, the California Psychological Inventory (CPI), the Comrey Personality Scales (CPS), the Dimensional Assessment of Personality Pathology–Basic Questionnaire (DAPP–BQ), the EAS Temperament Scales (EAS), the Guilford–Zimmerman Temperament Survey (GZTS), the HEXACO Personality Inventory (HEXACO), the Hogan Personality Inventory (HPI), the Jackson Personality Inventory (JPI), the Millon Clinical Multiaxial Inventory–III (MCMI–III), the Minnesota Multiphasic Personality Inventory–2 (MMPI–2), the Multidimensional Personality Questionnaire (MPQ), the Personality Assessment Inventory (PAI), the Personality Research Form (PRF), the Temperament and Character Inventory (TCI), and the Trait Emotional Intelligence Questionnaire (TEIQue).

The robustness of the GFP is attested to by the diversity of the inventories from which it has been extracted. A GFP emerged regardless of whether the inventory covered the domain of normal personality (the NEO–PI, FFI) or the domain of the personality disorders (the DAPP–BQ, MMPI–2, PAI, MMCI–III). A GFP emerged regardless of whether the inventory was based on theoretical criteria (the PRF, PAI) or aimed to be eclectic (the CPI, JPI). It emerged whether the inventory distinguished between scales of "temperament" and "personality" (the TCI), or between those of "personality disorders," "social conditions," and "attitudes toward therapy" (the PAI). A GFP also emerged regardless of whether the inventory used an *empirical* approach to scale construction and selected items based on the frequency of endorsement by criterion groups (the CPI, MMPI), an *inductive* approach and selected items based on their relation to each other (the PAI), or a *rational* approach based on writing items to fit traits defined in advance (the DAPP–BQ). A GFP similarly emerged when the inventory was constructed to minimize the effects of social desirability by selecting neutral items (the JPI, PRF).

There is nothing vague about the GFP. Quite the contrary; it is by definition the most internally consistent linear combination of all traits. Its location at the apex of the hierarchy should be almost completely fixed in any large data set. Nonetheless, we should make it clear that we are not at all implying that only one dimension will explain all manifestations of the rich and complex tapestry of the human personality. Nor does a general factor invalidate the utility or theoretical importance of lower-order factors. It is an empirical question as to which level provides the best predictor for a given criterion. The personality facets that exist *below* the Big Five, and so are closer to the behavior expressed, are sometimes better predictors than higher-order traits. If a person is experiencing anxiety over public speaking, it may be more beneficial to focus on his or her specific problem than on his or her general adjustment. But focusing on one specific lower-order trait should not obscure the existence of the hierarchical structure any more than it should obscure other relevant traits at the same level.

In conclusion, the theory and evidence presented here agrees with and extends the viewpoint of Darwin (1871), Wilson (1975), and others, that social competition and reproductive dynamics have helped direct human evolution. In particular, the evidence confirms a theoretical suggestion made by Rushton (1985, 1990) to the effect that much of the field of individual differences can be organized under a hierarchy of broad, heritable dimensions that, taken together, comprise a fast–slow ($r$–$K$) life history. This perspective provides increased coherence to the study of human behavior and makes unique predictions, not easily derivable from other approaches.

## Notes

1   Our results contradict Digman (1997), who reported that the Big Two were *uncorrelated*. We were surprised to find so many discrepancies between the values Digman reported in his Appendix B and those we found in the sources he cited in Appendix A (Rushton & Irwing, 2008, pp. 680–681). We surmised that Digman must have worked from subsets of raw data from which the original papers had been published. Regardless, Digman's published data do give rise to a *correlated* Alpha and Beta, which give rise to the GFP.
2   Galton (1887) listed the traits alphabetically: *Good temper* (amiable, buoyant, calm, cool, equable, forbearing, gentle, good, mild, placid, self-controlled, submissive, sunny, timid); *Bad temper* (acrimonious, aggressive, arbitrary, bickering, capricious, captious, choleric, contentious, crotchety, decisive, despotic, domineering, easily offended, fiery, fits of anger, gloomy, grumpy, harsh, hasty, headstrong, huffy, impatient, imperative, impetuous, insane temper, irritable, morose, nagging, obstinate, odd-tempered, passionate, peevish, peppery, proud, pugnacious, quarrelsome, quick-tempered, scolding, short, sharp, sulky, sullen, surly, uncertain, vicious, vindictive).
3   The Appendix in Menninger, Wayman, and Pruyser (1963) documents a unitary construct over centuries of evolving concepts in psychiatric nosology.
4   Decades later, Deary (1996) discovered a latent Big Five in Webb's (1915) data, thereby "pre-confirming" the hierarchical structure we present in the current chapter, albeit using an opposite procedure from ours by decomposing Webb's higher-order GFP into the lower-order Big Five.

## References

Anusic, I., Schimmack, U., Pinkus, R. T., & Lockwood, P. (2009). The nature and structure of correlations among Big Five ratings: The Halo-Alpha-Beta model. *Journal of Personality and Social Psychology, 97*, 1142–1156.

Ashton, M. C., Lee, K., Goldberg, L. R., & de Vries, R. E. (2009). Higher-order factors of personality: Do they exist? *Personality and Social Psychology Review, 13,* 7991.

Bäckström, M., Björklund, F., & Larsson, M. R. (2009). Five-factor inventories have a major general factor related to social desirability which can be reduced by framing items neutrally. *Journal of Research in Personality, 43,* 335–344.

Barbaranelli, C., Fida, R., Paciello, M., Di Giunta, L., & Caprara, G. V. (2008). Assessing personality in early adolescence through self-report and other-ratings: A multitrait–multimethod analysis of the BFQ–C. *Personality and Individual Differences, 44,* 876–886.

Block, J. (2010). The five-factor model framing of personality and beyond: Some ruminations. *Psychological Inquiry, 21,* 2–25.

Bogaert, A. F., & Rushton, J. P. (1989). Sexuality, delinquency and r/K reproductive strategies: Data from a Canadian university sample. *Personality and Individual Differences, 10,* 1071–1077.

Bouchard, T. J. Jr., & McGue, M. (2003). Genetic and environmental influences on human psychological differences. *Journal of Neurobiology, 54,* 4–45.

Buss, A. H., & Plomin, R. (1984). *Temperament: Early developing personality traits.* Hillsdale, NJ: Lawrence Erlbaum Associates.

Butcher, J. N., Dahlstrom, W. G., Graham, J. R., Tellegen, A., & Kaemmer, B. (1989). *MMPI–2: Manual for administration and scoring.* Minneapolis, MN: University of Minnesota Press.

Camperio Ciani, A. S., Capiluppi, C., Veronese, A., & Sartori, G. (2007). The adaptive value of personality differences revealed by small island population dynamics. *European Journal of Personality, 21,* 3–22.

Carroll, J. B. (2002). The five-factor personality model: How complete and satisfactory is it? In H. I. Braun, D. N. Jackson, & D. E. Wiley (Eds.), *The role of constructs in psychological and educational measurement* (pp. 97–126). Mahwah, NJ: Lawrence Erlbaum Associates.

Cloninger, C. R., Przybeck, T. R., Svrakic, D. M., & Wetzel, R. D. (1994). *The Temperament and Character Inventory (TCI): A guide to its development and use.* St. Louis, MO: Center for Psychobiology of Personality, Washington University.

Comrey, A. L. (1995). *Revised manual and handbook of interpretations for the Comrey Personality Scales.* San Diego, CA: Educational and Industrial Testing Service.

Costa, P. T., Jr., & McCrae, R. R. (1992). *NEO PI–R professional manual.* Odessa, FL: Psychological Assessment Resources.

Darwin, C. (1859). *The origin of species.* London: Murray.

Darwin, C. (1871). *The descent of man.* London: Murray.

Darwin, C. (1872). *The expression of the emotions in man and animals.* London: Murray.

Davenport, C. B. (1911). *Heredity in relation to eugenics.* New York: Holt.

Deary, I. J. (1996). A (latent) Big Five personality model in 1915? A reanalysis of Webb's data. *Journal of Personality and Social Psychology, 71,* 992–1005.

DeYoung, C. G., Peterson, J. B., & Higgins, D. M. (2002). Higher-order factors of the Big Five predict conformity: Are there neuroses of health? *Personality and Individual Differences, 33,* 53–552.

Digman, J. M. (1997). Higher-order factors of the Big Five. *Journal of Personality and Social Psychology, 73,* 1246–1256.

Erdle, S., & Rushton, J. P. (2010). The general factor of personality, BIS–BAS, expectancies of reward and punishment, self-esteem, and positive and negative affect. *Personality and Individual Differences, 48,* 762–766.

Erdle, S., Gosling, S. D., & Potter, J. (2009). Does self-esteem account for the higher-order factors of the Big Five? *Journal of Research in Personality, 43,* 921–923.

Erdle, S., Irwing, P., Rushton, J. P., & Park, J. (2010). The general factor of personality and its relation to self-esteem in 628,640 Internet respondents. *Personality and Individual Differences, 48*, 343–346.

Eysenck, H. J. (1970). *The structure of human personality* (3rd ed.). London: Methuen.

Eysenck, H. J. (1992). Four ways five factors are not basic. *Personality and Individual Differences, 13*, 667–673.

Falconer, D. S. (1989). *Introduction to quantitative genetics* (3rd ed.). London: Longman.

Figueredo, A. J., & Rushton, J. P. (2009). Evidence for shared genetic dominance between the general factor of personality, mental and physical health, and life history traits. *Twin Research and Human Genetics, 12*, 555–563.

Figueredo, A. J., Sefcek, J. A., & Jones, D. N. (2006). The ideal romantic partner personality. *Personality and Individual Differences, 41*, 431–441.

Figueredo, A. J., Vásquez, G., Brumbach, B. H., & Schneider, S. M. R. (2004). The heritability of life history strategy: The K-factor, covitality, and personality. *Social Biology, 51*, 121–143.

Figueredo, A. J., Vásquez, G., Brumbach, B. H., & Schneider, S. M. R. (2007). The K-factor, covitality, and personality: A psychometric test of life history theory. *Human Nature, 18*, 47–73.

Figueredo, A. J., Sefcek, J. A., Vásquez, G., Brumbach, B. H., King, J. E., & Jacobs, W. J. (2005). Evolutionary personality psychology. In D. M. Buss (Ed.), *The handbook of evolutionary psychology* (pp. 851–877). Hoboken, NJ: Wiley.

Fisher, R. A. (1954). *The genetical theory of natural selection* (2nd rev. ed.). New York: Dover.

Galton, F. (1869). *Hereditary genius.* London: Macmillan.

Galton, F. (1884). Measurement of character. *Fortnightly Review, 36*, 179–185.

Galton, F. (1887). Good and bad temper in English families. *Fortnightly Review, 42*, 21–30.

Gough, H. G. (1957). *California Psychological Inventory.* Mountain View, CA: Consulting Psychologists Press.

Gough, H. G., & Bradley, P. (1996). *CPI manual* (3rd ed.). Mountain View, CA: Consulting Psychologists Press.

Gray, J. A. (1970). The psychophysiological basis of introversion–extraversion. *Behavior Research and Therapy, 8*, 249–266.

Gray, J. A., & McNaughton, N. (2000). *The neuropsychology of anxiety.* Oxford: Oxford University Press.

Guilford, J. P., & Zimmerman, W. S. (1949). *The Guilford–Zimmerman Temperament Survey: Manual.* Beverly Hills, CA: Sheridan.

Guilford, J. S., Zimmerman, W. S., & Guilford, J. P. (1976). *The Guilford–Zimmerman Temperament Survey handbook: Twenty-five years of research and applications.* San Diego, CA: Edits.

Gutiérrez-Zotes, J. A., Gutiérrez, F., Valero, J., Gallego, J., Baillés, E., Torres, X., Labad, A., & Livesley, W. J. (2008). Structure of personality pathology in normal and clinical samples: Spanish validation of the DAPP–BQ. *Journal of Personality Disorders, 22*, 389–404.

Hathaway, S. R., & McKinley, J. C. (1943). *The Minnesota Multiphasic Personality Inventory.* Minneapolis, MN: University of Minnesota Press.

Hofstee, W. K. B. (2001). Intelligence and personality: Do they mix? In J. M. Collis & S. Messick (Eds.), *Intelligence and personality: Bridging the gap in theory and measurement* (pp. 43–60). Mahwah, NJ: Lawrence Erlbaum Associates.

Hofstee, W. K. B. (2003). Structures of personality traits. In I. B. Weiner (Series Ed.), T. Millon & M. J. Lerner (Vol. Eds.), *Handbook of psychology: Vol. 5. Personality and social psychology* (pp. 231–254). Hoboken, NJ: Wiley.

Irwing, P., & Rushton, J. P. (2010). *Just one general factor of personality (GFP): Consistent results from four test batteries.* Submitted for publication.

Jensen, A. R. (1998). *The g factor.* Westport, CT: Praeger.

Jöreskog, K. G. (1993). Testing structural equation models. In K. A. Bollen & J. S. Long (Eds.), *Testing structural equation models* (pp. 294-316). London: Sage.

Livesley, W. J., & Jackson, D. N. (2009). *Dimensional Assessment of Personality Pathology— Basic Questionnaire: Technical manual.* Port Huron, MI: Sigma Assessment Systems.

Livesley, W. J., & Larstone, R. M. (2008). The dimensional assessment of personality pathology (DAPP). In G. J. Boyle, G. Matthews, & D. H. Saklofske (Eds.), *The Sage handbook of personality theory and testing: Vol. 2. Personality measurement and assessment* (pp. 608–625). London: Sage.

McIntyre, H. H. (2010). Gender differences in the nature and linkage of higher-order personality factors to trait and ability emotional intelligence. *Personality and Individual Differences, 48,* 617–622.

Menninger, K., Wayman, M., & Pruyser, P. (1963). *The vital balance: The life process in mental health.* New York: Viking.

Miller, G. F. (2007). Sexual selection for moral virtues. *Quarterly Review of Biology, 82,* 97–125.

Millon, T. (2006). *Millon Clinical Multiaxial Inventory–III manual* (3rd ed.). Minneapolis, MN: NCS Pearson.

Morey, L. C. (2007). *The Personality Assessment Inventory professional manual* (2nd ed.). Odessa, FL: Psychological Assessment Resources.

Mount, M. K., Barrick, M. R., Scullen, S. M., & Rounds, J. (2005). Higher-order dimensions of the Big Five personality traits and the Big Six vocational interest types. *Personnel Psychology, 58,* 447–478.

Musek, J. (2007). A general factor of personality: Evidence for the Big One in the five-factor model. *Journal of Research in Personality, 41,* 1213–1233.

Pelissolo, A., Mallet, L., Baleyte, J.-M., Michel, G., Cloninger, C. R., Allilaire, J.-F., & Jouvent, R. (2005). The Temperament and Character Inventory–Revised (TCI–R): Psychometric characteristics of the French version. *Acta Psychiatrica Scandinavia, 112,* 126–133.

Petrides, K. V. (2009). *Technical manual for the Trait Emotional Intelligence Questionnaire (TEIQue).* London: London Psychometric Laboratory, University of London.

Pritchard, J. C. (1835). *A treatise on insanity and other disorders affecting the mind.* London: Sherwood, Gilbert, & Piper.

Rebello, I., & Boomsma, D. I. (2007). Personality: Possible effects of inbreeding depression on sensation seeking. *European Journal of Personality, 21,* 621–623.

Rushton, J. P. (1985). Differential K Theory: The sociobiology of individual and group differences. *Personality and Individual Differences, 6,* 441–452.

Rushton, J. P. (1990). Sir Francis Galton, epigenetic rules, genetic similarity theory, and human life history analysis. *Journal of Personality, 58,* 117–140.

Rushton, J. P., & Erdle, S. (2010). No evidence that social desirability response set explains the general factor of personality and its affective correlates. *Twin Research and Human Genetics, 13,* 131–134.

Rushton, J. P., & Irwing, P. (2008). A general factor of personality (GFP) from two meta-analyses of the Big Five: Digman (1997) and Mount, Barrick, Scullen, and Rounds (2005). *Personality and Individual Differences, 45,* 679–683.

Rushton, J. P., & Irwing, P. (2009a). A general factor of personality (GFP) from the Multidimensional Personality Questionnaire. *Personality and Individual Differences, 47,* 571–576.

Rushton, J. P., & Irwing, P. (2009b). A general factor of personality in 16 sets of the Big Five, the Guilford–Zimmerman Temperament Survey, the California Psychological Inventory, and the Temperament and Character Inventory. *Personality and Individual Differences, 47,* 558–564.

Rushton, J. P., & Irwing, P. (2009c). A general factor of personality in the Comrey Personality Scales, the Minnesota Multiphasic Personality Inventory–2, and the Multicultural Personality Questionnaire. *Personality and Individual Differences, 46,* 437–442.

Rushton, J. P., & Irwing, P. (2009d). A general factor of personality in the Millon Clinical Multiaxial Inventory–III, the Dimensional Assessment of Personality Pathology, and the Personality Assessment Inventory. *Journal of Research in Personality, 43,* 1091–1095.

Rushton, J. P., Bons, T. A., & Hur, Y.-M. (2008). The genetics and evolution of a general factor of personality. *Journal of Research in Personality, 42,* 1173–1185.

Rushton, J. P., Irwing, P., & Booth, T. (2010). A general factor of personality (GFP) in the personality disorders: Three studies of the Dimensional Assessment of Personality Pathology–Basic Questionnaire (DAPP–BQ). *Twin Research and Human Genetics, 13,* 301–311.

Rushton, J. P., Bons, T. A., Ando, J., Hur, Y-M., Irwing, P., Vernon, P. A., Petrides, K. V., & Barbaranelli, C. (2009). A general factor of personality from multitrait–multimethod data and cross-national twins. *Twin Research and Human Genetics, 12,* 356–365.

Schermer, J. A., & Vernon, P. A. (2010). The correlation between general intelligence (g), a general factor of personality (GFP), and social desirability. *Personality and Individual Differences, 48,* 187–189.

Spearman, C. (1927). *The abilities of man.* New York: Macmillan.

Strelau, J. (2008). *Temperament as a regulator of behavior.* Clinton Corners, NY: Eliot Werner.

te Nijenhuis, J., Cremers, M., Van der Linden, D., & van de Ven, C. (2010). *The General Factor of Personality: 17 individual military studies, a large meta-analysis, and 4 criterion-related validity studies.* Submitted for publication.

Tellegen, A. (1982). *A brief manual for the Differential Personality Questionnaire* [Unpublished manual]. Department of Psychology, University of Minnesota, MN.

Tellegen, A., & Waller, N. G. (2008). Exploring personality through test construction: Development of the Multidimensional Personality Questionnaire. In G. J. Boyle, G. Matthews, & D. H. Saklofske (Eds.), *The Sage handbook of personality theory and assessment: Vol. 2. Personality measurement and testing* (pp. 261–292). London: Sage.

Templer, D. I. (2008). Correlational and factor analytic support for Rushton's differential K life-history theory. *Personality and Individual Differences, 45,* 440–444.

Van der Linden, D., Bakker, A. B., & Serlie, A. (2010). *The general factor of personality and professional-level assessor ratings of job suitability in 2,700 candidates.* Submitted for publication.

Van der Linden, D., te Nijenhuis, J., & Bakker, A. B. (2010). The general factor of personality: A meta-analysis of Big Five intercorrelations and a criterion-related validity study. *Journal of Research in Personality. 44,* 315–327.

Van der Linden, D., Scholte, R. H. J., Cillessen, A. H. N., te Nijenhuis, J., & Segers, E. (2010). The general factor of personality and classroom ratings of likeability and popularity. *Journal of Research in Personality, 44,* 669–672.

Veselka, L., Schermer, J. A., Petrides, K. V., & Vernon, P. A. (2009). Evidence for a heritable general factor of personality in two studies. *Twin Research and Human Genetics, 12,* 254–260.

Veselka, L., Schermer, J. A., Petrides, K. V., Cherkas, L. F., Spence, T. D., & Vernon, P. A. (2009). A general factor of personality: Evidence from the HEXACO model and a measure of trait emotional intelligence. *Twin Research and Human Genetics, 12,* 420–424.

Webb, E. (1915). *Character and intelligence: An attempt at an exact study of character.* Cambridge: Cambridge University Press.

Wilson, E. O. (1975). *Sociobiology: The new synthesis.* Cambridge, MA: Harvard University Press.

Zawadzki, B., & Strelau, J. (2010). Structure of personality: The search for a general factor viewed from a temperament perspective. *Personality and Individual Differences, 49,* 77–82.

# 6

# Five into One Doesn't Go
## A Critique of the General Factor of Personality

### Eamonn Ferguson, Tomas Chamorro-Premuzic, Alan Pickering, and Alexander Weiss

Throughout the history of psychology the idea of the Big One, or *p*-factor (the Primordial One), or general factor of personality (GFP) has emerged and disappeared, the first mention going as far back as 1915 (Webb, 1915). The concept of the GFP has recently been discussed within the personality (e.g. Musek, 2007) and wider sociobiology literature (Figueredo, Vásquez, Brumbach, & Schneider, 2004, 2007). Musek (2007) provided a theoretical perspective on the GFP, suggesting (1) that it evolved to promote socially desirable characteristics; (2) that it is heritable; and (3) that high and low GFP are associated with the dopaminergic and serotonergic system, respectively. Subsequently, Rushton and colleagues marshaled a seemingly impressive array of psychometric and behavioral genetics evidence for a GFP, and further developed the GFP's theoretical framework (Rushton & Irwing, 2008, 2009a, 2009d; Rushton, Bons, & Hur, 2008; Rushton, Bons, Ando, et al., 2009). In this chapter we review the theory and evidence in support of the GFP, addressing the question of the extent to which they are consistent.

## The Theory of the General Factor of Personality

The observation that the domains of the five-factor model (FFM)[1]—neuroticism (N), extraversion (E), openness (O), agreeableness (A), and conscientiousness (C)—are empirically intercorrelated, despite being theoretically orthogonal, has led some to suggest that the "Big Five" are not the broadest taxonomy to describe or explain normal individual differences in personality (Digman, 1997; Eysenck, 1992). Some argued theoretically that fewer dimensions are required to explain normal personality, for instance Eysenck's "Giant 3" (neuroticism, extraversion, and psychoticism: Eysenck, 1992), whereas others developed higher-order factor solutions for the FFM. An example of the latter is Digman's (1997) derivation of the Big Two: α (low N,

*The Wiley-Blackwell Handbook of Individual Differences*, First Edition.
Edited by Tomas Chamorro-Premuzic, Sophie von Stumm, and Adrian Furnham.
© 2011 Blackwell Publishing Ltd. Published 2011 by Blackwell Publishing Ltd.

high A, and high C: reflecting socialization processes) and $\beta$ (high O and high E: reflecting agency and development)—which DeYoung (2006) developed theoretically in terms of their basic neuroscience, referring to them as *stability* and *plasticity*, respectively. Work on the GFP derives from a theoretical approach to personality based on Rushton's (1985) differential $K$ theory, with the GFP hypothesized to reside at the top of the personality hierarchy. Therefore a central question is, to what degree the GFP has greater explanatory power than the FFM in terms of the covariance among the five factors, their heritability, validity, and evolutionary plausibility.

Rushton and Irwing (2008, 2009b) report average meta-analytic correlations among FFM domains of .26 and .21 respectively. Given this degree of intercorrelation, it is a trivial observation to note that it is possible to derive higher-order factor solutions. The central question should be whether these higher-order solutions are substantive or artifactual (Ashton, Lee, Goldberg, & de Vries, 2009). Substantive correlations require that the covariation among factors is determined *causally* by a theoretically meaningful higher-order personality construct. The alternative is that the covariation is artifactual, reflecting influences not tied to a meaningful higher-order personality construct (e.g. shared method variance).

GFP proponents claim that covariation among the FFM domains is substantive and has a theoretical basis in life history theory. Rushton's (1985) differential $K$ theory is derived from the $r$–$K$ theory of reproductive strategies (MacArthur & Wilson, 1967). Organisms living in unpredictable environments adopt $r$ strategies (e.g. greater number of offspring, lower parental care), whereas organisms in predictable environments adopt $K$ strategies (e.g. fewer offspring, higher parental care). Rushton (1985) argues that $K$-selected individuals are also characterized by high intelligence, altruism, and cooperation. Figueredo and Rushton (2009) hypothesized that normal personality traits covary together and with other co-evolved adaptive life history traits, to meet the adaptive challenges of life, and that these factors are organized hierarchically, with a single higher-order factor at the apex. Rushton, Bons, and Hur (2008) propose that the GFP evolved via *directional selection*, to influence behavior across many different contexts, much as is proposed for the general factor of intelligence ($g$). Directional selection occurs when individuals at one end of a normally distributed trait are more likely to survive and reproduce; and, over generations, the distribution shifts toward that end of the distribution. One prediction of directional selection is the presence of genetic dominance effects, which reflect more recent natural selection (Rushton, Bons, & Hur, 2008; p. 1175).

Recently, Rushton, Bons, Ando et al. (2009; see also Musek, 2007) suggested that the GFP evolved through selection for desirable traits (see also Musek, 2007); indeed Rushton and Irwing (2009d, p. 1091) suggest that high scorers on the GFP were defined as "altruistic, emotionally stable, agreeable, conscientious, extraverted, and intellectually open, with high levels of well-being, satisfaction with life, self-esteem and emotional intelligence." This implies that sexual selection may be an additional route through which the GFP evolved (Figueredo & Rushton, 2009). As such, there should be mate preference for GFP characteristics, and GFP characteristics should be related to greater reproductive success. Finally, just as high GFP scores are hypothesized to reflect social advantage, low scores are hypothesized to reflect social challenge and personality disorder (Rushton & Irwing, 2009d).

We explore these claims. First, we examine the psychometric evidence. Second, we evaluate alternative explanations of why FFM domains are correlated, including the possibility of a statistical or methodological artifact. Third, we look at the relationship between the GFP and personality disorders. Fourth, we review theorizing about the evolution of personality, mate preference, and sexual selection, to see how these inform the evolutionary account of the GFP.

## Evidence for the GFP

The main evidence comes from Rushton and colleagues, who have presented a series of psychometric and behavioral genetic studies. These findings are in the form of: confirmatory factor analyses (CFA) of meta-analytically derived correlation matrices (Rushton & Irwing, 2008); exploratory factor analyses (EFA) of existing data sets (Rushton, Bons, & Hur, 2008); CFA analyses of multi-trait–multi-method (MTMM) twin data (Rushton, Bons, Ando et al., 2009); EFA analysis of twin data (Rushton, Bons, Ando et al., 2009); and CFA analysis of existing data or published matrices (Rushton & Irwing, 2009a, 2009d). In all analyses, the authors show evidence to support a GFP based on eigenvalues and loadings from EFAs, or a hierarchical structure indicating a general factor from CFA, or a sequence of exploratory models and MTMM analyses. Similar evidence, using EFA and CFA, is presented by Musek (2007), Schermer and Vernon (2010), and Rauthmann and Kolar (2010). Analysis of twin data demonstrated dominance effects in one study (Rushton, Bons, & Hur, 2008), but not in another (Rushton, Bons, Ando et al., 2009), while a third one found no difference between models which did and did not include dominance effects (Figueredo & Rushton, 2009). On the surface, and as interpreted by Rushton's team and others, these results provide evidence for the GFP. In the following sections we explore these results in detail and highlight several problems.

## Evaluating the Psychometric Evidence

We suggest the following criteria to evaluate the psychometric evidence presented for the GFP. First, when measures with known FFM solutions are used to explore normal personality, a theoretically driven sequence of CFAs should be used. Initially an orthogonal lower-order FFM model is compared to an oblique first-order FFM model. If the oblique model is better, a second-order model can be estimated, which should resemble Digman's or be otherwise theoretically specified. Similar steps should then be taken to determine whether a full GFP hierarchical model can be estimated. Alternatively, the second-order model could be the full GFP. Furthermore, models with factor-facet blends (as detailed by Ashton et al., 2009) should be compared to higher-order models. Second, when no a priori theoretical lower-order structure exists and exploratory analysis is required, then solutions should, where possible, be cross-validated on a separate sample. Third, post hoc modifications to improve the fit of CFA models should be avoided, as they lead to inflated alphas, poor generalizability, and weak cross-validation (MacCallum, Roznowski, & Necowitz, 1992). If modifications are used, cross-validation may help, but, at the least, Bentler (2007) argued that model parameters pre- and post-modification should be compared. Finally, scree plots, parallel analyses, and fit statistics for different exploratory models in M*plus* (Muthén & Muthén, 1998–2010) need to be reported for EFAs. Table 6.1 summarizes the evidence for the GFP in relation to these criteria.

As can be seen from Table 6.1, a mixed EFA–CFA approach was used most frequently. Interestingly, in many papers where measures known to conform to a structure are used (e.g. the NEO–PI–R),[2] EFA rather than CFA approaches are presented. EFA approaches involve either extracting a single factor and reporting the loadings (e.g. Rushton, Bons, Ando et al., 2009) or using a sequence of EFAs to identify lower-order factors, and the covariance among these is then used to derive second-order factors and, ultimately, a GFP (e.g. Schermer & Vernon, 2010). Often loadings of the domains on the GFP are low. For example, in Rushton, Bons, Ando et al. (2009), NEO–PI–R agreeableness loaded .20 and TCI novelty-seeking loaded .13. While it is possible to calculate the significance of loadings, these are low by all the conventional standards which suggest .3 or .4 as cut-offs. In addition, Table 6.1 reveals that basic statistical information for EFA is not reported, so the adequacy of some solutions cannot be determined.

For the mixed EFA–CFA procedure, M*plus* is used most frequently to develop an initial exploratory model of lower-order traits. This is then confirmed—and in many cases modified—with a CFA and a hierarchical model built on that basis. Cross-validation of these exploratory models is rarely reported, as many models are developed on a single matrix reported in manuals. It is also notable from Table 6.1 that, in most CFA studies, several model modifications are required to achieve good fit for the hierarchical solution, which causes real worries about capitalizing on chance (MacCallum et al., 1992). Also, these studies do not follow the sequence of CFA models described above—often the oblique FFM is not included, or just a single hierarchical GFP is reported (when one of these key models is omitted this is indicated by "partial" in Table 6.1). Interestingly, when an oblique FFM is included, it shows as good a fit as the GFP (Ruston & Irwing, 2009b, p. 573, Table 3). Furthermore, Rushton and Irwing (2009d) report excellent fit statistics for the higher-order GFP model (SRMSR of .047), but equally good—or slightly better—fit for the first-order FFM (SRMSR of .038). This suggests that the first-order model is a good explanation of the covariation among scales and that the hierarchical GFP model accounts for the covariation among first-order factors; but it does *not* show that the GFP solution is better than the first-order model.

There is also an issue concerning the MTMM analyses (Rushton, Bons, Ando et al., 2009). These authors used correlated errors among similar informants to model method variance. However, this approach prevents them from examining correlations among method factors (e.g. self-report) or from examining higher-order method factors (Widaman, 1985). Not partitioning out the effects of correlated method factors could lead to inflated correlations among FFM domains (Biesanz & West, 2004). It would have been more informative if they adopted an approach comparing a sequence of hierarchically nested models to delineate the effect of traits, methods, and error (Biesanz & West, 2004; Widaman, 1985).

**Table 6.1** Details of psychometric studies supporting the general factor of personality (GFP). BFI = Big Five Inventory; IPIP-300 = International Personality Item Pool–300; PRF = Personality Research Form; JPI = Jackson Personality Inventory; CPS = Comrey Personality Scales; MMPI–2 = Minnesota Multiphasic Inventory–2; MCPQ = Multicultural Personality Questionnaire; MCMI = Millon Clinical Multiaxial Inventory–III; DAPP = Dimensional Assessment of Personality Pathology; PAI = Personality Assessment Inventory; BFQ-C = Big Five Questionnaire – Children; GZTS = Guilford–Zimmerman Temperament Survey; CPI = California Psychological Inventory; TCI = Temperament and Character Inventory; MPQ = Multidimensional Personality Questionnaire; TEIQue = Trait Emotional Intelligence Questionnaire; PCA = Principal-Components Analysis; PAF = Principal Axis Factor Analysis; Mplus–LISREL = A sequence whereby Mplus is used to conduct exploratory analysis and LISREL the CFA.

| Paper | Measure | Purely EFA | Purely CFA | Theoretical CFA sequence | Mixed EFA-CFA on the same sample | MI used | Rotation | Basic Stats |
|---|---|---|---|---|---|---|---|---|
| Figueredo et al. (2004) | MIDUS survey | Yes (PAF) | | | | | | No |
| Figueredo et al. (2007) | MIDUS survey | Yes (PAF) | | | | | | No |
| Musek (2007) | BFI, IPIP–300 | | | No | Yes: PCA–LISREL | Yes: 2 correlated errors | Oblique | Yes |
| Rushton & Irwing (2008) | Meta-analysis of Digman (1997) and Mount et al. (2005) | | Yes | Partial | | Yes: 1 cross-loading | | |
| Rushton, Bons & Hur (2008) | Study 1: PRF & JPI | Yes (PCA & PAF) | | | | | Orthogonal & Oblique | No |
| | Study 2: 20 PRF scales plus 9 other scales | Yes | | | | | Orthogonal | |

| | | | | | |
|---|---|---|---|---|---|
| Rushton & Irwing (2009a) | Study 1: CPS | No | Yes: *Mplus*-LISREL (with cross-validation) | Yes: 2 correlated errors | No |
| | Study 2: MMPI–2 | No | Yes: PAF *Mplus*–LISREL | | No |
| | Study 3: MCPQ | No | Yes: PAF *Mplus*–LISREL | Yes: 2nd higher order factor | No |
| Rushton & Irwing (2009d) | Study 1: MCMI | No | *Mplus*–LISREL Yes: *Mplus*–LISREL | | No |
| | Study 2: DAPP | No | Yes: *Mplus*–LISREL | | No |
| | Study 3: PAI | No | Yes: *Mplus*–LISREL | Yes: 1 cross-loading | No |
| Rushton, Bons, Ando et al. (2009) | Study 1: BFQ–C (MTMM) | Yes | | | |
| | Study 2: NEO–PI–R & TCI | Yes (PAF) | No | | No |
| | Study 3: NEO–PI–R | Yes (PCA) | No | | No |

*(Continued)*

**Table 6.1** (*Continued*)

| Paper | Measure | Purely EFA | Purely CFA | Theoretical CFA sequence | Mixed EFA–CFA on the same sample | MI used | Rotation | Basic Stats |
|---|---|---|---|---|---|---|---|---|
| Rushton & Irwing (2009b) | Study 1: Meta-analysis of measures from DeYoung | | Yes | No | | | | |
| | Study 2: GZTS | | | No | Yes: *Mplus* – LISREL | Yes: 4 loadings & 4 correlated errors | | |
| | Study 3: CPI | | | No | Yes: *Mplus* – LISREL | Yes: 8 correlated errors and 7 factor loadings | | |
| | Study 4: TCI | | | No | Yes: *Mplus* – LISREL | Yes: 3 factor loading and 2 correlated errors | | |
| Rushton & Irwing (2009c) | Study 1: MPQ | | Yes | Partial | | Yes: 5 correlated errors | | |
| Schermer & Vernon (2010) | Study 1: PRF | Yes (PAF) | | Partial | | | | No |
| Rauthmann & Kolar (2010) | MIDUS survey | Yes (PAF & PCA) | | Partial | | | | No |
| Veselka et al. (2009) | HEXACO TEIQue | Yes (PCA) | | | | | | No |

There are other analytic concerns. Rushton and Irwing's (2009b) meta-analytic CFA of 16 data sets failed to meet the independence assumption, as many scales were collected on the same sample, which led to an artificial inflation of sample size. Rushton and Irwing (2009e) argued that there was a need to aggregate across measures of the FFM, as there is variability between the FFM domain associations across studies, and that this variability may arise from sampling error. While this is possible, the variability may also reflect something more systematic, such as the context in which the participants are assessed (van Oers, Klunder, & Drent, 2005). Rauthmann and Kolar (2010) reported low CFIs for the GFP derived from self- (.85) and other-ratings (.93), though they did not include a FFM for comparison. Finally, while Veselka et al. (2009) have access to item-level data, their analyses were conducted at scale level.

Finally, no consistent pattern or logic could be identified to explain why CFA or EFA were used, or why one is preferred over the other. For example, Rushton, Bons, and Hur (2008) used a sequence of EFAs to examine the JPI and PRF—both of which have a known structure—whereas Rushton, Bons, Ando et al. (2009) used CFA to explore another standard FFM index (BFQ–C).

It should also be noted that there have been failures to find the GFP (Ashton et al., 2009; DeYoung, 2006). Also, Rushton and Irwing (2009a) reported that a GFP needed to be supplemented by a "cultural-empathy" factor, and Jang et al. (2006) showed that a single factor was not the best fit in terms of genetic and environmental factors. Therefore the GFP has not been consistently replicated, as is required before any major theoretical changes or paradigm shifts are adopted.

In summary, there are real problems with the robustness of the psychometric data presented in support of the GFP. The use of numerous model modifications, a limited sequence of CFA models, the lack of cross-validation, and the mixed EFA–CFA procedures on the same data are all problematic and detract from a strong conclusion in favor of the existence of a GFP. The analysis of secondary data from manuals adds to these problems, as it does not allow for cross-validation. It is now time for new data to be collected, or for existing data, where access to primary data is available, to be analysed.

## Artifact or Substance?

That correlations are observed among FFM domains is not in dispute; the question is what they represent. One possibility is that they are *substantive* and describe higher-order latent variables causally leading to the lower-order domains. Another possibility is that they are *artifacts* reflecting, for example, the way personality is measured. In this section we summarize findings related to this question. If the covariance among the FFM domains results from, for example, measurement artifacts, then, once measurement variance is controlled, the covariance should disappear and the FFM would represent the highest point in the personality hierarchy. Social desirability is another factor that can result in inflated correlations between the FFM domains.

## Methods, schemas, and blends

Biesanz and West (2004) were the first to examine whether correlations among the FFM domains were substantive or artifactual by using an MTMM analysis of self-, peer-, and parent ratings. They showed that orthogonality depended on the "lens" through which personality is viewed. When multiple perspectives are used and method factors are included, orthogonality is observed, whereas this is not the case for self-ratings, which suggests that, when correlations are found among domains resulting from self-reports, they may reflect common method variance. DeYoung (2006) took this MTMM work further and showed that, while the five factors are intercorrelated, this may reflect people's expectations about how traits covary.

Recently, McCrae, Yamagata, Jang, Riemann, Ando, Ono, Angleitner, and Spinath (2008) used a mixture of twin and multi-informant data in order to test the extent to which correlations among the FFM domains reflect substance (correlations across twins or informants) or artifact (correlations within twins and informants). They found that the artifact model was a better explanation. However, they showed that a full model (containing substantive and artifact effects) had a marginally better fit than the artifact model.

Ashton et al. (2009) argued that simple structure is unlikely to be achieved at the lower facet level of personality measurement, and that this lower level is characterized by meaningful cross-loadings or positively valenced blends. That is, a facet like friendliness may not only load on its target factor (A), but also show a smaller but meaningful cross-loading on E. They showed that, if these blends are modelled, then orthogonality between the five factors is observed. Moreover, they found that models based on blends fit the data better, and were conceptually more parsimonious than models with higher-order factors. Importantly, they showed that this was not the case for cognitive ability, where models with a higher-order factor fit data better than blended models. The finding that cognitive ability, but not FFM traits, has a hierarchical structure is problematic for GFP theory, which argues that the two are conceptually similar.

Recently Anusic, Schimmack, Pinkus, and Lockwood (2009) provided evidence for a halo factor in personality measurement. They further showed that this halo factor reflects biases in how ratings of the FFM domains are made. They also demonstrated that the halo factor is not a meta-trait that causes covariation among the FFM domains, but rather one that produces covariation in how self-ratings (biases) of the FFM domains are made. Finally, they demonstrated that the halo factor influenced ratings of several relatively independent attributes (intelligence, athletic ability, attractiveness, and knowledge of trivia). These results suggest that covariation among FFM domains and personal attributes reflects a stable halo bias in how people make ratings rather than a halo trait that causes the FFM domains to be correlated.

In summary, Biesanz and West (2004), Ashton et al. (2009), and Anusic et al. (2009) suggest that the covariation among the FFM domains is artifactual. In contrast, DeYoung (2006) and McCrae et al. (2008) suggest that, while artifact is present, there is some substance to the observed covariance among domains. Thus, while not definitive, the results from these five papers collectively tend to show that the covariation among FFM domains reflects artifact more than substance. This artifact is most likely a reflection of shared schemas about personality and a general halo bias.

## Social desirability

Social desirability is another potential artifact that may account for covariation among the FFM domains. While proponents of the GFP argue that it evolved to favor traits that might be desirable to others (see Musek, 2007; Rushton, Bons, Ando et al. 2009), it is not unreasonable to hypothesize that GFP simply reflects positive self-presentation. Bäckström, Björklund, and Larson (2009) provided compelling evidence consistent with this hypothesis. These authors obtained a GFP solution when the standard FFM items were used. Critically, when standard FFM items are re-written to be phrased more neutrally, removing their social desirability content, evidence for the GFP all but disappeared with the mean factor loadings for the general factor dropping from .56 to .09. These researchers also found that participants who scored high on social desirability were more likely to distort their answers and to score higher on the standard FFM items, but not on the FFM items where the social desirability content has been removed. Thus, when a motivation to respond in a socially desirable way was combined with items that contained socially desirable content (thereby providing the opportunity to respond in a socially desirable way), responses were distorted.

Evidence from meta-analytic reviews of experimental (Viswesvaran & Ones, 1999) and correlational studies (Li & Bager, 2006), demonstrating that the FFM domains are associated with social desirability, suggests that social desirability effects generalize across FFM indices. Furthermore, social desirability is known to reflect impression management and self-deception (Paulhus, 1984). The former is associated with deliberate and conscious attempts by individuals to manipulate the way they present themselves in order to create the best impression. The latter is less likely to be conscious and reflects the person's inaccurate perceptions of his or her abilities. Li and Bagger (2006) have shown that low scores on N and high scores on A and C are associated with impression management, and that the FFM domains are associated with self-deception. In conjunction with Bäckström et al.'s (2009) results, this evidence strongly suggests that the GFP may reflect shared variance across the FFM domains relating to social desirability.

## Good Guys and Bad Guys

Even if the covariance reflected substance, there would still be a major concern over what a GFP would represent. Rushton and colleagues argued that those with high GFP scores are emotionally stable, sociable, trustworthy, creative, and hardworking (Rushton, Bons, Ando et al., 2009). This "profile" may be attractive to potential mates or may have other fitness benefits. Indeed, these authors suggest that the GFP "evolved as a result of natural selection for socially desirable behavior" (p. 356). They also argue that people with low GFP scores will be more likely to suffer from personality disorders (PDs; Rushton & Irwing, 2009d). Here we will examine some of these claims with respect to PDs and mate preference/selection.

## Personality disorder, psychopathology, and the GFP

Rushton and colleagues suggested that the GFP has some of the same basic properties of $g$. However, while the adaptive benefits of $g$ increase monotonically (Martin & Kubzansky, 2005), this is unlikely to be the case for personality (see Borghans, Duckworth, Heckman & ter Weel, 2008). Indeed, many have argued that scores at either extreme of a personality dimension are possibly maladaptive (MacDonald, 1995). Furthermore, several authors developed theoretical frameworks linking high scores on FFM domains with personality disorders (e.g. Lynam & Widiger, 2001; Widiger & Mullins-Sweatt, 2009). High scores on a GFP are, therefore, likely to be related to clinical manifestations of PDs. This contention is supported by numerous studies reporting bivariate correlations between the FFM domains and facets and PDs (see Samuels & Widiger, 2008, for a recent review).

Factor analytic evidence confirms the link between the FFM and PDs. Livesley, Jang, and Vernon (1998) identified four similar phenotypic and genetic factors from PD measures that resembled four FFM domains. They labeled these factors emotional dysregulation (linked to the high pole of N), inhibition (linked to the low pole of E), compulsivity (linked to high pole of C) and dissocial behavior (linked to the low pole of A; see also O'Connor, 2005). While these authors did not compare mean scores on these factors across clinical and general populations, or correlate the scores on these factors with FFM domains, they nonetheless showed, contrary to predictions made by GFP theory, that C is recoverable as a factor positively linked to PDs.

Consistent with the GFP perspective, high levels of N and some of its facets are positively related to paranoid, borderline, narcissistic, and avoidant PDs (Bagby, Costa, Widiger, Ryder, & Marshall, 2005; Samuels & Widiger, 2008). However, low N is related to maladaptive behavior such as "glib charm" (see Widiger & Mullins-Sweatt, 2009), which may relate to antisocial PD. With respect to the other FFM domains, high E is related to histrionic and dependent PDs (Bagby et al., 2005; Ball, Tennen, Poling, Kranzler, & Rounsaville, 1997) and all of the facets of E are positively related to histrionic PD (Samuels & Widiger, 2008). Obsessive–compulsive PD is related to high C and all its facets (Costa & McCrae, 1990; Samuels & Widiger, 2008). Finally, high A is related to dependent PD (Costa & McCrae, 1990). These associations show that, like extremely low scores, extremely high scores on E, A, and C are associated with several PDs, and that low N may also reflect maladaptive characteristics.

While these associations are informative, of more importance is how particular FFM profiles might relate to PDs. Theoretical profiles have been developed on the basis of expert researcher or clinician ratings concerning how the FFM domains and facets are linked to PDs (Lynam & Widiger, 2001; Widiger & Mullins-Sweatt, 2009). These theoretical profiles have then been empirically related to PD data, with a good degree of support for some of the PD profiles—including borderline and avoidant PD (see Samuels & Widiger, 2008). O'Connor and Dyce (2001) examined correlations between FFM vectors and PDs. Using this procedure they showed, for example, that histrionic PD was profiled as low in N and high in E, A, and C—that is, as high GFP without O—and is totally at odds to what GFP theory would predict.

While O is unrelated to PDs (Piedmont, Sherman, Sherman, Dy-Liacco, & Williams, 2009; Samuels & Widiger, 2008), O is related to disorders other than PDs. For example, Piedmont et al. (2009) suggest that O relates to disorders concerning (1) the inability to regulate the world of inner experiences with outer reality, (2) emphasizing inner experiences and ideations, and (3) being absorbed in personal images and ideas. Widiger and Mullins-Sweatt (2009) similarly suggest that high O should be associated with maladaptive traits of bizarre interests as well as with eccentric and peculiar behavior. Consistent with these findings, Piedmont et al. (2009) showed that high O is related to odd and eccentric behavior as assessed by self- and observer reports. Further evidence consistent with the idea of dysfunctional O comes from data showing a positive association between O and absorption (Glisky, Tatryn, Tobias, Kihlstrom, & McConkey, 1991), psychosis proneness (Camisa et al., 2005), depression (Wolfenstein & Trull, 1997), and a U-shaped relationship with hypochondriasis (Ferguson, 2001).

There is evidence that maladaptive behaviors are associated with high GFP scores. For example, drug and alcohol abuse, as well as proneness to traffic accident, have been linked to high E (Clarke & Robertson, 2005; Flory, Lynam, Milich, Leukefeld, & Clayton, 2002; McCrae, 1991), and workaholism to C (Clark, Vorhies & McEwen, 1994). DeYoung, Peterson, Seguin, and Tremblay (2008) have shown that "plasticity" (high E and high O) is associated with externalizing behavior (e.g. aggression). Finally, McCrae, Löckenhoff, and Costa (2005) developed a theoretical framework linking the FFM domains and facets with basic problems of living. These authors suggest that: (1) those low in N show too much emotional control; (2) those high in E are likely to be sexually promiscuous; (3) those high in O are likely to feel like outsiders; (4) those high in A are likely to be overly responsible for others' well-being; and (5) those high in C are likely to set unrealistic goals.

To summarize, FFM profiles consistent with the GFP and some profiles combining such high scores are linked to PDs, psychiatric outcomes, and maladaptive behavior. This is difficult to reconcile with the idea that low GFP scores are linked to PD and high scores to adaptive outcomes. It may be that the GFP is negatively related to a general PD factor, but this would lose all specificity of the type described above. Such a relationship would amount to little more than showing that having a generally positive view of the world is negatively associated with having a generally negative view of the world.

## Evolutionary Perspectives on the GFP

A central theoretical claim for the GFP is that it evolved via directional selection, as evolution favored desirable traits (through sexual selection) and normal personality traits covaried together and with other co-evolved adaptive life history traits (Figueredo & Rushton, 2009). These claims can be explored within current thinking in the evolutionary psychology of personality and mate selection. There are several questions we can ask. First, is the GFP positively related to other adaptive co-evolved traits, such as $g$? The prediction from the GFP theorists is that $g$ and the GFP should be correlated on the grounds of a shared evolutionary process. Second, what is the evidence that low scores on N and high scores on the other FFM domains are linked to increased fitness? GFP theory would predict that this profile would be positively correlated with several key fitness indictors (e.g. longevity and fertility). Third, do linear combinations of the FFM domains predict higher fitness? GFP theory claims that they should. Fourth, does the GFP show a higher level of heritability than lower-order traits? There is evidence that the higher-order factor associated with cognitive ability tests such as the Wechsler Adult Intelligence Scales (WAIS) exhibit higher levels of heritability than any single cognitive ability sub-test (Friedman et al., 2008). If, as proposed, the GFP shares characteristics with $g$, and the GFP provides the greatest explanatory power in the domain of healthy human personality, then the heritability of the GFP should be greater than that of lower-order traits. Another set of general questions relates to the hypothesis that the GFP reflects sexual selection. When choosing a mate, do people prefer mates who express a GFP profile of the FFM domains? Again, GFP theory would predict that they do. A final question is whether personality traits are changing in a prosocial direction. GFP theory might predict that the mean level of positive traits is increasing in the population. Apart from examining these main questions, we will also review current thinking on evolutionary theories of personality and how this informs the existence of a GFP.

## Is there a link between GFP and $g$?

Rushton, Bons, Ando et al. (2009) found no significant association between $g$ and the GFP, as assessed by the NEO–PI–R ($r = .11$) and TCI ($r = .03$). However, in line with others (Ackerman & Heggestad, 1997), they report a positive correlation between O and $g$ ($r = .33$). Schermer and Vernon (2010) report correlations of .256 and .279 between a GFP and $g$. However, they do not report correlations with the FFM domains and, in consequence, the extent to which these correlations are driven by associations of $g$ and O is unclear. As such, the evidence on the question is mixed. However, several reported associations between cognitive ability measures and the FFM go in the opposite direction of what GFP theory would predict. Notably, $g$ has been found to correlate negatively, rather than positively, with C in large-scale single studies and meta-analytic reviews, whilst introverts often outperform extraverts on cognitive ability tests (see Chamorro-Premuzic & Furnham, 2005, 2006 for reviews).

## Is the GFP linked to fitness?

Longevity is a general index of fitness, and there is evidence that C is related to longevity (Kern & Freidman, 2008). In terms of reproductive success, the evidence is much more limited. There is some evidence that high emotionality (N) and sociability (E) are related to reduced and increased reproductive success, respectively (Jokela, Kivimaki, Elovainio, & Keltikangas-Jarvinen, 2009). However, this same study found that having children leads to personality changes such as increased emotionality and sociability, suggesting that these relationships are likely to be bidirectional rather than unidirectional. Another index of fitness arises from disruptions to developmental stability, where the genomic blueprint is disrupted via environmental factors or mutations. If this occurs, organisms will not develop to conform to that blueprint (Penke, Denissen, & Miller, 2007, pp. 560–561). This concept can be operationalized in terms of bodily fluctuating asymmetries and, while there is evidence that $g$ is negatively associated with bodily fluctuating asymmetry (Bates, 2007; Luxen & Buunk, 2006; Prokosch, Yeo, & Miller, 2005; but see Johnson, Segal, & Bouchard, 2008), the FFM domains are not (Luxen & Buunk, 2006).

While there are links between specific traits and fitness indicators, the evidence does not sustain the idea that all personality domains are linked to fitness outcomes. The GFP predicts that traits add up monotonically, and proponents of GFP should test whether the GFP predicts fitness outcomes better than individual domains do.

## Do linear combinations of the FFM domains increase fitness?

Developing the above idea of links between personality and fitness, Dingemanse and Réale (2005) argue that it is vital that we examine how the correlation among traits predicts fitness. Only one study has examined the relationship between phenotypic trait correlations and fitness. Eaves, Martin, Heath, Hewitt, and Neale (1990) examined how the correlation between E and N was related to reproductive success. They showed that, while there was little relationship to fitness for E and N taken individually, for the two considered together there was a saddle-shaped relationship to fitness. Specifically, fitness for N varied along E, such that fitness was maximal for high N when E was low and maximal for high E when N was low. While the low N/high E finding is consistent with the GFP, the high N/low E finding is not.

## Is the GFP more heritable than lower-order traits?

Estimates indicate that 42 percent to 58 percent of the variance in the GFP is heritable (see Rushton, Bons & Hur, 2008; Rushton, Bons, Ando et al., 2009). This range of estimates is no higher than that of lower-order traits as reported by Rushton, Bons, Ando et al. (2009) and others (see Bouchard & Loehlin, 2001 for a review). In contrast, the heritability of executive functioning is higher at higher levels of the hierarchy, with a mean heritability of .10 at the level of individual tests, .33 at the level of first-order factors, and .99 at the level of the higher-order factor (Friedman et al., 2008).

## Do people prefer mating with those who express high levels of the GFP?

While high GFP scores are linked to maladaptive behaviors and to PDs, it is still possible to argue that aspects of this maladaptive pattern may be attractive, and therefore evolutionarily adaptive. The issue of mate choice and GFP can be examined from the perspective of the multiple mechanisms through which mate choice operates: (1) consensual—certain traits are desirable to all; (2) sex differences—some traits are likely to be more favored by men and others by women; and (3) individual differences—individuals differ in preferences for certain traits (e.g. some prefer high scores on kind–compassionate traits, others prefer religious traits), and these preferences may be associated with personality traits (Buss & Barnes, 1986). Drawing on sexual strategies theory, we also know that men and women express different preferences depending on the type of relationship they are seeking (short-term or long-term), physical attractiveness being more important for short-term relationships, and virtues (e.g. honesty) being more important for long-term relationships (Buss & Schmitt, 1993; Miller, 2007).

If GFP traits underlie mate preference, we would expect high GFP traits to show consensual agreement as preferred traits in a mate. There is evidence for consensual agreements using explicit (Buss & Barnes, 1986) and indirect measures (Wood & Brumbaugh, 2009), so-called gamma or communal traits (e.g. intelligence, soft heartedness) being preferred in the choice of a date. These traits may represent combinations of A, E, and O. Attractiveness ratings, however, are more associated with alpha or agentic traits (e.g. body shape, confidence; Wood & Brumbaugh, 2009). Thus aspects of the GFP profile are associated with mate preference. From the perspective of individual differences, however, Wood and Brumbaugh demonstrated that extraverted men and women showed a preference for alpha rather than gamma characteristics and for less intelligent and more physically attractive people. Thus extraverts tend not to express a preference for the GFP.

There is also the issue of whether these preferences translate into real choices. Do people end up with partners who possess these preferred traits? Buss and Barnes (1986) reported that women who preferred artistic–intelligent husbands ended up with highly N men, whereas men who preferred artistic–intelligent wives ended up with ambitious and self-accepting women. These findings suggest that desired traits are not always realized. There is also little evidence for assortative mating on the basis of the FFM domains (Ozer & Benet-Martinez, 2006). However, McCrae (1996) has shown that there is some assortative mating for O and a smaller amount of it for C.

There is also a large body of evidence for the view that mate preferences (Buss & Schmitt, 1993) and mate attraction (Griskevicius et al., 2007) reflect behavioral strategies. Griskevicius et al. (2007), for example, showed that men will adopt a strategy of conspicuous spending and displays of bravery, while women are more likely to make conspicuous displays of helping others. There is also evidence that people will alter their displays of "generosity" if they know such displays are public or that they will to be used to select them for future interactions, or if they happen in a potential sexual context (Barclay & Willer, 2007). On the other side of the equation—are these displays attractive to a long-term partner? Observations by Jensen-Campbell, Graziano, and West (1995) are informative here. They showed that: (1) women tend to rate potential mates who are low in kindness (low A) as less desirable, and they do so to a greater extent than men; (2) for short-term relationships, men rate agreeable women as more desirable, but women find desirable those men who are high both in agreeableness and in dominance (e.g. active, assertive, bold); and (3) for long-term relationships, both sexes rate as desirable potential mates who are agreeable and dominant. Thus people will strategically alter their behavior to attract a mate, and preferences may therefore not get translated into desired outcomes (Buss & Barnes, 1986).

Also confounding desired outcomes is the fact that people may "cheat" by presenting themselves in a desirable manner not aligned with their true personalities. Furthermore, people who score high on traits such as A and E are more likely to be exploited by others; thus high scores on these traits may not be advantageous in the context of sexual selection (Buss & Duntley, 2008). Cheating and how to detect and avoid it is a big problem for models of altruism (Buss & Duntley, 2008). As high GFP is theorized to be related to altruism, the theory of GFP has to deal with this problem. At present, this is absent from GFP theory. For example, while gamma-type traits are desirable in a mate, they may not be inherited through sexual selection if they are not genuinely present in the person displaying them—rather the ability to cheat, impression manage, and exploit may be inherited. Indeed, Miller (2007) argued that the evidence for sexual selection should show, among other characteristics, (1) heritability; (2) high trait variance in males; and (3) conspicuous courtship displays. Furthermore, the expressed trait and the preference for that trait should both be heritable and genetically correlated (Miller, 2000, 2007). While this pattern has been proved in the case of altruism (Philips, Ferguson, & Rijsdijk, 2010; Philips, Ferguson, Reeder & Barnard, 2008), it still needs to be established for the GFP.

## Are we becoming more prosocial?

While there are no data to examine if the personality profile of the population has changed on an evolutionary time scale, it is possible to examine how levels of personality traits have changed in recent history. Any theory suggesting that positive traits are selectively favored would also suggest that the expression of traits should become more positive over time. However, evidence from temporal meta-analyses shows that personality scores have changed in the direction of individualism rather than toward prosociality; today people score higher on narcissism, anxiety, extraversion, assertiveness, high expectations, and external locus of control (see Twenge, 2009 for a review; but see also Trzesniewski & Donnellan, 2010).

## What do evolutionary models of personality tell us?

A recent article (Penke et al., 2007) reviewed the theoretical mechanisms for the evolution of human personality and drew several conclusions. We will briefly review its main suggestions before returning to implications for the GFP.

Penke et al. (2007) reviewed three mechanisms for the evolution of human personality. The first mechanism, *selective neutrality*, concerns mutations that are neutral with respect to fitness and therefore invisible to natural selection. The authors argue that this mechanism is unlikely to account for variability in personality traits, as personality traits are related to a variety of outcomes that influence fitness (we noted some of these above). The second mechanism—*mutation–selection balance*—holds that natural selection acts to counteract mutation. Mutation increases variation, whereas the opposing force of natural selection works to decrease variation. The authors argue that this mechanism is plausible for higher-order traits such as *g*, which reflect overall functional integrity. The final mechanism, *balancing–selection*, suggests that extremes of a trait are equally favored by selection under different conditions.

Concerning the variants of balancing–selection, Penke et al. (2007) suggest that *frequency-dependent* selection is the most plausible for the evolution of personality. A frequency-dependent mechanism favors a particular ratio of traits within a population, in which a particular trait's fitness decreases as it increases in the population. This optimal ratio produces an evolutionary stable strategy (ESS); the ratio of men to women, or of altruists to free-riders, are examples of this. MacDonald (1995) argued that, for the FFM domains, different ESSs are established in different environmental niches, and Penke et al. (2007) extended this principle to suggest that these niches are most likely to be social.

The key feature of the *balancing–selection* approach is that extremes of a trait are equally favored by selection under different conditions. An implication of this idea is that traits will have evolved to exhibit a mixture of costs and benefits. This implication contradicts the GFP model, which suggests that desirable traits are favored. In this context Nettle (2006) presented a cost–benefit trade-off model of the evolution of human personality (see Smith & Blumstein, 2008 for a similar model). This model suggests that all traits have costs and benefits associated with them, the optimal balance depending on the context in which they are expressed. For example, while vigilance about dangers is a benefit of N, susceptibility to depression is a cost (Nettle, 2006). As contexts vary, then, within the population, traits will maintain a normal distribution of costs and benefits.

The idea that traits contain a mixture of costs and benefits implies that different characteristics of traits will be more or less adaptive in different contexts. Indeed, Penke et al. (2007) and Denissen and Penke (2008) have developed this idea in the context of reaction norms, and they suggest that the FFM domains reflect individual differences in the motivation to react to environmental contingencies.[3] Buss (2009) similarly suggested that personality traits evolved to help solve problems of adaptation.

Rushton, Bons, and Hur (2008), propose that the GFP evolved in response to *directional selection*, much as is proposed for *g*, to confer benefits across all environmental contingencies (see Rushton, Bons, & Hur, 2009, p. 1175). The above brief review suggests that higher-order personality traits and *g* are related to different evolutionary mechanisms: a mutation–selection model for *g* and a balancing–selection model for personality (Penke et al., 2007). This conclusion—plus the idea that personality traits evolved through cost–benefit trade-offs, which are likely to be more adapative in different contexts—suggests that a simple directional model is unlikely to explain the variability and complexity of personality traits.

## Additional Challenges

There are additional challenges that proponents of the GFP have to address if they are to make their case convincing. A basic consequence of the GFP is that it predicts that a simple, linear, monotonic combination of lower-order traits should be maximally predictive of future outcomes. However, some effects for personality reflect synergistic rather than monotonic combinations. For example, the GFP would predict that health prevention behaviors should be linked to lower N and higher E, A, C, and O. Or the GFP would suggest that depression should be linked to high N with low O (and/or low E). However, Ingledew and Brunning (1999) showed that the use of health prevention behaviors was strongest for a combination of high C and low O. Weiss et al. (2009) reported that trait combinations described as overly emotional (high N and high E) or hypersensitive (high N and high O) were risk factors for major depressive episodes. Thus non-monotonic combinations of traits are related to adaptive and maladaptive characteristics in a manner which is not consistent with the GFP.

The other main challenge to the GFP is to show predictive validity over and above the FFM domains, and to show predictive specificity rather than simply increased variance. For example, within the occupational psychology literature, there is evidence that C is related to most job outcomes, while E is linked to success in social jobs such as sales (Salgado, 1997). With a single GFP, this specificity would be lost. As Chamorro-Premuzic and Furnham (2006) argued, a single GFP or "intelligent personality" factor is unlikely to provide predictive validity across different settings. Yet "the fact that the same combination of personality traits may not be extrapolated across different performance criteria should not discourage researchers from conceptualizing and assessing the personality determinants of success in each context or setting" (p. 261).

## Conclusions

In this chapter we hope to have shown reasons why belief in the existence of the GFP should be strongly questioned.

1  There are concerns about the psychometric basis of the GFP, for instance the use of model modifications, or the lack of use of a full and systematic CFA sequence when testing model fits.
2  It is plausible that the covariation among the five domains of the FFM is artifactual, due to (a) implicitly held personality beliefs; (b) social desirability influences on responding; or (c) lower-level factor blends.
3  High GFP is linked to PDs and maladaptive behaviors.
4  It is hard to sustain the idea that a GFP may be associated with mate preference for a socially desirable trait, or with sexual selection.
5  The evidence that the GFP is linked to $g$ and fitness outcomes is not consistent.
6  There are non-linear relationships between traits predicting fitness-related outcomes.
7  A directional evolutionary model for personality is not supported by current evidence and thinking in the evolutionary psychology of personality, which specifically suggests that traits are a mix of costs and benefits, whose adaptability depends on context.

## Future Research Directions

Work on the GFP is in its infancy and we obviously feel that the case for the GFP is far from proven. We propose that the following research challenges will help to establish whether the GFP is a substantive concept.

First, data need to be collected to allow cross-validation by using a detailed theoretical sequence of CFA, as detailed above. If these data are collected from twins and using a MTMM design, then the artifacts and substance models proposed by Anusic et al. (2009), Ashton et al. (2009), Biesanz and West (2004), DeYoung (2006), and McCrae et al. (2008) should be tested.

Second, evidence for the incremental predictive validity of the GFP needs to be established. This is especially true with respect to key fitness indices as well as with respect to general outcomes where FFM domains are known to have differential prediction (e.g. occupational success).

Third, it is important to show that specificity and sensitivity are not lost by reduction to a single factor. That is, certain FFM domains may offer greater predictive power in some domains than others. This is important for theory-building as well as for developing potential interventions.

Fourth, GFP theorists need to examine developmental trends. Is the psychometric GFP present early on in life? If so, is it found in children's self-reports, or only in teacher or parent ratings? Such evidence would throw some light on the idea that the GFP reflects people's implicit personality theories. If the GFP is substantive, then it should be present in young people's self-ratings, as younger people will have had less time to develop implicit models.

Fifth, experimental studies should be conducted. In these studies, for example, manipulations could contrast certain contexts, where the desire to show a positive self-image would be high, with others, where it would not. If the GFP reflects socially desirable responding, then it is more likely be observed only in social-desirability enhanced contexts.

Sixth, it would be informative to explore the hierarchical structure of non-human personality. Is there a GFP present in data derived directly from the ratings of keepers of captive animals, and how does this compare with the structure derived from lay judgments for the same species? Would a GFP emerge from lay judgments of a species and from the keepers' judgments? If so, then this again suggests that stereotyping and implicit models are driving the covariance observed among the FFM domains.

Seventh, it would also be useful to consider conducting simulation work in order to examine the structure of the FFM when, for example, the nature of the distributions is changed to reflect faking, by for example positively skewing the distributions. Does the GFP emerge only when the data are skewed? If so, then, again, the GFP is likely to be an artifact.

The above are just some ideas and suggestions regarding broad areas that could be pursued. The aim of these proposals is to move away from simple psychometrics as a main source of evidence, and to take a much more theoretical and hypothesis-driven approach to interrogating the existence of the GFP.

## Notes

1   While the FFM and the Big Five are distinct (Goldberg, 1992), for simplicity we will treat them as synonymous in this chapter.

2   Acronyms are defined in Table 6.1.
3   The concept of reaction norms was put forward by biologists examining animal personality, to explain the relationship between genotype, phenotype, and the environment (see Penke et al., 2007). Van Oers, de Jong, van Noordwijk, Kempenaers, and Drent (2005) define reaction norms as the "function relating a phenotypic response of a genotype to a change in the environment" (p. 1197) and refer to a typical response function for an individual genotype to a specific context.

# References

Ackerman, P. L., & Heggestad, E. D. (1997). Intelligence, personality, and interests: Evidence for overlapping traits. *Psychological Bulletin, 121,* 219–245.

Anusic, I., Schmmack, U., Pinkus, R. T., & Lockwood, P. (2009). The nature and structure of the correlations among the Big Five ratings: The Halo–Alpha–Beta model. *Journal of Personality and Social Psychology, 97,* 1142–1156.

Ashton, M. C., Lee, K., Goldberg, L. R., & de Vries, R. E. (2009). Higher order factors of personality: Do they exist? *Personality and Social Psychological Review, 13,* 79–91.

Bäckström, M., Björklund, F., & Larson, M. R. (2009). Five factor inventories have a major general factor related to social desirability which can be reduced by framing items neutrally. *Journal of Research in Personality, 43,* 335–344.

Bagby, R. M., Costa, P. T., Jr., Widiger, T. A., Ryder, A. G., & Marshall, M. (2005). DSM–IV personality disorders and the five-factor model of personality: A multi-method examination of domain- and facet-level predictions. *European Journal of Personality, 19,* 307–324.

Ball, S. A., Tennen, H., Poling, J. C., Kranzler, H. R., & Rounsaville, B. J. (1997). Personality, temperament and character dimensions and the DSM–IV personality disorders in substance abusers. *Journal of Abnormal Psychology, 106,* 545–553.

Barclay, P., & Willer, R. (2007). Partner choice creates competitive altruism in humans. *Proceedings of the Royal Society B, 274,* 749–753.

Bates, T. C. (2007). Fluctuating asymmetry and intelligence. *Intelligence, 35,* 41–46.

Bentler, P. M. (2007). On tests and indices for evaluating structural models. *Personality and Individual Differences, 42,* 825–829.

Biesanz, J. C., & West, S. G. (2004). Towards understanding assessments of the Big Five: Multitrait–multimethod analyses of convergent and discriminant validity across measurement occasions and type of observer. *Journal of Personality, 72,* 845–876.

Borghans, L., Duckworth, A. L., Heckman, J. J., & ter Weel, B. (2008). The economics and psychology of personality traits. *Journal of Human Resources, 43,* 972–1059.

Bouchard, T. J., Jr., & Loehlin, J. C. (2001). Genes, evolution, and personality. *Behavior Genetics, 31,* 243–273.

Buss, D. M. (2009). How can evolutionary psychology successfully explain personality and individual differences? *Perspectives on Psychological Science, 4,* 359–366.

Buss, D. M., & Barnes, M. (1986). Preferences in human mate selection. *Journal of Personality and Social Psychology, 50,* 559–570.

Buss, D. M., & Duntley, J. D. (2008). Adaptations for exploitation. *Group Dynamics, 12,* 53–62.

Buss, D. M., & Schmit, D. P. (1993). Sexual strategies theory: An evolutionary perspective on human mating. *Psychological Review, 100,* 204–232.

Camisa, K. M., Bockbrader, M. A., Lysaker, P., Rae, L. L., Brenner, C. A., & O'Donnell, B. F. (2005). Personality traits in schizophrenia and related personality disorders. *Psychiatry Research, 133,* 23–33.

Chamorro-Premuzic, T., & Furnham, A. (2005). *Personality and intellectual competence.* Mahwah, NJ: Lawrence Erlbaum Associates.

Chamorro-Premuzic, T., & Furnham, A. (2006). Intellectual competence and the intelligent personality: A third way in differential psychology. *Review of General Psychology, 10,* 251–267.

Clark, L. A., Vorhies, L., & McEwen, J. L. (1994). Personality disorder sympomatology from the five-factor model perspective. In P. T. Costa, Jr. & T. A. Widiger (Eds.), *Personality disorder and the five-factor model of personality* (pp. 95–116). Washington, DC: American Psychological Association.

Clarke, S., & Robertson, I. T. (2005). A meta-analytic review of the Big Five personality factors and accident involvement in occupational and non-occupational settings. *Journal of Occupational and Organizational Psychology, 78,* 355–376.

Costa, P. T., Jr. & McCrae, R. R. (1990). Personality disorders and the five-factor model of personality. *Journal of Personality Disorders, 4,* 362–371.

Denissen, J. J. A., & Penke, L. (2008). Motivational individual reaction norms underlying the five-factor model of personality: First steps towards a theory-based framework. *Journal of Research in Personality, 42,* 1285–1302.

DeYoung, C. G. (2006). Higher-order factors of the Big Five in a multi-informant sample. *Journal of Personality and Social Psychology, 91,* 1138–1151.

DeYoung, C. G., Peterson, J. B., Seguin, J. R., & Tremblay, R. E. (2008). Externalizing behavior and the higher order factors of the Big Five. *Journal of Abnormal Psychology, 117,* 847–953.

Digman, J. M. (1997). Higher-order factors of the Big Five. *Journal of Personality and Social Psychology, 73,* 1246–1256.

Dingemanse, N. J., & Réale, D. (2005). Natural selection and animal personality. *Behaviour, 142,* 1159–1184.

Eaves, L. J., Martin, N. G., Heath, A. C., Hewitt, J. K., & Neale, M. C. (1990). Personality and reproductive fitness. *Behavior Genetics, 20,* 563–568.

Eysenck, H. J. (1992). Four ways five factors are not basic. *Personality and Individual Differences, 13,* 667–673.

Ferguson, E. (2001). Intellect and somatic health: Associations with hypochondriacal concerns, perceived threat and fainting. *Psychotherapy and Psychosomatics, 70,* 319–327.

Figueredo, A. J., & Rushton, J. P. (2009). Evidence for shared genetic dominance between the general factor of personality, mental and physical health, and life history traits. *Twin Research and Human Genetics, 12,* 555–563.

Figueredo, A. J., Vásquez, G., Brumbach, B. H., & Schneider, S. M. R. (2004). The heritability of life history strategy: The K-factor, covitality and personality. *Social Biology, 51,* 121–143.

Figueredo, A. J., Vásquez, G., Brumbach, B. H., & Schneider, S. M. R. (2007). The K-factor, covitality and personality. *Human Nature, 18,* 47–73.

Flory, K., Lynam, D., Milich, R., Leukefeld, C., & Clayton, R. (2002). The relations among personality, symptoms of alcohol and marijuana abuse, and symptoms of comorbid psychopathology: Results from a community sample. *Experimental and Clinical Psychopharmacology, 10,* 425–434.

Friedman, N. P., Miyake, A., Young, S. E., DeFries, J. C., Corley, R. P., & Hewitt, J. K. (2008). Individual differences in executive functions are almost entirely genetic in origin. *Journal of Experimental Psychology: General, 137,* 201–255.

Glisky, M. L., Tatryn, D., Tobias, B. A., Kihlstrom, J. F., & McConkey, K. M. (1991). Absorption, openness to experience and hypnotizability. *Journal of Personality and Social Psychology, 60,* 263–272.

Goldberg, L. R. (1992). The development of the markers for the Big-Five factor structure. *Psychological Assessment, 4,* 26–42.

Griskevicius, V., Tybur, J. M., Sundie, J. M., Cialdini, R. B., Miller G. F., & Kenrick, D. T. (2007). Blatant benevolence and conspicuous consumption: When romantic motives elicit strategic costly signals. *Journal of Personality and Social Psychology, 93,* 85–102.

Ingledew, D. H. K., & Brunning, S. (1999). Personality, preventative health behaviour and comparative optimism about health problems. *Journal of Health Psychology, 4,* 193–208.

Jang, K. L., Livesley, W. J., Ando, J., Yamagata, S., Suzuki, A., Angleitner, A., Ostendorf, F., Riemann, R., & Spinath, F. (2006). Behavioral genetics of the higher-order factors of the Big Five. *Personality and Individual Differences, 41,* 261–272.

Jensen-Campbell, L. A., Graziano, W. G., & West, S. G. (1995). Dominance, prosocial orientation, and female preferences: Do nice guys really finish last? *Journal of Personality and Social Psychology, 86,* 427–440.

Johnson, W., Segal, N. L., & Bouchard, T. J., Jr. (2008). Fluctuating asymmetry and general intelligence: No genetic or phenotypic association. *Intelligence, 36,* 279–288.

Jokela, M., Kivimaki, M., Elovainio, M., & Keltikangas-Jarvinen, L. (2009). Personality and having children: A two-way relationship. *Journal of Personality and Social Psychology, 96,* 218–230.

Kern, M. L., & Friedman, H. S. (2008). Do conscientious individuals live longer? A quantitative review. *Health Psychology, 27,* 505–512.

Li, A., & Bagger, J. (2006). Using the BIDR to distinguish the effects of impression management and self-deception on the criterion validity of personality measures: A meta-analysis. *International Journal of Selection and Assessment, 14,* 131–141.

Livesley, W. J., Jang, K. L., & Vernon, P. A. (1998). Phenotypic and genetic structure of traits delineating personality disorder. *Archives of General Psychiatry, 55,* 941–948.

Loehlin, J. C., McCrae, R. R., Costa, P. T., Jr. & John, O. P. (1989). Heritabilities of the common and measure-specific components of the Big Five personality factors. *Journal of Research in Personality, 32,* 431–453.

Luxen, M. F., & Buunk, B. P. (2006). Human intelligence, fluctuating asymmetry and the peacock's tail: General intelligence (*g*) as an honest signal of fitness. *Personality and Individual Differences, 41,* 897–902.

Lynam, D. R., & Widiger, T. A. (2001). Using the five-factor model to represent the DSM–IV personality disorders: An expert consensus approach. *Journal of Abnormal Psychology, 110,* 401–412.

MacArthur, R. H., & Wilson, E. O. (1967). *The theory of island biogeography.* Princeton, NJ: Princeton University Press.

MacCallum, R. C., Roznowski, M., & Necowitz, L. B. (1992). Model modifications in covariance structure analysis: The problem of capitalization on chance. *Psychological Bulletin, 111,* 490–504.

MacDonald, K. (1995). Evolution, the five-factor model, and levels of personality. *Journal of Personality, 63,* 525–567.

Martin, L. T., & Kubzansky, L. D. (2005). Childhood cognitive performance and risk of mortality: A prospective cohort study of gifted individuals. *American Journal of Epidemiology, 162,* 887–890.

McCrae, R. R. (1991). The five-factor model and its assessment in clinical settings. *Journal of Personality Assessments, 57,* 399–414.

McCrae, R. R. (1996). Social consequences of experiential openness. *Psychological Bulletin, 120,* 323–337.

McCrae, R. R., Löckenhoff, C. E., & Costa, P. T., Jr. (2005). A step toward DSM–V: Cataloguing personality-related problems in living. *European Journal of Personality, 19,* 269–286.

McCrae, R. R., Yamagata, S., Jang, K. L., Riemann, R., Ando, J., Ono, Y., Angleitner, A., & Spinath, F. M. (2008). Substance and artefact in the higher-order factors of the Big Five. *Journal of Personality and Social Psychology, 95,* 442–455.

Miller, G. F. (2000). *The mating mind: How sexual choice shaped the evolution of human nature.* New York: Doubleday.

Miller, G. F. (2007). Sexual selection for moral virtues. *Quarterly Journal of Biology, 82,* 97–125.

Musek, J. (2007). A general factor of personality: Evidence for the Big One in the five-factor model. *Journal of Research in Personality, 41,* 1213–1233.

Muthén, L. K., & Muthén, B. O. (1998–2010). *Mplus user's guide* (6th ed). Los Angeles, CA: Muthén & Muthén.

Nettle, D. (2006). The evolution of personality variation in humans and other animals. *American Psychologist, 61,* 622–631.

O'Connor, B. P. (2005). A search for consensus on the dimensional structure of personality disorders. *Journal of Clinical Psychology, 61,* 232–345.

O'Connor, B. P., & Dyce, J. A. (2001). Rigid and extreme: A geometric representation of personality disorder in five-factor space. *Journal of Personality and Social Psychology, 81,* 1119–1130.

Ozer, D. J., & Benet-Martinez, V. (2006). Personality and the prediction of consequential outcomes. *Annual Review of Psychology, 57,* 401–421.

Paulhus, D. L. (1984). Two-component models of socially desirable responding. *Journal of Personality and Social Psychology, 46,* 598–609.

Penke, L., Denissen, J. J. A., & Miller, G. F. (2007). The evolutionary genetics of personality. *European Journal of Personality, 21,* 549–587.

Philips, T., Ferguson, E., & Rijsdijk., F. (2010). A link between altruism and sexual selection: Genetic influence on altruistic behaviour and mate preference towards it. *British Journal of Psychology, 101,* 809–819.

Philips, T., Ferguson, E., Reeder, T., & Barnard, C. (2008). Mate preference towards altruistic traits suggests a link between human altruism and sexual selection. *British Journal of Psychology, 99,* 555–572.

Piedmont, R. L., Sherman, M. F., Sherman, N. C., Dy-Liacco, G. S., & Williams, J. E. G. (2009). Using the five-factor model to identify a new personality disorder domain: The case of experiential permeability. *Journal of Personality and Social Psychology, 96,* 1245–1258.

Prokosch, M. D., Yeo, R. A., & Miller, G. F. (2005). Intelligence tests with higher *g*-loadings show higher correlations with body symmetry: Evidence for a general fitness factor mediated by developmental stability. *Intelligence, 33,* 201–213.

Rauthmann, J. F., & Kolar, G. P. (2010). Implicit simplicity at low acquaintanceship: Evidence for a g-factor of personality in personality judgments. *Personality and Individual Differences, 48,* 522–526.

Rushton, J. P. (1985). Differential K theory: The sociobiology of individual and group differences. *Personality and Individual Differences, 6,*441–452.

Rushton, J. P., & Irwing, P. (2008). The general factor of personality (GFP) from two meta-analyses of the Big Five: Digman (1997) and Mount, Barrick, Scullen, and Rounds (2005). *Personality and Individual Differences, 45,* 679–683.

Rushton, J. P., & Irwing, P. (2009a). A general factor of personality in the Comrey Personality Scales, the Minnesota Multiphasic Personality Inventory–2, and the Multicultural Personality Questionnaire. *Journal of Research in Personality, 46,* 437–442.

Rushton, J. P., & Irwing, P. (2009b). A general factor of personality in 16 sets of the Big Five, the Guilford–Zimmerman Temperament Survey, the California Psychology

Inventory, and the Temperament and Character Inventory. *Personality and Individual Differences, 47*, 558–564.

Rushton, J. P., & Irwing, P. (2009c). A general factor of personality (GFP) from the Multidimensional Personality Questionnaire. *Personality and Individual Differences, 47*, 571–567.

Rushton, J. P., & Irwing, P. (2009d). A general factor of personality in the Millon Clinical Multiaxial Inventory–III, the Dimensional Assessment of Personality Pathology, and the Personality Assessment Inventory. *Journal of Research in Personality, 43*, 1091–1095.

Rushton, J. P. & Irwing (2009e). Is there a general factor of personality? *Paper presented at 14th Biennial Conference of the International Society for the Study of Individual Differences,* July 18–22, Evanston, IL.

Rushton, J. P., Bons, T. A., & Hur, Y. M. (2008). The genetics and evolution of the general factor of personality. *Journal of Research in Personality, 42*, 1173–1185.

Rushton, J. P., Bons, T. A., & Hur, Y. M. (2009). The genetics and evolution of the general factor of personality (corrigendum). *Journal of Research in Personality, 43*, 532.

Rushton, J. P., Bons, T. A., Ando, J., Hur, Y. M., Irwing, P., Vernon, P. A., Petrides, K. V., & Barbaranelli, C. (2009). A general factor of personality from multitrait–multimethod data and cross-national twins. *Twin Research and Human Genetics, 12*, 356–365.

Salgado, J. F. (1997). The five factor model of personality and job performance in the European community. *Journal of Applied Psychology, 82*, 30–43.

Samuel, D. B., & Widiger, T. A. (2008). A meta-analytic review of the relationship between the five-factor model and the DSM–IV–TR personality disorders: A facet level analysis. *Clinical Psychology Review, 28*, 1326–1342.

Schermer, J. A., & Vernon, P. A. (2010). The correlation between general intelligence ($g$), a general factor of personality (GFP), and social desirability. *Personality and Individual Differences, 48*, 187–189.

Smith, B. R., & Blumstein, D. T. (2008). Fitness consequences of personality: A meta-analysis. *Behavioral Ecology, 19*, 448–455.

Twenge, J. M. (2009). Generational changes and their impact in the classroom: Teaching Generation Me. *Medical Education, 43*, 398–405.

Trzesniewski, K. H., & Donnellan, M. B. (2010). Rethinking "Generation Me": A study of cohort effects from 1976–2006. *Perspectives in Psychological Science, 5*, 58–75.

Van Oers, K., Klunder, M., & Drent, P. J. (2005). Context dependence of personalities, risk-taking behavior in a social and a nonsocial situation. *Behavioral Ecology, 16*, 716–723.

Van Oers, K., de Jong, G., van Noordwijk, A. J., Kempenaers, B., & Drent, P. J. (2005). Contribution of genetics to the study of animal personalities: A review of case studies. *Behaviour, 142*, 1185–1206.

Veselka, L., Schermer, J. A., Petrides, K. V., Chaerkas, L. F., Spector, T. D., & Vernon, P. A. (2009). A general factor of personality: Evidence form the HEXACO model and a measure of trait emotional intelligence. *Twin Research and Human Genetics, 12*, 420–424.

Viswesvaran, C., & Ones, D. S. (1999). Meta-analyses of fakability estimates: Implications for personality measurement. *Educational and Psychological Measurement, 59*, 197–210.

Webb, E. (1915). Character and intelligence. *British Journal of Psychology Monograph Supplement* (Vol. 3, pp. 1–113). Cambridge: Cambridge University Press. [See also review in *Nature, 96*, 1800.]

Weiss, A., Sutin, A. R., Duberstein, P. R., Friedman, B., Bagby, R. M., & Costa, P. T., Jr. (2009). The personality domains and styles of the five-factor model are related on incident depression in medicare recipients aged 65–100. *American Journal of Geriatric Psychiatry,* *17,* 591–601.

Widaman, K. F. (1985). Hierarchically nested covariance structure models for multitrait–multimethod data. *Applied Psychological Measurement, 9,* 1–26.

Widiger, T. A., & Mullins-Sweatt, S. N. (2009). Five-factor model of personality disorder: A proposal for DSM–V. *Annual Review of Clinical Psychology, 5,* 197–220.

Wolfenstein, M., & Trull, T. J. (1997). Depression and openness to experience. *Journal of Personality Assessment, 69,* 614–632.

Wood, D., & Brumbaugh, C. C. (2009). Using revealed mate preferences to evaluate market forces and differential preference explanations for mate selection. *Journal of Personality and Social Psychology, 96,* 1226–1244.

# 7

# The Nature and Structure of "Intelligence"

## Charlie L. Reeve and Silvia Bonaccio

## 1   Introduction

The scientific study of how and why people differ in systematic ways arose in the late nineteenth century, spurred in part by the theorizing of natural variation by Charles Darwin, who wrote:

> the many slight differences which appear in the offspring from the same parents [...] may be called individual differences. [...] These individual differences are of the highest importance for us, for they are often inherited; [...] and they thus afford materials for natural selection to act on. (Darwin, 1958, p. 60)

Influenced heavily by this work, Darwin's cousin Sir Francis Galton would shortly thereafter play a major role in the founding of the field of inquiry known as the psychology of individual differences (or differential psychology). In contrast to experimental psychology, which seeks to discover general laws about human behavior, differential psychology seeks to understand how interindividual, intra-individual, and group differences in psychological characteristics interact with environmental affordances and demands, so as to produce differences in a variety of personal, occupational, educational, and social outcomes. The present book is concerned with this aspect of scientific psychology. The focus of this chapter is on the concept of intelligence.

The scientific study of intelligence plays a prominent role in the history of differential psychology, as these fields of inquiry were in essence born together. Indeed, it was Galton's theorizing about individual differences in intellectual achievement that helped found the field of differential psychology. In the intervening century, the scientific study of intellectual differences—a sub-discipline now referred to as the

*The Wiley-Blackwell Handbook of Individual Differences*, First Edition.
Edited by Tomas Chamorro-Premuzic, Sophie von Stumm, and Adrian Furnham.
© 2011 Blackwell Publishing Ltd. Published 2011 by Blackwell Publishing Ltd.

science of mental abilities—has been exceedingly successful as a scientific effort, as it amassed a wealth of empirical data concerning a number of exciting issues surrounding the nature and development of intelligence, the source of individual and group differences, and the broad and lasting impact of such differences on personal, educational, occupational, and social outcomes. Further, it was the attempt to measure and understand the structure of intelligence that spurred much of the early work in measurement theory and psychometrics. These quantitative domains have arguably made the largest contribution to the advancement of psychology as a scientific enterprise—a belief well summarized by Guilford, who stated:

> No other contribution of psychology has had the social impact equal to that created by the psychological test. No other technique and no other body of theory in psychology has been so fully rationalized from the mathematical point of view. (Guilford, 1954, p. 341)

The central purpose of this chapter is to discuss the nature and structure of intelligence as it is currently understood. Specifically, our goals are to provide the interested reader with (1) a cogent framework for understanding the broad and at times seemingly chaotic nature of this field; (2) an overview of the primary theories regarding the nature and structure of intelligence, including a historical overview of the developmental trajectory of theorizing on this subject; and (3) a description of the contemporary understanding of the psychometric structure of cognitive abilities.

## 1.1  Intelligence as a nomological network

The nature or meaning of "intelligence" is, at once, seemingly simple and ephemeral. Despite the common usage of the term, disagreement and confusion abound when one tries to ascribe a verbal definition to the term "intelligence." In fact, it has been noted that no other term in psychology seems as difficult to define as "intelligence" (Jensen, 1998, p. 46), and it is often noted that not even experts can agree upon such a definition (Sternberg & Detterman, 1986). Even a cursory perusal of the scientific literature makes it apparent that this term is often used to refer to different constructs and concepts. As such, it is important to understand that our goal here is not to contribute yet another verbal definition of intelligence. Indeed, as was elegantly described by Gottfredson (2009), an unwarranted focus on variations in verbal definitions of intelligence has occasionally led to fallacious ideas and to the dismissal of evidence about the reality of individual differences in intellectual behavior. Rather, we seek to encourage enhanced conceptual thinking about the nature of different phenomena, as these are reflected and validated by empirical evidence regardless of what labels are attached to them.

As a first step toward rectifying the "definition" problem, it is useful to recognize that "intelligence" is a generic term, which encompasses a variety of constructs and concepts such as cognitive abilities, cognitive skills, acculturated knowledge, and so on. In fact, some have suggested that the term "intelligence" is so broad as to be of no scientific value, and it has been recommended that this term be jettisoned from the scientific literature (e.g. Jensen, 1998, ch. 3; Spearman, 1927). We believe that the term "intelligence" might still have some limited value, but we suggest that it is best thought of as a term referring to a tightly knit nomological network of different constructs rather than to any specific construct within this network. From a scientific perspective, then, it is more useful to concern ourselves with the nature and structure of specific constructs within this network. To begin, we note that it is generally thought that there are two major components of "intelligence," which are distinguishable and amenable to precise operational or empirical descriptions (see Cattell, 1943; Chamorro-Premuzic & Furnham, 2005; Fleishman, 1967; Hebb, 1942; Jensen, 1998): (1) the *ability to learn* new things and solve novel problems (i.e. abilities; fluid intelligence), and (2) the *outcomes of learning*, namely the achievement of acquired knowledge and skills, which are dependent on prior experience within a specific cultural context (i.e. developed intellect; crystallized intelligence).

*1.1.1  Mental abilities*[1]   Carroll (1993) describes "ability" as the source of variance— that is, a latent trait—in the threshold levels of difficulty for successful performance on a class of tasks. Jensen (1998) adds that, to infer the existence of an ability from observed performance, the performance must (a) exhibit some specified degree of temporal stability (be repeatable, or show consistency over some time interval); (b) be amenable to being somehow objectively evaluated in terms of meeting some objective standard of proficiency (e.g. running a given distance in 10 seconds is faster than running it in 15 seconds; answering "four" to question "2 + 2 = ?" is correct, "five" is not); and (c) have some degree of generality, so that the performance can be repeated across equivalent but different trials.

Cognitive abilities (or "mental abilities") are thus reflected as sources of variance in performance on a task which requires one to mentally process, comprehend, and manipulate information. Examples might include such things as the ability to reason deductively or inductively, grasp general principles from observing behavior of objects, mentally rotate objects in one's mind, quickly and accurately comprehend what one is reading, or deal effectively with mathematical concepts. Finally, a cognitive capacity can be said to be an ability (rather than a skill or knowledge), to the extent that it is relatively stable over time and predicts the acquisition of new skills or knowledge, but is itself relatively resistant to training or to explicit education (Carroll, 1993; Jensen, 1998; Lubinski & Dawis, 1992). Further, abilities are the latent constructs posited to account for the correlated performances across different kinds of mental tasks. For example, consider that individual differences in performance on tests of verbal analogies, vocabulary, reading comprehension, and sentence completion are consistently and strongly correlated. If one were to posit that each task reflects a separate and specific skill that is learned, it would be difficult to explain what societal mechanism would lead to consistent rank-ordering in the development of each skill. On the other hand, it is theoretically more parsimonious to posit a verbal reasoning ability that is the underlying explanation for correlated performances.

Although some researchers appear to question the utility of general mental abilities as scientific constructs, a broad array of psychometric, biological, and behavioral genetic evidence (e.g. Carroll, 1993; Jensen, 1998) has given rise to a broad consensus among experts that mental abilities are not just a statistical artifact (Gottfredson, 1997a; Reeve & Charles, 2008; Snyderman & Rothman, 1987) and that they have a significant and meaningful influence on important real-world outcomes (e.g. Gottfredson, 1997b, 2004; Jensen, 1998; Kuncel, Hezlett, & Ones, 2004; Schmidt & Hunter, 1998; see also Gottfreddson, 1997c and Deary, 2009 [special issues of *Intelligence*], and Lubinski, 2004 [in a special section of the *Journal of Personality and Social Psychology*]).

*1.1.2  Knowledge and skills*  The Merriam-Webster dictionary defines knowledge as: (1) the fact or condition of knowing something with familiarity gained through experience or association; (2) the range of one's information or understanding; and (3) the circumstance or condition of apprehending truth or fact through reasoning. Similarly, as a psychological construct, knowledge reflects those specific facts, concepts, and ideas that a person has learned through personal experience (e.g. via study, investigation, observation) within a specific cultural context. Thus, whereas abilities refer to general capacities for learning and solving novel problems, knowledge refers to the acquired and retained information that can be drawn upon for use in domain-specific situations. Similarly, "skills" are reflected by proficiency in executing the sequence of responses required by a specific task (Fleishman, 1967). Like knowledge, mental skills are those capacities involved in the comprehension or apprehension of information that are acquired and improved by instruction, practice, or manipulation.

Admittedly, the distinction between abilities, skills, and knowledge is somewhat a matter of degree, and these categories often denote contrasting points of emphasis rather than indicating qualitatively distinct constructs (Carroll, 1993; Jensen, 1998; Lubinski & Dawis, 1992). The features emphasized as making the demarcation are degree of generality and sensitivity to training. Abilities are typically denoted by their generality, whereas skills and knowledge are denoted by their domain-specificity. To the extent that a behavioral capacity generalizes across domains, and in particular to novel content, we can consider it as reflecting an ability. The more a behavioral capacity seems to be limited to a specific type of task or context and is dependent on practice or training, the more we can think of it as reflecting an acquired skill or knowledge.

This distinction between intelligence-as-knowledge and intelligence-as-abilities is particularly useful for understanding some of the apparent discrepancy in definitions of "intelligence." For example, contextualists have argued that the set of acquired skills and knowledge that are of greatest relevance to success in a specific situation should be considered to be the essence of intelligence (see Berry, 1974; Sternberg & Grigorenko, 2006). These types of domain-specific "hot intelligences," as they have been called, focus on the outcome of learning from experience (i.e. intelligence-as-knowledge). In contrast, psychometric conceptualizations have tended to focus on the broad, cross-situational behavioral capacities (i.e. abilities). There is nothing inconsistent about these ideas; basic abilities give rise to individual differences in the capacity to learn valuable domain-specific knowledge and skills from experience (which by definition takes place in the culture in which one lives).

## 1.2  Approaches to the study of the structure of "intelligence"

Historically, there are two general approaches to the study of intelligence that correspond somewhat (but not entirely) to the distinction between basic abilities on the one hand, and the development of acquired skills and contextual knowledge on the other hand. The first approach, commonly referred to as the *psychometric tradition*, focuses on the number and nature of basic cognitive abilities. This approach has largely relied on the use of quantitative methods such as factor analysis and multidimensional scaling to identify the abilities that account for the pattern of correlated performances across various mental tasks. In contrast, others have taken a more developmental or holistic perspective, often focusing on the nature of acquired intellect.

While some continue to see these approaches as competing, others have noted their natural synergy and have made important advances in the development of theories that better integrate the various pieces in the network of intelligence (see Ackerman, 1996; Cattell, 1943). For example, Horn (1968) advanced the Cattellian *Gf/Gc* theory on the premise that it provides a meaningful framework for integrating the psychometric models with developmental and process theories. More recently, Ackerman's PPIK theory (see below) stands as a prime example of the potential natural synergy between these approaches, and one that gives rise to a more complete understanding of "intelligence" and of its connections to other individual difference domains. Nonetheless, because these two schools of thought have tended to focus on different constructs (abilities vs. developed knowledge and skills) and have tended toward independent histories, we discuss them separately below.

## 2 "Intelligence" as Cognitive Abilities: Psychometric Models

The debate over the psychometric structure of cognitive abilities is perhaps one of the most storied in differential psychology. At the risk of oversimplifying this voluminous history, the debate largely centered on the question of whether there is just a single, general cognitive ability or many independent specific abilities. Though there is not a universally accepted model of abilities, most experts today accept some form of a hierarchal model, with a single general cognitive ability factor at the apex – $g$ or "general mental ability" – in large part due to the exhaustive work of John Carroll (1993). Below this general factor there is a small number of specific abilities (also referred to as "group factors"); and each of these abilities, in turn, subsumes a large number of task-specific skills reflecting the effects of experience and learning (ibid., pp. 633–634). Different models arrange the number and nature of the lower strata in different ways. Some conceive of the second level as having eight to ten abilities, whereas others appear to define an intermediate stratum with three broad kinds of ability, which typically reflect verbal, quantitative (or perceptual), and visual–spatial ability (see Johnson & Bouchard, 2005; Süß & Beauducel, 2005; Vernon, 1961). However, before describing the nature of a contemporary model of cognitive abilities in detail, it is useful to consider the history of this field, in order to appreciate and understand fully the roots of this model and why most researchers subscribe to something akin to it.

## 2.1  A historical overview of the psychometric tradition

Under the influence of his cousin Charles Darwin, Galton (2006 [1869], 1907) was among the first to conceive of a general mental ability as the primary characteristic differentiating individuals engaged in intellectual endeavors. Among his many contributions, Galton (2006 [1869]) introduced the concept of a general mental ability factor into psychology. Largely on the basis of his study of eminence within family lines, Galton suggested that a general intellectual ability, rather than specialized ones, was responsible for achievement:

> People lay too much stress on apparent specialties, thinking that because a man is devoted to some particular pursuit he would not have succeeded in anything else. They might as well say that, because a youth has fallen in love with a brunette, he could not possibly have fallen in love with a blonde. As likely as not, the affair was mainly or wholly due to a general amorousness. (Galton, 2006, p. 64)

Although Galton's theorizing was crucial to the founding of a science of mental abilities, it was not until Spearman (1904) and his students (Garnett, 1919; El Koussy, 1935) introduced factor analysis that the psychometric structure of cognitive abilities could be explored in a more systematic fashion. Indeed, the use of factor analysis in the study of cognitive abilities is in many ways equivalent to the use of the telescope in the study of astrological bodies. Each one is a primary tool for its respective science, and it is hard to imagine the latter having advanced in any meaningful way without this tool. Observing that individual differences in performance on cognitive tasks exhibited what he called a "positive manifold" (a phrase referring to a correlation matrix comprised of only positive correlations), Spearman (1904) initially proposed a two-factor theory, positing that the variance in true scores on any intellectual task could be explained by two types of factors: a single general factor, common to all tests, which he labeled $g$, and a specific factor, $s$, which was unique to each and every test. Because $g$ and $s$ were said to be uncorrelated (as were the multitude of $s$ factors with each other), the principle of aggregation dictates that any composite score would primarily reflect the cumulated influence of $g$, whereas the unique $s$ factors would tend to cancel each other out. Thus the early expectation stemming from the influence of Galton and Spearman was that individual differences in a broad, general factor were of primary importance in explaining a wide variety of outcomes, and that there was presumably little to be gained from assessing more specific aspects.

Breaking from the British school of thought, Thurstone (1938) proposed a multifactor model of so-called primary mental abilities (PMAs)—a model that explicitly rejected any common or general factor. Using a meaningfully different method of factor analysis, Thurstone proposed seven specialized, orthogonal dimensions of ability, all of the same limited degree of generality. Spearman (1927, 1939) criticized the PMA model because Thurstone's orthogonal rotation method prohibited the extraction of a general factor, if one existed. His re-analysis of Thurstone's data, undertaken using different factor-analytic methods, which allowed for (but did not require) a higher-order general factor, showed that $g$ could be extracted in addition

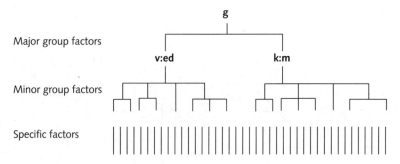

**Figure 7.1**   Vernon's hierarchical model. Source: Vernon, 1961, p. 22. Reproduced with permission

to multiple PMA-type factors. On the basis of this, Spearman (and later Burt, 1949) proposed a multifactor, hierarchical model of cognitive abilities. Likewise, after refining his methods to allow for oblique rotation, Thurstone (1947) eventually granted that his primary factors were in fact correlated, and he admitted that a second-order general factor, consistent with Spearman's *g* factor, was plausible. Thus the (eventual) Spearman and Thurstone models of cognitive abilities appear to be highly consistent with each other, the primary difference between them being in the relative importance they attach to the general factor and to group factors.

In a Both Spearman's and Thurstone's models should probably be considered as hierarchical; but Vernon (1950, 1961) is widely recognized as one of the first to postulate, specifically, a hierarchical model (see Burt, 1949). Shown in Figure 7.1, Vernon's four-stratum model is typically discussed as consisting of two major second-order factors: *v:ed* (verbal:educational), which accounts for relations among the verbal facility, the numerical facility, logical reasoning, attention, and fluency factors; and *k:m* (spatial : mechanical), which is associated with a range of knowledge factors in technical or mechanical areas, psychomotor coordination, and spatial ability. The two group factors are in turn dominated by a higher-order *g* factor. At the lowest level reside the task-specific skills. Vernon (1961) attributes substantial weight to *g* in predicting individual differences in any domain; but he appears strongly to support the assumption that intra-individual differences in specific abilities and interests will be important determinants of individual differences in domain-specific educability.

In a somewhat different vein, Guilford (1967) proposed a taxonomic model of cognitive abilities, known as the structure of intellect (SOI) model (see Figure 7.2). Guilford classified mental tests according to the content of the test, the operation required of the respondent, and the product. Specifying four types of content, five types of operations, and six types of products, he claimed that 120 distinct ability factors could be identified. Importantly, Guilford rejected the possibility of a hierarchical model, arguing that all of the abilities in the SOI model are independent (i.e. uncorrelated); thus he ruled out the possibility of a general factor. Despite its appeal as a potential categorization system for measures of cognitive abilities, the SOI model

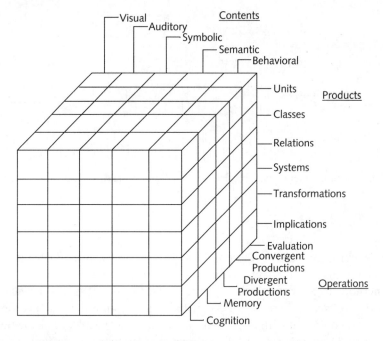

**Figure 7.2**   Guilford's structure of intellect (SOI) model. Source: Guilford, 1967, p. 63.
Reproduced with permission

has been characterized as "fundamentally defective," on account of its illogical nature
and inconsistency with empirical evidence (Carroll, 1993; Horn & Knapp, 1973;
Jensen, 1998). In particular, it has been shown that, when corrections are made for
artifacts (e.g. range restriction and unreliability), all the correlations in Guilford's own
data are above zero, with a mean of $r = .45$ (Alliger, 1988).

Although Guilford's model has fallen out of favor for empirical reasons, the application of facet theory to the study of intelligence continued. The most prominent
application, Snow and colleagues' radex model of cognitive abilities (Snow, Kyllonen,
& Marshalek, 1984), stems from Guttman's (1965) faceted view of intelligence. A
key feature of this perspective is the contiguity hypothesis, which predicts that the
more facet elements (e.g. operations, content, products) two tests have in common,
the more they will covary as a result of common variance (See Süß & Beauducel,
2005, for a detailed presentation of Guttman's theorizing). Using non-metric multidimensional scaling techniques, Snow's model (shown in Figure 7.3) is essentially
a circular grid in which the manifest indicators appear to be closer to the center of
the circle the more they require the inductive and deductive reasoning abilities, and
cluster together in different sectors of the grid depending on similarity of content.
Although facet models appear to have significant value for both theoretical and
psycho-educational efforts, they have not been as well integrated into the mainstream
psychometric literature on intelligence as traditional factor-analytic models have (Süß
& Beauducel, 2005).

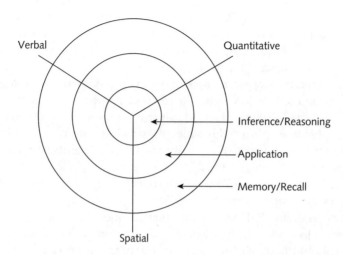

Verbal

Quantitative

Inference/Reasoning

Application

Memory/Recall

Spatial

**Figure 7.3** Schematic representation of the radex model of cognitive abilities

Coming from a developmental perspective, Cattell (1943) proposed what has evolved into one of the most influential psychometric models of intelligence, one based on two basic forms of "intelligence": (1) "fluid" intelligence (*Gf*), which reflects basic reasoning abilities and the ability to solve novel problems, for which prior knowledge and skills are of little use; and (2) "crystallized" intelligence (*Gc*), which reflects accumulated declarative knowledge gained through experience and education. Cattell theorized that *Gc* would reflect the extent to which an individual was able to profit from his or her investment of *Gf* in the immediate sociocultural context. Although the *Gf/Gc* model appears to have been broadly accepted as a theoretical approach to understanding the development of adult intellect, it was largely untested until the 1960s, when Cattell's student John Horn began his program of research. Through this effort, the model has been refined several times, the most recent version consisting of a hierarchical model with nine specific factors subsumed by the broad *Gf* and *Gc* factors (Horn & Noll, 1997).

An important distinction between the Horn–Cattell model and other contemporary models is that Horn does not concede the existence of a higher-order *g* factor despite evidence that the broad factors are positively correlated. He states:

This well-documented finding of generally positive intercorrelations—a positive manifold—among intellectual abilities has been accepted widely as evidence in support of a hypothesis of a general intelligence factor underlying observed performances. While this evidence cannot be discounted and there is a sense in which it indicates a general intelligence, too much should not be inferred from it. Positive manifold is not equivalent to hierarchical order among intercorrelations [...] Hierarchical order may be interpreted parsimoniously as indicating one and only one influence, but positive manifold permits the possibility of many influences only loosely inter-related. (Horn, 1968, pp. 255–256)

Thus Horn's version of the *Gf/Gc* model is somewhat reminiscent of the early PMA model. Others have shown, however, that, when a *g* factor is extracted, the *Gf* and *g* factors are correlated near unity, and, when the second stratum factors are residualized, *Gf* disappears (Gustafsson, 1988; Jensen, 1998).

The most comprehensive attempt to model the psychometric structure of abilities was conducted by the late John Carroll. In an exhaustive survey and re-analysis of factor-analytic studies, Carroll (1993) analyzed over 400 data sets spanning more than 60 years of research. From this endeavor, which is reported in a comprehensive tome, a three-stratum structure of cognitive abilities was identified in which a general mental ability factor (*g*) in the third stratum subsumes eight broad group factors located in the second stratum. Below the group factors, in the first stratum, lie 69 narrow abilities. Although Carroll's "strata" are graphically depicted in a higher-order fashion, shown in Figure 7.4, he cautions that the model should not be interpreted as a strict hierarchy, as the factors within each stratum are not necessarily of equal generality. It should be noted that some of the latter group factors are not as well defined as others and Carroll cautions that some slight modifications or further refinement to those factors may be in order.

In light of the close similarity between Carroll's model and the *Gf/Gc* model, McGrew (1997, 2009) has developed a conceptual synthesis known as the Carroll–Horn–Cattell (CHC) model. In particular, McGrew noted that a number of the second-stratum factors in Carroll's model have direct counterparts in the Horn–Cattell *Gf/Gc* model, whereas other second-stratum factors appear to be mixed components of Horn–Cattell factors. Most of the discrepancies between the two models were resolved by making slight revisions to the specification of the group factors and to the specific location of narrow factors under the group factors. A key feature of McGrew's synthesized framework is the inclusion of a third-order general ability factor consistent with Carroll's model.

Finally, Johnson and Bouchard (2005) have recently provided a direct empirical comparison between the relative fit of Cattell's *Gf/Gc*, of Vernon's *v:ed* and *k:m*, and of Carroll's models. While all three models provided reasonable descriptions of the structure of cognitive abilities, none seems to meet their criteria for a well-fitted model. Vernon's (1961) four-stratum *v:ed* and *k:m* model appeared to fare better than the predictions from the *Gf/Gc* model; however, it lacked the specification of memory and image rotation factors found in the lower stratum of Carroll's model. On the basis of these findings, Johnson and Bouchard (2005) proposed a new hierarchical model referred to as the VPR model, which is shown in Figure 7.5. In addition to some changes to the specification of the narrow abilities in the second stratum, the key feature of their model is the inclusion of a third stratum between *g* and the second stratum of narrow abilities. This new stratum consists of three broad factors, namely a verbal factor, a perceptual factor, and a factor related to image rotation.

## 2.2   A contemporary model of cognitive abilities and their scientific significance

Figure 7.6 displays a four-stratum framework of the structure of cognitive abilities. Our framework is primarily a synthesis of McGrew's (1997, 2009) CHC model and of Johnson and Bouchard's (2005) VPR model; but it is also informed by radex models (see Snow et al., 1984) as well as by some recent factor-analytic models (e.g. Johnson & Bouchard, 2005; Reeve & Blacksmith, 2009; Süß & Beauducel, 2005), which reveal a stratum consisting of three broad domains. Before discussing the factors within the model, we want to emphasize, as McGrew (2009) and Carroll (1993) did, that there remain some discrepancies among theorists regarding the exact specification of the narrow abilities; and refining of the precise organization or narrow abilities is expected to continue. Also, we emphasize Carroll's point that the precise, "tree-like" structure typically depicted is not likely to be an accurate reflection of reality. Any given specific skill or narrow ability need not be related to (or be a function of) only one higher-stratum ability. Nor is there any expectation that the abilities encompassed within any given stratum will necessarily be of the same breadth or importance. Again, we emphasize that this is a conceptual model.

*2.2.1   Stratum I: Task-specific skills*   The lowest stratum contains the task-specific skills. In theory, there are an unknown multitude of these skills. In practice, the size of the test battery being analyzed typically restricts the number realized in any analysis. Typically, these are of little theoretical interest.

*2.2.2   Stratum II: Specific abilities (aka, group factors, narrow abilities)*   Stratum II is comprised of domain-specific cognitive abilities often referred to as "group factors," "narrow abilities," or "specific abilities." As just noted, there remains some slight disagreement across models and theorists regarding the ideal specification of specific abilities. Below we offer a description of the specific abilities included in most factor models of cognitive abilities. Our list should not be taken as the final word, but rather an example of a typical list.

- *Fluid intelligence/reasoning (Gf):* ability to apply rules and premises so as to reach a solution; ability to discover underlying characteristics that govern problems. (Note that this factor appears to be equivalent to $g$ and typically disappears once variance due to $g$ has been removed. Hence it likely does not exist as a unique specific factor. We include it here because of its prominence in Horn's models.)
- *Quantitative reasoning/skills (Gq):* ability to reason, either inductively or deductively, with mathematical concepts, relations, and properties; general knowledge of mathematical concepts.
- *Crystallized intelligence (Gc):* size and sophistication of vocabulary; ability to comprehend and communicate orally and to use communication skills with fluency; range of general and acculturated knowledge.
- *Verbal (reading/writing) ability (Grw):* ability to recognize and decode words or disguised words; ability to comprehend, and to communicate with clarity of thought and expression, in oral and written discourse; general understanding of rules in one's native language.
- *Visual-spatial processing (Gvs):* ability to manipulate objects or visual patterns mentally, such as in mentally rotating multidimensional objects in space; ability to discern quickly a meaningful object from partially obscured or vague patterns and stimuli.

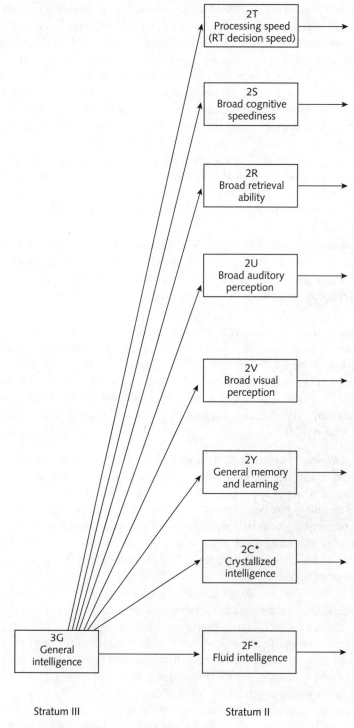

Stratum III                              Stratum II

**Figure 7.4**  Carroll's three-stratum model of cognitive abilities. Source: Carroll, 1993, p. 626. Reproduced with permission

Speed factors:
  Simple reaction time (R1); Choice reaction time (R2); Semantic processing speed (R4);
  Mental comparison speed (R7)

Speed factors:
  Rate of test taking (R9); Numerical facility (N); [Perceptual speed (P) – also listed under 2V]

Level factors:
  Originality/Creativity (FD)
Speed factors:
  Ideational fluency (FI); Naming facility (NA); Associational fluency (FA); Expressional fluency (FE);
  Word fluency (FW); Sensitivity to problems (SP); Figural fluency (FF); Figural flexibility (FX)

Level factors:
  Hearing and speech threshold factors (UA, UT, UU); Speech sound discrimination (US);
  General sound discrimination (U3); Sound-frequency discrimination (U5);
  Sound-intensity/Duration discrimination (U6); Musical discrimination & judgment (UI, U9);
  Resistance to auditory stimulus distortion (UR); Temporal tracking (UK);
  Maintaining & judging rhythm (UB); Memory for sound patterns (UM); Absolute pitch (UP);
  Sound localization (UL)

Level factors:
  Visualization (VZ)
Speed factors:
  Spatial relations (SR); Closure speed (CS); Flexibility of closure (CF); Serial perception integration (PI);
  Spatial scanning (SS); Perceptual speed (P)
Miscellaneous:
  Imagery (IM); Length estimation (LE); Perception of illusions (IL); Perceptual alternations (PN)

Level factors:
  Memory span (MS)
Rate factors:
  Associative memory (MA); Free recall memory (M6); Meaningful memory (MM);
  Visual memory (MV); Learning ability (L1)

Level factors:
  Language development (LD); Verbal (printed) language comprehension (V); Lexical knowledge (VL);
  Reading comprehension (RC); Reading decoding (RD); Cloze ability (CZ); Spelling ability (SG);
  Phonetic coding (PC); Grammatical sensitivity (MY); Foreign language aptitude (LA);
  Communication ability (CM); Listening ability (LS); Foreign language proficiency (KL)
Speed factors:
  Reading speed (RS); Oral production and fluency (OP); Writing ability (WA)

Level factors:
  General sequential reasoning (RG); Induction (I); Quantitative reasoning (RQ);
  Piagetian reasoning (RP)
Speed factors:
  Speed of reasoning (RE?)

Stratum I

* In many analyses, factors 2F and 2C cannot be distinguished;
  they are represented, however, by a factor designated 2H,
  a combination of 2F and 2C.

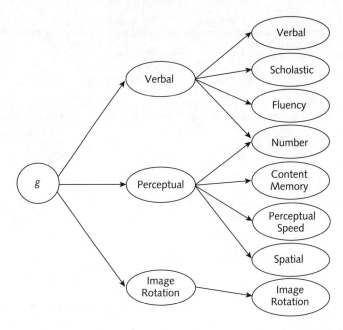

**Figure 7.5** Structural representation of the visual–perceptual–rotational (VPR) model. Source: Johnson & Bouchard, 2005, p. 408. Copyright Elsevier. Adapted with permission

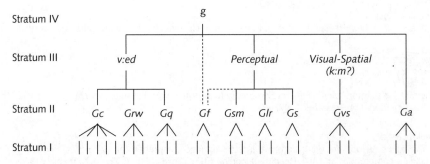

**Figure 7.6** Schematic representation of the contemporary thinking on the structure of mental abilities

- *Short-term memory (Gsm):* ability to form and store mental representations of stimuli and then to recognize or recall them after a short duration.
- *Long-term associative storage and retrieval (Glr):* ability to store and recall previously learned material, whether meaningful or not; ability to rapidly produce series of ideas, words, or other elaborative information related to a specific theme or object; ability to rapidly make connections among stimuli.
- *Cognitive speededness (Gs):* ability to react quickly to stimuli or to make quick decisions which require the encoding of and manipulation of stimulus information.

- *Auditory processing (Ga):* ability to process speech sounds; phonological aware-ness; ability to discriminate speech sounds in normal and distorted contexts, ability to discriminate tones, tonal patterns, pitch, and other variations in sound qualities; ability to localize sounds in space.

Intuitively it is often assumed that measures of specific abilities can be an important source of information, which estimates of $g$ alone cannot provide. However, for many years, the general trend was to find little if any incremental validity due to specific abilities over and above $g$. As Thorndike (1991) stated it, "there can be little doubt that [...] most of the prediction that is possible from cognitive ability measures is provided by a single general ability factor" (p. 298). More recently, a number of researchers (e.g. Gustafsson & Snow, 1997; Reeve, 2004) have questioned this con-clusion, suggesting that the inability to discover substantive relationships between specific abilities and certain theoretical outcomes may be a result of inappropriate methodology. For example, the relative contribution of narrow abilities (but not of $g$) may have been obscured in prior research due to a theoretically and methodologi-cally deficient consideration of the construct(s) underlying observed criteria (Reeve, 2004). Subsequent improvements in methodology and theory have helped recast the role and value of specific abilities for theoretical and psychoeducational use. For example, occupational research on the ability profiles of persons pursuing and main-taining careers indicate that, given open access to a variety of occupations, people "identify, seek, are selected for, and remain in occupations with work tasks that are congruent with their specialized abilities" (Prediger, 1989, p. 4).

*2.2.3 Stratum III: Broad abilities*  This stratum is comprised of the broad verbal: educational, perceptual, and visual–spatial abilities, as posited by Johnson and Bouchard (2005). The verbal:educational domain encompasses narrow capacities reflecting verbal and linguistic abilities, ideational fluency, and various forms of crys-tallized intelligence—including quantitative abilities. The perceptual domain appears to encompass perceptual speed, speed of reasoning, and memory factors. Their visual–spatial factor appears to encompass visualization and mental rotation abilities (Vernon would include mechanical abilities in this domain as well).

The scientific and practical significance of broad abilities has been well established through the work of Lubinski and Benbow (see Benbow, 1992; Lubinski & Benbow, 2000; Park, Lubinski, & Benbow, 2008; Wai, Lubinski, & Benbow, 2009), which shows that profile differences in broad abilities are especially important determinants of the particular domain in which high-$g$ individuals realize their potential and find occupational success. Hence, compared to Thorndike's (1991) assessment of the value of abilities beyond $g$, the contemporary view seems to be well captured by Lubinski (2000), who stated:

> quantitative, spatial, and verbal reasoning abilities all possess psychological import beyond $g$. This is especially true for predicting educational and career tracks that people self-select, but also for individual differences in criterion performance. [...] This becomes especially true at higher $g$ levels. (Lubinski, 2000, p. 412)

*2.2.4   Stratum IV: The "g" factor*   Finally, at the apex is a broad general cognitive ability, typically referred to as *g*. Arguably, no other psychometric question has been scrutinized and empirically tested more than the existence of *g*. And the evidence is unequivocal: there is a *g* factor that underlies human mental functioning (Carroll, 1993; Gottfredson, 1997a; Jensen, 1998; Spearman, 1904; Thurstone, 1947). Formally, *g* is defined as the "eduction of relations and correlates" (Spearman, 1927, Jensen, 1998)—that is, the ability to infer or deduce meaningful principles and concepts from abstractness and from novel situations. In short, the *g* factor essentially reflects the general ability to learn. The *g* factor is indicated by the pervasive positive manifold among any set of tests or tasks that require any form of cognitive manipulation or processing of information. The *g* factor has been shown to be remarkably invariant, across (1) different test batteries (Thorndike, 1987); (2) the method of factor extraction (Jensen & Weng, 1994; Reeve & Blacksmith, 2009); and (3) racial, cultural, ethnic, and nationality groups (Carroll, 1993; Jensen, 1985, 1998; Jensen & Reynolds, 1982).

Perhaps because of its pervasiveness, the construct of *g* has been, and continues to be, a major object of scrutiny. Some critics have argued that *g* is purely an arbitrary mathematical artifact and that, by conducting research on *g*, psychologists are guilty of "reification" (e.g. Gould, 1996). However, this argument is fallacious (Jensen, 1986; Jensen & Weng, 1994). All constructs are abstractions, purposely invoked to describe coherent classes of phenomena that co-occur in nature. For instance, gravity is a mathematical construct that describes one of the four classes of forces associated with matter. Similarly, *g* is a psychometric and psychological construct that describes a class of phenomena associated with results of human mental functioning. Both of these constructs are abstract ideas; both are latent. However, because the phenomena ascribed to these constructs can be observed, the constructs are subject to conceptual refinement, measurement, and verification. Constructs need not be "hard objects" to be real in a scientific sense (Meehl, 1991). Additionally, research on the biological and neurological basis for *g* confirms that the *g* factor reflects something "real" (in a physical sense) about the brain (see Haier, 2009 [special issue of *Intelligence*]). For example, *g* scores have been shown to correlate with brain size and volume (Rushton & Ankney, 2009), with complexity of average evoked potentials (Eysenck & Barrett, 1985), and with nerve conduction velocity (Reed & Jensen, 1993).

Other critics continue to question the scientific significance of *g* as a construct, typically arguing that *g* does not account for meaningful amounts of variation in important outcomes (Vasquez & Jones, 2006). Again, such arguments have been shown to be vacuous, being typically predicated on a selective and biased review of the empirical literature (Kuncel & Sackett, 2007). Rather, just as Spearman (1904) postulated over a century ago, empirical research has shown that this "fundamental factor" manifests itself in virtually all life functions for which intellectual activity is required. Many large-scale studies and meta-analyses have demonstrated that individual differences in *g* are a strong determinant of an array of behaviors, such as job performance and academic achievement (Kuncel & Hezlett, 2007; Kuncel et al., 2004; Salgado, Anderson, Moscoso, Bertua, & de Fruyt, 2003; Schmidt & Hunter, 1998) as well as of epidemiological phenomena (Batty, Deary, & Gottfredson, 2007;

Deary, Whalley & Starr, 2009), health-related behaviors (Anstey, Low, Christensen & Sachdev, 2009; Deary et al., 2009; Gottfredson, 2004), and religious beliefs (Lynn, Harvey, & Nyborg, 2009; Nyborg, 2009). The importance of $g$ was perhaps best summed up by Brand (1987), who stated that "$g$ is to psychology as carbon is to chemistry" (p. 257).

# 3   Intelligence as Developed Intellect and Other Models

The alternative approach to the study of the structure of "intelligence" has typically focused on the developed adult intellect. Our coverage is not exhaustive; rather we focus on the approaches that are, arguably, the most well known and have received the most attention (either in the scientific literature or in the popular press). A key feature of many of these theories is their potential for generating useful ideas regarding how abilities and personality (or other non-cognitive factors) interact within a specific cultural context to produce knowledge and skills.

## 3.1   Sternberg's triarchic theory of intelligence

Central to Sternberg's (1985) triarchic theory of intelligence is the division of the various components of this network into categories, which he labels "practical intelligence," "analytic/academic intelligence," and "creative intelligence." In this model, cognitive abilities appear to be largely contained within the analytic/academic category, whereas knowledge and skills are primarily contained within the other two categories. Sternberg's description of his model clearly shows that he places more importance on the last two categories than on the first, but this model does not appear to contradict the basic conceptualization or psychometric structure of abilities (what he calls "analytic/academic intelligence") as we have presented it above.

Creative intelligence purportedly involves the individual's ability to respond to, and cope with, novel situations and tasks. Central to creative functioning is a concept which Sternberg calls "synthetic ability," which is the capacity to generate novel ideas that are of high quality and relevant to the task (Sternberg & O'Hara, 2000). This requires three related processes: selective encoding (attending to the relevant information and not attending to the irrelevant), selective combination (combining information in innovative ways), and selective comparison (combining new and old information in innovative ways). On the basis of this description, creative intelligence appears to capture the idea of a trait constellation: it consists, namely, in the application of reasoning abilities and acquired domain-specific knowledge to task-specific demands. The finding that creative thinking is moderately related to measures of reasoning ability is consistent with this description (ibid.).

Finally, on the basis of a distinction first advanced by Neisser (1976), Sternberg postulates a third category, which he calls "practical intelligence" and he defines as the ability to adapt to, and shape, one's environment. Practical intelligence is often referred to as "street smart" or "common sense" (Sternberg & Hedlund, 2002, p. 145) and requires what Sternberg refers to as "tacit knowledge," meaning knowledge acquired through unstructured personal experiences, with limited help from others. In addition, tacit knowledge is said to be largely procedural in that it guides context-specific performance and it is related to individuals' goals.

From a purely conceptual standpoint, Sternberg's theory appears to be consistent with the long tradition of distinguishing between abilities and knowledge and with the conception that adult intellectual behavior draws heavily upon acquired knowledge and skills. However, unlike other theories of intelligence which distinguish between abilities and knowledge (e.g. Cattell, 1943), Sternberg posits that practical intelligence is independent of analytic/academic ability (i.e. of cognitive abilities). Sternberg and colleagues have reported some evidence which they interpret as supportive of this claim; however, their claim has been contradicted by independent evaluations (see Gottfredson, 2003). In addition, many have criticized the conceptualization of practical intelligence. One of the most comprehensive critical evaluations of practical intelligence was done by Gottfredson (2003), who pointed out that, as a scientific concept, practical intelligence suffers from a lack of proper empirical testing and, as a theory, it ignores decades of scientific evidence regarding the nature, existence, and importance of $g$. This was similarly acknowledged by Chamorro-Premuzic and Furnham (2005), who state that "there is little empirical evidence for the existence of testable individual differences in practical intelligence, particularly in terms of psychometric instruments" (p. 40). The lack of empirical evidence to support the validity of practical intelligence as a construct, as well as the validity of key claims of the theory (such as the idea that practical intelligence would have larger validities than the established abilities), has been noted by others as well (Brody, 2003; Kline, 1998; Messick, 1992).

Though not all aspects of the triarchic theory have fared well from an empirical standpoint, Jensen points out that it does draw attention to the consideration of higher-order meta-cognitive process—such as the deployment and coordination of basic cognitive process and declarative knowledge for problem-solving within specific contexts (Jensen, 1998, p. 132). Similarly, the theory could yet prove to be useful as a framework for understanding how different individuals invest $g$ in their personal activities according to how they are affected by their particular opportunities, interests, personality traits, and motivations (Gottfredson, 2003; Jensen, 1998). Unfortunately, as Gottfredson notes, some of this potential has presumably been tempered by continuing efforts to "spin illusions of a wholly new intelligence that defies the laws of evidence" (2003, p. 392).

## 3.2   Gardner's multiple intelligences

A contextualist view of intelligence that has received significant attention in the popular press is Gardner's (1983) theory of multiple intelligences. Gardner defines "an intelligence" as "the ability to solve problems or fashion products that are of consequence in a particular cultural setting or community" (Gardner, 2006, p. 6). As such, Gardner posits the existence of eight independent "intelligences" corresponding to particular activities or situations: linguistic, logical–mathematical, spatial, musical, bodily–kinesthetic, interpersonal, intra-personal, and naturalistic (the latter being the latest addition to the theory). Importantly, Gardner denies the existence of any positive manifold in intellectual behavior.

Briefly, linguistic intelligence implies verbal fluency in all its aspects (semantic, syntactic, phonological, and so on). Logical–mathematical intelligence refers to one's reasoning ability, logic, and numerical fluency. Musical intelligence refers to musical ability and sensitivity to pitch, rhythm, and timbre. Bodily–kinesthetic intelligence refers to the ability to use one's body in expressive ways, as well as to the capacity to work with external entities. Spatial intelligence comprises the ability to perceive objects, mentally to manipulate them, and to reproduce them. Interpersonal intelligence is the ability to make sense of others, particularly of their emotions and feelings; while intra-personal intelligence is the capacity to understand oneself, to be introspective. Finally, naturalistic intelligence refers to having empathy for, and an understanding of, nature. In more recent iterations of the theory, the two personal intelligences have been combined into one, and other possible intelligences have been advanced but not formally added to the list (e.g. existential intelligence).

Gardner's theory of multiple intelligences has been criticized on several fronts. First, many of the multiple intelligences identified by Gardner have significant correlations with each other and with traditional measures of ability (Chamorro-Premuzic & Furnham, 2005). Thus the relative independence of these abilities, as originally articulated by Gardner, has been refuted. In addition, Jensen (1998) argues that many of the intelligences Gardner articulates correspond closely to the group factors—that is, to the specific abilities—outlined in the previous section and many are highly $g$-loaded—in particular logical–mathematical, linguistic, and spatial intelligence. Finally, many have noted that the empirical evidence to support the theory of multiple intelligences has been scarce at best, and non-existent at worse (Allix, 2000; Waterhouse, 2006). This is, in part, due to a lack of construct clarity and measurement devices for many of the multiple intelligences (Waterhouse, 2006). In conclusion, from a scientific perspective, Gardner's theory has not fared well. Nonetheless, its appeal likely stems from its "holistic" perspective. Indeed, though not actual constructs in any scientific sense, many of Gardner's "intelligences" seem to correspond to lay notions of important skills or competencies (or, in some cases, to admirable personality traits). To the extent that theories such as Gardner's encourage thinking about the development of trait constellations, they may yet prove to be of some scientific value.

## 3.3 Emotional intelligence

Perhaps the best known recent extension of the nomological network of intelligence is the concept of emotional intelligence (EI). Although there are various conceptualizations of EI, current thinking suggests that EI involves the ability to perceive and understand emotions accurately, the ability to manage one's own emotional reactions, the ability to appraise emotions in situations and identify them in others, and the ability to use emotions for reasoning (Mayer, Roberts, & Barsade, 2008). Thus, within our conceptualization of intelligence as a nomological network, EI can likely be defined as acquired or developed skills involving emotional perception and emotional understanding. In this respect EI is thought to fall at the interface of emotions and intelligence (Matthews, Zeidner, & Roberts, 2002).

In terms of its scientific and practical significance, EI appears to be an important predictor of positive interpersonal relationships in both childhood and adulthood. For example, it has been reported that children and adults with higher emotional intelligence tend to feel more competent in interpersonal relationships, and also tend to be perceived more positively by others (see e.g. Denham et al., 2003; Lopes et al., 2004). Additionally, the competencies captured by EI appear to have some practical value, as is revealed by correlates with work-related behaviors such as supervisory rating of performance and organizational citizenship behaviors (Côté & Miners, 2006). However, it should be noted that even proponents of EI caution that in many cases these correlates are modest to begin with and tend to shrink even further when one controls for general mental ability and personality traits (Cherniss, 2010). Indeed, while EI appears to be related to teachers' *perceptions* of their students' academic ability, it is not related to actual academic achievement after controlling for differences in general mental ability and personality (e.g. Barchard, 2003; Izard et al., 2001). Thus, while EI may have scientific significance in the sense that it captures some important aspects of socially adaptive behavior not fully represented in existing models of personality or intelligence, its practical value as an important and independent predictor of academic and occupational outcomes remains to be proved.

As in other theories that use the term "intelligence" and take it to designate a distinct construct, here too a number of conceptual and psychometric concerns about EI have been identified. First, as noted above, EI does not appear to be intellectual ability per se (in the traditional sense of a cognitive ability); rather, EI is better conceptualized as an acquired competence or achievement (Jensen, 1998; Locke, 2005). As such, EI likely reflects an achievement that is best thought of as the confluence of basic cognitive abilities, motivations, and personality traits. Indeed a number of contemporary definitions (though perhaps not the most favored ones: see Mayer et al., 2008) do in fact highlight the social competence aspect of EI (cf. also Cherniss, 2010). Consistent with these definitions, it has been shown that variance on EI measures are typically well accounted for by established personality traits and abilities such as verbal abilities (Davies, Stankov, & Roberts, 1998; Roberts, Schulze, & MacCann, 2008). In addition, others have conceptualized EI as a compound personality trait (e.g. Petrides, Pita, & Kokkinaki, 2007) or as introspective skills (Locke, 2005). These latter perspectives would seem to place EI in the domain of personality rather than in that of intelligence.

Second, from a psychometric perspective, EI has been problematic (see Conte, 2005 for a detailed review). For example, if EI is to be conceptualized within the intelligence domain (i.e. as an ability or skill), then it should be amenable to assessment via *power* tests (i.e. tests containing questions that have a specified correct answer) rather than via self-report forms akin to personality inventories (Chamorro-Premuzic & Furnham, 2005). To date, only Mayer and colleagues have successfully developed an EI measure that appears to meet traditional psychometric standards (Mayer, Caruso, & Salovey, 1999). Perhaps most damagingly, despite claims by EI proponents, EI does not seem to enhance our ability to predict important outcomes, such as work and academic performance, above and beyond established constructs such as a $g$, personality traits, and technical knowledge (Landy, 2005).

### 3.4 Ackerman's PPIK theory

Drawing on earlier theories of intelligence—most notably, but not exclusively, that of Cattell (1943) and Hebb (1942)—as well as on a variety of evidence regarding the central role of knowledge in adult intellectual functioning, Ackerman (1996) has proposed an investment theory of intelligence, shown in Figure 7.7, which orchestrates the concomitant influence of abilities, personality, and interests in the acquisition of knowledge and skills. In particular, Ackerman theorizes that abilities and interests develop in tandem, such that ability level determines the probability of success in a particular task domain, and personality and interests determine the motivation for attempting the task. Subsequent to successful attempts at task performance, interest in the task domain increases along with task- and domain-specific knowledge. Conversely, unsuccessful attempts result in a decrement in interest for that domain and they likely limit or hinder any further increase in domain-specific knowledge.

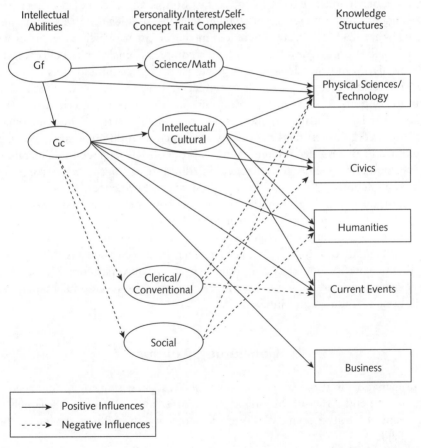

**Figure 7.7** Illustration of the constructs and influences in the PPIK theory. Source: Ackerman, Bowen, Beier, & Kanfer, 2001, p. 799. Copyright American Psychological Association. Reprinted with permission

Thus individual differences in $g$ and other domain-relevant broad abilities will impact the rate, depth, and sophistication of acquired knowledge, while affective factors (such as personality) and conative ones (such as interests) guide the allocation of those cognitive resources toward various opportunities for particular knowledge acquisition.

The theory is called PPIK, which reflects its four central components: intelligence-as-process (reflecting basic cognitive abilities); personality; interests; and intelligence-as-knowledge. In contrast to other recent theories that have struggled with conceptual problems, PPIK conceives of personality and interests as being distinct from intelligence-as-abilities and intelligence-as-knowledge, yet these components function interactively, to yield changes in intellect. Because of the conceptual clarity and strong empirical basis of PPIK, its tenets have been well supported by subsequent research (see Ackerman & Beier, 2005 for a review), and the theory appears to coalesce with other theoretical work in the development of expertise and talent (e.g. Lubinski & Benbow, 2000; Simonton, 1999). For example, PPIK is consistent with research on the development of expertise, which shows domain-specific deliberate practice to be essential (Ericsson, Krampe, & Tesch-Römer, 1993). PPIK suggests that differences in domain-relevant abilities, interests, and affective tendencies are likely to create differences in the extent to which experiences within a domain afford positive reinforcement. In a complex domain, initial efforts to learn, made by high-$g$ individuals, are more likely to be successful and thus evaluated as positive, interesting, and pleasurable experiences. This will bolster interest and motivation to continue to seek out opportunities for further skill acquisition within that domain; that is, to engage in, and sustain, deliberate practice. Thus differences in knowledge, skill, interest, and personality associated with differences in general abilities ultimately give rise to differences in the propensity to engage in deliberate practice, which in turn give rise to differences in adult intellect over the life span (see also Lubinski & Benbow, 2000 for similar arguments and evidence).

In addition to highlighting the importance of intelligence-as-knowledge as a determinant of adult intellectual performance, PPIK places heavy emphasis on understanding the coordination of cognitive, motivational, and social processes that give rise to differentiated knowledge structures. That is, theories such as PPIK provide a useful framework for understanding how a common, universal core of basic psychological characteristics function cross-culturally to give rise to culturally differentiated and personally unique adult intellects.

# 4   Concluding Comments

Our primary goal in this chapter was to provide readers with a cogent understanding of the nature and structure of intelligence. To do so, our chapter has largely been retrospective up to this point. We conclude with some thoughts regarding the future of this field.

We feel it is safe to conclude that a fairly comprehensive picture of the psychometric structure of cognitive abilities has been established. A century's worth of psychometric investigation appears to have converged on a consensus structure.

Though not insignificant from a scientific perspective, debate regarding the remaining distinctions among models is likely to be perceived by those outside the field largely as "narcissisms of subtle difference" (Lubinski, 2000, p. 7). Thus, we believe that the most productive and important work in this area will involve the investigation of issues other than the psychometric structure of cognitive abilities. Three issues appear to be of particular importance and poised for significant progress.

The first one involves the consideration of the scientific significance of lower-order dimensions of human abilities (those beyond $g$) and how best to appraise their scientific worth (see Lubinski, 2000 for an excellent discussion on this theme). There is no question that individual differences in $g$ are important. Yet, as discussed above, there remains some doubt about the scientific significance of specific abilities, and this is due to a number of methodological considerations. Recent work appears to confirm the position that specific abilities are in fact of importance (see Park et al., 2008). However, we caution against what might be termed the "horse race" mentality occasionally seen in the past. Indeed, the value of specific abilities or skills can be demonstrated without futile attempts to discredit $g$. Rather, as was noted by Carroll (1993), the scientific significance of various abilities comes in degrees: "[A]bilities are analogous to elements in the periodic table: Some, like fluid intelligence ['$g$'], are obviously as important as carbon or oxygen; others are more like rare earth elements [...]" (p. 689).

The second issue involves the attempt to further develop the vertical and horizontal aspects of the $g$ nexus (Jensen, 1998; Lubinski, 2000). The vertical line of inquiry refers to the effort to uncover more fundamental (that is, biological and neurological) bases for $g$, and to develop more ultimate (that is, evolutionary) explanations. A recent special issue of *Intelligence* (Deary, 2009) highlighted the exciting progress of this area of work. The horizontal aspect refers to efforts to better understand the practical significance of $g$ via the breadth of its associations with an array of social–psychological and health-related variables. The potential value and importance of this line of investigation have recently been realized with the emergence of the field of cognitive epidemiology (Deary, 2009; Gottfredson & Deary, 2004).

Third, we expect that much progress will be made in the next few decades in two areas; (1) the conceptualization of developed intellect (i.e. acquired knowledge and skills), and (2) the development of "meta-theories" that account for the interplay between the three broad domains of individual differences (intelligence, personality, and conative factors) on the one hand, and environmental affordances and demands in the development of that intellect on the other. These more comprehensive models are likely not only to provide a more complete understanding of the nature and development of "intelligence," but also to help reintegrate the various domains of differential psychology. Among these are three important examples we believe to be the most well-validated and theoretically coherent (and hence, hopefully, the most influential): Snow's (2002) final work regarding a comprehensive theory of aptitude, Ackerman's (1996) PPIK theory, and Chamorro-Premuzic and Furnham's (2005) emerging model of intellectual competence.

However, in this endeavor, we caution against losing touch with our greatest strength—psychometrics. In the same breath in which he cautioned against assuming a general intelligence factor on the basis of the positive manifold alone, Horn (1968) also noted that "this does not mean that we should move to the other extreme of separately measuring every aspect of human intellectual ability [...] nor does it mean that ability distinctions defined purely, or mainly, on the basis of logic alone [...] should constitute a basis for applied use or theoretical formulation" (p. 256). We concur with Horn's sentiment; scientific innovation is to be encouraged, but efforts to fashion new models of developed intellect must eventually stand up to psychometric scrutiny. Although new ideas should be given adequate time to demonstrate their worth, it has been noted that some concepts such as Gardner's multiple intelligences have continuously failed the criterion of scientific significance (Jensen, 1998; Visser, Ashton, & Vernon, 2006). By the same token, new names need not be given to existing constructs, and existing terms should not be applied to different concepts. For example, renaming domain-specific knowledge and skills is unlikely to be scientifically productive, as it simply serves to muddy the waters. The recent trend to recast various domain-specific skills as "intelligences" is one example of where such behavior has led to much unnecessary and unwarranted controversy.

Finally, we would be remiss in our duty to write a chapter on the nature of intelligence if we did not acknowledge that scientific research on intelligence has often met with fierce public opposition and criticism. Even within the scientific community, there have occasionally been false claims and criticisms based on misconstrued or misunderstood evidence. Part of the reason for this was noted by Arthur Jensen in his 1999 Galton Lecture. In that lecture he discussed the link in the public's mind between eugenics and the horrific acts committed in its name during the Second World War, which subsequently "contributed to making research on intelligence [...] stigmatized to a degree not seen for scientific research on other natural phenomena, save perhaps for evolution as perceived by biblical fundamentalists" (quoted in Holden, 1999). A second reason, we believe, stems from the recognition of the great import that intelligence has for individuals and society. Although the intensity and longevity of the debate surrounding the nature and importance of intelligence might be evidence that others share our passion, it seems that this energy is often driven more by dogmatic opinions and political criticism than by a genuine enthusiasm for greater understanding. This wastes valuable resources, time, and energy. As we noted above, few of the contemporary theories of intelligence are truly incompatible. Yet, occasionally, a new model is presented as a radical new alternative that contradicts the status quo. While such approaches may feed the popular press's appetite for supposed controversy, they are unlikely to be productive from a scientific perspective. Thus we call upon the scientific community to embrace what might be called "passionate dispassion." That is, one should seek the truth with passion, but one must remain dispassionate about what that truth might be.

## Acknowledgments

This work was supported by the Social Sciences and Humanities Research Council of Canada.

## Note

1  It should be noted that different authors use the terms "ability" and "aptitudes" differently. Carroll (1993) for example uses the term "ability" in a generic sense, simply to refer to individual differences in behavioral capacities, and uses the term "aptitude" for what we define as "ability." In contrast, Snow (2002) seems to define "aptitude" very broadly, noting that it refers to a person's readiness to perform in a given domain, and he explicitly includes personality and motivation as components of these developed skills. In fact, Snow explicitly discusses the role of "abilities" in the development of aptitudes, clearly indicating that he conceives of abilities as domain-independent capacities to learn. Similarly, Fleishman (1967) uses the term "ability" as we have done in this chapter; and this use corresponds to Carroll's use of the term "aptitude." Jensen (1998) also seems to favor the use of the term "ability" as we have used it here. The use of the same term to refer to different things, and the use of different terms to refer to the same thing, have no doubt contributed to some of the apparent confusion in this literature. We do not wish to contribute any further to it; in consequence we are explicit about our use of the term "ability" in this chapter.

## References

Ackerman, P. L. (1996). A theory of adult intellectual development: Process, personality, interests, and knowledge. *Intelligence, 22,* 227–257.

Ackerman, P. L., & Beier, M. E. (2005). Knowledge and intelligence. In O. Wilhelm & R. W. Engle (Eds.), *Handbook of understanding and measuring intelligence* (pp. 125–139). Thousand Oaks, CA: Sage.

Ackerman, P. L., Bowen, K. R., Beier, M., & Kanfer, R. (2001). Determinants of individual differences and gender differences in knowledge. *Journal of Educational Psychology, 93,* 797–825.

Alliger, G. M. (1988). Do zero correlations really exist among measures of different intellectual abilities? *Educational and Psychological Measurement, 48,* 275–280.

Allix, N. M. (2000). The theory of multiple intelligences: A case of missing cognitive matter. *Australian Journal of Education, 44,* 272–288.

Anstey, K. J., Low, L-F., Christensen, H., & Sachdev, P. (2009). Level of cognitive performance as a correlate and predictor of health behaviors that protect against cognitive decline in late life: The path through life study. *Intelligence, 37,* 600–606.

Barchard, K. A. (2003). Does emotional intelligence assist in the prediction of academic success? *Educational and Psychological Measurement, 63,* 840–858.

Batty, G. D., Deary, I. J., & Gottfredson, L. (2007). Premorbid (early life) IQ and later mortality risk: Systematic review. *Annals of Epidemiology, 17,* 278–288.

Benbow, C. P. (1992). Academic achievement in mathematics and science of students between ages 13 and 23: Are there differences among students in the top one percent of mathematical ability? *Journal of Educational Psychology, 84,* 51–61.

Berry, J. W. (1974). Radical cultural relativism and the concept of intelligence. In J. W. Berry & P. R. Dasen (Eds.), *Culture and cognition: Readings in cross-cultural psychology* (pp. 225–229). London: Methuen.

Brand, C. (1987). The importance of general intelligence. In S. Modgil & C. Modgil (Eds.), *Arthur Jensen: Consensus and controversy* (pp. 251–265). New York: Falmer Press.

Brody, N. (2003). Construct validation of the Sternberg Triarchic Abilities Test (STAT): Comment and reanalysis. *Intelligence, 31,* 319–329.

Burt, C. (1949). The structure of the mind: A review of the results of factor analysis. *British Journal of Educational Psychology, 19,* 176–199.

Carroll, J. B. (1993). *Human cognitive abilities: A survey of factor-analytic studies.* New York: Cambridge University Press.

Cattell, R. B. (1943). The measurement of adult intelligence. *Psychological Bulletin, 40,* 153–193.

Chamorro-Premuzic, T., & Furnham, A. (2005). *Personality and intellectual competence.* Mahwah, NJ: Lawrence Erlbaum Associates.

Cherniss, C. (2010). Emotional intelligence: Towards clarification of a concept. *Industrial and Organizational Psychology: Perspectives on Science and Practice, 3,* 110–126.

Conte, J. M. (2005). A review and critique of emotional intelligence measures. *Journal of Organizational Behavior, 26,* 433–440.

Côté, S., & Miners, C. T. H. (2006). Emotional intelligence, cognitive intelligence, and job performance. *Administrative Science Quarterly, 51,* 1–28.

Darwin, C. (1958). *The origin of species by means of natural selection or the preservation of the favoured races in the struggle for life* [1859]. New York: Penguin Books.

Davies, M., Stankov, L., & Roberts, R. (1998). Emotional intelligence: In search of an elusive construct. *Journal of Personality and Social Psychology, 75,* 989–1015.

Deary, I. (Ed.) (2009). Intelligence, health and death: The emerging field of cognitive epidemiology. *Intelligence, 37*(6) [Special Issue].

Deary, I. J., Whalley, L. J., & Starr, J. M. (2009). *A lifetime of intelligence: Follow-up studies of the Scottish mental surveys of 1932 and 1947.* Washington, DC: American Psychological Association.

Denham, S. A., Blair, K. A., DeMulder, E., Levitas, J., Sawyer, K., & Auerbach-Major, S. (2003). Preschool emotional competence: Pathway to social competence. *Child Development, 74,* 238–256.

El Koussy, A. A. H. (1935). Visual perception of space. *British Journal of Psychology Monograph Supplement, 7,* No. 20.

Eysenck, H. J., & Barrett, P. (1985). Psychophysiology and the measurement of intelligence. In C. R. Reynolds & P. C. Wilson (Eds.), *Methodological and statistical advances in the study of individual differences* (pp. 1–49). New York: Plenum Press.

Ericsson, K. A., Krampe, R. T., & Tesch-Römer, C. (1993). The role of deliberate practice in the acquisition of expert performance. *Psychological Review, 100,* 309–324.

Fleishman, E. A. (1967). Development of a behavior taxonomy for describing human tasks: A correlational–experimental approach. *Journal of Applied Psychology, 51,* 1–10.

Galton, F. (2006). *Hereditary genius: An enquiry into its laws and consequences* [1869]. Amherst, NY: Prometheus Books.

Galton, F. (1907). *Inquiries into human faculty and its development.* London: J. M. Dent & Co.

Gardner, H. (1983). *Frames of mind.* New York: Basic Books.

Gardner, H. (2006). *Multiple Intelligences: New horizons.* New York: Basic Books.

Garnett, J. C. M. (1919). General ability, cleverness and purpose. *British Journal of Psychology, 9,* 345–366.

Gottfredson, L. (1997a). Editorial: Mainstream science on intelligence: An editorial with 52 signatories, history, and bibliography. *Intelligence, 24,* 13–23.

Gottfredson, L. (1997b). Why *g* matters: The complexity of everyday life. *Intelligence, 24,* 79–132.

Gottfredson, L. (Ed.) (1997c). Intelligence and social policy. *Intelligence, 24*(1) [Special Issue].

Gottfredson, L. (2003). Dissecting practical intelligence theory: Its claims and evidence. *Intelligence, 31,* 343–397.

Gottfredson, L. (2004). Intelligence: Is it the epidemiologists' elusive "fundamental cause" of social class inequalities in health? *Journal of Personality and Social Psychology*, *86*, 174–199.

Gottfredson, L. (2009). Logical fallacies used to dismiss the evidence on intelligence testing. In R. Phelps (Ed.), *Correcting fallacies about educational and psychological testing* (pp. 11–65). Washington, DC: American Psychological Association.

Gottfredson, L., & Deary, I. J. (2004). *Intelligence* predicts health and longevity: But why? *Current Directions in Psychological Science*, *13*, 1–4.

Gould, S. J. (1996). *The mismeasure of man*. New York: Norton.

Guilford, J. P. (1954). *Psychometric methods* (2nd ed.). New York: McGraw-Hill,

Guilford, J. P. (1967). *The nature of human intelligence*. New York: McGraw-Hill.

Gustafsson, J.-E. (1988). Hierarchical models of individual differences in cognitive abilities. In R. J. Sternberg (Ed.), *Advances in the psychology of human intelligence* (Vol. 4, pp. 35–71). Hillsdale, NJ: Lawrence Erlbaum Associates.

Gustafsson, J.-E., & Snow, R. E. (1997). Ability profiles. In R. F. Dillion's (Ed.), *Handbook on Testing* (pp. 107–135). Westport, CT: Greenwood Press.

Guttman, L. (1965). A faceted definition of intelligence. In R. Eiferman (Ed.), *Studies in psychology, scripta heirosolymitana* (Vol. 14, pp. 166–181). Jerusalem: The Hebrew University.

Haier, R. J. (2009). Neuro-intelligence, neuro-metrics and the next phase of brain imaging studies. *Intelligence*, *37*, 121–123.

Hebb, D. O. (1942). The effect of early and late brain injury upon test scores and the nature of normal adult intelligence. *Proceedings of the American Philosophical Society*, *85*, 275–292.

Holden, C. (1999, November 12). The IQ taboo. *Science*, *286*, 1285.

Horn, J. L. (1968). Organization of abilities and the development of intelligence. *Psychological Review*, *75*, 242–259.

Horn, J. L., & Knapp, J. R. (1973). On the subjective character of the empirical base of Guilford's structure-of-intellect model. *Psychological Bulletin*, *80*, 33–43.

Horn, J. L., & Noll, J. (1997). Human cognitive capabilities: Gf-Gc theory. In D. P. Flanagan, J. L. Genshaft, & P. L. Harrison's (Eds.), *Contemporary intellectual assessment: Theories, tests, and issues* (pp. 53–90). New York: Guilford Press.

Izard, C. E, Fine, S., Schultz, D., Mostow, A. J., Ackerman, B., & Youngstrom, E. (2001). Emotion knowledge as a predictor of social behavior and academic competence in children at risk. *Psychological Sciences*, *12*, 18–23.

Jensen, A. R. (1985). The nature of the black–white difference on various psychometric tests: Spearman's hypothesis. *Behavioral and Brain Sciences*, *8*, 193–219.

Jensen, A. R. (1986). *g*: Artifact or reality? *Journal of Vocational Behavior*, *29*, 301–331.

Jensen, A. R. (1998). *The g factor: The science of mental ability*. Westport, CT: Praeger.

Jensen, A. R., & Reynolds, C. R. (1982). Race, social class and ability patterns on the WISC–R. *Personality and Individual Differences*, *3*, 423–438.

Jensen, A. R., & Weng, L.-J. (1994). What is a good *g*? *Intelligence*, *18*, 231–258.

Johnson, W., & Bouchard, T. J. (2005). The structure of human intelligence: It is verbal, perceptual and image rotation, not fluid and crystallized. *Intelligence*, *33*, 393–416.

Kline, P. (1998). *The new psychometrics: Science, psychology and measurement*. London: Routledge.

Kuncel, N. R., & Hezlett, S. A. (2007). Standardized tests predict graduate students' success. *Science*, *315*, 1080–1081.

Kuncel, N. R., & Sackett, P. R. (2007). Selective citation mars conclusions about test validity and predictive bias. *American Psychologist*, *62*, 145–146.

Kuncel, N. R., Hezlett, S. A., & Ones, D. S. (2004). Academic performance, career potential, creativity, and job performance: Can one construct predict them all? *Journal of Personality and Social Psychology, 86,* 148–161.

Locke, E. A. (2005). Why emotional intelligence is an invalid concept. *Journal of Organizational Behavior, 26,* 425–431.

Lopes, P. N., Brackett, M. A., Nezlek, J. B., Schutz, A., Sellin, I., & Salovey, P. (2004). Emotional intelligence and social interaction. *Personality and Social Psychology Bulletin, 30,* 1018–1034.

Lubinski, D. (2000). Scientific and social significance of assessing individual differences: "Sinking shafts at a few critical points." *Annual Review of Psychology, 51,* 405–444.

Lubinski, D. (Ed.) (2004). Cognitive abilities: 100 years after Spearman's (1904) "'General intelligence,' objectively determined and measured." *Journal of Personality and Social Psychology, 86*(1), 96–199 [Special Section].

Lubinski, D., & Benbow, C. P. (2000). States of excellence. *American Psychologist, 55,* 137–150.

Lubinski, D., & Dawis, R. V. (1992). Aptitudes, skills, and proficiencies. In M. D. Dunnette & L. Hough (Eds.), *Handbook of industrial and organizational psychology* (Vol. 2, pp. 1–59). Palo Alto, CA: Consulting Psychologists Press.

Lynn, R., Harvey, J., & Nyborg, H. (2009). Average intelligence predicts atheism rates across 137 nations. *Intelligence, 37,* 11–15.

Matthews, G., Zeidner, M., & Roberts, R. D. (2002). *Emotional intelligence: Science and myth.* Cambridge, MA: MIT Press.

Mayer, J. D., Caruso, D. R., & Salovey, P. (1999). Emotional intelligence meets traditional standards for an intelligence. *Intelligence, 27*(4), 267–298.

Mayer, J. D., Roberts, R. D., & Barsade, S. G. (2008). Human abilities: Emotional intelligence. *Annual Review of Psychology, 59,* 507–536.

McGrew, K. S. (1997). Analysis of the major intelligence batteries according to a proposed comprehensive Gf-Gc framework. In D. P. Flanagan, J. L. Genshaft, & P. Harrison (Eds.), *Contemporary intelligence assessment: Theories, tests, and issues* (pp. 151–179). New York: Guilford Press.

McGrew, K. S. (2009). CHC theory and the human cognitive abilities project: Standing on the shoulders of the giants of psychometric intelligence research. *Intelligence, 37,* 1–10.

Meehl, P. E. (1991). Four queries about factor reality. *History and Philosophy of Psychology Bulletin, 3,* 16–18.

Messick, S. (1992). Multiple intelligences or multilevel intelligence? Selective emphasis on distinctive properties of hierarchy: On Gardner's *Frames of mind* and Sternberg's *Beyond IQ* in the context of theory and research on the structure of human abilities. *Psychological Inquiry, 3,* 365–384.

Neisser, U. (1976). General, academic, and artificial intelligence. In L. Resnick (Ed.), *Human intelligence: Perspectives on its theory and measurement* (pp. 179–189). Norwood, NJ: Ablex.

Nyborg, H. (2009). The intelligence–religiosity nexus: A representative study of white adolescent Americans. *Intelligence, 37,* 81–93.

Park, G., Lubinski, D., & Benbow, C.P. (2008). Ability differences among people who have commensurate degrees matter for scientific creativity. *Psychological Science, 19,* 957–961.

Petrides, K. V., Pita, R., & Kokkinaki, F. (2007). The location of trait emotional intelligence in personality factor space. *British Journal of Psychology, 98,* 273–289.

Prediger, D. J. (1989). Ability differences across occupations: More than *g. Journal of Vocational Behavior, 34,* 1–27.

Reed, T. E., & Jensen, A. R. (1993). Choice reaction time and visual pathway nerve conduction velocity both correlate with intelligence but appear not to correlate with each other: Implications for information processing. *Intelligence, 17*, 191–203.

Reeve, C. L. (2004). Differential ability antecedents of general and specific dimensions of declarative knowledge: More than *g*. *Intelligence, 32*, 621–652.

Reeve, C. L., & Blacksmith, N. (2009). Equivalency and reliability of vectors of *g*-loadings across different methods of estimation and sample sizes. *Personality and Individual Differences, 47*, 968–972.

Reeve, C. L., & Charles, J. E. (2008). Survey of opinions on the primacy of *g* and social consequences of ability testing: A comparison of expert and non-expert views. *Intelligence, 36*, 681–688.

Roberts, R. D., Schulze, R., & MacCann, C. (2008). The measurement of emotional intelligence: a decade of progress? In G. Boyle, G. Matthews, & D. Saklofske (Eds.), *The SAGE handbook of personality theory and assessment: Personality measurement and testing* (Vol. 2, pp. 461–482). Thousand Oaks, CA: Sage.

Rushton, J. P., & Ankney, C. D. (2009). Whole-brain size and general mental ability: A review. *International Journal of Neuroscience, 119*, 691–731.

Salgado, J. F., Anderson, N., Moscoso, S., Bertua, C., & De Fruyt, F. (2003). International validity generalization of GMA and cognitive abilities: A European community meta-analysis. *Personnel Psychology, 56*, 573–605.

Schmidt, F. L., & Hunter, J. E. (1998). The validity and utility of selection methods in personnel psychology: Practical and theoretical implications of 85 years of research findings. *Psychological Bulletin, 124*, 262–274.

Simonton, D. K. (1999). Talent and its development: An emergenic and epigenetic model. *Psychological Review, 106*, 435–457.

Snow, R. E. (2002). *Remaking the concept of aptitude: Extending the legacy of Richard E. Snow* (work completed by L. Corno, L. J. Cronbach, H. Kupermintz, D. F. Lohman, E. B. Mandinach, A. W. Porteus, & J. E. Talbert). Mahwah, NJ: Lawrence Erlbaum Associates.

Snow, R. E., Kyllonen, P. C., & Marshalek, B. (1984). The typography of ability and learning correlations. In R. J. Sternberg (Ed.), *Advances in the psychology of human intelligence* (Vol. 2, pp. 47–103). Hillsdale, NJ: Lawrence Erlbaum.

Snyderman, M., & Rothman, S. (1987). Survey of expert opinion on intelligence and aptitude testing. *American Psychologist, 42*, 137–144.

Spearman, C. (1904). "General intelligence," objectively determined and measured. *American Journal of Psychology, 15*, 201–292.

Spearman, C. (1927). *The abilities of man: Their nature and measurement*. New York: Macmillan.

Spearman, C. (1939). Thurstone's work reworked. *Journal of Educational Psychology, 30*, 1–16.

Sternberg, R.J. (1985). *Beyond IQ: A triarchic theory of human intelligence*. New York: Cambridge University Press.

Sternberg, R. J., & Detterman, D. K. (1986). *What is intelligence?* Norwood, NJ: Ablex.

Sternberg, R. J., & Grigorenko, E. L. (2006). Cultural intelligence and successful intelligence. *Group and Organization Management, 31*, 27–39.

Sternberg, R. J., & Hedlund, J. (2002). Practical intelligence, *g*, and work psychology. *Human Performance 15*, 143–160.

Sternberg, R. J., & O'Hara, L. A. (2000). Intelligence and creativity. In R. J. Sternberg (Ed.), *Handbook of intelligence* (pp. 609–628). New York: Cambridge University Press.

Süß, H. M., & Beauducel, A. (2005). Faceted models of intelligence. In O. Wilhelm & R. W. Engle (Eds.), *Handbook of understanding and measuring intelligence* (pp. 313–332). Thousand Oaks, CA: Sage.

Thorndike, R. L. (1987). Stability of factor loadings. *Personality and Individual Differences, 8*, 585–586.

Thorndike, R. L. (1991). Is there any future for intelligence? In R. E. Snow & D. E. Wiley (Eds.), *Improving inquiry in social science* (pp. 285–303). Hillsdale, NJ: Lawrence Erlbaum Associates.

Thurstone, L. L. (1938). Primary mental abilities. *Psychometric Monographs*, No. 1.

Thurstone, L. L. (1947). *Multiple factor analysis: A development and expansion of* The Vectors of the Mind. Chicago: University of Chicago Press.

Vasquez, M., & Jones, J. M. (2006). Increasing the number of psychologists of color: Public policy issues for affirmative diversity. *American Psychologist, 61*, 132–142.

Vernon, P. E. (1950). *The structure of human abilities.* London: Methuen.

Vernon, P. E. (1961). *The structure of human abilities* (2nd ed.). London: Methuen.

Visser, B. A., Ashton, M. C., & Vernon, P. A. (2006). Beyond g: Putting multiple intelligences theory to the test. *Intelligence, 34*, 487–502.

Wai, J., Lubinski, D., & Benbow, C. P. (2009). Spatial ability for STEM domains: Aligning over 50 years of cumulative psychological knowledge solidifies its importance. *Journal of Educational Psychology, 101*, 817–835.

Waterhouse, L. (2006). Multiple intelligences, the Mozart effect, and emotional intelligence: A critical review. *Educational Psychologist, 41*, 207–225.

# 8

# Re-Visiting Intelligence–
# Personality Associations
## *Vindicating Intellectual Investment*
## Sophie von Stumm, Tomas Chamorro-Premuzic, and Phillip L. Ackerman

Intelligence and personality share many common features other than their seminal role in individual differences research. First, they both refer to cognitive, affective, and behavioral differences that are quantifiable through the use of standardized psychometric instruments (Funder, 2001). Second, they are both genetically determined, albeit to different degrees (e.g. Spinath & Johnson, 2011: this volume). Third, both constructs show great temporal stability, manifested as stable patterns of behavior throughout the life span (e.g. Caspi, 2000; Deary, Whalley, Lemmon, Crawford, & Starr, 2000). Fourth, intelligence and personality predict individual differences in a wide range of outcomes, including educational and occupational performance, health, and longevity (Barrick & Mount, 1991; Calvin, Batty, & Deary, 2011: this volume; Kern & Friedman, 2011: this volume; Poropat, 2009).

Notwithstanding these similarities, intelligence and personality differ in multiple aspects. First, intelligence is usually measured in terms of maximal performance or of what an individual *can* do, whereas personality measures are concerned with general tendencies of behavior or with what an individual *will typically* do (Cronbach, 1949; Fiske & Butler, 1963; Wallace, 1966)—in fact personality can be defined as the "tendency to do x." In line with this disparity, psychometric assessment tools differ in their test-completion instructions: ability tests ask us to do our best, but non-ability tests are based on the request for candid, truthful responses (Zeidner & Matthews, 2000). Second, intelligence is unidirectional, ranging from "little of" to "much of," whereas most personality traits are bidirectional, with opposing poles of extreme dispositions (Zeidner & Matthews, 2000). Third, intelligence and personality are traditionally validated by using different sets of criteria; that is, personality measures

*The Wiley-Blackwell Handbook of Individual Differences*, First Edition.
Edited by Tomas Chamorro-Premuzic, Sophie von Stumm, and Adrian Furnham.
© 2011 Blackwell Publishing Ltd. Published 2011 by Blackwell Publishing Ltd.

are employed to predict clinical, interpersonal, and intra-personal outcomes, whereas intelligence tests are applied to forecast individual differences in achievement, such as educational and occupational performance (and particularly school success). Fourth, intelligence and personality have enjoyed uneven degrees of attention in individual differences research. Despite the fact that both constructs are frequently referred to as the core pillars of individual differences research (e.g. Chamorro-Premuzic & Furnham, 2006), it is intelligence that has been famously dubbed "one of the most central phenomena in all of behavioral science, with broad explanatory powers" (Jensen, 1998, p. xii). Indeed, there is general agreement amongst mainstream individual differences researchers (and such agreement is rare in any scientific discipline) on how to measure intelligence and on its psychometric structure, its genetic and neurological etiology, and its role in many real-life outcomes (e.g. Gottfredson, 1994; Neisser et al., 1996). Personality, in contrast, continues to face problems that intelligence has long overcome. For example, recent research often emphasized an alleged convergence of academics on the five-factor approach as an adequate taxonomy of personality. Yet the current volume clearly illustrates the variety of theoretical conceptualizations of personality (e.g. Smillie, Avery, & Laxton, 2011, this volume; Strobel & Brocke, 2011: this volume) and its psychometric structure (e.g. Ferguson, Chamorro-Premuzic, Pickering, & Weiss, 2011: this volume; Rushton & Irwing, 2011: this volume). Furthermore, personality research often relies on self-report measures, which may be of meager psychometric quality and only tap into the *explicit* (accessible by introspection) personality, but not into the *implicit* (inaccessible by introspection) personality (James, 1998).[1] These and other arguments on personality assessment continue to obstruct progress on research into the etiology and consequences of personality traits.

The aforementioned differences and similarities between personality and intelligence have led individual differences researchers to adopt, albeit not explicitly, one of three theoretical perspectives on intelligence–personality associations (IPA; Figure 8.1). A first, traditional approach emphasizes the conceptual and empirical independence of both constructs. That is, intelligence and personality are believed to have no meaningful relationship and are best studied by distinctive methods, in separate contexts, and following different research agendas. A second perspective assumes an association at the measurement level, whereby personality traits affect performance on intelligence *tests*, for example leading to individual differences in response accuracy and speed (or the trade-off between them). This approach has been largely supported by experimental studies that manipulate test-takers' mental and physical status as well as the conditions of test administration. Finally, a third perspective postulates a developmental relationship between personality and intelligence, such that personality traits influence *how, when,* and *where* individuals apply and invest their cognitive ability, and hence they shape the maturity and the life-course development of the intellect. We believe that this third approach constitutes the most promising avenue for integrating achievement-related individual differences in both personality and intelligence. Such an integrative approach is essential to advance our understanding of the role of individual differences in real-life outcomes (e.g. educational and occupational achievement, status attainment, health, and longevity), and also of the nature of personality and intelligence.

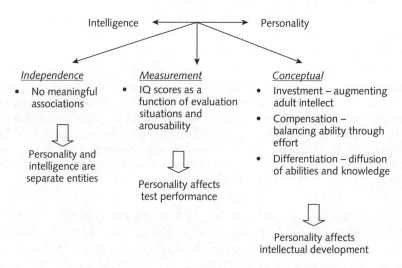

**Figure 8.1** Theoretical perspectives on IPA

In this chapter we will provide an up-to-date review of the literature on each of the above-mentioned perspectives on the IPA. Subsequently we will highlight some of the obstacles that currently stand in the way of progress for research on the IPA, and we will give some ideas on how to overcome them.

# 1 Theoretical Perspectives

## 1.1 Independence

Traditionally, intelligence and personality have been treated as separate entities and were studied independently of each other. This autonomy is often traced back to Webb's (1915) doctoral thesis and monograph, entitled "Character and intelligence." Webb asked 10 advanced students to rate 194 male teacher trainees on 45 mental abilities and personality traits; each trainee was rated by two raters over a college term of approximately 10 weeks. Influenced by Spearman's (1904) notion of general intelligence (*g*), Webb speculated that there should be an analogous general factor of personality. Therefore Webb extracted Spearman's *g* factor of intelligence from positively interrelated ratings of trainees' intellectual qualities, and, subsequently, searched for a second general factor to emerge from the ratings of "non-intellective" attributes, after partialing out the variance due to *g* (Deary, 1996). Webb concluded that "a second factor, of wide generality, exists; and that this factor is prominent on the 'character' side of mental activity (as distinguished from the purely intellective side)" (1915, p. 58). Accordingly, there should be a character side as well as an intellective one to mental activity. Closely mimicking Webb's study, Alexander (1935) extracted an independent dimension in addition to *g* and to a verbal ability factor, which he referred to as practical facility in performance contexts. Both Webb and Alexander forced their factor solutions to be mathematically orthogonal, but the nomological independence of extracted factors is warranted neither by their evidence nor by their conclusions. Thus Thorndike stated:

> With few or no exceptions superiority in one desirable trait implies superiority in any other. The various sorts of intelligence [...] are positively related; intelligence in general is correlated with virtue and goodwill toward men; both are correlated with skill in control of hand, eye, voice, etc.; all these are correlated with health, poise, sanity, and sensitiveness to beauty. Some of these intercorrelations are low [...] but they are rarely zero or negative. There is, I think, no demonstrated case of a negative correlation in all the work so far done. (Thorndike, 1940, pp. 273–274)

Such early speculations on the breadth of factors that are embedded in Spearman's (1904) "positive manifold" find contemporary support in a growing body of evidence for a general fitness factor as well as for the "discovery" of a general personality factor (e.g. Arden, Gottfredson, & Miller, 2009; Deary, 2008; Miller, 2000; Rushton & Irwing, 2011: this volume). However, previous reports of non-significant zero-order correlations between intelligence and personality initially supported the assumption of the constructs' independence (e.g. Eysenck, 1971; Holland, Dollinger, Holland, & MacDonald, 1995; Zeidner, 1995).

Low correlations between personality and intelligence and their distinctive conceptual features have therefore discouraged most researchers from studying IPA, but without real justification. For one, low correlations are nonetheless evident correlations; in line with this, the psychometric approach has repeatedly shown that cognitive abilities and personality traits are modestly but consistently associated (e.g. Ackerman & Heggestad, 1997; Judge, Jackson, Shaw, Scott, & Rich, 2007; Poropat, 2009). For the other, a certain amount of heterogeneity amongst psychometric constructs does not necessarily recommend studying both as independent entities, but rather the opposite is advisable. That is, studying personality and intelligence in conjunction will transfer ideas and research findings from one area of interest to the other, and thereby enhance the understanding of both domains.

Measures of intelligence have been shown to effectively predict individual differences in academic performance for children and adolescents, but personality measures seem to be less meaningful (Chamorro-Premuzic & Furnham, 2006). Mandatory educational settings represent a relatively strong situational press, which undermines the effects of personality on academically relevant behaviors (Ackerman, in press), and their influence is most likely at the margins—that is, at extremes of personality traits or temperament difficulties (e.g. Colom, Escorial, Shih, & Privado, 2007). However, the situational press is somewhat diminished when people reach post-secondary education, because here the emphasis has shifted from basic demonstrations of ability to advanced task execution and performance. Therefore individual differences in personality can be expected to play a larger role in determining outcomes such as level of educational qualification, persistence, and work performance or attendance (Chamorro-Premuzic & Furnham, 2010). In this way one can expect a seesaw of importance between the influence of ability and non-ability factors: when the situation is strong (e.g. in a high-stakes task), intellectual abilities will have more importance, but when the situation is weak (e.g. in a continuous task demand), personality and other individual traits (e.g. interests, values) will gain in weight (Ackerman, in press). High intelligence does not directly lead one to work long hours at a job, seek additional training, or strive for competitive success in business, but rather one's values, interests, and personality do so. However, intellectual abilities will partly determine the success of individuals who engage in any of those behaviors.

## 1.2 Associations at the measurement level

Furnham, Forde, and Cotter (1998, p. 187) noted that, "under certain circumstances, personality and intelligence scores are logically and significantly related. Much depends upon the type of test, specifically how long it is and whether it is timed, and on the test-taking attitude of the test-taker." Indeed, IPAs at the measurement level address how personality may affect intelligence test performance rather than ability per se, and they focus mostly on the trait dimensions of extraversion and neuroticism, as well as on closely related trait scales (e.g. anxiety). In the following pages, the theoretical rationales and empirical evidence for these associations will be reviewed.

*1.2.1 Extraversion/introversion* Within a psychobiological model of personality, Eysenck (1957, 1967, 1970; Eysenck & Eysenck, 1985) hypothesized that variability in the extraversion/introversion dimension is rooted in the differential reactivity of the ascending reticular activating system. That is, extraverts have low cortical arousability and show small phasic change responses to cortical activity stimulation, whereas introverts have high levels or arousal and arousability (see Strobel & Brocke, 2011: this volume for further details). This understanding of individual differences in personality, together with the Yerksen–Dodson law, which dictates that performance is best at intermediate levels of arousal (Yerkes & Dodson, 1908), has led to the notion that intelligence test scores are a function of extraversion and situational arousal level (Humphreys & Revelle, 1984). Eysenck (1967) also hypothesized that extraverts differed from introverts in their test-taking style: the former would trade off accuracy for speed to increase excitement and arousal, but the latter would work at a slower rate, increasing accuracy and avoiding over-stimulation. Bates and Rock (2004) concluded that such different test-taking styles would have a zero net effect on the total score. Indeed, the current empirical evidence, which is admittedly rather sparse, does not confirm a meaningful speed–accuracy trade-off among extraverts and introverts (e.g. Malhotra, Malhotra, & Jerath, 1989; Sočan & Bucik, 1998).

Revelle, Amaral, and Turriff (1976) tested extraverts' and introverts' verbal intelligence under three differently stressful test-taking conditions, in a sample of 101 students. In the first condition, participants were allowed to take as much time as they wished to complete the verbal ability test; in the second condition, a strict time limit was imposed and participants were administered placebo caffeine pills; in the third condition, test completion was again strictly timed, and actual caffeine was administered. Introverts' performance dropped drastically from the relaxed condition to those of time pressure and caffeine, whereas extraverts' performance remained stable in the relaxed and time-pressured condition, but markedly peaked in the caffeine consumption setting. Ambiverts, who are at the mid-point of the extraversion/introversion dimension, showed the smallest variance in test scores across testing conditions compared to the other two groups; on average, they performed at mid-range across all three conditions and never reached extreme levels of low or high achievement. The results clearly support the view that individual differences in arousal and arous-ability affect test performance: over-stimulating introverts reduces their verbal test scores, but extraverts only begin to show their potential stressful situations.

Using a somewhat different research design, Bates and Rock (2004) analyzed the performance of 56 students on Raven's matrices across five conditions of auditory distraction, including a base level of silence (low arousal), white noise, and domestic conversations with moderate emotional content (medium arousal), and excerpts from action and horror movies (high arousal). Introverts performed best in silence and substantially worse than extraverts and ambiverts in the high arousal condition. Extraverts showed a steady increment in scores with increasing auditory stimulation, and ambiverts had the least amount of variance in scores across conditions, with no meaningful increases or decreases in performance, supporting Revelle et al.'s (1976) earlier findings.

Rawlings and Carnie (1989) tested 40 students on extraversion and administered sub-tests of the Wechsler Adult Intelligence Scale, including arithmetic, information, digit span, and picture arrangement, under timed and untimed conditions; the results showed that introverts were more adversely influenced by time pressure than their extraverted counterparts were. Rawlings and Carnie concluded that intelligence tests with strictly timed conditions generally favor extraverts over introverts, who perform better on less restrictively timed measures, such as information and verbal tests.

It has been noted that several studies have failed to replicate interactions between extraversion and situational arousal value (e.g. Wolf & Ackerman, 2005). In particular, Rawlings and Skok (1993) and Saklofske and Kostura (1990) found no meaningful association of extraversion and intelligence in samples of children. In order to clarify the nature of intelligence–extraversion associations, Wolf and Ackerman (2005) conducted a comprehensive meta-analysis, which included a wide range of extraversion measures as well as social potency, social closeness, and third- and second-stratum factors of cognitive ability, in correspondence with Ackerman and Heggestad's (1997) meta-analytic approach. Wolf and Ackerman (2005) reported a significant coefficient across ability factors and extraversion measures of .06 from 166 samples; however, meta-analytic coefficients with specific intelligence factors were fairly inconsistent. The authors highlighted the importance of three moderating variables in the intelligence–extraversion relationship: differences in measurement instruments, the sample's age, and the year of publication. Overall, their results exemplify the complexity of assessing and explaining IPAs, emphasizing subtle associations between intelligence test scores and extraversion at the measurement level.

*1.2.2 Neuroticism and test anxiety* The relationship between neuroticism and psychometric intelligence is consistently found to be negative, implying that intelligence increases with decreasing negative affectivity (e.g. Furnham et al., 1998; Reeve, Meyer, & Bonaccio, 2006). Ackerman and Heggestad (1997) reported a meta-analytic coefficient of −.33 between neuroticism and general intelligence; however, Judge and colleagues (2007) recently reported a considerably lower meta-analytic coefficient of .09 for general mental ability and emotional stability.

Chamorro-Premuzic and Furnham (2005) pointed out that neurotic individuals may not be inherently less intelligent, but rather the typical emotions and cognitions experienced by neurotics, such as anxiety and worry, would impair their ability test performance (see also Zeidner & Matthews, 2000). In this respect, Eysenck (1981) distinguished worry, construed as a cognitive component of neuroticism, from emotionality, construed as neuroticism's emotional aspect. Worry and negative expectations, such as fear of failure, are assumed to obscure neurotics' focus on the task at hand and particularly to affect working memory systems by triggering task-irrelevant processing (Chamorro-Premuzic & Furnham, 2005; Eysenck, 1979). Thus previous research often focused on the role of test anxiety, which refers to the psychological distress a person experiences prior to or during an evaluative situation (Spielberger, Anton, & Bedell, 1976) and is closely related to neuroticism (Chamorro-Premuzic, Ahmetoglu, & Furnham, 2008). In an extensive meta-analysis of 562 studies, Hembree (1988) found that test anxiety was strongly correlated both with state and with trait anxiety at .45 and .53, respectively; he also confirmed a stable negative association of test anxiety with intelligence test performance of −.23. Three possible scenarios have been suggested to explain this association (see Wicherts & Scholten, 2010 for a comprehensive summary): a *deficit* model, whereby test anxiety relates solely to a latent trait of general ability; an *interference* model, which implies that test anxiety affects ability test scores but not general intelligence; and a *full* model of test anxiety, affecting general intelligence as well as individual test scores. Comparing two nested structural equation models, Reeve and Bonaccio (2008) showed that test anxiety was related to a latent trait of ability but not to item parcels of observed test scores; they concluded that a deficit model best described the conceptual association of test anxiety and ability. That is, test anxiety may cause a latent ability deficit, or it may also be a byproduct of low ability because of an awareness of, or insight into, one's lower intelligence. Furthermore, Wicherts and Scholten (2010) recently showed that test anxiety improved criterion-related validity over and above the effects of general intelligence, when the criterion is also related to test anxiety.

It remains unclear, however, whether neuroticism results in reduced general intelligence (i.e. task-irrelevant processing) or is indeed a characteristic of low-ability individuals (i.e. an awareness of low ability). What does seem clear is that negative affect is not only reflected in intelligence test scores or latent traits of ability, but is also linked to real-life performance outcomes. As correctly pointed out by Sternberg's little princess on the Piagetica planet: "[…] how can you really know a person's competence except through their performance?" (Sternberg, 1992, p. 386). That is, the extraversion/introversion dimension and negative affectivity affect real aptitude rather than distorting evaluation situations because performance is necessarily ability— no one will excel in any given task because of non-performed ability.

## 1.3  Associations at the conceptual level

Conceptual associations between personality and intelligence hypothesize a developmental relationship between intelligence and personality, whereby personality traits affect *when, where,* and *how* individuals apply and invest their cognitive abilities (Chamorro-Premuzic & Furnham, 2006). That is, individual differences in the application of ability as directed by non-ability factors are expected to have long-term consequences for behaviors and life-course development. In this context, three possible mechanisms have been studied—investment, compensation, and differentiation. Investment of ability is assumed to result in knowledge gain; this model dates back to Cattell's (1943, 1971, 1987) investment theory, which was later extended and fully developed by Ackerman's (1996) model of intelligence-as-process, personality, interests, and intelligence-as-knowledge (PPIK). Compensation refers to the adaptation of dispositions and habits that balance and complement ability; in particular, related research has focused on compensating for low intelligence via increments in diligence and zeal (Chamorro-Premuzic & Furnham, 2005). Finally, differentiation refers to life-course intellectual development and the uncoupling of cognitive abilities (e.g. Spearman, 1927), which has been shown to occur with increasing ability and age but is also proposed to depend on personality. In what follows we review each of these frameworks for understanding conceptual IPA.

*1.3.1 Investment*  Spearman's (1927) law of diminishing returns, as well as age-related performance declines in specific cognitive ability tests (Jones & Conrad, 1933; see also McArdle, Ferrer-Caja, Hamagami, & Woodcock, 2002; Tucker-Drob & Salthouse, 2011: this volume), had led Cattell (1941, 1943, 1971, 1987)[2] to speculate about the alleged one dimensional nature of intelligence, and he proposed to differentiate fluid (*Gf*) from crystallized intelligence (*Gc*):

> 1  Adult mental capacity is of two kinds, [...] which may be best connoted by the use of the terms "fluid" and "crystallized."
> 2  Fluid ability has the character of a purely general ability to discriminate and perceive relations between any fundaments, new or old. It increases until adolescence and then slowly declines. It is associated with the action of the whole cortex. It is responsible for the intercorrelations, or general factor, found among children's tests and among the speeded or adaptation-requiring tests of adults.
> 3  Crystallized ability consists of discriminatory habits long established in a particular field, originally through the operation of fluid ability, but not longer requiring insightful perception for their successful operation. (Cattell, 1943, p. 178; quotation marks as in original)

Cattell (1943) outlined that psychometric tests of intelligence at all ages combined aspects of *Gf* and *Gc* and that the dominance of these components shifted from childhood to adulthood and old age. Hayes (1962) believed that intelligence was the totality of abilities acquired through experiences over time. In his perspective, individual differences in intelligence resulted from genetic variations in motivation or drive, which caused differential experiences across individuals. Hayes concluded that individual differences in intellectual development were due to "inherent differences in the tendency to engage activities conducive to learning" (p. 335). Therefore, manifest intelligence was nothing more than the accumulation of facts and skills, whereas general intelligence or intellectual potential consisted of cognitive engagement and activity. Similarly, Ackerman (1996) proposed a causal linkage from intelligence-as-process to intelligence-as-knowledge, whereby speeded aspects of intelligence decline during normal adulthood development, but content or knowledge components become more influential. Individual differences in intelligence-as-knowledge are partially due to ability, but are also determined by interests and personality traits to the extent that the latter determine intellectual investment (Ackerman, 1996).

1.3.1.1 WHAT ARE INVESTMENT TRAITS? Intellectual investment traits refer to stable individual differences in the tendency to seek out, engage in, enjoy, and continuously pursue opportunities for effortful cognitive activity (von Stumm, 2010). Within the five-factor approach, openness to experience has been most frequently studied as an adequate proxy of an intellectual investment trait (Ackerman, 1996; Ackerman & Heggestad, 1997; Bates & Shieles, 2003; Beier, Campbell, & Crook, 2010; Chamorro-Premuzic & Furnham, 2006). However, investment traits are not limited only to the Big-Five realm, but also include measures that attempt to map the personality space around intelligence. To date, these scales comprise "isolated personality measures [...] with no linkage to any personality theory", and a unifying research endeavor is yet to be undertaken (Ackerman & Heggestad, 1997, p. 222).

1.3.1.2 OPENNESS TO EXPERIENCE The trait openness entails intellectual curiosity, esthetic awareness, and artistic interests, which are reflected in the six facet scales of fantasy, feelings, esthetics, action, ideas, and values (Costa & McCrae, 1992). Individuals with these characteristics prefer intellectually stimulating environments and therefore enjoy a wealth of learning experiences, which plausibly result in greater knowledge and *Gc*. Furthermore, open behaviors are encouraged in more able individuals, who understand and adapt to new information and environments more easily than less intelligent people (Chamorro-Premuzic & Furnham, 2005). Indeed, openness and general intelligence have been repeatedly shown to correlate positively, for example Judge and colleagues (2007) reported a meta-analytic correlation of .22. Ackerman and Heggestad's (1997) earlier meta-analysis also reviewed associations at the second-stratum level of intelligence, showing a non-significant association of openness with *Gf* at .08, and a significant correlation with *Gc* at .30. Further evidence for the effects of openness on *Gc* comes from an experimental study by Bates and Shieles (2003). In 64 students, openness was unrelated to inspection time and to *Gf*, assessed by Raven's matrices, but it sustained a meaningful positive effect on *Gc* after partialing out general intelligence. Even though the majority of evidence is not longitudinal and reported effect sizes are generally modest, these results give initial support to investment theories. In line with the findings, openness may also be expected to have positive effects on indicators of intellectual accomplishment other than *Gc* tests, for example on academic and professional performance. However, three recent meta-analyses estimated the association of openness and academic performance at .06 and .13 (O'Connor & Paunonen, 2007; Poropat, 2009; Trapmann, Hell, Hirn, & Schuler, 2007); similarly, openness was not found to relate significantly to job performance ratings (Barrick & Mount, 1991; Salgado, 1997).

In a recent series of studies, DeYoung and colleagues empirically substantiated previous notions of openness by incorporating two related, but distinct, aspects of this trait (e.g. Saucier, 1992): intellect, reflecting intellectual engagement and perceived intelligence—with the facet ideas as main marker—and openness, comprising artistic and contemplative qualities related to engagement in sensation and perception, including facets of fantasy, esthetics, feelings, and actions (DeYoung, Quilty,

& Peterson, 2007). Noteworthy is that the facet scale of values was not found to be a distinct marker of either aspect of openness (DeYoung, Peterson, & Higgins, 2005). Using fMRI in a sample of 104 community members from the Washington area, DeYoung, Shamosh, Green, Braver, and Gray (2009) showed that intellect was associated with brain activity in neural systems of working memory, but openness was not. The authors concluded that openness to experience comprised two separable, neurally distinctive aspects of one larger domain of personality. Further evidence for the two dimensionality of openness comes from behavior genetics. Wainwright and colleagues (Wainwright, Wright, Luciano, Geffen, & Martin, 2008) analyzed data from 754 families on intelligence, academic achievement, and six facets of openness, to examine the possibility of one underlying genetic factor. A specific genetic openness factor had loadings of .30 and above for fantasy, esthetics, feelings, and actions, but lower loadings for ideas and values, after controlling for a general genetic factor that was associated with five openness facets (actions being the exception), intelligence, and academic performance. From all openness scales, ideas loaded most strongly on the general genetic factor, followed by values; it was these two that did not load substantially on a specific openness factor. This finding suggests that intellect, marked by ideas, is genetically closer to intelligence and academic performance than openness, which is marked by fantasy, esthetics, feelings, and actions. The lack of evidence for an effect of openness on intellectual accomplishments at the phenotypic level is likely to be due to studying such associations on the higher-order factor rather than at facet level. Therefore, the aforementioned results are not understood to invalidate investment theories, but they should initiate a novel conceptualization and more research on the openness dimension.

1.3.1.3  SPECIFIC INVESTMENT TRAITS: A HUNGRY MIND  Openness to experience taps individual differences in a broad context, much broader than dispositions of intellectual investment (McCrae, 1994). Beyond the Big Five, an abundance of measures exists which capture more precisely individual differences in the desire to comprehend and engage in intellectual problems. In an attempt to review and unify these investment scales, von Stumm (2010) identified 30 relevant trait measures from the literature, for example inquiring intellect (Fiske, 1949), intellectual efficiency (Gough, 1953), and intellectence (Welsh, 1975). To discuss each of them is beyond the scope of this chapter; therefore, we will selectively focus on the two most frequently studied scales—typical intellectual engagement (TIE; Goff & Ackerman, 1992) and need for cognition (NFC; Cacioppo & Petty, 1982). Openness to experience is related to NFC and TIE, all of which are conceptually similar and also empirically correlated; however, a significant part of their variance is non-shared and they are thought to cover different parts of the personality realm (Arteche, Chamorro-Premuzic, Ackerman, & Furnham, 2009; Goff & Ackerman, 1992; see also Rocklin, 1994 for a different view).

Cacioppo and Petty (1982) proposed that there are stable individual differences in people's tendency to engage in and enjoy cognitive effort, and thus they developed the concept of "need for cognition," defined as a bipolar trait dimension that stretches from "cognitive misers to cognizers" (Cacioppo, Petty, Feinstein, & Jarvis, 1996, p. 197). They recognized that NFC was to covary with, but also to be distinct from, intelligence. Albeit independent of abstract reasoning ability (e.g. Cacioppo, Petty, & Morris, 1983), NFC is related to other indicators of intellect, such as *Gc* and academic performance (Bors, Vigneau, & Lalande, 2006). Recently, von Stumm (2010) meta-analyzed bivariate associations of NFC and indicators of adult intellect, including *Gc*, academic performance (e.g. grade point average and final exam grades), college entry tests, and general knowledge and found coefficients of .32, .20, .26, and .29, respectively. Although these associations are only of low to medium effect size, they substantiate the positive effects of NFC for intellectual development supporting investment theories. Furthermore, they are considerably higher than corresponding estimates for the effects of openness.

Goff and Ackerman (1992) developed a scale of Typical Intellectual Engagement (TIE) to measure "a dispositional construct that [...] is associated with intelligence as typical performance" (p. 539). The TIE scale aims to differentiate individuals' typical expression of engaging and understanding their environment, as well as their desire to comprehend, solve, and absorb complex topics and intellectual problems (Goff & Ackerman, 1992). To that effect, TIE specifically refers to settings of advanced stages of education, in which the predictive validity of maximal intelligence is diminished. TIE has been shown to be mostly independent of abstract reasoning ability (Chamorro-Premuzic, Furnham, & Ackerman, 2006; Furnham, Swami, Arteche, & Chamorro-Premuzic, 2008; Goff & Ackerman, 1992) but significantly associated with indicators of adult intellect: meta-analytic correlations are .39 with *Gc*, .28 with academic performance, .21 with college entry tests, and .38 with general knowledge (von Stumm, 2010). Furthermore, von Stumm, Hell, and Chamorro-Premuzic (2010) showed that TIE sustained a significant, independent effect on academic performance after adjusting for general intelligence and conscientiousness. In a structural equation model fitted to a meta-analytic correlation matrix, TIE's effect on academic performance was equal to the impact of conscientiousness (von Stumm, Hell, & Chamorro-Premuzic, 2010), which is an important, positive predictor of performance in educational and occupational settings (e.g. Barrick & Mount, 1991; Poropat, 2009). In contrast, openness to experience was found to have a negative effect on academic performance after controlling for its intercorrelations with general intelligence, conscientiousness and TIE, which suggested again that the openness dimension entailed two distinctive trait components (von Stumm et al., 2010). These models illustrate the importance of TIE for intellectual accomplishments over and above the power of pure reasoning ability and applied efforts, as well as the inadequacy of openness as proxy of an intellectual investment trait.

So far, TIE and NFC have been treated as distinctive constructs and were mostly studied in different contexts; that is, TIE is predominantly employed in the context of skill and knowledge acquisition (i.e. investment theories), whereas NFC is more commonly examined in personality and social psychology. Recently Woo, Harms, and Kuncel (2008) showed that TIE and NFC were interchangeable scales because of their high intercorrelation of .78 and their similar correlation profile across the Big Five, learning styles, and self-reported knowledge. Furthermore, both scales include a substantial number of literally and content-wise identical items (von Stumm, 2010). Therefore traditional measurements of individual differences in the tendency to engage in and enjoy effortful cognitive activity may be best summarized in terms of a hungry mind. Dewey (1910, p. 31) stated that "the curious mind [is] constantly alert and exploring [and] seeking material for thought, as a vigorous and healthy body is on the *qui vive* for nutriment." In this spirit, we propose a hungry mind to constitute a powerful force that underlies specifically academic performance, and skill and knowledge acquisition (cf. Hayes, 1962) but will also have broader long-term consequences.

*1.3.2 Compensation* Another developmental perspective on IPA is the notion of compensation, to which research has so far paid less attention in comparison to other investment models. The trait of interest in this context is conscientiousness, which entails dispositions of zeal, effort, and diligence.[3] It has been argued that "less" able individuals may become increasingly more conscientious in order to compensate for their lower levels of cognitive ability, whereas more intelligent people rely to a greater extent on their intelligence and can "afford" to be less dutiful and organized and nevertheless excel (Chamorro-Premuzic & Furnham, 2005, p. 65). Intelligence and conscientiousness have been shown to be largely independent, although some studies reported negative, albeit modest correlations (e.g. Ackerman & Heggestad, 1997; Moutafi, Furnham, & Crump, 2006; Poropat, 2009). Recently, Postlethwaite and colleagues (Postlethwaite, Robbins, Rickerson, & McKinniss, 2009) investigated the role of intelligence and conscientiousness in the prediction of work-related safety behaviors. In a sample of 219 employees, the positive relationship of conscientiousness and safety behaviors was moderated by cognitive ability; that is, conscientiousness was a stronger predictor of safety behavior in individuals of low cognitive ability compared to high-ability individuals. Intelligence is predictive of a wide range of outcomes, including risk of injury and accidents (Gottfredson & Deary, 2004); avoiding the latter by compensating with heightened conscientiousness may seem a far cry from life-course intellectual development. Nonetheless, future research may investigate whether this interaction also holds true for intellectual accomplishments in educational and occupational settings.

*1.3.3 Differentiation: Spearman's law of diminishing returns* In the early 1960s, Lienert (1963), Shure and Rogers (1963), and Eysenck and White (1964, re-analysing Lienert's data) proposed a specific type of intelligence–personality associations, namely differentiation. Spearman (1927) was the first to report that correlations of ability test scores reduced in magnitude with increasing levels of intelligence because of a greater differentiation of intellectual abilities; this phenomenon has been termed Spearman's law of diminishing returns (SLODR). That is, the higher an individual's general intelligence or *g* score, the smaller the amount of variance in the matrix of ability test scores that is attributable to a general factor. The ability differentiation was recently confirmed in several studies testing various samples (e.g. Deary et al., 1996; Detterman & Daniel, 1989; Legree, Pifer, & Grafton, 1996), prompting suggestions that *g* represented stupidity rather than intelligence

(Detterman, 1991). Spearman (1927) metaphorically referred to general intelligence as fuel for engines that perform task-specific functions; fuel, however, does not make the engine work faster, but it drives it for longer. That is, higher ability allows one to benefit from learning opportunities, and it is the unique, individual learning experiences that, over time, result in the specialization of abilities (Ferguson, 1954). To incorporate the time aspect, Garrett (1938, 1946) expanded Spearman's (1927) original law and proposed the age differentiation hypothesis, whereby "an amorphous general ability" gradually transforms "into a group of fairly distinct aptitudes" with increasing age (Garrett, 1946, p. 375). Several studies have empirically supported the age differentiation hypothesis (e.g. Atkin et al., 1977; Facon, 2006, 2008; but see also Tucker-Drob, 2009), suggesting yet another perspective on life-course cognitive development. With regard to personality, two possible mechanisms of differentiation have been studied: intelligence by personality and personality by intelligence.

1.3.3.1 INTELLIGENCE BY PERSONALITY DIFFERENTIATION  Eysenck and White (1964) suggested that the structure of cognitive abilities varied as a function of neuroticism, whereby intelligence is less differentiated at increased levels of neuroticism. In other words, $g$ should account for more of the total observed variance in a battery of ability tests at high levels of neuroticism than at low levels. So far, the empirical evidence for this notion has been inconsistent (e.g. Austin, Deary, & Gibson, 1997; Austin et al., 2002). Austin and colleagues (1997) compared correlations of a fluid and a crystallized intelligence test across two groups of neurotics (low versus high) and found a significant difference in the magnitude of correlation coefficients, with a higher $r$ value for the high neuroticism group; this finding was confirmed in a later study of two large samples of US police applicants and US felons (Austin, Hofer, Deary, & Eber, 2000). In addition, Austin et al. (2002) tested effects of Eysenck's Gigantic Three and of Costa and McCrae's Big Five on ability differentiation in four longitudinal samples of overall more than 4,000 adults aged 50 years and above. In two samples, ability was less differentiated at higher levels of neuroticism, but no other personality trait affected the differentiation of intelligence; in the remaining two, no significant effects were observed. Finally, in a sample of 322,535 high school students, Bonaccio and Reeve (2006) showed that the variance–covariance matrices of an ability test battery were invariant across neuroticism levels. Similarly, in a sample of 569 teenage students, Escorial, García, Cuevas, and Juan-Espinosa (2006) found no change in the amount of variance accounted for by a general intelligence factor across personality level groups of the Big Five. Overall, these findings suggest that neuroticism most likely only had a spurious effect on the structure of cognitive ability.

With reference to investment theories of intelligence, it is odd that previous research has not established effects for openness to experience, which theoretically predicts a greater differentiation of intelligence (Austin et al., 2002; Escorial et al., 2006). This null finding may be partially due to the distinctiveness of openness subfactors (DeYoung et al., 2005); but further research is needed to fully understand the role of personality traits in ability differentiation.

1.3.3.2   PERSONALITY BY INTELLIGENCE DIFFERENTIATION   The personality by intelligence differentiation derives from the idea that higher levels of general intelligence encourage developing more, or more differentiated, personality dimensions (Austin et al., 1997; Brand, Egan, & Deary, 1994). It has been hypothesized that, in less intelligent individuals, fewer personality factors or trait dimensions suffice to explain the variance in the self-report questionnaires. Conversely, it may also be that the number of trait dimensions is equal across ability groups, but that high-ability individuals are more variable within given trait dimensions (Austin et al., 1997). Austin and colleagues (2000) suggested that more intelligent individuals understand personality questionnaire items better or more accurately, which results in extreme scores and in a larger standard deviation by comparison to the scores of their less intelligent counterparts. It is equally possible that intelligent individuals view the personality questionnaire as more comprehensive, increasing scale variability; that is, such people may aim to provide broader information about themselves when assessed for personality (Austin et al., 2000).

    The hypothesis of personality by intelligence differentiation has only been studied sporadically and has produced inconsistent results. For example, in a sample of 210 East Scottish farmers, Austin and colleagues (1997) found that the standard deviations of all Big-Five dimensions were larger in a high-ability group than in a low-ability group; these differences were significant for neuroticism and openness. Conversely, Harris, Vernon, and Jang (2005) showed, in a large-scale study of 516 adult twins and siblings from the Western Ontario Twin Project, that high-ability groups were significantly more variable in their personality scores across 20 self-report trait scales from the Personality Research Form (Jackson, 1989). That is, more intelligent individuals seem to be equipped with "more" personality traits (Brand et al., 1994). It may be, however, that this association merely exists at the measurement level, because less intelligent individuals read personality test items differently from more intelligent individuals, rather than because their personality profiles are actually made of more traits. Yet another explanation, which applies to all empirical studies of differentiation, roots in a serious methodological problem. Most ability tests are not constructed to have a uniform distribution of item difficulties, and therefore their discriminatory quality varies across levels of ability. The psychometric characteristics of personality measures tend to be less well understood, but they are likely to have even less consistent measurement precision across trait levels. Therefore, splitting a sample on the basis of its test scores, be they ability or non-ability test scores, will result in scales with unequal reliabilities and validities when correlated with other measures. That is, the changes in correlation coefficients may be entirely due to test design characteristics rather than proving Spearman's law true.

## 1.4   A hungry mind outside the ivory tower

Throughout this chapter we stressed the importance of intellectual investment in understanding associations between intelligence and personality, as well as in pursuing intellectual accomplishments and life-span cognitive development. Most research evaluating the role and the predictive validity of so-called intellectual investment traits has focused on indicators of adult intellect as outcome variable (e.g. Ackerman, 1996; Ackerman & Goff, 1994; Ackerman, Kanfer, & Goff, 1995; Beier et al., 2010; Chamorro-Premuzic et al., 2006). This observation holds particularly true for TIE. For NFC, however, a multitude of associations across a wide range of outcomes has been reported (see Cacioppo et al., 1996 for a comprehensive overview). We propose to expand the research realm of investment traits that characterize a "hungry mind" beyond intellectual development, and also to consider differences in health and health behaviors as a consequence of dispositions toward intellectual engagement. Investment traits such as openness, TIE, and NFC have been repeatedly shown to be positively associated with skill and knowledge acquisition, including health knowledge (e.g. Beier & Ackerman, 2003). Likewise, better health knowledge will help the realization of a healthier lifestyle and discourage health-hazardous habits, such as smoking or drinking. Some variance in health outcomes is accounted for by the cognitive ability (Calvin et al., 2011: this volume; Gottfredson & Deary, 2004), and some is due to social inequalities (Marmot et al., 1991). However, causes and determinants of health outcomes are presently far from being fully understood, and it is plausible that investment traits incrementally add to the explained variance. Tentative evidence for such notions comes from communication research that focuses on the persuasiveness of preventive health messages showing that individuals high in NFC are more receptive to various types of health warnings (e.g. Braverman, 2008). NFC is also negatively related to risk-taking (Meertens & Lion, 2008), stress (Petty & Jarvis, 1996), and alcohol consumption (Hittner, 2004).Therefore, NFC and conceptually similar scales may be important factors in health research and add yet another individual differences variable to the novel field of (cognitive) epidemiology.

A hungry mind may also be expected to have a positive effect on life satisfaction, which people commonly rated as the most important element of their life (Diener, 2000). Life satisfaction is only partially determined by major life events, political factors, and economic status (Diener, Lucas, & Scollon, 2006), leaving plenty of variance for individual differences to account for (see also Pavot & Diener, 2011: this volume). Recently, Gow and colleagues (2005) showed in the Lothian birth cohort that life satisfaction was unrelated to cognitive ability at age 11 and at age 79, as well as to the decline of intelligence across the life span. Conversely, Weiss, Bates, and Luciano (2008) found that personality was reliably correlated with subjective well-being, and also that the Big Five and subjective well-being shared the same genetic origin. Therefore life satisfaction is a personality rather than an intelligence factor, and we propose four possible pathways through which intellectual investment traits may enhance it (Figure 8.2).

First, investment traits exert a positive effect on predictors of social status attainment, such as academic achievement and job performance (e.g. Deeter-Schmelz & Sojka, 2007; von Stumm, 2010). On the one hand, this may simply be inherently satisfactory; on the other, higher status leads to better living conditions, for example to safe, non-stressful employment settings, higher income, and better housing provisions, which in turn uplift life satisfaction. Second, intellectual investment traits may have a protective effect on health, as outlined above. Better health is associated with greater life satisfaction (Koivumaa-Honkanen et al., 2000), and

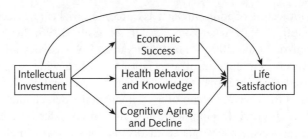

**Figure 8.2**   Theoretical pathways through which intellectual investment affects life-satisfaction

thus intellectual investment may operate on life satisfaction via health. Third, life-course intellectual engagement may result in better functioning brains across the life span, and therefore it may buffer the decline of mental abilities, leading to better cognition in old age—in correspondence with Schooler's "use it, or lose it" theory (Schooler, 2001; Tucker-Drob & Salthouse, 2011: this volume). As a final pathway, pleasure in intellectually stimulating activities and the pursuit of the latter may simply be of intrinsic value for people with a heightened tendency to engage in effortful cognitive activity. That is, intellectual investment may have a direct impact on life satisfaction, as well as mediated effects via economic success, health, and cognitive reserve. At present, the outlined pathways remain largely speculative and future research must further explore their validity. There has been, however, one recent study that reported a significant positive correlation between life satisfaction and NFC in a sample of 192 American students and community members, providing early, tentative support (Gauthier, Christopher, Walter, Mourad, & Marek, 2006).

## 2   (Overcoming) Current Research Obstacles

Although intellectual investment is a promising dimension of individual differences to explain IPA as well as variance in outcomes beyond knowledge and skill acquisition, it has received insufficient attention by the individual differences research community and is largely understudied. IPAs have proven to be of greater complexity than simple linear relationships, suggesting that a large bulk of existing correlational evidence is of limited use. In particular, what this field of enquiry lacks is experimental studies that probe interactions, mediation, and moderation mechanisms in IPAs. Moreover, intellectual investment traits are rarely included in assessment batteries of large-scale longitudinal studies with representative population samples. On one hand, this is due to the misconception that intellectual investment is not relevant to "real-life" outcomes, such as educational and occupational performance or health status. On the other hand, very few studies have employed genetic, psychobiological, and neurological research methods to disentangle the etiology of intellectual investment, and thus the construct is often not perceived to be a meaningful marker of adult intellectual competence. The accumulation of correlational evidence (or IPA research at the measurement level) presently confines investment traits to the status of obscure psychometric instruments, which loiter on the side of the present individual differences research paradigm. This paradigm dictates that the study of any phenotype be done in the context of (1) colorful photographs representing brain activity; (2) twin study designs decomposing any given (or not given) variance into additive genetic, shared and non-shared environment components; and (3) genome-wide association studies identifying non-replicable single nucleotide polymorphisms. Such—admittedly polemic—perspective prompts the question of how a phenotype actually "jumps on the wagon of variables" that are worthy of neurological and genotypic dissection. It seems that a crucial step in becoming a successful phenotype is to secure the recognition, acceptance, and appraisal of the established scholars of individual differences research. Such acknowledgment is typically based on empirical evidence demonstrating that a trait represents an important dimension of individual differences, with an adequate definition and corresponding measures of such differences, resulting in quantifiable long-term consequences for behavior, affect, and cognition. In this chapter, we hope to have demonstrated that intellectual investment traits matter, as is evidenced in their associations with academic performance and general knowledge, and as is hypothesized with regard to health and life satisfaction. With this, we hope to have laid out a starting point from which to take intellectual investment theories, and with that the exploration of IPAs, into the twenty-first century of individual differences research.

## Notes

1  See also Hogan and Chamorro-Premuzic (2011: this volume) for a distinction between identity and reputation aspects of personality.
2  Cattell (1941, 1943) was not the first to hypothesize that intelligence was a two-dimensional construct (e.g. Binet & Simon, 1961; Hebb, 1942; Hemnon, 1921; see Ackerman, 1996, for a historical review); however, he contributed the most influential theoretical principles, as well as early empirical evidence for the *Gf–Gc* distinction.
3  Conscientiousness is widely used in research of IPA as a proxy for effort and trait motivation. There is, however, an abundance of alternative measures of (achievement) motivation, for example self-efficacy, ambition, and drive, whose consideration will benefit research on IPA.

## References

Ackerman, P. L. (1996). A theory of adult intellectual development: Process, personality, interests, and knowledge. *Intelligence, 22,* 227–257.
Ackerman, P. L. (in press). Personality and cognition. In S. Kreitler (Ed.), *Cognition and motivation: Forging an interdisciplinary perspective.* Cambridge: Cambridge University Press.

Ackerman, P. L., & Goff, M. (1994). Typical intellectual engagement and personality: Reply to Rocklin (1994). *Journal of Educational Psychology*, *86*, 150–153.

Ackerman, P. L., & Heggestad, E. D. (1997). Intelligence, personality, and interests: Evidence for overlapping traits. *Psychological Bulletin*, *121*, 219–245.

Ackerman, P. L., Kanfer, R., & Goff, M. (1995). Cognitive and noncognitive determinants and consequences of complex skill acquisition. *Journal of Experimental Psychology: Applied*, *1*, 270–304.

Alexander, W. P. (1935). Intelligence, concrete and abstract: A study in differential traits. *British Journal of Psychology Monograph*, *6*(19).

Arden, R., Gottfredson, L. S., & Miller, G. (2009). Does a fitness factor contribute to the association between intelligence and health outcomes? Evidence from medical abnormality counts among 3,654 US veterans. *Intelligence*, *37*, 581–591.

Arteche, A., Chamorro-Premuzic, T., Ackerman, P. L., & Furnham, A. (2009). Typical intellectual engagement as a byproduct of openness, learning approaches, and self-assessed intelligence. *Educational Psychology*, *29*, 357–367.

Atkin, R., Bray, R., Davison, M., Herzberger, S., Humphreys, L. G., & Selzer, U. (1977). Ability factor differentiation, grades 5 through 11. *Applied Psychological Measurement*, *1*, 65–76.

Austin, E. J., Deary, I. J., & Gibson, G. J. (1997). Relationships between ability and personality: Three hypotheses tested. *Intelligence*, *25*, 49–70.

Austin, E. J., Hofer, S. M., Deary, I. J., & Eber, H. W. (2000). Interactions between intelligence and personality: Results from two large samples. *Personality and Individual Difference*, *29*, 405–427.

Austin, E. J., Deary, I. J., Whiteman, M. C., Fowkes, F. G. R., Pedersen, N., Rabbitt, P., Bent, N., & McInnes, L. (2002). Relationships between ability and personality: Does intelligence contribute positively to personal and social adjustment? *Personality and Individual Differences*, *32*, 1391–1411.

Barrick, M. R., & Mount, M. K. (1991). The Big Five personality dimensions and job performance: A meta-analysis. *Personnel Psychology*, *44*, 1–26.

Bates, T., & Rock, A. (2004). Personality and information processing speed: Independent influences on intelligent performance. *Intelligence*, *32*, 33–46.

Bates, T. C., & Shieles, A. (2003). Crystallized intelligence as a product of speed and drive for experience: The relationship of inspection time and openness to *g* and *Gc*. *Intelligence*, *31*, 275–287.

Beier, M. E., & Ackerman, P. L. (2003). Determinants of health knowledge: An investigation of age, gender, abilities, personality, and interests. *Journal of Personality and Social Psychology*, *84*, 439–447.

Beier, M. E., Campbell, M., & Crook, A. E. (2010). Developing and demonstrating knowledge: Individual differences determinants of learning and performance. *Intelligence*, *38*, 176–184.

Binet, A., & Simon, T. (1961). Méthodes nouvelles pour le diagnostic du niveau intellectuel des anormaux [New methods for the diagnosis of the intellectual levels of abnormals] [1961]. Translated by E. S. Kite. In J. J. Jenkins, & D. G. Paterson (Eds.), *Studies in individual differences: The search for intelligence* (pp. 90–96). New York: Appleton–Century–Crofts. [Originally published in *L'Année Psychologique*, *11*, 191–244.]

Bonaccio, S., & Reeve, C. L. (2006). Differentiation of cognitive abilities as a function of neuroticism level: A measurement equivalence/invariance analysis. *Intelligence*, *34*, 403–417.

Bors, D. A., Vigneau, F., & Lalande, A. (2006). Measuring the need for cognition: Item polarity, dimensionality, and the relation with ability. *Personality and Individual Differences*, *40*, 819–828.

Brand, C. R., Egan, V., & Deary, I. J. (1994). Intelligence, personality and society: "constructivist" versus "essentialist" possibilities. In D. Detterman (Ed.), *Intelligence and society* (pp. 29–42). Norwood, NJ: Ablex.

Braverman, J. (2008). Testimonials versus informational persuasive messages. *Communication Research*, *35*, 666–694.

Cacioppo, J. T., & Petty, R. E. (1982). The need for cognition. *Journal of Personality and Social Psychology*, *42*, 116–131.

Cacioppo, J. T., Petty, R. E., & Morris, K. (1983). Effects of need for cognition on message evaluation, recall, and persuasion. *Journal of Personality and Social Psychology*, *45*, 805–818.

Cacioppo, J. T., Petty, R. E., Feinstein J. A., & Jarvis, B. G. (1996). Dispositional differences in cognitive motivation: The life and times of individuals varying in need for cognition. *Psychological Bulletin*, *119*, 197–253.

Calvin, C., Batty, G. D., & Deary, I. J. (2011: in this volume). Cognitive epidemiology: Concepts, evidence, and future directions. In T. Chamorro-Premuzic, S. von Stumm, & A. Furnham (Eds.), *Handbook of individual differences*. Oxford: Wiley–Blackwell.

Caspi, A. (2000). The child is father of the man: Personality continuities from childhood to adulthood. *Journal of Personality and Social Psychology*, *78*, 158–172.

Cattell, R. B. (1941). Some theoretical issues in adult intelligence testing [Abstract]. *Psychological Bulletin*, *38*, 592.

Cattell, R. B. (1943). The measurement of adult intelligence. *Psychological Bulletin*, *40*, 153–193.

Cattell, R. B. (1971). *Abilities: Their structure, growth, and action*. Boston, MA: Houghton Mifflin.

Cattell, R. B. (1987). *Intelligence: Its structure, growth and action*. Amsterdam: North-Holland.

Chamorro-Premuzic, T., & Furnham, A. (2005). *Personality and intellectual competence*. Mahwah, NJ: Lawrence Erlbaum Associates.

Chamorro-Premuzic, T., & Furnham, A. (2006). Intellectual competence and the intelligent personality: A third way in differential psychology. *Review of General Psychology*, *10*, 251–267.

Chamorro-Premuzic, T., & Furnham, A. (2010). *The psychology of personnel selection*. New York: Cambridge University Press.

Chamorro-Premuzic, T., & Ahmetoglu, G., & Furnham, A. (2008). Little more than personality: Trait determinants of test anxiety. *Learning and Individual Differences*, *18*, 258–263.

Chamorro-Premuzic, T., Furnham, A., & Ackerman, P. (2006). Ability and non-ability correlates of general knowledge. *Personality and Individual Differences*, *41*, 419–429.

Colom, R., Escorial, S., Shih, P. C., & Privado, J. (2007). Fluid intelligence, memory span, and temperament difficulties predict academic performance of young adolescents. *Personality and Individual Differences*, *42*, 1503–1514.

Costa, P. T., Jr., & McCrae, R. R. (1992). *Revised NEO Personality Inventory (NEO–PI–R) and NEO Five-Factor Inventory (NEO–FFI): Professional manual*. Odessa, FL: Psychological Assessment Resources.

Cronbach, L. J. (1949). *Essentials of psychological testing*. New York: Harper.

Deary, I. J. (1996). A (latent) big five personality model in 1915? A re-analysis of Webb's data. *Journal of Personality and Social Psychology, 71*, 992–1005.

Deary, I. J. (2008). Why do intelligent people live longer? *Nature, 456*, 175–176.

Deary, I. J., Whalley, L. J., Lemmon, H., Crawford, J. R., & Starr, J. M. (2000). The stability of individual differences in mental ability from childhood to old age: Follow-up of the 1932 Scottish Mental Survey. *Intelligence, 28*, 49–55.

Deary, I. J., Egan, V., Gibson, G. J., Austin, E. J., Brand, C. R., & Kellaghan, T. (1996). Intelligence and the differentiation hypothesis. *Intelligence, 23*, 105–132.

Deeter-Schmelz, D. R., & Sojka, J. Z. (2007). Personality traits and sales performance: Exploring differential effects of need for cognition and self-monitoring. *Journal of Marketing Theory & Practice, 15*, 147–159.

Detterman, D. K. (1991). Reply to Deary and Pagliari: Is *g* intelligence or stupidity? *Intelligence, 15*, 251–255.

Detterman, D. K., & Daniel, M. H. (1989). Correlations of mental tests with each other and with cognitive variables are highest in low-IQ groups. *Intelligence, 13*, 349–359.

DeYoung, C. G., Peterson, J. B., & Higgins, D. M. (2005). Sources of openness/intellect: Cognitive and neuropsychological correlates of the fifth factor of personality. *Journal of Personality, 73*, 825–858.

DeYoung, C. G., Quilty, L. C., & Peterson, J. B. (2007). Between facets and domains: 10 aspects of the Big Five. *Journal of Personality and Social Psychology, 93*, 880–896.

DeYoung, C. G., Shamosh, N. A., Green, A. E., Braver, T. S., & Gray, J. R. (2009). Intellect as distinct from openness: Differences revealed by fMRI of working memory. *Journal of Personality and Social Psychology, 97*, 883–892.

Dewey, J. (1910). *How we think.* Lexington, MA: Heath.

Diener, E. (2000). Subjective well-being: The science of happiness, and a proposal for a national index. *American Psychologist, 55*, 34–43.

Diener, E., Lucas, R., & Scollon, C. N. (2006). Beyond the hedonic treadmill: Revising the adaptation theory of well-being. *American Psychologist, 61*, 305–314.

Escorial, S., García, L. F., Cuevas, L., & Juan-Espinosa, M. (2006). Personality level on the Big Five and the structure of intelligence. *Personality and Individual Differences, 40*, 909–917.

Eysenck, H. J. (1957). *Sense and nonsense in psychology.* Harmondsworth: Penguin.

Eysenck, H. J. (1967). *The biological basis of personality.* Springfield, IL: Thomas.

Eysenck, H. J. (1970). *The structure of human personality.* London: Methuen.

Eysenck, H. J. (1971). Relation between intelligence and personality. *Perceptual and Motor Skills, 32*, 637–638.

Eysenck, H. J. (1979). *The structure and measurement of intelligence.* Berlin: Springer-Verlag.

Eysenck, H. J. (1981). Psychoticism as a dimension of personality: A reply to Kasielke. *Zeitschrift für Psychologie, 189*, 381–386.

Eysenck, H. J., & Eysenck, M. W. (1985). *Personality and individual differences: A natural science approach.* New York: Plenum.

Eysenck, H. J., & White, P. O. (1964). Personality and the measurement of intelligence. *British Journal of Educational Psychology, 24*, 197–201.

Facon, B. (2006). Does age moderate the effect of IQ on the differentiation of cognitive abilities during childhood? *Intelligence, 34*, 375–386.

Facon, B. (2008). How does the strength of the relationships between cognitive abilities evolve over the life-span for low-IQ vs high-IQ adults? *Intelligence, 36*, 339–349.

Ferguson, G. A. (1954). On learning and human ability. *Canadian Journal of Psychology, 8,* 95–112.

Ferguson, E., Chamorro-Premuzic, T., Pickering, A., & Weiss, A. (2011: this volume). Five into One Doesn't Go: A critique of the general factor of personality. In T. Chamorro-Premuzic, S. von Stumm, & A. Furnham (Eds.), *Handbook of individual differences.* Oxford: Wiley–Blackwell.

Fiske, D. W. (1949). Consistency of the factorial structures of personality ratings from different sources. *Journal of Abnormal and Social Psychology, 44,* 329–344.

Fiske, D. W., & Butler, J. M. (1963). The experimental conditions for measuring individual differences. *Educational and Psychological Measurement, 23,* 249–266.

Funder, D. C. (2001). Personality. *Annual Review of Psychology, 52,* 197-221.

Furnham, A., Forde, L., & Cotter, T. (1998). Personality scores and test-taking style. *Personality and Individual Differences, 24,* 19–23.

Furnham, A., Swami, V., Arteche, A., & Chamorro-Premuzic, T. (2008). Cognitive ability, learning approaches, and personality correlates of general knowledge. *Educational Psychology, 28,* 427–437.

Garrett, H. E. (1938). Differentiable mental traits. *Psychological Record, 2,* 259–298.

Garrett, H. E. (1946). A developmental theory of intelligence. *American Psychologist, 1,* 372–378.

Gauthier, K. J., Christopher, A. N., Walter, M. I., Mourad, R., & Marek, P. (2006). Religiosity, religious doubt, and the need for cognition: Their interactive relationship with life satisfaction. *Journal of Happiness Studies, 7,* 139–154.

Goff, M., & Ackerman, P. (1992). Personality–intelligence relations: Assessment of typical intellectual engagement. *Journal of Educational Psychology, 84,* 537–552.

Gottfredson, L. (1994). Mainstream science on intelligence. *Wall Street Journal,* December 13, p. A18.

Gottfredson, L., & Deary, I. J. (2004). Intelligence predicts health and longevity: But why? *Current Directions in Psychological Science, 13,* 1–4.

Gough, H. G. (1953). A nonintellectual intelligence test. *Journal of Consulting Psychology, 17,* 242–246.

Gow, A. J., Whiteman, M. C., Pattie, A., Whalley, L. J., Starr, J. M., & Deary, I. J. (2005). Lifetime intellectual function and satisfaction with life in old age: Longitudinal cohort study. *British Medical Journal, 331,* 141–142.

Harris, J. A., Vernon, P. A., & Jang, K. L. (2005). Testing the differentiation by intelligence hypothesis. *Personality and Individual Differences, 38,* 277–286.

Hayes, K. J. (1962). Genes, drives, and intellect. *Psychological Reports, 10,* 299–342.

Hebb, D. O. (1942). The effects of early and late brain injury upon test scores, and the nature of normal adult intelligence. *Proceedings of the American Philosophical Society, 85,* 275–292.

Hembree, R. (1988). Correlates, causes, and treatment of test anxiety. *Review of Educational Research, 58,* 47–77.

Hemnon, V. A. C. (1921). Intelligence and its measurement. A Symposium—VIII. *Journal of Educational Psychology, 12,* 195–198.

Hittner, J. B. (2004). Alcohol use among American college students in relation to need for cognition and expectations of alcohol's effects on cognition. *Current Psychology: Developmental, Learning, Personality, Social, 23,* 173–187.

Hogan, R., & Chamorro-Premuzic, T. (2011: this volume). Leadership. In T. Chamorro-Premuzic, S. von Stumm, & A. Furnham (Eds.), *Handbook of individual differences.* Oxford: Wiley–Blackwell.

Holland, D., Dollinger, S., Holland, C., & MacDonald, D. (1995). The relationship between psychometric intelligence and the five-factor model of personality in a rehabilitation sample. *Journal of Clinical Psychology, 51*, 79–88.

Humphreys, M. S., & Revelle, W. (1984). Personality, motivation, and performance: A theory of the relationship between individual differences and information processing. *Psychological Review, 91*, 153–184.

Jackson, D. N. (1989). *Personality research form manual* (3rd ed.). Port Huron, MI: Sigma Assessment Systems.

James, L. R. (1998). Measurement of personality via conditional reasoning. *Organizational Research Methods*, 1, 131–163.

Jensen, A. R. (1998). *The g factor: The science of mental ability.* Westport, CT: Praeger.

Jones, H. E., & Conrad, H. S. (1933). The growth and decline of intelligence: A study of a homogeneous group between the ages of ten and sixty. *Genetic Psychology Monographs, 13*, 223–275.

Judge, T., Jackson, C., Shaw, J., Scott, B., & Rich, B. (2007). Self-efficacy and work-related performance: The integral role of individual differences. *Journal of Applied Psychology, 92*, 107–127.

Kern, M., & Friedman, H. (2011: this volume). Personality and health. In T. Chamorro-Premuzic, S. von Stumm, & A. Furnham (Eds.), *Handbook of individual differences.* Oxford: Wiley–Blackwell.

Koivumaa-Honkanen, H., Honkanen, R., Viinamaki, H., Heikkila, K., Kaprio, J., & Koskenvuo, M. (2000). Self-reported life satisfaction and 20-year mortality in healthy Finnish adults. *American Journal of Epidemiology, 152*, 983–991.

Legree, P. J., Pifer, M. E., & Grafton, F. C. (1996). Correlations among cognitive abilities are lower for higher ability groups. *Intelligence, 23*, 45–57.

Lienert, G. A. (1963). Die Faktorenstruktur der Intelligenz als Funktion des Neurotizismus. *Zeitschrift für Experimentelle und Angewandte Psychologie, 10*, 140–159.

Malhotra, L., Malhotra, D., & Jerath, J. M. (1989). Speed and accuracy in learning as a function of personality. *Journal of Personality and Clinical Studies, 5*, 5–8.

Marmot, M. G., Davey Smith, G., Stansfeld, S., Patel, C., North, F., Head, J., White, I., Brunner, E., & Feeney, A. (1991). Health inequalities among British civil servants: The Whitehall II study. *The Lancet, 337*, 1387–1393.

McArdle, J. J., Ferrer-Caja, E., Hamagami, F., & Woodcock, R. W. (2002). Comparative longitudinal structural analyses of the growth and decline of multiple intellectual abilities over the life-span. *Developmental Psychology, 38*, 115–142.

McCrae, R. R. (1994). Openness to experience: Expanding the boundaries of Factor V. *European Journal of Personality, 8*, 251–272.

Meertens, R. M., & Lion, R. (2008). Measuring an individual's tendency to take risks: The risk propensity scale. *Journal of Applied Social Psychology, 38*, 1506–1520.

Miller, G. F. (2000). Sexual selection for indicators of intelligence. In G. Bock, J. A. Goode, & K. Webb (Eds.), *The nature of intelligence* (Vol. 233, pp. 260–275). Chichester: John Wiley & Sons.

Moutafi, J., Furnham, A., & Crump, J. (2006). What facets of openness and conscientiousness predict fluid intelligence score? *Learning and Individual Differences, 16*, 31–42.

Neisser, U., Boodoo, G., Bouchard, T., Boykin, A. W., Brody, N., Ceci, S. J., Halpern, D. F., Loehlin, J. C., Perloff, R., Sternberg, R. J., & Urbina, S. (1996). Intelligence: Known and unknown. *American Psychologist, 51*, 77–101.

O'Connor, M. C., & Paunonen, S. V. (2007). Big Five personality predictors of post-secondary academic performance. *Personality and Individual Differences, 43*, 971–990.

Pavot, W., & Diener E. (2011: this volume). Personality and happiness: Predicting the experience of subjective well-being. In T. Chamorro-Premuzic, S. von Stumm, & A. Furnham (Eds.), *Handbook of individual differences*. Oxford: Wiley–Blackwell.

Petty, R. E., & Jarvis, B. G. (1996). An individual differences perspective on assessing cognitive processes. In N. Schwarz & S. Sudman (Eds.), *Answering questions: Methodology for determining cognitive and communicative processes in survey research* (pp. 221–257). San Francisco: Jossey-Bass.

Poropat, A. (2009). A meta-analysis of the five-factor model of personality and academic performance. *Psychological Bulletin, 135*, 322–338.

Postlethwaite, B., Robbins, S., Rickerson, J., & McKinniss, T. (2009). The moderation of conscientiousness by cognitive ability when predicting workplace safety behaviour. *Personality and Individual Differences, 47*, 711–716.

Rawlings, D., & Carnie, D. (1989). The interaction of EPQ extroversion and WAIS Subtest performance under timed and un-timed conditions. *Personality and Individual Differences, 10*, 453–458.

Rawlings, D., & Skok, M. (1993). Extraversion, venturesomeness and intelligence in children. *Personality and Individual Differences, 15*, 399–396.

Rocklin, T. (1994). Relation between typical intellectual engagement and openness: Comment on Goff & Ackerman. *Journal of Educational Psychology, 86*, 145–149.

Reeve, C. L., & Bonaccio, S. (2008). Does test anxiety induce measurement bias in cognitive ability tests? *Intelligence, 36*, 526–538.

Reeve, C. L., Meyer, R., & Bonaccio, S. (2006). Intelligence–personality associations reconsidered: The importance of distinguishing between general and narrow dimensions of intelligence. *Intelligence, 34*, 387–402.

Revelle, W., Amaral, P., & Turriff, S. (1976). Introversion/extraversion, time stress, and caffeine. *Science, 192*, 149–150.

Rushton, J. P., & Irwing, P. (2011: this volume). The general factor of personality: Normal and abnormal. In T. Chamorro-Premuzic, S. von Stumm, & A. Furnham (Eds.), *Handbook of individual differences*. Oxford: Wiley–Blackwell.

Salgado, J. F. (1997). The 5-factor model of personality and job-performance in the European Community. *Journal of Applied Psychology, 82*, 30–43.

Saklofske, D. H., & Kostura, D. D. (1990). Extraversion–introversion and intelligence. *Personality and Individual Differences, 11*, 547–551.

Saucier, G. (1992). Openness versus intellect: Much ado about nothing? *European Journal of Personality, 6*, 381–386.

Shure, G. H., & Rogers, M .S. (1963). Personality factor stability for three ability levels. *Journal of Psychology, 55*, 445–456.

Smillie, L. D., Loxton., N. J., & Avery, R. (2011: this volume). Reinforcement sensitivity theory: Research, applications, and future. In T. Chamorro-Premuzic, S. von Stumm, & A. Furnham (Eds.), *Handbook of individual differences*. Oxford: Wiley–Blackwell.

Sočan, G., & Bucik, V. (1998). Relationship between speed of information-processing and two major personality dimensions—extraversion and neuroticism. *Personality and Individual Differences, 25*, 35–48.

Schooler, C. (2007). Use it—And keep it, longer, probably: A reply to Salthouse (2006). *Perspective on Psychological Sciences, 2*, 24–29.

Spearman, C. E. (1904). "General intelligence" objectively determined and measured. *American Journal of Psychology, 15*, 201–293.

Spearman, C. E. (1927). *The abilities of man*. London: Macmillan.

Spielberger, C. D., Anton, W. D., & Bedell, J. (1976). The nature and treatment of test anxiety. In M. Zuckerman & C. D. Spielberger (Eds.), *Emotions and anxiety: New concepts, methods, and applications* (pp. 57–81). New York: Wiley.

Spinath, F., & Johnson, W. (2011: this volume). Behaviour genetics. In T. Chamorro-Premuzic, S. von Stumm, & A. Furnham (Eds.), *Handbook of individual differences*. Oxford: Wiley–Blackwell.

Sternberg, R. J. (1992). The princess grows up: A satiric fairy tale about intellectual development. In R. J. Sternberg & C. A. Berg (Eds.), *Intellectual development* (pp. 381–394). New York: Cambridge University Press.

Strobel, A., & Brocke, B. (2011: this volume). Molecular genetics of personality. In T. Chamorro-Premuzic, S. von Stumm, & A. Furnham (Eds.), *Handbook of individual differences*. Oxford: Wiley–Blackwell.

von Stumm, S. (2010). Intelligence, investment and intellect: Re-examining intelligence–personality associations. Unpublished doctoral dissertation. Goldsmiths University of London.

von Stumm, S., Hell, B., & Chamorro-Premuzic, T. (2010, September). Neugier als dritte Saeule der Studieneignung. Oral presentation at the Deutsche Gesellschaft für Psychologie, Bremen, Germany.

Thorndike, E. L. (1940). *Human nature and the social order*. New York: Macmillan.

Trapmann, S., Hell, B., Hirn, J. O., & Schuler, H. (2007). Meta-analysis of the relationship between the Big Five and academic success at university. *Zeitschrift für Psychologie/Journal of Psychology, 215*, 132–151.

Tucker-Drob, E. M. (2009). Differentiation of cognitive abilities across the lifespan. *Developmental Psychology, 45*, 1097–1118.

Tucker-Drob, E. M., & Salthouse, T. (2011: this volume). Cognitive aging. In T. Chamorro-Premuzic, S. von Stumm, & A. Furnham (Eds.), *Handbook of individual differences*. Oxford: Wiley–Blackwell.

Wainwright, M. A., Wright, M. J., Luciano, M., Geffen, G. M., & Martin, N. G. (2008). Genetic covariation among facets of openness to experience and general cognitive ability. *Twin Research and Human Genetics, 11*, 275–286.

Wallace, J. (1966). An abilities conception of personality: Some implications for personality measurement. *American Psychologist, 21*, 132–138.

Webb, E. (1915). Character and intelligence. Unpublished doctoral dissertation. Goldsmiths University of London.

Welsh, G., S. (1975). *Creativity and intelligence: A personality approach*. Chapel Hill, NC: Institute for Research in Social Science.

Weiss, A., Bates, T. C., & Luciano, M. (2008). Happiness is a personal(ity) thing: The genetics of personality and well-being in a representative sample. *Psychological Science, 19*, 205–210.

Wicherts, J. M. & Scholten, A. (2010). Test anxiety and the validity of cognitive tests: A confirmatory factor analysis perspective and some empirical findings. *Intelligence, 38*, 169–178.

Wolf, M. B., & Ackerman, P. L. (2005). Extraversion and intelligence: A meta-analytic investigation. *Personality and Individual Differences, 39*, 531–542.

Woo, S. E., Harms, P. D., & Kuncel, N. R. (2008). Integrating personality and intelligence: Typical intellectual engagement and need for cognition. *Personality and Individual Differences, 43*, 1635–1639.

Yerkes, R. M., & Dodson, J. D. (1908). The relation of strength of stimulus to rapidity of habit-formation. *Journal of Comparative Neurology and Psychology, 18*, 459–482.

Zeidner, M. (1995). Personality trait correlates of intelligence. In D. Saklofske & M. Zeidner (Eds.), *International handbook of personality and intelligence* (pp. 299–319). New York: Plenum.

Zeidner, M., & Matthews, G. (2000). Personality and intelligence. In R. J. Sternberg (Ed.), *Handbook of human intelligence* (2nd ed., pp. 581–610). New York: Cambridge University Press.

# 9

# Individual Differences in Cognitive Aging

## Elliot M. Tucker-Drob and Timothy A. Salthouse

As populations of healthy adults grow older, average levels of performance in many different areas of cognitive functioning gradually decrease. Recently, however, researchers have begun moving beyond conceptualizing cognitive aging merely as a population-level phenomenon. Instead, there is a growing appreciation for person-to-person *individual differences* in the cognitive aging process. The two quotes that follow exemplify this shift.

> Researchers are recognizing increasingly that the study of mean change with age does not give a full account of cognitive change across the life span. Although the average performance on most tasks may decline with age, studies have suggested that many older individuals may change very little, whereas others deteriorate dramatically. (Christensen et al., 1999, p. 365)

> In some people cognition declines precipitously, but in many others cognition declines only slightly or not at all, or improves slightly. Determining the factors that contribute to this variability is likely to require detailed knowledge about individual differences in patterns of change in different cognitive abilities in old age. (Wilson et al., 2002, p. 179)

There are seven questions that we believe to be foundational to this burgeoning area of inquiry. These are:

1  To what extent do individual differences exist in aging-related cognitive changes?
2  How many explanations are needed for cognitive aging?
3  What are the moderators of cognitive aging?
4  What can improve cognitive performance in adulthood?
5  How does cognitive aging relate to real-world functioning?

6   What are the neurobiological substrates of individual differences in cognitive aging?
7   What are the genetic risk factors for cognitive aging?

In this chapter we summarize the progress that has been made toward answering each of these questions and discuss prospects for future research. First, we describe the pattern of cognitive aging at the population level.

## When Does Cognitive Aging Begin and for What Cognitive Abilities?

Before addressing questions about individual differences in cognitive aging, it is useful to describe the basic population-level phenomenon in question. Lay intuition might suggest that aging-related cognitive decline only occurs for memory, that decline only occurs later in life, and that decline only occurs for the small segment of the population that experiences neurological disease. However, there is now strong evidence that declines occur for a number of different abilities apart from memory (e.g. reasoning, speed of processing, and spatial visualization); that these declines begin in early adulthood; and that declines occur for healthy, disease-free adults (Salthouse, 2004a).

### Cross-sectional evidence

The most abundant sources of information about age-related effects on cognitive functioning come from cross-sectional studies, in which people of many different ages are tested during the same general period of time and compared to one another in their test performance. Among the first reports of cross-sectional age trends for cognitive abilities was an article published by Jones and Conrad in 1933. This study was based on a community sample of close to 1,200 rural New England residents between 10 and 60 years of age. Jones and Conrad observed that on nearly all of the sub-tests of the Army Alpha Intelligence Test, including Numerical Completion, Common Sense, and Analogies, mean levels of performance increased until approximately 18 years of age, at which point they declined continuously throughout adulthood. Two exceptions were the Opposites sub-test (i.e. antonym vocabulary) and the General Information sub-test, mean levels of which increased steeply in childhood and then leveled off in adulthood. Nearly identical cross-sectional trends in similar cognitive tests have been reported over the 75 years since Jones's and Conrad's original observations (e.g. Cattell, 1987; Li et al., 2004, Tucker-Drob, 2009; Wechsler, 1958). For tests that require effortful processing at the time of assessment (i.e. tests of *processing abilities*), mean levels of performance are highest during late adolescence and young adulthood, and monotonically decline with advancing adult age. For tests that require the production of previously acquired information (i.e. declarative knowledge) and/or highly automatized forms of processing (i.e. procedural knowledge), mean levels of performance peak in middle adulthood, after which point they remain relatively stable. These trends are illustrated in Figure 9.1, which is based on data

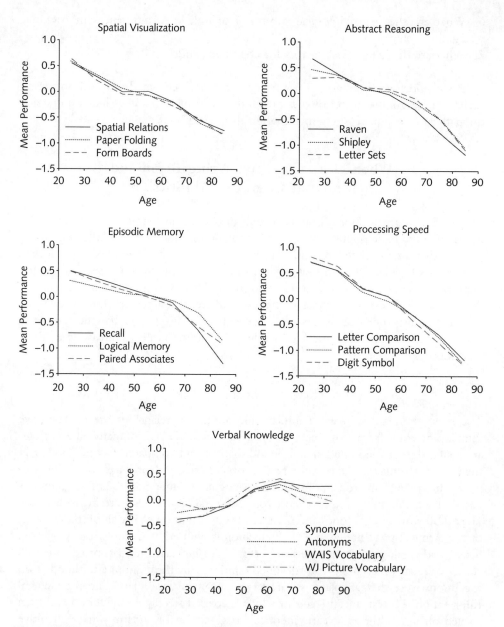

**Figure 9.1** Cross-sectional age trends from the Virginia Cognitive Aging Project at the University of Virginia. VCAP; *N* = 2,541. All variables have been standardized to have a mean of 0 and a standard deviation of 1 in the entire sample

from the Virginia Cognitive Aging Project at the University of Virginia (VCAP; *N* = 3,560; Salthouse, 2004b; Salthouse, Pink, & Tucker-Drob, 2008; Tucker-Drob, in press a; Tucker-Drob & Salthouse, 2008, 2009). These data were collected over 16 tests representative of five different cognitive abilities, four of which (spatial visualization, abstract reasoning, episodic memory, and processing speed) require effortful processing and begin declining in early adulthood, and one of which (verbal knowledge) reflects stores of previously acquired information and increases until approximately 65 years of age. It can be inferred that these patterns are not attributable to age trends in the prevalence of dementia, as the correlations between abilities and age are very similar, both before and after the exclusion of individuals with scores below 27 out of 30 on the Mini Mental State Examination (a popular dementia screening instrument; Folstein, Folstein, & McHugh, 1975). For composite scores representing each ability, these are:

- spatial visualization ($r_{\text{full sample}} = -.474$, $r_{\text{MMSE}\geq 27} = -.477$);
- abstract reasoning ($r_{\text{full sample}} = -.482$, $r_{\text{MMSE}\geq 27} = -.477$);
- episodic memory ($r_{\text{full sample}} = -.433$, $r_{\text{MMSE}\geq 27} = -.427$);
- processing speed ($r_{\text{full sample}} = -.629$, $r_{\text{MMSE}\geq 27} = -.627$); and
- verbal knowledge ($r_{\text{full sample}} = .245$, $r_{\text{MMSE}\geq 27} = .311$).[1]

## Longitudinal evidence

Whereas cross-sectional data clearly demonstrate declines in multiple domains of effortful processing beginning in early adulthood, results of a number of longitudinal studies appear to indicate that declines do not begin to transpire until middle to late adulthood. Because logistic issues make it very difficult for longitudinal studies to span an entire lifetime, longitudinal evidence typically comes from what are termed "accelerated" or "sequential" designs, in which participants of different ages are followed over a few years (although see McArdle, Grimm, Hamagami, Bowles, & Meredith, 2009 for a notable exception). Figure 9.2 illustrates some typical findings. Data come from the Seattle Longitudinal Study (reproduced from Salthouse, 2005). It can be seen that, for longitudinal changes in inductive reasoning, for which

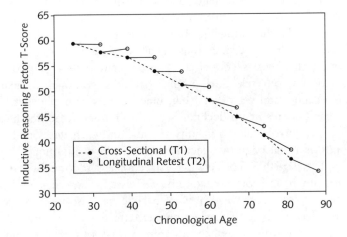

**Figure 9.2** Cross-sectional and longitudinal age trends in inductive reasoning from the Seattle Longitudinal Study. Reproduced from Salthouse (2005, p. 553). The factor has been standardized to have a mean of 50 and standard deviation of 10 in the entire sample

cross-sectional studies indicate declines beginning in early adulthood, mean levels of performance actually increase until approximately 50 years of age, only after which point they begin to decline. How can the discrepancy between cross-sectional deficits and longitudinal gains be reconciled?

A number of factors, or validity threats, have the potential to contribute to the differences typically observed between cross-sectional and longitudinal studies (Salthouse, 2010b). One potential validity threat is the existence of cohort differences in cognitive functioning. If, all else being equal, individuals born in later generations begin adulthood with higher overall levels of performance (see e.g. Flynn, 1987) than those born in earlier generations, then these younger participants will outperform older participants (i.e. the participants born earlier) at any given time point, not because of aging-related changes, but because of historical differences (e.g. in nutrition or education). A second potential validity threat is non-random selection. If older participants in a cross-sectional study tend to be more positively selected than younger participants are, aging-related deficits could actually be masked in cross-sectional data. A related validity threat, selective attrition, involves lower-functioning participants being less likely to return for a longitudinal assessment (due either to lack of interest or to a relation between cognitive functioning and illness or death; Lindenberger, Singer, & Baltes, 2002), which would lead to an underestimation of aging-related deficits in longitudinal data. A final validity threat, and the one that we believe is the largest contributor to the empirically observed discrepancies between cross-sectional and longitudinal age trends, is that longitudinal research inherently requires the repeated testing of individuals and is therefore contaminated by practice-related learning as a result of individuals' accumulating experiences with the tests (Salthouse & Tucker-Drob, 2008).

How can we evaluate the contributions of each of these possibilities and their alternative implications for the validity of cross-sectional versus longitudinal research? A tremendous amount of work has been published on this topic (Baltes, Reese, & Nesselroade, 1977; Baltes & Schaie, 1976; Horn & Donaldson, 1976; Yang, Schullhofer-Wohl, Fu, & Land, 2008), and we cannot possibly attempt to summarize it all here. We do make the following observations. First, the validity threats do not all bias inferences in the same directions. That is, while some threats (e.g. cohort differences) imply that cross-sectional comparisons may overestimate decline, other threats (e.g. non-random selection) imply that cross-sectional comparisons may underestimate decline, and yet others (e.g. practice effects) imply that longitudinal comparisons may underestimate decline. Second, a number of different approaches have been used to correct for the validity threats, and each tends to be consistent with the proposition that cognitive decline begins in early adulthood. For example, when Rönnlund et al. (2005) corrected cross-sectional data for cohort differences in educational attainment and corrected longitudinal data for experience-related practice effects, results were consistent with early life declines in episodic memory. Salthouse (2009) has provided evidence that, when practice effects are removed either by comparing twice-tested individuals to once-tested individuals or by statistically correcting for the number of previous testing occasions that individual participants have experienced, aging-related deficits were apparent in early adulthood for episodic memory, spatial visualization, processing speed, and abstract reasoning. Third, neurobiological indices thought to be related to cognition, such as brain size, begin declining in early adulthood in both cross-sectional and longitudinal data (Dennis & Cabeza, 2008). Fourth, continuous aging-related cognitive deficits have been documented in controlled studies of animals (Herndon, Moss, Rosene, & Killiany, 1997; Le Bourg, 2004), in which the threats to validity that are common to studies with human participants are not applicable. On the basis of these observations, we believe that there is conclusive evidence that, on average, aging-related declines in processing abilities begin in early adulthood, as suggested by cross-sectional age trends. Nevertheless, we value longitudinal approaches for the information they provide about individual differences in change, particularly when statistical methods for controlling for practice effects are applied.

## To What Extent Do Individual Differences Exist in Aging-Related Cognitive Changes?

The most basic question of direct relevance to the topic of individual differences in cognitive aging is the question of whether appreciable individual variation actually exists in aging-related cognitive changes. That is, are there some people who decline more steeply than others, or, put differently, are there some people who experience little decline (or even increase) and others who experience much decline? We make two points of clarification here. First, this section is concerned with the simple existence of individual difference in changes in processing abilities. We address predictors of these individual differences in later sections. Second, we focus on the continuous distribution of individual differences in cognitive aging across normal healthy adults. We acknowledge that there are, very likely, large differences in cognitive declines between healthy adults and those who experience dementia. However, this chapter is only concerned with how normal adults differ from one another, not with how they differ from patient populations.

### Cross-sectional evidence

One simple, albeit fairly crude, means of examining whether individual differences exist in cognitive aging is to examine whether there are age differences in the magnitude of between-person variation in cognitive performance. That is, one might expect the differences between individuals to increase with age, as some maintain high levels of performance while others experience large declines (note, however, that, if the most able decline the steepest, one might actually expect a pattern of decreasing variation in cognitive performance with age). Evidence appears to be mixed for the existence of age-related increases in between-person variation in adulthood. Morse (1993) analyzed data from studies published in *Psychology and Aging* and the *Journal of Gerontology* over a five-year period and concluded that adult age was related to increased variability in reaction time, memory, and reasoning, but not in verbal knowledge. On the basis of data from the WAIS–III standardization sample and of scaling standard deviations relative to mean performance (which we are critical of, because it confounds variation with performance level), Ardila (2007, p. 1010) similarly concluded that aging-related declines in test scores were associated with increased test score heterogeneity. However, in analyzing data from a community sample of 1,424 adults, Salthouse (2004a, p. 141) alternatively concluded that the variation in speed, reasoning, and memory scores evidenced nearly constant variability, and that the entire distributions of scores shifted downward with advancing adult age. Moreover, in analyzing data from the Berlin Aging Study, Lindenberger and Baltes (1997) similarly found no evidence for age-related differences in variation in perceptual speed, fluency, memory, or general intelligence. Finally, in surveying the published statistics from the nationally representative norming samples from a number of standardized cognitive testing batteries, Salthouse (2010a) was unable to find clear evidence for systematic cross-sectional age trends in between-person variation in cognitive test performance. To judge from these findings, there does not appear to be much evidence that between-person variation in cognitive test performance increases with adult age. We do note, however, that cross-sectional differences in between-person variability are likely to be quite sensitive to age differences in the participation rates of adults of different levels of functioning (a validity threat known as "selectivity") and to failures of the assumption of interval measurement of the cognitive tests (of which ceiling and floor effects can be considered severe examples).

## Longitudinal evidence

Given the limitations of cross-sectional approaches for making inferences about individual differences in cognitive changes, we turn to evidence derived from longitudinal data. In a longitudinal study, individual differences in cognitive aging would be directly reflected by individual differences in (i.e. variation in) rates of cognitive change. While variation in simple difference scores is likely to be disproportionately attributable to the existence of measurement error (Cronbach & Furby, 1970), new growth curve modeling and latent difference score modeling approaches enable researchers to produce estimates of variation in changes that are theoretically error-free. On the basis of these new methods, there is accumulating evidence for systematic and statistically significant variation in longitudinal cognitive change (e.g. Wilson et al., 2002). Even with measurement error removed, however, it is possible that individual differences in longitudinal change reflect a mixture of individual differences in true maturational change and individual differences in practice-related learning. We therefore emphasize studies that have examined whether between-person variation in longitudinal change persists after statistically correcting for estimates of between-person variation in practice effects. These include McArdle, Ferrer-Caja, Hamagami, and Woodcock (2002), Tucker-Drob, Johnson, and Jones (2009), and Tucker-Drob (in press a). Each study has reported significant variation in longitudinal slopes that is independent of variation in the practice effects (interestingly, variation in the practice effects was in many cases not statistically significant). What is the magnitude of this variation? Tucker-Drob (in press a) has reported that, in longitudinal data from VCAP, the ratio of the standard deviation of yearly maturational change to the standard deviation of individual differences at baseline was 9 percent, 8 percent, 12 percent, and 8 percent for reasoning, spatial visualization, episodic memory, and processing speed respectively. While this variation in yearly change may appear to be modest, it is important to realize that compounding it across multiple years or decades can result in substantial heterogeneity in the cognitive aging process.

Finally, we call attention to evidence that individual differences in maturational cognitive change are reliable and systematic. Evidence comes from recent studies by Ferrer, Salthouse, McArdle, Stewart, and Schwartz (2005), Wilson et al. (2002), Tucker-Drob et al. (2009), and Tucker-Drob (in press a), all of which have reported moderate correlations (approximately r = .5 in magnitude) among rates of change in different cognitive variables, even after accounting for practice effects. Because correlations can only exist in the presence of systematic variability (see e.g. Hertzog, von Oertzen, Ghisletta, & Lindenberger, 2008), this is strong evidence that individual differences in cognitive change are systematic. We discuss the topic of correlated longitudinal changes in further detail in the next section.

## How Many Explanations Are Needed for Cognitive Aging?

That age-related deficits are apparent on multiple measures representative of multiple domains of cognitive functioning raises the question of whether each of these deficits reflect a distinct developmental process, or they are all simply symptomatic of a fewer number of more general deficits. The former, *multidimensional* possibility would suggest the operation of a heterogeneous variety of causes of cognitive aging, with different causes affecting different functions. The latter, *few-dimensional* or *unidimensional* possibility would suggest a relatively smaller set of "common causes" (Baltes & Lindenberger, 1997), each one of which influences many different functions.

### Shared influence approaches

Shared influence approaches derive from two observations. First, many different cognitive variables evidence moderate to large negative correlations with adult age. Second, all reliably measured cognitive variables evidence moderate to large positive correlations with one another. These two observations allow for the possibility that mean age differences on each of the different cognitive variables can be accounted for by way of the influences of age on just a few common factors.

Salthouse and colleagues have tested shared influence models in a number of large cross-sectional data sets (Salthouse, 2004b, 2009; Salthouse & Davis, 2006; Salthouse & Ferrer-Caja, 2003). The general finding is that the mean age-related deficits that are observed on a variety of different cognitive variables can be parsimoniously accounted for by way of age differences on a very small number of dimensions. This is illustrated as a path diagram in Figure 9.3 for cross-sectional data from the Virginia Cognitive Aging Project. In this case, the negative effects of age on 12 different cognitive variables can be well accounted for by the influences of age on three dimensions: a common factor (often termed "*g*"), an episodic memory factor, and a speed of processing factor.

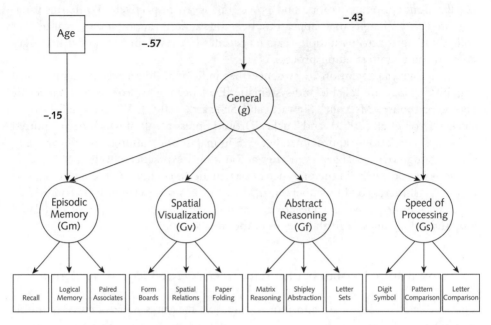

**Figure 9.3**   Localizing cross-sectional aging-related differences in a hierarchical structure

## Correlated changes approaches

In the past decade, researchers have begun to estimate correlations amongst individual differences in longitudinal changes in different cognitive variables. In contrast to cross-sectional shared influences models, which examine the extent to which mean age differences are shared across different cognitive variables, these correlated change approaches examine the extent to which individuals' rates of cognitive changes relative to their peers tend to be similar for different variables. Correlated changes approaches help to answer a question posed most plainly by Rabbitt (1993): "Does it all go together when it goes?"

Evidence is beginning to accumulate to suggest that the answer to Rabbitt's question is a qualified "yes." Rates of change in a variety of different indices of cognitive functioning tend to be moderately correlated with one another, such that a large proportion (although not all) of the individual differences in changes in different cognitive domains are shared. Such correlations have been reported by Anstey, Hofer, and Luszcz (2003), Lemke and Zimprich (2005), Sliwinksi and Buschke (2004), and Sliwinski, Hofer, and Hall (2003). Ferrer et al. (2005), Tucker-Drob (in press a), Tucker-Drob et al. (2009), and Wilson et al. (2002) have reported that these correlations largely persist when practice effects are statistically controlled for.

Five studies (Hertzog, Dixon, Hultsch, & MacDonald, 2003; Lindenberger & Ghisletta, 2009; Reynolds Gatz, & Pederson, 2002; Tucker-Drob, in press a; and Wilson et al., 2002) have employed factor-analytic methods to examine the extent to which the changes in a broad variety of cognitive variables can be attributable to a common underlying dimension of individual differences in changes. Results have been quite consistent with one another, with a single common factor accounting for between approximately 35 percent and 60 percent of individual differences in cognitive changes. Tucker-Drob (in press a) has, moreover, demonstrated that a hierarchical factor model can be fit to longitudinal cognitive changes. In such a hierarchical factor model, approximately 40 percent of individual differences in longitudinal changes in 12 tests of cognitive processing from VCAP (the same tests depicted in Figure 9.3) could be accounted for by a domain-general change factor, approximately 30 percent could be accounted for by domain-specific factors (reasoning, spatial visualization, memory, or processing speed), and approximately 30 percent was variation in change specific to the individual tests. These results, together, suggest that individual differences in cognitive aging are attributable to a mixture of a domain-general factor and multiple domain-specific factors.

It is of note that nearly all examinations of correlated changes have been based on data from middle-aged and older adults. The question of whether correlated changes also exist in young adulthood is, however, relevant to at least two major issues. First, as was described earlier, there is still some controversy regarding whether meaningful age-related deficits indeed begin in early adulthood. If abilities remain stable and do not decline during early adulthood, one would not expect individual differences in change to exist in healthy young adults. Alternatively, establishing that similar patterns of individual differences in change pertain to younger and older adults would suggest that the meaning of change does not differ with age (see Salthouse, 2010c), and therefore it would undermine the view that cognitive aging does not begin until middle to late adulthood. Second, a number of researchers (Baltes & Lindenberger, 1997; de Frias, Lövden, Lindenberger, & Nilsson, 2007; Lövdén & Lindenberger, 2005; McDonald, 2002) have argued that, even though idiosyncratic function-specific cognitive declines may indeed begin in young adulthood, general deficits that pervade many domains of functioning are only prominent in later life. Tucker-Drob (in press a) produced one of the first examinations of the extent to which global patterns of correlated cognitive changes are evident in younger adults. Participants were divided into three groups, the younger group containing adults between 18 and 49 years of age, the middle group containing adults between 50 and 69 years of age, and the older group containing adults between 70 and 95 years of age. A common factor model was fit to longitudinal slopes representing changes in four domains of cognition: fluid reasoning, spatial visualization, episodic memory, and processing speed. The resulting patterns were consistent across age groups, with moderate to large positive loadings on a global change factor in all three groups. Furthermore, constraining the unstandardized factor variances and factor loadings to be equivalent across groups did not significantly decrease model fit—in other words, there was no evidence that the pattern was significantly different across the three groups. These findings suggest that the global and pervasive patterns of cognitive declines that are typically experienced in older adulthood originate in early adulthood.

## What Are the Moderators of Cognitive Aging?

One question that is of great interest not only to cognitive aging researchers, but to the public at large, is: *Who* are the people who stave off decline, and how do they differ from those who do not? Here we follow the lead of Hertzog, Kramer, Wilson, and Lindenberger (2009) and focus on social environments and individual behaviors that have been hypothesized to protect against cognitive declines. We do not consider hypotheses relating chronic illness or unhealthy behaviors (e.g. smoking) to individual differences in cognitive decline, nor do we review work on the roles of nutrition or pharmaceuticals. Instead, we focus on two broad classes of popular hypotheses. The first hypothesis has often been termed the *cognitive reserve* hypothesis. It predicts that advantages afforded by educational and socioeconomic opportunities in early life can serve to slow the rates of aging-related cognitive decline. The second hypothesis has frequently been termed the *"use it or lose it"* hypothesis. It predicts that mental exercise and maintenance of an engaged lifestyle can help to slow the rates of aging-related cognitive declines.

Before reviewing the scientific evidence pertaining to the two above-described hypotheses, it is important to make a conceptual clarification. Relations between hypothesized protective factors and late-life cognitive function might be observed for one of two distinct possible reasons. The first possibility is what Salthouse and colleagues (Salthouse 2006; Salthouse, Babcock, Skovronek, Mitchell, & Palmon, 1990) have referred to as "differential preservation." Differential preservation, which is illustrated in the left panel of Figure 9.4, describes a situation in which individuals who differ in their level of a hypothesized protective factor also predictably differ in their rate of cognitive decline (i.e. the preservation of cognitive function is differential). The second possibility is what Salthouse and colleagues (Salthouse 2006; Salthouse et al., 1990) have referred to as "preserved differentiation." Preserved differentiation, which is illustrated in the right panel of Figure 9.4, describes a situation in which individuals who differ in their level of a hypothesized protective factor begin adulthood at different levels of cognitive ability, but do not differ in their rate of cognitive decline (the differentiation between people is preserved across time). Therefore, under preserved differentiation, the differences that exist between groups at the beginning of adulthood are preserved into later adulthood, but do not widen.

Consider the implications of differential preservation and preserved differentiation for interpreting the finding relating a risk factor (e.g. education) to the incidence rate

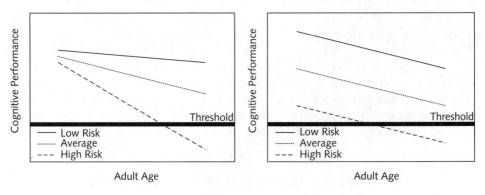

**Figure 9.4** Illustration of differential preservation (left) and preserved differentiation (right) scenarios. The horizontal line depicts a diagnostic threshold beyond which the level of cognitive functioning is considered pathological

of dementia, or otherwise clinically severe levels of functioning. Dementias and related disorders are often identified by using cognitive tests: if real-world functioning is deemed to be impaired and performance on the cognitive test falls below a diagnostic threshold, diagnosis is probable (American Psychiatric Association, 2000). An increased risk of dementia is therefore likely to reflect at least one of two general possibilities. The first is that individuals high on the risk factor decline more steeply in their cognitive performance than those low on the risk factor (this possibility reflects differential preservation). The second possibility, however, is that individuals high on the risk factor decline in their cognitive performance at similar rates to those of individuals who are low on the risk factor (a possibility that reflects preserved differentiation), but they begin adulthood at lower levels of cognitive performance, such that they are closer to the diagnostic threshold. To illustrate these possibilities, a threshold is superimposed atop the differential preservation and preserved differentiation patterns in Figure 9.4. It can be seen that those who are high on the risk factor surpass the threshold the earliest, regardless of whether the risk factor is related or not to the rate of cognitive decline. In the preserved differentiation scenario, the risk factor is related to the incidence of dementia simply because high-risk individuals begin adulthood closer to the threshold beyond which their performance is considered clinically severe or pathological. Because of the ambiguity associated with examining prevalence and incidence rates for inferring differential preservation versus preserved differentiation, we only review here studies that examine cognition measured on a continuous scale, and we do not review studies that focus on presence versus absence outcomes.

The *cognitive reserve hypothesis* generally refers to the prediction that those who have experienced more enriched socioeconomic environments during childhood and early adulthood have more resilient cognitive and/or neurobiological architectures, which protect against aging-related cognitive deficits. The number of years of educational attainment is among the most popular indices of such advantages. Multiple versions of the cognitive reserve hypothesis currently exist, and they can generally be classified either as passive models or as active models (Stern, 2009). Passive models are more frequently conceptualized at the neurobiological level. These models generally view high-reserve (i.e. more educated) individuals as having more resilient brains, whose functions are less affected by neurodegeneration than those of low-reserve (less educated) individuals are. One such basis for these models is the hypothesis that high-reserve individuals have more redundant brain networks. Therefore, if a single network is damaged but the redundant network is not, functioning is unaffected. Active models, alternatively, are most often—although not exclusively—conceptualized at the cognitive level. These models generally view high-reserve individuals as better able to compensate for neurodegeneration, through a reorganization of information-processing networks and/or through a shift in reliance on unaffected cognitive processes or knowledge structures to support functions that were previously supported by the now-affected processes. Under active models, high-reserve individuals should have more flexible brain structures, cognitive processes, and/or knowledge structures.

The cognitive reserve hypothesis has frequently been tested by examining the relation between educational attainment and rates of longitudinal cognitive changes.

While some studies have reported statistically significant positive relations, more highly educated individuals exhibiting smaller declines than less educated individuals, many of these studies suffer from major methodological limitations (see Tucker-Drob et al., 2009 for a discussion). The main limitation is that studies have relied upon measures that are not very sensitive to the task of discriminating between individuals at the higher ranges of functioning. Because education is consistently related to levels of functioning at the beginning of a longitudinal study, the change amongst the more highly educated will be harder to detect with crude instruments, and an artifactual positive relation between educational attainment and cognitive change will arise. We therefore emphasize the results from studies that have made use of sensitive cognitive measures. Such studies include those by Christensen et al. (2001), Hofer et al. (2002), Mackinnon, Christensen, Hofer, Korten, and Jorm (2003), Tucker-Drob et al. (2009), and Van Dijk, van Gerven, van Boxtel, van der Elst, and Jolles (2008), all of which have failed to find positive education–cognitive changes relations. We therefore conclude that there currently exists little persuasive evidence that educational attainment (or any factors for which it may act as a surrogate) protects against normative cognitive declines. We do emphasize, however, that there is substantial evidence that those with higher levels of education have higher average levels of cognitive functioning throughout adulthood (likely as the result of preserved differentiation). Educational attainment may therefore still have important real-world implications for cognitive functioning in adulthood, even if it does not protect against aging-related cognitive decline.

The *"use it or lose it" hypothesis*, also known as the mental exercise hypothesis, predicts that those who maintain a mentally engaged and mentally active lifestyle will experience relatively less cognitive decline than those who do not. Mentally stimulating activities that have been hypothesized as protective against cognitive aging include recreational activities such as doing crossword puzzles and playing chess, learning a new skill such as how to play an instrument or speak a foreign language, and having an intellectually demanding job.

Salthouse (2006) has comprehensively reviewed cross-sectional evidence for the "use it or lose it" hypothesis. As he explains, observing that older adults who are more mentally active tend to have higher cognitive functioning is not very informative, because (1) the mental activity–mental ability relation may have existed in childhood and therefore have nothing to do with aging; and (2) mental activity may be an outcome of ability level rather than a determinant of ability level. Examination of mental activity-related differences in aging trajectories is therefore much more informative than examination of simple mental activity-cognitive function correlations. Such examinations of mental activity-related differences in aging trajectories can help to distinguish between the preserved differentiation and differential preservation scenarios with respect to the "use it or lose it" hypothesis. Salthouse (2006) has reviewed a large body of such evidence, comparing pre-existing groups known to engage in different levels of mental activity. One exemplary study (Salthouse et al., 1990) found that architects, who regularly employ spatial reasoning in their day-to-day jobs, exhibited age-related deficits in the visual–spatial test performance comparable to those of unselected adults. Another representative study (Hambrick, Salthouse, & Meinz, 1999) found no statistically significant differences in age-related cognitive trends as a function of time spent per week completing crossword puzzles. It is of note that there was a large degree of variation in the amount of time spent completing crossword puzzles, with the bottom quartile completing 1.1 hours per week, and the top quartile completing 10.2 hours per week. Salthouse (2006) reviewed work on age differences in cognitive performance as a function of self-reports on the time spent being engaged in cognitively demanding activities (sometimes scaled by the participant's subjective demands of each activity), and additionally as a function of self-reported dispositions toward engaging in cognitively stimulating activities. He concluded that there was little evidence supportive of a differential preservation pattern. In a 2009 paper, Hertzog and colleagues criticized Salthouse's conclusion for its overreliance on cross-sectional data. They cited six longitudinal studies that, they argued, produced evidence consistent with a differential preservation pattern. We note that, for the majority of these studies, the differential preservation pattern only held for small subsets of the hypothesized risk factors and cognitive outcomes examined (and therefore may have been spurious); the cognitive outcomes were measured with tests of questionable validity; or large portions of participants who were in the process of converting to dementia were included. Our view is therefore that there does not currently appear to be persuasive evidence for the differential preservation of cognitive abilities with respect to mental activity in normal healthy adults.

## What Can Improve Cognitive Performance in Adulthood?

Related to the question of what individual characteristics and behaviors might moderate the rate of cognitive change, there is also the question of what interventions might be applied to boost an overall level of cognitive performance. Here the question is not whether the rate of cognitive change can be altered, but whether overall performance can be improved. Research on interventions is relevant to individual differences in cognitive aging for at least two reasons. First, individual differences in late-life cognition can arise because some people have undergone an effective (naturally occurring) intervention, whereas others have not. Second, individual differences in late-life cognition can arise because some benefit more from an intervention than others do. While not much research has currently been done on the latter topic to date, we anticipate that this topic will gain more attention with the increasing appreciation of individual differences in cognitive aging, combined with recent methodological developments for examining individual differences in experiments (Muthén & Curran, 1997; Tucker-Drob, in press b). Here we focus on two categories of interventions: (1) cognitive training interventions; and (2) physical activity interventions. Medical and pharmacological interventions are beyond the scope of the current chapter.

### Cognitive training interventions

In the history of cognitive aging research, cognitive training interventions have been popular among researchers seeking to determine whether declining cognitive functions in old age can be remediated (see e.g. Schaie & Willis, 1986; Willis & Schaie, 1986, 1994). The Advanced Cognitive Training for Independent and Vital Elderly

(ACTIVE; Ball et al., 2002; Willis et al., 2006) serves as a recent and representative example of some of the latest attempts at improving late-life cognition through training.

Cognitive training interventions have conventionally been based on the premise that older adults can be taught skills and strategies that can be used to increase cognitive performance. In ACTIVE, 2,832 participants were randomized either to a no-contact control condition or to one out of three different cognitive training interventions, each one of which was conducted in small groups of 10, for 60- to 75-minute sessions, over up to six weeks. The memory-training intervention involved learning mnemonic strategies for remembering word lists, sequences of items, text material, and main ideas and details of stories. Application of these mnemonics was practiced on lab-based memory tasks and on everyday memory tasks (such as recalling a list of groceries), which were similar to those used as outcome measures. The reasoning training involved learning strategies designed to identify serial patterns. Application of these strategies was practiced on abstract reasoning tasks and on everyday reasoning tasks similar to those used as outcome measures. Speed of processing training involved learning visual search skills and strategies for identifying and localizing visual information quickly. Participants practiced speeded tasks that varied in complexity on the computer. A subset (60 percent) of the intervention group participants were offered booster training after 11 months. Booster training consisted of four 75-minute sessions over up to three weeks. Outcomes were assessed at pretraining baseline, posttest, one year, two years, three years, and five years. Outcomes included psychometric tests of memory, reasoning, and processing speed, self-reports on activities of daily living, and ecologically face-valid tests of everyday problem-solving, activities of everyday living, and everyday processing speed.

At face value, results from ACTIVE might appear to indicate that the training was a success. Relative to controls, participants improved on the psychometric tests of the abilities on which they were trained (participants trained in memory improved in memory, participants trained in reasoning improved in reasoning, and so forth). Moreover, the differences between control and intervention groups were still detectable after over five years. However, these results are not very surprising, as the skills and strategies taught as part of the training were tailored toward these specific outcomes. For example, participants who received the reasoning intervention were taught strategies to identify the pattern in a letter or word series, and indeed they improved on psychometric measures of letter series and word series completion. We believe that a more interesting and important question is whether the skills transferred, such that performance would improve on psychometric tasks that were not trained, or on ecologically face-valid measures of everyday functions. Results suggest that such a transfer did not occur. Training did not transfer across domains (e.g. participants trained in reasoning did not improve in memory relative to controls), nor did it transfer to objective measures of everyday functioning (e.g. relative to controls, participants receiving training interventions did not improve in their abilities to understand medication directions, to pay bills, or to follow food recipes). It is of note that, at the fifth-year follow-up, participants in the reasoning training group reported less difficulty with everyday tasks relative to controls. Given that this effect was only found on self-report measures of everyday functions but not on objective measures of everyday functions, it is likely that it represents an effect of training on personal beliefs about functioning, rather than actual functioning. A major challenge for future cognitive training intervention work will be to demonstrate the transfer of benefits to objective indices of cognitive performance and everyday functioning that may not share the same superficial qualities as the tasks on which the training occurred (McArdle & Prindle, 2008).

## Physical activity interventions

Over the past decade, results from randomized experiments have provided evidence supportive of a causal effect of aerobic exercise on cognitive function in older adults. A particularly rigorous study on this topic was conducted by Kramer et al. (1999), who randomly assigned 124 previously sedentary older adults to an aerobic walking intervention group or to a stretching and toning control group. They found that, compared to those in the stretching and toning group, those in the walking group exhibited enhanced performance on switching, distracter interference, and response inhibition tasks. Colcombe and Kramer (2003) later identified 18 articles reporting on cognitive change during randomized controlled fitness interventions. They meta-analyzed these studies, which in total included 197 effect sizes for a total of 96 control group participants and 101 exercise group participants. Exercise-related gains were observed in all cognitive domains: executive functioning, controlled processing, spatial visualization, and processing speed, with the largest gains ($d$ = approximately .6) observed in executive functioning, and the smallest gains ($d$ = approximately .2) observed in processing speed. It is not yet clear what mechanisms underlie the cognitive benefits of increased exercise, but some possibilities may include enhanced cerebral blood flow, stimulation of neurotransmitter activity, enhanced hormonal activity or regulation, stabilized mood, or automation of physical functions that would otherwise require effortful cognitive resources. We discuss research on the neurobiological bases of cognitive aging in a later section. However, one interesting possibility is that the mechanisms that underlie exercise-related cognitive benefits might be the mechanisms that degrade with age. In other words, exercise may help to restore functions that deteriorate as a result of normal aging. On the basis of this assumption, one might expect larger exercise benefits for older participants and for those who have exhibited particularly pronounced declines. Finally, of interest is whether these effects are simply immediate, or also result in altered rates of cognitive decline. Unfortunately, there is currently little work on this topic.

## How Does Cognitive Aging Relate to Real-World Functioning?

One is likely to wonder about the real-world implications of the rather dramatic age-related decreases in performance on cognitive tasks that occur during adulthood. Because the jobs, decisions, and even everyday activities that people perform in their lives often involve high levels of complexity and sophisticated thought, the conclusion that real-world functioning decreases substantially with old age might appear to be rather straightforward. Alternatively, studies of the self-appraisals of real-world functioning by older adults, as well as the observations of a number of cognitive aging researchers, suggest that the effects of cognitive aging on real-world function are rather minimal. For example Park (1998, p. 61) has written that "older adults function well and that cognitive declines documented in the lab do not impact as negatively as one would expect on everyday domains of behavior."

Do everyday functions, such as balancing a checkbook, following a food recipe, looking up a telephone number, or understanding medication adherence directions, decline along with cognitive declines in adulthood? These functions have received a great deal of attention from researchers, because they are crucial for independent living, and because failures of these functions (following medication instructions in particular) can have major negative consequences. Interestingly, contradictory findings are often produced by studies in which everyday functions are subjectively measured versus studies in which everyday functions are objectively measured. Self-reports of the subjective difficulty that adults experience in performing daily tasks typically exhibit only very weak relations to age, or to cognitive abilities for that matter. Alternatively, objectively measured performance on ecologically face-valid tests of everyday functions typically exhibit strong relations to age and to cognitive abilities. A recent study by Tucker-Drob illustrates these contradictory findings and produces evidence that may help to resolve them. Tucker-Drob (in press c) analyzed five-year longitudinal data from adults aged 65 years and older, who were living independently and were dementia-free at enrollment. He found that, although self-reports of everyday functions were indeed only weakly related to cognitive abilities and to age, objective, ecologically valid measures of everyday functions were negatively related to age, strongly related to cognitive abilities, and, most importantly, they declined in tandem with cognitive abilities (i.e. individual differences in changes in everyday functions were strongly correlated with individual differences in changes in cognitive abilities). These new results suggest that the reason why the effects of cognitive aging are not apparent on everyday functions is that people are poor at appraising their own levels of functioning, not that cognitive aging and everyday functioning are truly independent.

A related question concerns whether on-the-job performance declines with adult age. Rather than surveying many specific studies of many different types of job performance, we summarize this issue conceptually. Industrial/organizational psychologists have established that the efficient and successful performance of different jobs requires different mixtures of knowledge, skills, abilities, and "other" (Schmitt & Chan, 1998). "Other" includes aspects of personality, such as conscientiousness, extraversion, motivation, curiosity, and interests. Therefore, whether a person's job performance decreases, remains stable, or even increases with age is likely to be determined by a combination of the extent to which that individual changes in his or her levels of knowledge, skills, abilities, and "other," weighted by the extent to which that person's job requires each of these four factors (cf. Salthouse & Maurer, 1996). It is important to appreciate that, as individuals age and their processing abilities decline on average, their experience on the job accumulates. For many jobs, this experience results in the accumulation of knowledge and skills that positively impact performance, and overall job performance may continue to increase for much of adulthood (Skirbekk, 2004). Alternatively, for jobs that are especially high in cognitive demands, accumulating experience may not be sufficient to offset declines in processing abilities, and job performance may not increase with age, or may even begin to decline early in adulthood. Job performance may also decline early in adulthood for jobs that require cognitive effort but little knowledge or skill. These statements of course simplify the situation, as "other" factors (e.g. personality factors) may also change with age and therefore play roles in age-related changes in job performance.

## What Are the Neurobiological Substrates of Individual Differences in Cognitive Aging?

A complete understanding of the factors that underlie individual differences in cognitive aging will certainly require an understanding of individual differences in changes in the neurobiological factors that underlie cognitive performance. Indeed, numerous aspects of brain physiology have been found to change with age (Dennis & Cabeza, 2008; Raz et al., 2005; Raz & Rodrigue, 2006). Age-related decreases in overall brain volume and in regional brain volumes have been reported for both cross-sectional and longitudinal data. Gray matter shrinkage appears to be most pronounced for the frontal lobes, followed by the parietal lobes, and then by the medial temporal lobes (Dennis & Cabeza, 2008). Age-related degradation of white matter volume and integrity and of dopamine function appear to be similarly disproportionately concentrated in the frontal brain regions. There is evidence that each of these measures is correlated with cognitive function in older adults, suggesting that they are indeed plausible substrates of cognitive aging. However, future work will need to be done to link individual differences in longitudinal changes in the various neurobiological indices with those in various cognitive functions. Moreover, given the evidence that different cognitive functions change together (Tucker-Drob, in press a) and emerging evidence that different aspects of brain anatomy change together (Raz et al., 2005), it will be important to take multivariate approaches to the neurobiology–cognition link, such that commonalities among predictors and among outcomes can be taken into account.

## What Are the Genetic Risk Factors for Cognitive Aging?

A complete treatment of the topic of individual differences in cognitive aging necessitates that some attention be paid to the extent to which between-person genetic variation underlies individual differences in cognitive aging trajectories. As Turkheimer (2000) has stated, the finding that psychological traits are heritable is so pervasive that it can be considered "the first law of behavioral genetics." Cognitive abilities in adulthood are no exceptions to this law. In fact, genetic influences have been estimated to account for as much 80 percent of individual differences in cognitive abilities during later adulthood (Pederson, Plomin, Nesselroade, & McLearn, 1992). However, the finding that cognitive ability is highly heritable in adulthood is not a direct indication of the extent to which cognitive aging is genetically influenced. That is, because individual differences on cognition in adulthood reflect a combination of individual differences in cognitive development in addition to individual differences in cognitive aging, the heritability of cognitive ability potentially reflects the combination of genetic influences on development and genetic influences on cognitive aging. As such, it is much more informative to examine the heritability of individual differences in longitudinal cognitive changes that actually occur during adulthood. Only a few longitudinal twin studies of cognitive aging exist, and conclusions with respect to the heritability of cognitive changes are therefore somewhat tentative. Some of the best data come from the Swedish Adoption/Twin Study of Aging, for which Reynolds, Finkel, McArdle, Gatz, Berg, and Pedersen (2005) fit quadratic growth curve models to 13-year longitudinal data on 10 different cognitive variables representative of either verbal, spatial, memory, or processing speed abilities. The median reported heritability of the linear component of change was 16 percent, and of the quadratic component of change the median reported heritability was 41 percent. In the same data, Finkel, Reynolds, McArdle, and Pedersen (2005) reported the heritability of the linear components of change in verbal ability, spatial ability, memory, and processing speed composite scores to be 5 percent, 19 percent, 23 percent, and 32 percent respectively, and heritabilities for the quadratic components to be 5 percent, 57 percent, 69 percent, and 82 percent respectively. While these heritability estimates of aging-related cognitive changes are somewhat lower than the corresponding estimates for levels of cognitive functioning, there still appears to be ample room for genes to contribute to individual differences in cognitive aging.

A number of specific genetic polymorphisms have been identified as potential risk factors for cognitive decline. McGue and Johnson (2008) provide an accessible review of research on candidate genes for aging-related cognitive changes. As they explain, the gene for which the most robust and compelling evidence exists for a link to late-life cognition is the Apolipoprotein E (APOE) gene, which has been implicated in lipid transport and neuronal repair. The ε4 allele of APOE, which is present in approximately 15 percent of individuals with European ancestry, has been identified as a potential risk for cognitive decline. The ε4 allele of APOE has been robustly associated both with the age of dementia onset and with normal-range variation in cognitive functioning during later adulthood. Significant meta-analytic associations between APOE variation and general cognitive ability, episodic memory, and executive functioning in cognitively intact adults have been reported (Small, Rosnick, Fratiglioni, & Bäckman, 2004), and evidence is accumulating from studies to the effect that APOE is related to the rate of cognitive decline (Bretsky, Guralnik, Launer, Albert, & Seeman, 2003; Deary et al., 2004; Hofer et al., 2002). A number of other genetic polymorphisms have been proposed as candidates for risk of cognitive decline. These include Angiotensin I Converting Enzyme (ACE; implicated as a risk factor for hypertension), Catechol-O-Methyltransferase (COMT; involved in the degradation of released catecholamines), and Methionine Synthase (MTR; involved in the metabolism of homocysteine). McGue and Johnson (2008), however, conclude that current evidence for a systematic association between these genes and late-life cognitive functioning is inconsistent.

It is important to note that the population-genetic and molecular–genetic research on cognitive aging that has been conducted to date has primarily been concerned with the main additive effects of genes and has paid comparatively little attention to the possibilities of gene-by-environment interaction (i.e. of genetic influences varying as a function of specific environmental conditions) and of gene–environment correlation (i.e. of different environmental protective or risk factors varying systematically with different individual genotypes). There is, however, growing emphasis on gene-by-environment interaction and on gene–environment correlation in current research and theory (Deater-Deckard & Mayr, 2005; Shanahan & Hofer, 2005).

## Conclusions, Outlook, and Future Directions

Given that the ultimate goal of research in the psychological sciences is to understand, and perhaps even ultimately to affect, processes that occur for individuals, it is appropriate that research on cognitive aging is moving toward an increased appreciation of individual differences. In this chapter we have presented and summarized the progress that has been made toward answering seven major questions that we believe to be fundamental to the study of individual differences in cognitive aging. Much progress has already been made, but the answers to the questions are far from complete. Here we describe what we believe to be the next major steps that need to be taken in this important area of inquiry.

First, an increasing focus on individual differences in cognitive aging will entail an increased reliance on longitudinal data derived from sensitive measures. High-quality longitudinal data, paired with appropriate analytical methodologies for modeling change and for removing retest effects, will serve as the basis for better characterizing the progression of cognitive aging and for robustly identifying its correlates and consequences.

Second, in light of recent findings that large proportions of individual differences in aging-related changes in many different cognitive functions are overlapping, it will be important for future work to integrate the diverse findings and models that have been established for individual tasks and functions across those tasks and functions. This will entail increased collection of multivariate data and increased application of multivariate methodologies.

Third, there is a need to integrate findings from cognitive aging with findings from cognitive development. Although we do not believe that there is currently strong evidence consistent with differential preservation patterns with respect to popularly hypothesized moderators of cognitive aging, we note that there are ubiquitous socoidemographic correlates of levels of cognitive function at all stages of adulthood (i.e. preserved differentiation is well supported for many popularly hypothesized risk factors). It will therefore be crucial to understand the developmental processes that give rise sociodemographic disparities in cognitive functioning in childhood, which in turn persist throughout adulthood. In fact, it has even been suggested that the most cost-effective interventions to boost adult levels of cognitive functioning are likely to be those that target cognitive development during childhood (Heckman, 2006).

Fourth, crucial to intervention work will be the construction and evaluation of interventions that do not simply have proximal effects on test performance, but which reliably result in far transfer to many different abilities, and most importantly to real-world outcomes. Training adults in specific strategies that can be applied to specific sorts of tasks is not likely to produce gains that generalize to many functions. For cognitive training interventions, far transfer may be more likely to occur when general skills and functions, rather than specific strategies, are targeted.

Fifth, it will be crucial to empirically link the neurobiological changes that are thought to underlie cognitive aging with actual cognitive changes. That neurobiological variables degrade on average with age does not necessarily imply that such declines underlie aging-related cognitive declines, even if the neurobiological variables correlate with cognitive functions at a given period of time. Rather, it will be crucial to examine the longitudinal relations between individual differences in neurobiological variables and in cognitive variables. Longitudinal relations can take the form of (1) level of one variable preceding and predicting change in another variable; (2) changes in two or more variables being concurrently related; or (3) change in one variable preceding and predicting later change in another variable. Moreover, given that multiple neurobiological variables change with age, it will be important to examine the unique influences of different neurobiological variables on cognition, controlling for other neurobiological variables. This will help to map different aspects of cognitive aging to their specific neurobiological substrates.

Sixth, it is clear that conceptualizing genetic influences as uncorrelated and additive with environmental influences on cognition grossly oversimplifies reality. Future population–genetic and molecular–genetic work should test specific hypotheses regarding gene-by-environment interaction and the gene–environment correlation. The existence of gene-by-environment interaction may help to explain why candidate environmental risk factors are inconsistently linked with cognitive decline. That is, the relation between risk factor and outcome may be different for different people.

Finally, while the current chapter has primarily treated cognitive aging as an outcome in need of explanation, there is much work on how individual differences in cognitive functioning and cognitive aging predict individual differences in health and epidemiological outcomes. *Why* individual differences in cognitive functioning and in cognitive change relate to individual differences in health outcomes is a fundamental issue, which will need to be resolved in future research (Deary, 2008).

## Note

1   $r_{full\ sample}$ refers to the correlation between age and the ability in the full sample. $r_{MMSE≥27}$ = refers to the correlation between age and the ability when individuals with scores below 27 out of 30 on the Mini Mental State Examination are excluded.

# References

American Psychiatric Association (2000). *Diagnostic and statistical manual of mental disorders* (4th rev. ed.). Washington, DC: American Psychiatric Association.

Anstey, K. J., Hofer, S. M., & Luszcz, M. A. (2003). Cross-sectional and longitudinal patterns of dedifferentiation in later-life cognitive and sensory function: The effects of age, ability, attrition, and occasion of measurement. *Journal of Experimental Psychology: General, 132,* 470–487.

Ardila, A. (2007). Normal aging increases cognitive heterogeneity: Analysis of dispersion in WAIS-III scores across age. *Archives of Clinical Neuropsychology, 22,* 1003–1011.

Ball, K., Berch, D. B., Helmers, K. F., Jobe, J. B., Leveck, M. D., Marsiske et al. (2002). Advanced Cognitive Training for Independent and Vital Elderly Study Group (ACTIVE): Effects of cognitive training interventions with older adults: A randomized controlled trial. *Journal of the American Medical Association, 288,* 2271–2281.

Baltes, P. B., & Lindenberger, U. (1997). Emergence of a powerful connection between sensory and cognitive functions across the adult life span: A new window to the study of cognitive aging? *Psychology and Aging, 12,* 12–21.

Baltes, P. B., & Schaie, K. W. (1974). The myth of the twilight years. *Psychology Today, 7,* 35–38, 40.

Baltes, P. B., Reese, H.W., & Nesselroade, J. R. (1977). *Life-span developmental psychology: Introduction to research methods.* Monterey, CA: Brooks/Cole.

Bretsky, P., Guralnik, J. M., Launer, L., Albert, M., & Seeman, T. E. (2003). The role of APOE–4 in longitudinal cognitive decline: MacArthur studies of successful aging. *Neurology, 60,* 1077–1081.

Cattell, R. B. (1987). *Intelligence: Its structure, growth, and action.* [Revised and reprinted from *Abilities: Their structure, growth and action,* 1971.] Amsterdam: North-Holland.

Christensen, H., Hofer, S. M., Mackinnon, A. J., Korten, A. E., Jorm, A. F., & Henderson, A. S. (2001). Age is no kinder to the better educated: Absence of an association established using latent growth techniques in a community sample. *Psychological Medicine, 31,* 15–27.

Christensen, H., Mackinnon, A. J., Korten, A. E., Jorm, A. F., Henderson, A. S., Jacomb, P., & Rodgers, B. (1999). An analysis of diversity in the cognitive performance of elderly community dwellers: Individual differences in change scores as a function of age. *Psychology and Aging, 14,* 365–379.

Colcombe, S., & Kramer, A. F. (2003). Fitness effects on the cognitive function of older adults: A meta-analytic study. *Psychological Science, 14,* 125–130.

Cronbach, L. J., & Furby, L. (1970). How should we measure "change"—or should we? *Psychological Bulletin, 74,* 8–80.

Deary, I. (2008). Why do intelligent people live longer? *Nature, 456,* 175–176.

Deary, I. J., Whiteman, M. C., Pattie, A., Starr, J. M., Hayward, C., Wright, A. F. et al. (2004). Apolipoprotein E gene variability and cognitive functions at age 79: A follow-up of the Scottish Mental Survey of 1932. *Psychology and Aging, 19,* 367–371.

Deater-Deckard, K., & Mayr, U. (2005). Cognitive change in aging: Identifying gene–environment correlation and nonshared environment mechanisms. *Journal of Gerontology: Series B, 60,* 24–31.

Dennis, N.A., & Cabeza, R. (2008). Neuroimaging of healthy cognitive aging. In F. E. M. Craik & T. Salthouse (Eds.), *Handbook of aging and cognition* (3rd ed., pp. 1–54). New York: Psychology Press.

Ferrer, E., Salthouse, T. A., McArdle, J. J., Stewart, W. F., & Schwartz, B. S. (2005). Multivariate modeling of age and retest in longitudinal studies of cognitive abilities. *Psychology and Aging, 20*, 412–422.

Flynn, J. R. (1987). Massive IQ gains in 14 nations: What IQ tests really measure. *Psychological Bulletin, 101*, 171–191.

Folstein, M. F., Folstein, S. E., & McHugh, P. R. (1975). "Mini-mental state." A practical method for grading the cognitive state of patients for the clinician. *Journal of Psychiatric Research, 12*, 189–198.

de Frias, C. M., Lövden, M., Lindenberger, U., & Nilsson, L.-G. (2007). Revisiting the dedifferentiation hypothesis with longitudinal multi-cohort data. *Intelligence, 35*, 381–392.

Hambrick, D. Z., Salthouse, T. A., & Meinz, E. J. (1999). Predictors of crossword puzzle proficiency and moderators of age-cognition relations. *Journal of Experimental Psychology: General, 128*, 131–164.

Heckman, J. J. (2006). Skill formation and the economics of investing in disadvantaged children. *Science, 312*, 1900–1902.

Herndon, J. G., Moss, M. B., Rosene, D. L., & Killiany, R. J. (1997). Patterns of cognitive decline in aged rhesus monkeys. *Behavioural Brain Research, 87*, 25–34.

Hertzog, C., Dixon, R. A., Hultsch, D. F., & MacDonald, S. W. S. (2003). Latent change models of adult cognition: Are changes in processing speed and working memory associated with changes in episodic memory? *Psychology and Aging, 18*, 755–769.

Hertzog, C., Kramer, A. F., Wilson, R. S., & Lindenberger, U. (2009). Enrichment effects on adult cognitive development: Can the functional capacity of older adults be preserved and enhanced? *Psychological Science in the Public Interest, 9*, 1–65.

Hertzog, C., von Oertzen, T., Ghisletta, P., & Lindenberger, U. (2008). Evaluating the power of latent growth curve models to detect individual differences in change. *Structural Equation Modeling, 15*, 541–563.

Hofer, S. M., Christensen, H., MacKinnon, A. J., Korten, A. E., Jorm, A. F., Henderson, A. S., & Easteal, S. (2002). Change in cognitive functioning associated with apoE genotype in a community sample of older adults. *Psychology and Aging, 17*, 194–208.

Horn, J. L., & Donaldson, G. (1976). On the myth of intellectual decline in adulthood. *American Psychologist, 31*, 701–719.

Kramer, A. F., Hahn, S., Cohen, N. J., Banich, M. T., McAuley, E., Harrison, C. R., Chason, J., Vakil, E., Bardell, L., Boileau, R. A., & Colcombe, A. (1999). Ageing, fitness and neurocognitive function. *Nature, 400*, 418–419.

Le Bourg, E. (2004). Effects of aging on learned suppression of photopositive tendencies in Drosophila melanogaster. *Neurobiology of Aging, 25*, 1241–1252.

Lemke, U., & Zimprich, D. (2005). Longitudinal changes in memory performance and processing speed in old age. *Aging, Neuropsychology, and Cognition, 12*, 57–77.

Li, S.-C., Lindenberger, U., Hommel, B., Aschersleben, G., Prinz, W., & Baltes, P. B. (2004). Transformations in the couplings among intellectual abilities and constituent cognitive processes across the life span. *Psychological Science, 15*, 155–163.

Lindenberger, U., & Baltes, P. B. (1997). Intellectual functioning in old and very old age: Cross-sectional results from the Berlin Aging Study. *Psychology and Aging, 12*, 410–432.

Lindenberger, U., & Ghisletta, P. (2009). Cognitive and sensory declines in old age: Gauging the evidence for a common cause. *Psychology and Aging, 24*, 1–16.

Lindenberger, U., Singer, T., & Baltes, P. B. (2002). Longitudinal selectivity in aging populations: Separating mortality-associated versus experimental components in the Berlin Aging Study (BASE). *Journal of Gerontology: Psychological Sciences, 57*, 474–482.

Lövdén, M., & Lindenberger, U. (2005). Development of intellectual abilities in old age: From age gradients to individuals. In O. Wilhelm & R. Engle (Eds.), *Understanding and measuring intelligence* (pp. 203–221). Thousand Oaks, CA: Sage.

Mackinnon, A., Christensen, H., Hofer, S. M., Korten, A., & Jorm, A. F. (2003). Use it and still lose it? The association between activity and cognitive performance established using latent growth techniques in a community sample. *Aging, Neuropsychology, and Cognition*, *10*, 215–229.

McArdle, J. J., & Prindle, J. J. (2008). A latent change score analysis of a randomized clinical trial in reasoning training. *Psychology and Aging*, *23*, 702–719.

McArdle, J. J., Ferrer-Caja, E., Hamagami, F., & Woodcock, R.W. (2002). Comparative longitudinal multilevel structural analyses of the growth and decline of multiple intellectual abilities over the life-span. *Developmental Psychology*, *38*, 115–142.

McArdle, J. J., Grimm, K. J., Hamagami, F., Bowles, R. P., & Meredith, W. (2009). Modeling life-span growth curves of cognition using longitudinal data with multiple samples and changing scales of measurement. *Psychological Methods*, *14*, 126–149.

McDonald, R. J. (2002). Multiple combinations of co-factors produce variants of age-related cognitive decline: A theory. *Canadian Journal of Experimental Psychology*, *56*, 221–239.

McGue, M. & Johnson, W. (2008). Genetic research and cognitive aging. In F. Craik & T. Salthouse (Eds.), *Handbook of aging and cognition* (3rd ed., pp. 55–96). New York: Psychology Press.

Morse, C. K. (1993). Does variability increase with age? An archival study of cognitive measures. *Psychology and Aging*, *8*, 156–164.

Muthén, B. O., & Curran, P. J. (1997). General longitudinal modeling of individual differences in experimental designs: A latent variable framework for analysis and power estimation. *Psychological Methods*, *2*, 371–402.

Park, D. C. (1998). Cognitive aging, processing resources, and self-report. In N. Schwarz, D. C. Park, B. Knaueper, & S. Sudman (Eds.), *Aging, cognition, and self-report*. Washington, DC: Psychology Press.

Pedersen, N. L., Plomin, R., Nesselroade, J. R., & McClearn, G. E. (1992). A quantitative genetic analysis of cognitive abilities during the second half of the life span. *Psychological Science*, *3*, 346–353.

Rabbitt, P. (1993). Does it all go together when it goes? The Nineteenth Bartlett Memorial Lecture. *The Quarterly Journal of Experimental Psychology*, *46*, 385–434.

Raz, N., & Rodrigue, K. M. (2006). Differential aging of the brain: Patterns, cognitive correlates, and modifiers. *Neuroscience and Biobehavioral Reviews*, *30*, 730–748.

Raz, N., Lindenberger, U., Rodrigue, K. M., Kennedy, K. M., Head, D., Williamson, A., Dahle, C., Gerstorf, D., & Acker, J. D. (2005). Regional brain changes in aging healthy adults: General trends, individual differences and modifiers. *Cerebral Cortex*, *15*, 1676–1689.

Reynolds, C. A., Gatz, M., & Pederson, N. L. (2002). Individual variation for cognitive decline: Quantitative patterns for describing patterns of change. *Psychology and Aging*, *17*, 271–287.

Reynolds, C. A., Finkel, D., McArdle, J. J., Gatz, M., Berg, S., & Pedersen, N. L. (2005). Quantitative genetic analysis of latent growth curve models of cognitive abilities in adulthood. *Developmental Psychology*, *41*, 3–16.

Rönnlund, M., Nyberg, L., Bäckman, L., & Nilsson, L.-G. (2005). Stability, growth, and decline in adult life-span development of declarative memory: Cross-sectional and longitudinal data from a population-based sample. *Psychology and Aging 20*, 3–18.

Salthouse, T. A. (2004a). What and when of cognitive aging. *Current Directions in Psychological Science*, *13*, 140–144.

Salthouse, T. A. (2004b). Localizing age-related individual differences in a hierarchical structure. *Intelligence, 32,* 541–561.

Salthouse, T. A. (2005). Book review: K. Warner Schaie, *Developmental influences on adult intelligence: The Seattle Longitudinal Study. Intelligence, 33,* 551–554.

Salthouse, T. A. (2006). Mental exercise and mental aging: Evaluating the validity of the "use it or lose it" hypothesis. *Perspectives on Psychological Science, 1,* 68–87.

Salthouse, T. A. (2009). When does age-related cognitive decline begin? *Neurobiology of Aging, 30,* 507–514.

Salthouse, T. A. (2010a). *Major issues in cognitive aging.* New York: Oxford.

Salthouse, T. A. (2010b). Influence of age on practice effects in longitudinal neurocognitive change. *Neuropsychology, 24,* 563–572.

Salthouse, T. A. (2010c). Does the meaning of neurocognitive change change with age? *Neuropsychology, 24,* 273–278.

Salthouse, T. A., & Davis, H. P. (2006). Organization of cognitive abilities and neuropsychological variables across the lifespan. *Developmental Review, 26,* 31–54.

Salthouse, T. A., & Ferrer-Caja, E. (2003). What needs to be explained to account for age-related effects on multiple cognitive variables? *Psychology and Aging, 18,* 91–110.

Salthouse, T. A., & Maurer, T. J. (1996). Aging, job performance and career development. In J. E. Birren & K. W. Schaie (Eds.), *Handbook of the psychology of aging* (4th ed., pp. 353–364). New York: Academic Press.

Salthouse, T. A., & Tucker-Drob, E. M. (2008). Implications of short-term retest effects for the interpretation of longitudinal change. *Neuropsychology, 22,* 800–811.

Salthouse, T. A., Pink, J. E., & Tucker-Drob, E. M. (2008). Contextual analysis of fluid intelligence. *Intelligence, 36,* 464–486.

Salthouse, T. A., Babcock, R. L., Skovronek, E., Mitchell, D. R. D., & Palmon, R. (1990). Age and experience effects in spatial visualization. *Developmental Psychology, 26,* 128–136.

Schaie, K. W., & Willis S. L. (1986). Can intellectual decline in the elderly be reversed? *Developmental Psychology, 22,* 223–232.

Shanahan, M. J., & Hofer, S. M. (2005). Social context in gene–environment interactions: Retrospect and prospect. *Journals of Gerontology: Series B, 60,* 65–76.

Schmitt, N., & Chan, D. (1998). *Personnel selection: A theoretical approach.* Thousand Oaks, CA: Sage.

Skirbekk, V. (2004). Age and individual productivity: A literature survey. *Vienna Yearbook of Population Research.* Vienna: Austrian Academy of Sciences Press.

Sliwinksi, M., & Buschke, H. (2004). Modeling intraindividual cognitive change in aging adults: Results from the Einstein aging studies. *Aging, Neuropsychology, and Cognition, 11,* 196–211.

Sliwinski, M., Hofer, S., & Hall, C. B. (2003). Correlated cognitive change in older adults with and without preclinical dementia. *Psychology and Aging, 18,* 672–683.

Small, B. J., Rosnick, C. B., Fratiglioni, L., & Bäckman, L. (2004). Apolipoprotein E and cognitive performance: A meta-analysis. *Psychology and Aging, 19,* 592–600.

Stern, Y. (2009). Cognitive reserve. *Neuropsychologia, 47,* 2015–2028.

Tucker-Drob, E. M. (2009). Differentiation of cognitive abilities across the lifespan. *Developmental Psychology, 45,* 1097–1118.

Tucker-Drob, E. M. (in press a). Global and domain-specific changes in cognition throughout adulthood. *Developmental Psychology.*

Tucker-Drob, E. M. (in press b). Individual differences methods for randomized experiments. *Psychological Methods.*

Tucker-Drob, E. M. (in press c). Neurocognitive functions and everyday functions change together in old age. *Neuropsychology.*

Tucker-Drob, E. M., & Salthouse, T. A. (2008). Adult age trends in the relations among cognitive abilities. *Psychology and Aging, 23,* 453–460.

Tucker-Drob, E. M., & Salthouse, T. A. (2009). Confirmatory factor analysis and multidimensional scaling for construct validation of cognitive abilities. *International Journal of Behavioral Development, 33,* 277–285.

Tucker-Drob, E. M., Johnson, K. E., & Jones, R. N. (2009). The cognitive reserve hypothesis: A longitudinal examination of age-associated declines in reasoning and processing speed. *Developmental Psychology, 45,* 431–446.

Turkheimer, E. (2000). Three laws of behavior genetics and what they mean. *Current Directions in Psychological Science, 9,* 160–164.

Van Dijk, K. R. A, van Gerven, P. W. M., van Boxtel, M. P. J., van der Elst, W., & Jolles, J. (2008). No protective effects of education during normal cognitive aging: Results from the 6-year follow-up of the Maastricht Aging Study (MAAS), *Psychology and Aging, 23,* 119–130.

Wechsler, D. (1958). *The measurement and appraisal of adult intelligence* (4th ed.). Baltimore, MD: Williams and Wilkins.

Willis, S. L., & Schaie, K. W. (1986). Training the elderly on the ability factors of spatial orientation and inductive reasoning. *Psychology and Aging. 1,* 239–247.

Willis, S. L., & Schaie, K. W. (1994). Cognitive training in the normal elderly. In F. Forette, Y. Christen, & F. Boiler (Eds.), *Plasticité cérébrale et stimulation cognitive [Brain plasticity and cognitive stimulation]* (pp. 91–113). Paris: Fondation Nationale de Gérontologie.

Willis, S. L., Tennsteadt, S. L., Marsiske, M., Ball, K., Elias, J., Koepke, K. et al. (2006). Long-term effects of cognitive training on everyday functional outcomes in older adults. *Journal of American Medical Association, 296,* 2805–2814.

Wilson, R. S., Beckett, L. A., Barnes, L. L., Schneider, J. A., Bach, J., Evans, D. A., & Bennett, D. A. (2002). Individual differences in rates of change in cognitive abilities of older persons. *Psychology and Aging, 17,* 179–193.

Yang, Y., Schulhofer-Wohl, S., Fu, W., & Land, K. (2008). The intrinsic estimator for age-period-cohort analysis: What it is and how to use it? *American Journal of Sociology, 113,* 1697–1736.

# Part III
# Biological Causes of Individual Differences

# 10

# Behavior Genetics

## Frank M. Spinath and Wendy Johnson

## Introduction

Behavior genetics, the study of genetic and environmental origins of individual differences in behavior, is an interdisciplinary area combining the behavioral sciences and genetics. It is also arguably one of the most rapidly evolving scientific fields today, characterized by a breathtaking pace of discoveries and methodological advances that continues to accelerate. A generation ago, it seemed that the outcome of the nature–nurture debate depended on the degree to which twin and adoption studies revealed substantial genetic contributions to important domains of human behavior. This research has yielded almost unanimous results indicating that individual differences in all behavior, be it related to personality or ability or even to particular activities, is subject to genetic influence. As a consequence, the field of behavior genetics has accomplished a paradigm shift in psychology, biology, and sociology. It is now generally accepted that genetic influences on behavior are ubiquitous, so much so that Turkheimer (2000) summarized this fact as "the first law of behavior genetics." This general prevalence of genetic influences is of critical importance for our understanding that major sources of behavior lie in individual differences intrinsic to the individual. But what does it mean, specifically, with regard to the underlying biology? What role does the environment play? And, even more interestingly, how do nature and nurture transact in shaping people's developments over the life-course?

The present chapter discusses the ways in which genetic and environmental influences are involved in individual differences and in the quantitative and molecular genetic methodologies that have been used to explore them. In our account of the quantitative genetic approach we focus primarily on twin studies, although we acknowledge the importance of adoption designs as alternative or complementary approaches, which are discussed in detail elsewhere (Plomin, DeFries, McClearn, &

*The Wiley-Blackwell Handbook of Individual Differences*, First Edition.
Edited by Tomas Chamorro-Premuzic, Sophie von Stumm, and Adrian Furnham.
© 2011 Blackwell Publishing Ltd. Published 2011 by Blackwell Publishing Ltd.

McGuffin, 2008). We begin by defining the major concepts, and then summarize the overall findings of the past 40 years in the areas of ability and personality. In describing the findings, we explain the methods that have been used to obtain them and the assumptions that underlie those methods. In doing so, we stress that the development of new methods has been driven by the ongoing goal of behavior geneticists to relax and test the assumptions that underlie methods used in the past.

## The Twin Method, Its Underlying Assumptions, and a Cautionary Note

The formation of behavior genetics as a field was influenced by Charles Darwin and Francis Galton. Darwin's descriptions of individual differences in behavior within species (Darwin, 1859) and Galton's interest in the inheritance of physiological and psychological human characteristics (Galton, 1869) mark the beginning of systematic investigation into the sources of individual psychological differences. Today's field of behavior genetics encompasses diverse research strategies—such as twin and adoption studies, called *quantitative genetics*, which investigate the relative importance of genetic and environmental influences, as well as strategies to identify specific genes associated with trait-like patterns of behavior, called *molecular genetics* (Plomin et al., 2008). The development of the twin method is usually also ascribed to Galton (1876) although it is uncertain whether Galton was aware of the distinction between monozygotic and dizygotic twins (Rende, Plomin, & Vandenberg, 1990).

### Classical twin design

It was not until more than 50 years after Darwin's and Galton's original writings that explicit descriptions of the classical twin method were published (Merriman, 1924; Siemens, 1924). The classical twin study compares the phenotypic resemblances of identical or monozygotic (MZ) and fraternal or dizygotic (DZ) twins. MZ twins derive from the splitting of one fertilized zygote, and therefore they inherit identical genetic material. DZ twins are first-degree relatives, because they develop from separately fertilized eggs. They share on average 50 percent of the genes that differ among humans—as do full singleton siblings. It follows that a greater within-pair similarity in MZ compared to DZ twins suggests that genetic variance influences the trait under study. Comparing the phenotypic or observable resemblance of MZ and DZ twins for a trait or measure under study offers a first estimate of the extent to which genetic variance is associated with phenotypic variation of that trait. This is typically measured by using a statistic called heritability. Heritability is defined as the proportion of phenotypic differences among individuals that can be attributed to genetic differences in a particular population. The heritability ($h^2$) of the trait can be estimated by doubling the difference between MZ and DZ correlations, that is, $h^2 = 2(r_{MZ} - r_{DZ})$ (Falconer, 1960).

Shared environmental effects index the extent to which people are similar independently of genetic effects, because they share some environmental influence such as parental socioeconomic status. The proportion of the variance that is due to shared environmental effects ($c^2$) can be derived by calculating $c^2 = r_{MZ} - h^2$, where $r_{MZ}$ is the correlation between MZ twins—because MZ similarity can be conceptualized as $h^2$ (similarity due to genetic influences) + $c^2$ (similarity due to shared environmental influences). Substituting $2(r_{MZ}-r_{DZ})$ for $h^2$ offers another way of calculating shared environmental effects ($c^2 = 2r_{DZ} - r_{MZ}$). In other words, the presence of shared environmental influences on a certain trait is suggested if DZ twin similarity exceeds half the MZ twin similarity for that trait. DZ twin similarity which is less than half the MZ twin correlation indicates the presence of non-additive genetic effects. In contrast to additive genetic effects, which occur when the effects of alleles at a particular locus and across loci act independently of each other and thus additively, non-additive genetic effects occur when the effects of alleles differ in the presence of other alleles either at the same locus (dominance) or at other loci (epistasis). Non-shared environmental effects index the extent to which family members are different, despite sharing genetic material and growing up together. Examples include having different peers, attending different classes, participating in different leisure activities, and receiving different parental treatment. Non-shared environmental influences ($e^2$) can be estimated from $e^2 = r_{tt} - r_{MZ}$, where $r_{tt}$ is the test–retest reliability of the measure. If $1 - r_{MZ}$ is used to estimate $e^2$ instead, the resulting non-shared environmental influences are confounded with measurement error.

For example, in studies of more than 10,000 MZ and DZ twin pairs on general cognitive ability (*g*), the average MZ correlation is .86, which is near the test–retest reliability of the measures, in contrast to the DZ correlation of .60 (Plomin & Spinath, 2004). On the basis of these data, application of the above formulae results in a heritability estimate of $h^2 = .52$, shared environmental estimate of $c^2 = .34$, and non-shared environmental influence/measurement error estimate of $e^2 = .14$. Thus, given that MZ and DZ twin correlations are available, this straightforward set of formulae can be used to derive estimates of genetic and environmental influences on any given trait under study. Instead of the Pearson product–moment correlation coefficient, twin similarity is typically calculated by using intra-class correlation (ICC1.1; Shrout & Fleiss, 1979) because this form of correlation eliminates any bias due to non-random ordering of twins within pairs.

## Requirements and assumptions

Interpretation of twin correlations in the described manner relies on a number of assumptions: the absence of assortative mating for the trait in question; the absence of G(enotype)—E(nvironment) correlation (rGE) and interaction (G × E); and the viability of the equal environments assumption (EEA). Each of these assumptions is addressed briefly below.

*Assortative mating* describes non-random mating that results in similarity or dissimilarity between spouses. When a trait shows genetic influences and spouses are more similar than randomly paired couples, the spouses show some correlation for the trait and their offspring show higher correlations due to increased genetic similarity resulting from the transmission of similar genes from both parents. Assortative mating can result from social stratification for similar traits, and thus, at the individual level, from simple propinquity (people tend to select their spouses from those most immediately around them socially), and/or from active social selection, as when people of a given religious faith in a religiously mixed society select their spouses specifically from among those of their own faith. Assortative mating tends to be low for some psychological traits (e.g. personality), but can be substantial for others (e.g. intelligence, with average spouse correlations of about .40; Jensen, 1998). In twin studies, unrecognized assortative mating can result in underestimates of heritability, because it raises the DZ correlation but does not affect the MZ correlation, thus mimicking shared environmental influences.

*Gene–environment correlation* (rGE) describes the phenomenon that genetic propensities can be correlated with individual differences in experience. This occurs when either there is genetic control of exposure to environmental circumstances or there is environmental control of gene frequency, or both; this phenomenon will be treated in greater detail below. Previous research indicates that genetic factors often contribute substantially to measures of the environment, especially the family environment (Plomin, 1994). In the classic twin study, however, rGE is assumed to be zero.

*Genotype–environment interaction (G×E)* is often conceptualized as the genetic control of sensitivity to the environment (Kendler & Eaves, 1986) or, alternatively, as environmental control of differential gene effects. Heritability that is conditional on environmental exposure can indicate the presence of a G × E. The classic twin study is based on the assumption that there is no G × E.

The classic twin model is based on the assumed equality of pre- and postnatal environmental influences within the two types of twins. In other words, under the *equal environments assumption* we assume that environmentally caused similarity is roughly the same for both types of twins reared in the same family. Violations of the EEA because MZ twins experience more similar environments than DZ twins inflate estimates of genetic influences. The EEA has been tested in a number of studies. Even though MZ twins appeared to experience more similar environments than DZ twins, these differences did not seem to be responsible for the twins' differential similarity (Bouchard & Propping, 1993).

In recent years, the prenatal environment among twins has received increasing attention (e.g. Carlier & Spitz, 2000). About two-thirds of MZ twin pairs are monochorionic (MC). All DZ twins are dichorionic (DC). The type of placentation in MZ twins is a consequence of timing in zygotic diversion. If the division occurs at an early stage (up to day 3 after fertilization), the twins will develop separate fetal membranes (chorion and amnion), that is, they will be dichorionic (DC) diamniotic. When the division occurs later (between days 4 and 7), the twins will be monochorionic (MC) diamniotic. For anthropological measures (such as height), a "chorion effect" has been documented: Within-pair differences are larger in MC–MZs than in DC–MZs. Findings for cognitive and personality measures are less consistent. If possible, chorionicity should be taken into account in twin studies even if failure to discriminate between MC– and DC–MZ twin pairs does not necessarily lead to an overestimate of heritability. The importance of the prenatal maternal environment on IQ has been demonstrated in a meta-analysis (Devlin, Daniels, & Roeder, 1997). Accurate information about chorionicity is not always available, however, particularly in older twin samples. This is partly due to a long-standing misimpression that the presence of two chorions is a specific marker of the fact that the twins are DZ.

## Structural equation modeling

The comparison of intra-class correlations between MZ and DZ twins can be regarded as a reasonable first step in our understanding of the etiology of particular traits. This approach, however, cannot accommodate the effects of variations in the sizes of MZ and DZ samples, or mean or variance differences between types of twins. Nor can it accommodate the effect of gender on variances and covariances of opposite-sex DZ twins. To model genetic and environmental effects as the contribution of unmeasured (latent) variables to phenotypic differences, structural equation modeling (SEM) is required. Analyzing univariate data from MZ and DZ twins by means of SEM offers numerous advances over the mere use of correlations; these advances include an overall statistical fit of the model for the greater MZ twin compared to DZ twin similarity; tests of parsimonious sub-models; maximum likelihood confidence intervals for each latent influence included in the model; and use of maximum likelihood to incorporate information on participants with incomplete data. The true strength of SEM, however, lies in its application to multivariate and multi-group data. During the last two decades, powerful models and programs to estimate these models efficiently have been developed (Neale, Boker, Xie, & Maes, 1999). Extended twin designs and the simultaneous analysis of correlated traits are among the most important developments that go beyond the classic twin designs, yet still use the information inherently available in twins (Boomsma, Busjahn, & Peltonen, 2002).

## A cautionary note

As a ratio of genetic to total (genetic plus environmental) variance, heritability is dependent on the magnitudes of both genetic and environmental variances. With the same magnitude of genetic variance, heritability can be high because environmental variance is relatively low, or low because environmental variance is relatively high. This again points to the importance of the environment in what is measured in heritability. Where relevant environmental circumstances are tightly constrained, heritability will be high even if there is little genetic variance. And where relevant environmental circumstances vary widely, heritability will be low even with substantial genetic variance. Because of this fluctuation in heritability with environmental variation, changes in environmental circumstances that also impact variation in environmental circumstances can have dramatic effects on heritability in a population group. For the same reason, heritability can only be informative about reasons for between-group differences when we can be reasonably sure that the environments experienced by the groups are similar in ways that actually affect the development of the trait.

# Individual Psychological Differences and Behavior Are Heritable

## Intelligence

Genetic and environmental influences on intelligence have been the focus of many behavioral genetic studies. The evidence converges on the conclusion that individual differences in intelligence are substantially heritable (e.g. Plomin & Spinath, 2004). Heritability increases from a low value of about 30 percent in early childhood to well over 50 percent in adulthood, which continues into old age. Shared environmental effects ($c^2$) explain most of the individual variation in early childhood, but by the time children enter school, genetic influences and non-shared environmental effects ($e^2$) become increasingly important.

Extensive reviews of the genetic literature on intelligence are available (see Deary, Johnson, & Houlihan, 2009; Deary, Spinath, & Bates, 2006), providing overviews of the biometric and molecular genetic studies of human psychometric intelligence. We focus on selective results from twin studies here. Interestingly enough, earlier reviews of the world literature on the genetic influence on intelligence (Bouchard & McGue, 1981; Nichols, 1978) have only been corroborated by more recent studies. Thus, more recent studies have been aimed at more specific questions and have typically involved structural equation modeling procedures to estimate genetic and environmental contributions. For example, an analysis of 1st to 6th grade twins (148 MZ pairs, 135 same-sex DZ pairs) from the Western Reserve Twin Project suggested that specific aspects of abilities may be differentially affected by genetic and environmental variation (Luo, Petrill, & Thompson, 1994). However, these differential patterns may simply have reflected the degree to which the specific ability tests measure general intelligence. Analyzing 17 measures of specific cognitive abilities grouped into two test batteries, Luo and colleagues found that all the tests were influenced by genetic sources common to all tests: in other words, they found a *genetic g*. They also found some genetic effects that were specific to domains of cognitive functioning such as verbal, spatial, and perceptual speed, and memory functions. Correlations between phenotypic *g* loadings and genetic *g* loadings were .88 and .76 for the two mental-test batteries.

This topic was investigated further, in a Dutch Twin Study (Rijsdijk, Vernon, & Boomsma, 2002) in which 194 18-year-old Dutch twin pairs took Raven's Progressive Matrices and the Wechsler Adult Intelligence Scale (WAIS). A hierarchical model with three group-factors (verbal comprehension, perceptual organization, and freedom from distractability) and a higher-order *g* factor fit the phenotypic data and the additive genetic influences best, yielding heritability estimates of .84, .68, and .66, respectively for the three group-factors. There were no significant shared environmental effects. There were, however, substantial unique environmental contributions, specific to each sub-test. The general genetic factor contributed a mean of 30 percent of the variance in all tests. There were modest contributions from genetic factors at the level of the cognitive domain and of the individual test. Summing genetic contributions from all sources, the heritabilities of the individual tests ranged from 27 percent to 76 percent, with a mean of 56 percent. The contributions of unique environment to sub-tests ranged from 24 percent to 73 percent, with a mean of 44 percent. The authors concluded that the factorial structures of the various sub-tests were determined by individual differences in genetic structure (phenotypic *g* being strongly related to genetic *g*), and that the covariation among the WAIS sub-tests and the covariation between the sub-tests and the Raven in their data were predominantly influenced by a second-order genetic factor. They claimed that this finding strongly supported the notion of a biological basis of *g*.

Analyses of a Dutch twin study addressed the changing genetic contribution to intelligence with age. A total of 209 twin pairs were assessed by the RAKIT-test battery at ages 5, 7, and 10 years, and on the WISC–R at age 12 (Bartels, Rietveld, van Baal, & Boomsma, 2002). For full-scale IQ at ages 5, 7, 10, and 12, the contributions (percents of variance) were as follows: genetics, 26, 39, 54, 64; shared environment, 50, 30, 25, 21 (for the latter three values the 95 percent confidence interval included zero); and non-shared environment, 24, 31, 21, 15. This decrease in the shared environmental contribution and increase in genetic influence with age, from childhood to adolescence, was consistent with an earlier summary indicating differences between MZ and DZ twin correlations for *g* increase during adolescence and into adulthood (McGue, Bouchard, Iacono, & Lykken, 1993). The best fitting model in the Dutch longitudinal study showed an additive genetic influence, which was a common factor, but one with age-specific factor loadings; thus "continuity in cognitive abilities is mainly due to additive genetic factors" (p. 245). Shared environment contributed to continuity and change in cognition, and non-shared environment contributed to change in development.

The relatively low heritability of mental ability in young children was replicated in the Twins Early Development Study (TEDS; Spinath, Ronald, Harlaar, Price, & Plomin, 2003). The $h^2$ for verbal ability and parents' reports of children's nonverbal abilities in 6,963 pairs of twins at ages 2, 3, and 4 ranged from .25 to .30. The shared environmental estimates ($c^2$) were .61 to .65. Parents' socioeconomic status and chaos in the home mediated an independent and significant, but modest, portion of the shared environmental variance associated with cognitive functioning, accounting for 10 percent or less of the total variance in test scores (Petrill, Pike, Price, & Plomin, 2004).

The increase in importance of genetic effects from infancy to childhood has also been demonstrated in TEDS. For example, in data from 2,824 twins analyzed using a genetic longitudinal latent *g* model, heritability increased from .17 for a composite score across ages 2, 3, and 4 to .47 at age 7 (Spinath & Plomin, 2003). Since multivariate analyses indicated that the same genes appeared to affect IQ across age, this result pattern is compatible with what has been described as (genetic) "amplification" (Plomin & DeFries, 1985). Another mechanism that could explain it is the correlation between genetic and shared environmental influences in infancy and young childhood, which shifts gradually to a correlation between genetic and non-shared environmental influences as individuals increasingly make their own choices with respect to educational and intellectual activities, career occupations, and social environments. A systematic series of genetic analyses of learning abilities for the entire TEDS sample at 7, 9, and 10 years for both the low extremes and the entire sample yielded similarly high heritabilities and modest shared environmental influences across school domains, despite major changes in content across these years (Kovas, Haworth, Dale, & Plomin, 2007). Genetic effects appeared to contribute strongly to stability and to similarity in performance within and across domains, whereas environmental influences primarily contributed to change from age to age and to differences in performance.

Most of the studies described above concern ages up to adolescence. A Dutch study with several hundred adult subjects from extended twin families contained two cohorts, aged around 26 and 50 years (Posthuma, de Geus, & Boomsma, 2001; Posthuma et al., 2003). They were given a Dutch version of the Wechsler Adult Intelligence Scale III. Genetic factors accounted for 85 percent of the variation in verbal IQ and 69 percent of the variation in performance IQ (Posthuma et al., 2001). The remainder was accounted for by non-shared environmental effects. There were no significant shared environmental effects.

Studies that have assessed intelligence in twins over 75 years of age typically find substantial heritabilities as well (e.g. McClearn et al., 1997; McGue & Christensen, 2001). For example, general and specific cognitive abilities were studied in 110 Swedish MZ and 130 same-sex DZ twin pairs aged 80 or more, for whom neither twin had major cognitive, sensory, or motor impairment. Heritability estimates from structural equation modeling were .62 for general cognitive ability, .55 for verbal ability, .32 for spatial ability, .62 for speed of processing, and .52 for memory (McClearn et al., 1997). The authors also found evidence for the significant influence of idiosyncratic experience as the single environmental component that most determined individual differences in cognitive abilities late in life.

## Motivation

There is growing interest in non-cognitive factors that predict academic achievement. It is widely accepted that intelligence is the single most important predictor in this domain (Gustafsson & Undheim, 1996). However, the role of motivational factors in the prediction of academic achievement has recently been investigated not only with a focus on the incremental validity of motivational variables beyond intelligence (e.g. Spinath, Spinath, Harlaar, & Plomin, 2006), but also with regard to the genetic and environmental contributions to individual differences in motivation (Greven, Harlaar, Kovas, Chamorro-Premuzic, & Plomin, 2009; Johnson, McGue, & Iacono, 2006, 2007a; Spinath, Toussaint, Spengler, & Spinath, 2008). Spinath, Toussaint, and colleagues (2008) studied self-perceived ability and intrinsic values, key variables from the expectancy-value approach by Eccles and her associates (Eccles [Parsons] et al., 1983; Wigfield & Eccles, 2000) in a sample of 407 German twin pairs aged 7 to 11 years. Interestingly, in the over 20 years since the Eccles model was published, not a single twin or adoption study has looked at the genetic and environmental influences on the main constructs in this model. This is all the more surprising as the authors have formulated a model that aims to explain the development of individual differences in self-perceived ability and intrinsic values. In this model, children's self-concepts of ability are primarily influenced by their parents' beliefs, expectations, attitudes, and behavior. In brief, parents are regarded as expectancy socializers. The possibility of genetic influences has long been neglected and it is only recently that a direct influence from individual differences in aptitude on motivation has been acknowledged (Eccles & Wigfield, 2002).

Structural equation modeling of the available German twin data yielded an average $h^2$ across school domains of .55 for self-perceived ability and .42 for intrinsic values. The remaining variance was entirely due to non-shared environmental factors. These results were replicated in a genetic analysis (Spinath, Spinath, & Plomin, 2008) of self-perceived abilities and intrinsic values assessed in a large sample of 4,464

9-year-old UK twins from the Twins' Early Development Study (TEDS; Oliver & Plomin, 2007), yielding an average $h^2$ across school domains of .38 for self-perceived ability and .33 for intrinsic values. Greven and colleagues (2009) studied 3,785 pairs of twins from TEDS longitudinally. In a multivariate genetic analysis that included intelligence at age 7, self-perceived ability at age 9, and teacher-assessed school achievement at ages 9 and 10, they demonstrated not only substantial genetic influences on self-perceived ability ($h^2 = .51$), but also the fact that self-perceived ability predicted school achievement independently of intelligence, for genetic rather than environmental reasons.

Johnson, McGue, and Iacono (2006) investigated parents' effects on school achievement, incorporating the construct of engagement as a motivational measure, which encompassed different attitudinal and behavioral aspects of school-related motivation but referred to no particular motivational theory. Findings indicated substantial genetic influences on all the investigated variables, including motivation, and only modest shared environmental influences.

## Personality

More than three decades ago, Loehlin and Nichols (1976) published a landmark study, concluding that nearly all personality traits show moderate genetic influence. This conclusion was based on the observation that MZ twins consistently showed greater similarity than DZ twins for various traits in a sample of nearly 800 pairs of adolescent twins. Since then, this observation has been replicated extensively by using twin samples from many different populations, cultures, and age ranges, reared both together and apart, and by using a wide variety of personality measures reflecting both self-report and peer ratings (Bouchard & Loehlin, 2001; Caspi, 1998; Goldsmith, 1983; Loehlin, 1992; Riemann, Angleitner, & Strelau, 1997; Tellegen et al., 1988). In his meta-analysis, Loehlin (1992) concluded that additive genetic effects accounted for 22–46 percent of the phenotypic variance, that non-shared environment accounted for another 44–55 percent, and that shared environmental influences were negligible, accounting for 0–11 percent of individual differences in personality. Results for extraversion and neuroticism were based on five large twin studies from five different countries, with a total sample size of 24,000 twin pairs. Plomin and colleagues (2008) summarized the genetic results for personality traits, ascribing 40 percent of the inter-individual variance to genetics and 60 percent to non-shared environmental effects. In addition, two recent handbook chapters (Krueger & Johnson, 2008; Krueger, Johnson, & Kling, 2006) covered the state of behavioral genetic research in the area of personality in more extensive detail.

What has puzzled researchers in behavior genetics over the years is the fact that there were no real systematic differences in heritability estimates by particular personality trait. A second surprise was the seeming absence of shared environmental influences. It was argued that most genetic studies on personality utilized self-report questionnaires, which can introduce systematic bias in the modeling of genetically informative data (e.g. Brody, 1993; Heath, Neale, Kessler, Eaves, & Kendler, 1992). For this reason, the German Observational Study of Adult Twins (GOSAT) assessed personality for 168 MZ and 132 DZ twins on the basis of actual behavior (Borkenau,

Riemann, Angleitner, & Spinath, 2001). Personality ratings were provided by 120 judges who never met the twins but observed videotaped behaviors of one twin of each pair in one out of 15 different settings. SEM analyses of the aggregated video-based trait ratings suggested about 40 percent genetic, 25 percent shared environmental, and 35 percent non-shared environmental influence. In fact, for all personality traits from the five-factor model except for extraversion, shared environmental effects were found. Suggestive evidence that shared environmental effects might play a more important role in determining personality deviance was reported in a study of 2,796 female adolescent twins who had completed the Junior Eysenck Personality Questionnaire (Pergadia et al., 2006). For high neuroticism and high social non-conformity, SEM indicated moderate to substantial shared environmental estimates which were not found in continuous trait analyses.

Conceptual considerations have been brought forward to reconcile the absence of shared environmental effects in self-reports of personality. Low shared environmental effects for personality traits mean that, beyond their genetic similarity, people are not similar in personality within families. One interpretation of this finding is that parents do not have much impact on the personalities of their offspring (Harris, 1998). This interpretation is reasonable if the only way in which parents make an impact on their offspring is by making them more similar to each other than they would be on the strength of their genetic endowments alone. Another possibility is that the impact of parents is not an entirely shared environmental phenomenon (Krueger, South, Johnson, & Iacono, 2008). For example, parenting could act to make children within the same family different in ways that are not correlated with genetic endowments. In this scenario, parenting is a non-shared environmental phenomenon encompassed by the E component—a component of variation that, for personality, is as large as the genetic component (Krueger & Johnson, 2008). Yet another possibility is that, when people rate themselves, they think about how they differ from everyone they know, including members of their family. But when others rate them, those others see the familially influenced similarity because they look across everyone in the sample they are rating.

Genetically informative longitudinal studies have begun to investigate the stability of personality over time (for a review, see Krueger et al., 2006). The literature points to the role of genetic factors in maintaining stability and of environmental factors in promoting change. Particularly when data from adults are analyzed, a strong stabilizing effect of genetic influences on personality is found, but the environment also appears to help maintain personality stability. For example, Johnson, McGue, and Krueger (2005) studied a sample of 833 twins from the Minnesota Twin Study of Adult Development and Aging who completed the Multidimensional Personality Questionnaire (MPQ; Tellegen, 1982) twice. The average age of the twins was 59 years at the first measurement, and the average retest interval was 5 years. Phenotypic rank-order stability was high (r = .76 on average). Bivariate biometric analyses showed that the genetic influences on most of the scale scores were almost perfectly correlated across the two waves. However, non-shared environmental influences were also highly correlated across the two assessments (ranging from .53 to .73). Taking into consideration attenuation due to measurement error, these correlations were as strong as the genetic correlations.

Recently, Kandler and colleagues (2010) utilized data from the first, third, and fifth wave of the Bielefeld Longitudinal Study of Adult Twins (BiLSAT; Bleidorn, Kandler, Riemann, Angleitner, & Spinath, 2009; Spinath, Wolf, Angleitner, Borkenau, & Riemann, 2005), including twin pairs in young and middle adulthood (average age at the first wave 23 and 39 years, respectively). At three, approximately equidistant measurement occasions self- and peer reports were gathered on the NEO five-factor inventory, covering a time period of 13 years. Data from 696 MZ and 387 DZ twin pairs reared together were analyzed. Correcting for measurement error, the model made it possible to disentangle genetic and environmental effects on long- and short-term stability, on occasional influences, and on self- and peer report-specific stability. Consistent with other studies reviewed by Krueger and colleagues (2006), genetic factors represented the main source contributing to phenotypic long-term stability of personality in young and middle adulthood, whereas change was predominantly attributable to environmental factors. Furthermore, phenotypic continuity increased as a function of cumulative environmental effects, which became manifest in stable trait variance and in decreasing occasion-specific effects with age. These findings suggested that environmental factors were the primary sources of change within and across young and middle adulthood.

Bleidorn and colleagues (2009) examined the patterns and sources of 10-year stability and change of adult personality assessed by the 5 domains and 30 facets of the Revised NEO Personality Inventory in 126 MZ and 61 DZ twins from the BiLSAT. Consistent with previous research, analyses revealed significant mean-level changes in domains and facets suggesting maturation of personality, but there were also substantial individual differences in the change trajectories of both domain and facet scales. Ten-year stability and change of personality were influenced by both genetic and environmental factors.

# New Developments

## Evaluating the assumptions of quantitative genetic studies

Increasingly, we are understanding that the assumptions underlying behavior genetic analyses based on twin and adoption studies are probably often violated (Moffitt, Caspi, & Rutter, 2006; Rutter, 2007). It is possible that the violations of these assumptions may help to explain both the differences in heritability estimates from these two most commonly used kinds of samples and the greater than expected difficulty in identifying the specific genes associated with psychological traits. Among psychologists, behavior genetic researchers have been particularly aggressive in examining the accuracy of the assumptions underlying their methodologies, which has led to the development of new areas of investigation and increasingly sophisticated methods. For example, the equal environments assumption has been tested in several ways. The early tests generally indicated that it is reasonable (Bouchard & Propping, 1993), but more recent and sensitive tests have cast some doubt on this view (Mitchell et al., 2007) and increased awareness that the bias that such violation can introduce in heritability estimates may not be unimportant.

This is an ongoing process, of course, and it always remains possible that the tests that have been run have not been sensitive to the issues actually involved. For example, the typical tests run on the equal environments assumption have centered around the extent to which the twins' environments were equal: whether they were dressed alike as children, whether they shared a bedroom, whether they were in the same classroom and had the same friends at school, etc., and whether the extent to which these environmental circumstances were shared mattered to the trait of interest. It is possible, however, that what is relevant to the equal environments assumption is not whether these circumstances were shared in the abstract, but exactly what these circumstances were. For example, it is very unlikely that the way one is dressed matters in the same way to all individuals and for any outcome, if it matters at all. How it might matter would depend on some combination of genetically and environmentally influenced personality traits that contribute to the individual's sensitivity to whatever environmental response the choice of clothing evokes. Whether or not parents dress their young twins alike, it is very unlikely that the two have completely different wardrobes. If wearing T-shirts and jeans when everyone else is dressed up matters for some outcome, it may very well not matter particularly whether the twins are wearing identical T-shirts and jeans or not; and MZ twins likely will respond to whatever the environment does about their attire more similarly than DZ twins will. The measures used to date have not picked this up. In other words, the degree of equality of the environment is partly in the eyes of the people experiencing it.

## Gene–environment correlation

Tests of the absence of a gene–environment correlation have fared even worse than those of the equal environments assumption. The requirement to carry out tests for the absence of gene–environment correlation came up early in behavior genetic attempts to identify the specific environmental cimrcumstances that account for the substantial non-shared environmental variance that most psychological traits display. That is, most ostensibly environmental measures also show substantial genetic influences in both adoption and twin samples. For example, the Home Observation for Measurement of the Environment (HOME; Caldwell & Bradley, 1978) is a widely used observational and interview measure that assesses aspects of children's home environments such as parental responsivity, encouragement of development, and material provisions. Sibling HOME scores were more similar in non-adoptive families than in adoptive families, and indicated heritability of about 40 percent, a result which is very similar to the estimates for personality (Braungart, Fulker, & Plomin, 1992). This study led in part to the development of the Nonshared Environment Adolescent Development Project (NEAD; Reiss, Neiderhiser, Hetherington, & Plomin, 2000), which showed substantial heritability for all measures of family relationship interactions observed. Heritability has also been observed for environmental measures extending beyond the family, including characteristics of children's play groups (e.g. Manke, McGuire, Reiss, Hetherington, & Plomin, 1995), classroom environments (e.g. Jacobson & Rowe, 1999), work environments (e.g. Herschberger, Lichtenstein, & Knox, 1994), life events (e.g. Kendler, Neale, Kessler, Heath, & Eaves, 1993), and even exposure to trauma (e.g. Lyons et al., 1993).

The omnipresence of genetic influences on ostensibly environmental measures was initially surprising, and it led to consideration of the possibility that the traits that had traditionally been considered the province of individual differences psychology (intelligence, personality, psychopathology) mediate effects that had been attributed to the environment. Even more importantly, however, this omnipresence suggested that it might be the genetic influences on these traits that contribute to the ability of environmental measures to predict psychological outcomes. To the extent that this is the case, the assumption that underlies most behavior genetic studies—namely that there is no gene–environment correlation—is violated.

Three kinds of gene–environment correlation are typically distinguished (Plomin et al., 2008). Passive correlation occurs when heritable parenting practices that foster the development of heritable traits in children are correlated with those traits. The children need play no active role in the gene–environment correlation they experience. For example, reading to children may be heritable and may help to develop their intelligence. If more intelligent parents are more likely to do it, then the children experience a passive gene–environment correlation. But parenting is clearly a reciprocal function: parents respond (to varying degrees) to what their children do and appear to need. Evocative gene–environment correlation expresses the extent to which parental responses (and those of anyone else in the child's environment) are tailored to traits that are genetically influenced in the children. For example, even parents very dedicated to reading consistently to their children may often let the children select the books. Some children may prefer to hear the same book repeatedly, while others would prefer something new. To the extent that wider or deeper exposure to books is more or less helpful in developing intelligence, the parental responses to the children's preferences induce evocative gene–environment correlation. And children make active choices about their activities, whether these involve other people or not. Active gene–environment correlation takes place when people's selections of activities that relate to trait maintenance or to development are themselves genetically influenced. For example, particularly as they grow older, some children may choose to read on their own much more than others, and this may build intelligence. The distinctions among these kinds of gene–environment correlation are not clear-cut. For example, parents may respond to children's active expression of interest in specific activities by giving them lessons in those activities, mixing active and evocative gene–environment corelation. And parents with certain characteristics may be more likely than others to take their children to museums, but some of the children who have these experiences may learn much more from them than others, mixing passive and active gene–environment correlations.

Samples including adoptive families can be used in at least two ways to detect the presence of a gene–environment correlation (Plomin, DeFries, & Loehlin, 1977). The first way compares correlations between environmental measures and traits known to be genetically influenced in adoptive and non-adoptive families. In adoptive families we can be sure that there is no passive gene–environment correlation, though we cannot be sure there is no active or evocative gene–environment correlation. In non-adoptive families, gene–environment correlations may be of all three types. Thus, if correlations are systematically higher in non-adoptive than in adoptive families, there is evidence for passive gene–environment correlation. Studies that sample both adoptive and non-adoptive families are not very common, and those that exist have not tended to be used in this way. Still, evidence for passive gene–environment correlation came from the Colorado Adoption Project in the form of higher correlations between the HOME and general cognitive and language abilities in 2-year-olds from non-adoptive than from adoptive families (Plomin, Loehlin, & DeFries, 1985) and in the form of higher correlations between SES and school achievement in non-adoptive than in adoptive families in the Sibling Interaction and Behavior Study (Johnson, McGue, & Iacono, 2007b).

Samples that include both biological and adoptive parents of adopted children, though rather unusual, can indicate active and evocative gene–environment correlations where there are correlations between traits of biological parents and the environments in which their adopted-away offspring live. This method is weak, however, as traits of biological parents are, at best, poor indicators of offspring genotype. Despite this, the method has provided some evidence for gene–environment correlation involving adolescent antisocial behavior. For example, Ge and colleagues (1996) found that adoptive offspring whose biological parents displayed antisocial personality disorder or drug abuse had adoptive parents who were parented more negatively than adoptive parents of offspring who did not display such traits. The effect was mediated by the adolescent adoptees' own antisocial behavior.

Samples including twins can also be used to detect the presence of gene–environment correlation. The most common method involves calculation of the extent to which a phenotypic correlation between a genetically influenced trait and an environmental measure can be attributed to common genetic influences. This has been demonstrated repeatedly, for pairs of variables such as parenting and school achievement (Johnson et al., 2007a), personality and life events (Saudino, Pedersen, Lichtenstein, McClearn, & Plomin, 1997), socioeconomic status and general cognitive ability (Rowe, Vesterdal, & Rodgers, 1999), socioeconomic status and health (Lichtenstein, Harris, Pedersen, & McClearn, 1992), and social support and depression or well-being (Kessler, Kendler, Heath, Neale, & Eaves, 1992). Another approach is to compare correlations between genetically influenced traits and environmental measures in singleton samples and in monozygotic twins discordant for the environmental measure (McGue, Osler, & Christensen, 2010). When correlations are less strong in MZ twins than in DZ twins, and less strong in DZ twins than in singletons (and/or they even change sign), gene–environment correlation is indicated. This has also been demonstrated repeatedly for many pairs of variables (e.g. Harden, Mendle, Hill, Turkheimer, & Emery, 2008; Johnson, Hicks, McGue, & Iacono, 2009; Osler, McGue, & Christensen, 2008).

Still a third approach also makes use of discordant twins but allows greater distinction between gene–environment correlation and shared environmental influences in some cases. Using this approach, levels of traits in the children of MZ and DZ twins who are discordant for some environmental circumstance are examined. Because the children of MZ twins are genetically half-siblings, while those of DZ twins are effectively cousins and most adult co-twins do not share households, when rates in children of MZ twins do not differ by affected status of the twin parent but those in children of DZ parents are lower when the parent co-twin is not affected, a gene–environment correlation is indicated (D'Onofrio et al., 2003). This has also been demonstrated in several studies. For example, D'Onofrio and colleagues (2006) found evidence for gene–environment correlation between parental divorce and adolescent drug use, but not between parental divorce and emotional adjustment in the offspring. In the latter, the association appeared to be directly environmental.

Though all of these methods can reveal the presence of gene–environment correlation, none is very good at illuminating the processes actually involved, or even at providing a very clear indication of the magnitude of the effect on overall variance (Plomin et al., 1977).

## Gene–environment interaction

Tests of the absence of gene–environment interaction have also not fared well. Gene–environment interaction appears to be rather common, though its magnitudes tend to vary across samples, particularly when the interaction is reduced to the level of interaction between specific genetic polymorphisms and measured environments (e.g. Munafo, Durrant, Lewis, & Flint, 2009; Risch et al., 2009). To a large degree, this lack of replicability of specific gene–environment interaction effects makes sense: if genetic expression is dependent on environmental conditions *within* a population or sample group, then we should expect that, given differences in gene frequencies, differences in the extent to which various genes may be linked, differences in rates of various specific environmental circumstances, and differences in combinations of environmental circumstances from population group to population group, there should also be differences in the extent of gene–environment interaction *across* samples.

Adoption studies can be used to investigate the presence of gene–environment interaction when information is available about the genetic status of the adoptees, often through the traits of the biological parents. This approach has been especially useful in demonstrating gene–environment interaction with respect to antisocial behavior. For example, adoptees whose biological parents had criminal convictions were more likely to display antisocial behavior in adolescence than those whose biological parents did not (Brennan, Mednick, & Jacobsen, 1996), and adoptees whose adoptive parents had criminal convictions also were more likely to display antisocial behavior than those who did not. The latter was primarily true, however, when the adoptees also had biological parents with criminal convictions. This general pattern has been reported in several other studies as well (e.g. Cadoret, Cain, & Crowe, 1983; Cadoret, Yates, Troughton, & Woodworth, 1995; Crowe, 1974; Mednick, Gabrielli, & Hutchings, 1984). The method has not, however, always indicated gene–environment interaction for other traits (see Capron & Duyme, 1989; Capron & Duyme, 1996; Duyme, Dumaret, & Tomkiewicz, 1999, for parental education or socioeconomic status and offspring IQ). As when investigating gene–environment correlation, the method is not very powerful because traits in the biological parents are poor indicators of offspring genotype. Thus it is not clear whether failure to observe gene–environment interaction in other combinations of traits and environments indicates that the interaction is not there.

Twin studies can also be used to investigate the presence of gene–environment interaction. One way to do this is to use one twin's phenotype as an indicator of the other twin's genetic risk, comparing the effects of measured environments. This has generated observations that stressful life events have greater effects on those at genetic risk for depression (Kendler et al., 1995), and physical maltreatment has greater effects on those at genetic risk for conduct problems (Jaffee et al., 2005), among other results. Another way, more commonly applied, is to compare heritabilities or genetic variance in different environments. This can be done either discretely, by grouping environmental circumstances categorically, or by defining the environmental measure continuously. One question of perennial interest in this area is whether heritability of intelligence varies with parental socioeconomic status. Several studies have suggested that it does, that heritability is higher in those with parents of high status (Harden, Turkheimer, & Loehlin, 2007; Kremen et al., 2005; Turkheimer, Haley, Waldron, D'Onofrio, & Gottesman, 2003). Other studies, however, have shown either no or the opposite effect (Asbury, Wachs, & Plomin, 2005; van der Sluis, Willemsen, de Geus, Boomsma, & Posthuma, 2008). This may be because effects vary with the specific way of measuring parental socioeconomic status or other environmental conditions, but it also may be because, to date, the models used in these studies to estimate the genetic and environmental variance components have not made provision for the parents' genetic contribution to both their own socioeconomic status and their offspring's intelligence.

Several studies reporting interactions between specific genetic polymorphisms and measured environments in singleton samples have generated considerable attention as well (Caspi et al., 2002; Caspi, Moffitt et al., 2005; Caspi et al., 2003). In these studies, presence of particular alleles of specific single nucleotide polymorphisms was associated with higher levels of types of psychopathology than presence of the other alleles was, but only in more stressful environments. Like most genetic association studies and most studies of interactions more generally, these studies have been replicated with mixed success (Kim-Cohen et al., 2006; Munafo et al., 2009; Risch et al., 2009). Nevertheless, they document that gene–environment interaction, though perhaps not stable with environmental conditions, may be common (Moffitt et al., 2006). Researchers are also starting to use genome-wide associations to explore gene–environment interaction (e.g. Harlaar, Butcher, Meaburn, Craig, & Plomin, 2006).

## The impact of gene–environment correlation and interaction on standard estimates of genetic and environmental influences

As noted, most estimates of genetic and environmental influences on psychological traits rely on the assumptions that there are no important correlations or interactions between genetic and environmental influences. When these assumptions are violated, the violations introduce systematic distortions in the estimates from twin studies that are the most common sources of such estimates. These distortions have different effects, depending on the specific kinds of gene–environment correlation and/or interaction that exist (Purcell, 2002). Correlation between genetic and shared environmental influences acts to overstate estimates of shared environmental influences, while correlation between genetic and non-shared environmental influences acts to overstate estimates of genetic influences. This is because gene–environment correlation of either kind increases both MZ and DZ twin correlations, but, when the correlation involves shared environmental influences, it increases both MZ and DZ correlations to the same degree—because the extent of increase is based on the shared environmental variance parameter. In contrast, when the correlation involves non-shared environmental influences, it increases the DZ correlation only half as much as the MZ correlation, because the extent of increase is based on the genetic parameter. Interaction between genetic and shared environmental influences has almost the opposite effects: interaction between genetic and shared environmental influences acts to overstate estimates of genetic influences because the extent of increase is based on the genetic parameter, while interaction between genetic and non-shared environmental influences acts to overstate estimates of non-shared environmental influences because the extent of increased variance introduces no additional covariance between members of twin pairs, but does introduce additional overall variance. If gene–environment correlations and interactions are in fact rather common, these distortions underlie many of the estimates of genetic and environmental influences that have been presented for psychological traits.

## Recognizing the importance of development in understanding genetic and environmental influences on psychological traits

Developmental and evolutionary biologists have long argued that genetic and environmental correlations and interactions are likely to be important in understanding phenotypic outcomes in any trait that shows genetic variation (Hogben, 1932; Schmalhausen, 1949; Waddington, 1942). Because their focus has been on developmental processes, they have been aware that genetically influenced traits emerge over time and that individuals who are indistinguishable at one point in development may take on very different characteristics later on in development. Within the laboratory, where conditions are controlled, developmental and evolutionary biologists used model organisms such as *Drosophila*, to test how variations in specific environmental conditions were involved in the emergence of differences in outcomes among individuals known to have the same genotype, and to test how individuals with different genotypes responded to the same environmental conditions. Their experiments led them to the conclusions that gene–environment interactions were common and that they directly involved environmental triggers of gene expression in some circumstances—triggers that in other circumstances would remain silent (Tabery, 2008). In some cases, the experiments demonstrating this fact were carried out before the discovery of DNA, so the understanding that emerged was clearly on the level of principle rather than one of specific molecular mechanisms. Nevertheless, this result is consistent with the currently developing understanding among geneticists that much of genetic influence, whether between or within species, is tied up in differences in the regulation of gene expression rather than in differences in the genes that are available to be expressed (Amaral & Mattick, 2008). The same result is also consistent with the current focus of interest on the mechanisms of differences in genetic expression that are summarized under the term "epigenetics" (Gottesman & Hanson, 2005; Masterpasqua, 2009; Petronis, 2001).

The developmental and evolutionary biologists could demonstrate the importance of gene–environment interactions in the controlled conditions of the laboratory, where they could dictate the environmental circumstances their model organisms experienced. They recognized, however, that the natural environment of any organism capable of locomotion differed from the laboratory in the fundamental sense that the organism always has at least some choice over the environmental circumstances experienced. This opportunity to make some choice about the environment always exists in the presence of differential genetic sensitivity to environmental circumstances and of genetically influenced individual differences in motivation and capacity to make use of the opportunity. The developmental and evolutionary biologists understood that, in principle, this meant that organisms will move to avoid noxious environmental circumstances and to capitalize on favorable environmental circumstances to varying degrees (Schmalhausen, 1949). This in turn creates gene–environment correlations and links them to gene–environment interactions (Johnson, in press). Modern treatment has extended this observation, and offers increasing ability to measure the extent to which the phenomenon actually takes place (Johnson, 2007; Price & Jaffee, 2008; Purcell, 2002; Rathouz, van Hulle, Rodgers, Waldman, & Lahey, 2008), though further methodological advances would be helpful, particularly in recognizing and estimating the roles of active and evocative gene–environment correlation in the presence of gene–environment interaction (e.g. Purcell & Koenen, 2005; Turkheimer, D'Onofrio, Maes, & Eaves, 2005). All else being equal, those organisms most sensitive to the prevailing environmental conditions and most able to move will move first. Because all else is rarely equal, however, the most sensitive may not be the most able to move, and the most able to move may not be the most sensitive. This means that gene–environment interactions and correlations will be linked in systematic ways, and the correlations will generally be incomplete: they will generally be stronger in some environmental circumstances than in others (Johnson, 2007).

## Developmental theories incorporating gene–environment correlation and interaction

Three developmental theories in psychology have addressed the transactions between genetic and environmental influences in the emergence of individual differences in psychological traits. First, Sandra Scarr (Scarr, 1989; 1992; 1996; Scarr & McCartney, 1983) has been particularly direct in postulating a strong role for gene–environment correlation in the development of individual differences in psychological traits. She has posited that, within broad ranges of normality, differences in environmental circumstances have few (if any) systematic effects on developmental outcomes, because individuals respond to these environmental circumstances differently, on the basis of their differing genotypes. Although this implies the existence of gene–environment interaction, Scarr has focused instead on the attendant gene–environment correlation. According to her genotype → environment theory, individual differences among children emerge over time explicitly as a result of the passive gene–environment correlations that exist, because biological parents both pass on behaviorally related genes to their offspring and orchestrate the kinds of environments their offspring experience; because people evoke from others responses correlated with the characteristics that stimulated those responses; and because people actively select environments correlated with their interests, aptitudes, and personality characteristics. Accordingly, she has maintained, the balance of these genotype → environment effects changes from passive to active as developmental maturity brings increasing responsibility and opportunity to make choices among various activities available for pursuit, making genetic differences in personality among individuals increasingly important with increasing age. She recognized that the relevance of this theory was dependent on the ability of each person to select from some range of available environmental circumstances, and that the extent of this available range might vary over time and place.

Bouchard and colleagues (Bouchard, 1997; Bouchard, Lykken, Tellegen, & McGue, 1996) have argued similarly, extending Hayes's (1962) experience-producing drive theory to encompass psychological traits in general and to incorporate an evolutionary perspective. Hayes made two fundamental propositions regarding the development of intelligence: that "a) manifestation of intelligence is nothing more than an accumulation of facts and skills, and b) innate intellectual potential consists of tendencies to engage in activities conducive to learning, rather than inherited intellectual capacities as such" (p. 337). As Bouchard (1997) noted, increased understanding of brain function since Hayes's time has made it clear that motivations, affect, and attentional biases are involved in learning, rendering unlikely the hypothesis of a single, general-purpose, and independently functioning learning mechanism. Thus Bouchard posited a range of genetically influenced species-specific affective–motivational systems involving specialized features of the brain, which mediate both capacity and preferences and which have been shaped by the environment of evolutionary adaptation. As he noted, this is consistent with Darwin's view that natural selection has its effects through the organisms' actions rather than through the existence of characteristics that simply await environmental stimulation. Bouchard argued that genetic variation around these systems persists because it makes it possible for individuals within the species to seek individually optimal circumstances from a range of environmental conditions, which again implies the imporance of gene–environment correlation. Importantly, like Scarr, he stressed that actualizing full development of these systems depends on the existence of opportunities to select environmental circumstances, and he added that the choices of activity made by organisms, expressly including humans, may not always be adaptive. This might be due to constraints on the kinds of opportunities for choice of activity available, and to conflicts between constraints and opportunities and to conflicts between the kinds of circumstances that foster the development of different psychological characteristics.

Roberts and Caspi (e.g. Roberts & Caspi, 2003; Caspi, Roberts, & Shiner, 2005) have outlined similar developmental themes with respect to personality. They suggest that three fundamental principles underlie observations to date about changes in personality through the life course. First, people tend to become more dominant, agreeable, conscientious, and emotionally stable with age, which Roberts and Caspi have termed the "maturity principle." Second, these authors' "continuity principle" has been used to summarize the finding that individual differences in personality are remarkably consistent throughout the life span, though personality is by no means fixed. Caspi and Roberts have attributed this consistency to stable genetic influences that reinforce a "setpoint" around which environmentally induced fluctuations may take place; but they have also specifically attributed it to what they have termed "niche-building." To them, niche-building describes the processes through which people create, seek out, or end up in environments that are correlated with their traits. They have suggested that, once people are in trait-correlated environments, the environment acts to reinforce the persistence of the trait behaviors and to minimize opportunities for change.

Relatedly, consistency of personality is maintained because people tend to commit to some socially recognized identity, often involving an occupation or a social role such as parent. Of course, genetically influenced individual differences contribute to the process of selecting the identity to which the individual commits, and, once he or she has committed, the environment associated with the identity reinforces its relevant traits. Third, though they have not expressed it this way, Roberts and Caspi have proposed that even the change in personality that takes place does so within the context of correlations between genetically influenced traits and environmental influences. They have used the phrase "corresponsive principle" to capture the observation that life experiences tend to deepen the personality characteristics that had led individuals to those experiences in the first place. Thus, people who tend to be responsible and careful tend to be trusted with situations requiring those characteristics, which helps them to build experience in dealing with the kinds of problems that do arise and leaves them with increased capability to manage such situations in future. Roberts and Caspi have tended to write about this in positive terms: socially valued characteristics are deepened and strengthened by their manifestation. But, as also noted by Bouchard (1997), it is likely that sometimes psychological characteristics that are not socially valued are reinforced and accentuated by environmental responses to their expression as well. Expressions of psychopathology such as aggressive and criminal behavior, depression, poor attitudes toward school, and substance abuse may be examples of this (Moffitt, Caspi, Dickson, Silva, & Stanton, 1996).

The idea that people sort themselves into environments on the basis of their pre-existing aptitudes, interests, and personality characteristics has long been familiar also to industrial/organizational psychologists, though they have not expresssed their ideas in behavior genetic terms.

## Testing these developmental theories

Testing these developmental theories is difficult. This is because, as noted earlier, available behavior genetic methods are better at revealing the presence of gene–environment correlation and/or interaction than at illuminating the processes involved in their creation, or even at quantifying the magnitude of their effects. And samples that do not recognize genetic relationship suffer from the problem that unmeasured genetic and shared environmental confounds always lurk in the background. Moreover, these theories inherently posit ongoing reciprocal effects between variables intrinsic and extrinsic to the individual, making it necessary constantly to expect and thus to model reverse causation. As with studies of development in general, longitudinal samples are essential. But the issues in testing these theories are more complex than can be readily addressed simply by making use of genetically informative longitudinal samples. All three theories imply that the manifestation of traits depends on the existence of the kinds of environmental stimuli that make trait development possible. Exactly what stimuli these might be, however, is not clear, particularly since all the theories include recognition that individual differences arise in rather ordinary environments. Measures such as sensation-seeking or openness to experience might be expected to capture them, but these measures are intended to capture general curiosity and interest in novelty, and many intrinsic motivations, interests, and attentional biases may be much more narrowly focused. This means that the people most strongly motivated to build their own environmental niches could even be among those who score lowest on them.

For example motivation, attentional bias, and aptitude might orient a developing child toward the manipulation of spatial configuration. Such a child might become a dance choreographer if the opportunity were present, in the process assimilating much of the cultural identity associated with dance. But this child might also be so focused on dance patterns that s/he had little interest in trying a new food, experiencing another culture, or understanding why water expands when it freezes. At the same time, the orientation itself may be capable of quite flexible expression. Another child with the same orientation but a very different environment might become an American football quarterback, in the process assimilating much of a very different cultural identity. We thus need measures that can identify both the narrow and the broad intensity of exploratory activities, and that can do so in very primitive form, in infants, while still tracking how both narrow and broad intensities of exploratory activities develop as infants grow into children and then adults.

Despite these difficulties, some evidence at least consistent with these developmental theories does exist. For example, as noted earlier, Scarr's genotype → environment theory predicts that genetic influences should become stronger with age for psychological traits affected systematically by gene–environment correlation. Within the theory, this would take place for two reasons. First, as also predicted by Scarr's theory (Scarr & McCartney, 1983), correlation between genetic and environmental influences would shift from shared to non-shared environmental influences as children move from parental control of much of their environments to independence. The biases inherent in our most commonly made estimates of the proportions of variance attributable to genetic and environmental influences would thus shift from overstatement of shared environmental influences to overstatement of genetic influences (Deary et al., 2009; Johnson, in press). Second, with development, people would become increasingly successful at creating their environmental niches, thus limiting the variance in the environmental circumstances they experience and allowing their genetic proclivities to be more clearly manifested. This phenomenon of the increasing importance of genetic influences with age is well documented for several traits, including intelligence (e.g. Deary et al., 2009) and antisocial behavior (e.g. Carey & DiLalla, 1994). For example, for intelligence, genetic influences increase from perhaps 30 percent in young childhood to as much as 80 percent in adulthood, while shared environmental influences decrease from as much as 35 percent in young childhood to 0 percent in adulthood.

Studies more directly exploring the association between activity and trait development implied by these developmental theories have not been common, though there have been a few. For example, Hayes and colleagues (1989) found that, over a 4-week period, children with higher IQs read 50 percent more from popular children's books than their peers with lower IQs did, and that the material they read was both lexically more complex and longer. Of course, this study would only be consistent with the developmental theories if the reading activity were genetically influenced (though most traits and activities are; Turkheimer, 2000) and if it were shown that reading activity contributed directly to later increases in IQ. Another study (Raine, Reynolds, Venables, & Mednick, 2002) of stimulation-seeking and cognitive abilities between the ages of 3 and 11 found correlations ranging from .20 to .44 between stimulation-seeking at age 3 and various aspects of cognitive ability at age 11. The correlations with general intelligence ranged from .33 to .44. This study also failed directly to pinpoint the source of the link between stimulation-seeking and later IQ as genetic influences, and the lack of precise means of measuring intelligence limited the ability to address whether its variance actually increased between the ages of 3 and 11. Verifying this would be important in providing evidence for the developmental theories.

Again, industrial/organizational psychologists have been at the forefront of documenting the existence of niche-building processes with respect to occupational selection. For example, Wilk and Sackett (1996) showed that, across their careers, people tend to change jobs in ways that increasingly match their IQs. That is, those who have higher IQs than required by their jobs tend to move toward more intellectually challenging jobs, while those who have IQs that are lower than those of most of their colleagues tend to move toward less intellectually challenging jobs. Roberts, Caspi, and Moffitt (2003) documented similar processes with respect to the contribution of work experience to personality development. These kinds of studies, however, also leave the genetic contribution to inference or guesswork.

## Molecular Genetics

Advances in molecular biology and genetics during the past decade have included techniques that make it possible to search the entire genome for genetic variants that may be related to disease states or psychological traits (see also Brocke & Strobel, this volume). Humans share as much as 50 percent of their genetic material with organisms such as bacteria and worms, and approximately 98 percent with chimpanzees, our closest interspecific relatives. Within the human species, therefore, we share over 99.9 percent of our genetic material. Still, given the size of the human genome, this leaves room for over 3 million expected genetic differences between any two unrelated individuals. These differences are called "polymorphisms" (when they are found in more than 1 percent of the population). Polymorphisms are variations in DNA sequence that occur on average once every 300 to 500 base pairs. Some of these variations get translated directly into proteins that control the production of observable individual differences, such as differences in eye color, blood type, and disease susceptibility. Most variations, however, occur in sections of the DNA called "introns," and do not code directly for proteins, though they may have regulatory effects on other DNA segments that do. The effects of these polymorphisms on an organism's appearance or function are generally unknown, but the polymorphisms themselves are detectable at the DNA level and can be used as markers. Examples of polymorphisms include single-nucleotide polymorphisms (SNPs), in which a single nucleotide base is substituted for another at a single location in DNA. They also include "variable number of tandem repeats" (VNTR), or certain sequences of nucleotides that are repeated within a gene; but the number of repeats varies across individuals. And they include insertion/deletion polymorphisms, in which a sequence of nucleotides is present in one variant, but absent in another (Canli, 2008).

## Linkage

Traditional linkage analysis is a technique that detects associations between DNA markers and traits. For single-gene disorders such as Huntington disease, such associations can be identified by using a few large family pedigrees, in which the co-transmission of a DNA marker and of a trait can be traced (Plomin et al., 2008). We can search for the genes associated with the trait by establishing a panel of different, essentially random, DNA markers, spread across the entire genome. The linkage analysis capitalizes on the fact that recombination, the exchange of chromosomal parts during meiosis, occurs on average once per chromosome, and more or less at random. If there is a large distance between two DNA sequences on a chromosome, the likelihood that recombination between them will occur is high. In contrast, if two DNA sequences are very close together, they will recombine only rarely. When a DNA marker is found to be associated with a trait, potential genes actually associated with the trait are mapped by measuring recombination potential with the nearest markers. In most cases, recombination will occur frequently, indicating that the disease gene and the marker are far apart. Some markers, however, due to their proximity, will tend not to recombine with the trait gene. These are said to be linked to it. The LOD score (logarithm [base 10] of odds) is a statistical test often used for linkage analysis in human populations. It compares the likelihood of obtaining the empirical results if the genetic marker is associated with the trait to the likelihood of observing the same data purely by chance. Ideally, markers are identified that define a small candidate region of the genome in which the trait gene lies. Exact identification of the gene itself, however, can still be cumbersome. In the case of the gene that causes Huntington disease, it took 10 years from the initial finding of the marker linkage to the gene's identification in 1993 (Bates, 2005). Linkage analysis of large pedigrees has been effective for locating genes for single-gene disorders. For quantitative traits that involve several, up to many, genes of small effect size, however, traditional linkage analysis is not powerful enough.

## Genetic association studies

Molecular genetics has given us considerable knowledge about the genes that produce many specific proteins. Sometimes this knowledge can be used to develop ideas about genes that may be good candidates for involvement in the expression of a trait, because we also have some molecular understanding that their protein products are involved in the trait. Studies that explore this are known as "candidate genetic association studies." They compare frequencies of selected DNA markers for groups such as individuals with a disorder (cases) versus controls or low-scoring versus high-scoring individuals on a quantitative trait (Sham, Cherny, Purcell, & Hewitt, 2000). If association is present, a particular polymorphism or combination of polymorphisms will be seen more often in individuals carrying the trait than would be expected if it were to occur by chance. The weakness of such studies is that an association can only be detected if the genetic marker is itself the functional gene (direct association) or very close to it (indirect association or linkage disequilibrium). The candidate gene approach therefore requires strong hypotheses as to which genes are good candidates, and we often lack this knowledge (Plomin et al., 2008), since individual differences in complex traits very likely involve the influence of many genes of small effect, any single one of which may not be sufficient or necessary to associate reliably with the trait (Plomin, Owen, & McGuffin, 1994).

## Genome-wide association studies (GWAS)

Genome-wide association studies (GWAS) have become possible and affordable only recently (Hirschhorn & Daly, 2005). Through the use of probes for large numbers of SNPs that require only little DNA, systematic scans of the entire genome (DNA) and of the entire transcriptome (RNA) are feasible (Plomin & Schalkwyk, 2007). The first major GWAS was a search for type II diabetes variants published in *Nature* in February 2007 by Robert Sladek and colleagues. The group tested 392,935 SNPs in a French case-control cohort and identified several associations, including some that had never been considered candidates (Sladek et al., 2007). By 2008, nearly 100 loci for as many as 40 common diseases and traits had been identified and replicated in GWAS, many in genes not previously suspected of having a role in the diseases under study, and some in genomic regions containing no known genes (Pearson & Manolio, 2008). A recent review article on GWAS of SNP associations for complex diseases summarized more than 450 GWAS published since 2005, reporting more than 2,000 findings (Ku, Loy, Pawitan, & Chia, 2010). The same review also found that most of the risk alleles identified in GWAS for various complex diseases had small effect sizes (odds ratio <1.5) and accounted, taken together, for very small amounts of variance in the traits in question. To detect associations with SNPs of such small effect size requires extremely dense searches, which can be problematic because the denser the search, the larger the number of statistical tests performed. Testing 500,000 to 1 million SNPs for association, which has become common, presents an unprecedented potential for false-positive results, leading to new stringency in acceptable levels of statistical significance and requirements for replication of findings (Hunter & Kraft, 2007).

The GWAS strategy has resulted in the identification of reliable links between SNPs and a variety of phenotypes (Johnson & O'Donnell, 2009). However, for most complex traits, these specific SNP effects have been small in magnitude. To this day, GWAS on well-established heritable traits such as human height (e.g. Weedon, et al., 2008), intelligence (e.g. Butcher, Davis, Craig, & Plomin, 2008), and personality (e.g. Krueger et al., 2009) have yielded disappointing results, despite fine-grained approaches with up to 1 million SNPs in the analysis and increasingly large samples. It remains to be seen whether future genome-wide scans will be able to identify replicable associations.

## Conclusions and Future Directions

In this chapter we have documented the importance of genetic influences on individual differences in psychological traits, along with the methods that have been used to establish this importance. As has been common in behavior genetics, we have also focused on the limitations of these methods. In doing so, we do not mean in any way to question the importance or accuracy of the ubiquitous observation that genes make substantial contributions to psychological traits. Rather, we mean to emphasize the challenges and opportunities that confront the coming generation of behavioral genetic research. Developments in molecular genetics are suggesting that rare genetic variants, copy number variations, epigenetic mechanisms controlling gene expression, gene–gene and gene–environment interactions, and genetically influenced canalization of development all may be important in explaining the pervasive genetic influences on individual differences in psychological traits, beyond the additive genetic influences that have traditionally been presumed to explain most of them. At the social and individual levels, recognition of the likely importance of selection processes that create gene–environment correlation is also increasing. We believe that this is an exciting time for behavior genetics: re-examination of, and challenge to, the assumptions underlying traditional methods, along with extension of those methods to relax those assumptions, may go further than molecular genetics toward making possible the illumination of the social and psychological processes that underlie the development of individual differences in psychological outcomes.

Though we have highlighted the challenges involved in unraveling the traditional assumption that genetic and environmental influences are independent and involve no gene–environment correlations or interactions, other assumptions that underlie the classical twin method also warrant attention, especially the assumptions that traits involve no assortative mating and that genetic influences are primarily additive. Extended twin family designs, which incorporate siblings, parents, and offspring of twins as well as other relatives such as aunts, uncles, and cousins, can be very helpful in this regard. Extremely large samples are necessary for this, however, as the subsamples of each kind of relationship pair must be substantial. In addition, such sub-samples must be recruited so that they are consistently representative of the populations of interest.

Today there is remarkable consensus across scientific disciplines, including psychology, sociology, and economics, that genetically informed studies constitute a major advance in social science research (e.g. Freese, 2008; Guo & Stearns, 2002). The growing acceptance of genetic approaches in the social sciences has been clearly documented in recent special issues of the influential journals *Nature* (2008), *Sociological Methods and Research* (2008), *American Journal of Sociology* (2008), and *Developmental Psychology* (2009), all dealing comprehensively with the interaction between biology and the environment. Sociologists are beginning to combine longitudinal panel studies with biomarker approaches, thus studying the effects of social contexts on individuals that might depend on genetic differences among individuals. A recent publication from the special issue of the *American Journal of Sociology* illustrates this development. Drawing on the National Longitudinal Study of Adolescent Health, Shanahan and colleagues (Shanahan, Vaisey, Erickson, & Smolen, 2008) studied the effects of social capital and of the DRD2 dopamine receptor gene on educational continuation beyond secondary school. For boys, they found that DRD2 risk was associated with a decreased likelihood of school continuation. Parental socioeconomic status, high parental involvement in school, and a high-quality school compensated for this negative relationship, consistent with environmental contingency. However, the DRD2 risk allele was also less commonly observed in settings that were rich in social capital, which suggested that boys who were at genetic risk had a lower probability of benefiting from environmental compensation. Like all studies, this one clearly requires replication; but if it reports a robust phenomenon, it documents an important example of the kinds of gene–environment correlations and interactions that are likely to pervade the phenomena of interest to behavioral scientists, and the fusion of molecular and quantitative genetics that is going to be required to understand them.

# References

Amaral, P. P., & Mattick, J. S. (2008). Non-coding RNA in development. *Mammalian Genome, 19*, 454–492.

Asbury, K., Wachs, T. D., & Plomin, R. (2005). Environmental moderators of genetic influence on verbal and non-verbal abilities in early childhood. *Intelligence, 33*, 643–661.

Bartels, M., Rietveld, M. J. H., van Baal, G. C. M., & Boomsma, D. I. (2002). Genetic and environmental influences on the development of intelligence. *Behavior Genetics, 32*, 237–249.

Bates, G. P. (2005). History of genetic disease: The molecular genetics of Huntington disease–A history. *Nature Reviews Genetics, 6*, 766–773.

Bleidorn, W., Kandler, C., Riemann, R., Angleitner, A., & Spinath, F. M. (2009). Patterns and sources of adult personality development: Growth curve analyses of the NEO–PI–R scales in a longitudinal twin study. *Journal of Personality and Social Psychology, 97*, 142–155.

Boomsma, D. I., Busjahn, A., & Peltonen, L. (2002). Classical twin studies and beyond. *Nature Reviews Genetics, 3*, 872–882.

Borkenau, P., Riemann, R., Angleitner, A. & Spinath, F. M. (2001). Genetic and environmental influences on observed personality: Evidence from the German Observational Study of Adult Twins. *Journal of Personality and Social Psychology, 80*, 655–668.

Bouchard, T. J. (1997). Experience producing drive theory: How genes drive experience and shape personality. *Acta Paediatrica Supplement, 422*, 60–64.

Bouchard, T. J., & Loehlin, J. C. (2001). Genes, evolution, and personality. *Behavior Genetics, 31*, 243–273.

Bouchard, T. J., & McGue, M. (1981). Familial studies of intelligence: A review. *Science, 212*, 1055–1059.

Bouchard, T. J., & Propping, P. (1993). *Twins as a tool of behavior genetics.* Chichester: John Wiley & Sons.

Bouchard, T. J., Lykken, D. T., Tellegen, A., & McGue, M. (1996). Genes, drives, environment, and experience: EPD theory revised. In C. P. Benbow & D. Lubinski (Eds.),

*Intellectual talent: Psychometric and social issues* (pp. 5–43). Baltimore, MD: Johns Hopkins University Press.

Braungart, J. M., Fulker, D. W., & Plomin, R. (1992). Genetic mediation of the home environment during infancy: A sibling adoption study of the HOME. *Developmental Psychology*, *28*, 1048–1055.

Brennan, P. A., Mednick, S. A., & Jacobsen, B. (1996). Assessing the role of genetics in crime using adoption cohorts. In G. R. Bock & J. A. Goode (Eds.), *Genetics of criminal and antisocial behavior* (pp. 115–128). Chichester: John Wiley & Sons.

Brody, N. (1993). Intelligence and the behavioral genetics of personality. In R. Plomin & G. E. McClearn (Eds.), *Nature, nurture, and psychology* (pp. 161–178). Washington, DC: American Psychological Association.

Butcher, L. M., Davis, O. S., Craig, I. W., & Plomin, R. (2008). Genome-wide quantitative trait locus association scan of general cognitive ability using pooled DNA and 500 K single nucleotide polymorphism microarrays. *Genes, Brains and Behavior*, *7*, 435–446.

Cadoret, R. J., Cain, C. A., & Crowe, R. R. (1983). Evidence for gene–environment interaction in the development of adolescent antisocial behavior. *Behavior Genetics*, *13*, 301–310.

Cadoret, R. J., Yates, W. R., Troughton, E., & Woodworth, G. (1995). Genetic–environmental interaction in the genesis of aggressivity and conduct disorders. *Archives of General Psychiatry*, *52*, 916–924.

Caldwell, B. M., & Bradley, R. H. (1978). *Home Observation for Measurement of the Environment*. Little Rock, AR: University of Arkansas.

Canli, T. (2008). Toward a "molecular psychology" of personality. In L. A. Pervin, O. P. John, & R. W. Robins (Eds.), *Handbook of personality: Theory and research* (3rd ed., pp. 311–327). New York: Guilford Press.

Capron, C., & Duyme, M. (1989). Assessment of the effects of socioeconomic status on IQ in a full cross-fostering study. *Nature*, *340*, 552–554.

Capron, C., & Duyme, M. (1996). Effect of socioeconomic status of biological and adoptive parents on WISC–R subtest scores of the French adopted children. *Intelligence*, *22*, 259–275.

Carey, G., & DiLalla, D. L. (1994). Personality and psychopathology: Genetic perspectives. *Journal of Abnormal Psychology*, *103*, 32–43.

Carlier, M. & Spitz, E. (2000). The twin method. In B. C. Jones & P. Mormède (Eds.), *Neurobehavioral genetics: Methods and applications* (pp. 151–159). Boca Raton, FL: CRC Press.

Caspi, A. (1998). Personality development across the life course. In W. Damon & N. Eisenberg (Eds.), *Handbook of child psychology: Vol. 3. Social emotional, and personality development* (pp. 311–388). New York: Wiley.

Caspi, A., Roberts, B. W., & Shiner, R. L. (2005). Personality development: Stability and change. *Annual Review of Psychology*, *56*, 453–484.

Caspi, A., McClay, J., Moffitt, T. E., Mill, J., Martin, J., Craig, I. W. et al. (2002). Role of genotype in the cycle of violence in maltreated children. *Science*, *297*, 851–854.

Caspi, A., Moffitt, T. E., Cannon, M., McClay, J., Murray, R., Harrington, H. et al. (2005). Moderation of the effect of adolescent-onset cannabis use on adult psychosis by a functional polymorphism in the catechol-O-methyltransferase gene. *Biological Psychiatry*, *57*, 1117–1127.

Caspi, A., Sugden, K., Moffitt, T. E., Taylor, A., Craig, I. W., Harrington, H. et al. (2003). Influence of life stress on depression: Moderation by a polymorphism in the 5–HTT gene. *Science*, *301*, 386–389.

Crowe, R. R. (1974). An adoption study of antisocial personality. *Archives of General Psychiatry*, *31*, 785–791.

Darwin, C. (1859). *The origin of species by means of natural selection*. London: Murray.

Deary, I. J., Johnson, W., & Houlihan, L. (2009). Genetic foundations of human intelligence. *Human Genetics, 126*, 215–232.

Deary, I. J., Spinath, F. M., & Bates, T. C. (2006). Genetics and IQ. *European Journal of Human Genetics, 14*, 690–700.

Devlin, B., Daniels, M., & Roeder, K. (1997). The heritability of IQ, *Nature, 388*, 468–471.

D'Onofrio, B. M., Turkheimer, E., Emery, R. E., Slutzke, W. S., Heath, A. C., & Madden, P. A. (2006). A genetically informed study of the processes underlying the association between parental marital instability and offspring adjustment. *Developmental Psychology, 42*, 486–499.

D'Onofrio, B. M., Turkheimer, E. N., Eaves, L. J., Corey, L. A., Berg, K., Solaas, M. H. et al. (2003). The role of the Children of Twins Design in elucidating causal relations between parent characteristics and child outcomes. *Journal of Child Psychology and Psychiatry and Allied Disciplines, 44*, 1130–1144.

Duyme, M., Dumaret, A. C., & Tomkiewicz, S. (1999). How can we boost IQ of "dull children"? A late adoption study. *Proceedings of the National Academy of Sciences of the United States of America, 96*, 8790–8794.

Eccles, J. S., & Wigfield, A. (2002). Motivational beliefs, values, and goals. *Annual Review of Psychology, 53*, 109–132.

Eccles (Parsons), J., Adler, T. F., Futterman, R., Goff, S. B., Kaczala, C. M., Meece, J. L. et al. (1983). Expectancies, values, and academic behaviors. In J. T. Spence (Ed.), *Achievement and achievement motives* (pp. 75–146). San Francisco: Freeman.

Falconer, D. S. (1960). *Introduction to quantitative genetics*. New York: Ronald Press.

Freese, J. (2008). Genetics and the social science explanation of individual outcomes. *American Journal of Sociology, 114*, 1–35.

Galton, F. (1869). *Hereditary genius*. London: Macmillan.

Galton, F. (1876). The history of twins as a criterion of the relative powers of nature and nurture. *Royal Anthropological Institute of Great Britain and Ireland Journal, 6*, 391–406.

Ge, X., Conger, R. D., Cadoret, R. J., Neiderhiser, J. M., Yates, W., Troughton, E. et al. (1996). The developmental interface between nature and nurture: A mutual influence model of child antisocial beahavior and parenting. *Developmental Psychology, 32*, 574–589.

Goldsmith, H. H. (1983). Genetic influences on personality from infancy to adulthood. *Child Development, 54*, 331–355.

Gottesman, I. I., & Hanson, D. R. (2005). Human development: Biological and genetic processes. *Annual Review of Psychology, 56*, 271–286.

Greven, C. U., Harlaar, N., Kovas, Y., Chamorro-Premuzic, T., & Plomin, R. (2009). More than just IQ: School achievement is predicted by self-perceived abilities—but for genetic rather than environmental reasons. *Psychological Science, 20*, 53–762.

Guo, G., & Stearns, E. (2002). The social influences on the realization of genetic potential for intellectual development. *Social Forces, 80*, 881–910.

Gustafsson, J.-E., & Undheim, J. O. (1996). Individual differences in cognitive functions. In D. C. Berliner & R. C. Calfee (Eds.), *Handbook of educational psychology* (pp. 186–242). New York: Prentice Hall International.

Harden, K. P., Turkheimer, E., & Loehlin, J. C. (2007). Genotype by environment interaction in adolescents' cognitive aptitude. *Behavior Genetics, 37*, 273–283.

Harden, K. P., Mendle, J., Hill, J. E., Turkheimer, E., & Emery, R. E. (2008). Rethinking timing of first sex and delinquency. *Journal of Youth and Adolescence, 37*, 373–385.

Harlaar, N., Butcher, L., Meaburn, E., Craig, I. W., & Plomin, R. (2006). A behavioral genomic analysis of DNA markers associated with general cognitive ability in 7-year-olds. *Journal of Child Psychology and Psychiatry, 46,* 1097–1107.

Harris, J. R. (1998). *The nurture assumption: Why children turn out the way they do.* New York: Free Press.

Hayes, D., Whitehead, F., Wellings, A., Thompson, W., Marschlke, C., & Moran, M. (1989). *How strongly do genes drive children's choice of experiences?* Ithaca, NY: Technical Report Service 89–13, Cornell University.

Hayes, K. J. (1962). Genes, drives, and intellect. *Psychological Reports, 10,* 299–342.

Heath, A. C., Neale, M. C., Kessler, R. C., Eaves, L. J., & Kendler, K. S. (1992). Evidence for genetic influences on personality from self-reports and informant ratings. *Journal of Personality and Social Psychology, 63,* 85–96.

Herschberger, S. L., Lichtenstein, P., & Knox, S. S. (1994). Genetic and environmental influences on perceptions of organizational climate. *Journal of Applied Psychology, 79,* 24–33.

Hirschhorn, J. N., & Daly, M. J. (2005). Genomewide association studies for common diseases and complex traits. *Nature Reviews Genetics, 6,* 95–108.

Hogben, L. (1932). *Genetic principles in medicine and social science.* New York: Alfred A. Knopf.

Hunter, D. J., & Kraft, P. (2007). Drinking from the fire hose: Statistical issues in genomewide association studies. *New England Journal of Medicine, 357,* 436–439.

Jacobson, K. C., & Rowe, D. C. (1999). Genetic and environmental influences on the relationship between family connectedness, school connectedness, and adolescent depressed mood: Sex differences. *Developmental Psychology, 35,* 926–939.

Jaffee, S. R., Caspi, A., Moffitt, T. E., Dodge, K. A., Rutter, M., & Taylor, A. (2005). Nature × nurture: Genetic vulnerabilities interact with physical maltreatment to promote conduct problems. *Development and Psychopathology, 17,* 67–84.

Jensen, A. R. (1998). *The g-factor: The science of mental ability.* London: Praeger.

Johnson, A. D., & O'Donnell, C. J. (2009). An open access database of genome-wide association results. *BMC Medical Genetics, 10,* 6.

Johnson, W. (2007). Genetic and environmental influences on behavior: Capturing all the interplay. *Psychological Review, 114,* 423–440.

Johnson, W. (in press). What do genes have to do with cognition? In S. Kreitler (Ed.), *Cognition and motivation.* New York: Cambridge University Press.

Johnson, W., McGue, M., & Iacono, W. G. (2006). Genetic and environmental influences on academic achievement trajectories during adolescence. *Developmental Psychology, 42,* 514–532.

Johnson, W., McGue, M., & Iacono, W. G. (2007a). How parents influence school grades: Hints from a biological and adoptive sample. *Learning and Individual Differences, 17,* 201–219.

Johnson, W., McGue, M., & Iacono, W. G. (2007b). Socioeconomic status and school grades: Placing their association in broader context in a sample of biological and adoptive families. *Intelligence, 35,* 526–541.

Johnson, W., McGue, M., & Krueger, R. F. (2005). Personality stability in late adulthood: A behavior genetic analysis. *Journal of Personality, 73,* 523–551.

Johnson, W., Hicks, B. M., McGue, M., & Iacono, W. G. (2009). How intelligence and education contribute to substance use: Hints from the Minnesota Twin Family Study. *Intelligence, 37,* 613–624.

Kandler, C., Bleidorn, W., Riemann, R., Spinath, F. M., Thiel, W., & Angleitner, A. (2010). Sources of cumulative continuity in personality: A longitudinal multiple-rater twin study. *Journal of Personality and Social Psychology, 98,* 995–1008.

Kendler, K. S., & Eaves, L. J. (1986). Models for the joint effects of genotype and environment on liability to psychiatric illness. *American Journal of Psychiatry, 143,* 279–289.

Kendler, K. S., Neale, M. C., Kessler, R. C., Heath, A. C., & Eaves, L. J. (1993). A twin study of recent life events and difficulties. *Archives of General Psychiatry, 49,* 789–796.

Kendler, K. S., Kessler, R. C., Walters, E. E., MacLean, C. J., Neale, M. C., Heath, A. C. et al. (1995). Stressful life events, genetic liability, and onset of an episode of major depression in women. *American Journal of Psychiatry, 152,* 833–842.

Kessler, R. C., Kendler, K. S., Heath, A. C., Neale, M. C., & Eaves, L. J. (1992). Social support, depressed mood, and adjustment to stress: A genetic epidemiological investigation. *Journal of Personality and Social Psychology, 62,* 257–272.

Kim-Cohen, J., Caspi, A., Taylor, A., Williams, B., Newcombe, R., Craig, I. W. et al. (2006). MAOA, maltreatment, and gene-environment interaction predicting children's mental health: New evidence and a meta-analysis. *Molecular Psychiatry, 11,* 903–913.

Kovas, Y., Haworth, C. M. A., Dale, P. S., & Plomin, R. (2007). The genetic and environmental origins of learning abilities and disabilities in the early school years. *Monographs of the Society for Research in Child Development, 72,* 1–144.

Kremen, W. S., Jacobson, K. C., Xian, S., Eisen, S. A., Waterman, B., & Toomey, R. (2005). Heritability of word recognition in middle-aged men varies as a function of parental education. *Behavioral Genetics, 35,* 417–433.

Krueger, R. F., & Johnson, W. (2008). Behavioral genetics and personality. In L. A. Pervin, O. P. John, & R. W. Robins (Eds.), *Handbook of personality: Theory and research* (3rd ed., pp. 287–310). New York: Guilford Press.

Krueger, R. F., Johnson, W., & Kling, K. C. (2006). Behavior genetics and personality development. In D. Mroczek & T. Little (Eds.), *Handbook of personality development* (pp. 81–108). Mahwah, NJ: Lawrence Erlbaum Associates.

Krueger, R. F., South, S., Johnson, W., & Iacono, W. (2008). The heritability of personality is not always 50%: Gene–environment interactions and correlations between personality and parenting. *Journal of Personality, 76,* 1485–1521.

Krueger, R. F., Agrawal, A., Derringer, J., Grucza, R. A., Saccone, S., Lynskey, M. T. et al. (2009). *A Genome Wide Association Study (GWAS) of the five factor model (FFM) of personality.* Paper presented at the Ist stand-alone Conference of the Association of Research in Personality (ARP), Evanston, IL, 17–18th July.

Ku, C. S., Loy, E. Y., Pawitan, Y., & Chia, K. S. (2010). The pursuit of genome-wide association studies: Where are we now? *Journal of Human Genetics, 55,* 195–206.

Lichtenstein, P., Harris, J. R., Pedersen, N. L., & McClearn, G. E. (1992). Socioeconomic status and physical health, how are they related? An empirical study based on twins reared apart and twins reared together. *Social Science and Medicine, 36,* 441–450.

Loehlin, J. C. (1992). *Genes and environment in personality development.* Newbury Park, CA: Sage.

Loehlin, J. C., & Nichols, J. (1976). *Heredity, environment, and personality.* Austin, TX: University of Texas Press.

Luo, D., Petrill, S. A, & Thompson, L. A. (1994). An exploration of genetic *g*: Hierarchical factor analysis of cognitive data from the Western Reserve Twin Project. *Intelligence, 18,* 335–347.

Lyons, M. J., Goldberg, J., Eisen, S. A., True, W., Tsuang, M. T., Meyer, J. M. et al. (1993). Do genes influence exposure to trauma? A twin study combat. *American Journal of Medical Genetics (Neuropsychiatric Genetics), 48,* 22–27.

Manke, B., McGuire, S., Reiss, D., Hetherington, E. M., & Plomin, R. (1995). Genetic contributions to adolescents' extra-familial social interactions: Teachers, best friends, and peers. *Social Development, 4*, 238–256.

Masterpasqua, F. (2009). Psychology and epigenetics. *Review of General Psychology, 13*, 194–201.

McClearn, G. E., Johansson, B., Berg, S., Pedersen, N. L., Ahern, F., Petrill, S. A. et al. (1997). Substantial genetic influence on cognitive abilities in twins 80+ years old. *Science, 276*, 1560–1563.

McGue, M., & Christensen, K. (2001). The heritability of cognitive functioning in very old adults: Evidence from Danish twins aged 75 years and older. *Psychology and Aging, 16*, 272–280.

McGue, M., Osler, M., & Christensen, K. (2010). Causal inferences and observational research: The utility of twins. *Perspectives on Psychological Science, 5*, 546–556.

McGue, M., Bouchard, T. J., Iacono, W. G., & Lykken, D. T. (1993). Behavioral genetics of cognitive ability: A life-span perspective. In R. Plomin & G. E. McClearn (Eds.), *Nature, nurture, and psychology* (pp. 59–76). Washington, DC: American Psychological Association.

Mednick, S. A., Gabrielli, W. F., & Hutchings, B. (1984). Genetic factors in criminal behavior: Evidence from an adoption cohort. *Science, 224*, 891–893.

Merriman, C. (1924). The intellectual resemblance of twins. *Psychological Monographs, 33*, 1–58.

Mitchell, K. S., Mazzeo, S. E., Bulik, C. M., Aggen, S. H., Kendler, K. S., & Neale, M. C. (2007). An investigation of twins' equal environments. *Twin Research and Human Genetics, 6*, 840–847.

Moffitt, T. E., Caspi, A., & Rutter, M. (2006). Measured gene–environment interactions in psychopathology: Concepts, research strategies, and implications for research, intervention, and public understanding of genetics. *Perspectives in Psychological Science, 1*, 5–27.

Moffitt, T. E., Caspi, A., Dickson, N., Silva, P., & Stanton, W. (1996). Childhood-onset versus adolescent-onset of antisocial conduct problems in males: Natural history from 3 to 18 years. *Developmental Psychopathology, 8*, 399–424.

Munafo, M., Durrant, C., Lewis, G., & Flint, J. (2009). Gene × environment interactions at the serotonin transporter locus. *Biological Psychiatry, 65*, 211–219.

Neale, M. C., Boker, S. M., Xie, G., & Maes, H. (1999). *Mx: Statistical modeling* (5th ed.). VCU Box 900126, Department of Psychiatry, Richmond, 23298.

Nichols, R. C. (1978). Twin studies of ability, personality, and interests. *Homo, 29*, 158–173.

Oliver, B. R., & Plomin, R. (2007). Twins' Early Development Study (TEDS). A multivariate, longitudinal genetic investigation of language, cognition and behavior problems from childhood through adolescence. *Twin Research and Human Genetics, 10*, 96–105.

Osler, M., McGue, M., & Christensen, K. (2008). Marital status and twins' health and behavior: An analysis of middle-aged Danish twins. *Psychosomatic Medicine, 70*, 482–487.

Pearson, T. A., & Manolio, T. A. (2008). How to interpret a genome-wide association study. *Journal of the American Medical Association, 299*, 1335–1344.

Pergadia, M. L., Madden, P. A. F., Lessov, C. N., Todorov, A. A., Bucholz, K. K., Martin, N. G., & Heath, A. C. (2006). Genetic and environmental influences on extreme personality dispositions in adolescent female twins. *Journal of Child Psychology and Psychiatry, 47*, 902–909.

Petrill, S. A, Pike, A., Price, T., & Plomin, R. (2004). Chaos in the home and socio-economic status are associated with cognitive development in early childhood: Environmental mediators identified in a genetic design. *Intelligence, 32*, 445–460.

Petronis, A. (2001). Human morbid genetics revisited: Relevance of epigenetics. *Trends in Genetics, 17*, 142–146.

Plomin, R. (1994). *Genetics and experience: The interplay between nature and nurture.* Thousand Oaks, CA: Sage.

Plomin, R., & DeFries, J. C. (1985). *Origins of individual differences in infancy: The Colorado Adoption Project.* Orlando, FL: Academic Press.

Plomin, R., & Schalkwyk, L. C. (2007). Microarrays. *Developmental Science, 10,* 19–23.

Plomin, R., & Spinath, F.M. (2004). Intelligence: Genetics, genes, and genomics. *Journal of Personality and Social Psychology, 86,* 112–129.

Plomin, R., DeFries, J. C., & Loehlin, J. C. (1977). Gene–environment interaction and correlation in the analysis of human behavior. *Psychological Bulletin, 84,* 309–322.

Plomin, R., Loehlin, J. C., & DeFries, J. C. (1985). Genetic and environmental components of "environmental" influences. *Developmental Psychology, 21,* 391–402.

Plomin, R., Owen, M. J., & McGuffin, P. (1994). The genetic basis of complex human behaviors. *Science, 264,* 1733–1739.

Plomin, R., DeFries, J. C., McClearn, G. E., & McGuffin, P. (2008). *Behavioral genetics* (5th ed.). New York: Worth.

Posthuma, D., de Geus, E. J. C., & Boomsma, D. I. (2001). Perceptual speed and IQ are associated through common genetic factors. *Behavior Genetics, 31,* 593–602.

Posthuma, D., Baaré, W. F., Hulshoff Pol, H. E., Kahn, R. S., Boomsma, D. I., & de Geus, E. J. C. (2003). Genetic correlations between brain volumes and the WAIS–III dimensions of verbal comprehension, working memory, perceptual organization, and processing speed. *Twin Research, 6,* 131–139.

Price, T. S., & Jaffee, S. R. (2008). Effects of the family environment: Gene–environment interaction and passive gene–environment correlation. *Developmental Psychology, 44,* 305–315.

Purcell, S. (2002). Variance component models for gene–environment interaction in twin analysis. *Twin Research, 5,* 554–571.

Purcell, S., & Koenen, K. C. (2005). Environmental mediation and the twin design. *Behavior Genetics, 35,* 491–498.

Raine, A., Reynolds, C., Venables, P. H., & Mednick, S. A. (2002). Stimulus seeking and intelligence: A prospective longitudinal study. *Journal of Personality and Social Psychology, 82,* 663–674.

Rathouz, P. J., van Hulle, C. A., Rodgers, J. L., Waldman, I. D., & Lahey, B. B. (2008). Specification, testing, and interpretation of gene-by-measured-environment interaction models in the presence of gene–environment correlation. *Behavior Genetics, 38,* 301–315.

Reiss, D., Neiderhiser, J. M., Hetherington, E. M., & Plomin, R. (2000). *The relationship code: Deciphering genetic and social patterns in adolescent development.* Cambridge, MA: Harvard University Press.

Rende, R. D., Plomin, R., & Vandenberg, S. G. (1990). Who discovered the twin method? *Behavior Genetics, 20,* 277–285.

Riemann, R., Angleitner, A., & Strelau, J. (1997). Genetic and environmental influences on personality: A study of twins reared together using the self- and peer-report NEO–FFI scales. *Journal of Personality, 65,* 449–476.

Rijsdijk, F. V., Vernon, P. A., & Boomsma, D. I. (2002). Application of hierarchical genetic models to Raven and WAIS subtests: A Dutch twin study. *Behavior Genetics, 32,* 199–210.

Risch, N., Harrell, R., Lehner, T., Liang, K. Y., Eaves, L., Hoh, J. et al. (2009). Interaction between the serotonin transporter gene, stressful life events, and risk of depression: A meta-analysis. *Journal of the American Medical Association, 301,* 2462–2471.

Roberts, B. W., & Caspi, A. (2003). The cumulative continuity model of personality development: Striking a balance between continuity and change in personality traits across the life course. In U. Staudinger & U. Lindenberger (Eds.), *Understanding human development: Lifespan psychology in exchange with other disciplines*. Dordrecht, The Netherlands: Kluwer Academic.

Roberts, B. W., Caspi, A., & Moffitt, T. E. (2003). Work experiences and personality development in young adulthood. *Journal of Personality and Social Psychology, 84*, 582–593.

Rowe, D. C., Vesterdal, W. J., & Rodgers, J. L. (1999). Herrnstein's syllogism: Genetic and shared environmental influences on IQ, education, and income. *Intelligence, 26*, 405–423.

Rutter, M. (2007). Proceeding from observed correlation to causal inference. *Perspectives in Psychological Science, 2*, 377–395.

Saudino, K. J., Pedersen, N. L., Lichtenstein, P., McClearn, G. E., & Plomin, R. (1997). Can personality explain genetic influences on life events? *Journal of Personality and Social Psychology, 72*, 196–206.

Scarr, S. (1989). How genotypes and environments combine: Development and individual differences. In G. Downey, A. Caspi, & N. Bolger (Eds.), *Interacting systems in human development* (pp. 217–244). New York: Cambridge University Press.

Scarr, S. (1992). Developmental theories for the 1990s: Development and individual differences. *Child Development, 63*, 1–19.

Scarr, S. (1996). How people make their own environments: Implications for parents and policy makers. *Psychology of Public Policy and the Law, 2*, 204–228.

Scarr, S., & McCartney, K. (1983). How people make their own environments: A theory of genotype–environment effects. *Child Development, 54*, 424–435.

Schmalhausen, I. I. (1949). *Factors of evolution: The theory of stabilizing selection*. Philadelphia: The Blakiston Company.

Sham, P. C., Cherny, S. S., Purcell, S., & Hewitt, J. (2000). Power of linkage versus association analysis of quantitative traits, by use of variance-components models, for sibship data. *American Journal of Human Genetics, 66*, 1616–1630.

Shanahan, M. J., Vaisey, S., Erickson, L. D., & Smolen, A. (2008). Environmental contingencies and genetic propensities: Social capital, educational continuation, and Dopamine Receptor Gene DRD2. *American Journal of Sociology, 114* Suppl., S260–S286.

Shrout, P. E., & Fleiss, J. L. (1979). Intraclass correlations: Uses in assessing rater reliability. *Psychological Bulletin, 86*, 420–428.

Siemens, H. W. (1924). Die *Zwillingspathologie: Ihre Bedeutung, ihre Methodik, ihre bisherigen Ergebnisse*. [Twin pathology: Importance, methodology, and results.] Berlin: Springer.

Sladek, R., Rocheleau, G., Rung, J., Dina, C., Shen, L., Serre, D. et al. (2007). A genome-wide association study identifies novel risk loci for type 2 diabetes. *Nature, 445*, 881–885.

Spinath, B., Spinath, F. M., Harlaar, N., & Plomin, R. (2006). Predicting school achievement from intelligence, self-perceived ability, and intrinsic value. *Intelligence, 34*, 363–374.

Spinath, F. M., & Plomin, R. (2003). Amplification of genetic influence on g from early childhood to the early school years. Paper presented at the IVth Meeting of the International Society for Intelligence Research (ISIR), Irvine, USA, December 4–6.

Spinath, F. M., Spinath, B., & Plomin, R. (2008). The nature and nurture of intelligence and motivation in the origins of sex differences in elementary school achievement. *European Journal of Personality, 22*, 211–229.

Spinath, F. M., Toussaint, A., Spengler, M., & Spinath, B. (2008). Motivation als Element schulbezogener Selbstregulation: Die Rolle genetischer Einflüsse. [Motivation as an element of self-regulation: The role of genetics.] *Unterrichtswissenschaft, 36*, 3–16.

Spinath, F. M., Ronald, A., Harlaar, N., Price, T., & Plomin, R. (2003). Phenotypic *g* early in life: On the etiology of general cognitive ability in a large population sample of twin children aged 2 to 4 years. *Intelligence, 31,* 195–210.

Spinath, F. M., Wolf, H., Angleitner, A., Borkenau, P., & Riemann, R. (2005). Multimodale Untersuchung von Persönlichkeit und kognitiven Fähigkeiten. Ergebnisse der deutschen Zwillingsstudie BiLSAT und GOSAT. [A multimodal investigation of personality and cognitive ability: Results from the German twin studies BiLSAT and GOSAT.] *Zeitschrift für Soziologie in der Erziehung, 25,* 146–161.

Tabery, J. (2008). R. A. Fisher, Lancelot Hogben, and the origin(s) of genotype–environment interaction. *Journal of the History of Biology, 41,* 717–761.

Tellegen, A. T. J. (1982). *Brief manual for the Differential Personality Questionnaire.* Unpublished manual, Department of Psychology, University of Minnesota, MN.

Tellegen, A. T. J., Bouchard, T. J., Wilcox, K. J., Segal, N. L., Lykken, D. T., & Rich, S. (1988). Personality similarity in twins reared apart and together. *Journal of Personality and Social Psychology, 54,* 1031–1039.

Turkheimer, E. (2000). Three laws of behavior genetics and what they mean. *Current Directions in Psychological Science, 9,* 160–164.

Turkheimer, E., D'Onofrio, B. M., Maes, H. H., & Eaves, L. J. (2005). Analysis and interpretation of twin studies including measures of the shared environment. *Child Development, 76,* 1217–1233.

Turkheimer, E., Haley, A., Waldron, M., D'Onofrio, B. M., & Gottesman, I. I. (2003). Socioeconomic status modifies heritability of IQ in young children. *Psychological Science, 14,* 623–628.

van der Sluis, S., Willemsen, G., de Geus, E. J., Boomsma, D. I., & Posthuma, D. (2008). Gene–environment interaction in adults' IQ scores: Measures of past and present environment. *Behavior Genetics, 38,* 348–360.

Waddington, C. H. (1942). The epigenotype. *Endeavor, 1,* 18–20.

Weedon, M. N., Lango, H., Lindgren, C. M., Wallace, C., Evans, D. M., Mangino, M. et al. (2008). Genome-wide association analysis identifies 20 loci that influence adult height. *Nature Genetics, 40,* 575–583.

Wigfield, A., & Eccles, J. S. (2000). Expectancy-value theory of achievement motivation. *Contemporary Educational Psychology, 25,* 68–81.

Wilk, S. E., & Sackett, P. R. (1996). Longitudinal analysis of ability–job complexity fit and job change. *Personnel Psychology, 49,* 937–967.

# 11

# Molecular Genetic Aspects of Personality

## Alexander Strobel and Burkhard Brocke

## 1 Introduction

Personality psychology and behavior genetics share a common theme: the investigation of given interindividual differences. Because genetic variations belong to the most powerful influences on behavioral dispositions and human behavior, behavior genetics can be seen as one of the core areas of differential and personality psychology. The more we know about genetic mechanisms underlying individual differences, the more promising it will be to look for neurobiological pathways, which explain individual differences in human behavior and which may be generalized to explanations of the behavior of all individuals (the "modal" person).

Modern behavior genetics is primarily characterized by three basic questions, which coevally delineate the main fields of this research area:

1 Which kinds of behavior and behavioral dispositions are influenced, and to what extent, by genetic factors and, respectively, by environmental factors? (*quantitative behavior genetics*)
2 What specific genes are important for specific kinds of behavioral dispositions or traits? (*molecular behavior genetics*)
3 How and by what mechanisms and behavior genetic pathways do genes impact on behavior? (*functional genomics*)

Important foundations of genetics had already been realized in the middle of the nineteenth century (Mendel, Galton). Its further development progressed smoothly for a long period. At the beginning of the twentieth century Mendel's laws were rediscovered, twin and adoption studies developed, and the extension to complex traits with multiple genetic and environmental influences began with Fisher (e.g.

*The Wiley-Blackwell Handbook of Individual Differences*, First Edition.
Edited by Tomas Chamorro-Premuzic, Sophie von Stumm, and Adrian Furnham.
© 2011 Blackwell Publishing Ltd. Published 2011 by Blackwell Publishing Ltd.

Fisher, 1918). In the second half of the twentieth century the detection of the structure of DNA and the detection of the genetic code were milestones in the further
development of molecular genetics. The vast decoding of the genome at the beginning of twenty-first century marks the apex of this development. A breathtaking
development and new, powerful tools characterize present molecular genetics: linkage
analysis, positional cloning, and candidate gene studies dominated molecular genetic
research in the 1990s; genome-wide association analyses, genome-wide sequencing,
endophenotype analyses, epigenetics, transcriptomics, and proteomics are going to
mark the research of the coming decade.

    With the establishment of differential psychology at the beginning of the past
century, the nearest relative of behavior genetics emerged early on. This chapter is
intended to provide a current overview of the *molecular genetics* approach of behavior
genetics. In the following pages we will introduce the foundations and methods of the
molecular genetic approach to the study of individual differences (Section 2). Then
we will give an overview of theories and models in personality psychology, which
provide one necessary basis for deductive candidate gene studies (Section 3). In the
main part of our overview (Sections 4 and 5), we will delineate important findings on
genetic variations and environmental factors influencing personality. The last section
outlines current developments and future directions in molecular genetic approaches.

## 2   Foundations and Methods

This section will introduce basic concepts and methods of the molecular genetics of
individual differences. First, conceptual issues (what genetic polymorphisms are,
whether and how they impact on behavior) will be summarized shortly to further
the understanding of methodological approaches of molecular genetics, i.e. how can
genetic polymorphisms be studied and linked to individual differences? These
approaches will be outlined in the second part of the section, where the main focus
will be on association studies.

### 2.1   Genes, genetic variations, and their potential impact
on behavior

Our genes—strands of deoxyribonucleic acid (DNA) located on 23 pairs of chromosomes in the cell nucleus—code for proteins, e.g. enzymes responsible for the synthesis or degradation of certain neurotransmitters. A gene complex consists not only
of coding regions or exons—that is, sequences of so-called triplets of nucleotide bases
(adenine, thymine, guanine, and cytosine), which code for certain amino acids and
their sequence in the final protein—but also of non-coding regions or introns, which
can have some regulatory function, and finally of transcriptional control regions, or
promoters, located upstream of a gene. These promoters have a regulatory function
and are important regulators of the transcription of a gene.

    If, on the basis of cellular mechanisms, a signal is generated that more of a given
protein is needed, then transcription factors bind to certain recognition sites within
the gene promoters. This allows a ribonucleic acid (RNA) polymerase protein complex

to bind to the DNA and to start the gene transcription at the so-called start codon (i.e. the nucleotide sequence ATG). The DNA sequence is subsequently transcribed into RNA via an assembly of nucleotide bases, according to the DNA template sequence. Afterwards, during the so-called splicing, messenger RNA (mRNA) is generated from the RNA: in other words, intronic information is cut and only exonic information is retained. Then the mRNA is transferred to the ribosomes for translation, that is, for the mRNA code-based assembly of amino acids into the final protein.

With the exception of the sex chromosomes of males, each gene has a corresponding gene on the partner chromosome, one from each parent. Such corresponding gene variants are called alleles. These alleles can be identical or can differ with regard to their nucleotide sequence. Importantly, the term "allele" is also used to refer to interindividual variation in one gene's nucleotide sequence, and such variation is frequent throughout the genome. Genetic variation can be due to errors during DNA replication or to external factors, and it can, but must not, have an impact on the function of the gene product—the protein. If alterations of the nucleotide sequence are found in more than 1 percent of a population, the term "polymorphism" should be used; otherwise the term "mutation" is commonly used to denote a rare genetic variation.

There are different kinds of possible genetic variations. First, single nucleotides can be substituted by another nucleotide. These *single-nucleotide polymorphisms* (SNPs) may affect a gene product's function if they are located in exonic regions and may change the code for a given amino acid. As already mentioned, three nucleotide bases form one coding element, for example AAC codes for the amino acid asparagine. If, due to some single nucleotide substitution, the code is changed to AAT, then the gene product will still be the same (a so-called silent variation), as AAT also codes for asparagine. If, however, the nucleotide sequence is changed to AAA or AAG, then the amino acid lysin is incorporated into the protein chain at the respective site (a missense variation), and this can affect the protein's structure, and hence function, which ultimately may affect some brain mechanism underlying a behavioral trait. SNPs can affect the function of a gene product also if they destroy or create a recognition site for transcription factors in the gene promoter, or if they reside in such intronic gene regions, which may have regulatory functions.

Second, nucleotides can be inserted into, or deleted from, a given sequence (*Ins/Del polymorphisms*), and, third, a certain nucleotide sequence can be multiplied, resulting in *repeat polymorphisms* (e.g. so-called variable number of tandem repeats, VNTR). Again, on the basis of the location of such variation in exons, introns, or promoters, changes in the function of a gene product are possible, but not mandatory.

The functional significance of a given genetic variation can be examined *in vitro*, for instance via expression studies using model cells, but also *in vivo*, for instance via postmortem expression studies, or finally *in silico*, on the basis of data base-driven information on whether, say, a given genetic variation creates or destroys a transcription factor recognition site. The demonstration of the actual or likely functional significance of a genetic variation provides a reasonable basis for investigations into the role of this genetic variation in the modulation of individual differences in behavioral phenotypes. Then we can move on and follow one of the approaches outlined in what follows, to relate genetic to phenotypic variation.

## 2.2   Molecular genetic approaches and methods

As stated above, genes do not code for behavior, but for proteins. How, then, can behavioral differences be associated with genetic variation? The logic is as follows: functional alteration in cellular mechanisms (i.e. neurotransmitter synthesis) may affect more global functions (e.g. the balance of the function of a given neurotransmitter within a certain neuronal circuit) and ultimately brain systems subserving complex behavior (e.g. systems involved in the processing of emotional stimuli), thereby impacting on individual differences in behavioral traits (e.g. affectivity) and vulnerability to psychopathology (e.g. depression). Despite this unifying logic, there are two, or rather three ways to close the gap between the two ends of the behavioral genetic pathway.

First, we can start at the behavioral level. We gather theory- or experience-based information on putative biological substrates of some behavioral trait such as a temperament dimension, or a cognitive function including associated psychological disorders. We then identify genetic variations, which are likely to impact on these biological substrates, and finally we associate these genetic variations with individual differences in the behavioral traits under question, for example via examination of mean differences of trait expressions between carriers of different variants of our preselected genetic polymorphisms. This top-down strategy is the so-called *candidate gene approach*, and it has been followed in the vast majority of molecular genetic investigations of individual differences so far.

Second, we can start with the observation of some gene exhibiting a high degree of polymorphism. Here, the very existence of such polymorphism seems reasonably due to some evolutionary fitness gain associated with certain forms of this variation. We then need to identify the biological mechanisms which are impacted by this genetic variation, and ultimately we may arrive at some behavioral trait which is likely to be influenced by this biological mechanism, and thus likely to be associated with the genetic variation under discussion. This bottom-up approach could be termed *candidate phenotype approach*, and it has been pursued much less frequently than the candidate gene approach.

Third, while the two above-mentioned approaches are deductive and hypothesis-testing in nature, we can also follow an inductive and *hypothesis-generating* approach and use as much information on genetic variation as possible in order to identify so far unknown genetic factors presumably impacting on behavioral differences. Here we can use so-called genome-wide association studies (see Section 6.1) and examine hundreds of thousands of polymorphic gene variants, spread across the whole genome, with respect to their role as marker variables for DNA regions possibly involved in individual differences in one or more of the behavioral traits under investigation. In the near future, we might also be able to examine every single data point of individual genomes with respect to its role in modulating individual differences in behavioral traits. This inductive *genome-wide approach* certainly has some appeal, but it also has several limitations, which will be outlined below (see Section 6.1).

Whatever approach we use, we need to determine both the genotypic and the phenotypic status of our subjects in order to perform association tests using, say, chi-square tests (in the case of binary traits such as the presence or absence of a disorder) or analyses of variance (in the case of a continuous trait such as a personality dimension). To genotype our subjects, individual DNA needs to be extracted from cell samples such as blood cells, or more conveniently from buccal cells or saliva, and to be subjected to a method which enables us to determine which variants of a given polymorphism can be identified in a given individual. There are numerous ways to achieve this, and even to mention and briefly describe all of them would require several further sections. Therefore only the simplest method will be described shortly in what follows: namely polymerase chain reaction (PCR) followed by electrophoresis.

PCR allows us to amplify segments of the DNA, which harbor a polymorphism of interest via "tagging" this segment by using so-called primers (i.e. short sequences of nucleotide bases, which match the nucleotide sequences flanking the segment of interest) and repeated duplication of the segment until a critical number of copies is achieved. Electrophoresis is used to determine the length of the amplified segments: the PCR products are tagged with an UV-marker and applied to a porous carrier substance, for instance an agarose gel. After application of voltage, the negatively charged DNA travels through the pores of the carrier substance, shorter DNA segments travelling faster. After a while one can differentiate between segments of different length by photographing the DNA on the carrier substance under UV light. In the case of repeat length polymorphisms, the fragment length directly informs about the genotype (e.g. a fragment of 300 base pairs [bp] in length might constitute a double repeat of a sequence of 150 bp, while a sequence of 450 bp identifies this fragment as a triple repeat). In the case of SNPs or short Ins/Del polymorphisms, an intermediate step becomes necessary: before electrophoresis, an enzyme is applied to the PCR product, which cuts the DNA if it recognizes a certain nucleotide sequence. The presence or absence of a given nucleotide base of a SNP, or an insertion or deletion, respectively, might create or delete such a recognition site, and hence the application of the enzyme results in cut or uncut fragments, which differ in length and may be distinguished after electrophoresis (e.g. the substitution of an A to a G at position 200 of a fragment of 600 bp in length might create a recognition site for a cutting enzyme; a carrier of two A alleles would therefore be identified by two shorter—cut—fragments, whereas a carrier of two G alleles would be identified by two long—uncut—fragments, and a carrier of an A/G genotype would be identified by one short and one long fragment). Hence, on the basis of PCR/electrophoresis, we can determine which variants of genetic polymorphisms are found in a given individual and can link this information with phenotypic measures.

To "phenotype" our subjects, we need to determine behavioral traits which, depending on our research topic, may be disease status, dimensions of cognitive functioning, or personality traits. Here we can refer to diagnostic criteria for mental disorders using the classifications provided in the *ICD–10* (World Health Organization, 1992) or in the *DSM* (American Psychiatric Association, 2000); to cognitive psychological theories and their operationalizations, in other words, to experimental paradigms; or to personality theories and their operationalizations, that is, self- and peer report questionnaires. The theories underlying the latter phenotypic measures will be outlined in what follows, so as to provide a basis for the assessment of the potential for top-down candidate gene approaches.

## 3   Candidate Gene Approaches: Theories Informing about Gene–Trait Associations

As outlined above, the effects of genetic variance are not expressed directly at the level of behavior. They are mediated by molecular and cellular effects on neural mechanisms and processes underlying behavior and behavioral dispositions or phenotypes, i.e. traits. Neurobiological theories of personality, explaining individual differences in emotional and cognitive behavior, inform about underlying neural processes and mechanisms, which offer hints as to the genetic influences possibly involved (*forward genetics*; Seyffert, 1998). Conversely, known genetic variation, e.g. of the serotonergic system, may provide a basis to identify neural processes and mechanisms associated with phenotypic individual differences yet to be detected (*reverse genetics*). This section gives an overview of relevant theoretical models in personality psychology, which have provided one necessary basis to identify candidate genes, thus enabling deductive candidate gene studies.

We will shortly describe in detail Eysenck's biopsychological PEN theory as the origin of this new kind of neurobiological theorizing in personality psychology; the reinforcement sensitivity theory (Gray); the five-dimensional model of personality (Depue); the biosocial theory of personality (Cloninger); as well as further approaches (Zuckerman, Davidson, Panksepp). We will close with an investigation of the presumptive relations of these theories to the five-factor model (FFM or "Big Five"), and we will discuss suggestions for integrating these models with respect to the question of how they can aid molecular genetic research into individual differences.

### 3.1   Correlational and biopsychological trait theories

Eysenck's PEN theory (Eysenck, 1967, 1981, 1997; Eysenck & Eysenck, 1985) was the first of the early influential models of personality (Cattell, Guilford) which transcended the limited potential of purely correlational systems by systematically specifying the causal neurobiological mechanisms underlying individual differences. While correlational theories only allow to describe, diagnose, and predict individual differences, causal theories allow to *explain* individual differences and to answer questions like: "Why do extraverts frequent societal situations?" (Brocke, 2000). In addition, Eysenck's paradigmatic kind of theory systematically combined a correlational description of the personality types—extraversion (E), neuroticism (N), and psychoticism (P) (the descriptive personality theory)—with a large body of neurobiological causal component theories explaining the behavioral characteristics of these types (the arousal/activation theory and its component theories). Further, this theory has been conceived as a twofold hierarchical system with a hierarchy of correlational assumptions describing the three "superfactors," or types E, N, and P, and 27 more specific factors ("traits") on the one hand, and a hierarchy of neurobiological assumptions on the mechanisms underlying these personality factors on the other hand (for a systematic description, see Brocke & Battman, 1992; Brocke, Hennig, & Netter, 2004). Thus the theory offers a rich body of information and a basis for the identification of genes potentially associated with the traits or phenotypes of the model.

In the neurobiological part of the PEN theory, Eysenck focused on the activity of the ascending reticular activating system (ARAS or reticulo-cortical circuit), the activation of which he called *arousal*. He postulated the differential reactivity of this system, differential *arousability*, as the basis of extraversion. The activity of the reticulo-limbic circuitry was labeled *activation*, and he hypothesized that differential *activation thresholds* are the basis of neuroticism. He postulated that extraverts have a lower arousability of the reticulo-cortical circuit than introverts, and therefore they seek more stimulating activities and sensations in order to achieve their preferred level of arousal. Neurotics are more easily *activated* by emotion-inducing stimuli (reticulo-limbic circuit) and, because of the association of the two circuits, they get eventually more *aroused* (reticulo-cortical circuit) than emotionally stable individuals are. The theory does not specify a systematic biological model of psychoticism, but Eysenck postulated a negative association of psychoticism with the serotonergic system and a positive association with dopaminergic function (Eysenck, 1997; Eysenck & Eysenck, 1985).

Eysenck's theory is of central importance as an origin of the new neurobiological personality theories integrating causal and correlational components. The valid parts of the theory offer a basis to identify candidate genes, thus enabling deductive candidate gene studies. However, parts of it are no longer in accordance with latest findings of neuroscience and have to be modified or adjusted, as happened with the concept of "unspecific arousal" and the underlying activity of the ascending reticular activating system (cf. Fischer, Langner, Birbaumer, & Brocke, 2008). Other parts have to be crucially revised and further developed, as is described below (Gray, Depue, Cloninger).

## 3.2   Revised reinforcement sensitivity theory (rRST)

Jeffrey Gray worked in close connection with Eysenck's approach, criticizing, modifying, and basically enhancing his main assumptions (Gray, 1982). He developed a conceptual nervous system encompassing three components (see Corr, 2004, 2009). The behavioral inhibition system (BIS) is sensitive to conditioned aversive stimuli, to omission or termination of expected reward, and to a class of diverse inputs, including extreme novelty, high-intensity stimuli, and innate fear stimuli (blood or snakes). The behavioral approach system (BAS) is postulated to be sensitive to conditioned appetitive stimuli and to the termination or omission of signals of punishment; and the fight–flight system (FFS) is sensitive to unconditioned aversive stimuli (innately painful stimuli). In a substantially revised version, Gray and McNaughton (2000) updated and elaborated the preceding version of Gray's theory and made different predictions in some essential respects.

In the revised version of the RST (rRST; for details, see Smillie, this volume), the former FFS includes "freezing" and is now called the "fight–flight–freeze" system (FFFS). It is responsible for reactions to *all* aversive stimuli, conditioned and unconditioned, and leads to active avoidance or attempted elimination (panic, flight, or fight). The BIS was the most modified system; it is now conceived of as being responsible for the resolution of goal conflict in general, for instance it responds to stimuli which arouse desire, but at the same time contain potential threat (approach–avoidance). Such conflicts may be induced by simultaneously activating the FFFS and the BAS, whereas the BIS acts as a detector of the resulting approach–avoidance conflict. Avoidance–avoidance and approach–approach conflicts can also trigger the BIS. Activation of this system produces vigilance and passive avoidance, and is involved in processes leading to anxiety-formation. The BAS is now responsible for reactions to *all* appetitive stimuli, conditioned and unconditioned, and produces approach behavior.

The neural basis of the BAS is postulated to be in the mesolimbic dopaminergic system; the neural basis of the BIS is postulated to be in the septo-hippocampal system and the amygdala; and the FFFS is linked to the amygdala, hypothalamus, and periaqueductal gray (see Corr, 2009). Originally, BIS and BAS reactivity were associated with anxiety and impulsivity, respectively; hence both traits were described as 30-degree rotations from neuroticism and extraversion. Meanwhile, along with the revision of the RST, Gray and McNaughton described neuroticism as sensitivity to general threat, associated with both BIS and FFFS activity. In addition, extraversion and not impulsivity is increasingly seen as being associated with BAS reactivity (e.g. Corr, 2009; Smillie, Pickering, & Jackson, 2006). Together with the problem that former measures of the RST traits (Carver & White, 1994; Torrubia, Ávila, Moltó, & Caser, 2001) do not represent the revised functions of the three neurobiological systems, the psychometric basis of the rRST is the weakest part of this theory.

### 3.3   Cloninger's biosocial theory of personality

Modifying and enhancing central concepts of the three-system RST, C. Robert Cloninger (1987) developed a theory which was similarly based on three distinct neurobiological systems underlying three basic personality traits: novelty-seeking (NS), harm avoidance (HA), and reward dependence (RD). In a later version of his theory, he included four further personality traits: persistence, cooperativeness, self-directedness, and self-transcendence. He postulated that the first four of the seven traits have a biological basis and should strongly be genetically influenced (being dimensions of the "temperament") and the latter three are primarily formed by experience and not by genes (they are dimensions of "character"). With regard to the intention to identify candidate genes influencing phenotypic variation, we focus on the neurobiologically founded temperamental traits. To measure the traits of his model, Cloninger developed the Tridimensional Personality Questionnaire (TPQ; Cloninger, Svrakic, & Przybeck, 1991) and later on the Temperament and Character Inventory (TCI; Cloninger, Przybeck, Svrakic, & Wetzel, 1994).

The three biological systems underlying the temperamental traits are activated by cues of novelty (behavioral activation system), danger (behavioral inhibition system), and reward (behavioral maintenance system) and produce approach and avoidance behavior (Cloninger, Svrakic, & Przybeck, 1993). They are primarily mediated by an individual neurotransmitter system. Cloninger postulated that the serotonergic system is associated with HA, the dopaminergic system with NS, and the norepinephrine system with RD.

Because of this one-trait–one-neurotransmitter hypothesis, the biosocial theory of personality became very popular as a basis for deductive candidate gene studies.

Variation of genes modulating an individual neurotransmitter system were hypothesized as candidate genes for the temperamental trait influenced by the respective neurotransmitter. However, this assumption, as well as the postulated seven-factor structure, could not be unambiguously confirmed; and there is some contradicting evidence (DeYoung & Gray, 2009).

### 3.4   Depue's five-dimensional model of personality

Depue started the development of his theory with a neurobiological differentiation of two kinds of the complex extraversion trait. He described agentic extraversion as primarily dopaminergic-modulated, and affiliative extraversion as modulated by opioids and peptides like oxytocin (Depue & Collins, 1999). Depue's theory in its recent version postulates five dimensional traits (Depue & Lenzenweger, 2005): (1) *agentic extraversion*, based on dopamine facilitation of the incentive of reward motivation; (2) *affiliation*, based on mu-opiate mediation of appetitive and consumatory reward processes; (3) *anxiety or neuroticism*, based on the activity of corticotrophin-releasing hormone in the limbic structures, in the bed nucleus of the stria terminalis (BNST), and in the rostral medulla; (4) *fear*, based on amygdala activity responding to particular localized threat, and (5) *non-affective constraint*, based on serotonergic modulation of the expression of other emotional traits.

The differentiation of neuroticism/anxiety from fear was proposed (White & Depue, 1999) concurrently with the differentiation of agentic extraversion and affiliative extraversion (Depue & Collins, 1999). In the final version of his approach, Depue dropped "extraversion" from the label of the latter trait and he presented a theory of "affiliative bonding" (Depue & Morrone-Strupinski, 2005). His most recent empirical work focuses on the interplay between pharmacologically facilitated neurotransmitters and neuropeptides and psychological processes related to temperament, with the goal of understanding differences in the behavioral expression of these traits.

Depue used the Multidimensional Personality Questionnaire (Tellegen & Waller, 1992) to measure his five dimensions: the MPQ scales of social closeness for affiliation, social potency for agentic extraversion, stress reaction for anxiety, and MPQ harm avoidance for fear. Finally he used MPQ impulsivity versus control to represent non-affective control.

### 3.5   Further approaches and an integration

Zuckerman (1994, 2005) has provided a rich body of knowledge of biosocial personality psychology. He developed a (correlational) five-factor model of personality, the *Alternative Five*, describing the personality factors of sociability, neuroticism–anxiety, aggression–hostility, impulsive sensation-seeking, and activity (Zuckerman, Kuhlman, Joireman, Teta, & Kraft, 1993). Starting in the 1960s and later on in parallel with work on his correlational model, Zuckerman developed a biosocial theory as a basis for his model, and primarily for sensation-seeking (Zuckerman, 2005). Contrary to Cloninger's approach, his biosocial theory is characterized by the assumption that neurobiological traits are mediated by multiple biological systems, rather than by individual neurotransmitter systems. Impulsive sensation-seeking is for example modulated by dopamine, serotonin, and norepinephrine, as well as by gonadal hormones and further mechanisms. A second characteristic of his approach is the view that only those personality traits which have a biological basis and substantial heritability can be seen as basic personality dimensions (Zuckerman, 2005, 1993). A third important feature of his approach is the hierarchical structure of the theory (Zuckerman, 1990; Brocke, 2004), a multi-level approach encompassing seven levels from genes to behavior.

Among further biopsychological theories of personality, two more approaches should be mentioned. Jaak Panksepp developed a neurobiological personality theory comprising six traits. He labeled them playfulness, seeking, caring, fear, anger, and sadness, and he postulated that they were influenced by six neurally based networks or emotional systems (Panksepp, 1998). Additionally, he developed an inventory for the psychometric operationalization of his neurobiological traits (Affective Neuroscience Personality Scales, ANPS; Davis, Panksepp & Normansell, 2003). Thus his model exhibits the same structure as the other neurobiological theories, containing a descriptive, psychometric, and mostly correlational component and an hypothetically causal biopsychological component.

On the basis of neuropsychological and psychophysiological findings, Richard J. Davidson postulated two separate brain systems, located in the right and left hemisphere, respectively, which are basically involved in behavior regulation (Davidson, 1992). The system located in the left prefrontal area is part of a motivational system and is responsible for approach behavior (see Amelang, Bartussek, Stemmler, & Hagemann, 2006). Apart from the left prefrontal cortex, this system comprises subcortical structures, especially the nucleus accumbens, and dopamine is involved in the modulation of approach behavior. Davidson postulated a complementary motivational system, located in the right prefrontal cortex and in limbic structures like the amygdala and hypothalamus, which is responsible for retreat behavior. Davidson assumes that not all individuals show a symmetric activity of both systems, but rather tend to exhibit either a left or right prefrontal base activity of the cortex. This frontal asymmetry is assumed to be a stable disposition and to be ascertainable by indicators of the spontaneous EEG. Individuals with a relatively left frontal asymmetry show a greater sensitivity to approach behavior and exhibit a marked positive emotionality. Individuals with a relatively right frontal asymmetry are predisposed to exhibiting retreat behavior and marked negative emotionality. The emotional traits of positive and negative emotionality corresponding to the respective frontal asymmetry are often measured with the Positive and Negative Affect Schedule (PANAS; Watson, Clark, & Tellegen, 1988).

The personality theories described above show considerable overlap and shared explanations. Not least for the purpose of obtaining an informative basis for the identification of candidate genes associated with phenotypic variation, an integration of these theories seems to be attractive. However, one has to be careful to avoid premature structuring of the field, which lacks sufficient evidence.

With respect to the goal of identifying candidate genes associated with phenotypic variation, a suggestion made by Revelle (1995) looks especially promising. Revelle describes three basic behavioral dimensions: approach, avoidance, and fight–flight behavior. These behavioral dimensions widely correspond to characteristic activity in the neurotransmitter systems: dopamine (approach behavior; e.g. extraversion, sensation-seeking, novelty-seeking); serotonin and noradrenaline (avoidance behavior; e.g. anxiety, neuroticism, negative emotionality); and serotonin, noradrenaline, and gamma-aminobutyric acid (fight–flight behavior; e.g. fear). Revelle's typology as a basis for integration might be helpful in generating suggestions for candidate genes. However, the presumptive associations with individual psychometric trait concepts still have to stand the test (cf. Sen et al., 2004).

DeYoung and others made the suggestion to translate the results from the models described above "into a single common language" (DeYoung & Gray, 2009) relating each model to the five-factor model of personality (FFM or Big Five; Costa & McCrae, 1992; Digman, 1990; Goldberg, 1990). However, there has been no sound authentic biological basis for the Big Five for long, which made the translation difficult. To import the neurobiological systems underlying the personality dimension of the theories described above may again be helpful in generating suggestions for candidate genes; however, it may again risk premature integration.

Only recently has a systematic, though preliminary, effort been undertaken to develop a biological basis for the FFM. Questioning the independence of the five domains (extraversion, neuroticism, agreeableness, conscientiousness, openness), some research results showed slight intercorrelations and demonstrated a higher-order factor structure (DeYoung, 2006; Jang et al., 2006). Neuroticism, agreeableness, and conscientiousness formed one higher trait, named $\alpha$ or *stability*, and extraversion and openness formed another, named $\beta$ or *plasticity*. Jang et al. (2006) provided data suggesting that the two higher-order traits are genetically influenced. DeYoung and Gray (DeYoung 2006; DeYoung & Gray, 2008) and Yamagata et al. (2006) suggest that stability is related to serotonin and plasticity may be related to dopamine. DeYoung and Gray (2008) see the identification of dopamine and serotonin as presumptive biological substrates for the higher-order traits as the beginning of a psychobiological model for the (hierarchical) FFM. In the context of a literature review, they generate hypotheses about biological substrates for the domains, substrates that would be unique for the individual domains, and they are looking for shared substrates for the higher-order traits. Thereby they primarily inspect the above-described biopsychological theories and additional material.

## 4 Molecular Genetic Main Effects

In this section we will sketch paradigmatic evidence on the potential role of genetic variation (1) in modulating personality traits, exemplified by the impact of genetic variation in serotonin transporter function on individual differences in anxiety- and depression-related personality traits; (2) in the development of psychopathology, again, by focusing on genetic variation of serotonin transporter function and its putative associations with affective and anxiety disorders; and (3) in modulating psychophysiological correlates of personality and psychopathology, e.g. genotypic differences in fMRI parameters of emotional processing.

## 4.1   Personality traits

The personality theories outlined in Section 3 suggest the existence of a general personality dimension of negative emotionality, comprising aspects of neuroticism *sensu* Costa and McCrae, of behavioral inhibition *sensu* Gray, of harm avoidance *sensu* Cloninger, and of related constructs. Taken together, negative emotionality can be conceptualized as a stable and heritable sensitivity to aversive stimuli (Clark, Watson, & Mineka, 1994). Given that negative emotionality can be viewed as a dimension of the vulnerability toward developing anxiety and affective disorders (Clark et al., 1994; Kendler, Gatz, Gardner, & Pedersen, 2006; Ormel, Oldehinkel, & Vollebergh, 2004), and given that negative emotionality shows high genetic correlations with these disorders (Carey & DiLalla, 1994), we may view anxiety and depression as extremes of normal variation in negative emotionality.

Hence, genetic variation impacting on the biological mechanisms involved in the development of affective and anxiety disorders may also modulate individual differences in the vulnerability dimension of negative emotionality. If we take into account that certain chemical compounds—like selective serotonin reuptake inhibitors (SSRIs)—can be used successfully to treat psychological conditions such as anxiety disorders or depression (see e.g. Nemeroff & Owens, 2002), some variation in the gene encoding the target site for SSRI action, the serotonin transporter, is likely to affect a biological mechanism involved in the vulnerability to develop these disorders. Therefore an association between genetic variation of serotonin transporter function and negative emotionality seems plausible.

This logic was applied in a seminal study by Lesch and colleagues (Lesch et al., 1996). The authors focused on a polymorphic sequence in the promotor of the serotonin transporter gene, previously detected by that group and termed serotonin (5–HT) transporter (5–HTT) linked polymorphic region (5–HTTLPR; Heils et al., 1996). 5–HTTLPR is an insertion/deletion polymorphism with a long (L) variant comprising 16 copies of a 20–23 base pair repeat sequence and a short (S) variant comprising 14 copies. Among Caucasians, the frequencies of the L and S alleles are about .60 and .40, respectively (Heils et al., 1996), although allele frequencies vary across different populations (Gelernter, Cubells, Kidd, Pakstis, & Kidd, 1999). The S allele is associated with lower transcriptional efficiency of the 5–HTT gene, and hence with lower levels of serotonin uptake (Heils et al., 1996; Lesch et al., 1996).

Interestingly, Lesch and colleagues (Lesch et al., 1996) observed carriers of the S allele to exhibit significantly higher scores in neuroticism as measured using the NEO–PI–R. This effect explained only 2–4 percent of the variance in neuroticism— an effect size which is typical for association studies of complex traits, because such traits are likely to be influenced by a large number of genes, which additively or interactively impact on a given trait. Nevertheless, such small effects can be of high value for the understanding of the neurogenetic underpinnings of behavioral differences, given that they are biologically plausible and can be replicated.

Concerning the biological plausibility of the association between the 5–HTTLPR S allele and neuroticism, this result might at first glance seem counterintuitive, as carriers of a gene variant associated with lower serotonin transporter function showed significantly higher scores in a vulnerability factor for affective and anxiety disorders, which can effectively be treated with SSRIs that inhibit serotonin transporter function. Here we must take into account that a genetic variation may impact on physiological processes in the long term, perhaps via a role during critical developmental phases. It seems likely that a genetically mediated reduction in serotonin transporter function might result in higher serotonin levels during critical developmental phases, which in turn might prompt counteracting inhibitory processes with regard to serotonin synthesis and release via the action of serotonin autoreceptors. This might ultimately result in a lower serotonin release and concentration in the synaptic cleft, which then needs to be raised using SSRIs and which may impact on the re-regulation of serotonin turnover and serotonin neuromodulation. Of course, alternative explanations exist.

Concerning the replicability of this association, it has to be noted that the finding of Lesch and colleagues has been replicated in a number of studies, mostly by using NEO–PI–R neuroticism or TPQ harm avoidance to assess variation in negative emotionality. While there are also conflicting results and non-replications, current meta-analyses point to a replicable effect of 5–HTTLPR variation of negative emotionality, given that negative emotionality is assessed by using the NEO–PI–R (Schinka, Busch, & Robichaux-Keene, 2004; Sen, Burmeister & Ghosh, 2004; see, however, Munafò, Clark, & Flint, 2005). These meta-analytic findings may indicate that the behavioral phenotype impacted by 5–HTTLPR-mediated variation in the function of brain systems may be more closely related to the five-factor model conceptualization of negative emotionality than to Cloninger's conceptualization of harm avoidance. Another possible reason for the inconsistency of the present findings can be seen in the fact that a recently discovered A to G single nucleotide substitution within the region designated as 5–HTTLPR impairs the transcriptional efficiency of the L allele (Hu et al., 2005), with only carriers of the common $L_A/L_A$ genotype exhibiting high 5–HTT gene transcription. Therefore, in earlier studies, several individuals with the rare $L_G$ variant may indeed have shown comparably low levels of 5–HTT transcription as carriers of the S allele.

## 4.2   Psychopathology

Given the association between the 5–HTTLPR S allele and a vulnerability dimension for the development of affective and anxiety disorders, it seems plausible that the 5–HTTLPR S allele should also be over-represented in individuals diagnosed with these disorders. Intriguingly, however, evidence from meta-analyses suggests small positive associations of the S allele with bipolar disorder and suicidal behavior, but not with depression itself (Levinson, 2006). Similarly inconclusive is the evidence concerning associations of 5–HTTLPR with anxiety-related disorders such as panic disorders (Maron & Shlik, 2006) or obsessive–compulsive disorder (Bloch et al., 2008).

This inconclusive evidence may in part be due, again, to methodological differences between studies. It may, however, also be explained by the possibility that common genetic variants such as 5–HTTLPR may imply some predisposition to develop psychopathology, but only in interaction with other genetic or environmental factors such as adverse life events. Before this issue is covered in more detail in Section

5, we will close the present one with exciting findings concerning the neurobiological underpinnings of the role of 5–HTTLPR in the modulation of information-processing networks assumed to be disturbed in anxiety and depression in order to show that, despite inconclusive evidence on a given polymorphism's role in modulating *phenotypic* behavioral expressions, we might be able to gather more consistent evidence at a so-called *endophenotypic* level.

## 4.3   Endophenotypes

The term *endophenotype*, reintroduced by Gottesman and Gould (2003), refers to some measure of individual differences at a more basic level, for instance the behavioral, cognitive, neurophysiological, biochemical, endocrinological, or neuroanatomical level, which is assumed to causally impact on, or at least to correlate with, a given phenotype—such as a disorder or a personality trait. Within the context of the present example, an endophenotype of negative emotionality as a vulnerability factor for the development of affective and anxiety disorders could, say, be a neurobiological substrate relevant for the processing of aversive stimuli. Promising endophenotypes for negative emotionality therefore are measures of the function of amygdala-relayed cortico-subcortical circuits, as the amygdala can be regarded as a key structure in emotional processing, especially of aversive events.

Following this logic, a seminal functional magnetic imaging (fMRI) study by Hariri and colleagues (Hariri et al., 2002) demonstrated that carriers of the 5–HTTLPR S allele exhibited a higher neuronal activation in the amygdala in response to negative facial expressions. This finding has been replicated and extended by showing that 5–HTTLPR genotype also impacts on the functional connectivity between the amygdala and ventromedial prefrontal and anterior cingulated regions (Heinz et al., 2005; Pezawas et al., 2005). Hence, the 5–HTTLPR S allele seems to play a role in amygdala responses to aversive stimuli, which may be regarded as one factor underlying the higher scores in negative emotionality observed for carriers of the S allele (see above). Thus this evidence points to a biologically plausible mechanism, which mediates between variation at the 5–HTT gene locus and behavioral expressions of a heightened sensitivity to aversive events, being the core feature of negative emotionality.

Another example of an endophenotype of negative emotionality is the startle reflex, that is, the reflex response of an organism to sudden high-intensity stimulation, which in itself may be of aversive nature. In our own studies (Armbruster et al., 2009; Brocke et al., 2006), we were able to show that 5–HTTLPR S allele carriers exhibit an elevated startle response. Hence this evidence suggests that, even at the level of basic reflexes, genetic variation in serotonin transporter function impacts on individual differences in responses to aversive events.

## 5   Gene–Gene and Gene–Environment Interactions, and Pleiotropic Gene Effects

Given that a main effect of a genetic variation on some biological substrate—e.g. the 5–HTTLPR-mediated heightened amygdala response, or the elevated startle reflex to aversive stimulation—has adverse behavioral consequences, such as the development of a psychopathology, the question arises why this variation has not been removed from the gene pool during evolution, due the resulting reduction in fitness.

The present section is therefore devoted to solutions to the evolutionary puzzle of the existence of genetic variations potentially predisposing to psychopathology, and consequently to fitness reductions. One promising answer to this puzzle is that, especially for common genetic variants—the 5–HTTLPR S allele is present in about 40 percent of Caucasian populations (see above)—a "risk allele" might bear some risk of psychopathology *only* in the presence of further modulating factors, such as other genetic variations (a gene–gene interaction effect, or epistasis, or a haplotype effect, only the first one of which is covered in the present section) or environmental factors (a gene–environment interaction effect); or it might have adverse effects on one trait, but be beneficial for some other trait (a so-called pleiotropic gene effect). A molecular genetic focus on the mechanisms underlying complex human traits and disorders therefore needs to take into account these modes of behavioral modulation. In the following, evidence on such effects is sketched—again, primarily with regard to 5–HTTLPR.

## 5.1    Gene–gene interactions

As early as 1998, Ebstein and colleagues (Ebstein et al., 1998) observed that temperament measures in neonates were modulated by an interaction between 5–HTTLPR and a variant in the gene encoding the dopamine D4 receptor (DRD4). The latter polymorphism is a VNTR within the third exon of DRD4, where a segment of 48 bp is repeated 2 to 10 times, which potentially affects D4 receptor function (see Oak, Oldenhof, & Van Tol., 2000). The DRD4 exon III 7-repeat allele has been the focus of considerable research efforts and has been associated with higher scores in novelty-seeking (e.g. Ebstein et al., 1996; Strobel, Wehr, Michel, & Brocke., 1999). Whereas meta-analyses do not suggest a significant association between DRD4 exon III and novelty-seeking (e.g. Kluger, Siegfried, & Ebstein, 2002; Schinka, Letsch, & Crawford, 2002), the evidence on the 7-repeat allele's role in a related phenotype, namely attention deficit/hyperactivity disorder, is rather consistent (see e.g. DiMaio, Grizenko, & Joober, 2003; Swanson et al., 2000).

In the Ebstein et al. (1998) study, the 5–HTTLPR S/S genotype was related to lower scores in orientation to novel stimuli in those neonates who did not carry the DRD4 exon III 7-repeat allele. Likewise, in a follow-up study, the scores in measures of negative emotionality were again higher in two-month-old infants who were carriers of the 5–HTTLPR S/S genotype but lacked the 7-repeat allele (Auerbach et al., 1999).

Even higher-order interactions have been reported. For the association between DRD4 exon III and novelty-seeking, it was reported that carriers of the DRD4 exon III 7–repeat allele showed higher scores in novelty-seeking especially when they also had the 5–HTTLPR L/L genotype and the Val/Val genotype of a SNP in the gene encoding the dopamine-catabolizing enzyme catechol O-methyltransferase (COMT; Benjamin et al., 2000). In a sample of our own, where we did not observe a main effect of DRD4 exon III on novelty-seeking, we could replicate the above-mentioned pattern (Strobel, Lesch, Jatzke, Paetzold, & Brocke., 2003).

These findings indicate that, even if a genetic variant does not show replicable main effects on a given temperament trait (as in the case of the inconsistent DRD4 exon III–novelty-seeking association), its effects may become visible if other polymorphisms are taken into account (such as 5–HTTLPR and COMT Val158Met in the example provided in the previous paragraph), or the genetic variant in question may influence the mode of action of another variant (like 5–HTTLPR in the evidence sketched in the penultimate paragraph) on another, perhaps related, temperament trait (negative emotionality, which to some extent is inversely related to novelty-seeking).

## 5.2   Gene–environment interactions

As outlined in Section 4.2, the role of the 5–HTTLPR S allele in the pathogenesis of depression is equivocal. However, as also noted, its role in modulating individual differences in neuroticism as a vulnerability factor for depression and in the function of neuronal circuits which are disturbed in depression is quite replicable. Hence the 5–HTTLPR S allele may not influence the development of depression per se, but rather impact on a vulnerability or diathesis variable, which only in interaction with stress leads to an increased risk of depression.

In a seminal study, Caspi et al. (2003) demonstrated that stressful life events such as adverse financial, medical, or psychosocial conditions were major factors impacting on the development of depressive symptoms, but that this effect was most pronounced in carriers of one or two copies of the 5–HTTLPR S. These results—which were later substantiated by the finding that a gene–environment interaction between 5–HTTLPR and stressful life events is observed even at the level of amygdala activation by aversive stimuli (Canli et al., 2006)—could be replicated in several, (though not all) subsequent studies (for a recent meta-analysis see Risch et al., 2009); the mode of assessing or defining a stressful life event is one likely reason for inconsistencies between studies: Uher & McGuffin, 2010). Interestingly, in a review by Belsky and colleagues (Belsky et al., 2009), it was convincingly argued that the available evidence on the interaction between 5–HTTLPR and stressful life events points to higher resilience of the S allele carriers when no stressful life events are present. Hence, common genetic variants may exert their behaviorally relevant effects in an environment-contingent fashion, which explains their existence in the gene pool, as their fitness-reducing effects in one environment are outweighed by fitness enhancing effects in another environment (see also Penke, Denissen, & Miller, 2007).

## 5.3   Pleiotropic gene effects

In another study by Canli and colleagues (Canli et al., 2005) it was found that 5–HTTLPR not only mediates the amygdala response to aversive stimuli, but also impacts on functional and structural differences in other brain regions, including prefrontal and motor areas; this suggests a broader role for 5–HTTLPR in brain function, including cognitive and motor processes. Indeed, there is emerging evidence that genetic variation in serotonin function impacts not only on emotional, but also on cognitive traits.

This is better illustrated using the example of another genetic variation along the serotonergic signaling pathway: the gene encoding the brain-expressed isoform of the serotonin-synthesizing enzyme, tryptophan hydroxylase 2 (TPH2), harbors a SNP in its promotor region, the TPH2 G–703T polymorphism. Although it is still a matter of debate whether this polymorphism itself affects the efficiency of gene transcription or whether it only resides near a functional variant (see Chen, Vallender, & Miller, 2008; Lin et al., 2007; Scheuch et al., 2007), the evidence on the behavioral correlates of this variant is currently quite consistent: the rare T/T genotype was associated with lower scores in measures of negative emotionality in a study by Reuter and colleagues (Reuter, Küpper, & Hennig, 2007), and a similar pattern was observed in an study of our own (Gutknecht et al., 2007). In another study, the T/T genotype was found to be associated with poorer performance in a task of executive attention (Reuter, Ott, Vaitl, & Hennig, 2007), which is in part substantiated by another finding of poorer executive control functions in T allele carriers (Strobel et al., 2007).

This evidence provides an illustrative example for a pleiotropic gene effect: a genetic variant of benefit with regard to one trait (i.e. negative emotionality) might be regarded as a vulnerability factor with regard to another trait (i.e. executive functioning) and vice versa, with the positive net effects potentially outweighing the negative ones in terms of evolutionary fitness. Hence, this example provides another explanation for the existence of common genetic variants.

# 6   Future Directions

This section finally sketches current directions in molecular genetic approaches to individual differences. We will briefly exemplify the potential of genome-wide association studies and epigenetic investigations (that is, studies on the role of, say, environmental factors in modulating gene expression), and will also provide a short overview of the emerging field of system genetics (that is, approaches implying systems translating genetic variation from genes to endophenotypes and behavior, for example transcriptomics, proteomics, or cellomics).

## 6.1   Genome-wide association studies

As mentioned in Section 2, genome-wide association studies (GWAS) provide a fresh approach to the study of molecular genetic influences on individual differences. Using DNA microarray technologies, it is now possible to genotype individuals not with regard to their genotype of one or several candidate polymorphisms, but with regard to hundreds of thousands of variants spread throughout the genome (current GWAS use 500,000 or 1,000,000 variants located on one DNA microarray). These variants then serve as markers for gene regions, which harbor genetic variability associated with a phenotype under discussion. Thus, this approach can aid the detection of genetic variability impacting on individual differences, even if we do not know the function of the respective polymorphic genes, and thereby it can help to generate hypotheses on new signaling pathways potentially involved in the modulation of a given phenotype.

Of course, when applying this technique, we need to consider several issues in order to avoid false positive findings. First, if we carry out, say, 1,000,000 association tests, one for each marker o the microarray, then 5 percent, —that is, 50,000 of these tests—might be significant just by chance. Hence we must apply a correction for multiple testing—e.g. the Bonferroni correction, which in the present example would require an effect being significant at an uncorrected level of $\alpha = 0.00000005$. Second, we need very large samples to detect effects at this stringent level of signifi-cance; and, third, we need one or more large replication samples to make sure that effects detected by a GWAS are not false positive effects. Fourth, after GWAS and the replication of one variant (which is to be associated with a given phenotype), ideally we should move on and detail the genetic variant(s) and signaling pathways responsible for the observed association.

With regard to negative emotionality there are so far at least three GWAS on the trait neuroticism: Shifman and colleagues (Shifman et al., 2008) observed an associa-tion of neuroticism with a variant in the gene encoding phosphodiesterase-4D (PDE4D, an enzyme involved in second-messenger signaling, which presumably has a role in modulating the effects of antidepressants (Zhang et al., 2002). Although the effect could not be replicated in internal replication samples of Shifman and col-leagues, the role of PDE4D in modulating negative emotionality was later substanti-ated by an independent group (Heck et al., 2008).

Unfortunately, in two further GWAS (van den Oord et al., 2008; Terracciano et al., 2010), PDE4D was not detected as one major factor influencing neuroticism. Rather, in these two studies, neuroticism was associated with variation in the gene encoding MAM domain containing glycosylphos-phatidylinositol anchor 2 (MAMDC1), which is involved in cell adhesion, and synaptosomal-associated protein 25 (SNAP25), which modulates vesicle–membrane fusion, respectively. Although these genes may point to interesting mechanisms underlying neuroticism, we need to await further studies and meta-analyses before we can rely on consistent evidence concerning promising signaling pathways involved in the modulation of negative emotionality, and hence in vulnerability to affective and anxiety disorders. Nevertheless, the GWAS approach has a high potential for hypothesis generation and likely will dominate the field over the next years—but certainly together with the approach outlined in the next section.

## 6.2   Epigenetic studies

The term *epigenetics* refers to changes in gene expression which are not due to variation of the DNA itself (i.e. genetic polymorphisms). Rather, remodeling of chromatin—a complex of DNA, wrapped around proteins called histones, and of non-histone proteins—can alter gene expression, as chromatin exists in an activated state (euchromatin), which allows gene transcription, and in an inactivated state (heterochromatin), which does not allow gene transcription. The latter repression of gene transcription can be due to methylation of histones or the DNA itself, which inhibits the binding of transcription factors (for an informative overview, see Tsankova,

Renthal, Kumar, & Nestler, 2007). It is important to note that such epigenetic modulation of gene transcription can be due to experiential/environmental factors in a region-/cell-specific way (i.e. DNA methylation in a cell cluster in the brain due to certain external factors will usually not be detectable if we examine the DNA methylation in blood cells).

An impressive demonstration of the crucial role of epigenetic mechanisms in the modulation of psychologically relevant phenomena can be found in a study by Weaver and colleagues (Weaver et al., 2004). They demonstrated that rats, which were raised under good rearing conditions (i.e. by "good mothers"), showed less methylation in the promotor region of the rat glucocorticoid receptor (GR) gene, and consequently, a higher GR expression than rats raised by "bad mothers." Importantly, a laboratory stress measure showed that the latter rats showed an exaggerated stress response (in terms of corticosterone levels) as compared to the former. Importantly, this effect was not observed in rats *born* by "bad mothers," but only in rats *reared* by "bad mothers."

Interestingly, comparable evidence could also be obtained in an examination of human postmortem brains (McGowan et al., 2009): it was shown that, in suicide victims who had experienced childhood abuse, hippocampal GR promotor methylation was higher and GR gene expression was lower than in control subjects or suicide victims without childhood abuse. Furthermore, it could be shown that behaviorally relevant epigenetic mechanisms can be studied even using peripheral tissue extracted from blood. Philibert and colleagues recently showed that childhood abuse is associated with higher methylation in the 5–HTT gene promotor (Beach, Brody, Todorov, Gunter, & Philibert, in press), with the 5–HTTLPR S allele possibly also impacting on higher methylation of the 5–HTT gene promotor (Philibert et al., 2007). Hence this evidence extends the findings of Weaver and colleagues, by showing a comparable effect of early adverse environmental factors on epigenetic mechanisms underlying stress responses and, putatively, negative emotionality. Moveover, the latter studies demonstrate that, until methods are available to examine epigenetic regulation in specific brain regions and cell assemblies of living humans, advances in the understanding of epigenetic mechanisms can already be made by using peripheral tissue.

## 6.3   Beyond genomics: system genetics

The more we learn about the role of genetic variation (including epigenetic remodeling) in the modulation of individual differences, the more it becomes obvious that we need to shift our focus from one or a handful of genetic variations to a systems view. Such systems include genetic/genomic networks (with gene–gene interactions as an example) impacting, over molecular and cellular networks, on tissue networks such as brain networks like the BIS described above, and ultimately on organismic networks comprising brain–periphery interactions. Thus, beyond genomics, the areas of transcriptomics, proteomics, and cellomics await exploration—which, however, requires sophisticated methods. In an interesting review, Sieberts and Schadt (2007) summarize such methods for a comprehensive integration of gene variation, gene expression/co-expression, and phenotypic data to understand the complex relationships among gene expression and individual differences at the trait level. These network approaches will soon add significantly to the knowledge gathered by genetic association studies.

The molecular genetics approach continues to generate new evidence on the neurobiology of individual differences, and at a fast pace. The evidence summarized in this chapter can be viewed only as an example designed to provide a first insight into the field. We nevertheless hope that we were able to generate (or further) the interest of our readers in this exciting area of research.

# References

Amelang, M., Bartussek, D., Stemmler, G., & Hagemann, D. (2006). *Differentielle Psychologie und Persönlichkeitsforschung* [Differential psychology and personality research] (6th ed.). Stuttgart: Kohlhammer.

American Psychiatric Association (2000). *Diagnostic and statistical manual of mental disorders* (4th rev. ed.). Washington, DC: American Psychiatric Association.

Armbruster, D., Moser, D. A., Strobel, A., Hensch, T., Kirschbaum, C., Lesch, K.-P., & Brocke, B. (2009). Serotonin transporter gene variation and stressful life events impact processing of fear and anxiety. *International Journal of Neuropsychopharmacology, 12*, 393–401.

Auerbach, J., Geller, V., Lezer, S., Shinwell, E., Belmaker, R. H., Levine, J., & Ebstein, R. P. (1999). Dopamine D4 receptor (D4DR) and serotonin transporter promoter (5–HTTLPR) polymorphisms in the determination of temperament in 2-month-old infants. *Molecular Psychiatry, 4*, 369–373.

Beach, S. R., Brody, G. H., Todorov, A. A., Gunter, T., D., & Philibert, R. A. (in press). Methylation at SLC6A4 is linked to family history of child abuse: An examination of the Iowa adoptee sample. *American Journal of Medical Genetics Part B.*

Belsky, J., Jonassaint, C., Pluess, M., Stanton, M., Brummet, B., & Williams, R. (2009). Vulnerability genes or plasticity genes? *Molecular Psychiatry, 14*, 746–754.

Benjamin, J., Osher, Y., Kotler, M., Gritsenko, I., Nemanov, L., Belmaker, R. H., & Ebstein, R. P. (2000). Association between Tridimensional Personality Questionnaire (TPQ) traits and three functional polymorphisms: Dopamine receptor D4 (DRD4), serotonin transporter promotor regions (5–HTTLPR) and catechol-O-methyltransferase (COMT). *Molecular Psychiatry, 5*, 96–100.

Bloch, M. H., Landeros-Weisenberger, A., Sen, S., Dombrowski, P., Kelmendi, B., Coric, V., Pittenger, C., & Leckman, J. F. (2008). Association of the serotonin transporter polymorphism and obsessive–compulsive disorder: Systematic review. *American Journal of Medical Genetics Part B, 147B*, 850–858.

Brocke, B. (2000). Das bemerkenswerte Comeback der Differentiellen Psychologie. Glückwünsche und Warnungen vor einem neuen Desaster. [The remarkable comeback of personality psychology: Congratulations and warnings against a new disaster.] *Zeitschrift für Differentielle und Diagnostische Psychologie, 21*, 5–30.

Brocke, B. (2004). The multilevel approach in sensation seeking: Potentials and findings of a four-level research program. In R. Stelmack (Ed.), *On the psychobiology of personality* (pp. 267–293). New York: Elsevier.

Brocke, B., & Battmann, W. (1992). The arousal-activation theory of extraversion and neuroticism: A systematic analysis and principal conclusions. *Advances in Behaviour Research and Therapy, 14*, 211–246.

Brocke, B., Hennig, J., & Netter, P. (2004). Biopsychologische Theorien der Persönlichkeit. [Biopsychological theories of personality.] In K. Pawlik (Ed.), *Die Enzyklopädie der*

*Psychologie: Vol. 5, Series VIII. Theorien und Anwendungsfelder der differenziellen Psychologie* (pp. 365–430). Göttingen: Hogrefe.

Brocke, B., Armbruster, D., Müller, J., Hensch, T., Jacob, C.-P., Lesch, K.-P., Kirschbaum, C., & Strobel, A. (2006). Serotonin transporter gene variation impacts innate fear processing: Acoustic startle response and emotional startle. *Molecular Psychiatry, 11,* 1106–1112.

Canli, T., Omura, K., Haas, B. W., Fallgatter, A. J., Constable, R. T., & Lesch, K. P. (2005). Beyond affect: A role for genetic variation of the serotonin transporter in neural activation during a cognitive attention task. *Proceedings of the National Academy of Sciences of the USA, 102,* 12224–12229.

Canli, T., Qiu, M., Omura, K., Congdon, E., Haas, B. W., Amin, Z., Herrmann, M. J., Constable, R. T., & Lesch, K. P. (2006). Neural correlates of epigenesis. *Proceedings of the National Academy of Sciences of the USA, 103,* 16033–16038.

Carey, G., & DiLalla, D. L. (1994). Personality and psychopathology: Genetic perspectives. *Journal of Abnormal Psychology, 103,* 32–43.

Carver, C. S., & White, T. L. (1994). Behavioral inhibition, behavioral activation, and affective responses to impending reward and punishment: The BIS/BAS scales. *Journal of Personality and Social Psychology, 67,* 319–333.

Caspi, A., Sugden, K., Moffitt, T. E., Taylor, A., Craig, I. W., Harrington, H., McClay, J., Mill, J., Martin, J., Braithwaite, A., & Poulton, R. (2003). Influence of life stress on depression: Moderation by a polymorphism in the 5–HTT gene. *Science, 301,* 386–389.

Chen, G. L., Vallender, E. J., & Miller, G. M. (2008). Functional characterization of the human TPH2 5′ regulatory region: Untranslated region and polymorphisms modulate gene expression in vitro. *Human Genetics, 122,* 645–657.

Clark, L. A., Watson, D., & Mineka, S. (1994). Temperament, personality, and mood and anxiety disorders. *Journal of Abnormal Psychology, 103,* 103–116.

Cloninger, C. R. (1987). A systematic method for clinical description and classification of personality variants. *Archives of General Psychiatry, 44,* 573–588.

Cloninger, C. R., Svrakic, D. M., & Przybeck, T. R. (1991). The Tridimensional Personality Questionnaire: U.S. normative data. *Psychological Reports, 69,* 1047–1057.

Cloninger, C. R., Svrakic, D. M., & Przybeck, T. R. (1993). A psychobiological model of temperament and character. *Archives of General Psychiatry, 50,* 975–990.

Cloninger, C. R., Przybeck, T. R., Svrakic, D. M., & Wetzel, R. D. (Eds.) (1994). *The Temperament and Character Inventory (TCI): A guide to its development and use.* St. Louis: Washington University, Center for Psychobiology of Personality.

Corr, P. J. (2004). Reinforcement sensitivity theory and personality. *Neuroscience and Biobehavioral Reviews, 28,* 317–332.

Corr, P. J. (2009). The reinforcement sensitivity theory of personality. In P. J. Corr & G. Matthews (Eds.), *Cambridge handbook of personality* (pp. 323–346). New York: Cambridge University Press.

Davidson, R. J. (1992). Emotion and affective style: Hemispheric substrates. *Psychological Science, 3,* 39–43.

Davis, K. L., Panksepp, J., & Normansell, L. (2003). The Affective Neuroscience Personality Scale: Normative data and implications. *Neuropsychoanalysis, 5,* 57–70.

Depue, R. A., & Collins, P. F. (1999). Neurobiology of the structure of personality: Dopamine, facilitation of incentive motivation, and extraversion. *Behavioral and Brain Sciences, 22,* 491–569.

Depue, R. A., & Lenzenweger, M. F. (2005). A neurobehavioral dimensional model of personality disturbance. In M. Lenzenweger & J. Clarkin (Eds.), *Theories of personality disorders* (2nd ed., pp. 391–454). New York: Guilford Press.

Depue, R. A., & Morrone-Strupinsky, J. V. (2005). A neurobehavioral model of affiliative bonding: Implications for conceptualizing a human trait of affiliation. *Behavioral and Brain Sciences, 28,* 313–350.

DeYoung, C. G. (2006). Higher-order factors of the Big Five in a multi-informant sample. *Journal of Personality and Social Psychology, 91,* 1138–1151.

DeYoung, C. G., & Gray, J. R. (2009). Personality neuroscience: Explaining individual differences in affect, behavior, and cognition. In P. J. Corr & G. Matthews (Eds.), *Cambridge handbook of personality* (pp. 323–346). New York: Cambridge University Press.

Digman, J. M. (1990). Personality structure: Emergence of the five-factor model. *Annual Review of Psychology, 41,* 417-440.

DiMaio, S., Grizenko, N., & Joober, R. (2003). Dopamine genes and attention-deficit hyperactivity disorder: A review. *Journal of Psychiatry and Neuroscience, 28,* 27–38.

Ebstein, R. P., Levine, J., Geller, V., Auerbach, J., Gritsenko, I., & Belmaker, R. H. (1998). Dopamine D4 receptor and serotonin transporter promoter in the determination of neonatal temperament. *Molecular Psychiatry, 3,* 238–246.

Ebstein, R. P., Novick, O., Umansky, R. Priel, B., Osher, Y., Blaine, D., Bennett, E. R., Nemanov, L., Katz, M., & Belmaker, R. H. (1996). Dopamin D4 receptor (D4DR) exon III polymorphism associated with the personality trait of novelty seeking. *Nature Genetics, 12,* 78–80.

Eysenck, H. J. (1967). *The biological basis of personality.* Springfield, IL: Thomas.

Eysenck, H. J. (1981). *A model for personality.* New York: Springer.

Eysenck, H. J. (1997). Personality and experimental psychology: The unification of psychology and the possibility of a paradigm. *Journal of Personality and Social Psychology, 73,* 1224–1237.

Eysenck, H. J., & Eysenck, M. W. (1985). *Personality and individual differences: A natural science approach.* New York: Plenum.

Fischer, T., Langner, R., Birbaumer, N., & Brocke, B. (2008). Arousal and attention: Self-chosen stimulation optimizes cortical excitability and minimizes compensatory effort. *Journal of Cognitive Neuroscience, 20,* 1443–1453.

Fisher, R. A. (1918). The correlation between relatives on the supposition of Mendelian inheritance. *Transactions of the Royal Society of Edinburgh, 52,* 399–433.

Gelernter, J., Cubells, J. F., Kidd, J. R., Pakstis, A. J., & Kidd, K. K. (1999). Population studies of polymorphisms of the serotonin transporter gene. *American Journal of Medical Genetics Part B, 88B,* 61–66.

Goldberg, L. R. (1990). An alternative "description of personality": The Big-Five factor structure. *Journal of Personality and Social Psychology, 59,* 1216–1229.

Gottesman, I. I., & Gould, T. D. (2003). The endophenotype concept in psychiatry: Etymology and strategic intentions. *American Journal of Psychiatry, 160,* 636–645.

Gray, J. A. (1982). *The neuropsychology of anxiety: An enquiry into the functions of the septo-hippocampal system.* New York: Oxford University Press.

Gray, J. A., & McNaughton, N. (2000). *The neuropsychology of anxiety: An enquiry into the functions of the septo-hippocampal system* (2nd ed.). New York: Oxford University Press.

Gutknecht, L., Jacob, C., Strobel, A., Müller, J., Reif, A., Mössner, R., Zeng, Y., Gross, C., Brocke, B., & Lesch, K. P. (2007). Tryptophan hydroxylase-2 gene variation influences personality traits and related disorders. *International Journal of Neuropsychopharmacology, 10,* 309–320.

Hariri, A. R., Mattay, V. S., Tessitore, A., Kolachana, B., Fera, F., Goldman, D., Egan, M. F., & Weinberger, D. R. (2002). Serotonin transporter genetic variation and the response of the human amygdala. *Science, 297,* 400–403.

Heck, A., Lieb, R., Unschuld, P. G., Ellgas, A., Pfister, H., Lucae, S., Erhardt, A., Himmerich, H., Horstmann, S., Kloiber, S., Ripke, S., Müller-Myhsok, B., Bettecken, T., Uhr, M., Holsboer, F., & Ising, M. (2008). Evidence for associations between PDE4D polymorphisms and a subtype of neuroticism. *Molecular Psychiatry, 13*, 831–832.

Heils, A., Teufel, A., Petri, S., Stöber, G., Riederer, P., Bengel, D., & Lesch K.-P. (1996). Allelic variation of human serotonin transporter gene expression. *Journal of Neurochemistry, 66*, 2621–2624.

Heinz, A., Braus, D. F., Smolka, M. N., Wrase, J., Puls, I., Hermann, D., Klein, S., Grüsser, S. M., Flor, H., Schumann, G., Mann, K., & Büchel, C. (2005). Amygdala-prefrontal coupling depends on a genetic variation of the serotonin transporter. *Nature Neuroscience, 8*, 20–21.

Hu, X., Oroszi, G., Chun, J., Smith, T. L., Goldman, D., & Schuckit, M. A. (2005). An expanded evaluation of the relationship of four alleles to the level of response to alcohol and the alcoholism risk. *Alcoholism, Clinical and Experimental Research, 29*, 8–16.

Jang, K. L., Livesley, W. J., Ando, J., Yamagata, S., Suzuki, A., Angleitner, A., Ostendorf, F., Riemann, R., & Spinath, F. (2006). Behavioral genetics of the higher-order factors of the Big Five. *Personality and Individual Differences, 41*, 261–272.

Kendler, K. S., Gatz, M., Gardner, C. O., & Pedersen, N. L. (2006). Personality and major depression: A Swedish longitudinal, population-based twin study. *Archives of General Psychiatry, 63*, 1113–1120.

Kluger, A. N., Siegfried, Z., & Ebstein, R. P. (2002). A meta-analysis of the association between DRD4 polymorphism and novelty seeking. *Molecular Psychiatry, 7*, 712–717.

Lesch, K.-P., Bengel, D., Heils, A., Sabol, S. Z., Greenberg, B. J., Petri, S., Benjamin, J., Müller, C. R., Hamer, D. H., & Murphy, D. L. (1996). Association of anxiety-related traits with a polymorphism in the serotonin transporter gene regulatory region. *Science, 274*, 1527–1531.

Levinson, D. F. (2006). The genetics of depression: A review. *Biological Psychiatry, 60*, 84–92.

Lin, Y. M., Chao, S. C., Chen, T. M., Lai, T. J., Chen, J. S., & Sun, H. S. (2007). Association of functional polymorphisms of the human tryptophan hydroxylase 2 gene with risk for bipolar disorder in Han Chinese. *Archives of General Psychiatry, 64*, 1015–1024.

Maron, E., & Shlik, J. (2006). Serotonin function in panic disorder: Important, but why? *Neuropsychopharmacology, 31*, 1–11.

McGowan, P. O., Sasaki, A., D'Alessio, A. C., Dymov, S., Labonté, B., Szyf, M., Turecki, G., & Meaney, M. J. (2009). Epigenetic regulation of the glucocorticoid receptor in human brain associates with childhood abuse. *Nature Neuroscience, 12*, 342–348.

Munafò, M. R., Clark, T., & Flint, J. (2005). Does measurement instrument moderate the association between the serotonin transporter gene and anxiety-related personality traits? A meta-analysis. *Molecular Psychiatry, 10*, 415–419.

Nemeroff, C. B., & Owens, M. J. (2002). Treatment of mood disorders. *Nature Neuroscience, 5* (Suppl), 1068–1070.

Oak, J. N., Oldenhof. J., & Van Tol, H. H. M. (2000). The dopamine D4 receptor: One decade of research. *European Journal of Pharmacology, 405*, 303–327.

Ormel, J., Oldehinkel, A. J., & Vollebergh, W. (2004). Vulnerability before, during, and after a major depressive episode: A 3-wave population-based study. *Archives of General Psychiatry, 61*, 990–996.

Panksepp, J. (1998). *Affective neuroscience: The foundations of human and animal emotion.* New York: Oxford University Press.

Penke, L., Denissen, J. J. A., & Miller, G. F. (2007). The evolutionary genetics of personality. *European Journal of Personality, 21*, 549–587.

Pezawas, L., Meyer-Lindenberg, A., Drabant, B. A., Verchinski, B. A., Munoz, K. E., Kolachana, B. S., Egan, M. F., Mattay, V.S., Hariri, A.R., & Weinberger, D.R. (2005). 5–HTTLPR polymorphism impacts human cingulate-amygdala interactions: A genetic suspectibility mechanism for depression. *Nature Neuroscience, 8*, 828–834.

Philibert, R. A., Madan, A., Andersen, A., Cadoret, R., Packer, H., & Sandhu, H. (2007). Serotonin transporter mRNA levels are associated with the methylation of an upstream CpG island. *American Journal of Medical Genetics Part B Part B, 144B*, 101–105.

Reuter, M., Küpper, Y., & Hennig, J. (2007). Association between a polymorphism in the promoter region of the TPH2 gene and the personality trait of harm avoidance. *International Journal of Neuropsychopharmacology, 10*, 401–404.

Reuter, M., Ott, U., Vaitl, D., & Hennig, J. (2007). Impaired executive control is associated with a variation in the promoter region of the tryptophan hydroxylase 2 gene. *Journal Cognitive Neuroscience, 19*, 401–408.

Revelle, W. (1995). Personality processes. *Annual Review of Psychology, 46*, 295–328.

Risch, N., Herrell, R., Lehner, T., Liang, K. Y., Eaves, L., Hoh, J., Griem, A., Kovacs, M., Ott, J., & Merikangas, K. R. (2009). Interaction between the serotonin transporter gene (5–HTTLPR), stressful life events, and risk of depression: A meta-analysis. *Journal of the American Medical Association, 301*, 2462–2471.

Scheuch, K., Lautenschlager, M., Grohmann, M., Stahlberg, S., Kirchheiner, J., Zill, P., Heinz, A., Walther, D. J., & Priller, J. (2007). Characterization of a functional promoter polymorphism of the human tryptophan hydroxylase 2 gene in serotonergic raphe neurons. *Biological Psychiatry, 62*, 1288–1294.

Schinka, J. A., Busch, R. M., & Robichaux-Keene, N. (2004). A meta-analysis of the association between the serotonin transporter gene polymorphism (5–HTTLPR) and trait anxiety. *Molecular Psychiatry, 9*, 197–202.

Schinka, J. A., Letsch, E. A., & Crawford, F. C. (2002). DRD4 and novelty seeking: Results of meta-analyses. *American Journal of Medical Genetics Part B, 114B*, 643–648.

Sen, S., Burmeister, M., & Ghosh, D. (2004). Meta-analysis of the association between a serotonin transporter promoter polymorphism (5–HTTLPR) and anxiety-related personality traits. *American Journal of Medical Genetics Part B, 127B*, 85–89.

Seyffert, W. (1998). *Lehrbuch der Genetik*. Stuttgart: Gustav Fischer.

Shifman, S., Bhomra, A., Smiley, S., Wray, N. R., James, M.R., Martin, N. G., Hettema, J. M. et al. (2008). A whole genome association study of neuroticism using DNA pooling. *Molecular Psychiatry, 13*, 302–312.

Sieberts, S. K., & Schadt, E. E. (2007). Moving toward a system genetics view of disease. *Mammalian Genome, 18*, 389–401.

Smillie, L. D., Pickering, A. D., & Jackson, C. J. (2006). The new reinforcement sensitivity theory: Implications for personality measurement. *Personality and Social Psychology Review, 10*, 320–335.

Strobel, A., Wehr, A., Michel, A., & Brocke, B. (1999). Association between the dopamine D4 receptor (DRD4) exon III polymorphism and measures of novelty seeking in a German population. *Molecular Psychiatry, 4*, 378–384.

Strobel, A., Lesch, K.-P., Jatzke, S., Paetzold, F., & Brocke, B. (2003). Further evidence for a modulation of novelty seeking by DRD4 exon III, 5–HTTLPR, and COMT val/met variants. *Molecular Psychiatry, 8*, 271–272.

Strobel, A., Dreisbach, G., Müller, J., Goschke, T., Brocke, B., & Lesch, K. P. (2007). Genetic variation of serotonin function and cognitive control. *Journal of Cognitive Neuroscience, 19*, 1923–1931.

Swanson, J. M., Flodman, P., Kennedy, J., Spence, M. A., Moyzis, R., Schuck, S., Murias, M., Moriarity et al. (2000). Dopamine genes and ADHD. *Neuroscience and Biobehavioral Reviews, 24*, 21–25.

Tellegen, A., & Waller, N. G. (1992) *Exploring personality through test construction: Development of the Multi-Dimensional Personality Questionnaire* (MPQ). Unpublished manuscript. Department of Psychology, University of Minnesota.

Terracciano, A., Sanna, S., Uda, M., Deiana, B., Usala, G., Busonero, F., Maschio, A., Scally, M. et al. (2010). Genome-wide association scan for five major dimensions of personality. *Molecular Psychiatry. 15*, 647–656.

Torrubia, R., Ávila, C., Moltó , J., & Caseras, X. (2001). The Sensitivity to Punishment and Sensitivity to Reward Questionnaire (SPSRQ) as a measure of Gray's anxiety and impulsivity dimensions. *Personality and Individual Differences, 31*, 837–862.

Tsankova, N., Renthal, W., Kumar, A., & Nestler, E. J. (2007). Epigenetic regulation in psychiatric disorders. *Nature Reviews Neuroscience, 8*, 355–367.

Uher, R., & McGuffin, P. (2010). The moderation by the serotonin transporter gene of environmental adversity in the etiology of depression: 2009 update. *Molecular Psychiatry, 15*, 18–22.

van den Oord, E. J., Kuo, P. H., Hartmann, A. M., Webb, B. T., Möller, H. J., Hettema, J. M., Giegling, I., Bukszár, J., & Rujescu, D. (2008). Genomewide association analysis followed by a replication study implicates a novel candidate gene for neuroticism. *Archives of General Psychiatry, 65*, 1062–1071.

Watson, D., Clark, L. A., & Tellegen, A. (1988). Development and validation of brief measures of positive and negative affect: The PANAS scales. *Journal of Personality and Social Psychology, 54*, 1063–1070.

Weaver, I. C. G., Cervoni, N., Champagne, F. A., D'Alessio, A. C., Sharma, S., Seckl, J. R., Dymov, S., Szyf, M., & Meaney, M. J. (2004). Epigenetic programming by maternal behavior. *Nature Neuroscience, 7*, 847–854.

White, T. L., & Depue, R. A. (1999). Differential association of traits of fear and anxiety with norepinephrine- and dark-induced pupil reactivity. *Journal of Personality and Social Psychology, 77*, 863–877.

World Health Organization (1992). *The ICD–10 classification of mental and behavioural disorders: Clinical descriptions and diagnostic guidelines.* Geneva: World Health Organization.

Yamagata, S., Suzuki, A., Ando, J., Ono, Y., Kijima, N., Yoshimura, K., Ostendorf, F., Angleitner, A., Riemann, R., Spinath, F. M., Livesley, W. J., & Jang, K. L. (2006). Is the genetic structure of human personality universal? A cross-cultural twin study from North America, Europe, and Asia. *Journal of Personality and Social Psychology, 90*, 987–998.

Zhang, H. T., Huang, Y., Jin, S. L., Frith, S. A., Suvarna, N., Conti, M., & O'Donnell, J. M. (2002). Antidepressant-like profile and reduced sensitivity to rolipram in mice deficient in the PDE4D phosphodiesterase enzyme. *Neuropsychopharmacology, 27*, 587–595.

Zuckerman, M. (1990). The psychophysiology of sensation seeking. *Journal of Personality, 58*, 313–345.

Zuckerman, M. (1993). P-impulsive sensation seeking and its behavioral, psychophysiological and biochemical correlates. *Neuropsychobiology, 28*, 30–36.

Zuckerman, M. (1994). *Behavioral expressions and biosocial bases of sensation seeking.* Cambridge: Cambridge University Press.

Zuckerman, M. (2005). *Psychobiology of personality* (2nd ed.). New York: Cambridge University Press.

Zuckerman, M., Kuhlman, D. M., Joireman, J., Teta, P., & Kraft, M. (1993). A comparison of three structural models of personality: The Big Three, the Big Five, and the Alternative Five. *Journal of Personality and Social Psychology, 65*, 757–768.

# 12

# Understanding Human Intelligence by Imaging the Brain

## Roberto Colom and Paul M. Thompson

This chapter reviews the biological basis of individual differences in human intelligence. However, we note from the outset that our review is based on results derived from the application of neuroimaging methods. Both structural and functional approaches are considered here. The first section discusses what we call "the brain connection," a phrase which designates the fact that genetic and non-genetic factors influencing intelligence play on the brain. Understanding this psychological factor requires deep knowledge regarding brain structure and function. Secondly, intelligence is defined and some implications are derived from the standardized measurement of this construct. The distinction among "constructs," "vehicles," and "measurements" is especially relevant in this context.

The section on methods presents the main structural and functional approaches employed so far for analyzing the intelligence construct. Neuroimaging studies involve creating models and maps of the brain. Typical data are cortical thickness, gray matter density, gyral pattern variability, hemispheric asymmetry, heritability, or fMRI signals. It is highlighted that the study of white matter is developing quickly and provides useful insights.

The next section discusses key findings within the framework defined by the parieto-frontal integration theory of intelligence (P–FIT, Jung & Haier, 2007). Interestingly, it is shown that this theory is also relevant for other psychological constructs, like working memory capacity or attention. This overlap underscores frontal and parietal brain areas, along with their connections, for understanding individual differences in cognition. The chapter ends by suggesting a movement from correlation to experimental approaches for studying the biological base of intelligence by means of techniques such as TMS (transcranial magnetic stimulation).

*The Wiley-Blackwell Handbook of Individual Differences,* First Edition.
Edited by Tomas Chamorro-Premuzic, Sophie von Stumm, and Adrian Furnham.
© 2011 Blackwell Publishing Ltd. Published 2011 by Blackwell Publishing Ltd.

## The Brain Connection

Thompson et al. (2001) reported, for the very first time, that regional brain structure is influenced by genetic differences. This brain structure was more alike in identical than in fraternal twins, and this latter group showed more similarities than genetically unrelated controls (Plate 1). The genetic maps revealed how genes contribute to individual differences: genes influenced structural variations in Broca's and Wernicke's areas as well as in the frontal lobes. Further, structural differences in the frontal lobes were related to IQ scores derived from four Wechsler sub-tests (vocabulary, similarities, block design, and digit symbol). Clearly, understanding phenotypic differences in measured intelligence requires attention to genetic factors impacting on individual differences in brain structure.

Nevertheless, brain structural differences are also sensitive to the influence of non-genetic factors. Draganski et al. (2004) demonstrated changes in brain structure after learning to juggle. Participants were scanned before practice, after 3 months of intensive practice, and 3 months after ending practice. The expansion of gray matter was found in the mid-temporal area bilaterally and in the left posterior intraparietal sulcus. Of note is that the observed expansion decreased in the third scan. Ilg et al. (2008) reported brain structural changes after only two weeks of daily practicing mirror reading. Increased gray matter was detected in the right dorsolateral occipital cortex. Haier, Karama, Leyba, and Jung (2009) have shown significant regional cortical thickness changes after 3 months of practice in a complex spatial task (TETRIS). Practice evoked structural changes in the superior frontal gyrus (Brodmann area, BA 6) and in the anterior superior temporal gyrus (BAs 22/38). Even when the physiological basis of differences in regional gray matter in healthy people is far from clear, the main conclusion that would be extracted from these training studies is that brain structural changes are related to human behavior.

The interplay between genes and behavior takes place in the brain. Therefore, learning the language of the brain would be crucial to understand how genes and behavior interact. Regarding this issue, Kovas and Plomin (2006) proposed the so-called "generalist genes" hypothesis, on the basis of multivariate genetic research findings showing significant genetic overlap among cognitive abilities such as the general factor of intelligence (*g*), language, reading, or mathematics. The hypothesis has implication for cognitive neuroscience, because of the concepts of pleiotropy (one gene affecting many traits) and polygenicity (many genes affecting a given trait). These genetic concepts suggest a "generalist brain": the genetic influence over the brain is thought to be general and distributed.

Kovas and Plomin discuss three mechanisms connecting genes, the brain, and cognitive processes: (1) a gene influences one area of the brain, which influences different cognitive processes; (2) a gene influences several areas of the brain, and each area affects a specific cognitive process; and (3) a gene influences several areas of the brain, and each area affects several cognitive processes. The third mechanism is favored by these researchers because it would lead to genetic correlations in the brain. It is noteworthy that this mechanism is in tension with cognitive neuroscience research favoring a modular view of the brain (Barrett & Kurzban, 2006).

# What Is Intelligence?

Intelligence is "a very general mental capability that, among other things, involves the ability to reason, plan, solve problems, think abstractly, comprehend complex ideas, learn quickly and learn from experience" (Gottfredson et al. [52 researchers], 1997, p. 13). This definition is consistent with the *positive manifold* phenomenon: all the correlations in a matrix comprised by several diverse cognitive ability tests are positive. The finding of generalized positive correlations among cognitive abilities is an empirical fact, and it underlies the extraction of the general factor of intelligence ($g$). As underscored by Jensen (1998) and Carroll (2003), the $g$ factor is a common source of individual differences in all cognitive ability tests.

There are some theories supporting the view of intelligence as a collection of separate cognitive abilities. Guilford's "structure-of-intellect" (SOI) postulates 180 independent cognitive abilities (Guilford, 1988). Cattell's *Gf–Gc* theory distinguishes culture-reduced (or fluid) and culture-specific (or crystallized) abilities (Cattell, 1987). Gardner's theory (Gardner, 2004) postulates several orthogonal intelligences (spatial, musical, verbal, and so forth). Sternberg's triarchic theory (Sternberg, 1988) discriminates among analytic, practical, and creative intelligence. All these theories share the view that group abilities are more prominent than the general intelligence factor ($g$).

However, the apparent conflict between group or specific cognitive abilities and $g$ is not real. The near-zero correlations reported by Guilford were the result of sampling error, restriction of range, measurement error, and the inclusion of tests of divergent production. When proper corrections are made for restriction of range and attenuation, all the correlations are around .45 (Jensen, 1998). The $g$ theory is required to understand the relationships among Sternberg's intelligences (Brody, 2003) and Gardner's taxonomy is arbitrary and without empirical foundation (Waterhouse, 2006).

The positive manifold is unavoidable when representative samples of the general population are considered. This is acknowledged by the most recent developments regarding the structure of human intelligence (Johnson & Bouchard, 2005; Johnson, Nijenhuis, J., & Bouchard, 2008; Johnson, Bouchard, Krueger, McGue, & Gottesman 2004; McGrew, 2009). McGrew favors the CHC (Cattell–Horn–Carroll) theory, which stands on the three-stratum theory proposed by Carroll (1993, 2003) and on Cattell's *Gf–Gc* theory. Johnson and Bouchard's VPR (verbal–perceptual–rotational) model is based on several confirmatory factor analyses testing three influential theories on the structure of human intelligence. They discarded the distinction between *Gf* and *Gc*, supporting the view that it makes much more sense, from a neuroscience perspective, to distinguish between verbal and spatial content domains. Even when both the left and right hemispheres of the brain are involved in any given cognitive task, the left is more prone to processing verbal information, whereas the right is more inclined to treat spatial information. Indeed, Johnson and Bouchard found a relatively low correlation between the verbal and image rotation factors identified in their VPR model. This finding suggests distinguishable involvement for the left and right hemispheres with respect to intellectual performance, "with some individuals more verbally than spatially adept, and vice versa. This has important implications for the development of a neurological understanding of intellectual performance" (Johnson & Bouchard, 2005, p. 413).

Hunt (2011) analyzed these models of the structure of human intelligence, concluding the following:

a   Looking at specific intelligence measurements, it is easy to find people displaying many specific abilities, because these measurements are not perfectly correlated.

b   The positive manifold is a statistical fact, but it is a more appropriate description of the data at the bottom than at the top of the intelligence distribution.

c   This manifold is compatible with the view that there are informative individual differences in several brain processes influencing human cognition.

d   People differ along cognitive dimensions (e.g. linguistic and spatial) that can be distinguished from the *g* factor.

## The Measurement of Intelligence: Implications for Neuroimaging Studies

The scientific construct of general intelligence (*g*) rests on the *correlations* among test scores, while IQ rests on the *summation* of standardized scores. Although IQ is usually considered a proper measure of general intelligence (*g*), IQ is actually an arbitrary variable (intelligence in general). Intelligence in general combines *g* plus specific cognitive abilities and skills. IQ is a mixture of those general and specific abilities and skills (Colom, Abad, Garcia, & Juan-Espinosa, 2002).

This can be demonstrated by submitting to a hierarchical factor analysis the scores obtained by a sample representative of the population. Table 12.1 shows the hierarchical factor matrix that can be obtained after the Spanish standardization of the latest version the Wechsler adult intelligence scale (WAIS–III).

Table 12.1 shows a powerful general factor of intelligence (*g*) accounting for almost 60 percent of the common variance (last row). In contrast, the four first-order factors (F1 to F4) account for much less variance (from 3 percent to 6 percent each). What this means is that intelligent performance is highly dependent on a general ability represented by the *g* factor. First-order factors, representing specific cognitive abilities such as verbal comprehension, perceptual organization, working memory, and processing speed, are also contributing to the observed variance, but they are much less important.

The 14 mental tests enumerated in Table 12.1 are remarkably different regarding their particular cognitive requirements, but a positive correlation emerges. Nevertheless, as noted by Hunt (2011), the correlation among intelligence tests is far from perfect. This underlies the numbers (loadings) that can be seen in Table 12.1. The "vocabulary" subtest shows a *g* loading of .74, but it also shows loadings on the remaining factors (.48, .01, .02, and .07). The commonality ($h^2$) for "vocabulary" is .79. This value represents the variance in "vocabulary" explained by the extracted common factors, including *g*. But there is also some uniqueness ($u^2 = .21$), which represents "vocabulary" specificity. Therefore individual differences in "vocabulary" must be attributed to *g*, to specific group factors (F1 to F4), and to its specificity ($u^2$).

**Table 12.1**  Hierarchical factor analysis of the sub-tests comprised in the WAIS–III

| Sub-tests | *g.* | *F1* | *F2* | *F3* | *F4* | *h2* | *u2* |
|---|---|---|---|---|---|---|---|
| *Verbal comprehension* | | | | | | | |
| Vocabulary | .744 | .478 | .015 | .017 | .070 | .79 | .21 |
| Similarities | .737 | .413 | .032 | .001 | .027 | .72 | .28 |
| Information | .725 | .369 | .093 | .053 | .106 | .68 | .32 |
| Comprehension | .661 | .509 | .046 | .000 | .010 | .70 | .30 |
| *Perceptual organization* | | | | | | | |
| Picture completion | .752 | .127 | .197 | .018 | .078 | .63 | .37 |
| Block design | .815 | .040 | .364 | .007 | .023 | .80 | .20 |
| Matrix reasoning | .847 | .051 | .252 | .039 | .059 | .79 | .21 |
| Picture arrangement | .790 | .089 | .205 | .010 | .097 | .68 | .32 |
| Object assembly | .748 | .014 | .287 | .012 | .060 | .65 | .35 |
| *Working memory* | | | | | | | |
| Arithmetic | .738 | .133 | .107 | .206 | .058 | .62 | .38 |
| Digit span | .724 | .011 | .004 | .407 | .009 | .69 | .31 |
| Letter–number sequencing | .815 | .011 | .001 | .392 | .088 | .83 | .17 |
| *Processing speed* | | | | | | | |
| Coding | .785 | .012 | .045 | .040 | .426 | .80 | .20 |
| Symbol search | .779 | .006 | .096 | .025 | .368 | .75 | .25 |
| % Variance | 58.2% | 6% | 2.8% | 2.6% | 2.6% | | |

Importantly, these numbers could change for different samples. This corresponds to point (b) highlighted by Hunt (2011). Thus, for instance, Colom, Abad et al. (2002) found that the *g* factor accounts for 50 percent of the common variance in participants with low levels of education, whereas it accounts for 25 percent of the common variance in participants with high levels of education. Increasing values for the *g* factor involve less relevance for group ability factors, and vice versa.

These distinctions are important for cognitive neuroscience. Haier, Colom et al. (2009) stated several recommendations in this regard:

1  Use several diverse measures tapping abstract, verbal, numerical, and spatial content domains.

2  Use three or more measures to define each group factor. These group factors should fit the main abilities comprised in models such as those proposed by McGrew (2009) and by Johnson and Bouchard (2005).

3  Measures for each group factor should not be based solely on speeded or non-speeded tests. Both types should be used to achieve high degrees of representativeness for the constructs of interest.

4  Use three or more group factors to define the higher-order factor representing the general factor of intelligence (*g*). Measurement models should reveal that non-verbal, abstract, or fluid reasoning is the group factor best predicted by *g*. Drawing inferences, concept formation, classification, generating and testing hypotheses,

identifying relations, comprehending implications, problem-solving, extrapolating, and transforming information are the abilities more closely related to $g$ (Carroll, 2003).

5   Find a way for separating sources of variance contributing to participants' performance on the measures. The influence of $g$ is pervasive, but it changes for different group (lower-order) factors and specific measures. As noted above, participants' scores result from $g$, cognitive abilities (group factors), and cognitive skills (test specificities). Brain correlates for a given cognitive ability, like verbal or non-verbal ability, are influenced by all these sources of variance.

In short, psychometrics and cognitive neuroscience should work in tandem to find the most likely biological correlates of individual differences in human intelligence. As highlighted by Jensen (1998), any given psychological *construct* (the general factor of intelligence, verbal ability, spatial ability, and so forth) can be represented by distinguishable *vehicles* (intelligence tests, laboratory tasks, or biological indices) yielding different *measurements*. Changes in the measurements may or may not involve changes in the construct. The former changes implicate different sources of variance (Figure 12.1). Unfortunately, these theoretical distinctions are frequently neglected in the scientific analysis of the biological basis of human intelligence.

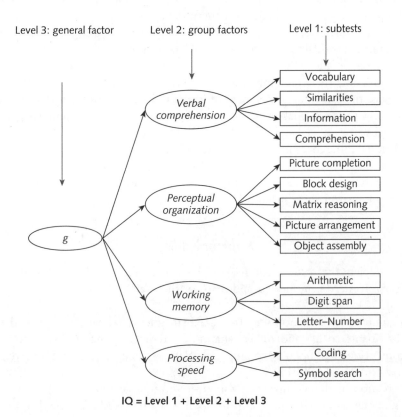

IQ = Level 1 + Level 2 + Level 3

**Figure 12.1**   IQ scores combine sources of variance from level 1 (measurements), level 2 (group or first-order factors), and level 3 (higher-order factor). However, these sources of variance should be distinguished to achieve proper neuroimaging data

# Imaging Intelligence: Methods

Thompson et al. (2004) reviewed several neuroimaging methods currently available to the scientific community. The development of mathematical and computational algorithms contributes to improve the quality of the window through which we look at the living brain. Brain mapping techniques are currently applied to longitudinal follow-up of large groups of people for studying normal development, disease detection, the spontaneous evolution of diseases such as Alzheimer disease (AD), or changes following the administration of a given drug.

Imaging intelligence must take into account the complexity of the cortical geometry and the huge individual differences evident in this geometry. Therefore mathematical techniques are required to model these individual differences without loss of relevant information. Computational anatomy of group differences relies on differential geometry, numerical analysis, and the theory of partial differential equations for modeling objects and processes in brain images.

There are three main and usual steps followed in imaging research: (1) generating average patterns of brain structure for a group of people; (2) encoding individual differences in brain structure and identifying germane variations (groups differences, changes over time, and so forth); and (3) generating imaging data bases comprising demographic, cognitive, genetic, or clinical data.

Individual differences in brain structure can be treated using geometric models, using parametric surfaces, and building deformation maps that would relate cortical regions across people. This allows the construction of average models of cortical anatomy preserving their anatomic-relevant features. These average models (or templates) save the individual differences of interest. This process for matching anatomy erases noisy variance, making easier the identification of consistent structural and functional patterns.

Individual differences in cortical variability can be analyzed by building maps that deform various cortices. The statistical analysis of these deformation maps shows up regions with significant differences in several cortical attributes, such as cortical thickness or gray matter distribution (Thompson et al., 1997).

## Structural analyses

Plate 2 depicts the stages required for a standard structural neuroimaging study, which involves creating models and maps of the brain:

a   alignment (linear or non-linear) of MRI (magnetic resonance imaging) data from participants to a standardized anatomical template (the ICBM—International Consortium for Brain Mapping—template is an usual frame of reference; see Mazziotta et al., 2001);
b   correction of aligned images for intensity inhomogeneities;
c   segmentation into gray matter (GM), white matter (WM), and cerebrospinal fluid (CSF);
d   parcellation of GM and WM volumes for regional quantification of tissue volumes;

e   comparison of these brain volume measures by means of statistical techniques such as multiple regression or creating maps of anatomical differences.

This last step involves the extraction of cortical surface models from each image, along with the flattening and warping of cortical features to improve data alignment across participants (Thompson et al., 2003). GM thickness, GM density, or cortical pattern asymmetry can be computed from here (Good et al., 2001; Sowell et al., 2002; Thompson et al., 2001).

Cortical pattern matching can be thought of as a non-linear registration method for pooling data from a group of people. Typical data are cortical thickness, GM density, gyral pattern variability, hemispheric asymmetry, heritability, or fMRI signals (Plate 3). Cortical measures are sensitive to different attributes of cortical anatomy, so they can be useful for assessing individual differences in brain structure and function.

For cortical thickness analyses applied at the Laboratory of Neuroimaging (LONI, UCLA) the MRI scan is segmented into GM, WM, CSF, and a background class. Quantifying cortical GM thickness requires using the three-dimensional (3D) distance measured from the cortical WM boundary in the tissue-classified brain volumes to the cortical surface (GM–CSF boundary) for each participant. Distance measures assess GM thickness at subvoxel spatial resolution (thousands of homologous cortical locations are considered), and individual differences in this thickness are averaged at each cortical surface location for building spatial maps of local thickness differences.

GM density analyses are much less demanding than the cortical thickness protocol summarized above. This explains why most work studying GM differences in the last decade has focused on GM density (Ashburner & Friston, 2000; Thompson et al., 2003). GM density shows high correlations with cortical thickness measures. Furthermore, GM density allows the quantification of subcortical structures.

Beyond GM, the study of WM is developing quickly. Diffusion tensor imaging (DTI) is an imaging technique for characterizing the directional properties of the process of diffusion of water molecules in the brain. Two types of parameters are usually considered: (a) diffusion anisotropy (= amount of directionality); and (b) orientation of the axis along which water molecules move. DTI provides relevant information regarding white matter architecture. The integrity of white matter tracts can be assessed by fractional anisotropy (FA), usually regarded as an indicator of myelination and axonal thickness.

Color mapping allows the visualization of WM tracts: (a) image brightness represents diffusion anisotropy; and (b) red–blue–green color indicates tract orientations. Wakana, Jiang, Nagae-Poestcher, van Zijl, and Mori (2004) published WM atlases showing 17 WM tracts that fall into five functional categories: (1) the brainstem; (2) projection fibers (cortex–spinal cord, cortex–brainstem, and cortex–thalamus connections); (3) association fibers (cortex–cortex connections); (4) limbic systems tracts; and (5) commissural fibers (right–left hemispheric connections).

Although the information provided by DTI techniques is exciting, it is important to keep in mind that they show the averaged water diffusion property within a pixel and that this is an indirect approach to the axonal structures (Wedeen, Reese, & Tuch, 2000).

## Functional analyses

PET and fMRI are hemodynamic techniques with a good spatial resolution, but with low temporal resolution (neural events lasting less than 1 second may evoke a blood flow change lasting 10 seconds). Both techniques analyze neural activity, measuring changes in blood flow, and they are apt to identify large-scale distributed networks in the brain (Buckner & Logan, 2001).

PET measures hemodynamic changes by marking blood with a radioactive tracer, whereas fMRI measures changes in blood flow on the basis of changes in blood oxygenation. The so-called BOLD (blood–oxygen-level dependent) signal is crucial for fMRI: brain activations increase oxyhemoglobin beyond the current oxygen requirements, so the related decrease in deoxyhemoglobin evokes a signal registered by the MRI machine.

fMRI is more affected by motion artifacts than PET; but it is less invasive than PET, provides structural information, and lends itself to event-related experiments. The experimental designs usually compare blood flow in a task of interest (target task) and a control task (reference task). Thus, for instance, the task of interest could be items from the Raven Advanced Progressive Matrices Test (RAPM), comprising the demanding distribution of three rules, whereas the reference task could be items from this same test that can be solved by using simple perceptual strategies. Brain regions displaying significantly more activity in the target task with respect to the reference task define the activations of interest. However, because this subtraction method comprises some arguable assumptions (Friston et al., 1996), parametric designs are frequently applied. If we are interested in getting knowledge about the neural correlates of the reasoning processes that take place during solving the RAPM, it is possible to organize its items by their cognitive complexity (Carpenter, Just, & Shell, 1990; Colom & Abad, 2007). Only brain regions showing higher levels of activation with the increased complexity of the items would be nominated as relevant from a psychological standpoint. It is possible to overcome the problems derived from the subtraction paradigm by using event-related designs. For instance, an item from the RAPM can be decomposed in rows and columns, separated into domain (the matrix itself) and range (the alternative of response), and so forth.

PET and fMRI outputs show up brain regions related to the mental activity of interest, but are silent with respect to the relationships among regions. This requires network analyses correlating brain activations across regions (Cole & Schneider, 2007; Nyberg & McIntosh, 2001). The resulting correlation maps are thought to reveal the functional connectivity (Friston, 1994).

Nevertheless, as noted by Toga and Thompson,

> functional brain imaging has been widely applied to map brain activation [...] However, the cause of individual differences in hemodynamic based functional measures—their heritability, for example—is largely unknown. Although it is clear that functional imaging provides the link between anatomic maps and cognitive measures, the present paucity of data using fMRI may be due to the vagaries of neurovascular coupling, the variability of the response or the limitations of instrumentation, and protocols to date [...] Structural brain mapping, in contrast, has already shown specific patterns related to intelligence

and, as with other brain mapping studies, can provide the anatomic framework to achieve improved sensitivity in functional studies. (Toga & Thompson, 2005, p. 5)

# Findings

Jung and Haier (2007) reviewed 37 structural and functional neuroimaging studies published between 1988 and 2007. The reviewed studies in their revision identify a wide variety of brain areas: (a) 32 brain areas in structural studies; (b) 22 areas in PET studies; and (c) 26 areas in fMRI studies. However, as noted by Colom (2007), (a) only regions belonging to Brodmann areas (BAs) 10 and 39/40 reach a reasonable 50 percent of convergence in the structural studies; (b) only regions within BAs 18/19 and 46–47 show 50 percent of convergence in PET studies; and (c) only regions at BAs 6, 7, 9, 19, and 40 reach 50 percent of convergence in fMRI studies. Further, structural and functional results are not consistent. Of those brain areas approaching 50 percent of convergence, none overlaps across neuroimaging research strategies.

This disturbing evaluation results from the large heterogeneity of the available evidence. But why is the evidence so heterogeneous? We can think of (a) the influence of sociodemographic factors (age, sex, etc.); (b) the representativeness of the analyzed samples (groups of convenience vs. representative samples); and (c) the measurement of the "construct" of intelligence (reasoning, verbal ability, spatial ability, etc.).

Colom (2007) emphasized that neuroimaging studies on human intelligence must refine the way this psychological construct is measured. Finding commonalities among studies is interesting. However, different measures provide sharply distinct structural and functional correlates, so we are required to discover the causes underlying the discrepancies found among studies.

In this regard, the study reported by Colom, Jung, and Haier (2006) underscored the relevance of the "vehicle" used to elicit the "construct" of intelligence (see above). These researchers showed that, as the $g$ loading of a given intelligence measure increases, more widespread discrete brain areas become involved (Plate 4). What is even more important, this increased recruitment was not related to the superficial characteristics of the measurements, for instance their verbal or non-verbal nature.

## The P–FIT model

On the basis of the commonalities underscored in their revision, Jung and Haier (2007) proposed the parieto-frontal integration theory of intelligence (P–FIT). This theory identifies several brain areas relevant for human intelligence, which are distributed across the entire brain. These P–FIT regions support distinguishable information-processing stages (Figure 12.2).

Temporal and occipital areas process sensory information in the first processing stage: the extrastriate cortex (BAs 18 and 19) and the fusiform gyrus (BA 37), involved in recognition, imagery, and elaboration of visual inputs, as well as Wernicke's area (BA 22), for analysis and elaboration of syntax of auditory information. The second stage involves the integration and abstraction of sensory information by parietal BAs 39 (angular gyrus), 40 (supramarginal gyrus), and 7 (superior parietal lobule). These parietal areas interact with the frontal lobes in the third processing stage, and this interaction underlies problem-solving, evaluation, and hypothesis testing. Frontal BAs 6, 9, 10, 45, 46, and 47 are underscored by the model. Finally, the anterior cingulate (BA 32) is implicated for response selection and inhibition of alternative responses, once the best solution is determined in the previous stage.

White matter, especially the arcuate fasciculus, is thought to play a critical role for a reliable communication of information across these brain processing units.

Frontal, parietal, temporal, and occipital areas are depicted in Figure 12.2. So, why is this theory "parieto-frontal"? Jung and Haier (2007) suggest that not all the nominated brain areas are equally necessary in all individuals for intelligence. They predict that only discrete brain regions of the dorsolateral prefrontal cortex (BAs 9, 45, 46, and 47) and of the parietal cortex (BAs 7 and 40) might be considered core areas for human intelligence.

The review published by Shaw (2007) is consistent with the P–FIT model: "the weight of the evidence suggests intelligence is a distributed property of multiple interconnected cortical regions" (p. 964). Gray and Thompson (2004) also underscored the relevance of a fronto-parietal network, noting that these brain regions are also implicated in working memory tasks. In this regard, the study reported by Gray, Chabris, and Braver (2003) tested whether fluid or reasoning ability (*Gf*) was mediated by neural mechanisms supporting working memory. Participants performed verbal and non-verbal working memory tasks. They had to indicate if a current item matched the item they saw three items previously (3-back). Brain activity was measured by event-related fMRI. The demand for working memory varied across trials. Interestingly, (a) participants scoring higher on the Progressive Matrices Test (the measure of *Gf*) were more accurate in the 3-back task; and (b) only lateral prefrontal and parietal regions mediated the correlation between *Gf* and 3-back performance.

These fMRI results are largely consistent with the structural study reported by Colom, Jung, and Haier (2007). In light of the well-established fact that the general factor of intelligence (*g*) and working memory capacity are very highly correlated (Colom, Abad, Rebollo, & Shih, 2005; Colom, Abad, Quiroga, Shih, & Flores-Mendoza 2008; Colom, Rebollo, Palacios, Juan-Espinosa, & Kyllonen, 2004; Engle, 2002; Kane, Hambrick, & Conway, 2005; Oberauer, Schulze, Wilhelm, & Süb, 2005), these researchers predicted that *g* and working memory would share common neural systems. Therefore, using a VBM (voxel-based morphometry) approach, they quantified the overlap in brain areas where regional gray matter was correlated to measures of general intelligence and to working memory, finding a common neuroanatomic framework, supported by frontal gray matter regions belonging to BA 10 and by the right inferior parietal lobule (BA 40) (Plate 5). These results were interpreted after the theory proposed by Cowan (2005): parietal regions support "capacity limitations," whereas frontal areas underlie the "control of attention."

Lee et al. (2006) used an fMRI approach to investigate the neural bases of superior intelligence. Eighteen gifted and 18 non-gifted adolescents were analyzed. These participants solved reasoning problems showing high and low loadings on the $g$. Increased bilateral fronto-parietal activations (lateral prefrontal, anterior cingulate, and posterior parietal cortices) were found for both groups, but the gifted adolescents showed greater activations in the posterior parietal cortex. Furthermore, activations at regions belonging to BAs 7 and 40 (superior and intraparietal cortices) correlated with intelligence differences. The authors interpreted their findings by stating that high intelligence involves "functional facilitation of the fronto-parietal network driven by the posterior parietal activation" (Lee et al., 2006, p. 578).

Gläscher et al. (2010) investigated the neural substrates of $g$ in 241 patients with focal brain damage, using voxel-based lesion-symptom mapping. These researchers found statistically significant associations between $g$ and damage within a distributed network in frontal and parietal brain regions. Further, white matter association tracts were also related to the identified frontopolar areas. They suggested that $g$ draws on connections between regions integrating verbal and visuospatial processes, working memory processes, and executive processes.

The structural studies reported by Colom et al. (2009) and Karama et al. (2009) are also reasonably consistent with the P–FIT model. In the first study, $g$ was estimated after nine diverse measures of reasoning, verbal, and non-verbal intelligence. Their measurement model fitted quite well the recommendations provided by Haier, Colom et al. (2009). Their VBM approach revealed several clusters of voxels correlating with individual differences in $g$ scores. The main regions included the dorsolateral prefrontal cortex, Broca's and Wernicke's areas, the somato-sensory association cortex, and the visual association cortex. The design matrix in this study controlled for sex. However, when total gray matter is controlled for instead of sex, significant correlations are concentrated in frontal and parietal areas only (Plate 6): superior, middle, and frontal gyrus, along with the postcentral gyrus and the superior parietal lobule.

Karama et al. (2009) used an automated cortical thickness protocol (CIVET: Ad-Dab'bagh et al., 2006) to analyze a large sample of children and adolescents representative of the population. The most consistent areas of association between $g$ scores and cortical thickness were found in lateral prefrontal, occipital extrastriate, and para-hippocampal areas. As in the study reported by Colom et al. (2009), results found by Karama et al. (2009) identified more brain regions related to $g$ than the P–FIT model proposed.

There are two other studies that applied a cortical thickness approach, one of them (Narr et al., 2007) following the refined guidelines proposed by the Laboratory of Neuroimaging (LONI, UCLA, see above). Shaw et al. (2006) analyzed the trajectory of change in the thickness of the cerebral cortex after a big sample of 307 children and adolescents. Intelligence was measured by four sub-tests from the Wechsler scales (vocabulary, similarities, block design, and matrix reasoning). They found that changes in thickness are more related to intelligence than thickness itself is. Specifically, negative correlations were found in early childhood, whereas the correlation was positive in late adolescence (these positive correlations were identified in frontal BAs 4, 6, 8, 10, 11, and 44–46, in parietal BAs 1–3, 5, 39, 40, in temporal BAs 21, 37, and

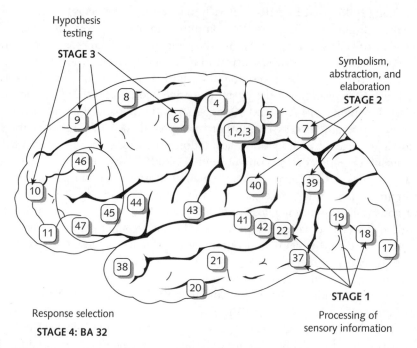

Hypothesis
testing
STAGE 3
Symbolism,
abstraction, and
elaboration
STAGE 2
Response selection
STAGE 4: BA 32
Processing of
sensory information
STAGE 1

**Figure 12.2**  Processing stages proposed by the P–FIT model. Source: Colom, Haier et al., 2009, Figure 1, p. 125

in occipital BAs 17, 18, and 19). Further, intelligence differences were associated with the trajectory of cortical development in frontal brain regions. Finally, children with higher scores on intelligence showed more plasticity in the developmental process.

In the second study, Narr et al. (2007) analyzed a sample of 65 participants. They found positive associations between cortical thickness and intelligence bilaterally, in prefrontal BAs 10/11 and 47, as well as in posterior temporal BAs 36/37. These researchers also analyzed males and females separately, finding that the former showed correlations in temporal–occipital association cortices, whereas the latter exhibited correlations in prefrontal and temporal association cortices. It must be noted that these results depart from the parieto-frontal framework:

> these findings contrast with VBM findings of strong intelligence correlations in frontal and parietal regions in male subjects. Female-specific associations, however, were observed in prefrontal cortices (BA 10) as consistent with our results, but associations were not detected in temporal association regions. (Narr et al., 2007, p. 2170)

Using an fMRI approach, Bishop, Fossella, Croucher, and Duncan (2008) reported a study based on previous evidence showing that a polymorphism (val[158]met) in the Catechol-O-Methyltransferase (COMT) gene regulates catecholaminergic signaling in prefrontal cortex. The val[158] allele is associated with higher COMT activity than the met[158] allele. Twenty-two participants, genotyped for the COMT val[158]met polymorphism, performed verbal and spatial fluid intelligence (*Gf*) items. These were classified according to their cognitive complexity, as estimated from the loadings on the general factor of intelligence ($g$) (see Duncan et al., 2000). The researchers were particularly interested in the analysis of the fronto-parietal network related to fluid intelligence (the lateral prefrontal cortex, the presupplementary motor area/anterior cingulate cortex, and the intraparietal sulcus). The findings revealed a positive effect of COMT val allele load upon the BOLD signal in regions belonging to this brain network when items showing distinguishable cognitive complexity were compared. This result suggests that the COMT val[158]met polymorphism impacts on the neural network supporting fluid intelligence.

Conceptually, this latter finding implies that the effect of single genes might be detected at the level of analysis proper of fMRI studies. Catecholamine modulation within the identified network contributes to explain individual differences in the neural response to high levels of cognitive complexity, irrespective of the content domain (verbal or non-verbal).

## White matter

The association between individual differences in intelligence and variations in total and regional gray matter is well established (Luders, Narr, Thompson, & Toga, 2009). However, the relationship between human intelligence and the integrity of white matter is much less investigated. As noted above, diffusion tensor imaging (DTI) is based on the random motion of water molecules in the brain, and their behavior provides information about the size, orientation, and geometry of brain tissue. The integrity of white matter tracts can be assessed by means of an index called fractional anisotropy (FA). FA approaches myelination and axonal thickness. Further, white matter tracts can be visualized and extracted from the surrounding structures using tractography techniques.

In this regard, Schmithorst, Wilke, Dardzinski, and Holland (2005) analyzed the relationship between intelligence and white matter structure. The sample was comprised of 47 children and adolescents (age range 5–18). White matter structure was studied by means of a DTI approach, using fractional anisotropy (FA) and mean diffusivity (MD) indices. These indices were correlated with intelligence scores obtained from the Wechsler scales. These researchers found positive correlations bilaterally for FA in white matter association areas (frontal and parieto-occipital areas). These correlations were thought to reflect a positive relationship between fiber organization density and intelligence.

Also using a DTI approach, Yu et al. (2008) computed correlations between the integrity of several tracts (corpus callosum, cingulum, uncinate fasciculus, optic radiation, and corticospinal tract) and intelligence. After their scores on the Wechsler scales, 79 participants were divided into two groups: average intelligence and high intelligence. White matter integrity was assessed by fractional anisotropy (FA). The results showed that high intelligence participants display more white matter integrity than average intelligence participants only in the right uncinate fasciculus. The authors concluded that the right uncinate fasciculus is an important neural basis of intelligence differences. These researchers also analyzed a sample of 15 participants with mental retardation. These participants were compared with the 79 healthy controls and they showed extensive damage in the integrity of the next brain white matter tracts: corpus callosum, uncinate fasciculus, optic radiation, and corticospinal tract.

Pol et al. (2006) analyzed the heritability of focal white matter. They explored the genetic influence on focal white matter densities after a sample of 54 identical and 58 fraternal twin pairs, along with 34 of their siblings. They applied a VBM approach, finding that intelligence shares a common genetic origin with superior occipito-frontal, callosal, and left optical radiation.

Chiang et al. (2009) have reported the very first study combining a genetically informative design and a DTI approach for analyzing the relationships between white matter integrity and human intelligence. Intelligence was assessed by the Multidimensional Aptitude Battery, which provides measures of general intelligence, verbal (information, vocabulary, and arithmetic), and non-verbal intelligence (spatial and object assembly). The sample was comprised of 23 pairs of identical twins and 23 pairs of fraternal twins. White matter integrity, quantified using FA, was used to fit structural equation models (SEM) at each point in the brain. After doing that, Chiang et al. generated three-dimensional maps of heritability. White matter integrity was found to be under powerful genetic control in bilateral frontal, bilateral parietal, and left occipital lobes. FA measures were correlated with the estimate of general intelligence and with non-verbal intelligence in the cingulum, optic radiations, superior fronto-occipital fasciculus, internal capsule, callosal isthmus, and the *corona radiata*. Further, common genetic factors mediated the correlation between intelligence and white matter integrity. This latter finding suggested a common physiological mechanism and a common genetic determination.

## Networks for human intelligence

Recently, Li et al. (2009) reported an exciting study testing the hypothesis that high levels of intelligence involve more efficient information circulation in the brain (Neubauer & Fink, 2009). Specifically, studying a sample of 79 participants, these researchers constructed brain anatomical networks by means of diffusion tensor tractography. These networks were comprised by both intra-hemispheric and inter-hemispheric connections. Six white matter tracts were further constructed: the *genu* ("knee," i.e. the anterior part) of the corpus callosum, the body of the corpus callosum, the splenium of the corpus callosum, the cingulum, the corticospinal tract, and the inferior fronto-occipital fasciculus. Thereafter they calculated the topological properties of the networks for every participant. The sample was divided into average and high intelligence according to scores on the Wechsler scales. Higher global efficiencies were revealed for the latter group. Furthermore, higher intelligence was found to display shorter characteristic path length and a higher global efficiency of the networks. This was interpreted as a symptom of a more efficient parallel information transfer in the brain. In consequence, the efficiency of brain structural organization would be an important biological basis for human intelligence.

Song et al. (2008) analyzed 59 adults to study the relationships between spontaneous brain activity at rest and individual differences in intelligence. Intelligence was assessed on the Wechsler scales. Using fMRI, the bilateral dorsolateral prefrontal cortices were the seed regions for investigating the correlations across subjects between individual intelligence scores and the strength of the functional connectivity between the seed regions and the remaining brain regions. These researchers found that brain regions in which the strength of the functional connectivity significantly correlated with intelligence scores were distributed in the frontal, parietal, occipital, and limbic lobes. Furthermore, functional connectivity within the frontal lobe and between the frontal and the posterior brain regions predicted differences in intelligence. These results are consistent with the relevance of a network view for human intelligence.

Finally, van den Heuvel, Stam, Kahn, and Pol (2009) used graph analysis for exploring the presumed organization of the brain network. Functional connections of this brain network were analyzed computing correlations among the spontaneous signals of different brain regions during rest. The sample was composed of 19 subjects, and intelligence was measured on the Wechsler scales. The researchers found negative associations between path length and individual differences in intelligence. This was interpreted as suggesting that how efficiently the brain integrates information between brain regions provides support to human intelligence. The strongest effects were found in the frontal and parietal regions. Furthermore, intelligence differences were not related to the level of local information processing and to the total number of functional connections of the brain network.

## Sex differences?

Neuroimaging studies could shed new light regarding the sensitive issue of the discussed average sex differences in intelligence. Whereas some research indicates that there is no sex difference in general intelligence (Colom, García, Juan-Espinosa, & Abad, 2002; Colom, Juan-Espinosa, Abad, & García, 2000; Jensen, 1998) other approaches insist that, although small, there is a real difference (Lynn, 1999; Lynn & Irwing, 2004, 2008).

Several reports show sex differences in brain structure and function (Chen, Sachdev, Wen, & Anstey, 2007; Jordan, Wüstenberg, Heinze, Peters, & Jäncke, 2002; Luders et al., 2005, 2006; Schmithorst & Holland, 2007; Sowell et al., 2007). These group differences may or may not be related to intelligence differences between males and females.

Haier, Jung, Yeo, Head, and Alkire (2005) examined the relationship between structural brain variation and intelligence using a VBM approach. They found that females showed more white matter and less gray matter correlated with intelligence than males. For females, the strongest correlations between intelligence and gray matter were found in BA 10 and in Broca's area. For males, the most prominent correlations were found in the frontal and parietal regions (BA 8, 9, 39, 40). The main message was that males and females show equivalent intelligence levels in different brain regions, and therefore these human groups display different brain designs.

However, the mean intelligence for males was 118.8, whereas the mean intelligence for females was 113.5. So the average intelligence difference in Haier et al.'s sample was equivalent to 5 IQ points favoring males. This average difference (a) is pretty close to the difference reported by those favoring the existence of a sex difference in intelligence; and (b) raises doubts about the genuine support for the statement that males and females use different brain designs to achieve the same level of intelligence.

The debate appears unsolvable if one relies on standardized intelligence measures. Jensen (1998) and Colom, García et al. (2002) accept that there is a small average sex difference in IQ (intelligence in general), but this difference may not reflect a genuine difference in the scientific construct of general intelligence ($g$). Lynn and Irwing (2004) equate IQ and $g$ on this basis they claim that there is a real difference between males and females. Because this approach appears to arrive at a dead end, recently Lynn and Irwing (2008) proposed a different perspective. These researchers reasoned that, if working memory and $g$ are almost isomorphic constructs (see above) and if there is a sex difference in working memory, then the sex difference in $g$ must be accepted.

A recent neuroimaging study published by Schmidt et al. (2009) contains an answer to this latter challenge. Using an fMRI approach, these researchers investigated sex differences (25 males and 25 females, matched for age and education) in patterns of brain activation during a parametric version of the $n$-back task. They found that both groups showed identical performance levels (in terms of accuracy and response times) and, more importantly, used similar brain regions to the same degree. Bilateral activations were observed in the superior frontal gyrus (BA 6), middle frontal gyrus (BAs 9 and 10), inferior frontal gyrus (BA 47), and inferior parietal lobule (BA 40).

In conclusion, there is no sex difference in working memory capacity, and males and females use the same brain design for coping with this paradigmatic experimental task. These results are in tension both with Lynn and Irwing's (2008) approach and with the main conclusion drawn by Haier et al. (2005) regarding the relevance of the sex variable in understanding human intelligence.

## Final Remarks

The significance of a fronto-parietal network for supporting individual differences in intelligence goes far beyond this psychological construct. Wager and Smith (2003) computed a meta-analysis of 60 PET and fMRI studies of working memory. They analyzed the effect of three content domains (verbal, spatial, and object) and of three executive functions (updating, temporal order, and manipulation) along with their interactions. The brain areas most involved in all these cognitive facets were located in the frontal and parietal lobes: (a) spatial and non-spatial contents were separated in posterior but not anterior areas; (b) executive manipulation evoked more frontal activations, but with some exceptions; and, importantly, (c) the parietal cortex was always implicated in executive processing. The meta-analysis by Wager, Jonides, and Reading (2004) after 31 PET and fMRI studies of shifting attention also highlights this fronto-parietal network (medial prefrontal, superior and inferior parietal, medial parietal, and premotor cortices).

Marois and Ivanoff (2005) analyzed the fascinating issue of the limits of the brain's capacity for information processing. Specifically, these researchers focused on three basic limitations: for perception, for working memory, and for action. The paradigmatic tasks reflecting these limitations are the attentional blink, visual short-term memory, and the psychological refractory period. Their revision was based mainly on fMRI evidence and it led to the following conclusions: (1) perception and action limitations are related to fronto-parietal brain networks; and (2) working memory capacity limitations are associated to parieto-occipital brain networks. The lateral prefrontal cortex may support "general" target consolidation and response selection, using a flexible coding system for processing relevant information in any given task. In contrast, the lateral parietal cortex might provide support for more specific processing goals. Thus, for instance, this brain region is more sensitive to perception than to action.

Therefore some basic cognitive functions (especially working memory) and intelligence share the discussed fronto-parietal brain network. Nevertheless, experimental confirmatory approaches should be welcome. In this regard, TMS (transcranial magnetic stimulation) may help to test hypotheses aimed at checking whether or not these brain regions are really important for understanding individual differences in human intelligence. TMS induces transient changes in brain activity non-invasively. Changes on a magnetic field induce electric currents in the brain, which promote the depolarization of cellular membranes. Cognitive neuroscience mainly relies on a correlation approach, whereas TMS allows studying causal brain–behavior relationships in high cognitive functions (Pascual-Leone, Bartres-Faz, & Keenan, 1999; Sack, 2006).

The study reported by Aleman and van't Wout (2008) exemplifies this approach by using a working memory task (forward and backward digit span). As noted above, working memory (and intelligence) performance is supported by the dorsolateral prefrontal cortex. Using repetitive transcranial magnetic stimulation (rTMS) over the right dorsolateral prefrontal cortex, these researchers found a significant decrease of performance in the forward and backward digit span test.

Regardless of the use of exploratory or confirmatory approaches, we predict that improvements in the available neuroimaging tools will reveal, sooner or later, the most likely biological basis of individual differences in human intelligence. This advancement in our knowledge would allow an increasing understanding of both normal and abnormal variation.

# References

Ad-Dab'bagh, Y., Einarson, D., Lyttelton, O., Muehlboeck, J.-S., Mok, K., Ivanov, O., Vincent, R. D., Lepage, C., Lerch, J., Fombonne, E., & Evans, A. C. (2006). The CIVET Image-Processing Environment: A fully automated comprehensive pipeline for anatomical neuroimaging research. *Proceedings of the Twelfth Annual Meeting of the Organization for Human Brain Mapping. NeuroImage, 31* (Supplement 1), p. S–45.

Aleman, A., & van't Wout, M. (2008). Repetitive transcranial magnetic stimulation over the right dorsolateral prefrontal cortex disrupts digit span task performance. *Neuropsychobiology, 57,* 44–48.

Ashburner, J., & Friston, K. J. (2000). Voxel-based morphometry—The methods. *Neuroimage, 11,* 805–821.

Barrett, H. C., & Kurzban, R. (2006). Modularity in cognition: Framing the debate. *Psychological Review, 113,* 628–647.

Bishop, S. J., Fossella, J., Croucher, C. J., & Duncan, J. (2008). COMT val[158]met genotype affects recruitment of neural mechanisms supporting fluid intelligence. *Cerebral Cortex.* doi:10.1093/cercor/bhm240.

Brody, N. (2003). Construct validation of the Sternberg Triarchic Abilities Test. Comment and reanalysis. *Intelligence, 31,* 319–329.

Buckner, R. L., & Logan, J. M. (2001). Functional neuroimaging methods: PET and fMRI. In R. Cabeza & A. Kingstone (Eds.), *Handbook of functional neuroimaging of cognition* (pp. 27–48). Cambridge, MA: MIT Press.

Carpenter, P. A., Just, M. A., & Shell, P. (1990). What one intelligence test measures: A theoretical account of the processing in the Raven Progressive Matrices test. *Psychological Review, 98,* 404–431.

Carroll, J. B. (1993). *Human cognitive abilities. A survey of factor analytic studies.* Cambridge: Cambridge University Press.

Carroll, J. B. (2003). The higher-stratum structure of cognitive abilities: Current evidence supports *g* and about 10 broad factors. In H. Nyborg (Ed.), *The scientific study of general intelligence: Tribute to Arthur R. Jensen* (pp. 5–21). Amsterdam: Pergamon.

Cattell, R. B. (1987). *Intelligence: Their [sic] structure, growth and action.* Amsterdam: North-Holland.

Chen, X., Sachdev, P. S., Wen, W., & Anstey, K. J. (2007). Sex differences in regional gray matter in healthy individuals aged 44–48 years: A voxel-based morphometric study. *Neuroimage, 36,* 691–699.

Chiang, M., Barysheva, M., Shattuck, D. W., Lee, A. D., Madsen, S. K., Avedissian, C. et al. (2009). Genetics of brain fiber architecture and intellectual performance. *The Journal of Neuroscience, 29,* 2212–2224.

Cole, M. W., & Schneider, W. (2007). The cognitive control network: Integrated cortical regions with dissociable functions. *NeuroImage, 37,* 343–360.

Colom, R. (2007). Intelligence? What intelligence? *Behavioural and Brain Sciences, 30,* 155–156.

Colom, R., Jung, R. E., & Haier, R. J. (2006). Distributed brain sites for the *g*-factor of intelligence. *Neuroimage, 31,* 1359–1365.

Colom, R., Jung, R. E., & Haier, R. J. (2007). General intelligence and memory span: Evidence for a common neuro-anatomic framework. *Cognitive Neuropsychology, 24,* 8, 867–878.

Colom, R., Abad, F. J., García, L. F., & Juan-Espinosa, M. (2002). Education, Wechsler's Full Scale IQ, and *g. Intelligence, 30,* 449–462.

Colom, R., Abad, F. J., Rebollo, I., & Shih, P. C. (2005). Memory span and general intelligence: A latent-variable approach. *Intelligence, 33,* 623–642.

Colom, R., García, L. F., Juan-Espinosa, M., & Abad, F. J. (2002). Null sex differences in general intelligence: Evidence from the WAIS–III. *Spanish Journal of Psychology, 5,* 29–35.

Colom, R., Juan-Espinosa, M., Abad, F., & García, L. F. (2000). Negligible sex differences in general intelligence. *Intelligence, 28,* 57–68.

Colom, R., Abad, F. J., Quiroga, Mª. A., Shih, P. C., & Flores-Mendoza, C. (2008). Working memory and intelligence are highly related constructs, but why? *Intelligence, 36,* 584–606.

Colom, R., Rebollo, I., Palacios, A., Juan-Espinosa, M., & Kyllonen, P. C. (2004). Working memory is (almost) perfectly predicted by *g. Intelligence, 32,* 277–296.

Colom, R., Haier, R. J., Head, K., Alvarez-Linera, J., Quiroga, Mª. A., Shih, P. C., & Jung, R. E. (2009). Gray matter correlates of fluid, crystallized, and spatial intelligence: Testing the P–FIT model. *Intelligence, 37,* 124–135.

Cowan, N. (2005). *Working memory capacity*. New York: Psychology Press.

Draganski, B., Gaser, C., Busch, V., Schuierer, G., Bogdahn, U., & May, A. (2004). Changes in grey matter induced by training. *Nature, 427*, 311–312.

Duncan, J., Seitz, J. R., Kolodny, J., Bor, D., Herzog, H., Ahmed, A. et al. (2000). A neural basis for general intelligence. *Science, 289*, 457–460.

Engle, R. W. (2002). Working memory capacity as executive attention. *Current Directions in Psychological Science, 11*, 19–23.

Friston, K. J. (1994). Functional and effective connectivity: A synthesis. *Human Brain Mapping, 2*, 56–78.

Friston, K. J., Price, C. J., Fletcher, P., Moore, C., Frackowiak, R. S., & Dolan, R. J. (1996). The trouble with cognitive subtraction. *Neuroimage, 4*, 97–104.

Gardner, H. (2004). Audiences for the theory of multiple intelligences. *Teachers College Record, 106*, 212–220.

Gläscher, J., Rudrauf, D., Colom, R., Paul, L. K., Tranel, D., Damasio, H., & Adolphs, R. (2010). The distributed neural system for general intelligence revealed by lesion mapping. *Proceedings of the National Academy of Sciences, 107*(10), 4705–4709.

Good, C. D., Johnsrude, I. S., Ashburner, J., Henson, R. N., Friston, K. J., & Frackowiak, R. S. J. (2001). A voxel-based morphometric study of ageing in 465 normal adult human brains. *NeuroImage, 14*, 21–36.

Gottfredson, L., Arvey, R. D., Bouchard, T. J., Carroll, J. B., Cohen, D. B., Dawis, R. W., Detterman, D. K., Dunnette, M. et al. (1997). Mainstream science on intelligence: An editorial with 52 signatories, history, and bibliography. *Intelligence, 24*, 1, 13–23.

Gray, J., & Thompson, P. (2004). Neurobiology of intelligence: Science and ethics. *Nature Reviews, 5*, 471–482.

Gray, J., Chabris, C., & Braver, T. (2003). Neural mechanisms of general fluid intelligence. *Nature Neuroscience, 6*, 316–322.

Haier, R. J., Karama, S., Leyba, L., & Jung, R. E. (2009). MRI assessment of cortical thickness and functional activity changes in adolescent girls following three months of practice on a visual–spatial task. *BMC Research Notes.* doi:10.1186/1756-0500-2-174.

Haier, R. J., Jung, R. E., Yeo, R. A., Head, K., & Alkire, M. T. (2005). The neuroanatomy of general intelligence: Sex matters. *NeuroImage, 25*, 320–327.

Haier, R. J., Colom, R., Schroeder, D., Condon, C., Tang, C., Eaves, E., & Head, K. (2009). Gray matter and intelligence factors: Is there a neuro-*g*? *Intelligence, 37*, 136–144.

Hunt, E. B. (2011). *Human intelligence*. Cambridge: Cambridge University Press.

Ilg, R., Wohlschlager, A. M., Gaser, C., Liebau, Y., Dauner, R., Woller, A., Zimmer, C., Zihl, J., & Muhlau, M. (2008). Gray matter increase induced by practice correlates with task-specific activation: A combined functional and morphometric magnetic resonance imaging study. *The Journal of Neuroscience, 28*, 4210–4215.

Jensen, A. R. (1998). *The g factor. The science of mental ability*. Westport, CT: Praeger.

Johnson, W., & Bouchard, T. (2005). The structure of human intelligence: It is verbal, perceptual, and image rotation (VPR), not fluid and crystallized. *Intelligence, 33*, 393–416.

Johnson, W., Nijenhuis, J., & Bouchard, T. (2008). Still just 1 *g*: Consistent results from five test batteries. *Intelligence, 36*, 81–95.

Johnson, W., Bouchard, T., Krueger, R. F., McGue, M., & Gottesman, I. I. (2004). Just one *g*: Consistent results from three test batteries. *Intelligence, 32*, 95–107.

Jordan, K., Wüstenberg, T., Heinze, H., Peters, M., & Jäncke, L. (2002). Women and men exhibit different cortical activation patterns during mental rotation tasks. *Neuropsychologia, 40*, 2397–2408.

Jung, R. E., & Haier, R. J. (2007). The parieto-frontal integration theory (P–FIT) of intel-ligence: Converging neuroimaging evidence. *Behavioral and Brain Sciences*, *30*, 135–187.

Kane, M. J., Hambrick, D. Z., & Conway, A. R. A. (2005). Working memory capacity and fluid intelligence are strongly related constructs: Comment on Ackerman, Beier, and Boyle (2005). *Psychological Bulletin*, *131*, 66–71.

Karama, S., Ad-Dab'bagh, Y., Haier, R. J., Deary, I., Lyttelton, O. C., Lepage, C., Evans, A. C., & the Brain Development Cooperative Group (2009). Positive association between cognitive ability and cortical thickness in a representative US sample of healthy 6 to 18 year-olds. *Intelligence*, *37*, 145–155.

Kovas, Y., & Plomin, R. (2006). Generalist genes: Implications for the cognitive sciences. *Trends in Cognitive Sciences*, *10*, 198–203.

Lee, K. H., Choi, Y. Y., Gray, J. R., Cho, S. H., Chae, J., Lee, S., & Kim, K. (2006). Neural correlates of superior intelligence: Stronger recruitment of posterior parietal cortex. *Neuroimage*, *29*, 578–586.

Li, Y., Liu, Y., Li, J., Qin, W., Li, K., Yu, C., & Jiang, T. (2009). Brain anatomical network and intelligence. *Computational Biology*, *5*, 1–17.

Luders, E., Narr, K. L., Thompson, P. M., & Toga, A. W. (2009). Neuroanatomical correlates of intelligence. *Intelligence*, *37*, 156–163.

Luders, E., Narr, K. L., Zaidel, E., Thompson, P. M., Jancke, L., & Toga, A. W. (2006). Parasagittal asymmetries of the corpus callosum. *Cerebral Cortex*, *16*, 346–354.

Luders, E., Narr, K. L., Thompson, P. M., Woods, R. P., Rex, D. E., Jancke, L., Steinmetz, H., & Toga, A. W. (2005). Mapping cortical gray matter in the young adult brain: Effects of gender. *Neuroimage*, *26*, 493–501.

Lynn, R. (1999). Sex differences in intelligence and brain size: A developmental theory. *Intelligence*, *27*, 1–12.

Lynn, R., & Irwing, P. (2004). Sex differences on the progressive matrices: A meta-analysis. *Intelligence*, *32*, 481–498.

Lynn, R., & Irwing, P. (2008). Sex differences in mental arithmetic, digit span, and *g* defined as working memory capacity. *Intelligence*, *36*, 226–235.

Marois, R., & Ivanoff, J. (2005). Capacity limits of information processing in the brain. *Trends in Cognitive Sciences*, *9*(6), 296–305.

Mazziotta, J. C., Toga, A. W., Evans, A. C., Fox, P. T., Lancaster, J., Zilles, K. et al. (2001). A probabilistic atlas and reference system for the human brain. [Invited Paper, 29 August.] *Journal of the Royal Society*, *356*(1412), 1293–1322.

McGrew, K. (2009). CHC theory and the human cognitive abilities project: Standing on the shoulders of the giants of psychometric intelligence research. *Intelligence*, *37*, 1–10.

Narr, K. L., Woods, R. P., Thompson, P. M., Szeszko, P., Robinson, D., Dimtcheva, T., Gurbani, M., Toga, A. W., & Bilder, R. M. (2007). Relationships between IQ and regional cortical gray matter thickness in healthy adults. *Cerebral Cortex*, *17*, 2163–2171.

Neubauer, A. C., & Fink, A. (2009). Intelligence and neural efficiency: Measures of brain activation versus measures of functional connectivity in the brain. *Intelligence*, *37*, 223–229.

Nyberg, L., & McIntosh, A. R. (2001). Network analyses of functional neuroimaging data. In R. Cabeza & A. Kingstone (Eds.), *Handbook of functional neuroimaging of cognition* (pp. 49–72). Cambridge, MA: MIT Press.

Oberauer, K., Schulze, R., Wilhelm, O., & Süß, H. (2005). Working memory and intelligence—Their correlation and their relation: Comment on Ackerman, Beier, and Boyle (2005). *Psychological Bulletin*, *131*, 61–65.

Pascual-Leone, A., Bartres-Faz, D., & Keenan, J. P. (1999). Transcranial magnetic stimulation: Studying the brain–behaviour relationship by induction of "virtual lesions." *Philosophical Transactions of the Royal Society, London B, 354*, 1229–1238.

Pol, H. E. H., Schnack, H. G., Posthuma, D., Mandl, R. C. W., Baaré, W. F., Oel, C. et al. (2006). Genetic contributions to human brain morphology and intelligence. *The Journal of Neuroscience, 26*, 10235–10242.

Sack, A. T. (2006). Transcranial magnetic stimulation, causal structure–function mapping and networks of functional relevance. *Current Opinion in Neurobiology, 16*, 593–599.

Schmidt, H., Jogia, J., Fast, K., Christodoulou, T., Haldane, M., Kumari, V., & Frangou, S. (2009). No gender differences in brain activation during the n-back task: An fMRI study in healthy individuals. *Human Brain Mapping, 30*, 3609–3615.

Schmithorst, V. J., & Holland, S. K. (2007). Sex differences in the development of neuroanatomical functional connectivity underlying intelligence found using Bayesian connectivity analysis. *Neuroimage, 35*, 406–419.

Schmithorst, V. J., Wilke, M., Dardzinski, B. J., & Holland, S. K. (2005). Cognitive functions correlate with white matter architecture in a normal pediatric population: A diffusion tensor MRI study. *Human Brain Mapping, 26*, 139–147.

Shaw, P. (2007). Intelligence and the developing human brain. *BioEssays, 29*, 962–973.

Shaw, P., Greenstein, D., Lerch, J, Clasen. L., Lenroot, R., Gogtay, N. et al. (2006). Intellectual ability and cortical development in children and adolescents. *Nature, 440*, 676–679.

Song, M., Zhou, Y., Li, J., Liu, Y., Tian, L., Yu, C., & Jianga, T. (2008). Brain spontaneous functional connectivity and intelligence. *NeuroImage, 41*, 1168–1176.

Sowell, E. R., Thompson, P. M., Peterson, B. S., Mattson, S. N., Welcome, H.-C., Henkenius, A. L., Riley, E. P., Jernigan, T. L., & Toga, A. W. (2002). Mapping cortical gray matter asymmetry patterns in adolescents with heavy prenatal alcohol exposure. *NeuroImage, 17*, 1807–1819.

Sowell, E. R., Peterson, B. S., Kan, E., Woods, R. P., Yoshii, J., Bansal, R., Xu, D., Zhu, H., Thompson, P. M., & Toga, A. W. (2007). Sex differences in cortical thickness mapped in 176 healthy individuals between 7 and 87 years of age. *Cerebral Cortex, 17*, 1550–1560.

Sternberg, R. (1988). *The triarchic mind*. London: Penguin Books.

Thompson, P. M., MacDonald, D., Mega, M. S., Holmes, C. J., Evans, A. C., & Toga, A. W. (1997). Detection and mapping of abnormal brain structure with a probabilistic atlas of cortical surfaces. *Journal of Computer Assisted Tomography, 21*, 567–581.

Thompson, P. M., Cannon, T. D., Narr, K. L., van Erp, T., Poutanen, V. P., Huttunen, M. et al. (2001). Genetic influences on brain structure. *Nature Neuroscience, 4*, 1253–1258.

Thompson, P. M., Hayashi, K. M., de Zubicaray, G., Janke, A. L., Rose, S. E., Semple, J. et al. (2003). Dynamics of gray matter loss in Alzheimer's disease. *Journal of Neuroscience, 23*, 994–1005.

Thompson, P. M., Hayashi, K. M., Sowell, E. R., Gogtay, N., Giedd, J. N., Rapoport, J. L. et al. (2004). Mapping cortical change in Alzheimer's disease, brain development, and schizophrenia. *Neuroimage, 23*, S2–S18.

Toga, A. W., & Thompson, P. M. (2005). Genetics of brain structure and intelligence. *Annual Reviews of Neuroscience, 28*, 1–23.

van den Heuvel, M. P., Stam, C. J., Kahn, R. S., & Pol, H. (2009). Efficiency of functional brain networks and intellectual performance. *The Journal of Neuroscience, 29*, 7619–7624.

Wager, T. D., & Smith, E. E. (2003). Neuroimaging studies of working memory: A meta-analysis. *Cognitive, Affective, and Behavioral Neuroscience, 3*, 255–274.

Wager, T. D., Jonides, J., & Reading, S. (2004). Neuroimaging studies of shifting attention: A meta-analysis. *NeuroImage, 22,* 1679–1693.

Wakana, S., Jiang, H., Nagae-Poestcher, L. M., van Zijl, P. C. M., & Mori, S. (2004). Fiber tract-based atlas of human white matter anatomy. *Radiology, 230,* 77–87.

Waterhouse, L. (2006). Multiple intelligences, The Mozart effect, and emotional intelligence: A critical review. *Educational Psychologist, 41,* 207–226.

Wedeen, V., Reese, T. G., Tuch, D. S., Weigel, M. R., Dou, J. G., Weiskoff, M. R. et al. (2000). Mapping fiber orientation spectra in cerebral white matter with Fourier-transform diffusion MRI (abstract). In *Proceedings of the Eighth Meeting of the International Society for Magnetic Resonance in Medicine* (p. 82). Berkeley, CA: International Society for Magnetic Resonance in Medicine.

Yu, C., Li, J., Liu, Y., Qin, W., Li, Y., Shu, N., Jiang, T., & Li, K. (2008). White matter tract integrity and intelligence in patients with mental retardation and healthy adults. *Neuroimage, 40,* 1533–1541.

# 13

# Evolutionary Psychology and Individual Differences

## Satoshi Kanazawa

The two subfields of psychology—evolutionary psychology and individual differences—have largely stood separately despite the fact that both subfields take biological and genetic influences on human behavior and cognition seriously. In some sense, this is understandable. Evolutionary psychology focuses on universal human nature, which is shared by all humans, or on sex-specific male human nature or female human nature, which is shared by all men or by all women. In contrast, differential psychology focuses on what makes individuals different from each other. Psychometrics, for example, is concerned with the accurate measurement of intelligence precisely because individuals vary in their level of intelligence, largely (though not entirely) as a result of their different genetic makeup.

Yet, as Tooby and Cosmides (1990a) articulate, the concept of universal human nature is not inimical to or incompatible with individual differences. While individual differences have yet to be fully integrated into evolutionary psychology (Buss, 1995; Nettle, 2006), some evolutionary psychologists have incorporated heritable or "reactively heritable" (Tooby & Cosmides, 1990a) individual differences into personality (Buss, 1991; MacDonald, 1995; Nettle, 2005), sociosexuality (Gangestad & Simpson, 1990, 200), and attachment and reproductive strategies (Belsky, Steinberg, & Draper, 1991; Buss & Greiling, 1999). Scarr (1995) and Bailey (1998) call for the incorporation of behavior genetics into evolutionary psychology in order to emphasize heritable individual and group differences and to provide a fuller explanation of human behavior.

In this chapter I will first discuss how evolutionary psychology can accommodate individual differences. I will then present Gross's (1996) typology of individual differences and two evolutionary models of them. The remainder of the chapter is devoted to extensive discussion of how to synthesize evolutionary psychology and individual differences, taking the effect of general intelligence on the universal constraints on the human brain as an example. The synthesis leads to a refinement of

*The Wiley-Blackwell Handbook of Individual Differences*, First Edition.
Edited by Tomas Chamorro-Premuzic, Sophie von Stumm, and Adrian Furnham.
© 2011 Blackwell Publishing Ltd. Published 2011 by Blackwell Publishing Ltd.

the concept of novelty and to the distinction between evolutionary novelty and experiential novelty.

## Individual Differences in Evolved Adaptations

Some critics (Borsboom & Dolan, 2006) believe that individual differences variables cannot be evolved adaptations, and evolved adaptations cannot have individual differences. Adaptations are universal and constant features of a species, shared by all its members. There thus cannot be any heritable individual differences in such universal features. These critics argue that adaptations and heritable individual differences are mutually exclusive.

These criticisms betray a profound misunderstanding of the nature of adaptations. A trait could simultaneously be an evolved adaptation and an individual difference variable. In fact, *most adaptations exhibit such individual differences*. Full-time bipedalism is a uniquely human adaptation, yet some individuals walk and run faster than others. The eye is a complex adaptation, yet some individuals have better vision than others. Language is an adaptation, yet some individuals learn to speak their native language at earlier ages and have greater linguistic facility than others.

Individual differences in evolved adaptations are what Tooby and Cosmides (1990a) call "random quantitative variation on a monomorphic design." "Because the elaborate functional design of individuals is largely monomorphic [shared by all members of a species], our adaptations do not vary in their architecture from individual to individual (*except quantitatively*)" (Tooby & Cosmides, 1990a, p. 37, emphasis added).

Intraspecific (interindividual) differences in such traits pale in comparison to interspecific differences. Carl Lewis and I run at virtually identical speed compared to cheetahs or sloths. Similarly, Einstein and I have virtually identical intelligence compared to cheetahs or sloths. It is therefore possible for a trait to be both universal and species-typical evolved adaptations (exhibiting virtually no variation in the architecture in a cross-species comparison) *and* to manifest vast individual differences in the quantitative performance among members of a single species.

Tooby and Cosmides (1990a, pp. 38–39) make this exact point, using "a complex psychological mechanism regulating aggression" as their example. They contend that aggression is an adaptation, even though there are heritable individual differences in the mechanism's threshold of activation, whether one has a "short fuse" or not. Tooby and Cosmides suggest that a complex psychological mechanism regulating aggression "is (by hypothesis) universal and therefore has zero heritability," even though "the *variations* in the exact level at which the threshold of activation is set are probably not adaptations." They contend that "nonadaptive, random fluctuations in the monomorphic design of a mental organ can give rise to heritable individual differences *in nearly every manifest feature of human psychology*" (1990a, p. 57, emphasis added). We would therefore expect some individual differences in all evolved psychological adaptations.

For example, the cheater detection module—the ability to tell when someone is not honoring an explicit or implicit social contract and is therefore behaving unfairly—was among the first evolved psychological mechanisms to be discovered (Cosmides, 1989). It is clearly an adaptation, in that all human beings have the evolutionarily given and innate ability to detect when they might be cheated out of a fair exchange in a social contract. But are there individual differences in how well individuals can detect cheaters? Are some individuals inherently better at it than others? If so, are such individual differences heritable? Are some individuals genetically predisposed to fall victims to cons and scams?

Theory of mind is another evolved psychological mechanism; adult humans have the ability to infer the mental states of others. However, we already know that some individuals with pathological conditions (autism, Asperger's syndrome) have a weakened or absent capacity for theory of mind (Baron-Cohen, 1995). Can developmentally normal individuals also vary in their theory of mind? Dunbar (2005) suggests that there are individual differences in *higher-order* theory of mind ("I think that you think that Sally thinks that Anne thinks that ..."), and that good writers like Shakespeare are rare because great dramas like *Othello* require writers to possess a sixth-order theory of mind. If individuals can vary in their capacity for higher-order theory of mind, it seems reasonable to suggest that they might also vary in their capacity for first-order theory of mind, where some are better than others at inferring the mental states of another person accurately. If so, can such individual differences in the evolved psychological mechanism of theory of mind be heritable, since we already know that autism and Asperger's syndrome may be heritable (Bailey, Le Couteur, Gottesman, & Bolton, 1995; Folstein & Rutter, 1988)?

## Typology of Individual Differences

In his classic paper, Gross (1996) provides a useful way of classifying individual differences into three distinct types: alternative strategies, conditional strategies, and mixed strategies. Although Gross's original typology refers specifically to reproductive strategies, the typology can easily be generalized and extended to all individual differences.

Figure 13.1 delineates how one can classify individual differences into one of the three types. In this endeavor, the first question to ask is: *Is there phenotypic polymorphism?* Do individuals differ in phenotypes? If the answer is "No," if there is no phenotypic polymorphism, then there are obviously no individual differences to talk about and explain. The trait in question is a constant among members of a given species.

If the answer to the first question is "Yes," then there are individual differences to classify and explain. The next question to ask is: *Is there genetic polymorphism?* Do individuals differ in their genotypes that affect the trait (phenotype) in question? Some individual differences are caused by underlying and corresponding genetic differences between individuals, while others are caused by environmental triggers during development that differentially activate the identical genes. If the answer is "Yes," if there is genetic polymorphism, then the individual differences we are talking about are classified as *alternative strategies*. Individuals are genetically different from each other, and individuals who differ in the affected alleles implement and employ different strategies.

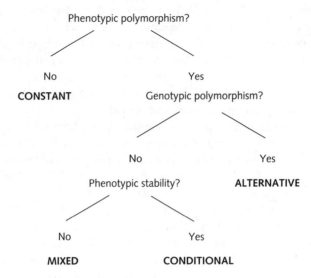

**Figure 13.1**  Typology of individual differences in strategy

If the answer to the second question is "No," if there is no genetic polymorphism, then the next question to ask is: *Is there phenotypic stability?* Do individuals employ the same strategy or tactic repeatedly over time? Some individual differences are temporally stable and the individuals employ the same strategy across situations and over time, while other individual differences are not temporally so stable and the individuals employ different strategies in different situations and at different times. If the answer is "Yes," if there is phenotypic stability, then the individual differences we are talking about are classified as *conditional strategies*. Individuals are genetically identical but respond differently to early developmental conditions and environmental cues. Once a given conditional strategy is adopted, however, individuals continue to employ it over time and across situations.

If the answer to the third question is "No," if there is no phenotypic stability, then the individual differences we are talking about are classified as *mixed strategies*. Individuals engage in a random mixture of strategies and tactics with known frequencies across situations and over time.

Let's say that the phenotype of interest is the mode of reproduction. Is there phenotypic pluralism for this trait (the first question)? Among humans (and most other species), the answer is "No." All humans, for example, reproduce sexually. While there are other species, which reproduce asexually, and still others, which combine sexual and asexual reproduction, for humans there is absolutely no phenotypic pluralism in this trait. So the trait in question is a constant and there are no individual differences.

But what about, say, reproductive strategies among females? Then the answer to the first question—Is there phenotypic pluralism?—is "Yes"; some women pursue a relatively restricted ("Madonna") strategy while others pursue a relatively unrestricted ("whore") strategy (Gangestad & Simpson, 1990).

Female reproductive strategy correlates with the age of menarche; relatively unrestricted women undergo menarche much earlier than relatively restricted women, so that they may start their reproductive career earlier (Belsky et al., 1991). Roughly 30–50 percent of the variance in individual differences in the age of menarche is heritable, while 20–50 percent of the variance is environmental (Ellis, 2004, pp. 922–924). So the answer to the next question—Is there genetic polymorphism?—is both "Yes" and "No." Women are partly different genetically, and their genes determine 50–80 percent of the variance in the age of menarche and reproductive strategy, but environmental conditions in early childhood determine 20–50 percent of the variance even among women who are genetically monomorphic. Women who are genetically different pursue restricted or unrestricted reproductive strategy as *alternative* strategies.

Women who are genetically monomorphic may employ their reproductive strategy stably over their life course (*conditional* strategies) or not (*mixed* strategies). However, Gross (1996, p. 92) notes that "there is no documented case of such a mixed reproductive strategy within a sex." If this is true, then all individual differences in reproductive strategy among women who are genetically monomorphic must be stable over time, and thus they must be conditional strategies. A truly mixed female reproductive strategy would require women to employ a sexually unrestricted strategy some of the time, with some potential sexual partners, and a sexually restricted strategy at other times, with other potential sexual partners. That would indeed be odd.

One of the major determining factors of conditional reproductive strategies among women is father absence; girls whose parents divorce before the girl has reached the age of 5, and who thus grow up without their biological father or with an unrelated stepfather in the household, undergo menarche earlier and are more likely to employ unrestricted sexual strategy later in life (Belsky et al., 1991; Ellis et al., 2003). Note, however, that, in order to determine whether women pursue variant reproductive strategies as *alternative* or as *conditional* adaptive strategies, one would need to look at their genes. In practice, such determination would require behavior genetic methods that control for genetic differences between individuals (Tither & Ellis, 2008).

Table 13.1 summarizes the three types of individual differences. The first two columns ("Genotype" and "Phenotype") recapture Figure 13.1. All individual differences are phenotypically polymorphic; conditional and mixed strategies are genetically monomorphic, while alternative strategies are genetically polymorphic.

**Table 13.1**  Summary of individual differences in strategy

| Strategy | Phenotype | Genotype | Locus of phenotypic variation | Selection mechanism |
|---|---|---|---|---|
| **Conditional** | Polymorphic | Monomorphic | Between individuals (obligate) | Status-dependent |
| **Alternative** | Polymorphic | Polymorphic | Between individuals (obligate) | Frequency-dependent |
| **Mixed** | Polymorphic | Monomorphic | Within individuals (facultative) | Frequency-dependent |

Because both conditional and alternative strategies are temporally and situationally stable, the individual differences in them are *obligate*; individuals do not really have a "choice" in how to behave. In contrast, mixed strategies are temporally and situationally varied, so individuals exercise "choice" (conscious or otherwise) in their behavior. Such individual differences are *facultative*. According to Gross (1996), the mechanism responsible for producing individual differences in conditional strategies is *status-dependent selection*, while for alternative and mixed strategies it is *frequency-dependent selection*.

The major difference between status-dependent selection and frequency-dependent selection as a mechanism for producing individual differences is that *different strategies produced by frequency-dependent selection necessarily have average equal fitnesses (they are equally adaptive on average), while those produced by status-dependent selection need not be*. Under frequency-dependent selection, the variants that are more successful increase in frequency and those that are less successful decrease in frequency until a stable equilibrium is achieved. The classic example of frequency-dependent selection is that of the "hawk" and "dove" in a game (Maynard Smith, 1982). While a hawk does better than a dove in a direct confrontation, the hawks' average fitness decreases if there are too many hawks in the population, and eventually the proportion of doves increases. But if there are too many doves, then the hawks can invade the population, because they are more likely to encounter doves than hawks in such a population. Eventually a stable equilibrium is reached, where hawks and doves have equal average fitnesses.

In status-dependent selection of conditional strategies, the average fitnesses of different variants may not necessarily be equal. A classic example of conditional strategies is offspring sex allocation (Trivers & Willard, 1973). The Trivers–Willard hypothesis (TWH) predicts that, among humans, upper-class families are more likely to have sons, because sons from upper-class families are expected to have greater reproductive success than their sisters. Historically, men from wealthy families could attract a large number of mates (wives, concubines, mistresses), whereas women from wealthy families could only have so many children. The TWH predicts that, in contrast, lower-class families are more likely to have daughters, because their sons would not be expected to attract any mate (and would thus be expected to become total reproductive losers), whereas their daughters could still attain some reproductive success through hypergamy. Figure 13.2 depicts the relationship between social class and the expected reproductive success of sons and daughters.

The TWH posits *conditional* reproductive strategies. Humans are genetically monomorphic—there are no genes that predispose men and women to having more sons or more daughters—but they respond to their social status and become more likely to produce sons if they find themselves in wealthy families and daughters if they find themselves in poor families. Notice that, in Figure 13.2, the average fitnesses of families in different social classes are not equal. Children from upper-class families are on average expected to have greater reproductive success than children from lower-class families, as even daughters from upper-class families (who are expected to have lower reproductive success than their brothers) are still expected to have greater reproductive success than daughters from lower-class families (who are expected to have higher reproductive success than their brothers).

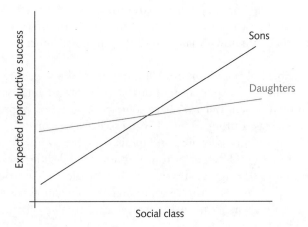

**Figure 13.2** Expected reproductive success of sons and daughters by social class: the Trivers–Willard hypothesis

Under status-dependent selection, all individuals *do the best they can, under the (developmental or environmental) circumstances.* If they happen to be wealthy, they should "bet" on sons; if they happen to be poor, they should "bet" on daughters. However, the conditional strategy of biasing their offspring sex ratios toward daughters among poor families still has lower average fitness than the conditional strategy of biasing their offspring toward sons among wealthy families. Variants in conditional strategies under status-dependent selection need not have equal average fitnesses.

## Evolutionary Explanations of Individual Differences

Individual differences present a theoretical challenge to evolutionary psychology, which focuses on a species-typical universal human nature (or on sex-specific male and female human natures). If all humans (or all men and all women) share a universal human nature, how can we explain persistent individual differences? There are two major approaches to evolutionary explanations of individual differences (Nettle, 2007): the fluctuating selection model and the fitness indicator model.

### The fluctuating selection model

Nettle (2005, 2006) is the primary proponent of the fluctuating selection model of individual differences in personality. The model focuses on *variations in selection pressure*, either over time or by geographical locations, as the cause of individual differences. Different ecological niches select for different personality types. For example, in safe and predictable environments, relatively free of predators, extraversion may be selected, because the exploration of unknown environments may bring benefits in terms of additional resources and mating opportunities. However, the same tendency to explore the environment may harm extraverts in dangerous and unpredictable environments, because extraverts are then more likely to come into contact with predators and other unknown dangers. So such environments may select for introverts.

The same principle holds for temporal variations in the same geographical location. During times of plenty, the exploration of unknown environments may produce relatively little additional benefit but may have some cost (in terms of predation, injury, and accidents), whereas, during times of scarcity, extraverts may be more likely to locate new food sources, undiscovered and undiscoverable by introverts. So different geographical locations and different historical times may select for different personality types. If, however, one aggregates across all ecological niches occupied and all historical times lived by humans, the distribution of personality types would probably turn out to be a normal one, with sufficient variance to allow for individual differences in personality.

## Fitness indicator model

Miller (2000c, 2009) is the primary proponent of the fitness indicator model of individual differences, principally in general intelligence. Miller argues that general intelligence and other fitness indicators such as height and physical attractiveness are indicators of underlying genetic and developmental health, which he calls the $f$ factor. Those who have healthier and higher-quality genes are able to have higher general intelligence, greater height, and greater physical attractiveness than those who have less healthy and lower-quality genes. Since it is difficult for everyone to have perfectly healthy genes, and since different individuals have different mutation loads, which simultaneously affect the quality of their genes and the fitness indicators (the greater the mutation loads, the lower the general intelligence, for example), there must be natural variance in the levels of general intelligence and in the other fitness indicators.

Both men and women may prefer to mate with those who have better genes; so, for example, men prefer to mate with physically attractive women, and women prefer to mate with tall and intelligent men. However, not everyone succeeds in mating with the ideal mates, endowed with the perfect genes. In addition, more mutations are introduced every generation. Hence there will always be natural variations and individual differences in all the fitness indicators, for instance in general intelligence— hence individual differences in all such traits.

## How to Synthesize Evolutionary Psychology and Individual Differences: An Illustration

In this section I discuss in great detail one example of how the fields of evolutionary psychology and individual differences can be merged, using general intelligence as an example of a trait which is simultaneously a domain-specific evolved psychological mechanism and an individual differences variable.

## Evolutionary psychology: the nature and limitations of the human brain

Adaptation, physical or psychological, is designed for and adapted to the conditions of the environment of evolutionary adaptedness, not necessarily to those of the current environment (Tooby & Cosmides, 1990b). This is easiest to see in the case of physical adaptations, such as vision and the color recognition system.

What color is a banana? A banana is yellow in the sunlight and in the moonlight. It is yellow on a sunny day, on a cloudy day, on a rainy day. It is yellow at dawn and at dusk. The color of a banana appears constant to the human eye under all these conditions, despite the fact that the actual wavelengths of the light reflected by the surface of the banana under these varied conditions are different. Objectively, they do not produce the same color all the time. However, the human eye and the color recognition system can compensate for these varied conditions because they all occurred during the course of evolution of the human vision system, and the eye can perceive the objectively varied colors as constantly yellow (Cosmides & Tooby, 1999, pp. 17–19; Shepard, 1994).

So a banana looks yellow under all conditions, *except in a parking lot at night*. Under the sodium vapor lights commonly used to illuminate parking lots, a banana does not appear natural yellow. This is because the sodium vapor lights did not exist in the ancestral environment, during the course of the evolution of the human vision system, and the visual cortex is therefore incapable of compensating for the change they produce.

Fans of the 1989 James Cameron movie *The Abyss* may recall a scene toward the end, where it is impossible for a diver to distinguish colors under artificial lighting in the otherwise total darkness of the deep oceanic basin. Regular viewers of the TV show *Forensic Files* (formerly known as *Medical Detectives*) and other real-life crime shows may further recall that eyewitnesses often misidentify the colors of cars on freeways, leading the police to either rule in or rule out potential suspects incorrectly, because highways and freeways are often lit with sodium vapor lights and other evolutionarily novel sources of illumination.

The same principle that holds for physical adaptations like the color recognition system also holds for psychological adaptations. Pioneers of evolutionary psychology (Crawford, 1993; Symons, 1990; Tooby & Cosmides, 1990b) all recognized that the evolved psychological mechanisms are designed for and adapted to the conditions of the environment of evolutionary adaptedness, not necessarily to the conditions of the current environment. Kanazawa (2004a) systematizes these observations into what he calls the Savanna Principle: *The human brain has difficulty comprehending and dealing with entities and situations that did not exist in the ancestral environment.* Burnham and Johnson (2005, pp. 130–131) refer to the same observation as *the evolutionary legacy hypothesis*, while Hagan and Hammerstein (2006, pp. 341–343) call it *the mismatch hypothesis*.

The Savanna Principle can explain why some otherwise elegant scientific theories of human behavior, such as the subjective expected utility maximization theory and game theory in microeconomics, often fail empirically, because they posit entities and situations that did not exist in the ancestral environment. For example, nearly half the players of one-shot Prisoner's Dilemma games make the theoretically irrational choice to cooperate with their partner (Sally, 1995). The Savanna Principle suggests that this may possibly be because the human brain has difficulty comprehending completely anonymous social exchange and absolutely no possibility of knowing future interactions (which, together, make the game truly one-shot) (Kanazawa, 2004a, pp. 44–45). Neither of these situations existed in the ancestral environment; however, they are crucial for the game-theoretic prediction of universal defection.

Fehr and Henrich (2003) suggest that one-shot encounters and exchanges might have been common in the ancestral environment. In their response to Fehr and Henrich, Hagen and Hammerstein (2006) point out that, even if *one-shot* encounters were common in the ancestral environment, *anonymous* encounters could not have been common, and the game-theoretic prediction of defection in one-shot games requires both non-iteration and anonymity. A lack of anonymity can lead to reputational concerns even in non-repeated exchanges.

As another illustration of the Savanna Principle, individuals who watch certain types of TV shows are more satisfied with their friendships, just as they are if they had more friends, or socialized with them more frequently (Derrick, Gabriel, & Hugenberg, 2009; Kanazawa, 2002). This may possibly be because realistic images of other humans, such as those displayed on television, in movies, videos, and photographs, did not exist in the ancestral environment, where all realistic images of other humans were other humans. As a result, the human brain may have implicit difficulty distinguishing "TV friends" (the characters repeatedly seen on TV shows) from real friends.

Van Beest and Williams's (2006) highly ingenious experiment provides yet another example of the Savanna Principle in operation. In their experiment, human subjects play a variant of a computer game called Cyberball, in which three players interact virtually and toss a ball back and forth between them on their computer screen. In one condition, the subjects are included in a fair share of the ball tosses, whereas in the other condition they are completely excluded from them after a couple of initial tosses. Independently of this manipulation, some subjects are paid when they are included in a ball toss (the "inclusion pays" condition), whereas other subjects are paid when they are excluded from a ball toss (the "exclusion pays" condition). Van Beest and Williams's results show that the subjects are much more satisfied and happier when they are included in the ball tosses than when they are excluded, *regardless* of whether they are in the "inclusion pays" or "exclusion pays" condition. In other words, those who are in the "exclusion pays" condition are happier and more satisfied if they lost money and less happy and satisfied if they made money.

While these results do not make sense from a purely economic perspective, they are perfectly consistent with the prediction of the Savanna Principle. Throughout the course of human evolution, exclusion from a group was *always* costly and inclusion was *always* beneficial. These two factors always covaried throughout evolutionary history, because there were no evil experimental psychologists in the ancestral environment to manipulate them independently. There were no such things as beneficial exclusion or costly inclusion, and the human brain therefore cannot comprehend these categories. It implicitly assumes that all inclusion is beneficial and all exclusion is costly.

Most evolutionary psychologists and biologists concur that humans have not undergone significant evolutionary changes in the last 10,000 years, since the end of the Pleistocene epoch, as the environment during this period has not provided a stable background against which natural and sexual selection can operate over many generations (Miller & Kanazawa, 2007, pp. 25–28). This is the assumption behind the Savanna Principle. More recently, however, some scientists have voiced the opinion that human evolution has continued and even accelerated during the Holocene epoch (Evans et al., 2005; Cochran & Harpending, 2009). While these studies conclusively demonstrate that new alleles have indeed emerged in the human genome since the end of the Pleistocene epoch, the implication and importance of such new alleles for evolutionary psychology are not immediately obvious. In particular, with the sole exception of lactose tolerance, it is not clear whether these new alleles have led to the emergence of new evolved psychological mechanisms in the last 10,000 years.

## Individual differences: the evolution of general intelligence

General intelligence refers to the ability to reason deductively or inductively, think abstractly, use analogies, synthesize information, and apply it to new domains (Gottfredson, 1997; Neisser et al., 1996). The $g$ factor, which is often used synonymously with general intelligence, is a latent variable which emerges in a factor analysis of various cognitive ("IQ") tests. They are not exactly the same thing. $g$ is an *indicator* or *measure* of general intelligence; it's not general intelligence itself.

The concept of general intelligence poses a problem for evolutionary psychology (Chiappe & MacDonald, 2005; Cosmides & Tooby, 2002; Miller, 2000a). Evolutionary psychologists contend that the human brain consists of domain-specific psychological mechanisms, which evolved to solve specific adaptive problems (problems of survival and reproduction) in specific domains. If the contents of the human brain are domain-specific, how can evolutionary psychology explain general intelligence, which is seemingly domain-general?

Miller (2000b, 2000c) equates general intelligence with mating intelligence and explains its emergence as an indicator of underlying genetic fitness in the process of sexual selection. Cosmides and Tooby (2002) explain general intelligence as an emergent exaptation of the sum total of dedicated and domain-specific evolved psychological mechanisms, from which general intelligence receives specific informational contents. Chiappe and MacDonald (2005) suggest that general intelligence evolved as a genuinely domain-general learning mechanism, in the face of the uncertainty and unpredictability of the ancestral environment.

In contrast to these views, Kanazawa (2004b) proposes that what is now known as general intelligence may have originally evolved as a domain-specific adaptation designed to deal with evolutionarily novel, non-recurrent problems. The human brain consists of a large number of domain-specific evolved psychological mechanisms, to solve recurrent adaptive problems. In this sense, our ancestors did not really have to *think* in order to solve such problems. Evolution has already done all the thinking, so to speak, and has equipped the human brain with the appropriate psychological mechanisms, which engender preferences, desires, cognitions, and emotions, and motivate adaptive behavior in the context of the ancestral environment.

Even in the extreme continuity and constancy of the ancestral environment, however, there were likely occasional problems that were evolutionarily novel and non-recurrent, which required our ancestors to think and reason in order to solve. Such problems may have included the following examples:

1  Lightning has struck a tree near the camp and set it on fire. The fire is now spreading to the dry underbrush. What should I do? How could I stop the spread of the fire? How could I and my family escape it? (Since lightning never strikes the same place twice, this is guaranteed to be a non-recurrent problem.)

2  We are in the middle of the severest drought in a hundred years. Nuts and berries at our normal places of gathering, which are usually plentiful, are not growing at all, and animals are scarce as well. We are running out of food because none of our normal sources of food is working. What else can we eat? What else is safe to eat? How else can we procure food?

3  A flash flood has caused the river to swell to several times its normal width, and I am trapped on one side of it while my entire band is on the other side. It is imperative that I rejoin them soon. How can I cross the rapid river? Should I wade across it? Or should I construct some sort of buoyant vehicle to use to get across it? If so, what kind of material should I use? Wood? Stones?

To the extent that these evolutionarily novel, non-recurrent problems happened frequently enough in the ancestral environment (a different problem each time) and had serious enough consequences for survival and reproduction, any genetic mutation that allowed its carriers to think and reason would have been selected for, and what we now call "general intelligence" could have evolved as a domain-specific adaptation for the domain of evolutionarily novel, non-recurrent problems, which did not exist in the ancestral environment and therefore for which there are no dedicated modules.

From this perspective, general intelligence may have become universally important in modern life (Gottfredson, 1997; Herrnstein & Murray, 1994; Jensen, 1998) only because our current environment is almost entirely evolutionarily novel. The new theory suggests, and empirical data confirm, that more intelligent individuals are better than less intelligent individuals at solving problems *only if* these are evolutionarily novel. More intelligent individuals are *not better* than less intelligent individuals at solving evolutionarily familiar problems, such as those in the domains of mating, parenting, interpersonal relationships, and wayfinding (Kanazawa, 2004b, 2007), *unless* the solution involves evolutionarily novel entities. For example, more intelligent individuals are no better than less intelligent individuals at finding and keeping mates, but they may be better at using computer dating services. Three recent studies, employing widely varied methods, have all shown that the average intelligence of a population appears to be a strong function of the evolutionary novelty of its environment (Ash & Gallup, 2007; Bailey & Geary, 2009; Kanazawa, 2008).

## Synthesis: how general intelligence modifies the evolutionary limitations of the human brain

The logical conjunction of the Savanna Principle and the theory of the evolution of general intelligence suggests a qualification of the Savanna Principle. If general intelligence evolved to deal with evolutionarily novel problems, then the human brain's difficulty in comprehending and dealing with entities and situations that did not exist in the ancestral environment (proposed in the Savanna Principle) should interact with general intelligence, such that the Savanna Principle holds stronger among less intelligent individuals than among more intelligent individuals. More intelligent individuals should be better able to comprehend and deal with evolutionarily novel (but *not* evolutionarily familiar) entities and situations than less intelligent individuals.

Thus the *Savanna–IQ Interaction Hypothesis* (Kanazawa, 2010) suggests that less intelligent individuals have greater difficulty comprehending and dealing with evolutionarily novel entities and situations that did not exist in the ancestral environment than more intelligent individuals do; in contrast, general intelligence does not affect individuals' ability to comprehend and deal with evolutionarily familiar entities and situations that existed in the ancestral environment.

Evolutionarily novel entities that more intelligent individuals are better able to comprehend and deal with may include ideas and lifestyles, which form the basis of their values and preferences; it would be difficult for individuals to prefer or value something that they cannot truly comprehend. Hence, applied to the domain of preferences and values, the hypothesis suggests that more intelligent individuals are more likely to acquire and espouse evolutionarily novel preferences and values that did not exist in the ancestral environment than less intelligent individuals are; but general intelligence has no effect on the acquisition and espousal of evolutionarily familiar preferences and values that existed in the ancestral environment (Kanazawa, 2010).

## Empirical evidence for the Savanna–IQ Interaction Hypothesis

The Savanna–IQ Interaction Hypothesis, derived from the synthesis of evolutionary psychology and individual differences, offers one potential way to account for some known individual differences and to predict novel ones. There has been accumulating evidence for the hypothesis in numerous and varied domains.

*TV Friends* Consistent with the Savanna Principle, Kanazawa (2002) and Derrick et al. (2009) show that individuals who watch certain types of TV shows are more satisfied with their own friendships, suggesting that they may possibly have implicit difficulty distinguishing the evolutionarily novel realistic images of actors, which they repeatedly see on TV, from their real friends. Kanazawa's (2006) re-analysis of the same data from the General Social Surveys shows, however, that this seeming difficulty in distinguishing between "TV friends" and real friends appears to be limited to men and women below median intelligence. Those who are above median in intelligence do not report greater satisfaction with their own friendships as a function of watching more TV; only those below median intelligence do. This seems to suggest that the evolutionary constraints on the brain suggested by the Savanna Principle, whereby individuals have implicit difficulty recognizing realistic electronic images on TV for what they are, appear to be weaker or altogether absent among more intelligent individuals. Since truly enjoying the experience of watching TV requires suspension of disbelief and *not* really understanding that characters repeatedly seen on

the screen are highly paid actors hired to play scripted roles, this finding can potentially explain why less intelligent individuals tend to enjoy the experience of watching
TV more than more intelligent individuals.

*Political Ideology*   It is difficult precisely to define a whole school of political ideology, but one may reasonably define liberalism (as opposed to conservatism) in the
contemporary United States as *the genuine concern for the welfare of genetically unrelated others and the willingness to contribute larger proportions of private resources for
the welfare of such others.* In the modern political and economic context, this willingness usually translates into paying higher proportions of individual incomes in taxes
toward the government and its social welfare programs.

Defined as such, liberalism is evolutionarily novel. Humans (like other species) are
evolutionarily designed to be altruistic toward their genetic kin (Hamilton, 1964),
their repeated exchange partners (Trivers, 1971), and members of their deme (a
group of intermarrying individuals) or ethnic group (Whitmeyer, 1997). They are
not designed to be altruistic toward an indefinite number of complete strangers,
whom they are not likely ever to meet or exchange with. This is largely because
our ancestors lived in small bands of 50–150 genetically related individuals, and
large cities and nations with thousands and millions of people are themselves evolutionarily novel.

The examination of the 10-volume compendium *The encyclopedia of world cultures*
(Levinson, 1991–1995), which describes *all* human cultures known to anthropology
(more than 1,500) in great detail, as well as extensive primary ethnographies of traditional societies (Chagnon, 1992; Cronk, 2004; Hill & Hurtado, 1996; Whitten,
1976), reveals that liberalism as defined above is absent in these traditional cultures.
While sharing of resources, especially food, is quite common and often normatively
prescribed among hunter–gatherer tribes, and while trade with neighboring tribes
often takes place (Ridley, 1996), there is no evidence that people in contemporary
hunter–gatherer bands *freely* share resources with *members of other tribes.* Because all
members of a hunter–gatherer tribe are genetic kin, or at the very least repeated
exchange partners (friends and allies for life), sharing of resources among them does
not qualify as an expression of liberalism as defined above. Given its absence in the
contemporary hunter–gatherer tribes, which are often used as modern-day analogs
of our ancestral life, it may be reasonable to infer that sharing of resources with total
strangers whom one has never met or is not ever likely to meet—liberalism—was not
part of our ancestral life. Liberalism may therefore be evolutionarily novel, and the
hypothesis would predict that more intelligent individuals are more likely to espouse
liberalism as a value than less intelligent individuals are.

Analyses of large representative American samples from the National Longitudinal
Study of Adolescent Health (Add Health) and from the General Social Surveys (GSS)
confirm this prediction (Kanazawa, 2010). Net of age, sex, race, education, earnings,
and religion, more intelligent individuals are more liberal than their less intelligent
counterparts. For example, among the Add Health respondents, those who identify
themselves as "very liberal" in early adulthood have a mean childhood IQ of 106.4,
whereas those who identify themselves as "very conservative" in early adulthood have
a mean childhood IQ of 94.8. Even though past studies show that women are more

liberal than men (Lake & Breglio, 1992; Shapiro & Mahajan, 1986; Wirls, 1986), and that blacks are more liberal than whites (Kluegel & Smith, 1989; Sundquist, 1983), the analyses show that the effect of childhood intelligence on adult liberalism is twice as large as the effect of sex or race.

*Religiosity* While religion is a cultural universal and its practice is observed in every known human society (Brown, 1991), recent evolutionary psychological theories (Atran, 2002; Boyer, 2001; Guthrie, 1993; Haselton & Nettle, 2006; Kirkpatrick, 2005) suggest that religiosity may not be an adaptation in itself, but may be a byproduct of other evolved psychological mechanisms, variously called "animistic bias" (Guthrie, 1993) or "the agency-detector mechanisms" (Atran, 2002). These theories contend that the human brain has been selected to *overinfer* agency—personal, animate, and intentional forces—behind otherwise natural phenomena whose exact causes cannot be known. This is because *overinferring* agency—and making a Type I error of being a bit paranoid—is more adaptive and conducive to survival than *underinferring* it—and making a Type II error and, as a result, being killed and maimed by predators and enemies who were incorrectly assumed not to exist. Religiosity—belief in higher powers—may be a byproduct of such overinference of agency behind natural phenomena.

If these theories are correct, then it means that religiosity—belief in higher powers—may have an evolutionary origin. It is evolutionarily familiar and natural to believe in God, and evolutionarily novel not to be religious. Out of more than 1,500 distinct cultures throughout the world described in *The encyclopedia of world cultures* (Levinson, 1991–1995), only 19 contain any reference to atheism. Not only do all these 19 cultures exist far outside of our ancestral home in sub-Saharan Africa, but all 19, without an exception, are former Communist societies. There are no non-former-Communist cultures described in *The encyclopedia* as containing any significant segment of atheists. Nor is there any reference to individuals who do not subscribe to the local religion in any of the monograph-length ethnographies consulted above (Chagnon, 1992; Cronk, 2004; Hill & Hurtado, 1996; Whitten, 1976).

It may therefore be reasonable to conclude that atheism may not be part of the universal human nature, and widespread practice of atheism may have been a recent product of Communism in the twentieth century. The Hypothesis would therefore suggest that more intelligent individuals are more likely to be atheist than less intelligent individuals. Consistent with the prediction, analyses of the Add Health and GSS data show that, net of the same control variables as in the analyses of liberalism, more intelligent individuals are more likely to be atheist than less intelligent individuals (Kanazawa, 2010). For example, among the Add Health respondents, those who identify themselves as "not at all religious" in early adulthood have a mean childhood IQ of 103.1, whereas those who identify themselves as "very religious" in early adulthood have a mean childhood IQ of 97.1. Even though past studies show that women are much more religious than men (Miller & Hoffmann, 1995; Miller & Stark, 2002), the analyses show that the effect of childhood intelligence on adult religiosity is twice as large as that of sex. It is remarkable that childhood intelligence is a significant and strong determinant of adult religiosity when religion itself is statistically controlled for (with "no religion" as the reference category).

*Sexual Exclusivity (only for Men)*  Throughout evolutionary history, humans were mildly polygynous. A species-typical degree of polygyny correlates with the extent of sexual dimorphism in size; the more sexually dimorphic the species is (where males are larger than females), the more polygynous the species (Alexander, Hoogland, Howard, Noonan, & Sherman, 1977; Leutenegger & Kelly, 1977). This is either because males of polygynous species become larger in order to compete with other males and monopolize females (Alexander et al., 1977; Leutenegger & Kelly, 1977) or because females of polygynous species become smaller in order to mature early and start mating (Harvey & Bennet, 1985; Kanazawa & Novak, 2005; Pickford, 1986). Thus strictly monogamous gibbons are sexually monomorphic (males and females are about the same size), whereas highly polygynous gorillas are equally highly sexually dimorphic in size. On this scale, humans are *mildly* polygynous, not as polygynous as gorillas, but not strictly monogamous like gibbons.

Consistent with this comparative evidence, an analysis of the Standard Cross-Cultural Sample (Murdock, 1967) shows that an overwhelming majority of traditional cultures in the world (83.39 percent) practice polygyny, with only 16.14 percent practicing monogamy and 0.47 percent practicing polyandry. Once again, while present-day hunter–gatherer societies are not exactly the same as our ancestors in every detail, they are our best analogs available for us to study. The fact that polygyny is widespread in such societies, combined with the comparative evidence discussed above, strongly suggests that our ancestors might have practiced polygyny throughout most of human evolutionary history.

Of course, polygynous marriage in any society is mathematically limited to a minority of men; most men in polygynous societies either have only one wife or no wife at all. However, at least some men throughout evolutionary history were polygynous, and we are disproportionately descended from polygynous men with a large number of wives (because they had more children than monogamous or wifeless men). Nor does the human evolutionary history of mild polygyny mean that women always remained faithful to their legitimate husband. There is anatomical evidence to suggest that women have always been mildly promiscuous (Baker & Bellis, 1995; Gallup et al., 2003).

Under polygyny, one man is married to several women, so a woman in a polygynous marriage still (legitimately) mates only with one man, just as a woman in a monogamous marriage does. In contrast, a man in a polygynous marriage concurrently mates with several women, quite unlike a man in a monogamous marriage, who mates with only one woman. So, throughout human evolutionary history, men have mated with several women while women have mated with only one man. Sexual exclusivity prescribed under socially imposed monogamy today is therefore evolutionarily novel for men, but not for women. The hypothesis would therefore suggest that more intelligent men may value sexual exclusivity more than less intelligent men, but intelligence may not affect women's likelihood of espousing the value of sexual exclusivity.

Consistent with this prediction, the analysis of Add Health data shows that, net of age, race, education, earnings, religion, and number of marriages, more intelligent boys are more likely to grow up to value sexual exclusivity in early adulthood than less intelligent boys, but intelligence does not affect girls' value on sexual exclusivity in early adulthood. The effect of intelligence on the value of sexual exclusivity is more than four times as strong among men than among women.

*Circadian Rhythms* Choice is not incompatible with or antithetical to genetic influence. As long as heritability $h^2 < 1.0$, individuals can still exercise some choice within broad genetic constraints. For example, political ideology has been shown to be partially genetically influenced; some individuals are genetically predisposed to be liberal or conservative (Alford, Funk, & Hibbing, 2005; Eaves & Eysenck, 1974). Nonetheless, individuals can still choose to be liberal or conservative within broad genetic constraints, and, as discussed above, more intelligent individuals are more likely to choose to be liberal than less intelligent individuals.

Another example of choice within genetic constraints is circadian rhythms— whether one is a "morning lark" or a "night owl." Virtually all species in nature, from single-cell organisms to mammals, including humans, exhibit a daily cycle of activity called the circadian rhythm (Vitaterna, Takahashi, & Turek, 2001). The circadian rhythm in mammals is regulated by two clusters of nerve cells called the suprachiasmatic nuclei (SCN) in the anterior hypothalamus (Klein, Moore, & Reppert, 1991). Geneticists have by now identified a set of genes that regulate the SCN, and thus the circadian rhythm, among mammals (King & Takahashi, 2000). "Humans, however, have the unique ability to cognitively override their internal biological clock and its rhythmic outputs" (Vitaterna et al., 2001, p. 90).

While there are some individual differences in the circadian rhythm, where some individuals are more nocturnal than others, humans are basically a diurnal (as opposed to nocturnal) species. Humans rely very heavily on vision for navigation but, unlike genuinely nocturnal species, they cannot see in the dark or under little lighting, and our ancestors did not have artificial lighting during the night until the domestication of fire. Any human in the ancestral environment up and about during the night would have been at risk of predation by nocturnal predators.

Once again, ethnographic evidence from traditional societies available from *The encyclopedia of world cultures* (Levinson, 1991–1995) and from extensive ethnographies (Chagnon, 1992; Cronk, 2004; Hill & Hurtado, 1996; Lee, 1979; Whitten, 1976) suggests that people in traditional societies usually rise shortly before dawn and go to sleep shortly after dusk, to take full advantage of the natural light provided by the sun. There is no indication that there are any sustained nocturnal activities, other than occasional conversations and singing, in these tribes. It is therefore reasonable to infer that our ancestors must also have limited their daily activities to daylight, and sustained nocturnal activities are largely evolutionarily novel. The hypothesis would therefore predict that more intelligent individuals are more likely to be nocturnal than less intelligent individuals.

Analysis of a large representative sample from Add Health confirms this prediction (Kanazawa & Perina, 2009). Net of age, sex, race, marital status, parenthood, education, earnings, religion, whether or not currently a student, and number of hours worked in a typical week, more intelligent children grow up to be more nocturnal as adults than less intelligent children. Compared to their less intelligent counterparts, more intelligent individuals go to bed later on weeknights (when they have to get up at a certain time the next day) and on weekend (when they don't), and they wake up later on weekdays (but not on weekend, for which the positive effect of childhood intelligence on nocturnality is not statistically significant). For example, those with childhood IQ of less than 75 go to bed around 23:42 on weeknight in early adulthood, whereas those with childhood IQ of over 125 go to bed around 00:30.

*Crime and Punishment*   Criminologists have long known that criminals on average have lower intelligence than the general population (Wilson & Herrnstein, 1985; Herrnstein & Murray, 1994). From the perspective of the hypothesis, there are two important points to note (Kanazawa, 2009). Much of what we call interpersonal crime today, such as murder, assault, robbery, and theft, were probably routine means of intra-sexual male competition in the ancestral environment. This is how men likely competed for resources and mating opportunities for much of human evolutionary history; they beat up and killed each other, and they stole from each other if they could get away with it. We may infer this from the fact that behavior that would be classified as criminal if engaged in by humans, like murder, rape, assault, and theft, are quite common among other species (Ellis, 1998), including other primates such as chimpanzees (de Waal, 1989), bonobos (de Waal, 1992), and capuchin monkeys (de Waal, Luttrell, & Canfield, 1993).

At the same time, the institutions that control, detect, and punish criminal behavior in society today—the police, the courts, the prisons—are all evolutionarily novel; there was very little formal third-party enforcement of norms in the ancestral environment, only second-party enforcement (victims and their kin and allies) or informal third-party enforcement (ostracism). Thus it makes sense, from the perspective of the Savanna–IQ Interaction Hypothesis, that men with low intelligence may be more likely to resort to evolutionarily familiar means of competition for resources (theft rather than full-time employment) and mating opportunities (rape rather than computer dating) and not to comprehend fully the consequences of criminal behavior imposed by evolutionarily novel entities of law enforcement.

## General intelligence and openness to experience

Research in personality psychology has shown that one of the five-factor model personality factors—openness to experience—is significantly positively (albeit moderately) correlated with intelligence (Ackerman & Heggestad, 1997). The similarity and overlap between intelligence and openness are apparent from the fact that some researchers call this personality factor "intellect" rather than "openness" (Goldberg, 1992; McRae, 1994). While it is widely accepted by personality psychologists that intelligence and openness covary across individuals, it is not known *why* (Chamorro-Premuzic & Furnham, 2006). The Savanna–IQ Interaction Hypothesis can potentially provide one explanation for why more intelligent individuals are more open to new experiences and are therefore more prone to seek novelty. It is instructive to note from this perspective that only the actions, ideas, and values facets of openness to experience are significantly correlated with general intelligence, not the fantasy, esthetics, and feelings facets (Gilles, Stough, & Loukomitis, 2004; Holland, Dollinger, Holland, & MacDonald, 1995).

At the same time, the hypothesis suggests a possible need to refine the concept of novelty and to distinguish between *evolutionary novelty* (entities and situations that did not exist in the ancestral environment) and *experiential novelty* (entities and situations that individuals have not personally experienced in their own lifetime). While the five-factor model does not specify the type of novelty that open individuals are more likely to seek, the Savanna–IQ Interaction Hypothesis suggests that more intelligent individuals are more likely to seek only evolutionary novelty, not necessarily experiential novelty.

For example, everybody who is alive in the United States today has lived their entire lives in a strictly monogamous society, and very few contemporary Americans have any personal experiences with polygyny. Therefore monogamy is *experientially familiar* for most Americans, whereas polygyny is *experientially novel*. The five-factor model may therefore predict that more intelligent individuals are more likely to be open to polygyny as an experientially novel idea or action.

In contrast, humans have been mildly polygynous throughout their evolutionary history (Alexander et al., 1977; Leutenegger & Kelly, 1977), and socially imposed monogamy is a relatively recent historical phenomenon (Kanazawa & Still, 1999). Therefore polygyny is *evolutionarily familiar* whereas monogamy is *evolutionarily novel*. The Savanna–IQ Interaction Hypothesis would therefore predict that more intelligent individuals are more likely to be open to monogamy and less open to polygyny. In fact, as discussed above, the evidence suggests that more intelligent men are more likely to value monogamy and sexual exclusivity than less intelligent men (Kanazawa, 2010).

As another example, for most contemporary Americans, traditional names derived from the Bible, such as John and Mary, are experientially more familiar than untraditional names like OrangeJello and LemonJello (Levitt & Dubner, 2005). So the five-factor model may predict that more intelligent individuals are more likely to name their children untraditional names like OrangeJello and LemonJello than less intelligent individuals. From the perspective of the Hypothesis, however, both John and OrangeJello are equally evolutionarily novel (because the Bible itself and all the traditional names derived from it are evolutionarily novel), so it would not predict that more intelligent individuals are more likely to name their children untraditional names. In fact, there is no evidence at all that more intelligent individuals are more likely to prefer untraditional names for their children (Fryer & Levitt, 2004; Lieberson & Bell, 1992).

The Savanna–IQ Interaction Hypothesis underscores the need to distinguish between evolutionary novelty and experiential novelty. It can potentially explain why more intelligent individuals are more likely to seek evolutionary novelty, but not necessarily experiential novelty. It further suggests that the established correlation between openness and intelligence may be limited to the domain of evolutionary novelty, not necessarily encompassing experiential novelty, but the current measures of openness do not adequately address this proposal.

## Conclusion

Focused as it is on the central theoretical concept of the species-typical universal human nature (or sex-typical male human nature and female human nature), evolutionary psychology has not traditionally dealt well with individual differences. This is rapidly changing, however. Nettle's (2005, 2006) fluctuating selection model and Miller's (2000c, 2009) fitness indicator model are two primary evolutionary models of individual differences. Kanazawa's (2010) work on the Savanna–IQ Interaction Hypothesis also illustrates how the two fields of evolutionary psychology and individual differences can be merged, by focusing on the effect of general intelligence on individual differences in preferences and values. The new field of *evolutionary differential psychology* or *evolutionary personality psychology* (Buss, 1991) is wide open and awaits further theoretical and empirical contributions.

# References

Ackerman, P. L., & Heggestad, E. D. (1997). Intelligence, personality, and interests: Evidence for overlapping traits. *Psychological Bulletin, 121,* 219–245.

Alexander, R. D., Hoogland, J. L., Howard, R. D., Noonan, K. M., & Sherman, P. W. (1979). Sexual dimorphisms and breeding systems in pinnipeds, ungulates, primates and humans. In N. A. Chagnon & W. Irons (Eds.), *Evolutionary biology and human social behavior: An anthropological perspective* (pp. 402–435). North Scituate, RI: Duxbury Press.

Alford, J. R., Funk, C. L., & Hibbing, J. R. (2005). Are political orientations genetically transmitted? *American Political Science Review, 99,* 153–167.

Ash, J., & Gallup, Jr., G. G. (2007). Paleoclimatic variation and brain expansion during human evolution. *Human Nature, 18,* 109–124.

Atran, S. (2002). *In gods we trust: The evolutionary landscape of religion.* Oxford: Oxford University Press.

Bailey, J. M. (1998). Can behavior genetics contribute to evolutionary behavioral science? In C. Crawford & D. L. Crebs (Eds.), *Handbook of evolutionary psychology: Ideas, issues, and applications* (pp. 211–233). Mahwah, NJ: Lawrence Erlbaum Associates.

Bailey, D. H., & Geary, D. C. (2009). Hominid brain evolution: Testing climatic, ecological, and social competition models. *Human Nature, 20,* 67–79.

Bailey, A., Le Couteur, A., Gottesman, I., & Bolton, P. (1995). Autism as a strongly genetic disorder: Evidence from a British twin study. *Psychological Medicine, 25,* 63–77.

Baker, R. R., & Bellis, M. A. (1995). *Human sperm competition: Copulation, masturbation and infidelity.* London: Chapman and Hall.

Baron-Cohen, S. (1995). *Mind blindness: An essay on autism and theory of mind.* Cambridge, MA: MIT Press.

Belsky, J., Steinberg, L., & Draper, P. (1991). Childhood experiences, interpersonal development, and reproductive strategy: An evolutionary theory of socialization. *Child Development, 62,* 647–670.

Borsboom, D., & Dolan, C. V. (2006). Why *g* is not an adaptation: A comment on Kanazawa (2004). *Psychological Review, 113,* 433–437.

Boyer, P. (2001). *Religion explained: The evolutionary origins of religious thought.* New York: Basic Books.

Brown, D. E. (1991). *Human universals.* New York: McGraw-Hill.

Burnham, T. C., & Johnson, D. D. P. (2005). The biological and evolutionary logic of human cooperation. *Analyse und Kritik, 27,* 113–135.

Buss, D. M. (1991). Evolutionary personality psychology. *Annual Reviews of Psychology, 42,* 459–491.

Buss, D. M. (1995). Evolutionary psychology: A new paradigm for psychological science. *Psychological Inquiry, 6,* 1–30.

Buss, D. M., & Greiling, H. (1999). Adaptive individual differences. *Journal of Personality*, *67*, 209–243.

Chagnon, N. (1992). *Yanomamö* (4th ed.). Fort Worth, TX: Harcourt Brace Jovanovich.

Chamorro-Premuzic, T., & Furnham, A. (2006). Intellectual competence and the intelligent personality: A third way in differential psychology. *Review of General Psychology*, *10*, 251–267.

Chiappe, D., & MacDonald, K. (2005). The evolution of domain-general mechanisms in intelligence and learning. *Journal of General Psychology*, *132*, 5–40.

Cochran, G., & Harpending, H. (2009). *The 10,000 year explosion: How civilization accelerated human evolution*. New York: Basic Books.

Cosmides, L. (1989). The logic of social exchange: Has natural selection shaped how humans reason? Studies with the Wason Selection Task. *Cognition*, *31*, 187–276.

Cosmides, L., & Tooby, J. (1999). What is evolutionary psychology? Available at www.psych.ucsb.edu/research/cep/254/WEP254.PDF.

Cosmides, L., & Tooby, J. (2002). Unraveling the enigma of human intelligence: Evolutionary psychology and the multimodular mind. In R. J. Sternberg & J. C. Kaufman (Eds.), *The evolution of intelligence* (pp. 145–198). Mahwah, NJ: Lawrence Erlbaum Associates.

Crawford, C. B. (1993). The future of sociobiology: Counting babies or proximate mechanisms? *Trends in Ecology and Evolution*, *8*, 183–186.

Cronk, L. (2004). *From Mukogodo to Maasai: Ethnicity and cultural change in Kenya*. Boulder, CO: Westview.

Derrick, J. L., Gabriel, S., & Hugenberg, K. (2009). Social surrogacy: How favored television programs provide the experience of belonging. *Journal of Experimental Social Psychology*, *45*, 352–362.

Dunbar, R. I. M. (2005). Why are good writers so rare? An evolutionary perspective on literature. *Journal of Cultural and Evolutionary Psychology*, *3*, 7–21.

Eaves, L. J., & Eysenck, H. J. (1974). Genetics and the development of social attitudes. *Nature*, *249*, 288–289.

Ellis, B. J. (2004). Timing of pubertal maturation in girls: An integrated life history approach. *Psychological Bulletin*, *130*, 920–958.

Ellis, B. J., Bates, J. E., Dodge, K. A., Fergusson, D. M., Horwood, L. J., Pettit, G. S., & Woodward, L. (2003). Does father absence place daughters at special risk for early sexual activity and teenage pregnancy? *Child Development*, *74*, 801–821.

Ellis, L. (1998). Neodarwinian theories of violent criminality and antisocial behavior: Photographic evidence from nonhuman animals and a review of the literature. *Aggression and Violent Behavior*, *3*, 61–110.

Evans, P. D., Gilbert, S. L., Mekel-Bobrov, N., Vallender, E. J., Anderson, J. R., Vaez-Azizi, L. M., Tishkoff, S. A., Hudson, R. R., & Lahn, B. T. (2005). Microcephalin, a gene regulating brain size, continues to evolve adaptively in humans. *Science*, *309*, 1717–1720.

Fehr, E., & Henrich, J. (2003). Is strong reciprocity a maladaptation? On the evolutionary foundations of human altruism. In P. Hammerstein (Ed.), *Genetic and cultural evolution of cooperation* (pp. 55–82). Cambridge, MA: MIT Press.

Folstein, S. E., & Rutter, M. L. (1988). Autism: Familial aggregation and genetic implications. *Journal of Autism and Developmental Disorders*, *18*, 3–30.

Fryer, Jr., R. G., & Levitt, S. D. (2004). The causes and consequences of distinctly black names. *Quarterly Journal of Economics*, *119*, 767–805.

Gallup, Jr., G. G., Burch, R. L., Zappieri, M. L., Parvez, R. A., Stockwell, M. L., & Davis, J. A. (2003). The human penis as a semen displacement device. *Evolution and Human Behavior*, *24*, 277–289.

Gangestad, S. W., & Simpson, J. A. (1990). Toward an evolutionary history of female socio-sexual variation. *Journal of Personality, 58,* 69–96.

Gangestad, S. W., & Simpson, J. A. (2000). The evolution of human mating: Trade-offs and strategic pluralism. *Behavioral and Brain Sciences, 23,* 573–644.

Gilles, G. E., Stough, C., & Loukomitis, S. (2004). Openness, intelligence, and self-report intelligence. *Intelligence, 32,* 133–143.

Goldberg, L. R. (1992). The development of markers for the Big-Five factor structure. *Psychological Assessment, 4,* 26–42.

Gottfredson, L. S. (1997). Why *g* matters: The complexity of everyday life. *Intelligence, 24,* 79–132.

Gross, M. R. (1996). Alternative reproductive strategies and tactics: Diversity within sexes. *Trends in Evolution and Ecology, 11,* 92–98.

Guthrie, S. E. (1993). *Faces in the clouds: A new theory of religion.* New York: Oxford University Press.

Hagen, E. H., & Hammerstein, P. (2006). Game theory and human evolution: A critique of some recent interpretations of experimental games. *Theoretical Population Biology, 69,* 339–348.

Hamilton, W. D. (1964). Genetical evolution of social behavior. *Journal of Theoretical Biology, 7,* 1–52.

Harvey, P. H., & Bennett, P. M. (1985). Sexual dimorphism and reproductive strategies. In J. Ghesquiere, R. D. Martin, & F. Newcombe (Eds.), *Human sexual dimorphism* (pp. 43–59). London: Taylor and Francis.

Haselton, M. G., & Nettle, D. (2006). The paranoid optimist: An integrative evolutionary model of cognitive biases. *Personality and Social Psychology Review, 10,* 47–66.

Herrnstein, R. J., & Murray, C. (1994). *The bell curve: Intelligence and class structure in American life.* New York: Free Press.

Hill, K., & Hurtado, A. M. (1996). *Ache life history: The ecology and demography of a foraging people.* New York: Aldine.

Holland, D. C., Dollinger, S. J., Holland, C. J., & MacDonald, D. A. (1995). The relationship between psychometric intelligence and the five-factor model of personality in a rehabilitation sample. *Journal of Clinical Psychology, 51,* 79–88.

Jensen, A. R. (1998). *The g factor: The science of mental ability.* Westport, CT: Praeger.

Kanazawa, S. (2002). Bowling with our imaginary friends. *Evolution and Human Behavior, 23,* 167–171.

Kanazawa, S. (2004a). The Savanna Principle. *Managerial and Decision Economics, 25,* 41–54.

Kanazawa, S. (2004b). General intelligence as a domain-specific adaptation. *Psychological Review, 111,* 512–523.

Kanazawa, S. (2006). Why the less intelligent may enjoy television more than the more intelligent. *Journal of Cultural and Evolutionary Psychology, 4,* 27–36.

Kanazawa, S. (2007). Mating intelligence and general intelligence as independent constructs. In G. Geher & G. Miller (Eds.), *Mating intelligence: Sex, relationships, and the mind's reproductive system* (pp. 283–309). Mahwah, NJ: Lawrence Erlbaum Associates.

Kanazawa, S. (2008). Temperature and evolutionary novelty as forces behind the evolution of general intelligence. *Intelligence, 36,* 99–108.

Kanazawa, S. (2009). Evolutionary psychology and crime. In A. Walsh & K. M. Beaver (Eds.), *Biosocial criminology: New directions in theory and research* (pp. 90–110). New York: Routledge.

Kanazawa, S. (2010). Why liberals and atheists are more intelligent. *Social Psychology Quarterly, 73,* 33–57.

Kanazawa, S., & Novak, D. L. (2005). Human sexual dimorphism in size may be triggered by environmental cues. *Journal of Biosocial Science, 37*, 657–665.

Kanazawa, S., & Perina, K. (2009). Why night owls are more intelligent. *Personality and Individual Differences, 47*, 685–690.

Kanazawa, S., & Still, M. C. (1999). Why monogamy? *Social Forces, 78*, 25–50.

King, D. P., & Takahashi, J. S. (2000). Molecular genetics of circadian rhythms in mammals. *Annual Review of Neuroscience, 23*, 713–742.

Kirkpatrick, L. A. (2005). *Attachment, evolution, and the psychology of religion*. New York: Guilford Press.

Klein, D. C., Moore, R. Y., & Reppert, S. M. (1991). *Suprachiasmatic nucleus: The mind's clock*. New York: Oxford University Press.

Kluegel, J. R., & Smith, E. R. (1986). *Beliefs about inequality: Americans' view of what is and what ought to be*. New York: Aldine.

Lake, C. C., & Breglio, V. J. (1992). Different voices, different views: The politics of gender. In P. Ries & A. J. Stone (Eds.), *The American woman, 1992–93: A status report* (pp. 178–201). New York: Norton.

Leutenegger, W., & Kelly, J. T. (1977). Relationship of sexual dimorphism in canine size and body size to social, behavioral, and ecological correlates in anthropoid primates. *Primates, 18*, 117–136.

Levinson, D. (Editor in Chief) (1991–1995). *Encyclopedia of world cultures* (10 vols.). Boston, MA: G. K. Hall.

Levitt, S. D., & Dubner, S. J. (2005). *Freakonomics: A rogue economist explores the hidden side of everything*. London: Penguin.

Lieberson, S., & Bell, E. O. (1992). Children's first names: An empirical study of social taste. *American Journal of Sociology, 98*, 511–554.

MacDonald, K. (1995). Evolution, the five-factor model, and levels of personality. *Journal of Personality, 63*, 525–567.

Maynard Smith, J. (1982). *Evolution and the theory of games*. Cambridge: Cambridge University Press.

McRae, R. R. (1994). Openness to experience: Expanding the boundaries of Factor V. *European Journal of Personality, 8*, 251–272.

Miller, A. S., & Hoffmann, J. P. (1995). Risk and religion: An explanation of gender differences in religiosity. *Journal for the Scientific Study of Religion, 34*, 63–75.

Miller, A. S., & Kanazawa, S. (2007). *Why beautiful people have more daughters*. New York: Penguin.

Miller, A. S., & Stark, R. (2002). Gender and religiousness: Can socialization explanations be saved? *American Journal of Sociology, 107*, 1399–1423.

Miller, G. F. (2000a). How to keep our metatheories adaptive: Beyond Cosmides, Tooby, and Lakatos. *Psychological Inquiry, 11*, 42–46.

Miller, G. F. (2000b). Sexual selection for indicators of intelligence. In G. R. Bock, J. A. Goode, & K. Webb (Eds.), *The nature of intelligence* (pp. 260–275). New York: John Wiley.

Miller, G. F. (2000c). *The mating mind: How sexual choice shaped the evolution of human nature*. New York: Doubleday.

Miller, G. F. (2009). *Spent: Sex, evolution, and consumer behavior*. New York: Viking.

Murdock, G. P. (1967). *Culture and society*. Pittsburgh, PA: University of Pittsburgh Press.

Neisser, U., Boodoo, G., Bouchard, Jr., T. J., Boykin, A. W., Brody, N., Ceci, S. J., Halpern, D. F., Loehlin, J. C., Perloff, R., Sternberg, R. J., & Urbina, S. (1996). Intelligence: Known and unknowns. *American Psychologist, 51*, 77–101.

Nettle, D. (2005). An evolutionary approach to the extraversion continuum. *Evolution and Human Behavior, 26*, 363–373.

Nettle, D. (2006). The evolution of personality variation in humans and other animals. *American Psychologist, 61,* 622–631.

Nettle, D. (2007). Individual differences. In R. I. M. Dunbar & L. Barrett (Eds.), *Oxford handbook of evolutionary psychology* (pp. 479–490). Oxford: Oxford University Press.

Pickford, M. (1986). On the origins of body size dimorphism in primates. In M. Pickford & B. Chiarelli (Eds.), *Sexual dimorphism in living and fossil primates* (pp. 77–91). Florence: Il Sedicesimo.

Ridley, M. (1996). *The origins of virtue: Human instincts and the evolution of cooperation.* New York: Viking.

Sally, D. (1995). Conversation and cooperation in social dilemmas: A meta-analysis of experiments from 1958 to 1992. *Rationality and Society, 7,* 58–92.

Scarr, S. (1995). Psychology will be truly evolutionary when behavior genetics is included. *Psychological Inquiry, 6,* 68–71.

Shapiro, R. Y., & Mahajan, H. (1986). Gender differences in policy preferences: A summary of trends from the 1960s to the 1980s. *Public Opinion Quarterly, 50,* 42–61.

Shepard, R. N. (1994). Perceptual–cognitive universals as reflections of the world. *Psychonomic Bulletin and Review, 1,* 2–28.

Sundquist, J. L. (1983). *Dynamics of the party system* (rev. ed.). Washington, DC: Brookings Institution.

Symons, D. (1990). Adaptiveness and adaptation. *Ethology and Sociobiology, 11,* 427–444.

Tither, J. M., & Ellis, B. J. (2008). Impact of fathers on daughters' age of menarche: A genetically and environmentally controlled sibling study. *Developmental Psychology, 71,* 1409–1420.

Tooby, J., & Cosmides, L. (1990a). On the universality of human nature and the uniqueness of the individual: The role of genetics and adaptation. *Journal of Personality, 58,* 17–67.

Tooby, J., & Cosmides, L. (1990b). The past explains the present: Emotional adaptations and the structure of ancestral environments. *Ethology and Sociobiology, 11,* 375–424.

Trivers, R. L. (1971). The evolution of reciprocal altruism. *Quarterly Review of Biology, 46,* 35–57.

Trivers, R. L., & Willard, D. E. (1973). Natural selection of parental ability to vary the sex ratio of offspring. *Science, 179,* 90–92.

van Beest, I., & Williams, K. D. (2006). When inclusion costs and ostracism pays, ostracism still hurts. *Journal of Personality and Social Psychology, 91,* 918–928.

Vitaterna, M. H., Takahashi, J. S., & Turek, F. W. (2001). Overview of circadian rhythms. *Alcohol Research and Health, 25,* 85–93.

de Waal, F. B. M. (1989). Food sharing and reciprocal obligations among chimpanzees. *Journal of Human Evolution, 18,* 433–459.

de Waal, F. B. M. (1992). Appeasement, celebration, and food sharing in the two *Pan* species. In T. Nishida, W. C. McGrew, & P. Marler (Eds.), *Topics in primatology: Human origins* (pp. 37–50). Tokyo: University of Tokyo Press.

de Waal, F. B. M., Luttrell, L. M., & Canfield, M. E. (1993). Preliminary data on voluntary food sharing in brown capuchin monkeys. *American Journal of Primatology, 29,* 73–78.

Whitmeyer, J. M. (1997). Endogamy as a basis for ethnic behavior. *Sociological Theory, 15,* 162–178.

Whitten, Jr., N. E. (1976). *Sacha Runa: Ethnicity and adaptation of Ecuadorian jungle Quichua.* Urbana, IL: University of Illinois Press.

Wilson, J. Q., & Herrnstein, R. J. (1985). *Crime and human nature: The definitive study of the causes of crime.* New York: Touchstone.

Wirls, D. (1986). Reinterpreting the gender gap. *Public Opinion Quarterly, 50,* 316–330.

# Part IV

# Individual Differences and Real-World Outcomes

# Section 1    Work

# 14

# Individual Differences at Work
## Deniz S. Ones and Chockalingam Viswesvaran

This chapter examines the role that individual differences play in work settings. There is a multitude of individual differences that are relevant for work environments, including physical abilities, occupational interests, among others. We focus on two domains of great import: cognitive abilities and personality.

Cognitive ability

is a very general mental capability that, among other things, involves the ability to reason, plan, solve problems, think abstractly, comprehend complex ideas, learn quickly and learn from experience. It is not merely book learning, a narrow academic skill, or test-taking smarts. Rather, it reflects a broader and deeper capability for comprehending our surroundings—"catching on," "making sense" of things, or "figuring out" what to do. (Gottfredson, 1997, p. 13)

Personality traits

are enduring dispositions and tendencies of individuals to behave in certain ways. Personality is not one single thing. Instead, personality refers to a spectrum of individual attributes that consistently distinguish people from one another in terms of their basic tendencies to think, feel, and act in certain ways. The enduring nature and consistency of personality characteristics are manifested in predictable tendencies of individuals to behave in similar ways across situations and settings. (Ones, Viswesvaran, & Dilchert, 2005b, p. 390)

Even though thousands of nuanced personality characteristics can be used to distinguish individuals from one another, here we limit our discussion to the Big-Five factors of personality and their facets, as well as compound personality traits (see Ones et al., 2005b).

---

*The Wiley-Blackwell Handbook of Individual Differences,* First Edition.
Edited by Tomas Chamorro-Premuzic, Sophie von Stumm, and Adrian Furnham.
© 2011 Blackwell Publishing Ltd. Published 2011 by Blackwell Publishing Ltd.

# Usefulness in Prediction and Explanation

The usefulness of individual differences attributes in work settings is best characterized by the relationships that have been documented for a broad spectrum of behaviors and outcomes at work. Such behaviors and outcomes constitute the *criteria* in criterion-related validity studies. Criterion-related validity is relied upon to demonstrate the usefulness of individual differences variables in work settings. We organize our chapter around important criteria or behavioral domains at work such as job performance, counterproductivity, job satisfaction, career success, and so on. The criterion construct domains covered in our review include variables that are important both from an organizational (business) and from an individual point of view. (Given other chapters devoted to the topics of individual differences and leadership and goal-setting in this volume, we do not devote space to these themes.)

We summarize the relationships between individual differences criteria on the basis of meta-analytic summaries of the vast literature on the topic. Our reasons for doing so are twofold. First, industrial, work, and organizational psychologists have been documenting such relationships for a good part of the past century in virtually all imaginable industries and jobs. As such, thousands of studies, published and unpublished (theses, doctoral dissertations, technical reports), form the basis of our scientific knowledge. Only comprehensive meta-analyses are capable of reflecting unbiased conclusions from the vast body of individual differences literature in work psychology. Second, each individual study is biased, due to a variety of statistical artifacts influencing its results (Schmidt, 2010). Sampling error, unreliability of measures, range restriction or artificially reduced variability, and dichotomization in the variables under study influence all primary studies, even large-scale ones. Furthermore, the degree to which such artifacts influence study results varies across studies, creating artifactual differences across study results. Psychometric meta-analyses of the sort summarized in this chapter distinguish such artifactual variation in results from true variation, thus informing researchers of the generalizability of findings (Hunter & Schmidt, 2004).

In the world of work, perhaps no other behavioral domain is more important than job performance. We first provide an overview of the relationships between individual differences variables and job performance. Then we summarize research on the relevance of individual differences for determinants of job success such as job knowledge and motivation. Next, we review meta-analyses pertaining to job satisfaction and withdrawal behaviors (e.g. absenteeism). Finally, we provide an overview of the relevance of individual differences for career movements and career success. Our narrative focuses on findings and conclusions. Accompanying tables provide the appropriate references supporting them.

## Job performance

Job performance is a vital construct for organizations, individuals, and economies at large. Organizations hire their employees to perform a job and then train, develop, and motivate them to sustain and increase job performance. The success of organizations depends on the productivity of their workforces. Job performance is a key behavioral domain for individuals, as, at the very least, their employment success and income depend on it. For many individuals, work performance also offers a major source of identity and meaning. For economies, national productivity is partly and, some would argue most importantly, a function of individual-level work performance of the labor force.

Job performance can be defined as "scalable actions, behavior, and outcomes that employees engage in or bring about that are linked with and contribute to organizational goals" (Viswesvaran & Ones, 2000, p. 216). The construct of job performance is hierarchically organized, with global job performance at the apex (Viswesvaran & Ones, 2005). Most measures of job performance tap strongly into this general factor by aggregating ratings across sub-domains of job performance (Viswesvaran & Ones, 2007). These primary performance domains are task performance, organizational citizenship behaviors, and avoidance of counterproductive work behaviors.

*Overall job performance*    Relationships of major individual differences characteristics with *overall* job performance have been examined. Overall job performance measures either assess the construct directly, using global evaluation items rated by supervisors or by aggregating items across performance sub-dimensions and domains. Either way, overall job performance reflects global and typical performance of employees.

In the prediction of job performance, cognitive ability is a more potent predictor than personality variables. Cognitive ability correlates in the .50s with overall job performance, whereas the strongest single personality variable can correlate only in the .40s (more often in the .20s and .30s) with overall job performance. Given low overlap between cognitive abilities and most personality variables, personality measures provide substantial incremental validity to the prediction of job performance.

For cognitive ability, the overview we provide here is based on and buttressed by the tables and data offered in Ones, Viswesvaran, and Dilchert (2004, 2005a) and Ones, Dilchert, Viswesvaran, and Salgado (2010). Even though there is a large number of cognitive abilities that can be assessed depending on the content and requirements of the jobs that employees perform (e.g. verbal abilities for jobs with large communications requirements), general mental ability (*g*) test scores are more strongly related to overall job performance than specific abilities. General mental ability is general information processing capacity, and it is associated with job-related knowledge and skill acquisition as well as with reasoning and judgment as job duties are performed. Thus individuals with higher levels of general cognitive ability know more about what to do on their jobs and how to do it. Key workplace competencies such as accurate and expeditious decision-making and communicating also depend on general cognitive ability. General cognitive ability influences all aspects of job performance and is therefore particularly powerful in predicting overall job performance. This is why general cognitive ability relates more strongly to overall job performance than specific abilities, and why specific abilities yield little incremental validity over *g* for the criterion of overall job performance.

The importance of cognitive ability increases as job complexity increases. Cognitive ability tests are most closely related to overall job performance in highly complex jobs (e.g. of attorney, or of medical doctor). For medium complexity jobs, relationships are somewhat weaker, but still tend to be impressive (in the .50s). For lowest complexity jobs, correlations are yet weaker, but nonetheless in the useful range (in the .20s).

A number of potential moderators of cognitive test validities for overall job performance have been extensively examined across multiple meta-analyses. Their effects
on cognitive ability–overall job performance relationships are negligible. Such rejected
moderators include the race, ethnicity, and sex of employees, as well as the situational
and organizational setting. Cognitive ability tests predict well for African Americans,
Hispanics, and women, as they do for Caucasians and men. They are valid in military
and civilian settings as well as in different industries and organizations. The hypothesis
of situational specificity does not hold for cognitive ability–overall job performance
relationships. Validities have been found to be similar in meta-analyses based on
concurrent and predictive validation studies; and there is good evidence that, when
the criterion is overall job performance, cognitive ability tests retain their validity up
to five years. Meta-analyses from individual European countries (e.g. France, Germany,
Belgium, the Netherlands, Spain, and the UK) as well as across Europe have produced
validity estimates similar to those reported from North American studies. The relevance and importance of cognitive ability is not likely to diminish in different cultural
contexts either. Cross-culturally, the organization of work, the content of jobs, and
the cultural milieu in which work takes place may change, but the capacity to learn
and adapt, to deal with complexity, and to process job-relevant information is universally essential.

Personality attributes also provide key insights into performance at work. The
review we provide here is based on Barrick, Mount, and Judge (2001), as well as on
updates offered in Ones et al. (2005b) and in Ones, Dilchert, Viswesvaran, and Judge
(2007). Over a dozen meta-analytic investigations have documented relationships
of personality variables for overall job performance within and across occupational
groups. Of the Big-Five personality factors, conscientiousness usefully predicts overall
job performance (operational validities are in .20s). What is more remarkable about
conscientiousness is the consistency of its predictive power. Virtually identical levels
of meta-analytically estimated validities (.19–.22) have been reported for skilled jobs,
semi-skilled jobs, sales, customer service, managerial, professional, and law enforcement jobs. Analyses across heterogeneous sets of jobs yield virtually identical results.
These findings hold both in the US and European countries. Other Big-Five personality dimensions are less consistent in their usefulness. For overall job performance,
extraversion is predictive of overall job performance for sales and managerial jobs;
agreeableness is predictive for customer service jobs; emotional stability is predictive
for customer service, skilled, and semi-skilled jobs. The research evidence is clear,
however, that conscientiousness bears the weight of prediction for overall job performance. We should note that achievement and dependability facets of conscientiousness predict overall job performance similarly. However, across occupational
groups, order and cautiousness facets of conscientiousness display trivial relationships
(.09 and −.01), with overall job performance, although there is validity evidence of
these two conscientiousness facets for overall performance in sales, skilled and semi-
skilled (only order), and customer service jobs. Evidence for Big-Five facets has been
sporadically examined. For sales, law enforcement jobs, and managerial jobs, some
facets (e.g. dominance and energy facets of extraversion, for sales and managerial
jobs) appear to be as predictive as, if not more so than, the Big-Five factor domain
they are part of.

However, the most powerful personality attributes in the prediction of overall job performance are compound personality traits defined by multiple dimensions of personality. The largest amount of research evidence has accumulated for integrity tests which assess conscientiousness, agreeableness, and emotional stability. The construct assessed by integrity tests corresponds to the socialization construct, or Digman's (1997) factor Alpha (Ones & Viswesvaran, 1998). Predictive validities for integrity tests obtained by meta-analytically pooling data from studies with true predictive validation design indicate that integrity test scores correlate .41 with overall job performance across a wide variety of jobs (Ones, Viswesvaran, & Schmidt, 1993). Interestingly, integrity tests add incremental validity over conscientiousness, the single best Big-Five predictor of overall job performance, whereas conscientiousness scales do not add incremental validity over integrity tests. Furthermore, simply combining items that assess the three Big-Five traits that integrity tests tap into does not result in validities higher than those found for conscientiousness scales alone. Predictive power of factor Alpha appears to be directly and best captured by integrity tests.

Other scales, which also assess the same compound trait defined by conscientiousness, agreeableness, and emotional stability, by using varying weights for the three components, also display validities in the .40s (Ones & Viswesvaran, 2001a). These scales are customer service scales, violence scales, and stress tolerance scales. Fascinatingly, other personality measures assessing compound traits also yield validities superior both to the Big-Five personality factors and to their facets. Examples include core self-evaluations scales (Bono & Judge, 2003) and managerial potential scales (Ones, Viswesvaran, Hough, & Dilchert, 2005). All in all, in the personality domain, the evidence is clear: superior prediction from the personality domain is achieved by compound traits.

Overall, when the criterion of interest is overall job performance, the heft of prediction is provided by cognitive ability, particularly general cognitive ability, even though measures of compound personality traits such as integrity also carry much weight. Useful but lower levels of prediction and explanation are contributed by conscientiousness and emotional stability (Schmidt, Schaffer, & Oh, 2008).

*Task performance*   Task performance has been defined as "the proficiency with which incumbents perform activities that are formally recognized as part of their jobs; activities that contribute to the organization's technical core either directly by implementing a part of its technology process, or indirectly by providing it with needed materials and services" (Borman & Motowidlo, 1997).

Measures of task performance can be obtained using ratings from supervisors and other individuals who have an opportunity to observe the performance of the employee being rated. Work samples and other hands-on performance measures have often been relied upon to measure task performance or task proficiency (e.g. Knapp, Campbell, Borman, Pulakos, & Hanson, 2001). They capture can-do aspects of performance and assess maximal performance. Objective productivity indexes also aim to capture task performance, albeit via measurement of results and outcomes (Viswesvaran & Ones, 2000). They can also be deficient indicators of task performance, to the extent that a multitude of tasks comprise the job duties and requirements.

Both cognitive ability and personality variables are related to task performance. The relationships are summarized in Tables 14.1 and 14.2, respectively. The relationships between cognitive ability and work sample performance are stronger than for cognitive ability and supervisory ratings of overall job performance (Nathan & Alexander, 1988). In fact, it can be argued that cognitive ability influences overall job performance most strongly because the performance of job *tasks* depends on it. Structural

**Table 14.1**  Summary of meta-analyses: Cognitive ability–task performance relationships. Key: N = total sample size; $\rho_{op}$ = operational validity estimate; a = from Nathan and Alexander, 1988; b = from Schmidt, Gast-Rosenberg, and Hunter, 1980; c = from Schmidt and Hunter, 1977; d = from Funke, Krauss, Schuler, and Stapf, 1987; e = from McHenry et al., 1990; f = from Schmitt et al., 1984; g = not corrected for range restriction; h = corrected for unreliability in the predictor; i = not corrected for unreliability in the criterion; j = not corrected for range restriction or unreliability in the criterion

| Predictor/criterion | Job | N | $\rho_{op}$ | Source and status |
|---|---|---|---|---|
| **Production quality** | | | | |
| General mental ability | Clerical jobs | 438 | −.01 | agh |
| Memory | Clerical jobs | 462 | .32 | aghi |
| Quantitative ability | Clerical jobs | 647 | .17 | agh |
| Verbal ability | Clerical jobs | 1,134 | .15 | aghi |
| **Production quality** | | | | |
| General mental ability | Clerical jobs | 1,116 | .35 | agh |
| Memory | Clerical jobs | 274 | .38 | aghi |
| Quantitative ability | Clerical jobs | 630 | .44 | agh |
| Verbal ability | Clerical jobs | 931 | .28 | aghi |
| **Proficiency** | | | | |
| Arithmetic reasoning | Computer programmers | 535 | .57 | b |
| Figure analogies | Computer programmers | 535 | .46 | b |
| General mental ability | General clerks | | .67 | c |
| Number series | Computer programmers | 535 | .43 | b |
| Programmer aptitude test | Computer programmers | 1,299 | .73 | b |
| **Soldiering proficiency** | | | | |
| General mental ability | 9 military job families | 4,039 | .65 | ei |
| **Technical proficiency** | | | | |
| General mental ability | 9 military job families | 4,039 | .63 | ei |
| **Research achievement** | | | | |
| General mental ability | Research and science | 949 | .16 | dg |
| **Work samples** | | | | |
| General mental ability | Clerical jobs | 747 | .60 | agh |
| General mental ability | Heterogeneous jobs | 1,793 | .43 | fj |
| Memory | Computer programmers | 171 | .53 | aghi |
| Quantitative ability | Clerical jobs | 1,114 | .55 | aghi |
| Specific abilities | Heterogeneous jobs | 1,793 | .28 | fj |
| Verbal ability | Clerical jobs | 1,387 | .50 | aghi |

**Table 14.2** Summary of meta-analyses: Personality–task performance relationships. Key: *N* = total sample size; ρ = meta-analytic effect size estimate; a = from Hurtz and Donovan, 2000; b = from Alonso and Viswesvaran, 2009; c = from Barrick et al., 2001; d = from Ones et al., 1993

| Predictor/criterion | N | ρ | Source |
|---|---|---|---|
| **Task performance** | | | |
| Emotional stability | 1,243 | .13 | a |
| Extraversion | 1,839 | .06 | a |
| Openness | 1,176 | −.01 | a |
| Agreeableness | 1,754 | .07 | a |
| Conscientiousness | 2,197 | .15 | a |
| Emotional stability | 5,169 | .12 | b |
| Extraversion | 1,636 | −.03 | b |
| Openness | 5,167 | .12 | b |
| Agreeableness | 1,640 | .08 | b |
| Conscientiousness | 9,922 | .14 | b |
| **Objective measures** | | | |
| Emotional stability | 6,219 | .09 | c |
| Extraversion | 7,101 | .11 | c |
| Openness | 4,401 | .02 | c |
| Agreeableness | 4,969 | .13 | c |
| Conscientiousness | 6,905 | .19 | c |
| Integrity | 2,210 | .28 | d |

analyses have found evidence that cognitive ability is a direct, proximal determinant of task performance (e.g. as assessed by work samples) and a distal determinant of overall job performance. Meta-analyses of specific abilities have not reported notably higher criterion-related validities than general cognitive ability (Schmitt, Gooding, Noe, & Kirsch, 1984). Relationships for cognitive ability tend to be somewhat weaker when task performance is assessed using ratings/subjective evaluations and objective measures (e.g. production quantity) than when work sample measures are used.

Cognitive ability is a stronger correlate of task performance than personality variables. However, conscientiousness, emotional stability, and openness to experience are correlated with task performance. Individuals scoring higher on measures of these constructs are more successful in the performance of their tasks. Operational validities for conscientiousness have been reported in the .14 (for supervisory ratings of task performance, Hurtz & Donovan, 2000) to .20 (for objective performance measures, Barrick et al., 2001) range. These findings suggest that conscientiousness–task performance linkages cannot be brushed aside as supervisory evaluation bias. It appears that the achievement facet of conscientiousness is a stronger predictor of task performance than the conscientiousness global dimension (operational validity = .22). Motivational underpinnings of the achievement facet are likely to contribute to this finding. Emotional stability and openness to experience are slightly more weakly related to task performance across jobs (Alonso, Viswesvaran, & Sanchez, 2008). The relationship with emotional stability likely arises due to the behavioral inhibition that is associated with the negative pole of the construct, neuroticism. As such, emotional stability's influence on task performance in work settings is likely mediated through motivation. Few compound personality attributes have been examined as predictors of task performance. The operational validity of integrity tests for predicting objective measures of task performance is .28. Integrity tests also predict work sample performance with substantial validity (Viswesvaran & Ones, 2007). Given that the socialization (or stability [Alpha]) construct assessed by integrity tests is the unifying construct behind conscientiousness, agreeableness, and emotional stability, and given that two of these constructs are motivationally implicated, typical task performance in organizational settings can be profitably predicted by using integrity tests.

*Organizational citizenship behaviors*   Discretionary work behaviors in work settings are referred to as organizational citizenship behaviors (OCBs) or contextual performance. OCB has been originally defined as "individual behavior that is discretionary, not directly or explicitly recognized by the formal reward system, and in the aggregate promotes the efficient and effective functioning of the organization" (Organ, 1988, p. 4). Lower-level dimensions of the construct are OCBs directed at others in the organization, such as altruism and courtesy, and directed at the organization itself, such as civic virtue, conscientiousness (e.g. compliance with rules and regulations), and sportsmanship (Williams & Anderson, 1991). Although OCB and its dimensions are strongly correlated with task performance (observed correlations in the .45–.65 range; true score correlations over .70; Hoffman, Blair, Meriac, & Woehr, 2007), the constructs are distinct (Conway, 1999). There has also been a movement away from the original definition of the construct, as many behaviors assembled under the OCB umbrella can be implicitly or explicitly required by organizations.

Theoretically, organizational citizenship behaviors can be expected to relate to personality variables and less to cognitive abilities. Research to date has largely followed and borne this expectation. Few studies have examined relationships between cognitive ability and OCB (e.g. LePine & VanDyne, 2001). A meta-analysis of the relationship, based on 13 studies ($N = 9,797$), reports the unreliability corrected correlation as .05. By contrast, several meta-analyses incorporating data from dozens of studies have examined personality–OCB relationships. The Big-Five dimensions of personality as a set predict well a generalized compliance facet and overall citizenship performance (operational R = .23 and .31, respectively; Ones et al., 2007). Meta-analytic estimates for specific personality attributes are summarized in Table 14.3. Conscientiousness is particularly useful in predicting the global citizenship construct, generalized compliance, and job dedication. Relationships with job dedication are somewhat weaker, and with altruism they are negligible. Both achievement and dependability facets of conscientiousness are almost twice as strong as the global conscientiousness construct in predicting job dedication. For other facets of conscientiousness, relationships are not substantially stronger either with the global OCB construct or with its facets. As can be expected on conceptual grounds, job dedication is also correlated with emotional stability. Negative affectivity appears to contribute lower levels of OCB. Agreeableness is an important correlate of interpersonal facilitation, although both emotional stability and conscientiousness appear to play an equally important role. Extraversion also plays a role, even though stronger influences from the extraversion domain are via positive affect.

**Table 14.3** Summary of meta-analyses: Individual differences–organizational citizenship behaviors (OCB) relationships. Key: $N$ = total sample size; $\rho_{op}$ = operational validity estimate; a = from Alonso and Viswesvaran, 2009; b = from Borman, Penner, Allen, and Motowidlo, 2001; c = from Dalal, 2005; d = from LePine, Erez, and Johnson, 2002; e = from Hurtz and Donovan, 2000; f = from Dudley, Orvis, Lebiecki, and Cortina, 2006; g = from Organ and Ryan, 1995

| Predictor/criterion | $N$ | $\rho_{op}$ | Source |
|---|---|---|---|
| **Contextual performance** | | | |
| General mental ability | 9,797 | .05 | a |
| Emotional stability | 7,907 | .13 | a |
| Extraversion | 4,882 | .03 | a |
| Openness | 7,905 | .11 | a |
| Agreeableness | 4,889 | .12 | a |
| Conscientiousness | 16,696 | .10 | a |
| **Citizenship performance** | | | |
| Extraversion | 1,728 | .06 | b |
| Agreeableness | 1,554 | .13 | b |
| Conscientiousness | 1,963 | .19 | b |
| **OCB** | | | |
| Conscientiousness | 3,280 | .30 | c |
| Conscientiousness | 848 | .23 | d |
| **Job dedication** | | | |
| Emotional stability | 2,581 | .13 | e |
| Extraversion | 3,130 | .05 | e |
| Openness | 2,514 | .01 | e |
| Agreeableness | 3,197 | .08 | e |
| Conscientiousness | 3,197 | .18 | e |
| Conscientiousness | 3,197 | .20 | f |
| Achievement | 2,330 | .39 | f |
| Dependability | 979 | .46 | f |
| Order | 1,658 | .10 | f |
| Cautiousness | 878 | .08 | f |
| **Interpersonal facilitation** | | | |
| Emotional stability | 3,685 | .16 | e |
| Extraversion | 4,155 | .10 | e |
| Openness | 3,539 | .05 | e |
| Agreeableness | 4,301 | .17 | e |
| Conscientiousness | 4,301 | .16 | e |
| Conscientiousness | 4,301 | .18 | f |
| Achievement | 3,264 | .11 | f |
| Dependability | 627 | .23 | f |
| Order | 3,011 | −.02 | f |
| Cautiousness | 2,187 | .00 | f |
| **Generalized compliance** | | | |
| Agreeableness | 916 | .11 | g |
| Conscientiousness | 1,818 | .30 | g |
| **Altruism** | | | |
| Agreeableness | 916 | .13 | g |
| Conscientiousness | 2,172 | .22 | g |

*Counterproductive work behaviors*   A counterproductive or deviant behavior is a voluntary behavior that violates "significant organizational norms and in so doing threatens the well being of an organization, its members, or both" (Robinson and Bennett, 1995, p. 556). Counterproductive work behaviors (CWBs) constitute a general umbrella that spans organizational rule-breaking, disobedience, misconduct, wrongdoing, and transgressions. Such behaviors detract from the productive behaviors at work, disrupt work-related activities, violate social norms, and diverge from organizationally desired behaviors. There is a variety of CWBs that employees can engage in in organizations. These include theft and related behavior, destruction of property, misuse of information, misuse of time, white-collar crime, absenteeism, tardiness, drug and alcohol abuse, disciplinary problems, poor-quality work, sabotage, inappropriate physical and verbal actions, sexual harassment, violence, accidents, and unsafe behaviors, among others. These individual indicators of CWB are related positively and markedly to one another (Ones & Viswesvaran, 2003). However, they relate weakly to task performance (e.g. maintaining discipline; Viswesvaran, Schmidt, & Ones, 2005).

CWBs can be grouped under two facets, which specify to whom the deviant employee's behavior is targeted: organizational CWBs and interpersonal CWBs (Robinson & Bennett, 1995). The distinction has initially emerged from a multi-dimensional scaling study and has been confirmed in factor analyses based on self-reports and organizational measures of CWB (Bennett & Robinson, 2000). Meta-analytically estimated convergent validity for organizational CWB and interpersonal CWB is .62 (corrected for unreliability in the measures; Berry, Ones, & Sackett, 2007; the value is .70, based on Dalal, 2005). Although CWB correlate negatively and moderately with measures of OCB, it is clear that the two constructs do not lie along the same construct continuum (Berry et al., 2007; Dalal, 2005).

Despite the usefulness of cognitive ability in predicting overall job performance as well as crime (Gottfredson & Hirschi, 1990), there have been very few examinations of cognitive ability and deviant behaviors in work settings. Adult criminal behaviors and CWB are likely to share common individual differences antecedents, including cognitive ability. In support of this hypothesis, three large-scale examinations of ability–CWB have reported moderate relationships between general cognitive ability and avoiding CWB that have explanatory and applied usefulness (McHenry, Hough, Toquam, Hanson, and Ashworth, 1990 for 4,049 Army enlisted personnel; Oppler, McCloy, and Campbell, 2001 for 1,454 supervisory Army personnel; Dilchert, Ones, Davis, & Rostow, 2007 for 816 police officers). The conceptual arguments that support such an effect involve the role of cognitive ability in moral reasoning as well as (perhaps more importantly) its inhibitory effect of considering possible consequences and outcomes of norm-violating behaviors before engaging in them (Dilchert et al., 2007). Incidentally, interpreting cognitive ability–CWB relationships as evidence of individuals with higher cognitive ability being able to better hide their misdeeds is no longer feasible on the basis of the available evidence. Cognitive ability correlates similarly with organizational and interpersonal CWB. All interpersonal CWBs are, by definition, unconcealed, public behaviors: they involve performance of the counterproductive behavior in the presence of at least one other individual.

In contrast to the scant research on cognitive ability, personality attributes have extensively been examined in explaining CWB. Table 14.4 provides an overview of

**Table 14.4**  Summary of meta-analyses: Big-Five personality–counterproductive work behaviors (CWB) relationships and outcomes. Key: $N$ = total sample size; $\rho_{op}$ = operational validity estimate; a = from Salgado, 2002; b = from Berry et al., 2007—operational validities obtained by attenuating reported true-score correlations using predictor reliability estimates; c = from Dudley et al., 2006—operational validities obtained by attenuating reported true-score correlations using predictor reliability estimates; d = from Clarke and Robertson, 2005—operational validities obtained by attenuating reported true-score correlations using predictor reliability estimates

| Predictor/criterion | N | $\rho_{op}$ | Source |
|---|---|---|---|
| **Overall CWB** | | | |
| Emotional stability | 3,107 | −.06 | [a] |
| Emotional stability | 2,300 | −.21 | [b] |
| Extraversion | 2,383 | .01 | [a] |
| Extraversion | 1,836 | −.08 | [b] |
| Openness | 1,421 | .14 | [a] |
| Openness | 1,772 | −.03 | [b] |
| Agreeableness | 1,299 | −.20 | [a] |
| Agreeableness | 2,934 | −.28 | [b] |
| Conscientiousness | 6,276 | −.26 | [a] |
| Conscientiousness | 2,934 | −.38 | [b] |
| Achievement | 1,026 | .00 | [c] |
| Dependability | 2,195 | −.30 | [c] |
| Order | 1,311 | −.06 | [c] |
| Cautiousness | 2,251 | −.10 | [c] |
| **Organizational CWB** | | | |
| Emotional stability | 2,842 | −.22 | [b] |
| Extraversion | 2,360 | .02 | [b] |
| Openness | 2,360 | −.08 | [b] |
| Agreeableness | 3,336 | −.39 | [b] |
| Conscientiousness | 3,458 | −.21 | [b] |
| **Interpersonal CWB** | | | |
| Emotional stability | 2,300 | −.21 | [b] |
| Extraversion | 1,836 | −.08 | [b] |
| Openness | 1,772 | −.03 | [b] |
| Agreeableness | 2,934 | −.28 | [b] |
| Conscientiousness | 2,934 | −.38 | [b] |
| **Workplace accidents** | | | |
| Emotional stability | 1,958 | −.25 | [c] |
| Extraversion | 1,524 | −.08 | [c] |
| Openness | 570 | −.43 | [c] |
| Agreeableness | 420 | −.53 | [c] |
| Conscientiousness | 1,125 | −.27 | [c] |
| **Absenteeism** | | | |
| Emotional stability | 2,491 | .04 | [a] |
| Extraversion | 1,799 | .08 | [a] |
| Openness | 1,339 | .00 | [a] |
| Agreeableness | 1,339 | .04 | [a] |
| Conscientiousness | 2,155 | −.06 | [a] |

the relationships for Big-Five personality dimensions. Overall, two of the Big-Five dimensions are consistently related to CWB across meta-analyses: conscientiousness and agreeableness. Weaker and less consistent relationships are found for emotional stability. The dependability facet of conscientiousness is stronger in explaining variance in CWB than the order or achievement facets of the construct are. However, facet-level relationships for conscientiousness are not stronger than the factor-level findings. Interestingly, in predicting interpersonally directed CWB, the most powerful Big-Five personality attributes are agreeableness, conscientiousness, and emotional stability, in that order. However, in predicting organizationally directed CWB, the most powerful Big-Five personality attributes are conscientiousness, agreeableness, and emotional stability, in that order. The involvement of the same three personality factors in both types of CWB suggests the same source trait: socialization, or Digman's factor Alpha. Yet the different weights on the constructs suggest potentially different pathways in the expression of the deviant behaviors, depending on the profile pattern suggested by the three variables. That is, the findings from meta-analyses are consistent with the idea that profile levels (elevation) across conscientiousness, agreeableness, and emotional stability would yield best predictive power for CWB; however, personality profile patterns would explain the types of CWB that employees engage in (see Davison & Davenport, 2002; Dilchert, 2007 for discussions of profile level and pattern effects).

In addition to CWB, specific outcomes associated with unsafe work behaviors are also related to personality variables. As is noted in Table 14.4, the same three personality variables implicated in the prediction of overall CWB and of dimensions of CWB are also key factors in predicting and explaining workplace accidents. Individuals who are low on conscientiousness, low on agreeableness, and low on emotional stability (high neuroticism) tend to get involved in accidents in their workplaces. Although sizable relationships with openness to experience have been reported, these are not consistent across individual studies (i.e. extremely large variabilities accompany meta-analytic estimates). Extraversion appears to be unrelated to accident involvement.

Employee absences are a specific form of CWB. A portion of Table 14.4 summarizes the relationships between the Big Five and absenteeism. The scant empirical literature on the topic suggests a limited role for the Big Five in explaining variance in absenteeism. Table 14.4 includes compound personality trait relationships with absenteeism. Personality-based integrity tests can be used to forecast employee absenteeism, and the effect sizes associated with personality-based integrity tests are strong.

As can be expected from the patterns of reviewed results for CWB, compound personality variables, particularly those tapping into socialization, can be expected to be especially useful in understanding and predicting CWB. As can be seen in Table 14.5, integrity tests, both overt and personality-based (Ones & Viswesvaran, 1998), violence scales, stress tolerance scales, drug and alcohol scales, and customer service scales are all substantially predictive of CWB. Operational validities are strong. Specific indices of CWB such as theft, property damage, drug and alcohol use, and workplace violence are also correlated with the same set of compound personality scales. However, validities for these are weaker, due to the fact that narrower slices of the CWB are represented. It may be important to recall that all the compound personality traits listed in Table 14.5 assess the same underlying personality construct defined by conscientiousness, agreeableness, and emotional stability.

**Table 14.5** Summary of meta-analyses: Compound personality scale–counterproductive work behaviors (CWB) relationships and outcomes. Key: $N$ = total sample size; $\rho_{op}$ = operational validity estimate; a = from Ones, Viswesvaran, and Schmidt, 1993; b = from Ones and Viswesvaran, 2001c; c = from Ones and Viswesvaran, 2001b; d = from Ones and Viswesvaran, 2008; e = from Ones and Viswesvaran, 1996; f = from Ones, Viswesvaran, and Schmidt, 2003

| Predictor/criterion | | $N$ | $\rho_{op}$ | Source |
|---|---|---|---|---|
| **Overall CWB** | | | | |
| Integrity tests (personality-based) | | 93,092 | .29 | a |
| Integrity tests (overt) | | 5,598 | .39 | a |
| Drug and alcohol scales | | 665 | .29 | b |
| Violence scales | | 533 | .46 | c |
| Stress tolerance scales | | 594 | .42 | c |
| Customer service scales | | 740 | .42 | d |
| **Facets of CWB** | | | | |
| Integrity tests (overt) | Detected theft | 2,434 | .13 | a |
| Integrity tests (overt) | Admitted theft | 68,618 | .42 | a |
| Integrity tests | Workplace accidents | 759 | .52 | e |
| Integrity tests | Property damage | 1,970 | .69 | e |
| Drug and alcohol scales | Drug use | 931 | .33 | b |
| Violence scales | Violent behaviors | 1,265 | .48 | c |
| Integrity tests (personality-based) | Absenteeism | 5,435 | .36 | f |
| Integrity tests (overt) | Absenteeism | 8,537 | .09 | f |

As is evident from the foregoing discussion, both cognitive ability and personality are important as individual differences determinants of CWB. However, in this behavioral domain, personality attributes, particularly socialization (conscientiousness, agreeableness, and emotional stability) play the leading role. In work settings, personnel selection and placement decisions can be improved and CWB can be stemmed by assessing job applicants on these personality characteristics.

## Determinants of job performance

Major proximal determinants of job performance are knowledge (declarative and procedural) and motivation. All individual differences predictors of performance are hypothesized to act through the constructs of job knowledge and motivation. In this section we provide an overview of the relationships between individual differences traits and job knowledge, as well as motivation.

*Job knowledge and its acquisition in training* Acquisition of job knowledge often takes place during education and, more specifically, during job training. Training success is a proximal outcome of learning. Both cognitive abilities and personality characteristics contribute to the prediction of learning. As skill acquisition is covered in another chapter of this volume, we will only provide an overview of relationships for training success.

Jobs have knowledge and information processing demands that necessitate the use of cognitive abilities in performing work behaviors (Reeve & Hakel, 2002). General cognitive ability is a key determinant of job knowledge, which in turn is a strong determinant of overall and task performance. Cognitive ability, which has often been referred to as "the ability to learn" (Schmidt, 2002), is an excellent predictor of educational success (e.g. Kuncel, Hezlett, & Ones, 2001, 2004). Ones, Viswesvaran, and Dilchert (2004) have summarized the extant evidence for cognitive ability–learning success in educational settings. Table 14.6 provides an overview of cognitive ability test validities for training success.

**Table 14.6** Summary of meta-analyses: General mental ability–training success relationships. Key: $N$ = total sample size; $\rho_{op}$ = operational validity estimate; a = not corrected for unreliability in the criterion; b = not corrected for range restriction; c = corrected for criterion unreliability using conservative criterion reliability estimates. Adapted from Ones, Viswesvaran, and Dilchert, 2005a, Table 1 (which lists individual sources)

| Job/settings | | N | $\rho_{op}$ | Status |
|---|---|---|---|---|
| **General mental ability (GMA)** | | | | |
| GMA | Heterogeneous jobs | 6,496 | .55 | |
| GMA | Heterogeneous jobs, Europe | 16,065 | .54 | |
| GMA | Heterogeneous jobs, Spain | 2,405 | .47 | |
| GMA | Heterogeneous jobs, UK | 20,305 | .56 | |
| GMA | Heterogeneous jobs, Spain + UK | 22,710 | .53 | |
| GMA | Heterogeneous jobs; military | 472,539 | .62 | a |
| GMA | High complexity jobs (CJ) | 235 | .65 | |
| GMA | High CJ | 64 | .60 | bc |
| GMA | High CJ, Europe | 2,619 | .74 | |
| GMA | Moderately high CJ | 1,863 | .50 | |
| GMA | Medium CJ | 3,823 | .57 | |
| GMA | Medium CJ | 347 | .33 | c |
| GMA | Medium CJ, Europe | 4,304 | .53 | |
| GMA | Moderately low CJ | 575 | .54 | |
| GMA | Moderately low CJ | 3,169 | .40 | bc |
| GMA | Low CJ | 106 | .00 | bc |
| GMA | Low CJ, Europe | 4,731 | .36 | |
| GMA | Apprentices, Europe | 1,229 | .49 | |
| GMA | Chemical workers, Europe | 1,514 | .72 | |
| GMA | Clerical jobs | 32,157 | .71 | |
| GMA | Clerical jobs; military | 42,832 | .58 | a |
| GMA | Drivers, Europe | 2,252 | .40 | |
| GMA | Electrical assistants, Europe | 353 | .63 | |
| GMA | Electronic jobs; military | 92,758 | .67 | a |
| GMA | Engineers, Europe | 1,051 | .74 | |
| GMA | General technical jobs; military | 180,806 | .62 | a |
| GMA | Information jobs, Europe | 579 | .69 | |
| GMA | Mechanical jobs; military | 156,143 | .62 | a |
| GMA | Mechanics, Europe | 549 | .40 | |
| GMA | Petroleum industry | 1,694 | .54 | |
| GMA | Policemen, Europe | 392 | .25 | |

**Table 14.6** (*Continued*)

| Job/settings | | N | $\rho_{op}$ | Status |
|---|---|---|---|---|
| GMA | Skilled workers, Europe | 2,276 | .27 | |
| GMA | Typists, Europe | 1,651 | .57 | |
| **Specific abilities** | | | | |
| Verbal and reasoning ability | Policemen and detectives | 1,151 | .71 | |
| Cognitive + mechanical comprehension | Firefighters | 1,027 | .77 | |
| Computerized cognitive ability battery | 17 jobs; military | | .73 | a |
| Arithmetic reasoning | 35 jobs, time 1; military | 10,488 | .56 | a |
| Arithmetic reasoning | 35 jobs, time 2; military | 10,534 | .57 | a |
| Arithmetic reasoning | Petroleum industry | 1,378 | .52 | |
| Quantitative ability | Heterogeneous jobs, Europe | 10,860 | .48 | |
| Quantitative ability | Clerical jobs | 50,751 | .70 | |
| Quantitative ability | Police and detectives | 1,206 | .63 | |
| Reasoning ability | Clerical jobs | 4,928 | .39 | |
| Reasoning ability | Internships in graduate school | 300 | .22 | |
| Reasoning ability | Police and detectives | 4,374 | .61 | |
| Verbal ability | Heterogeneous jobs, Europe | 11,123 | .44 | |
| Verbal ability | Clerical jobs | 44,478 | .64 | |
| Verbal ability | Police and detectives | 3,943 | .64 | |
| Vocabulary | 35 jobs, time 1; military | 10,488 | .51 | a |
| Vocabulary | 35 jobs, time 2; military | 10,534 | .52 | a |
| Short-term memory test | Heterogeneous jobs | 16,521 | .49 | |
| Memory | Heterogeneous jobs, Europe | 3,323 | .34 | |
| Memory | Police and detectives | 801 | .41 | |
| Automotive information | 35 jobs, time 1; military | 10,488 | .41 | a |
| Automotive information | 35 jobs, time 2; military | 10,534 | .38 | a |
| Chemical comprehension | Petroleum industry | 1,378 | .47 | |
| Clerical speed | 35 jobs, time 1; military | 10,488 | .39 | a |
| Clerical speed | 35 jobs, time 2; military | 10,534 | .42 | a |
| Electronics information | 35 jobs, time 1; military | 10,488 | .45 | a |
| Electronics information | 35 jobs, time 2; military | 10,534 | .44 | a |
| Mechanical aptitude | 35 jobs, time 1; military | 10,488 | .51 | a |
| Mechanical aptitude | 35 jobs, time 2; military | 10,534 | .50 | a |
| Mechanical comprehension | Firefighters | 869 | .62 | |
| Mechanical comprehension | Petroleum industry | 1,419 | .52 | |
| Radio information | 35 jobs, time 1; military | 10,488 | .32 | a |
| Radio information | 35 jobs, time 2; military | 10,534 | .32 | a |
| Radiocode aptitude | 35 jobs, time 1; military | 10,488 | .34 | a |
| Radiocode aptitude | 35 jobs, time 2; military | 10,534 | .35 | a |
| Shop mechanics | 35 jobs, time 1; military | 10,488 | .48 | a |
| Shop mechanics | 35 jobs, time 2; military | 10,534 | .48 | a |
| Programmer aptitude test | Computer programmers | 1,635 | .91 | |
| Cognitive ability—unspecified | Firefighters | 2,007 | .77 | |
| Cognitive ability—unspecified | Craft jobs; utility industry | 5,872 | .67 | |
| Aptitude—unspecified | Military | | .27 | |

**Table 14.7**　Summary of meta-analyses: Personality–training success relationships. Key: $N$ = total sample size; $\rho$ = meta-analytic effect size estimate; a = from Barrick et al. 2001; b = from Ones and Viswesvaran, 1998)

| Predictor/criterion | N | $\rho$ | Source |
|---|---|---|---|
| **Big Five** | | | |
| Emotional stability | 3,753 | .08 | a |
| Extraversion | 3,484 | .23 | a |
| Openness | 3,177 | .24 | a |
| Agreeableness | 4,100 | .11 | a |
| Conscientiousness | 3,909 | .23 | a |
| **Compound personality scales** | | | |
| Integrity tests | 2,364 | .38 | b |

As job complexity or the complexity of knowledge to be acquired increases, the usefulness of cognitive ability as a determinant increases. Criterion-related validities are substantial for both military and private sector jobs. Data supporting the validity of cognitive ability tests produce similarly large effect sizes in the US and in European countries. Validities for general cognitive ability and for specific abilities are not drastically different, and there are indeed several studies that have shown that specific ability tests add little to the prediction that can be derived from tests of general mental ability.

Acquisition of knowledge, learning, and therefore training performance are necessarily cognitive abilities; therefore cognitive variables are extraordinarily successful in the prediction of such criteria. The usefulness of personality measures is weaker by comparison. However, when the Big-Five dimensions of personality are used to predict training performance, the operational multiple correlation is .40 (See Table 1 in Ones et al., 2007). The validities for individual dimensions are summarized in Table 14.7. Similarly moderate relationships are found for extraversion, openness, and conscientiousness (in the .20s). The former two dimensions are part of the higher-order plasticity construct (Digman's [1997] factor Beta) and may conceptually reflect approach patterns to material to be learned. Conscientiousness is likely to contribute to training performance through the influences of hard work, time of task, persistence, and industriousness. The achievement motivation aspect of conscientiousness is only weakly related to skill acquisition, but strongly related to motivation to learn (Colquitt, LePine, & Noe, 2000).

Only one compound personality scale has been used in the prediction of training performance: integrity tests. As is indicated in Table 14.7, their operational criterion-related validity for training success is .38. As integrity tests assess the socialization construct, which is defined by conscientiousness, agreeableness, and emotional stability, we suspect that part of the predictive value of integrity tests for this criterion domain arises due to conscientiousness. However, the higher validity of integrity tests (.38) compared to that found for conscientiousness (.23) suggests that there is more to the construct of integrity that is predictively valuable in training settings. Yet the incremental variance explained is unlikely to stem from emotional stability and agreeableness, which display poor validities for training performance. One plausible hypothesis involves the emergent properties of the integrity construct. Another plausible hypothesis involves the measurement of training performance using instructor ratings, and the question whether such ratings also reflect avoidance of deviant behaviors in training settings.

*Motivation*  Theories of motivation at work abound. Other chapters in this volume are devoted to detailing research on the relevance of individual differences to specific motivational theories (e.g. goal-setting). Therefore here we provide a bird's eye view of the topic, for completeness sake.

Even though motivational constructs are not conceptually aligned with cognitive abilities, substantial relationships between cognitive ability tests and behaviors involving effort have been reported. In Project A, the effort and leadership dimension of job performance was found to be strongly related to scores on the ASVAB (Armed Services Vocational Aptitude Battery), a cognitive ability test for entry-level soldiers (Oppler, McCloy, Peterson, Russell, & Campbell, 2001). Similarly, criteria reflecting achievement and effort were moderately related to ASVAB scores for supervisors (Oppler, McCloy, & Campbell, 2001). These relationships can be interpreted as "more capable people are more motivated ones" (McCloy, Campbell, & Cudeck, 1994, p. 498). In other words, the general factor of job performance permeating all performance ratings, including ratings of motivation, is in part the result of cognitive ability influences.

Conceptually, motivation at work is inextricably related to individual differences in personality. The most detailed theoretical discussion of personality–motivation linkages is provided by Kanfer and Heggestad (1997). We refer the interested reader to their work. Instead, in Table 14.8 we summarize the relationships between the Big-Five dimensions of personality and three motivational theories/approaches: goal-setting, expectancy, and self-efficacy. All three are moderately linked with the Big-Five factors (multiple Rs = .20s; see Table 1 in Ones et al., 2007). However, links with goal-setting appear to be stronger (multiple R = .26). Both the individual personality relationships summarized in Table 14.8 and these multiple correlations attest to the dispositional influences on work motivation. For all three theories of motivation, strong robust relationships for emotional stability and conscientiousness empirically confirm the conceptual arguments that these two traits would relate to avoidance and approach, respectively. Emotional instability is likely to exert its influence through anxiety, and therefore avoidance; and conscientiousness is likely to exert its influence through achievement motivation, fueling approach.

## Individual differences and careers

Success at work does not just involve performing well, but also being happy with work (job satisfaction). Employee well-being and happiness are important variables for organizations, as well as for the employees themselves. For example, dissatisfied employees leave. How individuals fare across their career span is also of significance. Career success includes two major aspects: intrinsic career success (career satisfaction) and extrinsic career success (promotions and income). The next few sections highlight the relevance of individual differences for these variables.

**Table 14.8**  Summary of meta-analyses: Personality–motivation to perform relationships. Key: $N$ = total sample size; $\rho$ = true-score correlation; a = from Judge and Ilies, 2002

| Predictor/criterion | N | ρ | Source |
|---|---|---|---|
| **Goal setting** | | | |
| Emotional stability | 2,780 | .29 | a |
| Extraversion | 498 | .15 | a |
| Openness | 262 | .18 | a |
| Agreeableness | 373 | −.29 | a |
| Conscientiousness | 2,211 | .28 | a |
| **Expectancy** | | | |
| Emotional stability | 1,770 | .29 | a |
| Extraversion | 663 | .10 | a |
| Openness | 567 | −.08 | a |
| Agreeableness | 875 | .13 | a |
| Conscientiousness | 1,487 | .23 | a |
| **Self-efficacy** | | | |
| Emotional stability | 6,730 | .35 | a |
| Extraversion | 2,067 | .33 | a |
| Openness | 755 | .20 | a |
| Agreeableness | 1,099 | .11 | a |
| Conscientiousness | 3,483 | .22 | a |

*Job satisfaction*   Job satisfaction is an attitudinal variable. Dissatisfaction with one's job is associated with low morale and poorer performance (Judge, Thoresen, Bono, & Patton, 2001). Dissatisfied employees tend to engage in more counterproductive behaviors in their workplaces (Greenberg, 1990). Various aspects of the job or situational factors (e.g. pay, working conditions, characteristics of the work being performed, and relations with co-workers) are related to job satisfaction. Yet it has also long been recognized that satisfaction with one's work is in part dispositional (Judge, Heller, & Mount, 2002). Employees meaningfully vary from one another in terms of their job satisfaction, and such differences are temporally stable, even across jobs and organizations (e.g. Staw & Ross, 1985). Both personality and affective variables have been linked with job satisfaction. Table 14.9 summarizes the relationships with personality variables, both for Big-Five and for compound scales. Emotional stability and extraversion are the key personality determinants of job satisfaction. Relationships with neuroticism and negative affect, as well as with extraversion and positive affect, are implicated in explaining job satisfaction (Connolly & Viswesvaran, 2000; Judge, Heller et al., 2002). Surprisingly, conscientiousness is also related to job satisfaction, and almost as strongly. Although conscientiousness–job satisfaction relationships have been reported and meta-analytically summarized, little has been offered by way of a theoretical rationale to explain the relationship. We hypothesize that jobs provide individuals opportunities to demonstrate responsibility; and, to the extent that employees draw meaning from responsible work (and higher

**Table 14.9**  Summary of meta-analyses: Personality–job satisfaction relationships. Key: *N* = total sample size; ρ = true-score correlation; a = Judge, Heller et al., 2002; b = from Judge and Bono, 2001; c = from Bruk-Lee, Khoury, Nixon, Goh, and Spector, 2009; d = uncorrected sample size weighted mean correlation

| Predictor | N | ρ | Source and status |
|---|---|---|---|
| **Big Five and facets** | | | |
| Emotional stability | 24,527 | .29 | a |
| Emotional stability | 7,658 | .24 | b |
|   Self-esteem | 20,819 | .26 | b |
| Extraversion | 20,184 | .25 | a |
| Openness | 15,196 | .02 | a |
| Agreeableness | 11,856 | .17 | a |
| Conscientiousness | 21,719 | .26 | a |
|   Achievement striving | 732 | .20 | cd |
| **Compound traits** | | | |
| Internal locus of control | 18,491 | .32 | a |
| Internal locus of control | 3,020 | .16 | cd |
| Type A | 6,083 | −.05 | cd |
| Narcissism | 789 | −.14 | cd |
| Machiavellianism | 1,241 | −.26 | cd |

conscientiousness individuals will do that to a greater extent), conscientiousness will be related to job satisfaction. Conscientiousness relationships noted in Table 14.9 (for conscientiousness and achievement striving) are consistent with such a theoretical explanation. In the prediction of job satisfaction, compound traits do not appear to provide an advantage over the Big Five, although direct tests of this have yet to be conducted.

*Turnover*  Turnover is an outcome rather than a behavioral criterion. Accordingly, it has been traditionally modeled as being the result of attitudinal variables such as low job satisfaction and/or performance (Johns, 2001). Turnover undoubtedly is a complexly determined outcome, and individual differences have only recently been acknowledged as important determinants.

Cognitive ability is not a strong predictor of voluntary turnover (e.g. Trevor, 2001). However, it does strongly relate to the types of jobs that individuals gravitate toward (see the section on careers, below). Personality variables provide a more fruitful venue for understanding turnover in organizations.

The most comprehensive meta-analysis of the personality–turnover literature to date reveals substantial roles for three of the Big-Five dimensions: emotional stability, agreeableness, and conscientiousness (Zimmerman, 2008). Emotional stability is the best predictor of intentions to turnover (true score correlation = −.29, *N* = 15.075). Particularly, individuals who score high on negative affect report greater intentions to quit. Intent to turnover relationships is weaker for other dimensions of the Big

Five. For actual turnover, agreeableness and conscientiousness, followed by emotional stability, are useful predictors. Operational validities are – .27 for agreeableness, – .22 for conscientiousness, and – .20 for emotional stability (Ns ranging between 1,532 and 1,824). Path analyses based on meta-analytic correlations simultaneously tested whether personality–turnover relationships were mediated by job satisfaction, job performance, and intention to turnover. Emotional stability's relationship with intention to quit was direct, as well as indirect—through job satisfaction. Employees who score high on neuroticism express intent to quit regardless of their performance or satisfaction levels. Both agreeableness and openness to experience had direct influences on actual turnover (recall also that, across jobs, agreeableness and openness are not as strongly related to job performance and job satisfaction as other dimensions of the Big Five). In contrast, most of the conscientiousness–turnover relationship could be explained by relations with job satisfaction and performance. Surprisingly, once these relationships were taken into account, the link between conscientiousness and turnover was a weak positive one. Other authors have noted that conscientiousness, particularly its achievement orientation facet, is related to changing jobs somewhat more often across a career span (Vinson, Connelly, & Ones, 2007). Perhaps another key finding from the meta-analytic literature is that personality–turnover relationships are stronger than those found for non-self-report measures of job characteristics/job complexity (Zimmerman, 2008).

*Career success*    Real or perceived achievements that individuals have accumulated as a result of their work experiences are referred to as career success (Judge, Cable, Boudreau, & Bretz, 1995). Intrinsic success and extrinsic career success are two relatively independent constructs, which have been studied as components of career success. *Intrinsic* career success refers to the individual's subjective reactions to his/her career. *Extrinsic* career success reflects relatively objective, observable outcomes such as pay and promotions (Judge et al., 1995; Seibert, Kraimer, & Liden, 2001).

INTRINSIC CAREER SUCCESS: CAREER SATISFACTION    Intrinsic career satisfaction is a subjective evaluation that reflects an individual's career satisfaction or career-related well-being. No meta-analytic investigations have examined the relationship between cognitive ability and career satisfaction. Perhaps this is because satisfaction is an attitudinal or affective variable, and one less likely to demonstrate strong relations with traits from the cognitive domain. To the extent that cognitive ability is tied to extrinsic career success and other positive occupational outcomes, cognitive ability can indirectly relate to career satisfaction.

On the other hand, personality variables have extensively been studied in relation to career satisfaction. The first part of Table 14.10 presents the meta-analytically derived relationships with the Big Five, some facets of the Big Five, and a two compound personality attributes. Similar to job satisfaction, the strongest Big-Five correlates of career satisfaction are emotional stability and extraversion. The self-esteem facet of emotional stability is also substantially related to career satisfaction. Relationships with the other Big-Five traits are weaker, but still positive. Proactive personality, a compound trait assessing conscientiousness, extraversion, and openness

**Table 14.10** Summary of meta-analyses: Individual differences–career success relationships. Key: $N$ = total sample size; $\rho$ = true-score correlation; a = from Ng, Eby, Sorensen, and Feldman, 2005; b = Judge and Bono, 2001; c = from Bruk-Lee et al., 2009; d = uncorrected sample size weighted mean correlation; e = Fuller and Marler, 2009

| Predictor/criterion | N | $\rho_{true}$ | Source and status |
|---|---|---|---|
| **Career satisfaction** | | | |
| Emotional stability | 10,566 | .36 | a |
| Emotional stability | 7,658 | .24 | b |
| Self-esteem | 20,819 | .26 | b |
| Extraversion | 10,566 | .27 | a |
| Openness | 10,962 | .12 | a |
| Agreeableness | 4,634 | .11 | a |
| Conscientiousness | 10,566 | .14 | a |
| Achievement striving | 732 | .20 | cd |
| Locus of control | 5,911 | −.03 | a |
| Proactive personality | 2,680 | .31 | e |
| **Salary** | | | |
| Cognitive ability | 9,560 | .27 | a |
| Emotional stability | 6,433 | .12 | a |
| Extraversion | 6,610 | .10 | a |
| Openness | 6,800 | .04 | a |
| Agreeableness | 6,286 | −.10 | a |
| Conscientiousness | 6,286 | .07 | a |
| Locus of control | 2,495 | .06 | a |
| Proactive personality | 3,031 | .14 | e |
| **Promotions** | | | |
| Emotional stability | 4,575 | .11 | a |
| Extraversion | 4,428 | .18 | a |
| Openness | 4,942 | .01 | a |
| Agreeableness | 4,428 | −.05 | a |
| Conscientiousness | 4,428 | .06 | a |
| Locus of control | 5,911 | −.03 | a |
| Proactive personality | 1,737 | .11 | e |

to experience (Fuller & Marler, 2009), is also an excellent predictor of career satisfaction. In fact, the relationship between proactivity and career satisfaction exceeds most bivariate relations of career satisfaction with the Big-Five domain, an exception being emotional stability.

EXTRINSIC CAREER SUCCESS: SALARY AND PROMOTIONS   In contrast to career satisfaction, extrinsic career satisfaction is measured by using objective indicators such as salary and promotions. Relationships between individual differences characteristics and both salary and promotions are summarized in the second portion of Table 14.10. Cognitive ability is the best predictor of salary and income, likely because individuals sort themselves into higher paying, more complex, and more prestigious jobs on the basis of their cognitive ability (Wilk & Sackett, 1996; Wilk, Desmarais, & Sackett, 1995) and because cognitive ability is the best predictor of overall job performance. In other words, brighter individuals end up in better (more complex, more prestigious, higher paying) jobs and, even within the same occupational group, cognitive ability is a key in determining who performs better and achieves more and therefore earns better. Personality variables fare less well against the salary criterion, as mostly weak relationships have been reported, unless there is naturally occurring range enhancement on the predictor or the criterion that magnifies weak effects (Dilchert & Ones, 2008).

Promotions are moderately related to promotions. In fact, among managers, the dominance/ascendancy facet of extraversion has been found to be an even stronger predictor of promotions (Ones, Hough, & Viswesvaran, 2000). The rest of the Big-Five factors and the proactive personality are weak predictors of promotions.

## Current and Future Directions for Individual Differences Workplace Applications

As the previous sections of this chapter highlighted, thousands of studies have documented the usefulness of individual differences in work settings. The findings vary by the criterion to be predicted and understood. Cognitive ability is the single best determinant of overall job performance, task performance, learning, and training success (job knowledge acquisition). Personality variables are particularly useful in explaining organizational citizenship behaviors, counterproductive work behaviors, motivation, and effort, as well as job satisfaction. When complex, real-world behaviors and criteria are to be predicted, compound personality traits are more potent than individual dimensions of the Big Five.

There are five areas that we would like to highlight for their importance in workplace applications. The first area involves group differences. Race, ethnic group, sex, and age differences have been reported for both cognitive ability (e.g. Roth, Bevier, Bobko, Switzer, & Tyler, 2001; Ones et al., 2010) and personality variables (Foldes, Jackson, Duehr, & Ones, 2008). The findings from these meta-analyses and large-scale studies suggest that the use of many individual differences scale scores in organizational decision-making can potentially lead to differential outcomes for various groups of employees. However, it is important to keep in mind and educate organizational stakeholders that unequal outcomes are the natural result of unequal distributions of underlying traits and, as long as such traits are related to important work behaviors (i.e. are job-related), discrimination need not be invoked as an explanation.

The second area involves linearity of relationships. In the cognitive ability domain, it has been argued that, beyond a certain threshold level, cognitive ability differences do matter. Empirical investigations of this clearly conclude that the ability–performance relationships are linear throughout the range of ability, even at the very high ends of the bell curve (see Kuncel, Ones, Sackett, 2010, for a summary). In the personality domain, the argument takes the form that, for a given trait, "too much of a good thing" may not be desirable. That is, it is hypothesized that personality–job behavior relationships are in one direction for the normal range and that they reverse direction when a certain threshold is reached (e.g. performance decrements occur). There is no persuasive evidence for this hypothesized non-linearity effect for personality variables when the same criterion is investigated.

The third area involves the stability of relationships and longitudinal effects. For cognitive ability, it has been suggested that criterion-related validities decline over time. When the criterion is overall job performance, there is no evidence for this. Substantial validities have been reported for overall job performance up to five years of employment (Schmidt, Hunter, Outerbridge, & Goff, 1988). In addition, concurrent validity studies of cognitive ability include employees of varying tenure in the validation sample. Substantial concurrent validities that approximate predictive validities in this domain suggest that the role of cognitive ability does not decline as employee tenure increases. For task performance, validities of cognitive ability tests decline for consistent tasks, but not for inconsistent tasks (Ackerman, 1988). Personality variables have also been examined for their longitudinal effects and relationships with behaviors, and outcomes appear to remain strong, even after several decades (Judge, Higgins, Thoresen, & Barrick, 1999). There is even some limited evidence that validities of personality variables increase in the long run (Lievens, Ones, & Dilchert, 2009).

The fourth issue involves whether new individual differences constructs exist and are warranted for improving prediction. There has been a proliferation of constructs that have been suggested for workplace applications. These have included a variety of intelligences (practical, emotional, cultural) and personality characteristics (integrity, core self-evaluations, proactive personality). The former have met with limited success, as general cognitive ability carries the bulk of predictive variance for overall job performance as well as for task performance (Van Rooy, Dilchert, Viswesvaran, & Ones, 2006). In contrast, "new" personality constructs have tended to be compound traits and have shown consistently superior predictive power to that of the Big Five, as well as incremental validity (e.g. Ones & Viswesvaran, 2001a; Judge, Erez, Bono, & Thoresen, 2002).

The fifth issue involves alternative ways of measuring individual differences constructs. Here the constructs to be measured stay the same, but the methods of assessing them are new. Such new approaches have included contextualized cognitive measures, situational judgment tests, and conditional reasoning measures. Here the evidence to date suggests that improvements to predictive power are unlikely to occur through format change alone. However, such format changes can alter assessee perceptions and acceptance.

In the domain of work, individual differences are strong and useful. They are incorporated into organizational decision-making, because there are bottom-line reasons for doing so. The research base that supports the use of both cognitive ability and personality variables for work applications is vast. Thousands of studies summarized in meta-analyses attest to the strength of cognitive abilities. Thousands of studies support the use of personality variables at work. Individuals, organizations, economies, and ultimately societies benefit from harnessing the knowledge regarding the role that individual differences play at work.

## Authors' Note

Both authors contributed equally to this chapter; the order of authorship is alphabetical.

## References

Ackerman, P. L. (1988). Determinants of individual differences during skill acquisition: Cognitive abilities and information processing. *Journal of Experimental Psychology: General, 117*, 288–318.

Alonso, A., Viswesvaran, C., & Sanchez, J. I. (2008). The mediating effects of task and contextual performance. In J. Deller (Ed.), *Research contributions to personality at work*. Munich, Germany: Rainer Hampp.

Barrick, M. R., Mount, M. K., & Judge, T. A. (2001). Personality and performance at the beginning of the new millennium: What do we know and where do we go next? *International Journal of Selection and Assessment, 9*, 9–30.

Bennett, R. J., & Robinson, S. L. (2000). Development of a measure of workplace deviance. *Journal of Applied Psychology, 85*, 349–360.

Berry, C. M., Ones, D. S., & Sackett, P. R. (2007). Interpersonal deviance, organizational deviance, and their common correlates: A review and meta-analysis. *Journal of Applied Psychology, 92*, 410–424.

Bono, J. E., & Judge, T. A. (2003). Core self-evaluations: A review of the trait and its role in job satisfaction and job performance. *European Journal of Personality, 17*, S5–S18.

Borman, W. C., & Motowidlo, S. J. (1997). Task performance and contextual performance: The meaning for personnel selection research. *Human Performance, 10*, 99–109.

Borman, W. C., Penner, L. A., Allen, T. D., & Motowidlo, S. J. (2001). Personality predictors of citizenship performance. *International Journal of Selection and Assessment, 9*, 52–69.

Bruk-Lee, V., Khoury, H. A., Nixon, A. E., Goh, A., & Spector, P. E. (2009). Replicating and extending past personality/job satisfaction meta-analyses. *Human Performance, 22*, 156–189.

Clarke, S., & Robertson, I. T. (2005). A meta-analytic review of the Big Five personality factors and accident involvement in occupational and non-occupational settings. *Journal of Occupational and Organizational Psychology, 78*, 355–376.

Colquitt, J. A., LePine, J. A., & Noe, R. A. (2000). Toward an integrative theory of training motivation: A meta-analytic path analysis of 20 years of research. *Journal of Applied Psychology, 85*, 678–707.

Connolly, J. J., & Viswesvaran, C. (2000). The role of affectivity in job satisfaction: A meta-analysis. *Personality and Individual Differences, 29*, 265–281.

Conway, J. M. (1999) Distinguishing contextual performance from task performance for managerial jobs. *Journal of Applied Psychology, 84*(1), 3–13.

Dalal, R. S. (2005). A meta-analysis of the relationship between organizational citizenship behavior and counterproductive work behavior. *Journal of Applied Psychology, 90*, 1241–1255.

Davison, M. L., & Davenport, E. C. (2002). Identifying criterion-related patterns of predictor scores using multiple regression. *Psychological Methods, 7*, 468–484.

Digman, J. M. (1997). Higher-order factors of the Big Five. *Journal of Personality and Social Psychology, 73*, 1246–1256.

Dilchert, S. (2007). Peaks and valleys: Predicting interests in leadership and managerial positions from personality profiles. *International Journal of Selection and Assessment, 15,* 317–334.

Dilchert, S., & Ones, D. S. (2008). Personality and extrinsic career success: Predicting managerial salary at different organizational levels. *Journal of Personnel Psychology* [formerly *Zeitschrift für Personalpsychologie*], *7,* 1–23.

Dilchert, S., Ones, D. S., Davis, R. D., & Rostow, C. D. (2007). Cognitive ability predicts objectively measured counterproductive work behaviors. *Journal of Applied Psychology, 92,* 616–627.

Dudley, N. M., Orvis, K. A., Lebiecki, J. E., & Cortina, J. M. (2006). A meta-analytic investigation of conscientiousness in the prediction of job performance: Examining the intercorrelations and the incremental validity of narrow traits. *Journal of Applied Psychology, 91,* 40–57.

Foldes, H. L. Jackson, Duehr, E. E., & Ones, D. S., (2008). Group differences in personality: Meta-analyses comparing five U.S. racial groups. *Personnel Psychology, 61,* 579–616.

Fuller, B., Jr., & Marler, L. E. (2009). Change driven by nature: A meta-analytic review of the proactive personality literature. *Journal of Vocational Behavior, 75,* 329–345.

Funke, U., Krauss, J., Schuler, H., & Stapf, K. H. (1987). Zur Prognostizierbarkeit wissenschaftlich-technischer Leistung mittels Personvariablen: Eine Metaanalyse der Validität diagnostischer Verfahren im Bereich Forschung und Entwicklung. [Predictability of scientific–technical achievement through personal variables: A meta-analysis of the validity of diagnostic procedures in research and development.] *Gruppendynamik, 18,* 407–428.

Gottfredson, L. S. (1997). Mainstream science on intelligence: An editorial with 52 signatories, history and bibliography. *Intelligence, 24,* 13–23.

Gottfredson, M. R., & Hirschi, T. (1990). *A general theory of crime.* Stanford, CA: Stanford University Press.

Greenberg, J. (1990). Employee theft as a reaction to underpayment inequity: The hidden cost of pay cuts. *Journal of Applied Psychology, 75,* 561–568.

Hoffman, B. J., Blair, C. A., Meriac, J. P., & Woehr, D. J. (2007). Expanding the criterion domain? A quantitative review of the OCB literature. *Journal of Applied Psychology, 92*(2), 555–566.

Hunter, J. E., & Schmidt, F. L. (2004). *Methods of meta-analysis.* Thousand Oaks, CA: Sage.

Hurtz, G. M., & Donovan, J. J. (2000). Personality and job performance: The Big Five revisited. *Journal of Applied Psychology, 85,* 869–879.

Johns, G. (2001). The psychology of lateness, absenteeism, and turnover. In N. Anderson, D. S. Ones, H. Sinangil Kepir, & C. Viswesvaran (Eds.), *Handbook of industrial, work, and organizational psychology. Vol. 2: Organizational Psychology* (pp. 232–252). Thousand Oaks, CA: Sage.

Judge, T. A., & Bono, J. E. (2001). Relationship of core self-evaluations traits—self-esteem, generalized self-efficacy, locus of control, and emotional stability—with job satisfaction and job performance: A meta-analysis. *Journal of Applied Psychology, 86,* 80–92.

Judge, T. A., & Ilies, R. (2002). Relationship of personality to performance motivation: A meta-analytic review. *Journal of Applied Psychology, 87,* 797–807.

Judge, T. A., Heller, D., & Mount, M. K. (2002). Five-factor model of personality and job satisfaction: A meta-analysis. *Journal of Applied Psychology, 87,* 530–541.

Judge, T. A., Cable, D. M., Boudreau, J. W., & Bretz, R. D. (1995). An empirical investigation of the predictors of executive career success. *Personnel Psychology, 48,* 485–519.

Judge, T. A., Erez, A., Bono, J. E., & Thoresen, C. J. (2002). Are measures of self-esteem, neuroticism, locus of control, and generalized self-efficacy indicators of a common core construct? *Journal of Personality and Social Psychology, 83*, 693–710.

Judge, T. A., Higgins, C. A., Thoresen, C. J., & Barrick, M. R. (1999). The Big Five personality traits, general mental ability, and career success across the life span. *Personnel Psychology, 52*, 621–652.

Judge, T. A., Thoresen, C. J., Bono, J. E., & Patton, G. K. (2001). The job satisfaction–job performance relationship: A qualitative and quantitative review. *Psychological Bulletin, 127*, 376–407.

Kanfer, R., & Heggestad, E. D. (1997). Motivational traits and skills: A person-centered approach to work motivation. In L. L. Cummings & B. M. Staw (Eds.), *Research in organizational behavior* (Vol. 19, pp. 1–56). Greenwich, CT: JAI Press.

Knapp, D. J., Campbell, C. H., Borman, W. C., Pulakos, E. D., & Hanson, M. A. (2001). Performance assessment for a population of jobs. In J. P. Campbell & D. J. Knapp (Eds.), *Exploring the limits in personnel selection and classification* (pp. 181–235). Mahwah, NJ: Lawrence Erlbaum Associates.

Kuncel, N. R., Hezlett, S. A., & Ones, D. S. (2001). A comprehensive meta-analysis of the predictive validity of the Graduate Record Examinations: Implications for graduate student selection and performance. *Psychological Bulletin, 127*, 162–181.

Kuncel, N. R., Hezlett, S. A., & Ones, D. S. (2004). Academic performance, career potential, creativity, and job performance: Can one construct predict them all? *Journal of Personality and Social Psychology, 86*, 148–161.

Kuncel, N. R., Ones, D. S., & Sackett, P. R. (2010). Individual differences as predictors of work, educational, and broad life outcomes. *Personality and Individual Differences, 49*, 331–336.

LePine, J. A., Erez, A., & Johnson, D. E. (2002). The nature and dimensionality of organizational citizenship behavior: A critical review and meta-analysis. *Journal of Applied Psychology, 87*, 52–65.

LePine, J. A., & Van Dyne, L. (2001). Voice and cooperative behavior as contrasting forms of contextual performance: Evidence of differential relationships with Big Five personality characteristics and cognitive ability. *Journal of Applied Psychology, 86*, 326–336.

Lievens, F., Ones, D. S., & Dilchert, S. (2009). Personality scale validities increase throughout medical school. *Journal of Applied Psychology. 94*(6), 1514–1535.

McCloy, R. A., Campbell, J. P., & Cudeck, R. (1994). A confirmatory test of a model of performance determinants. *Journal of Applied Psychology, 79*, 493–505.

McHenry, J. J., Hough, L. M., Toquam, J. L., Hanson, M. A., & Ashworth, S. (1990). Project A validity results: The relationship between predictor and criterion domains. *Personnel Psychology, 43*, 335–354.

Nathan, B. R., & Alexander, R. A. (1988). A comparison of criteria for test validation: A meta-analytic investigation. *Personnel Psychology, 41*, 517–535.

Ng, T. W. H., Eby, L. T., Sorensen, K. L., & Feldman, D. C. (2005). Predictors of objective and subjective career success. A meta-analysis. *Personnel Psychology, 58*, 367–408.

Ones, D. S., & Viswesvaran, C. (1996). Bandwidth-fidelity dilemma in personality measurement for personnel selection. *Journal of Organizational Behavior, 17*, 609–626.

Ones, D. S., & Viswesvaran, C. (1998). Integrity testing in organizations. In S. B. Bacharach, A. O'Leary-Kelly, J. M. Collins, & R. K. Griffin (Eds.), *Dysfunctional behavior in organizations: Violent and deviant behavior.* (pp. 243–276). London: JAI Press.

Ones, D. S., & Viswesvaran, C. (2001a). Integrity tests and other criterion-focused occupational personality scales (COPS) used in personnel selection. *International Journal of Selection and Assessment, 9*, 31–39.

Ones, D. S., & Viswesvaran, C. (2001b). Personality at work: Criterion-focused occupational personality scales used in personnel selection. In B. W. Roberts & R. Hogan (Eds.), *Personality psychology in the workplace* (pp. 63–92). Washington, DC: American Psychological Association.

Ones, D. S., & Viswesvaran, C. (2003). Personality and counterproductive work behaviors. In A. Sagie, S. Stashevsky, & M. Koslowsky (Eds.), *Misbehavior and dysfunctional attitudes in organizations* (pp. 211–249). Basingstoke: Palgrave Macmillan.

Ones, D. S., & Viswesvaran, C. (2007). A research note on the incremental validity of job knowledge and integrity tests for predicting maximal performance. *Human Performance*, *20*, 293–303.

Ones, D. S., & Viswesvaran, C. (2008). Costumer service scales: Criterion-related, construct, and incremental validity evidence. In J. Deller (Ed.), *Research contributions to personality at work* (pp. 19–46). Mering, Germany: Hampp.

Ones, D. S., Hough, L. M., & Viswesvaran, C. (2000, August). Personality predictors of performance for managers and executives. In L. M. Hough & D. S. Ones (Chairs), *Personality and performance in leadership positions: Presidents, CEO's and managers.* Symposium conducted at the annual conference of the American Psychological Association, Washington, DC.

Ones, D. S., Viswesvaran, C., & Dilchert, S. (2004). Cognitive ability in selection decisions. In O. Wilhelm & R. W. Engle (Eds.), *Handbook of understanding and measuring intelligence* (pp. 431–468). Thousand Oaks, CA: Sage.

Ones, D. S., Viswesvaran, C., & Dilchert, S. (2005a). Cognitive ability in personnel selection decisions. In A. Evers, O. Voskuijl, & N. Anderson (Eds.), *Handbook of selection* (pp. 143–173). Oxford: Blackwell.

Ones, D. S., Viswesvaran, C., & Dilchert, S. (2005b). Personality at work: Raising awareness and correcting misconceptions. *Human Performance*, *18*, 389–404.

Ones, D. S., Viswesvaran, C., & Schmidt, F. L. (1993). Comprehensive meta-analysis of integrity test validities: Findings and implications for personnel selection and theories of job performance. *Journal of Applied Psychology*, *78*, 679–703.

Ones, D. S., Viswesvaran, C., & Schmidt, F. L. (2003). Personality and absenteeism: A meta-analysis of integrity tests. *European Journal of Personality*, *17*, S19–S38.

Ones, D. S., Dilchert, S., Viswesvaran, C., & Judge, T. A. (2007). In support of personality assessment in organizational settings. *Personnel Psychology*, *60*, 995–1027.

Ones, D. S., Dilchert, S., Viswesvaran, C., & Salgado, J. F. (2010). Cognitive abilities. In J. L. Farr & N. T. Tippins (Eds.), *Handbook of employee selection* (pp. 255–275). Mahwah, NJ: Lawrence Erlbaum Associates.

Ones, D. S., Viswesvaran, C., Hough, L. M., & Dilchert, S. (2005). Managers, leaders, and executives: Successful personality. In J. Deller, & D. S. Ones (Eds.), *International symposium on Personality at Work: Proceedings* (p. 8). Lüneburg: University of Applied Sciences.

Oppler, S. H., McCloy, R. A., & Campbell, J. P. (2001). The prediction of supervisory and leadership performance. In J. P. Campbell & D. J. Knapp (Eds.), *Exploring the limits in personnel selection and classification* (pp. 389–409). Mahwah, NJ: Lawrence Erlbaum.

Oppler, S. H., McCloy, R. A., Peterson, N. G., Russell, T. L., & Campbell, J. P. (2001). The prediction of multiple components of entry-level performance. In J. P. Campbell & D. J. Knapp (Eds.), *Exploring the limits in personnel selection and classification* (pp. 349–388). Mahwah, NJ: Lawrence Erlbaum Associates.

Organ, D. W. (1988). *Organizational citizenship behavior: The good soldier syndrome.* Lexington, MA: Lexington Books.

Organ, D. W., & Ryan, K. (1995). A meta-analytic review of attitudinal and dispositional predictors of organizational citizenship behavior. *Personnel Psychology, 48,* 775–802.

Reeve, C. L., & Hakel, M. D. (2002). Asking the right questions about *g*. *Human Performance, 15,* 47–74.

Robinson, S. L., & Bennett, R. J. (1995). A typology of deviant workplace behaviors: A multidimensional scaling study. *Academy of Management Journal, 38,* 555–572.

Roth, P. L., Bevier, C. A., Bobko, P., Switzer, F. S., & Tyler, P. (2001). Ethnic group differences in cognitive ability in employment and educational settings: A meta-analysis. *Personnel Psychology, 54,* 297–330.

Salgado, J. F. (2002). The Big Five personality dimensions and counterproductive behaviors. *International Journal of Selection and Assessment, 10,* 117–125.

Schmidt, F. L. (2002). The role of general cognitive ability and job performance: Why there cannot be a debate. *Human Performance, 15,* 187–211.

Schmidt, F. L. (2010). Detecting and correcting the lies that data tell. *Perspectives on Psychological Science, 5*(3), 233–242.

Schmidt, F. L., & Hunter, J. E. (1977). Development of a general solution to the problem of validity generalization. *Journal of Applied Psychology, 62,* 529–540.

Schmidt, F. L., Gast-Rosenberg, I., & Hunter, J. E. (1980). Validity generalization results for computer programmers. *Journal of Applied Psychology, 65,* 643–661.

Schmidt, F. L., Shaffer, J. A., & Oh, I. S. (2008). Increased accuracy for range restriction corrections: Implications for the role of personality and general mental ability in job and training performance. *Personnel Psychology, 61*(4), 827–868.

Schmidt, F. L., Hunter, J. E., Outerbridge, A. N., & Goff, S. (1988). Joint relation of experience and ability with job performance: Test of three hypotheses. *Journal of Applied Psychology, 73,* 46–57.

Schmitt, N., Gooding, R. Z., Noe, R. A., & Kirsch, M. (1984). Meta-analyses of validity studies published between 1964 and 1982 and the investigation of study characteristics. *Personnel Psychology, 37,* 407–422.

Seibert, S. E., Kraimer, M. L., & Liden, R. C. (2001). A social capital theory of career success. *Academy of Management Journal, 44,* 219–237.

Staw, B. M., & Ross, J. (1985). Stability in the midst of change: A dispositional approach to job attitudes. *Journal of Applied Psychology, 70,* 469–480.

Trevor, C. O. (2001). Interactions among actual ease-of-movement determinants and job satisfaction in the prediction of voluntary turnover. *Academy of Management Journal, 44,* 621–638.

Van Rooy, D. L., Dilchert, S., Viswesvaran, C., & Ones, D. S. (2006). Multiplying intelligences: Are general, emotional, and practical intelligences equal? In K. R. Murphy (Ed.), *A critique of emotional intelligence: What are the problems and how can they be fixed?* (pp. 235–262). Mahwah, NJ: Lawrence Erlbaum Associates.

Vinson, G. A, Connelly, B. S., & Ones, D. S. (2007). Relationships between personality and organization switching: Implications for utility estimates. *International Journal of Selection and Assessment, 15,* 118–133.

Viswesvaran, C., & Ones, D. S. (2000). Perspectives on models of job performance. *International Journal of Selection and Assessment, 8,* 216–227.

Viswesvaran, C., & Ones, D. S. (2005). Job performance: Assessment issues in personnel selection. In A. Evers, O. Voskuijl, & N. Anderson (Eds.), *Handbook of selection* (pp. 354–375). Oxford: Blackwell.

Viswesvaran, C., & Ones, D. S. (2007). Job performance models. In S. G. Rogelberg (Ed.), *Encyclopedia of industrial organizational psychology.* Thousand Oaks, CA: Sage.

Viswesvaran, C., Schmidt, F. L., & Ones, D. S. (2005). Is there a general factor in ratings of job performance? A meta-analytic framework for disentangling substantive and error influences. *Journal of Applied Psychology, 90*, 108–131.

Wilk, S. L., & Sackett, P. R. (1996). Longitudinal analysis of ability–job complexity fit and job change. *Personnel Psychology, 49*, 937–967. doi:10.1111/j.1744-6570.1996.tb02455.x

Wilk, S. L., Desmarais, L. B., & Sackett, P. R. (1995). Gravitation to jobs commensurate with ability: Longitudinal and cross-sectional tests. *Journal of Applied Psychology, 80*, 79–85. doi: 10.1037/0021-9010.80.1.79

Williams, L. J., & Anderson, S. E. (1991). Job satisfaction and organizational commitment as predictors of organizational citizenship and in-role behaviors. *Journal of Management, 17*, 601–617.

Zimmerman, R. D. (2008). Understanding the impact of personality traits on individuals' turnover decisions: A meta-analytic path model. *Personnel Psychology, 61*, 309–348.

# 15

# Leadership

## Robert Hogan and Ghufran Ahmad

## 1  Introduction

Leadership is one of the most widely written about topics in business and social psychology; the enormous published literature can be neatly placed in two categories. By far the larger category is "the troubadour tradition"; these are popular business books and articles, written to justify past (often failed) practices and to make money. They are frequently interesting, but they are collections of opinions with minimal truth value—as we normally understand the term. The second, and much smaller, category is "the academic tradition"; these are articles in refereed journals. They are rarely fun to read, they contain various nuggets of empirical "truth," but cumulatively they don't add up to a comprehensive picture of leadership.

In our view, the academic study of leadership has largely failed (see Hamel, 2007; Khurana, 2007). As Kramer (2008, p. 28) notes, the leadership literature is "a strange mixture of alchemy, romantic idealism, and reason," and the lack of consistent practical findings prompts some business people "to wash their hands of the whole subject, talent shortage or no talent shortage." There are three primary reasons for this failure. First, the literature typically defines leadership in terms of the persons who are in charge of organizations (see Kaiser, Hogan, & Craig, 2008), and this is a mistake— the people at the top of large organizations are politicians and savvy organization players, but they only sometimes have talent for leadership. As the saying goes, Dwight Eisenhower didn't become a politician because he had been a general, he became a general because he was a politician. Second, the literature ignores the followers. Leadership is about getting work done through others, so it seems important to consider the psychology of followership in any discussion of leadership (Graen, 2009). And, third, the literature ignores the issue of return on investment (ROI). CEOs are a large source of variance in corporate profitability (Day & Lord, 1988;

*The Wiley-Blackwell Handbook of Individual Differences,* First Edition.
Edited by Tomas Chamorro-Premuzic, Sophie von Stumm, and Adrian Furnham.
© 2011 Blackwell Publishing Ltd. Published 2011 by Blackwell Publishing Ltd.

Joyce, Nohria, & Roberson, 2003; Thomas, 1988), and it seems odd to ignore ROI as a criterion of business leadership.

Although we lack a comprehensive, synoptic, or persuasive understanding of leadership, the problem is immensely important. Consider the following: In the twentieth century 167,000,000 people were murdered for political reasons. Of that number, invading armies killed 30,000,000 people, and 137,000,000 people were murdered by their own government (Rummel, 1994). Leadership is literally a matter of life or death. When good leadership is in place, organizations and their incumbents tend to prosper and benefit; when bad leadership is in place, organizations often fail and incumbents inevitably suffer.

The good news is that organizations and incumbents prosper when good leadership is in place. The bad news is that the estimated base rate for incompetent leadership in the corporate world, in both the private and the public sector, ranges from 30 percent to 67 percent, with an average of about 50 percent. These estimates come from different sources, including failure rates in publicly traded companies (e.g. Bentz, 1985; Shipper & Wilson, 1992), estimates provided by senior executives from for-profit and nonprofit organizations (e.g. Sessa, Kaiser, Taylor, & Campbell, 1998), and estimates provided by organizational consultants (e.g. Charan, 2005; Smart, 1999). We believe that two thirds of existing managers are incompetent and at least half will eventually be fired. The problem is important, and we have a problem.

We begin by reviewing how leadership is defined in the academic literature; we then present our views; we close by reviewing the major academic models of leadership. Given the size and complexity of the leadership literature, it is impossible to describe it in detail; consequently, we focus on current issues in the literature, which also coincide with emerging trends in the social sciences more generally.

## 2   Defining Leadership

Leadership concerns interactions between someone considered to be a leader and others considered to be followers, usually in order to reach a mutually desired outcome in a particular context. The interactions involve a process of mutual influence, which is affected by the characteristics of the people and situations involved. "Leadership is easy to identify in situ; however, it is difficult to define precisely" (Antonakis, Cianciolo, & Sternberg, 2004, p. 5).

The academic definition is imprecise for several reasons. Kaiser et al. (2008) note that, in 90 percent of the published literature, leadership is defined in terms of the persons who are in change—of a team, a department, or an organization. But, as Hogan, Hogan, and Kaiser (in press) note, about two thirds of these people are regarded as incompetent, which means that the talents needed to gain a leadership position are not the same as those needed to be effective in the role. We think the convention of defining leadership in terms of the persons in charge is an important reason why the leadership literature doesn't converge—different people get to the top of hierarchies for different (and usually political) reasons.

Second, by ignoring the needs of followers and the situations in which they are willing to accept leadership, the study of leadership is, by definition, conceptually inadequate (Dvir & Shamir, 2003; Grint, 2000; Välikangas & Okumura, 1997). Third, leadership researchers in sociology, social psychology, history, economics, and anthropology tend not to read one another's work. However, each discipline has a unique perspective, so that each specialist is like the proverbial blind man, who is happy with his version of the elephant. The study of leadership must become interdisciplinary in order to arrive at an adequate understanding of the subject (Bennis, 2007).

Evolutionary psychology provides an interdisciplinary perspective that can integrate the leadership literature (Van Vugt, 2006). Researchers from a variety of disciplines use Darwinian insights to interpret human behavior (Buss, 1999; Katz, 2000; Laurent & Nightingale, 2001; Markoczy & Goldberg, 1998; Schaller, Simpson, & Kenrick, 2006; Shane, 2009). We also prefer to think about social processes in terms of human origins (Van Vugt, Hogan, & Kaiser, 2008). Human beings are an old species, and much of our social behavior reflects our adaptation to perhaps 2,500,000 years of a hunter–gatherer lifestyle (cf. Wade, 2006). We have been living in "modern" circumstances for only a few hundred years, which means that we are unconsciously primed to respond to conditions that no longer exist—at least in the form that drove our evolution.

For most of our existence, we lived in semi-nomadic bands of 30 to 50 people; each band might be connected with two or three other bands, and this suggests that 150 people is the maximum number with whom an individual can identify. It is also the number that companies like Toyota use to structure themselves internally, and we don't think this is a coincidence. The physical conditions in which people evolved were quite challenging. Food supplies were rarely abundant, and dangerous predators were everywhere. Among the most dangerous of the predators were other people (Bowles, 2009). There was warfare between the groups and homicide within the groups. This suggests that persuading group members to cooperate had survival value, especially vis-à-vis hostile neighbors.

Boehm (1999) argues that, for about 2.5 million years, human groups were fundamentally egalitarian, there were no formal leaders, and the group collectively gave leaders power by choosing to follow. Bullies inevitably emerged in these groups (as in any other); when they tried to take over, they were sanctioned and, if necessary, killed. This reverse dominance hierarchy drove the evolution of specific patterns of leadership and followership. To understand leadership and followership, reflect on the survival benefits of social coordination—which is essential if one is to hunt large game or to defend against attacks from rival tribes. Social coordination is best facilitated through a decision-making process in which one person initiates a plan and the others agree to follow it. Thus leadership works best when followership is a rational strategy, when a plan maximizes the interests of both leaders and followers.

The foregoing is based on what we think we know about human origins. Living conditions changed at the end of the last ice age, about 13,000 years ago, when people on the eastern end of the Mediterranean Sea invented agriculture. Dependable food supplies fostered settled communities, the accumulation of surplus resources, individual differences in the control of resources (power), the emergence of cultural elites, and the subordination of the farmers/peasants. Agriculture spread slowly east and west in the middle latitudes (Diamond, 1997) such that, by the time of the

Roman Empire, about half of Europe was farming, while the rest of the population were hunter–gatherers. Feudalism is the term used to describe the agricultural social structure that existed for thousands of years, until the Industrial Revolution in the nineteenth century.

Another descriptor for feudalism is "warlord society." Societies dominated by warlords are the norm in pre-industrial societies such as medieval France (Johnson & Earle, 1987). A substantial part of the people today in parts of Asia, much of Africa, the Middle East, Central and South America live in societies ruled by warlords—it is the default position for human society when centralized government breaks down. Warlords are leaders—they retain loyal followers by granting them the possibility of gaining resources, privilege, and prestige in return for their support (Padilla, Hogan, & Kaiser, 2007)—and some warlords are more successful than others. All of them, however, exist by exploiting peasant masses, who are often little more than slaves.

The Industrial Revolution transformed living conditions for many of those who could join it; it led to the emergence of the modern state and modern organizations, some of which are more successful than others. Citizens of developed states and employees in organizations are relatively free from the predations of warlords, and may even be able to defect to other states or organizations. The ability to defect produces conditions that resemble the reverse dominance hierarchies of ancestral humanity—that is, leaders must pay some attention to the needs of the followers in order to retain them. Modern academic discussions of leadership concern social arrangements in the industrialized world (Wielkiewicz & Stelzner, 2005), conditions that have existed for less than 200 years. Modern organizational structures may make business sense, but they often conflict with our 2-million-year-old evolved psychology of leadership.

The foregoing considerations lead us to two conclusions. First, people are pre-wired to evaluate the leadership potential of the other members of their tribe or group, and this explains the power of implicit leadership theory (Lord, De Vader, & Alliger, 1986). Second, leadership should be defined in terms of the ability to build (and maintain) a high-performing team, relative to the other teams with which it is in competition. When leadership is defined in this way, the empirical literature begins to make sense (Van Vugt, 2006).

## 3 Leadership and Organizational Effectiveness

We believe that the data support the view that: (1) personality predicts leadership performance (who you are determines how you lead); and (2) leadership predicts business unit performance (how you lead affects organizational effectiveness). From a pragmatic perspective, the links between leadership and unit effectiveness are what matter; sadly, much published leadership research seems to have been conducted for its own sake, rather than to enhance organizational performance.

Before proceeding, we need to define personality, which is actually defined in two different ways. On the one hand, personality refers to your *identity*, the person you think you are—your goals, aspirations, passions, and dreads—the unseen factors inside you that explain why you act the way you do. On the other hand, personality

**Table 15.1**   The dimensions of the five-factor model

| Dimension | Definition |
| --- | --- |
| Adjustment: | Anxious, self-doubting, and fearful vs. confident, stable, and brave |
| Ascendance: | Shy, quiet, and restrained vs. outgoing, noisy, and assertive |
| Agreeableness: | Tough, insensitive, and critical vs. warm, charming, and tolerant |
| Prudence: | Spontaneous, limit testing, and irreverent vs. self-controlled, limit respecting, and conforming |
| Openness: | Conventional and incurious with narrow interests vs. unconventional and curious with wide interests |

refers to your *reputation*, the person we think you are—how you are described by people who have had the pleasure of your company.

Historically, personality research has almost exclusively focused on analyzing unseen factors inside people; but, after 100 years, there isn't much to report, especially relative to the effort spent studying these factors. There is no taxonomy of identity, there is no measurement base (to capture individual differences), and there are very few reliable generalizations to be found. However, reputation is easy to study using checklists and observer descriptions. The well-known five-factor model (FFM; Wiggins, 1996—see Table 15.1) is based on factor analyses of observer descriptions and it provides a robust taxonomy of individual differences in reputation. And measures based on, and research organized in terms of, the FFM have produced a veritable cornucopia of empirical findings (see Roberts, Kuncel, Shiner, Caspi, & Goldberg, 2007). In the remainder of this chapter we define personality in terms of reputation—specifically, how leaders are described by others.

## 4   Personality and Leadership

We have defined personality and leadership; the next question concerns the relationship between the two. To evaluate the links, we need scores for individual leaders on the dimensions of the five-factor model (see Table 15.1) and quantitative indices of performance in leadership roles. The more of this sort of data we can find, the better we can make the evaluation. In the best study yet done on this topic, Judge, Bono, Ilies, and Gerhardt (2002) reviewed 73 published studies of personality and leadership performance. These studies contained more than 25,000 managers from every level, in 5,000 organizations, across every industry sector. They found that four of the five dimensions of the five-factor model were significantly correlated with ratings for leadership emergence and effectiveness. Adjustment was the best predictor, agreeableness was the weakest predictor, and ascendance, prudence, and openness also significantly predicted leadership performance. The correlation between IQ and leadership performance was .23; the multiple correlation between personality and leadership was .53. In our view, multiple correlations are the best way to estimate the relationship between personality and rated leadership performance.

For people who believe in data, this landmark study ends the argument—personality predicts rated leadership performance across all organizational levels and industry sectors, and does so more powerfully than any known alternative. It is also important to note that this research concerns the links between personality (as captured by the five-factor model) and observers' ratings of a person's leadership performance. The study does not tell us about the links between leader personality and business unit or team performance. The study makes two more important points. First, people who seem confident (adjustment), assertive (ascendance), self-controlled (prudence), and open-minded (openness) are perceived as having talent for leadership independently of organization or organizational level—that is, individuals differ in their potential for leadership. Second, agreeableness seems to be irrelevant to the perceived leadership syndrome. Why this is so is an interesting and unresolved question.

A second way to study the links between personality and leadership involves implicit leadership theory. Implicit leadership theory assumes that people have shared cognitive prototypes regarding the characteristics of effective leaders (Kouzes & Posner, 2002; Lord et al., 1986), and then it tries to identify these prototypes. Kouzes and Posner (2002) provide an overwhelming amount of data showing that, if people are asked to describe the best and the worst bosses they have known, they describe them in terms of four categories of characteristics that anyone can replicate. The four categories are supported by data as well as by the five-factor model; but academic researchers have largely overlooked these findings.

The first and most important leadership characteristic is integrity; it is vital that people be able to trust their leaders not to lie to them, exploit them, betray them, or behave foolishly; the data also suggest that followers are often disappointed here. The second category is "decisiveness," the ability to make sound, defensible decisions in a timely way, usually on the basis of limited data. Good decision-making is crucial because the history of any business is the sum of the decisions that managers make over time (March & Simon, 1958), and some decisions (e.g. Napoleon's decision to invade Russia in the winter) can be disastrous. The third characteristic is competence— leaders need to be a resource for their groups, and a leader's legitimacy depends on his/her demonstrated expertise (French & Raven, 1959). Finally, the fourth characteristic concerns vision—good leaders project a vision that gives people confidence in the future and facilitates team performance by clarifying roles and goals (House, 1971).

To summarize, implicit leadership theory maintains that people are pre-wired to evaluate leaders in terms of four broad performance characteristics—integrity, good judgment, competence, and vision—and if leaders lack these attributes (as they often do), they also lack credibility as leaders. This generalization raises a further two questions. First, what is the relationship between implicit leadership theory and the five-factor model, both of which are taxonomies of reputation? And second, do good leaders (those who can build effective teams) in fact have the attributes identified by implicit leadership theory? The answer to both questions is, "We don't know."

The five-factor model concerns the reputations of people in general, it concerns what we would like to know about anyone before we meet that person—is he or she neurotic, approachable, charming, dependable, and/or imaginative? Similarly, implicit leadership theory concerns the reputations of leaders in general, it concerns what we would like to know about any candidate for a leadership position before we meet that person—is he or she honest, decisive, competent, and visionary?

The question about the empirical links between implicit leadership theory and the five-factor model has not been examined explicitly in the research literature. We suspect that integrity is a function of the dimensions of adjustment, prudence, and agreeableness (Ones, Viswesvaran, & Schmidt, 1993). Decisiveness is likely to be a function of adjustment and openness. Competence will be most closely related to experience and IQ or cognitive ability. Finally, vision is probably related to ascendance and openness. But these speculations remain to be evaluated.

## 5  Leadership and Business Unit Performance

The preceding section argues that personality and leadership style are related. This section concerns whether it matters, and asks three questions:

1  Is there such a thing as good management?
2  Does it matter?
3  If so, how?

Regarding the existence of good management and whether it matters, Bloom and Van Reenen (2007) studied the management practices at 732 manufacturing firms in the United States, Great Britain, France, and Germany; they found that a firm's financial performance was a function of the degree to which it followed "well-established management practices" in the areas of operations, performance management, and talent management. They then replicated these findings by using an additional 3,268 firms, including a large sample from Asia. Three of the conclusions from this important study are worth noting. First, there are, in fact, well-established principles of management, even though some academic psychologists don't believe this. Second, the companies that use these principles are more profitable than those that do not. Third, senior leadership decides what management practices will be used. This is one way in which leadership is linked to firm performance.

Regarding the effects of good leadership, Collins (2001) searched the data base for the Fortune 1,000 companies in order to identify companies that satisfied two conditions: (1) 15 years of performance significantly below the mean for their industry; then (2) 15 years of performance significantly above the mean for their industry. He found 11 companies matching that profile. That which distinguished those 11 companies was the CEO, each of whom was characterized as humble and relentlessly determined. Collins concluded that the personality of the CEO is a vital component of organizational effectiveness, and that the cult of the charismatic CEO is utterly wrongheaded. In our experience, the word "charisma" is often a synonym for narcissism, which is a known management derailer (cf. Hogan et al., in press).

A paper by Harter, Schmidt, and Hayes (2002) highlights the crucial role of followers for business unit performance. Specifically, Harter, Schmidt, and Hayes show that how employees view their supervisors (implicit leadership theory) determines their overall level of engagement and job satisfaction, and that, in turn, drives unit performance. In a study using 198,514 employees from 7,939 business units from all industry sectors, they report that employee engagement and satisfaction at the business-unit level correlate .37 and .38 respectively with a composite index of business unit performance that included turnover, customer loyalty, and financial performance. They have replicated these findings in subsequent research, published in non-academic sources.

Thus the way a manager treats his/her staff impacts staff morale. When morale is low, turnover goes up, and customer satisfaction and productivity go down; when morale is high, turnover goes down, and customer satisfaction and productivity go up. The data supporting this conclusion are beyond reproach, and indicate that the impact of leadership on business unit performance is mediated by staff morale. This puts the spotlight directly on the question of what the followers want.

# 6   What Do Followers Want?

For literally millions of years, humans lived in egalitarian hunter–gatherer societies with no formal leaders; individuals exercised leadership by persuading the group to follow their suggestions on the strength of their reputation for good judgment, integrity, expertise, and contributions to group welfare. Modern research shows that dominance is unrelated to leadership effectiveness in laboratory and real-world settings. Dominance may produce compliance, but at the cost of alienation and resentment. Leadership that creates voluntary commitment is best for engaging followers.

Ronald Reagan was fond of saying: "He governs best who governs least," and he may have been on to something. Several years ago, on a commercial flight, one of us sat next to a retired engineer who was a story-teller. After a few stories, he mentioned that he had been Ronald Reagan's boss during the Second World War, when they ran a logistic operation for the army. He added that Reagan was the best natural manager he had ever known. I pointed out that Reagan was often criticized for his "hands-off" leadership style, and the engineer snapped, "That's because he knows what he is doing." He noted that Reagan's transition into the White House had been the smoothest in memory—more so than that of the compulsively organized nuclear engineer Jimmy Carter—and this testified to Reagan's skill as a manager.

The fundamental dynamic in every organization is the individual search for power. This inevitably leads some managers to invent "projects for promotion"; ambitious managers, eager to advance their careers, propose initiatives—not to solve problems but to demonstrate their leadership talent. In this way, much energy and money are spent enhancing the legacy of push managers. We suspect that, at work, people mostly want to be left alone to do their jobs. Leadership is probably relevant in times of crisis and when organizations are confronted with internal or external threats. In any case, it is worth asking if, in the typical case (e.g. a middle manager), leadership is important.

Three considerations support the view that the importance of leadership is overblown. First, as noted above, in hunter–gatherer societies, which are proxies for the original social organization of humans, there are no leaders. We evolved in leaderless societies and, in ordinary circumstances, we may find leadership alienating.

Second, we estimate that the base rate for incompetent management in corporate America is 65 percent to 75 percent. On the basis of this percentage, if leadership were truly important, most organizations should fail; the fact that they don't fail suggests that factors other than leadership explain organizational performance. Third, anyone who has conducted job analyses in organizations knows that employees expend a lot of effort avoiding their managers.

Kelley argued that corporate success is not necessarily due to leaders. Followers who can manage themselves, are committed to the organization, and are courageous, honest, and credible, not only contribute to organizational success but also keep their leaders out of trouble: "Groups with many leaders can be chaos. Groups with none can be very productive" (1988, p. 148).

There are good data to support the case for minimal leadership. For example, Harter et al. (2002) show that leadership style impacts staff morale, and that staff morale then predicts business unit performance, which highlights the importance of staff morale. Leadership style correlates about .30 with staff morale. However, staff members' own scores on the five-factor model dimension of adjustment correlate above .50 with staff morale. This suggests that, although leadership style affects staff morale, it is not the most important determinant. The conclusion seems straightforward: the best way to enhance staff morale, and therefore business unit performance, is to hire staff with high scores for adjustment; leadership is a secondary consideration.

In Herzberg's (1964) study of employee motivation, he concluded that it is important to distinguish between motivator factors and hygiene factors. Motivator factors improve performance, whereas hygiene factors demotivate people. Removing hygiene factors eliminates sources of dissatisfaction, but does not actually enhance performance. The data suggest that leadership may be a hygiene factor—although bad leadership degrades employee performance, good leadership seems not to improve it. It is easy to conclude that leadership interventions should focus on weeding out the bad ones and not on worrying about the good ones.

Most research considers followers to be passive recipients of leader interventions and then measures their motivation, productivity, and satisfaction levels. Ahmad and Loch (2010) investigate the circumstances in which followers actually need a leader's input. Their results suggest that people mostly want to do their work and resolve their problems alone; sometimes, however, the nature of the work or the problems found therein require a leader's input. These findings help clarify what leaders do when facilitating collaborative outcomes. Rather than performing multiple functions, as suggested by Barnard (1948), Mintzberg (1973), and Fleishman et al. (1991), this research suggests that leaders should only intervene when there are coordination problems or conflict of interests among team members. A similar study by Gillet, Cartwright, and Van Vugt (2010) shows that leadership is a resource for the group, not a benefit for the leader; leaders incur personal costs when they assist group efforts, a finding that supports the notion of servant leadership.

We think that the key variable impacting leadership concerns the degree to which followers are free to defect. If they are free to defect, then leadership is essential to

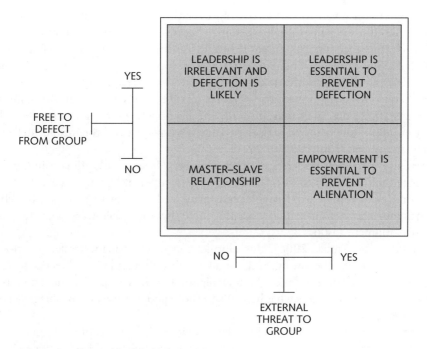

**Figure 15.1** Conditional leadership matrix

maintain their support. If they are not free to defect, then leadership primarily impacts follower engagement or alienation. Figure 15.1 illustrates this point.

## 7 Bad and Unethical Leadership

The effectiveness of leaders depends not only on their perceived competence, but also on their perceived integrity. The steady procession of corporate failures and financial scandals over the past several years has produced a line of inquiry focused on how leaders fail and what can be done about it. For readers who have not been paying attention, Kenneth Lay (CEO of Enron), Bernard Ebbers (CEO of WorldCom), and Dennis Koslowski (CEO of Tyco International) destroyed over US$300 billion of shareholder value (George, 2003b), and Bernard Madoff, an investment fund operator, duped his investors out of US$10–17 billion in a historically large but not uncommon Ponzi scheme (Shamir, 2009).

Kellerman (2004) identifies seven types of bad leaders as follows: incompetent leaders lack the ability to produce results; rigid leaders are unwilling to change; intemperate leaders lack self-control; callous leaders bully others; corrupt leaders lie, steal, or cheat to serve their own interests; insular leaders are unconcerned about the welfare of others; and, finally, evil leaders deliberately cause pain and suffering. However, malevolent leaders must rely on willing followers and supportive environments to enable their destructive personal agendas (Lipman-Blumen, 2006; Padilla et al., 2007).

The attention given to bad leadership over the past 20 years or so parallels the modern interest in charismatic leadership. Theories of charismatic, transformational, and visionary leadership, sometimes referred to as the "new" leadership (Bass, 2008), appeared in the late 1970s and mid-1980s and profoundly affected leadership research. From 1990 to 2000, one third of the articles in *The Leadership Quarterly* concerned charismatic and transformational theories (Lowe & Gardner, 2000). Similarly, Khurana (2002) describes what he calls the irrational quest for charismatic CEOs (who enjoyed huge compensation packages irrespective of the results delivered) during the period from 1980 to 2000.

Bass's (2008) new leadership theories concern how "extraordinary individuals" influence their followers toward "exceptional performance." Achieving excellence and delivering great results are desirable, but many leaders went to extremes to achieve or maintain the heroic status accorded them by their followers and the media (Lipman-Blumen, 2006).

According to Ciulla (2004), this glorification of charismatic leaders overlooked the fact that they can be wrong, and can take their followers in bad directions. Keeley (1995) notes that transformational leadership implies consensus on values and mission of the leaders, and wonders what happens to those people who do not share a leader's values and goals.

Leaders who, in conjunction with their followers, deliver exceptional results sometimes do so while causing harm to others, or to society at large (Price, 2000). Followers of such heroes are likely to overlook the not-so-ethical means employed in dealing with out-groups. And then the same leaders may relegate their followers to the out-group. So, charisma can be a double-edged sword.

Some scholars have proposed ideal models of leadership designed to counter these problems. Greenleaf and Spears (2002) propose that leaders should serve followers and uphold ethical principles even if their organizations incur financial losses. Other writers propose "authentic leadership"—the view that leaders should match their words and deeds with their values and that their values should include concern for others and for the community. These authentic individuals become leaders in order to enact their values rather than to obtain status and privileges (Gardner, Avolio, Luthans, May, & Walumbwa, 2005; George, 2003a; Price, 2003). These theories are prescriptive, not descriptive, and they lack clear measurement models (Cooper, Scandura, & Schriesheim, 2005) or empirical support (Yukl, 2006).

The concept of charisma is itself somewhat problematic. First, as noted earlier, the assessment literature suggests that charisma resembles narcissism. Measures of charisma correlate significantly with measures of narcissism, and persons with high scores on measures of charisma and narcissism are described in the same terms (Hogan & Fico, in press). Second, in Collins' (2001) study of effective CEOs, all of them were described as "humble"; humility is the antithesis of charisma. Finally, Chatterjee and Hambrick (2007) show that narcissistic CEOs are bad for business. These researchers assigned CEOs scores for narcissism on the basis of three criteria: (1) the degree to which marketing material contained pictures of the CEO alone; (2) the frequency with which the CEO used the word "I" in his/her public statements; and (3) the ratio of the CEO's salary to the next highest paid person in the organization. Companies with narcissistic CEOs had more volatility in their annual performance and the average performance of their companies was worse by comparison with companies with more humble CEOs. Charisma and narcissism are not identical, but they are more closely related than is often recognized.

# 8 Shared Team Leadership

Most current theories define leadership in terms of the people who are in charge, and then they analyze the characteristics, behaviors, styles, and methods these people use to produce results (Ayman, 2004; Bass & Riggio, 2006; Chemers, 2000; Marta, Leritz, & Mumford, 2005; Zaccaro, Kemp, & Bader, 2004). Thus these theories adopt a top-down approach (Pearce, 2004) to studying leadership, with leaders placed at the top and followers arrayed beneath them. This is the individualistic view of leadership, which we use when we think of nations in terms of their presidents (e.g. Barak Obama, Saddam Hussein), of corporations in terms of their CEOs (Jack Welch, Bill Gates, and Jeffrey Skilling), and of sports teams in terms of their coaches or star players. Leadership development programs mostly teach individual leadership skills such as how to advance on the job, and major organizations hire managers on the basis of their individual characteristics and skills.

Gibb (1954) proposed an early alternative to individualized models of leadership; he suggested thinking about leadership in terms of different team roles, distributed across the members of a team. As modern organizations become increasingly complex, the idea of sharing leadership tasks among team members becomes attractive (O'Toole, Galbraith, & Lawler, 2003). Flattening hierarchies, creating more fluid and democratic organizational structures, and shifting from industrial work to knowledge work increasingly makes individualized hierarchical leadership ineffective and suggests that it be reconsidered (Pearce, 2004).

Pearce and Conger suggest that shared leadership is

a dynamic, interactive influence process among individuals in groups for which the objective is to lead one another to the achievement of group or organizational goals or both. This influence process often involves peer, or lateral, influence and at other times involves upward or downward hierarchical influence. (Pearce & Conger, 2003, p. 1)

The shared approach sees leadership as the result of the team processes such as teamwork and team learning; leadership is a team resource that develops over time and allows a team to adapt to complex environments and to improve performance (Day, Gronn, & Salas, 2004).

Shared leadership is likely to develop in environments that offer team members a shared purpose and allow them to participate fully in team activities and to provide input on relevant matters (Carson, Tesluk, & Marrone, 2007). Shared leadership is an alternative to the traditional conception of leadership; but there are many issues to be resolved before it gains wider acceptance. For example, there is considerable confusion about what constitutes shared leadership and under what circumstances this form of leadership is likely to be effective (Pearce, Conger, & Locke, 2007). Obviously, such debates should be resolved using empirical studies and data to decide what formulations are best. Finally, individual team members always differ in terms of their personality characteristics. How different personality characteristics interact to produce high-functioning teams is an important topic for research.

## 9   Leadership Training

Leadership training is a multibillion dollar industry (Fulmer, 1997). Nonetheless, the failure rates for executives suggest that these leadership development programs are not fully effective. Ready and Conger (2003) identify three reasons for the failure of leadership development programs. First, leadership training typically creates a mindset preoccupied with control, power acquisition, and advancement rather than shared accountability. Second, many organizations buy off-the-shelf training programs that are based upon the latest consulting fad, without considering whether these programs are aligned with the strategic direction of the organization. Third, there are no effective systems available to evaluate the effectiveness of such training interventions.

According to Day (2000), it is important to distinguish between leader development and leadership development; the latter involves building the collective capacity of organizations to deploy leadership processes effectively (McCauley, Moxley, & Van Velsor, 1998). Leadership development is likely to be more effective when individuals are able to learn from their on-the-job experiences. Moreover, in rapidly flattening organizations that use interdependent networks to achieve their strategic objectives (Hernez-Broome & Hughes, 2004), "lone ranger" leaders are increasingly irrelevant.

The core task of leadership is to build and maintain a high-performing team. Bad managers are bad because they either destroy, or can't build, effective teams. Managers/leaders build teams by forging relationships between themselves and the individual team members. A core component of any leadership training effort, therefore, should concern evaluating a person's talent for building relationships—or for identifying his/her proclivities for destroying relationships.

It is important to acknowledge that some people are incapable of working as part of a team or of engaging with managers, no matter how skilled those managers might be. In athletics, these people are called "team killers." Such people are easy to identify by using standard psychometric screening procedures (cf. Hogan & Kaiser, 2010).

Every organizational intervention, including leadership training, should begin with an assessment. The assessment data will reveal an individual's strengths and shortcomings for performance in leadership roles, and can be used to construct training interventions. We believe the best and most efficient assessment model involves using well-validated measures of personality combined with subordinate appraisals. Consistent with our focus on leader reputation, for personality measures we favor the California Psychological Inventory (Gough, 1975), the Hogan Personality Inventory (Hogan & Hogan, 1995), and the Hogan Development Survey (Hogan & Hogan, 2009), because they are validated against observer descriptions. For subordinate appraisals, we favor the Leadership Versatility Index (Kaplan & Kaiser, 2006), on the grounds of its clear conceptualization and solid empirical support.

Scores on well-constructed personality measures change only slightly over time, and this stability creates a lot of confusion about training efforts. The scores on the personality inventories predict how a person will typically behave. Armed with this information, that person can then modify the undesirable aspects of his/her behavior. Bad managers can stop lying, playing favorites, bullying, hogging the credit, and cheating on credit card expenses, and can start treating their staff with respect. But, without feedback on their typical performance, they won't know what behaviors need changing.

It is also the case that, for training purposes, there is no news in good news. Good news means that you should continue doing what you are doing. Useful feedback for training purposes only comes from information about what you are doing wrong.

Ultimately, however, the key to training effectiveness is an individual differences variable called "coachability." Good athletes are always coachable; talented but underperforming athletes are uncoachable. Despite the importance of individual differences in coachability for training effectiveness, we seem to know very little about the characteristics of people who are coachable.

# 10 Conclusion

Over the years, views regarding the value of leadership research have alternated between optimism and skepticism. "For those who are not aware of the crises leadership researchers faced, image the following task: Take bits and pieces of several sets of jigsaw puzzles, mix them, and then ask a friend to put the pieces together into one cohesive picture" (Antonakis, et al., 2004, p. 4). In the early 1900s, scholars began compiling lists of traits associated with leadership; this approach assumes that there are individual differences in the talent for leadership, and that personality and leadership are organically related. Then, in an influential review, Stogdill (1948) challenged the importance of personality and shifted the focus of research to situational factors and associated leadership behaviors; this was followed by theories of "situational leadership," which minimized the importance of personality and individual differences in the talent for leadership. Later, Burns (1978) published a Pulitzer prize-winning book that dramatized the phenomenon of transformational/charismatic leadership. This view, which again emphasizes the importance of individual differences, influenced subsequent leadership research up to the present. More recently, widespread financial wrong-doing and corporate failures highlighted the importance of incompetent and unethical leadership, an emphasis that also concerns individual differences. Finally, the inexorable advance of globalization, information technology, and knowledge-based work and the distribution of operations across cultural boundaries have created interest in team-based models of leadership.

These changing emphases outlined above show how scholars have responded to changes in the social milieu; but these developments also reflect the fact that leadership research lacks a strong theoretical background or foundational principles. More importantly, each of these research traditions ignores the role of followers. But it is followers, people like the readers and authors of this chapter, who choose or accept people as leaders, and we know little about the process. Followership is "one of the most interesting omissions in theory and research on leadership" (Avolio, Walumbwa, & Weber, 2009, p. 434). Some scholars believe that a clearer picture is now emerging (Antonakis, et al., 2004), but we think that major pieces of the "puzzle" are still missing (e.g. followers) and other pieces have been highlighted inappropriately (e.g. individual leaders). If researchers are unable to resolve their disputes around definitional issues (Rost, 1991), unable to ask different questions (Hackman & Wageman, 2007), and unable to adopt an interdisciplinary perspective (Bennis, 2007), leadership studies will remain confused and unhelpful (Bennis, 1959; Glynn & DeJordy, 2010; Yukl, 1989).

Leaders play crucial and sometimes malevolent roles in modern life. To the degree that we are able to influence the choice of these leaders, we need to base our choices on a rational understanding of leaders and leadership. It is easy to think that, with so much at stake, the empirical analysis of leadership is too important a topic to be left to the academics. In any case, the problem is consequential and largely misunderstood; this is the challenge and opportunity of studying leadership as a scholarly discipline.

# References

Ahmad, M. G., & Loch, C. H. (2010). *The core functions of leadership.* Manuscript submitted for publication.

Antonakis, J., Cianciolo, A. T., & Sternberg, R. J. (2004). Leadership: Past, present, and future. In J. Antonakis, A. T. Cianciolo, & R. J. Sternberg (Eds.), *The nature of leadership* (pp. 3–15). Thousand Oaks, CA: Sage.

Avolio, B. J., Walumbwa, F. O., & Weber, T. J. (2009). Leadership: Current theories, research, and future directions. *Annual Review of Psychology, 60,* 421–449.

Ayman, R. (2004). Situational and contingency approaches to leadership. In J. Antonakis, A. T. Cianciolo, & R. J. Sternberg (Eds.), *The nature of leadership* (pp. 148–170). Thousand Oaks, CA: Sage.

Barnard, C. (1948). The nature of leadership. In C. Barnard (Ed.), *Organization and management, selected papers* (pp. 88–110). Cambridge, MA: Harvard University Press.

Bass, B. M. (2008). *The Bass handbook of leadership: Theory, research, and managerial applications* (4th ed.). New York: The Free Press.

Bass, B. M., & Riggio, R. E. (2006). *Transformational leadership.* Mahwah, NJ: Lawrence Erlbaum Associates.

Bennis, W. (1959). Leadership theory and administrative behavior: The problem of authority. *Administrative Science Quarterly, 4*(3), 259–301.

Bennis, W. (2007). The challenges of leadership in the modern world: Introduction to the special issue. *American Psychologist, 62*(1), 2–5.

Bentz, V. J. (1985). *A view from the top: A thirty-year perspective on research devoted to discovery, description, and prediction of executive behavior.* Paper presented at the 93rd Annual Convention of the American Psychological Association, Los Angeles.

Bloom, N., & Van Reenen, J. (2007). Measuring and explaining management practices across firms and countries. *Quarterly Journal of Economics, 122*(4), 1351–1408.

Boehm, C. (1999). *Hierarchy in the forest: The evolution of egalitarian behavior.* Cambridge, MA: Harvard University Press.

Bowles, S. (2009). Did warfare among ancestral hunter–gatherers affect the evolution of human social behaviors? *Science, 324*(5932), 1293–1298.

Burns, J. M. (1978). *Leadership.* New York: Harper & Row.

Buss, D. M. (1999). *Evolutionary psychology: The new science of the mind.* Boston, MA: Allyn & Bacon.

Carson, J. B., Tesluk, P. E., & Marrone, J. A. (2007). Shared leadership in teams: An investigation of antecedent conditions and performance. *Academy of Management Journal, 50*(5), 1217–1234.

Charan, R. (2005). Ending the CEO succession crisis. *Harvard Business Review, 83*(2), 72–81.

Chatterjee, A., & Hambrick, D. C. (2007). It's all about me: Narcissistic chief executive officers and their effects on company strategy and performance. *Administrative Science Quarterly, 52*(3), 351–386.

Chemers, M. M. (2000). Leadership research and theory: A functional integration. *Group Dynamics: Theory, Research, and Practice, 4*(1), 27–43.

Ciulla, J. B. (2004). Ethics and leadership effectiveness. In J. Antonakis, A. T. Cianciolo, & R. J. Sternberg (Eds.), *The nature of leadership* (pp. 302–327). Thousand Oaks, CA: Sage.

Collins, J. (2001). Level 5 leadership: The triumph of humility and fierce resolve. *Harvard Business Review, 79*(1), 66–79.

Cooper, C. D., Scandura, T. A., & Schriesheim, C. A. (2005). Looking forward but learning from our past: Potential challenges to developing authentic leadership theory and authentic leaders. *The Leadership Quarterly, 16*(3), 475–493.

Day, D. V. (2000). Leadership development: A review in context. *The Leadership Quarterly, 11*(4), 581–613.

Day, D. V., & Lord, R. G. (1988). Executive leadership and organizational performance: Suggestions for a new theory and methodology. *Journal of Management, 14*(3), 453–464.

Day, D. V., Gronn, P., & Salas, E. (2004). Leadership capacity in teams. *The Leadership Quarterly, 15*(6), 857–880.

Diamond, J. (1997). *Guns, germs, and steel: The fates of human societies.* New York: W. W. Norton.

Dvir, T., & Shamir, B. (2003). Follower developmental characteristics as predicting transformational leadership: A longitudinal field study. *The Leadership Quarterly, 14*(3), 327–344.

Fleishman, E. A., Mumford, M. D., Zaccaro, S. J., Levin, K. Y., Korotkin, A. L., & Hein, M. B. (1991). Taxonomic efforts in the description of leader behavior: A synthesis and functional interpretation. *The Leadership Quarterly, 2*(4), 245–287.

French, J. R. P., Jr., & Raven, B. (1959). The bases of social power. In D. Cartwright (Ed.), *Studies in social power* (pp. 150–167). Ann Arbor, MI: Institute for Social Research.

Fulmer, R. M. (1997). The evolving paradigm of leadership development. *Organizational Dynamics, 25*(4), 59–72.

Gardner, W. L., Avolio, B. J., Luthans, F., May, D. R., & Walumbwa, F. (2005). "Can you see the real me?" A self-based model of authentic leader and follower development. *The Leadership Quarterly, 16*(3), 343–372.

George, B. (2003a). *Authentic leadership—Rediscovering the secrets to creating lasting value.* San Francisco, CA: Jossey-Bass.

George, B. (2003b). Crisis and corporate ethics: Where have all the leaders gone? Retrieved February 11, 2010, from http://www.billgeorge.org/page/crisis-and-corporate-ethics-where-have-all-the-leaders-gone.

Gibb, C. A. (1954). Leadership. In G. Lindzey (Ed.), *Handbook of social psychology* (Vol. 2, pp. 877–917). Reading, MA: Addison-Wesley.

Gillet, J., Cartwright, E., & Van Vugt, M. (2010). *Selfish or servant leadership? Evolutionary predictions on leadership personalities in coordination games.* Manuscript submitted.

Glynn, M. A., & DeJordy, R. (2010). Leadership through an organization behavior lens. In N. Nohria & R. Khurana (Eds.), *Handbook of leadership theory and practice* (pp. 119–157). Boston, MA: Harvard Business Press.

Graen, G. B. (2009). Early identification of future executives: a functional approach. *Industrial and Organizational Psychology, 2*, 437–441.

Greenleaf, R. K., & Spears, L. C. (2002). *Servant leadership: A journey into the nature of legitimate power and greatness* (25th anniversary ed.). Mahwah, NJ: Paulist Press.

Grint, K. (2000). *The arts of leadership.* Oxford: Oxford University Press.

Gough, H. G. (1975). *Manual for the California Psychological Inventory.* Palo Alto, CA: Consulting Psychologists Press.

Hackman, J. R., & Wageman, R. (2007). Asking the right questions about leadership: Discussion and conclusions. *American Psychologist, 62*(1), 43–47.

Hamel, G. (2007). *The future of management.* Boston, MA: Harvard Business School Press.

Harter, J. K., Schmidt, F. L., & Hayes, T. L. (2002). Business-unit-level relationship between employee satisfaction, employee engagement, and business outcomes: A meta-analysis. *Journal of Applied Psychology, 87*(2), 268–279.

Hernez-Broome, G., & Hughes, R. J. (2004). Leadership development: Past, present, and future. *Human Resource Planning, 27*(1), 24–32.

Herzberg, F. (1964). The motivation–hygiene concept and problems of manpower. *Personnel Administration, 27*(1), 3–7.

Hogan, R., & Fico, J. (in press). Narcissism and leadership. In W. K. Campbell & J. Miller (Eds.), *The handbook of narcissism and narcissistic personality disorder.* New York: Wiley.

Hogan, R., & Hogan, J. (1995). *Manual for the Hogan Personality Inventory.* Tulsa, OK: Hogan Assessment Systems.

Hogan, R., & Hogan, J. (2009). *Manual for the Hogan Development Survey.* Tulsa, OK: Hogan Assessment Systems.

Hogan, R., & Kaiser, R. B. (2010). Personality. Evidence-based practices for selecting and developing organizational talent. In J. C. Scott & D. H. Reynolds (Eds.), *Handbook of workplace assessment: Selecting and developing organizational talent* (pp. 81–108). New York: Pfeiffer.

Hogan, J., Hogan, R., & Kaiser, R. B. (in press). Management derailment. In Sheldon Zedeck (Ed.), *American Psychological Association Handbook of Industrial and Organizational Psychology.* Washington, DC: American Psychological Association.

House, R. J. (1971). A path goal theory of leader effectiveness. *Administrative Science Quarterly, 16*(3), 321–339.

Johnson, A. W., & Earle, T. (1987). *The evolution of human societies: From foraging group to agrarian state.* Stanford, CA: Stanford University Press.

Joyce, W. F., Nohria, N., & Roberson, B. (2003). *What really works.* New York: Harper Business.

Judge, T. A., Bono, J. E., Ilies, R., & Gerhardt, M. W. (2002). Personality and leadership: A qualitative and quantitative review. *Journal of Applied Psychology, 87*(4), 765–780.

Kaiser, R. B., Hogan, R., & Craig, S. B. (2008). Leadership and the fate of organizations. *American Psychologist, 63*(2), 96–110.

Kaplan, B., & Kaiser, R. (2006). *The versatile leader.* San Francisco, CA: Pfeiffer.

Katz, L. D. (Ed.). (2000). *Evolutionary origins of morality: Cross-disciplinary perspectives.* Bowling Green, OH: Imprint Academic.

Keeley, M. (1995). The trouble with transformational leadership: Toward a federalist ethic for organizations. *Business Ethics Quarterly, 5*(1), 67–96.

Kellerman, B. (2004). *Bad leadership: What it is, how it happens, why it matters.* Boston, MA: Harvard Business School Press.

# Plates

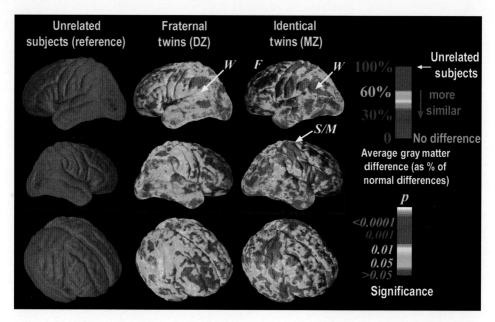

**Plate 1**  Genetic continuum of similarity in brain structure. Differences in the quantity of gray matter at each region were computed for identical and fraternal twins, averaged and compared with the average differences that would be found between pairs of unrelated individuals (blue, left). Color-coded maps show the percentage reduction in intra-pair variance for each cortical region. Fraternal twins exhibit only 30% of the normal differences (red, middle), and these affinities are restricted to perisylvian language and spatial association cortices. Genetically identical twins display only 10–30% of normal differences (red and pink) in a large anatomical band spanning frontal (F), sensorimotor (S/M), and Wernicke's (W) language cortices, suggesting strong genetic control of brain structure in these regions, but not in others (blue; the significance of these effects is shown on the same color scale). Source: P. M. Thompson et al. (2001)

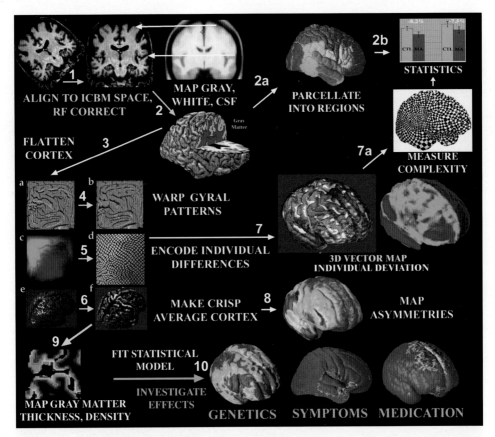

**Plate 2** Image analysis steps for detecting differences in cortical anatomy. An image analysis pipeline is shown here. It can be used to create maps that reveal how brain structure varies in large populations, differs in disease, and is modulated by genetic or therapeutic factors. 3D MRI scans from patients and controls are aligned (1) with an average brain template based on a population. Tissue classification algorithms generate maps of gray matter, white matter, and CSF (2). In a simple analysis, these tissue maps can be parcellated into lobes (2a) and their volumes assessed with analysis of variance or other statistics (2b). Or, to compare cortical features from subjects whose anatomy differs, individual cortical surfaces can be flattened (3) and aligned with a group average gyral pattern (4). If a color code indexing 3D cortical locations is flowed along with the same deformation field (5), a crisp group average model of the cortex can be made (6). Relative to this average, individual gyral pattern differences (7), measures of cortical complexity (7b), or cortical pattern asymmetry (8) can be computed. Once individual gyral patterns are aligned to the mean template, differences in gray matter density or thickness (9) can be mapped after pooling data across subjects from homologous regions of cortex. Correlations can be identified between differences in gray matter density or cortical thickness and genetic risk factors (10). Maps may also be generated visualizing regions in which linkages are detected between structural deficits and clinical symptoms, cognitive scores, and medication effects.
Source: P. M. Thompson et al. (2004)

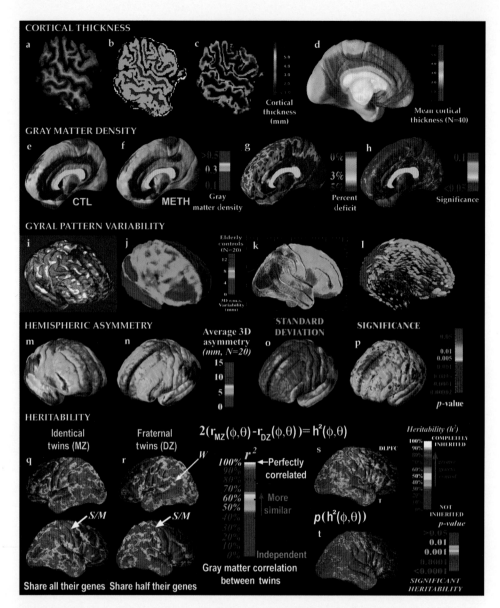

**Plate 3** Statistical maps of cortical structure. A variety of maps can be made that describe different aspects of cortical anatomy. These include maps of cortical thickness (a–d), gray matter density (e–h), gyral pattern variability (i–l), hemispheric asymmetry (m–p), and heritability of brain structure (q–t). These maps are sensitive to changes in development or disease and can be used to pinpoint regions where structure is abnormal or where it correlates with clinical or treatment parameters. Source: P. M. Thompson et al. (2004)

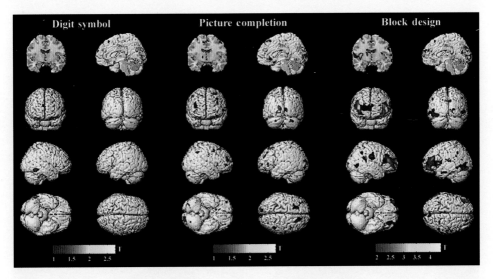

**Plate 4**  Correlations between regional gray matter and digit symbol scores, picture completion, and block design ($N = 48$). Color bar shows $t$ values; maximum $r = .36, .39,$ and $.57$ respectively. Source: Colom, Jung, & Haier, 2006, Figure 2, p. 1362

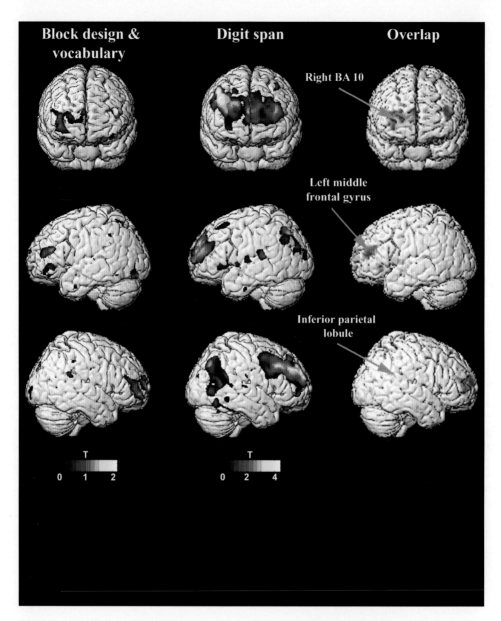

**Plate 5** Correlations between gray matter and measures of *g* (conjunction of block design and vocabulary; left panel), working-memory capacity (WMC; total digit span score; middle panel), and the overlap between the two (right panel) are shown on standard magnetic resonance imaging (MRI) templates (frontal, left, and right, respectively). Correlations with *g* and WMC are shown at $p < .0001$; overlap correlations are at $p < .000001$ (i.e. the square of .001). The three overlap correlations labelled are significant at $p < .05$ corrected for multiple comparisons. Source: Colom, Jung, & Haier, 2007

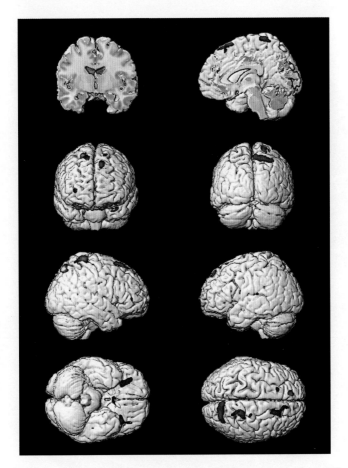

**Plate 6**  Regional correlations between gray matter density and individual differences in *g* (*N* = 104). The design matrix controls for total gray matter

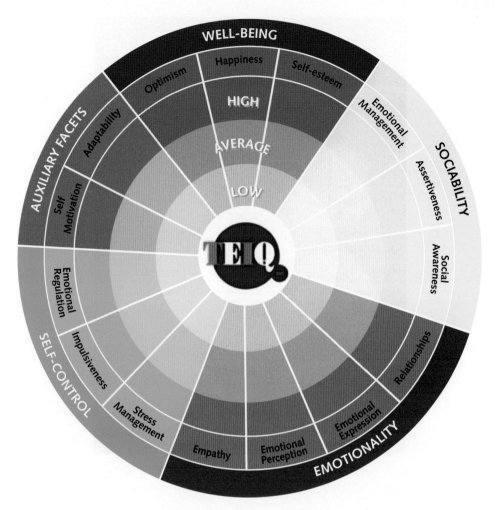

**Plate 7** The 15 facets of the TEIQue positioned with reference to their corresponding factor. Note that adaptability and self-motivation ("auxiliary" or "independent" facets) are not keyed to any factor, but feed directly into the global trait EI score. A brief description of the facets is given in Table 25.2

Kelley, R. E. (1988). In praise of followers. *Harvard Business Review*, 66(6), 142–148.

Khurana, R. (2002). *Searching for a corporate savior: The irrational quest for charismatic CEOs*. Princeton, NJ: Princeton University Press.

Khurana, R. (2007). *From higher aims to hired hands: The social transformation of American business schools and the unfulfilled promise of management as a profession*. Princeton, NJ: Princeton University Press.

Kouzes, J. M., & Posner, B. Z. (2002). *The leadership challenge* (3rd ed.). San Francisco, CA: Jossey-Bass.

Kramer, R. J. (2008). Have we learned anything about leadership development? *The Conference Board Review*, 45(May/June), 26–30.

Laurent, J., & Nightingale, J. (2001). *Darwinism and evolutionary economics*. Cheltenham: Edward Elgar.

Lipman-Blumen, J. (2006). *The allure of toxic leaders: Why we follow destructive bosses and corrupt politicians–And how we can survive them*. Cambridge, MA: Oxford University Press.

Lord, R. G., De Vader, C. L., & Alliger, G. M. (1986). A meta-analysis of the relation between personality traits and leadership perceptions: An application of validity generalization procedures. *Journal of Applied Psychology*, 71(3), 402–410.

Lowe, K. B., & Gardner, W. L. (2000). Ten years of *The Leadership Quarterly*: Contributions and challenges for the future. *The Leadership Quarterly*, 11(4), 459–514.

March, J. G., & Simon, H. (1958). *Organizations*. New York: Wiley.

Markoczy, L., & Goldberg, J. (1998). Management, organization and human nature: An introduction. *Managerial and Decision Economics*, 19(7/8), 387–409.

Marta, S., Leritz, L. E., & Mumford, M. D. (2005). Leadership skills and the group performance: Situational demands, behavioral requirements, and planning. *The Leadership Quarterly*, 16(1), 97–120.

McCauley, C. D., Moxley, R. S., & Van Velsor, E. (Eds.) (1998). *The Center for Creative Leadership handbook of leadership development*. San Francisco, CA: Jossey-Bass.

Mintzberg, H. (1973). *The nature of managerial work*. New York: Harper & Row.

O'Toole, J., Galbraith, J., & Lawler, E. E. I. (2003). The promise and pitfalls of shared leadership: When two (or more) heads are better than one. In C. L. Pearce & J. A. Conger (Eds.), *Shared leadership: Reframing the hows and whys of leadership* (pp. 250–267). Thousand Oaks, CA: Sage.

Ones, D. S., Viswesvaran, C., & Schmidt, F. L. (1993). Comprehensive meta-analysis of integrity test validities: Findings and implications for personnel selection and theories of job performance. *Journal of Applied Psychology*, 78(4), 679–703.

Padilla, A., Hogan, R., & Kaiser, R. B. (2007). The toxic triangle: Destructive leaders, susceptible followers, and conducive environments. *The Leadership Quarterly*, 18(3), 176–194.

Pearce, C. L. (2004). The future of leadership: Combining vertical and shared leadership to transform knowledge work. *Academy of Management Executive*, 18(1), 47–57.

Pearce, C. L., & Conger, J. A. (2003). All those years ago: The historical underpinnings of shared leadership. In C. L. Pearce & J. A. Conger (Eds.), *Shared leadership: Reframing the hows and whys of leadership* (pp. 1–18). Thousand Oaks, CA: Sage.

Pearce, C. L., Conger, J. A., & Locke, E. A. (2007). Shared leadership theory. *The Leadership Quarterly*, 18(3), 281–288.

Price, T. L. (2000). Explaining ethical failures of leadership. *Leadership and Organization Development Journal*, 21(4), 177–184.

Price, T. L. (2003). The ethics of authentic transformational leadership. *The Leadership Quarterly*, 14(1), 67–81.

Ready, D. A., & Conger, J. A. (2003). Why leadership-development efforts fail. *MIT Sloan Management Review*, *44*(3), 83–88.

Roberts, B. W., Kuncel, N. R., Shiner, R., Caspi, A., & Goldberg, L. R. (2007). The power of personality: The comparative validity of personality traits, socioeconomic status, and cognitive ability for predicting important life outcomes. *Perspectives on Psychological Science*, *2*(4), 313–345.

Rost, J. C. (1991). *Leadership for the twenty-first century*. Westport, CT: Praeger.

Rummel, R. (1994). *Death by government*. New Brunswick, NJ: Transaction Publishers.

Schaller, M., Simpson, J. A., & Kenrick, D. T. (2006). *Evolution and social psychology*. New York: Psychology Press.

Sessa, V. I., Kaiser, R., Taylor, J. K., & Campbell, R. J. (1998). *Executive selection: A research report on what works and what doesn't*. Greensboro, NC: Center for Creative Leadership.

Shamir, S. (2009). Extent of Madoff fraud now estimated at far below $50b. Retrieved February 18, 2010, from http://www.haaretz.com/hasen/spages/1069457.html

Shane, S. (2009). Introduction to the focused issue on the biological basis of business. *Organizational Behavior and Human Decision Processes*, *110*(2), 67–69.

Shipper, F., & Wilson, C. (1992). The impact of managerial behaviors on group performance, stress, and commitment. In K. E. Clark, M. B. Clark, & D. Campbell (Eds.), *Impact of leadership* (pp. 119–129). Greensboro, NC: Center for Creative Leadership.

Smart, B. D. (1999). *Topgrading: How leading companies win by hiring, coaching, and keeping the best people*. Upper Saddle River, NJ: Prentice-Hall.

Stogdill, R. M. (1948). Personal factors associated with leadership: A survey of the literature. *Journal of Psychology*, *25*, 35–71.

Thomas, A. B. (1988). Does leadership make a difference to organizational performance? *Administrative Science Quarterly*, *33*(3), 388–400.

Välikangas, L., & Okumura, A. (1997). Why do people follow leaders? A study of a U.S. and a Japanese change program. *The Leadership Quarterly*, *8*(3), 313–337.

Van Vugt, M. (2006). Evolutionary origins of leadership and followership. *Personality and Social Psychology Review*, *10*(4), 354–371.

Van Vugt, M., Hogan, R., & Kaiser, R. B. (2008). Leadership, followership, and evolution: Some lessons from the past. *American Psychologist*, *63*(3), 182–196.

Wade, N. (2006). *Before the dawn*. New York: Penguin.

Wielkiewicz, R. M., & Stelzner, S. P. (2005). An ecological perspective on leadership theory, research, and practice. *Review of General Psychology*, *9*(4), 326–341.

Wiggins, J. S. (1996). *The five-factor model of personality: Theoretical perspectives*. New York: Guilford Press.

Yukl, G. (1989). Managerial leadership: A review of theory and research. *Journal of Management*, *15*(2), 251–289.

Yukl, G. (2006). *Leadership in organizations* (6th ed.). New York: Pearson Education.

Zaccaro, S. J., Kemp, C., & Bader, P. (2004). Leader traits and attributes. In J. Antonakis, A. T. Cianciolo, & R. J. Sternberg (Eds.), *The nature of leadership* (pp. 101–124). Thousand Oaks, CA: Sage.

# Section 2    Health, Longevity, and Death

# 16

# Cognitive Epidemiology
## *Concepts, Evidence, and Future Directions*
### Catherine M. Calvin, G. David Batty, and Ian J. Deary

## Introduction

Cognitive epidemiology is a new field for the study of individual differences, attempting to understand associations between pre-morbid cognitive ability (we shall also use the terms and phrases "intelligence," "mental ability," "IQ") and health outcomes, particularly morbidity and mortality. The concept of intelligence in association with health may be a familiar one. Evidence from the field of cognitive aging has related somatic diseases to a subsequent decline in intellectual function (Arvanitakis, Wilson, & Bennett, 2006; Comijs et al., 2009; Kivipelto et al., 2005; Okereke et al., 2008; Rafnsson, Deary, Smith, Whiteman, & Fowkes, 2007; Yaffe et al., 2004). Cross-sectional studies pervade the health psychology literature, demonstrating that mental performance and physical health variables significantly correlate. Examining the influences of individual differences in cognitive ability upon health is a more recent endeavor, which has made rapid progress in the last five years. Cognitive epidemiology began with the observation that scores on mental ability tests were inversely correlated with the risk of all-cause mortality over a long-term follow-up. This finding has resonance in several disciplines. For differential psychologists, it offers further evidence for the predictive validity of general intelligence ($g$), the highly stable (Deary, Whalley, Lemmon, Crawford, & Starr, 2000) and heritable (Deary, Johnson, & Houlihan, 2009) trait that significantly correlates with other lifetime outcomes, including educational attainment and career success (Deary, Strand, Smith, &

*The Wiley-Blackwell Handbook of Individual Differences,* First Edition.
Edited by Tomas Chamorro-Premuzic, Sophie von Stumm, and Adrian Furnham.
© 2011 Blackwell Publishing Ltd. Published 2011 by Blackwell Publishing Ltd.

Fernandes, 2007; Gottfredson, 1997; Schmidt & Hunter, 2004). For epidemiologists, clinicians, and policy-makers, the observation has importance for its contribution to understanding health inequalities in populations. The field has gained momentum, and already a large body of empirical work exists which is helping to map out the underlying mechanisms relating cognitive ability to health outcomes.

This chapter presents the latest empirical evidence from the field, together with key issues that merit further investigation and understanding. Before doing so, two important areas are covered. First, a brief historical presentation of the context will be made—that is, a presentation of the events leading up to cognitive epidemiology becoming a defined area of research. Secondly, in recognition that the field brings together two main disciplines—differential psychology and epidemiology—we briefly introduce psychology readers to some key concepts and methods in epidemiology. Evidence from the best of the field's empirical work comes in the following order of presentation: pre-morbid intelligence in relation to all-cause mortality; cause-specific mortality and morbidities; and disease-risk factors. The final section of this chapter discusses the potential mechanisms that may explain these associations, and the methods that will help to consolidate such mechanisms for the field.

## A Brief History

A paper by Maller (1933) is cited as the first observational study to report an inverse association between childhood mental ability scores and risk of mortality (Deary & Batty, 2006; Gottfredson, 2004). This study took the average mental ability test scores of the schools distributed among 310 geographical areas of New York City, linking them to the mortality rates given in 1930 for each region. The correlation was $r = -.43$, such that higher IQ scores were associated with lower mortality risk. The study was important by virtue of registering a trend; but it was 55 years later that one of the first known peer-reviewed empirical studies to use individual data on pre-morbid intelligence and adult mortality was published. The Australian Veterans Health Study included data from over 2,300 servicemen born between 1947 and 1953, and linked their mental ability test scores from approximately 18 years of age with their mortality records spanning 17 subsequent years (O'Toole, Adena, & Jones, 1988). The results showed that ex-servicemen deceased before follow-up had significantly lower mean scores on the Army Classification Test compared to those who were still alive at follow-up. The next published evidence followed 13 years later, in the *British Medical Journal*, and also reported an inverse association between IQ and risk of mortality (Whalley & Deary, 2001). This study's cohort represented 80 percent of children ($N = 2,230$) born in Aberdeen, Scotland in 1921, who were part of the Scottish Mental Survey 1932 (SMS32). It was a population-wide study, which applied the same intelligence test to almost every child in Scotland born in 1921. The follow-up period for mortality was 65 years. The authors reported a significant hazard ratio of 0.79 (95 percent confidence interval [CI]: 0.75 to 0.84) for the risk of mortality by 76 years of age, given a one-SD (standard deviation) advantage in IQ scores at age 11, and a hazard ratio of 0.63 (0.56–0.71) for all-cause mortality, given a two-SD advantage in IQ. This study heralded several recent studies in the field, and it had some strengths: a population-representative cohort with long-term follow-up; publication in a general medical journal, which brought the IQ–mortality association to a wider readership; reporting of hazard ratios for the risk of mortality—statistics being more familiar to epidemiologists (see later section on measuring risk for an explanation of hazard ratios and related measures of risk)—which brought a measure of individual differences into the arena of public health.

The contribution that individual differences in general cognitive ability could make to understanding health inequalities had been suggested before, although it was recognized that epidemiologists might not readily embrace this idea:

[IQ]'s potential for informing public policy is grossly underappreciated. In part, this neglect is because intellectual assessment is typically focused on individuals (a hallmark of the psychometric approach) as distinct from populations (more of an epidemiological approach). (Lubinski & Humphreys, 1997, pp. 159–160)

Opinion pieces followed, emphasizing the importance of cognitive ability for health outcomes (Gottfredson & Deary, 2004) and proposing possible mechanisms to explain the association (Batty & Deary, 2004). A theoretical review posited that intelligence might be the underlying cause of the well-documented socioeconomic inequalities in health (Gottfredson, 2004). The empirical work has continued, and the existing large cohorts, which replicated the inverse intelligence–mortality link, give further credibility to the basic finding. In publication date order, these cohorts include: a second cohort of the SMS32, involving 922 men and women followed up for 69 years (Hart et al., 2003); the Danish Metropolit Study of 7,308 members, in which members completed IQ tests at 12 years and were followed up 33 years later (Osler et al., 2003); the Swedish Conscripts Birth Cohort 1949–1951, involving 49,262 men who took mental ability tests at 18 to 20 years and were followed up for 31 years (Hemmingsson, Melin, Allebeck, & Lundberg, 2006); a cohort of the Vietnam Experience Study (VES) with IQ test scores from the time of the military conscription of participants, who were followed up to a mean age of 53 years (Batty, Shipley et al., 2008).

A glossary of the field, including a description of common epidemiological and intelligence-related concepts, was published in the *Journal of Epidemiology and Community Health* (Deary & Batty, 2007). In the same year, a systematic review in *Annals of Epidemiology* collected the inverse associations between pre-morbid IQ and total mortality (Batty, Deary, & Gottfredson, 2007). Overview articles published in the journals *Intelligence* (Deary, 2009; Lubinski, 2009), *Maturitas* (Kilgour, Starr, & Whalley, 2009), and *Nature* (Deary, 2008) summarized research in the field and developed the discussion surrounding potential mechanisms of the intelligence–mortality link. Crucially, a special issue on *Cognitive Epidemiology* (Vol. 37, No. 6) was published in *Intelligence* in 2009: it advanced the understanding of issues that have emerged more recently, through articles covering: mediators along the intelligence–disease pathway, including behavior (Anstey, Low, Christensen, & Sachdev, 2009), medical compliance (Deary, Gale et al., 2009), substance use and abuse (Johnson, Hicks, McGue, & Iacono, 2009); the relation of cognitive ability to

specific morbidities such as cardiovascular disease (Singh-Manoux et al., 2009), metabolic syndrome (Richards et al., 2009), and psychiatric health (Gale, Hatch, Batty,
& Deary, 2009); the contribution of a "fitness factor" in understanding underlying
causes (Arden, Gottfredson, & Miller, 2009). The main findings of much of this
empirical work are presented after the next section on epidemiological practices.

## Finding Roots in Epidemiology

A definition of epidemiology is: "the study of the distribution and determinants of
health-related states and events in populations, and the application of this study to
control health problems" (Last, 1988, p. 159). For cognitive epidemiology to prosper
in this context, the disciplines of differential psychology and epidemiology should
each aim to establish roots in the other. The field asks that epidemiologists give
greater consideration to genetic influences on health inequalities rather than to established environmental factors only (Deary, 2010), and also, that psychometric intelligence tests, as valid and stable measures of general cognitive ability, are given
credence. Conversely, psychologists studying individual differences require understanding of fundamental principles of epidemiology, taking care, for example, to
distinguish claims of association from causation in observational research (Rothman
& Greenland, 2005). As this book is aimed at those interested in differential psychology, we highlight some key epidemiological concepts and methods that may be less
familiar to readers. More in-depth coverage of these concepts and methods can be
found in introductory (Rothman, 2002) or comprehensive textbooks (Bhopal, 1997;
Hennekens & Buring, 1987).

### Causation

Evaluating the evidence for the claim that cognitive ability is either a direct or an
indirect causal factor in health outcomes is a complex challenge, familiar to epidemiologists who must carefully interpret new associations between risk factors and
disease. Sets of guidelines available to observational epidemiology are useful tools in
deciding upon whether causation can be reliably deduced. Table 16.1 presents a
recent list of six such criteria (Bhopal, 2008), which find their origin in Bradford
Hill's (1965) nine "viewpoints," with some credit given to Evans' (1978) "rules of
evidence." Here we discuss each of these criteria in turn, emphasizing their relevance
to validating the likelihood of causation in cognitive epidemiology.

The first criterion, *temporality*, considers if the measure of exposure precedes the
signs or symptoms of a disease and can therefore be conceptualized as a predictor
variable. In cognitive epidemiology, the most robust means to evaluate this hypothesis comes from longitudinal cohort studies that link the cognitive ability scores of
children or young adults with their medical or mortality records in later adult life.
Although general cognitive ability scores show high stability across the life course
(Deary et al., 2000), the studies referenced in this chapter's introduction show
that the onset of certain somatic diseases, or their treatments, can result in changes
to the cognitive function. Therefore cohorts that are young at the time of IQ testing

**Table 16.1**  Six epidemiological questions for assessing the likelihood of causation. The list of guidelines originated from Bradford Hill, 1965, with distillation by Bhopal, 2008

| Causation guideline | Question |
| --- | --- |
| Temporality | Does the proposed causal factor precede the effect? |
| Strength | Does exposure variation influence incidence of outcome? |
| Specificity | Does the exposure relate more strongly to some outcomes over others? |
| Consistency | Is the association replicated between and within studies? |
| Experiment | Does altering exposure to the cause influence incidence? |
| Biological | Is the association biologically plausible? |

reduce the risk of reverse causation in studies that evaluate intelligence as a risk factor for disease.

The *strength* of an association is a second guideline for causation, which demands that variation in the exposure relates significantly to differences in the risk of disease. Large population data sets that have full, representative distributions of intelligence are best suited to evaluate this criterion, as are cohorts with longer periods of follow-up that increase the number of disease or mortality cases, ensuring adequate statistical power. Cognitive epidemiology has been fortunate to have such data sets available from several western or westernized countries, including Australia, Scandinavia, US, and the UK (Batty, Deary, & Gottfredson, 2007). In most cases these have been government initiatives via educational or military institutions. Such sizeable and representative cohorts are quite novel in psychological research, which often draws upon smaller convenience samples, including student populations. Detailed descriptions of many of these cohorts are available elsewhere (see Deary & Batty, in press). Two examples are the Scottish Mental Surveys of 1932 and 1947 (SMS32 and SMS47), which contain mental ability scores from the majority of 11-year-olds born in Scotland in 1921 and 1936 respectively, who were attending school at the time of testing (i.e. in 1932 and 1947; see Deary, Whalley & Starr, 2009 for cohort profile). Together, these cohorts involve over 150,000 individual children's data, and the follow-up period for health information on sub-samples of the cohorts has so far been 69 years. The second example of a population-based cohort is the Swedish Conscripts Study, which includes over 1.3 million men with IQ test scores taken at 18 years of age, at entry to national service; this figure represents nearly the entire Swedish male population born during 1950 to 1976 (Batty, Wennerstad et al., 2007). These data are linked to recent detailed Cause of Death registers from Sweden, and because the maximum age at follow-up (at the present time) is about 50 years, this cohort will continue to gain in value with increase in the number of mortality data. Evidence for the varying strength of the association between intelligence and mortality is discussed later on.

In support of causation is also the evidence for the *specificity* of an association: does intelligence relate more strongly to the risk of some diseases over others? Findings from single cohort studies can indicate differences in the risk of particular causes of death associated with mental ability scores. For example, in the Swedish

Conscripts Study, a one-SD decrease in IQ was associated with a 31 percent increased risk of coronary heart disease (CHD) mortality, a 22 percent increased risk of accident and suicide-related mortalities, and a 3 percent increased risk of total cancer deaths by middle age (Batty, Wennerstad et al., 2009). However, such findings require replication to support specificity. Evaluation of empirical data on cause-specific outcomes follows in the next section of this chapter.

A fourth guideline, *consistency*, demands that the association between exposure and outcome be replicated across cohorts of varying time, place, and circumstance if causation is to be inferred (Bradford Hill, 1965). So far, this has been supported by a systematic review of pre-morbid IQ and all-cause mortality, which reported a significant inverse association across nine cohorts from five countries. Mental ability scores came from a range of intelligence test batteries. Cohort members were born in various decades of the twentieth century, and were representative either of military personnel or more broadly of school children from their background populations (Batty, Deary, & Gottfredson, 2007).

The *biological* plausibility of an association between pre-morbid intelligence and morbidity is among the more challenging of Bradford Hill's criteria to test. A biological explanation for the intelligence–mortality association is presented by system integrity theory, which implies an underlying complex physiology that determines both cognition and health outcomes. This hypothesis may ultimately be addressed by the field of genetics. An alternative explanation would be that intelligence may act indirectly upon health outcomes, by determining health behaviors and socioeconomic factors in adulthood. These central theories are discussed in the final section of our chapter.

*Experimental* evidence for causation is another problematic guideline for the field of cognitive epidemiology to address. However, if a genetic or environmental exposure was identified that naturally showed changes to individuals' intelligence test scores, then exposed versus non-exposed participants of a cohort could theoretically be tested and followed up for the risk of disease.

## Real or artifact?

The problem of confounding is a perennial one in observational epidemiology, and the data must be continuously appraised and tested in order for us to avoid errors of interpretation. For example, childhood socioeconomic status (SES), commonly indicated by factors such as family income, parental occupation, or education, is often cited as a potential confounder in the association between pre-morbid intelligence and health. In social epidemiology, childhood SES is studied as an underlying factor of health inequalities within populations, where cognitive resources are largely ignored or regarded as mediators of a SES-health phenomenon (Bartley & Plewis, 2007; Gallo, Espinosa de los Monteros, & Shivpuri, 2009; Lleras-Muney, 2005). The converse view is that intelligence may be the underlying cause of social inequalities in health (Gottfredson, 2004). Whether the contribution of intelligence to health outcomes is a real phenomenon or an artifact of confounding SES factors is addressed by cohort studies that contain detailed childhood measures of both variables. Some of this evidence will be discussed here later.

## Measuring risk

Epidemiologists routinely use logistic regression or Cox proportional hazards regression when quantifying the relationship between a variable and disease risk. These methods are appropriate, given that a health outcome is nearly always binomial: disease or no disease, dead or alive. The odds ratio (OR) is the measure of risk probability derived from logistic regression (Cox, 1958), and in epidemiology it is the ratio between two likelihoods: of a health outcome occurring given a particular exposure, and of the health outcome not occurring given the same exposure. The hazard ratio (HR) is a similar proportional measure, derived from Cox proportional hazards regression (Cox, 1972); it is the statistic preferred by epidemiologists (Symons & Moore, 2002), because it takes into account the time to an event for each individual, rather than assuming that the magnitude of risk is constant in respect of time.

In cognitive epidemiology, a continuous exposure variable (such as IQ-type test score) may be represented as a unit (per-point) difference or as a one-SD difference in intelligence scores, in relation to the risk of the outcome. The hazard or odds ratios are reported with their 95 percent confidence interval, which gives an indication of the statistical significance of risk. Both effect sizes have null effects at 1, and a confidence interval that includes 1 indicates that there is no statistically significant association between the health outcome (disease) and the exposure (IQ) at $p < 0.05$. Conventionally, if the ratio and its confidence interval exceed 1, this indicates a significantly increased risk of disease, given a specified SD decrease or an increase in mental ability scores. Conversely, if an effect size and its confidence interval fall below 1, this indicates that risk of disease is significantly decreased, given the unit change in test scores.

The degree of risk is often reported as a percentage, so that, for example, if a HR for mortality, given one-SD increase in IQ, is 0.78, this can be expressed as a 22 percent reduced risk. Alternatively, a HR of 1.22 translates as a 22 percent increase in risk of disease. This expression offers a useful way of interpreting the degree of attenuation by covariates, for example when studies report the HR before and after adjustment for SES. In understanding the risks generated by such analyses, it is always important to attend to the units of the exposure variable.

## Pre-Morbid Intelligence and Risk of Total Mortality

A systematic review published in the *Annals of Epidemiology* identified nine unrelated longitudinal cohorts, each one reporting a significant association between lower premorbid intelligence test scores and increased risk of all-cause mortality in adulthood (Batty, Deary, & Gottfredson, 2007). The paper not only helped to validate the IQ–mortality association, but it raised a number of issues for the field to address, for example: What is the size and nature of confounding by early life factors? To what extent do adult SES factors mediate the association? Is the magnitude of the association the same for women as for men (most cohorts, being military, were male-only)? And what is the influence of pre-morbid cognitive ability on specific causes of death?

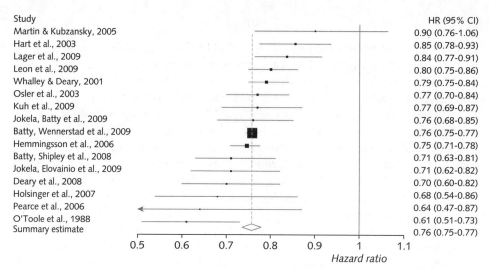

| Study | HR (95% CI) |
| --- | --- |
| Martin & Kubzansky, 2005 | 0.90 (0.76–1.06) |
| Hart et al., 2003 | 0.85 (0.78–0.93) |
| Lager et al., 2009 | 0.84 (0.77–0.91) |
| Leon et al., 2009 | 0.80 (0.75–0.86) |
| Whalley & Deary, 2001 | 0.79 (0.75–0.84) |
| Osler et al., 2003 | 0.77 (0.70–0.84) |
| Kuh et al., 2009 | 0.77 (0.69–0.87) |
| Jokela, Batty et al., 2009 | 0.76 (0.68–0.85) |
| Batty, Wennerstad et al., 2009 | 0.76 (0.75–0.77) |
| Hemmingsson et al., 2006 | 0.75 (0.71–0.78) |
| Batty, Shipley et al., 2008 | 0.71 (0.63–0.81) |
| Jokela, Elovainio et al., 2009 | 0.71 (0.62–0.82) |
| Deary et al., 2008 | 0.70 (0.60–0.82) |
| Holsinger et al., 2007 | 0.68 (0.54–0.86) |
| Pearce et al., 2006 | 0.64 (0.47–0.87) |
| O'Toole et al., 1988 | 0.61 (0.51–0.73) |
| Summary estimate | 0.76 (0.75–0.77) |

**Figure 16.1**　Hazard ratio estimates of all-cause mortality per one standard deviation increase in pre-morbid intelligence, for individual cohort studies and for all studies combined ($N = 16$). Squares mark cohort-specific effect sizes, which are proportional to the statistical weight (i.e. inverse variance), and diamond indicates the aggregate effect size. Horizontal lines represent 95% confidence intervals. Odds ratios from four studies are treated as hazard ratios (Holsinger et al., 2007; Jokela, Batty et al., 2009; Jokela, Elovainio et al., 2009; O'Toole et al., 1988). Source: Calvin et al., 2010

There has been a considerable increase in the publication frequency of intelligence versus all-cause mortality studies since the review. This has created the opportunity to quantify the association by using meta-analysis and to address some of the pertinent issues raised. Calvin et al. (2010) extracted 16 unrelated studies from systematic reviews that met strict inclusion criteria, including over 22,000 deaths among more than 1,100,000 participants for which individual intelligence test scores were available. Follow-up periods ranged from 17 to 69 years, and the cohorts represented populations in Australia, Europe, and the United States. Meta-analysis estimated that, across all studies, a one-SD increase in IQ was associated with a 24 percent reduced risk of mortality, with a 95 percent confidence interval of 23 percent to 25 percent (forest plot shown in Figure 16.1). Furthermore, a lack of heterogeneity between the studies indicated that differences in study characteristic or design did not affect the magnitude of the association (Sutton, Abrams, Jones, Sheldon, & Song, 2000). This means that cohorts of larger or smaller sample size, those with high or low attrition rates, with shorter or longer follow-up periods, and from military or school populations consistently reported similar hazard ratios for the association between IQ and all-cause mortality.

## Gender differentials in the intelligence–mortality relation

Gender differences in the onset, patterns, and prevalence of health behaviors, risk factors, and disease (Anand et al., 2008; Wingard, 1984) might contribute to sex differentials in intelligence–health gradients. The SMS32 cohort was the first study to estimate IQ–mortality effects by sex, reporting a stronger association between childhood IQ and risk of mortality in women (more than double) in comparison with men (Whalley & Deary, 2001). However, the increased rate of deaths among high IQ-scoring males during the Second World War may have reduced the effect size for men in this particular cohort. The UK's National Survey of Health and Development (NSHD) study provided a more recent birth cohort, born in 1946, with cognitive scores at age 8 and followed up at age 54. This study reported that, among male members with low cognitive scores, the risk of mortality was twice as high as among high scorers, whereas no effect was observed for women (Kuh, Richards, Hardy, Butterworth, & Wadsworth, 2004). However, the increased life expectancy of women when compared to men, which reduces the relative number of female to male deaths, may have lost statistical power to this study. Indeed, in a more recent follow-up of the same British cohort, with an increased number of female deaths the effect became significant, in that women scoring in the highest quartile for cognitive ability had a 51 percent reduced risk of mortality by follow-up, when compared to those in the lowest quartile (Kuh et al., 2009). Since then, meta-analysis of seven cohorts that reported on sex-specific effect sizes observed that the risk of mortality, given a one-SD increase in IQ, was equivalent for men and women: a reduced risk of 20 percent and 22 percent respectively (Calvin et al., 2010).

## Dose–response effects on all-cause mortality

Studies that report on the risk of mortality according to a one-SD difference in IQ-type scores assume a linear association. However, exploration of incremental effects on the intelligence–mortality slope could reveal a threshold beyond which an association no longer exists. The afore-described study of the 1946 cohort provided evidence that pre-morbid cognitive ability is only predictive of risk of death at the low end of the range for cognitive ability. Men who scored in the bottom quartile of the cognitive score distribution were reported to be at nearly twice the risk of mortality by comparison with those who scored in the top quartile, whereas between the second, third, and top quartile groups there were no statistically significant differences in risk of mortality (Kuh et al., 2004). After adjustment for educational attainment or adult SES, the effect was removed, which suggested that the influence of cognitive ability on mortality might be mediated by adverse socioeconomic factors more common among low scorers (or that intelligence is a causal factor in these outcomes, as well as in health). Two further studies have also supported a threshold effect of cognitive ability on risk of all-cause mortality above the lower end of the IQ distribution (Hart et al., 2003; Hemmingsson et al., 2006). However, a US study of "gifted" children—children with Stanford–Binet IQ scores in the high range (135 to 163)—reported a 32 percent decreased risk of mortality given one-SD increase in IQ (Martin & Kubzansky, 2005). This is evidence that an intelligence–mortality gradient is observed even at the highest end of the IQ distribution. Three population-representative cohorts support this conclusion (Batty, Wennerstad et al., 2009; Osler et al., 2003; Whalley & Deary, 2001), ruling out the possibility that the effect is driven by specific health problems associated with learning disabilities (Batty & Deary, 2004).

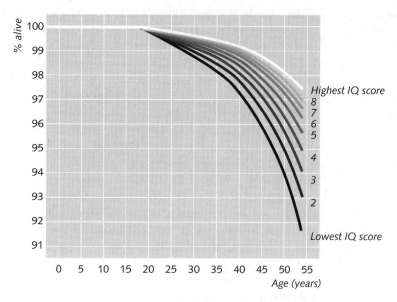

**Figure 16.2**   Survival rates of 1,133,712 Swedish men aged between 18 and 54, with IQ scores between 1 and 9. Compiled with permission from F. Rasmussen (personal communication), using the Swedish Cohort Data described in Batty, Wennerstad et al., 2007

In one study, over a million Swedish conscripts were divided evenly into nine groups of ascending intelligence scores, and a *monotonic* (linear) relationship was observed between IQ and risk of mortality (Batty, Wennerstad et al., 2009). This is shown in the time-to-survival curve in Figure 16.2, produced specifically for this chapter.

## "*g*" or specific cognitive function?

Despite recourse to different cognitive ability test batteries among the cohort studies used in cognitive epidemiology—including the Moray House Test, the Wechsler Adult Intelligence Scale, the Stanford–Binet, and Raven's Progressive Matrices tests (Deary and Batty, 2007)—the magnitude of the associations between their global IQ-type scores and risk of all-cause mortality shows consistency (Calvin et al., 2010). It is likely therefore that the general intelligence factor (*g*), which accounts for up to half of the total variance in batteries of diverse mental ability tests' scores (Carroll, 1993), is a better cognitive predictor of health outcomes than measures of specific cognitive function. In the Swedish Cohort Study, performance scores on four cognitive tests including verbal reasoning, visuo-spatial ability, logical reasoning, and technical ability were each inversely associated with all-cause mortality to the same magnitude as that of a global cognitive score (Batty, Wennerstad et al., 2009). However, among follow-up studies that have estimated the risk of mortality according to specific cognitive function measured in adulthood, a steeper gradient has been reported for fluid compared to crystallized intelligence (Batterham,

Christensen, & Mackinnon, 2009), and a significant inverse association was shown for executive function, but not for verbal and visuo-spatial reasoning abilities (Hall, Dubin, Crossley, Holmqvist, & D'Arcy, 2009). Still, until further cohort data of specific cognitive abilities in childhood become available, the issue remains undecided as to whether specific cognitive function could relate differentially to health outcomes.

One alternative indicator of cognitive function, which has been measured in childhood and could help to explain mechanisms underlying associations with health outcomes, is processing speed. Reaction-time tasks, which measure information processing efficiency, have been significantly associated with all-cause mortality, in that faster reaction times are associated with reduced risk (Deary & Der, 2005). In the UK adult cohort of 898 members reported by Deary and Der (2005), reaction time also very substantially attenuated the association between IQ and all-cause mortality after 14 years' follow-up. This finding lends support to the system integrity theory (Whalley & Deary, 2001) of intelligence's associations with health outcomes, if processing speed is an effective indicator of neurological integrity which reflects overall physiological integrity. However, without full understanding of why intelligence and reaction time correlate significantly, the interpretation of mechanisms remains problematic.

## Other psychological traits in cognitive epidemiology

Intelligence measures remain the strongest and most consistent predictors of death in differential psychology, and yet behavior traits such as personality may also be important risk factors for adult mortality, either independently or in interaction with intelligence. In the SMS47 6-day sample, 1,181 children who had IQ scores at age 11 and teacher-rated personality ratings at age 14 were followed up for a period of 55 years for all-cause mortality (Deary, Batty, Pattie, & Gale, 2008). A *dependability* factor extracted from item scores measuring perseverance, conscientiousness, and stability of mood was significantly associated with the reduced risk of death by follow-up. Furthermore, mortality risk was twice as great for children who scored in the bottom half of the IQ and dependability distributions, in comparison with those who scored in the top half of those distributions. High scores on a *neuroticism* factor among US military conscripts were also significantly related to an increased risk of mortality (Weiss, Gale, Batty, & Deary, 2009). Neuroticism showed independent effects from IQ in predicting risk of death, but an interaction effect was also reported: intelligence's effect on mortality was more pronounced at high levels of neuroticism; and neuroticism's effect on mortality was more pronounced at low levels of intelligence.

More recently, a delinquency factor measured by the Minnesota Multiphasic Personality Inventory was associated with the risk of mortality at age 75, after controlling for the influences of education and IQ (Trumbetta, Seltzer, Gottesman, & McIntyre, 2010). However in this analysis, mean imputation was applied to a quarter of participants with missing IQ data, which may have weakened the effect of IQ in the model, particularly if the missing cases were at the lower end of the distribution.

## Specific Causes of Morbidity and Mortality

A single theoretical basis for the association of intelligence with total mortality is unlikely, given that causes of death vary so widely. For example, intelligence's association with risk of accidental injury (a leading cause of mortality in early adulthood) may not be explained by the same mechanism that relates it to the risk of coronary heart disease (the main cause of death around by middle age in western and westernized countries)—unless it was shown that intelligence reflects a general propensity to look after oneself in the short and longer terms. Many cohorts relevant to cognitive epidemiology have linked to death records that include specific causes of death, or medical or hospital admission records that contain information on specific morbidities. In the next section, the most valuable contributions from empirical studies regarding the association between intelligence and specific causes of mortality and morbidity are presented, and the behavioral and psychological risk factors along these pathways are discussed.

### Cardiovascular disease (CVD)

The higher incidence of CVD-related deaths in midlife by comparison with deaths related to other causes has enabled several longitudinal studies to explore the risk of CVD according to pre-morbid intelligence. The first empirical data were from Scotland: 938 participants from the 1970s Midspan prospective cohort studies, whose IQ scores at age 11 were available from 1932, were followed up for a period of 25 years, by which time 43 percent had a CVD-related outcome (Hart et al., 2004). In this group, a 15-point decrease in IQ was related to 11 percent increased risk of hospital admission or death due to CVD; and the risk of those events occurring only up to and including 65 years was further increased (22 percent). Similar inverse associations for pre-morbid intelligence and risk of CVD diagnosis or cause-related death have been replicated by other well-characterized cohorts, including the SMS47 6-day sample (Deary, Whiteman, Starr, Whalley, & Fox, 2004), and the Swedish Conscripts Study 1940–1951, in which data on nearly 50,000 men were collected (Hemmingsson et al., 2006).

Coronary heart disease (CHD) and stroke are the most common causes of CVD-related deaths; but, albeit sharing some modifiable risk factors, they differ in their pathogenesis. It is therefore important to consider how intelligence might relate to each of these morbidities separately. In respect of risk of CHD outcomes, the magnitude of the association with pre-morbid intelligence has been fairly consistent. The Midspan study by Hart et al. (2004) has been the longest follow-up study for CHD outcomes, and it reported a 16 percent increased risk of CHD-related hospital admissions or deaths corresponding to a one-SD decrease in IQ. This figure increased to a 29 percent risk once CHD events occurring above age 65 were excluded. Further cohorts, with follow-up to midlife, report similar findings. The Danish Metropolit Study of 6,910 men born in 1953 in Copenhagen, with IQ test scores from the age of 12, traced cause-of-death and hospital discharge records of members up to age 47 (Batty, Mortensen, Nybo Andersen, & Osler, 2005). Relative to the highest IQ scoring quartile, the lowest, second, and third quartile groups had an increased risk of 170 percent, 143 percent, and 69 percent, respectively, for CHD events. These effects were little changed after adjusting for early life factors, including birth weight and childhood SES. In a similar cohort design, the Aberdeen Children of the 1950s study of 11,125 members reported a 30 percent reduced risk of fatal or non-fatal CHD, according to a one-SD advantage in intelligence (Lawlor, Batty, Clark, Macintyre, & Leon, 2008). The risk of CHD in association with intelligence test scores was greater in women (51 percent) than in men (21 percent), and was also shown to be incremental when hazard ratios were calculated separately for eight groups of increasing IQ test score. However, after adjusting for education, the effects reduced to non-significance. The Swedish Conscripts Study also reported attenuating effects of education on a 31 percent increased risk of CHD-mortality according to a one-SD decrease in IQ, although this was by 45 percent only, and the effect remained statistically significant (Batty, Wennerstad et al., 2009). Adjusting for early life and physical factors—including birth year, parental social class, BMI (body mass index) and blood pressure, and illness—made little change to the association between mental ability scores and risk of CHD-related death.

Studies of the association between pre-morbid intelligence and stroke have not been so definitive. This may be because the trend for an inverse association has not reached statistical significance in some cohorts (Batty, Mortensen, Nybo Andersen et al., 2005; Hart et al., 2004), owing to lack of power from low numbers of stroke events. However, in a sufficiently large study—the Aberdeen children of the 1950s—a one-SD advantage in intelligence was significantly associated with a 32 percent reduced risk of incident stroke (Lawlor et al., 2008), an effect which increased for women when compared to men. Furthermore, the Swedish Conscripts Cohort was large enough to permit researchers to estimate the effects of pre-morbid intelligence on risk of stroke sub-type. For each sub-type, the authors reported inverse associations for all fatal and non-fatal stroke events, which were statistically significant in most cases (Wennerstad, Silventoinen, Tynelius, Bergman, & Rasmussen, 2009). However, the strongest association was estimated for hemorrhagic strokes, and there was a weaker effect for ischemic strokes. Adjusting for childhood SES, BMI and systolic blood pressure, or education only modestly attenuated these effects.

Established risk factors for cardiovascular disease include medical conditions such as diabetes mellitus, obesity or overweight, metabolic syndrome, and hypertension. If pathways between intelligence and cardiovascular outcomes are to be understood, then it is important to evaluate cognitive ability in relation to each of these. Among 7,476 men and women from the US National Longitudinal Survey of Youth (1979) with intelligence test scores from adolescence, a one-SD increase in mental ability scores was associated with the significantly reduced odds of self-reported hypertension (16 percent), heart problems (16 percent), and diabetes (12 percent) at age 40 (Der, Batty, & Deary, 2009). Hypertension was also associated with childhood cognitive ability in the SMS32–Midspan cohort. Among 938 men and women, a one-SD increase in IQ was associated with a 3.15 mmHg reduction in systolic blood pressure and a 1.5 mmHg reduction in diastolic blood pressure (Starr et al., 2004).

Metabolic syndrome is characterized by a cluster of cardiovascular risk factors, including abdominal obesity, high blood pressure, high blood triglycerides, low HDL (high-density lipoprotein) cholesterol, and hyperglycemia. Data from the VES reported that pre-morbid intelligence scores were inversely associated with four out of five risk factors measured at midlife: blood triglycerides, blood pressure, blood glucose, and BMI. By adjusting for these, the risk of mortality from CVD according to IQ scores was attenuated by about a third. In the 1946 NSHD study, a one-SD increase in IQ at age 8 was associated with a 14 percent reduction in the odds of metabolic syndrome at 53 years of age (Richards et al., 2009). Of all the metabolic syndrome risk factors, lower IQ was most strongly associated with high blood pressure, blood triglycerides, and abdominal obesity. Education or adult income attenuated the size of risk to non-significance, and one interpretation of this phenomenon is that cognitive ability has an indirect effect on this cluster of risk factors. The inverse relationship between childhood IQ and risk of obesity and weight gain in midlife was also significant, according to data on nearly 10,000 men and women from the 1958 National Child Development Study (Chandola, Deary, Blane, & Batty, 2006). This study reported a stronger effect of risk of obesity in women (38 percent) than in men (26 percent), according to a SD difference in IQ, and all effects were attenuated to non-significance after adjusting for educational attainment.

More recent work has begun to investigate the association between intelligence and biochemical markers for CVD. For example, one study reported that lower childhood cognitive ability was significantly associated with increased levels of C-reactive protein and fibrinogen in blood samples taken from people between 67 and 71 years of age (Luciano, Marioni, Gow, Starr, & Deary, 2009). Both are inflammatory markers that are frequently raised in patients with vascular diseases. An understanding of the mechanisms underlying the relation between cognitive ability and biomarkers of disease is warranted, in particular whether pre-morbid intelligence leads to health behaviors that increase inflammatory components of cells, or whether inflammatory processes are an aspect of system integrity that underlie individual differences in intelligence.

## Cancers

Given that cancers share with CVD some common modifiable risk factors, including obesity and smoking, it might be expected that the association between pre-morbid intelligence and cancer morbidities is consistent with that manifested in the case of CVD. However, the evidence to date does not support this hypothesis. The Swedish Conscripts Study of nearly one million men reported a non-significant 3 percent increased risk of total cancer mortality according to a one-SD decrease in IQ (Batty, Wennerstad et al., 2009). Similar negligible findings were reported in the earlier Swedish Conscripts Study (1949–1951 birth cohort), which registered an increased risk of 4 percent for a one-SD decrease in IQ (Hemmingsson et al., 2006), and in the SMS32–Midspan cohort, where a 8 percent increased risk of all-cancer mortality related to the same unit change in IQ (Hart et al., 2003). However, one large US military cohort has estimated a significant inverse relationship between IQ and risk of all-cancer mortality. Data from the Vietnam Experience Study, in which IQ scores were available for 14,491 male conscripts at an average age of 20 years, were linked to cancer mortality records up to middle age. A 27 percent increase in risk of all-cancer mortality was reported according to a one-SD decrease in IQ (Batty,

Mortensen et al., 2009). This may be due to IQ's association with specific cancers, as the risk was found to be particularly high for smoking-related cancer deaths (37 percent).

Given the many different types of cancers, with multiple causes and risk factors, it has been appropriate to look at the effects of IQ in relation to specific types of cancers, rather than treating them as a homogeneous disease group. Hart et al. (2003) reported a 36 percent increased risk of lung cancer associated with a one-SD decrease in IQ, and a 46 percent increased risk in stomach cancer, although this failed to reach a level of statistical significance because of the small number of cases. No effects were observed for colorectal or breast cancers, but again, larger cohorts would be required to achieve adequate statistical power. By far the largest study found statistically significant weak associations between intelligence and carcinoma of stomach (where any protective effect of intelligence was seen only in the highest intelligence tertile), but not between intelligence and lung or other cancer death; the study also found that high intelligence was a risk factor for skin cancer (Batty, Wennerstad et al., 2007). This latter effect may be due to the relation between higher intelligence and job income and the resulting increased frequency of holidays spent in hot climates, although the effect was only slightly attenuated after controlling for SES and still remained significant. It is possible that negative health behaviors such as smoking and poor diets may help understand mechanisms underlying IQ's relation to particular malignancies. Future cohort studies with larger numbers of specific-cancer cases are required to evaluate this relation properly.

## Respiratory disease

Given the inverse association between IQ and smoking and the positive association between IQ and smoking cessation uptake (Batty, Deary, & Macintyre, 2007; Batty, Deary, Schoon, & Gale, 2007c; Taylor et al., 2003), it is perhaps unsurprising that higher pre-morbid IQ is also associated with the reduced risk of illnesses relating to respiratory function in adult life. For example, the NLSY79 cohort reported a 22 percent reduced risk of developing chronic lung disease at age 40, according to a one-SD increase in intelligence test scores (Der et al., 2009). Furthermore, two studies have demonstrated a significant association between childhood mental ability and improved lung capacity, based on forced expiratory volume (Deary, Whalley, Batty, & Starr, 2006; Richards, Strachan, Hardy, Kuh, & Wadsworth, 2005). This observation may be explained by IQ being positively related to height; also, by dint of their bodily habitus, taller people have high lung function, which may indicate a general fitness factor underlying the link between cognitive ability and these physical markers. However, in one study the positive association remained statistically significant after controlling for adult height in addition to birth weight, adult SES, and lifetime smoking (Richards et al., 2005).

## Intentional and unintentional injury

Unintentional injury or death can be the result of road traffic or industrial accidents—or falls, for example. In the Danish Metropolit Study, the higher childhood cognitive scores of 11,339 males were associated with a 22 percent reduced risk of fatal or non-fatal injury by road traffic accidents, falls, or unintentional self-poisoning by 48 years of age (Osler, Nybo Andersen, Laursen, & Lawlor, 2007). The effects of IQ on risk of falling and self-poisoning were still significant after adjusting for educational status. IQ exposure was also inversely related to injury mortality among over one million Swedish men (Batty, Gale, Tynelius, Deary, & Rasmussen, 2009). Low IQ scorers compared to the highest IQ scorers had a 482 percent increased risk of death by poisoning, a 339 percent increased risk of fire mortality, a 217 percent increased risk of fall mortality, a 216 percent higher risk of drowning, and a 117 percent increased risk of road injury mortality. The inverse association between cognitive ability and injury mortality was incremental across the IQ range, and SES inequalities explained about half of the total effects.

The association between pre-morbid intelligence and accidental injury is consistently higher than that seen for chronic disease, although so far this may only be true for serious injuries, which lead to hospitalization or death. However, studies that assess cognitive ability in relation to minor accidents or injuries can be complicated by problems of self-reporting. For example, reporting bias may have influenced results from the British birth cohort of 1970, in which higher childhood cognitive scores were related to an increased reporting of accidents in the home by age 30 (Batty, Deary, Schoon, & Gale, 2007a).

Injury can otherwise be intentional or death can be self-inflicted, for example in attempted suicide, or it can be the result of others' actions, including physical attack and homicide. Due to the low numbers of suicide and homicide cases in cohorts, only very large studies ensure sufficient statistical power with which to evaluate associations with pre-morbid intelligence. A cross-sectional ecological study of census data from 48 European and Asian countries had reported a positive association between mean literacy rates and incidence of suicide among older adults, in that the higher the literacy rate, the greater the incidence of suicide (Voracek, 2005). However, such study design fails to take account of individual differences and changes in populations over time. Published in the same year, longitudinal data from the Swedish Conscripts Study reported a significant inverse association between pre-morbid intelligence test scores and risk of death by suicide up to midlife (Gunnell, Magnusson, & Rasmussen, 2005). The authors suggested that lower cognitive ability might contribute to an increased risk of suicide either because it is a risk factor for psychiatric illness, or because of a disadvantage in being able to resolve problems or personal crises. Within the same cohort, Batty, Deary, Tengstrom, and Rasmussen (2008) related the Swedish conscripts' IQ scores to homicide mortality after 20 years of follow-up. A one-SD increase in pre-morbid IQ was associated with a 51 percent reduced risk of death by homicide, and the effect was incremental across the IQ range. This effect was marginally attenuated by early life social factors, height, and somatic and psychiatric illness. Explanations for this finding included: people with higher IQ scores being more able to negotiate and resolve conflicts, or having a higher perception of risk; lower IQ scorers being more frequently intoxicated with alcohol or drugs; there being an association between the intelligence of perpetrator and victim (perpetrators of homicide have lower than average IQ scores) (Batty, Deary, Tengstrom et al., 2008). Another explanation is the confounding influence of height, which, as described, has been positively associated with cognition (Gale, 2005; Vågerö & Modin, 2006), and may be protective against the threat of external physical attack (Batty, Deary, Tengstrom et al., 2008). These potential explanations deviate from the mechanistic pathways posited for other cause-specific mortalities, highlighting the need to evaluate multiple mechanistic models for intelligence and morbidity pathways.

## Behavioral risk factors for disease

Tobacco smoking, excessive alcohol consumption, and sedentary living are risk factors common to a range of life-threatening diseases, including CVD and cancers. Longitudinal cohorts have been used to evaluate associations between pre-morbid mental ability and these health behaviors, to explore how they might explain IQ–mortality pathways. Higher childhood intelligence is positively associated with a reduced risk of current or previous cigarette smoking in adults (Batty, Deary, & Macintyre, 2007; Batty, Deary, Schon, & Gale, 2007c; Taylor et al., 2003), an effect which is attenuated by educational attainment, and to a lesser degree by adult SES (Batty, Deary, & Macintyre, 2007; Batty, Deary, Schon, & Gale, 2007c). In two UK studies, smoking cessation in adulthood was more likely to be found among higher childhood intelligence test scorers, particularly women (Batty, Deary, & Macintyre, 2007), and controlling for deprivation index attenuated the effect (Taylor et al., 2003). However, in the Swedish Conscripts Study (1949–51), IQ was not associated with quitting smoking (Hemmingsson, Kriebel, Melin, Allebeck, & Lundberg, 2008). Members of this study would have been exposed to public health promotions in the 1970s to reduce smoking, at a younger age than cohort members of the previous two studies. This could suggest that higher intelligence leads to more adaptive behaviors, in response to new public health campaigns (Taylor et al., 2003).

The association between childhood IQ scores and excess alcohol consumption in adulthood is less consistent than for smoking. In a Scottish 1950s birth cohort, assessed for IQ at age 11, and followed up with alcohol-related questionnaires at age 44 and up to 53, there was a significant inverse relationship between childhood IQ and self-reported hangovers (Batty, Deary, & Macintyre, 2006). For a one-SD increase in IQ there was a 20 percent reduced odds of having regular alcohol-related hangovers in midlife—an indicator of regular binge drinking—that was attenuated after controlling for adult SES. However, in a different study from Denmark, a null association was reported between IQ and excess drinking in men (Mortensen, Sørensen, & Grønbæk, 2005). Furthermore, two studies have indicated that intelligence can positively correlate with excess alcohol consumption. Data on men and women from the 1946 NSHD study, including childhood cognitive scores from age 8 and self-assessment of alcohol abuse at age 53, reported that those whose cognitive scores were in the top half of the distribution were at 2.4 times greater risk of alcohol abuse (Hatch et al., 2007). A second British cohort of men and women, born in 1970, with cognitive scores at 10 years of age and information on alcohol use at age 30, reported that higher intelligence was positively related to increased regular intake of alcohol, as well as to perceived alcohol problems (Batty, Deary, Schoon et al. 2008). This association was stronger for women, and remained significant after controlling for education and social factors. Attrition or response bias could be causing these positive findings, but further studies are warranted to produce better understanding of alcohol drinking behaviors (including participants' choice of alcohol type) that are influenced by cognitive ability differences.

Childhood cognitive ability has also been related to taking more physical exercise, to consuming more healthy foods (including fruit, vegetables, and wholemeal bread) and less unhealthy foods (chips, cakes, and biscuits), and to vegetarianism, which could also mediate intelligence–disease pathways (Batty, Deary, Schoon, & Gale, 2007b; Gale, Deary, Schoon, & Batty, 2007). Better characterized cohorts, with detailed information on exercise and nutritional lifetime habits, are required in order to understand the contribution of these factors to IQ–disease associations.

## Psychiatric illness

Mental health problems are important to consider in cognitive epidemiology, because they pose greater health risks to individuals, are enduring throughout the life course, and lead to increased risk of comorbidities and mortality. For example, psychiatric illness is linked to more negative health behaviors, including smoking (Lawrence, Mitrou, & Zubrick, 2009), and is a risk factor for suicidal behavior (Moscicki, 1995) and cardiovascular disease (Phillips et al., 2009; Van der Kooy et al., 2007). Large, well-characterized cohort studies consistently show an inverse association between pre-morbid intelligence and risk of mental health problems, as characterized in Table 16.2. In Scotland and Denmark, lower cognitive scores were associated with the increased likelihood of developing a psychiatric disorder over long-term follow-up (Batty, Mortensen, & Osler, 2005; Walker, McConville, Hunter, Deary, & Whalley, 2002). Furthermore, in cohorts from New Zealand, Sweden, and the US, the association was significant for the development of a range of specific psychiatric diagnoses, including anxiety-related disorders, depression, and schizophrenia, by middle age (Gale, Batty, Tynelius, Deary, & Rasmussen, 2010; Gale et al., 2008) or at earlier stages (Koenen et al., 2009). For example, among over 1 million men from the Swedish Conscripts Study, lower IQ scores were associated with a greater risk of hospitalization for eight psychiatric disorders by midlife (Gale et al., 2010). Cases included a 60 percent increased risk of being admitted for schizophrenia, a 50 percent increased risk for mood disorders, and a 75 percent increased risk of alcohol-related disorders, associated with a one-SD decrease in IQ scores. In the VES cohort, intelligence was inversely related to the risk of alcohol disorders, depression, generalized anxiety disorder, and post-traumatic stress disorder (Gale et al., 2008), and the magnitude of these risks increased if more than one disorder was present, so that the likelihood of psychiatric comorbidity increased as participants moved toward the lower end of the IQ distribution.

At the less extreme end of psychiatric illness, higher cognitive ability at age 10 and 11 is also related to a reduced risk of self-reported psychological distress in early adulthood, according to a combined cohort of over 12,000 members from the 1958 National Child Development Survey and from the 1970 British Birth Cohort (Gale, Hatch et al., 2009). Adjusting for early life factors and SES in childhood and adulthood made no difference to this effect, but the inclusion of education in the model showed moderate attenuation.

**Table 16.2**  A summary of longitudinal studies on the inverse association between pre-morbid cognitive ability and adult mental health outcomes. Abbreviations: SMS32 = Scottish Mental Surveys 1932; NCDS58 = National Child Development Study 1958; BCS70 = British Cohort Study 1970; VES = Vietnam Experience Study; GAD = generalized anxiety disorder; PTSD = post-traumatic stress disorder. Arrows indicate the magnitude of effect, which here represents a significantly increased risk of a psychiatric outcome, per one standard deviation decrease in cognitive ability: ↑ indicates 10–39% increased risk; ↑↑, 40–69%; ↑↑↑, 70% or more

| Study | Reference | Age at IQ; follow-up (yrs) | Cohort N | | Psychiatric outcome |
|---|---|---|---|---|---|
| SMS32 | Walker et al., 2002 | 11; 76 | 4,199 | ↑ | Any psychiatric disorder |
| Danish cohort | Batty et al., 2005 | 12; 49 | 7,022 | ↑ | Any psychiatric disorder |
| NCDS58 | Gale et al., 2009 | 10; 33 | 6,369 | ↑↑ | Psychological distress |
| BCS70 | Gale et al., 2009 | 11; 30 | 6,074 | ↑ | Psychological distress |
| VES | Gale et al., 2008b | 20; midlife | 3,258 | ↑ | Alcohol-related disorder |
| | | | | ↑ | Depression |
| | | | | ↑↑ | GAD |
| | | | | ↑ | PTSD |
| Dunedin cohort | Koenen et al., 2009 | 11; 32 | 1,037 | ↑ | Depression |
| | | | | ↑ | GAD |
| | | | | ↑↑ | Schizophrenia |
| | | | | ↑↑ | Social phobia |
| Swedish Conscripts | Gale et al., 2010 | 18; midlife | 1,049,663 | ↑↑ | Adjustment disorder |
| | | | | ↑↑ | Alcohol-related disorder |
| | | | | ↑↑ | Mood disorder |
| | | | | ↑↑ | Neurotic disorder |
| | | | | ↑↑ | Non-affective psychosis |
| | | | | ↑↑↑ | Personality disorder |
| | | | | ↑↑ | Schizophrenia |
| | | | | ↑↑↑ | Substance-use disorder |

## Pathological cognitive decline and dementia

Lower pre-morbid intelligence is also associated with the risk of later pathological cognitive decline. A sample from the SMS32 cohort reported the inverse association with risk of late-onset, but not early-onset, dementia (Whalley et al., 2000). In the evaluation of associations with pre-morbid cognitive ability, a larger sample of the SMS32 enabled late-onset dementia cases to be separated into vascular dementia and Alzheimer's type dementia. The investigators reported that lower childhood intelligence was a significant risk factor for late-onset vascular dementia, but not Alzheimer's, suggesting that vascular processes rather than cognitive reserve are likely mediators in the pathway between early life intelligence and later cognitive decline (McGurn, Deary, & Starr, 2008). Whether this suggests an underlying biological mechanism consistent with system integrity theory, or can be explained by risk behaviors that damage vascular health, is an issue for future investigation.

## Intelligence–Disease Mechanisms, and the Future for Cognitive Epidemiology

The growing body of empirical studies reflected in this chapter has advanced the understanding of the likely mechanistic pathways that relate individual differences in cognitive ability scores to disease outcomes and death. Deary (2008) reflected that there is as yet "no clear chain of causation from intelligence to health" (p. 176). It is, however, likely that intelligence differences may play an important role as risk factor, mediator, *and* covariate in models that explain health outcomes. It could also prove to be a partial confounder for other early life or social factors. A mechanistic model for the associations between IQ and mortality (from Batty, Deary, & Gottfredson, 2007), based on earlier theoretical suggestions of Whalley and Deary (2001), is shown in Figure 16.3, indicating most of these possibilities. Additional to the model is the more explicit recognition of the potential contribution of genetic factors that underlie both individual differences in intelligence and health, which are yet to be adequately explored (Arden, Gottfredson, & Miller, 2009). The theory of system integrity, which is present in the model and posits that an underlying physiological make-up may explain the association between pre-morbid intelligence and health outcomes, incorporates the role of genetic factors, but these deserve prominence in future research. In this section, the tested theories for intelligence-to-disease mechanisms are evaluated in light of the latest empirical evidence and debate.

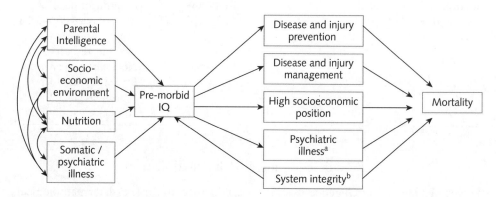

[a]Although psychiatric disease is shown as a possible mediating variable between IQ and mortality, it might also be an antecedent variable if, for example, sub-optimal neurodevelopment were the prior cause of both psychiatric disease and early mortality.

[b]Note that system integrity is shown as antecedent to both IQ and mortality. In this pathway, lower IQ is not a cause of mortality, but both IQ and mortality are influenced by this more fundamental physiological integrity. Double-pointed arrows indicate correlations between antecedent variables.

**Figure 16.3**  Simplified model of influences on pre-morbid IQ and potential pathways linking pre-morbid IQ with later mortality. Source: Batty, Deary, & Gottfredson, 2007. Reproduced and revised with permission

## Lifetime social and environmental factors: causation or mediation?

It is an ongoing debate whether it is intelligence (Gottfredson, 2004) or SES (Bartley & Plewis, 2007; Gallo et al., 2009) that makes the greater contribution in predicting health outcomes across populations. In social epidemiology, common indicators of SES are education, occupational income, or social class (Hackman & Farah, 2009) and advantages in these have been associated with lower risk of total or cause-specific mortality, and health morbidities, in longitudinal cohort studies (DeWalt, Berkman, Sheridan, Lohr, & Pignone, 2004; Huisman et al., 2005; Lleras-Muney, 2005; Singh-Manoux, Ferrie, Chandola, & Marmot, 2004; Torssander & Erikson, 2010)—although evidence suggests that these are not interchangeable factors for a latent social trait (Geyer, Hemstrom, Peter, & Vågerö, 2006; Torssander & Erikson, 2010). The issue is made more complex by the covariation between cognitive ability and socioeconomic indicators (Lubinski, 2009). Causal associations between intelligence and SES are obscured, and controlling for either IQ or SES when evaluating the other's relation to mortality can "weed out some of the very influence [...] we are trying to detect" (Deary, 2008, p. 176).

One theory is that early life influences, particularly SES, are total confounders of the association between pre-morbid mental ability and adult morbidities. However, meta-analysis of eight cohorts that controlled for parental occupational status or income in the association between pre-morbid intelligence and all-cause mortality reported a negligible 4 percent attenuation of the effect (Calvin et al., 2010). This is also the observed trend in many of the studies reported in the previous section of this chapter, which assessed cause-specific diseases in relation to cognitive abilities. One study that controlled for an alternative childhood SES factor—overcrowding in the home—also showed negligible attenuation of the IQ–mortality link (Whalley & Deary, 2001). It has been posited that adverse events in the prenatal period or early childhood, such as exposure to smoking and obesity, which are not captured by common indices of SES, may yet explain some of the association between pre-morbid cognitive function and adult health outcomes (Kilgour et al., 2009); but data for sustaining such an idea are as yet unavailable. A study of young infants who were adopted within the first year of life reported an inverse association between their adult mortality rates and the social class of their biological father, whereas a null association was found between risk of mortality and the adoptive fathers' social class (Osler, Petersen, Prescott, Teasdale, & Sørensen, 2006). This suggests that genetic factors more likely explain the intelligence–mortality link, unless environmental factors that carry their influence in the very early stages of development remain unaccounted for. So far, studies that have controlled for birth weight (an indicator of prenatal events) have reported negligible attenuation of the association between intelligence and mortality (Jokela, Elovainio, Singh-Manoux, & Kivimaki, 2009; Leon, Lawlor, Clark, Batty, & Macintyre, 2009; Osler et al., 2003), although this may not be surprising, given that correlations between birth weight and cognitive ability in childhood are modest (Shenkin, Starr, & Deary, 2004). Future cohort studies of more detailed early life measures, including maternal factors, would help clarify whether IQ-type scores may act in part as a surrogate for early life determinants of health.

Adult SES indicators may explain more of the influence of cognitive ability scores on health outcomes. It is well established that higher mental ability in childhood is predictive of better educational and socioeconomic successes (Deary et al., 2007; Schmidt & Hunter, 2004; Strenze, 2007; Von Stumm, Macintyre, Batty, Clark, & Deary, 2010; Zagorsky, 2007). These can lead to a "protective chain of events" for long life (Batty & Deary, 2004, p. 586): better working conditions in higher-ranking jobs provide safer and healthier environments; more comfortable, less hazardous home environments afforded by increased incomes; educational and/or occupational successes leading to improved heath literacy and the means to better understand medical advice and intervention; and greater exposure to accurate public health knowledge with which to engage. In meta-analysis, adjusting for adult occupation or income in five studies attenuated the IQ–all-cause mortality effect by about a third (Calvin et al., 2010). In the same study, the hazard ratio aggregate from six cohorts that adjusted for education found that the effect was attenuated by half. Furthermore, when studies have simultaneously controlled for occupational status and education, the association between pre-morbid intelligence and all-cause mortality is entirely diminished (Jokela, Batty, Deary, Gale, & Kivimaki, 2009; Jokela, Elovainio et al., 2009; Kuh et al., 2009). Home ownership has also been shown to have a significant attenuation effect on the risk of mortality according to intelligence test scores (Kuh et al., 2009).

An alternative way of evaluating intelligence along with SES in respect of health outcomes is to assess the potential attenuating effects of cognitive ability in relations between social inequalities and health outcomes. This helps test the theory that intelligence is the fundamental cause of social inequalities in health, as posited by Gottfredson (2004). In the west of Scotland Twenty-07 study, respective risks of CHD-related and total mortalities according to five child and adult SES indices were estimated both before and after adjusting for adult IQ scores (Batty, Der, Macintyre, & Deary, 2006). In support of a "fundamental cause" theory, controlling for intelligence scores entirely attenuated the inverse associations between years in education and the risk of CHD-related and total mortality (by 111 percent and 131 percent respectively), as well as the inverse association between adult SES and risk for these mortalities (94 percent and 106 percent respectively). However, for other SES indices, intelligence had less of an attenuating effect, reducing by about a third to a half the effects of childhood SES, income, and deprivation on CHD and total-mortality outcomes. Other health measures, including respiratory function, long-term illness, and poor self-perceived health, also saw varying attenuation effects by IQ scores in this study, and it was reported that low SES was still significantly predictive of some poor health outcomes after adjusting for intelligence in adulthood. In the Swedish Malmo Cohort, where intelligence test scores were measured in childhood, these were not found to fully explain social inequalities in health outcomes, although marked attenuation was apparent. Adjusting for IQ reduced the education–mortality gradient by only one quarter in men, and the size of the effect actually increased in women following controlling for cognitive ability (Lager, Bremberg, & Vågerö, 2009). The association between IQ and risk of mortality was not entirely explained either by childhood SES or by education, suggesting that intelligence has independent effects on health outcomes from those of SES.

It is possible that the attenuation effects observed in these studies may be caused by over-adjustment (Deary & Batty, 2007), rather than by mediation or confounding. A challenge for cognitive epidemiology is to separate these influences. Structural equation modeling (SEM) provides a statistical means by which to do this, as it at least controls for covariation. One paper to use SEM analyses, presented alongside standard regression, used the Vietnam Experience Study data, and it reported that the effect of IQ was entirely mediated by education, income, and poor physical health and had no direct effects on the risk of mortality (Weiss et al., 2009). However, this evidence cannot rule out the possibility that education acts as a proxy for intelligence. Future studies using SEM could help clarify whether or not IQ's main influence on morbidity and mortality is via socioeconomic influences. Evidence from sibling control studies could also further address the intelligence–SES confounding issue (Lubinski, 2009).

## Disease management and health behaviors

It is likely that individual differences in lifetime patterns of health behaviors and self-care management are on the pathway between pre-morbid cognitive ability and health outcomes, yet the extent of their mediation effects is not yet established. Although these differences are considered here separately, they are certainly not exclusive of socioeconomic factors and education but have strong associations in their effects on the IQ–mortality link. Indeed they may more accurately reflect the social and behavioral influences that interplay with cognitive processes, thereby affecting health outcomes.

Self-management of disease and treatment intervention is a cognitive undertaking (Gottfredson, 2004). Better health outcomes are more likely if people are able to understand and remember medical advice and instruction during the course of disease, if they can plan and execute necessary changes to their lifestyle to facilitate disease management or recovery, and if they recognize earlier on symptoms that are likely to necessitate further medical intervention. Within clinical populations, cognitive ability has been positively associated with correctly following medical regimens. In female patient groups with diabetes, breast cancer, and hyperlipidemia, better cognitive performance on memory, attention, and executive function tasks was associated with greater compliance with medication dosages (Stilley, Bender, Dunbar-Jacob, Sereika, & Ryan, 2010). Furthermore, in a randomized placebo-controlled trial of patients with atherosclerosis, verbal intelligence in adulthood was positively related to continuing with medication two years after treatment allocation (Deary, Gale et al., 2009). Those scoring in the lowest quartile for the verbal test were 2.5 times more likely to have stopped medication within two years, compared to those in the highest quartile group. Among the aging populations of many industrialized countries, it is recognized that patients may be increasingly burdened with a life-long involvement in their own complex disease management, the success of which may depend on effective cognitive processes (Gottfredson, 2004). So far, in cognitive epidemiology, however, the extent to which disease management mediates intelligence–morbidity associations has remained unexplored, due to the lack of such descriptive variables in longitudinal cohorts with pre-morbid cognitive test scores. Therefore this remains a pertinent area for the field to address.

Health behaviors are also integral to disease management or prevention. In the previous section of this chapter, associations between pre-morbid cognitive ability and health behaviors were discussed. However, there is little evidence so far that such behaviors account for the link between mental ability on the one hand, and morbidity or mortality on the other. For example, in the Vietnam Experience Study, the 29 percent reduced risk of all-cause mortality according to a one-SD increase in IQ was attenuated by 7 percent to 14 percent after separately adjusting for alcohol consumption and smoking (Batty, Shipley et al., 2008). Furthermore, cognitive performance is sometimes more strongly predictive of risk of mortality relative to behavioral risk factors, which suggests that these cannot account for the intelligence–mortality link. In the UK Health and Lifestyle Survey, cognitive function, as measured by using choice reaction time, was observed to be a stronger risk factor for CVD mortality than smoking, alcohol consumption, and physical exercise (Roberts, Der, Deary, & Batty, 2009). In the Twenty-07 study, cognitive ability in childhood was more strongly associated with all-cause mortality than all the established risk factors for CVD, with the exception of smoking (Batty, Deary, Benzeval, & Der, 2010). If health behaviors do account for some of the inverse association between intelligence and risk of disease or mortality, then their effects are likely to vary according to cultural and historical contexts. In industrialized countries for example, where health behaviors and lifestyle may be playing a role in epidemics of chronic disease, their mediation effects may be greater (Gottfredson, 2004).

## System integrity

The theory of general body integrity posits that the inverse association between pre-morbid cognitive ability and health outcomes can be explained by underlying physiological make-up. In this context, childhood mental ability is an early indicator of system integrity, and therefore a covariate with risk of disease rather than a causal factor acting upon it. This theory finds resonance with the field of cognitive aging, in which some empirical data show physical and cognitive deterioration acting in parallel (Deary, 2008). However, the theory presents challenges in its testing, particularly as indicators for system integrity remain imperfect. One putative marker for system integrity adopted by the field is reaction time, a measure of cognitive processing efficiency that may reflect neurological as well as general bodily integrity (Batty & Deary, 2004). Not only is faster reaction time significantly correlated with higher cognitive test scores (Neisser et al., 1996), but it is associated with the reduced risk of CHD, CVD, respiratory disease, lung cancer, digestive-related and all-cause mortalities (Gallacher et al., 2009; Roberts et al., 2009; Shipley, Der, Taylor, & Deary, 2006). As mentioned earlier, the Twenty-07 study reported that reaction time largely attenuated the inverse association between cognitive ability and all-cause mortality (Deary & Der, 2005), providing support for the system integrity theory. Another marker of system integrity is physical coordination, as measured by childhood upper and lower limb-related tasks. However, despite significant associations with both IQ and health outcomes, this indicator does not appear to explain the intelligence–mortality association (Gale, Batty, Cooper, & Deary, 2009). Other potential markers of system integrity that positively correlate with mental ability scores include low morning cortisol peaks (Power, Li, & Hertzman, 2008), semen quality (Arden,

Gottfredson, Miller, & Pierce, 2009), and indices of physical health that might indicate a "fitness factor," including cranial, motor, and peripheral sensory nerves, reflexes, head, and general physical health (Arden, Gottfredson, & Miller, 2009). It remains to be seen whether these may contribute to an understanding of the intelligence–mortality relation. A major contribution to this field is likely to come from future genetics research. One relevant study has identified a molecular genetic linkage between lower cognitive ability and a marker for inflammation, vagal tone (Frye, 2009). Reduced vagal nerve signalling is associated with an increased risk of total mortality, CVD, type 2 diabetes, metabolic syndrome, and depression, and so it may yet provide evidence for a system integrity theory of the IQ–mortality association, in which inflammatory processes could underlie neurological and physiological integrity.

## Conclusion

The field of cognitive epidemiology already lays claim to a significant body of empirical work, evaluating associations between pre-morbid intelligence and health outcomes, including risk factors for disease. The successful application of robust epidemiological practices to extremely large, well-characterized cohorts gives considerable validity to these findings and sets a high standard for continuing work in the field. This will bring intelligence differences to the attention of epidemiologists, who share an interest in understanding pathways of influence to health inequalities, and who link with policy-makers to affect change. It may still be common practice to put socioeconomic influences before intelligence differences in mapping out causal factors of disease (Gallo et al., 2009; Marmot, 2010; Marmot & Kivimäki, 2009), yet there remains compelling evidence for the independent effects of cognition on health outcomes.

The various theories that link intelligence to health outcomes require further consolidation. Investigating the effect in different nations and ethnic groups may prove important, taking account of differences in disease patterns and heritability, health behaviors and medical services. Evidence from behavioral genetics data and twin studies will be invaluable in the evaluation of the independent contributions made by genes and by the environment. Further studies of molecular genetics may also help to elucidate a shared genetic linkage between intelligence and health, if system integrity theory is to be supported.

Cognitive epidemiology has shown the convergence of two fields, yet future progress will depend upon wider cross-disciplinary collaborations, including contributions from behavioral genetics, gerontology, cognitive psychology, neurology, medical sociology, statistics, and economics. This is not a simple endeavor, but the end result is to enhance physical health and save lives, while reducing health inequalities.

## Acknowledgments

This work was undertaken by the University of Edinburgh Centre for Cognitive Ageing and Cognitive Epidemiology, which is part of the cross-council Lifelong

Health and Wellbeing Initiative (G0700704/84698). Funding from the Biotechnology and Biological Sciences Research Council (BBSRC), Engineering and Physical Sciences Research Council (EPSRC), Economic and Social Research Council (ESRC), and Medical Research Council (MRC) is gratefully acknowledged. David Batty is funded by a Wellcome Trust Fellowship (WBS Code U.1300.00.006.00012.01). The Medical Research Council (MRC) Social and Public Health Sciences Unit receives funding from the MRC and the Chief Scientist Office at the Scottish Government Health Directorates.

The authors wish to thank Finn Rasmussen of the Karolinska Institute in Stockholm, Sweden for giving permission to use data from the Swedish Conscripts Study on mental ability scores and mortality for the purpose of producing the time-to-survival chart in Figure 16.2.

# References

Anand, S. S., Islam, S., Rosengren, A., Franzosi, M. G., Steyn, K., Yusufali, A. H. et al. (2008). Risk factors for myocardial infarction in women and men: Insights from the INTERHEART study. *European Heart Journal, 29*(7), 932–940.

Anstey, K. J., Low, L.-F., Christensen, H., & Sachdev, P. (2009). Level of cognitive perform-ance as a correlate and predictor of health behaviours that protect against cognitive decline in late life: The path through life study. *Intelligence, 37*(6), 600–606.

Arden, R., Gottfredson, L. S., & Miller, G. (2009). Does a fitness factor contribute to the association between intelligence and health outcomes? Evidence from medical abnormality counts among 3654 veterans. *Intelligence, 37*(6), 581–591.

Arden, R., Gottfredson, L. S., Miller, G., & Pierce, A. (2009). Intelligence and semen quality are positively correlated. *Intelligence, 37*(3), 277–282.

Arvanitakis, Z., Wilson, R. S., & Bennett, D. A. (2006). Diabetes mellitus, dementia, and cognitive function in older persons. *Journal of Nutrition, Health and Aging, 10*(4), 287–291.

Bartley, M., & Plewis, I. (2007). Increasing social mobility: An effective policy to reduce health inequalities. *Journal of the Royal Statistical Society: Series A, 170*(2), 469–481.

Batterham, P. J., Christensen, H., & Mackinnon, A. J. (2009). Fluid intelligence is independ-ently associated with all-cause mortality over 17 years in an elderly community sample: An investigation of potential mechanisms. *Intelligence, 37*(6), 551–560.

Batty, G. D., & Deary, I. J. (2004). Early life intelligence and adult health. *British Medical Journal, 329*(7466), 585–586.

Batty, G. D., Deary, I. J., Benzeval, M., Der, G. (2010). Does IQ predict cardiovascular disease mortality as strongly as established risk factors? Comparison of effect estimates using the West of Scotland Twenty-07 cohort study. *European Journal of Cardiovascular Prevention and Rehabilitation, 17*(1), 24–27.

Batty, G. D., Deary, I. J., & Gottfredson, L. S. (2007). Premorbid (early life) IQ and later mortality risk: Systematic review. *Annals of Epidemiology, 17*(4), 278–288.

Batty, G. D., Deary, I. J., & Macintyre, S. (2006). Low childhood IQ and life course socioeco-nomic position in relation to alcohol induced hangovers in adulthood: The Aberdeen chil-dren of the 1950s study. *Journal of Epidemiology and Community Health, 60*(10), 872–874.

Batty, G. D., Deary, I. J., & Macintyre, S. (2007). Childhood IQ in relation to risk factors for premature mortality in middle-aged persons: The Aberdeen children of the 1950s study. *Journal of Epidemiology and Community Health, 61*(3), 241–247.

Batty, G. D., Mortensen, E. L., & Osler, M. (2005). Childhood IQ in relation to later psychiatric disorder: Evidence from a Danish birth cohort study. *British Journal of Psychiatry*, *187*, 180–181.

Batty, G. D., Deary, I. J., Schoon, I., & Gale, C. R. (2007a). Childhood mental ability in relation to cause-specific accidents in adulthood: The 1970 British Cohort Study. *QJM: Journal of the Association of Physicians*, *100*(7), 405-414.

Batty, G. D., Deary, I. J., Schoon, I., & Gale, C. R. (2007b). Childhood mental ability in relation to food intake and physical activity in adulthood: The 1970 British Cohort Study. *Pediatrics*, *119*(1), e38–e45.

Batty, G. D., Deary, I. J., Schoon, I., & Gale, C. R. (2007c). Mental ability across childhood in relation to risk factors for premature mortality in adult life: The 1970 British Cohort Study. *Journal of Epidemiology and Community Health*, *61*(11), 997–1003.

Batty, G. D., Deary, I. J., Tengstrom, A., & Rasmussen, F. (2008). IQ in early adulthood and risk of death by homicide: Cohort study of one million men. *British Journal of Psychiatry*, *193*(6), 461–465.

Batty, G. D., Der, G., Macintyre, S., & Deary, I. J. (2006). Does IQ explain socioeconomic inequalities in health? Evidence from a population based cohort study in the west of Scotland. *British Medical Journal*, *332*(7541), 580–584.

Batty, G. D., Mortensen, E. L., Nybo Andersen, A.-M., & Osler, M. (2005). Childhood intelligence in relation to adult coronary heart disease and stroke risk: Evidence from a Danish birth cohort study. *Paediatric and Perinatal Epidemiology*, *19*(6), 452–459.

Batty, G. D., Gale, C. R., Tynelius, P., Deary, I. J., & Rasmussen, F. (2009). IQ in early adulthood, socioeconomic position, and unintentional injury mortality by middle-age: Cohort study of over one million Swedish men. *American Journal of Epidemiology*, *169*(5), 606–615.

Batty, G. D., Deary, I. J., Schoon, I., Emslie, C., Hunt, K., & Gale, C. R. (2008). Childhood mental ability and adult alcohol intake and alcohol problems: The 1970 British Cohort Study. *American Journal of Public Health*, *98*(12), 2237–2243.

Batty, G. D., Gale, C. R., Mortensen, L. H., Langenberg, C., Shipley, M., & Deary, I. J. (2008). Pre-morbid IQ, the metabolic syndrome and mortality: The Vietnam Experience Study. *Diabetologia*, *51*(3), 436–443.

Batty, G. D., Mortensen, L. H., Gale, C. R., Shipley, M., Roberts, B. & Deary, I. J. (2009). IQ in early adulthood, risk factors in middle age, and later cancer mortality in men: The Vietnam Experience Study. *Psycho-Oncology*, *18*(10), 1122–1126.

Batty, G. D., Wennerstad, K. M, Davey Smith, G., Gunnell, G., Deary, I. J., Tynelius, P., & Rasmussen, F. (2007). IQ in early adulthood and later cancer risk: Cohort study of 1 million Swedish men. *Annals of Oncology*, *18*(1), 21–28.

Batty, G. D., Wennerstad, K. M., Davey Smith, G., Gunnell, D., Deary, I. J., Tylenius, P., & Rasmussen, F. (2009). IQ in early adulthood and mortality by middle age: Cohort study of one million Swedish men. *Epidemiology*, *20*(1), 100–109.

Batty, G. D., Shipley, M. J., Mortensen, L. H., Boyle, S. H., Barefoot, J., Gronbaek, M., Gale, C. R., & Deary, I. J. (2008). IQ in late adolescence/early adulthood, risk factors in middle age and later all-cause mortality in men: The Vietnam Experience Study. *Journal of Epidemiology and Community Health*, *62*(6), 522–531.

Bhopal, R. (1997). Which book? A comparative review of 25 introductory epidemiology textbooks. *Journal of Epidemiology and Community Health*, *51*(6), 612–622.

Bhopal, R. (2008). *Concepts of epidemiology: Integrating the ideas, theories, principles and methods of epidemiology* (2nd ed.). Oxford: Oxford University Press.

Bradford Hill, A. (1965). The environment and disease: Association or causation? *Proceedings of the Royal Society of Medicine*, *58*(5), 295–300.

Calvin, C. M., Deary, I. J., Fenton, C., Roberts, B., Der, G., Leckenby, N., & Batty, G. D. (2010). Early life intelligence and mortality in population-based studies: A systematic review with meta-analysis. *International Journal of Epidemiology.* Advance online publication. doi: 10.1093/ije/dyq190

Carroll, J. B. (1993). *Human cognitive abilities: A survey of factor-analytic studies.* Cambridge and New York: Cambridge University Press.

Chandola, T., Deary, I. J., Blane, D., & Batty, G. D. (2006). Childhood intelligence in relation to obesity and weight gain in adult life: Findings from the National Child Development (1958) Study. *International Journal of Obesity, 30*(9), 1422–1432.

Comijs, H. C., Kriegsman, D. M., Dik, M. G., Deeg, D. J., Jonker, C., & Stalman, W. A. (2009). Somatic chronic diseases and 6-year change in cognitive functioning among older persons. *Archives of Gerontology and Geriatrics, 48*(2), 191–196.

Cox, D. R. (1958). The regression analysis of binary sequences. *Journal of the Royal Statistical Society: Series B, 20*(2), 215–242.

Cox, D. R. (1972). Regression models and life tables (with discussion). *Journal of the Royal Statistical Society: Series B, 34*(2), 187–220.

Deary, I. J. (2008). Why do intelligent people live longer? *Nature, 456*(13), 175–176.

Deary, I. J. (2009). Introduction to the special issue on cognitive epidemiology. *Intelligence, 37*(6), 517–519.

Deary, I. J. (2010). Cognitive epidemiology: Its rise, its current issues, and its challenges. *Personality and Individual Differences, 49*(4), 337–343.

Deary, I. J., & Batty, G. D. (2006). Commentary: Pre-morbid IQ and later health—The rapidly evolving field of cognitive epidemiology. *International Journal of Epidemiology, 35*(3), 670–672.

Deary, I. J., & Batty, G. D. (2007). Cognitive epidemiology. *Journal of Epidemiology and Community Health, 61*(5), 378–384.

Deary, I. J., & Batty, G. D. (in press). Intelligence as a predictor of health, illness and death: "Cognitive epidemiology." In R. J. Sternberg & S. B. Kaufman (Eds.), *The Cambridge Handbook of Intelligence.* Cambridge: Cambridge University Press.

Deary, I. J., & Der, G. (2005). Reaction time explains IQ's association with death. *Psychological Science, 16*(1), 64–69.

Deary, I. J., Johnson, W., & Houlihan, L. M. (2009). Genetic foundations of human intelligence. *Human Genetics, 126*(1), 215–232.

Deary, I. J., Whalley, L. J., & Starr, J. M. (2009). *A lifetime of intelligence: Follow-up studies of the Scottish Mental Surveys of 1932 and 1947.* Washington, DC: American Psychological Association.

Deary, I. J., Batty, G. D., Pattie, A., & Gale, C. G. (2008). More intelligent, more dependable children live longer: A 55-year longitudinal study of a representative sample of the Scottish nation. *Psychological Science, 19*(9), 874–880.

Deary, I. J., Strand, S., Smith, P., & Fernandes, C. (2007). Intelligence and educational achievement. *Intelligence, 35*(1), 13–21.

Deary, I. J., Whalley, L. J., Batty, D., & Starr, J. M. (2006). Physical fitness and lifetime cognitive change. *Neurology, 67*(7), 1195–1200.

Deary, I. J., Whalley, L. J., Lemmon, H., Crawford, J. R., & Starr, J. M. (2000). The stability of individual differences in mental ability from childhood to old age: Follow-up of the 1932 Scottish Mental Survey. *Intelligence, 28*(1), 49–55.

Deary, I. J., Whiteman, M. C., Starr, J. M., Whalley, L. J., & Fox, H. C. (2004). The impact of childhood intelligence on later life: Following up the Scottish Mental Surveys of 1932 and 1947. *Journal of Personality and Social Psychology, 86*(1), 130–147.

Deary, I. J., Gale, C. R., Stewart, M. C. W., Fowkes, F. G. R., Murray, G. D., Batty, G. D., & Price, J. F. (2009). Intelligence and persisting with medication for two years: Analysis in a randomised controlled trial. *Intelligence, 37*(6), 607–612.

Der, G., Batty, G. D., & Deary, I. J. (2009). The association between IQ in adolescence and a range of health outcomes at 40 in the 1979 US National Longitudinal Study of Youth. *Intelligence, 37*(6), 573–580.

DeWalt, D. A., Berkman, N. D., Sheridan, S., Lohr, K. A., & Pignone, M. P. (2004). Literacy and health outcomes. A review of the literature. *Journal of General Internal Medicine, 19*(12), 1228–1239.

Evans, A. (1978). Causation and disease: A chronological journey. *American Journal of Epidemiology, 108*(4), 249–258.

Frye, R. A. (2009). Cognitive epidemiology of ethnic health and the CHRM2 vagal vigour hypothesis. *Nature Precedings*. Article retrieved July 1, 2009 from http://precedings.nature.com/documents/2862/version/1

Gale, C. (2005). Commentary: Height and intelligence. *International Journal of Epidemiology, 34*(3), 678–679.

Gale, C. R., Batty, G. D., Cooper, C., & Deary, I. J. (2009). Psychomotor co-ordination and intelligence in childhood and health in adulthood: Testing the system integrity hypothesis. *Psychosomatic Medicine, 71*(6), 675–681.

Gale, C. R., Deary, I. J., Schoon, I., & Batty, G. D. (2007). IQ in childhood and vegetarianism in adulthood: 1970 British Cohort Study. *British Medical Journal, 334*(7587), 245–248.

Gale, C. R., Hatch, S. L., Batty, G. D., & Deary, I. J. (2009). Intelligence in childhood and risk of psychological distress in adulthood: The 1958 National Child Development Survey and the 1970 British Cohort Study. *Intelligence, 37*(6), 592–599.

Gale, C. R., Batty, G. D., Tynelius, P., Deary, I. J., & Rasmussen, F. (2010). Intelligence in early adulthood and subsequent hospitalisation and admission rates for the whole range of mental disorders: Longitudinal study of 1,049,663 men. *Epidemiology, 21*(1), 70–77.

Gale, C. R., Deary, I. J., Boyle, S. H., Barefoot, J., Mortensen, L. H., & Batty, G. D. (2008). Cognitive ability in early adulthood and risk of 5 specific psychiatric disorders in middle life: The Vietnam Experience Study. *Archives of General Psychiatry, 65*(12), 1410–1418.

Gallacher, J., Bayer, A., Dunstan, F., Yarnell, J., Elwood, P., & Ben-Sholmo, Y. (2009). Can we understand why cognitive function predicts mortality? Results from the Caerphilly Prospective Study (CaPS). *Intelligence, 37*(6), 535–544.

Gallo, L. C., Espinosa de los Monteros, K., & Shivpuri, S. (2009). Socioeconomic status and health: What is the role of reserve capacity? *Current Directions in Psychological Science, 18*(5), 269–274.

Geyer, S., Hemstrom, O., Peter, R., & Vågerö, D. (2006). Education, income, and occupational class cannot be used interchangeably in social epidemiology. Empirical evidence against a common practice. *Journal of Epidemiology and Community Health, 60*(9), 804–810.

Gottfredson, L. S. (1997). Mainstream science on intelligence: An editorial with 52 signatories, history, and bibliography. *Intelligence, 24*(1), 13–23.

Gottfredson, L. S. (2004). Intelligence: Is it the epidemiologists' elusive "fundamental cause" of social class inequalities in health? *Journal of Personality and Social Psychology, 86*(1), 174–199.

Gottfredson, L. S., & Deary, I. J. (2004). Intelligence predicts health and longevity, but why? *Current Directions in Psychological Science, 13*(1), 1–4.

Gunnell, D., Magnusson, P. K. E., & Rasmussen, F. (2005). Low intelligence test scores in 18 year old men and risk of suicide: Cohort study. *British Medical Journal, 330*(7484), 167–170.

Hackman, D. A., & Farah, M. J. (2009). Socioeconomic status and the developing brain. *Trends in Cognitive Neuroscience, 13*(2), 65–73.

Hall, P. A., Dubin, J. A., Crossley, M., Holmqvist, M. E., & D'Arcy, C. (2009). Does executive function explain the IQ–mortality association? Evidence from the Canadian Study of Health and Aging. *Psychosomatic Medicine, 71*(2), 196–204.

Hart, C. L., Taylor, M. D., Davey Smith, G., Whalley, L. J., Starr, J. M., Hole, D. J., Wilson, V., & Deary, I. J. (2004). Childhood IQ and cardiovascular disease in adulthood: Prospective observational study linking the Scottish Mental Survey 1932 and the Midspan studies. *Social Science and Medicine, 59*(10), 2131–2138.

Hart, C. L., Taylor, M. D., Davey Smith, G., Whalley, L. J., Starr, J. M., Hole, D. J. et al. (2003). Childhood IQ, social class, deprivation, and their relationships with mortality and morbidity risk in later life: Prospective observational study linking the Scottish Mental Survey 1932 and the Midspan studies. *Psychosomatic Medicine, 65*(5), 877–883.

Hatch, S. L., Jones, P. B., Kuh, D., Hardy, R., Wadsworth, M. E., & Richards, M. (2007). Childhood cognitive ability and adult mental health in the British 1946 birth cohort. *Social Science and Medicine, 64*(11), 2285–2296.

Hemmingsson, T., Kriebel, D., Melin, B., Allebeck, P., & Lundberg, I. (2008). How does IQ affect onset of smoking and cessation of smoking—linking the Swedish 1969 conscription cohort to the Swedish survey of living conditions. *Psychosomatic Medicine, 70*(7), 805–810.

Hemmingsson, T., Melin, B., Allebeck, P., & Lundberg, I. (2006). The association between cognitive ability measured at ages 18–20 and mortality during 30 years of follow-up: A prospective observational study among Swedish males born 1949–51. *International Journal of Epidemiology, 35*(5), 665–670.

Hennekens, C. H., & Buring, J. E. (1987). *Epidemiology in Medicine.* Philadelphia, PA: Lippincott Williams & Wilkins.

Holsinger, T., Helms, M., & Plassman, B. (2007). Intelligence in early adulthood and life span up to 65 years later in male elderly twins. *Age and Ageing, 36*(3), 286–291.

Huisman, M., Kunst, A. E., Bopp, M., Borgan, J.-K., Borrell, C., Costa, G. et al. (2005). Educational inequalities in cause-specific mortality in middle-aged and older men and women in eight western European populations. *Lancet, 365*(9458), 493–500.

Johnson, W., Hicks, B. M., McGue, M., Iacono, W. G. (2009). How intelligence and education contribute to substance use: Hints from the Minnesota Twin Family Study. *Intelligence, 37*(6), 613–624.

Jokela, M., Elovainio, M., Singh-Manoux, A., & Kivimaki, M. (2009). IQ, socioeconomic status, and early death: The US National Longitudinal Survey of Youth. *Psychosomatic Medicine, 71*(3), 322–328.

Jokela, M., Batty, G. D., Deary, I. J., Gale, C. R., & Kivimaki, M. (2009). Low childhood IQ and early adult mortality: The role of explanatory factors in the 1958 British Birth Cohort. *Pediatrics, 124*(3), e380–e388.

Kilgour, A. H., Starr, J. M., & Whalley, L. J. (2009). Associations between childhood intelligence (IQ), adult morbidity and mortality. *Maturitas, 65*(2), 98–105.

Kivipelto, M., Nganda, T., Fratiglioni, L., Vittanen, M., Kåreholt, I., Winblad, B. et al. (2005). Obesity and vascular risk factors at midlife and the risk of dementia and Alzheimer disease. *Archives of Neurology, 62*(10), 1556–1560.

Koenen, K. C., Moffitt, T. E., Roberts, A. L., Martin, L. T., Kubzansky, L., Harrington, H., Poulton, R., & Caspi, A. (2009). Childhood IQ and adult mental disorders: A test of the cognitive reserve hypothesis. *American Journal of Psychiatry, 166*(1), 50–57.

Kuh, D., Richards, M., Hardy, R., Butterworth, S., & Wadsworth, M. E. J. (2004). Childhood cognitive ability and deaths until middle age: A post-war birth cohort study. *International Journal of Epidemiology, 33*(2), 408–413.

Kuh, D., Shah, I., Richards, M., Mishra, G., Wadsworth, M., & Hardy, R. (2009). Do childhood cognitive ability or smoking behaviour explain the influence of lifetime socioeconomic conditions on premature adult mortality in a British post war birth cohort? *Social Science and Medicine*, *68*(9), 1565–1573.

Lager, A., Bremberg, S., & Vågerö, D. (2009). The association of early IQ and education with mortality: 65 year longitudinal study in Malmo, Sweden. *British Medical Journal*, *339*(111), b5282.

Last, J. M. (1988). What is "clinical epidemiology"? *Journal of Public Health Policy*, *9*(2), 159–163.

Lawlor, D. A., Batty, G. D., Clark, H., Macintyre, S., & Leon, D. A. (2008). Association of childhood intelligence with risk of coronary heart disease and stroke: Findings from the Aberdeen Children of the 1950s cohort study. *European Journal of Epidemiology*, *23*(10), 695–706.

Lawrence, D., Mitrou, F., & Zubrick, S. R. (2009). Smoking and mental illness: Results from population surveys in Australia and the United States. *BMC Public Health*, *7*(9), 285.

Leon, D. A., Lawlor, D. A., Clark, H. Batty, G. D., & Macintyre, S. (2009). The association of childhood intelligence with mortality risk from adolescence to middle age: Findings from the Aberdeen children of the 1950s cohort study. *Intelligence*, *37*(6), 520–528.

Lleras-Muney, A. (2005). The relationship between education and adult mortality in the United States. *Review of Economic Studies*, *72*(1), 189–221.

Lubinski, D. (2009). Cognitive epidemiology: With emphasis on untangling cognitive ability and socioeconomic status. *Intelligence*, *37*(6), 625–633.

Lubinski, D., & Humphreys, L.G. (1997). Incorporating general intelligence into epidemiology and the social sciences. *Intelligence*, *24*(1), 159–201.

Luciano, M., Marioni, R. E., Gow, A. J., Starr, J. M., & Deary, I. J. (2009). Reverse causation in the association between C-reactive protein and fibrinogen levels and cognitive abilities in an aging sample. *Psychosomatic Medicine*, *71*(4), 404–409.

Maller, J. B. (1933). Vital indices and their relation to psychological and social factors. *Human Biology*, *5*(1), 94–121.

Marmot, M. (2010). The Marmot review. Strategic review of health inequalities in England post-2010. Article retrieved February 11, 2010 from http://www.marmot-review.org.uk

Marmot, M., & Kivimäki, M. (2009). Social inequalities in mortality: A problem of cognitive function? *European Heart Journal*, *30*(15), 1819–1820.

Martin, L. T., & Kubzansky, L. D. (2005). Childhood cognitive performance and risk of mortality: A prospective cohort study. *American Journal of Epidemiology*, *162*(9), 887–890.

McGurn, B., Deary, I. J., & Starr, J. M. (2008). Childhood cognitive ability and risk of late-onset Alzheimer and vascular dementia. *Neurology*, *71*(14), 1051–1056.

Mortensen, L. H., Sørensen, T. I. A., & Grønbæk, N. (2005). Intelligence in relation to later beverage preference and alcohol intake. *Addiction*, *100*(10), 1445–1452.

Moscicki, E. K. (1995). Epidemiology of suicidal behavior. *Suicide and Life-Threatening Behavior*, *25*(1), 22–35.

Neisser, U., Boodoo, G., Bouchard, T. J., Boykin, A. W., Brody, N., Ceci, S. J. et al. (1996). Intelligence: Knowns and unknowns. *American Psychologist*, *51*(2), 77–101.

O'Toole, B. I., Adena, M. A., & Jones, M. P. (1988). Risk factors for mortality in Australian Vietnam-era national servicemen: A case-control study. *Community Health Studies*, *12*(4), 408–417.

Okereke, O. I., Kang, J. H., Cook, N. R., Gaziano, J. M., Manson, J. E., Buring, J. E., & Grodstein, F. (2008). Type 2 diabetes mellitus and cognitive decline in two large cohorts of community-dwelling older adults. *Journal of the American Geriatrics Society, 56*(6), 1028–1036.

Osler, M., Nybo Andersen, A.-M., Laursen, B., & Lawlor, D. A. (2007). Cognitive function in childhood and early adulthood and injuries later in life: The Metropolit 1953 male birth cohort. *International Journal of Epidemiology, 36*(1), 212–219.

Osler, M., Petersen, L., Prescott, E., Teasdale, T. W., & Sørensen, T. I. A. (2006). Genetic and environmental influences on the relation between parental social class and mortality. *International Journal of Epidemiology, 35*(5), 1272–1277.

Osler, M., Andersen, A. M., Due, P., Lund, R., Damsgaard, M. T., & Holstein, B. E. (2003). Socioeconomic position in early life, birth weight, childhood cognitive function, and adult mortality. A longitudinal study of Danish men born in 1953. *Journal of Epidemiology and Community Health, 57*(9), 681–686.

Pearce, M. S., Deary, I. J., Young, A. H., & Parker, L. (2006). Childhood IQ and deaths up to middle age: The Newcastle Thousand Families Study. *Public Health, 120*(11), 1020–1026.

Phillips, A. C., Batty, G. D., Gale, C. R., Deary, I. J., Osborn, D., Macintyre, K., & Carroll, D. (2009). Generalized anxiety disorder, major depressive disorder, and their comorbidity as predictors of all-cause and cardiovascular mortality: The Vietnam Experience Study. *Psychosomatic Medicine, 71*(4), 395–403.

Power, C., Li, L., & Hertzman, C. (2008). Cognitive development and cortisol patterns in mid-life: Findings from the British birth cohort. *Psychoneuroendocrinology, 33*(4), 530–539.

Rafnsson, S. B., Deary, I. J., Smith, F. B., Whiteman, M. C., & Fowkes, F. G. R. (2007). Cardiovascular diseases and decline in cognitive function in an elderly community population: The Edinburgh Artery Study. *Psychosomatic Medicine, 69*(5), 425–434.

Richards, M., Strachan, D., Hardy, R., Kuh, D., & Wadsworth, M. (2005). Lung function and cognitive ability in a longitudinal birth cohort study. *Psychosomatic Medicine, 67*(4), 602–608.

Richards, M., Black, S., Mishra, G., Gale, C. R., Deary, I. J., & Batty, G. D. (2009). IQ in childhood and the metabolic syndrome in middle age: Extended follow-up of the 1946 British Birth Cohort Study. *Intelligence, 37*(6), 567–572.

Roberts, B. A., Der, G., Deary, I. J., & Batty, G. D. (2009). Reaction time and established risk factors for total and cardiovascular disease mortality: Comparison of effect estimates in the follow-up of a large, UK-wide, general-population based survey. *Intelligence, 37*(6), 561–566.

Rothman, K. J. (2002). *Epidemiology: An introduction.* Oxford: Oxford University Press.

Rothman, K. J., & Greenland, S. (2005). Causation and causal inference in epidemiology. *American Journal of Public Health, 95*(1), S144–S150.

Schmidt, F. L., & Hunter, J. (2004). General mental ability in the world of work: Occupational attainment and job performance. *Journal of Personality and Social Psychology, 86*(1), 162–173.

Shenkin, S. D., Starr, J. M., & Deary, I. J. (2004). Birth weight and cognitive ability in childhood: A systematic review. *Psychological Bulletin, 130*(6), 989–1013.

Shipley, B. A., Der, G., Taylor, M. D., & Deary, I. J. (2006). Cognition and all-cause mortality across the entire adult age range: Health and lifestyle survey. *Psychosomatic Medicine, 68*(1), 17–24.

Singh-Manoux, A., Ferrie, J. E., Chandola, T., & Marmot, M. (2004). Socioeconomic trajectories across the life course and health outcomes in midlife: Evidence for the accumulation hypothesis? *International Journal of Epidemiology, 33*(5), 1072–1079.

Singh-Manoux, A., Sabia, S., Kivimaki, M., Shipley, M. J., Ferrie, J. E., & Marmot, M. G. (2009). Cognition and incident coronary heart disease in late midlife: The Whitehall II study. *Intelligence, 37*(6), 529–534.

Starr, J. M., Taylor, M. D., Hart, C. L., Davey Smith, G., Whalley, L. J., Hole, D. J., Wilson, V., & Deary, I. J. (2004). Childhood mental ability and blood pressure at midlife: Linking the Scottish Mental Survey 1932 and the Midspan Studies. *Journal of Hypertension, 22*(5), 893–897.

Stilley, C. S., Bender, C. M., Dunbar-Jacob, J., Sereika, S., & Ryan, C. M. (2010). The impact of cognitive function on medication management: Three studies. *Health Psychology, 29*(1), 50–55.

Strenze, T. (2007). Intelligence and socioeconomic success: A meta-analytic review of longitudinal research. *Intelligence, 35*(5), 401–426.

Sutton, A. J., Abrams, K. R., Jones, D. R., Sheldon, T. A., & Song, F. (2000). *Methods for meta-analysis in medical research.* Chichester: John Wiley & Sons.

Symons, M. J., & Moore, D. T. (2002). Hazard rate ratio and prospective epidemiological studies. *Journal of Clinical Epidemiology, 55*(9), 893–899.

Taylor, M. D., Hart, C. L., Davey Smith, G., Starr, J. M., Hole, D. J., Whalley, L. J., Wilson, V., & Deary, I. J. (2003). Childhood mental ability and smoking cessation in adulthood: Prospective observational study linking the Scottish Mental Survey 1932 and the Midspan Studies. *Journal of Epidemiology and Community Health, 57*(6), 464–465.

Torssander, J., & Erikson, R. (2010). Stratification and mortality: A comparison of education, class, status, and income. *European Sociological Review, 26*(4), 465–474.

Trumbetta, S. L., Seltzer, B. K., Gottesman, I. I., & McIntyre, K. M. (2010). Mortality predictors in a 60-year follow-up of adolescent males: Exploring delinquency, socioeconomic status, IQ, high-school drop-out status, and personality. *Psychosomatic Medicine, 72*(1), 46–52.

Van der Kooy, K., van Hout, H., Marwijk, H., Marten, H., Stehouwer, C., & Beekman, A. (2007). Depression and the risk for cardiovascular diseases: Systematic review and meta analysis. *International Journal of Geriatric Psychiatry, 22*(7), 613–626.

Von Stumm, S., Macintyre, S., Batty, D. G., Clark, H., & Deary, I. J. (2010). Intelligence, social class of origin, childhood behavior disturbance and education as predictors of status attainment in midlife in men: The Aberdeen Children of the 1950s study. *Intelligence, 38*(1), 202–211.

Voracek, M. (2005). National intelligence, suicide rate in the elderly, and a threshold intelligence for suicidality: An ecological study of 48 Eurasian countries. *Journal of Biosocial Science, 37*(6), 721–740.

Walker, N. P., McConville, P. M., Hunter, D., Deary, I. J., & Whalley, L. J. (2002). Childhood mental ability and lifetime psychiatric contact: A 66-year follow-up study of the 1932 Scottish Mental Survey. *Intelligence, 30*(3), 233–245.

Weiss, A., Gale, C. R., Batty, G. D., & Deary, I. J. (2009). Emotionally stable, intelligent men live longer: the Vietnam Experience Study. *Psychosomatic Medicine, 71*(4), 385–394.

Wennerstad, K. M., Silventoinen, K., Tynelius, P., Bergman, L., & Rasmussen, F. (2009). Association between intelligence and type specific stroke: A population-based cohort study of early fatal and non-fatal stroke in one million Swedish men. *Journal of Epidemiology and Community Health, 64*(10), 908–912.

Whalley, L. J., & Deary, I. J. (2001). Longitudinal cohort study of childhood IQ and survival up to age 76. *British Medical Journal, 322*(7290), 819–822.

Whalley, L. J., Starr, J. M., Athawes, R., Hunter, D., Pattie, A., & Deary I. J. (2000). Childhood mental ability and dementia. *Neurology, 55*(10), 1455–1459.

Wingard, D. L. (1984). The sex differential in morbidity, mortality, and lifestyle. *Annual Review of Public Health, 5,* 433–458.

Yaffe, K., Kanaya, A., Lindquist, K., Simonsick, E.M., Harris, T., Shorr, R.I. et al. (2004). The metabolic syndrome, inflammation, and risk of cognitive decline. *Journal of the American Medical Association, 292*(18), 2237–2242.

Zagorsky, J. L. (2007). Do you have to be smart to be rich? The impact of IQ on wealth, income and financial distress. *Intelligence, 35*(5), 489–501.

# 17

# Personality and Differences in Health and Longevity

## Margaret L. Kern and Howard S. Friedman

## Personality and Differences in Health and Longevity

There are striking individual differences in health, well-being, and longevity. Some people are more likely to get sick, are less likely to recover when ill, and are less likely to live to a healthy old age. Although some of this variation is due to chance circumstances, there are systematic differences in disease proneness and longevity. The explanation for this variation is, however, much more complex than it first appears.

Modern scientific conceptions view personality as having biological, psychological, and social aspects. The individual is born with certain genetic predispositions and biologically influenced temperaments, is socialized to develop a self-identity and typical patterns of behavior, and lives in a social environment that encourages and elicits certain tendencies and reactions and discourages others. Personality is thus well-suited for studying modern conceptions of health that rely on a biopsychosocial model. That is, as it has become clearer that a full understanding of health, illness, and recovery requires adding psychosocial components to the biological ones, a biopsychosocial conception of personality is a natural conception to employ in sophisticated models and research.

## History and Background

It has long been observed that emotional aspects of personality, such as being angry, anxious, or depressed, are associated with disease. For the ancient Greeks—Hippocrates, Galen, and their followers—so-called bodily humors were the explanation. They postulated that health arose from a balance across four known fluids—blood, black bile, yellow bile, and phlegm—and imbalance led to disease. If you were chronically sad, with a splenic melancholia, it was not surprising that early cancer might

*The Wiley-Blackwell Handbook of Individual Differences*, First Edition.
Edited by Tomas Chamorro-Premuzic, Sophie von Stumm, and Adrian Furnham.
© 2011 Blackwell Publishing Ltd. Published 2011 by Blackwell Publishing Ltd.

accompany your depression. Treatments thus often involved attempts to restore humoral balance through bloodletting, emetics, dietary changes, purging, diuretics, and so on. Although the humoral elements and their relations to health were without any scientific justification and proved to be incorrect, this concept of balance, or homeostasis, has become a cornerstone for modern ideas of emotional patterns and health.

Two millennia later, the psychophysiological models of the French physiologist Claude Bernard (1880) and of the "fight-or-flight" discoverer Walter Cannon (1932) developed the idea of biological homeostasis, successfully applying the concept of internal balance to nerves and hormones. The body consists of a series of systems that respond and adapt to continual strains and changes in the body. Most clearly, under stress, the sympathetic nervous system activates, and then is complemented by the parasympathetic system to restore balance. Processes of homeostasis involving the hypothalamic–pituitary–adrenal axis, the autonomic nervous system, and the cardiovascular, metabolic, and immune systems are core to today's understanding of health. But how are they linked to individual differences?

The dominance of psychoanalytic and neo-analytic theory as the field of psychiatry developed in the first half of the twentieth century led to many interesting observations and ideas in so-called psychosomatic medicine, but empirical validation was next to impossible. The psychoanalyst Alexander (1950) suggested that various diseases are caused by specific unconscious emotional conflicts. For example, ulcers and a dependent personality might be caused by oral conflicts—an unconscious desire to have basic infantile needs satisfied. However, neither the unconscious conflicts nor their supposed links to personality traits and disease states could be studied in a rigorous scientific manner.

In reaction to this imprecise and weak investigation, cardiologists proposed the Type A behavior pattern (Chesney & Rosenman, 1985). Type A people are those involved in a constant competitive struggle to do more and more things in less and less time, and are often quite aggressive in their efforts. They are hasty, hurried, impatient, impulsive, hyper-alert, and tense. The cardiologists intentionally eschewed psychological (especially psychodynamic) concepts, and explicitly aimed to objectify their concept by choosing a neutral term ("Type A"), defined as a medical syndrome of coronary proneness. Individuals who did not show Type A characteristics were called "Type B," rather than given some psychological or behavioral description. As research on this topic continued, it became apparent that the disease-relevant characteristics and patterns of individuals cannot be adequately explained in such a barren way. Research soon turned to trying to understand the trait correlates, the emotional components, the developmental bases, and the various consequences of Type A behavior. It became popular to use the term "Type A personality" even though the originators specifically tried to avoid a personality-type approach.

As research began to examine the health correlates of Type A behavior beyond coronary disease, it became apparent that, in a formulation where Type A behavior is defined as practically synonymous with coronary proneness ("the Type A coronary-prone personality"), the concept begs the question of whether this type of personality does indeed predict coronary disease. Inconsistencies across studies in how the construct was defined and measured, the use of simple correlations, and numerous dead-end research programs only led to more confusion. After thousands of studies, research on Type A behavior nearly collapsed of its own dead weight. The missteps of the neo-analytic psychosomatic approaches and the atheoretical Type A syndrome approaches did, however, point the way to better concepts and better research designs.

## Disease-Prone Personalities and Self-Healing Personalities

To address the deficiencies and to develop a more complete perspective, which relies on a full nomological net (Campbell & Fiske, 1959; Cronbach & Meehl, 1955), Friedman and Booth-Kewley (1987) meta-analyzed the correlations between emotional aspects of personality and certain chronic diseases (including heart disease) thought to be especially influenced by psychosomatic factors. A notably similar pattern of associations appeared between personality predictors and various disease outcomes. That is, the results failed to confirm the existence of a "coronary-prone personality," a distinct "ulcer-prone personality," and so on. Rather, it appeared that various negative traits such as hostility, anxiety, depression, and aggressiveness are markers of increased risk for various diseases, although not always to the same extent or for the same reasons (see Smith & Gallo, 2001; Suls & Bunde, 2005). This broader pattern was termed the *disease-prone personality* (Friedman & Booth-Kewley, 1987).

One implication of this emerging conception was that it would be necessary to employ multiple and valid personality predictors in the same study. The second implication was that it would be wise to employ multiple health outcomes in the same study. More than a half-century ago, the World Health Organization (1948) defined health as a multifaceted construct, comprised of physical, mental, social, cognitive, and functional components. Many of the best studies now do indeed employ multiple predictors and multiple health and well-being outcomes (Friedman, 2007; Friedman, Kern, & Reynolds, 2010; Smith & Gallo, 2001), but it is only recently that attention has extended beyond the physical dimension. Rather than simultaneously analyzing multiple health outcomes, too many approaches have relied instead on an uninformative "Type B" default formulation, in which you are seen as healthy if you are not ill.

Another key implication of this broader perspective is that more attention has been paid not only to risks and disease proneness, but also to analysis of the potential health-promoting effects of often salutary traits. Much research is now considering the role of optimism, sociability, hardiness, and conscientiousness. Complementing the disease-prone personality, Friedman (1991) proposed the notion of a *self-healing personality*—a personality with a multidimensional emotional style providing a match or adjustment between the individual and the environment, which maintains a physiological and psychosocial homeostasis, and through which good mental health promotes good physical health. Although the construct is characterized in part by traits such as hardiness (control, commitment, and challenge; Maddi & Kobasa, 1984) and sociability, its core is the fit between the person and the environment that will best maintain biopsychosocial balance. For example, a driven, successful business executive may be quite content with her fast-paced lifestyle and may become ill and depressed if forced to slow down and take a long vacation. This inclusion of the socio-environmental context adds the "social" component to the biological and psychological elements, thus producing a true biopsychosocial approach.

## Measuring Personality

Personality can be conceptualized and measured at different levels, including broad dimensions of positive and negative affect, dispositional traits, and life-story narratives (McAdams & Olson, 2010). Lower levels (narrow traits) are often better predictors of specific outcomes and may highlight processes connecting personality and health. For example, in two community samples, preventative behaviors were best predicted by the industriousness and orderliness facets of conscientiousness, whereas risky behaviors were best predicted by the impulse control and conventionality sub-scales (Sixkiller et al., 2010). Still, higher-order factors better generalize across multiple samples and link more reliably to key health outcomes, including longevity. In health psychology research, the five-factor model has been the focus of much of the recent literature linking personality and health, and it offers a framework for structuring and understanding personality–health relations (Smith & Williams, 1992).

Following a lexical approach, there essentially are two five-factor models, one stemming from work by Costa and McCrae and captured by the NEO–PI–R (Costa & McCrae, 1992), and the other stemming from work by other personality pioneers in the field (Goldberg, 1993). There is dispute over the exact definitions and the lower-order facets and traits comprising each factor, but the five main factors are typically labeled extraversion (social, active, dominant, positive affect), neuroticism (tendency to experience the world as distressful, proneness toward anxiety and depression, emotional instability), intellect/openness to experience (intellectual, imaginative, creative, artistic), agreeableness (cooperative, trusting, kind, generous), and conscientiousness (orderly, achievement motivated, responsible, planful).

Notably, the five-factor model allows multiple personality traits to be considered with multiple health outcomes, can easily be measured by commonly available instruments, and has been linked to health, longevity, occupational success, education, social relationships, marital stability, and productive contributions to society (Ozer & Benet-Martinez, 2006; Roberts, Kuncel, Shiner, Caspi, & Goldberg, 2007). At the same time, inconsistent findings point to the complexity of personality–health relations, simultaneously providing direction to our studies and challenging the field to look beyond overly simple causal models. Personality is behaviorally manifested within the context of situations; it influences and is influenced by the sociocultural context over time.

## Measuring Health Outcomes

What does it mean to be healthy? In the traditional biomedical model, health is defined as a lack of disease and disability. The medical care system is mostly designed to treat disease symptoms to restore a state of "health." Yet many individuals live long, fulfilling, and/or productive lives while managing one or more chronic conditions (Holstein & Minkler, 2003; Minkler & Fadem, 2002). For example, one study classified elderly participants as healthy if they lacked any disease or disability, maintained cognitive function, and were actively engaged in society (Strawbridge, Wallhagen, & Cohen, 2002). Less than 19 percent could be categorized as healthy by this definition, but over half of the participants declared themselves as healthy agers. With a growing percent of the population developing one or more chronic illness conditions, the biomedical model—which works well for acute disease that can be easily diagnosed and treated—fails to adequately address the mental, social, and functional problems that many chronic conditions bring.

In addition, there is the often-confused matter of subjective well-being. From a lay perspective, health means feeling good—yet this involves a considerable degree of subjectivity. For one individual, mild nausea, occasional dizziness, and regular muscle pain indicate severe problems that require medical intervention; for another, such symptoms are considered normal elements of everyday life. Although self-perceived health, typically assessed by a single self-reported item (e.g. "in general how is your health—very poor, poor, fair, good, very good?"), is often a good predictor of mortality risk (Idler & Kasl, 1991), people vary in how the question is interpreted. Some individuals focus solely on physical symptoms, whereas others view health in a more holistic sense, which incorporates maintaining balance across physical, mental, social, cognitive, environmental, and spiritual dimensions (Kern, Horton, Tung, Rajec, & Friedman, 2008). Personality can offer a lens through which physiological, emotional, and behavioral states and changes are perceived and interpreted. For example, extraverted individuals may focus more on social elements when evaluating their health; conscientious individuals may focus more on functional ability; intellectual individuals may focus on cognitive dimensions; and neurotic individuals may focus more on emotional elements.

Depending on the theoretical conception of health, the size of the sample, the resources available, and the goals of the study, different measures of health are used. Physical health can be measured through self-report of symptoms or pain, doctor reports, medical records, physiological signs (such as blood pressure or diagnostic test results), and definable clinical events (e.g. heart attack, stroke). Psychological or "mental" aspects (such as happiness, life satisfaction, lack of depression, subjective well-being) are usually assessed via self-reported questionnaires or interviews. Social aspects (e.g. how well a person interacts with others) are measured through self-report, friend report, observation, or social network size. Functional abilities (daily activities and what a person accomplishes and contributes to society) are often assessed through self-reports of daily activities and goals, reports by others, and records of personal accomplishments and achievements. Cognitive function (e.g. mental strength, alertness, and lack of cognitive dysfunction such as dementia and Alzheimer's) is usually assessed through various cognitive tests.

Note that a significant problem with many studies of personality and health is that they rely on measures that share method and definitional variance—with predictors and outcomes often both being self-reported measures of the individual's feelings, self-perceived symptoms, complaints, and perceptions of health and well-being. It is thus desirable, when possible, to include length of life as a very important outcome.

Longevity is a valid, reliable health outcome that temporally follows other variables. From a public health perspective, the largest economic benefit occurs through optimizing life expectancy (that is, increased length of life) while reducing physical, psychological, and social morbidity that may occur with advanced life (in other words, compressing morbidity into the shortest period before death; Fries, 1990). A valuable, outcome-focused approach thus measures health as a combination of length of life and quality-life years, defined through a combination of chronic conditions, perceived satisfaction, and functional ability (Kaplan, 2003).

Health is often measured as if it were relatively stable, and it is assessed through single time-point assessments; but health clearly can be influenced by fluctuating moods, cognitions, and physical and social conditions. A better alternative is to understand health within the context of an individual's lifelong trajectory (Schultz & Heckhausen, 1996; Smith & Spiro, 2002). In this sense, we can assess how the person functions physically, mentally, cognitively, socially, and productively at different ages and examine different trajectories. Are people following positive, healthy trajectories, or are they set on negative pathways leading toward illness, depression, and/or disability? From this perspective, health entails maintaining homeostasis by adjusting to changes that may occur, often using one area to compensate for loss in another area to maintain a general sense of competence and well-being (Baltes, Lindenberger, & Staudinger, 2006). We can then examine what influences these trajectories, personality being an important moderator across life domains. For example, an extraverted individual who suddenly loses his job or social network may have a low quality of life, even though he initially has few physical problems. Another individual may have experienced physical health problems early on in young adulthood, but learned to deal with the illness or disability, live a productive life, maintain a sense of independence and control, and be content with her accomplishments.

## The Importance of Multiple Causal Linkages

A key reason for studying personality and health is to be able to design interventions to promote health and prevent disease. This usually will require a deep understanding of complex causes across time. In health studies, it is tempting to draw unfounded causal conclusions—equating correlations with causation. Even randomized control trials—the "true experiments" of health research—often cannot establish full and generalizable causality, as practical limitations (e.g. ethical considerations, sampling bias, non-adherence, attrition) arise. Personality and health links are therefore often best understood within a lifespan perspective. No single study answers all of our research questions, but when multiple short- and long-term studies, using different populations, measures, and methods, converge on similar answers, we build a valid understanding. Cross-sectional comparisons and short-term studies are helpful in uncovering what personality traits may link to what health outcomes, whereas long-term prospective studies allow us to consider the pathways involved, and often reveal relationships that otherwise are obscured by the methods and limitations of other studies.

In the past two decades, personality has been linked to multiple dimensions of health through multiple pathways. In curing acute disease, medicine aims to find a simple cause to treat, such as a virus, broken bone, or clogged artery, and it is tempting to look for such simple causal links between personality and health. Perhaps the most common model links personality and health through physiological dysregulation. This model postulates that emotional instability and negative affect lead to chronic high levels of stress, which wear down the physiological system, break down internal homeostasis, and eventually lead to illness. This model is evaluated by correlating levels of neuroticism and other negative traits with physiological markers of stress and subjective reports of poor health. Unfortunately, although such a model may be relatively easy to test statistically, multiple assumptions (often hidden) about simple causal pathways are made, leading to premature conclusions, mixed results, and greater confusion. A closer assessment suggests multiple pathways that function individually and synergistically.

Based on the concepts of homeostasis and allostasis, this distress and stress pathway involves a diathesis–stress process, in which personality characteristics influence stress, cause chronically elevated levels of stress and lack of regulation within different physiological systems, and lead to breakdown and disease. A growing body of literature is studying dysregulation at the physiological and neurological levels. For example, high levels of depression and hostility have been linked both to high levels of cortisol (an easily measured hormone that marks stress reactions) and to heart disease (Barefoot et al., 2000; Barefoot & Schroll, 1996; Ford et al., 1998; Januzzi, Stern, DeSanctis, & Pasternak, 2000; Rugulies, 2002; Suls & Bunde, 2005). Chronic stress predicts lowered resistance to infection (Cohen, Doyle, Turner, Alper, & Skoner, 2003). Levels and chronicity of stress can also moderate immunological parameters (Segerstrom & Miller, 2004). Still, although stress and dysregulation are linked to illness and mortality, studies have yet to test the entire process. Personality may both predict and moderate levels of stress, appraisals of circumstances, and coping responses. The field will benefit from examining biological, immunological, and neurological mechanisms within a causal model that links psychosocial influences on development to health outcomes (Friedman, 2008; Miller, Chen, & Cole, 2009).

A second prominent model links personality and health through behaviors— protective behaviors, such as eating a healthy diet, engaging in moderate exercise, getting sufficient sleep, flossing, wearing sunscreen, and sanitary practices, or risky behaviors, such as smoking, alcohol and drug abuse, promiscuous sex, and dangerous driving. In this model, personality characteristics influence the behaviors that people engage in, which subsequently lead to health or illness. Behaviors clearly affect risk for disease and many chronic conditions, accidents and injury, and early mortality. Smoking and tobacco use present the highest risk; their associated morbidity and mortality risk is higher than the effect of all other common health behaviors combined (Kassel, Stroud, & Paronis, 2003; Mokdad, Marks, Stroup, & Gerberding, 2004). To a lesser extent, other behaviors influence health outcomes. Personality may both predict and moderate health behaviors and subsequent health outcomes.

A third model links personality and health through a social pathway. In this model, personality influences the availability of social support, whom a person associates with, the activities that people engage in, the reactions evoked in others, the quality of relationships, and the amount of conflict within relationships. A large body of literature confirms the importance of social support for health and well-being (cf. Taylor, 2007), although the types of support and the mechanisms involved remain unclear. Social relationships may fulfill a basic human need to relate to others (Ryan & Deci, 2000). Conversely, although relationships can add a positive element to life, they can also cause stress, conflict, and related poor health outcomes. For example, divorce and marital conflict increase risk of morbidity and mortality (Hughes & Waite, 2009; Tucker, Friedman, Wingard, & Schwartz, 1996). Social relationships also feed into the other pathways. In the physiological pathway, social support may buffer stressful experiences, change appraisals of life experiences, and help the person successfully cope with stressors to maintain a sense of balance and well-being. In the behavioral pathway, others influence the behaviors that people engage in, positively or negatively. Adherence to medical regimes is higher when supported by others, and good health habits promoted by some individuals can influence others within the group toward a healthy lifestyle. By contrast, the adage "bad company corrupts good character" remains: individuals (especially adolescents, who are particularly prone to peer influences) can be drawn into risky situations and influenced toward unhealthy behaviors. Personality affects the degree to which people influence and are influenced by others; it affects the quality and quantity of social relationships and it may moderate responses within different relationships.

A fourth model links personality and health through biological third variables, including genetics, early social environments, and neurological differences. To a certain extent, early experiences based both on genetic proclivities and on the early social environment predispose individuals to various conditions and provide biological set points across physical and mental domains. For example, the body has a general set point for body weight, and the body attempts to maintain that weight. As weight increases, hunger decreases and metabolism speeds up; as weight significantly declines, hunger increases and metabolism slows down. Similarly, research from positive psychology suggests a set point for happiness that is about 50 percent genetically driven (Lyubomirsky, Sheldon, & Schkade, 2005). Such set points can change over time, but it takes persistence and gradual change. Genetic and early environmental aspects may predispose individuals toward certain personality-type dispositions and toward various physiological reactions and related disease. People may have a tendency to respond in a certain way or to develop various conditions, but symptoms do not appear until stress triggers the condition. Two individuals under intense chronic stress may both become ill, but one develops heart disease and the other develops cancer, depending on which disease they are prone toward. Similarly, risky family characteristics can disrupt psychosocial functioning and biological regulation, increasing the risk of mental health problems, chronic disease, and early mortality (Repetti, Taylor, & Seeman, 2002). In such third-variable models, it may appear that personality influences disease, but an underlying biological factor influences both the individual characteristics and the health outcomes.

A fifth, but closely related model links personality and health through the situations that people select or are drawn toward and the resulting trajectories that lead toward health and resilience or toward decline and morbidity (Friedman, 2000). This in turn feeds into the other pathways, by influencing the likelihood of stressful or non-stressful experiences, appraisal of stressors, coping strategies, behaviors that people engage in, and the social relationships that are developed (Carver & Connor-Smith, 2010; Vollrath, 2001). Studies in developmental psychology suggest that, although natural disasters and some major events cannot be controlled, most stressful life events do not occur randomly (Caspi & Roberts, 1999; Caspi, Roberts, & Shiner, 2005). Much of this is probably driven by genetics, early experiences, and the habitual response patterns that are developed fairly early in life.

A final model linking personality and health reverses the causal arrow. Certain medical conditions, mental illnesses, and various drugs and medications can cause radical personality changes. For example, in a four-year study that tracked individuals with hemiparkisonism, neural network changes were evident two years before motor signs appeared (Tang, Poston, Dhawan, & Eidelberg, 2010). Such neural changes may manifest as personality changes—an otherwise social, agreeable, conscientious individual may become hostile and impulsive—long before medical tests show the underlying cognitive decline. Similarly, many drugs, both legal and illegal, cause major changes in personality. Antidepressants, which mute emotional responses and impair cognitive functioning, are being prescribed at an alarming rate (Paulose-Ram, Safran, Jonas, Gu, & Orwig, 2007). Under the influence of alcohol, even conscientious individuals can become impulsive and irresponsible.

Each of these approaches offers a piece of the puzzle linking personality and health. These approaches are interrelated, and narrowly attributing relations to a specific part of the model only limits our understanding. Most likely, each of these plays a role some of the time for some people.

## The Five-Factor Model and Health Outcomes

We now turn to a focus on multiple health outcomes and the personality traits of conscientiousness, extraversion, agreeableness, and neuroticism. We include sections on optimism and hostility. The fifth factor in the five-factor approaches to personality—intelligence or openness to experience—is also relevant to health and longevity, but is beyond the scope of this chapter (see Batty, Deary, & Gottfredson, 2007; Batty et al., 2009; Deary, Batty, Pattie, & Gale, 2008 for work in this area). We employ the conceptual framework sketched above to review key findings, and we include illustrations from our own empirical research.

Over the past 20 years, we have worked with the Terman Life Cycle Study, a longitudinal project begun in 1922 by Lewis M. Terman and his colleagues at Stanford University, focusing on gifted children (IQ 135 and above). Over 1,500 children were first assessed and rated across a broad array of personality, psychosocial, and physical variables. They were then followed throughout their lives, completing written assessments every 5 to 10 years. We have gathered death information for about 90 percent of the sample, and have worked to refine and validate items and scales to assess various psychosocial variables, including child and adult personality, health behaviors, social relationships, stressful life events, health and well-being in youth, adulthood, old age, and longevity.

## Conscientiousness

A growing body of important literature not only illustrates how relevant conscientiousness is for health and longevity outcomes, but also underscores the limits of simple causal models of personality and health. In an initial study with the Terman sample, we examined childhood personality, rated by parents and teachers, and mortality risk across the lifespan (Friedman et al., 1993). Children who were rated high on conscientiousness were at a lower risk of dying at any given age across seven decades. This finding triggered multiple studies by others, with different samples and various measures of conscientiousness. For example, 174 patients with chronic renal insufficiency were assessed using the NEO–FFI; high conscientiousness predicted lower mortality risk over a four-year period (Christensen et al., 2002). Conscientiousness likewise predicted lower mortality risk in a sample of older clergy members followed for eight years (Wilson, Mendes de Leon, Bienias, Evans, & Bennett, 2004). In a sample of frail older individuals in the Medicare Demonstration Study, conscientiousness was protective over a 4- to 5-year period, with low impulsiveness and high self-discipline driving this relation (Weiss & Costa, 2005). Meta-analytically combining the results of 20 studies, we found that all studies reported a positive relation, and the overall effect was significant (Kern & Friedman, 2008). Subsequent studies have continued to find a health-protective effect of conscientiousness (Chapman, Fiscella, Kawachi, & Duberstein, 2010; Deary et al., 2008; Fry & Debats, 2009). Altogether, conscientiousness predicts up to a 2- to 4-year benefit in length of life.

Examining multiple health components is informative for understanding the potential pathways linking conscientiousness and health. In the Terman sample, we used adult personality, self-reported in early adulthood (average age 30), to predict multiple components of older age health 45 years later, when participants were in their 70s (Friedman et al., 2010). High conscientiousness predicted better physical health (including self-rated health and reports of disease), good social relationships, and productivity (active engagement in society), but was less relevant to subjective well-being. These findings point to several potential pathways: physiological resilience (suggesting a biological pathway), social resilience (suggesting a social pathway), and functional resilience (suggesting behavioral and situational pathways). Importantly, a growing body of research supports each of these pathways.

The most straightforward pathway is the behavioral one. Conscientious individuals are more likely to engage in protective behaviors and less likely to engage in risky behaviors (Bogg & Roberts, 2004). They are more adherent to treatment recommendations and structure their environments to be protective. However, although such healthy lifestyles are important, behavior alone is insufficient in explaining the health-protective effect. In the Terman study, the conscientiousness–longevity link was only partially mediated by health behaviors such as those related to smoking and alcohol use (Friedman et al., 1995). In the Hawaii Health and Personality Cohort Study, physical activity, education, healthy eating, not smoking, and moderate alcohol intake partially mediated a positive relationship between high conscientiousness (rated by teachers when the participants were children) and self-rated health (self-reported 40 years later; Hampson, Goldberg, Vogt, & Dubanoski, 2006, 2007).

In terms of an underlying third variable, genetic predispositions or early environments may lead both to a conscientious personality and to better health. Clear links with physical health and longevity (as compared to self-reports of well-being), including fewer reports of disease, are consistent with a biological pathway. For example, in a study of genetic polymorphic alleles, a variant in the gene sequence was related both to abnormal hypothalamic responses and to low conscientiousness (Wand et al., 2002). Higher levels of serotonin, a hormone important to regulation of sleeping and eating, have been linked with higher levels of conscientiousness (Carver & Miller, 2006, Evans & Rothbart, 2007; Kusumi et al., 2002; Manuck et al., 1998).

Conscientious individuals may experience fewer stressful events and may cope better with stress that does occur. In the males of the Terman study, conscientiousness attenuated the negative effects of an unsuccessful career (Kern, Friedman, Martin, Reynolds, & Luong, 2009). In a meta-analysis of 165 different samples, conscientious individuals appeared to be more likely to engage in problem-focused coping and cognitive restructuring, and less likely to cope by expressing negative emotion, using substances, and denying the problem (Connor-Smith & Flachsbart, 2007). Conscientious individuals may perceive daily life as less threatening; for example, conscientious students perceived fewer daily hassles and less academic pressure over a 3-year period (Vollrath, 2000). Conscientious individuals are also drawn toward circumstances that promote health, such as stable jobs and marriages. They are more likely to choose stable marriage partners and to maintain successful careers, which in turn can increase levels of conscientiousness and promote health. Thus, through both experiences and appraisals, conscientious individuals may better self-regulate and maintain homeostasis.

People high on conscientiousness are more likely to report active engagement in society. Self-determination theory suggests that people are driven by the needs of competence, relatedness, and autonomy (Ryan & Deci, 2000). Continued social engagement can help achieve these needs—active engagement maintains feelings of competence and provides a sense of meaning, social connections are developed and maintained, and the ability to complete daily tasks and contribute to society breeds a sense of control and independence. By fulfilling these needs in the right circumstances, physical and mental well-being improves.

All of these pathways are health-relevant and complementary, and together suggest that conscientiousness has far-reaching consequences. Is it possible to increase levels of conscientiousness, and, if so, would it always be beneficial? Although personality is considered a relatively stable part of the individual, it can and does change (Roberts & Del Vecchio, 2000). In a meta-analysis of 101 studies, conscientiousness showed little change from adolescence into college, but then it increased from age 20 to age 50 and from 60 to 70 (Roberts, Walton, & Viechtbauer, 2006), although there was much individual variation. Changes may also vary across lower-order facets; in two cross-sectional samples, industriousness increased early on, impulse control and reliability increased across the life course, and orderliness remained fairly stable (Jackson et al., 2009). In the Mills Longitudinal Study of Women, marital stability, increased work responsibility, and less substance use increased social responsibility over a 30-year period (Roberts & Bogg, 2004).

Potentially, by promoting psychological maturity, by discouraging unhealthy behavior patterns, and by structuring stable environments so as to develop a personal sense of responsibility, society can help individuals become more conscientious, with resulting health benefits. However, such a model has not been tested. To be successful, such an intervention must consider the multiple pathways through which conscientiousness and health may be linked. Interventions must carefully consider: (1) whether change is indeed possible; (2) which techniques work; (3) who would benefit from change; (4) what contextual factors are needed to support positive growth; (5) when it is appropriate to intervene; and perhaps most importantly, continually evaluate (6) whether changing levels of conscientiousness will translate into practical health benefits. Still, research findings from the past two decades evince hope that improvements in the psychological maturity and mental health of a population can have dramatic impacts on the physical health and longevity of that population.

## Extraversion

Extraversion has been inconsistently linked to physical health (Cloninger, 2005; Roberts et al., 2007; Wilson et al., 2004; Wilson et al., 2005), and recent evidence suggests that relations between extraversion and life satisfaction are weaker than was previously assumed (Luhmann & Eid, 2009; Rammstedt, 2007). Extraversion has strong biological and interpersonal components, and links with health may depend on the facet of extraversion, the type of health outcome, and the context in which characteristics are manifested. The main facets of extraversion are dominance, sociability, activity, and positive emotions (Davies, Connelly, & Ones, 2010), and preliminary evidence suggests that these domains relate to health differentially.

The dominance facet of extraversion is predictive of positive job outcomes, but links to other aspects of health may depend on an individual's biologically influenced tendencies toward dominance (such as those dictated by testosterone, estrogen, and other hormones), the particular social environment in which the trait is expressed, combinations with other traits such as neuroticism and agreeableness, and ongoing appraisals and reactions to stress. Males tend to be more dominant than females, and dominance and aggressive tendencies predict heart disease in males, but not in females (Ferraro & Nuriddin, 2006; Rasul, Stansfeld, Hart, & Smith, 2005). But whether or not dominance and health are related may depend on the context. In stable environments, dominance may be adaptive, whereas in unstable environments, where dominance cannot be established, risk may accrue. In a series of studies with cynomolgus monkeys, dominant male monkeys within unstable social groups were much more likely to develop atherosclerosis than subordinate monkeys in unstable social groups and than dominant and subordinate monkeys in stable groups (Manuck, Kaplan, Adams, & Clarkson, 1988).

At times, dominant individuals may use less adaptive coping mechanisms and may create more stressful social relationships, which lead to chronically elevated levels of stress, increased wear on the physiological system, and increased susceptibility to illness. For example, in a study of over 300 older adult couples, spouse ratings of higher levels of dominance predicted coronary artery calcification, a marker of coronary artery disease (Smith et al., 2008). When combined with agreeableness and positive affect, dominance can be an important component of effective leadership (Judge, Bono, Ilies, & Gerhardt, 2002); but, when combined with hostility, dominance may increase risk of heart disease and chronic illness, unstable social relationships, and poor mental health. This is another example of how personality—in this case dominance—is tied to the social context in which it is manifested.

The social aspects of extraversion are especially apparent in the sociability facet. High sociability generally is linked to good subjective and social health outcomes, but presents a mixed picture for objective physical health outcomes. In the Terman sample, extraversion predicted more social ties and high social competence 45 years later (Friedman et al., 2010), but it predicted physical health in women only. Extraverted individuals are more likely to use engagement coping strategies, including problem-solving (Connor-Smith & Flachsbart, 2007). In fact, sociability is characterized by an approach temperament, in which individuals pursue positive engagement with circumstances and people (Carver & Connor-Smith, 2010). In a study of personality and behaviors, extraverted individuals were more likely to expect positive outcomes from social interactions than introverted individuals were (Hensler & Wood, 2010). In a study of older adults, extraverted individuals were less likely to withdraw from social relationships, building more satisfying relationships and social support (Cukrowicz, Franzese, Thorp, Cheavens, & Lynch, 2008). In turn, social individuals may face fewer stressful experiences, appraise situations as less threatening, and have the ability to build and use resources to ameliorate stressful experiences (Fredrickson, 2001).

But here again, sociability can be a double-edged sword. Sociable individuals may be drawn toward positive environments with positive social relationships and healthy lifestyles, or they may be especially drawn toward social situations where alcohol or promiscuous sexual behavior is the norm, with subsequent negative outcomes. For example, extraverted college students are much more likely to smoke, consume alcohol and binge drink, get insufficient sleep, and have multiple sexual partners, increasing the risk of morbidity and mortality (Ploubidis & Grundy, 2009; Raynor & Levine, 2009).

The activity facet of extraversion is potentially beneficial across multiple dimensions of health outcomes. Extraversion has been linked to higher levels of physical activity (Kern, Reynolds, & Friedman, 2010; Rhodes & Smith, 2006), and it may be the activity facet of extraversion that drives this relation (Rhodes, Courneya, & Jones, 2002). Kaplan (1994) suggested that healthy aging can be defined as being alive and "doin' stuff" (p. 451)—that is, active engagement in life. In the Georgian Centenarian Study, extraverts lived a more engaged lifestyle, which in turn related to high mental status (Martin, Baenziger, MacDonald, Siegler, & Poon, 2009). Extraverts may have a biologically based drive for activity; when that need is filled, boosts in both positive affect and fitness levels occur. Extraverted individuals both objectively and subjectively engage in a greater quantity and quality of enjoyable activities, and experience greater positive arousal and energy from being physically active (Bolger & Zuckerman, 1995; Magnus, Diener, Fujita, & Payot, 1993; Miller & Krizan, 2010; Mroczek & Almeida, 2004; Roberts, Caspi, & Moffitt, 2003; Taylor, Repetti, & Seeman, 1997). In addition, physical activity can be an effective method for coping with stress, helping to restore balance to the physiological system.

The fourth facet of extraversion, positive affect, again presents a mixed picture. A growing literature suggests the importance for physical health of positive affect, life satisfaction, and happiness, although the degree to which positive affect influences physical health rather than subjective reports about health remains unclear (Pressman & Cohen, 2005; Salovey, Rothman, Detweiler, & Steward, 2000). A meta-analysis of over 300 studies found a small, positive correlation of trait levels of positive affect with subjective well-being, perceptions of health, symptom control, and survival in chronic disease conditions (Howell, Kern, & Lyubomirsky, 2007), but the causal links remain unspecified.

As with the other extraversion facets, there are multiple ways in which positive affect can be tied to health and disease. Biological differences may influence both the levels of positive affect and related health outcomes. Behaviorally, people are more likely to exercise and follow healthy habits when they are in a positive mood (Biddle, 2000). In terms of the stress pathway, positive affect may directly buffer the physiological system from stress by producing a muted response to stressors or by causing a faster return to baseline levels when stress occurs, thus preventing the accumulation of stress on the system (Pressman & Cohen, 2005); but this is not yet well established (Friedman, 2008). Positive affect relates to better social relationships (Lyubomirsky, King, & Diener, 2005) and may also affect perceptions of stressors, such that various experiences are viewed as challenging rather than threatening. Most likely, positive affect complements other traits. For example, in a population-based study in Nova Scotia, positive affect predicted lower incidence of heart disease across a 10-year period (Davidson, Mostofsky, & Whang, 2010), but positive affect was rated by nurses during an interview, making it unclear whether it was positive affect, social skills, or the many other unmeasured elements the interview, the person, and the situation that affected health outcomes.

Altogether, extraversion presents a mixed picture, which depends on the lifestyle that arises from social groups, appraisals of stress, and associated health behaviors. Most notably, positive emotionality will offer little physical benefit if it translates into dangerous activities or risky health behaviors.

## Dispositional optimism

A related positive trait is dispositional optimism. Optimism includes elements of neuroticism and extraversion, and encompasses three beliefs: positive outcome expectancies (the general tendency to have positive expectations for the future), positive efficacy expectancies (belief in the ability to cope across various circumstances), and positive unrealistic thinking (a bias toward believing good things are more likely and negative things are less likely to happen to you than to others; Carver & Connor-Smith, 2010; Fournier, de Ridder, & Bensing, 2002; Marshall, Wortman, Kusulas, Hervig, Vickers, 1992). Optimism relates to positive outcomes, including psychological well-being and self-rated physical health (Segerstrom, 2007). In many cases, optimism predicts faster recovery from surgery, less illness, and lower mortality risk (e.g. Fry & Debats, 2009). However, evidence is mixed for other objective outcomes, including immunological parameters and disease outcomes (Segerstrom, 2005). And there is no solid evidence that staying positive can shrink tumors or open clogged arteries.

Optimistic individuals tend to be persistent in pursuing goals and display greater ability to continue despite setbacks or difficulties (Scheier & Carver, 1985). In a study of cardiac rehab patients, optimists engaged in fewer maladaptive behaviors to cope, which resulted in better post-treatment physical functioning (Shen, McCreary, & Myers, 2004). However, optimists may not see themselves as at risk, thus creating a barrier to healthy behavior. Many individuals across age, gender, educational level, and occupation have an optimistic bias that they are less susceptible than the average person to diseases and negative outcomes (Weinstein, 1987). In turn, people feel immune to risk and will engage in unhealthy behavior until it is too late. For example, in the Terman sample, children who were rated as optimistic and cheerful were at an increased risk of dying at any given age, which could be partly explained by engagement in risky behaviors in adulthood (Friedman et al., 1993; Martin et al., 2002). Optimistic individuals may perceive that they are more adherent and maintaining healthier behaviors than they actually are. For example, in a weight loss study, dispositional optimism related to confidence in ability to lose weight but did not translate into actual weight loss (Benyamini & Raz, 2007).

Evidence for the psychophysiology and social pathways has yet to be established. Optimists are more likely to use engagement coping strategies and less likely to use disengagement strategies (Carver & Connor-Smith, 2010; Solberg Nes & Segerstrom, 2006). Optimism relates to positive social relationships, which can build resources that buffer stressful experiences (Segerstrom, 2007). It remains unclear whether and when optimism acts as a true buffer from stress, changes perceptions such that stress is appraised as less threatening, makes a helpful combination of the two, or does neither.

Optimism is more cognitively based than the other traits, reflecting a dispositional manner of thinking about life experiences. Depending on the circumstances, a pessimistic style may at times be beneficial. For example, law students with a pessimistic explanatory style outperformed students with an optimistic style (O'Grady, 2006; Satterfield, Monahan, & Seligman, 1997). When faced with a health threat, if information is presented in terms of risk, an optimist may become defensive and build an unrealistic perception of low risk, whereas, if the information is presented as an opportunity for positive growth, an optimist may appropriately regulate his or her behavior and be successful in protecting his or her health (Schwarzer, 1999). In addition, combinations with other traits may be relevant. Optimism may be especially protective when combined with high conscientiousness, as a person is driven toward achievement and has a high degree of self-efficacy for achieving those goals, whereas optimism may be detrimental when combined with impulsivity, as unrealistic biases become particularly powerful. Future research should consider how optimism fits with the main five factors to impact various health outcomes.

## Hostility and agreeableness

Much of the history of research on personality and health has been characterized by a focus on negative traits, especially depression and hostility. Although research on Type A behavior was often conceptually flawed, numerous studies have found that hostility, aggression, and anger predict heart disease, illness, and mortality risk (Booth-Kewley & Friedman, 1987; Matthews, 1988; Miller, Smith, Turner, Guijarro,

& Hallet, 1996; Ramsay, McDermott, & Bray, 2001; Suls & Bunde, 2005). Most explanations assume a physiological stress model, in which hostility chronically stresses the system and leads to disease (Smith & Ruiz, 2002; Vitaliano, Scanlan, Zhang, Savage, & Hirsch, 2002). However, health behaviors, biological third variables, and poor social relationships almost certainly play a role as well. In a meta-analysis of 27 studies, high hostility was associated with higher BMI, more alcohol consumption, smoking, and markers of heart disease, suggesting behavioral pathways (Bunde & Suls, 2006). Hostile individuals are also prone to poor social relationships. Rather than building a supportive social network, hostile individuals drive the others away, which leaves them with few resources in times of need.

Hostility has elements of both neuroticism (in the sense of being tense and discontented—considered in the section below) and agreeableness. Highly agreeable individuals are characterized by positive interpersonal traits—they are cooperative and trusting rather than cold and quarrelsome. Theoretically, they should have better social relationships and better health outcomes (Carver & Connor-Smith, 2010). Meta-analysis confirms that agreeableness does predict greater use of social support and more cognitive restructuring to cope with stress (Connor-Smith & Flachsbart, 2007). However, links with health outcomes are mixed, predicting subjective outcomes but inconsistently predicting objective physical health outcomes (Cloninger, 2005; Korotkov & Hannah, 2004; Roberts et al., 2007; Wilson et al., 2004, 2005). In the Terman sample, high agreeableness most strongly predicted social competence and subjective well-being, with mixed findings for physical health and longevity (Friedman et al., 2010). In a study of 100 elderly individuals, higher levels of trust related to functional health and longer life (Barefoot et al., 1998). In the MIDUS study, a nationally representative sample from the US, agreeableness predicted better self-perceived health and, in some cases, lower mortality risk (Goodwin & Endstrom, 2002; Weiss & Costa, 2005), but other studies have found no relation with mortality (Iwasa et al., 2008; Martin & Friedman, 2000; Wilson et al., 2004).

Although links between agreeableness and health may primarily occur through a social pathway, other pathways linking agreeableness and health are also relevant. Across cultures, women are more agreeable than men, a situation suggesting evolutionary biological underpinnings (Chapman, Duberstein, Sörensen, & Lyness, 2007; Costa, Terraciano, & McCrae, 2001; Jerram & Coleman, 1999), which in turn may influence health outcomes. Low agreeableness may be especially detrimental for women. For example, for many women in business, agreeable tendencies must be suppressed in order to gain the respect of male subordinates. This can create feelings of role conflict (known to be a significant workplace stressor), as women try to balance the desire to be friendly with a need to establish order and power.

Agreeableness may work in combination with other traits. In the MIDUS study, high agreeableness was protective for individuals high on conscientiousness, but it increased risk for individuals low on conscientiousness (Chapman et al., 2009). Individuals with a combination of self-disciplined behavior and friendly countenance may build good relationships and gain health benefits, by comparison with individuals who are driven but drive others away through hostility and selfish pursuit (i.e. have high conscientiousness, low agreeableness). Very agreeable individuals who lack self-discipline (i.e. have high agreeableness, low conscientiousness) may yield their own desires to others, and in the process of maintaining harmony build internal stress, which results in poor health outcomes.

Altogether, very low levels of agreeableness are risky, whereas high levels depend on the social context and other traits. A moderate degree of agreeableness may turn out to be optimal for good health, as a balance is developed between amiable relationships with others and self-interests. This remains an open question.

## Neuroticism

Neuroticism and negative emotionality are often seen as damaging traits that lead to ill-being, but the true picture is more complex. The strongest health links are evident between neuroticism and lower subjective well-being (DeNeve & Cooper, 1998). Neuroticism predicts increased susceptibility to pain, which may influence reports and experiences of poor health (Charles, Gatz, Kato, & Pedersen, 2008). Several reviews and meta-analyses indicate that negative emotionality, depression, and anxiety predict higher incidence of illness and coronary heart disease (Booth-Kewley & Friedman, 1987; Grippo & Johnson, 2002; Matthews, 1988; Miller et al., 1996; Rugulies, 2002; Smith & Gallo, 2001; Suls & Bunde, 2005; Wulsin & Singal, 2003). Across 19 studies, a meta-analysis found an increased mortality risk for emotional instability (Roberts et al., 2007). However, the evidence is mixed, as some studies report no relation or the reversed relation—neuroticism being health protective (e.g. Almada et al., 1991; Iwasa et al., 2008; Korten et al., 1999; Taga, Friedman, & Martin, 2009; Weiss & Costa, 2005). Neurotic tendencies, in light of social experiences and stresses, may have mixed effects.

Friedman (2000) suggested that there are two manifestations of individual neuroticism: one is a proneness toward pessimism, anxiety, depression, and resentment; the other is a "healthy neuroticism" that pays attention to all symptoms and so leads to a vigilance about taking care of one's health. The first can produce a negative trajectory toward depression, illness, and early mortality. The second may lead to reports of lower well-being, more psychosomatic symptoms, and more doctor's visits, but objectively lead to fewer diseases and longer life. In the Terman sample, higher levels of neuroticism predicted lower subjective well-being in older age for both men and women (Friedman et al., 2010). For women, neuroticism also predicted lower physical health and increased mortality risk. But, for men, neuroticism was less predictive of poor physical health, and it predicted *lower* mortality risk.

The effects of neuroticism may depend on other traits. For the Terman men, high neuroticism was protective when combined with high conscientiousness, whereas neuroticism conferred great risk at low levels of conscientiousness (Kern, Martin, & Friedman, 2010). That is, neurotic, conscientious men reported lower well-being, but were objectively healthier. In the MIDUS study, the mortality risk associated with high neuroticism depended on the combination of high or low agreeableness, conscientiousness, and socioeconomic status (Chapman et al., 2009). In the Vietnam Experience Study cohort, high neuroticism showed risk at low levels of cognitive ability, but not at high cognitive levels (Weiss, Gale, Batty, & Deary, 2009).

Neuroticism is partially biologically driven (Barker, Osmond, Forsén, Kajantie, & Eriksson, 2005; Bondy, 2007; McCaffery et al., 2006). For example, in a population-based sample in Italy, high levels of neuroticism related to interleukin-6, an inflammatory response marker that is often elevated in frail or morbid conditions (Sutin, Terracciano, Deiana, Naitza et al., 2010). A study of 289 male twins suggested that major depressive disorder and microvascular dysfunction (an indicator of early atherosclerosis) share a genetic pathway (Vaccarino et al., 2009). Women on average are more neurotic than men, and underlying physiological differences may also impact health risks. For example, in a community-based Italian sample, depression related to lower levels of high-density cholesterol (HDL—good cholesterol) for women, but not for men (Sutin, Terracciano, Deiana, Uda et al., 2010). In a nationally representative sample in Great Britain, neuroticism both directly and indirectly increased mortality risk for women, whereas for men risk was indirect, depending on levels of psychological distress and on smoking (Ploubidis & Grundy, 2009).

It is important to note, however, that such relations do not necessarily translate into disease. Cross-sectional relations can identify individuals potentially at risk for disease, but longitudinal studies tracing the same people over time are necessary to see if disease actually develops. Although there is evidence that inflammatory markers increase the risk of heart disease (Rodondi et al., 2010), other core factors, such as social relationships and health behaviors, are also relevant. In the Italian sample (Sutin, Terracciano, Deiana, Naitza et al., 2010), individuals with higher levels of IL–6 were also more likely to smoke and be overweight. In a Canadian study of over 700 community members, emotionally stable individuals were more likely to engage in healthy behavioral practices under stressful conditions, whereas neurotic individuals were less likely to engage in healthy behaviors (Korotkov, 2008). Many relationships between neuroticism and morbidity or mortality are significantly reduced or mediated when smoking, alcohol use, and other risky health behaviors are controlled. Other relations are biologically based and will not be fully altered by attempts to stop worrying or to reduce anxiety.

Neuroticism and health links influence and are influenced by the perception and occurrence of stressful experiences. Anxious individuals may interpret normal everyday circumstances as more negative and stressful, and report more daily hassles (cf. Vollrath, 2001). Neurotic individuals are more reactive to negative events and stressful experiences, and in turn tend to experience higher levels of negative affect and more cognitive difficulties when stress occurs (Bolger & Schilling, 1991; Gunthert, Cohen, & Armeli, 1999; Neupert, Mroczek, & Spiro, 2008). For example, in a large representative sample in Germany, neurotic individuals who experienced unemployment or repeated divorce reported stronger negative reactions than less neurotic individuals (Luhmann & Eid, 2009). Further, such individuals are less likely to use adaptive mechanisms for coping with stressors, such as problem-solving and cognitive restructuring, and are more likely to use less adaptive coping responses such as expressing negative emotion, withdrawing from others, using wishful thinking, and substance use (Connor-Smith & Flaschbart, 2007). High levels of chronic stress and maladaptive coping responses may further stress the physiological system, making the individual more susceptible to disease.

Further, psychophysiological effects most likely are bidirectional. Depression and anger increase the risk of disease and illness (Friedman & Booth-Kewley, 1987), but inflammatory responses, disease development, and neurological changes can cause depression, anxiety, anger, and other negative emotions (Kemeny, 2007; Räikkönen, Matthews, & Kuller, 2002). Thus, both psychologically and physiologically, a negative spiral may occur in which the person becomes more depressed and anxious, which in turn affects levels of neurotransmitters, stress reactions, and an accumulation of health risks, and these in turn make the person more depressed and anxious.

The trajectory of negative emotion is also important to consider. In the Normative Aging Study, mortality risk was highest for men who were high on neuroticism and became more neurotic, which suggests that both level *and* change are important (Mroczek & Spiro, 2007). In a 20-year longitudinal study, individuals who experienced a traumatic life event increased in neuroticism, especially on the anger and frustration facets, over the subsequent 5- to 10-year period (Lockenhoff, Terracciana, Patriciu, Eaton, & Costa, 2009). High neuroticism at baseline did not predict mental health 20 years later, whereas increasing levels of neuroticism did predict poor mental health, again suggesting that changes in neuroticism may be more consequential than levels alone. In another study with the Normative Aging Study, trajectory analyses suggest that anxiety and hostility may predispose individuals to maladjustment at some point in the lifespan, but the timing may depend on other psychosocial factors (Aldwin, Spiro, Levenson, & Cupertino, 2001).

In sum, although neuroticism is often considered an unhealthy trait, much depends on the social context and other characteristics. Optimism is not always protective, and negative emotionality is not always harmful.

## Conclusion

Individual differences in health, well-being, and longevity are commonly observed and are of obvious importance. Although variations in health are sometimes due to chance infections, accidental trauma, or random genetic changes, most individual differences in health and longevity are due to predictable but complex combinations of biological, psychological, and socio-environmental factors, which cumulatively develop as consistent patterns across time. Because modern scientific conceptions view personality as likewise having biological, psychological, and social aspects, the biopsychosocial approach to personality can be an excellent means of analyzing biopsychosocial influences on health.

Overall, we have repeatedly found that conscientiousness plays an important role in all aspects of health, both individually and interactively with other traits. For example, the combination of low conscientiousness and high neuroticism can be especially hazardous. Although high levels of agreeableness are often associated with self-reports of well-being, this relationship often fails to appear in more objective health outcomes, which suggests that third variables, especially aspects of the social context, may be influencing both agreeableness and health. A double-edged story may be true with extraversion, such that extraversion may positively or negatively influence health, depending on the life circumstances. Finally, neuroticism and optimism are probably the most misunderstood and misinterpreted aspects of personality with respect to their relation to health.

One important implication of this biopsychosocial perspective is that simultaneous consideration should be given to multiple aspects of personality *and* to multiple health outcomes. Traits of conscientiousness, extraversion, optimism, hostility, agreeableness, and neuroticism can all be relevant to physical health, subjective well-being, social accomplishment, and longevity. The second important implication of this perspective is that personality interacts with psychosocial contexts across time to affect health, and so the best conceptions and the optimal research designs and analyses will include trajectories of individuals within their social contexts. An individual may have a tendency toward emotional instability, but enter a supportive marriage, practice healthy behaviors, and develop good social skills. That individual may learn to filter her anxiety into productive areas, effectively manage stress, and experience positive health outcomes. Another individual may avoid social interactions, self-medicate with alcohol and tobacco, struggle with social relationships and employment stress, and slip into a pattern of ill-health. Biological predispositions, early experiences, and subsequent stressful and social experiences impact these trajectories. If one ignores the broader social context in which the trait unfolds, the simple paradigm of good and bad is insufficient for describing personality and health relationships. A deeper conception of the relevant issues and more appropriate models of health across the lifespan will facilitate the systematic accumulation of research findings into an understanding that more validity captures the causal relations and makes it possible to design the best interventions in order to improve health.

# References

Aldwin, C. M., Spiro, III, A., Levenson, M. R., & Cupertino, A. P. (2001). Longitudinal findings from the normative aging study III: Personality, individual health trajectories, and mortality. *Psychology & Aging, 16*, 450–465.

Alexander, F. (1950). *Psychosomatic medicine: Its principles and applications.* New York: Norton.

Almada, S. J., Zonderman, A. B., Shekelle, R. B., Dyer, A. R., Daviglus, M. L., Costa, P. T., Jr., & Stamler, J. (1991). Neuroticism and cynicism and risk of death in middle-aged men: The Western Electric Study. *Psychosomatic Medicine, 53*, 165–175.

Baltes, P. B., Lindenberger, U., & Staudinger, U. M. (2006). Life span theory in developmental psychology. In R. M. Lerner, & W. Damon (Eds.), *Handbook of child psychology: Vol 1. Theoretical models of human development* (6th ed., pp. 569–664). Hoboken, NJ: John Wiley & Sons.

Barefoot, J. C., & Schroll, M. (1996). Symptoms of depression, acute myocardial infarction, and total mortality in a community sample. *Circulation 93*, 1976–1980.

Barefoot, J. C., Brummett, B. H., Helms, M. J., Mark, D. B., Siegler, I. C., Williams, R. B. (2000). Depressive symptoms and survival of patients with coronary artery disease. *Psychosomatic Medicine 62*, 790–795.

Barefoot, J. C., Maynard, K. E., Beckham, J. C., Brummett, B. H., Hooker, K., & Sielger, I. C. (1998). Trust, health, and longevity. *Journal of Behavioral Medicine, 21*, 517–526.

Barker, D. J. P., Osmond, C., Forsén, T. J., Kajantie, E., & Eriksson, J. G. (2005). Trajectories of growth among children who have coronary events as adults. *New England Journal of Medicine, 353*, 1802–1809.

Batty, G. D., Deary, I. J., & Gottfredson, L. S. (2007). Premorbid (early life) IQ and later mortality risk: Systematic review. *Annals of Epidemiology, 17*, 278–288.

Batty, G. D., Wennerstad, K. M., Smith, G. D., Gunnell, D., Deary, I. J., Tynelius, P., & Rasmussen, F. (2009). IQ in early adulthood and mortality by middle age: Cohort study of 1 million Swedish men. *Epidemiology, 20*, 100–109.

Benyamini, Y., & Raz, O. (2007). "I can tell you if I'm really going to lose all that weight": Dispositional and situated optimism as predictors of weight loss following a group intervention. *Journal of Applied Social Psychology, 37*, 844–861.

Bernard, C. (1880). *Leçons de pathologie expérimentale: Et leçons sur les propriétés de la moelle épinière*. Paris: Librarie J.-B. Baillière et fils.

Biddle, S. J. H. (2000). Emotion, mood, and physical activity. In S. J. H. Biddle, K. R. Fox, & S. H. Boutcher (Eds.), *Physical activity and psychological well-being* (pp. 63–87). London: Routledge.

Bogg, T., & Roberts, B. W. (2004). Conscientiousness and health-related behaviors: A meta-analysis of the leading behavioral contributors to mortality. *Psychological Bulletin, 130*, 887–919.

Bolger, N. & Zuckerman, A. (1995). A framework for studying personality in the stress process. *Journal of Personality and Social Psychology, 69*, 890–902.

Bolger, N., & Schilling, E. A. (1991). Personality and problems of everyday life: The role of neuroticism in exposure and reactivity to daily stressors. *Journal of Personality, 59*, 356–386.

Bondy, B., (2007), Common genetic factors for depression and cardiovascular disease. *Dialogues in Clinical Neuroscience, 9*, 19–28.

Booth-Kewley, S., & Friedman, H. S. (1987). Psychological predictors of heart disease: A quantitative review. *Psychological Bulletin, 101*, 343–362.

Bunde, J., & Suls, J. (2006). A quantitative analysis of the relationship between the Cook–Medley Hostility Scale and traditional coronary artery disease risk factors. *Health Psychology, 25*, 493–500.

Campbell, D. T., & Fiske, D. W. (1959). Convergent and discriminant validation by the multitrait–multimethod matrix. *Psychological Bulletin, 56*, 81–105.

Cannon, W. B. (1932). *Wisdom of the body*. New York: W. W. Norton.

Carver, C. S., & Connor-Smith, J. (2010). Personality and coping. *Annual Review of Psychology, 61*, 679–704.

Carver, C. S., & Miller, C. J. (2006). Relations of serotonin function to personality: Current views and a key methodological issue. *Psychiatry Research, 144*, 1–15.

Caspi, A., & Roberts, B. W. (1999). Personality continuity and change across the life course. In L. A. Pervin & O. P. John (Eds.), *Handbook of personality: Theory and research* (2nd ed., pp. 300–326). New York: Guilford Press.

Caspi, A., Roberts, B. W., & Shiner, R. L. (2005). Personality development: Stability and change. *Annual Review of Psychology, 56*, 453–484.

Chapman, B. P., Duberstein, P. R., Sörenson, S., & Lyness, J. M. (2007). Gender differences in five factor model personality traits in an elderly cohort. *Personality and Individual Differences, 43*, 1594–1603.

Chapman, B. P., Fiscella, K., Kawachi, I., & Duberstein, P. B., (2010). Personality, socio-economic status, and all-cause mortality in the United States. *American Journal of Epidemiology, 171*, 83–92.

Charles, S. T., Gatz, M., Kato, K., & Pedersen, N. L. (2008). Physical health 25 years later: The predictive ability of neuroticism. *Health Psychology, 27*, 369–378.

Chesney, M. A., & Rosenman, R. H. (Eds.). (1985). *Anger and hostility in cardiovascular and behavioral disorders*. Washington: Hemisphere Publishing Corp.

Christensen, A. J., Ehlers, S. L., Wiebe, J. S, Moran, P. J., Raichle, K., Ferneyhough, K., & Lawton, W. J. (2002). Patient personality and mortality: A 4-year prospective examination of chronic renal insufficiency. *Health Psychology, 21*, 315–320.

Cloninger, C. R. (2005). How does personality influence mortality in the elderly? *Psychosomatic Medicine, 67*, 839–840.

Cohen, S., Doyle, W. J., Turner, R. B., Alper, C. M., & Skoner, D. P. (2003). Sociability and susceptibility to the common cold. *Psychological Science, 14*, 389–395.

Connor-Smith, J. K., & Flachsbart, C. (2007). Relations between personality and coping: A meta-analysis. *Journal of Personality and Social Psychology, 93*, 1080–1107.

Costa, P. T., & McCrae, R. R. (1992). *Revised NEO Personality Inventory (NEO PI–R) and NEO Five-Factor Inventory (NEO–FFI): Professional Manual.* Odessa, FL: Psychological Assessment Resources.

Costa, P. T., Terracciano, A., & McCrae, R. R. (2001). Gender differences in personality traits across cultures: Robust and surprising findings. *Journal of Personality and Social Psychology, 81*, 322–331.

Cronbach, L. J., & Meehl, P. E. (1955). Construct validity in psychological tests. *Psychological Bulletin, 52*, 281–302.

Cukrowicz, K. C., Franzese, A. T., Thorp, S. R., Cheavens, J. S., & Lynch, T. R. (2008). Personality traits and perceived social support among depressed adults. *Aging and Mental Health, 12*, 662–669.

Davidson, K. W., Mostofsky, E., & Whang, W. (2010). Don't worry, be happy: Positive affect and reduced 10-year incident coronary heart disease: The Canadian Nova Scotia Health Survey. *European Heart Journal, 31*, 1065–1070.

Davies, S. E., Connelly, B. S., & Ones, D. S. (January, 2010). *Differential prediction using extraversion facets.* Talk presented at the 11th Annual Convention of the Society of Personality and Social Psychology, Las Vegas, NV.

Deary, I., Batty, G. D., Pattie, A. & Gale, C. R. (2008). More intelligent, more dependable children live longer: A 55-year longitudinal study of a representative sample of the Scottish nation. *Psychological Science, 19*, 874–880.

DeNeve, K. M., & Cooper, H. (1998). The happy personality: A meta-analysis of 137 personality traits and subjective well-being. *Psychological Bulletin, 124*, 197–229.

Evans, D. E., & Rothbart, M. K. (2007). Developing a model for adult temperament. *Journal of Research in Personality, 41*, 868–888.

Ferraro, K. F., & Nuriddin, T. A. (2006). Psychological distress and mortality: Are women more vulnerable? *Journal of Health and Social Behavior, 47*, 227–241.

Ford, D. E., Mead, L. A., Chang, P. P., Cooper-Patrick, L., Wang, N., & Klag, M. J. (1998). Depression is a risk factor for coronary artery disease in men. *Archives of Internal Medicine 158*, 1422–1426.

Fournier, M., de Ridder, D., & Bensing, J. (2002). How optimism contributes to the adaptation of chronic illness: A prospective study into the enduring effects of optimism on adaptation moderated by the controllability of chronic illness. *Personality & Individual Differences, 33*, 1163–1183.

Fredrickson, B. L. (2001). The role of positive emotions in positive psychology: The broaden-and-build theory of positive emotions. *American Psychologist, 56*, 218–226.

Friedman, H. S. (1991). *The self-healing personality.* New York: Henry Holt.

Friedman, H. S. (2000). Long-term relations of personality, health: Dynamisms, mechanisms, and tropisms. *Journal of Personality, 68*, 1089–1107.

Friedman, H. S. (2007). Personality, disease, and self-healing. In H. S. Friedman & R. C. Silver (Eds.), *Foundations of health psychology* (pp. 172–199). New York: Oxford University Press.

Friedman, H. S. (2008). The multiple linkages of personality and disease. *Brain, Behavior, and Immunity, 22*, 668–675.

Friedman, H. S., & Booth-Kewley, S. (1987). The "disease-prone personality": A meta-analytic view of the construct. *American Psychologist, 42*, 539–555.

Friedman, H. S., Kern, M. L., & Reynolds, C. A. (2010). Personality and health, subjective well-being, and longevity as adults age. *Journal of Personality, 78*, 179–216.

Friedman, H. S., Tucker, J. S., Tomlinson-Keasey, C., Schwartz, J. E., Wingard, D. L., & Criqui, M. H. (1993). Does childhood personality predict longevity? *Journal of Personality and Social Psychology, 65*, 176–185.

Friedman, H. S., Tucker, J. S., Schwartz, J. E., Martin, L. R., Tomlinson-Keasey, C., Wingard, D., & Criqui, M. (1995). Childhood conscientiousness and longevity: Health behaviors and cause of death. *Journal of Personality and Social Psychology, 68*, 696–703.

Fries, J. F. (1990). Medical perspectives upon successful aging. In P. B. Baltes & M. M. Baltes (Eds.), *Successful aging: Perspectives from the behavioral sciences* (pp. 35–49). New York: Cambridge University Press.

Fry, P. S., & Debats, D. L. (2009). Perfectionism and the five-factor personality traits as predictors of mortality in older adults. *Journal of Health Psychology, 14*, 513–524.

Goldberg, L. R. (1993). The structure of phenotypic personality traits. *American Psychologist, 48*, 26–34.

Goodwin, R., & Engstrom, G. (2002). Personality and perception of health in the general population. *Psychological Medicine, 32*, 325–332.

Grippo, A. J., & Johnson, A. K. (2002). Biological mechanisms in the relationship between depression and heart disease. *Neuroscience and Biobehavioral Reviews, 26*, 941–962.

Gunthert, K. C., Cohen, L. H., & Armeli, S. (1999). The role of neuroticism in daily stress and coping. *Journal of Personality and Social Psychology, 57*, 731–739.

Hampson, S. E., Goldberg, L. R., Vogt, T. M., & Dubanoski, J. P. (2006). Forty years on: Teachers' assessments of children's personality traits predict self-reported health behaviors and outcomes at midlife. *Health Psychology, 25*, 57–64.

Hampson, S. E., Goldberg, L. R., Vogt, T. M., & Dubanoski, J. P. (2007). Mechanisms by which childhood personality traits influence adult health status: Educational attainment and healthy behaviors. *Health Psychology, 26*, 121–125.

Hensler, M., & Wood, D. (2010, January). Motives, abilities, and perceptions underlying the Big Five traits. Poster presented at the 11th annual convention of the Society of Personality and Social Psychology, Las Vegas, NV.

Holstein, M. B., & Minkler, M. (2003). Self, society, and the "new gerontology." *Gerontologist, 43*, 787–696.

Howell, R., Kern, M. L. & Lyubomirsky, S. (2007). Health benefits: Meta-analytically determining the impact of well-being on objective health outcomes. *Health Psychology Review, 1*, 83–136.

Hughes, M. E., & Waite, L. J. (2009). Marital biography and health at midlife. *Journal of Health and Social Behavior, 50*, 344–358.

Idler, E. L., & Kasl, S. (1991). Health perceptions and survival: Do global evaluations of health status really predict mortality? *Journals of Gerontology, 46*, S55–S65.

Iwasa, H., Masui, Y., Gondo, Y., Inagaki, H., Kawaai, C., & Suzuki, T. (2008). Personality and all-cause mortality among older adults dwelling in a Japanese community: A five-year population-based prospective cohort study. *American Journal of Geriatric Psychiatry, 16*, 399–405.

Jackson, J. J., Bogg, T. B., Walton, K. E., Wood, D., Harms, P. D., Lodi-Smith, J. et al., (2009). Not all conscientiousness scales changes alike: A multimethod, multisample study of age differences in the facets of conscientiousness. *Personality Processes and Individual Differences*, *96*, 446–459.

Januzzi, J. L., Stern, T. A., Pasternak, R., & DeSanctis, R. W. (2000). The influence of anxiety and depression on outcomes of patients with coronary artery disease. *Archives of Internal Medicine 160*, 1913–1921.

Jerram, K. L. & Coleman, P. G. (1999). The Big Five personality traits and reporting of health problems and health behaviour in old age. *British Journal of Health Psychology*, *4*, 181–192.

Judge, T. A., Bono, J. E., Ilies, R., & Gerhardt, M. W. (2002). Personality and leadership: A qualitative and quantitative review. *Journal of Applied Psychology*, *87*, 765–780.

Kaplan, R. M. (1994). The Ziggy theorem: Toward an outcomes-focused health psychology. *Health Psychology*, *13*, 451–460.

Kaplan, R. M. (2003). The significance of quality of life in health care. *Quality of Life Research*, *12*, 3–16.

Kassel, J. D., Stroud, L. R., & Paronis, C. A. (2003). Smoking, stress, and negative affect: Correlation, causation, and context across stages of smoking. *Psychological Bulletin*, *129*, 270–304.

Kemeny, M. E. (2007). Psychoneuroimmunology. In H. S. Friedman & R. C. Silver (Eds.), *Foundations of health psychology* (pp. 92–116). New York: Oxford University Press.

Kern, M. L., & Friedman, H. S. (2008). Do conscientious individuals live longer? A quantitative review. *Health Psychology*, *27*, 505–512.

Kern, M. L., Martin, L. R., & Friedman, H. S. (2010, January). *Personality and longevity across seven decades*. Poster presented at the 11th Annual Meeting of the Society of Personality and Social Psychology, Las Vegas, NV.

Kern, M. L., Reynolds, C. A., & Friedman, H. S. (2010). Physical activity stability across midlife: A growth curve analysis. *Personality and Social Psychology Bulletin*, *36*, 1058–1072.

Kern, M. L., Friedman, H. S., Martin, L. R., Reynolds, C. A., & Luong, G. (2009). Personality, executive functioning, career success, and longevity: A lifespan analysis. *Annals of Behavioral Medicine*, *37*, 154–163.

Kern, M. L., Horton, S., Tung, G., Rajec, A., & Friedman, H. S. (2008, April). *Conceptions of health: Qualitative vs. quantitative comparisons*. Poster presented at the 88th Annual Meeting of the Western Psychological Association, Irvine, CA.

Korotkov, D. (2008). Does personality moderate the relationship between stress and health behavior? Expanding the nomological network of the five-factor model. *Journal of Research in Personality*, *42*, 1418–1426.

Korotkov, D., & Hannah, T. E. (2004). The five-factor model of personality: Strengths and limitations in predicting health status, sick-role and illness behaviour. *Personality and Individual Differences*, *36*, 187–199.

Korten, A. E., Jorm, A. F., Jiao, Z., Letenneur, L., Jacomb, P. A., Henderson, A. S. et al. (1999). Health, cognitive, and psychosocial factors as predictors of mortality in an elderly community sample. *Journal of Epidemiology and Community Health*, *53*, 83–88.

Kusumi, I., Suzuki, K., Sasaki, Y., Kameda, K., Sasaki, T., & Koyama, T. (2002). Serotonin 5–HT–sub(2A) receptor gene polymorphism, 5–HT–sub(2A) receptor function and personality traits in healthy subjects: A negative study. *Journal of Affective Disorders*, *68*, 235–241.

Lockenhoff, C. E., Terracciana, A., Patriciu, N. S., Eaton, W. W., & Costa Jr., P. T. (2009). Self-reported extremely adverse life events and longitudinal changes in five-factor model personality traits in an urban sample. *Journal of Traumatic Stress*, *22*, 53–59.

Luhmann, M., & Eid, M. (2009). Does it really feel the same? Changes in life satisfaction following repeated life events. *Journal of Personality and Social Psychology*, *97*, 363–381.

Lyubomirsky, S., King, L., & Diener, E. (2005). The benefits of frequent positive affect: Does happiness lead to success? *Psychological Bulletin, 131*, 803–855.

Lyubomirsky, S., Sheldon, K. M., & Schkade, D. (2005). Pursuing happiness: The architecture of sustainable change. *Review of General Psychology, 9*, 111–131.

Maddi, S. R., & Kobasa, S. C. (1984). *The hardy executive: Health under stress.* Chicago: Dow Jones-Irwin.

Magnus, K., Diener, E., Fujita, F., & Payot, W. (1993). Extraversion and neuroticism as predictors of objective life events: A longitudinal analysis. *Journal of Personality and Social Psychology, 65*, 1046–1053.

Manuck, S. B., Flory, J. D., McCaffery, J. M., Matthews, K. A., Mann, J. J., & Muldoon, M. F. (1998). Aggression, impulsivity, and central nervous system serotonergic responsivity in a nonpatient sample. *Neuropsychopharmacology, 19*, 287–299.

Manuck, S. B., Kaplan, J. R., Adams, M. R., & Clarkson, T. B. (1988). Studies of psychosocial influences on coronary artery atherogenesis in cynomolgus monkeys. *Health Psychology, 7*, 113–124.

Marshall, G. N., Wortman, C. B., Kusulas, J. W., Hervig, L. K., Vickers, R. R., Jr. (1992). Distinguishing optimism from pessimism: Relations to fundamental dimensions of mood and personality. *Journal of Personality and Social Psychology, 62*, 1067–1074.

Martin, L. R., & Friedman, H. S. (2000). Comparing personality scales across time: An illustrative study of validity and consistency in life-span archival data. *Journal of Personality, 68*, 85–110.

Martin, P., Baenziger, J., MacDonald, M., Siegler, I. C., & Poon, L. W. (2009). Engaged lifestyle, personality, and mental status among centenarians. *Journal of Adult Development, 16*, 199–208.

Martin, L. R., Friedman, H. S., Tucker, J. S., Tomlinson-Keasey, C., Criqui, M. H., & Schwartz, J. E. (2002). A life course perspective on childhood cheerfulness and its relation to mortality risk. *Personality and Social Psychology Bulletin, 28*, 1155–1165.

Matthews, K. A. (1988). Coronary heart disease and Type A behaviors: Update on and alternative to the Booth-Kewley and Friedman (1987) quantitative review. *Psychological Bulletin, 104*, 373–380.

McAdams, D. P., & Olson, B. D. (2010). Personality development: Continuity and change over the life course. *Annual Review of Psychology, 61*, 517–542.

McCaffery, J. M., Frasure-Smith, N., Dubé, M. P., Théroux, P., Rouleau, G. A., Duan, Q., & Lespérance, F. (2006). Common genetic vulnerability to depressive symptoms and coronary artery disease: A review and development of candidate genes related to inflammation and serotonin. *Psychosomatic Medicine, 68*, 187–200.

Miller, G., Chen, E., & Cole, S. W. (2009). Health psychology: Developing biologically plausible models linking the social world and physical health. *Annual Review of Psychology, 60*, 501–524.

Miller, J., & Krizan, Z. (2010, January). *Exercise for extraverts: Do they feel even better than others afterwards?* Poster presented at the 11th Annual Convention of the Society of Personality and Social Psychology, Las Vegas, NV.

Miller, T. Q., Smith, T. W., Turner, C. W., Guijarro, M. L., & Hallet, A. J. (1996). Meta-analytic review of research on hostility and physical health. *Psychological Bulletin, 119*, 322–348.

Minkler, M., & Fadem, P. (2002). "Successful aging": A disability perspective. *Journal of Disability Policy Studies, Special Disabilities, and Aging, 12*, 229–235.

Mokdad, A. H., Marks, J. S., Stroup, D. F., & Gerberding, J. L. (2004). Actual causes of death in the United States, 2000. *Journal of the American Medical Association, 291*, 1238–1245.

Mroczek, D. K., & Almeida, D. M. (2004). The effects of daily stress, age, and personality on daily negative affect. *Journal of Personality 72*, 354–378.

Mroczek, D. K., & Spiro III, A. (2007). Personality change influences mortality in older men. *Psychological Science, 18*, 371–376.

Neupert, S. D., Mroczek, D. K., & Spiro III, A. (2008). Neuroticism moderates the daily relation between stressors and memory failures. *Psychology and Aging, 23*, 287–296.

O'Grady, C. G. (2006). Cognitive optimism and professional pessimism in the large-firm practice of law: The optimistic associate. *Law and Psychology Review, 30*, 23–55.

Ozer, D. J., & Benet-Martinez, V. (2006). Personality and the prediction of consequential outcomes. *Annual Review of Psychology, 57*, 401–421.

Paulose-Ram, R., Safran, M. A., Jonas, B. S., Gu, Q., & Orwig, D. (2007). Trends in psychotropic medication use among US adults. *Pharmacoepidemiology and Drug Safety, 16*, 560–570.

Ploubidis, G. B., & Grundy, E. (2009). Personality and all-cause mortality: Evidence for indirect links. *Personality and Individual Differences, 47*, 203–208.

Pressman, S. D., & Cohen, S. (2005). Does positive affect influence health? *Psychological Bulletin, 131*, 925–971.

Räikkönen, K., Matthews, K. A., & Kuller, L. H. (2002). The relationship between psychological risk attributes and the metabolic syndrome in healthy women: Antecedent or consequences? *Metabolism, 51*, 1573–1577.

Rammstedt, B. (2007). Who worries and who is happy? Explaining individual differences in worries and satisfaction by personality. *Personality and Individual Differences, 43*, 1626–1634.

Ramsay, J. M. C., McDermott, M. R., & Bray, C. (2001). Components of the anger–hostility complex and symptom reporting in patients with coronary artery disease: A multi-measure study. *Journal of Health Psychology, 6*, 713–729.

Rasul, F., Stansfeld, S. A., Hart, C. L., & Smith, G. D. (2005). Psychological distress, physical illness, and risk of coronary heart disease. *Journal of Epidemiology and Community Health, 59*, 140–145.

Raynor, D. A., & Levine, H. (2009). Associations between the five-factor model of personality and health behaviors among college students. *Journal of American College Health, 58*, 73–81.

Repetti, R. L., Taylor, S. E., & Seeman, T. E. (2002). Risky families: Family social environments and the mental and physical health of offspring. *Psychological Bulletin, 128*, 330–366.

Rhodes, R. E., & Smith, N. E. I. (2006). Personality correlates of physical activity: A review and meta-analysis. *British Journal of Sports Medicine, 40*, 958–965.

Rhodes, R. E., Courneya, K. S., & Jones, L. W. (2002). Personality, the theory of planned behavior, and exercise: A unique role for extroversion's activity facet. *Journal of Applied Social Psychology, 32*, 1721–1736.

Roberts, B. W., & Bogg, T. (2004). A longitudinal study of the relationships between conscientiousness and the social–environmental factors and substance-use behaviors that influence health. *Journal of Personality, 72*, 325–353.

Roberts, B. W., & Del Vecchio, W. F. (2000). The rank-order consistency of personality from childhood to old age: A quantitative review of longitudinal studies. *Psychological Bulletin, 126*, 3–25.

Roberts, B. W., Caspi, A., & Moffitt, T. (2003). Work experiences and personality development in young adulthood. *Journal of Personality and Social Psychology 84*, 582–593.

Roberts, B. W., Walton, K. E., & Viechtbauer, W. (2006). Patterns of mean level change in personality traits across the life course: A meta-analysis of longitudinal studies. *Psychological Bulletin, 132,* 1–25.

Roberts, B. W., Kuncel, N. R., Shiner, R., Caspi, A., & Goldberg, L. R. (2007). The power of personality: The comparative validity of personality traits, socioeconomic status, and cognitive ability for predicting important life outcomes. *Perspectives on Psychological Science, 2,* 313–345.

Rodondi, N., Marques-Vidal, P., Bitler, J., Sutton-Tyrrell, K., Cornuz, J., Satterfield, S. et al. (2010). Markers of atherosclerosis and inflammation for prediction of coronary heart disease in older adults. *American Journal of Epidemiology, 171,* 540–549.

Rugulies, R. (2002). Depression as a predictor for coronary heart disease: A review and meta-analysis. *American Journal of Preventive Medicine, 23,* 51–61.

Ryan, R. M., & Deci, E. L. (2000). Self-determination theory and the facilitation of intrinsic motivation, social development, and well-being. *American Psychologist, 55,* 68–78.

Salovey, P., Rothman, A. J., Detweiler, J. B., & Steward, W. T. (2000). Emotional states and physical health. *American Psychologist, 55,* 110–121.

Satterfield, J. M., Monahan, J., & Seligman, M. E. P. (1997). Law school performance predicted by explanatory style. *Behavioral Sciences and the Law, 15,* 95–105.

Scheier, M. F., & Carver, C. S. (1985). Optimism, coping, and health: Assessment and implications of generalized outcome expectancies. *Health Psychology, 4,* 219–247.

Schultz, R., & Heckhausen, J. (1996). A life span model of successful aging. *American Psychologist, 51,* 702–714.

Schwarzer, R. (1999). Self-regulatory processes in the adoption and maintenance of health behaviors. *Journal of Health Psychology, 4,* 115–127.

Segerstrom, S. C. (2005). Optimism and immunity: Do positive thoughts always lead to positive effects? *Brain, Behavior, & Immunity, 19,* 195–200.

Segerstrom, S. C. (2007). Optimism and resources: Effects on each other and health over 10 years. *Journal of Research in Psychology, 41,* 772–786.

Segerstrom, S. C., & Miller, G. E. (2004). Psychological stress and the human immune system: A meta-analytic study of 30 years of inquiry. *Psychological Bulletin 104,* 601–630.

Shen, B-J., McCreary, C. P., & Meyers, H. F. (2004). Independent and mediated contributions of personality, coping, social support, and depressive symptoms to physical functioning outcomes among patients in cardiac rehabilitation. *Journal of Behavior Medicine, 27,* 39–62.

Sixkiller, K., Takahashi, Y., Edmonds, G. W., Jackson, J. J., Bogg, T., Walton, K. E. et al. (2010, January). *Conscientiousness and health behaviors: Considerations of lower order facets and observer ratings of conscientiousness.* Poster presented at the 11th annual meeting of the Personality and Social Psychology Society, Las Vegas, NV.

Smith, T. W., & Gallo, L. C. (2001). Personality traits as risk factors for physical illness. In A. Baum, T. Revenson, & J. Singer (Eds.), *Handbook of health psychology* (pp. 139–172). Hillsdale, NJ: Lawrence Erlbaum Associates.

Smith, T. W., & Ruiz, J. M. (2002). Psychosocial influences on the development and course of coronary heart disease: Current status and implications for research and practice. *Journal of Consulting and Clinical Psychology. Special Issue: Behavioral medicine and clinical health psychology, 70,* 548–568.

Smith, T. W., & Spiro, A. (2002). Personality, health, and aging: Prolegomenon for the next generation. *Journal of Research in Personality, 36,* 363–394.

Smith, T. W., & Williams, P. G. (1992). Personality and health: Advantages and limitations of the five-factor model. *Journal of Personality, 60,* 395–423.

Smith, T. W., Uchino, B. N., Berg, C. A., Florsheim, P., Pearce, G., Hawkins, N. et al. (2008). Associations of self-reports versus spouse ratings of negative affectivity, dominance, and affiliation with coronary artery disease: Where should we look and who [*sic*] should we ask when studying personality and health? *Health Psychology, 27,* 676–684.

Solberg Nes, L., & Segerstrom, S. C. (2006). Dispositional optimism and coping: A meta-analytic review. *Personality and Social Psychology Review, 10,* 235–251.

Strawbridge, W. J., Wallhagen, M. I., & Cohen, R. D. (2002). Successful ageing and well-being: Self-rated compared with Rowe and Kahn. *Gerontologist, 42,* 727–733.

Suls, J, & Bunde, J. (2005). Anger, anxiety, and depression as risk factors for cardiovascular disease: The problems and implications of overlapping affective dispositions. *Psychological Bulletin, 131,* 260–300.

Sutin, A. R., Terracciano, A., Deiana, B., Naitza, S., Ferrucci, L., Uda, M. et al. (2010). High neuroticism and low conscientiousness are associated with interleukin-6. *Psychological Medicine, 40,* 1485–1493.

Sutin, A. R., Terracciano, A., Deiana, B., Uda, M., Schlessinger, D., Lakatta, E. G., & Costas, P. T., Jr. (2010). Cholesterol, tryglicerides, and the five-factor model of personality. *Biological Psychology, 84,* 186–191.

Taga, K. T., Friedman, H. S., & Martin, L. R. (2009). Early personality predictors of mortality risk following conjugal bereavement. *Journal of Personality, 77,* 669–690.

Tang, C. C., Poston, K. L., Dhawan, V., & Eidelberg, D. (2010). Abnormalities in metabolic network activity precede the onset of motor symptoms in Parkinson's disease. *The Journal of Neuroscience, 30,* 1049–1056.

Taylor, S. E. (2007). Social support. In H. S. Friedman & R. C. Silva (Eds.), *Foundation of health psychology* (pp. 145–171). New York: Oxford University Press.

Taylor, S. E., Repetti, R. L., & Seeman, T. (1997). Health psychology: What is an unhealthy environment and how does it get under the skin? *Annual Review of Psychology, 48,* 411–447.

Tucker, J. S., Friedman, H. S., Wingard, D. L., & Schwartz, J. E. (1996). Marital history at mid-life as a predictor of longevity: Alternative explanations to the protective effect of marriage. *Health Psychology, 15,* 94–101.

Vaccarino, V., Votaw, J., Faber, T., Veledar, E., Murrah, N. V., Jones, L. R. et al. (2009). Major depression and coronary flow researve detected by positron emission tomography. *Archives of Internal Medicine, 169,* 1668–1676.

Vitaliano, P. P., Scanlan, J. M., Zhang, J., Savage, M. V., & Hirsch, I. B. (2002). A path model of chronic stress, the metabolic syndrome, and coronary heart disease. *Psychosomatic Medicine, 64,* 418–435.

Vollrath, M. (2000). Personality and hassles among university students: A three-year longitudinal study. *European Journal of Personality, 14,* 199–215.

Vollrath, M. (2001). Personality and stress. *Scandinavian Journal of Psychology, 42,* 335–347.

Wand, G. S., McCaul, M., Yang, X., Reynolds, J., Gotjen, D., Lee, S., & Ali, A. (2002). The mu-opioid receptor gene polymorphism (A118G) alters HPA axis activation induced by opioid receptor blockade. *Neuropsychopharmacology, 26,* 106–114.

Weinstein, N. D. (1987). Unrealistic optimism about susceptibility to health problems: Conclusions from a community-wide sample. *Journal of Behavioral Medicine, 10,* 481–500.

Weiss, A., & Costa, P. T. (2005). Domain and facet personality predictors of all-cause mortality among Medicare patients aged 65 to 100. *Psychosomatic Medicine, 67,* 724–733.

Weiss, A., Gale, C. R., Batty, D., & Deary, I. J. (2009). Emotionally stable, intelligent mean live longer: The Vietnam Experience Study cohort. *Psychosomatic Medicine, 71,* 385–394.

Wilson, R. S., Mendes de Leon, C. F., Bienias, J. L., Evans, D. A., & Bennett, D. A. (2004).

Personality and mortality in old age. *Journals of Gerontology: Series B: Psychological Sciences and Social Sciences, 59B,* P110–P116.

Wilson, R. S., Krueger, K. R., Gu, L., Bienias, J. L., Mendes de Leon, C. F., & Evans, D. A. (2005). Neuroticism, extraversion, and mortality in a defined population of older persons. *Psychosomatic Medicine, 67,* 841–845.

World Health Organization (1948). Preamble to the constitution of the World Health Organization as adopted by the International Health Conference. *Official Records of the World Health Organization, 2,* 100.

Wulsin, L. R., & Singal, B. M. (2003). Do depressive symptoms increase the risk for the onset of coronary disease? A systematic quantitative review. *Psychosomatic Medicine, 65,* 201–210.

# Section 3  Society

# 18

# Personality and the Laws of History

## Robert Hogan and Tomas Chamorro-Premuzic

## Introduction

*Societies aren't made of sticks and stones, but of men whose individual characters, by turning the scale one way or another, determine the direction of the whole.* (Plato, *The republic*)

Alfred Kroeber (1952), the influential pioneer of cultural anthropology, argued that the study of history is fundamentally different from the study of natural science. History is not like biology or physics, he said, because historical events can only be understood in terms of specific cultural contexts, and the relations between such contexts are only sequential; history, like life, is just one damned thing after another.

There are two points to note about Kroeber's view. First, because science is about making generalizations, if Kroeber is right, there can be no general laws or real science of history. Second, Kroeber's emphasis on culture as the determinant of human affairs has inspired many social psychologists to interpret most human behaviors as a function of somewhat arbitrary situational contingencies. Indeed, Mischel's (1968) famous attack on personality psychology was based on the anarchic claim that there are no significant consistent patterns of intra-individual behavior, which is equivalent to saying that personality does not exist. Although this claim may seem ridiculous to most readers of this book, the current state of US personality psychology says a lot about the continuing influence of the situationalist argument and about how it is used to interpret historical events. Thus Zimbardo (2007) recently argued that the human capacity for evil is not a function of anything inherent to people, but something caused by "situational forces."

*The Wiley-Blackwell Handbook of Individual Differences,* First Edition.
Edited by Tomas Chamorro-Premuzic, Sophie von Stumm, and Adrian Furnham.
© 2011 Blackwell Publishing Ltd. Published 2011 by Blackwell Publishing Ltd.

The educated reader will realize that there is a deep connection between Kroeber's emphasis on culture as the determinant of social action and the emphasis that Hegel and Marx put on the dynamics of history as the cause of human affairs. For both philosophers, human action is explained by contextual factors and by the tide of history rather than by any salient human attributes. A moment's reflection should also reveal that Zimbardo's "situations" can be seen in Marxist terms as "micro-bursts of history" (which is equivalent to saying that history is formed of situational clusters). For these writers, situations, culture, and history refer to the same causal phenomena at different levels of aggregation, and Hegel's logic of causation is formally identical with the logic of causation in psychological situationism.

When one realizes that, in the twentieth century, over 137 million people were killed by their own governments (Rummel, 1994; see also Hogan & Ahmad 2011: this volume), it would seem to be important to understand the causes of human aggression. Can a serious science claim that these murders were the product of random situational factors? Can history or psychology be serious sciences if they are unable to explain the causes of major human disasters? Consider for example the holocaust. Zimbardo's conjectures aside, analyses of this (by no means unique) event inevitably point to the importance of the personalities of the principal actors.

This chapter has two goals: (1) to highlight the importance of personality as a determinant of historical events; and (2) to bridge the dichotomy between situational and personality-based approaches to interpreting history by examining interactions between personality and cultural context. In order to integrate the major units of analysis in social life—the person, small groups, and societies—we need a better understanding of how personality impacts history. This chapter provides the foundations for such an understanding.

## Some Simple Rules for Human Nature

All fields in the social and behavioral sciences depend on assumptions about human nature; for example, economics assumes that people are motivated by self-interest (Smith, 1991), sociology assumes that people are the creatures of their culture (Durkheim, 1960), political science assumes that people are the product of political systems or government (Goodin & Klingemann, 1996), and so on. The subject matter of personality psychology is human nature (Hogan, 2007), hence it provides a basis for evaluating the assumptions other sciences make about humans.

### Personality psychology

Personality psychology consists of three related activities. The first, personality *theory*, is a quasi-philosophical attempt to conceptualize human nature—to define what people are like, way down deep. The second activity, personality *assessment*, concerns identifying and measuring the most important individual differences in affect, cognition, and behavior. This is a practical exercise, which uses various psychometric procedures to predict significant life outcomes—academic or occupational performance (Chamorro-Premuzic & Furnham, 2006, 2010), health status (Allport, 1963;

Roberts & Bogg, 2004), romantic relationships (Ahmetoglu, Swami, & Chamorro-Premuzic, in press; Kelly & Conley, 1987), delinquency (Egan & Hamilton, 2008), and so forth. The third activity concerns personality *development*, or tracing how people change over the life span (McAdams & Olson, 2010). In sum, personality psychology concerns defining human nature, identifying and measuring the crucial ways in which people differ, and analyzing how these differences develop and what outcomes they predict.

Research in personality psychology replicates about as well as research in biology, and validity coefficients for well-constructed personality measures compare favorably with those for well-known medical screening procedures (Meyer et al., 2000). Further, personality psychologists can predict important outcomes, such as happiness (see Pavot & Diener 2011: this volume) and life expectancy (Roberts, Kuncel, Shiner, Caspi, & Goldberg, 2007), much better than economists, allegedly the most "scientific" of the social scientists.

We believe that personality theory is crucial for identifying the "syntax" or dynamics underlying human history. As seen in the study of chaos, complex behavior is driven by a few simple initial conditions, or rules (Gribben, 2002; Holland, 1992). Likewise, personality theory—in the present chapter, socioanalytic theory (Hogan, 1983)—can identify the rules that explicate the behavior of individuals in groups and, subsequently, the causal determinants of history. Socioanalytic theory links evolutionary theory, psychodynamics, and sociology (in other words it links Sigmund Freud and George Herbert Mead, John Bowlby and Erving Goffman, Irenaus Eibl-Ibesfeldt and Gustav Ichheiser) to derive a comprehensive account of human motivation (cf. Hogan, 1996, 2007).

## Two perspectives on personality: reputation and identity

Personality can be defined from two perspectives: that of the actor and that of the observer. Personality from the actor's perspective is the "you" that you know, your view of you—the view from the inside—and it can be summarized in terms of your *identity*. Freud would argue that the "you" that you know (your identity) is hardly worth knowing, because you made it up. We disagree; regardless of its truth status, and regardless of how hard it is to study rigorously, your identity is important because it guides and directs your social behavior (see McAdams, 1985).

Personality from the observer's perspective is the "you" that we know and can be summarized in terms of your *reputation* (Hogan, 1983). It is the result of how others evaluate your social behavior. Reputations directly affect lives because access to people, jobs, and financing depend on how others perceive you (Chamorro-Premuzic & Furnham, 2010). Moreover, it is easy to study reputation by using observer ratings (Mount, Barrick, & Strauss, 1994).

Reputation tells us what people typically do, identity tells us *why* they do such things. Personality psychologists use reputation to predict behavior (the best predictor of future behavior is past behavior, and reputation reflects past behavior), but we use identity to *explain* behavior.[1]

Consider, for example, Robert Mugabe, the dictator of Zimbabwe. Mugabe has a reputation for arrogance, economic incompetence, and ruthless suppression of dissent. Why does he behave like a dictator? Mugabe naturally explains his behavior in terms of his identity as a freedom fighter and a populist African leader, an identity that worked well when he fought against white control and led Zimbabwe's transition to self-rule. Having defeated white control, Mugabe then began to suppress "internal enemies" and to resist the destabilizing influence of neighboring states. Mugabe stole elections, ordered mass executions, and presided over the collapse of Zimbabwe's economy, while proclaiming himself to be a savior (Meredith, 2007).

By distinguishing between identity and reputation, we can escape the circularity inherent in trait theory. For instance, trait theory would argue that Mugabe is arrogant because he has a trait for arrogance (a circular statement). The present view maintains that Mugabe's reputation for arrogance is a function of the behavior that results from his motives of entitlement and self-righteous savior identity. Thus identifying people's motives should help us understand their identity, which, in turn, should help us explain the consistent patterns of behavior that create their reputations and predict their future behaviors.

## Master motives

Theories of personality always rest on models of motivation. If we think about humanity from the perspective of anthropology, sociology, and evolutionary theory, three general themes become apparent. First, people always live in groups. Second, every group has a status hierarchy. And, third, every group has a culture (including religion) which contains the rules for interaction. These three themes point to some important generalizations about human motivation—namely that people need social living, they need status and power, and they need a sense of predictability and order in their lives. Furthermore, these needs are biologically mandated, such that their satisfaction promotes individual survival and reproductive fitness (Lawrence & Nohria, 2002; Wilson, 1978). We refer to these needs as *getting along, getting ahead*, and *finding or imposing meaning*.[2]

Most psychologists understand the importance of getting along because they realize that normal people need love and friendship (Baumeister & Leary, 1995). For example, attachment theory begins with this assumption (Bowlby, 1969) and argues that, unless we develop a secure relationship with a primary caregiver, we will face persistent psychological impairment and be unable to form healthy relations with others during adulthood (Neustadt, Chamorro-Premuzic, & Furnham, 2006). Likewise, positive psychology suggests that people are happiest if they maintain meaningful social relations with others, including romantic bonds and close friendships (Seligman & Csikszentmihalyi, 2000). Moreover, even Freud thought there is little more to life than *lieben und arbeiten* (Erikson, 1950), and current conceptualizations of maladaptiveness agree (see Chamorro-Premuzic, 2007).

On the other hand, psychologists view getting ahead and status-seeking with considerable ambivalence. For Freud, ambition reflects an unconscious desire to kill one's father; for Adler, it is an unconscious compensation for feelings of inferiority. Furthermore, mainstream personality models fail to distinguish between getting along and getting ahead. For instance, several Big-Five taxonomies (Costa & McCrae, 1992; Wiggins, 1996) confound sociability and ambition in a factor variously labeled extraversion or surgency. Indeed, even business psychologists confuse these concepts and typically evaluate managers by using performance ratings—how much they are liked[3] (London & Smither, 1995). Sociability is about getting along with others, whereas ambition is about outperforming them and getting ahead, and measures of sociability and ambition predict different criteria (Hogan & Holland, 2003; see also Hogan, 2007).

As evidence for the importance of the human need for predictability and order, consider two observations. First, research in areas as diverse as cognitive dissonance (Festinger, 1957) and learned helplessness (Seligman, 1975) shows that people find inconsistency and a lack of predictability to be highly stressful. Second, consider the role of religion in human affairs. Although religion is a cultural universal[4] (Norbeck, 1974), its evolutionary significance is less clear (see, however, Wade, 2009). On the one hand, religion explains the meaning of life; on the other hand, religions provide collectives with the justification for a common set of social roles, customs, and rules for getting along and getting ahead (i.e. culture; Pinker, 2002). These beliefs and practices function as a sort of "social glue" that binds people together and provides a collective identity. Recent work also suggests that religions may have helped early societies defend against epidemics and diseases, for instance by dictating diets that prevent the spread of diseases (e.g. not eating pork avoids the spread of trichinosis and is prescribed by Islam and in Judaism). This is consistent with the fact that hot countries tend to have both an abundance of parasitic diseases and a great number of indigenous beliefs that promote healthy lifestyles (*The Economist*, July 31, 2008).

There are two final points to be noted about this model of motivation. First, getting along is a precondition for getting ahead, but both processes coexist in a dynamic state of tension (Bakan, 1966; Guisinger & Blatt, 1994). To get along with others, we must conform to their wishes (which often include controlling us) and repress the impulse to compete (which often includes controlling them). Moreover, if we are successful in getting ahead, we risk jealousy and backstabbing, and if we are really successful, we risk stalking and assassination—ask John Lennon, Robert and J. F. Kennedy, or Abraham Lincoln (or, outside the US, Archduke Franz Ferdinand and Julius Caesar).

Second, all three motives have a dark side. The desire to get along leads to group-think (McCauley, 1985) and mindless conformity (Latane, 1981). The desire to get ahead leads to a wide range of unscrupulous behaviors, from tax evasion to murder (this is what Bernard Madoff, Silvio Berlusconi, Ghengis Khan, and many wealthy residents of Monaco and Marbella have in common). Last but not least, the need for predictability and order can lead to religious fanaticism and genocide; Jonestown, 9/11, the Armenian genocide, the holocaust, and Scientology are examples.

Our main point concerning master motives is that, if we assume their importance, and if we accept that there are individual differences in people's ability to satisfy them, then we have an agenda for personality theory that contains a model for interpreting and predicting collective behavior, including history.

## Some Collective Dynamics

We now offer five generalizations about human collectives that are independent of the people who populate them, but nonetheless are a function of human nature. That is to say, we offer five examples of the point that every useful generalization we can make about group dynamics depends on understanding the master motives of personality, regardless of the people who are in the group at a particular point in time.

## Leadership matters

First, the success of any organization depends in part on the competency of its leadership (Kaiser, Hogan, & Kraig, 2008; see also Hogan & Ahmad 2011: this volume), and the principles of leadership are independent of the individuals who are actually in the role. The fundamental task of leadership is to build a constituency into an effective team that can outperform the competition (Hogan, Curphy, & Hogan, 1994). Effective leaders build coalitions of supporters and offer an attractive vision of the future (cf. Hogan & Kaiser, 2005). This generalization is true whether we are talking about the British prime minister or the manager of the Inter Milan soccer team. As Freud suggested, most people seem pre-programmed to respond to leadership, and those who are not responsive are either social isolates or power-hungry psychopaths who want to be in charge themselves.

## Rules calcify

Every organization becomes more bureaucratic and rule-bound with the passage of time (Hogan, 2007). The reason has to do with the fact that, in every organization, members make mistakes and/or cheat in order to advance their own interests (Ridley, 1997). New rules are put in place to prevent errors and to control the cheating; rules are non-biodegradable, so they accumulate. In mature organizations, there will be so many rules that, in order to respond rapidly to unexpected problems, one will have to break a rule—and that will provide one's critics with ammunition. The point is that the increasing rigidity of every organization is a function of human nature.

## All coalitions are temporary

Although people are both selfish and cooperative, these tendencies emerge at different times and in response to different demands (Wilson & Wilson, 2007, 2008). This means, among other things, that people will only work for the collective good for short periods; leadership may only enlist people in a common cause for a limited time (Hargreaves & Fink, 2004; Hogan et al., 1994, p. 493). At some point, people go back to pursuing their individual interests, leaving the group vulnerable to the predations of its competitors, or to the appeals of a leader with a more seductive vision. Consequently, as Robert Mugabe will discover, most political careers end in failure.

## Factions are inevitable

In any group the emergence of cabals and factions is inevitable. Individuals lose faith in the established leadership, or they sense an opportunity to enhance their own power and control. These like-minded individuals cluster together, and the result, as the executive branch of the US government or the department structure of University

College London shows, is an organization characterized by silos, fiefdoms, and entrenched pockets of self-interest. Tribalism is an ancient tendency, and people always identify with their local colleagues and form an "us versus them" view of other clusters (Levine & Campbell, 1972). One of the most important tasks of leadership is to combat these inevitable insular tendencies and to unite divided factions as one constituency. If unification fails, the group will be wracked by discord and left vulnerable to stronger and more cohesive rival groups.

### Free riders are inevitable and weaken the group

In every collectivity, from the "wrinkly spreader" bacteria (*Pseudomonas fluorescens*) floating in ponds to prides of lions to human groups, free riders inevitably emerge. Free riders are selfish individuals who enjoy the benefits of living in the group but contribute less than they consume. There are substantial benefits associated with free riding and, unless free riders are dealt with self-consciously, their numbers tend to grow. However, groups dominated by free riders are less able to compete compared to groups of cooperators (Wilson & Wilson, 2007, 2008). Over time, individuals who take more than they contribute tend to rise to the top and become the cultural elite. This undermines the group's fitness, leaving it vulnerable to rival groups. Turchin (2003),[5] a theoretical biologist who specializes in non-linear population dynamics, uses data to show how the free rider problem explains the fall of Rome and other civilizations.

## Collective Histories

In contrast with Marx and Kroeber, we believe that the "syntax" of history can be largely explained by a few reliable rules that operate at the level of individual actors. In a manner analogous to the behavior of neurons in the brain, these relatively simple rules of individual behavior are sufficient to give rise to complex behavior at the level of groups, which aggregate to create social events and later become history. Our empirical claim is that, within any human collective, during any chunk of history, the social dynamics will be the same, and these dynamics will be driven by the fundamental patterns of human nature.

The fact that humans evolved as group-living animals (Baumeister & Leary, 1995; Wilson, 1978) suggests that human history is best seen as the history of collectives rather than simply as the inexorable tide of a monolithic history. Moreover, the history of collectives, like individual lives, comes in chunks—the rise and fall of Athens, the British Empire, the Cold War and the Soviet Union, or the war on terror—and the histories of *some* collectives, like the histories of some individuals, are much more successful and consequential than others. Accordingly, history can be broken down into minor historical components, such that *history is composed of histories*, for example: the history of Napoleonic France, Ghandi's India, Mao's China.

The histories of today and tomorrow can seem arbitrary and random as they unfold, but perceptions of randomness depend on our level of analysis. For example,

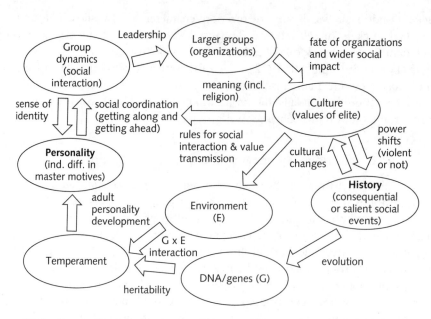

**Figure 18.1** Personality and the syntax of history: A bottom-up approach

many neuroscientists believe that human consciousness is the emergent byproduct of billions of interactions between neurons in the brain, but that each individual neuron follows straightforward laws of behavior (Koch, 2004; Pinker, 1997). This "bottom-up" approach is precisely what characterizes personality-based interpretations of history: from innate behavioral tendencies engraved in our DNA (and their interactions with the environment), to early individual differences in temperament during infancy and childhood, and to subsequent developments in personality throughout adolescence and into adulthood, the relative success or failure of human collectives is the relative success or failure of individuals; specifically, how they impact small groups and then larger groups (organizations and societies) and thereby shape historical cultural changes. Thus individual efforts to get along and get ahead in groups and in society, combined with differing levels of social coordination, are *the* key not only to the success of collectives but also to our evolutionary future (see Figure 18.1).

## Personality and Culture

Humans evolved as culture-producing and culture-consuming animals—language use and the capacity for collective action gave us an adaptive advantage over our primate competitors in the context of human origins (Diamond, 1992; Pinker, 1997). This means that we are pre-programmed to form collectives and to interact with others: the process of using culture to organize interaction is biologically mandated—something Kroeber did not understand.

## Social interaction

Every social interaction in every human institution (and this is how "situations" should be defined) has the same underlying structure, namely there must be: (a) an agenda; (b) rules for the interaction; and (c) roles to play (Mead, 1934). Without these structural elements, interaction is impossible, and without interaction there is no social life. Situations can, therefore, be defined in terms of their (overt and covert) agendas, rules, and roles, all of which organize interaction; thus personality, situations, culture, and interactions are inextricably intertwined. Culture prescribes the acceptable agendas, roles, and rules; situations are defined by combinations of these elements; and personality (defined as identity) dictates how an individual will play his/her roles. There is, therefore, no inherent conflict between biology and culture: our desire to interact comes from our biology, the manner in which we interact is regulated by our culture and our identities. Life is an extended series of interactions during which our major needs (for acceptance, status, and predictability) are frustrated or fulfilled.

So, to paraphrase Marshall McLuhan, the milieu is the message; interacting with others teaches us who we are—social interaction gives us our sense of identity. And our identities shape our subsequent interactions. But interactions are also vehicles for the pursuit of our individual agendas. In every social group, every interaction concerns individuals searching for acceptance, status, and control. This explains why even informal conversations about work with family and friends often resemble coaching sessions in which people seek support for their position ("They aren't treating me right") and develop strategies for advancing their agendas once they go back on the job. What goes on inside the General Electric Corporation, Deutsche Telekom, or Vivendi is formally identical with what goes on in the halls of the Vatican, the Kremlin, or Harvard University. Although it is possible to have a life outside such organizations, it is a life outside history.

## Integrating personality, context, and culture

The view that personal and contextual interpretations are mutually exclusive has substantially clouded the debate about the explanation of history (or social behavior in general). This fallacy has been around since the end of the nineteenth century and takes many forms—for example culture versus personality, nature versus nurture, person versus situation—and is often resolved (or not) by suggesting that the two classes of explanatory variables "interact" (see Magnusson & Endler, 1976), without specifying how. One reason for the persistence of the fallacy is that there are no clear definitions of "situations," let alone taxonomies for classifying them (Hogan, 2007). Indeed, as Hogan and Judge (in press) recently argued, conceptualizations of situations are largely based on the economists' notion of "imponderable contingencies," which make it virtually impossible to measure or study contextual influences on behavior in a rigorous way.

In our view, there is no conflict between the two forms of explanation. In fact, personality and contextual explanations of behaviors have been integrated in three ways, each of which has implications for our understanding of how personality affects the laws of history.

The first integrative model depends on the view that behavior is a function of both situational and personal factors (Ross & Nisbett, 1991). Moreover, as Mischel seems to say, when situational factors are pressing (an earthquake), personality factors will seem unimportant; in the absence of situational constraints, however, personality will prevail. In simple terms, this model implies that behavior (B) is a function of both a situation (S) and an individual's personality (P), that is, P + S = B. This *additive* approach parallels the historical divide between social and personality psychology, with social psychologists attributing behavior to situations (consistent with Kroeber's metaphysics) and personality psychologists attributing behavior to traits (consistent with Carlyle's view of history as the biography of great men). But there is a fundamental flaw in this model: namely, it assumes that personality and contextual factors are independent. Even historians integrate personal and contextual variables; for example Herbert Spencer (1896) "synthesized" the Marxist view of history in the "great man" approach, noting that "the genesis of the great man depends on the long series of complex influences which has produced the race in which he appears, and the social state into which that race has slowly grown. [...] Before he can remake his society, his society must make him" (p. 34). What this means is that the "situations" that moderate the influence of our personality on behavior have been shaped by other personalities beforehand.

The second way to integrate personality and context highlights the interplay between nature and nurture. Geneticists have long understood how behavior is the result of interactions between genetic and environmental causes of behaviors, but personality psychology still studies one or the other (unless it studies neither). Tryon (1942) was the first person explicitly to address this problem. In his artificial selection experiment in rats,[6] Tryon bred rats for maze-running ability and created two strains: maze bright and maze dull. However, the difference between the strains disappeared in a single generation if the slower rats were raised in a "richer" environment— one with more objects to explore. This study shows that genetic effects on running ability are only seen under certain environmental conditions. Similarly, clinical psychologists use the *diathesis–stress model* to demonstrate that a constitutional vulnerability to psychopathology (the diathesis) only creates psychological disorders in the presence of the "right" environmental triggers (the stress). The greater the underlying vulnerability, the less stress is needed to trigger the disorder; conversely, when the diathesis is smaller, greater life stress is required to produce psychopathology. This model differs from P + S = B in that, no matter how strong the diathesis, the disorder will only develop under stress, and vice versa (in other words, no matter how much stress individuals face, they will only develop a disorder if they have a constitutional vulnerability). Therefore this model, first used in Holmes and Rahe's (1967) social readjustment study, can be illustrated by a multiplicative formula, such that P + S = B becomes P × S = B.

As in the diathesis–stress model, personality only affects history in the presence of the "right" cultural events. Indeed, if we interpret "S" as the context and "B" as the salient historical outcomes (using the initials of the above formula), the equation implies that contextual variables determine how personality impacts history—that is, certain events potentiate the effects of certain personality characteristics on historical outcomes, and other events inhibit the impact of those same personality characteristics. Thus a combative temperament will be historically consequential during times of conflict, but will have trivial effects otherwise. As Nietzsche said, in peaceful times the violent man makes war on himself.

Finally, the third approach for integrating personality and contextual variables is *reciprocal determinism*. Common examples of this model include parents' responses to their children's genetically influenced behaviors—such as nurturing a child's musical talent with musical lessons; or nurturing intellectual curiosity with environments that feed hungry minds; or providing aggressive children with violent computer games and violent movies (see Plomin, DeFries, McClearn, & McGuffin, 2008, for a discussion of "active gene–environment correlations"). This approach has major implications for understanding how personality impacts history; it suggests that individual differences predispose to particular choices, and the *fit* between personality and contextual variables potentiates the effects of personality on historical events.

Personality also affects how events are interpreted (e.g. positive vs. negative bias, external vs. internal attribution, elaboration–likelihood routes, etc.), which means that contextual variables also *depend* on personality. Thus different people will experience the same environments differently. For example, emotionally unstable persons will experience stress in situations where well-adjusted persons will not, sensation-seekers will experience thrills where non-sensation-seekers may experience fear, and combative people will see provocations where most people see none. Einstein's famous remark that "great spirits have often encountered violent opposition from weak minds" can be interpreted using reciprocal determinism—the actual opposition great spirits encounter mainly depends on the way they interpret and experience adversity: where some see criticism, others see opportunities for getting ahead (via self-improvement, hard work, and competition).

Our subjective interpretations of reality affect ourselves and others; consider, for example, that changes in real-estate or oil prices are a function of collective market expectations, which are often driven by the views of single individuals—leaders. George Soros broke the Bank of England in 1992 by applying his knowledge of reflexivity and self-fulfilling prophecies (two well-known examples of reciprocal determinism) to making money (Soros, 1994). Indeed, Soros realized that economic transitions are marked by changes in investor *bias* (perceptions rather than any rational rules of the market). Just as investors' interpretations of capital markets may influence valuations of the market, the personalities of certain individuals will project onto historical events and shape them. Thus market valuations are little more than the perceptions of an elite group of personalities (which are financially consequential), cultures are little more than the values of ruling elites, and history is little more than a record of how leaders reacted to the events of their time. The events would have created different reactions in their competitors. But, more importantly, the desire and ability to change things, including the capacity to sell a different *Weltanschauung* to a social collective, is only in those who shall rule.

## How Individual Personality Shapes Collective History

In contrast with Kroeber, we do not believe that history is a long stream of stochastic events, one following the next in no fathomable order. History is organized at the next lower level of analysis, and is driven by individual humans striving in groups, pursuing three desires—to get along, to get ahead, to find or impose meaning (see, again, Figure 18.1). Indeed, this is why the same themes in human affairs seem to recur generation after generation—and why great art and literature transcend time and place, not to mention psychology.

Freud's (1959) *Group psychology and the analysis of the ego* provides an early, albeit partial, version of our argument. In his little book, Freud examined Le Bon's (1895) theory of crowd behavior and concluded that the actions of mobs and riots can be best understood in terms of the personality dynamics of individual actors. Specifically, every collectivity is composed of individual actors who are trying to get along and get ahead. These activities take place during social interaction inside social institutions, and some people are more successful at advancing their agendas than others. The winners succeed by building coalitions of supporters on the basis of their competence[7] in activities that matter to the group (George Washington, Fidel Castro), by providing answers to pressing group needs (Franklin Roosevelt), through persuasion (Abraham Lincoln) and inspiration (Martin Luther King, Jr., Barack Obama). Failing that, people can find success through flattery, bribery, deceit, betrayal, coercion, and phenomenal persistence. The most socially skilled and persistent individuals end up as politicians, company heads, team leaders, union officials, or the rulers of countries, and, as Freud suggested, in order to retain power, they must be constantly alert to the machinations of the ambitious people below them in the hierarchy.

## Cultural competition

Every collectivity has a ruler and a ruling class, but some collectivities are more successful than others, and the success of collectivities, relative to their competitors, depends on the qualities of the individuals who rule them (Kaiser et al., 2008). Anthropological research shows that marked cultural differences between groups emerge during times of rapid change (Richerson & Boyd, 2006), and intergroup competition subsequently favors those whose beliefs, practices, and values help them adapt to the change. History has to do with the rise and fall of ruling coalitions within specific collectives. At this level of analysis, the recent history of the various tribes in Somalia can be interpreted in precisely the same terms as the history of the British Empire in the nineteenth century. Most importantly, though, the dynamics of those collective histories will be explicable in terms of personality theory, the rise and fall of ruling elites, and the clash of the cultures they create. The following examples illustrate the point.

## Christian values in Rome

The cultures of the Roman pagans and early Christians were in competition, and their respective values served as both markers of identity and guides to appropriate behavior. From the death of Christ to about AD 260, the number of Christians increased from a tiny group to around 20 million. Roman culture had weak traditions of mutual aid, and the poor and sick were often ignored. The values of the Christian community, on the other hand, emphasized self-sacrifice, charity, and the requirement to support people who were sick or hurt. Such mutual assistance was especially attractive during the several plagues that struck the Roman Empire in late antiquity. Because healthy pagan Romans refused to help the sick or to bury the dead, disease spread further and some cities dissolved into anarchy (Boyd, 2006; Boyd & Richerson, 2006). The survival rates in Christian communities were much higher. Historians believe that Romans converted to Christianity because they were attracted to a better quality of life in the early Christian community (Ferguson, 2007). It is easy to see this shift as a form of cultural evolution driven by the pragmatic consequences of different sets of values and of their differential ability to serve biological needs.

## The history of fifteenth-century Florence

Florence was one of the wealthiest and most powerful city-states in fifteenth-century Italy, and the history of Florence was clearly shaped by the Medici family. Beginning with Cosimo dei Medici, the family controlled Florence from behind the scenes. Their power came from *amici degli amici* ("friends of friends"), a large patronage network, and a financial link with the Catholic Church, by which the Medici bank collected 10 percent of citizens' earnings on behalf of the Church, making their bank the most profitable business in Europe. Naturally, the Medici also had rivals, other wealthy Florentine families, whom they controlled by intimidation, torture, and murder (see Devillier Donegan Enterprises, 2004; Hale, 1977; Hibbert, 1999).

In 1434, Cosimo dei Medici named himself ruler of Florence to better protect his family's money. In so doing, he ended Florence's historic republic. Cosimo's son, Lorenzo, then inherited the leadership role and ruled Florence benevolently and competently until his death in 1492. Two years later, the Dominican preacher Savonarola led a revolt and threw the Medici out of the city. Savonarola reinstated the Florentine Republic, but one with a strong religious orientation. In 1498, tired of his excesses, the Florentines executed Savonarola and restored the secular republic. The republic lasted 14 years, during which time Florence was constantly threatened by the armies of France, Spain, the Holy Roman Empire, Milan, Genoa, Venice, Naples, powerful warlords, and other wealthy Florentine families. In 1512, Pope Julius II assembled the Holy League against France. He demanded that Florence join the League and restore the exiled Medici family to power. Giuliano dei Medici and his supporters marched into Florence, resumed control, and began extending their influence across Europe.

Both feared and admired by the populace (a leadership strategy no doubt learned from one of the first "spin doctors" of history, Niccolò Machiavelli), the Medici bought alliances, inter-married with other powerful families, intimidated rivals, supported art, literature, and science, and catalyzed the Enlightenment. Two Medici became popes. Lorenzo's great-granddaughter, Catherine, married the French king, Henri II, in 1533 and became queen of France. By the early sixteenth century, virtually every ruling house in Europe was related to the Medici.

Our point is that the history of fifteenth-century Florence is best understood in terms of the machinations of the Medici family. But, if the Medici had not existed, Florentine history would have been shaped by the activities of other ruling elites—who may or may not have been as successful and influential beyond Florence.

## Other examples of successful values: England goes Dutch and the Protestant ethic

In a book entitled *Going Dutch: How England plundered Holland's glory*, Jardine (2008) demonstrates how Dutch values transformed Britain. In the 1600s, Holland (with a population one tenth of the population of France) was the wealthiest and most advanced nation on earth, with a flourishing overseas trading empire (New York City), advanced arts and sciences (Rembrandt, Huygens) and great philosophers (Baruch Spinoza). Its culture was characterized by extreme openness, hostility toward hierarchy, and enthusiasm for innovation—it was the most open society on earth. In the same time period, England was a second-rate power, consumed by squabbles between the Protestants and the Catholics. In 1688, to protect the English Protestants, William of Orange invaded and conquered England, introduced Dutch values, and England swiftly became the dominant power on earth.

England's subsequent success has also been explained in terms of values. Most notably, Max Weber (1864–1920) argued in *The Protestant ethic and the spirit of capitalism* (1905) that the values of hard work, savings (putting off immediate gratification for the sake of long-term benefits), and striving for success explained the economic progress that defined the Industrial Revolution. Weber's thesis can be generalized: he argued that values drive the wealth of nations. His argument was nicely supported by the research of David McClelland (McClelland, Atkinson, Clark, & Lowell, 1953), the personality psychologist who popularized the concept of need for achievement—the embodiment of the Protestant ethic at the level of individual personality. McClelland coded achievement themes in children's story books, and found that the frequency of these themes was strongly correlated with quantitative indices of economic prosperity in the western world.[8]

In an important book, *A farewell to arms*, Clark (2007) returns to Weber's argument with new data, providing further support for the notion that values drive the wealth of nations. Using archival data, Clark reconstructs certain features of the English economy between 1200 and 1800. He shows conclusively that the economy was locked in the Malthusian trap before 1800—each new technology increased the efficiency of production a little, and that was followed by an increase in population size, which caused the standard of living to remain static (and poor). Clark's analyses involved ancient wills which he used to study the link between wealth and family size. He found a direct relationship—wealthier people had larger families, so they were outbreeding the poorer parts of the population. This led to a sort of downward mobility—the poor failed to reproduce and the children of the wealthy took their place. Clark concludes that the modern English population mostly descends from the economic upper classes of the Middle Ages. The upper classes differed from the lower classes primarily in terms of values. These values included working harder, saving money, valuing education, and using the law (as opposed to violence) to adjudicate disputes. By around 1800, these values came to dominate English society, and that dominance coincides very closely with the Industrial Revolution in England. Several points about these analyses are worth noting.

First, Clark's and Weber's data show that some values are associated with economic development and others are not. Second, counterproductive values characterize poor people and underdeveloped societies—*thus, not all values are equally valuable*. Third, the economic fate of nations (and the course of history) reflects the aggregate influence of individual values—individual values drive Adam Smith's "invisible hand" (see *The Wealth of Nations*, 1776, the founding text of economic theory). Fourth, these findings have immediate relevance for understanding organizational effectiveness. Organizational culture reflects the values of senior leadership, and not all organizational cultures are equally valuable. Finally, personality psychologists have more to say about the problems of poverty than do sociologists and economists. Yet, until recently, they have not even managed to define personality successfully.

## The Origins of the Capacity for Evil

Let us now consider an account of the holocaust that is an alternative to that provided by Freud (1959), Milgram (1974), Kohlberg (1969), and Zimbardo (2007). In *Group psychology and the analysis of the ego*, Freud explained crowd behavior in terms of individual conformity to authority. He distinguished between the psychology of leaders, who are mostly self-promoting narcissists and psychopaths, and the psychology of followers, who are the rest of us. Freud argued that, in a crowd, the strength of an individual's superego collapses and is replaced by the voice of the leader, who then becomes the individual's conscience and guide to action. Freud's unstated moral is that conformity to leaders often leads to immoral action, and that we should always be prepared to resist our leaders.

This is precisely the lesson of Milgram's famous studies (1974): normal people who conform and follow the dictates of authority are potential murderers of innocent strangers. In a direct extension of Milgram's argument, Kohlberg's theory of moral development states that people who base their actions on the dictates of authority are immature and capable of immoral behavior in the name of authority (Kohlberg, 1969). Likewise, Zimbardo (2007) explains the capacity for evil in terms of conformity to peer pressure or perverse leaders.

As seen, Freud, Milgram, Kohlberg, and Zimbardo all suggest that the behavior of the perpetrators of the holocaust should be explained in terms of their compliance with Hitler's racist and genocidal vision. A better explanation, it seems to us, is to see Hitler's staff, and the German government at the time, as composed of the usual cast of ambitious characters who were eager to succeed, and who understood that status in the Nazi hierarchy depended on pleasing Hitler. As Adams and Balfour (1998) note: "routine administrative processes [were central] to the implementation of the Holocaust [...] the nature and dynamics of these bureaucratic processes are not unique to Nazi Germany [...] but instead are entirely consistent with modern organizations and the technical–rational approach to administration" (p. 54).

Kershaw (2008), Hitler's best biographer, notes that the holocaust was just one part of a much larger agenda of ethnic cleansing in Eastern Europe, that killing Jews was a prelude to the primary objective of eradicating Poles. Furthermore, Kershaw notes that at no point did Hitler explicitly authorize or order the genocide. He set a tone, but much of what went on in the Third Reich involved Hitler's subordinates interpreting his objectives and devising ways to please him and to further their own agendas. Someone somewhere in the upper reaches of the Nazi hierarchy mentioned something like the Final Solution, and from that point certain officials began to compete with one another to implement, in an increasingly horrific manner, a policy designed to please the leader. As another historian noted: "Participation in the Final Solution did not result so much from explicit orders systematically disseminated, as through self-recruitment by the zealous and ambitious servants of the Third Reich in response to the impulses and hints they perceived emanating from the center of power" (Browning, 1989, pp. 98–99).

In this way, the dynamics of the holocaust were less a matter of mindless conformity, and more a function of deliberate individual efforts to get ahead and reinforce their worldview, with no concern for the human cost. But, more importantly, the same dynamics are at work in every large organization, and when those organizations have access to deadly force, the potential for atrocity is always present.

## Concluding Remarks

The eminent cultural anthropologist George Kroeber famously remarked that the events of history can only be understood in terms of specific cultural contexts; consequently, there can be no scientific study of history. If Kroeber was right, psychology becomes largely irrelevant as a way to analyze history; we believe otherwise. In response, this chapter has made three claims. First, history is the story of specific collectivities (e.g. Periclean Athens; Napoleon's France; the Medici's Florence). Second, the story of collectivities can be understood in terms of the machinations of their ruling elites. And, third, the machinations of the ruling elites can be understood in terms of personality psychology. Although the actors change, the principles of group behavior are formal and universal.

Despite its obvious importance for interpreting history, the scientific study of personality has a minority status in modern psychology. The reason for this, we believe, has to do with the discipline's failure to resolve the competing claims of personality versus contextual explanations of behavior. As seen in this chapter, contextual and individual explanations can be integrated in three ways, and each model has implications for understanding the relationship between personality and history.

Human behavior occurs in groups, and the laws underlying group dynamics are universal; in other words, they are as true for the tribe of a Pashtun warlord in Afghanistan as they are for the Romanovs in nineteenth-century Russia or for a present-day American political party. In every group someone will build a coalition, gain control, and work to maintain the coalition in order to remain in power, while competitors within and without the group constantly scheme to replace the ruling coalition (Hogan, 2007). When psychologists study a figure like Napoleon, they characterize him in terms of traits (e.g. narcissistic, intrepid, self-promoting, etc.), but trait attributions are missing the point. The point is not to the describe Napoleon's temperament, but to explain how he recruited his supporters, how he maintained their support, and why they finally abandoned him; these are the relevant personality questions that have historical repercussions.

We believe that history is always played out in terms of the personality dynamics within groups—that is, in terms of individual efforts to get along, get ahead, and make sense of the world. These dynamics exist at the level of individuals and give rise to intricate patterns of behaviors at the collective level. As humans seek status, approval, and control during interaction, they create religious movements, factions, splinter groups, corporations, and nation-states; they work to build these congeries, maintain them, extend them, or tear them down. In order to understand the role of personality psychology in human affairs, we must pay less attention to how people feel about themselves and more attention to their ability to develop social support and acquire power, and to the morality of the methods they use. The competing claims of Darwinians and cultural anthropologists (Boas, 1911; Kroeber, 1952) have never been reconciled, and people today still criticize personality theory for the same reasons that Boas criticized the early Darwinian psychologists. In order for personality theory to be taken seriously by the larger intellectual community (and not just readers by of this handook), this 100-year-old debate needs to be resolved.

## Acknowledgments

We thank David Winsborough and Rob Kaiser for their work on earlier versions of this draft. Parts of this chapter were presented as a keynote address at the 11th European Conference on Personality, Jena, July 23, 2002. Inquiries may be sent to rhogan@hoganassessments.com, Hogan Assessment Systems, 2622 E. 21st St., Tulsa, OK 74114.

## Notes

1 Prediction and explanation are logically distinct activities. Prediction is pragmatic and empirical; explanation is esthetic and theoretical. Debates in science concern explanations. Sutationists prefer contextual explanations; personality psychologists prefer intrapsychic and intentional explanations (cf. Peters, 1958).

2 Many scholars have noted these themes prior to us. For example, Charles Darwin (1871) argued that the most important human motives are "social instincts" or needs that fostered group living (e.g. sympathy and moral sentiment). William James (1890) argued that the most important human motives are instincts that fostered rivalry and competition, and that these instincts led to the co-evolution of hunting and warfare. Jean Piaget (Piaget & Inhelder, 1962) believed that people are powerfully motivated to understand and shape their environments (via a biologically based process called adaptation).

3 These evaluations largely concern the social impact of managers—how much others like working with them (Brown & Keeping, 2005)—which is predicted by sociability. Instead, more attention should be paid to what managers actually accomplish (cf. Kaiser, Hogan, & Craig, 2008)—which is better predicted by ambition (Hogan & Holland, 2003).

4 The average number of religions per country is apparently 36 (*The Economist*, July 31, 2008).

5 Turchin's work is quite unique in its ability to explain how humans became the ultrasocial species they are (cooperating in groups of millions of *genetically unrelated* members).

Turchin's theory of multi-level selection posits that exponential increases in human societies are the result of repeated transitions from lower-level groups to higher-level groups of groups ("meta-groups"), which are fostered primarily by warfare and values designed to maintain cultural variability.

6  Given that the title of this publication was "individual differences," it is somewhat ironic that the study is rarely quoted by individual differences researchers.

7  The alert reader will have noted that this chapter makes no reference to the concept of "IQ" (as understood by mainstream intelligence theory). The reason for this is that IQ provides a very limited account of individual differences in the ability to satisfy our master motives. For instance, the ability to get along is better explained by social or emotional competence (see Petrides, 2011: this volume); the ability to get ahead is better explained by ambition and achievement motivation (see Hogan & Hogan, 1991; Hogan & Ahmad, 2011: this volume); and the ability to find or impose meaning can be better understood in terms of intellect or need for cognition (see Chamorro-Premuzic & Furnham, 2006; von Stumm, Chamorro-Premuzic, & Ackerman 2011: this volume). In order to conceptualize a valid theory of human competence it is necessary to look beyond individual differences in informational processing or computational power capability and to develop robust tests for good social and business judgment, look at synergies between personality and abilities, and understand people's perceptions of others' abilities (intelligence as reputation); when it comes to shaping human history, these factors can be expected to be much more consequential than a high IQ.

8  Nonetheless, economic historians have dismissed these ideas and these data.

# References

Adams, G. B., & Balfour, D. L. (1998). *Unmasking administrative evil*. London: Sage.

Ahmetoglu, A., Swami, V., & Chamorro-Premuzic, T. (in press). The relationship between dimensions of love, personality, and relationship length. *Archives of Sexual Behavior*.

Allport, G. W. (1963). *Pattern and growth in personality*. New York: Holt, Rinehart & Winston.

Bakan, D. (1966). *The duality of human existence*. Chicago, IL: Rand-McNally.

Baumeister, R. F., & Leary, M. (1995). The need to belong: Desire for interpersonal attachments as a fundamental human motivation. *Psychological Bulletin, 117*, 497–529.

Boas, F. (1911). *The mind of primitive man*. New York: Macmillan.

Bowlby, J (1969). *Attachment: Attachment and loss* (Vol. 1). New York: Basic Books.

Boyd, R. (2006). The puzzle of human sociality. *Science, 314*, 1553.

Boyd, R. and Richerson, P. J. (2006). Culture and the evolution of the human social instincts. In S. Levinson and N. Enfield (Eds.), *Roots of human sociality* (pp. 143–162). Oxford: Berg.

Brown, D. J., & Keeping, L. M. (2005). Elaborating the construct of transformational leadership: The role of affect. *The Leadership Quarterly, 16*, 245–272.

Browning, C. (1989). The decision concerning the final solution. In F. Furet (Ed.), *Unanswered questions: Nazi Germany and the genocide of the Jews* (pp. 96–118). New York: Schocken.

Chamorro-Premuzic, T. (2007). *Personality and individual differences*. Oxford: Wiley-Blackwell.

Chamorro-Premuzic, T., & Furnham, A. (2006). Intellectual competence and the intelligent personality: A third way in differential psychology. *Review of General Psychology, 10*, 251–267.

Chamorro-Premuzic, T., & Furnham, A. (2010). *The psychology of personnel selection*. New York: Cambridge University Press.

Clark, G. (2007). *A farewell to arms: A brief economic history of the world*. Princeton, NJ: Princeton University Press.

Costa, P. T., Jr., & McCrae, R. R. (1992). *NEO PI–R and NEO–FFI professional manual*. Odessa, FL: Psychological Assessment Resources, Inc.

Darwin, C. (1871). *The descent of man and selection in relation to sex*. London: John Murray.

Devillier Donegan Enterprises (2004). *Medici: Godfathers of the Renaissance*. PBS television mini-series: Empires.

Diamond, J. (1992). *The third chimpanzee*. New York: HarperCollins.

Durkheim, E. (1960). The dualism of human nature and its social conditions [1914]. In E. Durkheim, *Emile Durkheim 1858–1917: A collection of essays with translations and biography* (pp. 206–221). Edited by K. H. Wolff. Columbus: Ohio State University Press.

Egan, V., & Hamilton, E. (2008). Personality, mating effort and alcohol-related violence expectancies. *Addiction Research and Theory, 16*, 369–381.

Erikson, E. H. (1950). *Childhood and society*. New York: W. W. Norton.

Ferguson, N. (2007). *War of the worlds*. London: Penguin.

Festinger, L. (1957). *A theory of cognitive dissonance*. Stanford, CA: Stanford University Press.

Freud, S. (1959). *Group psychology and the analysis of the ego* [1920]. New York: Norton.

Goodin, R. E., & Klingemann, H.-D. (1996). *A new handbook of political science*. Oxford and New York: Oxford University Press.

Gribben, J. (2002). *In search of Schrödinger's cat*. New York: Bantam.

Guisinger, S., & Blatt, S. J. (1994). Individuality and relatedness: Evolution of a fundamental dialectic. *American Psychologist, 49*, 104–111.

Hale, J. R. (1977). *Florence and the Medici: The pattern of control*. London: Thames & Hudson.

Hargreaves, A., & Fink, D. (2004). The seven principles of sustainable leadership. *Educational Leadership, 61*, 8–13.

Hibbert, C. (1999). *The house of Medici: Its rise and fall*. New York: Harper.

Holland, J. H. (1992). *Adaptation in natural and artificial systems*. Cambridge, MA: MIT Press.

Hogan, R. (1983). A socioanalytic theory of personality. In M. M. Page & R. Dienstbier (Eds.), *1982 Nebraska Symposium on Motivation*. Lincoln: University of Nebraska Press.

Hogan, R. (1996). A socioanalytic perspective on the five-factor model. In J. S. Wiggins (Ed.), *The five factor model of personality* (pp. 163–179). New York: Guilford Press.

Hogan, R. (2007). *Personality and the fate of organizations*. Mahwah, NJ: Lawrence Erlbaum Associates.

Hogan, R., & Ahmad, G. (2011: this volume). Leadership. In T. Chamorro-Premuzic, S. von Stumm, & A. Furnham (Eds.), *Handbook of individual differences*. Oxford: Wiley-Blackwell.

Hogan, R., & Hogan, J. (1991). Personality and status. In D. G. Gilbert & J. J Connolly (Eds.), *Personality, social skill, and psychology: An individual differences approach* (pp. 137–154). New York: Plenum Press.

Hogan, J., & Holland, B. (2003). Using theory to evaluate personality and job performance relations: A socioanalytic perspective. *Journal of Applied Psychology, 88*, 100–112.

Hogan, R., & Judge, T. (in press). Personality and leadership. In M. G. Rumsey (Ed.), *The many sides of leadership*. Oxford: Oxford University Press.

Hogan, R., & Kaiser, R. B. (2005). What we know about leadership. *Review of General Psychology, 9*, 169–180.

Hogan, R., Curphy, G. J., & Hogan, J. (1994). What we know about leadership. *American Psychologist, 49*, 493–504.

Holmes, T. H., & Rahe, R. H. (1967). The social readjustment rating scale. *Journal of Psychosomatic Research, 11,* 213–219.

James, W. (1890) *Principles of psychology.* New York: Holt.

Jardine, L. (2008). *Going Dutch: How England plundered Holland's glory.* New York: Harper.

Kaiser, R. B., Hogan, R., & Craig, S. B. (2008). Leadership and the fate of organizations. *American Psychologist, 63,* 96–110.

Kelly, E. L, & Conley, J. J. (1987). Personality and compatibility: A prospective analysis of marital stability and marital satisfaction. *Journal of Personality and Social Psychology, 52,* 27–40.

Koch, C. (2004). *The quest for consciousness: A neurobiological approach.* Englewood Cliffs, NJ: Roberts & Co.

Kohlberg, L. (1969). Stage and sequence: The cognitive developmental approach to socialization. In D. Goslin (Ed.), *Handbook of socialization theory and research* (pp. 347–380). Chicago, IL: Rand-McNally.

Kroeber, A. L. (1952). *The nature of culture.* Chicago, IL: University of Chicago Press.

Latane, B. (1981). The psychology of social impact. *American Psychologist, 36,* 343–365.

Lawrence, P. R., & Nohria, N. (2002). *Driven: How human nature shapes our choices.* San Francisco, CA: Jossey-Bass.

Le Bon, G. (1895). *La psychologie des foules.* Paris: Alcan.

Levine, R. A., & Campbell, D. T. (1972). *Ethnocentrism.* New York: Wiley.

London, M., & Smither, J. W. (1995). Can multi-source feedback change perceptions of goal accomplishment, self-evaluations, and performance-related outcomes? *Personnel Psychology, 48,* 803–839.

Magnusson, D., & Endler, N. S. (1976). *Personality at the crossroads: Current issues in interactional psychology.* Hillsdale, NJ: Lawrence Erlbaum Associates.

McAdams, D. P (1985). *Power, intimacy, and the life story: Personological inquiries into identity.* New York: Guilford Press.

McAdams, D. P., & Olson, B. D. (2010). Personality development: Continuity and change. *Annual Review of Psychology, 61,* 517–542.

McCauley, C. (1985). The nature of social influence in groupthink: Compliance and internalization. *Journal of Personality and Social Psychology, 57,* 250–260.

McClelland, D. C., Atkinson, J. W., Clark, R. A., & Lowell, E. L. (1953). *The achievement motive.* Princeton, NJ: Van Nostrand.

Mead, G. H. (1934). *Mind, self, and society.* Chicago, IL: University of Chicago Press.

Meredith, M. (2007). *Mugabe: Power, plunder, and the struggle for Zimbabwe's future.* New York: PublicAffairs.

Meyer, G. J., Finn, S. E., Eyde, L. D., Kay, G. G., Moreland, K. L., Dies, R. R., Eisman, E. J., Kubiszyn, T. W., & Reed, G. M. (2000). Psychological testing and psychological assessment: A review of evidence and issues. *American Psychologist, 56,* 128–165.

Milgram, S. (1974). *Obedience to authority.* New York: Harper & Row.

Mischel, W. (1968). *Personalitly and assessment.* New York: Wiley.

Mount, M. K., Barrick, M. R., & Strauss, J. P. (1994). Validity of observer ratings of the Big Five personality dimensions. *Journal of Applied Psychology, 79,* 272–280.

Neustadt, E., Chamorro-Premuzic, T., & Furnham, A. (2006). The relationship between personality traits, self-esteem, and attachment at work. *Journal of Individual Differences, 27,* 208–217.

Norbeck, E. (1974). *Religion in human life.* New York: Holt.

Pavot, B., & Diener, E. (2011: this volume). Personality and happiness: Predicting the experience of subjective well-being. In T. Chamorro-Premuzic, S. von Stumm, & A. Furnham (Eds.), *Handbook of individual differences.* Oxford: Wiley-Blackwell.

Peters, R. S. (1958). *The concept of motivation*. London: Routledge & Kegan Paul.

Petrides, K. V. (2011: this volume). Trait emotional intelligence. In T. Chamorro-Premuzic, S. von Stumm, & A. Furnham (Eds.), *Handbook of individual differences*. Oxford: Wiley-Blackwell.

Piaget, J., and Inhelder, B. (1962). *The psychology of the child*. New York: Basic Books.

Pinker, S. (1997). *How the mind works*. New York: Norton.

Pinker, S. (2002). *The blank slate*. London: Penguin Classics.

Plomin, R., DeFries, J. C., McClearn, G. E., & McGuffin, P. (2008). *Behavioral genetics* (5th ed.). New York: Worth.

Richerson, P. J., & Boyd, R. (2006). *Not by genes alone: How culture transformed human evolution*. Chicago, IL: Chicago University Press.

Ridley, M. (1997). *The origins of virtue*. London: Penguin.

Roberts, B. W., & Bogg, T. (2004). A 30-year longitudinal study of the relationships between conscientiousness-related traits, and the family structure and health-behavior factors that affect health. *Journal of Personality, 72*, 325–354.

Roberts, B. W., Kuncel, N. R., Shiner, R., Caspi, A., & Goldberg, L. R. (2007). The power of personality: The comparative validity of personality traits, socioeconomic status, and cognitive ability for predicting important life outcomes. *Perspectives on Psychological Science, 2*, 313–345.

Ross, L., & Nisbett, R. E. (1991). *The person and the situation: Perspectives on social psychology*. New York, McGraw-Hill.

Rummel, R. J. (1994). *Death by government*. New Brusnwick, NJ: Transaction.

Seligman, M. E. P. (1975). *Helplessness*. San Francisco, CA: W. H. Freeman.

Seligman, M. E. P., & Csikszentmihalyi, M. (2000). Positive psychology. An introduction. *American Psychologist, 55*, 5–14.

Smith, A. (1991). *The wealth of nations* [1776]. New York: Prometheus Books.

Soros, G. (1994). *The alchemy of finance: Reading the mind of the market*. New York: Wiley.

Spencer, H. (1896). *The study of sociology*. New York: D. Appleton.

Turchin, P. (2003). *Historical dynamics: Why states rise and fall*. Princeton, NJ: Princeton University Press.

Tryon, R. C. (1942). Individual differences. In F. A. Moss (Ed.), *Comparative psychology* (rev. ed., pp. 330–365). New York: Prentice-Hall.

Von Stumm, S., Chamorro-Premuzic, T., & Ackerman, P. L. (2011: this volume). Re-visiting intelligence–personality associations. In T. Chamorro-Premuzic, S. von Stumm, & A. Furnham (Eds.), *Handbook of individual differences*. Oxford: Wiley-Blackwell.

Wade, N. (2009). *The faith instinct: How religion evolved and why it endures*. New York: Penguin.

Weber, M. (1905). *The Protestant work ethic and the spirit of capitalism*. London: Unwin Hyman.

Wiggins, J. S. (1996). *The five-factor model of personality: Theoretical perspectives*. New York: Guilford Press.

Wilson, D. S., & Wilson, E. O. (2008). Evolution: for the good of the group. *American Scientist, 98*, 380–389.

Wilson, E. O. (1978). *On human nature*. Cambridge, MA: Harvard University Press.

Wilson, E. O., & Wilson, D. S. (2007). Rethinking the theoretical foundation of sociobiology. *The Quarterly Review of Biology, 82*, 327–48.

Zimbardo, P. (2007). *The Lucifer effect*. New York: Random House.

# 19

# Individual Differences and Antisocial Behavior

## Vincent Egan

## 1   Introduction

Misconduct in the workplace (Roberts, Harms, Caspi, & Moffitt, 2007), carrying weapons and violently assaulting someone who "disrespects" you (Barlas & Egan, 2006), sexual deviance (Egan, Kavanagh, & Blair, 2005), and being more likely to shoplift (Egan & Taylor, 2010) all reflect the actions of the same few personality traits, as individual differences in personality and intelligence saturate human behavior. These qualities are based on biological, heritable, and information-processing mechanisms covered elsewhere in this volume. Learned, sociological, and demographic influences also influence antisocial behavior, sometimes substantially—but rarely in the gross sense that crude nativists would imply, as nurture works through nature. Thus it is that a person's entertainment preferences (which, for some, are graphic and grotesque) are of no genuine forensic or clinical significance—unless considered in the context of that person's underlying disposition (Charles & Egan, 2009; Egan & Campbell, 2009). The current chapter discusses the influence of personality and intelligence on antisocial behavior.

"Antisocial" is not always "criminal," and criminal law is sometimes at variance with what is seen as antisocial. Thus rape was not a criminal offense in Haiti until 2005 (BBC News Website, 2005), whereas under Sharia law infidelity may lead to execution rather than simply to social disapproval. There are no laws against drink-driving in Ethiopia, Vietnam, or the Congo. It may seem odd to use a phrase such as "social construction" in a volume like the one you are currently reading, but the phrase is apposite, given global variations in criminal law. Nevertheless, if one considers generally acceptable and unacceptable social behavior, local cultural variations are roundly outweighed by human universals (Brown, 2000). Universals associated with antisocial behavior include rulings against breaching property rights, violence, rape,

*The Wiley-Blackwell Handbook of Individual Differences*, First Edition.
Edited by Tomas Chamorro-Premuzic, Sophie von Stumm, and Adrian Furnham.
© 2011 Blackwell Publishing Ltd. Published 2011 by Blackwell Publishing Ltd.

and murder; imposing communally generated punishments; and efforts to inhibit gratuitous physical and verbal conflict. Transgressing universal behavioral norms in the domestic sphere typically generates animosity and retaliation. Likewise, globally, the breaching of exclusive sexual pair-bonds once agreed upon between the parties and the maltreatment of children provoke animosity and admonishment.

Criminal and antisocial activities clearly have a substantial environmental component; if one is poor, the struggle for survival will be greater, and this may require at the very minimum some ethical flexibility. The social demographics of offending are blunt; young, poor, minority, and uneducated males are by far the persons most likely to offend (though most people in all of these categories are not offenders). A sociologist or a criminologist may see these gross demographic trends as being themselves the final explanation of offending (or, less helpfully, argues that the classifications or the crimes in the statistic are somehow flawed, so the very observation of the trends is spurious). But not all sociological work dismisses the real experience of crime and its ethnographic context. One plausible sociological construct is community cohesion. A city-wide study of Chicago suggested that pro-social community cohesion reduced street violence, and that areas with concentrated disadvantage and household instability can become less violent if the communal efficacy is raised in the region (Sampson, Raudenbush, & Earls, 1997). This is a practical study, which prompts ideas by which one might seek to raise the quality of urban communal life and reduce street violence. Nevertheless, the study did not consider psychological differences influencing the individuals that make up the social groups. Again, using Chicago as a natural experiment, Gibson, Sullivan, Jones, and Piquero (2010) examined reported effects of the neighborhood on children's self-control and found (1) that variation in self-control between communities explained little of the total variance, once individual levels of self-control were considered; and (2) that neighborhood structural characteristics had few direct effects on self-control relative to parenting competency. There are other individual–environment interaction effects; impulsivity is a stronger predictor of antisocial behavior in poorer communities than in more affluent contexts (Lynam et al., 2000). It thus seems that acknowledging and incorporating individual differences sharpens sociological observations. The current chapter will focus on the mediating role individual differences have on antisocial behavior.

## 2  Genetics, Crime, and Antisocial Behavior

A small number of individuals (typically 6 percent) are responsible for a large number of offenses, and this remains the case even within criminal cohorts (Farrington, Barnes, & Lambert, 1996). Antisocial contagion is often used to explain such effects, as an offender may have parents or siblings and half-siblings who also have criminal histories, and who may act as criminal role-models. The intergenerational transmission and continuity of antisocial behavior may occur via exposure to multiple social risk factors, associated with cycles of deprivation; or via differential association (where one allegedly learns to be antisocial due to reinforcing cues in the environment) and environmental contagion. Though both constructs are sometimes seen as sociological, these processes can be equally seen as indirectly heritable (Blazei, Iacono, &

Krueger, 2006). Heritability may occur through a quite straightforward process—for example phenotypic assortative mating, whereby a person with antisocial elements in his or her disposition forms a relationship with another antisocial person, potentially passing on genes associated with these antisocial tendencies to any resulting offspring. Though the assortative mating is often low for personality, it is higher for intelligence (van Leeuwen, van den Berg, & Boomsma, 2008), and substantial for antisocial behavior (Krueger, Moffitt, Caspi, Bleske, & Silva, 1998).

Behavior geneticists use A (additive genetic influences), C (common shared environment), and E (unique individual environment)—or ACE—models to analyse how genetics and environmental influences express themselves within the individual. There is a wealth of evidence for strong A and E effects in antisocial and criminal populations. Miles and Carey (1997) found large A and E effects for human aggression, but rather more substantial was Rhee and Waldman's (2002) meta-analysis of 51 twin and adoption studies. The best fitting ACE model found that additive genetic influence explained 32 percent of observed antisocial variance, non-additive genetic influences (where genes interact with each other) explained 9 percent, shared environmental influences accounted for 16 percent, and non-shared environmental influences explained 43 percent of variation in antisocial behavior. These proportions can be seen in both genders, although developmentally males are more vulnerable to environmental antisocial influences than females are, and there are differential genetic effects over time, heritable influences becoming stronger with age (Bergen, Gardner, & Kendler, 2007; Jacobson, Prescott, & Kendler, 2002).

Findings from ACE models of the behavioral genetics underlying antisocial behavior thus show that, though antisocial behavior is substantially heritable, the third law of behavioral genetics—that idiosyncratic experience is more important than shared experience—is also important. Almost half of the influences on aggression and other antisocial behaviors reflect unique experiences, which can include biological and social accidents, peer-related forces, sibling effects, individual disposition and choice, parent–child interaction effects, and downright bloody bad luck. Despite a substantial heritable dimension, there is ample room for psychological processes and interventions to be considered when researching or managing antisocial behavior.

# 3   Why *Is* Antisocial Behavior Heritable?

It is unlikely that there are exact genes for hitting people or stealing. But Malouff, Rooke, and Schutte (2008) observe unambiguous evidence for the heritability of genetic precursors to antisocial acts. For example, attention deficit hyperactivity disorder (ADHD) and related developmental difficulties are very common precursors to antisocial activity in young people and adults, and are themselves highly heritable (McLoughlin, Ronald, Kuntsi, Asherson, & Plomin, 2007); low intelligence (as covered in Section 7 of this chapter and in related chapters within this volume) is also heritable (Deary, Spinath, & Bates, 2006), as is a general vulnerability to addiction (Uhla et al., 2006). Addiction can be seen as an extreme of human pharmacophagy, as many recreational substances (including nicotine, betel nut, and tetrahydrocannabinol, which is the psychoactive part of cannabis) help the body to expel parasitic worms (Hagen et al., 2009). Individuals who lack a gene for liver enzymes to neutralize plant toxins (the cytochrome P450 system) may be more inclined to consume substances with effects that others find aversive. Once a psychoactive substance is beyond the barrier for physical rejection and has entered the central nervous system, effects that others experience as aversive may become pleasurable for the individuals in question; and, if something is overwhelmingly reinforcing, it may create chronic appetitive behavior (Sullivan, Hagen, & Hammerstein, 2008). A candidate gene for the transmission of antisocial behavior—there are doubtlessly dozens, though all need replicable associations—is DRD2, which is associated with substance misuse, criminal offending, and developmental behavioral disorders. Persons with polymorphisms of this gene (which means that the gene is not present in their DNA as a random error) who also have a criminal father are differentially more likely to be involved in serious violent delinquency longitudinally, and to also have a greater number of general convictions (Delisi, Beaver, Vaughn, & Wright, 2009).

Duntley and Shakelford (2008) distinguish ultimate and proximal causes of behavior, proximal causes being recent triggers for the act, whereas ultimate causes project causality back further. Modern civilized society's laws, equal rights, and technology are historically very recent, as recorded human history covers only about 5 percent of the time since *Homo sapiens* has existed. The adaptations that *Homo sapiens* made over the previously unrecorded 195,000 years are deep within us, and the mechanisms that evolved to help us survive in the ancestral environment remain, although the environment we now live within has radically changed (Pinker, 2002). In the ancient ancestral environment, persons who were resilient, strong, and opportunistic may have been advantaged relative to persons with surplus cognition, as a quicker recourse to fighting and copulation may well have proved advantageous in the struggle for survival. The term "crime" is inherently moral; and, outside of a socially constructed system of values (albeit one that has its roots in the survival of the group, and thus of the species and, ultimately, of the gene), an unsanctioned act is not a "crime," as much as an alternative way of surviving by acquiring the desired material, social, and sexual resources, or by asserting the need to maintain one's status (Rowe, 2002). Within this adaptive model of antisocial acts, aggression and violence are morally neutral, as the aggression used to harm an individual might be equally used to harm persons who threaten the cohesion and integrity of social rules, aiding the equilibrium, and even the survival of the community (Buss & Shackelford, 1997). Bioarchaeology shows interpersonal violence is a human constant and that, if anything, the contemporary world is rather less violent than antiquity (Eisner, 2001; Walker, 2001).

Not all persons have the competency to acquire survival resources through socially acceptable means, which may reflect the rise of standards in civilization that favor a more agreeable personality and higher intelligence. Persons who lack these qualities could be said to be disadvantaged in the competition for such resources, so may need to resort to a different set of behavioral strategies. Such strategies—force, cheating, stealing, fraudulent charm—may be unacceptable now, but they were unavoidable, socially acceptable, or tolerated in the past. Thus it is that competitively disadvantaged males are more likely to commit crimes (Mealey, 1995; Rowe 2002; Rowe, Vazsonyi, & Figueredo, 1997). Finlayson (2009) has observed that the pressures that have shaped us over millennia continue, and that civilizations rise and fall; in the event of societal collapse and global disaster, persons who are more aggressive, opportunistic, and promiscuous would be very effective at surviving unpredictable and dangerous environments—as has always been the case. These qualities are within all of us, otherwise our ancestors would never have had opportunities to pass on their genes to the next generation.

## 4   Possible Mechanisms for Antisocial Behavior

It is no longer sufficient to say that a particular phenotype is heritable. The question is now shifting to a much more complex issue: What is the mechanism? If we accept that antisocial behavior may be in many ways "normal," but is only now regarded as generally unacceptable, and that genetic coding causes propensities to impulsivity (observed in children and young adults with ADHD, oppositional–defiant disorder, or child conduct disorder) in persons who are often of lower IQ (thus poorer at problem-solving and at acquiring the educational attainment that is the modern world's entry ticket to success), it is easy to see how an environment of aggregated disfranchisement can lead to self-expression through criminal acts, which are designed to help the perpetrators obtain what other people appear to get apparently effortlessly. There is a variety of possible biological mechanisms known to reflect individual differences, which have been advanced as specific mechanisms underlying antisocial behavior.

### 4.1   Sex hormones

Though in non-human animals the relationship between testosterone and aggression is well established, the effect–size association for humans is surprisingly modest. It is intuitively attractive to think that sex hormones (androgens) drive to aggression by masculinizing the body and the brain. Ellis, Das, and Buker (2008) examined self-reported criminality and androgen-promoted physiological characteristics in a student sample and found that self-reported violence was associated with more masculine mannerisms, body appearance, physical strength, intensity of sex drive, voice depth, upper body strength, lower body strength, and amount of body hair; for males, self-reported penis size was found to be positively correlated with criminality. While it is the case that castration reduces sexual aggression in hamsters, the same drastic surgery does not appear to deter human sexual aggression. The loss of the testes may reduce sexual desire in men, but sexual desire is also cognitive, so men who have had prostate surgery or testicular cancer and subsequent orchiectomy are still able to have penile erections (Weinberger, Sreenivasan, Garrick, & Osran, 2005). A meta-analysis of the relationship between testosterone and aggression, by using 45 independent studies (a total $N = 9,760$), identified associations which ranged from $-.28$ (less testosterone means *more* aggression) to .71 (as testosterone increases, so does aggression). The mean weighted correlation across studies was .14 (later corrected to 0.08; Archer, Graham-Kevan & Davies, 2005), indicating a weak positive relationship between the two constructs. This association was stronger in adolescent boys and younger males, which suggests that the early flood of testosterone associated with puberty and young manhood either reduces with maturation, or is adapted to (Book, Starzyk & Quinsey, 2001). Females also show a peak of offending in early puberty, when they experience a rush of female-specific sex hormones and testosterone (Najman et al., 2009).

## 4.2 Neurocognitive processes

Modern cognitive neuroscience takes converging lines of evidence in its thinking about antisocial behavior. Such lines are: the heritability of offending and psychopathology; the typical neurodevelopmental patterns shown in serious offenders and manifest in their childhood histories (e.g. ADHD, child conduct disorder, and oppositional–defiant disorder); and, for some, specific information-processing impairments, which reflect dysfunctional neural circuits (Blair, Mitchell, & Blair, 2005). Autonomic functions control our automatic bodily responses, and it has been observed that some offenders literally fail to learn from their own mistakes, perhaps because they do not feel frightened when they do something exciting or dangerous, which others would find physically too uncomfortable to persevere with. One theory is that non-offenders may have a "somatic marker," which inhibits them from behaving in some ways and which offenders lack (Damasio, Everitt, & Bishop, 1996). This finding explains why offenders and risk-takers are routinely found to score higher in sensation-seeking.

If the somatic marker hypothesis is true, it should be evident in the very learning of unconscious associations. True psychopaths are persons who present us with a combination of antisocial behavior and lifestyle and an unpleasant, interpersonally manipulative, and emotionally cold personality (Vitacco, Neumann, & Jackson, 2005). Flor, Birbaumer, Hermann, Ziegler, and Patrick (2002) examined differential aversive classical conditioning in psychopaths, non-criminal psychopaths, and matched controls, acquiring a brain-evoked potential (that is, the response of the brain to the task, and an indication of normal information processing) as the subjects performed their task. Control participants had significant positive and negative conditioned stimulus differentiation, whereas psychopaths did not, while the unconditioned responses were comparable between groups. The evoked potentials for the conditioned stimuli revealed that psychopaths were processing the task itself normally. These results show that the deficit in association formation for psychopathic persons is possibly related to abnormalities in links between limbic–subcortical and cortical structures that form associations related to punishment.

## 5 Biopsychosocial Processes

As life is lived, there is a constant transaction between biological, psychological, and social processes, and at different times the emphasis may lie with some particular influences over others. However, all influences are compounded. Rather than dismissing this complex process as impossible to investigate, researchers using longitudinal designs have explored the dynamic biopsychosocial model that reflects the reality of existence. For example, Raine, Brennan, Mednick, and Mednick (1996) examined obstetric, neuromotor, social, and behavioral measures taken for 397 men between

1 and 22 years of age, coding these people for obstetric-, poverty-, and both obstetric- and poverty-related concerns. Persons with combined difficulties had twice the violence and theft rates found in the other groups, they encountered more behavioral and academic problems in adolescence, and they committed over 70 percent of all the crimes recorded in the sample.

How can biological influences such as genetic factors and neurotransmitters interact with psychosocial factors from the environment and give rise to variations in behavioral responses? The enzyme known as monoamine oxidase A (MAO–A) metabolizes transmitters such as dopamine, noradrenalin, and serotonin. When MAO–A is lowered in cloned mice, it makes them more aggressive. Humans missing this gene are more antisocial. Maltreatment often brings out aggression in persons, and antisocial persons often come from homes and environments where they may have experienced physical, emotional, or sexual abuse. Child sexual abuse covers a wide variety of offenses, ranging from the hands-off and remote to the hands-on and penetrative, and this is perhaps why generic descriptions of "abuse" are more weakly associated with later adjustment problems in the general population than one would perhaps expect (Tromovitch & Rind, 2008). Some people are profoundly harmed by the experience, and the same is true for other kinds of abuse. Caspi et al. (2002) followed 1,037 people from birth to 26 years of age, recording details of their known personal, medical, and criminal histories, along with how strongly MAO–A was expressed in their brain chemistry. Maltreated children with high levels of the gene for metabolizing MAO–A were nine times less likely to commit a violent crime than peers who had a low level of this gene. This finding does not negate the influence of abuse on an individual's later behavior so much as it emphasizes how critical it is to protect individuals from harm, as some are particularly badly affected by such experiences. An even larger study found that physical maltreatment increases risk of conduct problems by 24 percent for those at high genetic risk, compared to 2 percent for those at low genetic risk (Jaffee et al., 2005). Lastly, general family dysfunction also interacts with genetic influences to predict antisocial behavior; a large twin study of family environment and conduct problems found effects associated with genes, the environment, and the combination of these factors; persons with the risk genotype had a greater susceptibility to family dysfunction, and this best predicted later expression of antisocial behavior (Button, Scourfield, Martin, Purcell, & McGuffin, 2005).

This section of the chapter has presented a strong argument for the importance of biological influences on antisocial behavior, detailing genetic and neurological influences that drive the behavior and how these influences appear to interface with more psychological processes. Times have changed, and contemporary individual differences psychologists do not proclaim that all antisocial behavior is "biologically determined"—not that they ever did; earlier work was selectively and mendaciously read to produce a rhetorical travesty of what was really meant. That said, biological influences on behavior are very important, and certainly not to be dismissed. If one knows what is genuinely changeable and what influences can effect that change, appropriate interventions can be implemented. Acknowledging evolutionary, genetic, neurophysiological, and neurochemical influences on behavior and analyzing how these can be expressed in biopsychosocial development allows a better understanding of antisocial and criminal behavior. It is not nature versus nurture; it is nature AND nurture.

## 6  Personality and Antisocial Behavior

This volume provides a number of chapters covering the theory and basic science associated with personality, and how the literature has settled on the overarching dominance of, initially, Hans Eysenck's "Gigantic Three" of psychoticism (P), extraversion (E), and neuroticism (N) (Eysenck & Eysenck, 1985), and later Costa and McCrae's five-factor model (FFM, sometimes called the "Big Five," though Fiske 1949 is currently thought to be the first recent scholar to document the consistency of a five-factor structure for personality ratings across a variety of sources and methods). The FFM comprises five trait domains: the foregoing N and E, to which are added openness (O), agreeableness (A), and conscientiousness (C). Each dimension has sub-scales (facet scores) within the overall construct. The FFM can be assessed using the 240-item NEO–Personality Inventory (NEO–PI) (Costa & McCrae, 1992), or a shorter, facet-score free 60-item NEO–Five-Factor Inventory (NEO–FFI) (Costa & McCrae, 1992). To overcome problems of dimensional correlation between ostensibly orthogonal dimensions (Egan, Deary, & Austin, 2000), a slight revision of the NEO–FFI has been proposed (McCrae & Costa, 2004). Another way to measure the FFM is to use instruments produced by the International Personality Item Project, an Internet-based public domain family of Big-Five measures (Goldberg et al., 2006). Both systems capture aspects of personality associated with antisocial behavior.

### 6.1  Psychoticism

Structural models of personality such as the PEN and FFM have dimensions associated with antisocial acts. Through factor-analytic work on the personality of offenders and psychiatric probands, Hans and Sybil Eysenck proposed the concept of "psychoticism," P—tough-mindedness, hostility, aggression, coldness, egocentricity, impulsivity, and low empathy (Eysenck & Eysenck, 1976). P associated with broad-spectrum psychopathology of many kinds, and proved to be a more productive adjunct to explaining criminality than Eysenck's early theory that criminals were extraverted, which was revised when impulsivity ceased to be seen as a facet of E and more as an intermediate construct between P and N (Gudjonsson, 1997). Once impulsivity was removed from measures of E, criminals were found to be typically low in E—introverts. There has never been any confusion over the level of N in the antisocial; barring primary psychopaths, antisocial persons tend to be high in N and thus prone to variable and labile moods (which perhaps also accounts for the frequency of both mild and serious mental disorders in such persons).

Antisocial behavior has a particularly strong relationship with Eysenck's P (Miller & Lynam, 2001). Meta-analysis of Eysenck's PEN model in relation to antisocial behavior, involving 52 studies and 97 samples and using from 14,468 to 15,403 persons per dimension (Cale, 2006), found that P (reconstrued as impulsivity/ disinhibition) strongly linked to antisocial behavior (weighted mean effect size = .39, 95 percent confidence interval (CI) = .35 to .42). N also linked to it, but less so (weighted mean effect size = .19, 95 percent CI = .15 to .23). E's link to antisocial behavior was relatively minor (weighted mean effect size = .09, 95 percent CI = .06

to 0.12). Age was a moderating influence on these associations, whereas gender was not. This work strongly suggests that the optimal strategy for understanding how personality relates to antisocial behavior is to focus on P (or P-like constructs) and on N. The reason why P might be thought to be so overwhelmingly influential on antisocial behavior is that it is autocatalytic (in other words a reaction product of P can be a catalyst for a P-type reaction); in sum, P is a disposition which provokes interpersonal difficulties. For example persons who are higher in P are verbally more aggressive, argumentative, and inappropriately assertive in interpersonal communication (McCroskey, Heisel, & Richmond, 2001). Persons high in P are more likely to accept the use of violence in conflict resolution (Zillman & Weaver, 1997). There is also an interaction (both physiological and emerging from self-report) between P and sexual depictions for arousal, high-P men being more aroused by depictions of rape and less aroused by depictions of consensual sex, whereas the reverse is the case for men who are low in P (Barnes, Malamuth, & Check, 1984). Finally, difficulties with personal space cause more difficulties for low-IQ/high-P violent prisoners than for higher-IQ, lower-P non-violent prisoners (Eastwood, 1985). Persons high in P thus cause and provoke conflict.

Given these substantive effects and strong illustrative examples of how P is able to effectively predict antisocial behavior, why has P been perhaps less influential than it should be? There is a number of reasons, some conceptual, some practical. First, the very term "psychoticism" could be seen as a provocation, which explicitly (and perhaps intentionally) creates a confusion between persons who are suffering from psychosis, the sane but behaviorally disordered, and the immature and temporarily socially unconventional (see Charles & Egan, 2008). A more pragmatic concern is that P scales have lower internal reliability than the E and N dimensions, which are massively stable and valid; this limits the accuracy and replicability of P measurement (Caruso, Witkiewitz, Belcourt-Dittloff, & Gottlieb, 2001). Perhaps accurately (should one be familiar with the grotesque and sensationalist creations of UK artists Jake and Dinos Chapman), art students were found to score more highly on P than prisoners or the mentally disordered (Woody & Claridge, 1977); however, this implies that P captures qualities other than simply being antisocial, for example being audaciously creative (or, to the more sensitive eye, oblique and bizarre), as developed in Eysenck's theory of creativity and genius (Eysenck, 1995). Lastly, Eysenck declared that his dimensions were fundamental dimensions from which other emergent traits emerged, rather than the reverse. However, when having to explain why in his model the combination of low A and low C produced P rather than the reverse, he conceded that perhaps P was a higher-order construct, emerging from lower dimensions—so P was not a basic trait, like E and N (Eysenck, 1992a, 1992b).

## 6.2   The five-factor model

With the emergence of the FFM, the PEN model has gradually declined in influence, perhaps because of the problems with P described above. Heaven (1996) ran an early study examining the relationship between the Big-Five personality dimensions and self-reported delinquency, and his findings exemplify general findings in the field; delinquents are lower in A and C, and those higher in N report more violence, vandalism, and theft. Lower-A facet scores for trust, altruism, and compliance, together with greater excitement-seeking (within the E facet), predict violence, whereas vandalism and theft are predicted by lower trust and altruism (A facets), greater excitement-seeking (an E facet), and lower self-discipline (a C facet). The axiomatic influence of low A on antisocial behavior was reiterated in Miller, Lynam, and Leukefeld's (2003) study of the relationship between the FFM and antisocial activities committed by 481 individuals living in the community. As might by now be becoming familiar, N, A, and C predicted the stability, variety, and onset of conduct problems, aggression, and signs of antisocial personality disorder, low A being most consistently related to all five antisocial and aggressive outcomes, and N, A, and C facets adding significant contributions to predicting outcome, in particular low straightforwardness and compliance (A facets), and low deliberation (a C facet).

One important aspect of applied trait psychology is the degree to which personality at an earlier point predicts behavior at a later one. Samuels et al. (2004) presented the results on 611 participants from the US, initially assessed in 1981 and followed for up to 12 to 18 years. All participants were assessed for DSM–IV personality disorders, completed the full NEO–PI–R, and had their scores related to official criminal records. The most frequent personality disorders within the cohort were antisocial personality disorder, paranoid personality disorder, borderline personality disorder, and narcissistic personality disorder—in other words most of the more dramatic personality disorders presented in DSM (cluster B), and the ones most commonly seen in offenders. They found that the persons who had been arrested more frequently were high on the N facets of angry hostility, depression, and impulsiveness. Non-offenders were higher on the warmth facet of E, whereas offenders were higher on the excitement-seeking facet of E. Persons who had been arrested were lower in the A facets of trust, straightforwardness, compliance, and modesty. Violent arrestees were less gregarious (E) and less open to feelings (O). Lastly, offenders were lower in C facets like competence, dutifulness, and deliberation. O was not associated with either offending or non-offending. Overall, personality had an effect size of .5 for predicting offending, and this effect was not attributable to age, sex, race, substance misuse, or a diagnosis of personality disorder.

## 6.3   Personality and aggression

Of perennial interest in the forensic field is the degree to which personality traits predict aggression, as aggression itself reflects a variety of expressions and triggers. Aggression can be seen in acts ranging from an actual physical assault through to a verbal one, a (possibly) provoked tirade, or simple antagonism, not so much expressed as felt. Alcohol is sometimes seen as a trigger to hostility, but alcohol-related violence is very much moderated by personality (Holcomb & Adams, 1985), and alcohol–violence expectancies are, inevitably, correlated with lower A and C scores (Egan & Hamilton, 2008). A way to think about the relationship between personality and aggression is documented in the pooling of three data sets collected from members of the general British public, all of whom completed the Buss–Perry

Aggression Questionnaire (BPAQ; Buss & Perry, 1992) along with the NEO–FFI–R
(ibid.). The sample comprised 603 individuals (M: F = 267: 335, mean age 35.4
years, SD = 12.2); means, standard deviations, and reliabilities of the measures are
presented in Table 19.1, and all are highly satisfactory. With so many participants in
a study of this kind, almost any correlation is going to be significant, so the size of
the coefficient and the effect size it represents become important. Table 19.2 presents
simple correlations between the two measures and indicates that, although lower A
has a strong and systematic association with greater aggression (however defined),
there are trace influences of other dimensions on the construct. (A separate analysis
including age found significant but minor associations in the region of .10.)

A factor analysis of the scales clarifies aggression–personality associations (Table
19.3). To overcome the possibility of spurious factors being generated due to the
number of participants and variables, a parallel analysis was run, which suggested that
only factors with eigenvalues of 1.19 or above should be retained. Factor analysis of
the nine measures produced a Kaiser–Meyer–Olkin (KMO) sampling adequacy of .74
(P < .001), supporting the use of factor analysis; three factors were produced,

Table 19.1    Means, standard deviations, and reliability of personality and aggression
measures

|  | Mean | SD | Alpha reliability |
|---|---|---|---|
| Buss–Perry Aggression Questionnaire |  |  |  |
| Physical aggression | 14.8 | 7.7 | 0.81 |
| Verbal aggression | 12.3 | 4.8 | 0.72 |
| Anger | 11.1 | 5.5 | 0.80 |
| Hostility | 14.7 | 6.9 | 0.82 |
| NEO–FFI–R |  |  |  |
| Neuroticism | 34.3 | 8.0 | 0.84 |
| Extraversion | 42.5 | 6.3 | 0.78 |
| Openness | 42.0 | 6.7 | 0.78 |
| Agreeableness | 44.1 | 6.2 | 0.77 |
| Conscientiousness | 43.7 | 5.9 | 0.75 |

Table 19.2    Correlations between the BPAQ and the NEO–FFI–R ($N = 603$)

|  | Physical aggression | Verbal aggression | Anger | Hostility |
|---|---|---|---|---|
| Neuroticism | 0.10[a] | 0.07 | 0.29[a] | 0.42[a] |
| Extraversion | 0.05 | 0.07 | 0.02 | −0.20[a] |
| Openness | 0.02 | 0.10[a] | 0.08[b] | −0.03 |
| Agreeableness | −0.52[a] | −0.49[a] | −0.45[a] | −0.38[a] |
| Conscientiousness | −0.19[a] | −0.07 | −0.16[a] | −0.13[a] |

[a] P < .001 (one-tailed).
[b] P < .01.

**Table 19.3** Factor analysis on BPAQ and NEO–FFI–R. Oblique (and varimax) scale loadings

|  | *F1* | *F2* |
| --- | --- | --- |
| Verbal aggression | 0.86 (0.85) |  |
| Anger | 0.71 (0.82) |  |
| Physical aggression | 0.82 (0.82) |  |
| Hostility | 0.74 (0.71) | −0.42[a] |
| Agreeableness | −0.71 (−0.71) |  |
| Neuroticism |  | −0.76 (−0.77) |
| Extraversion |  | 0.73 (0.73) |
| Conscientiousness |  | 0.67 (0.66) |
| Openness |  |  |

[a] Variable just below 0.40 loading criterion for varimax rotation.

explaining 66 percent of the observed variance, though one factor was below the criterion set by the parallel analysis. The two retained factors had eigenvalues of 3.13 and 1.72 and explained 34 and 19 percent variance respectively. Though subject to oblique and varimax solutions, very similar solutions were presented, and only loadings of .4 or above were considered, in order to ensure a conservative interpretation.

All the aggression scales loaded on a single factor, upon which A was negatively loaded, at − .71. There was a split loading for the hostility sub-scale of the BPAQ, which also loaded on a personality super-factor comprising low N, high E, and high C (Table 19.3). There is some debate within current individual differences research as to whether there is a general factor of personality, such that the Big Five or the Gigantic Three (Eysenck's PEN) are underpinned by just one dimension (Rushton & Irwing, 2011: this volume). Some think that this hypothesized dimension is an example of the "over-inclusive one" and a consequence of measurement artifact (Ferguson, Chamorro-Premuzic, Pickering, & Weiss, 2011: this volume). One way to test matters in this regard is to run a structural equation model (SEM) that can accommodate this shared variance and more closely examine the relationship between specific and general latent aggression (Figure 19.1).

Figure 19.1 shows significant ($P < .001$) standardized regression weights for the measured variables in the model. Other personality dimensions have rather smaller associations, which contribute negligibly to the overall understanding of the model. The general aggression factor presented in Table 19.3 quite easily became a latent aggression factor. The A dimension had a strong direct relationship to general aggression, and a specific relationship to physical aggression that no other dimension of personality had. Though C contributed nothing of significance to the model, higher N and lower E had unique associations with the specific measures of anger and hostility, but no association with the general latent aggression factor. These results show direct aggression to be overwhelmingly related to low A, whereas anger and antagonism reflect a conflux of high N and low E, as well as general aggressiveness. These results confirm that aggression and the basis of aggression are best differentiated into affective and predatory forms of expression (McEllistrem, 2004).

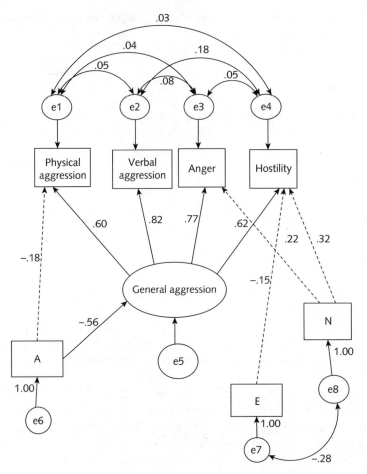

**Figure 19.1**  SEM fitting NEO–FFI–R data to BPAQ aggression. Squares represent measured variables, circles, error variance, and the large ellipse, a latent variable. Double-headed arrows represent covarying variables. Solid line reflects a significant relationship between the construct and the latent variable; dashed lines, significant direct relationships between measured variables other than explained by the latent construct. All regression coefficient weights are standardised and P < .001. Overall $\chi^2$ (10) = 44.5, P < .001, CMIN = 4.45, GFI = .98

## 6.4  Personality and its disorders

Personality disorders are in some ways the psychiatric expression of extremes of normal personality, and they are defined by clinical practitioners using either the American Psychiatric Association's (APA) DSM–IV, or the World Health Organization's ICD–10 (APA, 1994; WHO, 2007). Medicine derives from a differ-ent set of intellectual traditions from those of experimental and academic psychology, and it is only recently that the dimensional (rather than categorical) approach to personality has been embraced for clinical diagnosis (Widiger & Mullins-Sweatt, 2009). Although DSM–IV classifies the 10 currently recognized personality disorders into "odd," "dramatic," and "neurotic" disorders, it is the dramatic "externalizing" personality disorders (the borderline, histrionic, antisocial, and narcissistic personality disorders) that are disproportionately associated with aggression, violence, and other antisocial behaviors (Costa & Widiger, 2003; Egan & Lewis, 2011). In the UK, if you are unfortunate enough to be assaulted, there is a 50 percent chance of this being done by a person who is both drunk and diagnosed with a personality disorder: antisocial personality disorder if the assailant is male, borderline personality disorder if the assailant is female (Coid et al., 2006; Fazel & Danesh, 2002).

Comorbidity of personality disorders is the norm, and formal analyses of personality disorder ratings find that four factors ("the 4 As") rather than three ad hoc classifications best explain most of the variance shared between the 10 core DSM–IV personality disorders (Livesley, Jang, & Vernon, 1998). The 4As are *antisocial* (criminal, hostile), *asocial* (odd and withdrawn), *aesthenic* (inclined to personal distress), and *anankastic* (obsessive–compulsive) groups. Examining the 4A model in relation to Eysenck's PEN scheme, Deary, Peter, Austin, and Gibson (1998) found that the aesthenic dimension corresponded to Eysenck's N, antisociality was associated with Eysenck's P dimension, and the asocial factor correlated negatively with Eysenckian E. The anankastic dimension did not associate with any major dimension of personality. Joint factor analysis of the NEO–FFI and of the International Personality Disorder Examination (IPDE) self-report screening instrument for DSM–IV personality disorders (Loranger, 1999) by Egan, Austin, Elliot, Patel, and Charlesworth (2003) also derived a 4A model. In this model the asocial dimension had high positive loadings for high N and high negative loadings for E and C. The anxious dimension had a high positive loading for N. The antisocial dimension had high negative loadings for A and C.

Meta-analysis of the literature examining the FFM in relation to the 10 personality disorders defined by APA's DSM–IV also suggests that those affected by personality disorders are generally higher in N, lower in E, and routinely lower in A and C, with no replicable association between O and any personality disorder (Saulsman & Page, 2004). A recent meta-analysis of the FFM facets and of personality disorder further sharpens these general findings (Samuel & Widiger, 2008). Pooled mean weighted effect size correlations for the relationship between the personality disorder and the NEO–PI–R facet scores find no association of any significance between PD and O, which leaves 24 facet associations per disorder. Avoidant, borderline, paranoid, and antisocial personality disorders have the largest numbers of significant facet-level correlates; obsessive personality disorder (which is primarily related to C), the least. Of the facets which significantly affect PDs in 50 percent of cases, the N facets of anxiousness, angry hostility, depressiveness, self-consciousness, and vulnerability are cardinal, as are the E facets of (low) warmth, (low) gregariousness, and (low) positive emotions. The facet of low A most commonly seen in personality disorders is low trust, which may reflect the disturbed attachments so common in individuals afflicted by such disorders (Westen, Nakash, Thomas, & Bradley, 2006). The C facet of low self-discipline is also common in personality disordered persons, but reversed for persons with compulsive personality disorder (Samuel & Widiger, 2008).

Nevertheless, not all clinical personality disorder variance is captured by standard personality test measures. This is unsurprising; the modes of assessment and the cohorts of participants upon whom the underlying personality theories and measures have been validated are often quite different from one another. Researchers into the FFM themselves recognize that there is plenty beyond the Big Five (Paunonen & Jackson, 2000), just as there is plenty to study beyond gross heritability. Personality disorders are not exclusively extremes of normal personality; while N correlates at .67 (P < .001) with self-reported borderline personality disorder in mentally disordered offenders (Egan et al., 2003), borderline personality disorder is of a magnitude greater than high N. Persons with borderline personality disorder exhibit bodily dysmorphia and self-mutilation (Semiz et al., 2008) and are prone to dissociation when they are under stress; such moments may present themselves as brief episodes of apparent psychosis (Stiglmayr et al., 2008). It is for this reason that DSM–V will likely include a measure of clinical state and oddness (assessed by other DSM axes) along with any putative personality constructs in subsequent iterations of general clinical personality disorder assessments.

## 6.5   Psychopathy

Psychopathy is a higher-order personality construct, associated with antisocial behavior, the disorder being classically one of grandiosity, narcissism, deceitfulness, and callousness (Cleckley, 1941; Cooke & Michie, 2001). A longstanding researcher into psychopathy, Robert Hare, took this nucleus of general human characteristics (which are not inherently criminal as much as acutely obnoxious) and co-joined them to a similar nexus of antisocial behaviors, often observed concurrently in offenders. In this way he produced the Psychopathy Checklist (Hare, 1991), and eventually the revised Psychopathy Checklist (PCL–R; Hare, 2003). A massive research program now supports the validity of the psychopathy construct. For example, the PCL–R is about 80 percent effective in predicting predatory violence (McDermott, Quanbeck, Busse, Yastro, & Scott, 2008); and in conjunction with sexual deviance, high psychopathy predicts later reconviction for serious sexual offenses (Hildebrand, de Ruiter, & de Vogel, 2004). Psychopaths are not always violent; "snakes in suits" (psychopathic businessmen) are more inclined to commit fraud (Babiak & Hare, 2006; Haapasalo, 1994). Corporate psychopaths need not be criminal in order to gain what they want, and some work climates may even value mercenary and conspiratorial methods for providing a commercial edge; they would only show concern about personnel displaying such qualities when they find themselves in breach of professional standards and regulations. At a more routine, everyday level, persons higher on core psychopathic traits are more likely to be unfaithful to their partners (Egan & Angus, 2004).

Egan and Angus (2004) found that primary psychopathy (which reflects core psychopathic traits) loaded on a factor which also had a loading of – .68 for A. This finding was reiterated in a meta-analysis by Lynam and Derefinko (2006) showing psychopathy to be strongly and significantly correlated with low A, and, to a lesser degree, with low C, at – .52 and – .38 respectively. Like personality disorder, psychopathy has been examined in relation to the facets of the NEO–PI–R (Gaughan, Miller, Pryor, & Lynam, 2009). Four psychopathy factors—"callous and manipulative," "fearlessness and dominance," "dysregulation and disinhibition," and "broad antisocial behavior"— were extracted from a large undergraduate university sample, and all A facets routinely and systematically correlated negatively with these psychopathy factors. All six C facets correlated significantly, and negatively, with the "dysregulation and disinhibition" and "broad antisocial behavior" factors, but associated more erratically and nominally with the "callous and manipulative" and "fearlessness and dominance" dimensions. N is classically something of a diagnostic and classificatory fulcrum for differentiating the fearless quality of primary psychopathy from emotionally unstable secondary psychopathy (Blackburn, 1975). This distinction was found in Gaughan et al.'s study, where "fearlessness and dominance" was related negatively to four of the six N facets, whereas "dysregulation and dysinhibition" was correlated positively with four of the six N facets. E also had a differential effect; "fearlessness and dominance" was positively associated with all six E facets, whereas the "callous and manipulative" dimension was related to the E facets of lower warmth, lower gregariousness, and lower positive emotions. Unusually for the field of antisocial behavior, O was positively and broadly related to greater "fearlessness and dominance," and sporadically related to "callous and manipulative" qualities negatively, such persons having a lower esthetic sense and lower feelings. These findings open up psychopathy in intriguing ways, as psychopathy crosses more personality domains than some of the other personality disorders, a fact which perhaps explains why its Protean influence can be so malign.

The less attractive side of personality is sometimes said to have a dark triad— psychopathy, narcissism, and Machiavellianism—that is associated with antisocial and unpleasant behavior (Paulhus & Williams, 2002). Machiavellianism refers to interpersonal strategies that advocate self-interest, deception, and manipulation, so it would seem inherently related to core psychopathy and narcissism. Such observations led McHoskey, Worzel, and Szyarto (1998) to argue that, within the general population, Machiavellianism is a global measure of psychopathy comparable to primary and secondary psychopathy, and that the three elements of the dark triad are intercorrelated—which is precisely what they found. Paulhus and Williams (2002) examined the dark triad in relation to the FFM and found that A related negatively to all three elements, but they did not find N differentiated primary and secondary psychopathy, perhaps because their self-report measure of psychopathy was unable to make this differentiation. Using the Levenson measure of self-reported psychopathy to separate primary and secondary psychopathy along with standard measures of narcissism, Machiavellianism, and the NEO–FFI–R, Jakobwitz and Egan (2006) found that all the dark triad scales loaded highly negatively on a factor in which the only general personality dimension was A, secondary psychopathy having a split loading due to the fact that this dimension also loaded highly on a second factor, defined by high N and low C. Lastly, short-term sexual strategies are sometimes enjoyable for the parties involved (assuming that both are mindful that the seized moment is intended to be short, as otherwise one party may be unhappy that the early intimacy had no opportunity to grow stronger), and are more common in men higher on the dark triad (Jonason, Li, Webster, & Schmitt, 2009). Short-term sexual strategies are also associated with greater mating effort, itself associated with lower A and with delinquency (Charles & Egan, 2009). Thus it is that we find ourselves back to a consideration of evolutionary influences on our behavior and the centrality, whether we like it or not, of fighting and mating in the struggle for human existence and survival.

## 7   Intelligence, IQ, and Antisocial Behavior

A chapter on individual differences in antisocial behavior would be incomplete without a brief review of the importance of intelligence to the field. Intelligent people are quite able to be badly behaved, unpleasant, dishonest, and violent, particularly if their antisocial behavior is driven by a disagreeable personality, marked distress, or temporary disinhibition, such as that following substance misuse. Ego and arrogance (and possibly, stable psychopathy: Babiak & Hare, 2006) may lead educated and shrewd financiers to soberly decide to commit fraud, with huge material loss and social consequences for a nation. The losses incurred from such crimes exceed by far the average acquisitive criminals' petty larceny and prosaic dishonesty (irritating though such offenses are for the victim). In principle, most persons can think through the options open to them, consider the consequences of a given action, and anticipate the losses that could be incurred as a consequence of the antisocial act (Gordon, 1997); in practice, persons lower in IQ are poorer at a variety of everyday problems (Gottfredson, 1997), and thoughtlessness underlies many criminal cognitions (Egan, McMurran, Richardson, & Blair, 2000). The economic independence which a higher intelligence normally secures typically involves a better wage (Murray, 1998), if not actual freedom from debt or taxation (Zagorsky, 2007). If you are economically independent, you can buy drugs in foreign countries and explore international sex industries, which are free of the regulations against licentious crimes in your home nation. If your home life is unpleasant, you have the money to avoid your home or to create a new life, rather than end up in an unpleasant domestic incident (or put up with unpleasant behavior) because there is nowhere else to go. Persons with lower IQs and less money do not have the behavioral flexibility economic independence enables, so they may end up being prosecuted for crimes committed that the wealthier are able to avoid.

Crime is rarely genuinely remunerative; many drug dealers and petty criminals (who make up much of the prison population) live with their mothers and would make more money working in a fast-food restaurant (Levitt & Dubner, 2005; Venkatesh, 2009). When you have very little, small personal losses, whether material or personal, become differentially more important. The loss of face and consequent shame often creates or involves financial or material antecedents that provoke humiliation, anger, and reaction. A criminal's economic poverty is often a reflection of lower intelligence; unskilled manual occupations are far rarer nowadays than they were in the past, and persons with less education and intellectual ability are more likely to be unemployed than they used to be. In a recent study, 48 percent of British offenders were below level 1 in literacy, and 65 percent were below level 1 for numeracy (Clarke & Dugdale, 2008). Offenders generally show a marked discrepancy between their verbal (VIQ) and non-verbal (PIQ) IQ scores, VIQ being significantly lower than PIQ (Ellis & Walsh, 2003). Though one cannot easily increase IQ, one could reduce illiteracy and innumeracy rates (caused partly by conduct problems, which offenders typically show in the classroom) by increasing educational opportunities within jail, and thus occupational possibilities on release.

Hirschi and Hindelang (1977) reviewed the substantial literature on intelligence and crime and found unambiguous evidence for a strong inverse correlation between intelligence and involvement with delinquent and criminal behavior. The association was ubiquitous and robust. Their finding came during a colder section of the previously hot IQ wars so they were no longer physically assaulted for their statement of what Basil Fawlty would describe as "a statement of the bleeding obvious." But their commonplace observation was nevertheless inevitably challenged by reference to a variety of sociological, demographic, and psychological "third-variable" constructs, which might ostensibly explain a spurious crime–IQ correlation. A typical criticism was that of differential detection: clever offenders are better at getting away with a crime, when compared to their less able co-offenders; prisons are thus full of less intelligent criminals. This is incorrect. Moffitt and Sliva (1988) compared the IQs of two groups of delinquents from the same birth cohort, one which had been detected in delinquent acts by the police, and another which was not known to police, but was equivalent to the first in the amount and seriousness of self-reported delinquency. The groups did not differ significantly in IQ, but both were significantly below the IQ of non-delinquent cohort members. This finding roundly rejects the "differential detection" hypothesis.

Is the association between low IQ and crime due to class, race, test motivation, school failure, or poor self-control? Each of these post hoc constructs has a literature examining whether each one provides a third factor accounting for lower IQ in some vulnerable groups. In relation to the offending literature, Lynam, Moffitt, and Stouthamer-Loeber (1993) examined, in a longitudinal study, 13-year-old boys at high risk of becoming offenders. Analyses testing whether the IQ–crime relationship was spurious or was caused by social delinquency-related factors (which would have led to low IQ scores) failed. The systematic falsification of the various social theories for the causal direction between IQ and crime—such as race, class, and observed test motivation—is congruent with the most simple and obvious model: low IQ leads to delinquency. A more recent review of the intelligence and crime literature was conducted by Ellis and Walsh (2003). They found 60 out of the 68 studies of the IQ–crime association to be significant and negative for officially reported crime, as were 14 of the 17 studies for IQ and self-reported crime; 19 of 19 studies found that there is an association between low IQ and delinquency-associated developmental behavioral disorders such as ADHD, child conduct disorder, and antisocial personality disorder. Ellis and Walsh observed that historical factors reflected the direction of causality, in that child conduct disorder and ADHD diagnoses typically precede the onset of official delinquency, and that, even when one controls for parental SES, the IQ–crime association remains. Lastly and crucially, non-offending same-sex siblings have higher IQ than their offending sibling, despite a substantial shared familial environment.

Lower intelligence is common in some offender groups, for example sexual offenders; an extensive study aggregating IQ data from 236 samples (comprising 25,146 sexual offenders and controls) by Cantor, Blanchard, Robichaud, and Christensen (2005) found that sexual offenders tend to have lower IQs than non-sexual offender controls, and that the younger the child victim, the lower in IQ the offender; hands-on offenders against pre-pubescent children (much of the data coming from a time before the Internet was available for the downloading of indecent images) were on average 10 IQ points lower than sexual offenders targeting pubescent children. No difference in IQ was seen between intra-familial and extra-familial offenders, nor between offenders against males and offenders against females. Juvenile sexual offenders and juvenile non-sexual offenders did not differ in IQ from each other, and had lower IQs than the adult offenders. It has been suggested that those who commit sexual offenses against children do so out of emotional congruence; this is one in a "trinity" of constructs (along with cognitive distortions and poor victim empathy) that capture the cognitive core of pedophilic offending (Henry, Manderville-Norden, Hayes, & Egan, 2010). Cantor et al.'s findings offer an interpretation of emotional congruence beyond personality, suggesting that such congruence may also reflect a matched mental age between offender and victim.

## 8   Conclusions

This chapter has reviewed the literature on individual differences in antisocial behavior, starting with evidence for heritability of the behavior, and then discussing putative mechanisms (including hormonal, neurological, and biopsychosocial influences and synergies). The chapter continued to cover personality factors associated with antisocial behavior, reviewing Eysenck's model of P, some possible reasons why P was superseded, the FFM in relation to personality disorders and offending, and the *sine qua non* of antisocial personality, psychopathy. Finally, the influence of intelligence on offending—and possibly on not offending—was considered. Throughout, the social context of offending was recognized, and studies referring to integrations across different levels of explanation and meta-analyses were favored. Issues left undeveloped (for example evolutionary and intra-sexual competition influences on young offenders) can be chased up through the references cited.

Some readers may wonder why racial differences in offending have not been discussed; between assortative mating for antisocial tendencies, absent fathers and poor parenting skills, community disorder, extremes of personality, and the overall IQ–crime link, the color of a person's skin seems somewhat weak as an explanatory concept, particularly as the same processes drive high rates of offending, whether one is in the racially homogeneous (and white) east end of Glasgow, the African–American south side of Chicago, or the predominantly Hispanic east side of Los Angeles. Another issue that has remained underdeveloped is the corollary of the associations between low A and low IQ on the one hand and antisocial behavior on the other: namely that there is less offending in persons higher on these qualities. A resilience literature is emerging; adolescents with low N, high E, high A/low P, high C, and high O find it easier to eschew the vicissitudes and temptations to which their peers succumb (Davey, Eaker, & Walters, 2003). Longitudinal studies of violence in adolescents find that protective factors include connectedness to adults and school and better educational attainment (Resnick, Ireland, & Borowsky, 2004). As argued throughout, an overly moral perspective on human antisocial behavior is problematic, as the drives to survive, fight, and have sex reflect underlying biological drives that have evolved for millennia, and tend to push against human regulation. This tendency is the reason for the social rules that have evolved, and this is also why we are so impassioned against those who transgress them. But it is salutary to remember that the emotions offenders provoke may not be so different from those experienced by persons perceived as antisocial.

## Acknowledgments

I am indebted to Dr. Vickie Campbell and Meryl Lewis for providing me with the data for the analysis presented in Table 19.1. All tables and figures were generated for this chapter, and have not been previously published.

## References

APA [American Psychiatric Association] (1994). *Diagnostic and statistical manual of mental disorders* (4th ed.). Washington, DC: American Psychiatric Press.

Archer, J., Graham-Kevan, N., & Davies, M. (2005). Testosterone and aggression: A reanalysis of Book, Starzyk, and Quinsey's (2001) study. *Aggression and Violent Behavior, 10,* 241–261.

Babiak, P., & Hare, R. D. (2006). *Snakes in suits: When psychopaths go to work.* London: HarperCollins.

Barlas, J., & Egan, V. (2006). Weapons carrying in British teenagers: The role of personality, delinquency, sensational interests and mating effort. *Journal of Forensic Psychiatry and Psychology, 17,* 53–72.

Barnes, G., Malamuth, N., & Check, J. (1984). Psychoticism and sexual arousal to rape depictions. *Personality and Individual Differences, 5,* 273–279.

BBC News Website (2005). Rape looms large over Haiti slums. Retrieved February 24, 2010, from http://news.bbc.co.uk/nol/ukfs_news/hi/newsid_7750000/newsid_7750500/7750568.stm

Bergen, S. E., Gardner, C. O., & Kendler, K. S. (2007). Age-related changes in heritability of behavioral phenotypes over adolescence and young adulthood: A meta-analysis. *Twin Research and Human Genetics, 10,* 423–433.

Blackburn, R. (1975). An empirical classification of psychopathic personality. *British Journal of Psychiatry, 127,* 456–460.

Blair, J., Mitchell, D., & Blair, K. (2005). *The psychopath: Emotion and the brain.* Oxford: Blackwell.

Blazei, R. W., Iacono, W. G., & Krueger, R. F. (2006). Intergenerational transmission of antisocial behaviour: How do kids become antisocial adults? *Applied and Preventative Psychology, 11,* 230–253.

Book, A. S., Starzyk, K. B., & Quinsey, V. L. (2001). The relationship between testosterone and aggression: A meta-analysis. *Aggression and Violent Behavior 6,* 579–599.

Brown, D. E. (2000). Human universals and their implications. In N. Roughley (Ed.), *Being humans: Anthropological universality and particularity in transdisciplinary perspectives* (pp. 156–174). New York: Walter de Gruyter.

Buss, A. H., & Perry, M. (1992). The aggression questionnaire. *Journal of Personality and Social Psychology, 63,* 452–459.

Buss, D. M., & Shackelford, T. K. (1997). Human aggression in evolutionary psychological perspective. *Clinical Psychology Review, 17,* 605–619.

Button, T. M. M., Scourfield, J., Martin, N., Purcell, S., & McGuffin, P. (2005). Family dysfunction interacts with genes in the causation of antisocial symptoms. *Behavior Genetics, 35,* 115–120.

Cale, E. M. (2006). A quantitative review of the relations between the "Big 3" higher order personality dimensions and antisocial behavior, *Journal of Research in Personality, 40,* 250–284.

Cantor, J. M., Blanchard, R., Robichaud, L. K., & Christensen, B. K. (2005). Quantitative reanalysis of aggregate data on IQ in sexual offenders. *Psychological Bulletin, 131,* 555–568.

Caruso, J. C., Witkiewitz, K., Belcourt-Dittloff, A., & Gottlieb, J. D. (2001). Reliability of scores from the Eysenck Personality Questionnaire: A reliability generalization study. *Educational and Psychological Measurement, 61,* 675–689.

Caspi, A., McClay, J., Moffitt, T. E., Mill, J., Martin, J., Craig, I. W., Taylor, A., & Poulton, R. (2002). Role of genotype in the cycle of violence in maltreated children. *Science, 297,* 851–854.

Charles, K. E., & Egan, V. (2005). Mating effort correlates with self-reported delinquency in a normal adolescent sample. *Personality and Individual Differences, 38,* 1035–1045.

Charles, K. E., & Egan, V. (2008). Sensational and extreme interests in adolescents. In R. N. Koksis (Ed.), *The psychology of serial and violent crimes and their criminal investigation* (pp. 63–83). Totowa, NJ: The Humana Press.

Charles, K. E., & Egan, V. (2009). Military interests are not a simple predictor of adolescent offending: Evidence from a large normal British sample. *Personality and Individual Differences, 47,* 235–240.

Clarke, C., & Dugdale, G. (2008). *The role of literacy in offending behaviour: A discussion piece. Part 1.* London: National Literacy Trust.

Cleckley, H. (1941). *The mask of sanity.* St. Louis, MO: Mosby.

Coid, J., Yang, M., Roberts, A., Ullrich, S., Moran, P., Bebbington, P., Brugha, T., Jenkins, R., Farrell, M., Lewis, G., & Singleton, N. (2006). Violence and psychiatric morbidity in the national household population of Britain: Public health implications. *British Journal of Psychiatry, 189,* 12–19.

Cooke, D. J., & Michie, C. (2001). Refining the construct of psychopathy: Towards a hierarchical model. *Psychological Assessment, 13,* 171–188.

Costa, P. T., & McCrae, R. R. (1992). *Revised NEO Personality Inventory and NEO Five-Factor Inventory professional manual.* Odessa, FL: Psychological Assessment Resources.

Costa, P. T., & Widiger, T. A. (2003). *Personality disorders and the Five-Factor Model of Personality.* Washington, DC: American Psychological Association.

Damasio, A. R., Everitt, B. J., & Bishop, D. (1996). The somatic marker hypothesis and the possible functions of the prefrontal cortex. *Philosophical Transactions of the Royal Society: Biological Sciences, 351,* 1413–1420.

Davey, M., Eaker, D. G., & Walters, L. H. (2003). Resilience processes in adolescents: Personality profiles, self-worth, and coping. *Journal of Adolescent Research, 18,* 347–362.

Deary, I. J., Spinath, F. M., & Bates, T. C. (2006). Genetics of intelligence. *European Journal of Human Genetics, 14,* 690–700.

Deary, I. J, Peter, A., Austin, E., Gibson, G. (1998). Personality traits and personality disorders. *British Journal of Psychology, 89,* 647–661.

Delisi, M., Beaver, K. M., Vaughn, M. G., & Wright, J. P. (2009). All in the family: Gene × environment interaction between DRD2 and criminal father is associated with five antisocial phenotypes. *Criminal Justice and Behavior, 36,* 1187–1197.

Duntley, J. D., & Shackelford, T. K. (Eds.) (2008). *Evolutionary forensic psychology*. New York: Oxford University Press.

Eastwood, L. (1985). Personality, intelligence and personal space among violent and non-violent delinquents. *Personality and Individual Differences, 6,* 717–723.

Egan, V., & Angus, S. (2004). Is social dominance a sex-specific strategy for infidelity? *Personality and Individual Differences, 36,* 575–586.

Egan, V, & Campbell, V. (2009). Sensational interests, sustaining fantasies and personality predict physical aggression. *Personality and Individual Differences, 47,* 464–469.

Egan, V., & Hamilton, E. (2008). Personality, mating effort and alcohol-related violence expectancies. *Addiction Research and Theory, 16,* 369–381.

Egan, V., & Lewis, M. (2011). Neuroticism and agreeableness differentiate emotional and narcissistic expressions of aggression. *Personality and Individual Differences, 50.*

Egan, V., & Taylor, D. (2010). Shoplifting, unethical consumer behaviour, and personality: A naturalistic study. *Personality and Individual Differences, 48,* 878–883.

Egan, V., Deary, I. J., & Austin, E. (2000). The NEO–FFI: Emerging British norms and an item-analysis suggest N, A, and C are more reliable than O and E. *Personality and Individual Differences, 29,* 907–920.

Egan, V., Kavanagh, B., & Blair, M. (2005). Sexual offenders against children: The influence of personality and obsessionality on cognitive distortions. *Sexual Abuse, 17,* 223–240.

Egan, V., McMurran, M., Richardson, C., & Blair, M. (2000). Criminal cognitions and personality: What does the PICTS really measure? *Criminal Behaviour and Mental Health, 10,* 170–184.

Egan, V., Austin, E., Elliot, D., Patel, D., & Charlesworth, P. (2003). Personality traits, personality disorders and sensational interests in mentally disordered offenders. *Legal and Criminological Psychology, 8,* 51–62.

Eisner, M. (2001). Modernization, self-control and lethal violence. The long-term dynamics of European homicide rates in theoretical perspective. *British Journal of Criminology, 41,* 618–638.

Ellis, L., & Walsh, A. (2003). Crime, delinquency and intelligence: A review of the world-wide literature. In H. Nyborg (Ed.), *The scientific study of general intelligence* (pp. 343–365). London: Pergamon.

Ellis, L., Das, S., & Buker, H. (2008). Androgen-promoted physiological traits and criminality: A test of the evolutionary neuroandrogenic theory. *Personality and Individual Differences, 44,* 701–711.

Eysenck, H. J. (1992a). Four ways five factors are not basic. *Personality and Individual Differences, 13,* 667–673.

Eysenck, H. J. (1992b). A reply to Costa and McCrae. P or A and C—The role of theory. *Personality and Individual Differences, 13,* 867–868.

Eysenck, H. J. (1995). *Genius: The natural history of creativity*. Cambridge: Cambridge University Press.

Eysenck, H. J., & Eysenck, M. W. (1985). *Personality and individual differences: A natural science approach*. New York: Plenum.

Eysenck, H. J., & Eysenck, S. B. G. (1976). *Psychoticism as a dimension of personality*. London: Hodder & Stoughton.

Farrington, D. P., Barnes, G. C., & Lambert, S. (1996). The concentration of offending in families. *Legal and Criminological Psychology, 1,* 47–63.

Fazel, S., & Danesh, J. (2002). Serious mental disorder in 23000 prisoners: A systematic review of 62 surveys. *The Lancet, 359,* 545–550.

Finlayson, C. (2009). *The humans who went extinct: Why Neanderthals died out and we survived*. Oxford: Oxford University Press.

Ferguson, E., Chamorro-Premuzic, T., Pickering, A., & Weiss, A. (2011: this volume). Five into one doesn't go: A critique of the general factor of personality. In T. Chamorro-Premuzic, S. von Stumm, & A. Furnham (Eds.), *Handbook of individual differences*. Oxford: Wiley–Blackwell.

Fiske, D. W. (1949). Consistency of the factorial structures of personality ratings from different sources. *Journal of Abnormal and Social Psychology, 44*, 329–344.

Flor, H., Birbaumer, N. Hermann, C. Ziegler, & Patrick, C. J. (2002). Aversive Pavlovian conditioning in psychopaths: Peripheral and central correlates. *Psychophysiology, 39*, 505–518.

Gaughan, E. T., Miller, J. D., Pryor, L. R., & Lynam, D. R. (2009). Comparing two alternative measures of general personality in the assessment of psychopathy: A test of the NEO PI–R and the MPQ. *Journal of Personality, 77*, 965–996.

Gibson, C. L., Sullivan, C. J., Jones, S., & Piquero, A. R. (2010). "Does it take a village?" Assessing neighborhood influences on children's self-control. *Journal of Research in Crime and Delinquency, 47*, 31–62.

Goldberg, L. R., Johnson, J. A., Eber, H. W., Hogan, R., Ashton, M. C., Cloninger, C. R., & Gough, H. C. (2006). The International Personality Item Pool and the future of public-domain personality measures. *Journal of Research in Personality, 40*, 84–96.

Gordon, R. A. (1997). Everyday life as an intelligence test: Effects of intelligence and intelligence context. *Intelligence, 24*, 203–320.

Gottfredson, L. S. (1997). Why *g* matters: The complexity of everyday life. *Intelligence, 24*, 79–132.

Gudjonsson, G. H. (1997). Crime and personality. In H. Nyborg (Ed.), *The scientific study of human nature* (pp. 142–164). Oxford: Pergamon.

Haapasalo, J. (1994). Types of offense among the Cleckley psychopaths. *International Journal of Offender Therapy and Comparative Criminology, 38*, 59–67.

Hagen, E. H., Sullivan, R. J., Schmidt, R., Morris, G., Kempter, R., & Hammerstein, P. (2009). Ecology and neurobiology of toxin avoidance and the paradox of drug reward. *Neuroscience, 160*, 69–84.

Hare, R. D. (1991). The *Hare Psychopathy Checklist—Revised*. Toronto, Ontario: Multi-Health Systems.

Hare, R. D. (2003). *Manual for the Revised Psychopathy Checklist* (2nd ed.). Toronto, Ontario: Multi-Health Systems.

Heaven, P. C. L. (1996). Personality and self-reported delinquency: Analysis of the "Big Five" personality dimensions. *Personality and Individual Differences, 20*, 47–54.

Henry, O., Manderville-Norden, R., Hayes, E., & Egan, V. (2010). Do Internet sexual offenders reduce to normal, inadequate and deviant groups? *Journal of Sexual Aggression, 16*, 33–46.

Hildebrand, M., de Ruiter, C., & de Vogel, V. (2004). Psychopathy and sexual deviance in treated rapists: Association with sexual and nonsexual recidivism. *Sexual Abuse, 16*, 1–24.

Hirschi, T., & Hindelang, M. J. (1977). Intelligence and delinquency: A revisionist review. *American Sociological Review, 42*, 571–587.

Holcomb, W. R., & Adams, N. A. (1985). Personality mechanisms of alcohol related violence. *Journal of Clinical Psychology, 41*, 714–722.

Jacobson, K. C., Prescott, C. A., & Kendler, K. S. (2002). Sex differences in the genetic and environmental influences on the development of antisocial behaviour. *Development and Psychopathology, 14*, 395–416.

Jaffee, S. R., Caspi, A., Moffitt, T. E., Dodge, K. A., Rutter, M., Taylor, A., & Tully, L. A. (2005). Nature × nurture: Genetic vulnerabilities interact with physical maltreatment to promote conduct problems. *Development and Psychopathology, 17*, 67–84.

Jakobwitz, S., & Egan, V. (2006). The dark triad and normal personality traits. *Personality and Individual Differences, 40,* 331–339.

Jonason, P. K., Li, N. P., Webster, G. D., & Schmitt, D. P. (2009). The dark triad: Facilitating a short-term mating strategy in men. *European Journal of Personality, 23,* 5–18.

Krueger, R. F., Moffitt, T. E., Caspi, A., Bleske, A., & Silva, P. A. (1998). Assortative mating for antisocial behavior: Developmental and methodological implications. *Behavior Genetics, 28,* 173–186.

Levitt, S., & Dubner, S. J. (2005). *Freakonomics: A rogue economist explores the hidden side of everything.* New York: William Morrow/HarperCollins.

Livesley, W. J., Jang, K. L., & Vernon, P. A. (1998). Phenotypic and genetic structure of traits delineating personality disorder. *Archives of General Psychiatry, 55,* 941–948.

Loranger, A. W. (1999). *International personality disorder examination.* Odessa, FL: Psychological Assessment Resources.

Lynam, D. R., & Derefinko, K. J. (2006). Psychopathy and personality. In C. J. Patrick (Ed.), *Handbook of the psychopathy* (pp. 133–155). New York: Guilford Press.

Lynam, D. R., Moffitt, T. E., & Stouthamer-Loeber, M. (1993). Explaining the relation between IQ and delinquency: Class, race, test motivation, school failure, or self-control? *Journal of Abnormal Psychology, 102,* 87–196.

Lynam, D. R., Caspi, A., Moffit, T. E., Wikström, P.-O., Loeber, R., & Novak, S. (2000). The interaction between impulsivity and neighbourhood context on offending: The effects of impulsivity are stronger in poorer neighbourhoods. *Journal of Abnormal Psychology, 109,* 563–574.

Malouff, J. M., Rooke, S. E., & Schutte, N. S. (2008). The heritability of human behavior: Results of aggregating meta-analyses. *Current Psychology, 27,* 153–161.

McCrae, R. R., & Costa, P. T., Jr. (2004). A contemplated revision of the NEO Five-Factor Inventory. *Personality and Individual Differences, 36,* 587–596.

McCroskey, J., Heisel, A., & Richmond, V. (2001). Eysenck's Big Three and communication traits: Three correlational studies. *Communication Monographs, 68,* 360–366.

McDermott, B. E., Quanbeck, C. D., Busse, D., Yastro, K., & Scott, C. L. (2008). The accuracy of risk assessment instruments in the prediction of impulsive versus predatory aggression. *Behavioral Sciences and the Law, 26,* 759–777.

McEllistrem, J. E. (2004). Affective and predatory violence: A bimodal classification system of human aggression and violence. *Aggression and Violent Behaviour, 10,* 1–30.

McHoskey, J. W., Worzel, W., & Szyarto, C. (1998) Machiavellianism and psychopathy. *Journal of Personality and Social Psychology, 74,* 192–210.

McLoughlin, G., Ronald, A., Kuntsi, J., Asherson, P., & Plomin, R. (2007). Genetic support for the dual nature of attention deficit hyperactivity disorder: Substantial genetic overlap between the inattentive and hyperactive–impulsive components. *Journal of Abnormal Child Psychology, 35,* 999–1008.

Mealey, L. (1995). The sociobiology of sociopathy: An integrated evolutionary model. *Behavioral and Brain Sciences, 18,* 523–599.

Miles, D. R., & Carey, G. (1997). Genetic and environmental architecture on human aggression. *Journal of Personality and Social Psychology, 72,* 207–217.

Miller J. D., & Lynam, D. R. (2001). Structural models of personality and their relation to antisocial behaviour: A meta-analysis. *Criminology 39,* 765–798.

Miller, J. D., Lynam, D., & Leukefeld, C. (2003). Examining antisocial behavior through the lens of the five factor model of personality. *Aggressive Behavior, 29,* 497–514.

Moffitt, T. E., & Silva, P. A. (1988). IQ and delinquency: A direct test of the differential detection hypothesis. *Journal of Abnormal Psychology, 97,* 330–333.

Murray, C. (1998). *Income inequality and IQ.* Washington, DC: AEI Press.

Najman, J. M., Hayatbakhsh, M. R., McGee, T. R., Bor, W., O'Callaghan, M. J., & Williams, G. M. (2009). The impact of puberty on aggression/delinquency: Adolescence to young adulthood. *Australian and New Zealand Journal of Criminology*, 42, 369–386.

Paulhus, D. L. & Williams, K. M. (2002). The dark triad of personality: Narcissism, Machiavellianism and psychopathy. *Journal of Research in Personality*, 36, 556–563.

Paunonen, S. V., & Jackson, D. N. (2000). What is beyond the Big Five? Plenty! *Journal of Personality*, 68, 821–835.

Pinker, S. (2002). *The blank slate*. London: Penguin.

Raine, A., Brennan, P., Mednick, B., & Mednick, S. A. (1996). High rates of violence, crime, academic and behavioural problems in males with both early neuromotor deficits and unstable family environments. *Archives of General Psychiatry*, 53, 544–549.

Resnick, M. D., Ireland, M., & Borowsky, I. (2004). Youth violence perpetration: What protects? What predicts? Findings from the National Longitudinal Study of Adolescent Health. *Journal of Adolescent Health*, 35, 424.e1–424.e10.

Rhee, S. H., & Waldman, I. D. (2002). Genetic and environmental influences on antisocial behaviour: A meta-analysis of twin and adoption studies. *Psychological Bulletin*, 128, 490–529.

Roberts, B. W., Harms, P. D., Caspi, A., & Moffitt, T. E. (2007). Predicting the counterproductive employee in a child-to-adult prospective study. *Journal of Applied Psychology*, 92, 1427–1436.

Rowe, D. (2002). *Biology and crime*. Los Angeles, CA: Roxbury.

Rowe, D., Vazsonyi, A., & Figueredo, A. (1997). Mating-effort in adolescence: A conditional or alternative strategy. *Personality and Individual Differences*, 23, 105–115.

Rushton, J. P., & Irwing, P. (2011: this volume). The general factor of personality. In T. Chamorro-Premuzic, S. von Stumm, & A. Furnham (Eds.), *Handbook of individual differences*. Oxford: Wiley–Blackwell.

Sampson, R.J., Raudenbush, S.W., & Earls, F. (1997). Neighborhoods and violent crime: A multilevel study of collective efficacy. *Science*, 277, 918–924.

Samuel, D. B., & Widiger, T. A. (2008). A meta-analytic review of the relationships between the five-factor model and DSM–IV–TR personality disorders: A facet level analysis. *Clinical Psychology Review*, 28, 1326–1342.

Samuels, J., Bienvenu, J., Cullen, B., Costa, P. T., Eaton, W. W., & Nestadt, G. (2004). Personality dimensions and criminal arrest. *Comprehensive Psychiatry*, 45, 275–280.

Saulsman, L. M., & Page. A. C. (2004). The five-factor model and personality disorder empirical literature: A meta-analytic review. *Clinical Psychology Review*, 23, 1055–1085.

Semiz, U., Basoglu, C., Cetin, M., Ebrinc, S., Uzun, O., & Ergun, B. (2008). Body dysmorphic disorder in patients with borderline personality disorder: Prevalence, clinical characteristics, and role of childhood trauma. *Acta Neuropsychiatrica*, 20, 33–40.

Stiglmayr, C. E., Ebner-Priemer, U. W., Bretz, J., Behm, R., Mohse, M., Lammers, C.-H. et al. (2008). Dissociative symptoms are positively related to stress in borderline personality disorder. *Acta Psychiatrica Scandinavica*, 117, 139–147.

Sullivan, R. J., Hagen, E. H., & Hammerstein, P. (2008). Revealing the paradox of drug reward in human evolution. *Proceedings of the Royal Society, B: Biological Sciences*, 275, 1231–1241.

Tromovitch, P., & Rind, B. (2008). Child sexual abuse: Definitions, meta-analytic findings, and a response to the methodological concerns raised by Hyde (2003). *International Journal of Sexual Health*, 19, 1–13.

Uhla, G. R., Drgon, T., Johnson, C., Oluwatosin, O., Fatusina, Q., Contoreggi, C., Lic, C., Buck, K., & Crabbe, J. (2006). "Higher order" addiction molecular genetics: Convergent data from genome-wide association in humans and mice. *Biochemical Pharmacology, 75,* 98–111.

van Leeuwen, M., van den Berg, S. M., & Boomsma, D. I. (2008). A twin-family study of general IQ. *Learning and Individual Differences, 18,* 76–88.

Venkatesh, S. (2009). *Gang leader for a day: A rogue sociologist crosses the line.* London: Penguin.

Vitacco, M. J., Neumann, C. S., & Jackson, R. L. (2005). Testing a four-factor model of psychopathy: Associations with ethnicity, gender, intelligence, and violence. *Journal of Consulting and Clinical Psychology, 73,* 466–476.

Walker, P. L. (2001). A bioarcheological perspective on the history of violence. *American Review of Anthropology, 30,* 573–596.

Weinberger, L. E., Sreenivasan, S, Garrick, T., & Osran, H. (2005). The impact of surgical castration on sexual recidivism risk among sexually violent predatory offenders. *Journal of the American Academy for Psychiatry and the Law, 33,* 16–36.

Westen, D., Nakash, O., Thomas, C., & Bradley, R. (2006). Clinical assessment of attachment patterns and personality disorder in adolescents and adults. *Journal of Consulting and Clinical Psychology, 74,* 1065–1085.

WHO [World Health Organization] (2007). *International statistical classification of diseases and related health problems 10th revision version for 2007* (web). Geneva, Switzerland: World Health Organization. Retrieved February 26, 2010, from http://apps.who.int/classifications/apps/icd/icd10online/

Widiger T. A., & Mullins-Sweatt, S. N. (2009). Five-factor model of personality disorder: A proposal for DSM–V. *Annual Review of Clinical Psychology, 5,* 197–220.

Woody, E., & Claridge, G. (1977). Psychoticism and thinking. *British Journal of Social and Clinical Psychology, 16,* 241–248.

Zagorsky, J. L. (2007). Do you have to be smart to be rich? The impact of IQ on wealth, income and financial distress. *Intelligence, 35,* 489–501.

Zillmann, D., & Weaver, J. B. (1997). Psychoticism in the effect of prolonged exposure to gratuitous media violence on the acceptance of violence as a preferred means of conflict resolution. *Personality and Individual Differences, 22,* 613–627.

# 20

# Intelligence and Social Inequality
## *Why the Biological Link?*
### Linda S. Gottfredson

## 1 Introduction

Were he to survey life in western democracies today, the proverbial Man from Mars might conclude that the notions of *intelligence* and *inequality* are both profane. Many of my undergraduate students interpret the United States Declaration of Independence's premise that "all men are created equal" to mean, not that all individuals are born with the same freedoms and inalienable political rights, but rather with equal natural endowments. For them, to suggest otherwise is not only undemocratic, but a threat to the American polity.

Democracies seem particularly vexed by biologically based variation in general intelligence. Human groups have always had to accommodate the natural diversity of their members. Modern nations, however, are far larger and more anonymous than societies past, and hence their members' relations and social niches are more bureaucratized and regularized by cultural arrangements such as schools, workplaces, and layers of government. Nations expend increasing effort to measure, monitor, and manage these relations, as well as the unevenness in life outcomes they produce. They struggle with two contentious questions. One is empirical: Why is inequality so enduring? The second is political: How should a society react to it? This chapter addresses a more deeply contentious question: Why is socioeconomic inequality so entwined with a population's cognitive diversity?

Table 20.1, for fathers and sons, illustrates the typical pattern documented in hundreds, if not thousands, of studies. Son's IQ correlates modestly with father's education and occupational status (about .3, .3) and more strongly with son's own level of education, occupation, and earnings (.6, .5, .3), although most strongly with education and least with income. The particulars vary across studies, populations, time, ages, sex, and measures of family background, IQ, and status outcomes, but

*The Wiley-Blackwell Handbook of Individual Differences,* First Edition.
Edited by Tomas Chamorro-Premuzic, Sophie von Stumm, and Adrian Furnham.
© 2011 Blackwell Publishing Ltd. Published 2011 by Blackwell Publishing Ltd.

**Table 20.1**  Population-level perspective on human inequality and cognitive diversity. Entries are averages from four studies analyzed in Jencks et al., 1979, Tables A2.8, A2.9, A2.11, and A2.12

| | Father's occupation | Son's | | | |
|---|---|---|---|---|---|
| | | *IQ* | *Education* | *Occupation* | *Earnings* |
| Father | | | | | |
| Education | .48 | .27 | .40 | .28 | .20 |
| Occupation | | .29 | .38 | .31 | .22 |
| Son | | | | | |
| IQ | | | .57 | .46 | .28 |
| Education | | | | .61 | .38 |
| Occupation | | | | | .43 |

the pattern is always the same. Individuals who rise higher on one social ladder tend to rise higher on the others, and intelligence level predicts a rise on them all (the shaded entries in Table 20.1). Of particular concern to sociology, my native discipline, is that socioeconomic inequality is intergenerational. Specifically, children's differences in IQ and adult status outcomes are always correlated with those of their parents—only modestly so, yet substantially. This chapter focuses on how intelligence level might contribute to this parent–offspring similarity in adult socioeconomic attainments.

Philosophical debates about the natural relation between man and society help frame our analysis. For instance, in his *Discourse on the origin and foundations of inequality among men*, written in 1746, Jean-Jacques Rousseau (1964) argued that civil institutions magnify any natural differences among individuals. Thomas Henry Huxley (2009) argued the opposite in his 1871 and 1890 essays "Administrative nihilism" and "On the natural inequality of men"—namely that civil institutions work to level the human inequalities that exist in nature. Both men accepted that humans are born unequal, but they disagreed about whether social institutions exaggerate or ameliorate the social differences that natural ones create. Thus, while they both imply that social differences are unjust and hence should be minimized, if not eradicated, the two philosophers would seem to differ on whether civil institutions themselves are immoral or moral responses to natural human differences—Rousseau believing that civil institutions create unjust social differences and Huxley believing that they decrease them.

Their debate helps to frame our modern one in two ways. It points to social institutions as organized reactions to natural differences within populations, whether those reactions are designed to exaggerate or to moderate the differences. Next, by embodying the implicit assumption that inequality itself is unjust, this philosophical debate illustrates why empirical research on what creates and sustains it is so fraught with political tension. In fact, the all-too-common antipathy for the evidence in favor of the reality, importance, and durability of differences in intelligence may reflect just such a reaction to natural differences and to their social consequences.

Like variation in human height, cognitive diversity is a fact of nature. Every population exhibits a wide spread in general intelligence, and this takes a predictable form (something close to a bell curve, where most people cluster around the group average). As best we can tell, variation in phenotypic intelligence is fairly stable over time for the same population of genotypes. It likely oscillates within narrow limits, unless environmental effects on intelligence change dramatically. Average levels of ability may rise (or fall) over time, as is suggested by the secular increase in IQ scores during the twentieth century; but this will not necessarily change cohort variation in intelligence.

Although psychological measures do not yet allow the ratio level measurement required to know whether variation has changed, we can turn to secular increases in height, which have been comparable in magnitude in standard deviation (SD) units to the secular increases in IQ. The height of 18.5-year-old Dutch male military draftees (a compulsory draft) increased one SD between 1950 and 1978, but these males' variability in height remained the same (SD = 6.5 cm: van Wierungen, 1986, calculated from Table 11, p. 319). Dispersion in phenotypes might contract or expand in succeeding generations if the mix of genotypes changed, but changes would be glacial unless the group experienced a sudden shift in genotypes owing to rapid non-random loss or gain in members through war, disease, famine, migration, and the like.

## 1.1   Chapter topics and conceptual guide

This chapter focuses on a specific puzzle in the study of social inequality—why do differences in general intelligence, $g$, relate so pervasively, consistently, and substantially to different forms of socioeconomic status? Tackling it requires drawing evidence from the various disciplines that study individual differences in $g$—from their genetic sources, through their manifestations in the brain, to their practical consequences in social life. The following sections ask whether the evidence from these different disciplines forms systematic patterns (e.g. by age, type of task, or inequality), whether they replicate across different forms of evidence (psychometric, physiological, and so on), and whether they appear at both the phenotypic and genetic levels (for any of the above). Single studies are never dispositive, but patterns may be—but, even then, only when the full network of evidence has been considered.

Figure 20.1 provides a conceptual map by organizing questions and evidence according to the typical life-course model, essentially into a causal flowchart, used in status attainment modeling research. It adds two features to those models, however. It decomposes "background influences" (the leftmost column) into their genetic and environmental components, whereas status attainment research generally proceeds as if there were little or no genetic variance in family backgrounds or status attainment. Figure 20.1 also adds another phenomenon neglected in such models, which is that of differences in how well individuals actually perform jobs and other life tasks that might influence their status attainment (lower right of the figure).

Sections 2 and 3 of the present chapter examine the meaning and measurement of the two sides of the equation in question: social inequality and intelligence differences. Section 2 describes the social inequalities to be explained, which are depicted

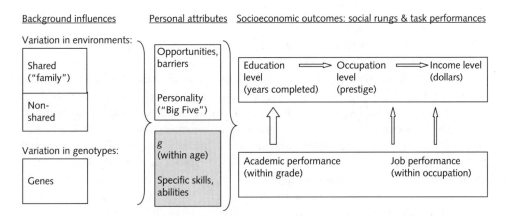

**Figure 20.1** Life course model of causes and consequences of social inequality

in the upper right of the figure. Section 3 turns to the key predictor of interest, cognitive diversity, which is represented in the shaded box under "personal attributes." To evaluate the meaning or *construct validity* of intelligence, Section 3 looks both backward and forward in Figure 20.1: back to the genetic and non-genetic roots of cognitive diversity ("background influences"), and forward to its manifestation in daily human performances outside mental test settings, particularly in school and at work ("task performances," to the lower right). Section 4 then introduces evidence on the phenotypic and genotypic links between the two realms, intelligence differences and social inequality, in order to test competing hypotheses about how cognitive diversity might generate social inequality as individuals compete to get ahead in life. The chapter concludes in Section 5 by revisiting the question of how societies attempt to accommodate cognitive diversity and why their efforts frequently have the opposite of their intended effects. The answer may be summarized as the *democratic dilemma*.

## 2   Meaning and Measurement of Social Inequality

Inequality is studied both at the individual and at the population level of analysis, referred to respectively as the study of *status attainment* ("who gets ahead") and of the *stratification* of populations into broad social classes.

### 2.1   Status attainment of individuals: level of education, occupation, and income

Research on individual differences in social inequality typically seeks to explain the spread of individuals across three social ladders: level of education, occupation, and income. These three achievements are sequentially contingent, as suggested by the life-course model in Figure 20.1. Advancing further in school increases one's chances of getting a good job, which in turn increases the odds of earning a good income.

Other things influence outcomes at each stage, but the range of possible outcomes is limited by achievements at earlier stages.

The education level (usually shortened to "education") is typically measured by self-reported years of schooling completed, ranges thereof (e.g. <8, 9–11, 12, 13–15, 16+), or highest degree earned (e.g. none, high school diploma, bachelor degree or more). Its meaning and causal significance usually remain vague and unspecified, or are supplied post hoc. Depending on the study, educational level may be interpreted as length of exposure to instruction, amount of information absorbed, level of cognitive skills inculcated, amount of human capital amassed, number of institutional hoops jumped, degree of acculturation or indoctrination, and so on. The shape of the distribution for years of schooling attained has changed radically across the twentieth century, from skewed right to skewed left. Only 10 percent of American 14–17-year-olds were attending secondary school in 1910, but over 90 percent were doing so by 1970; 2 percent and 36 percent of 18–24 year-olds were attending college in 1900 and 1970, and by 2008 half were in college (National Center for Education Statistics, 1993, Figure 7 and Table 24; 2010, Table A-1-1). These are culturally seismic changes.

Occupational level ("occupation") is usually measured in units of prestige level (e.g. 0–96 on the Duncan scale: Duncan, Featherman, & Duncan, 1972) or through a small set of ordered categories (e.g. Britain's socioeconomic classification, which ranges from I for professional to V for unskilled work). The distribution of workers by occupation has likewise shifted greatly over the last century, as economies evolved from primarily agricultural to mostly service-based ones. Almost 40 percent of the American civilian workforce worked in agriculture in 1900, under 5 percent in 1970, and less than 1.5 percent in 2008. In contrast, between 1970 and 2008 alone, the percentage of workers employed in the service sector (professional and business services [not financial], education, health and social assistance, leisure and household) rose from 26 percent to 46 percent (U.S. Bureau of the Census, 1990, Table 650; 2009, Table 607). Like many other sociologists, I see occupations as the key to understanding social inequality, so this chapter pays particular attention to that dimension of social inequality. This perspective focuses on how occupations differ hierarchically, as seen in Figure 20.2, in terms of both occupational prestige and their incumbents' typical intelligence level. Sociologists have tended to view occupations primarily as scaffolds on which societies hang social rewards, respect, and influence, but not as interesting entities in themselves. Section 3 will open up the black box of occupation to reveal a treasure trove of evidence. It shows that differences in task demands across these boxes matter a lot, and also influence the social ornaments attached to them.

Measuring income level ("income" or "earnings") is a more complicated matter, and economic inequality is the province of economists. There are many potentially relevant measures, but few are conceptually equivalent or typically available to the researcher. The latter include wages (for hourly workers), yearly salary (for many others), or self-employment income; income only from primary job versus all sources, including investments; and income of head of household versus all members. For some purposes, wealth of different sorts is counted (e.g. personal property or investments). Income data are highly skewed—a few individuals have huge incomes, but

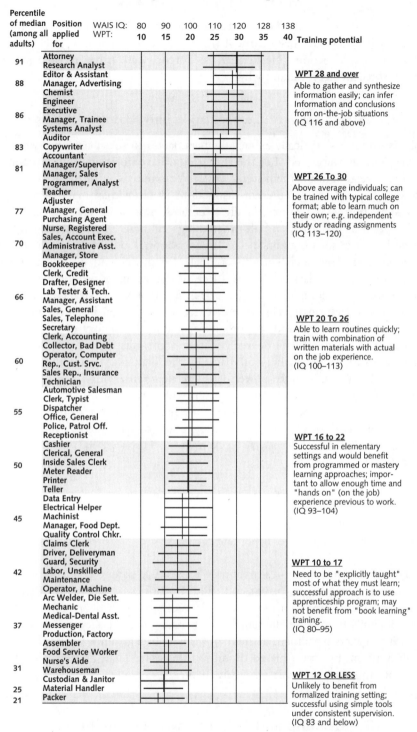

**Figure 20.2** Test scores by occupation applied for (1992). The bold horizontal line shows the range between the 25th and 75th percentiles. The bold crossmark shows the 50th percentile (median) of applicants to that occupation. Reprinted from Gottfredson, 1997, Figure 1. WPT = Wonderlic Personnel Test

the majority quite modest ones—so researchers often log-transform income data before analysis. They have been particularly interested in population-level changes in the distribution of income (Neckerman & Torche, 2007): has income inequality increased in recent decades, and why?

## 2.2   Stratification of the population into broad social classes

Sociologists do not statistically extract a general factor of social class, nor would that seem theoretically warranted. But the clustering of favorable versus unfavorable outcomes does create and maintain *social classes*. We often speak of the upper, middle, and lower classes. Classes represent distinctions in more than material well-being: also in social norms and mores, family structures, aspirations and expectations for children, political behavior, and all other things cultural. There is a rich legacy of theoretical work in sociology on social class formation. Conflict theories in that field have emphasized how social groups compete for power and privilege, and neo-Marxist ones have emphasized their relations to the means of production.

Sociologists have long studied the *permeability* of social strata by calculating rates of intergenerational *social mobility* across them. For instance, they might cross-tabulate fathers and sons by broad occupational category or self-designated social class, and then calculate degree of father–son similarity in category occupied. Greater similarity (more father–son pairs in the diagonal) is interpreted as lack of social mobility, or as more powerful *intergeneration transmission* of class. This inference rests on the assumption that parent–offspring similarity in adult status is not to be expected in a meritocratic society; it reflects an unfair transmission of social advantages or disadvantages from one generation to the next. A recent chapter in the *Annual Review of Sociology* (Neckerman & Torche, 2007, p. 339) states it explicitly:

> The most common measure of inequality of opportunity is the intergenerational associa-
> tion of income, earnings, class, or other resources. A weak parent–child association
> indicates that individual well-being is not highly determined by parental resources and
> it thus reflects high equality of opportunity in a society.

Although status attainment research tries to unpack parent–child correlations to determine what "mediates" parent and child similarities, it too tends to treat non-trivial parent–child correlations in socioeconomic status as evidence for unjust transmission of family resources. The same belief pervades social policy and debate today, when policy-makers presume that children from all backgrounds would rise or fall in equal proportion, but for a biased thumb on the scale. That, however, is a testable assumption, to be addressed later in this chapter.

## 3   Meaning and Measurement of Intelligence

In order to understand $g$'s role in social inequality, we must first understand its properties in everyday behavior, that is, as a behavioral phenotype. (Unless I specify otherwise, any mention of abilities or intelligence relates to phenotypes.) In terms of

Figure 20.1, we are now looking at the shaded box under "personal attributes." Some scholars use the term "intelligence" to refer to everything included there; others refer to *g* alone, as I do. This reflects just taste in labeling, and it makes no difference how the label is being used, as long as this is made clear. Our concern here is to understand the phenomena that mental tests capture and what they mean, operationally, in daily affairs.

## 3.1   Phenotypic structure of human cognitive differences

Perhaps the most important discovery about individual differences in psychological traits, when they are psychometrically assessed, is that they are highly *structured*. By structure or *architecture* I mean predictable form and the relatedness of diverse individual differences within a population—in this case, cognitive abilities (Carroll, 1993; Johnson et al., 2007). Beside being close to normally distributed, all cognitive abilities correlate with all others, and often substantially so, although some kinds (e.g. verbal, spatial) correlate more tightly among themselves than with others (see Reeve & Bonaccio, 2011: this volume). Clear order has emerged from the seeming welter of different human abilities, which is captured in their *hierarchical* organization, exemplified in Carroll's (1993) three-strata model (see, again, Reeve & Bonaccio, 2011: this volume). Four features of this hierarchical integration of the evidence are especially important for understanding why human cognitive diversity is so deeply and thoroughly entwined in social inequality, and why *g* in particular will hold the answer.

The first feature is that there is, in fact, only a single general latent factor (labeled *g*) at the top of the hierarchical model—stratum III in Carroll's model. Empirically, there is not a multiplicity of highly general abilities or "intelligences" comparable to *g*. Differentiation occurs only at lower levels of the hierarchy. In short, *g* seems to be the prime mover among abilities.

The second crucial feature is that *g* forms the thick core of all the narrower cognitive abilities in the strata below. There is often confusion on this point, because the phenomenon of *g* (the *construct*) is often mistakenly equated with the *scores* on tests used to gauge it. IQ scores are calculated by summing an individual's scores on the various sub-tests in an IQ battery, such as the Stanford–Binet. This summation procedure continues today, but not because intelligence is thought to be the sum of many independent specific abilities. Rather, IQ scores calculated in this manner happen to measure *g* well because, when sub-test scores are summed, their common variance (what they all measure in common) accumulates, while the more specific, non-*g* variances of each tend to cancel out. So *g* is not an amalgam of the separate specific abilities located lower in the hierarchical model. Instead, the lower are increasingly complex, multifaceted psychometric amalgams of the higher. This means that ability tests usually measure mostly *g*, regardless of their name or original intent. To illustrate, when a first factor is extracted from the 15 subtests of the WAIS–IV battery, 7 provide good measures of *g* (*g* loadings of .71–.78), another 7 provide fair measures (*g* loadings of .58–.70), and the 15th provides a poor measure (.44 for cancellation; Sattler & Ryan, 2009, Table 2–12, p. 49).

The third feature is that cognitive abilities are best distinguished by their *generality* or breadth of application. The *g* factor is most general because it enhances performance in the widest range of cognitive tasks, although not necessarily equally in all. In contrast, abilities at successively lower, more content-specific levels in the hierarchical model enhance performance in successively fewer, narrower ranges of task content. Whereas *g* has domain-general application, narrower abilities (stripped of their *g* component) have only domain-specific application (e.g. visual perception and auditory perception at stratum II level, and spatial scanning and temporal tracking at stratum I level; see Carroll, 1993, Figure 15.1).

Fourth, the structure of cognitive abilities seems largely independent of the structure of so-called non-cognitive traits (see Ferguson, Chamorro-Premuzic, Pickering, & Weiss, 2011: this volume; and von Stumm, Chamorro-Premuzic, & Ackerman, 2011: this volume). For instance, other than openness to experience, which reflects an interest in novel learning opportunities, there are few correlations of note between *g* and any of the Big-Five (or Three, or Eight) dimensions of personality. Personnel psychologists summarize these cognitive and non-cognitive realms as the "can do" and "will do" elements of human performance. Both are important in human affairs, but for different reasons and in different patterns. Both may be required to explain social inequality, but the influence of each would tend to be independent of *g*. This chapter focuses on the relation between cognitive diversity and social inequality, so the independence of the two realms of individual differences removes the need for us to examine the non-cognitive realm in the current context.

## 3.2   Universality of psychometric structure across human and non-human populations

The hierarchical organization of cognitive abilities would be of scant interest were it specific to time, place, or demographic group, or—as sometimes suggested—simply manufactured by psychometric techniques, patterns of social privilege, or educational practices in western schools.

Research to date indicates that intelligence test batteries actually do yield basically the same psychometric structure for different races and for both sexes (Gottfredson, 2005). As for *g* in particular, the *g* factors derived from different samples converge on the same true *g*. This convergence occurs not only across different broad batteries of tests, but also across different ages, sexes, races, cultures, and countries (Jensen, 1998; Johnson, te Nijenhuis, & Bouchard, 2008). A general factor is also found in other species, including mice, when they are administered batteries of diverse problem-solving tasks. Chabris (2007) refers to this as the "law of general intelligence." For instance, he describes how a general factor emerged among both 2–3-year-old rhesus monkeys (accounting for 35 percent of test variance) and among 5–6-year-old human children (accounting for 42 percent of the variance) when the two groups were administered the same five problem-solving tests. A general mental ability factor appears to be a pan-specific phenomenon—not in level, of course, but in having a domain-general core around which most within-species cognitive variation revolves.

These regularities refute any claim that recurring variation in general intelligence within human populations is just an epiphenomenon of their cultural activities, which might disappear if cultures organized themselves differently. A strictly socially induced cognitive inequality would not create phenotypic structures that are so consistent across time, place, and human groups, let alone species. This is not say that culture has no effect on intelligence (or height), but only that genetic diversity limits the range of effects culture might have on intelligence (or height) and the manner in which it achieves them.

## 3.3   Biological correlates of cognitive ability in human populations

If cognitive diversity truly is a biological fact, then phenotypes should be moderately heritable and correlated with physiological variation in the brain.

*3.3.1   Genetic architecture*   The heritability of $g$ (the ratio of genetic to phenotypic variation in $g$) increases linearly from .4 at age 9 to almost .7 at age 17 (Haworth et al., 2010), reaches .80 by mid-adulthood, and remains there into old-old age (Plomin, Pedersen, Lichtenstein, & McClearn, 1994). Some behavior geneticists speculate that the increase in heritability over the lifecycle results from individuals finding and creating personal niches that reinforce and magnify their genetic propensities—that is, from *gene–environment (g–e) correlation* (Bouchard, Lykken, Tellegen, & McGue, 1996; Scarr, 1996; see Spinath & Johnson, 2011: this volume).

The .7–.8 heritability of $g$ rivals that for weight (.7) and height (.9) in developed countries (Plomin, DeFries, McClearn, & McGuffin, 2008; see Towne, Demerath, & Czerwinski, 2002, for the heritability of other biometric measures). Variation in height and weight cannot be dismissed as just by-products of human imagination or social privilege, and neither can differences in $g$. Moreover, the phenotypic covariance among different major cognitive abilities (verbal, spatial, perceptual speed, memory, etc.) consists almost entirely of *genetic* variance in $g$, from adolescence into old-old age (Petrill et al., 1998; Spinath & Johnson, 2011: this volume). Each broad cognitive ability has other, independent sources of genetic or environmental influence, but those contributions are specific to that ability and, except for memory, they are small relative to genetic $g$.

Turning to strictly environmental influences on $g$, the only ones persisting into adulthood are those that affect each sibling uniquely (*non-shared* environmental influences), not those that affect siblings equally (*shared* environmental influences). That is, to the extent that differences in family advantage (e.g. higher parental education or income) have lasting influence on offspring intelligence, they do not affect all offspring equally or in the same way (see Spinath & Johnson, 2011: this volume). In statistical terms, differences in rearing environments have no main effect on adult intelligence. The lack of lasting shared environmental effects on intelligence certainly does not mean that "parents don't matter." As behavior geneticists are quick to point out, it means only that rearing environments within the typical range in today's western nations are "effectively equal" for supporting normal cognitive development (Scarr, 1996).

But might the systematic relatedness of abilities at the phenotypic level be socially induced? A growing body of research on the genetic correlations among cognitive abilities answers otherwise. The genetic architecture of cognitive abilities does, in fact, seem to mirror their phenotypic architecture: "It is a plausible working hypothesis that the taxonomic hierarchy of cognitive abilities is mirrored by (derived from?)

an isomorphic structure of genetic influences" (Brody, 2007, p. 439). Johnson et al. (2007) illustrate such isomorphism by using their verbal–perceptual–image rotation hierarchical model, an alternative to Carroll's. "Genetic correlations closely mirrored the phenotypic correlations" at all levels of the hierarchy, except for memory, revealing "high consistency [...] between the genetic and phenotypic structure" (pp. 542, 559). This suggests that any attempt to equalize intelligence phenotypes will eventually confront genetic resistance. Unless environmental advantages are arranged to correlate negatively with genetic ones, genetic variability will guarantee considerable phenotypic variability.

*3.3.2 Brain architecture*   Most research on the physiological manifestations of intelligence has focused on how psychometric *g* manifests itself in the physical realities of the brain. Investigators have recently begun examining whether the secondary dimensions of cognitive variation do too (Johnson et al., 2007). The most striking finding is that *g* has structural and functional correlates across the entire brain: volume of white matter, gray matter, and total brain; white matter lesions, organization, and integrity; rate of cerebral glucose metabolism and nerve conduction velocity; various characteristics of resting EEG and average evoked potentials; and much more (see Colom & Thompson, 2011: this volume; also Deary, Penke, & Johnson, 2010). General intelligence represents a distributed network, not isolated modules in the brain, and research is now apace to trace task performance in real time as it recruits different parts of the brain (Jung & Haier, 2007). Studies have used a mish-mash of tests, some more *g*-loaded than others or capturing more non-*g* variance, which makes the ubiquity of correlates all the more impressive.

As Jensen (1998) has suggested, the *g* factor is so thoroughly enmeshed in brain physiology that it may actually represent a property of the brain as a whole, for instance, its overall efficiency (capacity, speed, integration) or integrity (resilience, developmental stability), rather than an ability as such. The pattern of phenotypic covariation between *g* and brain attributes seems to be reflected in genetic covariation as well. Many specific aspects of brain structure and function are 70 percent to 90 percent heritable, and genetic influences on intelligence that are shared across brain regions are stronger than those specific to any one region (Deary et al., 2010). Revealing additional consilience across bodies of research, Deary, Johnson, and Houlihan (2009) note that age-related patterns of heritability in brain structure suggest a partial explanation for the age-related rise in the heritability of *g*.

Once again, non-genetic factors will influence brain phenotypes, in part by influencing how genotypes are expressed under different conditions—and some parts of the brain show more environmental variance than others (Deary et al., 2010); but non-genetic influences must work within the general confines laid down by the genetic substrate for brain physiology and typical human environments. There may be non-genetic means by which to decrease the environmental variance in phenotypic *g*, but they would likely have meaningful influence only if they altered brain physiology (e.g. drugs).

*3.3.3 Evolutionary robustness*   Evolution has left our species, like other surviving ones, with a genome that allows its members to physically weather or rebound from ever-present biological adversities, including starvation, injury, parasites, and infectious disease. The biological resistance of humans' mental prowess to lasting perturbation extends to typical features of modern social environments too, as confirmed by decades of socioeducational interventions intended to decrease inequalities (variance) in intelligence and academic achievement (Brody, 2007). All have failed to leave much mark on individual differences in $g$. It is also confirmed by adoption studies, perhaps the strongest social intervention of all, because adopted children become more similar to their biological relatives and less like their adoptive ones by the time they reach adolescence.

External, contextual influences do contribute to phenotypic variation, which increases spread in the population and somewhat alters the rank order of individuals within it. But these within-cohort influences on rank order tend to be modest and temporary in research to date. Examples include preschool interventions, malnutrition, and intestinal parasites (Sternberg & Grigorenko, 2001). When these influences are withdrawn, the good effects of the former "fade out" and the bad effects of the latter are usually reversed by "catch-up" growth (see also Tanner, 1986, on catch-up and catch-down growth in height after deprivation and interventions).

## 3.4   Meaning (construct validity) of $g$ as a behavioral phenotype

No longer is there dispute that psychometric $g$ predicts diverse life outcomes. It does, and pervasively so (Gottfredson, 1997; Herrnstein & Murray, 1994). The following findings help to narrow possible explanations concerning why it does.

*3.4.1   Three competing conceptions of* g *and its real-world utility*   Hypotheses have come in three main versions, the spirit of which may be captured, respectively, in Fischer et al. (1996), Sternberg and Wagner (1993), and Jensen (1980).

- *g-pretense conception: No latent trait, just the pretense of one*  IQ tests do not measure cognitive ability but something else, such as test-taking skill, past educational achievement, quality of instruction, or social class background. Society rewards these other things while seeming only to reward cognitive ability, because we mistakenly believe, or are falsely led to believe, that IQ tests measure something special.
- *g-academic conception: Narrow academic trait of limited practical value*  IQ tests measure only a narrow range of abilities, mostly academic aptitude ("book learning"), but not practical or creative intelligence. Academic abilities reap major rewards because modern industrialized societies have chosen to privilege them, despite their limited real-world utility.
- *g-general conception: Broad latent trait of pervasive practical value*  IQ tests measure a latent trait, $g$, which enhances performance in important life realms. Higher standing on the latent trait reaps more rewards because society values such performances and the social goods they generate for the group.

The first two conceptions have not stood up well against data amassed in recent decades. The biological evidence just reviewed rules out the first conception. Whatever *g* is, it exists as a biologically grounded axis of human differentiation. And, although phenotypic *g* is influenced by many genes and its physiological embodiment is suffused through the brain, it manifests itself as unitary in psychometric measurements and in everyday human performance. This favors the third hypothesis over the second, but not conclusively so, in explaining *g*'s role in status attainment.

*3.4.2 Attributes of tasks that put a premium on* g   We can get more purchase on *g* as a construct by identifying the attributes of life tasks and settings that call it forth most effectively (i.e. are most *g*-loaded) and therefore most clearly reveal individual differences in *g*. Analyses of tasks in three different realms of human performance—mental tests, school work, and jobs—all point to the same ingredient. It can be summarized as the complexity of information processing required for effective performance.

Looking first at mental tests, Jensen (1980, p. 231) describes how the most discriminating (most *g*-loaded) tests and test items are not distinguished by test format or surface content (words, pictures, etc.), but by something subtler and less concrete, namely the complexity of the information processing and mental manipulation they require for good performance.

> [T]ask complexity and the amount of conscious mental manipulation required seem to be the most basic determinants of the *g* loading of a task. If we distill this summary generalization still further, the amount of conscious mental manipulation set off by the input would seem to be the crucial element.

In order of increasing complexity, there are tasks requiring associative memory, reproduction, production, and eduction. Reasoning tests exemplify the latter, regardless of whether the information to be manipulated is verbal, mathematical, spatial, or pictorial. The following hypothetical number series items illustrate how task complexity can be increased with the same simple surface content: 2, 4, 6, __ vs. 2, 4, 8, __ vs. 2, 4, 6, 4, 6, __. The three require inferring increasingly complex rules to fill in the blank.

Jensen (1980, pp. 327–329) shows how school tasks, too, are more *g*-loaded when they require or allow more complex mental manipulation. For instance, success in learning is more highly correlated with *g* level when it is intentional, meaningful, insightful, age- (maturation-) related, permits or requires transfer from past learning, the material to be learned is hierarchical (as in science and math, which require mastery of building blocks), the material is moderately complex, learners are given the same fixed amount of time to learn, and they are at early stages of learning (material not already highly practiced).

Both the *g*-academic and *g*-general conceptions of *g* can claim to accommodate these findings, so we need to examine tasks performed outside of tests and schools. Job analysts in industrial–organizational psychology provide much data from employment settings. Jobs, not workers, are the units of analysis in their studies. Job incumbents and their supervisors rate the job in question according to a wide variety of characteristics. The same rating system is applied to a population of jobs, and factor analyses are performed on the ratings. The resulting factors reveal the underlying structure in the multitude of differences in task constellations and attendant aptitude and interest requirements. These factor analyses are thus parallel in aim and form to those performed by psychometricians on mental test scores for large groups of test-takers.

Job rating systems differ greatly, but all yield results that point to the centrality of task complexity and to the amount of intentional mental manipulation that jobs require of workers. Table 20.2 samples such results. When the focus is on behavioral requirements (top panel), the dominant factor is "judgment and reasoning" (learning, reasoning, quick understanding, making judgments, spotting and solving problems). When job duties and responsibilities are factor analyzed as well (lower panel), the dominant first factor is the "overall complexity" of information processing and decision-making (compiling, combining, analyzing information; writing, advising, negotiating, persuading). These separately derived first factors are just mirror images of each other, the first describing the behavioral manifestations of *g* and the second the stimuli that "set it off." When working conditions and needs for workers to

**Table 20.2** Correlations in two job analysis studies of selected job attributes with first factor. Sources: Arvey, 1986, p. 418 ("Judgment and reasoning" factor); Gottfredson, 1997, pp. 100–104 ("Job complexity" factor). Key: PAQ = Position Analysis Questionnaire; DOT = *Dictionary of Occupational Titles* (U.S. Department of Labor, 1984)

| Job attributes | Correlation with factor |
|---|---|
| "Judgment and reasoning" factor (140 jobs in petrochemical industry) | |
| Deal with unexpected situations | .75 |
| Able to learn and recall job-related information | .71 |
| Able to reason and make judgements | .69 |
| Able to identify problem situations quickly | .69 |
| React swiftly when unexpected problems occur | .67 |
| Able to apply common sense to solve problems | .66 |
| Able to learn new procedures quickly | .66 |
| Alert and quick to understand things | .55 |
| "Job complexity" factor (PAQ and DOT data for 276 broad Census occupations) | |
| Compiling information (importance) | .90 |
| Self-direction (amount) | .88 |
| Reasoning (level ), DOT | .86 |
| Advising (importance) | .86 |
| Update job knowledge (importance) | .85 |
| Complexity of dealings with data (level), DOT | .83 |
| Analyzing information (importance) | .83 |
| Planning/scheduling (amount) | .83 |
| Negotiating (importance) | .79 |
| Work under distractions (importance) | .78 |
| Frustrating situations (importance) | .77 |
| Criticality of position (degree) | .71 |
| Repetitive activities (importance) | −.49 |
| Supervision (level) | −.73 |

function independently are considered, the most complex jobs are also the ones requiring more self-direction, responsibility-taking, independent judgment, and continual need to update job knowledge, especially under distracting, frustrating, conflict-laden, time-sensitive, and changing conditions. All these increase the complexity of work, the cognitive load on the worker, and the need for more independent and more extensive mental manipulation of information.

Together, these findings echo descriptions of general intelligence itself (reasoning, judgment, problem-solving, facility in learning), tests of fluid $g$ (novel tasks, inferences required, spotting problems, integrating new information), and tests of crystallized $g$ (writing, display of independently accrued general knowledge). The job analysis data are especially compelling because their relevance to $g$ was neither of interest to, nor initially recognized by, job analysts (Arvey, 1986). These results for jobs' demands on workers converge with those for mental tests and school work, and the convergence is empirical, not by definition or design. It supports the $g$-general conception of intelligence by showing that mental tests, school work, and jobs are all distinguished primarily by the degree to which they require individuals to manipulate moderately complex information, regardless of content domain or of how academic they seem.

*3.4.3 g-Narrow vs. g-general predictions for external validity in non-academic work* The proof of the pudding is in the eating, however. Does the $g$-general conception fare any better than the $g$-academic conception in actually accounting for patterns in job performance? The two conceptions make opposing predictions about when and where $g$ will correlate most strongly with job performance.

Table 20.3 lists 10 pairs of competing predictions. Those for the $g$-academic conception are gleaned or inferred from well-known psychological and sociological writings that assert a more privilege-based view of why $g$ predicts so many life outcomes. Those listed for the $g$-general conception follow directly from what might be called $g$ theory, which I induce from the nomological network of empirical generalizations having $g$ at its core. The 10 pairs of predictions can be tested by turning to meta-analyses from a different literature: personnel selection psychology.

The $g$-general conception of intelligence predicts a very particular, non-obvious pattern of correlations between $g$ level and quality of job performance on the basis of what is known about the nature of $g$ and of the tasks that place a premium on it. As reviewed above, $g$ is a general proficiency in learning and reasoning, and tasks are more $g$-loaded when they require independent performance of moderately complex tasks (Chamorro-Premuzic & Furnham, 2010). The predictions from the $g$-academic conception follow from viewing $g$ as a narrow ability of limited practical value.

The two conceptions therefore differ in how pervasively they expect $g$ to correlate with on-the-job performance and how important other abilities will be relative to $g$ in predicting it. The $g$-academic conception predicts that $g$ will correlate with performance in only a small percentage of jobs, because only a minority are academic-like. The $g$-general conception, however, predicts a positive correlation in all jobs, because all jobs require some learning and reasoning (Prediction 1). The rationale is spelled out in Hunter's (1986) model of job performance. First, $g$ is an excellent

**Table 20.3** Differential predictions from competing conceptions of *g*'s practical utility: External validity by type of work, workforce, and performance criteria

| # | Correlations between g and performance | Competing conceptions of g's utility | | Reports on illustrative meta-analyses |
|---|---|---|---|---|
| | | g academic | g general | |
| Average correlations | | | | |
| 1 | correlations > 0 | low % | 100% | Schmidt & Hunter, 1998 |
| 2 | incremental validity of specific abilities | frequent & moderate | infrequent & small | Thorndike, 1986 |
| Moderators of correlations | | | | |
| *Work tasks* | | | | |
| 3 | more complex | no independent effect | higher | Hunter, 1986 |
| 4 | more academic | higher | no independent effect | see Figure 20.2 |
| 5 | more independently performed | no effect? | higher | Hunter, 1986 |
| *Performance criteria* | | | | |
| 6 | more objective | lower | higher | Hunter, 1986 |
| 7 | more exclusively technical | no effect? | higher | McHenry et al., 1990 |
| 8 | more exclusively citizenship | higher | lower | McHenry et al., 1990 |
| *Workforce* | | | | |
| 9 | more equal training | lower | higher | Hunter & Schmidt, 1996 |
| 10 | more equal experience | lower | higher | Schmidt, Hunter, Outerbridge, & Goff, 1988 |

predictor of job-specific knowledge for the same reason why it predicts learning in any other subject area, and job knowledge is the best predictor of who performs well once on the job. Second, jobs both allow and require workers to keep updating their knowledge, appropriately apply what they know, and continually spot and solve new problems—all of which tasks call for *g*.

The infrequent predictive value of *g* in the *g*-narrow view opens the door for other abilities to matter, especially in their own content areas. For instance, tests of mathematical reasoning will predict performance better in math-dependent jobs than in highly verbal work, and vice versa for tests of verbal ability, and both will predict performance substantially better than *g* alone in their own content realms (Prediction 2). In contrast, the *g*-general conception predicts only low or no incremental validity for specific abilities, after controlling for *g*, because *g* forms the core of all abilities and is domain-general. Because tests of broad abilities such as verbal and spatial ones tend to have only a fraction as much non-*g* variance as *g* variance, they are not likely to have much (if any) incremental validity in any content area.

Predictions 3–10 are more interesting because they deal with specific aspects of jobs and working conditions, which are expected to increase or decrease (i.e. *moderate*) the correlations between *g* and performance outcomes. Neither conception expects that the same difference in *g* (say, a 15-point IQ advantage) will confer the same competitive advantage in all circumstances where *g* matters. Table 20.3 lists three types of moderators: attributes of the jobs to be performed (Predictions 3–5), the criteria by which overall job performance is evaluated (Predictions 6–8), and variability among the workers in a job (Predictions 9–10). These may be conceptualized as three types of levers that, as the two conceptions predict, will ratchet *g*'s value up or down, the two differing only in the direction in which they expect the correlations to move.

The *g*-narrow conception mirrors prior expectations in personnel selection psychology, which once held to *specific aptitude theory* (Schmidt & Hunter, 2004), as well as still extant presumptions in sociology. It expects *g*'s predictive validity to rise under two conditions: first, when the job is more academic; and, second, when there are more opportunities for some sort of (usually unspecified) social privilege to affect performance outcomes. So, correlations should rise when jobs are more academic-like, say, for clerical rather than crafts work (Prediction 4), regardless of the complexity of work (Prediction 3). Next, supervisors will have more opportunity to bias their performance ratings in favor of higher-IQ workers, thus increasing the IQ–performance correlation, when they use more subjective means of rating performance (Prediction 6) and when they focus more exclusively on evaluating worker compliance and conformity (Prediction 8) rather than technical acumen (Prediction 7). Finally, proponents of social privilege theory predict that the competitive advantage of higher *g* will fall when workers have more equal job-specific training and experience (Predictions 9–10) because they believe differences in job knowledge result primarily from differences in opportunities to learn, not differences in learning proficiency or in problem-solving.

The *g*-general conception predicts the opposite. *g*'s correlations with job performance outcomes should increase monotonically with the complexity of the work performed, regardless of its academic-ness (Predictions 3–4), and when workers perform more independently (i.e. without help or hindrance; Prediction 5). They should also rise when performance is assessed more objectively (Prediction 6) and emphasizes "can do" technical performance rather than "will do" citizenship criteria such as self-discipline and professional bearing (Predictions 7–8).

Finally, the *g*-general conception predicts that *g*'s correlations with job performance should remain robust, not disappear, when workers have equal job-specific training and experience (Predictions 9–10) and, of course, when there is no artificial ceiling on job performance. *g* will continue to matter for reasons outlined earlier. Namely, it predicts the acquisition of job knowledge both during and after formal training, and it facilitates more effective exploitation of that knowledge in order to carry out job duties. Exposure to learning can be equalized, but knowledge gained per unit exposure cannot. Anticipated effects of equalizing workers' training and experience (exposure to learning opportunities) on the $g$-performance correlation will depend on whether workers' differences in exposure had been correlated with their $g$ levels. If not correlated (the typical situation; Schmidt, Hunter, Outerbridge, & Goff, 1988), then predictive validities will not change; if exposure had been negatively correlated with $g$, then validities will rise somewhat; if positively correlated, they will fall somewhat. This is what we would predict for any $g$-loaded test.

Note that all the work characteristics that the $g$-general conception expects will boost IQ–performance correlations are essential to creating a good test of $g$, so these eight predictions can be reduced to a single, more general one: the more closely that tasks and performance conditions mimic those of standardized tests of $g$, the better $g$ should predict on-the-job performance. This is not to say that jobs should mimic IQ tests, but only that performance is better predicted when they do.

### 3.4.4 *Evidence supports* g-*general predictions*  Meta-analytic studies (listed in Table 20.3) confirm all 10 predictions derived from $g$ theory. They contradict the competing $g$-academic conception, which has to invoke social privilege and bias to explain why $g$ seems to provide more social rewards than its supposedly limited functional utility would warrant. Moreover, the $g$-general predictions have also been confirmed for performance in education and training as well (see e.g. Jencks et al., 1979, chap. 4; 1986; Thorndike, 1986).

$g$ theory suggests that life itself can be conceptualized as a test (Gordon, 1997), so it should forecast patterned sets of $g$-performance correlations in other life areas as well, such as health self-care (Gottfredson, 2004; see also Calvin, Batty, & Deary, 2011: this volume). Life's tests are hardly standardized, nor do they hew to other essential psychometric requirements for test reliability and validity, but that is partly the point. If we knew how much or little they replicate the conditions for valid testing of $g$, we could predict when and where $g$ is likely to produce the most noticeable differences in performance and evoke differential rewards (Gordon, 1997).

### 3.4.5 *Statistical artifacts*  Meta-analysis in personnel selection warns us to anticipate statistical artifacts that would otherwise obscure the predicted pattern of $g$'s correlation with life outcomes: restriction in range, measurement error, and sampling error. Moreover, their effects are not random, because levels of all three often differ systematically over time, groups, or variables. This produces systematic biases in correlations we might wish to generalize to broader populations. To illustrate, it is hazardous to conclude that $g$ matters less and less at higher levels of education just because $g$'s observed correlations with academic performance progressively shrink at the higher levels (from .6– .7 in elementary school to .3– .4 in graduate school). The reason they do, of course, is that the spread in student $g$ levels has become successively narrowed at higher levels of schooling, precisely because $g$ mattered: it was a basis of selection or self-selection to the higher levels. It would likewise be hazardous to automatically assume that higher correlations signal stronger effects, when some variables were measured much less reliably than others.

The least recognized but most important of the three artifacts for the study of status inequality is restriction in range. Not only is restriction on $g$ range common in status attainment research samples (e.g. some exclude high school dropouts), but it is theoretically relevant for understanding status attainment itself. Restriction in range is the intended effect of institutionalized gatekeeping procedures, such as academic promotion, admissions, and credentialing, as well as of selection, placement, and promotion in military and civilian workplaces. It is the job of these institutions to filter, sort, channel, and segregate—to create restriction in range so as to meet operational needs. Sorting and self-segregation is also the aim of individuals seeking to get ahead (enter more exclusive social environments) or to find a comfortable and rewarding niche in life, where people like themselves can flourish, gain specialized expertise, and avoid conspicuous failure or displays of incompetence (Gordon, 1997). In short, systematic restriction in range is an inferential hazard when it remains unrecognized, but it can also provide valuable clues when viewed as evidence of social sorting machines at work.

## 4   Individual-Level Status Attainment Processes

Both the sociological study of social inequality and the psychological study of intelligence have amassed extensive nomological networks of evidence on what might be called their respective disciplines' master variables, social class and intelligence. Our question concerns how the two networks intersect and which direction the causal influences flow between them. In terms of Figure 20.1, we are now looking at the links (arrows) between "background influences," $g$, and "socioeconomic outcomes."

### 4.1   Status attainment modeling of phenotypic correlations

Research on status attainment (e.g. Duncan et al., 1972) is conducted on correlation matrices such as those shown in Table 20.1. Researchers make (though rarely test) assumptions about the causal ordering of variables, depict them in a path diagram, and then use statistical modeling to estimate parameters ("effect sizes") along each pathway (arrows)—say, from education to occupation. Pathways may be direct or indirect. In Figure 20.1, education would have an indirect path to income through occupation, but possibly also a direct path, not mediated (accounted for) by occupation. Non-significant paths are deleted from the final model.

Debate over $g$'s place in this nexus of correlations has taken the form of pitting IQ against family background in predicting adult status, especially since the publication of the *Bell Curve* (Herrnstein & Murray, 1994). The contest consists of seeing how large the direct "effects" of each are after partialing out their downstream indirect "effects" through other variables (e.g. education) and also controlling for the rest (IQ or family background). The winner is the one with the largest partial correlations left standing. The contest sometimes includes attempts to drive the direct effects of $g$ into statistical insignificance by controlling for a wide variety of family attributes (Fischer et al., 1996). Even when such attempts succeed (they rarely do), the results are causally ambiguous when conducted on genetically uninformative data, as the studies virtually always are. They usually commit the "partialing fallacy" besides (Gordon, 1968), which further muddies the interpretive waters. For instance, behavior geneticists would point out that family attributes and child's IQ are genetically correlated, because each is genetically correlated with a common cause, parents' *g* (see Spinath & Johnson, 2011: this volume). Controlling for family background thus removes valid genetic variance in child's IQ. However, this remains unacknowledged in most social science research, which usually attributes parent–child similarity in IQ to socialization (Scarr, 1996), even though a classic demonstration of this fundamental point appeared in the leading research journal in sociology over three decades ago (Scarr & Weinberg, 1978).

A recent meta-analysis (Strenze, 2007) confirms that son's IQ is a better predictor of son's educational, occupational, and income level than father's status is, when son's IQ was measured before age 19 and outcomes were measured after age 30. Corrected correlations for the three attainments were .42, .35, and .19 vs. .56, .45, and .23, with, respectively, father's occupation and son's IQ. Yet, as just noted, this means little without knowing why son's IQ correlates with his adult outcomes. This might reflect the functional value of higher *g*, but it could also reflect a "clubby snobbery" or irrational preference (Jencks et al., 1979, p. 84) on the part of institutional gate-keepers. The former process might be thought to be just, but the latter may not.

There is therefore only limited mileage to be gained from further modeling of phenotypic data from observational studies, one sample at a time—especially when the exercise is statistical more than theoretical, as tends to be the case (Gordon, 1968). Additional mileage might now be gained, however, by capitalizing on the nomological network for *g* to take a more theoretically informed approach. That is the approach taken below. How well do theories based on the *g*-academic and *g*-general conceptions of intelligence explain the *covariation* between *g* and successive outcomes shown in Figure 20.1, while respecting the larger network of evidence on *g*?

## 4.2 Social privilege theory vs. functional tool theory on *g*'s role in status attainment

Both sociology and psychology have actually offered the same competing explanations of *g*'s role in social inequality, which I label the *social privilege* ("privilege") and *functional tool* ("functional") theories. Neither has been an explicit theory, but I have fashioned them here to capture the key distinctions in causal assumptions and inferences I observe in both disciplines.

Social privilege theory views *g* as just one among other sorts of social inequality, which are manufactured or magnified by differences in advantages that siblings share (e.g. parental income). In contrast, the functional tool theory holds that *g* is a genetically conditioned phenotype which confers competitive advantages when performance, not mere privilege, governs social advancement; social privilege does not create differences in *g*, but it may affect whether individuals have the opportunity and encouragement to exploit their talents. Both theories agree that there are phenotypic differences in cognitive ability, as well as some genetic ones at birth. No theory that assumes otherwise would be viable, as some sociologists now argue

(Freese, 2008). They hold on to different conceptions of intelligence, however: social privilege theorists, to the narrower $g$-academic conception of intelligence, and functional tool theorists, to the $g$-general conception.

Thus the two theories generate competing predictions about how and why higher $g$ is translated into higher socioeconomic status over the life course. The most general difference concerns what would happen if a society provided all its members equal rearing environments and equal opportunity to succeed on the basis of individual merit. Social privilege theory predicts that it would drive down the correlation between IQ and socioeconomic success, possibly even to zero, because there would be no intergenerational transmission of social privilege. Functional tool theory predicts that it would drive up current IQ–outcome correlations and guarantee moderate intergenerational similarity *and* dissimilarity in status outcomes.

Table 20.4 lists 18 more specific pairs of predictions, which can be tested by extant evidence from behavior genetic research, longitudinal studies, and changes in public policy (natural "interventions"). I rely most heavily on the behavior genetic strategy of examining the genetic and non-genetic components of covariance between two measures, be they of traits, behaviors, environments, or life outcomes. I do so because the phenotypic correlations between (covariation of) IQ and socioeconomic success are precisely the phenomena to be explained (see Freese, 2008 on the value of this approach). Given its novelty in this context, the next section describes what it means to focus on the components of covariance between two variables.

### 4.3   Using components of covariance to test competing hypotheses

Each box in Figure 20.1 represents a pot of phenotypic variance, and the correlations between them constitute their covariation. Using Figure 20.3 as a conceptual aid, panel (a) depicts the variation in a particular variable, A. Of more interest, however, are its components (sources) of variation, as depicted in panel (b). Some proportion of the phenotypic variance may be genetic (the trait's heritability), and the rest will be non-genetic (plus measurement error). In turn, there may be two types of non-genetic variance: influences felt by all siblings in a family (shared environmental effects) and influences experienced by individual family members (non-shared effects).

Phenotypic correlations between different traits and outcomes are depicted in panel (c) of Figure 20.3 by the intersection of variables A and B. This is the variance they share in common. Most important for our purposes are the genetic and non-genetic components that make up that covariance as depicted by the intersection of A and B in panel (d). (See Jensen, 1971, for a psychometrically oriented discussion of how to interpret genetic covariance.)

*4.3.1   Cautions in interpreting genetic covariance*   It is crucial at this point to note that the components of covariance of two variables, panel (d), need not be found in the same proportions as the components of variance in either one alone, (b). This is illustrated in panel (e), where the heritability of B is considerably smaller than B's

**Table 20.4**  Opposing predictions on *g*'s role in social inequality: Social privilege vs. functional tool explanations (*g* = *g* level after adolescence). All predictions apply to broad populations, not to samples that may be restricted in range

| # | Predictions | Competing explanations | |
|---|---|---|---|
| | | Social privilege | Functional tool |
| **A. Components of genetic and environmental variation in g** | | | |
| 1 | early childhood | mostly shared | equally shared and genetic |
| 2 | adolescence | increasingly shared | decreasingly shared |
| 3 | adulthood | increasingly shared | not at all shared |
| **B. Covariation between g and socioeconomic success** | | | |
| | Phenotypic correlation | | |
| 4 | education level | moderately high | moderately high |
| 5 | occupation level | moderately high | moderately high, rises with age |
| 6 | income level | moderate | moderate, rises with age |
| | % of covariance that genetic | | |
| 7 | education level | low | high |
| 8 | occupation level | zero-low | high |
| 9 | income level | zero-low | high |
| | g-e component of genetic variance | | |
| 10 | education level | mostly evocative | mostly active |
| 11 | occupation level | mostly evocative | mostly active |
| 12 | income level | mostly evocative | mostly active |
| **C. Impact of social interventions on sorting process** | | | |
| | Interventions aimed at: | | |
| 13 | equalizing educational opportunity | *g*–education correlation falls | *g*–education correlation rises |
| 14 | equalizing educational opportunity | variance in educational outcomes shrinks | variability falls, heritability rises |
| 15 | equalizing educational opportunity | parent–child education correlation falls toward zero | parent–child correlation remains moderate, becomes 100% genetic |
| 16 | improving developmental environments for all | variability in outcomes narrows | variability in outcomes widens |
| 17 | weakening link of IQ to years of education | *g*–occupation correlation falls | education–occupation correlation falls |
| 18 | weakening link of education to occupation | *g*–occupation correlation falls | *g*–occupation correlation rises |

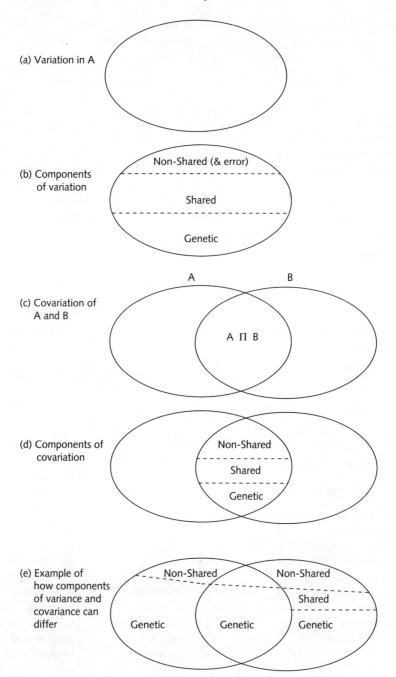

**Figure 20.3** Venn diagrams illustrating components of genetic and environmental variation and covariation

*bivariate* heritability with A. Bivariate heritability is the proportion of phenotypic *co*variance that is genetic. To take another example, if the covariance between A and B in e were mostly "shared family" rather than "genetic," then their bivariate heritability would be zero despite both A and B being moderately heritable.

A second caution is that, just as phenotypic correlations are not self-explanatory, neither are genetic ones. Even if we were sure that some genetically conditioned trait A is somehow influencing social outcome B (panel d), we still might not know why. Take, for instance, the .5 correlation between $g$ and occupational status (Table 20.1). Brighter individuals may end up in better jobs because their greater intelligence allows them to perform better in school and at work, but also because employers have an irrational or arbitrary preference for smart workers. The former would be an example of active gene–environment correlation (individuals seek out more intellectually compatible work environments), and the latter, a case of evocative (or "reactive") gene–environment correlation (gatekeepers select individuals into different environments on the basis of perceptions of their intelligence). The genetic correlation between family environment and child IQ, discussed earlier, is an example of a passive g–e correlation. In other contexts it might be called a spurious correlation, because child IQ and child's rearing environment correlate simply because both are independent results of the same parental genotype.

*4.3.2   Emergence of gene–environment (g–e) correlation between an adult's g and attainments*   The foregoing example of passive g–e correlation can be used to illustrate how active and evocative g–e correlations can emerge and increase the genetic covariation between $g$ and social outcomes. The passive g–e correlation between child's IQ and rearing environment comes about without any particular kind of activity on the part of the individuals involved. This might be the case, for example, if brighter parents read more to their pre-reading children than less bright parents do, without regard to whether the children ask to be read to or express any preferences about what to have read to them. Once children can read for themselves, purely passive g–e correlation is virtually impossible, because children begin to generate active g–e correlation when they choose different amounts and kinds of material to read. Relatives and teachers are likely to reinforce a bookish child's self-investment in reading by giving her books rather than other gifts—an example of evocation-type g–e correlation. The distinctions among the three types of g–e correlation become increasingly blurred with development, but both active and evocative g–e correlations serve to amplify the pre-existing genetic correlation, which is based on passive g–e correlation alone. If g–e correlations influence the development of intelligence itself, say, by recruiting environments that further develop and maintain differences in $g$, then the heritability of IQ will increase as development proceeds (because the active and evocative g–e correlations will add variance both to the numerator and to the denominator in calculating the heritability of $g$).

When g–e correlation between $g$ and status attainment magnifies differences in status outcomes, not in $g$, then their bivariate heritability should increase, as would the heritability of status outcomes, but not $g$. Some social scientists interpret this as environmental advantages being piled upon pre-existing genetic ones (thus Adkins & Vaisey, 2009, although they mistakenly refer to the process as *g–e* interaction).

So, in their view, some portion of the overall (*broad*) heritability of intelligence may actually reflect the influence of advantageous social contexts masquerading as genetic variance. Jensen (1969, pp. 38–39) anticipated this concern. He suggested that *narrow* heritability of intelligence (its additive genetic component) might therefore be used as a minimum estimate of genetic effects, but he also argued that its broad heritability has greater ecological validity for understanding the social consequences of genetic variation in intelligence, because it represents how genotypes actually operate in the real world. They are not passive, but generate their own advantages and disadvantages. He notes elsewhere (Jensen, 1981, pp. 121–123) that a society might be able to abolish passive g–e correlations by reassigning children to different rearing environments, and perhaps to discourage the emergence of g–e correlations of the evocative type; but it could never eliminate active g–e correlation. "No matter how hard we may try to create the same environmental opportunities for all children, we could never, even under the most rigidly totalitarian system of control, be able to eliminate the environmental differences that persons fashion for themselves in accord with their own particular genotypes."

## 4.4   Opposing assumptions of the two theories

The social privilege and functional tool theories of intelligence and social inequality predict different components of variance in all variables moving from left to right in Figure 20.1 and, in addition, different effects of social interventions on those variables' variance and covariance when social policies attempt to reduce $g$'s impact on status attainment. Those predictions, discussed shortly, rest on the following causal assumptions.

Social privilege theory postulates that: (1) differences in shared family resources (top box in leftmost column of Figure 20.1) create differences in all personal traits and circumstances (second column), including $g$; (2) these two sets of privileges— pre-existing familial and newly generated personal ones—provide the social credentials necessary for surmounting the many class barriers to advancement that gatekeepers erect for directing only the higher classes to higher rungs on the social ladder (outcomes in upper right); (3) differences in task performance (lower right) matter primarily to the extent that gatekeepers use them to reinforce or legitimate social privilege, not because good performance has any inherent value; and (4) therefore $g$ level matters to the extent that it transmits socioeconomic advantages from one generation to the next.

These and similar assertions pervade many sociological treatises. For instance, Adkins and Vaisey (2009) have attempted to reconcile the sociological and genetic perspectives on status attainment by portraying genes and family resources as being independent influences on cognitive ability and then arguing that social inequality makes it difficult to "translate" ability into status (Figure 20.1). Bowles and Gintis's (1972/1973) classic article "IQ in the U.S. class structure" is of particular interest, because it was written to rebut Jensen's (1969) conclusions about the importance of IQ in education, and hence economic success as well (but see also their recent conclusion that "the genetic inheritance of IQ explains little of the intergenerational transmission process [of income]," Bowles & Gintis, 2002, p. 13):

IQ is in fact *not* a crucial determinant of job adequacy. (p. 12)

[We do] not deny that for some individuals or for some jobs, cognitive skills are economically important. Rather, we assert for the vast majority of workers and jobs, selection, assessed job adequacy, and promotion are based on attributes other than IQ. (p. 7)

IQ is not an important cause of economic success [...] [Instead] the emphasis on intelligence as the basis for economic success serves to legitimize an authoritarian, hierarchical, stratified, and unequal economic system of production, and to reconcile the individual to his or her objective position within this system. (p. 2)

Functional theory emphasizes a different flow of influence across Figure 20.1: (1) shared environmental influences have no lasting impact on $g$, so the child's $g$ transmits only the genetic advantages of parents into adulthood; (2) differences in $g$ generate differences in performance on tasks having practical utility (lower right of Figure 20.1); (3) their functional utility encourages gatekeepers to sort and advance individuals somewhat on the basis of $g$-correlated traits and credentials; this (4) discourages their sole reliance on mere whim or social prejudice. In short, privilege theory minimizes the importance of genes and task performance, but functional theory emphasizes them. Where privilege theory would draw thick arrows across the top of Figure 20.1, functional theory would draw thin ones, and then add thick ones across the bottom of the figure.

## 4.5 Competing predictions from the two theories

Table 20.4 lists 18 pairs of predictions derived from the two theories' contrary assumptions. There are three types. Predictions 1–3 concern the components of variance in $g$—genetic, shared environmental, and non-shared environmental—to be expected at different ages. Predictions 4–12 concern the components of covariance between an individual's $g$ and own educational, occupational, and income attainments. Predictions 13–18 turn to a different matter: how social interventions intended to reduce differences in social advantage or to nullify their influence in later generations will change the degree of social inequality or its dependence on intelligence.

*4.5.1 Predictions 1–3: genetic and non-genetic variation in* g *at different ages*
Both theories predict that age will moderate the heritability of $g$, but in opposite directions. Privilege theorists believe that, although there may be a modest genetic component to intelligence differences in childhood, the impact of family privilege on $g$ cumulates and compounds with age, while genetic influences recede (Prediction 1). If modeling adults, they might erase any arrow from genes to $g$ (Prediction 3). As noted earlier, behavior genetic research (Haworth et al., 2010) has consistently provided evidence that the opposite is true, which is why functional theory states that shared environmental variance in $g$ will disappear by adulthood.

A few cautions are in order. Shared family influences (perhaps of schools, neighborhoods, and the like) account for as much variation in childhood intelligence as genetic differences do, although it remains unclear which particular aspects of rearing environments are responsible. It is clear, however, that even seemingly big differences in family advantage may have no effective influence on offspring intelligence, and that the impact they do have across all siblings in a family turns out to be temporary. This does not rule out the possibility that even temporary influences on intelligence might have lasting impact on *other* sorts of outcomes, such as selection into good private elementary schools. Nor does it rule out the possibility that one sibling will exploit the resources that were available to all in a family, such as good school instruction. When such exploitation is genetically driven, this generates a g–e correlation, and any resulting increase in *g* relative to age-mates will show up as non-additive genetic variance. When environmental influences on IQ are random with regard to both family origin and intelligence genotype, they will show up as non-shared environmental variance.

Social privilege theorists might claim that g–e correlations inflate the seeming importance of genes relative to environments by allotting their joint action to genes. This may be true in a purely statistical sense, but it does not enhance the plausibility of social privilege theory, because narrow heritability remains substantial. Nor is it clear how one can conceptualize the e in g–e correlations as a form of social "privilege" and, by implication, an unwarranted or socially manufactured advantage that might be leveled by social policy. Not only are these g–e correlations self-generated, but the e—the environmental influence—is non-shared and therefore uncorrelated with family background. Eradicating self-generated advantages would require restraining individuals from acting, or reacting differently toward other individuals on the basis of their individual genotypes, which are unknowable in any case.

*4.5.2 Predictions 4–12: genetic and non-genetic covariation between g and level of education, occupation and income* Both theories acknowledge the moderate to high correlations of *g* with the three outcomes, but they differ on whether to expect age-related shifts in this covariation (Predictions 4–6). Privilege theorists appear not to expect any, but functional theorists would, though most confidently for occupation and income. Their reasoning is that workers normally advance up job and pay ladders during their careers, which allows *g*-based performance differences to influence promotion (or demotion) over the decades.

Next, social privilege theorists would expect little or none of the covariance of *g* with education, occupation, and income to be genetic. This assumption is reflected in the practice, common in status attainment modeling, of ignoring genetic covariance on the apparent presumption that it is trivial. In contrast, functional theorists would expect most of *g*'s covariance with status to be genetic (Predictions 7–9). Further, privilege theorists would expect the environmental variance to be mostly of the shared variety, because it would originate in the cumulating effects of family privilege, which they expect to jointly influence *g* and adult status and increase over time. The functional tool theory would predict no shared environmental covariance between *g* and attainments, because *g* itself has no shared environmental component; any environmental covariance between the two would be of the non-shared type. Note that, although non-shared environmental influences cannot contribute to correlations between family members (say, in *g*), they can contribute to the covariance of different traits for the same individual (say, their own *g* and level of education).

Finally, to the extent that each of the theories expects some genetic covariation between *g* and socioeconomic status (for privilege theory, very little; for functional theory, a lot), they appear to differ in the type of g–e covariance they expect it to reflect: mostly evocative versus mostly active (Predictions 10–12). As noted before, social privilege theorists emphasize the social credentialing functions that intelligence and educational achievements serve. These reflect evocative (other-generated) g–e covariance if, as noted before, higher intelligence allows individuals to get ahead by eliciting favorable treatment from college admissions officers, employers, and other gatekeepers, not necessarily because higher intelligence matters per se, but because gatekeepers have a "clubby" taste for it. In this case, getting ahead on the basis of genetic $g$ would be similar to getting ahead on the basis of irrelevant physical traits (e.g. height, skin color, or sex): it matters only because of what others read into the phenotype (stereotypes or expectations), rather than on the strength of the true effects of the trait in question.

This is in keeping with the sociological perspective, which generally views individuals as passive objects of social influence. Those who rise less far were blocked from doing so on the basis of their *ascribed* (rather than *achieved*) characteristics. Adkins and Vaisey (2009) describe this as *social closure*—"the process by which social collectivities seek to maximize rewards by restricting access to resources and opportunities to a limited circle of eligibles. This entails the singling out of certain social or physical attributes as the justificatory basis of exclusion" (Adkins & Vaisey, 2009, p. 112, quoting Parkin, 1974).

In contrast, functional tool theorists would argue that differences in $g$ have instrumental value for the individual, and for society too, so $g$'s large genetic component thereby does, too. Moreover, they see individuals as active agents who shape their own environments in response to their internal, individualized, genetic propensities. That is, they are not passive creatures of either their genes or environments. Higher $g$ enhances performance (lower right of Figure 20.1), which in turn influences what individuals seek and attempt in life (see e.g. applicants in Figure 20.2), but also how successfully they negotiate or exploit the social sorting process (represented in the arrows between $g$, performance, and status outcomes). Thus, any g–e correlation between $g$ and social outcomes probably represents mostly active (self-generated) gene–environment correlation.

The evidence for testing Predictions 4–6 is sparse, but it favors functional tool theory because it shows age-related increases in the correlation between $g$ and status outcomes. Jencks et al.'s (1979, p. 121) analyses of multiple large datasets indicated that "the effects of test performance on earnings increase with age." The recent meta-analysis by Strenze (2007) also found that age moderated the correlations of attainment with IQ: they rose in the late 20s for occupation and in the early 30s for income. In testing the "gravitational hypothesis" for occupational advancement, industrial–organizational psychologists have found that, over time, brighter workers tend to move up job ladders, but less bright workers move downward (Wilk & Sackett, 1996).

Another large longitudinal study (Judge, Klinger, & Simon, 2010, p. 92) documented how, over 28 years, "the more intelligent achieve higher levels of extrinsic career success [income and occupational status] not only by realizing early career advantages but also by having steeper trajectories of success that unfold over time." One reason why they have steeper trajectories was that they got more education, more training, and gravitated toward more complex jobs. This finding implies not only a growing gene–environment correlation, but also one of the self-generated sort, whereby individuals increasingly shape and differentiate their life niches over time (Bouchard et al., 1996; Scarr, 1996). Judge et al. (2010, p. 92) suggest that it is this sort of $g$-related growth in skills that fuels the steeper ascension for higher-$g$ workers: "We argue that these trajectories provide environments in which high-GMA [general mental ability] individuals' skills are often reinforced and amplified, setting the stage for later academic and employee success."

A small but growing body of multivariate behavior genetic research (e.g. Lichtenstein & Pedersen, 1997; Rowe, Vesterdal, & Rodgers, 1998) decomposes the covariance between individuals' $g$ levels and their socioeconomic outcomes, so it provides evidence relevant to Predictions 7–9. It, too, remains sparse, but it also leans toward functional tool theory. Some of it (Rowe et al., 1998) has explicitly engaged the sociological debate over $g$'s role in social inequality. To begin with, level of education, occupation, and income appear to be moderately heritable in samples studied so far—respectively, about 60–70 percent, 50 percent, and 40–50 percent. The heritability of both $g$ and educational level increases with age, and their phenotypic correlation is driven mostly by their genetic correlation, even in childhood, when each is still substantially influenced by shared family effects (Petrill & Wilkerson, 2000). Half to two thirds of the heritability of education, occupation, and income level overlaps the heritability of IQ, which means that both $g$ and adult status are substantially influenced by the same genes. Rowe et al. (1998) calculated that two thirds of the .63 IQ–education correlation and of the .34 IQ–income correlation in their sample was genetic variance and one third was shared environment, which accords somewhat better with functional tool theory. (The authors also provide an excellent discussion of caveats in interpreting such evidence.)

Although evidence may exist for testing Predictions 10–12, I am not aware of it. They concern the relative amount of active vs. evocative g–e correlation that the two theories expect in the genetic covariance between $g$ and status outcomes. In light of the difficulty of distinguishing the two forms of g–e correlation in behavior genetic studies, data would have to be collected on specific mechanisms—worker and gatekeeper behaviors—that are thought to generate active or evocative g–e correlations.

It is important to note at this point that family background does, in fact, affect the degree to which individuals exploit higher $g$ for purposes of social advancement. This is illustrated by the fact that bright youngsters from lower-class backgrounds both aspire to and attain fewer years of education—they "invest" less of their $g$ in it—than equally bright peers from higher social class family backgrounds do (Gottfredson, 1981). They therefore earn a lower return on it. Although $g$ affects life chances more strongly than is often acknowledged, this clearly does not mean that social advantages lack importance independently of $g$. But that is not the question here. The question is why $g$ seems to play such a central role in status attainment.

*4.5.3 Predictions 13–18: impact of social interventions on variation and covariation in* g *and status attainment*   Another way to evaluate the theories is to compare what they expect social interventions to accomplish against what actually happens after they are implemented. There are now, in the United States and elsewhere, decades of experience with interventions guided by the assumptions of social privilege theory— principally, that inequality of outcomes is caused primarily or solely by inequality of opportunity and social capital. Our two philosophers would describe these interventions as attempts to use civic institutions to reduce social inequality.

Table 20.4 lists six pairs of predictions involving education, where the interventions aim either to equalize educational opportunities or to break the link between education and either IQ or occupation. Much policy targets schooling, because democracies view it as their "great equalizer." Accordingly, many educational interventions since the 1960s have sought to equalize students' quality and quantity of education, with the expectation that this would reduce their differences in $g$ and also weaken, if not eliminate, the intergenerational transmission of social inequality. This process would allow individuals to "learn their way out of poverty." By weakening the influence of family advantage and disadvantage, equalization would reduce the correlation between IQ and attainment (Prediction 13), shrink the variance in IQ and educational outcomes (e.g. raise low IQs, narrow social class differences in college-going; Prediction 14), and drive the parent–child correlation in education toward zero (i.e. increase "social mobility"; Prediction 15). Such policies may be desirable for various reasons, but the question here is whether they have the good effects that adherents of social privilege theory said they would.

Other policies, again rooted in social privilege theory, have aimed to shrink differences in socioeconomic outcomes by ensuring good developmental environments or services for all children and families (e.g. preschool interventions such as the Head Start Program, universal kindergarten, subsidized school lunches for the poor, more demanding curricula, national health care), on the assumption that this will shrink inequalities by bringing the disadvantaged bottom up closer to the privileged top (Prediction 16).

Next are the efforts, often driven by affirmative action policies in employment, to weaken the link between IQ and occupational level either by reducing the importance of IQ in obtaining essential educational credentials (Prediction 17) or by reducing the importance of academic credentials in getting good jobs (Prediction 18). Efforts to weaken the link between $g$ and educational attainment have included mastery learning, abolition of ability grouping for instruction, open admissions to college, and dropping the SAT as a requirement for college admissions. The social privilege theorists' two-part rationale for these expectations is, first, that educational sorting and credentialing places too much emphasis on narrow $g$-based entry criteria such as the SAT and too little on non-cognitive strengths such as leadership and, second, that initial, privilege-based academic weaknesses can be overcome when opportunities to learn are equalized.

Policies to weaken the link between past academic accomplishments and future occupational attainments have included scaling back the educational degrees required for job entry (e.g. no longer requiring a college degree to enter police work or fire fighting; a proposal for system-wide "de-credentialling," Collins, 1979), not using tests of basic skills to hire for seemingly non-academic jobs (again, police and fire fighting work), grouping scores on $g$-loaded tests of job aptitude into a few broad levels (e.g. test score "banding"), and altering employment test content to lower its *g* loading (Gottfredson, 1996). The rationale for these proposals is either that these academic credentials and skills are not relevant to performing the job (in legal terms, they are not "job-related"), or else that the vast majority of individuals could pick up the required skills once they are on the job (Collins, 1979). Requiring them discriminatorily screens out disadvantaged individuals who could do the work.

Note that these policy efforts target different nodes in the life-course model in Figure 20.1. Some aim to reduce the variance in some presumed or real predictor of educational attainment in the leftmost columns (e.g. family resources, IQ, school quality) or to reduce their influence on outcomes down the line, that is, by driving down their covariance. All are inspired by the notion that social inequality is the root cause of social inequality, differences in mental competence are overrated, and any reference to genetic differences is interpreted as blaming the victim. By this view, emphasizing intellectual competence is discriminatory. It rigs the competition against individuals from non-privileged social settings, while at the same time justifying the rigging as fair.

Functional tool theory predicts that these interventions will not only fail, but also have self-defeating side-effects. On Predictions 13–15, functional theorists would argue that high intelligence would still be an advantage and low intelligence a dis-advantage, even if environments were equalized, mental tests banned, everyone labeled equally intelligent, and all given the same level of education and training, because the business of living would continue to be complex and a higher *g* provides a competitive edge in dealing with complexity. Moreover, the edge provided by a higher *g* increases as the complexity of tasks and jobs increases. Family privilege matters; but cognitive diversity, especially within biological families, is constantly redistributing it. If non-genetic differences in social privilege are eradicated, socioeco-nomic inequalities may be reduced somewhat, but the correlation between *g* and outcomes would rise and become more heritable as a result.

Rates of intergenerational mobility would increase somewhat, but only to the limit imposed by genetic similarity, which is 50 percent between parent and child. A mod-erate parent–child correlation in socioeconomic fates would thus remain, for genetic reasons, as would moderate *differences* in siblings' attainments. On average, the genetic correlation between siblings is only .5, and their IQs differ by about 11 points (Jensen, 1980).

This chapter has already reviewed some of the pertinent evidence for Predictions 13–15. Jensen (1969) wrote his famous *Harvard Educational Review* article precisely because compensatory education was not having its expected benefits, and Brody's (2007) more recent assessment confirms a broader range of frustrated policy attempts. The intervening decades saw decade-to-decade oscillation between policies for pro-moting educational equality (e.g. 1960s compensatory education programs) and poli-cies for promoting educational excellence (e.g. the 1983 call for educational reform, *A Nation at Risk*). Such oscillation is a fact of life in education because the pursuit of one goal (reducing variance in outcomes) leads to institutional behavior that works against achieving the other goal (raising mean levels of performance): easing standards for high school graduation vs. raising them; not grouping students for instruction versus grouping them; investing education dollars in special education versus advanced placement classes. Other failed large-scale interventions, rarely mentioned, include efforts by the new Communist regime in post-Second World War Warsaw, Poland, to break the transmission of social class privilege. It assigned families to apartments and schools without regard to parental status, but this apparently had no discernible effect on the intergenerational transmission of $g$ (Firkowska et al., 1978).

On Prediction 16, functional tool theorists would predict that interventions to improve environments across the board would increase, not narrow, $g$-based differences in knowledge, performance, and socioeconomic attainment. Their rationale, given earlier, is encapsulated in Jensen's three laws of individual differences in $g$ (Sarich & Miele, 2004, p. 258): (1) individual differences (variance) in performance will increase as task complexity increases; (2) increases in mean levels of performance will be accompanied by increased variance in performance (the gap between top and bottom); and (3) individual differences in performance will increase as tasks are practiced over time (more education, training, experience), as long as there is no artificial ceiling on performance. From the social privilege perspective, these are perverse effects, but they are precisely what should follow interventions aimed to reduce variance, raise means, or do both at the same time. Ceci and Papierno describe such effects in their 2005 article, "The rhetoric and reality of gap closing—When the 'have-nots' gain but the 'haves' gain even more."

For recent evidence on efforts to "level up the playing field" in education, we might look at the cascade of events after enactment, in the United States, of the 2001 No Child Left Behind Act, whose stated aim is to reduce the long-standing demographic gaps in academic achievement (The White House, 2001). It attempts to do so by mandating that public schools bring all students up to the same high level of proficiency by 2014 and by punishing schools if they do not. Events unfolded just as functional tool theory would predict: school administrators started acknowledging that not all students learn equally proficiently even in the best of schools; state governments started (and kept) lowering the bar for what they counted as "proficient" performance; and any progress in closing demographic gaps was achieved primarily by lowering standards and restricting the range of student achievement through ignoring the needs of brighter students while concentrating on raising the lowest performing groups.

As for attempts to weaken the link between $g$ and occupational status (Predictions 17–18), functional tool theory predicts that lowering the $g$ loading of educational credentials will result in employers hiring less competent workers, to the extent that employers continue relying on such credentials. This will lead to higher rates of costly worker errors and subpar performance, which will generate skepticism about educational credentials and perhaps cause employers to turn to more $g$-loaded selection tools, including tests. If the $g$ loading of credentials is not restored first, this sequence of events would cause occupational attainment's correlation with education to fall and its correlation with $g$ to rise—just the opposite of what was originally intended.

*4.5.4 Burden of proof* We have now seen many sorts of evidence that converge in supporting the predictions of functional tool theory and in contradicting social privilege theory. Where the evidence has been ample, the patterns have been clear, consistent, and consilient—across the behavior genetic data and brain studies; the task attributes of tests, academic work, and jobs that call forth $g$; and predictive validity studies in employee selection. The burden of proof now lies with social privilege theory to demonstrate that it continues to offer a plausible explanation for why $g$ predicts who gets ahead. It is not enough to pick apart isolated bits in the web of evidence. The theory must account for the evidence in its entirety, and it must do so more effectively than functional tool theory currently does.

## 5 The Democratic Dilemma

Genetic differences in a population create dilemmas for democratic societies. Social inequality is inevitable when a society's members vary in a genetically conditioned trait, such as $g$, which is highly useful and therefore confers a competitive advantage and garners social rewards. Equal opportunity to use one's natural talents will guarantee unequal results.

### 5.1 The democratic passion for equality of condition

Even to suggest the necessity of such tradeoffs risks offending democratic sensibilities, so strong is the commitment to social equality in democratic regimes. The sense of offense may be observed especially in educational circles, which have sometimes flown the banner of EQuality to express the belief that educational excellence (Quality) and equality of outcomes (Equality) are mutually reinforcing goals, never conflicting ones.

These sensibilities are hardly new, as we learn from that early student of democracy, the Man from France, Alexis de Tocqueville. Although penned almost 200 years ago, his observations about inequality and natural differences in American life remain apt today. He observed that democratic societies have a love of freedom but an insatiable passion for equality of social condition that only grows as inequalities shrink.

> When inequality of conditions is the common law of society, the most marked inequalities do not strike the eye; when everything is nearly on the same level, the slightest are marked enough to hurt it. Hence the desire of equality always becomes more insatiable in proportion as equality is more complete. (de Tocqueville, 1972, p. 138)

He noted further (p. 138) that, "even if they unhappily attained that absolute and complete equality of position, the inequality of minds would still remain, which, coming directly from the hand of God, will forever escape the laws of man." Here is his stronger message to us.

> I think that democratic communities have a natural taste for freedom; left to themselves, they will seek it, cherish it, and view any privation of it with regret. But for equality their passion in ardent, insatiable, incessant, invincible; they call for equality in freedom; and if they cannot obtain that, they still call for equality in slavery. They will endure poverty, servitude, barbarism, but they will not endure aristocracy. (Ibid., p. 97)

So, while Rousseau and Huxley seem to judge the moral standing of civil society by its degree of inequality, Tocqueville would caution against elevating equality of condition above all else, as we are wont to do. The moral choice is not that simple, as we have seen, and assuming otherwise can harm the collective welfare. One such cost was alluded to earlier. Scholars of inequality and crusaders against it both focus tightly on variance in outcomes—"inequality"—with scant attention to means. However, as Jensen's laws of individual differences foretell and hard experience confirms (Ceci & Papierno, 2005), mean levels of performance tend to drop when variance shrinks, that is, when inequalities narrow. Conversely, when more information and resources are pumped into the system, mean levels of performance and well-being rise, but variance does, too, because some people exploit the new resources more effectively than others do (e.g. Gottfredson, 2004, on health knowledge, behavior, and outcomes). It is active g–e correlation at work.

## 5.2 Example of alternative responses to the democratic dilemma

Some commentators acknowledge the societal tradeoffs imposed by cognitive diversity and have pondered how a polity might best deal with them. Consider two books that tackle the conundrum from different ends of the political spectrum: *Excellence: Can We Be Equal and Excellent Too?* by John Gardner (1984) and *The End of Equality* by Mickey Kaus (1992). Both authors would refocus our efforts away from seeking equal outcomes only in the material, instrumental spheres of life, where $g$ matters most, and direct our attention to the socioemotional realms, where humans, as social beings, find deep meaning and satisfaction but $g$ matters least.

For Gardner, the challenge is how to "provide opportunities and rewards for individuals of every degree of ability so that individuals at every level will realize their full potentialities, perform at their best, and harbor no resentment toward those at any other level [of ability]" (p. 113). The rewards include not just self-respect, but the regard and gratitude earned in personal spheres of activity and influence for performing one's job well, whatever its nature (as he says, both a plumber's and philosopher's work must hold water), as well as serving as a leader and upstanding member of one's local communities. Kaus, on the other hand, looks to national governments to break down the sense of cultural separation and animosity between different economic classes. He would do this by ensuring equality in highly public spheres of national life. The federal government would provide everyone with the same level of basic services (universal health and child care) and create shared spaces where individuals from all social backgrounds would work in a common cause (mandatory national service). Kaus's approach—equal public services to individuals— would signal a nation's equal regard for all its citizens; and Gardner's approach—common public service by individuals—would break the barriers to mutual regard across economic lines.

One might protest that these solutions are no solutions at all, because socioeconomic inequality remains. But that misses their point. Although democracies cannot eliminate inequality of condition, they can find better ways to modulate it. To point out that cognitive diversity contributes to their dilemma does not signal that intelligence is "all important" or that it should be. However, the more important socioeconomic inequality is to us, the more it behooves us to understand its roots in human biological diversity, and in $g$ in particular.

# References

Adkins, D. E., & Vaisey, S. (2009). Toward a unified stratification theory: Structure, genome, and status across human societies. *Sociological Theory, 27*, 99–121.

Arvey, R. D. (1986). General ability in employment: A discussion. *Journal of Vocational Behavior, 29*(3), 415–420.

Bouchard, T., J., Jr., Lykken, D. T., Tellegen, A., & McGue, M. (1996). Genes, drives, environment, and experience: EPD theory revised. In C. P. Benbow & D. Lubinski (Eds.), *Intellectual talent: Psychometric and social issues* (pp. 5–43). Baltimore, MD: Johns Hopkins University Press.

Bowles, S., & Gintis, H. (1972/1973). IQ in the U.S. class structure. *Social policy, 3*(4/5), 65–96.

Bowles, S., & Gintis, H. (2002). The inheritance of inequality. *Journal of Economic Perspectives, 16*, 3–30.

Brody, N. (2007). Heritability and the nomological network of *g*. In M. J. Roberts (Ed.), *Integrating the mind: Domain general versus domain specific processes in higher cognition* (pp. 427–448). Hove: Psychology Press.

Carroll, J. B. (1993). *Human cognitive abilities: A survey of factor-analytic studies.* New York: Cambridge University Press.

Ceci, S. J., & Papierno, P. B. (2005). The rhetoric and reality of gap closing: When the "have-nots" gain but the "haves" gain even more. *American Psychologist, 60*(2), 149–160.

Chabris, C. E. (2007). Cognitive and neurobiological mechanisms of the law of general intelligence. In M. J. Roberts (Ed.), *Integrating the mind: Domain general versus domain specific processes in higher cognition* (pp. 449–491). Hove: Psychology Press.

Chamorro-Premuzic, T., & Furnham, A. (2010). *The psychology of personnel selection.* New York: Cambridge University Press.

Collins, R. (1979). *The credential society: An historical sociology of education and stratification.* New York: Academic Press.

Deary, I. J., Johnson, W., & Houlihan, L. M. (2009). Genetic foundations of human intelligence. *Human Genetics, 126*, 215–232.

Deary, I. J., Penke, L., & Johnson, W. (2010). The neuroscience of human intelligence differences. *Nature Reviews: Neuroscience, 11*, 201–211.

Duncan, O. D., Featherman, D. L., & Duncan, B. (1972). *Socioeconomic background and achievement.* New York: Seminar Press.

Firkowska, A., Ostrowska, A., Sokolowska, M., Stein, Z., Susser, M., & Wald, I. (1978). Cognitive development and social policy. *Science, 200*(4348), 1357–1362.

Fischer, C. S., Hout, M., Jankowski, M. S., Lucas, S. R., Swidler, A., & Voss, K. (1996). *Inequality by design: Cracking the bell curve myth.* Princeton, NJ: Princeton University Press.

Freese, J. (2008). Genetics and the social science explanation of individual outcomes. *American Journal of Sociology, 114* (Suppl.), S1–S35.

Gardner, J. (1984). *Excellence: Can we be equal and excellent too?* (rev. ed.). New York: Norton.

Gordon, R. A. (1968). Issues in multiple regression. *American Journal of Sociology, 73*(5), 592–616.

Gordon, R. A. (1997). Everyday life as an intelligence test: Effects of intelligence and intelligence context. *Intelligence, 24*(1), 203–320.

Gottfredson, L. S. (1981). Circumscription and compromise: A developmental theory of occupational aspirations. *Journal of Counseling Psychology* (Monograph), *28*(6), 545–579.

Gottfredson, L. S. (1996). Racially gerrymandering the content of police tests to satisfy the U.S. Justice Department: A case study. *Psychology, Public Policy, and Law, 2*(3/4), 418–446.

Gottfredson, L. S. (1997). Why *g* matters: The complexity of everyday life. *Intelligence, 24*(1), 79–132.

Gottfredson, L. S. (2004). Intelligence: Is it the epidemiologists' elusive "fundamental cause" of social class inequalities in health? *Journal of Personality and Social Psychology, 86,* 174–199.

Gottfredson, L. S. (2005). Implications of cognitive differences for schooling within diverse societies. In C. L. Frisby & C. R. Reynolds (Eds.), *Comprehensive handbook of multicultural school psychology* (pp. 517–554). New York: Wiley.

Haworth, C. M. A, Wright, M. J., Luciano, M., Martin, N. G., de Geus, E. J. C., & van Beijsterveldt, C. E. M. (2010). The heritability of general cognitive ability increases linearly from childhood to young adulthood. *Nature Communications: Molecular Psychiatry, 15,* 1112–20. doi:10.1038/mp.2009.55

Herrnstein, R. J., & Murray, C. (1994). *The bell curve: Intelligence and class structure in American life.* New York: Free Press.

Hunter, J. E. (1986). Cognitive ability, cognitive aptitudes, job knowledge, and job performance. *Journal of Vocational Behavior, 29,* 340–362.

Hunter, J. E., & Schmidt, F. L. (1996). Intelligence and job performance: Economic and social implications. *Psychology, Public Policy, and Law, 2*(3/4) 447–472.

Huxley, T. H. (2009). *Evolution and ethics.* Princeton, NJ: Princeton University Press.

Jencks, C., Bartlett, S., Corcoran, M., Crouse, J., Eaglesfield, D., Jackson, G. et al. (1979). *Who gets ahead? The determinants of economic success in America.* New York: Basic Books.

Jensen, A. R. (1969). How much can we boost IQ and scholastic achievement? *Harvard Educational Review, 39,* 1–123.

Jensen, A. R. (1971). Note on why genetic correlations are not squared. *Psychological Bulletin, 75,* 223–224.

Jensen, A. R. (1980). *Bias in mental testing.* New York: Free Press.

Jensen, A. R. (1981). *Straight talk about mental tests.* New York: Free Press.

Jensen, A. R. (1998). *The g factor: The science of mental ability.* Westport, CT: Praeger.

Johnson, W., te Nijenhuis, J., & Bouchard, T. J., Jr. (2008). Still just 1 *g*: Consistent results from five test batteries. *Intelligence, 36,* 81–95.

Johnson, W., Bouchard, T. J., Jr., McGue, M., Segal, N. L, Tellegen, A., Keyes, M., & Gottesman, I. J. (2007). Genetic and environmental influence on the verbal–perceptual–image rotation (VPR) model of the structure of mental abilities in the Minnesota study of twins reared apart. *Intelligence, 35,* 542–562.

Judge, T. A., Klinger, R. L., & Simon, L. S. (2010). Time is on my side: Time, general mental ability, human capital, and extrinsic career success. *Journal of Applied Psychology, 95*(1), 92–107.

Jung, R. E., & Haier, R. (2007). The parietal–frontal integration theory (P–FIT) of intelligence: Converging neuroimaging evidence. *Behavior and Brain Sciences, 30,* 135–154.

Kaus, M. (1992). *The end of equality.* New York: Basic Books.

Lichtenstein, P., & Pedersen, N. L. (1997). Does genetic variance for cognitive abilities account for genetic variance in educational achievement and occupational status? A study of twins reared apart and twins reared together. *Social Biology, 44*(1/2), 77–90.

McHenry, J. J., Hough, L. M., Toquam, J. L., Hanson, M. A., & Ashworth, S. (1990). Project A validity results: The relationship between predictor and criterion domains. *Personnel Psychology, 43,* 335–354.

National Center for Education Statistics (1993). *120 years of American education: A statistical portrait.* Washington, DC: U.S. Department of Education.

National Center for Education Statistics (2010). *The condition of education 2010.* Washington, DC: U.S. Department of Education.

Neckerman, K. M., & Torche, F. (2007). Inequality: Causes and consequences. *Annual Review of Sociology, 33,* 335–357.

Parkin, F. (1974). *The social analysis of class structure.* London: Tavistock.

Petrill, S. A., & Wilkerson, B. (2000). Intelligence and achievement: A behavioral genetic perspective. *Educational Psychology Review, 12*(2), 185–199.

Petrill, S. A., Plomin, R., Berg, S. Johansson, B., Pedersen, N. L., Ahern, F., & McClearn, G. E. (1998). The genetic and environmental relationship between general and specific cognitive abilities in twins age 80 and older. *Psychological Science, 9,* 183–189.

Plomin, R., DeFries, J. C., McClearn, G. E., & McGuffin, P. (2008). *Behavioral genetics* (5th ed.). New York: Worth.

Plomin, R., Pedersen, N. L., Lichtenstein, P., & McClearn, G. E. (1994). Variability and stability in cognitive abilities are largely genetic later in life. *Behavior Genetics, 24,* 207–215.

Rousseau, J. J. (1964). *Discourse on the origin and foundations of inequality among men* [Second discourse] [1755]. Translated by R. D. Masters and J. R. Masters. In *Jean-Jacques Rousseau: The first and second discourses,* edited by R. D. Masters. New York: St. Martin's Press.

Rowe, D. C., Vesterdal, W. J., & Rodgers, J. L. (1998). Herrnstein's syllogism: Genetic and shared environmental influences on IQ, education, and income. *Intelligence, 26*(4), 405–423.

Sarich, V., & Miele, F. (2004). *Race: The reality of human differences.* Boulder, CO: Westview Press.

Sattler, J. M., & Ryan, J. J. (2009). *Assessment with the WAIS–IV.* San Diego, CA: Jerome M. Sattler, Publisher, Inc.

Scarr, S. (1996). How people make their own environments: Implications for parents and policy makers. *Psychology, Public Policy, and Law, 2,* 204–228.

Scarr, S., & Weinberg, R. A. (1978). The influence of "family background" on intellectual attainment. *American Sociological Review, 43,* 674–692.

Schmidt, F. L., & Hunter, J. E. (2004). General mental ability in the world of work: Occupational attainment and job performance. *Journal of Personality and Social Psychology, 86,* 162–173.

Schmidt, F. L., Hunter, J. E., Outerbridge, A. N., & Goff, S. (1988). Joint relation of experience and ability with job performance: Test of three hypotheses. *Journal of Applied Psychology, 73,* 46–57.

Strenze, T. (2007). Intelligence and socioeconomic success: A meta-analytic review of longitudinal research. *Intelligence, 35*(5), 401–426.

Sternberg, R. J., & Grigorenko, E. L. (Eds.) ( 2001). *Environmental effects on cognitive abilities.* Mahwah, NJ: Lawrence Erlbaum Associates.

Sternberg, R. J., & Wagner, R. K. (1993). The g-ocentric view of intelligence and job performance is wrong. *Current Directions in Psychological Science, 2*(1), 1–5.

Tanner, J. M. (1986). Growth as a target-seeking function: Catch-up and catch-down growth in man. In F. Falkner & J. M. Tanner (Eds.), *Human growth: A comprehensive treatise* (2nd ed., Vol. 1, pp. 167–179). New York: Plenum.

Thorndike, R. L. (1986). The role of general ability in prediction. *Journal of Vocational Behavior, 29,* 332–339.

de Tocqueville, A. (1972). *Democracy in America: Volume 2* [1840]. New York: Vintage Books.

Towne, B. Demerath, E. W., & Czerwinski, S. A. (2002). The genetic epidemiology of growth and development. In N. Cameron (Ed.), *Human growth and development* (pp. 103–137). New York: Academic Press.

U.S. Bureau of the Census (1990). *Statistical abstract of the United States, 1990* (110th ed.). Washington, DC: U.S. Department of Commerce.

U.S. Bureau of the Census (2009). *Statistical abstract of the United States, 2010* (129th ed.). Washington, DC: U.S. Department of Commerce. Retrieved from <http://www.census.gov/statab/www/>.

U.S. Department of Labor (1984). *Dictionary of Occupational Titles* (4th ed.) Washington, DC: U.S. Government Printing Office.

van Wieringen, J. C. (1986). Secular growth changes. In F. Falkner & J. M. Tanner (Eds.), *Human growth: A comprehensive treatise* (2nd ed., Vol. 3, pp. 307–331). New York: Plenum.

The White House (2001). Foreword by President George W. Bush *[No Child Left Behind Act of 2001]*. Retrieved June 27, 2008, from http://www.whitehouse.gov/news/reports/no-child-left-behind.html

Wilk, S. L., & Sackett, P. R. (1996). Longitudinal analysis of ability–job complexity fit and job change. *Personnel Psychology, 49,* 937–967.

Wonderlic Personnel Test, Inc. (1992). *Wonderlic Personnel Test and Scholastic Level Exam: User's manual.* Libertyville, I: Wonderlic Personnel Test, Inc.

# Part V

# Motivation and Vocational Interests

# 21

# Goal-Setting
## *A State Theory, but Related to Traits*
### Gary P. Latham, Deshani B. Ganegoda, and Edwin A. Locke

A goal is an object or aim that an individual strives to attain (Locke & Latham, 1984). Goal-setting theory (Latham & Locke, 2007; Locke & Latham, 1990, 2002) states that goals are the immediate regulators of behavior. The theory was developed as a framework for predicting, explaining, and influencing an individual's motivation in the workplace. The theory states that: (1) a specific high goal leads to higher performance than an easy goal, no goal or a vague goal such as "do your best"; (2) given goal commitment, the higher the goal, the higher the performance; and (3) variables such as feedback or knowledge of results, participation in decision-making, competition, and incentives only affect an employee's performance to the extent that they lead to the setting of and commitment to a specific high goal.

The theory further states that four mediators explain the positive effect that a specific high goal has on job performance, namely choice, effort, persistence, and strategy. Whereas the first three are primarily motivational in nature, the fourth is more cognitive. In short, (1) the *choice* of goal focuses attention on goal-relevant and away from goal-irrelevant activity; the higher the goal, the greater (2) the *effort* and (3) *persistence* to attain it. Finally, goal pursuit compels an employee (4) to draw upon one or more extant *strategies* or to discover new knowledge that facilitates goal attainment.

Moderator variables included in goal-setting theory are a person's (1) ability, that is, knowledge and skill to reach the goal and (2) commitment to do so. In addition, (3) feedback is necessary for an individual to know whether to increase effort as well as to adhere to or change the strategy in order to ensure goal attainment. (4) Situational factors must be examined to ensure that an employee has the resources required for goal attainment. (5) Task complexity is a fifth moderator affecting the beneficial effects on performance due to goal-setting. As might be expected of a theory of motivation (as opposed to one of training), goal-setting has a greater effect

*The Wiley-Blackwell Handbook of Individual Differences,* First Edition.
Edited by Tomas Chamorro-Premuzic, Sophie von Stumm, and Adrian Furnham.
© 2011 Blackwell Publishing Ltd. Published 2011 by Blackwell Publishing Ltd.

on tasks that are straightforward rather than complex for people; however, this feature can be mitigated by ensuring that people working on complex tasks possess or acquire the needed skills.

Goal-setting theory is among the most, if not the most, practical theory for increasing performance (Latham & Pinder, 2005; Lee & Earley, 1992; Miner, 1984). More than 1,000 laboratory and field studies have found empirical support for it (Mitchell & Daniels, 2003).

## Individual Differences

With the exception of ability, goal-setting theory does not take into account individual differences in traits. This is because, as Adler and Weiss (1988) argued, goal-setting, as a state, creates a strong situation (Meyer, Dalal, & Hermida, 2010; Mischel, 1973). This is because the act of assigning a specific (clear) goal in the workplace leads employees to construe the goal in the same ways and, if there is commitment to the goal, to supersede trait influences. Traits, however, may be influential with self-set goals, as this is a weaker situation than the case where goals are assigned or set participatively.

With regard to incentives, people self-administer intrinsic rewards on the basis of their own appraisals of their accomplishments in relation to their goals (Bandura, 1986). Among the most consistent findings in goal-setting research is the relationship between goal attainment and performance satisfaction. Locke and Latham (1990) found that the mean correlation across 12 studies was .51. Subsequent research has shown that goal attainment increases self-efficacy, as well as imparting a sense of pride and achievement (Mento, Locke, & Klein, 1992). A review of the literature revealed that the increase in self-efficacy resulting from goal attainment and from the satisfaction derived from it leads to the setting of increasingly higher goals (Bandura, 1997; Latham, Locke, & Fassina, 2002). Extrinsic incentives for goal attainment include recognition from supervisors. Consistent goal attainment may also increase the likelihood of people (1) retaining their jobs during an economic downturn; (2) earning a promotion; and (3) receiving a monetary bonus, a salary increase, or both.

### Ability, knowledge and skill

When a person has the required knowledge or skill to perform a task, a specific high goal for job performance should be set (Winters & Latham, 1996). Moreover, setting a specific high-performance goal may have stronger effects on those with high rather than low ability (Locke, 1965, 1982). This is because those with high ability are able to draw upon more strategies for goal attainment than those who lack the requisite knowledge or skill are.

When a person lacks the requisite knowledge or skill to perform a task, Kanfer and Ackerman (1989) found that a vague goal, such as exhorting people to do their best, may result in higher performance than setting a specific, high-performance goal. This occurs when people scramble unsystematically to find ways to attain the goal before systematically exploring different strategies for attaining it. Mone and Shalley (1995) replicated this finding. Focusing just on the end result, goal attainment, interfered with learning the task-relevant strategies necessary for goal attainment.

Winters and Latham (1996) also replicated the above findings. People who were urged to do their best outperformed those who were given a specific high-performance goal. In contrast, those given a specific, high-learning goal had the highest performance. This is because a learning goal differs from a performance goal in that the emphasis of the former is on discovering or mastering new strategies, processes, or procedures—necessary strategies that people working on new, complex tasks may not initially possess. Winters and Latham's findings regarding the benefit of setting a learning rather than a performance goal for tasks, when people initially lack the required knowledge, has been replicated by others. Drach-Zahavy and Erez (2002) found that individuals with a learning goal (which is referred to as a "strategy goal" in their study) had higher levels of performance than those with a perform-ance goal on a highly complex stock-market prediction task. Seijts, Latham, Tasa, and Latham (2004) found that those who were assigned a specific high learning goal attained significantly more market share on an interactive, computer-based simulation of the US cellular telephone industry than those who were assigned a specific, high-performance goal did. Kozlowski and Bell (2006) showed that an assigned learning goal significantly improved both affective and cognitive self-regulatory processes relative to a specific high-performance goal. Noel and Latham (2006) found that participants who had a learning goal kept their simulated business running far longer than those with a performance goal did. Cianci, Klein, and Seijts (2010) reported that people with a learning goal experienced less tension and per-formed better following negative feedback than did those individuals who had a performance goal.

Unlike in the case of findings regarding ability as a moderator of the goal–performance relationship, a learning goal appears to benefit people with lower rather than higher cognitive ability. This is presumably because people with lower cognitive ability lack the requisite knowledge for goal attainment. The focus of a learning goal is knowledge acquisition, whereas the focus of a performance goal is to increase one's motivation to apply one's existing knowledge. Therefore, although both learning and performance goals are needed in order to be successful, performance goals should only be set after an employee has the ability to attain it (Seijts & Latham, 2005)—unless the employees can discover the needed knowledge on his or her own.

## Personality traits

Mitchell (1979) in his *Annual Review of Psychology* (ARP) chapter concluded that, despite their intuitive appeal, personality variables explained little in organizational behavior, let alone goal-setting. Similarly, in his ARP chapter, Schneider (1985) reached a similar conclusion regarding personality effects on goal-setting. As Locke, Saari, Shaw, and Latham (1981) had noted earlier, the only consistent finding regard-ing the relation of personality to goal-setting was inconsistency. Advances in the measurement of personality and the development of new theories in the 1990s, however, have led to more positive conclusions.

*Big Five* The five-factor model of personality (Wiggins, 1996), commonly referred to as the Big Five, assesses conscientiousness, extraversion, neuroticism, openness to experience, and agreeableness. In a meta-analysis that examined the relationships between this five-factor model and motivation, Judge and Ilies (2002) found that all five personality traits were significantly related to individuals' goal-setting motivation. The studies included in the meta-analysis were those that measured self-set goals either in terms of goal level (e.g. number of units salespeople targeted to sell; number of lines per week typists aimed to type) or in terms of difficulty (respondents' choice of tasks with varying difficulty levels). The results showed that the trait agreeableness displayed the strongest relationship with goal-setting ($\beta = -.51$), followed by conscientiousness ($\beta = .35$) and neuroticism ($\beta = -.31$). Extraversion ($\beta = .15$) and openness to experience ($\beta = .18$) displayed a weak, albeit a significant relationship with goal-setting motivation. The authors argued that the negative correlation between agreeableness and goal-setting motivation for self-set goals could be due to the fact that agreeable individuals set less ambitious performance goals because they are motivated more by communion (desire to be part of a larger group) than by agency (desire to achieve mastery and power; Graziano & Eisenberg, 1997). However, the authors also cautioned that the result in relation to agreeableness and goal-setting motivation might be due to the relatively small number of correlations analyzed in the meta-analysis ($k = 4$).

The trait of conscientiousness has been found to be particularly significant in jobs where employees are given a lot of autonomy (Mount & Barrick, 1995). Conscientious individuals are generally achievement-oriented, dependable, and orderly (Barrick & Mount, 1991; Costa & McCrae, 1992). Because of their need for achievement, conscientious employees are predisposed to set themselves, and to commit to, high goals. In a study of sales representatives, this trait correlated positively with goal commitment, which in turn correlated positively with sales volume and supervisory ratings of job performance (Barrick, Mount, & Strauss, 1993). This finding is consistent with previous studies that reported that those who score high on need for achievement set high goals. Yukl and Latham (1978), for example, found that word processing operators who scored high on need for achievement set more difficult goals than their colleagues who scored lower on this trait did.

*Core self-evaluations* Judge, Locke, and Durham (1997) developed a trait theory that they labeled "core self-evaluations"; it pertains to one's appraisals of people, events, and things in relation to self. Core evaluations are manifested in four highly correlated traits: self-esteem, locus of control, neuroticism/emotional stability, and "general" self-efficacy. Erez and Judge (2001) showed that core self-evaluations have a strong relationship with goal-setting motivation as well as with goal commitment. In fact, core self-evaluations explained 17 percent of the variance in goal-setting behavior and 3 percent of the variance in goal commitment.

Locus of control, one out of four variables in core evaluations theory, as well as need for achievement and conscientiousness, were also found by Hollenbeck and colleagues to be antecedents of goal commitment (Hollenbeck, Williams, & Klein, 1989; Hollenbeck, Klein, O'Leary, & Wright, 1989). Locus of control has also been shown to be a direct moderator of the relationship between self-set goals and performance, such that the goals were more predictive of performance when the person had a high level of locus of control (Lambert, Moore, & Dixon, 1999). In a study involving participatively set goals, employees who scored high on internal locus of control set more difficult goals than those who had an external locus of control (Yukl & Latham, 1978).

With regard to self-esteem, two studies found that self-esteem affected goal success. Employees with higher self-esteem attained their goals significantly more often than their peers with lower self-esteem (Dossett, Latham, & Mitchell, 1979; Yukl & Latham, 1978). Tang and Reynolds (1993) found that people with low self-esteem set lower goals and performed worse than people who scored high in this trait.

*Goal orientation*   Dweck's (1999) theory of goal orientation states that goal orientation is a relatively stable disposition. People who have a goal orientation toward performance (or a "performance goal orientation") choose goals that enable them to prove to others that they are competent. Because they fear failure, they find ways to avoid goals that are difficult; they fear, namely, that lack of goal attainment will lead to disapproval by those who are important to them. People who have a goal disposition toward learning (or a "learning goal disposition"), on the other hand, seek challenges. Therefore they choose goals that will enable them to increase their competence. Errors or mistakes are viewed by them as inherent to learning new competencies.

Brett and VandeWalle (1999) found that goal orientation does not have a direct relationship with performance. Rather it is mediated by the type of goal a person selects. Consistent with Dweck's theory, those with a learning goal orientation self-set a challenging or a learning goal, and those with a performance goal orientation self-set an easy goal—one they perceived as readily attainable.

Consistent with the earlier discussion of strong versus weak situations, *assigning* a specific high goal masks or mitigates the effect of goal orientation on behavior. On a task that was complex in that it required the acquisition of knowledge in order to master it, people with a learning goal orientation performed better than those with a performance goal orientation only in a "weak" situation, that is, in the experimental condition where people were instructed to do their best. But those who were assigned a specific, high-learning goal performed better than those with a goal to do their best on the task, regardless of their goal orientation (Seijts et al., 2004). In short, goal-setting as a state (when goals are assigned) appears to trump goal orientation as a trait on complex tasks.

*Regulatory focus*   Higgins's (1997, 1998) theory states that there are two dispositional regulatory systems: promotion and prevention. Like those with a learning goal orientation, people with a focus on promotion strive to grow and challenge themselves, whereas people with a focus on prevention, like those with a performance goal orientation, are motivated to take steps toward minimizing the loss of desired outcomes (e.g. the esteem of others). There is some evidence from one study that, to the extent that a person's regulatory focus (prevention vs. promotion) and goal (performance vs. learning) are consistent, the higher that person's task performance will be (Spiegel, Grant-Pillow, & Higgins, 2004). However, this relationship needs further study, especially in connection with other factors such as the complexity of the task at hand and the person's knowledge and skill to perform the task.

## Summary and Conclusions

Goal-setting is a powerful and effective state variable. Typical effect sizes range from .42 to .82 (Locke & Latham, 1990). In contrast, personality variables typically correlate with performance with an *r* of .20 or less (Cohen's *d* = .41 or less). This should not be surprising, given that traits are general and states are task- and situation-specific. Generally, task- and situation-specific variables, if they are relevant to the outcome in question, predict performance better than general ones. The only general trait that has been found to have a significant correlation with perform-ance across the vast majority of jobs and situations is intelligence (Schmidt, 2009)— but intelligence is not a personality trait. Assigned goals typically vitiate trait effects, because assigned goals constitute a strong situation. It might be that "strong traits" could offset strong situations created by assigned goals, but this has yet to be shown.

This does not mean that traits and states are unconnected, however. Traits, as we noted, have been found to affect goals. This occurs primarily in situations where goals are self-set rather than assigned. Goals can mediate trait effects because the specific typically mediates the general (Locke, 2001).

## Acknowledgments

Preparation of the chapter was funded in part by a grant from the Social Sciences and Humanities Research Council of Canada to the first author.

## References

Adler, S., & Weiss, H. M. (1988). Recent developments in the study of personality and organizational behavior. In C. L. Cooper & I. T. Robertson (Eds.), *International review of industrial and organizational psychology* (Vol. 3, pp. 307–330). Chichester: John Wiley & Sons.

Bandura, A. (1986). *Social foundations of thought and action: A social–cognitive view.* Englewood Cliffs, NJ: Prentice Hall.

Bandura, A. (1997). *Self-efficacy: The exercise of control.* New York: Freeman.

Barrick, M. R., & Mount, M. K. (1991). The Big Five personality dimensions and job per-formance: A meta-analysis. *Personnel Psychology, 44*, 1–26.

Barrick, M. R., Mount, M. K., & Strauss, J. P. (1993). Conscientiousness and performance of sales representatives: Test of the mediating effects of goal setting. *Journal of Applied Psychology, 78*, 715–722.

Brett, J. F., & VandeWalle, D. (1999). Goal orientation and goal content as predictors of performance in a training program. *Journal of Applied Psychology, 84*, 863–873.

Cianci, A. M., Klein, H. J., & Seijts, G. H. (2010). The effect of negative feedback on tension and subsequent performance: The main and interactive effects of goal content and conscientiousness. *Journal of Applied Psychology, 95,* 618–630.

Costa, P. T., Jr., & McCrae, R. R. (1992). *Revised NEO Personality Inventory (NEO–PI–R) and NEO Five-Factor Inventory (NEO–FFI) professional manual.* Odessa, FL: PAR.

Dossett, D. L., Latham, G. P., & Mitchell, T. R. (1979). The effects of assigned versus participatively set goals, KR, and individual differences when goal difficulty is held constant. *Journal of Applied Psychology, 64,* 291–298.

Drach-Zahavy, A., & Erez, M. (2002). Challenge versus threat effects on the goal–performance relationship. *Organizational Behavior and Human Decision Making, 88,* 667–682.

Dweck, C. S. (1999). *Self-theories: Their role in motivation, personality, and development.* Philadelphia, PA: Psychology Press.

Erez, A., & Judge, T. A. (2001). Relationship of core self-evaluations to goal setting, motivation, and performance. *Journal of Applied Psychology, 86,* 1270–1279.

Graziano, W. G., & Eisenberg, N. (1997). Agreeableness: A dimension of personality. In R. Hogan, J. Johnson & S. Briggs (Eds.), *Handbook of personality psychology* (pp. 795–824). San Diego, CA: Academic Press.

Higgins, E. T. (1997). Beyond pleasure and pain. *American Psychologist, 52,* 1280–1300.

Higgins, E. T. (1998). Promotion and prevention: Regulatory focus as a motivational principle. In M. P. Zanna (Ed.), *Advances in experimental social psychology* (Vol. 30, pp. 1–46). New York: Academic Press.

Hollenbeck, J. R., Williams, C. R., & Klein, H. J. (1989). An empirical examination of the antecedents of commitment to difficult goals. *Journal of Applied Psychology, 74,* 18–23.

Hollenbeck, J. R., Klein, H. J., O'Leary, A. M., & Wright, P. M. (1989). Investigation of the construct validity of a self-report measure of goal commitment. *Journal of Applied Psychology, 74,* 951–956.

Judge, T. A., & Ilies, R. (2002). Relationship of personality to performance motivation: A meta-analytic review. *Journal of Applied Psychology, 87,* 797–807.

Judge, T. A., Locke, E. A., & Durham, C. C. (1997). The dispositional causes of job satisfaction: A core evaluation approach. *Research in Organizational Behavior, 19,* 151–188.

Kanfer, R., & Ackerman, P. L. (1989). Motivation and cognitive abilities: An integrative aptitude treatment interaction approach to skill acquisition. *Journal of Applied Psychology, 74,* 657–690.

Kozlowski, S. W. J., & Bell, B. S. (2006). Disentangling achievement orientation and goal setting: Effects on self-regulatory processes. *Journal of Applied Psychology, 9,* 900–916.

Lambert, S. H., Moore, D. W., & Dixon, R. S. (1999). Gymnasts in training: The differential effects of self- and coach-set goals as a function of locus of control. *Journal of Applied Sport Psychology, 11,* 72–82.

Latham, G. P., & Locke, E. A. (2007). New developments in and directions for goal setting. *European Psychologist, 12,* 290–300.

Latham, G. P., & Pinder, C. C. (2005). Work motivation theory and research at the dawn of the twenty-first century. *Annual Review of Psychology, 56,* 485–516.

Latham, G. P., Locke, E. A., & Fassina, N. E. (2002). The high performance cycle: Standing the test of time. In S. Sonnentag (Ed.), *The psychological management of individual performance: A handbook in the psychology of management in organizations* (pp. 201–228). Chichester: John Wiley & Sons.

Lee, C., & Earley, P. C. (1992). Comparative peer evaluations of organizational behavior theories. *Organization Development Journal, 10,* 37–42.

Locke, E. A. (1965). The relationship of task success to task liking and satisfaction. *Journal of Applied Psychology, 49,* 379–385.

Locke, E. A. (1982). Relation of goal level to performance with a short work period and multiple goal levels. *Journal of Applied Psychology, 67,* 512–514.

Locke, E. A. (2001) Self-set goals and self-efficacy as mediators of incentives and personality. In M. Erez, U. Kleinbeck, & H. Thierry (Eds.), *Work motivation in the context of a globalizing economy* (pp. 13–26). Mahwah, NJ: Lawrence Erlbaum Associates.

Locke, E. A., & Latham, G. P. (1984). *Goal setting: A motivational technique that works!* Englewood Cliffs, NJ: Prentice Hall.

Locke, E. A., & Latham, G. P. (1990). *A theory of goal setting and task performance.* Englewood Cliffs, NJ: Prentice Hall.

Locke, E. A., & Latham, G. P. (2002). Building a practically useful theory of goal setting and task motivation: A 35-year odyssey. *American Psychologist, 57,* 705–717.

Locke, E. A., Saari, L. M., Shaw, K. N., & Latham, G. P. (1981). Goal setting and task performance: 1969–1980. *Psychological Bulletin, 90,* 125–152.

Mento, A. J., Locke, E. A., & Klein, H. J. (1992). Relationship of goal level to valence and instrumentality. *Journal of Applied Psychology, 77,* 395–405.

Meyer, R. D., Dalal, R. S., & Hermida, R. (2010). A review and synthesis of situational strength in the organizational sciences. *Journal of Management, 36,* 121–140.

Miner, J. B. (1984). The validity and usefulness of theories in emerging organizational science. *Academy of Management Review, 9,* 296–306.

Mischel, W. (1973). Toward a cognitive social learning reconceptualization of personality. *Psychological Review, 80,* 252–283.

Mitchell, T. R. (1979). Organizational behavior. *Annual review of psychology, 30,* 243–281.

Mitchell, T. R., & Daniels, D. (2003). Observations and commentary on recent research in work motivation. In L. Porter, G. Bigley, & R. Steers (Eds.), *Motivation and Work Behavior* (7th ed., pp. 26–44). New York: McGraw-Hill.

Mone, M. A., & Shalley, C. E. (1995). Effects of task complexity and goal specificity on change in strategy and performance over time. *Human Performance, 8,* 243–262.

Mount, M. K., & Barrick, M. R. (1995). The Big Five personality dimensions: Implications for research and practice in human resources management. *Research in Personnel and Human Resources Management, 13,* 153–200.

Noel, T., & Latham, G. P. (2006). The importance of learning goals versus outcome goals for entrepreneurs. *International Journal of Entrepreneurship and Innovation, 7,* 213–220.

Schmidt, F. (2009) Select on intelligence. In E. A. Locke (Ed.), *Handbook of principles of organizational behavior* (pp. 3–17). New York: Wiley.

Schneider, B. (1985). Organizational behavior. *Annual Review of Psychology, 36,* 573–611.

Seijts, G. H., & Latham, G. P. (2005). Learning versus performance goals: When should each be used? *Academy of Management Executive, 19,* 124–131.

Seijts, G. H., Latham, G. P., Tasa, K., & Latham, B. W. (2004). Goal setting and goal orientation: An integration of two different yet related literatures. *Academy of Management Journal, 47,* 227–239.

Spiegel, S., Grant-Pillow, H., & Higgins, E. T. (2004). How regulatory fit enhances motivational strength during goal pursuit. *European Journal of Social Psychology, 34,* 39–54.

Tang, T. L. P., & Reynolds, D. B. (1993). Effects of self-esteem and perceived goal difficulty on goal setting, certainty, task performance, and attributions. *Human Resource Development Quarterly, 4,* 153–170.

Wiggins, J. S. (1996). *The five-factor model of personality: Theoretical perspectives.* New York: Guilford Press.

Winters, D., & Latham, G. (1996). The effect of learning versus outcome goals on a simple versus a complex task. *Group and Organization Management, 21*, 236–250.

Yukl, G. A., & Latham, G. P. (1978). Interrelationships among employee participation, individual differences, goal difficulty, goal acceptance, goal instrumentality, and performance. *Personnel Psychology, 31*, 305–323.

# 22

# Personality and Approaches to Learning

## Adrian Furnham

## 1  Introduction

This chapter looks at the intersection of differential and educational psychology. These two sub-disciplines were once "happily married," though now they seem "amicably divorced." If one examines top journals in either discipline, neither seems very interested in the current agenda of the other. Some educational psychologists seem hostile to the very idea of individual differences, particularly to work on intelligence, because they believe that it reveals how little effect education has, compared to intelligence, in predicting educational outcomes. Equally, differential psychologists seem less interested in applying their work to learning settings, though this was not always the case. Some of the great differential psychologists, like R. B. Cattell and H. J. Eysenck, published many papers in educational psychology journals.

This chapter looks at individual differences in how people *approach* their learning, as well as in the *style* they adopt in learning. It is an area of research that has a long history, and there have been various attempts to review it both comprehensively and critically (Furnham, in press a, in press b). It is an area of application more than one of theory development, and there are various professionals such as accountants (Ballantine, Duff, & Larres, 2008; Flood & Wilson, 2008), engineers (Ellis, Goodyear, Calvo & Prosser, 2008), nurses (Snelgrove, 2004), teachers (Segers, Martens, & Van den Bossche, 2008), and students (Cano & Berben, 2009; Zhu, Valcke, & Schellens, 2008) eager to apply its ideas and measures to teaching and learning in their particular field.

Further, the field has "moved with the times" looking at such things as e-learning (Ellis, Ginns, & Piggott, 2009) and on-line peer assessment (Yang & Tsai, 2010). Thus Richardson (2009) found that a student's approach to learning and his or her

*The Wiley-Blackwell Handbook of Individual Differences*, First Edition.
Edited by Tomas Chamorro-Premuzic, Sophie von Stumm, and Adrian Furnham.
© 2011 Blackwell Publishing Ltd. Published 2011 by Blackwell Publishing Ltd.

studying behavior did not differ as a function of whether they received instruction face-to-face or on-line.

Approach to learning is mainly about *motivation* while style of learning (thinking) is about *preference*. Both the approach and the style literature seem to suggest that individuals adopt (willingly, consciously, "happily") both an approach and/or a style, though it is not clear why and how they do so. Certainly it seems conceivable that the approach that students take is more variable and situationally more determined than the style they "adopt." Approaches are mainly about the goals and perceptions of students in educational settings. As their motivation changes, possibly as a function of reward, so their whole approach to their studies can change. On the one hand it seems implicit in this literature that people (quite often, easily, and quickly) change their approach, yet the literature offers little evidence to that effect. However, there are longitudinal data to suggest that learning approaches do not change much over time and are relatively stable (Lietz & Matthews, 2010). The stability over time and the cross-situational consistency of an approach to learning speak to the origin of the motivation in the first place, and also to how easily learners may be modified by educators.

Both learning approach and style seem to be a function of many things, including a person's ability, personality, and values; how learning is evaluated; and the subject being studied. According to the presage–process–product model, certain character-istics of the student (including their prior educational experiences, their personality, and their ability) as well as their learning context (how they are taught and assessed) influence their perceptions of that context (clarity of goals, satisfaction with teaching)—which, in turn, influences their approach to learning, and hence their learning outcomes (Prosser & Trigwell, 1999). In this sense learning style partly influences approach to learning, and hence learning success.

The concept of *approach* is less well known than that of *style*. Indeed the style literature goes back well over 100 years. "Style" concerns the adoption or the assum-ing of a *characteristic manner*: a distinctive, recognizable, perhaps fashionable social behavior or appearance. The word implies a number of things. First, that styles seem relatively superficial, at least in the sense that they can be readily observed. Second, that the acquisition of a style is relatively simple and voluntaristic. Third, that styles may have an evaluative component to them, in the sense that some are "better," more appropriate, or more desirable than others.

The earliest literature in this area, now nearly 100 years old, is on cognitive style, which is how an individual thinks, processes information, or attempts to understand the world around him. The list of cognitive styles "discovered or described" by researchers is extensive. Thirty years ago, Messick (1976) listed 19 cognitive style variables, which he believed could be grouped under eight dimensions: broad versus narrow categorizing, cognitive complexity versus simplicity, field dependence versus independence, leveling versus sharpening, scanning versus focusing, converging versus diverging, automatization versus restructuring, and reflection versus impulsiv-ity. However, his list is not exclusive. Some reviewers have divided it into "best established" and "other" cognitive styles, which reflects the amount of research done in each area (Guilford, 1980). The list of styles continues to grow.

Cassidy (2004) noted:

> There is general acceptance that the manner in which individuals choose to or are
> inclined to approach learning situations has an impact on performance and achievement
> of learning outcomes. Whilst—and perhaps because—learning style has been the focus
> of such a vast number of research and practitioner-based studies in the area, there
> exist a variety of definitions, theoretical positions, models, interpretations and measures
> of the construct. To some extent, this can be considered a natural consequence of
> extensive empirical investigation and is to be expected with any continually developing
> concept which proves useful in gaining understanding of such a crucial and prevailing
> endeavour as learning. However, the level of ambiguity and debate is such that even the
> task of selecting an appropriate instrument for investigation is an onerous one, with
> the unifying of subsequent findings within an existing framework problematic, at best.
> (p. 419)

This skepticism is echoed by many in this field. Rayner and Peterson (2009, p. 107)
note: "The study of style differences in human psychology is regarded by many
academics as light-weight, problematic or even flawed." Furnham (in press a) has
argued:

> [M]any of the old questions remain in both areas. These include clarity of definition,
> and parsimony as well as verisimilitude of models. Most instruments in the area still
> appear to have not been subjected to the same rigour as those in ability and trait psy-
> chology. It seems researchers are too eager to "get to market" than [*sic*] to develop fine
> instruments with clear norms. More than anything else however the question still
> remains where these styles and concepts dwell in "individual differences" space. This is
> essentially about discriminant validity, then incremental validity.

The important issue for most psychologists comes to be how to differentiate the
concept of style from those two much more accepted individual characteristics of
ability (measured by power tests) and personality (measured by preference tests). One
important and fundamental issue is the difference between a style and a trait. Cynics
suggest that people often choose the former term only because it implies "ease of
change." You can change your style more easily than your personality traits. Further,
while some style theorists tend to be in favor of categorical measurement, trait theorists use a dimensional approach.

Many working in this area have argued that cognitive/learning/thinking styles
evolve both from individual personality and from ability (Furnham, 1995; Messick,
1984). They are thus related both to personality and to intelligence, and they are
similar to intellectual competencies. A person's style determines how they seek out,
perceive, and respond to various "information-processing task situations." Style can
therefore advantage or disadvantage a person in any particular situation.

Hence, quite logically, people seek out situations (courses) that advantage their
preferred style.

Learning style seems most closely linked to thinking or cognitive style. Moreover,
it may seem that it is also linked to attributional and coping style—namely to
how thinkers and learners explain and cope with their success and failure at learning.
Also, all these styles are linked fundamentally to the ability and temperament of
individuals.

Zhang and Sternberg (2009) believe that the styles literature deals with three main controversial issues: styles as value-laden or value-free; styles as traits versus states; and styles as different constructs versus similar constructs. They note six messages from their recently edited book: styles do matter; they are different from abilities; it is possible to build a common language of style; it is possible to situate the style literature within larger contexts (e.g. educational); many style issues (their malleability) are still open to debate; styles can be applied to other worlds. They also offer five answers to the "what next/where now" question: all style models or theories need to be empirically tested; we need to apply styles knowledge in applied settings and see if it has any benefit; we need to know the answers to some of the debates, for example whether styles are malleable; the styles literature needs to be better integrated with the wider academic fields; we need more cross-cultural studies.

## 2   Taxonomic and Measurement Consensus

Many areas of differential psychology have been wracked, and hence wrecked, by long-standing taxonomic debates and, worse, by authors seeking eponymous fame by constructing more and more similar overlapping instruments, while never bothering to provide either a robust theory/model or convincing evidence of test validity. Personality trait theory was dominated for around 30 years by the Eysenck–Cattell debate about the orthogonal, higher-order, "Giant Three" and the oblique, lower-order, comprehensive 16 traits. This was replaced by the Giant-Three versus Big-Five debate. Yet, although there remains lively debate the area, the general agreement about measuring personality traits by the Big Five has led to a renaissance of personality theory and to a distinct move forward. Whilst different measures of the Big Five remain—characterized by length, style, and format—there seems to be general agreement that they are all measuring the same thing. This general consensus has allowed the field to really go forward, though there is now considerable interest in a single factor of personality.

In intelligence research there has been much less debate about measurement, as most researchers agree that as there is impressive evidence for general intelligence ("$g$"), so that essentially most tests are tapping into the same construct. However, it was the debate around Herrnstein's *Bell Curve* book that led 50 of the world's most famous researchers in the area to agree on a 25-point summary of what was known (Gottfredson, 1999). This book, written by Herrnstein and Murray (1996), stresses the power of intelligence in predicting practically all life's major outcomes but partly because of a chapter on race led to an incredible response now called the "bell curve wars." However in many ways this helped intelligence researchers come together and agree some major issues. This "creed" (see Gottfredson, 1999) has also influenced the renaissance of work in intelligence. It would be an extremely useful exercise for style researchers to do the same: namely to meet and agree on what is known and understood in the area.

Agreement and consensus based on good theories and tests help a field consolidate. They make it easier for researchers inside and outside the area to summarize what is known, to ask good questions, and to move forward. Alas, neither the styles nor the approaches literature has benefited from this agreement and consensus.

Clinical, cognitive, differential, educational, and organizational psychologists have all expressed an interest in, and done research around, cognitive and learning styles. Yet all this interest and all this energy have not been rewarded with either consensus or great progress. There are few dominant systems or theories. In short, there is no paradigm. Peterson, Rayner, and Armstrong (2009) noted that the field of cognitive and learning style has been constantly criticized for conceptual confusion, contested definitions, poor measurement, and lack of validity. They e-surveyed 94 style researchers who seemed aware of all these criticisms but, rather depressingly, showed little resolve to address them.

# 3   Approaches to Learning (ATL)

The ATL literature is definitely alive and well (Ballantine et al., 2008; Cano & Berben, 2009; Ellis et al., 2008; Flood & Wilson, 2008: Segers, Martens, & Van den Bossche, 2008; Zhu et al., 2008), but it is very scattered in the applied and educational literature. It seems that practitioners want to use the concept before the psychometricians have really thoroughly sorted out the issues.

The ATL literature tends to be less complex and to show more agreement than can be seen in the cognitive style area. Whereas the "style" literature is essentially about how different people choose to *process* material, the "approaches" literature is clearly much more concerned with *motivation* and *assessment*. The issue is how people approach their learning task: how much time and effort they put into it, and how they go about preparing for exams. This may be a function of their personality, intelligence, and learning history, as well as of how they are taught, which in turn could be related to the approach in the first place.

Teachers and parents see it partly as their aim to shape a student's approach to his or her learning. Both tend to like to encourage students to be dedicated to learning and to do it efficiently, effectively, and with enjoyment. However, they may send contradictory signals. For instance they may say they want deep learning, but only encourage surface learning, because of the emphasis they place on grades. Indeed there may be cultural differences in educational philosophy, which shape whether students adopt various approaches. Thus some cultures value rote learning, while others stress the importance of students' ability to seek out and then critique the salient literature and facts.

One recent study of students on a placement showed that their approach to learning was a function of the number of students, educators, and assessors on the placement (Kell & Owen, 2009). That is, although there are differences in how students usually approach their learning, these preferences can easily be changed by the learning environment, particularly where students have little or no choice in how they are assessed.

Murray-Harvey (1994) pointed out the overlap/similarity between the learning styles and approaches to learning concepts: both are focused on individual differences in learning and both are directed to improving student learning. Both sets of

**Table 22.1** Characteristics of deep and surface approaches to learning. Adapted from various sources

| *Deep* | *Surface* |
| --- | --- |
| More critical | Less critical |
| More integrated | Less integrated |
| Active/involved | Passive/receiving |
| Interested in meaning | Interested in repeating |
| Focused on argument | Focused on "facts" |
| Interested in evidence | Less critical of evidence |
| Read for meaning/understanding | Read for memory storage |
| Applied to real issues/examples | Pragmatically exam-oriented |
| Motivated to understand | Motivated to pass exams |
| Intellectually engaged | Less engaged |

researchers talk of styles that seem a mixture of cognitive (ability and personality) individual differences factors. Nearly all researchers use either a processing or a systems approach. Approaches researchers are concerned with the learning strategy that students use, which is considered an important attribute that they bring to any learning situation.

Different ATL researchers, all working in the 1970s, came to similar categorizations and used comparable terminologies on the basis of their observations of learning processes. It was observed that, if students were given to read a text that they knew would be examined, some tried to understand, contextualize, and comprehend the "big picture" content, while others focused on remembering what they thought were the "facts" they would be examined on. These two very different approaches have been called *deep* versus *surface* approaches. To adopt the deep approach means to achieve a critical understanding and retention of concepts, which are integrated into a knowledge schema and used for problem-solving. The surface approach is based on a pragmatic, short-term memorization of salient facts, for examination or repetition.

*Deep* learning is about big picture, broad-view, evaluative, and crucial learning. Deep learners are intrinsically motivated, but also interested in applying their knowledge and in seeking evidence for its validity. Knowledge acquisition is thought of as both practical and enjoyable.

Most teachers and lectures argue that they try to encourage this style of learning.

*Surface* learners, on the other hand, are detailed and pragmatically focused on rote learning, memorization, and course assessment and requirements. Usually little effort is made to integrate the material into a wider knowledge base. Learning motivation is extrinsic and based more on fear of failure, success orientation, and even parent pressure.

Other approaches include the *achievement-oriented* or *strategic* approach. This is a highly pragmatic approach, aimed essentially at getting higher grades or at achieving some very specific target. Thus learners invest as much energy in studying past questions and in marking schemes and teacher's preferences as in studying the data themselves. They may be both deep and surface learners at different times, essentially to achieve different ends. Nearly all researchers in the area (Biggs, 1987; Entwistle, 1984, 1996; Marton & Saljo, 1976) have made the deep/surface distinction, but also added others. This distinction is similar to the intrinsic/extrinsic one, which is to be found in the motivational literature.

Nearly all the models and measures in the ATL literature make the surface/deep distinction, but questions remain as to what other different approaches may be usefully differentiated and whether these are in any sense "facets" of the Big Two or unique dimensions in their own right. A few sophisticated attempts have been made to answer these questions (Fox, McManus, & Winder, 2001).

# 4   Measures of Approaches to Learning

Different measures have been developed, but nearly all are based on Marton and Saljo's (1976) distinction between deep and surface learning styles. Many measures have been translated and validated in different languages and cultures (Valadas, Gonsalves, & Faisca, 2010). One well-known measure, the Approaches to Studying Inventory (ASI), has been well used, though more work has been done on the revised version (RASI; Entwistle, 1984; Entwistle & Ramsden, 1983; Entwistle & Tait, 1995; Entwistle, Hanley, & Hounsell, 1979).

The RASI is a 60-item questionnaire that assesses five dimensions: deep approach, surface approach, strategic approach, apathetic approach, and academic aptitude. A reduced version of this inventory, with 38 items, appeared in 1994; this time it was measuring five dimensions, labeled deep approach, surface approach, strategic approach, lack of direction, and academic self-confidence. A later version, produced in 1995, used 44 items, identifying a sixth dimension: meta-cognitive awareness of studying.

Duff (2004) reviewed various studies by using this instrument, and concluded that it could be successfully used to enhance the quality of learning in management students. However, in one study it was suggested that approach to learning, as measured by this instrument, was a "subset of personality" (p. 1907). Studies have continued to use this measure, showing for instance that it also has predictive validity, with workplace learning of a non-student sample (Geertshuis & Fazey, 2006). Others have adapted this measure to use in very specific contexts.

Perhaps the most widely used instrument developed from work conducted on surface and deep learning is Biggs' (1987, 1993) Study Process Questionnaire (SPQ). The deep/surface learning constructs formed the conceptual basis for the earlier work of Biggs, who subsequently used the terms "deep," "surface," and "achieving" to describe three qualitatively different approaches to studying. Each of these consists of a congruent motivational influence and a corresponding study strategy (see Table 22.2). A student using a predominantly surface approach is supposedly goal-oriented rather than deriving any intrinsic meaning from the task, and learns in a superficial manner (rote fashion) with the aim of achieving the minimum requirements. A student taking a deep approach is interested in obtaining a meaningful understanding of what is learned, and in doing so through extensive reading and research. A student

**Table 22.2**   Motive and strategy in approaches to learning and studying. Adapted from Biggs, 1987

| Approach | Motive | Strategy |
|---|---|---|
| SA: Surface | Surface motive (SM) is to meet exam requirements: a balancing act between failing and over-working. Pragmatic passing orientation | Surface strategy (SS) is to reproduce material through rote learning. Using any technique to maximize the ability to regurgitate material |
| DA: Deep | Deep motive (DM) is intrinsic interest in what is being learned; to develop competence/full understanding in particular disciplines subjects | Deep strategy (DS) is to discover and fully analyze meaning by reading widely, relating new ideas with previous relevant knowledge to integrate worldviews |
| AA: Achieving | Achieving motive (AM) is to enhance self-esteem through competition; simply to obtain highest grades, whether or not material is believed important or interesting | Achieving strategy (AS) is to be maximally efficient and effective in organizing time and working conditions; to behave as a "model student" so as to get maximum rewards |

undertaking an achieving approach is highly committed to gaining good grades and would use a systematic approach to her studies. Biggs (1987) maintained that students use predominantly one of these approaches to learning, and that these approaches are related to different performance outcomes.

A combination of deep and achieving approaches to learning is viewed by Biggs as resulting in a highly successful outcome and progression to further study. Students who continue to use a surface approach tend not to have such a successful outcome, and terminate their higher education after a first degree. Biggs (1987) noted that the identification of learning profiles on the basis of the assessment of approaches to learning is useful for identifying students' styles and their compatibility with a particular learning environment. These profiles would also be useful for identifying students with study strategies that are not congruent with academic success (ibid.).

Biggs' theory and measure have been successfully used in many studies (Duff, Boyle, Dunleavy, & Ferguson, 2004a, 2004b), and investigations of the psychometric properties of the instrument have shown it to be sound (Evans, Kirby, & Fabrigan, 2003; Snelgrove & Slater, 2003).

Often instruments get revised and adapted to be used for specific purposes. Thus Fox et al. (2001) devised a shortened version of the Biggs measure by using 18 of the 42 questions. In their study of 1,349 medical students they showed that the short version yielded the same factor structure. More interestingly, perhaps, in the longitudinal part of the study they showed that these learning approaches were partly stable over time, yet partly modifiable because of the educational experiences of the people involved.

Various strategies self-evidently encourage deep approaches: giving students a map of where they are going and how the information connects with other knowledge: involving the learner as an active participant in that learning. It is important both to give feedback and to encourage criticism of all that is learnt. Letting people know how they are doing, practicing assessment methods, and encouraging success all helps encouraging a strategic approach.

Approach to learning is not trait-like, in that it seems to vary to some extent over time and across situations. A learner who is intrinsically interested in a topic as well as having a teacher/instructor with a similar outlook and style may well be encouraged to adopt a deep learning approach. At the same time, he may become quite happily and effectively a strategic surface learner on a topic he is less interested in, and which "only requires a pass mark."

# 5  Personality and Approaches to Learning and Learning Style

A central question for "approach and style" researchers is the conceptual and empirical overlap between their measures and established personality traits. Approaches to learning measures have been related to many other different measures (Marrs & Benton, 2009; Yang & Tsai, 2010), but many have looked at the relation with personality (Swanberg & Martinsen, 2010).

Where does the approach concept sit in five-factor space? What is the overlap between these different measures? Both concepts are "preference-based" and measured. The question concerns the correlation between these measures; but, more than that, it concerns *incremental validity*. That is, if both trait and style measures are used to predict some criterion variable (like academic performance), is there evidence for the incremental validity of the one over the other? This nearly always boils down to the question of whether approaches, or style measures, "add anything" to the currently very well established Big-Five or Big-Three measures. This is particularly important as more psychometric work has gone into developing valid and reliable measures than has been the case with style and approach instruments.

Many studies have been done in this area over the years, usually comparing the scores of scholars or students in a variety of measures. In one paper, Furnham (1992) reported on three studies in this tradition: the Honey and Mumford (1982) Learning Style Questionnaire; the Whetten and Cameron (1984) Learning Style Instrument; and the Kolb (1984) Learning Style Inventory. Some correlations exceeded $r > .50$, but many were around $r = .30$, which made sense. Indeed it was primarily two traits—extraversion and psychoticism—that best predicted the learning cognitive styles.

Arteche, Chamorro-Premuzic, Ackerman, and Furnham (2009) looked at the correlation between the Big Five and the three scores derived from the Biggs measure in 300 students. They found that the surface learning style was correlated with neuroticism, conscientiousness, extraversion, and disagreeableness, while the deep learning approach was correlated with openness and agreeableness. The achievement approach was most strongly correlated with conscientiousness and extraversion, and negatively correlated with openness.

Swanberg and Martinsen (2010) looked at the relationship between the Big Five on the one hand and approaches to learning and actual grade achievement on the other, in 687 business school students. The highest correlations indicated that openness correlated with deep approaches ($r = .52$); strategic approaches with agreeableness ($r = .64$); and neuroticism ($r = .48$) and conscientiousness ($r = -.39$) correlated with surface approaches. They regressed sex, age, and school record, the Big Five, and the learning approaches onto the grade and found that the best predictor was school grade. They found that the relationship of conscientiousness and openness scores to grade achievement was mediated by the deep and strategic approach, while neuroticism had a direct and indirect effect on grade outcome through the surface approach. More importantly, they found that the three learning approaches explained variance in grade outcome beyond the Big Five, which suggested incremental validity.

Chamorro-Premuzic and Furnham (2009) attempted a review and study that looked at seven studies in the same area. The authors suggested three reasons for looking at this area. First, an examination of the psychometric overlap between these two measures (traits and approaches) may highlight the conceptual similarities between personality and learning approaches (Chamorro-Premuzic & Furnham, 2008; Furnham, 2008; Zhang, 2003)—a fact which has a number of practical and theoretical implications, as these approaches may help researchers and practitioners to compare the results of different investigations (by using personality or learning approaches measures). Second, personality traits have been conceptualized as less changeable and malleable than learning approaches (Furnham, 2008; Pedersen, Harris, Plomin, McClearn, & Nesselroade, in press), and interventions aimed at influencing students' learning approaches would benefit from knowing to what extent stable dispositions prevent or encourage changes in learning approach. Third, researchers or practitioners wishing to predict various educational outcomes, such as academic performance, vocational interests, or test anxiety, would benefit from knowing to what degree learning approaches and personality traits overlap.

Table 22.3 summarizes the results of the main studies devoted to the relationship between the Big Five and learning approaches. There was a number of consistent positive associations: neuroticism associated with surface learning and openness associated with deep learning. Inconsistencies may partly be attributed to the small and homogeneous samples, as well as to the different inventories used. Furthermore, most studies only reported bivariate correlations, which are insensitive to third-order variables and to the overlap among different predictors or outcomes. Duff et al. (2004a, 2004b) are the exception, as they tested a structural equation model (SEM), but their sample was small and the measures infrequently used. On the other hand, Busato, Frans, Elshout, and Hamaker (1999) did examine a large sample, but they looked at different learning styles and did not conduct a SEM. Indeed, our literature review identified only a single study (Shokri, Kadivar, Farzad, & Sangari, 2007) that simultaneously examined, via SEM, the combined effects of the Big Five on learning approaches in a relatively large sample, though the focus of that investigation was on assessing the extent to which learning approaches mediate the effects of the Big Five on academic achievement (see also Chamorro-Premuzic & Furnham, 2008).

Previous studies yielded inconsistent findings concerning the extent to which the combined personality traits and learning approaches factors overlap, some studies

**Table 22.3**  Summary of past correlations between Big Five traits and learning approaches

|                              | Surface | Deep       | Strategic |
|------------------------------|---------|------------|-----------|
| **Neuroticism**              | +++++   | –          | –/+       |
| Busato et al. (1999)         |         | –          |           |
| Zhang (2003a)                | ++      | –          | –         |
| Duff et al. (2004a)          | ++      | –          | –         |
| Furnham et al. (2007)        | +       |            | +         |
| Chamorro & Furnham (2008)    |         |            |           |
| **Extraversion**             | +       | ++++       | ++++      |
| Busato et al. (1999)         |         |            | +         |
| Zhang (2003a)                |         | +          | +         |
| Duff et al. (2004a)          |         | +          | ++        |
| Furnham et al. (2007)        | +       | +          |           |
| Chamorro & Furnham (2008)    |         | +          |           |
| **Openness**                 | –       | +++++++++  | +         |
| Busato et al. (1999)         |         | ++         |           |
| Zhang (2003a)                | –       | ++         | +         |
| Duff et al. (2004a)          |         | ++         |           |
| Furnham et al. (2007)        | –       | ++         |           |
| Chamorro & Furnham (2008)    |         | +          |           |
| **Agreeableness**            | –       | –          | ++/–      |
| Busato et al. (1999)         |         |            | +         |
| Zhang (2003a)                | –       |            | –         |
| Duff et al. (2004a)          |         | –          | +         |
| Furnham et al. (2007)        |         |            |           |
| Chamorro & Furnham (2008)    |         |            |           |
| **Conscientiousness**        | +/–     | ++++       | +++++     |
| Busato et al. (1999)         |         |            | +         |
| Zhang (2003a)                | –       | ++         | ++        |
| Duff et al. (2004a)          |         | +          |           |
| Furnham et al. (2007)        | +       | +          | ++        |
| Chamorro & Furnham (2008)    |         |            |           |

(Chamorro-Premuzic, Furnham, & Lewis, 2007; Zhang, 2003) concluding that learning approaches and personality traits are related, but distinct, constructs (about 25 percent overlap), and others (e.g. Duff et al., 2004a, 2004b) reporting a substantial overlap (about 45 percent). That said, the strength of the associations shown in Table 22.3 suggests that most of this overlap would be accounted for by the openness–deep learning approach relationship. In their study, Duff et al. (2004a) had a number of over 800 students. The results were clear. It was openness to experience that was clearly most predictive—positively for deep learning, but negatively for surface learning.

The results can be summarized thus. By far the strongest correlation between approaches and traits is that between openness and deep learning. Correlations often exceed $r = .5$. Studies have shown that numerous other psychological concepts relate to openness, for instance typical intellectual engagement and need for cognition (Furnham, Monsen, & Ahmetoglu, 2009). Further, openness is positively correlated with both cognitive ability and achievement success in educational settings. Clever, curious people are intrinsically interested in, and adopt, a deep approach, which satisfies their needs. However, the relationship between traits and the surface approach is less clear. This may suggest that the deep approach is more stable over time than the surface (or strategic) approach, and that students may be more easily encouraged to adopt a surface approach than a deep approach.

## 6   Educational Preferences

Any individual's learning style and approach to learning should have a direct and logical impact on many of that individual's educational preferences and on how she attempts to influence her learning environment (Jungert & Rosander, 2009). This would include the topic that students chose to study, given that they have a choice— such as between various lectures in school and at university; for the particular type of teacher they have; or between teaching styles or methods. The section will consider some recent research in this area.

## 7   Teaching Methods

Educational institutions offer a variety of teaching modalities, from formal lecturers to small discussion groups and individual tutorials. Some use videos; others encourage the students themselves to give the lectures. Methods vary as a function of the topic being taught, of the different assessment criteria, and of the personal preferences of the lecturers/teachers. Generally, it has been assumed that, if there is a "fit" between the student's preferred teaching style and method and those chosen by the lecturer/teacher/professor, the result would be both happier and academically more successful students. However, research often fails to support this hypothesis (Furnham, 1995), though there could be many reasons for this result. Possibly a surface teaching and learning style always results in weaker outcomes than a matched deep style. Equally, it may not always be possible to teach the students in the style they prefer. Third, if cognitive ability is linked both to an approach/style and to achievement, then the teacher's particular chosen style should seem less important.

Most research has concentrated on the relationship between students' personality traits and their preferred learning styles, rather than on their preferred teaching methods. Chamorro-Premuzic et al. (2007) got 221 medical students to complete a battery of tests including an approach to learning measure (Biggs, 1987), and a self-report scale designed for the purpose was used to assess participants' preference for different teaching modalities. A total of seven teaching modalities were included in the present questionnaire: (1) post-mortems/laboratory classes; (2) small group tutorials; (3) standard lectures; (4) independent study; (5) clinical/ward teaching; (6) group discussions/seminars; and (7) research projects. Ratings of preference were provided on a 10-point Likert-type scale ranging from 1 (least preferred) to 10 (most preferred). Participants rated their preferred teaching method for each of the subjects they were studying, namely geriatrics, surgery, obstetrics, psychiatry/neuroscience, general practitioner, pediatrics, anatomy, pathology, and physiology.

The most preferred teaching method was in small groups, and the least preferred teaching method was the research project, which also showed the smallest standard deviation. Correlations between personality traits and preferences for specific teaching methods showed a number of significant associations. Extraversion was negatively and significantly related to preferences for independent study (i.e. the more extraverted students were, the less they preferred to study independently). Neuroticism was negatively and significantly correlated with preferences for lab classes, small groups, clinical teaching, and group discussion (i.e. the more emotionally stable the students were, the more they preferred these teaching modalities). These four teaching methods were also significantly correlated with openness, though positively (i.e. the more open the students were, the more they preferred these teaching methods). Conscientiousness was positively and significantly related to preference for clinical teaching (i.e. the more conscientious the students were, the more they preferred clinical teaching). Finally, agreeableness—like openness—was positively and significantly correlated with preference for lab classes, small groups, clinical teaching, and group discussion (i.e. the more agreeable the students were, the more they preferred these four teaching methods). The deep motive and strategy were positively and significantly correlated with preference for lab classes, small groups, clinical teaching, and discussion groups. These teaching methods were also significantly correlated with surface motive and strategy, though negatively. Thus students with a deep approach to learning, being least likely to adopt a surface approach, enjoyed lab classes, small tutorial groups, clinical training, and discussion.

In a study of medical students, Papinczak (2009) considered whether deep and strategic learners enjoyed and supported problem-based learning and achieved well as a result of it. The results supported the hypothesis. Deep learners' intrinsic motivation and self-regulated learning made them able to cope with the time management and workload, and they made them uncertainly associated with self-directed learning well. Further, these students did better on written exams.

Another recent study of medical students looked at their approaches to learning anatomy (Smith & Mathias, 2010). The authors found, as predicted, a clear association between the students' perception of the anatomy learning environment, the approach they adopted, and the activities they engaged in. Those who adopted a deep approach were more interested in an exploratory, holistic approach; they were not only fact-driven, and they enjoyed the opportunity to use the language and terminology they had picked up.

In higher education, particularly at postgraduate levels, a wider variety of teaching methods are used apart from the traditional lecture. Furthermore, students can and do choose courses that specifically and explicitly offer different methods of teaching and assessment. Indeed, students appear to have a strong preference both for, and against, certain teaching methods, as they suit their temperament, ability, and experience. Whilst it may not always be possible for lecturers and teachers to use the teaching methods preferred by students, it is certainly interesting to get some idea of these preferences. More importantly, it would be interesting to get students to try to explain those preferences. The introduction of new teaching methods—for instance on-line and distance learning—suggests fruitful future areas of interest and research.

## 8 Assessment Method

There is now an extensive and growing literature on students' perceptions of assessment and evaluation in higher education (Birenbaum, 1997; Kniveton, 1996; Marlin, 1987). Much of this literature has concentrated on one particular assessment technique, namely multiple-choice questions (MCQs), and on one individual differences factor, namely approaches to learning. Scouller and Prosser (1994) showed that deep learners and achievement-oriented students had different perceptions of, and preparation strategies for, MCQs. Scouller (1998) later showed that students tended to employ a surface learning approach when examined by MCQ, and to perceive these tests as assessing knowledge-based lower levels of intellectual processing. Indeed deep learning approaches were associated with poorer performance in MCQs, but with the opposite in assignment essays. Birenbaum (2007) looked at students' test anxiety and learning strategies influence on their preference for type of instructon/teaching and assessment. He found evidence of a learning regulation dimension from self-regulation to instructor dependency and concluded by asserting the need for a dialogue between instructor and students, in order to structure expectations to make them fit the goals of higher education.

Others have looked at the possibility of using peer assessment. Thus Segers and Dochy (2001) compared students' own, their peers', and their tutors' assessments with examination scores. Interestingly, the highest correlations were between peer ratings and the examination score. Student assessment has been an active field of educational research and application. It has seen changes in ideas about the assessment *of* learning toward an assessment *for* learning. Further, new forms of assessment have been proposed, like peer or self-assessment (Scouller & Prosser, 1994).

Struyven, Dochy, and Janssens (2005) reviewed 35 salient papers on the topic. They concluded that a students' approach to learning is a clear and logical correlate of assessment preferences and that the assessment methods have an impact of the students' learning approach and vice versa. They noted that studies have focused on essay versus MCQ examinations and that students who are low in test-taking anxiety and in good learning skills prefer essays over MCQs, and, further, that highly anxious, poor learning-skill students prefer MCQs which elicit surface approaches to learning.

Some studies have looked at the consequences of changing the curriculum on the approach to learning of the students. Balasooriya, Hughes, and Toohey (2009), in a qualitative study, looked at how changes in an integrated medical syllabus aimed at deeper learning actually impacted on the student's behaviour. To their surprise, they found that the syllabus polarized students and that, while most responded, as the researchers had hoped, by adopting a deep style, some became more surface-oriented. The authors concluded: "It seems likely that individual characteristics such as previous learning experiences, learning preferences and level of cognitive development have as much or more influence on learning as curriculum design" (p. 299).

Pang, Ho, and Man (2009) also looked at how a move toward outcome-based teaching changed the learning approach in 512 Hong Kong-based business students. Around a third did not change their approach, but there was a clear movement toward an achievement approach. The authors argued that a students' choice of learning approach can be both deliberate and "unconscious," and that most business students adopt an achieving approach because of their values and goals.

Furnham and Chamorro-Premuzic (2005b) conducted a two-study examination of ability (IQ) and personality (Big Five) correlates of preference for assessment method. They found modest, but interpretable correlations between ability test scores, personality trait measures, and assessment preferences. The second study found that the students' academic performance had no relationship to their preference for assessment methods. Chamorro-Premuzic, Furnham, Dissou, and Heaven (2005) and Furnham and Chamorro-Premuzic (2005a) looked at the relationship between preferences for examination assessment methods, personalities, intelligence, and gender. Results replicated significant and negative associations between neuroticism and preference for both essay-type and oral exams. Extraversion was positively and significantly associated with preference for oral exams, while conscientiousness was positively and significantly related to preference for continuous assessment and dissertations. On the other hand, IQ was positively and significantly related to preference for multiple-choice exams.

Chamorro-Premuzic et al. (2005) replicated and extended this study with an Australian sample. Reliability analysis showed that participants tended to have consistent attitudes toward assessment methods across disciplines (e.g. history, biology, psychology). When these preferences were examined with regard to individual differences in personality, correlations revealed significant associations between three of the Big-Five personality dimensions and attitudes toward assessment methods. Neuroticism was negatively correlated with both preference for an oral exam and continuous assessment. Extraversion and openness to experience were both positively correlated with preference for oral examinations, and openness was significantly and negatively related to preference for multiple-choice exams. On the other hand, agreeableness and extraversion were both significantly and positively related to preference for group work. A series of hierarchical regressions examined the predictability of preferences for assessment methods by the Big-Five factors as well as self-assessed intelligence and gender. They showed that personality traits are significant predictors of preference for oral exams and group work, even when gender and self-assessed intelligence are considered.

More recently, Furnham, Batey, and Martin (2011) got more than 400 students from four universities in America and Britain to complete measures of approaches to learning, general knowledge (as a proxy for intelligence), and preference for examination method. Approach to learning was consistently associated with preferences: surface learners preferred multiple-choice and group-work options, and viewed essay-type and dissertation options less favorably. Deep learners, on the other hand, favored essay-type and oral exams as well as final dissertations. Males favored oral (*viva voce*) exams, and females favored coursework assessments. Extraverts preferred multiple-choice, oral, and group-work assessment, while openness was positively associated with essays and oral exams but negatively associated with multiple-choice and group work. Regression analysis showed that personality, learning style, general knowledge, and demographic factors accounted for 5–10 percent of the variance in preferred examination technique.

The results of these studies seem to indicate that the learning style and approach to learning any person has would influence the sort of assessment they would prefer. This remains in education a very controversial topic. There are pressures in some sectors to be more efficient and to examine large groups reliably. Thus some advocate machine-scored multiple tests, while other claim that frequently the way these tests are constructed leads to rote or surface learning. Certainly educators do believe that the most powerful way to alter a student's approach to learning is to vary the way in which she is assessed.

# 9   Conclusion

Differential psychologists have tried to identify individual differences in abilities, traits, and motivations. As can be seen from other chapters in this volume, there remain debates about taxonomization: are there more general abilities and traits— that is, general factors? The taxonomization debates have not been so noticeable in the area of motivation, primarily because of numerous problems associated with measuring motivation.

The literature on ATL has been less fractured than that on learning styles. There are fewer models and measures and more agreement about the terminology. The area remains at the periphery for most psychometricians. Most of the research in the ATL literature has been applied with relatively few sophisticated studies, which examine, and hence improve, the psychometric properties of the instruments used.

In a review of styles and approaches, Furnham (in press a) noted three trends:

> *First*, the business and commercial world seems particularly interested in the usefulness of styles instruments. This may be because of their disillusionment with more traditional IQ and personality tests (Furnham, 2008). Style concepts fit well into the current zeitgeist and appear to offer as much as, if not more than, some of the instruments used in the past. The major result of this interest has meant the styles literature is now more widely scattered than ever across academic disciplines. This makes the task harder for reviewers who still complain about the proliferation of confusion.
>
> *Second*, the approaches literature has both staid [*sic*] much more closely in the learning education world and progressed in terms of the further development of instruments. Further, it has been used to try to predict how individuals are attracted to and satisfied with particular institutions, courses, teachers, lecturing styles and assessment methods.
>
> *Third*, many of the old questions remain in both areas. These include clarity of definition, and parsimony as well as verisimilitude of models. Most instruments in the area still appear to have not been subjected to the same rigour as those in ability and trait psychology. It seems researchers are too eager to "get to market" than [*sic*] to develop fine instruments with clear norms. More than anything else however the question still remains where these styles and concepts dwell in "individual differences" space. This is essentially about discriminant validity, then incremental validity.

Most psychologists agree that we have developed reliable, robust, and valid measures of cognitive ability (Gottfredson, 2007) and (to a lesser extent) of personality (Furnham 2008), but that we are less successful in measuring motivation. Nevertheless, researchers in the ATL literature, which is reasonably narrow and applied to educational contexts, have developed relatively simple but useful models and measures for how people approach their education. It is now perhaps time to integrate this research into the wider arena of differential psychology to fully understand the etiology, structure, and consequences of adopting a particular approach to learning.

# References

Arteche, A., Chamorro-Premuzic, T., Ackerman, P., & Furnham, A. (2009). Typical intellectual engagement as a byproduct of openness, learning approaches, and self-assessed intelligence. *Educational Psychology, 29*, 357–367.

Balasooriya, C., Hughes, C., & Toohey, S. (2009). Impact of a new integrated medicine program on students' approaches to learning. *Higher Educational Research and Development, 28*, 289–302.

Ballantine, J., Duff, A., & Larres, P. (2008). Accounting and business students' approaches to learning. *Journal of Accounting Education, 26*, 188–201.

Birenbaum, M. (1997). Assessment preferences and their relationship to learning strategies and orientations. *Higher Education, 33*, 71–84.

Birenbaum, M. (2007). Assessment and instruction preferences and their relationship with test anxiety and learning strategies. *Higher Education, 53*, 749–768.

Biggs, J. (1987). *The Study Process Questionnaire manual.* Victoria: Australian Council for Educational Research.

Biggs, J. (1993). What do inventories of students' learning processes really measure? *British Journal of Educational Psychology, 3*, 3–19.

Busato, V. V., Frans, J. P., Elshout, J. J., & Hamaker, C. (1999). Intellectual ability, learning style, personality, achievement motivation and academic success of psychology students in higher education. *Personality and Individual Differences 29*, 1057–1068.

Cano, F., & Berben, A. (2009). University students' achievement goals and approaches to learning in mathematics. *British Journal of Educational Psychology, 79*, 131–153.

Cassidy, S. (2004). Learning styles: An overview of theories, models, and measures. *Educational Psychology, 24*, 419–440.

Chamorro-Premuzic, T., & Furnham, A. (2002). Neuroticism and "special treatment" in university examinations. *Social Behaviour and Personality, 30*, 807–812.

Chamorro-Premuzic, T., & Furnham, A. (2003). Personality predicts academic performance: Evidence from two longitudinal university samples. *Journal of Research in Personality, 37*, 319–338.

Chamorro-Premuzic, T., & Furnham, A. (2008). Personality, intelligence and approaches to learning as predictors of academic performance. *Personality and Individual Differences, 44*, 1596–1603.

Chamorro–Premuzic, T., & Furnham, A. (2009). Mainly openness: The relationship between the Big Five personality traits and learning approaches. *Learning and Individual Differences, 19*, 524–529.

Chamorro-Premuzic, T., Furnham, A., & Lewis, M. (2007). Personality and approaches to learning predict preference for different teaching methods. *Learning and Individual Differences, 17*, 341–350.

Chamorro-Premuzic, T., Furnham, A., Dissou, G., & Heaven, P. (2005). Personality and preferences for academic assessment. *Learning and Individual Differences, 15,* 246–255.

Duff, A. (2004). The Revised Approaches to Studying Inventory (RASI) and its use in management education. *Active Learning in Higher Education, 5,* 56–72.

Duff, A., Boyle, E., Dunleavy, K., & Ferguson, J. (2004a). The relationship between personality, approach to learning and academic performance. *Personality and Individual Differences, 36,* 1907–1920.

Duff, A., Boyle, E., Dunleavy, K., & Ferguson, J. (2004b). Erratum to "The relationship between personality, approach to learning and academic performance. *Personality and Individual Differences, 44,* 532." *Higher Education Research and Development, 28,* 303–318.

Ellis, R., Ginns, P., & Piggott, L. (2009). E-Learning in higher education: Some key aspects and their relationship to approaches to study. *Higher Education Research and Development, 28,* 303–318.

Ellis, R., Goodyear, P., Calvo, R., & Prosser, M. (2008). Engineering students' conceptions of and approaches to learning through discussions in face-to-face and online contexts. *Learning and Instruction, 18,* 267–282.

Entwistle, N. J. (1984). Contrasting perspectives on learning. In F. Marton, D. Hounsell, & N. Entwistle (Eds.), *The experience of learning* (pp. 1–18). Edinburgh: Scottish Academic Press.

Entwistle, N. J. (1996). *Styles of learning and teaching.* London: David Fulton Publisher.

Entwistle, N. J., & Ramsden, P. (1983). *Understanding student learning.* London: Croom Helm.

Entwistle, N. J., & Tait, H. (1995). *The Revised Approaches to Studying Inventory.* Edinburgh: University of Edinburgh Centre for Research on Learning and Instruction.

Entwistle, N. J., Hanley, M., & Hounsell, D. (1979). Identifying distinctive approaches to studying. *Higher Education, 8,* 365–380.

Evans, C., Kirkby, J., & Fabrigan, L. (2003). Approaches to learning, need for cognition, and strategic flexibility among university students. *British Journal of Educational Psychology, 73,* 507–538.

Eysenck, H. (1978). The development of personality and its relation to learning. In S. Murray-Smith (Ed.), *Melbourne studies in education* (pp. 134–181). Melbourne: Melbourne University Press.

Eysenck, H. J., & Cookson, D. (1969). Personality in primary school children, ability and achievement. *British Journal of Educational Psychology, 39,* 123–130.

Eysenck, M. (1981). Learning memory and personality. In H. J. Eysenck (Ed.), *A model for personality* (pp. 169–209). Berlin: Springer-Verlag.

Flood, B., & Wilson, R. (2008). An exploration of the learning approaches of perspective professional accountants in Ireland. *Accounting Forum, 32,* 225–239.

Fox, R., McManus, I., & Winder, B. (2001). The shortened Study Process Questionnaire. *British Journal of Educational Psychology, 71,* 511–530.

Furnham, A. (1992). Personality and learning style. *Personality and Individual Differences, 13,* 429–438.

Furnham, A. (1995). The relationship of personality and intelligence to cognitive learning style and achievement. In D. Saklofske & M. Zeidner (Eds.), *International handbook of personality and intelligence* (pp. 397–413). London: Plenum Press.

Furnham, A. (2008). *Personality and intelligence at work.* London: Routledge.

Furnham, A. (in press a). Learning style and approaches to learning. In T. Urdan, J. Roger, S. Graham, & M. Zeidner (Eds.), *APA educational psychology handbook.* Washington, DC: American Psychological Association.

Furnham, A. (in press b). Intelligence and intellectual styles. In L.-F. Zhang, R. Sternberg, & R. Rayner (Eds.), *Handbook of intellectual styles: Preferences in cognition, learning and thinking.* New York: Springer.

Furnham, A., & Chamorro-Premuzic, T. (2005a). Individual differences in students' preferences for lecturers' personalities. *Journal of Individual Differences, 26,* 170–184.

Furnham, A., & Chamorro-Premuzic, T. (2005b). Individual differences and beliefs associated with preference for university assessment methods. *Journal of Applied Social Psychology, 35,* 1–28.

Furnham, A., Batey, M., & Martin, N. (2011). How would you like to be evaluated? The correlates of students' preferences for assessment methods. *Personality and Individual Differences, 50,* 259–263.

Furnham, A., Monsen, J., & Ahmetoglu, G. (2009). Typical intellectual engagement, Big Five personality traits, approaches to learning and cognitive ability predictors of academic performance. *British Journal of Educational Psychology, 79,* 769–782.

Furnham, A., Christopher, A., Garwood, J., & Martin, G. (2007) Approaches to learning and the acquisition of general knowledge. *Personality and Individual Differences, 43,* 1563–1571.

Geertshuis, S., & Fazey, J. (2006). Approach to learning in the workplace. *Journal of Workplace Learning, 18,* 55–56.

Gottfredson, L. (1999). Mainstream science on intelligence. *Intelligence, 24,* 13–23.

Guilford, J. (1980). Some changes in the structure of intellect model. *Educational and Psychological Measurement, 48,* 1–4.

Honey, P., & Mumford, A. (1982). *The manual of learning styles.* Maidenhead: Honey Press.

Jungert, T., & Rosander, M. (2009). Relationship between students' strategies for influencing their study environment and their strategic approach to studying. *Studies in Higher Education, 34,* 139–152.

Kell, C., & Owen, G. (2009). Approaches to learning on placement: The students' perspective. *Physiotherapy Research International, 14,* 105–115.

Kolb, D. (1984). *Experimental learning.* Englewood Cliffs, NJ: Prentice-Hall.

Kniveton, B. (1996). Student perceptions of assessment methods. *Assessment and Evaluations in Higher Education, 21,* 229–238.

Lietz, P., & Matthews, B. (2010). The effects of college students' personal values on changes in learning approaches. *Research in Higher Education, 51,* 65–87.

Marlin, J. (1987). Student perception of end-of-course evaluations. *Journal of Higher Education, 58,* 704–716.

Marrs, H., & Benton, S. (2009). Relationship between separate and connected knowing and approaches to learning. *Sex Roles, 60,* 57–66.

Marton, E., & Saljo, R. (1976). On the qualitative differences in learning. *British Journal of Educational Psychology, 46,* 4–11.

Messick, S. (1984). The nature of cognitive styles: Problems and promises in educational practice. *Educational Psychologist, 19,* 59–74.

Messick, S. (Ed.) (1976). *Individuality in learning: Implications of cognitive styles and creativity for human development.* San Francisco, CA: Jossey-Bass.

Murray-Harvey, R. (1994). Learning styles and approaches to learning. *British Journal of Educational psychology, 64,* 373–388.

Pang, M., Ho., T., & Man, R. (2009). Learning approaches and outcome-based teaching and learning. *Journal of Teaching in International Business, 20,* 106–122.

Papinczak, T. (2009). Are deep strategic learners better suited to PBL? *Advances in Health Science Eduaction, 14,* 337–353.

Pedersen, N. L., Harris, J. R., Plomin, R., McClearn, G. E., & Nesselroade, J. R. (in press). Genetic and environmental stability for personality. *Psychology and Aging*.

Peterson, E., Rayner, S., & Armstrong, S. (2009). Researching the psychology of cognitive style and learning style: Is there really a future? *Learning and Individual Differences, 19,* 518–523.

Prosser, M., & Trigwell, K. (1999). *Understanding learning and teaching*. Milton Keynes: Open University Press.

Rayner, S., & Peterson, E. (2009). Reaffirming style as an individual difference. In L.-F. Zhang and R. Sternberg (Eds.), *Perspectives on the nature of intellectual styles* (pp. 107–134). New York: Springer.

Richardson, J. (2009). Face-to-face versus online tutoring support in humanities courses in distance education. *Arts and Humanities in Higher Education, 8,* 69–85.

Scouller, K. (1998). The influence of assessment method on students' learning approaches: Multiple choice question examination versus assignment essay. *Higher Education, 35,* 453–472.

Scouller, K., & Prosser, M. (1994). Students' experiences in studying for multiple choice question examinations. *Studies in Higher Education, 19,* 267–279.

Segers, M., & Dochy, F. (2001). New assessment forms in problem-based learning. *Studies in Higher Education, 26,* 327–343.

Segers, M., Martens, R., & Van den Bossche, P. (2008). Understanding how a case-based assessment instrument influences student teachers' learning approaches. *Teaching and Teacher Education, 24,* 1751–1764.

Shokri, O., Kadivar, P., Farzad, V., & Sangari, A. A. (2007). Role of personality traits and learning approaches on academic achievement of university students. *Psychological Research, 9,* 65–84.

Smith, C., & Mathias, H. (2010). Medical students' approaches to learning anatomy. *Clinical Anatomy, 23,* 106–114.

Snelgrove, S. (2004). Approaches to learning of student nurses. *Nurse Education Today, 24,* 605–614.

Snelgrove, S., & Slater, J. (2003). Approaches to learning. *Journal of Advanced Nursing, 43,* 496–505.

Struyven, K., Dochy, F., & Janssens, S. (2005). Students' perceptions about evaluation and assessment in higher education: A review. *Assessment and Evaluation in Higher Education, 30,* 325–341.

Swanberg, A., & Martinsen, O. (2010). Personality, approaches to learning and achievement. *Educational Psychology, 30,* 75–88.

Valadas, S., Gonsalves, F., & Faisca, L. (2010). Approaches to studying in higher education Portuguese students. *Higher Education, 59,* 259–275.

Yang, Y.-F., & Tsai, C.-C. (2010). Conceptions of and approaches to learning through online peer assessment. *Learning and Instruction, 20,* 72–83.

Zhang, L.-F. (2003). Does the Big Five predict learning approaches? *Personality and Individual Differences, 34,* 1431–1441.

Zhu, C., Valcke, M., & Schellens, T. (2008). A cross-cultural study of Chinese and Flemish university students: Do they differ in learning conceptions and approaches to learning? *Learning and Individual Differences, 18,* 120–127.

# 23

# Vocational Interests
## *The Road Less Traveled*
### Patrick Ian Armstrong, Rong Su, and James Rounds

Beginning with E. K. Strong's introduction of the Strong Vocational Interest Bank in the 1920s, the study of vocational interests has been driven by practical measurement concerns (Dawis, 1991). In fact, much of what we know about vocational interests can be found in books and manuals written by the Big Three developers and promoters (E. K. Strong, F. Kuder, and J. L. Holland) of interest inventories (Borgen, 1986). The narrowness of the literature is compounded by the fact that these authors centered their writings on their own vocational interest inventories, and did not consider the larger domain of interest measures. For the Strong Interest Inventory, we have Strong's (1943) book on the *Interests of men and women*, Campbell's (1971) *Handbook for the Strong Vocational Interest Blank*, and the Strong Interest Inventory technical manual by Harmon, Hansen, Borgen, and Hammer (1994). For the Kuder General Interest Survey (Kuder & Zytowski, 1988) and the Kuder Occupational Interest Survey (Kuder & Zytowski, 1991), we have Kuder's (1977) *Activity interests and occupation choice*. The last of the Big Three— Holland (1997), *Making vocational choices: A theory of vocational personalities and work environments*, summarizes research on the Vocational Preference Inventory (Holland, 1985) and on the Self-Directed Search (SDS; Holland, Fritzsche, & Powell, 1997). Within this almost exclusive focus on commercial interest inventories and their validities, a large body of literature has been established that is tied to predicting educational and vocational choice and occupational membership. This validity research, however, came at the expense of the development of interest theory and of the study of how vocational interests can contribute to the understanding of individual differences.

Savickas and Spokane (1999) attempted to remedy the narrow focus of interest scholarship on commercial measures through an edited book on interests. However, with a few exceptions, the edited chapters were on interest measurement and on the

---

*The Wiley-Blackwell Handbook of Individual Differences,* First Edition.
Edited by Tomas Chamorro-Premuzic, Sophie von Stumm, and Adrian Furnham.

application of interest inventories in counseling practice. The present chapter breaks with this practical, psychometric tradition in two ways—we discuss research that is not inventory centered, and we highlight recent interest research that links interests to the broader domain of individual differences and psychology in general.

Interest literature since the 1970s has primarily used Holland's RIASEC model to organize research results. Therefore, the present chapter begins with a review of Holland's (1997) structural formulations of interests. Next, we discuss gender differences in interests. In particular, Hyde and her colleagues (Hyde, 2005; Hyde & Linn, 2006) have argued, on the basis of an impressive array of meta-analyses, that gender differences in psychology are small or non-existent. We discuss how gender differences in interests are an exception to Hyde's conclusion, supporting Lubinski's (2000) assertion that interests show the "largest sex differences on major psychological dimensions" (p. 421). We then discuss continuity and change of interests across the life span. The assumption that interests are stable dispositional attributes is central to all considerations of the construct, especially in its primary motivational purpose of directing the fit between people and their environments. Recently, researchers have begun to propose that interests can form the structure for integrated models of individual differences. We provide a rationale and a theoretical underpinning for the development of integrated models of individual differences. Finally, beginning with Ackerman and Heggestad (1997), we review recent research on building models that integrate cognitive and non-cognitive individual differences measures.

## Holland's Structural Formulations

Holland's (1959, 1997) theory of vocational personalities and work environments is premised on a match between individuals and environments. Central to Holland's (1997) theory is the assumption that most individuals and environments can be categorized into one of six types: realistic (R), investigative (I), artistic (A), social (S), enterprising (E), and conventional (C), collectively referred to as RIASEC. In Holland's model, the person and the environment are described in commensurate ways. The link between the individual's personality and the environmental context is direct: for example, the individual's personality is manifested as preferences for work activities, and work environments are described in terms of the people who work in them and the activities they perform. Thus, it becomes possible to assess the environment in the same terms in which individuals are assessed. A simple way to do this is to describe the environment in terms of the percentage of the different RIASEC types. Holland's model, therefore, allows people and environments to be mapped in the same interest space. Both persons and educational–occupational settings have been described by using RIASEC codes. Typically, people and environments are described with three-letter codes, the first letter code being most descriptive. For example, fish farmers are characterized as REI and comedians are characterized as AES. For the individual, the six types consist of clusters of personality and behavioral repertories and are defined by vocational and avocational preferences, personality traits, life goals and values, self-beliefs, problem-solving styles, and competencies.

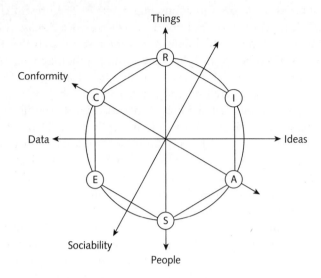

**Figure 23.1**  Prediger's (1982) data–ideas and people–things dimensions and Hogan's (1983) sociability and conformity dimensions embedded in Holland's RIASEC model. Key: R = realistic, I = investigative, A = artistic, S = social, E = enterprising, C = conventional

Holland's structural hypothesis is the cornerstone of the way in which the types are interrelated. As shown in Figure 23.1, the personality types and environments are related to each other in a circular fashion (Holland calls his model a hexagon). As in circumplex models in personality—such as Wiggins's (1982) interpersonal circle or, more recently, Schwartz's (Schwartz & Bilsky, 1987) value circumplex—the spatial proximity between types reflects the closeness of their conceptual relationships. Because of the circular nature of Holland's RIASEC model, it is expected that the relations decrease as the types move further away from each other. In other words, it is expected the relation between adjacent types, for example, the realistic type and the investigative type, to be larger than the relation between the alternate types realistic and artistic, which would be larger than the relation between the opposite types realistic and social. Similarly, since the types theoretically comprise a circular structure, one would expect that the relation between the realistic type and the conventional type (adjacent types) would be similar to the relation between the realistic and the investigative type.

Also illustrated in Figure 23.1 are the dimensional interpretations of the RIASEC circumplex proposed by Prediger (1982) and by Hogan (1983). Prediger (1982) proposed that two bipolar work-task dimensions underlie the interrelations among the six Holland types: working with things versus people and working with data versus ideas. Prediger's structural hypothesis uses two factors rather than a circumplex arrangement of types to account for why the responses to the RIASEC interests organize themselves as Holland hypothesized. In comparison, Hogan (1983) proposed that two personality-based dimensions, sociability and conformity, underlie the interrelations among the six Holland types.

## Gender Differences in Interests

The discussion of gender differences in vocational interests traditionally subsumes the study of interest measurement on the basis of Holland's RIASEC structure. Validation research of the Holland model has in general supported the circular order of RIASEC interest types for both males and females and the invariance of interest structure across gender. Anderson, Tracey, and Rounds (1997), for example, found the fit of the RIASEC data to be similar for both males and females who completed the Strong Interest Inventory. Day, Rounds, and Swaney (1998) examined the fit of Holland's model with large representative samples of students who completed the ACT Interest Inventory (UNIACT: ACT, 1995), and they found a good fit for the model with both male and female samples representing different US racial–ethnic groups. It should be noted that racial–ethnic differences in model–data fit appear when circular unidimensional scaling, a more rigorous method to evaluate circumplex models, is applied to RIASEC matrices (Armstrong, Hubert, & Rounds, 2003). Darcy and Tracey (2007), using a variety of analytic methods such as structural equation modeling (SEM), randomization tests, multidimensional scaling, and circular unidimensional scaling, also demonstrated relatively few differences in the circumplex structure of the UNIACT RIASEC scores across gender and age (from Grades 8 through 12), despite some variation across methods.

In contrast to the similarity of interest structure across gender, the existence of mean level gender differences for interest items and for RIASEC interest scales is widely acknowledged among vocational psychologists (e.g. Betz & Fitzgerald, 1987; Hackett & Lonborg, 1993). It is believed that women are more likely than men to report interest in social and artistic activities, whereas men are more likely than women to report interest in scientific, technical, and mechanical activities (Betz & Fitzgerald, 1987). However, only recently have researchers begun to systematically review the magnitude and pattern of gender differences in RIASEC interests. Su, Rounds, & Armstrong (2009) conducted a meta-analysis using technical manuals of historical and current inventories of interests and found substantial gender differences in vocational interests. Their results from 503,188 respondents showed that men tend to prefer careers involving working with things and women tend to prefer people-oriented careers, producing a large effect size ($d = .93$) on the things–people interest dimension. This mean difference of .93 indicates that only 46.9 percent of the male and female distributions of interest on the things–people dimension overlaps, or that up to 82.4 percent of men have stronger interests in things-oriented careers than an average woman. More specifically, men showed stronger realistic ($d = .84$) and investigative ($d = .26$) interests, and women showed stronger artistic ($d = .35$), social ($d = .68$), and conventional ($d = .33$) interests (see Figure 23.2 for an illustration of gender differences in interests by RIASEC types). Gender differences favoring men were also found for measures of interests in engineering ($d = 1.11$), science ($d = .36$), and mathematics ($d = .34$). In other words, 74.9 percent of female respondents showed stronger social interests than an average male, whereas only 13.3 percent of women were more interested in engineering than an average man. Such large gender differences have rarely been found on major

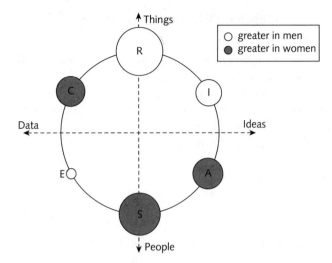

**Figure 23.2**  Effect sizes of gender differences in RIASEC interests. Adapted with permission from Su et al., 2009, p. 871. Key: R = realistic, I = investigative, A = artistic, S = social, E = enterprising, C = conventional

psychological dimensions (Lubinski, 2000). After reviewing 124 effect sizes from 46 meta-analyses of gender differences including measures of cognitive abilities, communication, social and personality variables, psychological well-being, motor behaviors, and a miscellaneous category that included moral behavior and job performance, Hyde (2005) concluded that gender differences in most individual differences domains are small to non-existent. Evidence from Su and colleagues' meta-analysis suggested that vocational interests are one of the exceptions to the gender similarity hypothesis, and that they are worth further attention from individual differences researchers.

It is crucial to view these gender differences in vocational interests in the broader context of career choices. Under-representation of women in certain occupational areas, particularly the STEM (science, technology, engineering, and mathematics) fields, has received intensive attention and has generated heated controversy regarding its causation (e.g. Ceci & Williams, 2007; Gallagher & Kaufman, 2005; Watt & Eccles, 2008). Despite the increasing number of women obtaining graduate degrees across a wide range of scientific disciplines over the past five decades, women remain a minority in fields like engineering and the physical sciences, and a disproportionately high number of women were found to switch out of math and science careers as they advanced (Preston, 2004). Research has generally found little gender differences in mathematical abilities and standardized test performance (e.g. Else-Quest, Hyde, & Linn, 2010; Hyde & Linn, 2006; Spekle, 2005). Some studies supported the effect of differential life values on men's and women's work preferences (e.g. Ferriman, Lubinski, & Benbow, 2009; Lubinski & Benbow, 2007). Eccles and colleagues (Eccles, 1994; Parsons, Adler, & Meece, 1984) proposed the expectancy-value model, which explains how the subjective task value associated with different work activities influences people's educational and occupational choices. Specifically, people-oriented careers are associated with higher subjective task value on the part of women, as these careers offer more opportunities of helping people and thus are preferred over things-oriented careers such as physical sciences and engineering. Vocational interests have been found to predict current occupation and future career aspirations very effectively (e.g. Donnay & Borgen, 1996; Hansen & Campbell, 1985), but interests have yet to receive the attention they deserve in the STEM gender debate. The gender differences in science, mathematics, and engineering interests were found to parallel the composition of men and women in corresponding educational programs and occupations (Su et al., 2009), suggesting the necessity for examining the role of vocational interests in occupational gender disparity.

The existence of large differences in interest scores between men and women unavoidably brings up the issue of the interpretation of these differences and of the consequential validity of interest measures (Messick, 1989). In particular, do these gender differences reflect sex-restrictiveness of interest inventories, and how does the development of sex-balanced interest inventories impact the validity of the measures? Traditionally, two opposing approaches have been taken to examining the validity of an interest inventory: an "opportunity approach to validation" (e.g. Prediger & Cole, 1975) and a "socialization approach to validation" (e.g. Gottfredson & Holland, 1978). The opportunity approach to validation argued that the primary purpose of using an interest inventory is occupational exploration. Its authors advocated removing gender differences from interest scores, in order to maximize career opportunities for individuals. In contrast, the socialization approach maintained that constructs measured by interest inventories are dependent on the differential socialization experiences of men and women. Its researchers argued against the removal of gender differences, in the belief that removing them would decrease the predictive validity of the measure.

Interest measures developed from these contrasting views tend to exhibit very different levels of gender differences in interest scores and have limited agreement in their career suggestions. Su et al. (2009) used interest-item development strategy as a moderator for examining the magnitude of gender differences in interest scales and found that using sex-balanced item development techniques substantially reduced gender differences. A large proportion of variances across interest inventories was explained by the item development techniques, especially for scales traditionally favoring men such as realistic interest, interest in science, and interest in engineering. For instance, the UNIACT–R (ACT, 1995) developed from the "opportunity approach of validation" showed a small to moderate gender difference in realistic interests ($d = .40$), as compared to the huge realistic interest difference ($d = 1.70$) in the SDS–R (Holland et al., 1997) developed from the "socialization approach to validation." Other studies have provided evidence for unsatisfactory convergence among interest inventories (e.g. Russell, 2007; Savickas, Taber, & Spokane, 2002). Russell (2007), for example, showed that the hit rate in the cross-classification of Holland RIASEC codes between the SDS–R (Holland et al., 1997) and the UNIACT–R (ACT, 1995) is only 50.16 percent, which means that on average half of the times an individual receives different career suggestions from the two inventories. These results indicate that minimizing gender differences in interest measures may be associated with change in the constructs being assessed. The consideration of social consequences of interest assessment needs to be addressed holistically, together with the achievement of construct and predictive validity.

More recently, under the impact of item response theory (IRT), research on gender differences in vocational interests has shifted focus from reducing the absolute level of gender differences to distinguishing gender bias from test impact (i.e. to reflect "true" gender differences in interest measures). Two studies have applied differential item functioning (DIF) techniques to examine item-level and scale-level gender bias, both using the Strong Interest Inventory (Harmon et al., 1994). In the first study, Aros, Henly, and Curtis (1998) used the Mantel–Haenszel log-odds ratios to examine differential responses to 28 occupational titles between males and females. They detected gender-related DIF in most of the items, even after controlling for measured gender differences at scale level. The authors also found the gender-related DIF to be significantly correlated with occupational gender stereotypes, which indicated that sex-typing of occupations may contaminate interest measurement and may bias the magnitude of measured gender differences of interests.

In another study, Einarsdóttir and Rounds (2009) applied SIBTEST (Stout & Roussos, 1996) to examine DIF in the full range of interest items from the Strong Interest Inventory. They detected DIF in 70 percent of all the items used to construct the RIASEC scales (mean absolute $\beta = .163$) with 33 percent of the items showing a large amount of DIF (i.e. an absolute $\beta > .200$). Moreover, they recalculated the gender difference effect sizes for each RIASEC scale only with items that did not display DIF. Interestingly, only the realistic scale and the investigative scale had reduced scale-level gender differences after being "purified" ($d$ changed from .86 to .64 and from .30 to .14, respectively); other scales all maintained the same amount of gender differences (recalculated gender differences for the artistic, social, enterprising, conventional scales were .44, .45, .11, and .29, respectively, as compared to .45, .45, .09, .24 before purification). Taken together, these results indicate that gender-related differential item functioning is prevalent and non-trivial; however, even after eliminating these biased items, a substantial amount of measured gender differences in interests at the scale level still persists.

The findings that gender differences in vocational interests are large and that they cannot be solely attributed to gender bias in measurement are important. They lead us beyond the traditional realm of interest measurement and bring up questions related to the broader domain of psychological research: Where do these differences come from? How are men's and women's interests developed? How much can interests change, and at what point of life do interests become stable? Future studies exploring these questions are necessary. In the following section, we provide a brief overview regarding the development and stability of interests, indicating that gender differences begin at an early age and are stable through the life course.

## Continuity and Change of Interests

The continuity and change of interests can be viewed from two theoretical perspectives: a situational perspective or a dispositional perspective (Silvia, 2006). Situational interests, primarily studied in educational setting, are defined as the context-specific state of emotional experience, curiosity, and momentary motivation (see Hidi, 1990; Schraw & Lehman, 2001). Therefore, situational interests are fluid and malleable and are contingent on factors such as learning tasks and classroom techniques (Knapp, 1999; Renninger, Hidi, & Knapp, 1992). Conversely, dispositional interests, most frequently examined in vocational psychology, are trait-like, reflecting a person's preferences for behaviors, situations, contexts in which activities occur, and/or the outcomes associated with the preferred activities (Rounds, 1995). Dispositional interests are relatively stable, being involved with an individual's identity and choice of environment. These two perspectives on interest stability are not, however, incompatible. Research has found large within-person variability, as well as strong central tendency for the behavioral manifestation of traits, indicating that trait contents are like a density function of states and can be non-conditional or context-specific (Fleeson, 2001). Yet it is only meaningful to examine how interests develop and stabilize over the life course when interests are viewed as dispositional attributes.

Scholars have identified several kinds of trait stability (see De Fruyt et al., 2006; Low & Rounds, 2007): rank-order, profile, mean-level, and structural stability. These forms of interest stability represent different aspects of interest development and are not necessarily related to each other conceptually or statistically. Changes in one or more of these types of stability can be present while the others remain constant. Next, we review research evidence for each of these types of stability.

Rank-order stability, or relative stability, refers to correlations between scale scores at different time points. It is typically indexed by test–retest reliability of scale scores, and it provides information about the changes in the relative ranking of individuals within a group, on a particular interest dimension. In comparison, profile stability refers to the correlations between interest configurations (or profiles) at different time points. Instead of examining the stability of an individual interest scale score, profile stability focuses on changes in the full profile of multiple interest scales. Also, it provides information about the relative ordering of interest types within an individual rather than rank-order between individuals. The examination of rank-order stability and profile stability is important because, when individuals choose educational or work environments, they tend to compare their interest in a certain area both with other people's interest in this area and with their own interests in other areas. From an interindividual perspective, people may choose a field when they perceive themselves as having a relatively higher interest in that field by comparison to others; from an inter-individual perspective, people may choose a field in which they have the strongest interest among all interest types. Rank-order and profile stability have a direct impact on person–environment fit.

Evidence for rank-order stability is abundant in interest measurement literature. Studies using test–retest correlations generally lead to the conclusion that interests are highly stable during adulthood (e.g. Campbell, 1971; Hansen, 1984; Swanson, 1999). More recent research involving children in elementary school and children transitioning into middle school (Grades 4 to 6) have found moderate levels of rank-order stability, and these indices increase as children age (Tracey, 2002; Tracey & Ward, 1998). Similar findings were obtained for profile stability, and the results were consistent across gender and ethnicity.

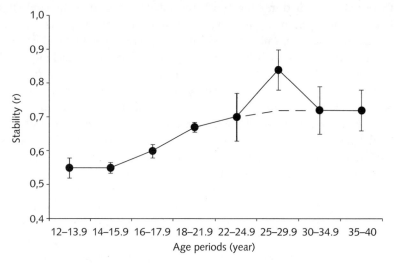

**Figure 23.3**  Estimates of mean interest stability across age categories. Adapted with permission from Low and Rounds, 2007, p. 29. Error bars indicate 95% confidence intervals for each age group. Dashed line indicates hypothesized stability

In a meta-analysis, Low, Yoon, Roberts, and Rounds (2005) summarized results from 66 longitudinal studies in order to evaluate rank-order and profile stability of interests at different life stages. The authors found that, for both males and females, interests remained reasonably stable from age 12 to age 40 ($\rho = .55–.83$). Stability estimates changed very little prior to graduation from high school (i.e. ages 12–13.9, ages 14–15.9 and ages 16–17.9; see Figure 23.3 for the development trend of interests across age periods). Interest stability increased dramatically during college years, peaked at ages 22–24.9, and subsequently plateaued for the remainder of adulthood with estimated stability above .70. Interestingly, the authors also compared meta-analytic estimates of rank-order stability between vocational interests and personality traits and showed that interests are consistently more stable than personality traits throughout the entire age period examined (see Figure 23.4). Overall, research examining rank-order stability indicates that interests are more stable than is commonly believed and that they stabilize at younger ages than was previously understood.

Mean-level stability, or absolute stability, refers to the absolute increase or decrease of a particular interest scale score over time. It can be measured at the individual level or at the group level. When a group of people shows consistent mean-level changes over a certain age period, we may infer that interests undergo normative growth which are consequences of maturational or historical processes shared by the group. Low (2009) conducted a meta-analytic review on the patterns of mean-level change in vocational interests, from early adolescence (age 12) to the end of emerging adulthood (age 24.9). Results showed that vocational interests exhibited a clear pattern of normative change, and this pattern of change was also moderated by gender. Specifically, investigative, artistic, social, and enterprising interests were found to increase across the studied period for both males and females, the greatest changes

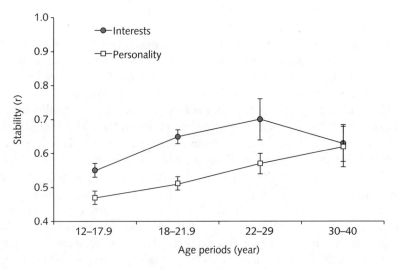

**Figure 23.4** Comparison between interest stability and personality consistency across age groups. Adapted with permission from Low and Rounds, 2007, p. 32. Error bars indicate 95% confidence intervals for each age group

of interest occurring during middle through late adolescence into emerging adulthood. Conventional interests were found to increase for females and to decrease for males during the same period. Contrary to stereotypes, realistic interests increased in females and decreased in males. Longitudinal studies examining the mean-level change of vocational interests before middle school are scarce.

Structural stability refers to the change of RIASEC structure, that is, the interrelationship between interest types, at different time points. It is indicated by the extent to which interest scales relate to one another in a consistent manner and to which the theoretical circumplex structure holds. Tracey and Ward (1998) found that the structure of interests is different in young children (elementary) and that the adherence to the circumplex structure increases during early to middle adolescence (Swaney & Flojo, 2001). Several studies based on samples of middle school and high school students have consistently shown that interest structure changed very little through Grade 8 to Grade 12 (e.g. Darcy & Tracey, 2007).

Research evidence from these four perspectives on interest stability demonstrates notable continuity. Such high stability can in part be attributed to genetic factors. Stability in interests can also be understood from the perspective of person–environment interaction. Interests, defined as preferences for certain activities and contexts, incentivize individuals to seek out environment and roles congruent with their predispositions. When they are not able to do so, individuals may try to change existing environments to better suit their preferences. In turn, experiences in the chosen environment, such as performing preferred tasks or interacting with similar people, further reinforce individuals' identity. It is through this iterative interaction process that increasing fit between person and environment is achieved. In other words, people "pick their niches" (Scarr & McCartney, 1983)—aligning their environments with their interests such that the environmental press is in the direction of maintaining the direction of their interests.

When compared to the other trait domain—personality—interests are traditionally viewed as the less stable "developmentally downstream" and are situated closer to behavior and its social context than personality (McCrae & Costa, 1999; Roberts & Wood, 2006). Research evidence reviewed in the current chapter may suggest otherwise. Low and colleagues' (2005) meta-analysis showed higher stability for interests over personality across all age periods, casting doubt on the claim that personality is the antecedent of vocational interests. Counterevidence for the claim may also come from research in developmental psychology, where studies showed that children are able to articulate their aspirations and to develop occupational gender stereotypes from as young as age 4 (Trice & Rush, 1995), while the perception of personality traits is developed much later (Rholes, Ruble, & Newman, 1990). An alternative explanation was offered by Low et al. (2005), suggesting that personality and vocational interests have different functions in person–environment interaction. In contrast to interests' motivational function in the selection of environment, personality traits appear to affect how a person copes with, or adapts to, an environment. McCrae and Costa (1999), for instance, argued that personality traits are central to problem-solving, influencing the ability to make strategic alliances and to compete with others for resources. In other words, personality traits influence individuals' behaviors toward adaptive functioning in an environment, after the environment has been selected, a role played by interests.

Setting aside the debate on the developmental sequence between personality and interests, it is worth noting that human functioning is a complex and inseparable process involving multiple individual difference traits, and these different aspects of individual identity are developed in a manner that interrelates them. In the next section we will present an integrative model of individual differences as a way to conceptualize traditionally separated domains of human dispositions.

Interests do change over time. Interests are shaped by environmental factors such as family, the school, and other aspects of the culture (Eccles, 1993). For example, Bandura, Barbaranelli, Caprara, and Pastorelli (2001) showed that, by controlling the type of activities to which their children are exposed, parents shape their children's interests. Helwig (1998) found that children's choices of occupations are influenced by parents' expectations and societal values. Presence of role models and availability of educational opportunities for female students were also shown to increase their non-traditional vocational interests (Betz & Schifano, 2000; Nauta, Epperson, & Kahn, 1998). The socialization process exerts a powerful influence on individuals' perception of self-identity and occupations, and plays an important role in interest development.

It is important to note, however, that changes in interests tend to occur very early. Previously reviewed empirical evidence showed that interests display a good deal of stability in childhood and early adolescence, and that crystallization of interests starts before middle school. Early stabilization of interests implies that any intervention on vocational interests needs to start at a much earlier age than the current focus (e.g. high school and college years), when interests are more malleable. In particular, efforts to increase girls' interests in the STEM fields, in order to bridge the gender gap, must be initiated at formative ages, as children are developing gender roles and perceptions of appropriate careers. Moreover, early stabilization of interests necessitates an appropriate method of interest measurement at an early age. Unfortunately, vocational psychologists rarely obtained samples from students younger than middle school, whereas developmental and educational psychologists working with younger samples usually focus on the study of situational interests without established interest measures. Future research bridging the gap between interest development and measurement for young children is needed to better understand the continuity and change of interests.

## Integrated Models

### Rationale

The call for the development of integrated models stems in part from the tendency for individual differences researchers to focus their research on a single domain. Research on the Holland model has focused on testing the structural model of the RIASEC types (Armstrong et al., 2003). Similarly, research on personality structure has focused on identifying the number and characteristics of broad personality traits (Goldberg, 1993), or on clarifying the nature of personality facets associated with each of the broad personality traits (Roberts, Bogg, Walton, Chernyshenko, & Stark, 2004). And research on intelligence structure has focused on testing alternative models of hierarchical structure (Carroll, 1993) and on the importance of general intelligence relative to domain-specific measures of intelligence (Carretta & Ree, 2000). In all three areas of individual differences research there is also an examination of the cross-cultural validity of measures. Most of the research that taps into more than one of these domains has focused primarily on the issue of incremental validity, that is, the extent to which individual differences measures from one domain can improve the prediction of an outcome over the established effectiveness of measures from another individual differences domain. For example, Roberts, Kuncel, Shiner, Caspi, and Goldberg (2007) found that personality traits had incremental validity over cognitive abilities and socioeconomic status for predicting mortality/longevity, divorce, and educational and occupational attainment.

With this tendency for researchers to focus on a single domain of individual differences, or on the incremental validity of using measures from multiple domains, the larger theoretical issue of how to conceptualize the interrelations among individual differences domains has received less attention. It should be noted that the tendency for researchers to focus their structural analyses on a single domain could be interpreted as assuming that the structural and theoretical conceptualizations of each domain are relatively independent. In other words, when developing a model of personality, the issue of interest or ability structure does not impact the identification of broad traits or their facets; or, when developing a hierarchical model of intelligence, Holland's circumplex structure of interests does not inform the number of domain-specific measures that are present or the magnitude of their loadings on a general factor of intelligence. When working within an individual differences domain, this practice is quite understandable—measures of intelligence are designed to measure objective performance on a task, which is separate from the question of how much the individual likes to perform a particular task, or from the question of which task will be chosen from a range of alternatives. However, when using individual differences measures to understand and predict behavior, the interrelations among the domains becomes more of an issue. As noted by Lubinski (2000), "a much richer picture of humanity and psychological diversity is brought into focus when constellations of individual-differences variables are assembled for research and practice" (p. 407).

The issue of how to represent the interrelations among individual differences domains in an integrated model is tied to larger theoretical issues, related to understanding how individuals choose environments that reflect their personalities, interests, and capabilities, and also to understanding how the learning experiences individuals obtain when interacting in an environment shape the development of individual differences. For example, the socio-analytic model of identity development (Hogan, 1983; Hogan & Roberts, 2000, 2004) hypothesizes that both personality traits and abilities will have an effect on the development of interests because individual differences in both personality and ability impact how an individual responds to opportunities and experiences in an environment, and it is these experiences (both successful and unsuccessful) in environments that help shape preferences. Conversely, interests will also have an effect on the development of personality and abilities over time, because preferences for different environments will impact the range of experiences an individual has (Ickes, Snyder, & Garcia, 1997; Scarr, 1996). In other words, there is a reciprocal feedback loop between interests, personality, and abilities, with personality and abilities contributing to interests by influencing how individuals function in environments, and interest-based self-selection of educational and work environments influencing which personality traits and abilities are developed and refined by new experiences (Roberts, Caspi, & Moffitt, 2003; Schooler, 2001).

This reciprocal feedback loop contributes to what Armstrong, Day, McVay, and Rounds (2008) refer to as "contextual convergence"—the finding that the distinct sets of constructs measured by personality, ability, and interest-based individual differences form a cohesive picture when examined from the perspective of educational and work environments. This tendency for educational and work environments to influence individual differences traits has also been referred to as "the gravitational hypothesis" (McCormick, DeNisi, & Shaw, 1979), which states that individuals will be pulled toward occupations that are matched to their level of cognitive ability. In this model, the source of gravity is the different levels of cognitive demands placed on individuals in various occupations. Individuals with relatively high levels of mental ability are pulled toward occupations with relatively high levels of cognitive demands, and are pulled away from occupations that lack sufficient levels of challenge. Conversely, individuals with less cognitive ability will be pulled away from occupations that are too challenging and toward occupations with cognitive demands that are commensurate with their level of ability. In addition to cognitive demands, the gravitational hypothesis has been implicated in other dimensions of the person–environment fit, including interests (Reeve & Heggestad, 2004). In other words, there is more than one gravitational field operating in the world of work: cognitive demands pull individuals toward occupations that are a good match for their mental abilities, personality traits pull individuals toward occupations where they can effectively express their personalities, and interests pull individuals toward occupations that reflect activity preferences.

One of the best known examinations of individual differences constellations is the meta-analysis by Ackerman and Heggestad (1997), which reported estimates of correlations between intelligence, personality, and Holland's model of interests. On the basis of their analysis, Ackerman and Heggestad identified four trait complexes. The first trait complex, social, combined interest in working with people from the social and enterprising Holland types with personality measures of extraversion and social potency, and also included measures of subjective well-being. The second trait complex, clerical/conventional, combined interest in the conventional interest types with personality measures of control, traditionalism, and conscientiousness, and with the ability measure of perceptual speed. The third trait complex, science/math, combined interest in working with things from the realistic and investigative interest types with the abilities of visual perception and math reasoning. And the fourth trait complex, intellectual/cultural, combined interest in the investigative and artistic types with the personality traits of openness to experience, typical intellectual engagement, and absorption and ability measures of ideational fluency and general cognitive ability.

Ackerman and Heggestad's (1997) results included two key contributions that have been continued in subsequent work on integrated models by Armstrong et al. (2008). The utility of Holland's theory as an organizational framework for trait complexes is established, and subsequent research has built on these findings by more explicitly testing the structural model of Holland's theory when identifying links between individual differences domains. Additionally, these results demonstrate that not all trait complexes combine the three domains of interest, personality, and abilities. Indeed, for two of the four complexes there is a missing element, as the social complex does not include any ability measures and the science/math complex does not include any personality measures. These results may reflect the limitations of current individual differences measures: namely the lack of personality measures associated with the science/math trait complex may indicate that the distinct personality traits of individuals who are interested in careers in math and science are not well represented by current measures. However, the lack of personality traits associated with the science/math complex may also reflect that multiple personality traits are compatible with this work environment, or that personality traits are not a critical factor for effective functioning in work environments that place an emphasis on math and science. Similarly, the lack of cognitive ability measures tied to the social trait complex may reflect a deficit in current ability measures: either the abilities used to work effectively with people are not captured by traditional cognitive ability measures, or cognitive abilities are not a critical factor for effective functioning in work environments that place an emphasis on interpersonal interactions.

## Using Holland as a framework

With the Atlas model of individual differences, Armstrong et al. (2008) proposed using interest-based structures, and Holland's (1997) model of interest structure in particular, as a template for developing integrated models of individual differences. In particular, they hypothesized that interests may provide an effective starting point for integrated models because, at the individual level, the process of interest development reflects the integration of personality traits and abilities with preferences for different educational and work environments. Holland's (1997) theory, which can be used to classify both individuals and work environments, provides a structure that can be used as a template for combining information from different sources. This approach builds on Ackerman and Heggestad's (1997) work by explicitly testing Holland's structural hypothesis when examining correlations between individual differences measures. In addition to statistical considerations, Holland's theory also has the advantage of being a well-established model in applied settings. In consequence, using the RIASEC model as an integrative framework provides information linking abilities and personality to career choices that may be useful when working with individuals who are making career-related decisions.

Armstrong et al. (2008) used the linear multiple regression-based technique of property vector fitting (Jones & Koehly, 1993; Kruskal & Wish, 1978) to model statistically the integration of individual differences variables into Holland's model. As illustrated in Figure 23.5, this technique allows for the placement of a variable into the RIASEC circumplex as a line, or property vector, emerging from the center point. The angle of the property vector is calculated from the regression coefficients

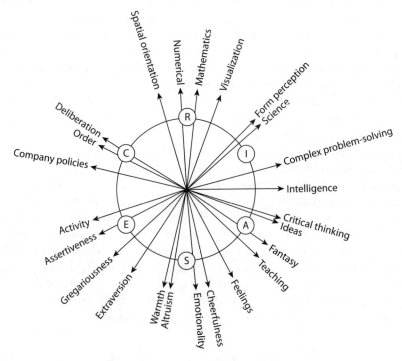

**Figure 23.5**   Illustrative results of property vector fitting analyses from Armstrong et al., 2008. Adapted with permission from Armstrong et al., 2008. Key: R = realistic, I = investigative, A = artistic, S = social, E = enterprising, C = conventional

obtained by regressing variable scores for each RIASEC type on the structural coordinates representing the interest structure. That is, when analyzing the relations between the individual differences measures and the Holland model, the property vector fitting technique examines the relative magnitude of relations across all six RIASEC types. In this approach, goodness of fit to the model reflects the extent to which the relative magnitude of the relations between a measure and all six types is consistent with the order-predictions in the Holland model. This builds on previous research, such as that of Ackerman and Heggestad (1997), which primarily focused on bivariate correlations. In other words, the integration process used in the Atlas model considers more than just the question of which ability or personality trait has the highest correlation with a particular RIASEC type. Property vector fitting results illustrate the structural relations among interests and other individual differences characteristics by indicating the orientation of characteristics in the interest structure and by comparing the relative orientations of different characteristics. Instead of focusing on the absolute magnitude of a particular bivariate relationship, this type of structural analysis systematically models the relative strength of associations between characteristics and the underlying interest structure. Subsequent research (Anthoney & Armstrong, 2010; Armstrong & Anthoney, 2009) has refined this approach by using a bootstrapping technique to develop confidence intervals for the magnitude of fit and orientation of property vectors in the RIASEC circumplex.

## Atlas-based studies

*People–things dimension* Research fitting personality and ability measures into the RIASEC model have consistently supported the people–things dimension of interest proposed by Prediger (1982) as underlying the inter-relations among the six types. This distinction between individuals who prefer involvement with other people and those who prefer involvement with things is, in fact, a recurrent theme in the interest literature dating back to Thorndike (1911), first demonstrated empirically by Thurstone (1931). Armstrong and colleagues (2008) found that a number of personality characteristics fit into the RIASEC structure in an arc encompassing the social type, which is the anchor for the people end of this dimension, and also encompassing the enterprising type. Personality measures of extraversion both from the five-factor model of personality and from the Myers–Briggs Type Indicator (MBTI; Myers & McCaulley, 1985) extravert–introvert scale were fit into the model, as were two measures of interpersonal confidence. Consistent with Ackerman and Heggestad (1997), Armstrong et al. (2008) found that results that fit ability requirements into the integrated model tended to be oriented toward the "things" end of the interest continuum, whereas the personality measures tend to emphasize the "people" end of the continuum.

At the facet level, Armstrong and Anthoney (2009) found that extraversion facets were oriented both toward the social and toward the enterprising type. When this analysis was done with NEO–PI–R (Costa & McCrae, 1992) extraversion facets, the range of the circumplex covered included both the extravert and the social type. However, when a second set of facets from the International Personality Item Pool (IPIP; Goldberg et al., 2006) was analyzed, the extraversion facets were more closely grouped around the social type. When comparisons were made between the two sets of results, Armstrong and Anthoney found that five of the six extraversion facets were embedded for both measures, with an average angle difference of 36°, suggesting a similar interpretation of the links between extraversion facets and interests across measures. These results were interpreted as supporting previous research, which linked extraversion with social and enterprising interests. However, the finding that extraversion is linked to both types raises potential problems with the dimensional interpretation of the RIASEC circumplex. In particular, Prediger's interpretation of people–things is anchored by the social and realistic types, which suggests that the social type has a stronger relation with people-oriented interests than the enterprising type. In comparison, Hogan (1983) has suggested that there is a sociability dimension that underlies the RIASEC circumplex and is oriented between the enterprising and the social type. As such, Armstrong and Anthoney's results tend to support Hogan's (1983) interpretation over that of Prediger (1982), in that the ordination of extraversion facets tended to fall between the enterprising and the social type, with no extraversion facets oriented toward the artistic type.

When comparing individual self-ratings and occupational requirements along the people–things dimension, Anthoney and Armstrong (2010) found that measures of mathematics, systems analysis, and technical skills were associated with working with things for individual self-ratings and for occupational requirements. However, for some things-oriented measures, the results were not consistent across individual self-ratings and occupational ratings. Spatial orientation and perceptual abilities were also related to the realistic area of the circumplex for women and for the occupational ratings. Visualization and selective attention abilities were linked to the realistic type by occupational ratings, but not by individual ratings. Quantitative ability and material resources management skills were significant for individual self-ratings, but not for occupational ratings. Despite this information on abilities required for environments that place an emphasis on interacting with things, there is comparatively little in the way of personality measures for things-oriented individuals.

In comparison, the range of environmental information for people-oriented work environments is smaller, but there is a number of personality measures reflecting an orientation toward people. For example, Anthoney and Armstrong (2010) found that service orientation, personnel resources management, and influencing skills are linked with the people dimension. Additionally, some verbal abilities and communication skills spanned the region between the artistic and social types, falling in the area between the people and the idea dimension-anchor in Prediger's model. Holland's theory associates verbal abilities with the A type, but also links speaking ability with E, which may result in an orientation of verbal abilities and communication skills between A and S when one is using property vector fitting. Teaching skills are associated with the S type for individuals and linked with the A type for occupations, suggesting dynamic work with people. Time management skill is people-oriented for occupations, yet did not fit the model for individual self-ratings. Overall, the differences between the individual self-ratings and the occupational ratings found by Anthoney and Armstrong suggest that there may be discrepancies between how individuals conceptualize working with people and more objective measures of workplace activities and ability requirements.

*Structured–dynamic dimension* Consistent with Ackerman and Heggestad's (1997) clerical/conventional and intellectual/cultural trait complexes, Armstrong et al. (2008) found that one of the dominant organizational dimensions that emerged when integrating individual differences measures into the RIASEC circumplex was a contrast between those individuals who prefer structured environments, where activities are regimented and tasks are clearly defined in advance, and those who prefer more dynamic environments, where specific tasks are not defined as clearly and an emphasis is placed on creative activities. For example, the five-factor model-based measure of openness to experience contrasted the artistic and the conventional type. The dynamic end of this dimension also included measures of independence, imagination, originality, creativity, and fluency of ideas.

At the facet level, Armstrong and Anthoney (2009) found that the most consistent pattern of relations between personality and interest across the two sets of facet measures emerged with the openness to experience facets, with an average angle difference of 24° between NEO–PI–R (Costa & McCrae, 1992) and IPIP (Goldberg et al., 2006) scales. The overall pattern of these results was consistent with that of previous studies, which examined these relations by using broader measures of the openness trait (e.g. Larson, Rottinghaus, & Borgen, 2002). However, Armstrong and Anthoney interpreted their findings as providing new information on links between personality and interests through the examination of the relative position of different facets of openness. For example, the feelings/emotionality facets were oriented more toward the social type, whereas the intellect/ideas facets were oriented more toward the investigative and artistic types. These results suggest that emotional openness may be tied more to social interests, and that intellectual openness may be tied to scientific and creative interests. Overall, measures of the broad personality trait of openness to experience are linked to the artistic type, but the various facets of openness span the investigative, artistic, and social types, reflecting the different ways individuals are open to experiences and to the work environments that best fit their openness.

In comparison, the structured end of this same dimension is oriented toward the conventional type. Armstrong et al. (2008) found that measures of conscientiousness, sensing, conformity, clerical ability, and need for supervision were oriented in that direction. At the personality facet level, Armstrong and Anthoney (2009) found that the NEO–PI–R (Costa & McCrae, 1992) conscientiousness facets were consistently linked with business-related interests, being oriented toward the C type and to the area between the E and C types. However, the results were less consistent with the IPIP (Goldberg et al., 2006) facet scales, where dutifulness and achievement were oriented toward the social type, and orderliness was oriented toward the enterprising type. Anthoney and Armstrong (2010) found that, when they compared individual self-ratings and occupational ratings, fewer property vectors were integrated consistently for the structured–dynamic dimension. Although there were skill vectors oriented toward individual self-ratings of the E and C types, there were no significant results for the occupational ratings.

Anthoney and Armstrong (2010) found that written communication skill is oriented in the dynamic direction for individuals and occupations, and that the generation of ideas (or, in the jargon, "idea generation") is linked with the dynamic dimension for men and occupations. Science skill is located between the I type and the R type, suggesting dynamic work with things. Additionally, there are several differences in the integration of individual and environmental ratings in the dynamic direction. Critical thinking and complex problem-solving skills are oriented in the dynamic dimension on the basis of environmental demands. Critical thinking is linked with working with things for women, and complex problem-solving is oriented in the structured dimension for men. Perceptual abilities are linked with the dynamic region for men, but they are linked with things for occupations, which suggests that, for men, perceptual abilities are viewed at a higher level of abstraction but are conceptualized more concretely in the occupational ratings. For women, perceptual abilities span the region between things and ideas.

## Conclusion

Vocational interests are more than just educational–occupational preferences. Interests are the affective and cognitive responses to critical features of environments and of the behaviors imposed or suggested by those environments. Interests are the perceived environmental affordances that constitute the means of attaining values and goals. Interests energize and direct action toward attaining and maintaining environments best suited to fulfill the individuals' needs. In that sense, interests describe the means by which and the environments in which people can function optimally.

Interests are important for the multiple decisions that are made prior to initial career choices, and they affect an individual's success and satisfaction with each of these choices. Since interests become stable early on in the life course, community support is necessary for the kinds of interests and early experiences that lead to educational choices in the STEM fields. Interests are an ideal candidate for classifying and understanding values, abilities, and personality characteristics. The interest foundation for integrative models of trait complexes may be different from the current circumplex models. For the development of new interest models, researchers need to continue to develop public-domain interest measures (Liao, Armstrong, & Rounds, 2008) rather than to rely on the liabilities of commercial interest inventories.

## References

Ackerman, P. L., & Heggestad, E. D. (1997). Intelligence, personality, and interests: Evidence for overlapping traits. *Psychological Bulletin, 121,* 219–245.

ACT [American College Testing Program] (1995). *Technical manual: Revised unisex edition of the ACT Interest Inventory (UNIACT).* Iowa City, IA: Author.

Anderson, M. Z., Tracey, T. J. G., & Rounds, J. (1997). Examining the invariance of Holland's vocational interest model across gender. *Journal of Vocational Behavior, 50,* 349–364.

Anthoney, S. F., & Armstrong, P. I. (2010). Individual and environments: Linking ability and skill ratings with interests. *Journal of Counseling Psychology, 57,* 36–51.

Armstrong, P. I., & Anthoney, S. F. (2009). Personality facets and RIASEC interests: An integrated model. *Journal of Vocational Behavior, 75,* 346–359.

Armstrong, P. I., Day, S. X, McVay, J. P., & Rounds, J. (2008). Holland's RIASEC model as an integrative framework for individual differences. *Journal of Counseling Psychology*, 55, 1–18.

Armstrong, P. I., Hubert, L., & Rounds, J. (2003). Circular unidimensional scaling: A new look at group differences in interest structure. *Journal of Counseling Psychology*, 50, 297–308.

Aros, J. R., Henly, G. A., & Curtis, N. T. (1998). Occupational sex type and sex differences in vocational preferences-measured interest relationships. *Journal of Vocational Behavior*, 53, 227–242.

Bandura, A., Barbaranelli, C., Caprara, G. V., & Pastorelli, C. (2001). Self-efficacy beliefs as shapers of children's aspirations and career trajectories. *Child Development*, 72, 187–206.

Betz, N. E., & Fitzgerald, L. F. (1987). *The career psychology of women*. Orlando, FL: Academic Press.

Betz, N. E., & Schifano, R. S. (2000). Evaluation of an intervention to increase realistic self-efficacy and interests in college women. *Journal of Vocational Behavior*, 56, 35–52.

Campbell, D. P. (1971). *Handbook for the strong vocational interest blank*. Stanford, CA: Stanford University Press.

Carretta, T., & Ree, M. J. (2000). General and specific cognitive and psychomotor abilities in personnel selection: The prediction of training and job performance. *International Journal of Selection and Assessment*, 8, 227–236.

Carroll, J. B. (1993). Human cognitive abilities. New York: Cambridge University Press.

Ceci, S. J., & Williams, W. M. (2007). *Why aren't more women in science? Top researchers debate the evidence*. Washington, DC: American Psychological Association.

Costa, P. T., & McCrae, R. R. (1992). *Revised NEO–Personality Inventory (NEO–PI–R) and NEO Five Factor Inventory (NEO–FFI): Professional manual*. Odessa, FL: Psychological Assessment Resources.

Dawis, R. V. (1991). Vocational interests, values, and preferences. In M. D. Dunnette & L. M. Hough (Eds.), *Handbook of industrial and organizational psychology* (Vol. 2, pp. 833–871). Palo Alto, CA: Consulting Psychologists.

Day, S. X., Rounds, J., & Swaney, K. (1998). The structure of vocational interests for diverse racial–ethnic groups. *Psychological Science*, 9, 40–44.

Darcy, M. U. A., & Tracey, T. J. G. (2007). Circumplex structure of Holland's RIASEC interests across gender and time. *Journal of Counseling Psychology*, 54, 17–31.

Deci, E. L., & Ryan, R. M. (1990). A motivational approach to self: Integration in personality. In R. Dienstbeir (Ed.), *Nebraska symposium on motivation: Vol. 38. Perspectives on motivation* (pp. 237–288). Lincoln, NE: University of Nebraska Press.

De Fruyt, F., Bartels, M.. Van Leeuwen, K. G., De Clercq, B., Decuyper, M., & Mervielde, I. (2006). Five types of personality continuity in childhood and adolescence. *Journal of Personality and Social Psychology*, 91, 538–552.

Donnay, D. A. C., & Borgen, F. H. (1996). Validity, structure, and content of the 1994 Strong Interest Inventory. *Journal of Counseling Psychology*, 43, 275–291.

Eccles, J. S. (1993). School and family effects on the ontogeny of children's interests, self-perceptions, and activity choice. In J. E. Jacobs & R. Dienstbier (Eds.), *Developmental perspectives on motivation* (Vol. 40, pp. 145–208). Lincoln, NE: University of Nebraska Press.

Eccles, J. S. (1994). Understanding women's educational and occupational choices: Applying the Eccles et al. model of achievement-related choices. *Psychology of Women Quarterly*, 18, 585–609.

Einarsdóttir, S., & Rounds, J. (2009). Gender bias and construct validity in vocational interest measurement: Differential item functioning in the Strong Interest Inventory. *Journal of Vocational Behavior, 74,* 295–307.

Else-Quest, N. M., Hyde, J. S., & Linn, M. C. (2010). Cross-national patterns of gender differences in mathematics: A meta-analysis. *Psychological Bulletin, 136,* 103–127.

Ferriman, K., Lubinski, D., & Benbow, C. P. (2009). Work preferences, life values, and personal views of top math/science graduate students and the profoundly gifted: Developmental changes and gender differences during emerging adulthood and parenthood. *Journal of Personality and Social Psychology, 97,* 517–532.

Fleeson, W. (2001). Toward a structure- and process-integrated view of personality: Traits as density distributions of states. *Journal of Personality and Social Psychology, 80,* 1011–1027.

Gallagher, A. M., & Kaufman, J. C. (2005). *Gender differences in mathematics: An integrative psychological approach.* New York: Cambridge University Press.

Goldberg, L. R. (1993). The structure of phenotypic personality traits. *American Psychologist, 48,* 26–34.

Goldberg, L. R., Johnson, J. A., Eber, H. W., Hogan, R., Ashton, M. C., Cloninger, C. R., & Gough, H. C. (2006). The International Personality Item Pool and the future of public-domain personality measures. *Journal of Research in Personality, 40,* 84–96.

Gottfredson, G. D., & Holland, J. L. (1978). Toward beneficial resolution of the interest inventory controversy. In C. K. Tittle & D. G. Zytowski (Eds.), *Sex-fair interest measurement: Research and implications* (pp. 43–51). Washington, DC: U.S. Government Printing Office.

Hackett, G., & Lonborg, S. D. (1993). Career assessment for women: Trends and issues. *Journal of Career Assessment, 1,* 197–216.

Hansen, J. C. (1984). The measurement of vocational interests: Issues and future directions. In S. D. Brown & R. L. Lent (Eds.), *Handbook of counseling psychology* (pp. 99–136). New York: Wiley.

Hansen, J. C., & Campbell, D. P. (1985) *Manual for the SVIB–SCII.* Palo Alto, CA: Consulting Psychologists Press.

Harmon, L. W., Hansen, J. C., Borgen, F. H., & Hammer, A. L. (1994). *Strong interest inventory: Applications and technical guide.* Stanford, CA: Stanford University Press.

Helwig, A. A. (1998). Developmental and sex differences in workers' functions of occupational aspirations of a longitudinal sample of elementary school children. *Psychological Reports, 82,* 915–921.

Hidi, S. (1990). Interest and its contribution as a mental resource for learning. *Review of Educational Research, 60,* 549–571.

Hogan, R. T. (1983). A socioanalytic theory of personality. In M. M. Page (Ed.), *Nebraska symposium on motivation: Vol. 30. Personality: Current theory and research* (pp. 55–89). Lincoln: University of Nebraska Press.

Hogan, R. T., & Roberts, B. W. (2000). A socioanalytic perspective on person/environment interaction. In W. B. Walsh, K. H. Craik, & R. H. Price (Eds.), *New directions in person–environment psychology* (pp. 1–24). Mahwah, NJ: Lawrence Erlbaum Associates.

Hogan, R. T., & Roberts, B. W. (2004). A socioanalytic model of maturity. *Journal of Career Assessment, 12,* 207–217.

Holland, J. L. (1959). A theory of vocational choice. *Journal of Counseling Psychology, 6,* 35–45.

Holland, J. L. (1985). *Vocational Preference Inventory (VPI) manual: 1985 edition.* Odessa, FL: Psychological Assessment Resources.

Holland, J. L. (1997). *Making vocational choices: A theory of vocational personalities and work environments* (3rd ed.). Odessa, FL: Psychological Assessment Resources.

Holland, J., Fritzsche, B., & Powell, A. (1997). *Self-Directed Search: Technical manual* (rev. ed.). Odessa, FL: Psychological Assessment Resources.

Hyde, J. S. (2005). The gender similarities hypothesis. *American Psychologist, 60*, 581–592.

Hyde, J. S., & Linn, M. C. (2006). Gender similarities in mathematics and science. *Science, 314*, 599–600.

Ickes, W., Snyder, M., & Garcia, S. (1997). Personality influences on the choice of situations. In R. Hogan, J. Johnson, & S. Briggs (Eds.), *Handbook of personality psychology* (pp. 165–195). New York: Academic Press.

Jones, L. E., & Koehly, L. M. (1993). Multidimensional scaling. In G. Kern & C. Lewis (Eds.), *A handbook for data analysis in the behavioral sciences: Methodological issues* (pp. 95–163). Hillsdale, NJ: Lawrence Erlbaum Associates.

Knapp, A. (1999). Interest, motivation and learning: An educational–psychological perspective. *European Journal of Psychology of Education, 14*, 23–40.

Kruskal, J. B., & Wish, M. (1978). *Multidimensional scaling*. Newbury Park, CA: Sage.

Kuder, F. & Zytowski, D. G. (1988). *Kuder General Interest Survey (Form E): Preliminary manual*. Adel, IA: National Career Assessment Services, Inc.

Kuder, F. & Zytowski, D.G. (1991). *Kuder Occupational Interest Survey (Form DD): General manual* (3rd ed.). Adel, IA: National Career Assessment Services, Inc.

Kuder, G. F. (1977). *Activity interests and occupational choice*. Chicago: Science Research Associates.

Larson, L. M., Rottinghaus, P. J., & Borgen, F. H. (2002). Meta-analyses of big six interests and Big Five personality factors. *Journal of Vocational Behavior, 61*, 217–239.

Liao, H.-Y., Armstrong, P. I., & Rounds, J. (2008). Development and initial validation of public domain basic interest markers [Monograph]. *Journal of Vocational Behavior, 73*, 159–183.

Low, K. S. D. (2009). *Patterns of mean-level changes in vocational interests: A quantitative review of longitudinal studies*. Unpublished doctoral dissertation, University of Illinois at Urbana-Champaign.

Low, K. S. D., & Rounds, J. (2007). Interest change and continuity from early adolescence to middle adulthood. *International Journal of Educational and Vocational Guidance, 7*, 23–36.

Low, K. S. D., Yoon, M., Roberts, B. W., & Rounds, J. (2005). The stability of vocational interests from early adolescence to middle adulthood: A quantitative review of longitudinal studies. *Psychological Bulletin, 131*, 713–737.

Lubinski, D. (2000). Scientific and social significance of assessing individual differences: "Sinking shaft at a few critical points." *Annual Review of Psychology, 51*, 405–444.

Lubinski, D. S., & Benbow, C. P. (2007). Sex differences in personal attributes for the development of scientific expertise. In S. J. Ceci & W. M. Williams (Eds.), *Why aren't more women in science? Top researchers debate the evidence* (pp. 79–100). Washington, DC: American Psychological Association.

McCormick, E. J., DeNisi, A. S., & Shaw, J. B. (1979) Use of the Position Analysis Questionnaire for establishing the job component validity of tests. *Journal of Applied Psychology, 64*, 51–56.

McCrae, R. R., & Costa, P. T., Jr. (1999). A five-factor theory of personality. In L. A. Pervin & O. P. John (Eds.), *Handbook of personality psychology* (pp. 139–153). New York: Guilford Press.

Messick, S. (1989). Meaning and values in test validation: The science and ethics of assessment. *Educational Researcher, 18*, 5–11.

Myers, I. B., & McCaulley, M. H. (1985). *Manual: A guide to the development and use of the Myers–Briggs Type Indicator.* Palo Alto, CA: Consulting Psychologists Press.

Nauta, M. M., Epperson, D. L., & Kahn, J. H. (1998). A multiple-groups analysis of predictors of higher level career aspirations among women in science and engineering. *Journal of Counseling Psychology, 45,* 483–496.

Parsons, J. E., Adler, T., & Meece, J. L. (1984). Sex differences in achievement: A test of alternative theories. *Journal of Personality and Social Psychology, 46,* 26–43.

Prediger, D. J. (1982). Dimensions underlying Holland's hexagon: Missing link between interests and occupations? *Journal of Vocational Behavior, 21,* 259–287.

Prediger, D. J., & Cole, N. S. (1975). Sex-role socialization and employment realities: Implications for vocational interest measures. *Journal of Vocational Behavior, 7,* 239–251.

Preston, A. E. (2004). *Leaving science: Occupational exit from scientific careers.* New York: Russell Sage Foundation.

Reeve, C. L., & Heggestad, E. D. (2004). Differential relations between general cognitive ability and interest–vocation fit. *Journal of Occupational and Organizational Psychology, 77,* 385–402.

Renninger, K. A., Hidi, S., & Knapp, A. (1992). *The role of interest in learning and development.* Hillsdale, NJ: Lawrence Erlbaum Associates.

Rholes, W. S., Ruble, D. N., & Newman, L. S. (1990). Children's understanding of self and other: Developmental and motivational aspects of perceiving persons in terms of invariant dispositions. In R. M. Sorrentino & E. T. Higgins (Eds.), *Handbook of motivation and cognition: Foundations of social behavior* (Vol. 2, pp. 369–407). Hillsdale, NJ: Lawrence Erlbaum Associates.

Roberts, B. W., & Wood, D. (2006). Personality development in the context of the neo-socioanalytic model of personality. In D. Mroczek & T. Little (Eds.), *Handbook of personality development* (pp. 11–39). Mahwah, NJ: Lawrance Erlbaum Associates.

Roberts, B. W., Caspi, A., & Moffitt, T. E. (2003). Work experiences and personality development in adulthood. *Journal of Personality and Social Psychology, 84,* 582–593.

Roberts, B. W., Bogg, T., Walton, K., Chernyshenko, O., & Stark, S. (2004). A lexical approach to identifying the lower-order structure of conscientiousness. *Journal of Research in Personality, 38,* 164–178.

Roberts, B. W., Kuncel, N. R., Shiner, R., Caspi, A., & Goldberg, L. R. (2007). The power of personality: The comparative validity of personality traits, socioeconomic status, and cognitive ability for predicting important life outcomes. *Perspectives in Psychological Science, 2,* 313–345.

Rounds, J. (1995). Vocational interests: Evaluation of structural hypotheses. In D. Lubinski & R. V. Dawis (Eds.), *Assessing individual differences in human behavior: New concepts, methods, and findings* (pp. 177–232). Palo Alto, CA: Consulting Psychologists Press.

Russell, M. (2007). *Assessing vocational interests: Convergence and divergence of inventories and informants.* Unpublished doctoral dissertation, University of Illinois at Urbana-Champaign.

Savickas, M. L., & Spokane, A. R. (Eds.) (1999). *Vocational interests: Meaning, measurement, and counseling use.* Palo Alto, CA: Davies-Black.

Savickas, M. L., Taber, B. J., & Spokane, A. R. (2002). Convergent and discriminant validity of five interest inventories [Monograph]. *Journal of Vocational Behavior, 61,* 139–184.

Scarr, S. (1996). How people make their own environments: Implications for parents and policy makers. *Psychology, Public Policy, and Law, 2,* 204–228.

Scarr, S., & McCartney, K. (1983). How people make their own environments: A theory of genotype–environment effects. *Child Development, 54,* 424–435.

Schooler, C. (2001). The intellectual effects of the demands of the work environment. In R. J. Sternberg & E. L. Grigorenko (Eds.), *Environmental effects on cognitive abilities* (pp. 363–380). Mahwah, NJ: Lawrence Erlbaum Associates.

Schraw, G., & Lehman, S. (2001). Situational interest: A review of the literature and directions for future research. *Educational Psychology Review, 13*, 23–52.

Schwartz, S. H., & Bilsky, W. (1987). Toward a universal psychological structure of human values. *Journal of Personality and Social Psychology, 53*, 550–562.

Silvia, P. J. (2006). *Exploring the psychology of interest.* New York: Oxford University Press.

Spekle, E. S. (2005). Sex differences in intrinsic aptitude for mathematics and science? A critical review. *American Psychologist, 60*, 950–958.

Strong, E. K., Jr. (1943). *Vocational interests of men and women.* Stanford, CA: Stanford University Press.

Stout, W., & Roussos, L. (1996). *SIBTEST manual.* University of Illinois at Urbana-Champaign: Authors.

Su, R., Rounds, J., & Armstrong, P. I. (2009). Men and things, women and people: A meta-analysis of gender and interests. *Psychological Bulletin, 135*, 859–884.

Swaney, K., & Flojo, J. (2001, June). *Age differences in vocational interest structure and clarity.* Paper presented at the annual meeting of the American Psychological Society, Toronto.

Swanson, J. L. (1999). Stability and change in vocational interests. In M. L. Savickas & R. L. Spokane (Eds.), *Vocational interests: Meaning, measurement, and counseling use* (pp. 135–158). Palo Alto, CA: Davies-Black.

Thorndike, E. L. (1911). *Individuality.* Boston, MA: Houghton Mifflin.

Thurstone, L. L. (1931). A multiple factor study of vocational interests. *Personnel Journal, 10*, 198–205.

Tracey, T. J. G. (2002). Development of interests and competency beliefs: A 1-year longitudinal study of fifth- to eighth-grade students using the ICA–R and structural equation modeling. *Journal of Counseling Psychology, 49*, 148–163.

Tracey, T. J. G., & Ward, C. C. (1998). The structure of children's interests and competence perceptions. *Journal of Counseling Psychology, 45*, 290–303.

Trice, A. D., & Rush, K. (1995). Sex-stereotyping in four-year-olds' occupational aspirations. *Perceptual & Motor Skills, 81*, 701–702.

Watt, H. M. G., & Eccles, J. S. (2008). *Gender and occupational outcomes: Longitudinal assessments of individual, social, and cultural influences.* Washington, DC: American Psychological Association.

# Part VI
# Competence beyond IQ

# Section 1   Special Abilities

# 24

# Exceptional Talent and Genius

## Dean Keith Simonton

## Introduction

Although Galton's 1869 *Hereditary genius* is often taken as the first scientific study of genius, his book was based directly on an earlier article, written in 1865 by the same author and entitled "Hereditary talent and character." This piece can be considered the first scientific study of talent. Hence, in Galton's mind, genius and talent were intimately related concepts. Both imply an individual ability that is truly *exceptional*, and perhaps, to some degree, *inherited*. Nevertheless, genius and talent are also seen as highly distinct. Potential contrasts are indicated by some common quotations, which can be gleaned by searching the Internet (e.g. by googling "genius talent quote"). My three personal favorites are: (1) "Genius does what it must, and Talent does what it can" (Owen Meredith); (2) "Mediocrity knows nothing higher than itself, but talent instantly recognizes genius" (Sir Arthur Conan Doyle); and (3) "Talent hits a target no one else can hit; Genius hits a target no one else can see" (Arthur Schopenhauer). It should be evident that genius enjoys the higher status of the two concepts. Genius is the more exceptional of the two.

Yet Galton's pioneering research is now very old, and the quotations are all speculations of writers and philosophers rather than conclusions of behavioral scientists. A great deal of more recent scientific research has been devoted to genius and talent (e.g. Albert, 1992; Eysenck, 1995; Simonton, 1997). It is the purpose of this chapter to provide an overview. I begin by defining the two terms. From there we can turn to the two key methods used to study these phenomena. Finally, I examine the three central issues that permeate the empirical and theoretical research: generic versus domain-specific profiles, nature versus nurture, and individual versus situation.

*The Wiley-Blackwell Handbook of Individual Differences*, First Edition.
Edited by Tomas Chamorro-Premuzic, Sophie von Stumm, and Adrian Furnham.
© 2011 Blackwell Publishing Ltd. Published 2011 by Blackwell Publishing Ltd.

## Genius versus Talent

Probably the best place to begin is a dictionary of the English language. Because I am a denizen of the United States, I will use the *American heritage electronic dictionary* (1992). Starting with genius, the most relevant definitions are the first two, namely: "1.a. Extraordinary intellectual and creative power. b. A person of extraordinary intellect and talent […] c. A person who has an exceptionally high intelligence quotient, typically above 140" and "2.a. A strong natural talent, aptitude, or inclination. b. One who has such a talent or inclination." In the case of talent, the first two dictionary definitions are again the most relevant: "1. A marked innate ability, as for artistic accomplishment" and "2.a. Natural endowment or ability of a superior quality. b. A person or group of people having such ability." It should be noted that, whereas talent sometimes crops up in the definition of genius, genius never appears in the definition of talent. This difference suggests that, while genius is often associated with talent, talent can potentially occur independently of genius, and perhaps most often does so.

To get a better idea of the distinction, I now need to examine the two concepts in more detail.

### Genius

The word "genius" actually goes back to antiquity, as it derives from Latin. In Roman mythology, each person was born with a guardian spirit called *genius*. Only later, and especially during the Italian Renaissance, did the word inherited from Latin come to designate something truly exceptional about the individual, something that set that person apart from the average person (Murray, 1989). This more exclusive usage intensified in the Romantic period in nineteenth-century Europe, and, finally, in the twentieth century, particularly in the United States, the term came to compass a number of distinctive meanings. These meanings can be grouped into two categories: superlative intelligence and extraordinary achievement.

*Superlative intelligence* As shown earlier, one recognized definition of genius relates to a person's intelligence quotient, or IQ score, a score of 140 or above providing the minimum threshold for the ascription. What the dictionary does not explain is where this magic cutoff originated. The source dates back to Terman's (1925–1959) five-volume *Genetic studies of genius*. Using his Stanford–Binet Intelligence Scale (Terman, 1916), Terman launched an ambitious longitudinal study, in which over 1,000 intellectually gifted children would be followed well into adulthood. Because a score of 140 represented the upper 1 percent of the intelligence distribution, that was taken as the criterion for inclusion; and, because these participants were explicitly identified as geniuses, this threshold eventually showed up in the dictionary. Yet it must be emphasized that this definition is utterly arbitrary. Among "genius societies," membership in Mensa requires an IQ that is only in the upper 2 percent, whereas the Mega Society requires an IQ that is attained by one in a million. Even Terman (1925) admitted into his sample some participants whose IQs were around 135, which is only a little above the Mensa standard.

The *Guinness book of world records* used to have a category for the highest IQ, an honor that was bestowed on Marilyn Vos Savant, who was purported to have an IQ of 228 (McFarlan, 1989). Whatever validity can be attributed to this certainly elevated score, it illustrates a critical problem with this particular definition: Although Vos Savant is definitely very bright, it is not likely that she would be identified as a genius. In fact, when college students are asked to identify people whom they consider highly intelligent, they do not pick her, but rather individuals like Albert Einstein, Isaac Newton, Thomas Edison, Wolfgang Amadeus Mozart, William Shakespeare, or Leonardo da Vinci (Paulhus, Wehr, Harms, & Strasser, 2002). What these six persons have in common is not a high IQ—indeed, none of them ever took an IQ test—but rather the fact that all can be credited with extraordinary achievements.

*Extraordinary achievement*   This second definition is actually older than the previous one. It dates back to Galton (1869), who, needless to say, could not define genius according to superlative performance on intelligence tests. That is not to say that he did not entertain an idea comparable to this conception. Galton believed that individuals differ greatly in "natural ability" and that these individual differences are normally distributed in the general population. Those whose ability put them at the upper tail of the distribution could then be styled geniuses. But, lacking a direct measure of natural ability, Galton relied on an indirect measure, namely eminence or reputation. He firmly believed that those at the tail end of the distribution would make a name for themselves in some major domain of human achievement. Therefore, to assess individual differences in achieved eminence would necessarily capture individual differences in the underlying natural ability. Yet what extraordinary achievements would count as indicators of genius? Galton considers several eligible domains, which can be grouped into three distinct categories: exceptional creativity, phenomenal leadership, and prodigious accomplishments (Simonton, 2009a).

EXCEPTIONAL CREATIVITY   Most researchers in the area of creativity would define a creative person as someone who can generate an idea that is both original and useful (Simonton & Damian, in press). Original ideas must be distinguished from mundane ideas, just as useful ideas must be separated from impractical, even insane ideas. Naturally, both originality and utility are quantitative variables that vary from zero to some unknown upper limit. At the upper end of the distribution of both variables, we can therefore begin to speak of truly exceptional creativity. Indeed, in the eighteenth century Immanuel Kant (1952) imposed another level of rigor by saying that creative genius must produce ideas that are not just original, but also *exemplary*—ideas worthy of admiration and even imitation by other creators. No doubt Einstein, Newton, Edison, Mozart, Shakespeare, and da Vinci, all mentioned earlier, would fall into this category. So would Charles Darwin, René Descartes, Miguel de Cervantes, Michelangelo Buonarroti, and Ludwig van Beethoven.

PHENOMENAL LEADERSHIP   Many of the extraordinary achievers studied in Galton's (1869) monumental work were exceptional creators. The work has chapters devoted to scientists, writers and poets, composers, and painters. Even so, he also devotes some chapters to a different guise of extraordinary achievement, namely leadership. In this group I include politicians and commanders as well as, perhaps, judges and divines. Thus it is possible to talk of political genius and military genius, and maybe even of judicial and religious genius. Nonetheless, phenomenal leadership has a somewhat more ambiguous relation with genius in comparison to exceptional creativity. In the first place, for creators it is often possible to identify the specific contributions that are responsible for their lasting reputation. These contributions most often take the form of particular masterpieces, such as Newton's *Principia mathematica philosophiae naturalis*, Michelangelo's *David*, Cervantes' *Don Quixote*, or Beethoven's Fifth Symphony. In contrast, it is often less easy to isolate the achievements on which a leader stakes his or her fame. That difficulty stems from the fact that a leader's impact is most often predicated on a lifetime of influence. Mahatma Gandhi, Martin Luther King, Jr., Mother Teresa, Nelson Mandela, and Aung San Suu Kyi provide examples. Furthermore, the ultimate eminence of a leader may not necessarily rest on achievements that are considered largely positive. Instead, some instances of phenomenal leadership may be viewed as "evil genius." Cases include Adolph Hitler, Joseph Stalin, and Benito Mussolini. Even less disreputable leaders may become most famous for the most infamous episodes of their careers. Napoleon's best-known battle is probably the one he fought at Waterloo—which he lost to the Duke of Wellington! That would be like Newton being most strongly associated with his misguided research on alchemy, or Beethoven being most conspicuously linked with his musical monstrosity *Wellington's Victory* (at Vitoria, not Waterloo).

PRODIGIOUS ACCOMPLISHMENTS   Beside exceptional creativity and phenomenal leadership, Galton (1869) included examples of extraordinary achievement that represent an entirely different category—sports. More specifically, he inserted chapters on both oarsmen and wrestlers. On first blush, this insertion might seem strange. Athletes would normally be considered talents rather than geniuses. Even so, this inclusion does fall within the dictionary meaning of the word. In this sense, all athletic champions might be considered geniuses in their sport. This would certainly include Olympic gold medalists, for example. Moreover, if this usage is allowed, we can add other types of prodigious performance, such as instrumental virtuosos. Thus Jimi Hendrix was a guitar genius, and Jasha Heifitz a violin genius. We also might include in this group chess geniuses, such as José Raúl Capablanca and Bobby Fisher, as well as great actors, such as Sir Laurence Olivier and Katharine Hepburn.

Although it is nice to be so generous with a qualifier like genius, such conceptual inclusiveness has a serious price. Representative geniuses then form a very heterogeneous group of people. Persons as diverse as Marie Curie, Sofia Kovalevskaya, Sylvia Plath, Indira Gandhi, Golda Meir, Wilma Rudolph, Jacqueline du Pré, Judit Polgár, and Meryl Streep can all be counted as exemplars of female genius. Yet, even after confining these cases to a single gender, can we really expect them to be very similar? This question is especially problematic when the psychologist focuses on individual differences variables. The cognitive abilities and dispositional traits may vary substantially for the three types of genius. As a consequence, in this chapter I will focus on exceptional creativity. Even when I treat phenomenal leadership or prodigious performance, it will be in the context of creative genius. It will be apparent soon enough that even creative geniuses form a very heterogeneous group from the standpoint of differential psychology.

## Talent

As just seen, one potential form of genius—the prodigious performer—might be viewed as talent instead. Olympic champions, virtuoso pianists, chess grandmasters, Oscar-winning actors, and even world-renowned comics, mimes, and jugglers might all be put into this category. That said, it is also possible to give talent a more inclusive definition, so as to make it encompass both exceptional creativity and phenomenal leadership. This is a conceptual shift, if we conceive of genius in terms of extraordinary achievement, but of talent in terms of remarkable innate potential for achievement. This usage is consistent with the dictionary definition. Indeed, it falls in line with the earlier observation that, while talent can be included in a definition of genius, genius need not be incorporated in a definition of talent. Talent alone is mere potential, whereas in genius that potential has been actualized. This definition also falls in line with the implicit assumption that genius is much less common than talent. The conversion of one into the other is a case of "many are called but few are chosen." On this view, finally, talent becomes more similar to the closely related concept of giftedness (Heller, Mönks, Sternberg, & Subotnik, 2000; see also Jensen, 1996).

I will have more to say about this potential, but right now it is important to recognize that the definition seems to exclude the first definition of genius—that concerning superlative intelligence. However, this exclusion might be remedied if we distinguish various kinds of talent. Along with creative talent, leader talent, and performance talent, we can conceive of intellectual talent (Benbow & Lubinski, 1996). The intellectually talented are those children or adolescents who very early on display the potential for unusually high adult general intelligence. Obvious examples are the children in Terman's (1925–1959) longitudinal study. The main objection to this usage is that it somewhat trivializes the concept of talent. Even in highly select samples, general intelligence is highly stable over the life span (Simonton, 1976; Terman & Oden, 1947), a stability no doubt partly linked to this variable's high heritability (e.g. Bouchard & McGue, 1981). This longitudinal stability is less interesting than trying to identify the individual differences variables that constitute talent in creativity, leadership, or performance. It is one thing to predict trait $X_t$ using a prior value of that trait, say, $X_{t-1}$, and quite another to use $X_{t-1}$ to predict $Y_t$, where the latter constitutes a measure of creative output, leader influence, or competitive performance.

## Psychometric versus Historiometric Methods

Although experimental methods dominate psychological research on a great many substantive topics, they play a minimal role in empirical inquiries into exceptional talent and genius. An infrequent exception is the occasional study of prodigal performance (e.g. Jensen, 1990). Far more useful are two kinds of method that have been long associated with investigations into individual differences, namely psychometric and historiometric methods.

## Psychometric methods

As noted earlier, although Galton (1869) identified genius with exceptional "natural ability," he did not measure that construct directly. He tried to remedy this deficiency some years later with his anthropometric instruments (Galton, 1883). Although these particular measures did not exhibit the expected predictive validity (Wissler, 1901), toward the end of the nineteenth century Cattell (1890) could introduce the concept of "mental tests." Early in the twentieth century, the outcome was the development of measures that could be used to study exceptional genius and talent— applications that expanded after the Second World War. These psychometric investigations fall into two broad categories, namely cross-sectional and longitudinal inquiries.

*Cross-sectional studies*   Occasionally exceptional creators can be persuaded to participate in empirical research concerning their origins and characteristics. Indeed, the very first study of this type was conducted by Galton in 1874, when he convinced over 100 Fellows of the Royal Society of London (to which he belonged) to fill out a questionnaire concerning their family background, education, and attitudes. Because the respondents included such notables as Charles Darwin, T. H. Huxley, Charles Lyell, James Clerk Maxwell, and Herbert Spencer, Galton was tapping into a truly elite sample (see Hilts, 1975, for the complete list). However, it was not until after the Second World War that this method began to take advantage of standardized psychometric instruments. One of the earliest examples was Anne Roe's (1953) study of 64 eminent scientists (one of whom was her own husband). Including luminaries in the physical, biological, and social sciences, she was able to administer intelligence tests as well as projective measures (see also Cattell & Butcher, 1968; Feist, 1993, 1994). On a much grander scale are the numerous studies carried out at the Institute for Personality Assessment and Research (IPAR) at the University of California, Berkeley (Barron, 1969; Helson & Crutchfield, 1970; MacKinnon, 1978). These investigations included famous creative writers, architects, and mathematicians, who were assessed on such instruments as the Minnesota Multiphasic Personality Inventory, as well as on several new measures devised by IPAR researchers (see Gough, 1979).

Cross-sectional research may not always include a comparison group of undistinguished colleagues. In that case, inferences regarding individual differences must often be based on the norms established when the measures where standardized. However, sometimes the investigator is interested in differences among creators in different domains, in which case comparison groups or norms are not always necessary (Chambers, 1964).

*Longitudinal studies*   An alternative approach is to obtain a sample of exceptional youths, subject them to a battery of tests, and then follow them sufficiently into adulthood to determine who made the transition from talent to exceptional achievement. I have already mentioned Terman's (1925–1959) classic longitudinal study of intellectually gifted children. Although none in the sample grew up to become a world-renowned genius, several notables did emerge, including the eminent psychologists Lee Cronbach and Robert R. Sears (who joined the research of which he was a participant; see Holahan & Sears, 1995). Naturally, longitudinal studies are seldom this ambitious, and often the research participants become known for less stellar achievements (see Subotnik & Arnold, 1994). Putting aside the labor and expense involved, the samples have to be very large in order to overcome the low base rates of extraordinary achievers. In light of such difficulties, we must look forward to the current longitudinal Study of Mathematically Precocious Youth (SMPY), initiated by Julian Stanley (1996) at Johns Hopkins University in the 1970s and now continued by Camille Benbow, David Lubinski, and their colleagues at Vanderbilt University (Lubinski & Benbow, 1994). Apart from the wide variety of psychometric measures being applied, what renders this inquiry especially impressive is that it combines a relatively large sample (in multiple cohorts) with high selectivity (the top 1 in 10,000), thereby increasing the odds of obtaining exceptionally creative mathematicians (Lubinski, Webb, Morelock, & Benbow, 2001). A case in point is Terence Tao, who in his 30s has already won the Fields Medal (the "Nobel Prize of Mathematics") as well as received a MacArthur Fellowship (the "genius award") and earned election as Fellow of the Royal Society and foreign associate of the United States National Academy of Sciences (Muratori et al., 2006). Judging from early indications, instances like this should multiply as the more recent cohorts reach adulthood (Wai, Lubinski, & Benbow, 2005).

## Historiometric methods

Historiometry applies objective and quantitative analyses to relatively large samples of historic figures, such as eminent creators and leaders (Simonton, 1990). It is to be carefully distinguished from other approaches to the study of exceptional talent and genius, including psychobiographical and comparative methods (Simonton, 1999b). Historiometry is also the oldest technique: the first historiometric study was published by the famous statistician Adolphe Quételet in 1835, three decades before Galton's first historiometric inquiry. Nonetheless, these early investigations concentrated on readily available biographical information (e.g. the age at which certain works were created, or the identity of family members who also attained eminence). It was not until the early twentieth century that researchers successfully assessed historic geniuses on individual differences variables comparable to those extracted by using psychometric methods (Woods, 1906). These historiometric assessments derive from four data sources: personality sketches, developmental histories, content analyses, and expert surveys (cf. Simonton, 2009b).

*Personality sketches* Biographical materials will often list adjectives and other descriptors of some of the core characteristics of the featured individual. These can be translated into individual differences measures. For example, Woods (1906) used such sketches to assess the intellect (intelligence) and virtue (morality) of European royalty on a 7-point scale (see also Thorndike, 1936). Later on, Thorndike used the same method to score 91 creators and leaders on 48 individual differences variables, both intellectual and dispositional (see Knapp, 1962; Simonton, 1991). This method has undergone considerable improvements since its first implementations.

Of particular importance are the following practices: (1) using multiple independent raters who are blind to the purpose of the investigation; (2) abstracting the biographical sketches with all identifying material removed; (3) adapting standard personality measures for the computation of scores; and (4) using statistical analyses to consolidate the scores to a subset of dimensions (see Deluga, 1997; Simonton, 1986). The Gough Adjective Check List, the Cattell 16 Personality Factors, and the NEO–R have all been adapted for this historiometric purpose (Cassandro & Simonton, 2010; Cattell, 1963; Hoffer, 1978; Simonton, 1986). This at-a-distance approach has proven especially useful in the historiometric study of phenomenal leadership (Song & Simonton, 2007).

*Developmental histories*   Terman's (1925–1959) longitudinal psychometric study contains an anomaly: Volume 2 is actually a retrospective historiometric study of 301 geniuses, conducted by Catharine Cox (1926) in the form of a doctoral dissertation under his supervision. Shortly after Terman (1916) had published the Stanford–Binet Intelligence Scale, he had conceived of a technique for estimating the IQ of one of his heroes, Francis Galton (Terman, 1916). This technique was predicated on the original definition of IQ as the ratio of mental age divided by chronological age multiplied by 100 (Stern, 1914). After Cox compiled detailed chronologies of intellectual accomplishments, she then had a team of independent raters use this information to compute estimated IQ scores. This distinctive approach has been applied and extended to other data sets and substantive problems (Simonton, 1991, 2008a; Walberg, Rasher, & Hase, 1978).

*Content analyses*   The previous two methods manage to extract individual difference variables from biographical materials. One could always argue that biographies may be contaminated by the biases and prejudices of biographers, who may either idolize or demonize their subject. Therefore it is always valuable to identify alternative data sources that are free of such contaminants. Fortunately, most extraordinary geniuses leave behind a wide assortment of primary sources that can be used just for this purpose—correspondence, diaries, speeches, poems, paintings, compositions, and so forth. These documents or artifacts can then be subjected to systematic and objective content-analytical methods (e.g. Smith, 1992). An excellent example is the extensive research on integrative complexity, a measure of an individual's capacity to both differentiate and integrate (Suedfeld, Tetlock, & Streufert, 1992). This coding scheme can be applied to any verbal material. Although often treated as a state variable, it can also be adopted as a trait variable (i.e. as the baseline around which the state fluctuates according to external circumstances). As such, it has been shown to predict performance in both leaders and creators (Suedfeld, 1985; Suedfeld, Corteen, & McCormick, 1986; see also Feist, 1994). A notable development is the advent of computerized content analysis, whereby primary material can be quantified in a totally objective and precise manner. For example, using Martindale's (1990) Regressive Imagery Dictionary, computers can differentiate charismatic and non-charismatic US chief executives (Emrich, Brower, Feldman, & Garland, 2001) by applying the same content categories that distinguish great and mediocre poetry (Simonton, 1989). Charismatic presidents are the poets of US politics.

*Expert surveys* Those who have attained a high level of genius will make such a name for themselves that they will become the object of academic scholarship. The consequence is the proliferation of experts who claim some special degree of knowledge regarding one or more exemplars of exceptional creativity, phenomenal leadership, or even prodigious accomplishments. These experts can then be sent questionnaires that ask them to assess the objects of their expertise on pertinent individual differences variables. These "observer-based" assessments have a long history, albeit their first employment was confined to peer evaluations of disciplinary impact. Cattell (1903) initiated this practice early in the twentieth century, and this procedure has been followed by many others, with respect to both exceptional creators (Farnsworth, 1969) and phenomenal leaders, US presidents receiving special attention (see Simonton, 2008b). Far more interesting is when experts are asked to assess individual differences on psychological variables. Because experts on US presidents are very numerous, this application is fairly commonplace. Maranell (1970) had 571 experts rate past presidents on such variables as flexibility and idealism, while Ridings and McIver (1997) asked 719 experts to rate largely the same chief executives on character and integrity. But, from the standpoint of differential psychology, the most fascinating application is that of Rubenzer and Faschingbauer (2004): they had presidential biographers rate their subjects on the Big-Five personality factors (see also Rubenzer, Faschingbauer, & Ones, 2000).

I should point out that the individual differences variables extracted from personality sketches, developmental histories, content analyses, and expert surveys display a considerable consensus (see e.g. Simonton, 1986, 2009b). This agreement is important insofar as each of the four methods has its own distinct set of potential artifacts. But no artifact is shared by all four approaches.

## Generic versus Domain-Specific Profiles

Presumably exceptional talent and genius can be characterized by a profile of cognitive abilities and dispositional traits. That is, with respect to the general population, they will score high on certain individual differences variables, low on other variables, and perhaps average on still other variables. Yet this neat expectation is disrupted by the fact that a one-size-fits-all profile may simply be impossible. The impossibility stems from studies of cognitive abilities and dispositional traits.

### Exclusive versus inclusive abilities

If talent and genius are defined according to exceptional scores on a standard intelligence test, then it becomes a tautology to say that talents and geniuses have high IQs. The only remaining question is what the tests themselves measure. Do they primarily assess general intelligence, such as Spearman's (1927) $g$, or do they gauge separate abilities, which may or may not be subsumed under a general factor? If the latter holds, then we should more properly talk about a person's intellectual profile. Two individuals might score 140 on a test, but one might score higher on verbal comprehension, whereas the other might score higher on perceptual reasoning. If so, we might then want to render the attribution more differentiated, such as by calling an individual a "genius at verbal comprehension." Yet, so long as the various sub-scales correlate fairly highly, it may still be meaningful to refer to "intellectual talent" and "genius IQ." That seems to be the case.

Matters become more interesting and difficult when we define talent and genius with respect to extraordinary achievement, whether potential or realized. The difficulty arises because general intelligence has a much more ambivalent relation with this alternative criterion (Simonton, 1994). This ambivalence is seen in both psychometric and historiometric research. The former case is illustrated by Roe's (1953) study of 64 eminent scientists: Although the mean scores on her intelligence tests were comparable to genius-level IQs, the ranges were very large, so that the least bright would not qualify for membership in Mensa. An illustration from historiometric research is Cox's (1926) study of 301 geniuses: Although the mean estimated IQs were clearly in the genius category, the range was also extensive, so the lower end of the distribution was not even a standard deviation above the presumed population mean (see also Song & Simonton, 2007). People at this level are not even considered intellectually gifted (Storfer, 1990).

To be sure, Cox (1960) calculated a positive correlation between the IQ estimates and Cattell's (1903) measure of achieved eminence (see also Simonton, 1976, 2008a; Walberg et al., 1978). Yet this very correlation raises another issue. Historiometric assessments of intelligence do not operate the same way as psychometric assessments do. While the latter are generic—everybody takes the same tests—the latter are more domain-specific. Mozart's score was based primarily on his precocity in music, whereas Pascal's score was founded mostly on his mathematical precocity. Both geniuses showed accelerated development in the domain in which they later achieved eminence. In this respect, Cox's assessments are comparable more to those of the mathematically precocious participants in the SMPY research (Wai, Lubinski, & Benbow, 2005). Hence, her correlations might be adopted as support for those researchers who argue that intelligence is truly multidimensional (e.g. Sternberg, 1996; Thorndike, 1927). The most conspicuous example of this point of view is Howard Gardner's (1983) theory of multiple intelligences. In its original formulation, there were just seven distinct intelligences (Gardner, 1998). Moreover, each of these intelligences could be characterized by a particular guise of genius (Gardner, 1993). More specifically, the highest intelligences are represented by Sigmund Freud (intra-personal), Albert Einstein (logical–mathematical), Pablo Picasso (spatial), Igor Stravinsky (musical), T. S. Eliot (linguistic), Martha Graham (bodily–kinesthetic), and Mahatma Gandhi (interpersonal). In this light, Cox merely assessed Mozart on musical intelligence and Pascal on mathematical intelligence. It should be obvious that most of these intelligences are not gauged by the typical intelligence test, requiring that the concept be rendered more inclusive.

I have just suggested that the concept of intelligence might have to be broadened when it is used to discuss exceptional genius and talent as achievement. Yet increasing the number of intelligences is not the only way in which the concept might have to be rendered more inclusive than the construct of general intelligence. This point becomes apparent when we look at phenomenal leadership. Psychometric research finds a positive association between intelligence and leadership (Ilies, Gerhardt, & Le, 2004; Simonton, 1995), and the same relation seems to be found in historiometric research (e.g. Simonton, 1983; Simonton & Song, 2009). Even so, the latter studies seem to indicate that intelligence measures correspond more strongly to leader performance when the measures of intelligence are inclusively more than exclusively defined.

For example, research on presidential leadership has found that performance evaluations are most strongly predicted by a variable called "intellectual brilliance" (Simonton, 1986, 2006). Although this variable is highly reliable ($\alpha = .90$), it is clear that it consists of a composite of two separate constructs, namely general intelligence and openness to experience. Yet intellectual brilliance is a better predictor of presidential greatness than either intelligence or openness alone (Simonton, 2006). The latter do not even have predictive utility after controlling for intellectual brilliance. This outcome implies that an inclusive measure is actually superior to a more precisely defined variable (cf. Chamorro-Premuzic & Furnham, 2006).

Thus we end up with something of a paradox. Measures of cognitive abilities are most likely to be predictive when they display some domain specificity, but they also can gain predictive power when they are broadened to include traits that might be considered dispositional more than cognitive.

## Convergent versus divergent traits

In the previous section I mentioned openness to experience, a well-known dimension among the Big-Five personality factors (John, 1990). Openness correlates not only with leadership but also with creativity (Simonton, 2009c; see also Ilies et al., 2004; McCrae, 1987). For exceptional creativity, this openness can assume the form of unusual versatility (Cassandro, 1998; Cassandro & Simonton, 2010; White, 1931). Genius-grade creators will often display proficiency in more than one domain (e.g. science and philosophy), or at least in more than one sub-domain (e.g. poetry and drama). It is hard to imagine someone more versatile and open than Johann Wolfgang von Goethe or Leonardo da Vinci. Nor is openness the sole trait almost universally associated with exceptional genius and talent. Most prominent is the impact of motivational factors such as drive, energy, determination, and persistence (Cox, 1926; Duckworth, Peterson, Matthews, & Kelly, 2007). Interestingly, Galton's (1869) initial conception of natural ability included not just intellect but also motivation.

Nevertheless, many other dispositional traits do not have the same impact across all forms of exceptional genius and talent. Both psychometric and historiometric studies have shown how trait profiles vary across domains of extraordinary achievement (e.g. Chambers, 1964; Cox, 1926; Feist, 1998). Probably the most striking illustration of these inter-domain differences concerns psychopathology.

The notion of the "mad genius" is very ancient, going back at least as far as Aristotle. Furthermore, connections between psychopathology and outstanding creativity have been suggested in historiometric (e.g. Ellis, 1926; Ludwig, 1992; Post, 1994; Raskin, 1936), psychometric (e.g. Barron, 1963; Götz & Götz, 1979a, 1979b; Rushton, 1990), and psychiatric (e.g. Andreasen, 1987; Andreasen & Canter, 1974;

Jamison, 1989) research. That is, creative geniuses not only exhibit higher rates and intensities of psychopathological symptoms, but they also are more likely to come from family lineages that display outright psychopathology (Andreasen & Canter, 1974; Juda, 1949; Karlson, 1970). Indeed, the genetic commonalities are now being isolated (Kéri, 2009). These findings should not be interpreted in the sense that genius is mad, but only that genius-level creativity shares some common cognitive and dispositional attributes with ordinary psychopathology (Eysenck, 1995). For instance, both groups are more likely to show a reduced capacity to filter out extraneous information; but, in the case of highly creative persons, this "defocused attention" is associated with moderating factors such as high intelligence and ego strength (Carson, Peterson, & Higgins, 2003; Eysenck, 1995).

The above conclusion notwithstanding, the accumulated research literature also indicates that the connection between genius and madness is not uniform across domains of extraordinary achievement (Ludwig, 1998; Post, 1994; Raskin, 1936). Not only are phenomenal leaders less likely to exhibit psychopathology than exceptional creators are (Ludwig, 1995), but major contrasts also appear within distinct areas of creativity (Post, 1994). For example, artistic creators have a higher propensity for psychopathology than scientific creators do (Ludwig, 1998; Raskin, 1936). These contrasts can become even more finely differentiated. Within the literary arts, poets exhibit more mental illness than novelists do, and these in turn exhibit more than non-fiction authors (Jamison, 1989; Karlson, 1970; Kaufman, 2000–2001; Ludwig, 1995; Simonton & Song, 2009). Within the sciences, not only are social scientists more vulnerable than natural scientists (Ludwig, 1995), but within paradigmatic disciplines psychopathology is more prominent in revolutionary scientists than in their more conventional and conforming colleagues (Ko & Kim, 2008).

All told, the expected trait profiles are highly contingent on the particular type of genius. Moreover, there is some tentative evidence that the same conclusion applies to exceptional talent. For instance, even in early childhood and adolescence, future poets are more disposed toward psychopathology than other forms of outstanding creativity or leadership are (Simonton & Song, 2009). So the poet's susceptibility to mental illness begins very early.

## Nature versus Nurture

The notion that genius is born, not made, is almost as old as the idea that genius is mad. Indeed, the two conceptions were intimately connected in the nineteenth century, when some suggested that geniuses suffered from a genetic disorder that could lead to outright madness (e.g. Babcock, 1895). Although Galton (1869) rejected the pathology, the title *Hereditary genius* is explicit about the fact that he thought that genius of all kinds—even "athletic genius"—was the upshot of biological inheritance. Of course, innateness is inherent in the very definition of talent, and I indicated above that Galton viewed talent and genius as almost interchangeable.

Shortly after Galton's 1869 work, Candolle (1873) published an empirical study, which challenged the conclusion that genius was born and not made. In particular, Candolle demonstrated that eminent scientists emerge under very specific and consistent sociocultural, economic, political, and religious circumstances. Candolle's book immediately inspired Galton to conduct his survey of Fellows of the Royal Society. The results of this survey were published in Galton's 1874 *English men of science: Their nature and nurture.* As the subtitle implies, Galton felt obliged to back off from his initial biological determinism. The environment (nurture), and not just inheritance (nature), had a part to play in the development of genius.

Unfortunately, Galton's 1874 compromise was swept away by later events in the history of psychology. First, behaviorists put the greatest stress on learning and conditioning at the expense of genetic endowment. Then cognitive psychologists continued this extreme nurture orientation by treating both genius and talent, no matter how extraordinary, as mere manifestations of domain-specific expertise acquisition, particularly expertise acquired through what was often called "deliberate practice" (Ericsson, 1996). One manifestation of this expertise theory was the "10-year rule," which predicted that a future genius could only produce first-class ideas after devoting a full decade to extensive practice and training (Hayes, 1989). Genius was not born, it was totally made, and a lot of personal effort had to be expended in that making (Howe, 1999). The very existence of "innate talent" was questioned, despite the fact that this expression would seem a tautology, on a par with "unmarried bachelor" (see e.g. Howe, Davidson, & Sloboda, 1998).

Happily, this shift toward the extreme nurture view has been countered by recent developments in behavior genetics (Lykken, 1998). While not denying the importance of environmental influences, including deliberate expertise acquisition, current research indicates that genetic factors cannot be ignored. Most obviously, almost all of the individual variables that predict exceptional genius and talent also happen to feature substantial heritabilities (Simonton, 2008c). Combining these heritability coefficients with their corresponding predictive validity coefficients, we can conservatively estimate that between a quarter and a third of the variance has some genetic foundation. This genetic endowment determines how fast a person can acquire domain-specific expertise, as well as how much creativity, leadership, or other performance can be manifested, given a particular level of acquired expertise.

In addition, contemporary research implies that the genetics may be far more complicated than Galton (1869) and others had originally envisioned (Lykken, 1998). More specifically, the genetic component of genius and talent may be (1) emergenic (multiplicative rather than additive); and (2) epigenetic (developmental rather than static). These complexities have critical consequences for such matters as the rarity of genius and talent, as well as for their anticipated developmental trajectories (Simonton, 1999c, 2001).

These contemporary findings from behavioral genetics strengthen the inference that individual differences variables do contribute directly to both genius and talent. Even so, it should have become obvious that these variables do not have a uniform impact, at least if that impact is defined as extraordinary achievement. Instead, each particular form of accomplishment is characterized by its own profile of cognitive abilities and dispositional traits, and each ability and trait have a corresponding heritability coefficient. Thus it is possible to say that artistic talent or genius has a higher degree of inheritability than scientific talent or genius has (Simonton, 2008c).

## Individual versus Situation

I have saved the best issue—or perhaps the worst issue—for the end. Ever since Mischel (1968) published his classic monograph, individual differences have had to be placed in the context of situational variables. There may be occasions where situational factors dominate over individual factors. Or there may be circumstances where the impact of an individual-level variable is significantly moderated by a situational variable. This issue has its counterpart in research on exceptional genius, namely in the debate over whether exceptional achievement is attributable to the "great person" or to the *Zeitgeist*—the "spirit of the times" (Simonton, 1994). On the former view, certain individuals have special characteristics that set them apart from everybody else. On the latter view, their accomplishments merely reflect the fact that they happened to be "in the right place at the right time." A classic illustration of this second position may be found in *War and Peace*, where Tolstoy argued that Napoleon's supposed military genius had no discernible impact on the French invasion of Russia in 1812.

Psychometric research is not well equipped to address this question. The reason is that the creators, leaders, and talents that make up any given cross-sectional sample are relatively homogeneous with respect to pertinent situational factors (Helson & Crutchfield, 1970; Roe, 1953; Terman, 1925). In other words, they all grew up and matured under pretty much the same sociocultural circumstances. In contrast, historiometric research has the advantage that its samples can be truly cross-cultural and trans-historical in extent (Candolle, 1873; Cox, 1926; Thorndike, 1950; Walberg et al., 1978). This often permits direct comparison between individual and situational factors, as well as tests for individual X situational interaction effects (Simonton, 1990). So what does the historiometric literature indicate?

First, the good news is that, for exceptional creativity, individual differences variables prove to be very important in predicting the magnitude of notable achievement (Simonton, 1999a). Only if we consider the domain of achievement as a situational factor does the domain have to be taken into consideration. Yet, given that individual differences variables likely influence the domain in which a creator contributes, it does not seem very probable that domain operates as a cause rather than an effect (Simonton, 2009c). A person becomes a great physicist rather than a notable poet because of his or her personality profile.

Second, the bad news: Phenomenal leadership operates differently from exceptional creativity (Simonton, 1995). For one thing, situational factors tend to explain more variance in leader performance than individual factors do. As an example, although political leaders are more effective if they are highly intelligent, the impact of intelligence is smaller than the circumstances under which the leaders rose to power (see Simonton, 1984, 1988b; and cf. Simonton, 1980). In addition, even when individual factors play a major role, their effects are often conditioned by situational factors. For instance, although a US president's flexibility has an impact on his performance as legislator, the effect of flexibility is moderated by such situational factors as the size of his electoral mandate and the degree to which his party controls Congress (Simonton, 1987). Thus superior performance as a leader may be more a matter of being the right person in the right place at the right time.

Nonetheless, both of the foregoing observations must be subjected to a serious qualification: Both conclusions are predicated on samples of historical geniuses— exceptional achievers whose accomplishments put their names in the history books. Such historiometric samples of necessity ignore all those exceptional talents who never managed to realize their full potential. Although part of this failure may reflect personal limitations, a much larger portion may be attributed to sociocultural context. Historiometric research indicates that genius is not randomly distributed across time and place, but rather tends to be clustered into certain "golden ages" and lesser "silver ages," separated by comparative "dark ages" (Kroeber, 1944; Murray, 2003; Simonton, 1988a; Sorokin & Merton, 1935). Examples include the Athenian Golden Age, the Gupta Empire of India, the early Tang Dynasty in China, the Abbasid Caliphate in Islamic civilization, the Heian period in Japan, Renaissance Italy, and the western European Scientific Revolution. Yet, unless we suppose that the genetic makeup of any population can undergo dramatic changes—an extremely unlikely assumption—these temporal and geographical fluctuations can only be explained by political, economic, social, and cultural factors that can change within a generation or two (Candolle, 1873; Murray, 2003; Simonton, 1975, 1992). Great talents were certainly born in the dark ages, but such periods were never able to convert that talent into full-fledged genius. Had the genetic twin of Isaac Newton been born in medieval England, he would probably not have become a great scientist and mathematician.

Hence it is reasonable to infer that situational factors are far more critical than individual factors in determining when and where exceptional talent becomes exceptional genius. This contingency helps us appreciate why geniuses of the highest order are much rarer than the assumed pool of talent. Each generation everywhere produces a vast supply of potential creators and leaders who live and die in an unsupportive world, leaving nothing behind except a weathering tombstone over some small plot. As Thomas Gray famously said in his *Elegy written in a country churchyard*, "Some mute inglorious Milton here may rest, / Some Cromwell, guiltless of his country's blood."

# References

Albert, R. S. (Ed.) (1992). *Genius and eminence* (2nd ed.). Oxford: Pergamon Press.

*American heritage electronic dictionary* (3rd ed.) (1992). Boston, MA: Houghton Mifflin.

Andreasen, N. C. (1987). Creativity and mental illness: Prevalence rates in writers and their first-degree relatives. *American Journal of Psychiatry*, *144*, 1288–1292.

Andreasen, N. C., & Canter, A. (1974). The creative writer: Psychiatric symptoms and family history. *Comprehensive Psychiatry*, *15*, 123–131.

Babcock, W. L. (1895). On the morbid heredity and predisposition to insanity of the man of genius. *Journal of Nervous and Mental Disease*, *20*, 749–769.

Barron, F. X. (1963). *Creativity and psychological health: Origins of personal vitality and creative freedom*. Princeton, NJ: Van Nostrand.

Barron, F. X. (1969). *Creative person and creative process*. New York: Holt, Rinehart & Winston.

Benbow, C. P., & Lubinski, D. (Eds.) (1996). *Intellectual talent: Psychometric and social issues*. Baltimore, MD: Johns Hopkins University Press.

Bouchard, T. J., Jr., & McGue, M. (1981, May 29). Familial studies of intelligence. *Science*, *212*, 1055–1059.

Candolle, A. de (1873). *Histoire des sciences et des savants depuis deux siècles*. Geneva: Georg.

Carson, S., Peterson, J. B., & Higgins, D. M. (2003). Decreased latent inhibition is associated with increased creative achievement in high-functioning individuals. *Journal of Personality and Social Psychology*, *85*, 499–506.

Cassandro, V. J. (1998). Explaining premature mortality across fields of creative endeavor. *Journal of Personality*, *66*, 805–833.

Cassandro, V. J., & Simonton, D. K. (2010). Versatility, openness to experience, and topical diversity in creative products: An exploratory historiometric analysis of scientists, philosophers, and writers. *Journal of Creative Behavior*, *44*, 1–18.

Cattell, J. M. (1890). Mental tests and measurements. *Mind*, *15*, 373–381.

Cattell, J. M. (1903). A statistical study of eminent men. *Popular Science Monthly*, *62*, 359–377.

Cattell, R. B. (1963). The personality and motivation of the researcher from measurements of contemporaries and from biography. In C. W. Taylor & F. Barron (Eds.), *Scientific creativity: Its recognition and development* (pp. 119–131). New York: Wiley.

Cattell, R. B., & Butcher, H. J. (1968). *The prediction of achievement and creativity*. Indianapolis, IN: Bobbs-Berrill.

Chamorro-Premuzic, T., & Furnham, A. (2006). Intellectual competence and intelligent personality: A third way in differential psychology. *Review of General Psychology*, *10*, 251–267.

Chambers, J. A. (1964). Relating personality and biographical factors to scientific creativity. *Psychological Monographs: General and Applied*, *78* (Whole No. 584), 1–20.

Cox, C. (1926). *The early mental traits of three hundred geniuses*. Stanford, CA: Stanford University Press.

Deluga, R. J. (1997). Relationship among American presidential charismatic leadership, narcissism, and related performance. *Leadership Quarterly*, *8*, 51–65.

Duckworth, A. L., Peterson, C., Matthews, M. D., & Kelly, D. R. (2007). GRIT: Perseverence and passion for long-term goals. *Journal of Personality and Social Psychology*, *92*, 1087–1101.

Ellis, H. (1926). *A study of British genius* (rev. ed.). Boston, MA: Houghton Mifflin.

Emrich, C. G., Brower, H. H., Feldman, J. M., & Garland, H. (2001). Images in words: Presidential rhetoric, charisma, and greatness. *Administrative Science Quarterly*, *46*, 527–557.

Ericsson, K. A. (1996). The acquisition of expert performance: An introduction to some of the issues. In K. A. Ericsson (Ed.), *The road to expert performance: Empirical evidence from the arts and sciences, sports, and games* (pp. 1–50). Mahwah, NJ: Lawrence Erlbaum Associates.

Eysenck, H. J. (1995). *Genius: The natural history of creativity*. Cambridge: Cambridge University Press.

Farnsworth, P. R. (1969). *The social psychology of music* (2nd ed.). Ames: Iowa State University Press.

Feist, G. J. (1993). A structural model of scientific eminence. *Psychological Science*, *4*, 366–371.

Feist, G. J. (1994). Personality and working style predictors of integrative complexity: A study of scientists' thinking about research and teaching. *Journal of Personality and Social Psychology*, *67*, 474–484.

Feist, G. J. (1998). A meta-analysis of personality in scientific and artistic creativity. *Personality and Social Psychology Review*, *2*, 290–309.

Galton, F. (1865). Hereditary talent and character. *Macmillan's Magazine, 12,* 157–166, 318–327.

Galton, F. (1869). *Hereditary genius: An inquiry into its laws and consequences.* London: Macmillan.

Galton, F. (1874). *English men of science: Their nature and nurture.* London: Macmillan.

Galton, F. (1883). *Inquiries into human faculty and its development.* London: Macmillan.

Gardner, H. (1983). *Frames of mind: A theory of multiple intelligences.* New York: Basic Books.

Gardner, H. (1993). *Creating minds: An anatomy of creativity seen through the lives of Freud, Einstein, Picasso, Stravinsky, Eliot, Graham, and Gandhi.* New York: Basic Books.

Gardner, H. (1998). Are there additional intelligences? The case for naturalist, spiritual, and existential intelligences. In J. Kane (Ed.), *Education, information, and transformation* (pp. 111–131). Upper Saddle River, NJ: Merrill.

Götz, K. O., & Götz, K. (1979a). Personality characteristics of professional artists. *Perceptual and Motor Skills, 49,* 327–334.

Götz, K. O., & Götz, K. (1979b). Personality characteristics of successful artists. *Perceptual and Motor Skills, 49,* 919–924.

Gough, H. G. (1979). A creative personality scale for the adjective check list. *Journal of Personality and Social Psychology, 37,* 1398–1405.

Hayes, J. R. (1989). *The complete problem solver* (2nd ed.). Hillsdale, NJ: Lawrence Erlbaum Associates.

Heller, K. A., Mönks, F. J., Sternberg, R. J., & Subotnik, R. F. (Eds.) (2000). *International handbook of research and development of giftedness and talent* (2nd ed.). Terrytown, NY: Pergamon.

Helson, R., & Crutchfield, R. S. (1970). Mathematicians: The creative researcher and the average Ph.D. *Journal of Consulting and Clinical Psychology, 34,* 250–257.

Hilts, V. L. (1975). *A guide to Francis Galton's* English men of science. Philadelphia, PA: American Philosophical Society.

Hoffer, P. C. (1978). Psychohistory and empirical group affiliation: Extraction of personality traits from historical manuscripts. *Journal of Interdisciplinary History, 9,* 131–145.

Holahan, C. K, & Sears, R. R. (1995). *The gifted group in later maturity.* Stanford, CA: Stanford University Press.

Howe, M. J. A. (1999). *Genius explained.* Cambridge: Cambridge University Press.

Howe, M. J. A., Davidson, J. W., & Sloboda, J. A. (1998). Innate talents: Reality or myth? *Behavioral and Brain Sciences, 21,* 399–442.

Ilies, R., Gerhardt, M. W., & Le, H. (2004). Individual differences in leadership emergence: Integrating meta-analytic findings and behavioral genetics estimates. *International Journal of Selection and Assessment, 12,* 207–219.

Jamison, K. R. (1989). Mood disorders and patterns of creativity in British writers and artists. *Psychiatry, 52,* 125–134.

Jensen, A. R. (1990). Speed of information processing in a calculating prodigy. *Intelligence, 14,* 259–274.

Jensen, A. R. (1996). Giftedness and genius: Crucial differences. In C. P. Benbow & D. J. Lubinski (Eds.), *Intellectual talent: Psychometric and social issues* (pp. 393–411). Baltimore, MD: Johns Hopkins University Press.

John, O. P. (1990). The "Big Five" factor taxonomy: Dimensions of personality in the natural language and in questionnaires. In L. A. Pervin (Ed.), *Handbook of personality theory and research* (pp. 66–100). New York: Guilford Press.

Juda, A. (1949). The relationship between highest mental capacity and psychic abnormalities. *American Journal of Psychiatry, 106,* 296–307.

Kant, I. (1952). *The critique of judgement* [1790]. Translated by J. C. Meredith. In R. M. Hutchins (Ed.), *Great books of the Western world* (Vol. 42, pp. 459–613). Chicago: Encyclopaedia Britannica.

Karlson, J. I. (1970). Genetic association of giftedness and creativity with schizophrenia. *Hereditas, 66*, 177–182.

Kaufman, J. C. (2000–2001). Genius, lunatics and poets: Mental illness in prize-winning authors. *Imagination, Cognition & Personality, 20*, 305–314.

Kéri, S. (2009). Genes for psychosis and creativity: A promoter polymorphism of the Neuregulin 1 gene is related to creativity in people with high intellectual achievement. *Psychological Science, 20*, 1070–1073.

Ko, Y., & Kim, J. (2008). Scientific geniuses' psychopathology as a moderator in the relation between creative contribution types and eminence. *Creativity Research Journal, 20*, 251–261.

Knapp, R. H. (1962). A factor analysis of Thorndike's ratings of eminent men. *Journal of Social Psychology, 56*, 67–71.

Kroeber, A. L. (1944). *Configurations of culture growth.* Berkeley: University of California Press.

Lubinski, D., & Benbow, C. P. (1994). The study of mathematically precocious youth: The first three decades of a planned 50-year study of intellectual talent. In R. F. Subotnik & K. D. Arnold (Eds.), *Beyond Terman: Contemporary longitudinal studies of giftedness and talent* (pp. 255–281). Norwood, NJ: Ablex.

Lubinski, D., Webb, R. M., Morelock, M. J., & Benbow, C. P. (2001). Top 1 in 10,000: A 10-year follow-up of the profoundly gifted. *Journal of Applied Psychology, 86*, 718–729.

Ludwig, A. M. (1992). Creative achievement and psychopathology: Comparison among professions. *American Journal of Psychotherapy, 46*, 330–356.

Ludwig, A. M. (1995). *The price of greatness: Resolving the creativity and madness controversy.* New York: Guilford Press.

Ludwig, A. M. (1998). Method and madness in the arts and sciences. *Creativity Research Journal, 11*, 93–101.

Lykken, D. T. (1998). The genetics of genius. In A. Steptoe (Ed.), *Genius and the mind: Studies of creativity and temperament in the historical record* (pp. 15–37). New York: Oxford University Press.

MacKinnon, D. W. (1978). *In search of human effectiveness.* Buffalo, NJ: Creative Education Foundation.

Maranell, G. M. (1970). The evaluation of presidents: An extension of the Schlesinger polls. *Journal of American History, 57*, 104–113.

Martindale, C. (1990). *The clockwork muse: The predictability of artistic styles.* New York: Basic Books.

McCrae, R. R. (1987). Creativity, divergent thinking, and openness to experience. *Journal of Personality and Social Psychology, 52*, 1258–1265.

McFarlan, D. (Ed.) (1989). *Guinness book of world records.* New York: Bantam.

Mischel, W. (1968). *Personality and assessment.* New York: Wiley.

Muratori, M. C., Stanley, J. C., Gross, M. U. M., Ng, L., Tao, T., Ng, J., & Tao, B. (2006). Insights from SMPY's greatest former prodigies: Drs. Terence ("Terry") Tao and Lenhard ("Lenny") Ng reflect on their talent development. *Gifted Child Quarterly, 50*, 307–324.

Murray, C. (2003). *Human accomplishment: The pursuit of excellence in the arts and sciences, 800 BC to 1950.* New York: HarperCollins.

Murray, P. (Ed.) (1989). *Genius: The history of an idea.* Oxford: Blackwell.

Paulhus, D. L., Wehr, P., Harms, P. D., & Strasser, D. I. (2002). Use of exemplar surveys to reveal implicit types of intelligence. *Personality and Social Psychology Bulletin*, 28, 1051–1062.

Post, F. (1994). Creativity and psychopathology: A study of 291 world-famous men. *British Journal of Psychiatry*, 165, 22–34.

Raskin, E. A. (1936). Comparison of scientific and literary ability: A biographical study of eminent scientists and men of letters of the nineteenth century. *Journal of Abnormal and Social Psychology*, 31, 20–35.

Ridings, W. J., Jr., & McIver, S. B. (1997). *Rating the presidents: A ranking of U.S. leaders, from the great and honorable to the dishonest and incompetent*. Secaucus, NJ: Citadel Press.

Roe, A. (1953). *The making of a scientist*. New York: Dodd, Mead.

Rubenzer, S. J., & Faschingbauer, T. R. (2004). *Personality, character, & leadership in the White House: Psychologists assess the presidents*. Washington, DC: Brassey's.

Rubenzer, S. J., Faschingbauer, T. R., & Ones, D. S. (2000). Assessing the U.S. presidents using the revised NEO Personality Inventory. *Assessment*, 7, 403–420.

Rushton, J. P. (1990). Creativity, intelligence, and psychoticism. *Personality and Individual Differences*, 11, 1291–1298.

Simonton, D. K. (1975). Sociocultural context of individual creativity: A transhistorical time-series analysis. *Journal of Personality and Social Psychology*, 32, 1119–1133.

Simonton, D. K. (1976). Biographical determinants of achieved eminence: A multivariate approach to the Cox data. *Journal of Personality and Social Psychology*, 33, 218–226.

Simonton, D. K. (1980). Land battles, generals, and armies: Individual and situational determinants of victory and casualties. *Journal of Personality and Social Psychology*, 38, 110–119.

Simonton, D. K. (1983). Intergenerational transfer of individual differences in hereditary monarchs: Genes, role-modeling, cohort, or sociocultural effects? *Journal of Personality and Social Psychology*, 44, 354–364.

Simonton, D. K. (1984). Leaders as eponyms: Individual and situational determinants of monarchal eminence. *Journal of Personality*, 52, 1–21.

Simonton, D. K. (1986). Presidential personality: Biographical use of the Gough Adjective Check List. *Journal of Personality and Social Psychology*, 51, 149–160.

Simonton, D. K. (1987). Presidential inflexibility and veto behavior: Two individual–situational interactions. *Journal of Personality*, 55, 1–18.

Simonton, D. K. (1988a). Galtonian genius, Kroeberian configurations, and emulation: A generational time-series analysis of Chinese civilization. *Journal of Personality and Social Psychology*, 55, 230–238.

Simonton, D. K. (1988b). Presidential style: Personality, biography, and performance. *Journal of Personality and Social Psychology*, 55, 928–936.

Simonton, D. K. (1989). Shakespeare's sonnets: A case of and for single-case historiometry. *Journal of Personality*, 57, 695–721.

Simonton, D. K. (1990). *Psychology, science, and history: An introduction to historiometry*. New Haven, CT: Yale University Press.

Simonton, D. K. (1991). Personality correlates of exceptional personal influence: A note on Thorndike's (1950) creators and leaders. *Creativity Research Journal*, 4, 67–78.

Simonton, D. K. (1992). Gender and genius in Japan: Feminine eminence in masculine culture. *Sex Roles*, 27, 101–119.

Simonton, D. K. (1994). *Greatness: Who makes history and why*. New York: Guilford Press.

Simonton, D. K. (1995). Personality and intellectual predictors of leadership. In D. H. Saklofske & M. Zeidner (Eds.), *International handbook of personality and intelligence* (pp. 739–757). New York: Plenum.

Simonton, D. K. (1997). *Genius and creativity: Selected papers.* Greenwich, CT: Ablex.

Simonton, D. K. (1999a). Creativity and genius. In L. A. Pervin & O. John (Eds.), *Handbook of personality theory and research* (2nd ed., pp. 629–652). New York: Guilford Press.

Simonton, D. K. (1999b). Significant samples: The psychological study of eminent individuals. *Psychological Methods, 4,* 425–451.

Simonton, D. K. (1999c). Talent and its development: An emergenic and epigenetic model. *Psychological Review, 106,* 435–457.

Simonton, D. K. (2001). Talent development as a multidimensional, multiplicative, and dynamic process. *Current Directions in Psychological Science, 10,* 39–43.

Simonton, D. K. (2006). Presidential IQ, openness, intellectual brilliance, and leadership: Estimates and correlations for 42 US chief executives. *Political Psychology, 27,* 511–639.

Simonton, D. K. (2008a). Childhood giftedness and adulthood genius: A historiometric analysis of 291 eminent African Americans. *Gifted Child Quarterly, 52,* 243–255.

Simonton, D. K. (2008b). Presidential greatness and its socio-psychological significance: Individual or situation? Performance or attribution? In C. Hoyt, G. R. Goethals, & D. Forsyth (Eds.), *Leadership at the crossroads: Vol. 1. Psychology and leadership* (pp. 132–148). Westport, CT: Praeger.

Simonton, D. K. (2008c). Scientific talent, training, and performance: Intellect, personality, and genetic endowment. *Review of General Psychology, 12,* 28–46.

Simonton, D. K. (2009a). *Genius 101.* New York: Springer.

Simonton, D. K. (2009b). The "other IQ": Historiometric assessments of intelligence and related constructs. *Review of General Psychology, 13,* 315–326.

Simonton, D. K. (2009c). Varieties of (scientific) creativity: A hierarchical model of disposition, development, and achievement. *Perspectives on Psychological Science, 4,* 441–452.

Simonton, D. K., & Damian, R. I. (in press). Creativity. In D. Reisberg (Ed.), *Oxford handbook of cognitive psychology.* New York: Oxford University Press.

Simonton, D. K., & Song, A. V. (2009). Eminence, IQ, physical and mental health, and achievement domain: Cox's 282 geniuses revisited. *Psychological Science, 20,* 429–434.

Smith, C. P. (Ed.) (1992). *Motivation and personality: Handbook of thematic content analysis.* Cambridge: Cambridge University Press.

Song, A. V., & Simonton, D. K. (2007). Studying personality at a distance: Quantitative methods. In R. W. Robins, R. C. Fraley, & R. F. Krueger (Eds.), *Handbook of research methods in personality psychology* (pp. 308–321). New York: Guilford Press.

Sorokin, P. A., & Merton, R. K. (1935). The course of Arabian intellectual development, 700–1300 AD. *Isis, 22,* 516–524.

Spearman, C. (1927). *The abilities of man: Their nature and measurement.* New York: Macmillan.

Stanley, J. C. (1996). In the beginning: The study of mathematically precocious youth. In C. P. Benbow & D. J. Lubinski (Eds.), *Intellectual talent: Psychometric and social issues* (pp. 225–235). Baltimore, MD: Johns Hopkins University Press.

Stern, W. (1914). *The psychological methods of testing intelligence.* Baltimore, MD: Warwick & York.

Sternberg, R. J. (1996). *Successful intelligence.* New York: Simon & Schuster.

Storfer, M. D. (1990). *Intelligence and giftedness: The contributions of heredity and early environment.* San Francisco, CA: Jossey-Bass.

Subotnik, R. F., & Arnold, K. D. (Eds.) (1994). *Beyond Terman: Contemporary longitudinal studies of giftedness and talent.* Norwood, NJ: Ablex.

Suedfeld, P. (1985). APA presidential addresses: The relation of integrative complexity to historical, professional, and personal factors. *Journal of Personality and Social Psychology*, *47*, 848–852.

Suedfeld, P., Corteen, R. S., & McCormick, C. (1986). The role of integrative complexity in military leadership: Robert E. Lee and his opponents. *Journal of Applied Social Psychology*, *16*, 498–507.

Suedfeld, P., Tetlock, P. E., & Streufert, S. (1992). Conceptual/integrative complexity. In C. P. Smith (Ed.), *Motivation and personality: Handbook of thematic content analysis* (pp. 393–400). Cambridge: Cambridge University Press.

Terman, L. M. (1916). *The measurement of intelligence: An explanation of and a complete guide for the use of the Stanford revision and extension of the Binet–Simon intelligence scale.* Boston, MA: Houghton Mifflin.

Terman, L. M. (1925). *Mental and physical traits of a thousand gifted children.* Stanford, CA: Stanford University Press.

Terman, L. M. (1925–1959). *Genetic studies of genius* (5 vols.). Stanford, CA: Stanford University Press.

Terman, L. M., & Oden, M. H. (1947). *The gifted child grows up.* Stanford, CA: Stanford University Press.

Thorndike, E. L. (1927). *The measurement of intelligence.* New York: Columbia University Teachers College.

Thorndike, E. L. (1936). The relation between intellect and morality in rulers. *American Journal of Sociology*, *42*, 321–334.

Thorndike, E. L. (1950). Traits of personality and their intercorrelations as shown in biographies. *Journal of Educational Psychology*, *41*, 193–216.

Wai, J., Lubinski, D., & Benbow, C. P. (2005). Creativity and occupational accomplishments among intellectually precocious youths: An age 13 to age 33 longitudinal study. *Journal of Educational Psychology*, *97*, 484–492.

Walberg, H. J., Rasher, S. P., & Hase, K. (1978). IQ correlates with high eminence. *Gifted Child Quarterly*, *22*, 196–200.

White, R. K. (1931). The versatility of genius. *Journal of Social Psychology*, *2*, 460–489.

Wissler, C. (1901). The correlation of mental and physical tests. *Psychological Monographs*, *3*(6): 1–62.

Woods, F. A. (1906). *Mental and moral heredity in royalty.* New York: Holt.

# 25

# Ability and Trait Emotional Intelligence

## K. V. Petrides

## History and Background

The distal roots of emotional intelligence (EI) can be traced back to the concept of "social intelligence," coined by E. L. Thorndike (1920) to refer to the ability to understand and manage people and to act wisely in human relations. Its proximal roots lie in Gardner's work on multiple intelligences and, more specifically, in his concepts of intra-personal and interpersonal intelligence. According to Gardner (1999), "*interpersonal intelligence* denotes a person's capacity to understand the intentions, motivations, and desires of other people and, consequently, to work effectively with others" (p. 43). By contrast, "*intrapersonal intelligence* involves the capacity to understand oneself, to have an effective working model of oneself—including one's own desires, fears, and capacities—and to use such information effectively in regulating one's own life" (p. 43).

As a phrase, EI has been present in the literature for a relatively long time (Leuner, 1966), although it was not until later that the construct was introduced in a form that resembles one of its current manifestations (Payne, 1985; Salovey & Mayer, 1990). EI was propelled into prominence by Goleman's (1995) best-selling book and by a subsequent lead article in *Time* magazine (Gibbs, 1995).

Theoretical accounts were soon followed by attempts to devise measures to assess the new construct (Bar-On, 1997; Mayer, Caruso, & Salovey, 1999; Schutte et al., 1998). The process of test construction, however, did not consider the fundamental psychometric distinction between measures of typical and maximum performance (Cronbach, 1949; Hofstee, 2001). Consequently, some measures were based on self-report (e.g. Schutte et al., 1998), whereas others attempted to develop items that can be responded to correctly or incorrectly (Mayer et al., 1999).

Petrides and Furnham (2000, 2001) noted this was problematic because different measurement approaches would almost certainly produce different results, even if the

*The Wiley-Blackwell Handbook of Individual Differences*, First Edition.
Edited by Tomas Chamorro-Premuzic, Sophie von Stumm, and Adrian Furnham.
© 2011 Blackwell Publishing Ltd. Published 2011 by Blackwell Publishing Ltd.

underlying model being operationalized is one and the same. It has since been demonstrated, in each and every empirical study investigating this issue, that the various methodologies used in the measurement of EI do not converge (Van Rooy, Viswesvaran, & Pluta, 2005; Warwick & Nettelbeck, 2004) and that it is imperative to draw a distinction between typical and maximal performance measurement in the field (Freudenthaler & Neubauer, 2007).

## Trait EI versus ability EI[1]

Two different EI constructs can be differentiated on the basis of the method of measurement used to operationalize them (self-report, as in personality questionnaires, or maximum performance, as in IQ tests; see Petrides & Furnham, 2000, 2001). *Trait EI* (or trait emotional self-efficacy) concerns emotion-related self-perceptions measured via self-report, whilst *ability EI* (or cognitive–emotional ability) concerns emotion-related cognitive abilities that ought to be measured via maximum-performance tests.

Table 25.1 summarizes the conceptual differences between the two constructs. Trait EI is defined as a constellation of self-perceptions located at the lower levels of personality hierarchies (Petrides, Pita, & Kokkinaki, 2007), whereas ability EI is defined as "the ability to perceive and express emotion, assimilate emotion in thought, understand and reason with emotion, and regulate emotion in the self and others" (Mayer & Salovey, 1997). As mentioned, correlations between measures of trait EI and ability EI are invariably low, thereby supporting the explicit distinction between them (Brannick, Wahi, Arce, & Johnson, 2009). The former belongs within the realm of personality, whereas the latter (theoretically, if not empirically) belongs within the domain of cognitive ability.

The distinction between trait EI and ability EI is now standard in the scientific literature, which helps to organize its development and the accumulation of knowledge in the field. Research that does not heed the distinction does, of course, exist, and there have also been cases where the distinction was acknowledged, but explicitly misinterpreted (e.g. Devonish & Greenidge, 2010 misconstrued a trait EI questionnaire as a measure of ability EI, thus undermining the interpretation of their own data). In any case, it is now generally acknowledged that trait EI and ability EI are different constructs. Their literatures are developing independently, and it is accepted that the operationalization of one does not have implications for the operationalization of the other.

# Problems with Ability EI: Why Emotional Intelligence Is Not a Real Intelligence

Maximum-performance measurement is a *sine qua non* for the assessment of genuine intelligence (Jensen, 1998). The operationalization of ability EI is problematic because the subjectivity of emotional experience (Matthews, Zeidner, & Roberts, 2007; Robinson & Clore, 2002) undermines the development of maximum-performance tests. The heart of the problem is the inability to create items or tasks

**Table 25.1** Trait EI versus ability EI

| Construct | Measurement | Conceptualization | Expected relationship to $g$ | Construct validity | Measures |
|-----------|-------------|-------------------|------------------------------|--------------------|----------|
| Trait EI | Self-report | Personality trait | Orthogonal Unimportant for construct validity | Consistent with models of differential psychology<br>Discriminant and incremental validity vis-à-vis personality<br>Concurrent and predictive validity with many criteria | TEIQue[a] |
| Ability EI | Maximum performance | Cognitive ability | Moderate to strong correlations Crucial for construct validity | Inconsistent with models of differential psychology<br>Awkward scoring procedures<br>Limited concurrent and predictive validity | MSCEIT<br>TEMNIT[b]<br>STEU/STEM[b] |

[a]The TEIQue is the only instrument that is explicitly based on trait EI theory and that covers the sampling domain of the construct comprehensively, but it is certainly not the only self-report measure of EI (see main text for details).
[b]Observations in the construct validity column do not necessarily apply to these measures, since they are relatively new and their properties are not yet fully established.

that can be scored according to truly objective criteria and that can cover the sampling domain of ability EI comprehensively. The use of alternative scoring procedures, such as "consensus" and "expert" scoring, to create correct responses among a number of equally logical alternatives leads to a host of problems repeatedly noted in the literature (Ortony, Revelle, & Zinbarg, 2007; O'Sullivan & Ekman, 2004; Roberts, Zeidner, & Matthews, 2001). These procedures yield scores that are not only foreign to cognitive ability, but also psychologically meaningless, as it is unclear whether they reflect confounding with vocabulary size (Wilhelm, 2005), conformity to social norms (Matthews, Emo, Roberts, & Zeidner, 2006), theoretical knowledge about emotions (Austin, 2010; Freudenthaler, Neubauer, & Haller, 2008), stereotypical judgments (O'Sullivan, 2007), or some unknown combination, or interaction, of some, or all, of these factors.

Conceptual challenges like the foregoing (see also Brody, 2004; Locke, 2005) also give rise to a bewildering range of empirical limitations. For readers wishing to explore these issues, the following references can provide a starting point: Austin (2010), Follesdal and Hagtvet (2009), Keele and Bell (2008, 2009), Rossen, Kranzler, and Algina (2008), and Zeidner and Olnick-Shemesh (2010). These publications describe in some detail the obstacles that arise from ignoring the inherently subjective nature of emotions. Emotional experience cannot be artificially objectified in order to be made amenable to IQ-style testing.

The core problem with the Mayer–Salovey–Caruso Emotional Intelligence Test (MSCEIT; Mayer, Salovey, & Caruso, 2002), as the most widely used test of ability EI, is not simply that it does not measure intelligence of any kind—as is constantly, albeit erroneously, claimed by its authors—but that it does not measure any coherent dimension of psychological interest. This is why it is scientifically barren to persist in the efforts to improve its psychometric properties and weak nomological net; for, even if these were to reach acceptable standards one day, the resultant scores would still be uninterpretable due to the nature of the underlying scoring system (Barchard & Russell, 2006; Brody, 2004; Keele & Bell, 2009; O'Sullivan & Ekman, 2004).

The avalanche of scientific criticism and negative findings on the MSCEIT has prompted the development of alternative measures of ability EI (Amelang & Steinmayr, 2006; MacCann & Roberts, 2008; Warwick, Nettelbeck, & Ward, 2010), whose empirical bases have not yet been fully developed (see Austin, 2010). Before proceeding with a full evaluation of the construct validity of any new ability-EI test, we must answer two questions: (1) Is it based on truly veridical scoring criteria (as opposed to novelty psychometrics)? (2) Does it provide comprehensive coverage of the sampling domain of the construct (as opposed to a handful of convenient facets)? Unless these two questions can be answered in the affirmative, it is not worthwhile to embark on the psychometric journey to establish criterion, discriminant, predictive, and incremental validity, because ultimately construct validity will remain elusive.

What can be said with relative certainty is that the model of ability EI (Mayer & Salovey, 1997) with the MSCEIT as its operationalization vehicle is a scientific cul-de-sac, for the reasons previously discussed. Instead, a tendency is unfolding to relabel almost any test with emotional content that does not rely on self-report methodologies as a measure of ability EI. Not only are these tests often inadequate in terms of their coverage of the content domain of this construct, focusing as they do on a few narrow and specific facets, but they do not even seem to correlate strongly, either with the MSCEIT or among themselves (Austin, 2010; Matthews, Emo, Funke et al., 2006). Another important issue that will need to be addressed is that of the often intentional blurring of the difference between *intelligence, behavioral effectiveness,* and mere *declarative knowledge,* which plagues tests of ability EI (for promising research on this front, see Freudenthaler & Neubauer, 2005, 2007; Freudenthaler, Neubauer, & Haller, 2008).

## Trait Emotional Intelligence

As noted, trait emotional intelligence concerns a constellation of emotional self-perceptions located at the lower levels of personality hierarchies (Petrides, Pita et al., 2007). An alternative label to describe the construct is *trait emotional self-efficacy.* Simply put, trait EI concerns people's perceptions of their own emotional abilities. Trait EI theory provides an operationalization that recognizes the inherent subjectivity of emotional experience.

Most research in the field is conducted within the broader domain of trait EI. We hasten to add that not all of this research is interpreted accordingly. Indeed, it remains common for researchers to use self-report questionnaires and then to go on to interpret their findings with reference to concepts of ability, competencies, and skills from the pop-psychology perspective of "EQ is good for you." Useful as documents of such research may be from an empirical point of view, the only way in which they can be connected to mainstream science in differential psychology is if they are interpreted with full reference to trait EI theory.

The trait EI label reflects the fact that the various notions that have been discussed in the literature under the descriptions "emotional intelligence" or "EQ" (Bar-On, 1997; Goleman, 1995; Payne, 1985; Salovey & Mayer, 1990) invariably describe permutations of personality traits, such as empathy, emotional expression, adaptability, and self-control, which are psychometrically orthogonal (unrelated) to mental ability. It should be clear by now that, in the case of models that are operationalized via pseudo maximum-performance tests, this claim is invalid, while in the case of models that are operationalized via self-report questionnaires the claim is absurd. Trait EI theory offers a way to redefine the latter models in order to link them, and the measures based on them, to scientific theories of psychology.

### Right and wrong answers: adaptive value of trait EI

Trait EI theory maintains that certain emotion profiles will be advantageous in some contexts, but not in others. For example, being reserved and non-supportive is not a mark of emotional dimness, but is a personality trait that happens to be more adaptive than sociability and emotional expression in, say, research contexts (Rushton, Murray, & Paunonen, 1983). Assessment in the field of emotional and other *intelligences fausses* will not be dramatically different from assessment in the field of personality, where individuals' profiles have to be matched to specific job descriptions, with different job descriptions calling for different personality profiles (Pervin, 1968). It follows that no magic profile of the "emotionally intelligent" individual, who will excel in all aspects of life, exists.

The notion that there is some archetypal "emotionally intelligent" individual who can be identified by proprietary tests and whom all leaders, managers, and employees should strive to emulate in order to succeed is, in all likelihood, a myth. Emotions are known to distort human judgment and decision-making (Shafir & LeBoeuf, 2002), as well as basic reasoning processes (Oaksford, Morris, Grainger, & Williams, 1996). The simplistic notion that "EQ is good for you" is also likely a myth. Emotion-based thinking tends to be intuitive, automatic, with low scientific rigor and low detail in judgment, in contrast to a more consciously analytic thinking, which is low in emotional valence (Croskerry & Norman, 2008).

It is vital to remember that high trait EI scores are not necessarily adaptive and low scores are not necessarily maladaptive. First, very high scores on trait EI instruments may be indicative of hubris and self-promotion. Beyond this, there are contexts in which high scores can have undesirable consequences. For example, in Petrides and Furnham (2003) participants with high trait EI scores showed greater mood deterioration following the presentation of a short distressing video segment when compared to participants with low scores, while in Sevdalis, Petrides, and Harvey (2007) high scorers showed greater mood deterioration following the recall of a poor real-life decision. Moreover, low trait EI scorers are more likely than their high-scoring counterparts to be straightforward and less likely to be afflicted by a need for self-verification and image management. Especially when it comes to predicting behavior, the desirability of particular trait EI profiles will always depend on the context and type of behavior that one seeks to predict.

## The sampling domain of trait EI

Table 25.2 presents the sampling domain of trait EI (i.e. its constituent elements) that was derived from a content analysis of early models of EI and related constructs, such as alexithymia, affective communication, emotional expression, and empathy (Petrides, 2009). The aim was to include core elements common to more than a single model, but to exclude peripheral elements appearing in only one specific conceptualization. This is analogous to procedures used in classical psychometric scale development, whereby the commonalities (shared core) of the various items comprising a scale are carried over into a total (internally consistent) score, their random or unique components (noise) being cancelled out in the process. The systematic nature of this method is to be contrasted with the haphazard procedures on which other models are based, whereby the inclusion or exclusion of facets is typically the outcome of unstated decisions.

## Trait EI theory as a general interpretative framework

Self-report questionnaires of EI and cognate variables operationalize a construct that is unrelated to capabilities, competencies, and skills. Rather, as we have argued in Petrides, Pita et al. (2007), these questionnaires provide coverage, of variable quality

**Table 25.2**  The sampling domain of trait EI in adults

| Facets | High scorers view themselves as ... |
|---|---|
| Adaptability | ... flexible and willing to adapt to new conditions. |
| Assertiveness | ... forthright, frank, and willing to stand up for their rights. |
| Emotion expression | ... capable of communicating their feelings to others. |
| Emotion management (others) | ... capable of influencing other people's feelings. |
| Emotion perception (self and others) | ... clear about their own and other people's feelings. |
| Emotion regulation | ... capable of controlling their emotions. |
| Impulsiveness (low) | ... reflective and less likely to give in to their urges. |
| Relationships | ... capable of maintaining fulfilling personal relationships. |
| Self-esteem | ... successful and self-confident. |
| Self-motivation | ... driven and unlikely to give up in the face of adversity. |
| Social awareness | ... accomplished networkers with superior social skills. |
| Stress management | ... capable of withstanding pressure and regulating stress. |
| Trait empathy | ... capable of taking someone else's perspective. |
| Trait happiness | ... cheerful and satisfied with their lives. |
| Trait optimism | ... confident and likely to "look on the bright side" of life. |

and adequacy, of emotion-related personality traits. In other words, we view these questionnaires as measures of trait EI, in contrast to their authors, who claim that they assess intelligence, competencies, or skills.

Trait EI theory is general and provides a platform for the correct interpretation of data from any EI questionnaire that would otherwise be interpreted through the homespun "EQ is good for you" accounts underpinning many EI models. We emphasize that EI-related questionnaires can be considered measures of trait EI *only in so far as their results are interpreted through the lens of trait EI theory*. Consequently, we urge researchers and practitioners to abandon the mushrooming number of models emanating from commercial test user manuals, in favor of trait EI theory.

We also urge caution in relation to the instruments chosen to operationalize trait EI. Although any EI-related questionnaire can (and should) be interpreted from the perspective of trait EI theory, the designated vehicle for operationalizing the construct is the Trait Emotional Intelligence Questionnaire (TEIQue). This is important for two reasons. First, investigations of the criterion and predictive validity based on measures that provide incomplete coverage of trait EI (e.g. Bar-On, 1997; Schutte et al., 1998; Wong & Law, 2002) can be misleading, usually underestimating the true validity of the construct (Martins, Ramalho, & Morin, 2010). Second, the use of instruments with proven psychometric flaws (Grubb & McDaniel, 2008) and messy factor structures (Gignac, Palmer, Manocha, & Stough, 2005; Palmer, Manocha, Gignac, & Stough, 2003) impedes the accumulation of evidence and the development of a nomological network, even when the results are appropriately interpreted with reference to trait EI theory.

## Trait emotional intelligence questionnaire (TEIQue)

The explosion in the number of trait EI measures may have given the impression that the construction of psychometrically sound instruments is an easy business. Anyone cognizant of the basic elements of psychometrics, particularly those relating to the validation process, understands that this is not the case. The fact is that few trait EI measures have been developed within a clear theoretical framework, and even fewer have solid empirical foundations. Indicative of the confusion in the field is the fact that most self-report questionnaires purport to measure EI as a cognitive ability. Such instruments are suitable neither for scientific inquiry nor for use in applied settings.

The TEIQue is predicated on trait EI theory, as described above. The latest version of the full form of the instrument comprises 153 items, providing scores on 15 facets, 4 factors, and global trait EI (see Plate 7). The TEIQue should be preferred over other EI-related questionnaires for three main reasons: first, it offers a direct route to the underlying theory of trait emotional intelligence; second, it provides comprehensive coverage of the trait EI sampling domain; and, third, it has greater predictive validity. Indeed, every study that has compared the TEIQue to other EI questionnaires has concluded that it has superior predictive validity and superior psychometric properties more generally (Freudenthaler, Neubauer, Gabler, & Scherl, 2008; Gardner & Qualter, 2010; Martins et al., 2010).

The TEIQue is based on a combination of the construct-oriented and inductive approaches to scale construction (Hough & Paullin, 1994) and has hitherto been translated into over 15 languages. It was designed to be factor-analyzed at the facet level in order to avoid the problems associated with item factor analysis (Bernstein & Teng, 1989). Its higher-order structure is explicitly hypothesized as oblique, in line with conceptions of multifaceted constructs. Consequently, factor overlap as well as cross-loadings are to be expected, and indeed they provide the justification for aggregating factor scores into global trait EI. According to the hierarchical structure of the TEIQue, the facets are narrower than the factors, which, in turn, are narrower than global trait EI.

Detailed psychometric analyses of the full form of the TEIQue are presented in Freudenthaler, Neubauer, Gabler et al. (2008; German adaptation), in Mikolajczak, Luminet, Leroy, and Roy (2007; French adaptation), and in Petrides (2009; English original). In addition to the full form, there are other TEIQue instruments, which we briefly describe below.

*TEIQue–short form*    This 30-item form is based on the full form and includes two items from each of the 15 facets of the TEIQue. Items were selected primarily on the basis of their correlations with the corresponding total facet scores, which ensured broad coverage of the sampling domain. The –SF can be used in research designs with limited experimental time, or wherein trait EI is a peripheral variable. Although it is possible to derive scores on the four trait EI factors, in addition to the global score, these tend to have lower internal consistencies (around .69) than in the full form. The –SF does not yield scores on the 15 trait EI facets. An Item Response Theory analysis of the short form of the inventory is presented in Cooper and Petrides (2010).

*TEIQue 360° and 360°–short*   These forms are used for collecting observer ratings and are available for both the full and the short forms of the TEIQue. They are especially useful for deriving rated (observation-based) trait EI profiles.

*TEIQue–adolescent form*   The –AF is modeled on the full form of the TEIQue and is intended to yield scores on the same facets and factors. The main target audience is adolescents between 13 and 17 years. Preliminary data (Petrides, 2009) suggest that its internal consistencies are strong at the facet, factor, and global level, although they are somewhat lower than the corresponding values of the full form.

*TEIQue–adolescent short form*   This is a simplified version, in terms of wording and syntactic complexity, of the adult short form of the TEIQue. The –ASF comprises 30 short statements, two for each of the 15 facets in Table 25.2 designed to measure global trait EI. In addition to the global score, it is possible to derive scores on the four trait EI factors; however, these tend to have considerably lower internal consistency than in the adolescent full form. This form does not yield scores on the 15 trait EI facets. The main target audience is adolescents between 13 and 17 years; however, the –ASF has been successfully used with children as young as 11 years. Example applications of the –ASF can be found in Mavroveli, Petrides, Rieffe, and Bakker (2007) and in Ferrando et al. (2010).

*TEIQue–child form*   The main aim of the –CF is to assess the emotion-related facets of child personality. Rather than a simple adaptation of the adult form, this variant is based on a sampling domain that has been specifically developed for children aged between 8 and 12 years. The children's sampling domain is presented, along with brief descriptions of the facets, in Table 25.3. It comprises 75 items, responded to on a 5-point scale, and measuring nine distinct facets (see Mavroveli, Petrides, Shove, & Whitehead, 2008).

## Location of trait EI in personality factor space

Petrides, Pita et al. (2007) carried out studies in order to locate trait EI in Eysenckian "Giant Three" and in Big-Five factor space. Locating trait EI in personality space is important, not least because we can thus connect the construct to the personality literature. Theorists who propose new individual differences constructs must demonstrate how these relate to extant knowledge in the field. This has been a major objective of our definition and development of trait EI. Furthermore, establishing the location of trait EI within existing taxonomies can provide empirical support for the construct's discriminant validity vis-à-vis the higher-order traits. If a distinct trait EI factor can be isolated in personality space, it means that a sufficient number of trait EI facets share enough common variance to define a separate factor in joint

**Table 25.3**   The sampling domain of trait EI in children

| Facets | Brief description | Example items |
|---|---|---|
| Adaptability | Concerns children's self-perceptions of how well they adapt to new situations and people. | "I find it hard to get used to a new school year." |
| Affective disposition | Concerns children's self-perceptions of the frequency and intensity with which they experience emotions. | "I'm a very happy kid." |
| Emotion expression | Concerns children's self-perceptions of how effectively they can express their emotions. | "I always find the words to show how I feel." |
| Emotion perception | Concerns children's self-perceptions of how accurately they identify their own and others' emotions. | "It's easy for me to understand how I feel." |
| Emotion regulation | Concerns children's self-perceptions of how well they can control their emotions. | "I can control my anger." |
| Low impulsivity | Concerns children's self-perceptions of how effectively they can control themselves. | "I don't like waiting to get what I want." |
| Peer relations | Concerns children's self-perceptions of the quality of their relationships with their classmates. | "I listen to other children's problems." |
| Self-esteem | Concerns children's self-perceptions of their self-worth. | "I feel great about myself." |
| Self-motivation | Concerns children's self-perceptions of their drive and motivation. | "I always try to become better at school." |

analyses with the "giant three" or the Big Five, which constitutes evidence of discriminant validity.

The results of the factor location analyses in Petrides, Pita et al. (2007) demonstrate that trait EI is a *distinct* (because it can be isolated in personality space) and *compound* (because it is partially determined by several personality dimensions) construct that lies at the *lower levels* of personality hierarchies (because the trait EI factor is oblique, rather than orthogonal to the Giant Three and the Big Five). This conclusion enables us to connect the trait emotional self-efficacy conceptualization of EI to the differential psychology literature: a major conceptual advantage, which integrates the construct into established models of personality. Moreover, this conceptualization appears to be consistent not only with hierarchical, but also with circumplex models of personality. Thus De Raad (2005) located trait EI within the abridged Big-Five circumplex and found that it comprises scattered aspects of the Big-Five domain and correlates with at least four of the five higher-order dimensions, conclusions that are fully in line with trait EI theory.

Recent research has established that the phenotypic correlations between trait EI and the Big-Five personality dimensions are attributable, primarily, to correlated genetic factors and, secondarily, to correlated non-shared environmental factors (Vernon, Villani, Schermer, & Petrides, 2008). This means that many of the genes that are responsible for the development of individual differences in the Big Five are also responsible for the development of individual differences in trait EI. Related studies have estimated the heritable proportion of global trait EI at about 40 percent, which is very similar to the estimates obtained for other broad bandwidth personality traits (Johnson, Vernon, & Feiler, 2008). Taken together, these findings provide solid support for the conceptualization of EI as a personality trait.

Trait EI theory is also relevant to the emerging literature on the general factor of personality (GFP; Figueredo & Rushton, 2009; Hofstee, 2001; Rushton & Irwing, 2009). In relation to research with the TEIQue, it has been shown that a general factor can be extracted from joint data sets with the HEXACO (Veselka, Schermer, Petrides, Cherkas et al., 2009) as well as with the NEO PI–R (Veselka, Schermer, Petrides, & Vernon, 2009). The fact that a GFP can be extracted from TEIQue data sets corroborates the view that EI ought to be integrated into multi-level personality hierarchies, somewhere between the highly specific traits at their base and the broad general factor at their apex (Petrides, Pita et al., 2007; Rushton et al., 2009).

## Applications of Trait Emotional Intelligence

Trait EI research has expanded significantly during the last few years. Recent data from children, adolescent, and adult samples show that trait EI scores predict teacher and peer ratings of prosocial and antisocial behavior (Mavroveli et al., 2007; Petrides, Frederickson, & Furnham, 2004; Petrides, Sangareau, Furnham, & Frederickson, 2006), adaptive coping styles and depressive affect (Mavroveli et al., 2007), leadership (Villanueva & Sanchez, 2007), happiness (Chamorro-Premuzic, Bennett, & Furnham, 2007), emotion regulation (Mikolajczak, Nelis, Hansenne, & Quoidbach, 2008), and affective decision-making (Sevdalis et al., 2007). A growing number of studies have revealed incremental trait EI effects over and above the higher-order personality dimensions (e.g. Kluemper, 2008; Petrides, Pita et al., 2007; Van Der Zee & Wabeke, 2004) and other emotion-related variables, such as alexithymia, optimism, and mood (Mikolajczak, Luminet, & Menil, 2006; Petrides, Pérez-González, & Furnham, 2007).

In the section that follows, we briefly discuss example applications of trait EI theory in organizational, clinical, health, educational, and social settings. A surge in the use of TEIQue specifically, and in the interpretation of other questionnaires from the perspective of trait EI theory more generally, means that it is now impossible to provide anything but a sketchy outline of relevant research in applied contexts. For continually updated material and developments, see www.psychometriclab.com.

### Organizational

One of the primary drivers of the initial spontaneous excitement about EI was the promise that it may be even more important than IQ in its ability to predict job performance (Goleman, 1995). On the basis of research conducted since then, it seems clear that its role in the workplace has been exaggerated in popular literature (Caruso & Salovey, 2004; Goleman, 1998). What little robust research has been carried out on this topic has revealed trait EI effects that are narrow and specific rather than broad and general, in line with the effects that other personality traits have in such contexts (Chamorro-Premuzic & Furnham, 2010). In organizational as in other domains, the relevance of trait EI in general and, more specifically, of the particular profile that will be conducive to superior performance will vary as a function of the context, and will therefore ideally require customized task analysis (Petrides & Furnham, 2003; Zeidner, Matthews, & Roberts, 2004).

In an early meta-analysis, Van Rooy and Visvesvaran (2004) reported a sample weighted mean correlation between EI and job performance of $\rho = .24$, although that research was not conducted in the context of the trait- versus ability-EI distinction. More recent studies have found that high trait EI is associated with lower levels of stress and higher levels of perceived job control, job satisfaction, and job commitment (Petrides & Furnham, 2006; Platsidou, 2010; Singh & Woods, 2008). Other research has suggested that high trait EI may be conducive to entrepreneurial behavior (Zampetakis, Beldekos, & Moustakis, 2009), protects against burnout (Platsidou, 2010; Singh & Woods, 2008), and predicts internal work locus of control (Johnson, Batey, & Holdsworth, 2009).

Perhaps more than any other topic, that of the links between trait EI and organizational performance requires more research, which should be predicated on theoretically driven hypotheses and comprehensive measures of the construct. Such research could also address the relevant topic of improving (from the perspective of trait EI theory, *optimizing*) EI, which is of particular interest in organizational contexts and on which there is a dearth of evidence (see Nelis, Quoidbach, Mikolajczak, & Hansenne, 2009, for an exception).

## Clinical

Trait EI, as operationalized by the TEIQue, is a very strong predictor of clinical variables. A lot of research is being carried out in clinical settings, and in this section we present indicative findings from only a few relevant studies. Petrides, Pérez-González et al. (2007) examined the possibility that very low trait EI levels may have psychopathological consequences. This study was conducted with reference to the personality disorders (PDs) in the 10th revision of the International Classification of Diseases (ICD–10; WHO, 1992). It was found that trait EI scores were negatively related to PDs, the relationships holding up after partialing out individual differences in dispositional mood (positive and negative affect), which are linked to psychopathology (Watson, 2000).

Other research along this line has corroborated the negative relationships between trait EI and various indicators of psychopathology (Leible & Snell, 2004; Malterer, Glass, & Newman, 2008). A notable recent study employed a small-scale longitudinal research design examining the effects of EI on psychopathology across the transition from primary to secondary school. The results showed that measures of trait EI were strong predictors of psychopathology (in contrast to measures of ability EI), concurrently as well as prospectively (notwithstanding an erroneous interpretation in the abstract; Williams, Daley, Burnside, & Hammond-Rowley, 2010a).

Mikolajczak, Petrides, and Hurry (2009) investigated the relationships between trait EI and self-harm in adolescence. Adolescents who deliberately harm themselves have become the focus of concerted research because of their greatly increased risk of suicide (Hawton & Zahl, 2003), but also because of the association between self-harm and a range of psychological disorders (Hurry, 2000).

The correlation between trait EI and self-harm in Mikolajczak et al.'s (2009) sample, which comprised 490 high-school students (mean age = 16.65 years; 57.3 percent girls), was negative and highly significant ($r = -.31$, $p < .01$). A probit regression analysis indicated that the likelihood of a self-harming adolescent is 75 percent if their TEIQue score is below 2.47, 50 percent if their TEIQue score is above 3.47, and only 25 percent if their TEIQue score is above 4.50.

## Health

There are many theoretical reasons to expect that trait EI will be related to both psychological and physical health (Austin, Parker, Petrides, & Saklofske, 2008). This is reflected in the large number of studies conducted in this area, which have been summarized in two meta-analyses (Martins et al., 2010; and Schutte, Malouff, Thorsteinsson, Bhullar, & Rooke, 2007). Overall, trait EI is a strong positive predictor of mental health and well-being (Johnson et al., 2009; Platsidou, 2010; Saklofske et al., 2003) and a negative predictor of psychopathology (Gardner & Qualter, 2009; Williams, Daley, Burnside, & Hammond-Rowley, 2010b).

Trait EI has been implicated in physical health, including in positive relationships with self-rated physical health (Tsaousis & Nikolaou, 2005) and in negative relationships with somatic complaints (Mavroveli et al., 2007). A range of associations has also been reported with health-related behaviors (for example, Saklofske, Austin, Rohr, & Andrews, 2007 found that trait EI has a significant, albeit weak, correlation with taking exercise). Related research has revealed links with addictive behaviors, ranging from gambling and Internet addiction (Parker, Taylor, Eastabrook, Schell, & Wood, 2008), to alcohol dependency (Austin, Saklofske, & Egan, 2005; Uva et al., 2010), and ecstasy use (Craig, Fisk, Montgomery, Murphy, & Wareing, 2010).

## Educational

Trait EI affects, directly or indirectly, a very wide range of variables in educational contexts. For example, high trait EI pupils tend to have fewer unauthorized absences and are less likely to have been expelled from school due to rule violations, in comparison to their low trait EI peers (Mavroveli et al., 2008; Petrides et al., 2004). Trait EI also influences children's peer relations at school (Petrides et al., 2006) and decreases the likelihood of aggressive and delinquent behavior (Santesso, Reker, Schmidt, & Segalowitz, 2006).

Trait EI theory posits that the construct will not show strong direct associations with cognitive ability or its close proxies, for instance academic performance. Indeed,

Petrides et al. (2004) did not find any such associations, although they demonstrated a moderating effect, according to which trait EI was positively related to performance in low-IQ pupils only. On this basis, they suggested that such effects as trait EI might have on academic performance are likely to assume prominence when the demands of a situation outweigh a pupil's intellectual resources. In contrast to their high-IQ counterparts, low-IQ pupils are more likely to be forced to draw on resources other than their cognitive ability in order to cope with the demands of their courses, which is why high trait EI may be an important asset for them.

Parker and colleagues (Parker, Summerfeldt, Hogan, & Majeski, 2004; Parker, Creque et al., 2004) reported modest correlations (e.g. $r = .20$, $p < .05$) between trait EI and academic performance in high school and university samples, raising the possibility that trait EI effects may vary across educational levels as well as across subjects, like the effects of other personality traits (e.g. Heaven, Ciarrochi, & Vialle, 2007). For example, Laidra, Pullmann, and Allik (2007) showed that agreeableness was an important predictor of academic performance (Grade Point Average) in primary school, but not in secondary school children. In contrast, neuroticism in their study predicted academic performance in secondary, but not primary, school-children. Overall, the picture emerging so far is consistent with the postulates of trait EI theory, indicating that the construct's impact on academic achievement is modest and likely to be more relevant to specific groups of vulnerable children (see Mavroveli & Sanchez-Ruiz, in press, for a comprehensive review).

## Social

Petrides et al. (2006) found that high trait EI facilitated prosocial and prevented antisocial behavior in children of primary school age. They also reported that pupils with high scores received more nominations from their classmates for being coopera-tive and for having leadership qualities, and fewer nominations for being disruptive, aggressive, and dependent. Similar results have been obtained in samples from dif-ferent countries and age groups (Mavroveli, Petrides, Sangareau, & Furnham, 2009; Mavroveli et al., 2007).

Significant research looking into the links between trait EI and interpersonal rela-tionships in adults has also been conducted. Examples include positive relationships with marital satisfaction, relationship quality, and constructive communication between partners, and negative relationships with detrimental communication pat-terns, including mutual avoidance and withholding (Schutte et al., 2001; Smith, Ciarrochi, & Heaven, 2008; Smith, Heaven, & Ciarrochi, 2008).

## Experimental Studies in Trait EI

Research has increasingly explored the role of trait EI in laboratory contexts, con-tributing toward the ultimate goal of integrating the experimental and correlational approaches to psychological science. Such is the level of activity that it cannot be meaningfully reviewed in this chapter. Rather, we briefly summarize promising find-ings from a few representative studies.

Mikolajczak, Bodarwe, Laloyaux, Hansenne, and Nelis (2010) provided impressive evidence of a relationship between individual differences in trait EI and differential frontal cortex activation. More specifically, high trait EI individuals showed significantly greater resting left frontal activation, which accords well with findings that left-frontal asymmetry is positively related to social competence and negatively related to shyness (Schmidt, 1999).

A number of studies have also demonstrated protective effects of trait EI vis-à-vis stress. For example, Mikolajczak and Luminet (2008) showed that high trait EI individuals are both more likely to appraise stressful events as challenges (as opposed to threats) and more confident that they can deal with such events. Furthermore, Mikolajczak, Roy, Luminet, Fillee, and de Timary (2007) found that high trait EI participants showed both less psychological reactivity (mood deterioration) and less physiological reactivity (salivary cortisol) in comparison with their low trait EI counterparts when exposed to a stressor (public speech task; see also Ciarrochi, Deane, & Anderson, 2002; Mikolajczak, Menil, & Luminet, 2007).

Austin (2004) explored the relationships between trait EI and performance on various experimental tasks, showing that certain (interpersonal) aspects of the construct correlated with performance on inspection time tasks involving emotional content. Within the same experimental paradigm, but using a different criterion, Austin (2009) found that global trait EI has an inverted U relationship with reaction times for responses to questionnaire items.

As noted, much more experimental research than we have been able to summarize has been conducted. Most of it has a strong theoretical basis, and its results have virtually always identified significant and meaningful trait EI effects. Going into the future, the sheer number of different criteria and the variations in the experimental methodologies across the various studies necessitate a two-fold focus on replication and on the systematic selection of criteria, in order to remove, as far as is possible, gratuitous sources of variation between studies.

## Extending the theory of trait emotional intelligence

Trait EI theory explains how the various EI models, where they are meaningful, mainly refer to established personality traits. It can be extended to cover other *intelligences fausses*, including in the first instance the intra-personal, interpersonal, and social. Focusing on personality traits related to emotions yields emotional "intelligence," focusing on traits related to social behavior yields social "intelligence," and so on. Through this strategy, the *intelligences fausses* can be integrated into existing personality taxonomies, which is where they belong conceptually.

In addition to linking the *intelligences fausses* to mainstream differential psychology, the trait intelligences framework offers concrete predictive and especially explanatory advantages. Carving up personality variance across specific content domains helps contextualize it, thus increasing its explanatory power. Instead of trying to explain findings on the basis of five broad and theoretically—yet not necessarily empirically—orthogonal personality dimensions, one relies on domain-specific, content-coherent constructs (see Petrides & Furnham, 2003).

The *trait intelligences* label emphasizes the aim of integrating the *intelligences fausses* into personality hierarchies, while the alternative, and in some respects preferable, labels of *trait self-efficacies* and *trait self-concepts* emphasize the aim of integrating the social–cognitive (Bandura, 2001) and self-concept literatures (Marsh, Trautwein, Ludtke, Koller, & Baumert, 2006) into the said hierarchies. Hitherto our research has focused on the former aim, even though the integration of the latter two literatures is possibly of greater interest, on account of their scientific origins and broader scope (Pervin, 1999).

Emotions are but a single, albeit fundamental, domain of personality, and it will be necessary to extend trait EI theory to encompass other important domains (e.g. social, personal, and meta-cognitive). The realization of this aim holds promise for the integration of self-concept, self-efficacy, and *intelligences fausses* models into the mainstream taxonomies of personality.

# Note

1 The distinction between trait EI and ability EI is based on the method used to measure the construct and *not* on the elements (facets) that the various models are hypothesized to encompass. It is, therefore, unrelated to the distinction between "mixed" and "ability" models of EI (Mayer, Salovey, & Caruso, 2000), which is based on whether a theoretical model "mixes" cognitive abilities and personality traits. Mayer et al.'s (2000) distinction is at odds both with psychometric theory, because it ignores the importance of measurement, and with the data, which clearly show that measures of trait EI intercorrelate strongly, irrespective of whether or not they are based on "mixed" or "ability" models. Also worth noting is that there is little evidence that some of the sub-scales of these measures have ability characteristics, while others have trait characteristics; in fact, all subscales clearly and consistently operate as personality traits.

# References

Amelang, M., & Steinmayr, R. (2006). Is there a validity increment for tests of emotional intelligence in explaining the variance of performance criteria? *Intelligence, 34,* 459–468.

Austin, E. J. (2004). An investigation of the relationship between trait emotional intelligence and emotional task performance. *Personality and Individual Differences, 36,* 1855–1864.

Austin, E. J. (2009). A reaction time study of responses to trait and ability emotional intelligence test items. *Personality and Individual Differences, 46,* 381–383.

Austin, E. J. (2010). Measurement of ability emotional intelligence: Results for two new tests. *British Journal of Psychology, 101,* 563–578.

Austin, E. J., Saklofske, D. H., & Egan, V. (2005). Personality, well-being and health correlates of trait emotional intelligence. *Personality and Individual Differences, 38,* 547–558.

Austin, E. J., Parker, J. D. A., Petrides, K. V., & Saklofske, D. H. (2008). Emotional intelligence. In G. J. Boyle, G. Matthews, & D. H. Saklofske (Eds.), *The SAGE handbook of personality theory and testing: Vol. 1. Personality theories and models* (pp. 576–596). Thousand Oaks, CA: Sage.

Bandura, A. (2001). Social cognitive theory: An agentic perspective. *Annual Review of Psychology, 52*, 1–26.

Barchard, K. A., & Russell, J. A. (2006). Bias in consensus scoring, with examples from ability emotional intelligence tests. *Psicothema, 18*, 49–54.

Bar-On, R. (1997). *Bar-On Emotional Quotient Inventory: Technical manual.* Toronto: Multi-Health Systems Inc.

Bernstein, I. H., & Teng, G. (1989). Factoring items and factoring scales are different: Spurious evidence for multidimensionality due to item categorization. *Psychological Bulletin, 105*, 167–177.

Brannick, M. T., Wahi, M. M., Arce, M., & Johnson, H. A. (2009). Comparison of trait and ability measures of emotional intelligence in medical students. *Medical Education, 43*, 1062–1068.

Brody, N. (2004). What cognitive intelligence is and what emotional intelligence is not. *Psychological Inquiry, 15*, 234–238.

Caruso, D. R., & Salovey, P. (2004). *The emotionally intelligent manager: How to develop and use the four key emotional skills of leadership.* San Francisco, CA: Jossey-Bass.

Chamorro-Premuzic, T., & Furnham, A. (2010). *The psychology of personnel selection.* Cambridge: Cambridge University Press.

Chamorro-Premuzic, T., Bennett, E., & Furnham, A. (2007). The happy personality: Mediational role of trait emotional intelligence. *Personality and Individual Differences, 42*, 1633–1639.

Ciarrochi, J. V., Deane, F. P., & Anderson, S. (2002). Emotional intelligence moderates the relationship between stress and mental health. *Personality and Individual Differences, 32*, 197–209.

Cooper, A., & Petrides, K. V. (2010). A psychometric analysis of the Trait Emotional Intelligence Questionnaire–Short Form (TEIQue–SF) using item response theory. *Journal of Personality Assessment, 92*, 449–457.

Craig, L., Fisk, J. E., Montgomery, C., Murphy, P. N., & Wareing, M. (2010). Is emotional intelligence impaired in ecstasy-polydrug users? *Journal of Psychopharmacology, 24*, 221–231.

Cronbach, L. J. (1949). *Essentials of psychological testing.* New York: Harper & Row.

Croskerry, P., & Norman, G. (2008). Overconfidence in clinical decision making. *American Journal of Medicine, 121*, S24–S29.

De Raad, B. (2005). The trait-coverage of emotional intelligence. *Personality and Individual Differences, 38*, 673–687.

Devonish, D., & Greenidge, D. (2010). The effect of organizational justice on contextual performance, counterproductive work behaviors, and task performance: Investigating the moderating role of ability-based emotional intelligence. *International Journal of Selection and Assessment, 18*, 75–86.

Ferrando, M., Prieto, M. D., Almeida, L. S., Ferrándiz, C., Bermejo, R., López-Pina, J. A., Hernández, D., Sáinz, M., & Fernández, M.-C. (2010). *Trait emotional intelligence and academic performance: Moderating effects of IQ, personality and self-concept.* Manuscript submitted for publication.

Figueredo, A. J., & Rushton, J. P. (2009). Evidence for shared genetic dominance between the general factor of personality, mental and physical health, and life history traits. *Twin Research and Human Genetics, 12*, 555–563.

Follesdal, H., & Hagtvet, K. A. (2009). Emotional intelligence: The MSCEIT from the perspective of generalizability theory. *Intelligence, 37*, 94–105.

Freudenthaler, H. H., & Neubauer, A. C. (2005). Emotional intelligence: The convergent and discriminant validities of intra- and interpersonal emotional abilities. *Personality and Individual Differences, 39,* 569–579.

Freudenthaler, H. H., & Neubauer, A. C. (2007). Measuring emotional management abilities: Further evidence of the importance to distinguish between typical and maximum performance. *Personality and Individual Differences, 42,* 1561–1572.

Freudenthaler, H. H., Neubauer, A. C., & Haller, U. (2008). Emotional intelligence: Instruction effects and sex differences in emotional management abilities. *Journal of Individual Differences, 29,* 105–115.

Freudenthaler, H. H., Neubauer, A. C., Gabler, P., & Scherl, W. G. (2008). Testing the Trait Emotional Intelligence Questionnaire (TEIQue) in a German-speaking sample. *Personality and Individual Differences, 45,* 673–678.

Gardner, H. (1999). *Intelligence reframed: Multiple intelligences for the 21st century.* New York: Basic Books.

Gardner, K., & Qualter, P. (2009). Emotional intelligence and Borderline personality disorder. *Personality and Individual Differences, 47,* 94–98.

Gardner, J. K., & Qualter, P. (2010). Concurrent and incremental validity of three trait emotional intelligence measures. *Australian Journal of Psychology, 62,* 5–13.

Gibbs, N. (1995, October 2). The EQ factor. *Time,* 60–68.

Gignac, G. E., Palmer, B. R., Manocha, R., & Stough, C. (2005). An examination of the factor structure of the schutte self-report emotional intelligence (SSREI) scale via confirmatory factor analysis. *Personality and Individual Differences, 39,* 1029–1042.

Goleman, D. (1995). *Emotional intelligence: Why it can matter more than IQ.* London: Bloomsbury.

Goleman, D. (1998). *Working with emotional intelligence.* London: Bloomsbury.

Grubb, W. L., & McDaniel, M. A. (2008). The fakability of Bar-On's Emotional Quotient Inventory Short Form: Catch me if you can. *Human Performance, 20,* 43–59.

Hawton, K., & Zahl, D. L. (2003). Suicide following deliberate self-harm: Long-term follow-up of patients who presented to a general hospital. *British Journal of Psychiatry, 182,* 537–542.

Heaven, P. C. L., Ciarrochi, J., & Vialle, W. (2007). Conscientiousness and Eysenckian psychoticism as predictors of school grades: A one-year longitudinal study. *Personality and Individual Differences, 42,* 535–546.

Hofstee, W. K. B. (2001). Personality and intelligence: Do they mix? In J. M. Collis & S. Messick (Eds.), *Intelligence and personality: Bridging the gap in theory and measurement* (pp. 43–60). Mahwah, NJ: Lawrence Erlbaum Associates.

Hough, L. M., & Paullin, C. (1994). Construct-oriented scale construction: The rational approach. In G. S. Stokes, M. D. Mumford, & W. A. Owens (Eds.), *The biodata handbook: Theory, research, and use of biographical information in selection and performance prediction* (pp. 109–145). Palo Alto, CA: Consulting Psychologists Press, Inc.

Hurry, J. (2000). Deliberate self-harm in children and adults. *International Review of Psychiatry, 12,* 31–36.

Jensen, A. R. (1998). *The g factor: The science of mental ability.* Westport, CT: Praeger.

Johnson, A. M., Vernon, P. A., & Feiler, A. R. (2008). Behavioral genetic studies of personality: An introduction and review of the results of 50+ years of research. In G. Boyle, G. Matthews, & D. Saklofske (Eds.), *Handbook of personality and testing.* Thousand Oaks, CA: Sage.

Johnson, S. J., Batey, M., & Holdsworth, L. (2009). Personality and health: The mediating role of trait emotional intelligence and work locus of control. *Personality and Individual Differences, 47,* 470–475.

Keele, S. M., & Bell, R. C. (2008). The factorial validity of emotional intelligence: An unresolved issue. *Personality and Individual Differences, 44,* 487–500.

Keele, S. M., & Bell, R. C. (2009). Consensus scoring, correct responses and reliability of the MSCEIT v.2. *Personality and Individual Differences, 47,* 740–747.

Kluemper, D. H. (2008). Trait emotional intelligence: The impact of core-self evaluations and social desirability. *Personality and Individual Differences, 44,* 1402–1412.

Laidra, K., Pullmann, H., & Allik, J. (2007). Personality and intelligence as predictors of academic achievement: A cross-sectional study from elementary to secondary school. *Personality and Individual Differences, 42,* 441–451.

Leible, T. L., & Snell, W. E. (2004). Borderline personality disorder and multiple aspects of emotional intelligence. *Personality and Individual Differences, 37,* 393–404.

Leuner, B. (1966). Emotionale Intelligenz und Emanzipation. [Emotional intelligence and emancipation.]. *Praxis der Kinderpsychologie und Kinderpsychiatrie, 15,* 196–203.

Locke, E. A. (2005). Why emotional intelligence is an invalid concept. *Journal of Organizational Behavior, 26,* 425–431.

MacCann, C., & Roberts, R. D. (2008). New paradigms for assessing emotional intelligence: Theory and data. *Emotion, 8,* 540–551.

Malterer, M. B., Glass, S. J., & Newman, J. P. (2008). Psychopathy and trait emotional intelligence. *Personality and Individual Differences, 44,* 735–745.

Marsh, H. W., Trautwein, U., Ludtke, O., Koller, O., & Baumert, J. (2006). Integration of multidimensional self-concept and core personality constructs: Construct validation and relations to well-being and achievement. *Journal of Personality, 74,* 403–456.

Martins, A., Ramalho, N., & Morin, E. (2010). A comprehensive meta-analysis of the relationship between emotional intelligence and health. *Personality and Individual Differences, 49,* 554–564.

Matthews, G., Zeidner, M., & Roberts, R. D. (2007). Emotional intelligence: Consensus, controversies, and questions. In G. Matthews, M. Zeidner, & R. D. Roberts (Eds.), *The science of emotional intelligence: Knowns and unknowns* (pp. 3–46). Oxford: Oxford University Press.

Matthews, G., Emo, A. K., Roberts, R. D., & Zeidner, M. (2006). What is this thing called emotional intelligence? In K. R. Murphy (Ed.), *A critique of emotional intelligence: What are the problems and how can they be fixed?* (pp. 3–36). Mahwah, NJ: Lawrence Erlbaum Associates.

Matthews, G., Emo, A. K., Funke, G., Zeidner, M., Roberts, R. D., Costa, P. T., Jr., & Schulze, R. (2006). Emotional intelligence, personality, and task-induced stress. *Journal of Experimental Psychology: Applied, 12,* 96–107.

Mavroveli, S., & Sanchez-Ruiz, M.-J. (in press). Trait emotional intelligence influences on academic performance and school behavior. *British Journal of Educational Psychology.*

Mavroveli, S., Petrides, K. V., Rieffe, C., & Bakker, F. (2007). Trait emotional intelligence, psychological well-being and peer-rated social competence in adolescence. *British Journal of Developmental Psychology, 25,* 263–275.

Mavroveli, S., Petrides, K. V., Sangareau, Y., & Furnham, A. (2009). Relating trait emotional intelligence to objective socioemotional outcomes in childhood. *British Journal of Educational Psychology, 79,* 259–272.

Mavroveli, S., Petrides, K. V., Shove, C., & Whitehead, A. (2008). Validation of the construct of trait emotional intelligence in children. *European Child and Adolescent Psychiatry, 17,* 516–526.

Mayer, J. D., & Salovey, P. (1997). What is emotional intelligence? In P. Salovey & D. Sluyter (Eds.), *Emotional development and emotional intelligence: Educational implications* (pp. 3–31). New York: Basic Books.

Mayer, J. D., Caruso, D. R., & Salovey, P. (1999). Emotional intelligence meets traditional standards for an intelligence. *Intelligence, 27*, 267–298.

Mayer, J. D., Salovey, P., & Caruso, D. R. (2000). Models of emotional intelligence. In R. J. Sternberg (Ed.), *Handbook of human intelligence* (pp. 396–420). New York: Cambridge University Press.

Mayer, J. D., Salovey, P., & Caruso, D. R. (2002). *Mayer–Salovey–Caruso Emotional Intelligence Test (MSCEIT): User's manual.* Toronto, Ontario: Multi-Health Systems, Inc.

Mikolajczak, M., Bodarwe, K., Laloyaux, O., Hansenne, M., & Nelis, D. (2010). Association between frontal EEG asymmetries and emotional intelligence among adults. *Personality and Individual Differences, 48*, 177–181.

Mikolajczak, M., & Luminet, O. (2008). Trait emotional intelligence and the cognitive appraisal of stressful events: An exploratory study. *Personality and Individual Differences, 44*, 1445–1453.

Mikolajczak, M., Luminet, O., Leroy, C., & Roy, E. (2007). Psychometric properties of the Trait Emotional Intelligence Questionnaire (TEIQue; Petrides & Furnham, 2003). *Journal of Personality Assessment, 88*, 338–353.

Mikolajczak, M., Luminet, O., & Menil, C. (2006). Predicting resistance to stress: Incremental validity of trait emotional intelligence over alexithymia and optimism. *Psicothema, 18*, 79–88.

Mikolajczak, M., Menil, C., & Luminet, O. (2007). Explaining the protective effect of trait emotional intelligence regarding occupational stress: Exploration of emotional labour processes. *Journal of Research in Personality, 41*, 1107–1117.

Mikolajczak, M., Nelis, D., Hansenne, M., & Quoidbach, J. (2008). If you can regulate sadness, you can probably regulate shame: Associations between trait emotional intelligence, emotion regulation and coping efficiency across discrete emotions. *Personality and Individual Differences, 44*, 1356–1368.

Mikolajczak, M., Petrides, K. V., & Hurry, J. (2009). Adolescents choosing self-harm as an emotion regulation strategy: the protective role of trait emotional intelligence. *British Journal of Clinical Psychology, 48*, 181–193.

Mikolajczak, M., Roy, E., Luminet, O., Fillee, C., & de Timary, P. (2007). The moderating impact of emotional intelligence on free cortisol responses to stress. *Psychoneuroendocrinology, 32*, 1000–1012.

Nelis, D., Quoidbach, J., Mikolajczak, M., & Hansenne, M. (2009). Increasing emotional intelligence: (How) is it possible? *Personality and Individual Differences, 47*, 36–41.

O'Sullivan, M. (2007). Trolling for trout, trawling for tuna: The methodological morass in measuring emotional intelligence. In G. Matthews, M. Zeidner, & R. Roberts (Eds.), *Emotional intelligence: Knowns and unknowns* (pp. 258–287). Oxford: Oxford University Press.

O'Sullivan, M., & Ekman, P. (2004). Facial expression recognition and emotional intelligence. In G. Geher (Ed.), *Measuring emotional intelligence: Common ground and controversy* (pp. 91–111). Hauppauge, NY: Nova Science Publishing.

Oaksford, M., Morris, F., Grainger, B., & Williams, J. M. G. (1996). Mood, reasoning, and central executive processes. *Journal of Experimental Psychology: Learning, Memory and Cognition, 22*, 476–492.

Ortony, A., Revelle, W., & Zinbarg, R. (2007). Why emotional intelligence needs a fluid component. In G. Matthews, M. Zeidner, & R. D. Roberts (Eds.), *The science of emotional intelligence. Knowns and unknowns* (pp. 288–304). Oxford: Oxford University Press.

Palmer, B. R., Manocha, R., Gignac, G., & Stough, C. (2003). Examining the factor structure of the Bar-On Emotional Quotient Inventory with an Australian general population sample. *Personality and Individual Differences, 35*, 1191–1210.

Parker, J. D. A., Creque, R. E., Barnhart, D. L., Harris, J. I., Majeski, S. A., Wood, L. M. et al. (2004). Academic achievement in high school: Does emotional intelligence matter? *Personality and Individual Differences*, *37*, 1321–1330.

Parker, J. D. A., Summerfeldt, L. J., Hogan, M. J., & Majeski, S. A. (2004). Emotional intelligence and academic success: Examining the transition from high school to university. *Personality and Individual Differences*, *36*, 163–172.

Parker, J. D. A., Taylor, R. N., Eastabrook, J. M., Schell, S. L., & Wood, L. M. (2008). Problem gambling in adolescence: Relationships with Internet misuse, gaming abuse and emotional intelligence. *Personality and Individual Differences*, *45*, 174–180.

Payne, W. L. (1985). A study of emotion: Developing emotional intelligence, self-integration, relating to fear, pain, and desire. *Dissertation Abstracts International*, *47*, 203.

Pervin, L. A. (1968). Performance and satisfaction as a function of the individual–environment fit. *Psychological Bulletin*, *69*, 56–68.

Pervin, L. A. (1999). Epilogue: Constancy and change in personality theory and research. In L. A. Pervin & O. P. John (Eds.), *Handbook of personality: Theory and research*. New York: Guilford Press.

Petrides, K. V. (2009). *Technical manual for the Trait Emotional Intelligence Questionnaires (TEIQue)*. London: London Psychometric Laboratory.

Petrides, K. V., Frederickson, N., & Furnham, A. (2004). The role of trait emotional intelligence in academic performance and deviant behaviour at school. *Personality and Individual Differences*, *36*, 277–293.

Petrides, K. V., & Furnham, A. (2000). On the dimensional structure of emotional intelligence. *Personality and Individual Differences*, *29*, 313–320.

Petrides, K. V., & Furnham, A. (2001). Trait emotional intelligence: Psychometric investigation with reference to established trait taxonomies. *European Journal of Personality*, *15*, 425–448.

Petrides, K. V., & Furnham, A. (2003). Trait emotional intelligence: Behavioural validation in two studies of emotion recognition and reactivity to mood induction. *European Journal of Personality*, *17*, 39–57.

Petrides, K. V., & Furnham, A. (2006). The role of trait emotional intelligence in a gender-specific model of organizational variables. *Journal of Applied Social Psychology*, *36*, 552–569.

Petrides, K. V., Pérez-González, J. C., & Furnham, A. (2007). On the criterion and incremental validity of trait emotional intelligence. *Cognition and Emotion*, *21*, 26–55.

Petrides, K. V., Pita, R., & Kokkinaki, F. (2007). The location of trait emotional intelligence in personality factor space. *British Journal of Psychology*, *98*, 273–289.

Petrides, K. V., Sangareau, Y., Furnham, A., & Frederickson, N. (2006). Trait emotional intelligence and children's peer relations at school. *Social Development*, *15*, 537–547.

Platsidou, M. (2010). Trait emotional intelligence of Greek special education teachers in relation to burnout and job satisfaction. *School Psychology International*, *31*, 60–76.

Roberts, R. D., Zeidner, M., & Matthews, G. (2001). Does emotional intelligence meet traditional standards for an intelligence? Some new data and conclusions. *Emotion*, *1*, 196–231.

Robinson, M. D., & Clore, G. L. (2002). Belief and feeling: Evidence for an accessibility model of emotional self-report. *Psychological Bulletin*, *128*, 934–960.

Rossen, E., Kranzler, J. H., & Algina, J. (2008). Confirmatory factor analysis of the Mayer–Salovey–Caruso Emotional Intelligence Test V 2.0 (MSCEIT). *Personality and Individual Differences*, *44*, 1258–1269.

Rushton, J. P., Bons, T. A., Hoor, Y.-M., Ando, J., Irwin, P., Vernon, P. A., Petrides, K. V., & Barbaranelli, C. (2009). A general factor of personality from cross-national twins and multi-trait multimethod data. *Twin Research and Human Genetics*, *12*, 356–365.

Rushton, J. P., & Irwing, P. (2009). A general factor of personality in 16 sets of the Big Five, the Guilford–Zimmerman Temperament Survey, the California Psychological Inventory, and the Temperament and Character Inventory. *Personality and Individual Differences*, *47*, 558–564.

Rushton, J. P., Murray, H. G., & Paunonen, S. V. (1983). Personality, research creativity, and teaching effectiveness in university professors. *Scientometrics*, *5*, 93–116.

Saklofske, D. H., Austin, E. J., & Minski, P. S. (2003). Factor structure and validity of a trait emotional intelligence measure. *Personality and Individual Differences*, *34*, 707–721.

Saklofske, D. H., Austin, E. J., Rohr, B. A., & Andrews, J. J. W. (2007). Personality, emotional intelligence and exercise. *Journal of Health Psychology*, *12*, 937–948.

Salovey, P., & Mayer, J. D. (1990). Emotional intelligence. *Imagination, Cognition, and Personality*, *9*, 185–211.

Santesso, D. L., Reker, D. L., Schmidt, L. A., & Segalowitz, S. (2006). Frontal electroencephalogram activation asymmetry, emotional intelligence, and externalising bahaviors in 10-year-old children. *Child Psychiatry and Human Development*, *36*, 311–328.

Schmidt, L. (1999). Frontal brain electrical activity in shyness and sociability. *Psychological Science*, *10*, 316–320.

Schutte, N. S., Malouff, J. M., Bobik, C., Coston, T. D., Greeson, C., Jedlicka, C., Rhodes, E., & Wendorf, G. (2001). Emotional intelligence and interpersonal relations. *Journal of Social Psychology*, *141*, 523–536.

Schutte, N. S., Malouff, J. M., Hall, L. E., Haggerty, D. J., Cooper, J. T., Golden, C. J. et al. (1998). Development and validation of a measure of emotional intelligence. *Personality and Individual Differences*, *25*, 167–177.

Schutte, N. S., Malouff, J. M., Thorsteinsson, E. B., Bhullar, N., & Rooke, S. E. (2007). A meta-analytic investigation of the relationship between emotional intelligence and health. *Personality and Individual Differences*, *42*, 921–933.

Sevdalis, N., Petrides, K. V., & Harvey, N. (2007). Trait emotional intelligence and decision-related emotions. *Personality and Individual Differences*, *42*, 1347–1358.

Shafir, E., & LeBoeuf, R. A. (2002). Rationality. *Annual Review of Psychology*, *53*, 491–517.

Singh, M., & Woods, S. A. (2008). Predicting general well being from emotional intelligence and three broad personality traits. *Journal of Applied Social Psychology*, *38*, 635–646.

Smith, L., Ciarrochi, J., & Heaven, P. C. L. (2008). The stability and change of trait emotional intelligence, conflict communication patterns, and relationship satisfaction: A one-year longitudinal study. *Personality and Individual Differences*, *45*, 738–743.

Smith, L., Heaven, P. C. L., & Ciarrochi, J. (2008). Trait emotional intelligence, conflict communication patterns, and relationship satisfaction. *Personality and Individual Differences*, *44*, 1314–1325.

Thorndike, E. L. (1920). Intelligence and its uses. *Harper's Magazine*, *140*, 227–235.

Tsaousis, I., & Nikolaou, I. (2005). Exploring the relationship of emotional intelligence with physical and psychological health functioning. *Stress and Health*, *21*, 77–86.

Uva, C. S. M., de Timary, P., Cortesi, M., Mikolajczak, M., du Roy de Blicquy, P., & Luminet, O. (2010). Moderating effect of emotional intelligence on the role of negative affect in the motivation to drink in alcohol-dependent subjects undergoing protracted withdrawal. *Personality and Individual Differences*, *48*, 16–21.

Van Der Zee, K., & Wabeke, R. (2004). Is trait-emotional intelligence simply or more than just a trait? *European Journal of Personality*, *18*, 243–263.

Van Rooy, D. L., & Viswesvaran, C. (2004). Emotional intelligence: A meta-analytic investiga-
    tion of predictive validity and nomological net. *Journal of Vocational Behavior*, *65*,
    71–95.
Van Rooy, D. L., Viswesvaran, C., & Pluta, P. (2005). A meta-analytic evaluation of construct
    validity: What is this thing called emotional intelligence? *Human Performance*, *18*,
    445–462.
Vernon, P. A., Villani, V. C., Schermer, J. A., & Petrides, K. V. (2008). Phenotypic and genetic
    associations between the Big Five and trait emotional intelligence. *Twin Research and
    Human Genetics*, *11*, 524–530.
Veselka, L., Schermer, J. A., Petrides, K. V., Cherkas, L. F., Spector, T. D., & Vernon, P. A.
    (2009). A general factor of personality: Evidence from the HEXACO model and a
    measure of trait emotional intelligence. *Twin Research and Human Genetics*, *12*,
    420–424.
Veselka, L., Schermer, J. A., Petrides, K. V., & Vernon, P. A. (2009). Evidence for a heritable
    general factor of personality in two studies. *Twin Research and Human Genetics*, *12*,
    254–260.
Villanueva, J. J., & Sanchez, J. C. (2007). Trait emotional intelligence and leadership self-
    efficacy: Their relationship with collective efficacy. *Spanish Journal of Psychology*, *10*,
    349–357.
Warwick, J., & Nettelbeck, T. (2004). Emotional intelligence is ...? *Personality and Individual
    Differences*, *37*, 1091–1100.
Warwick, J., Nettelbeck, T., & Ward, L. (2010). AEIM: A new measure and method of scoring
    abilities-based emotional intelligence. *Personality and Individual Differences*, *48*, 66–71.
Watson, D. (2000). *Mood and temperament*. New York: Guilford Press.
Wilhelm, O. (2005). Measures of emotional intelligence: Practice and standards. In R. Schulze,
    & R. D. Roberts (Eds.), *International handbook of emotional intelligence* (pp. 131–154).
    Seattle, WA: Hogrefe & Huber.
Williams, C., Daley, D., Burnside, E., & Hammond-Rowley, S. (2010a). Can trait emotional
    intelligence and objective measures of emotional ability predict psychopathology across
    the transition to secondary school? *Personality and Individual Differences*, *48*, 161–165.
Williams, C., Daley, D., Burnside, E., & Hammond-Rowley, S. (2010b). Does item overlap
    account for the relationship between trait emotional intelligence and psychopathology in
    preadolescents? *Personality and Individual Differences*, *48*, 867–871.
Wong, C. S., & Law, K. S. (2002). The effects of leader and follower emotional intelligence
    on performance and attitude: An exploratory study. *Leadership Quarterly*, *13*, 243–274.
WHO [World Health Organization] (1992). *International classification of diseases and related
    health problems* (10th rev. ed.). Geneva, Switzerland: World Health Organization.
Zampetakis, L. A., Beldekos, P., & Moustakis, V. S. (2009). "Day-to-day" entrepreneurship
    within organisations: The rote of trait emotional intelligence and perceived organisational
    support. *European Management Journal*, *27*, 165–175.
Zeidner, M., Matthews, G., & Roberts, R. D. (2004). Emotional intelligence in the workplace:
    A critical review. *Applied Psychology. An International Review—Psychologie Appliquée.
    Revue Internationale*, *53*, 371–399.
Zeidner, M., & Olnick-Shemesh, D. (2010). Emotional intelligence and subjective well-being
    revisited. *Personality and Individual Differences*, *48*, 431–435.

# 26

# Individual Differences in Creativity

## James C. Kaufman

What do we mean when we say the word "creative"? Although not quite as ubiquitous a concept as "love," creativity can mean many different things. It may refer to a creative product (such as a painting or a mathematical proof), a creative press (an environment that nurtures and encourages creativity), the creative process itself, or a creative person (Rhodes, 1962).

Some scholars (e.g. Beghetto & Kaufman, 2009) have argued that studying the creative products does a disservice to those who are potentially creative but have not articulated their thoughts into tangible evidence of creativity. Much of the research on the creative process is based in cognitive psychology (e.g. Finke, Ward, & Smith, 1992), and much of the work on the creative press is based in industrial/organizational psychology (e.g. Amabile, Barsade, Mueller, & Staw, 2005). Yet the creative person is studied across disciplines, and is of interest to nearly all researchers (see Kaufman, 2009, for a review). Much of the research on the creative person examines individual differences in creativity.

Sternberg and Lubart (1996) propose six key variables in determining whether a person is creative or not: intelligence, knowledge, personality, environment, motivation, and thinking styles. The studies on creativity and the environment naturally fall under the creative press. The research on creativity and thinking styles is limited; Pashler, McDaniel, Rohrer, and Bjork (2008) have even called into question the very existence of thinking (or learning) styles. Knowledge is a key component, but the role of domain-specific expertise in creativity is generally acknowledged (Ericsson, 1996). When the role of past expertise is called into question, it is typically at the group level (Ward, Patterson, Sifonis, Dodds, & Saunders, 2002). Similarly, there is an extensive body of research examining the relationship between intrinsic motivation and creativity (Amabile, 1996), but most of this work looks at how contextual factors increase or decrease a person's motivation (and thereby impact creativity). There has been much less work studying motivation as an individual trait.

*The Wiley-Blackwell Handbook of Individual Differences,* First Edition.
Edited by Tomas Chamorro-Premuzic, Sophie von Stumm, and Adrian Furnham.
© 2011 Blackwell Publishing Ltd. Published 2011 by Blackwell Publishing Ltd.

The remaining two components (personality and intelligence) will be discussed in detail in this chapter, along with the demographic components of gender and ethnicity.

# Personality

Hundreds of studies have been devoted to the relationship between personality and creativity. Whereas some findings are straightforward and consistent, there remain some places where questions persist. Many different theories of personality have been studied in relation to creativity; such is Eysenck's (1993) emphasis on the three superfactors (psychoticism and creativity being linked), or Barron's (1969) work with the MMPI and other instruments at the Institute for Personality Assessment and Research.

More recently, the five-factor personality model (McCrae & Costa, 1997) has been the focus of most of the empirical investigations. The five factors proposed by this theory are neuroticism, extraversion, openness to experience (sometimes just called openness), conscientiousness, and agreeableness. The names of these factors convey their meaning. Neuroticism measures an individual's emotional stability (or lack thereof). Extraversion indicates how outgoing and sociable someone is, whereas openness to experience conveys someone's intellectual and experiential curiosity. Conscientiousness taps into one's discipline, rule-orientation, and integrity, and agreeableness means friendliness and being good-natured (Kyllonen, Walters, & Kaufman, 2005; McCrae & Costa, 1997).

One of the most consistent findings in creativity research is the importance of the openness to experience factor. This relationship has been so consistently demonstrated that creative personality tests based heavily on openness to experience (e.g. Goldberg et al., 2006) have been used as a proxy measure of creativity (Baer & Oldham, 2006; Powers & Kaufman, 2004). The factor is split into openness to fantasy (showing a good imagination), to esthetics (being artistic), to feelings (experiencing and valuing feelings), to actions (trying new things, having many interests), to ideas (being curious, smart, liking challenges), and to values (being unconventional, liberal). More recently, DeYoung, Quilty, and Peterson (2007) argue that each of the Big Five can be split into two distinct factors. Openness to experience, they argue, can be broken into intellect and openness. They use conceptions of openness that are based on a multitude of tests, including the main one, which assesses the five-factor theory. Except for ideas, all of the specific sub-components of openness to experience are related to the openness component more than to the intellect component.

It is not surprising, then, that this relationship has been shown to hold across multiple measures of creativity, ranging from self-reports of creative acts (Griffin & McDermott, 1998) and self-estimates of creativity and scores on the Barron–Welsh Art Scale (Furnham, 1999), to verbal creativity (King, McKee-Walker, & Broyles, 1996), to studies of creative professions (Domino, 1974), to analysis of participants' daydreams (Zhiyan & Singer, 1996), to creativity ratings on stories (Wolfradt & Pretz, 2001) and autobiographical essays (Dollinger & Clancy, 1993), to creative activities and behaviors throughout life (Soldz & Vaillant, 1999), and to psychometric tests (McCrae, 1987). Silvia, Kaufman, and Pretz (2009) found that students with expertise in visual and performing arts were more open to experience than students without such accomplishments. This general finding of the power of openness to experience seems to extend across domains. Feist's (1998) extensive meta-analysis of personality and creativity found that creative scientists were more open to experience than less creative scientists, and artists were more open to experience than non-artists.

The relationship of the other four factors to creativity, however, is murkier and domain-dependent. The role of domains in creativity has fueled numerous debates in the literature (Baer, 1998; Plucker, 1998), although the two contrasting sides are converging in the middle. In essence, the question is whether there is a creativity factor *c*, analogous to intelligence's *g*, which transcends domains and enhances a person's creativity across many different areas. A comparable view in personality research is provided by the cognitive–social approach to personality coherence (Shoda, Mischel, & Wright, 1994; Smith, Shoda, Cumming, & Smoll, 2009). According to this approach, a person's behavior changes according to the situation. These behavioral changes are typically consistent across the same type of situation. For example, a student might be consistently conscientious across multiple classroom situations and consistently non-conscientious across multiple basketball-playing situations. If creativity and personality both seem to be domain-specific, then personality will presumably be related to creativity differently across different domains.

Indeed this type of discrepant pattern often emerges. Creative artists are unlikely to be conscientious. This finding was consistent across rated creativity (Wolfradt & Pretz, 2001) and biographical data (Walker, Koestner, & Hum, 1995). Students who scored *higher* on an arts-based creativity measure were also less conscientious (Furnham, Zhang, & Chamorro-Premuzic, 2006). Feist (1998) found that, although scientists were much more conscientious than non-scientists, creative scientists were not necessarily more conscientious than less creative scientists.

Extraversion is sometimes related to domain-general measures of creativity (Batey, Chamorro-Premuzic, & Furnham, 2009; Furnham, Crump, Batey, & Chamorro-Premuzic, 2009; Schuldberg, 2005) and sometimes it is not (Matthews, 1986; McCrae, 1987). Domain-specific investigations of artists and writers have found some evidence for an introversion–creativity connection (Mohan & Tiwana, 1987; Roy, 1996). Feist's (1998) meta-analysis shows that scientists were much more introverted than non-scientists—but creative scientists were more extraverted than less creative scientists. Feist (1998) also found that creative scientists were less agreeable than less creative scientists, and artists were less agreeable than non-artists (a result also obtained by Burch, Pavelis, Hemsley, & Corr, 2006).

Even openness to experience may have some domain dependence; Perrine and Brodersen (2005) examined openness to experience, interests, and artistic versus scientific creativity through a battery of survey measures. Five of the six sub-components—all but values—were related to artistic creativity, and the strongest relationship was found in esthetics. Ideas and values were the only sub-components related to scientific creativity. Another study investigated the potentially interactive relationship between openness to experience, conscientiousness, and creative behavior. George and Zhou

(2001) found that a supervisor's feedback and the structure of the task were essential in relating the two personality factors to creative behavior on the job. In situations where people received positive feedback from supervisors and had an open-ended task, those who were high on openness to experience produced more creative results. When a person's work is closely monitored, people who are high on conscientiousness will produce less creative results. In addition, people who are highly conscientious may be more likely to nitpick, be generally unhelpful, and create a negative work environment; these factors will then interact to produce a strikingly low level of creativity. Conscientiousness is typically associated with positive work outcomes (i.e. with people showing up for work on time, or getting projects completed by deadline), so this type of negative finding is fairly unusual.

Of the five factors, agreeableness has perhaps the mildest relationship to creativity. Feist's (1998) analysis found that creative scientists were less agreeable than less creative scientists, and artists were less agreeable than non-artists (the same was also found by Burch et al., 2006). Agreeableness has also been negatively correlated with creative accomplishments (King et al., 1996) and scores on divergent thinking tests (Batey et al., 2009). However the body of work associating this factor with creativity is not as extensive as for the other four factors.

The relationship between emotional stability and creativity veers into the frequent debate on the relationship between creativity and mental illness, with vociferous critics arguing either in favor of (Andreasen, 1987; Post, 1994) or against (Schlesinger, 2009) a link. Studies focusing on clinical levels of manic depression or schizophrenia are obviously discussing something more severe than neuroticism (or lack of emotional stability). The literature about hypomania and anxiety, however, seems to be quite relevant. Hypomania, as Furnham, Batey, Anand, and Manfield (2008) and as Lloyd-Evans, Batey, and Furnham (2006) argue, is a disorder related to bipolar depression (where there are periods of elevated mood, but they are less intense and shorter than their opposites); yet it does not necessarily lead to a diagnosis of "mentally ill." People with minor hypomania may be more creative, whereas people with extreme bipolar disorder may be less creative (see also Richards & Kinney, 1990). Another line of research focuses on the relationship between anxiety and creativity. Rubinstein (2008) found that anxious and depressed patients were more creative than schizophrenics, and shyness researchers have found links between diminished social anxiety and higher creativity (Cheek & Stahl, 1986; Kemple, David, & Wang, 1996).

The literature on personality and creativity is a mix of strong connections (openness to experience), conflicting results (extraversion), and domain-based differences (conscientiousness). A similarly extensive body of work exists for the relationship between intelligence and creativity.

# Intelligence

Like personality, intelligence comes with a theory that has clearly influenced most of the measures and tests. Unlike personality, there are extensive alternative theories, which are respected even if they are less mainstream. This section will first discuss the Cattell–Horn–Carroll (CHC) theory of intelligence and then explore other theories, which place creativity as a more central component of intellectual abilities.

Undoubtedly the theory of intelligence that is most often applied to IQ tests is the CHC theory, which is a combination of two earlier theories. The Cattell–Horn theory (see Horn & Cattell, 1966) initially proposed two types of intelligence: crystallized (*Gc*) and fluid (*Gf*). *Gc* is what a person knows and has learned, while *Gf* is how a person handles a new and different situation (in other words, problem-solving). Carroll's (1993) theory proposed a hierarchy of intellectual abilities. At the top of the hierarchy is general ability; in the middle there are various broad abilities (including learning, memory processes, and the effortless production of many ideas). At the bottom there are many narrow, specific abilities, such as spelling ability and reasoning speed.

The combined CHC theory incorporates both the concept of a general intelligence (all of the different aspects of intelligence are considered to be related to a common "*g*," although this aspect is not often emphasized; see Flanagan & Ortiz, 2002) and the concept of many different aspects of intelligence. Ten different broad factors of intelligence are proposed. These include *Gf* and *Gc* from the initial Cattell–Horn theory. The remaining are *Gq* (quantitative knowledge, typically math-related), *Grw* (reading and writing intelligence), *Gsm* (short-term memory intelligence), *Gv* (visual processing intelligence), *Ga* (auditory processing intelligence), *Glr* (long-term storage and retrieval intelligence), *Gs* (processing speed intelligence), and *Gt* (decision speed/reaction time intelligence). Of these 10, only seven are directly measured by today's intelligence tests: *Gq* and *Grw* are in the domain of academic achievement, and therefore are measured by achievement tests, and *Gt* is not measured by any major standardized test. Intelligence tests may indirectly measure some of these other skills, however. For example, intelligence tests indirectly measure achievements in various areas. The Stanford–Binet 5 (SB5, Roid, 2003) and the Woodcock–Johnson Revised (WJ–III; Woodcock, McGrew, & Mather, 2001) were the first intelligence tests to be built on *Gf*–*Gc* theory. Today nearly every major intelligence test is founded, either explicitly or implicitly, on the current version of the theory, namely CHC.

Although in the early stages of the Cattell–Horn *Gf*–*Gc* theory *Gf* (fluid intelligence) was hypothesized to be strongly linked to creativity (Cattell & Butcher, 1968), such a relationship is no longer explicitly part of the CHC theory. The current model, based on factor-analytic studies by Carroll (1993) and others, includes originality/creativity as a component of long-term storage and retrieval (*Glr*). According to the most recent presentation of CHC (McGrew, 2009), "[s]ome *Glr* narrow abilities have been prominent in creativity research (e.g., production, ideational fluency, or associative fluency)" (p. 6). In the detailed description of the model, this sentence contains the only mention of creativity, originality, or divergent thinking. Fluid intelligence (*Gf*) is discussed in terms of its relationship to problem-solving and coping with novel problems (both of which are considered to be highly related to creativity), yet the emphasis is on *Glr*.

Martindale (1999) proposed a differential relationship between *Gs* (processing speed) and creativity. According to Martindale's theory, people who are creative are selective with their speed of information processing. Early in the creative problem-solving stage, they widen their breadth of attention, allowing for a larger amount of information to be processed (and thereby lowering their speed). Later, when the problem is better understood, their attention span is shortened and their reaction time is quicker. This theory is reminiscent of Sternberg's (1981) distinction between global and local planning: According to Sternberg, brighter people spend more time in initial global planning, so that later they do not have to spend as much time in local planning.

Some have argued that the current CHC model shortchanges creativity (Kaufman, 2009). Placing all references to creativity and originality under *Glr* seems quite narrow. The ability to draw selectively on past experiences is essential for creating something new. But the connection between fluid intelligence and creativity is minimized in new conceptions of the model.

Most studies that look at creativity and intelligence use divergent thinking tests (such as the TTCT) or other related paper-and-pencil tests also scored for fluency, originality, or other divergent thinking-related methods of scoring. They have generally found that creativity is significantly associated with psychometric measures of intelligence (especially verbally oriented measures). This relationship is, typically, not a particularly strong one (Barron & Harrington, 1981; Kim, 2005; Wallach & Kogan, 1965), although Silvia (2008a, 2008b) argues that the relationship is underestimated because we are limited by looking at observable scores (i.e. by performance on an intelligence test).

Creativity's correlation with IQ is maintained up to a certain level of performance on a traditional individual intelligence test. Traditional research has argued for a "threshold theory," in which creativity and intelligence are positively correlated up to an IQ of approximately 120; in people with higher IQs, the two constructs show little relationship (e.g. Barron, 1963; Fuchs-Beauchamp, Karnes, & Johnson, 1993; Getzels & Jackson, 1962; Richards, 1976). More recently, however, the threshold theory has come under fire. Runco and Albert (1986) found that the nature of the relationship was dependent on the measures used and on the populations tested. Preckel, Holling, and Wiese (2006) looked at measures of fluid intelligence and creativity (as measured through divergent thinking tests), and found modest correlations across all levels of intellectual abilities. Wai, Lubinski, and Benbow (2005), in a longitudinal study of gifted (top 1 percent) 13-year-olds, found that differences in SAT scores—even within such an elite group—predicted creative accomplishments 20 years later. Kim (2005), in a meta-analysis of 21 studies, found virtually no support for the threshold theory, with small positive correlations found between measures of ability and measures of creativity and divergent thinking.

It is notable, however, that nearly all of these studies do not use traditional, individually administered intelligence tests. In Kim's (2005) meta-analysis, many of the studies were more than 30 years old, and therefore were conducted using IQ tests that do not reflect current IQ theory. In addition, most of the studies used group IQ tests. Although group IQ tests serve a strong purpose in research studies, they are not used by most school psychologists for psychoeducational assessment (Kaufman & Lichtenberger, 2006). One of the few research studies to use a modern and individually administered IQ test was that of Sligh, Conners, and Roskos-Ewoldsen (2005), who used the Kaufman Adolescent and Adult Intelligence Scale (Kaufman & Kaufman, 1993) and a creative invention task (there people would use shapes to create a possible object, and then would name and describe their invention; see Finke, 1990). Sligh et al. (2005) delved deeper into the intelligence–creativity relationship, by specifically examining the correlation between *Gf* (novel problem-solving) and *Gc* (acquired knowledge) and a measure of actual creative innovation. *Gc* showed the same moderate and positive relationship to creativity as found in the past studies mentioned above; in contrast, *Gf* showed the opposite pattern. IQ and creativity were significantly correlated for the high-IQ group, but they were not significantly correlated for people with average IQs. This finding implies that students who receive high *Gf* scores may be more likely to be creative than students who receive high *Gc* scores.

An interesting suggestion made by Batey and Furnham (2006) is that the roles of *Gf* and *Gc* in creativity may shift across the life span of a creative person. *Gf*, they argue, might be more important in early stages of a career (e.g. Kaufman & Beghetto, 2009). Conversely, a later-career creator may rely more on *Gc*—and, one might postulate, on *Glr*.

If the connection with intelligence is generally positive for people who are high both on *Gc* and on *Gf* but it is more complex at the extremes, the relationship between gender, ethnicity, and creativity offers a tapestry of similarities and differences across domains.

## Gender, Ethnicity, and Creativity

A wide variety of measures of intelligence and ability have shown lower scores for African–Americans and Hispanic Americans than for Caucasians (see Loehlin, 1999, and Weiss, Saklofske, Coalson, & Raiford, 2010, for overviews). Standardized tests such as the SAT, ACT, Graduate Record Examinations (GRE), and advanced placement (AP) exams have shown similar patterns of discrepancy among ethnic groups (Camara & Schmidt, 1999; Morgan & Maneckshana, 1996). The differences that are present between African–Americans and Whites on measures of ability and achievement are *not* found, by and large, in creativity, regardless of how it is measured (Kaufman, 2010). The Torrance Tests of Creative Thinking (TTCT; Torrance, 1966, 1974a, 1974b), discussed earlier, have been used along with other divergent thinking measures in these studies, with both verbal and figural forms (e.g. Glover, 1976; Iscoe & Pierce-Jones, 1964; Kaltsounis, 1974; Knox & Glover, 1978; Torrance, 1971, 1973). Torrance (1971, 1973) found that African–American children scored higher on the TTCT than White children, namely on the figural tests in fluency, flexibility, and originality; Whites scored higher on figural elaboration and on all the verbal sub-tests. The initial sample compared African–American children in Georgia with higher-SES children in Minnesota; when a subsequent study used Whites also from Georgia, all the differences were significantly reduced. Kaltsounis (1974) also found that African–Americans received higher fluency and originality scores on the TTCT. Troiano and Bracken (1983) gave measures of creative thinking to three kindergarten classes (Dutch Americans, African–Americans, and Native Americans). They found that African–Americans and Native Americans scored approximately one standard deviation higher on creative thinking, particularly in fluency, than the Dutch Americans.

Other studies that found no differences have utilized biographical questionnaires measuring creative accomplishments (Stricker, Rock, & Bennett, 2001), the ability to be trained on creativity tasks (Moreno & Hogan, 1976), and the development of divergent thinking abilities in adolescents from South Africa and the United States (Ripple & Jacquish, 1982). Kaufman, Baer, and Gentile (2004) studied poems, stories, and personal narratives written by African–American and White 8th-grade students. There were no differences in creativity scores as assigned by expert judges.

Although self-reported creativity can be of limited value, it is worth also noting that Kaufman (2006) asked 3,553 individuals (mostly high school and college students) to rate themselves in 56 different domains of creativity. African–Americans rated themselves as significantly higher than at least one other ethnicity on all factors. All ethnicities except for Asian Americans rated themselves higher than another ethnicity on at least one factor.

Further research has looked at Hispanic Americans and creativity. The key variable tends to be whether creativity is measured verbally or non-verbally. For example, Argulewicz and Kush (1984) found that Whites scored higher than Hispanic Americans on three out of four TTCT verbal forms, but they found no significant differences on the figural forms. It is worth noting, however, that the TTCT has been translated into Spanish (among many other languages), and has been shown to have validity in many Hispanic cultures (e.g. Wechsler, 2006). Studies using only non-verbal assessments have typically found no differences (e.g. Argulewicz, Elliott, & Hall, 1982), or they show a slight advantage for bilingual Hispanic Americans (Kessler & Quinn, 1987; Price-Williams & Ramirez, 1977). However, low-income Hispanic American elementary students scored below the norms on the TTCT (Mitchell, 1988), and teachers rated White students as being more creative than Hispanic American students, highly acculturated Hispanic Americans receiving higher marks than less acculturated Hispanic Americans (Masten, Plata, Wenglar, & Thedford, 1999).

Some researchers found that White parents had more favorable perceptions of creativity than Hispanic American parents (Strom & Johnson, 1989; Strom, Johnson, Strom, & Strom, 1992). However, they also found that Hispanic American parents were more likely to engage in play activities with their children and valued play more (Strom & Johnson, 1989). Make-believe play can be a valuable component of a child's developing imagination (Singer & Singer, 1990).

## Creativity across Culture: East versus West

Studies of the TTCT often show western cultures outperforming eastern cultures. Jellen and Urban (1989) administered a measure of creative thinking and drawing to children from several different countries. They found that, in general, western countries (such as Germany, England, and the United States) scored higher than eastern countries (such as China and India). American students outperformed Japanese students on the TTCT at the college (Saeki, Fan, & Van Deusen, 2001) and elementary school level (Ogawa, Kuehn-Ebert, & DeVito, 1991); the reverse findings were found, however, in a study of education majors (Torrance & Sato, 1979). Americans from five different age groups scored higher than similar people from Hong Kong (Jaquish & Ripple, 1984), and American school children outper-formed their peers in Taiwan, Singapore, and Germany on the TTCT–Verbal; the results on the TTCT–Figural were in reverse order. American graduate students outperformed their Chinese counterparts on divergent thinking tests (Zha, Walczyk, Griffith-Ross, Tobacyk, & Walczyk, 2006).

Plucker, Runco, and Lim (2006) found no difference in creative potential (as measured by the Runco Ideational Behavior Scale; Runco, Plucker, & Lim, 2001) between Korean students and American students; similarly, Lim and Plucker (2001) found that Koreans and Americans hold similar concepts of the nature of creativity. Results on comparing eastern and western self-assessments were mixed (Palaniappan, 1996). Studies have shown American students producing more creative artwork than Chinese students (Niu & Sternberg, 2001); others have found no differences (Chen et al., 2002; Cox, Perara, & Fan, 1998); a study that compared American and Japanese students favored the latter (Cox, Koyasu, Hiranuma, & Perara, 2001). In both studies, American and Chinese judges tended to agree on which products were creative and which products were not creative, although Niu and Sternberg (2001) found that the Chinese judges tended to give higher scores than their American counterparts.

Differences in styles and values among eastern and western cultures may explain some of the findings, namely the fact that westerners receive higher scores on creativ-ity assessments. Li (1997) proposed a horizontal and vertical tradition of creativity. Horizontal traditions, which are favored by western cultures, tend toward changing and modifying pre-existing structures—think of an artist like Picasso, constantly chal-lenging the limits of an art form. In vertical traditions, however, the nature of the work is much more constrained and consistent with past work. A piece's worth depends more on how well the artist is able to capture his or her subject matter (Li, 1997). Similarly, Averill, Chon, and Hahn (2001) propose that both eastern and western cultures value the effectiveness of a piece of creativity, but the West values the novelty of a piece much more than the East. Of much more interest to the East is whether a piece is authentic, representing the creator's personal values and beliefs.

Why does this difference occur between East and West? One answer may lie in the theory of an interdependent (or collectivistic) versus an independent (or individu-alistic) type of culture. This theory argues that northern Americans and western Europeans see themselves as independent. Their motivations and goals follow accord-ingly. In contrast, individuals in Asian cultures are more interdependent and have a higher sense of group responsibility. These cultures are motivated by different vari-ables, such as group harmony (Markus & Kitayama, 1991). Ng (2001; see also Ng & Smith, 2004) has argued that it is this emphasis that is responsible for East–West differences in creativity. People who are focused on group cohesiveness and are "nice" (a term Ng uses without specifically positive connotations) are less creative; people who are creative are less "nice." Goncalo and Staw (2006) examined individualistic and collectivistic-oriented people; when given instructions to be creative, individual-istic people generated both a higher number of ideas and more creative ideas than collectivistic people. With instructions to be practical, there were non-significant trends in the opposite direction.

Indeed, whether a person is part of an independent or interdependent culture can affect his or her personality and style. People from interdependent cultures are more likely to see themselves as fundamentally linked to others and to view themselves in the context of their social relationships (Cross & Markus, 1999). This view translates into cognitive style; Asians were found to be more field-dependent and more holistic than Americans, for example (Ji, Peng, & Nisbett, 2000; Nisbett, Peng, Choi, & Norenzayan, 2001). People who are more field-dependent have been found to score lower on tests of creativity (e.g. Chadha, 1985; Noppe, 1985).

There are many studies that compare Asians with Europeans or Americans. Fewer studies have compared Asian *Americans* to Americans of different ethnicities. Rostan, Pariser, and Gruber (2002) studied Chinese American and White students' artwork, with two groups in each culture: students with additional art training and classes and students with no such classes. Each group's artwork (one drawing from life and one drawing from imagination) was judged by both Chinese and American judges. There were no significant differences between cultures from either set of judges, only between art students versus non-art students. Wang (2007) studied Taiwanese and American student teachers and found that Whites outperformed Hispanic Americans, Asian Americans, and Taiwanese on the Torrance tests; however, Asian Americans were more creative than the Taiwanese. Differences in fluency, flexibility, and originality were minor, whereas differences in elaboration were larger.

Pornrungroj (1992) administered the figural form of the TTCT to Thai children and Thai American children and found that Thai children received significantly higher scores than Thai Americans. Yoon (2005) gave the TTCT to European American and Asian American middle school students (the latter being a mix of Chinese American, Korean American, Japanese American, and Southeastern Asian Americans). There were no significant differences either between the European Americans and Asian Americans or between the different sub-groups of Asian Americans.

A final note on cultural differences in creativity: having basic knowledge about other cultures may increase your own creativity. Leung, Maddux, Galinsky, and Chiu (2008) found that, when students were given information about another culture (China), they subsequently wrote more creative stories set in a different culture (Turkey) than students who had not been exposed. The authors infer that multicultural experiences enhance creativity. Similarly, studies from the industrial/organizational literature show that work teams that represent diverse backgrounds will be more innovative (Choi, 2007; Yap, Chai, & Lemaire, 2005).

## Gender Differences in Creativity

No simple conclusions can be drawn from examining the many studies that report gender differences (or lack thereof) in creativity tests. Some studies show that women do better; other studies show that men do better; still other studies show no difference. Baer and Kaufman (2008) reviewed the extensive literature on gender differences and found that most studies found no differences (21) or had mixed results (30). Four studies showed males doing better, and nine studies showed females doing better. Generally, there is a trend showing women scoring higher on verbal measures and men scoring higher on figural/mathematical measures (which mirrors the larger cognitive findings in achievement tests).

Most large-scale studies of personality do not show gender differences in openness to experience (Collins & Gleaves, 1998; Goldberg, Sweeney, Merenda, & Hughes, 1998). There is an interaction with education; women with higher levels of education tend to be more creative than less educated women—but there is no such difference in men (Matud, Rodríguez, & Grande, 2007).

It is important to note that there is a large inconsistency between gender differences on creativity tests and actual creative accomplishment. Although gender differences on creativity tests are minor or non-existent, differences in real-world creative accomplishment are large and significant (Simonton, 1994). Murray (2003), in a review of human accomplishment, notes that, out of 4,002 people he categorized as "significant," only 88 (2 percent) were female. He further points out that women comprised only 4 percent of all Nobel Prize winners from 1901 to 1950—and then only 3 percent of all winners from 1951 to 2000. The question is not simply one of having older sources, or biased accounts; current awards show just as much male dominance.

Why do women not reach the same creative peaks as men? Helson (1990) argued that cultural values, social roles, and sexist thinking are now recognized as key reasons for the comparative lack of creative accomplishment by women. Piirto (1991) notes that girls do not show less creative achievement until *after* high school and college, which indicates that the key issue may be a conflict between personal and professional demands.

Another possibility is suggested by the motivation literature. There is a steady stream of research indicating that extrinsic motivation may actually decrease creativity (Amabile, 1979; Amabile, Goldfarb, & Brackfield, 1990; Amabile, Hill, Hennessey, & Tighe, 1994; but see Eisenberger & Shanock, 2003).

Female creativity may be more susceptible to the negative effects of evaluation (and subsequent loss of intrinsic motivation). Baer (1997) asked 8th-grade subjects (66 girls, 62 boys) to write original poems and stories under conditions favoring both intrinsic and extrinsic motivation. In the intrinsic motivation conditions, subjects were told that their poems and stories would not be evaluated; in the extrinsic condition, subjects were led to expect evaluation, and the importance of the evaluation was made highly salient. The poems and stories were judged for creativity by experts. There was a significant gender by motivational interaction effect. For boys, there was virtually no difference in creativity ratings under intrinsic and extrinsic conditions, but for the girls the difference was quite large. This was confirmed in a follow-up study (Baer, 1998) that used students of the same age, in which the negative impact of both rewards and anticipated evaluation were shown to be largely confined to female subjects. More recently, Conti, Collins, and Picariello (2001) found that girls were less creative in competitive situations and boys were more creative in competitive situations.

## Conclusion

Individual differences can come in the form of preferences or abilities (e.g. personality and intelligence), or they can be based on such predetermined concepts as gender or ethnicity. For performance and abilities, certain types of individual differences are quite straightforward—people who are more open to experience and (broadly) smarter will also be more likely to be creative. There are also a number of vague and contradictory findings. Conscientiousness seems to have a notable relationship with creativity, but the specific nature of this link varies by domain. The exact nature of the intelligence–creativity relationship has been shown to vary by type of intelligence (fluid vs. crystallized), and generally to yield a wide pattern of results.

Examining creativity in relation to gender and ethnicity, there are some trends (for instance, women perform particularly well on creative tasks in the verbal domain), but the dominant message seems to be that most people have the potential to be creative regardless of gender or ethnicity. This theme—of the possibilities of human-kind to create and of the existence of a relatively level playing field—is a nice one to end on for a chapter focusing on individual differences.

## Acknowledgments

I would like to thank Arielle White for help in preparing the chapter.

## References

Amabile, T. M. (1979). Effects of external evaluation on artistic creativity. *Journal of Personality and Social Psychology, 37*, 221–233.

Amabile, T. M. (1996). *Creativity in context: Update to "The social psychology of creativity."* Boulder, CO: Westview Press.

Amabile, T. M., Goldfarb, P., & Brackfield, S. (1990). Social influences on creativity: Evaluation, coaction and surveillance. *Creativity Research Journal, 3*, 6–21.

Amabile, T. M., Barsade, S. G., Mueller, J. S., & Staw, B. M. (2005). Affect and creativity at work. *Administrative Science Quarterly, 50*, 367–403.

Amabile, T. M., Hill, K. G., Hennessey, B. A., & Tighe, E. M. (1994). The Work Preference Inventory: Assessing intrinsic and extrinsic motivational orientations. *Journal of Personality and Social Psychology, 66*, 950–967.

Andreasen, N. C. (1987). Creativity and mental illness: Prevalence rates in writers and their first-degree relatives. *American Journal of Psychiatry, 144*, 1288–1292.

Argulewicz, E. N., & Kush, J. C. (1984). Concurrent validity of the SRBCSS Creativity Scale for Anglo-American and Mexican–American gifted students. *Educational and Psychological Research, 4*, 81–89.

Argulewicz, E. N., Elliott, S. N., & Hall, R. (1982). Comparison of behavioral ratings of Anglo-American and Mexican–American gifted children. *Psychology in the Schools, 19*, 469–472.

Averill, J. R., Chon, K. K., & Hahn, D. W. (2001). Emotions and creativity: East and West. *Asian Journal of Social Psychology, 4*, 165–184.

Baer, J. (1997). Gender differences in the effects of anticipated evaluation on creativity. *Creativity Research Journal, 10*, 25–31.

Baer, J. (1998). Gender differences in the effects of extrinsic motivation on creativity. *Journal of Creative Behavior, 32*, 18–37.

Baer, J., & Kaufman, J. C. (2008). Gender differences in creativity. *Journal of Creative Behavior, 42*, 75–106.

Baer, M., & Oldham, G. R. (2006). The curvilinear relation between experienced creative time pressure and creativity: Moderating effects of openness to experience and support for creativity. *Journal of Applied Psychology, 91,* 963–970.

Barron, F. (1963). *Creativity and psychological health.* Princeton, NJ: D. Van Nostrand Company.

Barron, F. (1969). *Creative person and creative process.* New York: Holt, Rinehart & Winston.

Barron, F., & Harrington, D. M. (1981). Creativity, intelligence, and personality. *Annual Review of Psychology, 32,* 439–476.

Batey, M., & Furnham, A. (2006). Creativity, intelligence and personality: A critical review of the scattered literature. *Genetic, Social, and General Psychology Monographs, 132,* 355–429.

Batey, M., Chamorro-Premuzic, T. & Furnham, A. (2009). Intelligence and personality as predictors of divergent thinking: The role of general, fluid and crystallized intelligence. *Thinking Skills and Creativity, 4,* 60–69.

Beghetto, R. A., & Kaufman, J. C. (2009). Intellectual estuaries: Connecting learning and creativity in programs of advanced academics. *Journal of Advanced Academics, 20,* 296–324.

Burch, G., Pavelis, C., Hemsley, D. R. & Corr, P. J. (2006). Schizotypy and creativity in visual artists. *British Journal of Psychology, 97,* 177–190.

Camara, W. J., & Schmidt, A. E. (1999). *Group differences in standardized testing and social stratification.* (College Board Rep. No. 99–5). New York: College Board.

Carroll, J. B. (1993). *Human cognitive abilities: A survey of factor-analytic studies.* New York: Cambridge University Press.

Cattell, R. B., & Butcher, H. (1968). *The prediction of achievement and creativity.* Indianapolis, IN: Bobbs-Merrill.

Chadha, N. K. (1985). Creativity and cognitive style. *Psycho Lingua, 15,* 81–88.

Cheek, J. M., & Stahl, S. S. (1986). Shyness and verbal creativity. *Journal of Research in Personality, 20,* 51–61.

Chen, C., Kasof, J., Himsel, A. J., Greenberger, E., Dong, Q., & Xue, G. (2002). Creativity in drawings of geometric shapes: A cross-cultural examination with the consensual assessment technique. *Journal of Cross Cultural Psychology, 33,* 171–187.

Choi, J. N. (2007). Group composition and employee creative behaviour in a Korean electronics company: Distinct effects of relational demography and group diversity. *Journal of Occupational and Organizational Psychology, 80,* 213–234.

Collins, A. J., & Gleaves, D. (1998). Race, job applicants, and the five-factor model of personality: Implications for Black psychology, industrial/organizational psychology, and the five-factor theory. *Journal of Applied Psychology, 83,* 531–544.

Conti, R., Collins, M., & Picariello, M. (2001). The impact of competition on intrinsic motivation and creativity: Considering gender, gender segregation, and gender role orientation. *Personality and Individual Differences, 30,* 1273–1289.

Cox, M. V., Perara, J., & Fan, X. (1998). Children's drawing ability in the UK and China. *Psychologia Society, 41,* 171–182.

Cox, M. V., Koyasu, M., Hiranuma, H., & Perara, J. (2001). Children's human figure drawings in the UK and Japan: The effects of age, sex, and culture. *British Education, 16,* 47–56.

Cross, S. E., & Markus, H. R. (1999). The cultural constitution of personality. In L. Pervin & O. John (Eds.), *Handbook of personality* (2nd ed., pp. 378–396). New York: Guilford Press.

DeYoung, C. G., Quilty, L. C., & Peterson, J. B. (2007). Between facets and domains: 10 aspects of the Big-Five. *Journal of Personality and Social Psychology, 93,* 880–896.

Dollinger, S. J., & Clancy, S. M. (1993). Identity, self, and personality 2. Glimpses through the autophotographic eye. *Journal of Personality and Social Psychology, 64,* 1064–1071.

Domino, G. (1974). Assessment of cinematographic creativity. *Journal of Personality and Social Psychology, 30,* 150–154.

Eisenberger, R., & Shanock, L. (2003). Rewards, intrinsic motivation, and creativity: A case study of conceptual and methodological isolation. *Creativity Research Journal, 15,* 121–130.

Ericsson, K. A. (Ed.) (1996). *The road to expert performance: Empirical evidence from the arts and sciences, sports, and games.* Mahwah, NJ: Lawrence Erlbaum Associates.

Eysenck, H. J. (1993). Creativity and personality: Suggestions for a theory. *Psychological Inquiry, 4,* 147–178.

Feist, G. J. (1998). A meta-analysis of personality in scientific and artistic creativity. *Personality and Social Psychology Review, 2,* 290–309.

Finke, R. A. (1990). *Creative imagery: Discoveries and inventions in visualization.* Hillsdale, NJ: Lawrence Erlbaum Associates.

Finke, R. A., Ward T. B., & Smith, S. M. (1992). *Creative cognition: Theory, research, and applications.* Cambridge, MA: MIT Press.

Flanagan, D. P., & Ortiz, S. O. (2002). Best practices in intellectual assessment: Future directions. In A. Thomas & J. Grimes (Eds.), *Best practices in school psychology IV* (pp. 1351–1372). Washington, DC: National Association of School Psychologists.

Fuchs-Beauchamp, K. D., Karnes, M. B., & Johnson, L. J. (1993). Creativity and intelligence in preschoolers. *Gifted Child Quarterly, 37,* 113–117.

Furnham, A. F. (1999). Personality and creativity. *Perceptual and Motor Skills, 88,* 407–408.

Furnham, A. F., Zhang, J., & Chamorro-Premuzic, T. (2006). The relationship between psychometric and self-estimated intelligence, creativity, personality, and academic achievement. *Cognition and Personality, 25,* 119–145.

Furnham, A. F., Crump, J., Batey, M. & Chamorro-Premuzic, T. (2009). Personality and ability predictors of the consequences test of divergent thinking in a large non-student sample. *Personality and Individual Differences, 46,* 536–540.

Furnham, A. F., Batey, M., Anand, K., & Manfield, J. (2008). Personality, hypomania, intelligence and creativity. *Personality and Individual Differences, 44,* 1060–1069.

George, J. M. & Zhou, J (2001). When openness to experience and conscientiousness are related to creative behavior: An interactional approach. *Journal of Applied Psychology, 86,* 513–524.

Getzels, J. W., & Jackson, P. W. (1962). *Creativity and intelligence: Explorations with gifted students.* New York: Wiley.

Glover, J. A. (1976). Comparative levels of creative ability in Black and White college students. *Journal of Genetic Psychology, 128,* 95–99.

Goldberg, L. R., Sweeney, D., Merenda, P. F., & Hughes, J. E., Jr. (1998). Demographic variables and personality: The effects of gender, age, education, and ethnic/racial status on self-descriptions of personality attributes. *Personality and Individual differences, 24,* 393–403.

Goldberg, L. R., Johnson, J. A., Eber, H. W., Hogan, R., Ashton, M. C., Cloninger, C. R., & Gough, H. C. (2006). The International Personality Item Pool and the future of public-domain personality measures. *Journal of Research in Personality, 40,* 84–96.

Goncalo, J. A., & Staw, B. M. (2006). Individualism–collectivism and group creativity. *Organizational Behavior and Human Decision Processes, 100,* 96–109.

Griffin, M., & McDermott, M. R. (1998). Exploring a tripartite relationship between rebelliousness, openness to experience and creativity. *Social Behavior and Personality, 26,* 347–356.

Helson, R. (1990). Creativity in women: Outer and inner views over time. In M. A. Runco & R. S. Albert, *Theories of creativity* (pp. 46–58). Newbury Park, CA: Sage.

Horn, J. L., & Cattell, R. B. (1966). Refinement and test of the theory of fluid and crystallized intelligence. *Journal of Educational Psychology, 57*, 253–270.

Iscoe, I., & Pierce-Jones, J. (1964). Divergent thinking, age, and intelligence in White and Negro children. *Child Development, 35*, 785–797.

Jaquish, G. A., & Ripple, R. E. (1984). A life-span developmental cross-cultural study of divergent thinking abilities. *International Journal of Aging and Human Development, 20*, 1–11.

Jellen, H. G., & Urban, K. K. (1989). Assessing creative potential world-wide: The first cross-cultural application for the Test of Creative Thinking—Drawing Production. *Gifted Education International, 6*, 78–86.

Ji, L., Peng, K., & Nisbett, R. E. (2000). Culture, control, and perception of relationships in the environment. *Journal of Personality and Social Psychology, 78*, 943–955.

Kaltsounis, B. (1974). Race, socioeconomic status and creativity. *Psychological Reports, 35*, 164–166.

Kaufman, A. S., & Kaufman, N. L. (1993). *Kaufman Adolescent and Adult Intelligence Test (KAIT).* Circle Pines, MN: American Guidance Service.

Kaufman, A. S., & Lichtenberger, E. O. (2006). *Assessing adolescent and adult intelligence* (3rd ed.). New York: Wiley.

Kaufman, J. C. (2006). Self-reported differences in creativity by gender and ethnicity. *Journal of Applied Cognitive Psychology, 20*, 1065–1082.

Kaufman, J. C. (2009). *Creativity 101.* New York: Springer.

Kaufman, J. C. (2010). Using creativity to reduce ethnic bias in college admissions. *Review of General Psychology, 14*, 189–203.

Kaufman, J. C., & Beghetto, R. A. (2009). Beyond big and little: The Four C Model of Creativity. *Review of General Psychology, 13*, 1–12.

Kaufman, J. C., Baer, J., & Gentile, C. A., (2004). Differences in gender and ethnicity as measured by ratings of three writing tasks. *Journal of Creative Behavior, 39*, 56–69.

Kemple, K. M., David, G. M., & Wang, Y. (1996). Preschoolers' creativity, shyness, and self-esteem. *Creativity Research Journal, 9*, 317–326.

Kessler, C., & Quinn, M. E. (1987). Language minority children's linguistic and cognitive creativity. *Journal of Multilingual and Multicultural Development, 8*, 173–186.

Kim, K. H. (2005). Can only intelligent people be creative? *Journal of Secondary Gifted Education, 16*, 57–66.

King, L. A., McKee-Walker, L., & Broyles, S. J. (1996). Creativity and the five factor model. *Journal of Research in Personality, 30*, 189–203.

Knox, B. J., & Glover, J. A. (1978). A note on preschool experience effects on achievement, readiness, and creativity. *Journal of Genetic Psychology, 132*, 151–152.

Kyllonen, P. C., Walters, A. M., & Kaufman, J. C. (2005). Noncognitive constructs and their assessment in graduate education. *Educational Assessment, 10*, 153–184.

Leung, A. K., Maddux, W. W., Galinsky, A. D., & Chiu, C. (2008). Multicultural experience enhances *creativity:* The when and how. *American Psychologist, 63*, 169–181.

Li, J. (1997). Creativity in horizontal and vertical domains. *Creativity Research Journal, 10*, 107–132.

Lim, W., & Plucker, J. (2001). Creativity through a lens of social responsibility: Implicit theories of creativity with Korean samples. *Journal of Creative Behavior, 35*, 115–130.

Lloyd-Evans, R., Batey, M., & Furnham, A. (2006). Bipolar disorder and creativity: Investigating a possible link. *Advances in Psychology Research, 40*, 11–142.

Loehlin, J. C. (1999). Group differences in intelligence. In R. J. Sternberg (Ed.), *Handbook of intelligence* (pp. 176–193). Cambridge: Cambridge University Press.

Markus, H., & Kitayama, S. (1991). Culture and the self: Implications for cognition, emotion, and motivation. *Psychological Review, 98*, 224–253.

Martindale, C. (1999). Biological bases of creativity. In R. J. Sternberg (Ed.), *Handbook of creativity* (pp. 137–152). New York: Cambridge University Press.

Masten, W. G., Plata, M., Wenglar, K., & Thedford, J. (1999). Acculturation and teacher ratings of Hispanic and Anglo-American students. *Roeper Review, 22*, 64–65.

Matthews, G. (1986). The interactive effects of extraversion and arousal on performance: Are creativity tests anomalous? *Personality and Individual Differences, 7*, 751–761.

Matud, M. P., Rodríguez, C., & Grande, J. (2007). Gender differences in creative thinking. *Personality and Individual Differences, 43*, 1137–1147.

McCrae, R. R. (1987). Creativity, divergent thinking, and openness to experience. *Journal of Personality and Social Psychology, 52*, 1258–1265.

McCrae, R. R., & Costa, P. T., Jr. (1997). Personality trait structure as a human universal. *American Psychologist, 52*, 509–516.

McGrew, K. S. (2009). CHC theory and the human cognitive abilities project: Standing on the shoulders of the giants of psychometric intelligence research. *Intelligence, 37*, 1–10.

Mitchell, B. M. (1988). Hemisphericity and creativity: A look at the relationships among elementary-age low-income Hispanic children. *Educational Research Quarterly*, 2–5.

Mohan, J., & Tiwana, M. (1987). Personality and alienation of creative writers: A brief report. *Personality and Individual Differences, 8*, 449.

Moreno, J. M., & Hogan, J. D. (1976). The influence of race and social-class level on the training of creative thinking and problem-solving abilities. *Journal of Educational Research, 70*, 91–95.

Morgan, R., & Maneckshana, B. (1996). *The psychometric perspective: Lessons learned from 40 years of constructed response testing in the Advanced Placement Program.* Paper presented at the Annual Meeting of the National Council of Measurement in Education in New York.

Murray, C. (2003). *Human accomplishment: The pursuit of excellence in the arts and sciences, 800 BC to 1950.* New York: HarperCollins.

Ng, A. K. (2001). *Why Asians are less creative than westerners.* Singapore: Prentice-Hall.

Ng, A. K., & Smith, I. (2004). Why is there a paradox in promoting creativity in the Asian classroom? In L. Sing, A. Hui, and G. Ng (Eds.), *Creativity: When East meets West* (pp. 87–112). Singapore: World Scientific Publishing.

Nisbett, R. E., Peng, K., Choi, I., & Norenzayan, A. (2001). Culture and systems of thought: Holistic vs. analytic cognition. *Psychological Review, 108*, 291–310.

Niu, W., & Sternberg, R. J. (2001). Cultural influence of artistic creativity and its evaluation. *International Journal of Psychology, 36*(4), 225–241.

Noppe, L. D. (1985). The relationship of formal thought and cognitive style to creativity. *Journal of Creative Behavior, 19*, 88–96.

Ogawa, M., Kuehn-Ebert, C., & DeVito, A. (1991). Differences in creative thinking between Japanese and American fifth grade children. *Ibaraki University Faculty of Education Bulletin, 40*, 53–59.

Palaniappan, A. K. (1996). A cross-cultural study of creative perceptions. *Perceptual and Motor Skills, 82*, 96–98.

Pashler, H., McDaniel, M., Rohrer, D., & Bjork, R. (2008). Learning styles: Concepts and evidence. *Psychological Science in the Public Interest, 9*, 105–119.

Perrine, N. E., & Brodersen, R. M. (2005). Artistic and scientific creative behavior: Openness and the mediating role of interests. *Journal of Creative Behavior, 39*, 217–236.

Piirto, J. (1991). Why are there so few? (Creative women: Visual artists, mathematicians, musicians). *Roper Review, 13*, 142–147.

Plucker, J. A. (1998). Beware of simple conclusions: The case for the content generality of creativity. *Creativity Research Journal, 11*, 179–182.

Plucker, J., Runco, M., & Lim, W. (2006). Predicting ideational behavior from divergent thinking and discretionary time on task. *Creativity Research Journal, 18*, 55–63.

Pornrungroj, C. (1992). *A comparison of creativity test scores between Thai children in a Thai culture and Thai–American children who were born and reared in an American culture.* Unpublished doctoral dissertation, Illinois State University.

Post, F. (1994). Creativity and psychopathology: A study of 291 world-famous men. *British Journal of Psychiatry, 165*, 22–34.

Powers, D. E., & Kaufman, J. C. (2004). Do standardized tests penalize deep-thinking, creative, or conscientious students? Some personality correlates of Graduate Record Examinations test scores. *Intelligence, 32*, 145–153.

Preckel, F., Holling, H., & Wiese, M. (2006). Relationship of intelligence and creativity in gifted and non-gifted students: An investigation of threshold theory. *Personality and Individual Differences, 40*, 159–170.

Price-Williams, D. R., & Ramirez III, M. (1977). Divergent thinking, cultural differences, and bilingualism. *The Journal of Social Psychology, 103*, 3–11.

Rhodes, M. (1962). An analysis of creativity. *Phi Delta Kappan, 42*, 305–311.

Richards, R. L. (1976). A comparison of selected Guilford and Wallach–Kogan creative thinking tests in conjunction with measures of intelligence. *Journal of Creative Behavior, 10*, 151–164.

Richards, R. L., and Kinney, D. K. (1990). Mood swings and creativity. *Creativity Research Journal, 3*, 202–217.

Ripple, R. E., & Jaquish, G. A. (1982). Developmental aspects of ideational fluency, flexibility, and originality: South Africa and the United States. *South African Journal of Psychology, 12*, 95–100.

Roid, G. H. (2003). *Stanford–Binet Intelligence Scales, fifth edition: Technical manual.* Itasca, IL: Riverside Publishing.

Rostan, S. M., Pariser, D., & Gruber, H. E. (2002). A cross-cultural study of the development of artistic talent, creativity and giftedness. *High Ability Studies, 13*, 123–155.

Roy, D. D. (1996). Personality model of fine artists. *Creativity Research Journal, 9*, 391–394.

Rubinstein, G. (2008). Are schizophrenic patients necessarily creative? A comparative study between three groups of psychiatric inpatients. *Personality and Individual Differences, 45*, 806–810.

Runco, M. A., & Albert, R. S. (1986). The threshold theory regarding creativity and intelligence: An empirical test with gifted and nongifted children. *Creative Child and Adult Quarterly, 11*, 212–218.

Runco, M. A., Plucker, J., & Lim, W. (2001). Development and psychometric integrity of a measure of ideational behavior. *Creativity Research Journal, 13*, 393–400.

Saeki, N., Fan, X., & Van Deusen, L. (2001). A comparative study of creative thinking of American and Japanese college students. *Journal of Creative Behavior, 35*, 24–36.

Schlesinger, J. (2009). Creative myth conceptions: A closer look at the evidence for "mad genius" hypothesis. *Psychology of Aesthetics, Creativity, and the Arts, 3*, 62–72.

Schuldberg, D. (2005). Eysenck personality questionnaire scales and paper-and-pencil tests related to creativity. *Psychological Reports, 97*, 180–182.

Shoda, Y., Mischel, W., & Wright, J. C. (1994). Intraindividual stability in the organization and patterning of behavior: Incorporating psychological situations into the idiographic analysis of personality. *Journal of Personality and Social Psychology, 67,* 674–687.

Silvia, P. J. (2008a). Another look at creativity and intelligence: Exploring higher-order models and probable confounds. *Personality and Individual Differences, 44,* 1012–1021.

Silvia, P. J. (2008b). Creativity and intelligence revisited: A latent variable analysis of Wallach and Kogan (1965). *Creativity Research Journal, 20,* 34–39.

Silvia, P. J., Kaufman, J. C., & Pretz, J. E. (2009). Is creativity domain-specific? Latent class models of creative accomplishments and creative self-descriptions. *Psychology of Aesthetics, Creativity, and the Arts, 3,* 139–148.

Simonton, D. K. (1994). *Greatness: Who makes history and why.* New York: Guilford Press.

Singer, D. G., & Singer, J. L. (1990). *The house of make-believe: Children's play and the developing imagination.* Cambridge, MA: Harvard University Press.

Sligh, A. C., Conners, F. A., & Roskos-Ewoldsen, B. (2005). Relation of creativity to fluid and crystallized intelligence. *Journal of Creative Behavior, 39,* 123–136.

Smith, R. E., Shoda, Y., Cumming, S. P., & Smoll, F. L. (2009). Behavioral signatures at the ballpark: Intraindividual consistency of adults' situation–behavior patterns and their interpersonal consequences. *Journal of Research in Personality, 43,* 187–195.

Soldz, S., & Vaillant, G. E. (1999). The Big Five personality traits and the live course: A 50-year longitudinal study. *Journal of Research in Personality, 33,* 208–232.

Sternberg, R. J. (1981). Intelligence and nonentrenchment. *Journal of Educational Psychology, 73,* 1–16.

Sternberg, R. J., & Lubart, T. I. (1996). *Defying the crowd.* New York: Free Press.

Stricker, L. J., Rock, D. A., & Bennett, R. E. (2001). Sex and ethnic-group differences on accomplishment measures. *Applied Measurement in Education, 14,* 205–218.

Strom, R., Johnson, A., Strom, S. & Strom. P. (1992). Designing curriculum for parents of gifted children. *Journal for the Education of the Gifted, 15,* 182–200.

Strom, R., & Johnson, A. (1989). Rural families of gifted preschool and primary grade children. *Journal of Instructional Psychology, 14,* 32–38.

Torrance, E. P. (1966). *Torrance Tests of Creative Thinking: Directions manual and scoring guide.* Bensenville, IL: Scholastic Testing Service.

Torrance, E. P. (1971). Are the Torrance Tests of Creative Thinking biased against or in favour of disadvantaged groups? *Gifted Child Quarterly, 15,* 75–80.

Torrance, E. P. (1973). Non-test indicators of creative talent among disadvantaged children. *Gifted Child Quarterly, 17,* 3–9.

Torrance, E. P. (1974a). *Torrance Tests of Creative Thinking: Directions manual and scoring guide.* Verbal test booklet A. Bensenville, IL: Scholastic Testing Service.

Torrance, E. P. (1974b). *Torrance Tests of Creative Thinking: Norms—Technical manual.* Bensenville, IL: Scholastic Testing Service.

Torrance, E. P., & Sato, S. (1979). Differences in Japanese and United States styles of thinking. *Creative Child and Adult Quarterly, 4,* 145–151.

Troiano, A. B., & Bracken, B. A. (1983). Creative thinking and movement styles of three culturally homogeneous kindergarten groups. *Journal of Psychoeducational Assessment, 1,* 35–46.

Wai, J., Lubinski, D., & Benbow, C. P. (2005). Creativity and occupational accomplishments among intellectually precocious youth: An age 13 to age 33 longitudinal study. *Journal of Educational Psychology, 97,* 484–492.

Walker, A. M., Koestner, R., & Hum, A. (1995). Personality correlates of depressive style in autobiographies of creative achievers. *Journal of Creative Behavior, 29,* 75–94.

Wallach, M. A., & Kogan, N. (1965). *Modes of thinking in young children: A study of the creativity–intelligence distinction.* New York: Holt, Rinehart and Winston.

Wang, A. Y. (2007). *Contexts of creative thinking: Teaching, learning, and creativity in Taiwan and the United States.* Unpublished doctoral dissertation, The Claremont Graduate University.

Ward, T. B., Patterson, M. J., Sifonis, C. M., Dodds, R. A., & Saunders, K. N. (2002). The role of graded category structure in imaginative thought. *Memory and Cognition, 30,* 199–216.

Wechsler, S. (2006). Validity of the Torrance Tests of Creative Thinking to the Brazilian culture. *Creativity Research Journal, 18,* 15–25.

Weiss, L. G., Saklofske, D. H., Coalson, D. L., & Raiford, S. E. (Eds.) (2010). *WAIS-IV clinical use and interpretation.* San Diego, CA: Academic Press.

Wolfradt, U., & Pretz, J. E. (2001). Individual differences in creativity: Personality, story writing, and hobbies. *European Journal of Personality, 15,* 297–310.

Woodcock, R. W., McGrew, K. S., & Mather, N. (2001). *Woodcock–Johnson III.* Itasca, IL: Riverside Publishing.

Yap, C., Chai, K., & Lemaire, P. (2005). An empirical study on functional diversity and innovation in SMEs. *Creativity and Innovation Management, 14,* 176–190.

Yoon, S. N. (2005). *Comparing the intelligence and creativity scores of Asian American gifted students with Caucasian gifted students.* Unpublished doctoral dissertation, Purdue University.

Zha, P., Walczyk, J. J., Griffith-Ross, D. A., Tobacyk, J. J., & Walczyk, D. F. (2006). The impact of culture and individualism–collectivism on the creative potential and achievement of American and Chinese adults. *Creativity Research Journal, 18,* 355–366.

Zhiyan, T., & Singer, J. L. (1996). Daydreaming styles, emotionality, and the big five personality dimensions. *Imagination, Cognition, and Personality, 16,* 399–414.

Section 2    Relationships and
Subjective Well-Being

## 27

# Personality and Happiness
## Predicting the Experience of
## Subjective Well-Being

### William Pavot and Ed Diener

Despite both the pervasive desire of most members of the species to achieve happiness and considerable philosophical speculation about it (Haybron, 2008), the empirical study of human happiness has been slow to develop. Research on happiness, or, to use the preferred terminology of many researchers, on subjective well-being (SWB), was only occasionally conducted in the first half of the twentieth century (see Wilson, 1967, for a review of this early research). Real momentum in the study of SWB and other variables related to "positive psychology" (Seligman & Csikszentmihalyi, 2000, p. 5) did not become apparent until the 1970s. It now seems, however, that psychology and other social sciences are moving to make up for lost time; literally thousands of studies focused on understanding the experience of SWB have been conducted in the past two decades.

Many of these relatively recent studies have been conducted with the goal of identifying variables or factors that are strongly associated with SWB. An impressive array of potentially influential variables have thus far been examined. Modest correlations have been found between SWB and a number of situational factors such as marital status, income level, and the form of government under which an individual lives (for a review, see Diener, Suh, Lucas, & Smith, 1999). Although it is intuitively appealing that such variables would exert considerable influence on an individual's level of happiness, generally the connections between situational or life circumstance variables and SWB have been weaker than many would expect.

Standing in some contrast to the findings noted above, research examining the links between SWB and personality constructs has revealed some substantial and

*The Wiley-Blackwell Handbook of Individual Differences,* First Edition.
Edited by Tomas Chamorro-Premuzic, Sophie von Stumm, and Adrian Furnham.
© 2011 Blackwell Publishing Ltd. Published 2011 by Blackwell Publishing Ltd.

stable relations, indicating that personality exerts a pervasive and broadly based influence on the experience of well-being. At the same time, however, it must be noted that, while personality appears to account for a substantial proportion of the individual variation in SWB, no study has indicated that personality can account for all such variance. Thus the full understanding of these personality/SWB connections represents an essential step toward the greater goal of achieving a more general understanding of the experience of well-being, with the hope that such understanding can lead to possible positive intervention strategies. This review is intended to facilitate future research efforts aimed at furthering the understanding of the relation between personality and SWB.

In the early sections of this chapter we will briefly review the construct of SWB and its major sub-components, and consider their relation to one another. We will then examine some of the relevant theoretical formulations that have been advanced, and consider several of the methodological and measurement issues involved in the study of SWB. In subsequent sections we will review a few of the major findings linking personality constructs to the experience of SWB, moving from broad, temperament-level dispositions to more specific traits and personality processes. Underlying mechanisms with the potential for explaining the relation between personality and happiness (e.g. heritability) will be discussed. Concluding sections will examine issues such as stability and change in SWB, the overall influence of personality on SWB relative to other factors, and some potential areas for future investigation.

## The Construct of SWB

As interest in positive psychology and related constructs has grown, a number of conceptualizations of "well-being" have gradually emerged. From among these concepts, two have received considerable research interest: psychological well-being (PWB; Ryff, 1989; Ryff & Keyes, 1995) and subjective well-being (SWB; Diener, 1984, 2000). Grounded in the eudaimonic tradition, PWB generally is taken to represent a sense of well-being stemming from personal growth, autonomy, mastery of the environment, positive interpersonal relationships, and a sense of life purpose (Ryff, 1989). The basis of the construct of SWB (Diener, 2000) lies more within the hedonic tradition, with the experience of positive affect and life satisfaction as its central focus. Although the definitions and hypothesized sources of PWB and SWB differ, they tend to be complementary, and together they provide a more comprehensive view of well-being (Ryan & Deci, 2001). The emphasis for the present chapter will be on SWB rather than on PWB.

Reasonable consensus for a three-component model of the construct of SWB has gradually emerged, although this model is not universally embraced (see Kahneman, 1999). The "tripartite theory" structure (Arthaud-Day, Rode, Mooney, & Near, 2005, p. 449) includes positive affect (PA), negative affect (NA), and life satisfaction. The affective components of PA and NA reflect ongoing evaluations of emotions and mood states, whereas the life satisfaction component represents a "global evaluation by the person of his or her life" (Pavot, Diener, Colvin, & Sandvik, 1991, p. 150).

Intuitively, it is appealing to assume that PA and NA are highly (inversely) correlated, but considerable research has demonstrated that the two components show substantial independence, particularly when average levels are measured over time (Bradburn, 1969; Diener & Emmons, 1984; Emmons & Diener, 1985; Watson, Clark, & Tellegen, 1988). Therefore it is desirable to treat them as independent and to assess them separately. The third component, life satisfaction, represents a cognitive evaluation or judgment, made by the individual, concerning the quality of her or his life circumstances and of life as a whole (Pavot & Diener, 2008). When measured concurrently with PA and NA, life satisfaction typically will be observed to correlate with the two affective components, as the emotional state of the individual tends to influence her or his cognitive processes (Crooker & Near, 1998; Suh, Diener, Oishi, & Triandis, 1998). Nonetheless, self-reports of life satisfaction will typically show considerable independent variance as well (Schimmack, 2008). Using structural equation modeling for the analysis of data from multiple large samples, Arthaud-Day et al. (2005) found that a three-factor model (PA, NA, and life satisfaction) of SWB showed a better fit than a one- or two-factor model. On the basis of evidence such as this, it is highly desirable to treat life satisfaction as a unique component of SWB and to assess it accordingly.

Under some circumstances, and depending upon the goals of the researcher, additional measures might be considered. For example, the assessment of satisfaction with specific domains, such as housing, employment, income, relationships, and marriage, can provide a more intricate description of an individual's experience of SWB. Generally, such assessments are important within the specific context of a particular sample or research question, and may not be needed for inclusion in all studies.

From a temporal perspective, SWB shows considerable overall stability. For example, Lucas, Diener, and Suh (1996) reported stability coefficients for PA, NA, and life satisfaction ranging from .56 to .61 for a 3-year period. Magnus, Diener, Fujita, and Pavot (1993) reported a test–retest reliability coefficient of .54, over a 4-year interval, for the Satisfaction With Life Scale (Diener, Emmons, Larsen, & Griffin, 1985)—a global measure of satisfaction. In an analysis of data from a large-scale panel study (the German Socio-Economic Panel, GSOEP), Fujita and Diener (2005) found that the stability of life satisfaction, even when assessed by a simple one-item measure, was an estimated .25 over a 17-year interval.

Although the above results indicate moderately high stability for SWB, they do not indicate invariance. In addition to finding evidence for stability, for example, Fujita and Diener (2005) found that 24 percent of the respondents reported significant change in their level of SWB from their early baseline (comprising the first five years of the study) to the last five years. Further, they found that the stability of life satisfaction in the GSOEP sample dropped more quickly than the estimated stability of personality (Roberts & DelVecchio, 2000). Vaidya, Gray, Haig, and Watson (2002) compared the stability of affect to the stability of the Big-Five personality traits over a 2.5-year interval, and found that personality showed more stability than affect across that period. In a later section we will further discuss the stability of SWB within the context of heritability.

In sum, the construct of SWB is multi-faceted, encompassing, and evolving, rather than fixed and unitary in nature. Self-reports of SWB show moderately strong stability over time, but at the same time they show sensitivity in response to the individual's experience of major life events and changing circumstances.

## Theoretical Perspectives on SWB

A number of theoretical models focused on SWB have been proposed over time; generally these can be grouped into two categories: bottom-up theories and top-down theories (Diener, 1984; Schimmack, 2008). The general assumption of the bottom-up theories is that an individual's overall sense of SWB represents the sum of a number of evaluative judgments relevant to multiple life domains and to ongoing life experiences. Satisfaction with each component of a set of personally relevant domains is determined, and this process results in an overall aggregate judgment of SWB. Thus, according to this perspective, judgments of SWB are built from the bottom up.

In contrast, top-down models are based on the assumption that some underlying processes (usually identified as personality processes) set an overall affective tone, which tends to exert a ubiquitous influence on how a person judges his or her life experiences. These models tend to assume that SWB is largely stable, and that the effect of life events and changes in one's circumstances tends to be transitory in nature. An additional consideration is the influence of personality on life events (Magnus et al., 1993); this indirect influence can contribute to the strength of the personality/SWB relation.

Considerable debate has focused on the relative validity of top-down versus bottom-up theoretical models. A relatively recent meta-analytic effort (Heller, Watson, & Ilies, 2004) produced evidence that was not supportive of an overall top-down model for SWB; path analyses did support a temperament-based top-down model of life satisfaction, and an integrative model which included the influence of domain satisfaction on life satisfaction. These results indicate a mixture of both top-down and bottom-up influences and suggest that a comprehensive model is needed. In a review of relevant recent studies, Schimmack (2008) concludes that changes in specific domains can influence overall life satisfaction (bottom-up influences), but the evidence for top-down effects on life satisfaction is not as clear. Personality traits, such as extraversion and neuroticism, exert a stronger influence on the affective components of SWB (a top-down influence); further, the relation between personality and life satisfaction appears to be strongly mediated by the affective component (Schimmack, 2008).

Overall, the existing evidence indicates that a complexity of influences shape an individual's experience of SWB. Personality plays an important role, both in terms of the direct, top-down effects of temperament, and in terms of the less direct effects that personality has on life events (Magnus et al., 1993) and on behavioral patterns associated with major life outcomes—such as the association between conscientiousness and health (Roberts, Walton, & Bogg, 2005). But satisfaction with specific life domains and life events that are not influenced by personality also contribute to overall SWB.

A long-standing theoretical principle that has been frequently evoked as an explanation for the observed modest impact of life events and demographic circumstances on SWB is the "hedonic treadmill" (Brickman & Campbell, 1971). Based on the principle of adaptation-level (Helson, 1948, 1964), the hedonic treadmill proposes that, although life events and changes in life circumstances may have an initial impact on an individual's SWB, people tend to get quickly habituated to their new circumstances, and the ultimate effect of the life change on long-term SWB is nil. The implication is that people tend to return to a hedonically neutral point, and that interventions or attempts to increase happiness will not have lasting effects. Initially, the theory of adaptation received support from a number of empirical demonstrations. Brickman, Coates, and Janoff-Bulman (1978), for example, presented evidence that they interpreted to mean that powerful life events, such as winning a lottery or developing paraplegia after a trauma, did not result in long-term differences in the levels of happiness for the groups that experienced these events relative to others, who did not have such experiences. And, although the events studied were much less powerful than those of Brickman et al. (1978), Suh, Diener, and Fujita (1996) found that only recent good or bad events—events of the past two months—affected happiness.

As an explanation both for the apparent leveling power of adaptation and for the persistently observed correlation between personality and SWB, Headey and Wearing proposed dynamic equilibrium theory (Headey & Wearing, 1989), which has also come to be labeled "set-point theory" (SPT; Headey, 2008). Essentially, SPT, in its early form, asserted that adaptation to life events and changes does occur, but that, rather than returning to a hedonically neutral level after such events, individuals return to a set-point level of SWB, which is largely determined by the temperament-level traits of extraversion and neuroticism. SPT could therefore account for the relatively small impact of life events on SWB, and also for individual differences in SWB.

Subsequent evidence has gradually emerged, which suggests that some modifications to adaptation theory (Diener, Lucas, & Scollon, 2006) and to SPT (Headey, 2008) are needed. One problem with adaptation theory is that, rather than predominantly experiencing hedonic neutrality, most people are generally happy (Diener & Diener, 1996). In addition, individuals show considerable variation in set-points; at least a portion of the variance between them is due to personality-based influences (Diener & Lucas, 1999), and these personality-based influences appear to extend beyond extraversion and neuroticism, to other inherited characteristics (Lykken & Tellegen, 1996). A third objection is that happiness can change over time (Fujita & Diener, 2005), and at least some life events, such as becoming a widow or becoming unemployed (Lucas, Clark, Georgelllis, & Diener, 2004), do seem to produce long-term changes in the level of SWB of those who experience them.

Another issue is perhaps most relevant to the present discussion: individual differences in adaptation. It has gradually become clear that there are substantial differences in the degree to which individuals experience adaptation to life events. Longitudinal studies of adaptation to major life events such as marriage (Lucas, Clark, Georgelllis, & Diener, 2003) have revealed a wide range of effects on SWB, some individuals showing adaptation, whereas others showed lasting increases in SWB, and still others reported decreases. Some of these individual differences may stem from differences in coping with stress, and these differences, in turn, are related to personality characteristics. Individuals with relatively high levels of neuroticism tend to use ineffective coping strategies (Ferguson, 2001), which in turn might prolong the return to baseline after a stressful life event, whereas those higher in optimism tend to use strategies such as seeking social support, which are more likely to promote a quick recovery (Scheier, Weintraub, & Carver, 1986).

Along with the previously noted discrepancies, the evidence for individual differences in adaptation represents a challenge to the view of hedonic level adaptation as a universal and inexorable process. On the basis of these and additional findings, Diener et al. (2006) have suggested that the adaptation theory of SWB requires modification in order to accommodate them. The process of adaptation generally exerts a powerful influence, but it does not appear to be absolute, or impervious to intervention.

## Research Methods in the Study of SWB

Given the subjective nature of the construct, the dominant methodology of SWB researchers has involved self-reported assessments (Diener, 1994). With the exception of Bradburn's (1969) affect scale, early assessment efforts often employed very brief, single-item measures (e.g. Andrews & Withey, 1976), which were generally focused on the cognitive component or on the life satisfaction component of SWB. These assessments were typically embedded within a larger survey.

These very simple early measures were popular with survey researchers because of their brevity, but that advantage also represented a potential threat to their validity. Using data from a series of studies, Schwarz and Strack (1999) constructed a strong argument to the effect that contextual influences surrounding the self-report response, such as the momentary mood of the respondent or some unexpected occurrence, such as finding a small coin, can influence global reports of SWB. Responses to global measures can also be influenced by item-order effects (e.g. the content of the item(s) placed before such global measures of SWB in a larger survey questionnaire). Depending upon the circumstances, these contextual influences can be substantial (Strack, Martin, & Schwarz, 1988), although a meta-analysis by Schimmack and Oishi (2005) indicated that the effects of irrelevant factors such as item-order effects are generally small, relative to chronically accessible information, particularly in the formation of life satisfaction judgments. Still, investigators should be aware of these potential influences and should actively try to minimize their effects. At least two potential remedies to contextual influences have been pursued. One remedy is to obtain multiple SWB reports on separate occasions, and then to average these measures in a composite index, thereby presumably canceling out the effects of momentary mood or context in any single report (Pavot & Diener, 2003). A second strategy involves the use of more complex, multiple-item measures, which tend to have greater reliability and less vulnerability to contextual effects (Pavot & Diener, 1993). Combining these two strategies should work to further reduce the potential for immediate contextual effects to contaminate SWB assessments.

In addition to the problem of contextual effects, many of the early measures of SWB did not adequately distinguish between the components of PA, NA, and life satisfaction. Some of these early measures (see Bradburn, 1969) focused on the affective components of SWB and did not separately assess life satisfaction, whereas others focused on the cognitively oriented life satisfaction component, without specifically assessing PA and NA. Researchers using such unidimensional assessment instruments were reporting that they had measured "subjective well-being," but they were in fact often only measuring a sub-component of the construct. This situation eventually led to confusing and sometimes conflicting results, as the affective components of SWB often showed somewhat different relations with other variables that life satisfaction did (Pavot, 2008). It is now clear that the complete assessment of SWB requires either a multidimensional measure that assesses each of the components of SWB, or several separate component-specific measures.

Although much current research relies on established, traditional self-report instruments, additional methodologies have gradually emerged. One such approach, the experience-sampling method (ESM), involves obtaining reports of ongoing affective experiences from respondents, at random moments in their everyday lives, usually over a period of weeks (e.g. Sandvik, Diener, & Seidlitz, 1993). By obtaining these immediate, naturalistic reports of affective experience, some of the memory and contextual biases that are inherent in reports based on recalled experiences are reduced. With the advent of modern cue/response methods, such as Palm Pilot, the collection of ESM data is easier and more reliable. Some researchers, for instance Kahneman (1999), have suggested that assessments obtained by using ESM represent the best measure of "objective happiness" (p. 3). But ESM assessments can involve large amounts of data and complex analyses (Scollon, Kim-Prieto, & Diener, 2003). Further, the ability of the respondents to select their own criteria and to differentially weigh those criteria in the formation of a summary SWB judgment is diminished (Pavot & Diener, 2008). A more recent innovation, the Day Reconstruction Method (DRM; Kahneman, Krueger, Schkade, Schwarz & Stone, 2004), represents a "hybrid approach" (p. 1776). Using DRM, respondents are asked to revive memories of the previous day, and then construct a diary based on these recalled episodes. The affective content of these episodes is evaluated in a manner similar to that of ESM. The DRM is less disruptive and bothersome to respondents and provides a more holistic assessment, rather than a series of moment samples (Kahneman et al., 2004). It thus reduces some of the problems and complexities of the ESM, but it also moves away from the immediate response feature of the ESM.

In addition to obtaining direct self-reports of SWB, a number of indirect assessments have been demonstrated to have reasonable validity and utility. Probably the most common among these is the use of informant reports. Ratings of SWB by informants have been found to be moderately to highly correlated with self-reported SWB (Pavot et al., 1991; Sandvik et al., 1993). Pavot et al. (1991), for example, observed correlations in the range of .54 to .64 between self-reports on the Satisfaction with Life Scale and informant ratings completed by using the same instrument. This convergence serves to provide cross-method validation for self-report measures of SWB, and also represents evidence that SWB is a relatively stable phenomenon, rather than merely a momentary reaction to the immediate context or transient mood of the respondent. (For a meta-analysis of studies using self ratings and informant ratings of SWB, see Schneider & Schimmack, 2009.)

Other indirect measures have shown some validity in the assessment of SWB. Clinical-style interviews, memory bias measures (Sandvik et al., 1993), and the analysis of writing samples for emotional content (Danner, Snowdon, & Friesen, 2001) have all been used as alternatives to direct self-reports of SWB. At the physiological level, measures of neural activity in the prefrontal areas of the cortex have been shown to correlate with various components of SWB (Davidson, 2004). These measures will be discussed in a later section of this chapter.

A wide array of assessment instruments and methodologies focused on the measurement of SWB have emerged over time. When multiple measures and/or multiple methodologies are combined with longitudinal designs, most of the threats to the validity of SWB measurement (e.g. momentary mood or contextual effects) can be greatly reduced or eliminated. The available methodologies have the potential to yield reliable and valid assessments of SWB in a variety of conditions and settings.

## SWB and Temperament-Level Personality Traits

Among the personality traits and processes that have been examined for their association with SWB, the temperament-level traits of extraversion and neuroticism have been the subject of what is by far the largest portion of research efforts (Diener & Lucas, 1999). Although the relations between SWB and both high extraversion and low neuroticism (or being "worry-free") had been noted earlier (Wilson, 1967, p. 294), an influential paper authored by Costa and McCrae (1980) brought much attention to the SWB/temperament connection. In this paper Costa and McCrae presented data from a series of studies, including longitudinal data spanning a 10-year interval. These data indicated that extraversion was consistently correlated with PA, but not with NA, and neuroticism was consistently associated with NA, but not with PA. Together, neuroticism and extraversion represented independent influences on the experience of SWB. Using structural equation modeling, Fujita (1991) found an extraversion latent variable to be highly correlated (.71) with a positive affect latent trait, and neuroticism and negative affect formed a single factor. Many other studies (Argyle & Lu, 1990; Diener, Larsen, & Emmons, 1984; Diener, Sandvik, Pavot, & Fujita, 1992; Emmons & Diener, 1985; Hayes & Joseph, 2003; Pavot, Diener, & Fujita, 1990; Schimmack, Oishi, Furr, & Funder, 2004) have replicated the correlations between extraversion, neuroticism, and SWB.

At least two major meta-analytic efforts have focused on the relations between personality and SWB, and the results have shown some divergence, particularly with regard to the relations between extraversion, neuroticism, and SWB. In an influential paper, DeNeve and Cooper (1998) reported the results of a large-scale meta-analysis, in which they examined the correlations of 137 traits with SWB. Although the previously observed personality/SWB correlations were generally confirmed, the strength of the relations were modest. The observed correlations of SWB with extraversion (.17), neuroticism (−.22), agreeableness (.17), conscientiousness (.21), and openness to experience (.11) (DeNeve & Cooper, 1998) were in the expected directions, but not of the expected magnitude, to judge by previous empirical findings. These modest correlations were not indicative of personality as strongly predictive of SWB, accounting for a relatively small percentage (4 percent) of the variance of indices of SWB (DeNeve & Cooper, 1998).

Some 10 years later, and with the benefit of a much larger number of relevant studies, Steel, Schmidt, and Shultz (2008) again used meta-analysis to revisit the personality/SWB connection. Using techniques of categorization designed to reduce the effects of commensurability (that is, grouping dissimilar studies together) and a multivariate approach, Steel et al. (2008) found much stronger relations between SWB and personality; estimates reached as high as 39 percent of the variance (63 percent disattenuated) between personality and quality of life measures.

With the linkage between personality and SWB well established, it remains to provide a comprehensive explanation for the observed association. Most theoretical explanations fall into one of two general categories. One category of explanation posits a direct link between personality and SWB; in this view, temperament-level traits exert an unmediated influence on an individual's experienced affect. These explanations have been identified by McCrae and Costa (1991) as "temperament theories." The second general category, summarized by McCrae and Costa as "instrumental theories," posits an indirect pathway between personality and SWB; from this perspective, personality predisposes an individual toward particular life events and activities, and it is the experience of these activities that creates an emotional response, which in turn influences the individual's level of SWB.

From the temperament theory perspective, a prominent explanation for the personality/SWB relation has been offered by Jeffrey Gray (1981, 1991). Gray's work focuses on three basic motivational systems: the behavioral activation system (BAS), the behavioral inhibition system (BIS), and the fight–flight system (FFS). The BAS is hypothesized to regulate reactions to environmental signals of conditioned reward and non-punishment; the BIS is believed to regulate reactions to signals of conditioned punishment and non-reward; and the FFS regulates reactions to unconditioned punishment and non-reward. Among these systems, the first two, the BAS and the BIS, appear to map onto the traits of extraversion and neuroticism, respectively. Individuals higher in extraversion are believed to possess a stronger BAS, which predisposes them to be more reactive to signals of reward. These greater reactions in turn generate more cognitive processing and greater levels of positive emotion. Individuals higher in neuroticism possess a stronger BIS, and are believed to be more reactive to signals of punishment and to the accompanying negative emotions.

In an examination of temperament effects, Larsen and Ketelaar (1991) used laboratory mood induction procedures to test the sensitivity of individuals to positive and negative stimuli. In this study, extraverts showed greater sensitivity than introverts to positive mood induction procedures, and individuals high on neuroticism showed greater sensitivity to negative mood induction procedures than low-neuroticism participants. These effects have been replicated (Gomez, Cooper, & Gomez, 2000; Rusting & Larsen, 1997), but some failures in replication have also occurred, particularly with regard to the positive emotional reactivity associated with extraversion (Lucas & Baird, 2004). Thus some empirical support for the direct influence of temperament on the experience of SWB has accumulated, but the relative power of temperament mechanisms (e.g. of the BAS and BIS systems) is somewhat unclear. It remains for investigators also to uncover the biological and physiological mechanisms that underlie individual differences in temperament.

# Heredity, Temperament, and SWB

The influence of heritability on both personality and SWB has been examined in a number of behavior-genetic studies. The participants in these studies are usually members of monozygotic (identical) or dizygotic (fraternal) twin pairs. These individuals complete measures of personality and/or SWB, and the results are compared with those obtained from their twins for similarity. The estimated influence of genetic effects can thus be examined. The additive effects of genetics would be expected to produce cross-twin correlations approximately twice as large for MZ twins as those observed for DZ twins. The relative influence of genes versus environmental factors can be estimated if twins reared in the same family environment are compared to twins who were adopted shortly after birth and reared in separate environments.

In an early study utilizing behavior-genetic techniques, Tellegen et al. (1988) found evidence for the substantial influence of genetics on personality characteristics relevant to the affective components of SWB. The researchers estimated that genes account for about 40 percent of the variance in positive emotionality and for 55 percent of the variance in negative emotionality, which is much larger than the percentages accounted for by shared family environment (22 percent and 2 percent, respectively). A later re-analysis by Lykken and Tellegen (1996) indicated that approximately 40 to 55 percent of current SWB, and 80 percent of stable long-term well-being, can be attributed to heritability. On the basis of these findings, Lykken and Tellegen concluded that attempts to change an individual's level of SWB would be futile. There are several factors, however, such as the relatively small sample size and some inconsistency in replication (Lucas, 2008), which indicate the need for caution in the interpretation of the re-analysis by Lykken and Tellegen, particularly the remarkably high heritably estimate for long-term well-being. Still more recent efforts have produced evidence that is supportive of the more moderate estimates of the heritability of current SWB. Although the original study by Tellegen et al. (1988) did not utilize specific measures of SWB, later studies that did include measures intended to specifically assess global well-being (Roysamb, Harris, Magnus, Vitterso, & Tambs, 2002) and life satisfaction (Stubbe, Posthuma, Boomsma, & De Geus, 2005) have found similar effects of heritability on SWB.

In addition to the evidence from behavioral-genetic studies, some evidence relevant to the biological origins of SWB is emerging from direct genetic research. In what has become a classic study for the area, the Dunedin longitudinal study (Caspi et al., 2003), the investigators examined the relative roles that genetic variation and exposure to stressful life events (across a 20-year period) potentially might have in determining risk of depression. Differences in the serotonin transporter (5–HTT) gene were found to interact with the number of stressful life events experienced by the individual at the level of risk for depression. When the number of experienced stressful life events was low, genotype differences were not predictive of depression. Among individuals with a high frequency of stressful events, however, there were genotype effects such that individuals whose genotype included the low serotonin transporter gene were at greater risk for depression. The study by Caspi et al. (2003) is a clear demonstration of a gene-by-environment interaction; the impact of environmental factors on an individual's risk for disorder is moderated by his or her genotype. In another examination of the behavioral consequences of polymorphic variance in the human serotonin (5–HTT) gene, Lesch et al. (1996) found associations between the 5–HTT polymorphism and anxiety-related personality traits. Lesch et al.'s (1996) study provides direct evidence for a link between genotype and personality.

The findings from direct genetic research are intriguing, but research in this area is still in its infancy. Some findings in the area, for example those of Caspi et al. (2003), have not been consistently replicated (Risch et al., 2009). The effect sizes for many studies are small, often accounting for less than 1 percent of the variance. These small effect sizes seem to imply that many genetic factors might be involved in any particular trait or behavioral pattern, or that the genetic action is complex—or perhaps both of these factors are at work.

An expression of this complexity is emerging from the relatively new field of social genomics (Cole, 2009). The focus of this area is on identifying particular types of genes that are subject to social regulation and the mechanisms through which this regulation occurs. In a demonstration of these social effects, Cole et al. (2007) found that, among 22,283 genes assayed, 209 showed systematically different levels of expression among people who reported feelings of persistent, long-term social isolation, and the affected genes generally were involved in immune system function. Demonstrations such as these indicate that, as challenging as it may be to unravel the human genome, such knowledge will likely be insufficient without additional understanding of the effects of social feedback on genetic material. It appears that, at least in some instances, environmental factors can exert an influence on gene expression.

Taken as a whole, the evidence from studies focused on establishing the heritability of SWB indicates that approximately 40–50 percent of the variance of SWB can be attributed to genetic influences. The precise pathways of genetic expression are less clear and will likely require considerably more study before being completely understood, but the preponderance of evidence now favors a model of SWB that includes a substantial biological component.

Given the evidence for a substantial genetic contribution to SWB, some underlying physiological process or mechanism must be influential on affective experience. Whether there is an overall direct or indirect influence of genetic material on SWB is unclear, but some evidence of specific physiological correlates of SWB has emerged. One area that has generated considerable interest is research on asymmetrical hemispheric activation in the prefrontal cortex (Davidson, 2004). In a long-standing program of research, Davidson and other researchers, using electroencephalogram technology, have found evidence for a correlation between asymmetrical activity in the left versus right prefrontal areas of the cortex and the experience of affective states. Generally, heightened activity in the left prefrontal cortex (relative to the corresponding area in the right hemisphere) is associated with the experience of positive affect states, whereas relatively high activity in the right prefrontal area is associated with negative affective experience. These differences have been observed in both infants and adults. In one study (Fox & Davidson, 1987), 10-month-old infants were separated into groups on the basis of expressed distress (crying), which occurred when they were subjected to an anxiety-producing procedure, during which their mothers left them alone in a room, and then a stranger entered the room. They found that the infants who expressed distress showed more activity in the right prefrontal area than in the corresponding area in the left hemisphere, compared to infants who did not show distress. Similar patterns of frontal asymmetry have been found to be stable across a period of several months, both in infants (Fox, Bell, & Jones, 1992) and in adults (Davidson, 1993; Wheeler, Davidson, & Tomarken, 1993). The stability of these activity patterns is suggestive of a dispositional individual difference related to the experience of SWB. The pattern of asymmetrical hemispheric activation appears to align well with a general two-system model of temperament comparable to the BAS/BIS system of Gray, or perhaps even to the extraversion/neuroticism dimensions of Eysenck. Interestingly, this pattern of activity has shown some association not only with components of SWB, but also with PWB (Urry et al., 2004). Ultimately, research on such neural correlates of well-being may contribute to the eventual understanding of the confluence of these distinct conceptualizations.

## SWB and Other Personality Traits

Research focused on SWB and on the temperament-level traits of extraversion and neuroticism has dominated the literature, but a number of additional personality traits have been shown to be associated with SWB as well. In their meta-analysis, DeNeve and Cooper (1998) observed correlations between SWB and the additional "Big-Five" personality traits; these correlations were presented in an earlier section of this chapter. In their later meta-analysis, Steel, Schmidt, and Shultz (2008) reported generally larger coefficients, with correlations of .25, .30, and .13 between happiness and conscientiousness, agreeableness, and openness to experience, respectively. Sandvik et al. (1993), using a variety of self-report and non-self-report measures of SWB, found correlations ranging between .36 and .72 for optimism and SWB. Lucas, Diener, and Suh (1996) found a similar range of correlations between optimism and SWB and between self-esteem and SWB; these correlations were stable across intervals of 4 weeks and 2 years. Thus there is evidence that a number of other personality traits, in addition to extraversion and neuroticism, are associated with SWB.

## Ongoing Issues for Future Research

Research on personality and SWB has produced a number of robust and informative findings since Costa and McCrae's (1980) influential report appeared. As is often true, however, this body of research has gradually produced at least as many new questions as it has resolved. One issue involves the question of how to best characterize SWB. Is SWB a trait? In some respects, it shares many of the features of other, more established personality dispositions, which are commonly labeled "traits." There are clear individual differences in SWB. SWB has demonstrated reasonable stability over relatively long intervals (Fujita & Diener, 2005; Magnus et al., 1993), although the level of stability that SWB has exhibited is somewhat lower than that typically observed for the Big-Five personality traits. The components of SWB appear to have reliable physiological correlates. These findings tend to indicate that SWB meets several of the traditional criteria for establishing a "trait." On the other hand, SWB has also been shown to have variability over time, and some life events and life circumstances appear to produce long-term changes in the level of SWB for some individuals. But the same can be said of personality traits such as extraversion and neuroticism (Scollon & Diener, 2006). From the standpoint of individual-level stability and change, it is perhaps fair to say that SWB shows similar stability as compared to other personality traits, most notably the Big Five—although somewhat lower than them.

From another perspective, Veenhoven (1994) considers the dynamics of levels of SWB at the societal or national rather than individual level. In an examination of nation-level SWB, he points out that SWB is generally stable, but that profound changes in SWB can occur over relatively short periods, changes that are inexplicable if SWB is a largely stable personality trait. From a societal or nation-level viewpoint, SWB is very much a malleable entity. Additional research examining SWB at the societal level of analysis represents an important complement to work at the individual difference level, and could potentially offer new insights into the interaction of personality characteristics with societal dynamics in the experience of SWB.

Another area that requires some further study is the role of adaptation in the experience of SWB. For a number of years, adaptation was viewed as a formidable stabilizing factor in the experience of SWB; and, to some extent, that is still true today. But recent research has revealed some important exceptions and limitation to the rule of adaptation (Diener et al., 2006). It will be important for future researchers to determine more clearly, for example, the circumstances where adaptation is likely to be limited and the situations where individual differences in adaptation are likely to be most influential.

It will also be important to observe the ongoing developments in the area of behavioral genetics and to direct genetic research for findings potentially relevant to the understanding of both personality and SWB. This will likely be a challenging area of investigation, given the complexity of the variables involved; yet such efforts may well yield sizable dividends in the overall understanding of the biological mechanisms underlying personality processes and SWB.

Another area of potential future focus involves the development of valid and reliable new assessment techniques and measures. Although many brief measures of SWB have appeared in recent years, relatively few of them have undergone comprehensive evaluation with regard to their reliability and validity. All too often in the past, the assessment of SWB in many studies has been haphazard or incomplete (Pavot, 2008). The development of psychometrically strong, comprehensive measures of well-being would represent a significant advancement of the area. Two new measures were recently presented by Diener et al. (2010). The Flourishing Scale is a brief (8-item) summary measure of the respondent's self-perceived success in important life domains (e.g. relationships, purpose, self-esteem). The Scale of Positive and Negative Experience (SPANE) is a 12-item instrument designed to assess positive and negative feelings, and these two sub-scales can be used to produce a balance score.

The development of valid, reliable new measures of SWB will be an ongoing concern, but it will also be critical for future researchers to improve upon the research designs within which these specific measures are employed. In far too many instances, studies focused on SWB have not employed optimal research designs and have used measures that are not adequate to comprehensively assess SWB (Diener & Seligman, 2004; Pavot, 2008). As a consequence, although a large body of data relevant to the understanding of SWB has accumulated, the overall state of the database still appears to be rather "haphazard" (Diener & Seligman, 2004, p. 4). In an attempt to remedy this situation, Diener (2005) has proposed a set of guidelines and recommendations focused on the development and use of measures of both subjective well-being and ill-being. These proposed standards have been endorsed by many researchers interested in research on SWB and related constructs. The guidelines contain recommendations regarding both the psychometric quality of SWB measures and the methodology by which these measures might be most effectively employed. They also include definitions of SWB and of its major components. The primary intent of the guidelines was to aid researchers in the development of national indicators of SWB (Diener, 2000), but these guidelines represent a set of standards that are also generally applicable to basic research efforts. Adherence to these standards should result in data sets that have greater reliability and validity and are more directly comparable to the results of other studies.

## Summary

The relation between personality and SWB has been well established and is robust. A significant portion of the overall variance in levels of SWB between individuals can be accounted for by temperament-level personality characteristics. It is important to remember, however, that an additional large fraction of variance is due to external forces, which range from non-normative life events and circumstances to the effect of an individual's society and cultural context. Acknowledging the effects of personality on SWB should not serve as justification for the lack of an intervention designed to enhance individual well-being. SWB levels can and often do change, as does a component of personality itself.

## References

Andrews, F. M., & Withey, S. B. (1976). *Social indicators of well-being: America's perception of life quality.* New York: Plenum Press.

Argyle, M., & Lu, L. (1990). The happiness of extraverts. *Personality and Individual Differences, 11*, 1011–1017.

Arthaud-Day, M. L., Rode, J. C., Mooney, C. H., & Near, J. P. (2005). The subjective well-being construct: A test of its convergent, discriminant, and factorial validity. *Social Indicators Research, 74*, 445–476.

Bradburn, N. M. (1969). *The structure of psychological well-being*. Chicago: Aldine.

Brickman, P., & Campbell, D. T. (1971). Hedonic relativism and planning the good society. In M. H. Appley (Ed.), *Adaptation-level theory: A symposium* (pp. 287–305). New York: Academic Press.

Brickman, P., Coates, D., & Janoff-Bulman, R. (1978). Lottery winners and accident victims: Is happiness relative? *Journal of Personality and Social Psychology, 36,* 917–927.

Caspi, A., Sugden, K., Moffitt, T. E., Taylor, A., Craig, I. W., Harrington et al. (2003). Influence of life stress on depression: Moderation by a polymorphism in the 5–HHT gene. *Science, 301,* 386–389.

Cole, S. W. (2009). Social regulation of human gene expression. *Current Directions in Psychological Science, 18,* 132–137.

Cole, S. W., Hawkley, L. C., Arevalo, J. M., Sung, C. Y., Rose R. M., & Cacioppo, J. T. (2007). Social regulation of gene expression in human leukocytes. *Genome Biology, 8,* R189.

Costa, P. T., Jr., & McCrae, R. R. (1980). Influence of extraversion and neuroticism on subjective well-being: Happy and unhappy people. *Journal of Personality and Social Psychology, 38,* 668–678.

Crooker, K. J., & Near, J. P. (1998). Happiness and satisfaction: Measures of affect and cognition. *Social Indicators Research, 44,* 195–224.

Danner, D. D., Snowdon, D. A., & Friesen, W. V. (2001). Positive emotions in early life and longevity: Findings from the nun study. *Journal of Personality and Social Psychology, 80,* 804–813.

Davidson, R. J. (1993). The neuropsychology of emotion and affective style. In M. Lewis & J. M. Haviland (Eds.), *Handbook of emotions* (pp. 143–154). New York: Guilford Press.

Davidson, R. J. (2004). Well-being and affective style: Neural substrates and bio-behavioral correlates. *Philophical Transactions of the Royal Society of London B, 359,* 1395–1411.

DeNeve, K. M., & Cooper, H. (1998). The happy personality: A meta-analysis of 13 personality traits and subjective well-being. *Psychological Bulletin, 124,* 197–229.

Diener, E. (1984). Subjective well-being. *Psychological Bulletin, 95,* 542–575.

Diener, E. (1994). Assessing subjective well-being: Progress and opportunities. *Social Indicators Research, 31,* 107–157.

Diener, E. (2000). Subjective well-being: The science of happiness and a proposal for a national index. *American Psychologist, 55,* 34–43.

Diener, E. (2005). Guidelines for national indicators of subjective well-being and ill-being. *Social Indicators Network News, 84,* 4–6.

Diener, E., & Diener, C. (1996). Most people are happy. *Psychological Science, 7,* 181–185.

Diener, E., & Emmons, R. A. (1984). The independence of positive and negative affect. *Journal of Personality and Social Psychology, 47,* 1105–1117.

Diener, E., & Lucas, R. E. (1999). Personality and subjective well-being. In D. Kahneman, E. Diener, & N. Schwarz (Eds.), *Well-being: The foundations of hedonic psychology* (pp. 213–229). New York: Russell Sage Foundation.

Diener, E., & Seligman, M. E. P. (2004). Beyond money: Toward an economy of well-being. *Psychological Science in the Public Interest, 5,* 2–31.

Diener, E., Larsen, R. J., & Emmons, R. A. (1984). Person × situation interactions: Choice of situations and congruence response models. *Journal of Personality and Social Psychology, 47,* 580–592.

Diener, E., Lucas, R. E., & Scollon, C. N. (2006). Beyond the hedonic treadmill: Revising the adaptation theory of well-being. *American Psychologist, 61,* 305–314.

Diener, E., Emmons, R. A., Larsen, R. J., & Griffin, S. (1985). The Satisfaction with Life Scale. *Journal of Personality Assessment, 49,* 71–75.

Diener, E., Sandvik, E., Pavot, W., & Fujita, F. (1992). Extraversion and subjective well-being in a U.S. national probability sample. *Journal of Research in Personality, 26,* 205–215.

Diener, E., Suh, E. M., Lucas, R. E., & Smith, H. L. (1999). Subjective well-being: Three decades of progress. *Psychological Bulletin, 125,* 276–302.

Diener, E., Wirtz, D., Tov, W., Kim-Prieto, C., Choi, D., Oishi, S., & Biswas-Diener, R. (2010). New well-being measures: Short scales to assess flourishing and positive and negative feelings. *Social Indicators Research, 97,* 143–156.

Emmons, R. A., & Diener, E. (1985). Personality correlates of subjective well-being. *Personality and Social Psychology Bulletin, 11,* 89–97.

Ferguson, E. (2001). Personality and coping traits: A joint factor analysis. *British Journal of Health Psychology, 6,* 311–325.

Fox, N. A., & Davidson, R. J. (1987). Electroencephalogram asymmetry in response to the approach of a stranger and maternal separation. *Developmental Psychology, 23,* 233–240.

Fox, N. A., Bell, M. A., & Jones, N. A. (1992). Individual differences in response to stress and cerebral asymmetry. *Developmental Neuropsychology, 8,* 165–184.

Fujita, F. (1991). *An investigation of the relation between extraversion, neuroticism, positive affect, and negative affect.* Unpublished master's thesis, University of Illinois at Urbana-Champaign.

Fujita, F., & Diener, E. (2005). Life satisfaction set point: Stability and change. *Journal of Personality and Social Psychology, 88,* 158–164.

Gomez, R., Cooper, A., & Gomez, A. (2000). Susceptibility to positive and negative mood states: Test of Eysenck's, Gray's, and Newman's theories. *Personality and Individual Differences, 29,* 351–366.

Gray, J. A. (1981). A critique of Eysenck's theory of personality. In H. J. Eysenck (Ed.), *A model for personality* (pp. 246–276). New York: Springer-Verlag.

Gray, J. A. (1991). Neural systems, emotion, and personality. In J. Madden (Ed.), *Neurobiology of learning, emotion, and affect* (pp. 273–306). New York: Raven Press.

Haybron, D. M. (2008). Philosophy and the science of subjective well-being. In M. Eid & R. J. Larsen (Eds.), *The science of subjective well-being* (pp. 17–43). New York: Guilford Press.

Hayes, N., & Joseph, S. (2003). Big 5 correlates of three measures of subjective well-being. *Personality and Individual Differences, 34,* 723–727.

Headey, B. (2008). Life goals matter to happiness: A revision of set-point theory. *Social Indicators Research, 86,* 213–231.

Headey, B., & Wearing, A. (1992). *Understanding happiness: A theory of subjective well-being.* Melbourne, Australia: Longman Cheshire.

Heller, D., Watson, D., & Ilies, R. (2004). The role of person versus situation in life satisfaction: A critical examination. *Psychological Bulletin, 130,* 574–600.

Heller, D., Watson, D., & Ilies, R. (2006). The dynamic process of life satisfaction. *Journal of Personality, 74,* 1421–1450.

Helson, H. (1948). Adaptation-level as a basis for a quantitative theory of frames of reference. *Psychological Review, 55,* 297–313.

Helson, H. (1964). Current trends and issues in adaptation-level theory. *American Psychologist, 19,* 26–38.

Kahneman, D. (1999). Objective happiness. In D. Kahneman, E. Diener, & N. Schwarz (Eds.), *Well-being: The foundations of hedonic psychology* (pp. 3–25). New York: Russell Sage Foundation.

Kahneman, D., Krueger, A., Schkade, D., Schwarz, N., & Stone, A. (2004). A survey method for characterizing daily life experience: The Day Reconstruction Method (DRM). *Science, 306,* 1776–1780.

Larsen, R. J., & Ketelaar, T. (1991). Personality and susceptibility to positive and negative emotional states. *Journal of Personality and Social Psychology, 61,* 132–140.

Lucas, R. E. (2008). Personality and subjective well-being. In M. Eid & R. J. Larsen (Eds.), *The Science of Subjective Well-Being* (pp. 171–194). New York: Guilford Press.

Lucas, R. E., & Baird, B. M. (2004). Extraversion and emotional reactivity. *Journal of Personality and Social Psychology, 86,* 473–485.

Lucas, R. E., Diener, E., & Suh, E. (1996). Discriminant validity of well-being measures. *Journal of Personality and Social Psychology, 71,* 616–628.

Lucas, R. E., Clark, A. E., Georgellis, Y., & Diener, E. (2003). Reexamining adaptation and the set-point model of happiness: Reactions to changes in marital status. *Journal of Personality and Social Psychology, 84,* 527–539.

Lucas, R. E., Clark, A. E., Georgellis, Y., & Diener, E. (2004). Unemployment alters the set point for life satisfaction. *Psychological Science, 15,* 8–13.

Lesch, K. P., Bengel, D., Heils, A., Sabol, S. Z., Greenberg, B. D., Petri, S., Benjamin, J., Muller, C. R., Hamer, D. H., & Murphy, D. L. (1996). Association of anxiety-related traits with a polymorphism in the serotonin transporter gene regulatory region. *Science, 274,* 1527–1531.

Lykken, D., & Tellegen, A. (1996). Happiness is a stochastic phenomenon. *Psychological Science, 7,* 186–189.

Magnus, K., Diener, E., Fujita, F., & Pavot, W. (1993). Personality and events: A longitudinal analysis. *Journal of Personality and Social Psychology, 65,* 1046–1053.

McCrae, R. R., & Costa, P. T., Jr. (1991). Adding Liebe and Arbeit: The full five-factor model and well-being. *Personality and Social Psychology Bulletin, 17,* 227–232.

Muller, C. R., Hamer, D. H., & Murphy, D. L. (1996). Association of anxiety-related traits with a polymorphism in the serotonin transporter gene regulatory region. *Science, 274,* 1527–1531.

Pavot, W. (2008). The assessment of subjective well-being: Successes and shortfalls. In M. Eid & R. J. Larsen (Eds.), *The science of subjective well-being* (pp. 124–140). New York: Guilford Press.

Pavot, W., & Diener, E. (1993). The affective and cognitive context of self-reported measures of subjective well-being. *Social Indicators Research, 28,* 1–20.

Pavot, W., & Diener, E. (2008). The Satisfaction with Life Scale and the emerging construct of life satisfaction. *Journal of Positive Psychology, 3,* 137–152.

Pavot, W., Diener, E., & Fujita, F. (1990). Extraversion and happiness. *Personality and Individual Differences, 11,* 1299–1306.

Pavot, W., Diener, E., Colvin, C. R., & Sandvik, E. (1991). Further validation of the Satisfaction with Life Scale: Evidence for the cross–method convergence of well-being measures. *Journal of Personality Assessment, 57,* 149–161.

Risch, N., Herrell, R., Lehner, T., Liang, K., Eaves, L., Hoh, J., Griem, A., Kovacs, M., Ott, J., & Merikangas, K. R. (2009). Interaction between the serotonin transporter gene (5–HTTLPR), stressful life events, and risk of depression. *Journal of the American Medical Association, 301,* 2462–2471.

Roberts, B. W., & DelVecchio, W. F. (2000). The rank-order consistency of personality traits from childhood to old age: A quantitative review of longitudinal studies. *Psychological Bulletin, 126,* 3–25.

Roberts, B. W., Walton, K. E., & Bogg, T. (2005). Conscientiousness and health across the life course. *Review of General Psychology, 9,* 156–168.

Roysamb, E., Harris, J. R., Magnus, P., Vitterso, J., & Tambs, K. (2002). Subjective well-being: Sex-specific effects of genetic and environmental factors. *Personality and Individual Differences, 32,* 211–223.

Rusting, C. L., & Larsen, R. J. (1997). Extraversion, neuroticism, and susceptibility to positive and negative affect: A test of two theoretical models. *Personality and Individual Differences, 22,* 607–612.

Ryan, R. M., & Deci, E. L. (2001). On happiness and human potentials: A review of research on hedonic and eudaimonic well-being. *Annual Review of Psychology, 52,* 141–166.

Ryff, C. D. (1989). Happiness is everything, or is it? Explorations on the meaning of psychological well-being. *Journal of Personality and Social Psychology, 57,* 1069–1081.

Ryff, C. D., & Keyes C. L. M. (1995). The structure of psychological well-being revisited. *Journal of Personality and Social Psychology, 69,* 719–727.

Sandvik, E., Diener, E., & Seidlitz, L. (1993). Subjective well-being: The convergence and stability of self-report and nonself-report measures. *Journal of Personality, 61,* 317–342.

Scheier, M. F., Weintraub, J. K., & Carver, C. S. (1986). Coping with stress: Divergent strategies of optimists and pessimists. *Journal of Personality and Social Psychology, 51,* 1257–1264.

Schimmack, U. (2008). The structure of subjective well-being. In M. Eid & R. J. Larsen (Eds.), *The science of subjective well-being* (pp. 97–123). New York: Guilford Press.

Schimmack, U., & Oishi, S. (2005). The influence of chronically and temporarily accessible information on life satisfaction judgments. *Journal of Personality and Social Psychology, 89,* 395–406.

Schimmack, U., Oishi, S., Furr, R. M., & Funder, D. C. (2004). Personality and life satisfaction: A facet-level analysis. *Personality and Social Psychology Bulletin, 30,* 1062–1075.

Schneider, L., & Schimmack, U. (2009). Self-informant agreement in well-being ratings: A meta-analysis. *Social Indicators Research, 94,* 363–376.

Schwarz, N., & Strack, F. (1999). Reports of subjective well-being: Judgmental processes and their methodological implications. In D. Kahneman, E. Diener, & N. Schwarz, N. (Eds.), *Well-Being: The foundations of hedonic psychology* (pp. 61–84). New York: Russell Sage Foundation.

Scollon, C. N., & Diener, E. (2006). Love, work, and changes in extraversion and neuroticism over time. *Journal of Personality and Social Psychology, 91,* 1152–1165.

Scollon, C. N., Kim-Prieto, C., & Diener, E. (2003). Experience sampling: Promises and pitfalls, strengths and weaknesses. *Journal of Happiness Studies, 4,* 5–34.

Seligman, M. E. P., & Csikszentmihalyi, M. (2000). Positive psychology: An introduction. *American Psychologist, 55,* 5–14.

Steel, P., Schmidt, J., & Shultz, J. (2008). Refining the relationship between personality and subjective well-being. *Psychological Bulletin, 134,* 138–161.

Strack, F., Martin, L. L., & Schwarz, N. (1988). Priming and communications: Social determinants of information use in judgments of life satisfaction. *European Journal of Social Psychology, 18,* 429–442.

Stubbe, J. H., Posthuma, D., Boomsma, D. I., & De Geus, E. J. C. (2005). Heritability of life satisfaction in adults: A twin-family study. *Psychological Medicine, 35,* 1–8.

Suh, E., Diener, E., & Fujita, F. (1996). Events and subjective well-being: Only recent events matter. *Journal of Personality and Social Psychology, 70,* 1091–1102.

Suh, E. M., Diener, E., Oishi, S., & Triandis, H. C. (1998). The shifting basis of life satisfaction judgments across cultures: Emotions versus norms. *Journal of Personality and Social Psychology, 74,* 482–493.

Tellegen, A., Lykken, D. T., Bouchard, T. J., Wilcox, K. J., Segal, N. L., & Rich, S. (1988). Personality similarity in twins reared apart and together. *Journal of Personality and Social Psychology, 54,* 1031–1039.

Urry, H. L., Nitschke, J. B., Dolski, I., Jackson, D. C., Dalton, K. M., Mueller, C. J., Rosenkranz, M. A., Ryff, C. D., Singer, B. H., & Davidson, R. J. (2004). Making a life worth living: Neural correlates of well-being. *Psychological Science, 15,* 367–372.

Vaidya, J. G., Gray, E. K., Haig, J., & Watson, D. (2002). On the temporal stability of personality: Evidence for differential stability and the role of life experiences. *Journal of Personality and Social Psychology, 83,* 1469–1484.

Veenhoven, R. (1994). Is happiness a trait? Tests of the theory that a better society does not make people any happier. *Social Indicators Research, 32,* 101–160.

Watson, D., Clark, L. A., & Tellegen, A. (1988). Development and validation of brief measures of positive and negative affect: The PANAS scales. *Journal of Personality and Social Psychology, 54,* 1063–1070.

Wheeler, R. E., Davidson, R. J., & Tomarken, A. J. (1993). Frontal brain asymmetry and emotional reactivity: A biological substrate of affective style. *Psychophysiology, 30,* 82–89. Available at http://brainimaging.waisman.wisc.edu/publications/1993/Frontal%20 brain%20asymmetry%20and%20emotional%20reactivity.pdf

Wilson, W. (1967). Correlates of avowed happiness. *Psychological Bulletin, 67,* 294–306.

# 28

# Self-Esteem
## *Enduring Issues and Controversies*
### M. Brent Donnellan, Kali H. Trzesniewski, and Richard W. Robins

Self-esteem is one of the most widely studied constructs in the social and behavioral sciences. It is also one of the most controversial. Persistent debates surround nearly every aspect of self-esteem, including whether it is more trait- or state-like, whether it is causally related to important life outcomes, whether there is a dark side to high self-esteem, and whether it is distinct from constructs such as depression, neuroticism, and narcissism. In addition to discussing these debates, the goal of this chapter is to provide an overview of the definition, assessment, nomological network, and development of this important individual differences variable. We are necessarily selective in our review, given the sheer size of the literature. A PsycINFO search with the keyword "self-esteem" yielded more than 30,000 hits (over 6,000 in the past five years), and 35 percent of the respondents to a recent survey of prominent personality psychologists indicated that they study self-esteem (Robins, Tracy, & Sherman, 2007). Anyone who attempts to review this literature faces a daunting task of sifting through a vast set of measures, theories, controversies, and empirical findings. Consequently, we focus on foundational issues and current debates surrounding self-esteem as an individual differences construct.

## What Is Self-Esteem?

Self-esteem is one of the oldest constructs in psychology; historically, it has been conceptualized in terms of an individual's phenomenological experience. *Specifically, self-esteem is an individual's subjective evaluation of her or his worth as a person.* From this perspective, if a person believes that she is a person of worth and value, then she has high self-esteem, regardless of whether her self-evaluation is validated by others or corroborated by some external criteria. Researchers often distinguish between global and domain-specific self-evaluations, the former referring to an individual's

*The Wiley-Blackwell Handbook of Individual Differences*, First Edition.
Edited by Tomas Chamorro-Premuzic, Sophie von Stumm, and Adrian Furnham.
© 2011 Blackwell Publishing Ltd. Published 2011 by Blackwell Publishing Ltd.

overall evaluation of his or her worth as a person and the latter referring to an evaluation of a specific domain or facet of the self, such as academic competence or physical appearance. In this chapter we will focus on global self-esteem, a construct that seems to have important affective, motivational, and behavioral consequences.

The definition of global self-esteem has changed little over the past century. Late in the nineteenth century, William James (1985) defined self-esteem as the degree to which people perceive their accomplishments as consistent with their goals and aspirations. He offered the now famous formula that global self-esteem is "determined by the ratio of *our actualities* to *our supposed potentialities*" (italics added, p. 54). Morris Rosenberg (e.g. 1989), creator of the most widely used measure of global self-esteem, extended this definition by adding that self-esteem involves feelings of self-respect and self-acceptance. He offered this perspective:

> When we speak of high self-esteem, then, we shall simply mean that the individual respects himself, considers himself worthy; he does not necessarily consider himself better than others, but he definitely does not consider himself worse; he does not feel that he is the ultimate in perfection but, on the contrary, recognizes his limitations and expects to grow and improve. Low self-esteem, on the other hand, implies self-rejection, self-dissatisfaction, self-contempt. The individual lacks respect for the self he observes. (Rosenberg, 1989, p. 31)

Rosenberg's definition of global self-esteem is widely accepted; however, some authors have attempted to broaden it, suggesting a somewhat different perspective, which moves the construct beyond its roots in phenomenology. Baumeister, Campbell, Krueger, and Vohs (2003) define self-esteem as "the evaluative component of self-knowledge" (p. 2; see also Baumeister, Smart, & Boden, 1996, pp. 5–6). However, these authors also suggest that self-esteem should best serve as an accurate estimate of one's characteristics (Baumeister et al., 2003, pp. 37–38). This conceptualization requires the existence of an "external yardstick" against which to judge the accuracy of judgments about the self (see e.g. Robins & John, 1997; Tangney & Leary, 2003, p. 670). For classic writers like James and Rosenberg and more recent writers like Harter (e.g. 1999, 2006), the notion of judging the accuracy of one's self-esteem by reference to objective criteria is at odds with the phenomenological nature of the construct. James (1985) noted that "our self-feeling in this world depends entirely on what we *back* ourselves to be and do" (p. 54). The idea of tying self-esteem to an objective "third party" external yardstick leads to thorny questions involving the imposition of a set of values used to judge the self. Tangney and Leary (2003) expressed this concern by asking: "Is the suggestion here that the average college freshman, unemployed person, or mentally retarded individual *shouldn't* on the whole take a positive attitude toward themselves?" (p. 670; italics in original).

In light of these concerns, we endorse the more traditional and circumscribed phenomenological perspective on self-esteem offered by James and Rosenberg. From this perspective, it is irrelevant how a person's self-esteem compares to some external yardstick or validity criterion. If Sam likes himself and sees himself as a worthy person, then Sam necessarily has high self-esteem, regardless of his actual abilities, traits, or level of social acceptance. Researchers who are concerned with the possibility that

Sam is overly positive in his assessments of his actual likeability or intellectual capability would be studying self-enhancement rather than self-esteem. Likewise, researchers concerned that Sam is arrogant, egotistical, or has an otherwise grandiose sense of self would be studying constructs linked with narcissism. Adopting this classic perspective makes it easier to draw conceptual distinctions between high self-esteem and narcissism, as Rosenberg long ago made it clear that high self-esteem was not synonymous with egotism (e.g. Donnellan, Trzesniewski, Robins, Moffitt, & Caspi, 2005). Such clarity is often lost when researchers blur the distinctions between self-esteem and narcissism in discussions about the potential dark side of self-esteem (e.g. Baumeister et al., 1996; see Tangney & Leary, 2003). Another advantage of adopting the classic perspective is that it bypasses the need for a multi-method approach to assessing self-esteem, because the only true gauge of a person's self-worth is his/her self-evaluation.

## How Is Self-Esteem Measured?

The assessment of self-esteem is a long-standing issue, which dates back to William James's writings. Researchers have since developed a diverse set of measures, which includes self-report measures, informant report measures, "experience sampling" measures, picture and puppet-based measures for children, complicated self-ideal discrepancy measures, and implicit measures based on reaction times and preferences for the letters in one's name. Despite the wide range of options, the majority of research on self-esteem typically uses one of a handful of self-report scales containing face-valid items that directly ask about overall evaluations of the self. By far the most commonly used self-report measure is the Rosenberg Self-Esteem Scale (RSE; Rosenberg, 1989), which contains items such as "I take a positive attitude toward myself" and "One the whole, I am satisfied with myself." In this section we describe the RSE in detail, and then we provide a brief discussion of other self-report measures and implicit measures.

### The Rosenberg Self-Esteem Scale (RSE)

In work with adolescents, college students, and older adults, the RSE is by far the most widely used measure of self-esteem (see Blascovich & Tomaka, 1991). In light of its widespread use, it has received more psychometric analysis and empirical validation than perhaps any other self-esteem measure. The RSE is made up of 10 face-valid items, five positively worded and five negatively worded. Most researchers use a 4-, 5-, or 7-point Likert-type scale, with the end points labeled "strongly disagree" and "strongly agree." Scores for the RSE typically have a high level of internal consistency (i.e. alpha coefficients typically exceed .80 or .85; see e.g. Chen, 2008; Gray-Little, Williams, & Hancock, 1997; Robins, Hendin, & Trzesniewski, 2001).

The RSE is usually thought to assess a single construct, but there is some ongoing controversy about its factor structure (Marsh, 1996; Quilty, Oakman, & Risko, 2006; Tafarodi & Milne, 2002; Tomás & Oliver, 1999). Some investigators propose that there are facets of global self-esteem linked with self-acceptance that can be separated from facets linked with self-liking embedded within the RSE (Tafarodi & Milne, 2002). However, evidence for this distinction emerged from a fairly complicated confirmatory factor model involving five latent factors. Indeed, Tafarodi and Milne (2002, p. 456) noted that "a common factor accounted for the lion's share of reliable variance across items." Other investigators have proposed that method factors account for covariation among the positively keyed and negatively keyed items above and beyond a general factor (e.g. Tomás & Oliver, 1999). Although some researchers have attributed substantive meanings to the method factors (Quilty et al., 2006), we tend to view these as artifacts of item-wording (see also Carmines & Zeller, 1979; Greenberger, Chen, Dmitrieva, & Farruggia, 2003; Pullmann & Allik, 2000). In other words, we take the position that the RSE assesses an essentially unidimensional construct (see e.g. Donnellan & Trzesniewski, 2009; Gray-Little et al., 1997; Greenberger et al., 2003; Pullmann & Allik, 2000). This view is consistent with the vast majority of self-esteem research that is based on the composite score of responses to the 10 RSE items.

## Other self-report measures

There are several longer self-esteem inventories that are also used frequently in the literature. These include the Coopersmith Self-Esteem Inventory (Coopersmith, 1967), the Harter Self-Perception Profile (Harter & Pike, 1984), and the Marsh Self-Descriptive Questionnaire (Marsh, Ellis, Parada, Richards, & Heubeck, 2005). The latter two measures include different forms for children, adolescents, and adults, which makes them well-suited for longitudinal research. The Harter and Marsh measures are particularly noteworthy, because they contain global self-esteem scales as well as domain-specific scales that are developmentally appropriate (e.g. competence in romantic relationships is asked of adolescents and adults, but not of children in the Harter measures). The global scales from these other measures tend to be strongly correlated with the RSE (e.g. the RSE and the Harter Global scale correlate .74; Donnellan, Trzesniewski, Conger, & Conger, 2007). Robins, Hendin, and Trzesniewski (2001) even developed and validated a single-item measure (the single-item self-esteem measure, or SISE), which simply asks participant to rate the statement "I have high self-esteem" using a 5-point Likert-type scale. These different self-report measures of global self-esteem tend to be moderately to strongly intercorrelated (the correlations range from 40 to .70; see e.g. Zeigler-Hill, 2010).

## Implicit measures

One concern is that direct, simple, and face-valid self-report scales may not tap true, deep-seated feelings about the self. Issues of social desirability may affect how participants respond to the questions on self-report measures, given the pressure for high self-esteem in certain cultures. Moreover, individuals may not have conscious awareness of deep-seated feelings of inadequacy and worthlessness. These considerations motivated the development of implicit measures of self-esteem designed to assess global self-evaluations that are assumed to be automatic, over-learned, and outside of consciousness (see Bosson, Swann, & Pennebaker, 2000 for a review). The implicit association test (IAT) is one of the most commonly used implicit measures of self-esteem (Greenwald, McGhee, & Schwarz, 1998). The IAT uses a computerized reaction time procedure to assess the degree to which individuals associate the self with a positive as opposed to a negative concept. The underlying assumption is that a person with a high implicit self-esteem will be quicker to link positive words to the self than negative words. Because the task requires the individual to respond extremely quickly, the associations assessed through this procedure are assumed to be automatic and unconscious. The ultimate score is based on the difference in reaction times to the positive as opposed to the negative words.

One of the concerns in the current literature is that correlations between self-report scales and implicit measures are generally low and variable across studies (see Hofmann, Gawronski, Gschwendner, Le, & Schmitt, 2005). The level of convergence between implicit and explicit self-esteem measures is far below the level of convergence expected for two different measures of the same construct. These findings have led to debates about whether implicit and explicit self-esteem are psychologically distinct constructs. However, even different implicit measures of self-esteem do not correlate highly with each other (e.g. Bosson et al., 2000), pointing to potential problems with the validity of these measures. Given these concerns, we restrict our review to findings based on measures of explicit global self-esteem. Interested readers should consult Hofmann et al. (2005) for an extended discussion of the issues of convergence between implicit and explicit measures.

## What Are the Basic Demographic Correlates of Self-Esteem?

In this section we review research on gender, racial/ethnic, and social class differences in self-esteem. (Age differences in self-esteem are reviewed in a subsequent section explicitly devoted to developmental issues.) Fortunately, a number of recent meta-analyses have helped to summarize the enormous literature on the demographic correlates of self-esteem. The general message of this research is that demographic groups show smaller differences in self-esteem than would be anticipated by many classic theories of self-esteem.

Gender differences are a source of perennial interest and debate in psychology (Hyde, 2005). In terms of self-esteem, there appears to be a widespread cultural belief that girls are plagued by insecurities and tend to have much lower self-esteem than boys (see Hyde, 2005, p. 590). However, the actual gender difference in self-esteem is quite small (Kling, Hyde, Showers, & Buswell, 1999). Meta-analytic research on group differences typically summarizes standardized mean differences using a $d$-metric effect size. The strategy is to divide the absolute difference between women and men by the pooled standard deviation. Using conventions proposed by Cohen (1988; see also McCartney & Rosenthal, 2000), researchers often interpret these coefficients using the following rule of thumb: $d$s around .20 reflect "small" differences; $d$s around .50 reflect "moderate" differences; whereas $d$s around .80 reflect "large" differences (similar conventions exist for interpreting correlations in the range of .10, .30, and .50 as small, moderate, and large, respectively). The overall meta-analytic gender difference for self-esteem was .21 in favor of men (Kling et al.,

1999); however, this difference was qualified by developmental stage. The largest gender differences were found for individuals aged 11–14 ($d = .23$) and 15–18 ($d = .33$). The difference for individuals aged 23–59 was very small ($d = .10$) and virtually zero for those over 60 ($d = -.03$). In short, the gender difference in self-esteem, although somewhat more pronounced during adolescence, is relatively trivial throughout most of the life span.

In addition to gender, there has been a considerable amount of interest in racial/ethnic differences in self-esteem (Bachman & O'Malley, 1984; Bachman, O'Malley, Freedman-Doan, Trzesniewski, & Donnellan, in press; Gray-Little & Hafdahl, 2000; Twenge & Crocker, 2002). Ethnic differences tend to be small to moderate in magnitude. Rosenberg (1989) acknowledged that he was "astonished" that ethnic differences in self-esteem were more subtle than he expected in his classic work on adolescent self-esteem (pp. xvi–xvii). In particular, he expected that African American youth in the United States would report substantially lower levels of self-esteem than White youth, given that the former group was socially stigmatized, especially in the 1960s. He originally assumed that reflected appraisals (the internalization of how one is perceived by others) and social comparison processes would create these pronounced group differences. However, subsequent research convinced him that such a simplistic assumption was not appropriate given the actual data. Rosenberg suggested that the perceived opinions of "significant others" such as close family members, peers, and teachers, were more strongly linked to self-esteem than one's impression of how one is evaluated by people in general, or by the "generalized other." In addition, he noted that social comparisons might be based on within-group comparisons and affected by what contemporary social-personality psychologists refer to as self-enhancement biases (see also Crocker & Major, 1989).

As the matter stands, two meta-analyses indicate that African Americans score higher on measures of self-esteem than Whites (Gray-Little & Hafdahl, 2000; Twenge & Crocker, 2002). Twenge and Crocker (2002) found that Asians report the lowest level of self-esteem, and Latinos fall between Whites and Asians. These broad trends have been replicated by Bachman et al. (in press). An important point, again, is that the racial/ethnic differences are not large. For example, Bachman et al. (in press) examined self-esteem levels for high school seniors in the United States by gender and racial/ethnic group. The difference between young African American men and young White men yielded a $d$ around .10—a very small difference. The difference between young African American men and young Asian-American men was larger, but still modest by existing conventions ($d = .38$). Similar differences were observed when comparing scores for young women from different racial and ethnic groups.

Nonetheless, the observed ethnic differences require an explanation, and this is yet another contentious area of self-esteem research. Bachman et al. (in press; see also Bachman & O'Malley, 1984) suggest that such racial/ethnic differences might be explained by differences in cultural norms and standards for expressing high self-esteem. African American youth are perhaps encouraged to express high self-esteem, given the cultural belief that this helps young people cope with discrimination (reviewed in Hughes et al., 2006). Asian Americans, on the other hand, might be socialized to express humility and modesty, given the cultural importance of group harmony (Cai, Brown, Deng, & Oakes, 2007; Kim & Markus, 1999). In other words,

African Americans are socialized to communicate pride, whereas Asian Americans are socialized to communicate humility. Importantly, however, the cultural influence argument is agnostic as to whether or not the ethnic groups actually differ in their underlying levels of self-esteem (see Chen, 2008).

Turning to SES, the overall link with self-esteem is generally small according to a large meta-analysis (Twenge & Campbell, 2002). The overall effect of SES and self-esteem in the $r$-metric was .08 (referring to effect sizes in correlational metrics is useful in this context because both SES and self-esteem are continuous variables). The connection between SES and self-esteem was qualified by a number of moderators, chiefly age. The correlation between SES and self-esteem was strongest for young adults (ages 23–39; $r = .11$) and middle-aged adults (ages 40–59; $r = .13$) and small to virtually non-existent for elementary school students ($r = .04$), junior high students ($r = .06$), high school students ($r = .07$), college students ($r = .05$), and older adults ($r = .08$). These results point to a connection between earned status and self-esteem, as opposed to a connection between self-esteem and the SES of the family of origin. A current interpretation of these findings is that they reflect a connection between elevated social status in groups and feelings of self-worth (i.e. they reflect a social indicator model; see Twenge & Campbell, 2002). However, as was discussed for the effects for ethnicity, the actual strength of this association is weaker than would be anticipated by existing theories.

## How Is Self-Esteem Related to Other Individual Differences Constructs?

As reviewed in the previous section, the links between self-esteem and demographic variables are typically quite small. Are there more robust predictors or antecedents of self-esteem? Many classic developmental accounts emphasize the role of environmental factors such as parent and peer influences (e.g. Harter, 2006). Recent studies in quantitative genetics, however, have challenged a purely environmental explanation for the origins of self-esteem by showing that genetic factors account for about 40 percent of the observed variability in self-esteem (Kendler, Gardner, & Prescott, 1998; McGuire et al., 1999; Neiss, Sedikides, & Stevenson, 2002; Neiss, Stevenson, Legrand, Iacono, & Sedikides, 2009). Of course the relatively high heritability of self-esteem, which approaches that found for basic personality traits, could still fit with accounts that assume a central role for socializing agents such as parents and peers. The point is that something about individual variation in self-esteem is tied to genetic differences between people. Self-esteem no doubt emerges from intricate person–environment transactions as they occur across the life span. Genetic factors likely influence self-esteem through a complicated process, and no one claims that there is a single gene that codes for high (or low) self-esteem. Genetically influenced differences in temperament, intelligence, physical attractiveness, health, and so on will shape the social contexts the individual seeks out, the reactions they elicit from parents, peers, relationship partners, and other important figures in their lives, and their capacity to attain success in work and relationship contexts; collectively these interpersonal processes and environmental influences may in turn shape the individual's level of self-esteem (Robins, Donnellan, Widaman, & Conger, 2010). This account naturally leads to questions as to which aspects of temperament and core personality dispositions are most strongly associated with levels of self-esteem.

The task of summarizing these kinds of findings is facilitated by drawing on the well-known Big-Five domains, because they provide an organizing framework for the vast array of personality traits. Using data from an extremely large Internet study ($N = 326,641$), Robins, Tracy, Trzesniewski, Potter, and Gosling (2001) found a strong correlation between self-esteem and neuroticism ($r = -.50$) and relatively weaker relations with extraversion ($r = .38$), conscientiousness ($r = .24$), openness to experience ($r = .17$), and agreeableness ($r = .13$). Very similar coefficients were reported in an update of this data set (Erdle, Gosling, & Potter, 2009), which was based on an even larger sample size ($N = 628,640$), which was collected after the initial publication of Robins, Tracy et al. (2001). All in all, self-esteem is most strongly associated with neuroticism, and secondly with extraversion.

The associations reported by Robins, Tracy et al. (2001) are consistent with other recent studies, which also find that neuroticism is the strongest predictor of self-esteem (Graziano, Jensen-Campbell, & Finch, 1997; Heimpel, Elliot, & Wood, 2006; Judge, Erez, Thoresen, & Bono, 2002; Watson, Suls, & Haig, 2002). It is relatively straightforward to see how such a dispositional tendency could contribute to negative opinions about the self—both directly and due to the connections between neuroticism and impaired relationships, physical health, and diminished quality of life (Lahey, 2009). For instance, individuals high in neuroticism are easily distressed, as they have a low threshold for emotions such as hostility, fear, and sadness; thus they are regularly subjected to more frequent and/or more intensely aversive emotional experiences compared to individuals low in this disposition. This tendency can color self-judgments (Watson & Clark, 1984) and impair adaptation to the challenges of life, especially in terms of interpersonal relationships. Such a view is also consistent with McCrae and Costa's five-factor theory (e.g. 2008), which posits that basic dimensions of temperament influence people's self-conceptions.

An alternative to the perspective that self-esteem emerges, in part, from person–environment transaction is the idea that global self-esteem is simply a lower-order facet of a broader personality trait. Watson et al. (2002) proposed that global self-esteem defines the positive end of a continuum that measures trait depression, a lower-order facet of neuroticism. Judge et al. (2002) argued that global self-esteem and neuroticism are both indicators of "core self-evaluations"—an umbrella construct that also includes locus of control and self-efficacy.

Although further work is needed to completely evaluate these proposals, several recent studies do not support the claim that global self-esteem is nothing but a facet of a broader negative affect/neuroticism construct. First, there is growing evidence that self-esteem predicts life outcomes after controlling for depression (see Trzesniewski, Donnellan, Moffitt, Robins, Poulton, & Caspi, 2006). Second, low self-esteem predicts depression in cross-lagged longitudinal analyses, whereas depression does not predict low self-esteem (Orth, Robins, & Roberts, 2008; Orth, Robins, & Meier, 2009; Orth, Robins, Trzesniewski, Maes, & Schmitt, 2009); this asymmetry suggests that self-esteem serves as a vulnerability factor for depression and is not simply an alternative indicator of depression. Third, a study of Mexican American youth failed to find any connection between negative emotionality and self-esteem (Robins et al., 2010), which suggests that there might be a developmental aspect to the connection between neuroticism and self-esteem. Together, these findings are difficult to reconcile with the idea that self-esteem is simply an indicator of a more general common factor related to negative affect and neuroticism. Moreover, Trzesniewski (2009) conducted behavioral genetic analyses on the aspects of self-esteem that are distinct from depression, neuroticism, general affectivity, and anxiety. She found that this isolated component had unique genetic and environmental influences, which provided evidence for the uniqueness of the construct. In other words, "pure" self-esteem that was independent of these other dimensions was not simply random error or noise.

Nonetheless, researchers should keep in mind the moderate to strong associations between neuroticism, depression, and self-esteem. Including measures of these additional constructs as well as the components of core self-evaluations (such as self-efficacy and locus of control) could help to resolve these ongoing debates and to determine whether self-esteem still has predictive power while controlling for these variables. However, we suggest that theory and research on self-esteem would still be necessary in order to *understand* such relations. Accounting for variance in a phenomenon is not the same as explaining it in psychological terms. It is also worth noting that several researchers have claimed that the effects of personality on life outcomes might be mediated by self-esteem (see also Graziano et al., 1997; Heimpel et al., 2006).

A related issue surrounding the distinctions between self-esteem and other individual differences concerns the construct of narcissism. There has been an unfortunate tendency to conflate high self-esteem with narcissism in some of the discussion over the costs and benefits associated with self-esteem (see the review in the next section). For example, Baumeister et al. (1996) noted that "an effective and valid [self-esteem] scale would identify the arrogant, conceited narcissist just as well as the person who holds an unbiased appreciation of his or her own well-recognized good qualities" (pp. 28–29). Viewing self-esteem and narcissism as interchangeable constructs leads to the concern that "the societal pursuit of high self-esteem for everyone may literally end up doing considerable harm" (ibid., p. 29). These concerns may not be warranted, because it is possible to draw a distinction between healthy self-regard and narcissistic self-views. For example, Rosenberg (1989) noted that, "when we deal with self-esteem, we are asking whether the individual considers himself adequate—a person of worth—not whether he considers himself superior to others" (p. 62).

The empirical link between self-esteem and narcissism also suggests that these are distinct constructs. The vast majority of research in social and personality psychology uses the Narcissistic Personality Inventory (NPI; Raskin & Terry, 1988) to assess the multi-faceted construct of narcissism (see Cain, Pincus, & Ansell, 2008). The summary score for the NPI has a small to moderate association with global self-esteem (e.g. $r = .29$; Trzesniewski, Donnellan, & Robins, 2008). One concern is that this overall correlation masks some important distinctions for the sub-scales of the NPI. Indeed, it is often overlooked that the NPI assesses a number of constructs rather than a single, unidimensional construct (e.g. Bradlee & Emmons, 1992; Raskin & Terry, 1988). Some of the dimensions embedded within the NPI are more closely tied to classic ideas about narcissism, such as a sense of entitlement, whereas other dimensions look more like aspects of extraversion, which seem to be psychologically benign, or even adaptive (e.g. leadership/authority; see Emmons, 1987). Trzesniewski et al. (2008) found that self-esteem was virtually unrelated to the Psychological Entitlement Scale from the NPI ($r = -.04$), the dimension that seems to be more strongly associated with problematic outcomes. In contrast, self-esteem had larger associations with authority ($r = .33$) and self-sufficiency ($r = .32$), dimensions which seem to capture adaptive psychological functioning.

All in all, there seems to be little evidence that self-esteem is linked with the more socially toxic aspects of personality assessed by the NPI (Trzesniewski et al., 2008). Moreover, researchers sometimes find that the predictive validity of the NPI summary scale and self-esteem increases when controlling for their shared variance (Donnellan et al., 2005; Paulhus, Robins, Trzesniewski, & Tracy, 2004). The tentative interpretation of these findings is that controlling for the NPI helps to purify self-esteem measures of aspects of social dominance (see Brown & Zeigler-Hill, 2004), whereas controlling for self-esteem helps to isolate the socially toxic aspects of personality embedded in the NPI from the more adaptive aspects (see Sedikides, Rudich, Gregg, Kumashiro, & Rusbult, 2004). Regardless of how one conceptualizes self-esteem and narcissism, commonly used measures of the two constructs do not show the level of convergent validity expected for measures of the same construct, and the degree of convergence tends to fluctuate depending on the facet of the NPI examined.

## Is Self-Esteem Associated with Life Outcomes?

High self-esteem is generally viewed as an important component of psychological health and well-being (Jahoda, 1958; Rogers, 1961). One of the most contentious debates in the self-esteem literature, however, concerns whether self-esteem exerts any causal influence on life outcomes (Baumeister et al., 2003; Marsh & Craven, 2006; Swann, Chang-Schnieder, & McClarty, 2007; Trzesniewski et al., 2006). This is an extraordinarily difficult question to answer, given that much of the research literature on self-esteem is correlational and such designs have well-known limitations for constraining causal inferences. On the other hand, lab studies have limitations in terms of their ability to manipulate levels of trait self-esteem and in terms of their ability to evaluate the causal impact of any manipulation on long-term real-world outcomes. These facts place legitimate constraints on the confidence that can be invested in the existing literature.

Baumeister et al. (2003) published an extensive critique of the causal importance of self-esteem. They noted several broad concerns with the existing literature including: (1) the possibility that common method effects inflate observed correlations between self-reports of self-esteem and self-reports of life outcomes; (2) the possibility that general negativity effects create spurious connections between low self-esteem and negative outcomes; and (3) general problems of causal inference from correlational studies. They conducted a qualitative review of the studies that evaluated connections between self-esteem and significant life outcomes—such as school performance, task performance, interpersonal relationships, happiness, depression, and antisocial behavior. They ultimately concluded that, except for happiness, self-esteem is "not a major predictor or cause of almost anything" (p. 37).

Swann et al. (2007) responded to the Baumeister et al. (2003) report with a more optimistic review concerning the importance of self-esteem and other positive self-views. A main focus of their review was the importance of evaluating the evidence for the predictive validity of narrower self-related constructs rather than focusing on global self-esteem (see also Marsh & Craven, 2006). Swann and colleagues also directly countered Baumeister et al. (2003) by suggesting that global self-esteem is a generally reliable predictor of global outcomes, and they ultimately concluded that "people with negative self-views think and behave in ways that diminish their quality of life" (p. 92). They also suggested that it was worthwhile to continue to search for ways to improve negative self-views. One reading of the existing self-esteem literature in light of this review from Swann and colleagues is that there is a need for additional, but much more rigorous studies investigating the connections between self-esteem and life outcomes.

Consistent with the perspective that global self-esteem is a broad (albeit modest) predictor of a wide range of life outcomes in well-designed longitudinal studies, Trzesniewski et al. (2006) found that adolescents with higher self-esteem had better mental and physical health, better economic prospects, and lower levels of criminal behavior during adulthood, compared to adolescents with low self-esteem. These long-term consequences of self-esteem were also evident in models that had controls for adolescent depression, gender, and socioeconomic status. Moreover, the findings held when the outcome variables were assessed using objective measures (e.g. criminal reports, graduation rates) and informant reports; therefore the findings cannot be explained by shared method variance in self-report data. In short, there is compelling evidence that self-esteem is prospectively linked with important life outcomes. The task for future research is to develop a better understanding of the processes linking self-esteem to important life outcomes.

In line with this perspective, recent work by Ford and Collins (2010) points to a connection between self-esteem and the psychological and biological systems that respond to stress. In particular, they found evidence to suggest that self-esteem plays a role in regulating threats to social acceptance (that is, rejection). In an experimental paradigm, participants first read about the attributes of a potential interaction partner. They were also led to believe that the interaction partner was reading about them. Participants were then assigned to an ambiguous social rejection condition, where they were told that their anticipated partner chose not to continue, but were not told why or to a control condition, where they were told that the anticipated partner was ill. Compared to individuals with high self-esteem, individuals in the rejection condition with low self-esteem tended to blame themselves for the rejection. They also tended to form a more negative evaluation of their potential partner's personality. These low self-esteem participants also showed more physiological stress in response to the rejection. This work suggests that self-esteem moderates the relation between a potentially stressful event (social rejection) and physiological outcomes.

The idea that self-esteem plays a role in physiological processes linked to stress is also consistent with research conducted by O'Donnell, Brydon, Wright, and Steptoe (2008). They found that individuals with high self-esteem had lower heart rates, reduced inflammatory responses, and lower reports of subjective stress following stressful mental tasks. It appears that individuals with high self-esteem have more adaptive physiological and psychological responses to stress than those with low self-esteem. This biologically informed work helps to provide a potential physiological mechanism for some of the longitudinal associations between self-esteem and health reported in Trzesniewski et al. (2006). The observation that self-esteem may play a role in regulating adverse reactions to stressors could explain why self-esteem is linked with positive life outcomes.

In light of this more optimistic reading of the self-esteem literature, it is useful to address a persistent issue with respect to the potential dark side of high self-esteem. Although Baumeister et al. (2003) were generally pessimistic about the causal importance of self-esteem, this group has also suggested that high (not low) self-esteem might cause aggressive behavior (see also Baumeister et al., 1996; Bushman & Baumeister, 1998). The actual evidence for this claim is fairly weak. In one study, Bushman and Baumeister (1998) attempted to test, in a laboratory-based aggression task, whether "self-love" or "self-hate" was related to aggressive tendencies. Although they found no evidence connecting global self-esteem with aggression in two studies of college students (see also Konrath, Bushman, & Campbell, 2006), they did find that narcissism, as assessed by the Narcissistic Personality Inventory (Raskin & Terry, 1988), was linked to aggressive retaliation in response to negative feedback. Subsequent work seems to suggest that the NPI entitlement sub-scale is more strongly linked than the NPI summary score to laboratory aggression (Konrath et al., 2006).

Critics of self-esteem have seemingly based their conclusion that self-esteem has a "dark side" on the assumption that high self-esteem is conceptually similar, if not identical, to narcissism and psychological entitlement. In contrast to these laboratory-based studies of aggression, other studies focused on real-world outcomes have found evidence that low self-esteem is prospectively related to antisocial behavior (e.g. Donnellan et al., 2005). This relation held for self- and informant reports, for participants from different nationalities (United States and New Zealand), and across age groups (adolescents and college students). Given the bulk of the evidence, we are not convinced that high self-esteem has an appreciable dark side, especially given that self-esteem is virtually uncorrelated with psychological entitlement. The few studies that are interpreted as providing evidence for the dark side of self-esteem are usually based on either a conflation of self-esteem and narcissism, or on some type of statistical interaction between self-esteem and narcissism (e.g. Thomaes, Bushman, Stegge, & Olthof, 2008).

## Further Reflections on the Debate over the Benefits of Self-Esteem

The debate surrounding the causal power of self-esteem is reminiscent of an earlier debate about the validity of personality traits, which fomented throughout the 1970s and 1980s. Indeed, there are interesting parallels between Baumeister et al.'s (2003) review and the arguments against global personality traits advanced by Mischel

(1968), Ross and Nisbett (1991), and others. This is especially true regarding issues of effect size. For example, Baumeister et al. (2003) were occasionally inconsistent in their interpretations of effect sizes. On one occasion, they classified correlations around .25 as "weak" (p. 12), whereas in other places they considered an assortative mating coefficient of .23 (i.e. the correlation between husbands and wives) as an indication that spouses have "similar levels of self-esteem" (p. 18). Regardless of such inconsistencies, those who interpret effect sizes in the neighborhood of .20 as incon-sequential or weak overlook the fact that the mean situational effect size is about .22 on the basis of a meta-analytic review (Richard, Bond, & Stokes-Zoota, 2003, p. 337). Correlations of around .20 are perhaps given a different meaning when viewed against such a benchmark.

Likewise, Baumeister et al. did not clearly specify what level of correlation should be expected when evaluating the connections between self-esteem and multiply determined outcomes. This is an important issue, because researchers have long recognized that that there are limits on the predictive validity of any single trait in such conditions (e.g. Ahadi & Diener, 1989; Sarason, Smith, & Diener, 1975). The point here is that researchers need to carefully approach the interpretation of effect sizes when dealing with multiply determined outcomes.

It is also the case that many qualitative reviews of the self-esteem literature over-look meta-analytic reviews of self-esteem intervention programs, which demonstrate that "it is possible to significantly improve children's and adolescents' levels of [self-esteem/self-concept] and to obtain concomitant positive changes in other areas of adjustment" (Haney & Durlak, 1998, p. 429). Likewise, O'Mara, Marsh, Craven, and Debus (2006) found that self-concept enhancing programs benefited children and adolescents. These authors also reported that programs targeting specific aspects of self-evaluation (rather than global self-esteem) tied to a particular outcome tended to have larger effect sizes. For example, programs designed to improve grades were more effective when they targeted academic self-worth as opposed to global self-esteem. Nonetheless, O'Mara et al. (2006) reported positive effect sizes for global intervention efforts as well.

A final issue regarding the role of multivariate analyses in the current self-esteem debate is worth exploring. Critics of the effects of self-esteem often go to extreme lengths to explain away the effects of self-esteem in multivariate analyses (e.g. Boden, Fergusson, & Horwood, 2007, 2008). Anderson and Anderson (1996) offered a useful framework for understanding the point of such multivariate analyses by way of their philosophy of destructive testing. The point of many of these analyses is to introduce "competitors" (i.e. alternative explanations for links between self-esteem and life outcomes) into a prediction equation, so as to evaluate when such variables reduce the predictive validity of the focal construct to near-zero levels. Anderson and Anderson suggest that the relevant issue is how much "stress" the focal predictor can stand when one adds competing predictors into the model, the assumption being that there will usually be a point at which virtually every predictor variable is "broken" (i.e. it is no longer a significant predictor of the outcome).

Consider, for example, the work of Boden and colleagues (2007, 2008), which has been interpreted as consistent with the claim that measures of self-esteem lack predictive validity. In both articles, the authors report statistically significant zero-order effects between self-esteem and a range of important life outcomes. They then introduce a considerable number of covariates to their prediction models, to make the point that the independent effects of self-esteem often become non-significant after these variables are incorporated into the analysis. The rationale for including all of those covariates was not well specified, and there was no information about the correlations between the predictors. For example, Boden et al. (2008) predicted depression at ages 18, 21, and 25 from self-esteem at age 15, with a model that included 23 presumably correlated variables such as neuroticism (assessed at age 14) and depression (assessed at age 15). Neither depression at age 15 nor self-esteem at age 15 had a statistically significant independent effect in the multivariate model. Such results are quite difficult to interpret in conceptual terms. Nonetheless, the authors interpreted their results as showing that self-esteem was unrelated to subsequent depression, yet they neglected to point out that those same models, which included 23 other predictors, also failed to find a relation between prior levels of depression and future levels of the same construct. In other analyses, Boden et al. (2008) found that self-esteem at age 15 independently predicted suicidal ideation, life satisfaction, and peer attachment, even after controlling for the 23 other predictors. Thus they were not able to completely destroy the predictive validity of self-esteem in all cases. Using a similar approach, Boden et al. (2007) reported that self-esteem at age 15 still independently predicted self-reported hostility at ages 18 to 25. The coefficient for self-esteem was not statistically significant ($p = .06$) in the model that predicted self-reported violence from ages 18 to 25. However, all of these independent effects were reported for models that included 13 other variables, including conduct problems at age 13. In sum, the results of these two recent studies are ambiguous given the challenges that accompany the interpretation of complicated multivariate longitudinal models.

In general, researchers who use multivariate approaches to evaluate statistical effects need to clearly differentiate between confounding variables and potential mediators (MacKinnon, Krull, & Lockwoood, 2000). Such conceptual distinctions are statistically indistinguishable and therefore must be made on theoretical grounds. For example, Stamatakis et al. (2003) used a large longitudinal study of Finnish men to evaluate connections between self-esteem and mortality. They reported that self-esteem was associated with an elevated risk of age-adjusted mortality. They then showed that the effect of self-esteem was no longer statistically significant once a variable representing hopelessness was included in the model. On the basis of these results, they concluded that self-esteem "does not appear to be a strong etiologic factor for mortality" (p. 64). The alternative perspective, however, is that the effect of self-esteem on mortality is transmitted (i.e. mediated) by hopelessness (see O'Donnell et al., 2008); that is, low self-esteem individuals are more likely to die early because they are prone to feelings of hopelessness. This interpretation would be broadly consistent with work by Orth and Robins (e.g. Orth et al., 2008; Orth, Robins, & Meier, 2009; Orth, Robins, Trzesniewski et al., 2009), which shows that self-esteem is a risk factor for depressive thoughts and feelings, including hopelessness about the future. The point is that the interpretation of multivariate results should occur in the context of conceptual models about underlying processes rather than being based on a blind reading of *p*-values.

# Is Self-Esteem a State or a Trait?

Another persistent debate concerns whether self-esteem is best conceptualized as a state-like or trait-like psychological construct (e.g. Conley, 1984; Harter, 2006; Harter & Whitesell, 2003; Trzesniewski, Donnellan, & Robins, 2003). Various positions exist on the issue, and some authors have even denied the relevance of the question. For example, Harter (2006) concluded that "the construct of self-esteem (or self-worth), in and of itself, is neither a trait nor a state per se" (p. 554) and further argued that attempting to address this question was "false and misguided" (ibid.).

In contrast to Harter (2006), we believe whether self-esteem is more trait-like or state-like is an important empirical question. Drawing on contemporary conceptualizations of traits (e.g. Caspi & Roberts, 2001; Funder, 1991), we consider differential (i.e. rank-order) consistency over time to be the major criterion for determining whether a construct is trait-like or state-like (see also Conley, 1984). Differential consistency refers to the degree to which the relative ordering of individuals is preserved over time (e.g. do adolescents with low levels of self-esteem, when compared to their peers, continue to have relatively low levels in young adulthood?), and is typically operationalized by test–retest correlations. This definition allows constructs that show normative changes over time, such as basic personality dimensions and cognitive abilities, to be considered stable psychological traits. Quite simply, constructs that exhibit a relatively high degree of rank-order consistency over time are considered more trait-like, whereas constructs that do not are more state-like (see e.g. Roberts, 2009, p. 140).

Trzesniewski et al. (2003) conducted a meta-analytic review of self-esteem test–retest correlations and concluded that self-esteem is a stable individual-differences construct for much of the life span. In fact, the overall level of stability is similar to that found for the Big-Five traits (Roberts & DelVecchio, 2000). Interestingly, the stability of self-esteem shows systematic changes across the life span; it increases from adolescence to adulthood and then declines in old age. Although the increase in consistency during adulthood is consistent with findings for the Big-Five traits, the old age decline seems to be unique to self-esteem.

More recently, Donnellan, Kenny, Trzesniewski, Lucas, and Conger (2010) applied Kenny and Zautra's (2001) Stable Trait–Autoregressive Trait State (STARTS) model to 10 waves of self-esteem data collected from a sample followed from ages 13 to 32. This model explicitly recognizes that psychological attributes can involve a mixture of completely state-like and trait-like attributes. In particular, the model decomposes repeated measures assessments into three latent (i.e. unobserved) sources of variance. The stable trait factor captures individual differences that are completely stable across all time points whereas the autroregressive trait factor captures enduring variability that persists across adjacent assessment occasions. State factors reflect fleeting individual variability that is unique to any single measurement occasion (including measurement error in many models). In addition to providing estimates of the proportion of these three sources of variability, the model provides an estimate of the stability of the autoregressive trait factor from one measurement occasion to the next.

Donnellan et al. (2010) argued that the STARTS approach offers a more precise understanding of the consistency of self-esteem than has been provided by previous studies that focus on retest correlations. They reasoned that, if self-esteem were best conceptualized as a transitory state, then the model should indicate that state factors account for a substantial amount of variance in repeated measures of self-esteem. In contrast, if self-esteem were a relatively enduring individual difference, then the stable trait and the autoregressive trait should account for a large amount of variance in self-esteem scores taken over time. Consistent with this prediction, they found that the autoregressive trait factor and the stable trait factor accounted for most of the variance in self-esteem assessments. For example, a completely stable trait accounted for 35 percent of the variance, whereas the autoregressive trait factor accounted for 49 percent of the variance in a model that was able to separate measurement error from reliable but completely transitory variance that did not carry over from one occasion to the next. State variance was around 16 percent in this analysis. They also found that the autoregressive trait aspects of self-esteem become much more stable with age. For instance, the stability coefficient for adjacent autoregressive traits was around .50 between the ages of 13 and 14, but increased to .94 between the ages of 31 and 32.

Self-esteem thus seems to behave like many other personality traits, which also show a pattern of increasing consistency with age (Roberts & DelVecchio, 2000). This general pattern, whereby psychological traits become even more consistent with age, has been formalized into the *cumulative continuity* generalization about personality development (see Caspi, Roberts, & Shiner, 2005). Nonetheless, these descriptive findings for self-esteem demand an explanation. Why does the longitudinal consistency of self-esteem increase for much of the life span, and then perhaps decrease during the later stages of life?

Lower levels of consistency are expected when the individual is faced with dramatic environmental and/or maturational changes (Alsaker & Olweus, 1992; Trzesniewski et al., 2003; Wiggins & Pincus, 1992). The transition to adolescence typically involves substantial changes in the social, cognitive, and biological domains. Individuals often experience rapid physical changes attributable to puberty, along with changes in their educational settings and peer relations. Such changes may impact individuals in different ways, thereby shifting the relative ordering of individual differences. These considerations may explain why stability coefficients are lower in adolescence than in adulthood. During adulthood maturational changes are relatively minimal and environmental changes are increasingly subject to individual control. These factors would seem to promote consistency over time. However, the end phases of the life span often involve health-related decline, cognitive decline, changes in social role due to retirement, and the loss of spouses due to mortality. These less positive changes may also impact individuals in different ways and thus might account for declining stability at the end of the life span.

In summary, the evidence indicates that self-esteem is much like a personality trait for most of the life span in terms of its differential consistency. The one caveat is that self-esteem might exhibit less stability in old age relative to the core personality dispositions captured by the Big Five. This trait-like perspective on self-esteem might seem to be at odds with previous studies that focus on its state-like aspects.

Unfortunately, the state self-esteem literature is often difficult to interpret in a broader context. For example, researchers have developed separate, single time-point measures to capture state-like aspects of self-esteem (e.g. Heatherton & Polivy, 1991), but such measures are often strongly correlated with trait measures (Bosson & Swann, 2009, p. 532). Other studies have modified existing measures to detect more transitory fluctuations in self-esteem by changing the wording of items (e.g. Denissen, Penke, Schmitt, & van Aken, 2008; Kernis, Cornell, Sun, Berry, & Harlow, 1993). However, this practice usually assumes that the rewording of items necessarily transforms a given "trait" assessment into a "state" assessment, which might be problematic given the observed correlations between even explicit state and trait measures. Given these concerns, we have concluded that self-esteem is best characterized as an enduring trait rather than as a fleeting psychological state.

## What Are the Age-Related Differences in Self-Esteem across the Life Span?

Although self-esteem seems to be best conceptualized as a relatively trait-like construct, there is still the possibility that it shows normative developmental changes across the life span. The question here is whether average levels of self-esteem systematically increase or decrease across different life stages (e.g. is self-esteem lower in adolescence than in early adulthood?). As with other aspects of self-esteem, this issue has proven controversial (e.g. Demo, 1992; McCarthy & Hoge, 1982; O'Malley & Bachman, 1983; Orth, Trzesniewski, & Robins, 2010; Pullmann, Allik, & Realo, 2009; Robins, Trzesniewski, Tracy, Gosling, & Potter, 2002; Wylie, 1979). However, research accumulating over the last decade or two suggests that there are reliable age differences in self-esteem across the life span. A broad generalization, drawn across different longitudinal, cross-sectional, and meta analytic studies that have examined specific phases of the life span, is that self-esteem increases during the transition to adulthood, then reaches a relative peak somewhere in middle adulthood, and then declines in old age (Galambos, Barker, & Krahn, 2006; Orth et al., 2010; Robins & Trzesniewski, 2005; Twenge & Campbell, 2001). Orth et al. (2010) conducted one of the most extensive cohort-sequential analyses of mean levels of self-esteem across the life span and found that such a quadratic trend was a reasonable approximation of the age trend from 25 to age 104. Importantly, this study was based on the Americans' Changing Lives study (House, 1986), which used probability-based sampling methods, a design feature that addresses concerns about the use of convenience samples in this literature (Pullmann et al., 2009). Such a trend toward positive psychological development is broadly consistent with the *maturity principle* of personality development (Caspi et al., 2005). Gove, Ortega, and Style (1989) noted: "during the productive adult years, when persons are engaged in a full set of instrumental and social roles, their sense of self will reflect the fullness of this role repertoire [...] levels of life satisfaction and self-esteem will also be high" (p. 1122).

The normative pattern of self-esteem development from childhood to adolescence is more complicated. Robins et al. (2002) reported the results of a large

Internet-based study and found that self-esteem scores in children aged between 9 and 12 were relatively high compared to the rest of the life span. There are concerns, however, as to whether assessments of global self-esteem in children have validity and whether self-judgments in children are influenced by cognitive limitations (Davis-Kean & Sandler, 2001; Harter, 1999; Marsh, Craven, & Debus, 1991; Marsh, Ellis, & Craven, 2002; Trzesniewski, Kinal, & Donnellan, 2010). Nonetheless, average levels of self-esteem typically decline during the transition to adolescence (Robins et al., 2002; Seidman, Allen, Aber, Mitchell, & Feinman, 1994; Simmons, Blyth, Van Cleave, & Bush, 1979; Wigfield, Eccles, Mac Iver, Reuman, & Midgley, 1991; for exceptions, see Hirsch & Rapkin, 1987; Nottlemann, 1987). There are several potential explanations for this decline. For instance, Harter (2006) argues that the changes in self-esteem from childhood to adolescence stem from underlying cognitive changes that cause self-evaluations to be more strongly based on objective criteria and more strongly tied to social comparison processes (see also Cole et al., 2001). It is also possible that changes in educational practices and the kinds of feedback given to adolescents contribute to declines in self-esteem (see e.g. Eccles et al., 1993).

Perhaps more positively, self-esteem levels tend to increase from adolescence into adulthood, as indicated by a number of longitudinal analyses (Donnellan et al., 2010; Galambos et al., 2006; Twenge & Campbell, 2001; Young & Mroczek, 2003). This finding raises intriguing questions about the psychological impact of the transition to adulthood. It seems clear that the shift to adulthood is gradual in contemporary societies, a fact that leads some scholars to posit a stage in the life span known as emerging adulthood, which spans the years between ages 18 and 25 or so (Arnett, 2000). Although adolescence may not be an absolute time of storm and stress, as depicted in classic accounts (e.g. Hall, 1904), it might be a *relatively* difficult period in the life span (see Arnett, 1999), given limitations on freedom and the so-called maturity gap (Moffitt, 1993). To be sure, there are limits on individual agency during adolescence, because most adolescents live with their parents and attend secondary school. For much of this time, individuals are reproductively and cognitively mature, but they are given fairly limited opportunities to express their maturity. The greater freedom of emerging adulthood may facilitate increases in self-esteem because individuals are able to select environments in accordance with their individual attributes and gradually assume important and meaningful adult roles. This process may end up promoting psychological health and maturity, as illustrated by the increase in self-esteem.

## Is Self-Esteem a Universal Construct or a By-Product of Individualistic Cultures?

Yet another controversy surrounds the question of whether or not self-esteem is a predominantly culture-bound construct that applies more to individualistic than to collectivistic cultures (Heine, Lehman, Markus, & Kitayama, 1999; Sedikides, Gaertner, & Toguchi, 2003). Heine et al. (1999) even speculated that "self-esteem, as it is conventionally researched and understood, may be, in significant ways, a North

American phenomenon" (p. 768). This debate is often discussed as part of a broader and very contentious exchange over the universality of self-enhancement (e.g. Heine, Kitayama, & Hamamura, 2007; Sedikides, Gaertner, & Vevea, 2007). At issue, for the present purposes, is whether self-esteem has the same meaning and external correlates in collectivistic countries (e.g. Japan) as it does in individualistic countries (e.g. the United States).

The existing data seem to support a universalistic perspective on self-esteem. For example, the Rosenberg Self-Esteem Scale (RSE) has acceptable psychometric properties and similar relations with extraversion and neuroticism in Japan, India, and the United States (Schmitt & Allik, 2005). Using principal components analyses, Schmitt and Allik found that the Rosenberg scale has a similar structure across 53 samples taken from around the world. The only caveat is that negatively worded items were sometimes interpreted differently across cultures. One negatively worded RSE item ("I wish I could have more respect for myself") was particularly problematic, and occasionally had a negative loading on the first principal component in some samples. However, this item also tends to perform poorly in US samples; it was one of the worst items in an item response theory analysis of a large sample of American college students (Gray-Little et al., 1997). Overall, Schmitt and Allik (2005) concluded that "most people have an internally consistent conception of self-worth and can rate, both in the West and in the East, their position on this personality dimension" (p. 637). Moreover, the external correlates of self-esteem tended to be similar across cultures. In general, people who reported high self-esteem also reported being more extraverted and less neurotic, regardless of whether they were living in Finland, Mexico, Romania, Taiwan, the United States, or Zimbabwe. On the basis of their findings, Schmitt and Allik concluded that "the theoretically relativistic position that self-esteem is a socially constructed phenomenon, which primarily depends on cultural norms, values, and practices, may be overstated" (p. 638).

Although the structure and correlates of self-esteem tend to generalize across cultures, there do seem to be cultural differences in average levels of self-esteem (Schmitt & Allik, 2005). For example, the sample from the United States had a higher mean score (32.21; SD = 5.01) than the sample from Japan (25.50; SD = 4.37). Despite this seemingly substantial difference, Schmitt and Allik (2005) noted that the observed cultural differences in mean levels did not conform to a simple and clear pattern, in which scores would be higher in more individualistic countries than in collectivistic and eastern countries. They concluded that there was little justification for a "clear and wide division" between western and eastern countries.

A word of caution, however, is warranted when interpreting the existing results for mean-level cross-cultural comparisons. Beyond the fact that all of the samples were convenience samples in Schmitt and Allik (2005), there is a deeper concern about measurement equivalence or invariance (Chen, 2008). At issue is whether the Rosenberg scale has the degree of measurement invariance across cultures required to make definitive claims of mean-level differences in self-esteem (ibid.). This level of measure equivalence was not formally evaluated in the Schmitt and Allik (2005) study. In fact, it is a psychometric truism that many (if not most) psychological measures are better at ranking people from relatively higher to relatively lower levels than at weighing people—that is, at giving a precise score that is invariant across cultures and measurement occasions; see e.g. Gottfredson, 2009). It might be that the Rosenberg scale only ranks people in similar ways across cultures. Donnellan (2009), for example, tested the measurement equivalence of the Rosenberg scale in a large sample of ethnically diverse college students from multiple universities in the United States. He found indications of generally similar factor loadings for most of the items for Asian American as compared with European American students (i.e. metric invariance). In contrast, the evidence for the proposition that item intercepts could be constrained to the same value (i.e. scalar invariance) for both groups was less compelling. This more demanding level of measurement invariance is required for making definitive statements about mean-level group differences, and therefore these findings for ethnic differences within the United States raise potential concerns about the validity of cross-cultural mean-level comparisons. Accordingly, it is an open question whether existing measures of self-esteem have the psychometric equivalence to permit strong inferences about absolute differences across cultures (Chen, 2008).

## Conclusions

Although we have identified several ongoing controversies with respect to self-esteem, we believe that the field has made considerable progress since William James first introduced the construct to scientific psychology, well over 100 years ago. Accordingly, we suggest that there are several tentative conclusions that can serve as a foundation for future work. These take-home messages are summarized in Table 28.1. In short, self-esteem seems to be a universal trait that can be assessed validly and reliably across cultures by using reasonably short self-report scales. The construct of self-esteem is conceptually and empirically distinct from that of narcissism, as it is understood and operationalized in social and personality psychology. In light of this fact, the actual evidence that high self-esteem has a dark side is weak; we believe instead that there is good evidence pointing to a connection between low self-esteem and a range of negative life outcomes. Nonetheless, we acknowledge that this is a controversial and unresolved issue. Self-esteem is related to extraversion, neuroticism, and depression, and researchers are currently debating the magnitude and meaning of these associations. Self-esteem shows much more consistency across the life span than would be expected from a "state" conceptualization. All in all, self-esteem seems to behave much like other personality traits in terms of the size of its genetic under-pinnings, of its increasing pattern of consistency from childhood to adulthood, and of its tendency to show a normative developmental trajectory.

The conclusions in Table 28.1 naturally reflect our interpretations of the literature and should be viewed with the appropriate caveats. As we have stressed throughout this chapter, research about self-esteem is contentious. The existence of vigorous unresolved controversies suggests that the scientific study of self-esteem will continue for decades to come. In particular, we anticipate that genetically informed studies and explorations into the physiological correlates of self-esteem will provide important insights into the nature of the construct in the near future. Likewise, we antici-pate that rigorous evaluations of theoretically based self-esteem enhancement programs will help to resolve ongoing controversies about the value of promoting

**Table 28.1**   Summary of core themes regarding global self-esteem

| | |
|---|---|
| **Conceptualization** | Self-esteem is an individual's subjective evaluation of her or his overall worth as a person. |
| **Measurement** | Explicit self-esteem can be measured with a high degree of reliability and validity using even very brief self-report scales. The 10-item Rosenberg Self-Esteem Scale (Rosenberg, 1965) is the most commonly used self-report scale. |
| **Demographic differences** | Men have slightly higher self-esteem than women, especially during adolescence; African Americans have slightly higher levels of self-esteem than Whites, followed by Latinos, and then by Asian Americans; High SES adults have slightly higher self-esteem than low SES adults. |
| **Genetic influences** | About 40 percent of the observed variability in self-esteem is due to genetic factors. |
| **Big Five correlates** | Self-esteem is most strongly related to extraversion and (low) neuroticism. |
| **Narcissism** | Self-esteem and narcissism are moderately correlated, as assessed with common measures in social and personality psychology ($r \leq .30$). However, they are conceptually distinct, and care should be taken to avoid conflating them. |
| **Life outcomes** | Such findings are controversial and the subject of intense debate. However, there is evidence that low self-esteem is prospectively associated with better mental and physical health, better economic prospects, and lower levels of criminal behavior even after controlling for depression and other relevant variables. Emerging research suggests that low self-esteem is a vulnerability factor for the development of depression. |
| **State vs. trait** | Self-esteem is a stable trait that exhibits test–retest correlations as high as most personality traits for most of the life span. |
| **Developmental considerations** | Mean self-esteem levels tend to decline from childhood to adolescence, to increase from adolescence through adulthood, and then to decline in old age. |
| **Cultural variability** | Cultures differ in their reported levels of self-esteem, but the factor structure (i.e. factor loadings) and external correlates of self-esteem tend to generalize across cultures. Whether measures are psychometrically invariant across cultures in terms of scaling (i.e. whether a "3" or a "4" on a scale has the same absolute meaning in Japan vs. the United States) is unknown. |

self-esteem. In the end, Rosenberg (1989, p. 313) summarized his work on self-esteem with sentiments that are still very much relevant today:

> That the student of human behavior must take account of the self-image seems obvious. It is equally obvious that the problems in this field are sufficiently abundant and exciting to challenge the energy, imagination, and skill of research investigators for years to come.

# References

Ahadi, S., & Diener, E. (1989). Multiple determinants and effect size. *Journal of Personality and Social Psychology, 56,* 398–406.

Alsaker, F. D., & Olweus, D. (1992). Stability of global self-evaluations in early adolescence: A cohort longitudinal study. *Journal of Research on Adolescence, 2,* 123–145.

Anderson, C. A., & Anderson, K. B. (1996). Violent crime rate studies in philosophical context: A destructive testing approach to heat and southern culture of violence effects. *Journal of Personality and Social Psychology, 70,* 740–756.

Arnett, J. J. (1999). Adolescent storm and stress, reconsidered. *American Psychologist, 54,* 317–326.

Arnett, J. J. (2000). Emerging adulthood: A theory of development from the late teens through the twenties. *American Psychologist, 55,* 469–480.

Bachman, J. G., & O'Malley, P. M. (1984). Black–white differences in self-esteem: Are they affected by response styles? *American Journal of Sociology, 90,* 624–639.

Bachman, J. G., O'Malley, P. M., Freedman-Doan, P., Trzesniewski, K. H., & Donnellan, M. B. (in press). Adolescent self-esteem: Differences by race/ethnicity, gender, and age. *Self and Identity.*

Baumeister, R. F., Smart, L., & Boden, J. M. (1996). Relation of threatened egotism to violence and aggression: The dark side of high self-esteem. *Psychological Review, 103,* 5–33.

Baumeister, R. F., Campbell, J. D., Krueger, J. I., & Vohs, K. E. (2003). Does high self-esteem cause better performance, interpersonal success, happiness, or healthier lifestyles? *Psychological Science in the Public Interest, 4,* 1–44.

Blascovich, J., & Tomaka, J. (1991). Measures of self-esteem. In J. P. Robinson, P. R. Shaver, & L. S. Wrightsman (Eds.), *Measures of personality and social psychological attitudes* (pp. 115–160). New York: Academic Press.

Boden, J. M., Fergusson, D. M., & Horwood, L. J. (2007). Self-esteem and violence: Testing links between adolescent self-esteem and later hostility and violent behavior. *Social Psychiatry and Psychiatric Epidemiology, 42,* 881–891.

Boden, J. M., Fergusson, D. M., & Horwood, L. J. (2008). Does adolescent self-esteem predict later life outcomes? A test of the causal role of self-esteem. *Development and Psychopathology, 20,* 319–339.

Bosson, J. K., & Swann, W. B., Jr. (2009). Self-esteem. In M. R. Leary & R. H. Hoyle (Eds.), *Handbook of individual differences in social behavior* (pp. 527–546). New York: Guilford Press.

Bosson, J. K., Swann, W. B., Jr., & Pennebaker, J. W. (2000). Stalking the perfect measure of implicit self-esteem: The blind men and the elephant revisited? *Journal of Personality and Social Psychology, 79,* 631–643.

Bradlee, P. M., & Emmons, R. A. (1992). Locating narcissism within the interpersonal circumplex and the five-factor model. *Personality and Individual Differences, 13,* 821–830.

Brown, R. P., & Zeigler-Hill, V. (2004). Narcissism and the non-equivalence of self-esteem measures: A matter of dominance? *Journal of Research in Personality, 38,* 585–592.

Bushman, B. J., & Baumeister, R. F. (1998). Threatened egotisim, narcissism, self-esteem, and direct and displaced aggression: Does self-love or self-hate lead to violence? *Journal of Personality and Social Psychology, 84,* 1027–1040.

Cai, H., Brown, J. D., Deng, C., & Oakes, M. A. (2007). Self-esteem and culture: Differences in cognitive self-evaluations or affective self-regard? *Asian Journal of Social Psychology, 10,* 162–170.

Cain, N. M., Pincus, A. L., & Ansell, E. B. (2008). Narcissism at the crossroads: Phenotypic description of pathological narcissism across clinical theory, social/personality psychology, and psychiatric diagnosis. *Clinical Psychology Review, 28*, 638–656.

Carmines, E. G., & Zeller, R. A. (1979). *Reliability and validity assessment*. Thousand Oaks, CA: Sage.

Caspi, A., & Roberts, B. W. (2001). Personality development across the life course: The argument for change and continuity. *Psychological Inquiry, 12*, 49–66.

Caspi, A., Roberts, B. W., & Shiner, R. L. (2005). Personality development: Stability and change. *Annual Review of Psychology, 56*, 453–484.

Chen, F. F. (2008). What happens if we compare chopsticks with forks? The impact of making inappropriate comparisons in cross-cultural research. *Journal of Personality and Social Psychology, 95*, 1005–1018.

Cohen, J. (1988). *Statistical power analysis for the behavioral sciences* (2nd ed.). Hillsdale, NJ: Lawrence Erlbaum Associates.

Cole, D. A., Maxwell, S. E., Martin, J. M., Peeke, L. G., Seroczynski, A. D., Tram, J. M. et al. (2001). The development of multiple domains of child and adolescent self-concept: A cohort sequential longitudinal design. *Child Development, 72*, 1723–1746.

Conley, J. J. (1984). The hierarchy of consistency: A review and model of longitudinal findings on adult individual differences in intelligence, personality, and self-opinion. *Personality and Individual Differences, 5*, 11–25.

Coopersmith, S. (1967). *The antecedents of self-esteem*. San Francisco, CA: Freeman.

Crocker, J., & Major, B. (1989). Social stigma and self-esteem: The self-protective properties of stigma. *Psychological Review, 96*, 608–630.

Davis-Kean, P. E., & Sandler, H. M. (2001). A meta-analysis for preschool self-concept measures: A framework for future measures. *Child Development, 72*, 887–906.

Demo, D. H. (1992). The self-concept over time: Research issues and directions. *Annual Review of Sociology, 18*, 303–326.

Denissen, J. J. A., Penke, L., Schmitt, D. P., & van Aken, M. A. G. (2008). Self-esteem reactions to social interactions: Evidence for sociometer mechanisms across days, people, and nations. *Journal of Personality and Social Psychology, 95*, 181–196.

Donnellan, M. B. (2009, October). Using the MUSIC Database to study the nature of self-esteem and its correlates across diverse groups of college students. In M. B. Donnellan & S. Schwartz (Co-Chairs), *A multi-site collaboration to better understand development in college students: The MUSIC Study*. Fourth Conference on Emerging Adulthood. Atlanta, GA.

Donnellan, M. B., & Trzesniewski, K. H. (2009). How should we study generational change— or should we? A critical examination of the evidence for "Generation Me." *Social and Personality Compass, 3*, 775–784.

Donnellan, M. B., Trzesniewski, K. H, Conger, K. J., & Conger, R. D. (2007). A three-wave longitudinal study of self-evaluations during young adulthood. *Journal of Research in Personality, 41*, 453–472.

Donnellan, M. B., Kenny, D. A., Trzesniewski, K. H., Lucas, R. E., & Conger, R. D. (2010). *Using trait–state models to examine the longitudinal consistency of global self-esteem from adolescence to adulthood*. Unpublished manuscript. Michigan State University.

Donnellan, M. B., Trzesniewski, K. H., Robins, R. W., Moffitt, T. E., & Caspi, A. (2005). Low self-esteem is related to aggression, antisocial behavior, and delinquency. *Psychological Science, 16*, 328–335.

Eccles, J. S., Midgley, C., Wigfield, A., Buchanan, C. M., Reuman, D., Flanagan, C., & Mac Iver, D. (1993). Development during adolescence: The impact of stage–environment fit on young adolescents' experience in schools and in families. *American Psychologist, 48,* 90–101.

Emmons, R. A. (1987). Narcissism: Theory and measurement. *Journal of Personality and Social Psychology, 52,* 11–17.

Erdle, S., Gosling, S. D., & Potter, J. (2009). Does self-esteem account for the higher-order factors of the Big Five? *Journal of Research in Personality, 43,* 921–922.

Ford, M. B., & Collins, N. L. (2010). Self-esteem moderates neuroendocrine and psychological responses to interpersonal rejection. *Journal of Personality and Social Psychology, 98,* 405–419.

Funder, D. C. (1991). Global traits: A neo-Allportian approach to personality. *Psychological Science, 2,* 31–39.

Galambos, N. L., Barker, E. T., & Krahn, H. J. (2006). Depression, self-esteem, and anger in emerging adulthood: Seven-year trajectories. *Developmental Psychology, 42,* 350–365.

Gottfredson, L. S. (2009). Logical fallacies used to dismiss the evidence on intelligence testing. In R. P. Phelps (Ed.), *Correcting fallacies about educational and psychological testing* (pp. 11–66). Washington, DC: American Psychological Association.

Gove, W. R., Ortega, S. T., & Style, C. B. (1989). The maturational and role perspectives on aging and self through the adult years: An empirical evaluation. *American Journal of Sociology, 94,* 1117–1145.

Gray-Little, B., & Hafdahl, A. R. (2000). Factors influencing racial comparisons of self-esteem: A quantitative review. *Psychological Bulletin, 126,* 26–54.

Gray-Little, B., Williams, V. S. L., & Hancock, T. D. (1997). An item response theory analysis of the Rosenberg Self-Esteem Scale. *Personality and Social Psychology Bulletin, 23,* 443–451.

Graziano, W. G., Jensen-Campbell, L. A., & Finch, J. F. (1997). The self as a mediator between personality and adjustment. *Journal of Personality and Social Psychology, 73,* 392–404.

Greenberger, E., Chen, C., Dmitrieva, J., & Farruggia, S. P. (2003). Item-wording and dimensionality of the Rosenberg self-esteem scale: Do they matter? *Personality and Individual Differences, 35,* 1241–1254.

Greenwald, A. G., McGhee, D. E., & Schwartz, J. K. L. (1998). Measuring individual differences in implicit cognition: The Implicit Association Test. *Journal of Personality and Social Psychology, 74,* 1464–1480.

Hall, G. S. (1904). *Adolescence: Its psychology and its relation to physiology, anthropology, sociology, sex, crime, religion, and education* (Vols. 1–2). Englewood Cliffs: NJ: Prentice Hall.

Haney, P., & Durlak, J. A. (1998). Changing self-esteem in children and adolescents: A meta-analytic review. *Journal of Clinical Child Psychology, 27,* 423–433.

Harter, S. (1999). *The construction of the self: A developmental perspective.* New York: Guilford Press.

Harter, S. (2006). The self. In W. Damon & R. M. Lerner (Eds.), *Handbook of child psychology: Vol. 3. Social, emotional, and personality development* (6th ed., pp. 505–570). New York: Wiley.

Harter, S., & Pike, R. (1984). The pictorial scale of perceived competence and social acceptance for young children. *Child Development, 55,* 1969–1982.

Harter, S., & Whitesell, N. R. (2003). Beyond the debate: Why some adolescents report stable self-worth over time and situation, whereas others report changes in self-esteem. *Journal of Personality, 71,* 1027–1058.

Heatherton, T. F., & Polivy, J. (1991). Development and validation of a scale for measuring state self-esteem. *Journal of Personality and Social Psychology, 60,* 895–910.

Heimpel, S. A., Elliot, A. J., & Wood, J. V. (2006). Basic personality dispositions, self-esteem, and personal goals: An approach–avoidance analysis. *Journal of Personality, 74,* 1293–1320.

Heine, S. J., Kitayama, S., & Hamamura, T. (2007). Inclusion of additional studies yields different conclusions: Comment on Sedikides, Gaertner, & Vevea (2005), *Journal of Personality and Social Psychology. Asian Journal of Social Psychology, 10,* 49–58.

Heine, S. J., Lehman, D. R., Markus, H. R., & Kitayama, S. (1999). Is there a universal need for positive self-regard? *Psychological Review, 106,* 766–794.

Hirsch, B. J., & Rapkin, B. D. (1987). The transition to junior high school: A longitudinal study of self-esteem, psychological symptomology, school life, and social support. *Child Development, 58,* 1235–1243.

Hofmann, W., Gawronski, B., Gschwendner, T., Le, H., & Schmitt, M. (2005). A meta-analysis on the correlation between the Implicit Association Test and explicit self-report measures. *Personality and Social Psychology Bulletin, 31,* 1369–1385.

House, J. S. (1986). Americans' Changing Lives, Waves I and II, 1986 and 1989 [Data File]. University of Michigan, Survey Research Center [Producer]. Ann Arbor, MI: Inter-University Consortium for Political and Social Research [Distributor].

Hughes, D., Rodriguez, J., Smith, E. P., Johnson, D. J., Stevenson, H. C., & Spicer, P. (2006). Parents' ethnic–racial socialization practices: A review of research and directions for future study. *Developmental Psychology, 42,* 747–770.

Hyde, J. S. (2005). The gender similarities hypothesis. *American Psychologist, 60,* 581–592.

Jahoda, M. (1958). *Current concepts of positive mental health.* New York: Basic Books.

James, W. (1985). *Psychology: The briefer course* [1892]. Notre Dame, IN: University of Notre Dame Press.

Judge, T. A., Erez, A., Thoresen, C. J., & Bono, J. E. (2002). Are measures of self-esteem, neuroticism, locus of control, and generalized self-efficacy indicators of a common core construct? *Journal of Personality and Social Psychology, 83,* 693–710.

Kendler, K. S., Gardner, C. O., & Prescott, C. A. (1998). A population-based twin study of self esteem and gender. *Psychological Medicine, 28,* 1403–1409.

Kenny, D. A., & Zautra, A. (2001). The trait–state models for longitudinal data. In L. M. Collins & A. G. Sayer (Eds.), *New methods for the analysis of change* (pp. 243–263). Washington, DC: American Psychological Association.

Kernis, M. H., Cornell, D. P., Sun, C.-R., Berry, A. & Harlow, T. (1993). There's more to self-esteem than whether it is high or low: The importance of stability of self-esteem. *Journal of Personality and Social Psychology, 65,* 1190–1204.

Kim, H., & Markus, H. R. (1999). Deviance or uniqueness, harmony, or conformity? A cultural analysis. *Journal of Social and Personality Psychology, 77,* 785–800.

Kling, K. C., Hyde, J. S., Showers, C. J., & Buswell, B. N. (1999). Gender differences in self-esteem: A meta-analysis. *Psychological Bulletin, 125,* 470–500.

Konrath, S., Bushman, B. J., & Campbell, W. K. (2006). Attenuating the link between threatened egotism and aggression. *Psychological Science, 17,* 995–1001.

Lahey, B. B. (2009). Public health significance of neuroticism. *American Psychologist, 64,* 241–256.

MacKinnon, D. P., Krull, J. L., & Lockwood, C. M. (2000). Equivalence of the mediation, confounding, and suppression effect. *Prevention Science, 1,* 173–181.

Marsh, H. W. (1996). Positive and negative self-esteem: A substantively meaningful distinction or artifactors? *Journal of Personality and Social Psychology, 70,* 810–819.

Marsh, H. W., & Craven, R. G. (2006). Reciprocal effects of self-concept and performance from a multidimensional perspective. *Perspectives on Psychological Science, 1,* 133–163.

Marsh, H. W., Craven, R. G., & Debus, R. (1991). Self-concepts of young children 5 to 8 years of age: Measurement and multidimensional structure. *Journal of Educational Psychology, 83,* 377–392.

Marsh, H. W., Ellis, L. A., & Craven, R. G. (2002). How do preschool children feel about themselves? Unraveling measurement and multidimensional self-concept structure. *Developmental Psychology, 38,* 376–393.

Marsh, H. W., Ellis, L. A., Parada, R. H., Richards, G., & Heubeck, B. G. (2005). A short version of the Self-Description Questionnaire II: Operationalizing criteria for short-form evaluation with new applications of confirmatory factor analysis. *Psychological Assessment, 17,* 81–102.

McCarthy, J. D., & Hoge, D. R. (1982). Analysis of age effects in longitudinal studies of adolescent self-esteem. *Developmental Psychology, 18,* 372–379.

McCartney, K., & Rosenthal, R. (2000). Effect size, practical importance, and social policy for children. *Child Development, 71,* 173–180.

McCrae, R. R., & Costa, P. T., Jr. (2008). The five-factor theory of personality. In O. P. John, R. W. Robins, & L. A. Pervin (Eds.), *Handbook of personality* (3rd ed., pp. 159–181). New York: Guilford Press.

McGuire, S., Manke, B., Saudino, K. J., Reiss, D., Hetherington, E. M., & Plomin, R. (1999). Perceived competence and self-worth during adolescence: A longitudinal behavior genetic study. *Child Development, 6,* 1283–1296.

Mischel, W., (1968). *Personality and assessment.* New York: Wiley.

Moffitt, T. E. (1993). Adolescence-limited and life course-persistent antisocial behavior: A developmental taxonomy. *Psychological Review, 100,* 674–701.

Neiss, M. B., Sedikides, C., & Stevenson, J. (2002). Self-esteem: A behavioural genetic perspective. *European Journal of Psychology, 16,* 351–367.

Neiss, M. B., Stevenson, J., Legrand, L. N., Iacono, W. G., Sedikides, C. (2009). Self-esteem, negative emotionality, and depression as a common temperamental core: A study of mid-adolescent girls. *Journal of Personality, 77,* 1–20.

Nottlemann, E. D. (1987). Competence and self-esteem during transition from childhood to adolescence. *Developmental Psychology, 23,* 441–450.

O'Donnell, K., Brydon, L., Wright, C. E., & Steptoe, A. (2008). Self-esteem levels and cardiovascular and inflammatory response to acute stress. *Brain, Behavior, & Immunity, 22,* 1241–1247.

O'Malley, P. M., & Bachman, J. G. (1983). Self-esteem: Change and stability between ages 13 and 23. *Developmental Psychology, 19,* 257–268.

O'Mara, A. J., Marsh, H. W., Craven, R. G., Debus, R. L. (2006). Do self-concept interventions make a difference? A synergistic blend of construct validation and meta-analysis. *Educational Psychologist, 41,* 181–206.

Orth, U., Robins, R. W., & Meier, L. L. (2009). Disentangling the effects of low self-esteem and stressful events on depression: Findings from three longitudinal studies. *Journal of Personality and Social Psychology, 97,* 307–321.

Orth, U., Robins, R. W., & Roberts, B. W. (2008). Low self-esteem prospectively predicts depression in adolescence and young adulthood. *Journal of Personality and Social Psychology, 95,* 695–708.

Orth, U., Trzesniewski, K. H., & Robins, R. W. (2010). Self-esteem development from young adulthood to old age: A cohort-sequential longitudinal study. *Journal of Personality and Social Psychology, 98,* 645–658.

Orth, U., Robins, R. W., Trzesniewski, K. H., Maes, J., & Schmitt, M. (2009). Low self-esteem is a risk factor for depression across the lifespan. *Journal of Abnormal Psychology, 118,* 472–478.

Paulhus, D. L., Robins, R. W., Trzesniewski, K. H., & Tracy, J. L. (2004). Two replicable suppressor situations in personality research. *Multivariate Behavioral Research, 39*, 303–328.

Pullmann, H., & Allik, J. (2000). The Rosenberg Self-Esteem Scale: Its dimensionality, stability and personality correlates in Estonian. *Personality and Individual Differences, 28*, 701–715.

Pullmann, H., Allik, J., & Realo, A. (2009). Global self-esteem across the life span: A cross-sectional comparison between representative and self-selected Internet samples. *Experimental Aging Research, 35*, 20–44.

Quilty, L. C., Oakman, J. M., & Risko, E. (2006). Correlates of the Rosenberg self-esteem scale method effects. *Structural Equation Modeling, 13*, 99–117.

Raskin, R., & Terry, H. (1988). A principal-components analysis of the Narcissistic Personality Inventory and further evidence of its construct validity. *Journal of Personality and Social Psychology, 54*, 890–902.

Richard, F. D., Bond, C. F., Jr., & Stokes-Zoota, J. J. (2003). One hundred years of social psychology quantitatively described. *Review of General Psychology, 7*, 331–363.

Roberts, B. W. (2009). Back to the future: *Personality and assessment* and personality development. *Journal of Research in Personality, 43*, 137–145.

Roberts, B. W., & DelVecchio, W. F. (2000). The rank-order consistency of personality traits from childhood to old age: A quantitative review of longitudinal studies. *Psychological Bulletin, 126*, 3–25.

Robins, R. W., & John, O. P. (1997). The quest for self-insight: Theory and research on accuracy and bias in self-perception. In R. T. Hogan, J. A. Johnson, & S. R. Briggs (Eds.), *Handbook of personality psychology* (pp. 649–679). New York: Academic Press.

Robins, R. W., & Trzesniewski, K. H. (2005). Self-esteem development across the lifespan. *Current Directions in Psychological Science, 14*, 158–162.

Robins, R. W., Hedin, H. M., & Trzesniewski, K. H. (2001). Measuring global self-esteem: Construct validation of a single-item measure and the Rosenberg Self-Esteem Scale. *Personality and Social Psychology Bulletin, 27*, 151–161.

Robins, R. W., Tracy, J. L., & Sherman, J. W. (2007). What makes a personality psychologist? A survey of journal editors and editorial board members. In R. W. Robins, R. C. Fraley, & R. F. Krueger (Eds.), *Handbook of research methods in personality psychology* (pp. 673–678) New York: Guilford Press.

Robins, R. W., Donnellan, M. B., Widaman, K. F., & Conger, R. D. (in press). Evaluating the link between self-esteem and temperament in Mexican origin early adolescents. *Journal of Adolescence, 33*, 403-410.

Robins, R. W., Tracy, J. L., Trzesniewski, K. H., Potter, J., & Gosling, S. D. (2001). Personality correlates of self-esteem. *Journal of Research in Personality, 35*, 463–482.

Robins, R. W., Trzesniewski, K. H., Tracy, J. L., Gosling, S. D., & Potter, J. (2002). Global self-esteem across the lifespan. *Psychology and Aging, 17*, 423–434.

Rogers, C. R. (1961). *On becoming a person*. Boston, MA: Houghton Mifflin.

Rosenberg, M. (1989). *Society and adolescent self-image* (rev. ed.) [1965]. Middletown, CT: Wesleyan University Press.

Ross, L., & Nisbett, R. (1991). *The person and the situation: Perspectives of social psychology*. New York: McGraw-Hill.

Sarason, I. G., Smith, R. E., & Diener, E. (1975). Personality research: Components of variance attributable to the person and the situation. *Journal of Personality and Social Psychology, 32*, 199–204.

Schmitt, D. P., & Allik, J. (2005). Simultaneous administration of the Rosenberg Self-Esteem Scale in 53 nations: Exploring the universal and culture-specific features of global self-esteem. *Journal of Personality and Social Psychology, 89*, 623–642.

Sedikides, C., Gaertner, L., & Toguchi, Y. (2003). Pancultural self-enhancement. *Journal of Personality and Social Psychology, 84,* 60–79.

Sedikides, C., Gaertner, L., & Vevea, J. L., (2007). Inclusion of theory-relevant moderators yield the same conclusions as Sedikides, Gaertner, and Vevea (2005): A meta-analytical reply to Heine, Kitayama, and Hamamura (2007). *Asian Journal of Social Psychology, 10,* 59–67.

Sedikides, C., Rudich, E. A., Gregg, A. P., Kumashiro, M., & Rusbult, C. (2004). Are normal narcissists psychologically healthy? Self-esteem matters. *Journal of Personality and Social Psychology, 87,* 400–416.

Seidman, E., Allen, L., Aber, J. L., Mitchell, C., & Feinman, J. (1994). The impact of school transitions on the self-system and perceived social context of poor urban youth. *Child Development, 65,* 507–522.

Simmons, R. G., Blyth, D. A., Van Cleave, E. F., & Bush, D. M. (1979). Entry into early adolescence: The impact of school structure, puberty, and early dating on self-esteem. *American Sociological Review, 44,* 948–967.

Stamatakis, K. A., Lynch, J., Everson, S. A., Raghunathan, T., Salonen, J. T., & Kaplan, G. A. (2003). Self-esteem and mortality: Prospective evidence from a population-based study. *Annals of Epidemiology, 14,* 58–65.

Swann, W. B., Jr., Chang-Schnieder, C., & McClarty, K. L. (2007). Do people's self-views matter? Self-concept and self-esteem in everyday life. *American Psychologist, 62,* 84–94.

Tafarodi, R. W., & Milne, A. B. (2002). Decomposing global self-esteem. *Journal of Personality, 70,* 443–483.

Tangney, J. P., & Leary, M. R. (2003). The next generation of self research. In M. R. Leary & J. P. Tangney (Eds.), *Handbook of self and identity* (pp. 667–674). New York: Wiley.

Thomaes, S., Bushman, B. J., Stegge, H., & Olthof, T. (2008). Trumping shame by blasts of noise: Narcissism, self-esteem, shame, and aggression in young adolescents. *Child Development, 79,* 1792–1801.

Tomás, J. M., & Oliver, A. (1999). Rosenberg's self-esteem scale: Two factors or method effects. *Structural Equation Modeling, 6,* 84–98.

Trzesniewski, K. H. (2009, July). Clarifying the relation between self-esteem and depression: New evidence from a behavioral genetic investigation. In K. Trzesniewski & R. Krueger (Co-Chairs), symposium *Personality and behavioral genetics* held at the annual conference of the Association for Research in Personality, Chicago, IL.

Trzesniewski, K. H., Donnellan, M. B., & Robins, R. W. (2003). Stability of self-esteem across the lifespan. *Journal of Personality and Social Psychology, 84,* 205–220.

Trzesniewski, K. H., Donnellan, M. B., & Robins, R. W. (2008). Is "Generation Me" really more narcissistic than previous generations? *Journal of Personality, 76,* 903–918.

Trzesniewski, K. H, Kinal, P. A., & Donnellan, M. B. (2010). Self-enhancement and self-protection in developmental context. In M. Alicke & C. Sedikides (Eds.), *The Handbook of self-enhancement and self-protection.* (pp. 341–357) New York: Guilford Press.

Trzesniewski, K. H., Donnellan, M. B., Moffitt, T. E., Robins, R. W., Poulton, R., & Caspi, A. (2006). Low self-esteem during adolescence predicts poor health, criminal behavior, and limited economic prospects during adulthood. *Developmental Psychology, 42,* 381–390.

Twenge, J. M., & Campbell, W. (2001). Age and birth cohort differences in self-esteem: A cross-temporal meta-analysis. *Personality and Social Psychology Review, 5,* 321–344.

Twenge, J. M., & Campbell, W. (2002). Self-esteem and socioeconomic status: A meta-analytic review. *Personality and Social Psychology Review, 6,* 59–71.

Twenge, J. M., & Crocker, J. (2002). Race and self-esteem: Meta-analyses comparing Whites, Blacks, Hispanics, Asians, and American Indians and comment on Gray-Little and Hafdahl (2000). *Psychological Bulletin, 128*, 371–408.

Watson, D., & Clark, L. (1984). Negative affectivity: The disposition to experience aversive emotional states. *Psychological Bulletin, 96*, 465–490.

Watson, D., Suls, J., & Haig, J. (2002). Global self-esteem in relation to structural models of personality and affectivity. *Journal of Personality and Social Psychology, 83*, 185–197.

Wigfield, A., Eccles, J. S., Mac Iver, D., Reuman, D. A., & Midgley, C. (1991). Transitions during early adolescence: Changes in children's domain specific self-perceptions and general self-esteem across the transition to junior high school. *Developmental Psychology, 27*, 552–565.

Wiggins, J. S., & Pincus, A. L. (1992). Personality: Structure and assessment. *Annual Review of Psychology, 43*, 473–504.

Wylie, R. C. (1979). *The self-concept.* Lincoln, NE: University of Nebraska Press.

Young, J. F., & Mroczek, D. K. (2003). Predicting intraindividual self-concept trajectories during adolescence. *Journal of Adolescence, 26*, 586–600.

Zeigler-Hill, V. (2010). The interpersonal nature of self-esteem: Do different measures of self-esteem possess similar interpersonal content? *Journal of Research in Personality, 44*, 22–30.

# 29

# Love at First Sight?
## *Individual Differences and the Psychology of Initial Romantic Attraction*
### Viren Swami

Florentino Ariza, a young apprentice at the postal agency "with Indian hair plastered down with scented pomade and eyeglasses for myopia," who also suffered from chronic constipation, is sent one afternoon on a seemingly impossible mission: to deliver a telegram to a man named Lorenzo Daza, with no known place of residence. Ariza finds him, somehow, in an old house half in ruins in the Park of Evangels; he hears "no human sound as he follow[s] the barefoot maid under the arches of the passageway [...] At the far end of the patio [is] a temporary office where a very fat man, whose curly sideburns grew into his mustache, [sits] behind a desk, taking a siesta."

The resting man is in fact Lorenzo Daza, who receives the telegram "as if it were the continuation of an ominous dream," reads it quickly before handing Ariza some money, and sends the postal apprentice away with a handshake. Then the maid accompanies Ariza back to the street door, "more to keep an eye on him than to lead the way," and they make their way back along the arcaded passageway. Only, this time, Ariza knows

> that there [is] someone else in the house, because the brightness in the patio [is] filled with the voice of a woman repeating a reading lesson. As he passe[s] the sewing room, he [sees] through the window an older woman and a young girl sitting very close together on two chairs and following the reading in the book that the woman [holds] open on her lap ... The lesson was not interrupted, but the girl raise[s] her eyes to see who [is] passing by the window, and that casual glance [is] the beginning of a cataclysm of love that still had not ended half a century later. (García Márquez, 1989, pp. 54–55)

This scene, from Gabriel García Márquez's novel *Love in the time of cholera*, sets up one of the most common and powerful premises in western literature: that of love

*The Wiley-Blackwell Handbook of Individual Differences*, First Edition.
Edited by Tomas Chamorro-Premuzic, Sophie von Stumm, and Adrian Furnham.
© 2011 Blackwell Publishing Ltd. Published 2011 by Blackwell Publishing Ltd.

at first sight. This theme can be traced back at least to the ancient Greeks (Sternberg, 1998; Tallis, 2005). It appears, for example, in Ovid's *Metamorphoses* (1998), where the Boeotian hero Narcissus falls in love with a reflection in a pool, not realizing it is his own, and in Achilles Tatius's *Leucippe and Clitophon* (1989, p. 179), where Clitophon laments that "[b]eauty's wound is sharper than any weapon's, and it runs through the eyes down to the soul."

The latter brings to mind the concept of "love arrows," which are said to originate from mythological deities (usually Eros or Cupid, though sometimes also Rumor) or from the image of the object of affection itself. Later Renaissance writers like Giovanni Boccaccio believed that love was conveyed on bright beams of light from the eyes of the person being gazed upon, which sped through the eyes of the lover to his heart. Contemporary scholars, in contrast, have attempted to explain the phenomenon of love at first sight more rationally, suggesting that it is predicated on a distorted or idealized perception of a potential partner: in Sternberg's (1986, 1988) triangular theory of love, for example, love at first sight is an instance of infatuated love, devoid of intimacy and commitment.

Even so, the phenomenon of love at first sight offers scholars a useful means of understanding the psychological processes involved in initial romantic attraction (Graziano & Bruce, 2008). Specifically, in this chapter I want to suggest that an individual differences approach, when considered alongside traditional perspectives, affords potentially unique insights into the psychology of initial attraction. In this sense, an individual differences approach simply seeks to establish whether there are certain traits in the observer or in the observed that make relationship initiation more likely. To return to *Love in the time of cholera*, is it possible that there are certain psychological traits that increase the chances that Florentino Ariza will fall in love with Fermina Daza, daughter of Lorenzo Daza?

Before I attempt to answer this question, two caveats need to be introduced. First, in this chapter I limit myself to two related issues: on the one hand, those individual difference factors associated, in the process of early attraction, with the observer (Florentino Ariza, in the case of García Márquez's novel); and, on the other hand, those associated with the observed (Fermina Daza). Second, my focus here is on personality and individual differences traits, and, for reasons of space, I must forgo the increasingly large body of research that has examined, within the context of initial attraction, the role of physical cues (e.g. facial and bodily attractiveness) and of the social context (e.g. proximity; for extended discussions of these topics, see Swami, 2007; Swami & Furnham, 2007, 2008a; Swami & Salem, in press).

## Attraction as a Dynamic Process

Historically, the philosophy of esthetics has been plagued by what Zangwill (2000) has termed an "aesthetic realism." The most basic claim of esthetic realism is that "there are mind-independent aesthetic facts or states of affairs—where a mind-independent aesthetic fact or state of affairs is a structured entity, consisting of an object or event which possesses a mind-independent aesthetic property" (Zangwill, 2000, p. 595). The object or event could be anything from a breaking wave to a human being or a particular work of art (or even a specific performance of a work of art), but the basic point of an esthetically realist worldview is that beauty is essentially skin-deep: only the surface properties are relevant to our perception of beauty.

The alternative view is one in which esthetic properties are non-rigidly response-dependent. In this view, beauty is not an objective, external reality, but rather "depends on the character of our actual experience of colors, sounds, and perhaps smells and tastes" (Zangwill, 2000, p. 618). In short, beauty is not skin-deep, it is rather in the eye of the beholder. This short philosophical digression has at least one important implication for psychological research on interpersonal attraction: rather than viewing the attraction process simply as a function of physical beauty, which continues to be the dominant paradigm in the psychological sciences, researchers need also to consider the influence of non-physical factors, which include personality and other individual differences traits (Swami, 2007).

Traditionally, psychologists have been averse to studying non-physical factors in interpersonal attraction, believing that such factors do not play a major role in attraction, are more difficult to measure than static or physical attractiveness, or simply cannot be isolated from physical attractiveness (see Swami & Furnham, 2008a, Ch. 9). This occurs despite repeated calls by social psychologists, who have proposed that interpersonal attraction should be considered a multi-faceted phenomenon and that its definition should be expanded to include variables of "dynamic" attractiveness (Graziano & Bruce, 2008; Osborn, 2004, 2006; Riggio, Widaman, Tucker, & Salinas, 1991; Swami, 2007).

To be sure, the components of "dynamic" attractiveness are wide-ranging; they could include an individual's conversational skills, reputation, sense of humor, prosocial behavior, expressive movement, facial expressions and body language, and so on (e.g. Friedman, Riggio, & Casella, 1988; Jensen-Campbell, Graziano, & West, 1995; Miller, Berg, & Archer, 1983; Riggio, 1986; Riggio & Friedman, 1986; Riggio & Throckmorton, 1988; Rucas et al., 2006). Clearly, not all of these will be relevant to an individual differences approach to initial attraction. In the remainder of this chapter, therefore, I focus on those individual differences traits that have been identified as having an impact on interpersonal attraction and on the initiation of romantic relationships, beginning with traits associated with the observer.

## The Case of Florentino Ariza, or the Observer

The question I have set myself in this section is straightforward enough: Are there any individual differences traits on the part of the observer (Florentino Ariza, in the example that opened this chapter) that influence interpersonal attraction? While it seems plausible enough that there should be (Swami, 2007), readers may be surprised to learn that very few studies have empirically tested this possibility, and those that have done so have typically focused on the relation between individual differences traits and attraction toward different physical cues (e.g. different facial or bodily characteristics). In this section I consider some of the more important traits that have been discussed in the extant literature.

## Sociosexuality

Several authors have recently noted that the majority of studies of interpersonal attraction have neglected the broader framework of motivations that give rise to esthetic preferences (e.g. Schmalt, 2006). One such factor is the mating strategy of the observer (Brase & Walker, 2004), which has been operationalized as an individual differences trait in some studies (Swami, Miller, Furnham, Penke, & Tovée, 2008). Mating strategy, or sociosexuality, serves to distinguish between individuals who follow a short-term mating strategy (that is, pursuing low-commitment, transient sexual relationships with multiple partners) and individuals who follow a long-term mating strategy (pursuit of a single, high-investment relationship) (Buss & Schmitt, 1993).

Of course, in reality, the two mating strategies are unlikely to be mutually exclusive (Gangestad & Simpson, 2000); still, when asked, individuals tend to evaluate potential partners from one of these two viewpoints (Buss & Schmitt, 1993). For instance, individuals tend to be more selective and to compromise on physical attractiveness when they seek a long-term partner (Kenrick, Sadalla, & Groth, & Trost, 1990; Regan, 1998; Stewart, Stinnett, & Rosenfeld, 2000), but emphasize physical attractiveness and compromise on interpersonal and emotional responsiveness when they seek a short-term partner (Penke, Todd, Lenton, & Fasolo, 2007). Similarly, individuals who favor an "unrestricted" mating strategy (that is, who pursue short-term relationships) tend to value physical attractiveness more than "restricted" individuals (Fletcher, Simpson, Thomas, & Giles, 1999; Simpson & Gangestad, 1992), and some evidence suggests that the basic cognitive processes of more unrestricted individuals are better "attuned" to the perception of attractiveness (Maner, Galliot, & DeWall, 2007; Maner et al., 2003).

Some studies have also looked at whether preferences for a potential partner's body shape and body weight are influenced by sociosexuality, but results have been mixed. For example, two early studies using line drawings of the female figure reported no significant differences in preferred body shape between men who endorsed long- and short-term mating strategies (Furnham, Moutafi, & Baguma, 2002; Singh & Young, 1995). These studies, however, have been criticized on methodological grounds (specifically, the line drawings used in these studies demonstrate very poor ecological validity; see e.g. Bateson, Cornelissen, & Tovée, 2007; Swami, 2007; Swami, in press). Perhaps more relevant for our consideration here is that these studies have typically operationalized sociosexuality on the basis of single-item measures, which fails to capture the full dimension of this trait.

Other relevant work has sought to operationalize sociosexuality as an individual differences trait. For example, using the Sociosexual Orientation Inventory (SOI), a measure of an individual's willingness to engage in sexual activity in the absence of a committed relationship, Brase and Walker (2004) still failed to find major differences in men's preferences for female body shape as a function of sociosexuality. More recently, Swami, Miller et al. (2008), using a revised version of the SOI, reported that unrestricted men were more likely than restricted men to perceive thinner women as being more attractive, healthy, and fertile. The authors went on to suggest that unrestricted men may have perceived thinner women as more physically attractive because of the perceived and real association between thinness, health, and reproductive potential (Swami, Miller et al., 2008).

## Sexism

Since the 1970s, a number of feminist scholars have postulated that beauty ideals and practices arise due to pressures that women face in male-dominated societies (e.g. Bartky, 1990; Bordo, 1993; Dworkin, 1974; Jeffreys, 2005; Wolf, 1990). Beauty standards, in this view, reduce women to the status of sex objects, causing them to feel that their bodies are inadequate and forcing them to engage in practices that leave them feeling inauthentic if they do not live up to the idealized image of femininity (Dworkin, 1974; Wolf, 1990). This being the case, women in patriarchal societies do not have any real control over their bodies, and the body remains an important site for oppression (Baker-Sperry & Grauerholz, 2003; Murnen & Smolak, 2009; Smolak & Murnen, 2007).

Certainly there exists a great deal of cross-cultural evidence supporting the association between the subordination of women and the promotion of beauty ideals. For example, various authors have discussed the practice of foot-binding in China precisely in terms of the rejection of the natural body (e.g. Jeffreys, 2005) and of the "eroticisation of artificially modified (mutilated) body parts which become necessary in order to attain social and economic rewards" (Calogero, Boroughs, & Thompson, 2007, p. 283). Moreover, a number of authors have commented on the similarities between such cross-cultural traditions and contemporary practices among women in the West, including the wearing of high-heeled shoes (which, like the bound foot, increases the risk of injury and maintains the subjugation of women through cultural messages of objectified beauty; Brownmiller, 1984).

The reason why such feminist perspectives are relevant to an individual differences approach to interpersonal attraction is that it is possible to operationalize the notion that beauty ideals are oppressive as an individual differences trait (Forbes, Collinsworth, Jobe, Braun, & Wise, 2007). More specifically, several studies have operationalized this notion in terms of such individual differences traits as gender role orientation, sexism, and hostility toward women. Some research, for example, has suggested that masculine gender orientation and conservatism are associated with body size and body shape preferences, both at individual (Beck, Ward-Hull, & McLear, 1976; Lavrakas, 1975; Maier & Lavrakas, 1984; Wiggins, Wiggins, & Conger, 1968) and national levels (Furnham & Nordling, 1998; Swami, Antonakopoulos, Tovée, & Furnham, 2006; Swami, Caprario, Tovée, & Furnham, 2006; Swami, Smith et al., 2007).

A growing body of research has similarly examined the association between interpersonal attraction and attitudes toward women. For example, several studies have shown that the endorsement of the importance of thinness as well as the preference for thinness in a potential partner are both associated with more hostile and sexist attitudes toward women (Forbes et al., 2007; Swami, Coles et al., 2010). This is corroborated by work showing that pro-feminist attitudes are associated with the perception of a wider range of body sizes as being physically attractive (Swami, Salem, Furnham, & Tovée, 2008; but see Swami & Tovée, 2006).

Other related work has examined the association between sexist attitudes and preferences for height in a potential partner. This is an interesting area of contemporary research, because studies conducted in the West have reliably documented a "male-taller norm," such that both women and men prefer to be in relationships where the man is taller than the woman (see Fink, Neave, Brewer, & Pawłowski, 2007; Jackson & Ervin, 1992; Pawłowski & Jasieńska, 2005; Pawłowski & Koziel, 2002). Traditionally this norm has been explained in terms of evolutionary adaptations (e.g. Nettle, 2002a, 2002b; Salska et al., 2008). As argued by Swami, Furnham and colleagues (2008), however, an individual differences approach to height preferences has the potential to extend our understanding of such gendered norms.

For example, to the extent that height preferences reflect the cultural transmission of gender-appropriate behaviors, where tall men are socially constructed as being "masculine" and fulfilling gender norms and tall women as violating those norms (Helgeson, 1994), it should be expected that individual differences traits associated with attitudes toward women should show significant associations with height preferences (Swami, Furnham et al., 2008). Indeed, studies that have examined this possibility have reported weak correlations with endorsement of traditional male roles (Salska et al., 2008; Swami, Furnham et al., 2008) and stronger correlations with sexist attitudes and hostility toward women (Swami, Coles et al., 2010).

Finally, a rather interesting line of research has also documented significant associations between sexist attitudes and individual use of cosmetics on the one hand (Forbes, Jung, & Haas, 2006; Franzoi, 2001), the perceived need for potential partners to use cosmetics on the other (Swami, Coles et al., 2010). In general, the research on attraction and sexism remains relatively novel, and there remains some debate as to the strength and practical implications of the reported associations (Coles & Swami, 2010). Nevertheless, the available literature suggests that there may be reliable associations between sexist attitudes and the perception of potential partners, at least in terms of what would be considered an attractive body size or an appropriate height.

## The Big Five

One rather neglected area of research, which has only recently begun to receive some coverage, concerns the associations between the personality of the observer and the phenomenon of initial attraction. In recent work, my colleagues and I have speculated that observer personality traits may have the potential to explain at least some of the variance in within-culture differences in initial attraction (Swami & Tovée, 2009; Swami, Furnham et al., in press). Specifically, when personality is operationalized by using the Big-Five taxonomy (McCrae & Costa, 1997), it might be suggested that Openness to Experience should be associated with the perception of a wider range of potential partners as being attractive, particularly to the extent that this personality trait is correlated with an acceptance of unconventional societal norms (Swami & Tovée, 2009). The trait of Agreeableness might likewise be associated with perceiving a wider range of potential partners as attractive, given that agreeable individuals are more likely to have positive interpersonal interactions (Swami, Buchanan, Furnham, & Tovée, 2008).

To date, however, only a few studies have examined these possibilities, and the available results are mixed. In one study, Wood and Brumbaugh (2009) reported that each of the Big-Five personality traits were associated with revealed preferences for a target, where the latter was operationalized through the provision of 98 photographs of women and men (see Table 29.1). Wood and Brumbaugh went on to suggest that their findings demonstrated the existence of meaningful individual differences in preferences, although there was also a high degree of consensus across their 4,308 participants as to whom they found attractive and unattractive.

Another online study of almost 1,000 participants, in which personality was operationalized using the International Personality Item Pool (Buchanan, Johnson, & Goldberg, 2005), showed that Openness to Experience was correlated with the perception of a wider range of body sizes as being physically attractive (Swami, Buchanan et al., 2008), which may serve to widen the pool of potential partners. In contrast, one other study has reported no significant association between openness and body size preferences (Swami, Furnham et al., in press), although in this study the Big Five was measured by using a brief scale with low internal consistencies.

The available research has also reported significant associations between body size perceptions in a potential partner and Agreeableness (Swami, Buchanan et al., 2008) and extraversion (Swami, Furnham et al., in press). Other relevant work has shown that the trait of Neuroticism is significantly associated with a preference to be in a relationship where the male is taller than the woman (Swami, Furnham et al., 2008), possibly because more neurotic individuals are keen to avoid any negative emotions associated with contravening gendered or social norms (such as displayed in height preferences). Overall, however, it has to be noted that the reported associations between observer personality and self-reported attractiveness preferences are weak (reported *r*s range between .10 and .28), and there remains a dearth of reliable research in the area.

## The Case of Fermina Daza, I: Perceived Traits

So far, I have considered several individual differences traits associated with the observer that may influence the attraction process: Florentino Ariza is attracted to Fermina Daza because, I conjecture, he has certain individual traits that make that attraction more likely. We might consider, conversely, whether individual traits associated with the observed person also make attraction more likely; that is, are there traits associated with Fermina Daza that make it more likely that others will be attracted to her? In this regard, it is possible to distinguish between two separate phenomena: first, perceived traits that increase the likelihood of attraction; and, second, real traits that influence the attraction process. I briefly consider the first of these phenomena in this section, and I return to perceived traits in the next.

### What is beautiful is good

In the absence of any social interaction, observers have been shown to rely on physical cues (particularly facial cues) of the observed individual in making inferences about

**Table 29.1** The association between the Big-Five personality traits and partner preferences. Adapted from Wood & Brumbagh, 2009, pp. 1238–1239

| Observer Big-Five trait | Sex-typical | Preferred partner traits |
| --- | --- | --- |
| Extraversion | Both sexes | Higher preference for targets "who looked seductive, shapely (curvaceous or toned), confident, sex-typic (i.e., feminine female targets and masculine male targets) […] [and] who appeared well-groomed." Lower preference for targets "who appeared thin or intelligent." |
| | Male participants | Higher preference for women "who appeared trendy." |
| | Female participants | Higher preference for men "who were smiling" and lower preference for men "who looked formal or classy." |
| Agreeableness | Both sexes | Higher preference for members of the opposite sex who "were smiling" and lessened preference for targets who "were thin." |
| | Male participants | Higher preference for women "who appeared sexually suggestive, confident, or trendy." |
| | Female participants | Slightly higher preference for men "who appeared well groomed." |
| Conscientiousness | Both sexes | Higher preference for targets "who were formal and conventional […] well-groomed and smiling" and lower preference for "thin targets." |
| | Male participants | Higher preference for women who were "soft-hearted." |
| | Female participants | Higher preference for men "who appeared muscular and toned, confident, and masculine" and lower preference for men "who looked trendy or stylish." |
| Emotional stability | Both sexes | Higher preference for targets "who looked classy and well groomed, and who were smiling." |
| | Male participants | Higher preference for women "who looked soft-hearted." |
| | Female participants | Higher preference for men "who looked conventional, confident, masculine, and muscular or toned," and lower preference for men "who looked thin." |
| Openness to Experience | Both sexes | Higher preference for targets "who appeared trendy and thin" and lower preference for targets "who appeared conventional." |
| | Male participants | Lower preference for women "who were smiling." |
| | Female participants | Lower preference for "masculine men." |

the latter's personality (Hassin & Trope, 2000). The most obvious example of such attributions is what Dion, Berscheid, and Walster (1972) termed the "what is beautiful is good" phenomenon: attractive individuals, compared to unattractive individuals, are generally perceived as having more socially desirable and positive personality traits (for reviews, see Eagly, Ashmore, Makhijani, & Longo, 1991; Feingold, 1992; Langlois et al., 2000; Swami & Furnham, 2008a, Ch. 2). Paunonen (2006, p. 238) offers two practical examples of what this phenomenon entails:

> [S]omeone who is particularly attractive might be expected to have had a history of positive interpersonal experiences which, in turn, could have predictable effects on his or her characteristic behaviors. An attractive person could thus be rationally predicted to be extraverted, confident and happy (Snyder, Tanke, & Berscheid, 1977). Another example, with reference to a more specific physical attribute, might be someone with a wrinkled brow. That person could be reasonably judged to frown a lot and, therefore, be high in anxiety, depression, and hostility.

For our purposes in this chapter, however, the "what is beautiful is good" phenomenon only matters if it reliably influences relationship initiation. Put differently, the question is: Do personality judgments based on physical cues influence partner selection? The enquiry here is not whether such judgments are accurate (for discussions, see Gosling, Sandy, & Graham 2011: this volume; Hassin & Trope, 2000), but rather whether individuals use personality stereotypes to select partners with personalities that they desire. The evidence in this regard is mixed.

First, at a rather abstract level, personality traits are among the most important factors in partner selection, for both sexes and across cultures (Buss, 1989; Buss & Barnes, 1986), which might lead to the suggestion that perceived traits play a role in the attraction process. Certainly, at least one study reported that faces perceived to possess desired personality traits were rated as more attractive than faces perceived not to possess that trait (Little, Burt, & Perrett, 2006). In other words, desired personality traits were found to influence perceptions of opposite-sex facial attractiveness. Say, for example, that Florentino Ariza desires an extraverted partner; he may therefore be attracted to Fermina Daza because she is perceived by him to be extraverted on the basis of her facial appearance (even if the actual association between Daza's facial features and her extraversion is unreliable).

Even so, this possibility needs to be considered in light of the similarity–attraction hypothesis, which suggests that two individuals are more likely to form romantic affiliations to the extent that they share characteristics that include political and religious attitudes, socioeconomic background, level of education and intelligence (Buston & Emlen, 2003; Furnham, 2009; Klohnen & Luo, 2003; Luo & Klohnen, 2005; see also Hatfield, Singelis, Bachman, Muto, & Choo, 2007), but also personality. Studies that have examined the similarity–attraction hypothesis in relation to personality and romantic attraction have returned equivocal results, consensus now suggesting that the effects of similarity of personality are weak at best (Buunk, Dijkstra, Kenrick, & Warntjes, 2001; Caspi & Herbener, 1990; Gattis, Berns, Simpson, & Christensen, 2004; Thiessen, Young, & Delgado, 1997).

For example, using the Big-Five taxonomy of personality, Barelds (2005) reported only a small significant correlation between spouses' levels of Extraversion ($r = .12$).

Interestingly, it also appears to be the case that partners who fall in love at first sight show rather dissimilar personality profiles, particularly in relation to Extraversion, Neuroticism, and autonomy, although this dissimilarity did not appear to have a detrimental effect on perceived relationship quality (Barelds & Barelds-Dijkstra, 2007). Overall, then, it appears that, although perceived personality traits may influence romantic attraction to potential partners, partner personality similarity only has a weak effect on relationship initiation.

## But love is blind

Before leaving this section and moving on to consider the effects of real traits on relationship initiation, it may be worth pondering what some authors have termed the "love is blind" bias (Swami & Furnham, 2008b; see also Swami, 2009; Swami, Furnham, Georgiades, & Pang, 2007). This formulation refers to a tendency for individuals in romantic relationships to perceive their partners as physically more attractive than themselves. Formulated in this way, the "love is blind" bias is not an individual differences trait; it really refers to individuals who are already in committed relationships, rather than to potential partners. Nevertheless, the "love is blind" principle could just as easily be applied to the latter group. Let us return to *Love in the time of cholera*, where Florentino Ariza has not yet spoken with Fermina Daza; instead, he watches her every day:

> From seven o'clock in the morning, he sat on the most hidden bench in the little park, pretending to read a book of verse in the shade of the almond trees, until he saw the impossible maiden walk by [...] At her side, struggling to keep up with her, the aunt with the brown habit and rope of St. Francis did not allow him the slightest opportunity to approach. Florentino Ariza saw them pass back and forth four times a day and once on Sunday when they came out of High Mass, and just seeing the girl was enough for him. Little by little he idealized her, endowing her with improbable virtues and imaginary sentiments ... (García Márquez, 1989, p. 56)

Just as Florentino Ariza idealizes Fermina Daza, it is possible that individuals, in the early stages of romantic involvement, idealize their potential partner and imbue them with imagined qualities (Berscheid & Walster, 1978). As Swami and Furnham (2008b, p. 110) have noted:

> [P]ositive illusions in others help us steer through the "dangerous waters" of initial romance. By focusing on a potential partner's positive qualities, we feel optimistic that our chosen one lives up to ideals we hold about romance, falling in love and the ideal partner. In this sense, our initial liking for a person may not be for the actual individual we chase after, but rather for some ideal image that we have formed of her or him ...

The reason why the "love is blind" bias may be interesting from an individual differences perspective is that at least one previous study has reported significant associations between this bias and individual traits such as love styles and the Big-Five personality factor of Extraversion (Swami, Stieger, Haubner, Voracek, & Furnham, 2009). This study, however, included participants who had been in relationships for a relatively long period of time ($M = 144.70$ months, $SD = 179.69$). Here I report on a novel data set, which examines individual differences correlates of the "love is blind" bias in a community sample of participants involved in newly initiated dating relationships (length of relationship $M = 7.05$ weeks, $SD = 3.85$).

The participants in this study were 26 women and 40 men recruited from the community in Greater London (age $M = 35.38$, $SD = 11.93$). As in Swami, Stieger et al. (2009), participants completed a questionnaire in which they completed certain relationship demographics, estimated their own and their partner's overall physical attractiveness (a measure of the "love is blind" bias was computed as the difference between self- and partner ratings of attractiveness), and completed measures of their Big-Five personality factors, love styles, and sociosexual orientation.[1] All participants were recruited by the author of this chapter, provided informed consent, completed the questionnaire individually, took part on a voluntary basis (they were not remunerated for participation), and were verbally debriefed.

Means and standard deviations for each of the measured variables are reported in Table 29.2, as are inter-scale correlations. Initial analysis showed that participants who reported that their relationships were a case of "love at first sight" showed a significantly stronger "love is blind" bias than those who did not (Yes: $M = -18.64$, $SD = 17.01$; No: $M = 6.91$, $SD = 19.24$), $F(1, 65) = 6.88$, $p = .011$, $\eta_p^2 = .09$. This would seem to suggest that participants who entered intimate relationships more shortly after they met were more likely to hold positive illusions about their partners' physical attractiveness than those who got involved more gradually.

In addition, inter-scale correlations for the whole sample showed that the "love is blind" bias was significantly and positively correlated with Extraversion, Conscientiousness, and Openness, and negatively correlated with ludic love styles. When the variables were entered into a multiple regression model, with the "love is blind" bias as the dependent variable and all other variables as predictors, the results showed a significant prediction: $F(10, 55) = 3.23$, $p = .002$, adjusted $R^2 = .26$. Of the variables entered into the model, however, the only significant predictors were Extraversion (st. $\beta = .35$, $t = 2.40$, $p = .020$) and Conscientiousness (st. $\beta = .27$, $t = 2.09$, $p = .042$).

Setting aside the obvious limitations of a small sample, these results suggest that the Big-Five personality factors may be associated with idealized partner perceptions in the initial stages of romantic involvement. As Swami, Stieger et al. (2009) have suggested, the association of the "love is blind" bias with Extraversion may be related to the fact that extraverts are more oriented toward obtaining external gratification from romantic relationships, and hence are more likely to idealize their partners, possibly for egoistic reasons (self-esteem enhancement) or for reasons to do with the relationship (enhancing romantic satisfaction). The association with Conscientiousness, on the other hand, may be predicated on the association between this personality factor and emotional intelligence or intimacy (Engel, Olson, & Patrick, 2002), which similarly serves to enhance perceptions of the relationship (Swami & Furnham, 2008b).

**Table 29.2** Means and standard deviations for all measured variables as well as inter-scale correlations. $N = 66$, $*p < .05$, $**p < .001$

| | (1) | (2) | (3) | (4) | (5) | (6) | (7) | (8) | (9) | (10) | (11) |
|---|---|---|---|---|---|---|---|---|---|---|---|
| (1) Love is blind bias | | | | | | | | | | | |
| (2) Relationship satisfaction | .02 | | | | | | | | | | |
| (3) Eros-R | -.04 | .77** | | | | | | | | | |
| (4) Ludus-R | -.29* | -.47** | -.42* | | | | | | | | |
| (5) Friendship-based love | -.05 | .80** | .86** | -.50** | | | | | | | |
| (6) Conscientiousness | .35* | -.29* | -.35* | .03 | -.29* | | | | | | |
| (7) Extraversion | .41* | -.01 | -.26* | .03 | -.10 | .39* | | | | | |
| (8) Neuroticism | -.03 | -.46** | -.20 | -.01 | -.19 | .32* | .01 | | | | |
| (9) Agreeableness | -.19 | -.14 | .04 | -.21 | .21 | .01 | .15 | .32* | | | |
| (10) Openness | .30* | -.31* | -.36* | .25* | -.46** | .18 | .28* | -.03 | -.36* | | |
| (11) Sociosexual orientation | .08 | -.01 | -.17 | .25* | -.04 | .14 | .20 | -.03 | .17 | -.05 | |
| M | -12.77 | 5.40 | 5.78 | 2.57 | 5.92 | 9.71 | 9.98 | 8.62 | 10.38 | 8.59 | 22.36 |
| SD | 18.97 | 0.93 | 0.99 | 1.06 | 1.11 | 1.69 | 1.94 | 2.33 | 1.69 | 1.56 | 3.33 |

## The Case of Fermina Daza, II: Real Traits

In the previous section I considered the effects of partner traits, perceived on the basis of physical cues, on romantic involvement. However, for any relationship to be initiated, some degree of social interaction is necessary. Whereas, in the example from *Love in the time of cholera*, Florentino Ariza is already deeply in love with Fermina Daza, in more banal situations it might be suggested that individuals will be attracted to those who demonstrate real traits that are socially or individually valued (Albada, Knapp, & Theune, 2002). That is, individuals may be attracted to potential partners who show real personality or individual differences traits, which are sought after by the observer (or in the observer's culture). In this section I consider two examples of this possibility, first in relation to the "nice guys finish last" phenomenon and second in relation to personality traits.

### Do nice guys finish last?

A common phenomenon in the attraction process, one that is widely reported in general public discourse and in popular culture, is the "nice guys finish last" phenomenon (Desrochers, 1995; McDaniel, 2005; Urbaniak & Kilmann, 2003, 2006). Simply put, this formula registers a discrepancy between individuals' stated desire for sensitive and emotionally stable potential partners and their actual choice of not so nice partners (McDaniel, 2005). In terms of the available research, however, studies examining the "nice guys finish last" phenomenon have presented mixed results (for a review, see Graziano & Bruce, 2008).

For example, a number of experiments have presented women with vignettes of men with different personality types and asked them to rate the likelihood of a relationship initiation for each vignette (Herold & Milhausen, 1999; McDaniel, 2005; Urbaniak & Kilmann, 2003). These studies have generally reported a female preference for "nice guys," although the use of verbal scripts possibly resulted in a social desirability bias in favor of "niceness" over insensitivity (ibid.). Other work has reported that dominant men are not rated as more desirable than non-dominant men, although dominance does appear to enhance the physical attractiveness of men who are also high in prosocial tendencies (that is, men who are agreeable and altruistic) (Graziano, Jensen-Campbell, Finch, & Todd, 1997; Jensen-Campbell, Graziano, & West, 1995; see also Hardy & van Vugt, 2006).

In contrast, other studies have reported that dominant men are rated as sexually more attractive than non-dominant men. In a series of four studies in which dominance was manipulated by having a confederate engage in specific dominant or non-dominant behaviors, Sadalla, Kenrick, and Vershure (1987) reported that dominance increased the attractiveness of men, but not that of women. The authors also reported that this effect was specific to dominance, but not to related constructs (e.g. aggressiveness), although dominance did not increase the likeability of men. Similarly, recent studies have shown that men who use more expressive body language are rated as sexually more attractive (Ahmetoglu & Swami, 2010) and are more successful at courtship initiation (Renninger, Wade, & Grammer, 2004).

Interestingly, it appears that the observer's personality does not affect the preference for dominant men: Ahmetoglu and Swami (2010) showed that both extraverted and introverted women were just as likely to perceive dominant men as sexually attractive. The authors suggested that male dominance, as an interpersonal trait, is desirable in a potential partner, regardless of the observer's personality (although it is also possible that extraverts place a greater emphasis on dominance when seeking a short-term rather than a long-term partner). Other related work has reported significant associations between a man's number of sexual partners and traits such as dominance, hyper-masculinity, and sensation-seeking, all of which suggests that traits of the observed individual affect relationship initiation (Bogaert & Fisher, 1995).

## Humor

Although a good sense of humor appears to be a highly valued social trait in many cultures (Buss, 1988), only a handful of studies have assessed the importance of humor in relationship initiation. Certainly, studies of social desirability have shown that a good sense of humor is one the most favored personality traits for oneself (Anderson, 1968; Apte, 1987; Craik, Lampert, & Nelson, 1996): individuals claimed to possess this trait in numbers that exceeded objective possibilities (Lefcourt & Martin, 1986). But, of course, humor is more readily appreciated in the presence of others (Chapman, 1973; Chapman & Chapman, 1974; Martin & Kuiper, 1999; Provine, 1993), and the question remains as to the extent to which a sense of humor is involved in partner selection.

Several studies have suggested that a sense of humor in others is a desirable trait, participants reporting that they prefer individuals with a good sense of humor as both friends and relationship partners (Goodwin, 1990; Kenrick et al., 1990; Smith, Waldorf, & Trembath, 1990; Sprecher & Regan, 2002; Todosijevic, Snezasa, & Arancic, 2003). Hansen (1977), for example, reported that, out of 33 potential qualities, a good sense of humor was ranked third for a relationship and ninth for a potential mate. Moreover, the importance of a good sense of humor appears to increase as the level of commitment to the relationship increased (Kenrick et al., 1990; Murstein & Brust, 1985).

To directly test the effects of humor on partner preferences, McGee and Shevlin (2009) had participants rate, for attractiveness and suitability as a long-term partner, six vignettes that varied in the degree of possessing a good sense of humor and sex (see Table 29.3). Their results showed that targets with a good sense of humor received more favorable ratings than targets with an average or no sense of humor. Interestingly, McGee and Shevlin (2009) reported no interaction between target sex and sense of humor, although an earlier study found that only women evaluating men chose humorous individuals (this was operationalized by the presentation of autobiographic statements about two stimulus persons who were either funny or not) as preferred relationship partners (Bressler & Balshine, 2006).

Although these studies suggest that individuals with a good sense of humor may be perceived as more attractive potential partners, a good sense of humor may in fact be valued because it covaries with other desired traits. For example, Cann and Calhoun (2001) found that individuals described as "well above average" in sense of

**Table 29.3** Sense of humor vignettes used in the study by McGee and Shevlin, 2009 (reported on pp. 70–71)

| Condition | Vignette |
| --- | --- |
| Good sense of humor | One person who knows James/Chloe well said, "I have known James/Chloe a long time and s/he has a great sense of humor." |
| Average sense of humor | One person who knows James/Chloe well said, "I have known James/Chloe a long time and I wouldn't say s/he has either a great or poor sense of humor. S/he's kind of average." |
| No sense of humor | One person who knows James/Chloe well said, "I have known James/Chloe a long time and I can say that in relation his/her sense of humor—s/he doesn't have one." |

humor were perceived by participants as being lower in Neuroticism and higher in Agreeableness than others, who were described as "typical" or "below average" in sense of humor. A good sense of humor may also be reliably associated with lower levels of loneliness and greater perceived social popularity (Wanzer, Booth-Butterfield, & Booth-Butterfield, 1996).

## Personality traits

In the course of social interactions, individuals may also be attracted to potential partners endowed with certain desired personality traits; that is to say, personality information may have a causal influence on perceptions of attractiveness in relationship initiation (for longer-term effects, see Kniffin & Wilson, 2004). This can occur in two ways: first, as suggested above, individuals may prefer partners who have personality traits that are similar to their own (e.g. extraverted individuals may prefer partners who are outgoing); second, there may be traits that are socially or culturally desirable in general. Concerning the latter, for example, early studies have shown that certain personality dimensions, particularly Extraversion and exhibitionism, were positively associated with favorable attraction ratings in initial encounters (Friedman et al., 1988; Riggio, Friedman, & DiMatteo, 1981).

A larger body of work has examined the effects of presenting personality information concurrently with stimuli coming from the potential partners. In one early study of this kind, Gross and Crofton (1977) had participants rate the physical attractiveness of targets on the basis of a profile containing personality-related and physical information. They showed that both the attractiveness of the target and the favorability of the personality profile had an influence on ratings of physical attractiveness (see also Owens & Ford, 1978). Another study employed a within-subjects design, where participants rated the attractiveness of opposite-sex facial photographs, participated in a distraction task, and then rated the same photographs again, but paired with desirable, undesirable, or no personality information (Lewandowski, Aron, & Gee, 2007). Results showed that positive personality information produced significant changes in the ratings for physical attractiveness, such that targets were perceived as more desirable as friends and dating partners.

Two recent studies have utilized a similar design in examining the influence of personality information on body size perceptions. Swami, Greven, and Furnham (2007) presented participants with line-drawn stimuli that varied in body shape and body weight, as well as two levels of personal information (Extraversion vs. Introversion). They reported that, while there was an independent effect of each of the three variables, the variables also interacted to determine a figure's physical attractiveness. Similarly, on the basis of ratings of line-drawn stimuli, Fisak, Tantleff-Dunn, and Peterson (2007) showed that participants chose a wider range of body sizes as being attractive for female figures described as having a positive personality, by comparison with figures described as having a negative personality or not provided with any personality information.

However, it should be noted that, in much of this work, there has not been any consistency in the personality vignettes paired with stimuli: Fisak et al. (2007) and Lewandowski et al. (2007) used personality traits derived from previously compiled lists, whereas Swami, Greven et al. (2007) used polar opposites of the Big-Five personality factor of Extraversion. While both approaches are equally valid, Swami, Furnham et al. (in press) have argued that the Big-Five personality framework offers the most comprehensive means of examining the causal influence of personality on attractiveness ratings. In their study, they used a between-subjects design to examine the influence of each of the Big-Five personality traits on men's ratings of women who varied in body size. Specifically, participants in their study rated stimuli that were paired with vignettes of positive or negative personality information (polar opposites of the Big-Five traits).

The results of the study carried out by Swami, Furnham et al. (in press) showed that there were few significant differences in the figure whom participants found most physically attractive as a function of the provision of personality information; that is, whether or not participants were given personality information about the women they were rating, or whether they received positive or negative personality information, they generally agreed on the figure whom they found most physically attractive. Nevertheless, their results also showed that personality information did have a significant effect on the range of body sizes that participants judged to be physically attractive. Overall, the provision of positive Big-Five information resulted in a wider range of figures being perceived as attractive, by comparison with a control group whose members received no personality information; whereas the negative personality information resulted in a constriction of the range of figures perceived as attractive (see Figure 29.1).

Indeed, the results of Swami, Furnham et al. (in press) showed that, in comparison to negative personality poles, positive personality poles invariably resulted in a wider range of figures being rated as attractive, with the exception of Conscientiousness versus Unconscientiousness. Swami, Furnham et al. (in press) suggested that the availability of positive personality information possibly leads to larger figures being judged as physically attractive, and that personality may moderate the effect of body size on attractiveness. That is, positive personality information may reduce the salience of body size in interpersonal judgments, possibly because it compensates for less attractive physical traits.

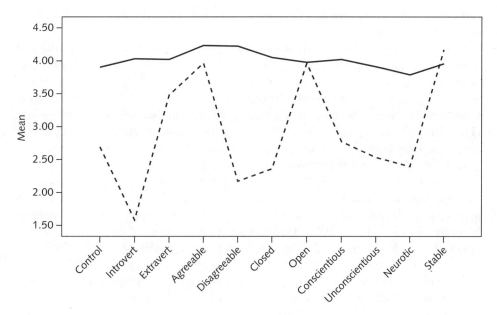

**Figure 29.1** The physically most attractive figure (solid line), as it appeared to a group of participants; the attractiveness range (dotted line) is a function of the provision of positive or negative Big-Five personality information. Derived from Swami et al. (in press), where participants were asked to rate the figure they found physically most attractive, as well as the thinnest and largest figures they perceived as attractive (the latter two ratings were used to calculate an "attractiveness range")

## Conclusion

In this chapter I have argued that an individual differences approach has the potential to further our understanding of romantic relationship initiation. More generally, such a perspective may offer researchers a useful means of examining and understanding within-culture differences among various perceptions of the attractiveness of a potential partner. Of course, it should be remembered that the extant literature suggests that individual differences account for only a small proportion of the phenomena associated with relationship initiation (such as the "love is blind" bias, or partner personality similarity), although effect sizes appear to be larger once social interaction has taken place (as in the case of the effects of real traits on partner perceptions).

A second problem with much of this research is that there remains a large discrepancy between stated and actual preferences. Certainly, the available research has documented certain individual differences in preference which are based on self-reported data, but researchers have also noted that self-reported preferences often do not show much congruence with the actual variation in attraction in the real world (Eastwick & Finkel, 2008; Todd, Penke, Fasolo, & Lenton, 2007). Indeed, some authors have suggested that variation in self-reported preferences is perceptual noise, and that actual preferences are relatively similar across individuals within the same cultural or sub-cultural group (Kurzban & Weeden, 2005; Penke et al., 2007; see also Coles & Swami, 2010).

Nevertheless, given that much of this work is in its infancy, there is the potential to extend an individual differences approach to related areas of research. For example, recent work has sought to examine personality and individual difference correlates of such phenomena as attitudinal dispositions toward cosmetic surgery (Swami, Chamorro-Premuzic, Bridges, & Furnham, 2009) and body image (e.g. Swami, Hadji-Michael, & Furnham, 2008; Swami, Taylor, & Carvalho, in press). Using observation methods (e.g. Gueguen, 2007; Swami & Barrett, 2010) may also help to overturn some of the limitations I have noted above.

In general, further research is urgently required on the influence of personality and individual differences factors on relationship initiation (and also on relationship maintenance; for relevant work, see for example Ahmetoglu, Swami, & Chamorro-Premuzic, 2010; Barelds, 2005; Davila, Karney, Hall, & Bradbury, 2003; Heaven, Smith, Prabhakar, Abraham, & Mete, 2006; Karney & Bradbury, 1995). Until such research is done, it may just be worth remembering García Márquez's (1989) warning that the lovesickness that afflicted Florentino Ariza is not something to be admired, but is rather a literal disease, comparable to cholera (Booker, 1993).

## Note

1   Specifically, participants completed their demographic details (sex and age) and three relationship demographic measures, namely length of the relationship in weeks, whether or not it was a case of "love at first sight" (1 = *Yes*, 2 = *No*), and a 7-item measure of relationship satisfaction (for details, see Swami, Stieger et al., 2009). In addition, participants completed the Revised Lovestyle Perceptions Survey (Grote & Frieze, 1994), the Abbreviated, 15-item Big Five Questionnaire (Furnham, McManus, & Scott, 2003), and the Revised Sociosexual Orientation Inventory (Penke & Asendorpf, 2008).

## References

Achilles Tatius (1989). *Leucippe and Clitophon*. Translated by J. J. Winkler. Edited by B. P. Reardon, *Collected ancient Greek novels* (pp. 121–233). Berkeley, CA: University of California Press.

Ahmetoglu, G., & Swami, V. (2010). *Where do nice guys finish? The effect of male dominance behaviour on women's ratings of sexual attractiveness*. Manuscript submitted for publication.

Ahmetoglu, G., Swami, V., & Chamorro-Premuzic, T. (2010). The relationship between dimensions of love, personality, and relationship length. *Archives of Sexual Behavior, 39*, 1181–1190.

Albada, K., Knapp, M. L., & Theune, K. E. (2002). Interaction appearance theory: Changing perceptions of physical attractiveness through social interaction. *Communication Theory, 12*, 8–40.

Anderson, N. H. (1968). Likeableness ratings of 555 personality-trait terms. *Journal of Personality and Social Psychology, 9*, 272–279.

Apte, M. (1987). Ethnic humor versus "sense of humor": An American cultural dilemma. *American Behavioral Scientist, 30,* 27–41.

Baker-Sperry, L., & Grauerholz, L. (2003). The pervasiveness and persistence of the feminine beauty ideal in children's fairy tales. *Gender and Society, 15,* 711–726.

Barelds, D. P. H. (2005). Self and partner personality in intimate relationships. *European Journal of Personality, 19,* 501–518.

Barelds, D. P. H., & Barelds-Dijkstra, P. (2007). Love at first sight or friends first? Ties among partner personality trait similarity, relationship onset, relationship quality, and love. *Journal of Social and Personal Relationships, 24,* 479–496.

Bartky, S. L. (1990). *Femininity and domination: Studies in the phenomenology of oppression.* New York: Routledge.

Bateson, M., Cornelissen, P. L., & Tovée, M. J. (2007). Methodological issues in studies of female attractiveness. In V. Swami & A. Furnham (Eds.), *Body beautiful: Evolutionary and sociocultural perspectives* (pp. 46–62). Basingstoke: Palgrave Macmillan.

Beck, S. P., Ward-Hull, C. I., & McLear, P. M. (1976). Variables related to women's somatic preferences of the male and female body. *Journal of Personality and Social Psychology, 34,* 1200–1210.

Berscheid, E., & Walster, E. H. (1978). *Interpersonal attraction* (2nd ed.). Reading, MA: Addison-Wesley.

Bogaert, A. F., & Fisher, W. A. (1995). Predictors of university men's number of sexual partners. *Journal of Sex Research, 32,* 119–130.

Booker, M. K. (1993). The dangers of gullible reading: Narrative as seduction in García Márquez's *Love in the time of cholera. Studies in Twentieth Century Literature, 17,* 181–195.

Bordo, S. (1993). *Unbearable weight: Feminism, western culture and the body.* Berkeley, CA: University of California Press.

Brase, G. L., & Walker, G. (2004). Male sexual strategies modify ratings of female models with specific waist-to-hip ratios. *Human Nature, 15,* 209–224.

Bressler, E. R., & Balshine, S. (2006). The influence of humor on desirability. *Evolution and Human Behavior, 27,* 29–39.

Brownmiller, S. (1984). *Femininity.* New York: Ballantine Books.

Buchanan, T., Johnson, J. A., & Goldberg, L. R. (2005). Implementing a five-factor personality inventory for use on the Internet. *European Journal of Psychological Assessment, 21,* 115–127.

Buss, D. M. (1988). The evolution of human intrasexual competition: Tactics of mating attraction. *Journal of Personality and Social Psychology, 54,* 616–628.

Buss, D. M. (1989). Sex differences in human mate preferences: Evolutionary hypotheses tested in 37 cultures. *Behavioural and Brain Sciences, 12,* 1–49.

Buss, D. M., & Barnes, M. (1986). Preferences in human mate selection. *Journal of Personality and Social Psychology, 50,* 559–570.

Buss, D. M., & Schmitt, P. (1993). Sexual strategies theory: An evolutionary perspective on human mating. *Psychological Review, 100,* 204–232.

Buston, P. M., & Emlen, S. T. (2003). Cognitive processes underlying human mate choice: The relationship between self-perception and mate preference in western society. *Proceedings of the National Academy of Sciences, 100,* 8805–8810.

Buunk, B. P., Dijkstra, P., Kenrick, D. T., & Warntjes, A. (2001). Age preferences for mates as related to gender, own age, and involvement level. *Evolution and Human Behavior, 22,* 241–250.

Calogero, R. M., Boroughs, M., & Thompson, J. K. (2007). The impact of western beauty ideals on the lives of women: A sociocultural perspective. In V. Swami & A. Furnham

(Eds.), *The body beautiful: Evolutionary and sociocultural perspectives* (pp. 259–298). Basingstoke: Palgrave Macmillan.

Cann, A., & Calhoun, L. G. (2001). Perceived personality association with differences in sense of humor: Stereotypes of hypothetical others with high or low senses of humor. *Humor, 14*, 117–130.

Caspi, A., & Herbener, E. S. (1990). Continuity and change: Assortative marriage and the consistency of personality in adulthood. *Journal of Personality and Social Psychology, 58*, 250–258.

Chapman, A. J. (1973). Social facilitation of laughter in children. *Journal of Experimental Social Psychology, 9*, 528–541.

Chapman, A. J., & Chapman, W. A. (1974). Responsiveness to humor: Its dependency upon a companion's humorous smiling and laughter. *Journal of Psychology, 88*, 245–252.

Coles, R., & Swami, V. (2010). *Feminism and body image: A qualitative investigation.* Manuscript submitted for publication.

Craik, K. H., Lampert, M. D., & Nelson, A. J. (1996). Sense of humor and styles of everyday humorous conduct. *Humor, 9*, 273–302.

Davila, J., Karney, B. R., Hall, T. W., & Bradbury, T. N. (2003). Depressive symptoms and marital satisfaction: Within-subject associations and the moderating effects of gender and neuroticism. *Journal of Family Psychology, 17*, 557–570.

Desrochers, S. (1995). What types of men are most attractive and most repulsive to women? *Sex Roles, 32*, 375–391.

Dion, K. K., Berscheid, E., & Walster, E. (1972). What is beautiful is good. *Journal of Personality and Social Psychology, 24*, 285–290.

Dworkin, A. (1974). *Woman hating.* New York: E. P. Dutton.

Eagly, E. H., Ashmore, R. D., Makhijani, M. G., & Longo, L. C. (1991). What is beautiful is good, but … A meta-analytic review of research on the physical attractiveness stereotype. *Psychological Bulletin, 110*, 109–128.

Eastwick, P. W., & Finkel, E. J. (2008). Sex differences in mate preferences revisited: Do people know what they initially desire in a romantic partner? *Personality and Social Psychology, 94*, 245–264.

Engel, G., Olson, K. R., & Patrick, C. (2002). The personality of love: Fundamental motives and traits related to components of love. *Personality and Individual Differences, 32*, 839–853.

Feingold, A. (1992). Good-looking people are not what we think. *Psychological Bulletin, 111*, 304–341.

Fink, B., Neave, N., Brewer, G., & Pawłowski, B. (2007). Variable preferences for sexual dimorphism in stature (SDS): Further evidence for an adjustment in relation to own height. *Personality and Individual Differences, 43*, 2249–2257.

Fisak, B., Jr., Tantleff-Dunn, S., & Peterson, R. D. (2007). Personality information: Does it influence attractiveness ratings of various body sizes? *Body Image, 4*, 213–217.

Fletcher, G. J. O., Simpson, J. A., Thomas, G., & Giles, L. (1999). Ideals in intimate relationships. *Journal of Personality and Social Psychology, 76*, 72–89.

Forbes, G. B., Jung, J., Haas, K. B. (2006). Benevolent sexism and cosmetic use: A replication with three college samples and one adult sample. *The Journal of Social Psychology, 146*, 635–640.

Forbes, G. B., Collinsworth, L. L., Jobe, R. L., Braun, K. D., & Wise, L. M. (2007). Sexism, hostility toward women, and endorsement of beauty ideals and practices: Are beauty ideals associated with oppressive beliefs? *Sex Roles, 5*, 265–273.

Franzoi, S. L. (2001). Is female body esteem shaped by benevolent sexism? *Sex Roles, 44*, 177–188.

Friedman, H. S., Riggio, R. E., Casella, D. F. (1988). Nonverbal skill, personal charisma, and initial attraction. *Journal of Personality and Social Psychology, 14,* 203–211.

Furnham, A. (2009). Sex differences in mate selection preferences. *Personality and Individual Differences, 47,* 262–267.

Furnham, A., & Nordling, R. (1998). Cross-cultural differences in preferences for specific male and female body shapes. *Personality and Individual Differences, 25,* 635–648.

Furnham, A., McManus, I. C., & Scott, D. (2003). Personality, empathy, and attitudes to animal welfare. *Anthrozoös, 16,* 135–146.

Furnham, A., Moutafi, J., & Baguma, P. (2002). A cross-cultural study on the role of weight and waist-to-hip ratio on judgements of women's attractiveness. *Personality and Individual Differences, 32,* 729–745.

Gangestad, S. & Simpson, J. A. (2000). The evolution of human mating: Trade-offs and strategic pluralism. *Behavioral and Brain Sciences, 2,* 573–587.

García Márquez, G. (1989). *Love in the time of cholera.* Translated by E. Grossman. London: Penguin.

Gattis, K. S., Berns, S., Simpson, L. E., & Christensen, A. (2004). Birds of a feather or strange birds? Ties among personality dimensions, similarity, and marital quality. *Journal of Family Psychology, 18,* 564–574.

Goodwin, R. (1990). Sex differences among partner preferences: Are the sexes really very similar? *Sex Roles, 23,* 501–513.

Graziano, W. G., & Bruce, J. W. (2008). Attraction and the initiation of relationships: A review of the empirical literature. In S. Sprecher, A. Wenzel, & J. Harvey (Eds.), *Handbook of relationship initiation* (pp. 269–294). New York: Psychology Press.

Graziano, W. G., Jensen-Campbell, L. A., Finch, J., & Todd, M. (1997). Interpersonal attraction from an evolutionary psychology perspective. In J. A. Simpson & D. Kenrick (Eds.), *Evolutionary social psychology* (pp. 141–167). Hillsdale, NJ: Lawrence Erlbaum Associates.

Gross, A. E., & Crofton, C. (1977). What is good is beautiful. *Sociometry, 40,* 85–90.

Grote, N. K., & Frieze, I. H. (1994). The measurement of friendship-based love in intimate relationships. *Personal Relationships, 1,* 275–300.

Gueguen, N. (2007). Women's bust size and men's courtship solicitation. *Body Image, 4,* 386–390.

Hansen, S. L. (1977). Dating choices of high school students. *Family Coordinator, 26,* 133–138.

Hardy, C. L., & van Vugt, M. (2006). Nice guys finish last: The competitive altruism hypothesis. *Personality and Social Psychology Bulletin, 32,* 1402–1414.

Hassin, R., & Trope, Y. (2000). Facing faces: Studies on the cognitive aspects of physiognomy. *Journal of Personality and Social Psychology, 78,* 837–852.

Hatfield, E., Singelis, T., Bachman, G., Muto, K., & Choo, P. (2007). Love schemas, preferences in romantic partners, and reactions to commitment. *Interpersona, 1,* 1–24.

Heaven, P. C. L., Smith, L., Prabhakar, S. M., Abraham, J., & Mete, M. E. (2006). Personality and conflict communication patterns in cohabiting couples. *Journal of Research in Personality, 40,* 829–840.

Helgeson, V. S. (1994). Prototypes and dimensions of masculinity and femininity. *Sex Roles, 31,* 653–682.

Herold, E. S., & Milhausen, R. R. (1999). Dating preferences of university women: An analysis of the nice guy stereotype. *Journal of Sex and Marital Therapy, 25,* 333–343.

Jackson, L. A., & Ervin, K. S. (1992). Height stereotypes of women and men: The liabilities of shortness for both sexes. *Journal of Social Psychology, 132,* 433–445.

Jeffreys, S. (2005). *Beauty and misogyny: Harmful cultural practices in the West.* London: Routledge.

Jensen-Campbell, L., Graziano, W. G., & West, S. G. (1995). Dominance, prosocial orientation, and female preferences: Do nice guys really finish last? *Journal of Personality and
Social Psychology, 68,* 427–440.

Kenrick, D. T., Sadalla, E. K., Groth, G., & Trost, M. (1990). Evolution, traits, and the stages
of human courtship: Qualifying the parental investment model. *Journal of Personality, 58,*
97–116.

Klohnen, E. C., & Luo, S. (2003). Interpersonal attraction and personality: What is attractive—
self similarity, ideal similarity, complementarity, or attachment security? *Journal of
Personality and Social Psychology, 85,* 706–722.

Kniffin, K. M., & Wilson, D. S. (2004). The effect of non-physical traits on the perception of
physical attractiveness: Three naturalistic studies. *Evolution and Human Behavior, 25,*
88–101.

Kurzban, R., & Weeden, J. (2005). HurryDate: Mate preferences in action. *Evolution and
Human Behavior, 26,* 227–244.

Langlois, J. H., Kalakanis, L. E., Rubenstein, A. J., Larson, A. D., Hallam, M. J., & Smoot,
M. T. (2000). Maxims and myths of beauty: A meta-analytic and theoretical review.
*Psychological Bulletin, 126,* 390–423.

Lavrakas, P. J. (1975). Female preferences for male physique. *Journal of Research in Personality,
9,* 324–334.

Lefcourt, H. M., & Martin, R. A. (1986). *Humor and life stress: Antidote to adversity.* New
York: Springer-Verlag.

Lewandowski, G. W., Aron, A., & Gee, J. (2007). Personality goes a long way: The malleability
of opposite-sex physical attractiveness. *Personal Relationships, 14,* 571–585.

Little, A. C., Burt, D. M., & Perrett, D. I. (2006). What is beautiful is good: Face
preference reflects desired personality. *Personality and Individual Differences, 41,*
1107–1118.

Luo, S., & Klohnen, E. C. (2005). Assortative mating and marital quality in newlyweds: A
coupled-centred approach. *Journal of Personality and Social Psychology, 65,* 56–68.

Maier, R., & Lavrakas, P. J. (1984). Attitudes towards women, personality rigidity, and idealized physique preferences in males. *Sex Roles, 11,* 425–433.

Maner, J. K., Galliot, M. T., & DeWall, C. N. (2007). Adaptive attentional attunement:
Evidence for mating-related perceptual bias. *Evolution and Human Behavior, 28,*
28–36.

Maner, J. K., Kenrick, D. T., Becker, D., Delton, A. W., Hofer, B., Wilbur, C. J. et al. (2003).
Sexually selective cognition: Beauty captures the mind of the beholder. *Journal of
Personality and Social Psychology, 85,* 1107–1120.

Martin, R. A., & Kuiper, N. (1999). Daily occurrence of laughter: Relationships with age,
gender, and type A personality. *Humor, 12,* 355–384.

McCrae, R. R., & Costa, P. T. Jr. (1997). Personality trait structure as a human universal.
*American Psychologist, 52,* 509–516.

McDaniel, A. K. (2005). Young women's dating behavior: Why/why not date a nice guy? *Sex
Roles, 53,* 347–259.

McGee, E., & Shevlin, M. (2009). Effect of humor on interpersonal attraction and mate selection. *The Journal of Psychology, 143,* 67–77.

Miller, L. C., Berg, J. H., & Archer, R. L. (1983). Openers: Individuals who elicit intimate
self-disclosure. *Journal of Personality and Social Psychology, 44,* 1234–1244.

Murnen, S., & Smolak, L. (2009). Are feminist women protected from body image problems?
A meta-analytic review of relevant research. *Sex Roles, 60,* 186–197.

Murstein, B. I., & Brust, R. G. (1985). Humor and interpersonal attraction. *Journal of
Personality Assessment, 49,* 637–640.

Nettle, D. (2002a). Height and reproductive success in a cohort of British men. *Human Nature, 13*, 473–491.

Nettle, D. (2002b). Women's height, reproductive success and the evolution of sexual dimorphism in modern humans. *Proceedings of the Royal Society of London B, 269*, 1919–1923.

Osborn, D. R. (2004, May 27–30). *A biological, cultural, and interactional (BIC) model of physical attractiveness judgements*. Poster presented at the 16th Annual Convention of the American Psychological Society, Chicago.

Osborn, D. (2006, May 28–31). *Historico-cultural factors in beauty judgments: 16th-century courtesans judged against 21st-century media ideals*. Poster presented at the Annual Meeting of the Association for Psychological Science, New York.

Ovid (1998). *Metamorphoses*. Translated by A. D. Melville. Oxford: Oxford University Press.

Owens, G., & Ford, J. G. (1978). Further considerations of the "What is good is beautiful" finding. *Social Psychology, 41*, 73–75.

Paunonen, S. V. (2006). You are honest, therefore I like you and find you attractive. *Journal of Research in Personality, 40*, 237–249.

Pawłowski, B., & Jasieńska, G. (2005). Women's preferences for sexual dimorphism in height depend on menstrual cycle phase and expected duration of relationship. *Biological Psychology, 70*, 38–43.

Pawłowski, B., & Koziel, S. (2002). The impact of traits offered in personal advertisements on response rates. *Evolution and Human Behavior, 23*, 139–149.

Penke, L., & Asendorpf, J. B. (2008). Beyond global sociosexual orientations: A more differentiated look at sociosexuality and its effects on courtship and romantic relationships. *Journal of Personality and Social Psychology, 95*, 1113–1135.

Penke, L., Todd, P. M., Lenton, A., & Fasolo, B. (2007). How self-assessments can guide human mating decisions. In G. Geher & G. F. Miller (Eds.), *Mating intelligence: Sex, relationships, and the mind's reproductive system* (pp. 37–75). Mahwah, NJ: Lawrence Erlbaum Associates.

Provine, R. R. (1993). Laughter punctuates speech: Linguistic, social, and gender contexts of laughter. *Ethology, 95*, 291–298.

Regan, P. C. (1998). What if you can't get what you want? Willingness to compromise ideal mate selection standards as a function of sex, mate value, and relationship context. *Personality and Social Psychology Bulletin, 24*, 1294–1303.

Renninger, L. A., Wade, T. J., & Grammer, K. (2004). Getting that female glance: Patterns and consequences of male nonverbal behavior in courtship contexts. *Evolution and Human Behaviour, 25*, 416–431.

Riggio, R. E. (1986). Assessment of basic social skills. *Journal of Personality and Social Psychology, 51*, 649–660.

Riggio, R. E., & Friedman, H. S. (1986). Impression formation: The role of expressive behavior. *Journal of Personality and Social Psychology, 50*, 421–427.

Riggio, R. E., & Throckmorton, B. (1988). The relative effects of verbal and nonverbal behavior, appearance and social skills on evaluations made in hiring interviews. *Journal of Applied Social Psychology, 18*, 331–348.

Riggio, R. E., Friedman, H. S., & DiMatteo, M. R. (1981). Nonverbal greetings: Effects of the situation and personality. *Personality and Social Psychology Bulletin, 7*, 682–689.

Riggio, R. E., Widaman, K. F., Tucker, J. S., & Salinas, C. (1991). Beauty is more than skin deep: Components of attractiveness. *Basic and Applied Social Psychology, 12*, 423–439.

Rucas, S., Kaplan, H., Winking, J., Gurven, M., Gangestad, S., & Crespo, M. (2006). Female intrasexual competition and reputational effects on attractiveness among the Tsimane of Bolivia. *Evolution and Human Behavior, 27*, 40–52.

Sadalla, E. K., Kenrick, D. T., & Vershure, B. (1987). Dominance and heterosexual attraction. *Journal of Personality and Social Psychology, 52,* 730–738.

Salska, I., Frederick, D. A., Pawłowski, B., Reilly, A. H., Laird, K. T., & Rudd, N. A. (2008). Conditional mate preferences: Factors influencing preferences for height. *Personality and Individual Differences, 44,* 203–215.

Schmalt, H.-D. (2006). Waist-to-hip ratio and female physical attractiveness: The moderating role of power motivation and the mating context. *Personality and Individual Differences, 41,* 455–465.

Simpson, J. A., & Gangestad, S. W. (1992). Sociosexuality and romantic partner choice. *Journal of Personality, 60,* 31–51.

Singh, D., & Young, R. K. (1995). Body weight, waist-to-hip ratio, breasts, and hips: Role in judgements of female attractiveness and desirability for relationships. *Ethology and Sociobiology, 16,* 483–507.

Smith, J. E., Waldorf, V. A., & Trembath, D. L. (1990). "Single white male looking for thin, very attractive ..." *Sex Roles, 23,* 675–685.

Smolak, L., & Murnen, S. K. (2007). Feminism and body image. In V. Swami & A. Furnham (Eds.), *Body beautiful: Evolutionary and sociocultural perspectives* (pp. 236–258). Basingstoke: Palgrave Macmillan.

Snyder, M., Tanke, E. D., & Berscheid, E. (1977). Social perception and interpersonal behavior: On the self-fulfilling nature of social stereotypes. *Journal of Personality and Social Psychology, 35,* 656–666.

Sprecher, S., & Regan, P. (2002). Loving some things (in some people) more than others: Partner preferences in romantic relationships and friendships. *Journal of Social and Personal Relationships, 19,* 463–481.

Sternberg, R. J. (1986). A triangular theory of love. *Psychological Bulletin, 93,* 119–138.

Sternberg, R. J. (1988). Triangulating love. In R. J. Sternberg & M. L. Barnes (Eds.), *The psychology of love* (pp. 119–138). New Haven, CT: Yale University Press.

Sternberg, R. J. (1998). *Cupid's arrow: The course of love through time.* Cambridge: Cambridge University Press.

Stewart, S., Stinnett, H., & Rosenfeld, L. B. (2000). Sex differences in desired partner characteristics of short-term and long-term relationship partner. *Journal of Social and Personal Relationships, 17,* 843–853.

Swami, V. (in press). Methodological and conceptual issues in the science of physical attraction. In F. Columbus (Ed.), *Visual perception: New research.* New York: Nova Science Publishers.

Swami, V. (2007). *The missing arms of Vénus de Milo: Reflections on the science of physical attractiveness.* Brighton: Book Guild.

Swami, V. (2009). An examination of the love-is-blind bias among gay men and lesbians. *Body Image, 6,* 149–151.

Swami, V., & Barrett, S. (2010). *Men's hair colour preferences: An assessment of courtship solicitation and stimulus ratings.* Manuscript submitted for publication.

Swami, V., & Furnham, A. (2008a). *The psychology of physical attraction.* London: Routledge.

Swami, V., & Furnham, A. (2008b). Is love really so blind? *The Psychologist, 21,* 108–111.

Swami, V., & Furnham, A. (Eds.) (2007). *Body beautiful: Evolutionary and sociocultural perspectives.* Basingstoke: Palgrave Macmillan.

Swami, V., & Salem, N. (in press). The evolutionary psychology of human beauty. In V. Swami (Ed.), *Evolutionary psychology: A critical introduction.* Oxford: Wiley–Blackwell.

Swami, V., & Tovée, M. J. (2006). The influence of body weight on the physical attractiveness preferences of feminist and non-feminist heterosexual women and lesbians. *Psychology of Women Quarterly, 30,* 252–257.

Swami, V., & Tovée, M. J. (2009). Big beautiful women: The body size preferences of male fat admirers. *Journal of Sex Research, 46,* 89–96.

Swami, V., Greven, C., & Furnham, A. (2007). More than just skin-deep? A pilot study integrating physical and non-physical factors in the perception of physical attractiveness. *Personality and Individual Differences, 42,* 563–572.

Swami, V., Hadji-Michael, M., & Furnham, A. (2008). Personality and individual difference correlates of positive body image. *Body Image, 5,* 322–325.

Swami, V., Taylor, R., & Carvalho, C. (in press). Associations between body dissatisfaction, sociocultural attitudes toward appearance, celebrity worship, the Big Five personality factors, and weight status. *Scandinavian Journal of Psychology.*

Swami, V., Furnham, A., Georgiades, C., & Pang, L. (2007). Evaluating self and partner physical attractiveness. *Body Image, 4,* 97–101.

Swami, V., Antonakopoulos, N., Tovée, M. J., & Furnham, A. (2006). A critical test of the waist-to-hip ratio hypothesis of female physical attractiveness in Britain and Greece. *Sex Roles, 54,* 201–211.

Swami, V., Buchanan, T., Furnham, A., & Tovée, M. J. (2008). Five-factor personality correlates of perceptions of women's body sizes. *Personality and Individual Differences, 45,* 697–699.

Swami, V., Caprario, C., Tovée, M. J., & Furnham, A. (2006). Female physical attractiveness in Britain and Japan: A cross-cultural study. *European Journal of Personality, 20,* 69–81.

Swami, V., Chamorro-Premuzic, T., Bridges, S., & Furnham, A. (2009). Acceptance of cosmetic surgery: Personality and individual difference predictors. *Body Image, 6,* 7–13.

Swami, V., Salem, N., Furnham, A., & Tovée, M. J. (2008). The influence of feminist ascription on judgements of women's physical attractiveness. *Body Image, 5,* 224–229.

Swami, V., Miller, R., Furnham, A., Penke, L., & Tovée, M. J. (2008). The influence of men's sexual strategies on perceptions of women's bodily attractiveness, health, and fertility. *Personality and Individual Differences, 44,* 98–107.

Swami, V., Stieger, S., Haubner, T., Voracek, M., & Furnham, A. (2009). Evaluating the physical attractiveness and oneself and one's romantic partner: Individual and relationship correlates of the love-is-blind bias. *Journal of Individual Differences, 30,* 35–43.

Swami, V., Coles, R., Salem, N., Wilson, E., Wyrozumska, K., & Furnham, A. (2010). Oppressive beliefs at play: Associations among beauty ideals and practices and individual differences in sexism, objectification of others, and media exposure. *Psychology of Women Quarterly, 34,* 365–379.

Swami, V., Furnham, A., Balakumar, N., Williams, C., Canaway, K., & Stanistreet, D. (2008). Factors influencing preferences for height: A replication and extension. *Personality and Individual Differences, 45,* 395–400.

Swami, V., Furnham, A., Chamorro-Premuzic, T., Akbar, K., Gordon, N., Harris, T., Finch, J., & Tovée, M. J. (in press). More than skin deep? Personality information influences men's ratings of the attractiveness of women's body sizes. *The Journal of Social Psychology.*

Swami, V., Smith, J., Tsiokris, A., Georgiades, C., Sangareau, Y., Tovée, M. J., & Furnham, A. (2007). Male physical attractiveness in Britain and Greece: A cross-cultural study. *The Journal of Social Psychology, 147,* 15–26.

Tallis, F. (2005). Crazy for you. *The Psychologist, 18,* 72–74.

Thiessen, D., Young, R. K., & Delgado, M. (1997). Social pressures for assortative mating. *Personality and Individual Differences, 22,* 157–164.

Todd, P. M., Penke, L. Fasolo, B., & Lenton, A. P. (2007). Different cognitive processes underlie human mate choices and mate preferences. *Proceedings of the National Academy of Sciences, 104,* 15011–15016.

Todosijevic, B., Snezasa, L., & Arancic, A. (2003). Mate selection criteria: A trait desirability assessment study of sex differences in Serbia. *Evolutionary Psychology, 1,* 116–126.

Urbaniak, G. C., & Kilmann, P. R. (2003). Physical attractiveness and the "nice guys paradox": Do nice guys really finish last? *Sex Roles, 49,* 413–426.

Urbaniak, G. C., & Kilmann, P. R. (2006). Niceness and dating success: A further test of the nice guy stereotype. *Sex Roles, 55,* 209–224.

Wanzer, M. B., Booth-Butterfield, M., & Booth-Butterfield, S. (1996). Are funny people popular? An examination of humor orientation, loneliness, and social attraction. *Communication Quarterly, 44,* 42–52.

Wiggins, J., Wiggins, N., & Conger, J. (1968). Correlates of heterosexual somatic preferences. *Journal of Personality and Social Psychology, 10,* 82–90.

Wolf, N. (1990). *The beauty myth.* London: Chatto & Windus.

Wood, D., & Brumbaugh, C. C. (2009). Using revealed mate preferences to evaluate market force and differential preference explanations for mate selection. *Journal of Personality and Social Psychology, 96,* 1226–1244.

Zangwill, N. (2000). Skin deep or in the eye of the beholder? The metaphysics of aesthetics and sensory properties. *Philosophy and Phenomenological Research, 61,* 595–618.

# 30

# Manifestations of Individual Differences in Physical and Virtual Environments

## Lindsay T. Graham, Carson J. Sandy, and Samuel D. Gosling

Individual differences are important to the extent that they have effects on the social and physical world. People care about intelligence and neuroticism in themselves and in others because these traits predict consequential behaviors: Who will complete an assignment effectively? Who will be a reliable business partner? Who will provide a thoughtful analysis? Who will make a suitable social companion?

Most research focuses on how individual differences exert their impact on social domains such as personal and professional relationships, on domains of achievement such as scholastic and occupational success, and on other life outcomes such as health and delinquency. However, many individual differences are also expressed in the quotidian contexts of everyday life. For example, individual differences can be expressed in the way individuals decorate their offices and bedrooms, in the possessions they own, and, more recently, in the features of the online worlds they occupy.

These everyday contexts are consequential for daily interactions and may serve as significant intermediate mechanisms driving longer-term effects. For example, the physical chaos and clutter associated with individuals low on conscientiousness may contribute to the fact that individuals low on this trait tend to fare relatively poorly in most occupational contexts when they are compared to highly conscientious individuals.

In this chapter we focus on the relatively neglected topic of how individual differences are expressed in daily life. To provide a broad framework within which to organize the varied findings, we start by describing a model for conceptualizing the different ways in which individuals can have an impact on their everyday environments. Then we review and summarize the research on how individual differences are expressed in three domains: physical environments, possessions, and virtual spaces. We conclude by identifying major themes in the literature and directions for future research.

*The Wiley-Blackwell Handbook of Individual Differences,* First Edition.
Edited by Tomas Chamorro-Premuzic, Sophie von Stumm, and Adrian Furnham.
© 2011 Blackwell Publishing Ltd. Published 2011 by Blackwell Publishing Ltd.

# How Do Individual Differences Impact Everyday Contexts?

Individual differences are expressed in an enormously wide array of daily contexts, including what people look like (Naumann, Vazire, Rentfrow, & Gosling, 2009; Vazire, Naumann, Rentfrow, & Gosling, 2008), what they do (Mehl & Pennebaker, 2003), where they go (Mehl & Pennebaker, 2003), where they live (Jokela, 2009; Rentfrow, Gosling, & Potter, 2008), what they say (Pennebaker, Mehl, & Niederhoffer, 2003), what they own (Gosling, Craik, Martin, & Pryor, 2005b), and what they like (Rentfrow, Goldberg, & Zilca, in press).

But what are the mechanisms connecting individual differences to these outcomes? Why is it that people high on the trait of openness tend to have diverse collections of music and reading materials (Gosling et al., 2005b; Gosling, Ko, Mannarelli, & Morris, 2002; Rentfrow & Gosling, 2003)? Why do students in danger of dropping out of college decorate their dorm rooms differently from students who are more likely to stay (Hansen & Altman, 1976; Vinsel, Brown, Altman & Foss, 1980)? Why is it that individuals high on emotional stability show a tendency to have email addresses that are more self-enhancing (Back, Schmukle, & Egloff, 2008), and individuals high on extraversion belong to more Facebook groups than introverts do (Buffardi & Campbell, 2008; Gosling et al., 2010; Orr et al., 2009; Ross et al., 2009)?

In the context of examining the impact of the effects of personality on bedrooms and offices, Gosling and colleagues proposed three mechanisms by which individuals affect the spaces they occupy (Gosling, 2008; Gosling, Gaddis, & Vazire, 2008; Gosling et al., 2002). Individuals want to broadcast information about themselves, they want to affect how they think and feel, and they inadvertently affect their spaces in the course of their everyday behaviors. The model was originally developed in the context of physical spaces such as bedrooms and offices, but, as we shall see, it can be applied to many contexts of daily life. The model posits three mechanisms: identity claims, thought and feeling regulators, and behavioral residue.

## Identity claims

Identity claims are statements made by an individual with the aim of communicating his or her values, attitudes, goals, and identity. These statements are deliberate and tend to be directed toward others. Prototypical examples would be a bumper sticker that explicitly broadcasts a specific political message, a t-shirt that signals allegiance to a university, a tattoo that reveals an association with a genre of music, or a prominently displayed photo of an individual engaging in an activity with which she identifies.

To be effective, identity claims tend to utilize symbols, statements, and motifs with shared meaning, so the target audiences can easily interpret them. The specific content of identity claims may vary according to the identity of the anticipated "other," with different audiences evoking different self-presentational motives—items that impress friends may not have the same effect on co-workers.

It should be noted that, although identity claims are deliberate statements, it cannot be assumed that the statements are disingenuous or manipulative. In fact, a large body of research in the self literature suggests that individuals strive to be known; people tend to be happier, healthier, and more productive if they can bring others to see them as they see themselves (Swann & Bosson, 2008).

## Thought and feeling regulators

Many activities performed in everyday contexts—from relaxing and reminiscing to working and playing—are affected by the physical and ambient qualities of the space. It can be hard to relax with a lot of noise around, and it is difficult to concentrate when surrounded by distractions. The environmental features conducive to one activity are not always the same as those conducive to another. A meal at a romantic restaurant is more often associated with candle-lit lighting, quiet sophisticated music, and an arrangement of tables that permits intimate conversations, than it is with flashing disco lights and a blaring techno beat.

Many items within an environment owe their presence to their ability to affect the feelings and thoughts of the occupant. Elements used to regulate emotions and thoughts could include photos of family, keepsakes, the color and pattern of the walls, and the music playing on the stereo. Each one of these elements can be used to affect how the occupant feels, serving such diverse purposes as allowing the occupant to unwind from a long day's work, brainstorm for an upcoming project, or get energized for an evening out with friends.

Thus thought and feeling regulators are similar to identity claims, in that both involve deliberate changes made to the environment. However, they are different in that only identity claims are designed to send signals to others. Although communication is not the primary purpose of thought and feeling regulators, observers may notice them and use them to draw conclusions about the occupant.

## Behavioral residue

A broad array of activities are performed in daily life. A subset of those behaviors leave a discernible residue in their wake. For example, the act of organizing one's space may result in the residue of an alphabetized CD collection, whereas the act of practicing one's violin may leave the occupant's sheet music and instrument case lying on the bed. "Behavioral residue" refers to the traces left in the environment by behavioral acts. Sometimes residue is a consequence of the absence of a behavior. For example, the dirty clothing scattered across the floor testifies to the fact that the occupant did not put them in the hamper after wearing them.

Behavioral residue tends to reflect repeated behaviors. Thus, a truly organized person does not organize her books just once; she keeps them organized, putting them back in their proper place after use, and she also organizes her CDs and keeps her filing drawers in order. So behaviors that occur repeatedly are more likely to leave residue than are behaviors that appear only occasionally. This is why behavioral residue tends to reflect consistent individual differences.

Behavioral residue can reflect activities undertaken within the space where they are found, as well as behaviors performed elsewhere. For example, gardening gloves, rubber boots, and sunhat stacked near the back door suggest an occupant who enjoys nature and the outdoors. Residue also includes items that signal anticipated behaviors because the items in the space and their arrangement reflect potential or envisaged behavior; so an unopened bottle of tequila and triple sec, accompanied by fresh limes and a set of glasses ready for salting, suggests someone is planning to entertain.

## Disentangling the three mechanisms

It should be noted that different behaviors can result in similar environmental manifestations—a messy room could indicate sloth, or it could indicate a person who is overwhelmed with other responsibilities. Moreover, the mechanisms described above are not mutually exclusive. For example, the genre of music playing in a passing car may truly reflect the occupant's self-regulation of emotions, but his decision to turn up the volume and roll down the windows may also reflect a desire to make other-directed identity claims.

# Scope and Methodology of Review

Gosling's model suggests some major mechanisms by which individual differences could be expressed in everyday life. To examine the extent to which individual differences really are reflected in everyday contexts, we next review the research linking characteristics of individuals to three major domains of daily life.

Our choice of these contexts is guided by two considerations. First, we follow Holleran and Mehl's (2010) conceptualization of "realistic everyday environments" and Funder's (1995) "realistic environments," to focus on the kinds of manifestations an individual could plausibly encounter in ordinary daily life. Second, building on the residue metaphor, we limit the review to everyday manifestations that naturally leave a discernible trace within physical and virtual spaces. We acknowledge that individual differences are also manifested in an enormous array of domains where no trace is left (e.g. in the way a person walks, the speed at which she drives, the timbre of her voice, the firmness of her handshake).

We admit that our focus on discernible traces is somewhat arbitrary; but, without drawing this line, our review would have to include every behavior ever performed in daily life. So our review does not include the words a person uses if those words are spoken, because no trace of them is left behind (without the unnatural intervention of researchers recording the words). However, our review would include the words a person uses if they were written in an email, where they could be detected in daily life.

Our review has focused only on individual differences in personality, intelligence, and gender. Gender was the only demographic variable we included, because it was the only one that was examined sufficiently frequently to allow us to draw some conclusions about it.

Studies of everyday manifestations of personality are dispersed across many disciplines, including psychology, marketing, and anthropology. Therefore, to capture as many relevant articles as possible, we used a broad search strategy. First, we searched for articles from previous reviews of first impressions within environments (Gosling et al., 2008) and personality judgments (Holleran & Mehl, 2010). Second, we conducted keyword searches for personality, personal spaces, possessions, or virtual spaces in the PsychInfo, Web of Science, and Google Scholar databases. Third, we searched the references cited by the articles identified in the first two steps. From the pool of articles identified by the searches, we selected only the empirical studies and broad reviews.

## Physical environments

FBI investigators and the famous detectives of crime-fiction have long held that physical spaces are useful sources of information about the individuals who dwell in them. Crime-fighters have focused on traces of criminal behavior, but the same principles can be applied by behavioral scientists interested in learning about less nefarious behaviors. The seminal volumes by Webb and colleagues on unobtrusive measurement (Webb, Campbell, Schwartz, & Sechrest, 1966; Webb, Campbell, Schwartz, & Sechrest, 2000; Webb, Campbell, Schwartz, Sechrest & Below Grove, 1981) described classic studies on trace measures, showing how people's behavior could be detected from the clues they left behind. One widely cited example, perhaps apocryphal, was the realization that the hatching-chicks exhibit at the Chicago Museum of Science and Industry must be the most popular due to the fact that the floor tiles in front of it had to be replaced more often than those in front of other exhibits.

Traditionally trace measures have been used to evaluate differences between groups of individuals. For example, to examine socioeconomic differences in levels of hostility, Sechrest and Olson (1971) examined the amount and content of graffiti in public restrooms at a variety of school types (e.g. trade schools, four-year colleges, universities, professional schools); in such studies investigators do not need to tie specific traces to specific individuals. In contrast, individual differences researchers need to measure specific individuals and specific spaces and connect the two.

To characterize spaces that tend to be occupied by specific individuals, Gosling and colleagues (Gosling, Craik, Martin & Pryor, 2005a; Gosling et al., 2005b) introduced the concept of the "personal living space" (PLS). PLSs are generally smaller spaces found within larger buildings, but designated for a specific individual; a PLS can be any space ranging from a room within a household or retirement center, to a corner of a dorm room or a cubical, or even a desk within an office building. Individuals may also leave clues to their personalities in shared spaces and in spaces they occupy temporarily; but, given the methodological and practical advantages of studying spaces habitually occupied by a single individual, it is not surprising that most research has focused on spaces that could be characterized as PLSs.

Most past research on manifestations of individual differences in physical environments has focused on bedrooms and offices. For example, one study examined the ways in which adolescents decorated their bedrooms, focusing on the differences between the items found in boys' and girls' rooms (Rheingold & Cook, 1975). To summarize the past research in this domain, Table 30.1 shows the 12 studies we found on physical environments that provided information both on individual differences and on features of physical spaces. For each study, the table provides a brief description of the kinds of spaces assessed and some details on which individual

**Table 30.1** Past research on individual differences manifested in physical spaces. Underlined variables denote traits for which manifestations were identified. Key: E = extraversion; A = agreeableness; C = conscientiousness; N = neuroticism; O = openness

| Study | Type of Space Assessed | Individual Differences | | | Manifestations | |
| --- | --- | --- | --- | --- | --- | --- |
| | | Method | Variables | | Method | Variables |
| Rheingold & Cook (1975) | Bedrooms (children's rooms: kids age 6 and younger) | • Self-report | Gender | | • Photos taken of room<br>• Researcher coding of possessions in photos | Personalization (e.g. stuffed animals, books, dolls, musical objects, sports equipment, etc.) |
| Hansen & Altman (1976) | Bedrooms (dorm rooms—only males assessed) | • University records | College drop-out rates per semester, GPA | | • Photos taken of space above bed<br>• Researcher coding of possessions in photos<br>• Volume of personalization measured | Personalization: diversity (e.g. abstract, reference objects, personal relationships, values, entertainment, etc.) and volume |
| Vinsel, Brown, Altman & Foss (1980) | Bedrooms (dorm rooms) | • Self-reports | Gender, college drop-out rates, privacy regulation behaviors within dorm | | • Photos taken of space above bed<br>• Volume of personalization measured<br>• Researcher coding of possessions in photos | Personalization: diversity (e.g. personal relationships, abstract, music/theater, sports, reference items, etc.) and volume |
| Gosling, Ko, Mannarelli & Morris (2002) | Bedrooms (dorms and apartments) | • Self-reports<br>• Informant reports | E, A, C, N, O, gender | | • Researcher coding of possessions | Personalization: items in space (e.g. clock, flowers, stuffed animals, books, CDs, etc.) and attributes of items and space (e.g. level of decoration, level of neatness, type of CDs, level of organization, level of clutter, etc.) |

| Study | Setting | Method | Variables | Coding | Personalization |
|---|---|---|---|---|---|
| Gosling, Craik, Martin & Pryor (2005a) | Bedrooms (dorms and apartments) | • Participants listed items in a room thought to be reflective of personality | E, A, C, N, O | • Raters categorized items | Personalization: items in space (e.g. clock, flowers, stuffed animals, books, CDs, etc.) and attributes of items (e.g. level of decoration, level of neatness, amount of CDs, level of organization, level of clutter, etc.) |
| Gosling, Craik, Martin & Pryor (2005b) | Bedrooms (dorms and apartments) | • Self-reports<br>• Informant reports | O, gender | • Researcher coding of possessions | Personalization: items in space (e.g. clock, flowers, stuffed animals, books, CDs, etc.) and attributes of items and space (e.g. level of decoration, level of neatness, type of CDs, level of organization, level of clutter, etc.) |
| Jones, Taylor, Dick, Singh & Cook (2007) | Bedrooms (adolescents' rooms) | • Self-reports | Gender, personalization influences, activities done in space | • Participant coding of possessions from checklist | Personalization: items (e.g. stuffed animals, photos, sports-related things, personally built items, building materials, etc.), room activities |
| McElroy, Morrow & Ackerman (1983) | Workspaces | • Self-reports | E, locus of control, need for interpersonal relationships | • Researchers measure of chair and desk placement | Desk placement (e.g. open or closed), seating arrangement (e.g. open or closed) |

(Continued)

**Table 30.1** (*Continued*)

| Study | Type of Space Assessed | Individual Differences | | Manifestations | |
|---|---|---|---|---|---|
| | | *Method* | *Variables* | *Method* | *Variables* |
| Wells (2000) | Workspaces | • Self-reports<br>• Researchers interview subset of employees about personalization | <u>Gender, status, need for affiliation, need for privacy, creativity</u> | • Employees self-reported coding of possession<br>• Researcher coding of possessions | Personalization (e.g. express identities individuality, emotions, improve the feel of the workspace, symbols of personal relationships, sports-related items, etc.) |
| Wells & Thelen (2002) | Workspaces | • Employee self-reports<br>• Owner/Manager self-report | <u>E, A, C, N, O, gender, status, type of workspaces</u> | • Employees self-reported coding of possession | Personalization (e.g. displays of friends, coworkers, pets, display of activities, the arts, etc.) |
| Gosling, Ko, Mannarelli & Morris (2002) | Workspaces | • Self-reports<br>• Informant reports | <u>E, A, C, N, O, gender</u> | • Researcher coding of possessions | Personalization: items in space (e.g. clock, flowers, stuffed animals, books, CDs, etc.) and attributes of items and space (e.g. level of decoration, level of neatness, type of books, level of organization, level of clutter, etc.) |
| Wells, Thelen & Ruark (2007) | Workspaces | • Employee self-reports<br>• Owner/Manager self-report | <u>Gender, status</u> | • Employees self-reported coding of possession | Personalization (e.g. display of family members, coworkers, artwork, trinkets, CD players, etc.) |

differences and which features of the physical environments were measured. The underlined variables are the ones for which the relevant study identified at least some specific manifestations. The table is organized first by the sub-domain in which the environment is examined (bedrooms and offices) and then chronologically within those categories.

Of the 12 studies presented in Table 30.1, 7 (58 percent) focused on bedrooms or dorm rooms and 5 (42 percent) examined office spaces. Some studies uncovered by our initial searches examined the connections between organizations and buildings (Arnell & Sloan Devlin, 2002; Maxwell & Chmielewski, 2007; Miwa & Hanyu, 2006; Sloan Devlin, 2008), but were excluded from the table because they did not draw connections between specific individuals and their spaces. Also note that some studies relevant to the present discussion are not included in the table because they did not contain enough relevant elements; for example, Laumann and House's (1970) analysis of living rooms described an instrument designed to document the features of PLSs, but it did not present estimates of individual differences in the occupants.

Together, the findings indicate that a broad range of individual differences are expressed in physical spaces. Several studies framed their analyses in terms of the widely used Big-Five model (John, Naumann, & Soto, 2008). The evidence suggests that all five dimensions can be manifested in PLSs, but openness and conscientiousness appear to leave the biggest imprint (Gosling et al., 2002). High-openness individuals tend to occupy spaces that are classified as "distinctive" and contain a high diversity of content items (e.g. books, magazines) and indicators of interest in various places and cultures (e.g. maps, souvenirs). The spaces occupied by conscientious occupants tend to be clean, organized, neat, and uncluttered. Although openness and conscientiousness were the traits most clearly manifested in physical spaces, others did get expressed. For example, extraverts engaged in more personalization and had offices that were classified as more inviting than offices occupied by introverts (ibid.). One way the invitingness can be expressed is in terms of a relatively open chair and desk arrangement (McElroy, Morrow, & Ackeman, 1983).

The environmental manifestations of the Big-Five traits are consistent with the logic of behavioral residue—the idea that certain traits are associated with certain behaviors, and that a subset of those behaviors leave a trace in physical spaces. For example, people high on openness engage in creative behaviors and have a wide range of interests, people high on conscientiousness are concerned with order, and people high on extraversion enjoy promoting social interactions.

In addition to the Big Five, a varied assortment of other traits has been examined, including status, need for interpersonal relationships, and locus of control. In one study, the likelihood of dropping out of college was predicted from the degree of personalization within a room (Hansen & Altman, 1976); specifically, individuals who personalized their rooms had lower drop-out rates than individuals who personalized them less did. When the drop-outs did personalize their spaces, their décor tended to be related to family and the loved ones. A similar study conducted some years later at the same university showed the opposite effect—drop-outs used decoration more than non-drop-outs (Vinsel et al., 1980). The discrepancies in these findings were explained in terms of the small size and composition (only males were assessed) of the sample in the Hansen and Altman study (ibid.). However, like the older study, the newer 1980 study did find similarities in the types of personalization that drop-outs utilized—photos of family and friends. The obvious interpretation is that the dorm-room décor consisted of identity claims, expressing commitment to the new college life in the non-drop-outs (who decorated with college-related emblems) and thought and feeling regulators designed to counter feelings of loneliness and isolation and reluctance to commit to college life in the drop-outs (who decorated with reminders of home).

One study of workspaces (Wells & Thelen, 2002) examined the connections between how a space was personalized and individual differences such as status. Occupants recorded the items in their workspace and gave details regarding their job, such as position and tenure within the company, and how many hours per week they worked. Status in the organization was a strong predictor of the amount of personalization in an office space. But these individual difference variables were only part of the story. Other factors such as the type of workspace (e.g. a private, enclosed space vs. an open cubical) and the company's personalization policies also influenced the types and amount of personalization of the workspaces.

Several studies identified substantial differences in the ways in which males and females personalized their bedrooms and office spaces. In general, women tend to decorate their spaces more than men do. In terms of specific items, compared with men, women tend to have more stuffed animals, candles, lotions, trinkets, and photos of close others such as family and friends. Men tend to have more sports equipment, CDs, stereos, and achievement-related items.

These trends have been identified in several populations, including young children (Rheingold, & Cook, 1975), adolescents (Jones, Taylor, Dick, Singh, & Cook, 2007), and college-age adults (Gosling et al., 2005b; Hansen & Altman, 1976; Vinsel et al., 1980). For example, in one study, adolescents listed all of the items in their rooms, described the activities done in the rooms, and gave reasons for personalizing the spaces the way they had (Jones et al., 2007). Girls had more stuffed animals and photos of people, whereas boys had more items relating to sports and to building things. Both boys' and girls' décor was influenced by things such as friends and pop culture; however, boys were also influenced by other sources such as parents, girlfriends, and extracurricular actives.

The differences in décor between the spaces occupied by men and women are so consistent that perceivers can readily identify the gender of an occupant on the basis of décor alone, especially in the case of bedrooms (Gosling et al., 2002). The perceivers may then use gender-stereotypes to make inferences about the occupants, even for traits about which they have no direct evidence. For example, a visitor to an office may realize that the occupant is male and, consistent with gender stereotypes, infer that he is relatively low on agreeableness and neuroticism. Of course, the accuracy of the perceiver's impressions will be boosted only to the extent that the stereotypes hold a kernel of truth (Jussim, Cain, Crawford, Harber, & Cohen, in press).

## Approaches to characterizing physical spaces

Three broad approaches have been taken to characterizing physical spaces. The first approach, used by 4 (33 percent) of the 12 studies, relied on participants to report on the kinds of personalization that they have displayed. This approach has the advantage of being easy to administer to large samples, but it is subject to self-reporting biases.

The second approach, used in three (25 percent) studies, relied on photographs of the whole space or portions of it. For example, both Hansen and Altman (1976) and Vinsel et al. (1980) investigated personalization within dorm rooms by examining photos of the space above a person's bed. Hansen and Altman (1976) measured the volume of personalization by placing a clear plastic sheet with cubic measures on top of the photograph, to measure the actual volume of decoration present, whereas Vinsel's team (1980) measured the amount of personalization by conducting a content analysis of the specific items. This photo-based approach is probably more accurate and easier to compare across spaces than the self-report approach, but there are many details that would be hard to discern from a photograph.

The third approach to characterizing spaces, used in five (42 percent) of the studies, was the most labor-intensive—measuring the spaces themselves. Gosling et al. (2002, 2005a, 2005b) and Wells (2000) assembled teams of trained researchers who entered the spaces and recorded the levels and types of personalization. In one study, specific items—chair and desk placement within an office—were recorded by a research team (McElroy et al., 1983). These studies, which relied on trained coders, probably provided the most trustworthy and fine-grained analyses of spaces, but they required great investments of time and resources and high levels of cooperation from the occupants.

## Possessions

The presence, state, and location of personal possessions can provide clues about the owner's individual differences. Possessions are often to be found in a person's physical space, so the domain of possessions can overlap with the domain of physical environments. However, we treat possessions separately from physical environments here, because many possessions (e.g. cars) are not found in personal living spaces, and in many cases they have been studied in isolation.

Research on how individual differences are manifested in personal possessions has been fairly limited. In the 1950s, 1960s, and 1970s, researchers emphasized the personality correlates of possessions and consumer behavior, but more recent papers have focused on concepts such as brand personality (e.g. Aaker, 1997) and identity signaling (e.g. Berger & Heath, 2007; Mittal, 2006).

There are many potential ways of organizing possessions. Some researchers organize them in terms of price, ranging from inexpensive everyday products such as chewing gum to big-ticket items such as cars. Other researchers prefer to organize the domain in terms of possessions' symbolic value, for instance treasured items or keepsakes versus instrumental, or utilitarian items that are used on a daily basis (e.g. television set, toothpaste). Items that carry instrumental or utilitarian value are referred to as "consumer items" in some fields. These different ways of conceptualizing possessions are driven, in large part, by the different methods and theories associated with consumer research and psychology. Consumer researchers tend to focus on demographic differences as well as on differences in self-concept among the buyers of various brands. Psychologists are more interested in the individual and personality differences related to the value that people place on certain possessions.

The differences in how possessions have been conceptualized create obstacles to summarizing the findings, because researchers have not classified possessions in consistent ways and they have focused on different sets of individual differences. For example, although there have been numerous studies of personality characteristics, there are few common threads in how they have been measured. Alarmingly, only a single study of possessions measured individual differences using the dimensions of the five-factor model.

Despite these discrepancies, we have summarized the studies in Table 30.2. On the basis of our review, we characterize possessions in terms of the three sub-domains that have been studied most extensively: cars, consumer products (also called utilitarian or instrumental items), and symbolic possessions (i.e. personally meaningful items).

Of the 10 studies presented in Table 30.2, four (40 percent) focused purely on automobile ownership. This minor flurry of studies reflects a wider interest in automobile model and brand preferences, which occurred in marketing research in the late 1950s and 1960s (Evans, 1959; Westfall, 1962). Another three studies (30 percent) focused on consumer products. This sample of studies taps only a tiny amount of the large research literature on consumer behavior; however, these studies were the only ones that examined individual differences as valid predictors of product choices. The remaining three studies (30 percent) conceptualized possessions in terms of their symbolic value (e.g. a photo album, or a childhood blanket). In the context of Gosling et al.'s (2002) model, described above, symbolic possessions would tend to be used as feeling regulators or as identity claims. Many other studies conceptualized possessions in terms of identity signaling (Berger & Heath, 2007) or as extensions of the self (Belk, 1988; Holman, 1980). But these studies did not explicitly measure the link between personality and possessions, so they are beyond the scope of this review.

As mentioned earlier, only one of the studies assessed individual differences in terms of the Big Five. Instead of personality traits, several studies focused on motivational constructs, such as needs. The claim, at least among early researchers, was that an individual's pattern of needs may be expressed through the objects he or she acquires. The most common measure of these "needs" was the Edwards Personal Preference Schedule (Edwards, 1959), yielding scores on such needs as exhibition (a need to be the center of attention in a group), autonomy, affiliation, and dominance. Several early studies linked these needs to preferred brands of automobile. One study suggested that owners of Fords were high on the needs for dominance and exhibition, whereas owners of Chevrolets were high on the needs for autonomy and affiliation (Evans, 1959). Another study showed that people scoring high on responsibility were more likely to own cars made by Mercury, Ford, and Plymouth than by Corvette or Thunderbird (Tucker & Painter, 1961). Subsequent researchers paid more attention to factors that could mediate the links between needs and preferences. For example, measures of certainty about how a brand will perform or perceptions of how differentiated the brands are increased the ability of personality variables to predict preferences for some brands and products (Brody & Cunningham, 1968).

The 1960s and 1970s saw a group of studies focused on a diverse array of consumer products, such as headache remedies, vitamins, cigarettes, deodorant, and

**Table 30.2** Past research on individual differences manifested in possessions. Underlined variables denote traits for which manifestations were identified. Key: E = extraversion; A = agreeableness; C = conscientiousness; N = neuroticism; O = openness; EPPS = Edward Personality Preference Scale; PRF = Personality Research Form

| Study | Type of Space Assessed | Individual Differences | | Manifestations | |
|---|---|---|---|---|---|
| | | Method | Variables | Method | Variables |
| Evans (1959) | Cars | • Self-report | EPPS (e.g. dominance, nurturance, aggression) | • Self-report | Own a Ford or a Chevrolet |
| Westfall (1962) | Cars | • Self-report | Thurstone Temperament Schedule (e.g. active, vigorous, impulsive, dominant) | • Self-report | Car models: standard, convertible, compact |
| Grubb & Hupp (1968) | Cars | • Self-report | Self-concept | • Self-report | Own a Pontiac or a Volkswagen |
| Alpert (1972) | Cars | • Self-report | EPPS (e.g. dominance, nurturance, aggression), gender | • Self-report | Automobile type, Movie preferences, Place of residence |
| Tucker & Painter (1961) | Consumer products | • Self-report | Gordon Personality Profile (ascendency, responsibility, emotional stability, sociability) | • Self-report | Sales and Marketing Personality Index (e.g. headache remedies, cigarettes, chewing gum) |
| Brody & Cunningham (1968) | Consumer products | • Self-report | EPPS (e.g. dominance, nurturance, aggression), gender | • Self-report | Coffee brand preference |
| Worthing, Venkatesam, & Smith (1973) | Consumer products | • Self-report | Jackson's PRF (e.g. affiliation, aggression, dominance, exhibition) | • Self-report | Product use (e.g. cigarettes, razor blades, radios, beer) |

(Continued)

**Table 30.2** (*Continued*)

| Study | Type of Space Assessed | Individual Differences | | Manifestations | |
|---|---|---|---|---|---|
| | | Method | Variables | Method | Variables |
| Horton (1979) | Consumer products | • Self-repot | Social anxiety, general anxiety, impulsiveness | • Self-report | Product use: Bath soap, instant coffee, toothpaste, aspirin, deodorant |
| Hirsh and Dolderman (2007) | Consumer products | • Self-report | E, A, C, N, O | • Self-report | Consumerism |
| Prentice (1987) | Symbolic possessions | • Self-report | Values: symbolic (e.g. a world at peace, family security), instrumental (e.g. ambition, courage) | • Self-report | Possession preference: Symbolic (e.g. family heirlooms), Instrumental (e.g. stereo) |
| Dittmar (1989) | Symbolic possessions | • Self-report | Gender | • Self-report | Possession preference: Symbolic (e.g. family heirlooms), Instrumental (e.g. stereo) |
| Burroughs, Drews, & Hallman (1991) | Symbolic possessions | • Self-report | Activity scales (e.g. energetic, relaxed), potency scales (e.g. strong, masculine), evaluation scales (e.g. logical, simple) | • Researchers coding from photos of clothing and dorm room<br>• Self-report academic courses and record albums | Preference in: Clothing, Academic courses, Record albums, Dorm rooms |
| Kamptner (1991) | Symbolic possessions | • Self-report | Gender, age | • Self-report | Early treasured items, Music, TV, Books |
| Richins (1994) | Symbolic possessions | • Self-report | Materialism | • Self-report | Possession preference: Symbolic (e.g. family heirlooms), Instrumental (e.g. stereo) |

chewing gum. For example, those scoring high on psychological ascendency (i.e. those who were assertive and self-assured in their relationships with others) were less likely to use remedies for headaches than low scorers were. Consumption of beer and cigarettes was linked to the needs for affiliation, aggression, dominance, exhibition, and social recognition (Worthing, Venkatesam, & Smith, 1973).

A subset of studies focused on attitudes and values (e.g. Kamptner, 1991; Prentice, 1987; Richins, 1994). For example, Prentice (1987) found that individuals who valued symbolic possessions (e.g. a family heirloom) over instrumental possessions (e.g. a television set) were more likely to endorse symbolic appeals and values (e.g. a world at peace) than instrumental values (e.g. being ambitious). Self-ratings on materialism also mediated a person's orientation toward the symbolic versus instrumental value of a possession (Richins, 1994). Those low on materialism emphasized the symbolic value and the hedonic (or pleasure-seeking) potential of possessions, whereas those high on materialism emphasized instrumental (or utilitarian) concerns. Males tended to prefer the active, physical, and instrumental qualities of possessions, whereas females were generally more drawn to the symbolic and interpersonal features of possessions (Dittmar, 1989; Kamptner, 1991).

Given the great diversity of individual differences, possessions, and methodologies in this domain, few meaningful substantive conclusions can be drawn. Broadly, there is evidence that a person's choice of possessions is linked to a variety of individual differences; but that is about all than can be said. It is clear that some degree of standardization needs to be brought to the field, so that the findings can build on one another and yield some conclusions of substance. One good place to start would be the creation of a comprehensive taxonomy of possessions. When combined with standard measures of personality, the possessions taxonomy could be used to chart the basic topography of how individual differences are manifested in preferences for, and ownership of, personal possessions.

## Approaches to characterizing possessions

Researchers working in the domain of possessions have overwhelmingly relied on self-reports to quantify individuals' possessions. With one exception, in which researchers coded items from photos of dorm rooms (Burroughs, Drews, & Hallman, 1991), none of the studies in Table 30.2 coded, or took an independent inventory of, participants' possessions. Instead, participants self-reported on consumer behavior (e.g. what type of beer they purchased) or on their preferences for symbolic versus instrumental items. The personality inventories (e.g. Gordon Personality Profile, or Jackson's PRF) were also all collected by using self-report. Clearly, the findings summarized here are qualified to the extent that participants are willing and able to provide accurate reports about their own possessions.

## Virtual spaces

As in the physical world, individual differences can be manifested in virtual worlds too. Virtual spaces refer to the environments and media in which individuals interact, communicate, and express themselves on-line. Traces of individual differences within these virtual contexts can be found across a variety of sub-domains including on-line social networking sites (OSNs), personal websites, blogs, and various forms of computer-mediated communication (CMC; e.g. email). Table 30.3 summarizes research within the four virtual sub-domains. The table is organized first by sub-domain (OSNs, personal websites, forms of CMC, and blogs) and then chronologically within these categories.

Manifestations of the Big Five can be found in each of the four sub-domains; however, the traits that are expressed and the ways in which they are expressed differ across sub-domains. For instance, research on perceptions of people on the basis of their Facebook profiles suggests that the profiles contain valid information on the profile owners' levels of extraversion, agreeableness, conscientiousness, and openness— but not neuroticism (Back et al., 2010). In contrast, blog posts do provide textual clues as to the bloggers' levels of neuroticism (Argamon, Koppel, Pennebaker, & Schler, 2009).

The search for valid indicators of personality traits on OSNs has largely focused on the features of Facebook profiles. For example, studies suggest that individuals high on openness are particularly likely to engage in behaviors such as commenting and posting on walls, and to belong to a large number of networks (Gosling et al., 2010; Ross et al., 2009). Other Facebook research indicates that extraverts display more unique photos, belong to more groups, and have more friends than introverts do (Gosling et al., 2010; Kramer & Winter, 2008). Facebook profiles must contain information about agreeableness and conscientiousness too, because perceivers are able to judge these traits with some accuracy on the strength of the profiles alone (Back et al., 2010); however, researchers have yet to uncover which specific clues convey information about these traits in OSN profiles.

All five of the Big-Five dimensions are expressed on a person's personal website. Accurate impressions can be made on all five dimensions on the basis of an individual's personal website (Vazire & Gosling, 2004). Individual differences can be detected from features such as the personal information the owner provides, the content of the site, and the links and photographs the owner displays (Marcus, Machilek, & Schütz, 2006). For example, higher levels of neuroticism were associated with photos of one's pets, conscientiousness was related to photos of family, openness was associated with the number of links relating to the visual arts, and extraversion was signaled by the inclusion of newsletters on the websites.

Blogs are another prevalent context for manifestations of individual differences in virtual space. Again, there is evidence that dimensions of the Big Five are expressed in this context. One study of more than 19,000 blogs examined the ways in which text was reflective of the author's level of neuroticism and gender, among other characteristics (Argamon et al., 2009). Bloggers high on neuroticism tended to refer to themselves relatively frequently, whereas the less neurotic bloggers displayed writing that was less concrete and precise. Another study focused on a random sample of nearly 700 blogs (Yarkoni, in press). It extended previous studies in two respects. First, the study differed from past studies, which had focused on word categories (e.g. positive or negative emotion words), by analyzing the frequencies of individual words. Second, in addition to examining linguistic markers of the broad Big-Five dimensions, the study analyzed the narrower facets that make up each broad

**Table 30.3** Past research on individual differences manifested in virtual spaces. Underlined variables denote traits for which manifestations were identified. E = extraversion; A = agreeableness; C = conscientiousness; N = neuroticism; O = openness

| Study | Type of Space Assessed | Individual Differences | | Manifestations | |
| | | Method | Variables | Method | Variables |
| --- | --- | --- | --- | --- | --- |
| Kramer & Winter (2008) | On-line Social Networking Site (StudiVZ) | • Self-report | <u>E</u>, self-esteem, <u>self efficacy</u> | • Content analysis of profiles | Features of profile (e.g. number of virtual friends, number of groups number of photos, number of completed fields, number of words, use of real name, display of political orientation and relationship status, style of text, type of photo) |
| Buffardi & Campbell (2008) | On-line Social Networking Site (Facebook) | • Self-reports | <u>Narcissism</u> | • Objective (standard features of profile) and subjective (research assistant coding) content analysis of profiles | Features of profile (e.g. quantity of social interactions, main photo self-promotion, main photo attractiveness, self-promotion of main photo, sexiness of main photo, etc.) |
| Ross, Orr, Sisic, Arseneault, Simmering & Orr (2009) | On-line Social Networking Site (Facebook) | • Self-reports | <u>E</u>, A, C, N, <u>O</u> | • Self-reports | Facebook behaviors (e.g. use of the Wall, posting photos, sending private messages, use of "poke" function, participation in groups, etc.), attitudes toward Facebook, on-line sociability |

(*Continued*)

**Table 30.3** (*Continued*)

| Study | Type of Space Assessed | Individual Differences | | | Manifestations | |
|---|---|---|---|---|---|---|
| | | Method | Variables | | Method | Variables |
| Orr, Sisic, Ross, Simmering, Arseneault & Orr (2009) | On-line Social Networking Site (Facebook) | • Self-reports | Shyness | | • Self-reports | Time spent on Facebook, attitudes toward Facebook, number of friends |
| Gosling, Augustine, Vazire, Holtzman & Gaddis (*under review*) | On-line Social Networking Site (Facebook) | • Self-reports | E, A, C, N, <u>O</u> | | • Content analysis of profiles | Features of profile (e.g. number of photos, number of photo albums, number of groups, number of wall posts, network, etc.) |
| Dominick (1999) | Personal websites | • Self-reports | Gender | | • Content analysis of websites | Self-presentation (e.g. biographical info, spouse/partner info, family info, job description, friend's information, etc.) |
| Marcus, Machilek & Schutz (2006) | Personal websites | • Self-reports | E, A, C, N, O, narcissism, self-esteem, self-presentation styles, self-monitoring, gender | | • Content analysis of websites | Personal website, content of site (e.g. personal info provided by owner, contact info, photographs, external links, misc. items) |
| Jung, Youn & McClung (2007) | Personal Websites (Cyworld website) | • Self-reports | Self-presentation strategies, motivations | | • Content analysis of site | Homepage items (e.g. background music, photos—number of albums and types of photos presented), management of site (e.g. expenditure of homepage maintenance, frequency of updates, representation of mood/thought on page) |

| Study | Domain | Method | Variables | Analysis | Features |
|---|---|---|---|---|---|
| Colley, Todd, Bland, Holmes, Khanom & Pike (2004) | Computer-mediated communication (emails and letters) | • Self-report<br>• Targets wrote emails to a friend | Gender | • Style and content of email analyzed | Style (e.g. formality, excitability, nonessentials, relationship devices), content (e.g. activities categories—sports, holidays, work, etc. and relationships categories—family, specific same-sex friends, specific opposite-sex friends, etc.) |
| Back, Schmukle & Egloff (2008) | Computer-mediated communication (email addresses) | • Self-reports<br>• Email addresses | E, A, C, N, O, narcissism, gender | • Specific cues of email addresses coded | Features of email address (e.g. number of characters and dots, email provider, use of humor, self-enhancing content, etc.) |
| Argamon, Koppel, Pennebaker & Schler (2009) | Blogs | • Writing samples collected<br>• Self-reports | Gender, N | • Style and content features of text analyzed | Word use: style (e.g. personal pronoun, determiner, preposition-matter, subject pronoun, reflexive pronoun etc.) and content (e.g. cute, mom, software, boyfriend, system, etc.) |
| Yarkoni (in press) | Blogs | • Writing samples collected<br>• Self reports | E, A, C, N, O (and facets of Big Five) | • Style and content features of text analyzed | Word use: categories (e.g. negative emotion, positive emotion, swear words, anger words, sexual words, etc.) and individual words (e.g. stressful, bar, harmony, joy, boring, etc.) |

dimension (Yarkoni, in press). Facets of agreeableness were negatively related to swearing and anger-related words, facets of extraversion were related to use of social and positively emotional words, and most facets of neuroticism were associated with negative word use. However, unlike the other neuroticism facets, the self-consciousness facet showed no positive correlation with negative affect categories and was the only facet of neuroticism to correlate negatively with categories related to interpersonal interaction (Yarkoni, in press). These findings are significant, because they show that the patterns of manifestations can differ across the facets within a single domain, and that the manifestations at the facet level may not always match the manifestations associated with the broader traits.

OSN profiles, websites, and blogs are already quite limited in terms of the information they provide. But how minimal could the information be and still reflect an individual's characteristics? One recent study (Back et al., 2008) suggests that four of the Big Five (all except extraversion) are reflected even in tiny fragments of information, such as the email address an individual creates for himself or herself. People low on neuroticism and agreeableness tend to use self-enhancing features (e.g. ladiessloveme@gmail.com), people high on conscientiousness tend to have addresses that are less funny (e.g. ilovemovies@yahoo.com), and people high on openness tend to have relatively creative email addresses (e.g. TobyornotToby@mac.com).

Beyond the Big Five, researchers have identified several other variables that get expressed in virtual environments; these include shyness, self-efficacy, self-presentation, and narcissism. For example, people high on shyness tend to spend more time on Facebook and have positive attitudes toward the platform when compared with non-shy people (Orr et al., 2009). Further, shyness is negatively related to the number of friends a person has within the Facebook site (ibid.). Also, within OSNs, people high on self-efficacy are likely to have profile photos that are rated as having striking or bold poses and as being "party" related (i.e. depicting socially oriented situations), to have many friends, and to have completed many profile fields (Kramer & Winter, 2008).

Many forms of virtual expression seem to afford opportunities for self-promotion, so it is not surprising that several investigators have researched the extent to which narcissism is expressed in virtual contexts. In one Facebook study, individuals high on narcissism were found to have main profile photos that were sexier, more attractive, and more self-promoting than non-narcissists had (Buffardi & Campbell, 2008). Also, narcissistic people tend to post more fun photos overall, but, contrary to the results regarding main profile pictures, they do not post more provocative or self-promoting non-profile photos. Additionally, narcissistic people are particularly prone to engage in social interactions on OSNs. However, contrary to what one might expect, they do not post more information about themselves than individuals low in narcissism do. Narcissism also shows up in email addresses, those high on the trait displaying more self-enhancing and salacious features (Back et al., 2008). There is no evidence to suggest that narcissism is reflected in personal websites (Marcus et al., 2006).

As in physical environments, there is considerable evidence that gender is expressed in virtual environments too. For example, in the context of personal websites, men and women differ in the kinds of information they display about themselves. Both men and women display descriptive biographies, job descriptions, and resumés; but the content of these items differs across the genders. Women tend to display more introspective biographies and information about family and their significant others (Dominick, 1999). Gender differences are also reflected in the content of emails and blogs. For instance, when emailing, women are more likely than men to mention things such as shopping and family (Colley et al., 2004). Women are also more likely than men to begin their emails with personal enquires and end the correspondence with affectionate signatures. In contrast, men tend to use more offensive language and less punctuation. In blogs, word content and style vary across genders (Argamon et al., 2009). Men use more prepositions and women use more personal pronouns. In terms of content, the biggest predictor of gender is the use of technological words (e.g. software, system, site) by males and of words about personal life (e.g. boyfriend, mom, feel) by females.

## Approaches to characterizing virtual spaces

Similar to the way research characterized various features of spaces in physical environments, research on virtual environments has tended to code and itemize the specific features of the virtual domains. This coding process is easier in virtual contexts than in physical worlds, because the features within the space are more limited and less varied than those found in physical spaces, and they can all be coded from a single location (namely from one's computer). In the majority of the studies presented here (8 of the 10 studies), researchers conducted some form of content analysis and feature coding procedure.

# The Expression of Individual Differences in Everyday Environments

The past research on the manifestations of individual differences in everyday life paints a picture that is provocative but far from conclusive. The picture is provocative because in nearly every domain that has been examined, from bedrooms to email addresses, researchers have identified manifestations of individual differences. The picture is inconclusive because the research is sparse and non-programmatic; the studies are dispersed across numerous disciplines and span a period of 50 years, each study sharing very little with the others in terms of background theory, methods, and constructs examined.

## The need for standardization

The difficulty of drawing specific substantive conclusions results from the fact that few studies have been done, and those that have vary in the psychological constructs they measure and in the methods they use. For example, the questions driving research on possessions and physical spaces are very similar—essentially, how do people use artifacts to express themselves deliberately and inadvertently?—but there is virtually no consistency across the fields in the ways the artifacts are classified and examined. Here we discuss the challenges associated with character-izing individuals and the features of everyday contexts, along with potential solutions.

## Characterizing individual differences

As the field moves forward, researchers should focus on measuring the same elements of personality, so that findings may accumulate within a single framework. The advent of the Big-Five personality dimensions has brought some degree of coherence to the more recent studies. Given its widespread use and acceptance in the field, the Big-Five model is the most obvious candidate for providing a common currency for the studies. However, the Big-Five framework should not be used so religiously that researchers may neglect demographic variables (gender, age, occupation, ethnicity) and other potentially relevant narrower constructs (likeability, political orientation, narcissism, self-esteem).

There are two good strategies for achieving the twin aims of making the research comparable with other studies and at the same time tapping the narrower constructs that might be of particular relevance to a domain. The first strategy is to assess the Big Five by using a very brief Big-Five instrument and to augment it with measures that tap relevant narrower constructs. Back et al. (2008) used this strategy in their analyses of email addresses. They measured the Big Five using a very short 10-item measure, and they also assessed narcissism using a standard measure. This strategy allowed the researchers to slot their findings into the context of other studies, and also to focus on a construct thought to be particularly relevant to the domain of email addresses.

A second strategy for balancing comparability with specificity is to measure the lower-order facets of the Big Five. The lower-order facets are useful because they allow researchers to tap constructs that are narrower than the broad dimension levels, but at the same time they can easily be slotted into the Big-Five framework for the purpose of comparing findings across studies. Yarkoni (in press) used this strategy in his analyses of blogs. He measured the Big Five using a 315-item questionnaire, which included facet-level scales. This strategy allowed him to highlight similarities with previous research at the broad dimension level as well as differences from previ-ous research at the narrower facet level. Instruments that generate facet-level scores tend to be longer than standard Big-Five instruments, but several shorter facet-level inventories have recently been developed (e.g. Yarkoni, 2010).

Despite the general lack of standardization, the common framework provided by the Big Five allows some broad conclusions to be drawn about which dimensions tend to get expressed in everyday contexts. Of the five dimensions, extraversion and openness were the ones most commonly expressed: extraversion was examined in 12 studies and found to have environmental manifestations in 10 (83 percent) of them; and manifestations of openness were found in all 11 (100 percent) studies that examined it. Manifestations of the other dimensions were identified as follows: agreeableness in 8 studies (out of the 10 that assessed it; 80 percent); conscientious-ness in 7 studies (out of 10; 70 percent); and neuroticism in 8 studies (out of 11; 73 percent).

## Characterizing the elements of everyday contexts

There are challenges to characterizing the features of all everyday contexts. However, quantifying the items in physical spaces is particularly challenging because of the enormous number of items that could be found in a space. An inventory that indexed every potential item would need to be enormous if it were to capture every possibility. The most ambitious attempt to document every item in a space is the Personal Living Space Cue Inventory (PLSCI; Gosling et al., 2005a). After several steps designed to generate possible items and categorize them (e.g. into books, toys, photos, posters, trophies and awards, sports equipment, stationery), the PLSCI contained 725 specific items, but even that list was not remotely sufficient to capture everything in the space.

Some researchers have attempted to solve the problem of the overwhelming number of cues by sampling just a few key items, thought to be relevant to the research question. For example, Laumann and House's (1970) Living Room Checklist itemized 53 individual items in the space, such as "large potted plants," "French furniture," and "sunburst clock." The instrument was designed for use by an interviewer during a 10-minute break of an interview conducted in the interviewee's home. The drawback was that the checklist was far from comprehensive, so it risked missing a huge array of objects and resulted in scores that were difficult to interpret (e.g. what should the interviewer do if the potted plants were only of medium size?).

Another approach to characterizing a space consists of using broad descriptors to capture higher-order features of the space (e.g. "organized," "distinctive"). For example, Kasmar's (1970) Environment Description Scale (EDS) consisted of ratings on 66 adjective pairs (appealing vs. unappealing, expensive vs. cheap) allowing users to quantify broad, global elements of architectural spaces. One concern with rating instruments like the EDS is that the raters might have idiosyncratic conceptions of how the descriptors should be defined, which results in unreliable assessments of the spaces. However, analyses of global descriptors on the PLSCI showed that raters can reach respectable levels of consensus (Gosling et al., 2005a): across the 42 global attributes examined, the coefficient Alpha reliability averaged .72, with more than half the attributes having a value of .70 or greater. According to the Spearman–Brown prophesy formula, the addition of one more judge would increase the Alpha reliability of the composites such that 30 of the 42 attributes (71 percent) would reach Alpha levels of at least .70.

Are the two approaches—coding individual items and global ratings—redundant, or does each method capture unique features of a space? To examine this question, Gosling et al. (2005a) also analyzed case studies and discovered that the two approaches are complementary, not redundant. That is, two spaces listed as very similar on a broad measure (e.g. organized) could contain very different items. It is for future research to determine which of the two approaches is better suited for picking up the kinds of manifestations that reflect the individual differences of occupants. This question is important, because the procedures of coding individual items are much more time-consuming and labor-intensive than the operation of collecting broad ratings of the global features of the spaces. Future studies would be more viable if the labor-intensive codings were not required.

The challenges of quantifying physical spaces are particularly great because the quantity, state, and location of items in those spaces are so varied. However, each of the domains reviewed here poses unique challenges. Just as standardized instruments are needed to characterize individual differences in people, robust standardized methods are needed to capture the features of the contexts in which the individual differences are expressed.

## Limitations in methods and samples

Like many areas of individual differences, the research reviewed here relied heavily on the self-report method. Self-reports are used widely, both for the individual differences measures and for the environmental manifestations of those individual differences. This reliance on self-reports raises the possibility that some of the convergent findings from the research literature may be attributed to shared method variance. To garner greater confidence in the findings, researchers must increase their efforts to collect data from sources other than self-reports (say, from informant reports).

The studies reviewed here have also relied heavily on college student samples. The reliance on undergraduate students is widespread in psychology (Gosling et al., 2004), but in the contexts examined here (e.g. in bedroom décor, or in OSNs), which vary considerably across different ages and demographic groups, the lack of diversity imposes a serious limitation on the generalizability of the results. It is imperative that future research makes efforts to extend the research to other populations.

## Future directions

New contexts of everyday expression are constantly emerging. As shown by the research on OSNs, these new domains are potentially rich contexts for the expression of individual differences. There are even some enormously popular virtual domains, such as massively multiplayer online role-playing games (e.g. World of Warcraft) and virtual worlds (e.g. Second Life), which have yet to be studied. So some of the most productive contexts for future research may be domains that have yet to be invented or become popular. If the goal is to understand how individual differences are expressed in everyday life, researchers must be ready to examine new fora of expression as they emerge.

Research is also needed to investigate how traits are manifested in shared spaces, and how an individual manifests his or her traits consistently across different contexts (e.g. are people with tidy homes also tidy at the office?). The overlap between manifestations across everyday domains has also yet to be fully understood. How do possessions vary from home to office? Are the objects one acquires in a virtual world such as Second Life similar to the ones one acquires in non-virtual contexts?

In short, the research on everyday manifestations is so sparse that this review has taught us more about what remains to be learned than about what has been learned. The findings are encouraging because they reveal that a wealth of information about individuals is expressed in everyday contexts. But much further exploration of these environments is needed in order to identify the specific ways in which individual differences are manifested in daily life. The findings from that research will provide the foundation on which to build models to explain how everyday manifestations mediate the links between individual differences and major life outcomes.

# References

Aaker, J. L. (1997). Dimensions of brand personality. *Journal of Marketing Research, 34,* 347–356.

Alpert, M. I. (1972). Personality and the determinants of product choice. *Journal of Marketing Research, 9,* 89–92.

Argamon, S., Koppel, M., Pennebaker, J. W., & Schler, J. (2009). Automatically profiling the author of an anonymous text. *Communications of the ACM, 52,* 119–123.

Arnell, A. B., & Sloan Devlin, A. (2002). Perceived quality of care: The influence of the waiting room environment. *Journal of Environmental Psychology, 22,* 345–360.

Back, M. D., Schmukle, S. C., & Egloff, B. (2008). How extraverted is honey.bunny77@hotmail.de? Inferring personality from e-mail addresses. *Journal of Research in Personality, 42,* 1116–1122.

Back, M. D., Stopfer, J. M., Vazire, S., Gaddis, S., Schmukle, S. C., Egloff, B., & Gosling, S. D. (2010). Facebook profiles reflect actual personality, not self-idealization. *Psychological Science, 21,* 372–374.

Belk, R. (1988). Possessions and the extended self. *Journal of Consumer Research, 15,* 139–168.

Berger, J. & Heath, C. (2007). Where consumers diverge from others: Identity signaling and product domains. *Journal of Consumer Research, 34,* 121–134.

Brody, R. P., & Cunningham, S. M. (1968). Personality variables and the consumer decision process. *Journal of Marketing Research, 5,* 50–57.

Buffardi, L. E., & Campbell, W. K. (2008). Narcissism and social networking web sites. *Personality and Social Psychology Bulletin, 34,* 1303–1314.

Burroughs, W. J., Drews, D. R., & Hallman, W. K. (1991). Predicting personality from personal possessions: A self-presentational analysis. *Journal of Social Behavioral and Personality, 6,* 147–163.

Colley, A., Todd, Z., Bland, M., Holmes, M., Khanom, N., & Pike, H. (2004). Style and content in emails and letters to male and female friends. *Journal of Language and Social Psychology, 23,* 369–378.

Dittmar, H. (1989). Gender identity-related meanings of personal possessions. *British Journal of Social Psychology, 28,* 159–171.

Dominick, J. R. (1999). Who do you think you are? Personal homepage and self-presentation on the World Wide Web. *Journal and Mass Communication Quarterly, 76,* 646–658.

Edwards, A. L. (1959). *Edwards Personal Preference Schedule* [manual] (rev. ed.). New York: Psychological Corp.

Evans, F. E. (1959). Psychological and objective factors in the prediction of brand choice Ford versus Chevrolet. *The Journal of Business, 32,* 340–369.

Funder, D. C. (1995). On the accuracy of personality judgment: A realistic approach. *Psychological Review, 102,* 652–670.

Gosling, S. D. (2008). *Snoop: What your stuff says about you.* New York: Basic Books.

Gosling, S. D., Gaddis, S., & Vazire, S. (2008). First impressions from the environments that we create and inhabit. In J. Skowronski & N. Ambady (Eds.), *First impressions* (pp. 334–356). New York: Guilford Press.

Gosling, S. D., Augustine, A. A., Vazire, S., Holtzman, N. S., & Gaddis, S. (2010). *Manifestations of personality in behaviors and features associated with Facebook profiles.* Manuscript submitted for publication.

Gosling, S. D., Craik, K. H., Martin, N. R., & Pryor, M. R. (2005a). The Personal Living Space Cue Inventory: An analysis and evaluation. *Environment and Behavior, 37,* 683–705.

Gosling, S. D., Craik, K. H., Martin, N. R., & Pryor, M. R. (2005b). Material attributes of personal living spaces. *Home Cultures, 2,* 51–88.

Gosling, S. D., Ko, S. J., Mannarelli, T., & Morris, M. E. (2002). A room with a cue: Judgments of personality based on offices and bedrooms. *Journal of Personality and Social Psychology, 82,* 379–398.

Gosling, S. D., Vazire, S., Srivastava, S., & John, O. P. (2004). Should we trust Web-based studies? A comparative analysis of six preconceptions about Internet questionnaires. *American Psychologist, 59,* 93–104.

Grubb, E., & Hupp, G. (1968). Perception of self, generalized stereotypes and brand selection. *Journal of Marketing Research, 5,* 58–63.

Hansen, W. B., & Altman, I. (1976). Decorating personal places: A descriptive analysis. *Environment and Behavior, 8,* 491–504.

Hirsh, J., & Dolderman, D. (2007). Personality predictors of consumerism and environmentalism: A preliminary study. *Personality and Individual Differences, 43,* 1583–1593.

Holleran, S. E., & Mehl, M. R. (2010). *The accuracy of personality judgments at zero-acquaintance: A meta-analysis of studies using realistic everyday environments.* Manuscript submitted for publication.

Horton, R. (1979). Some relationships between personality and consumer decision making. *Journal of Marketing Research, 16,* 233–246.

John, O. P., Naumann, L. P., & Soto, C. J. (2008). Paradigm shift to the integrative big-five trait taxonomy: History, measurement, and conceptual issues. In O. P. John, R. W. Robins, & L. A. Pervin (Eds.), *Handbook of personality: Theory and research* (pp. 114–158). New York: Guilford Press.

Jokela, M. (2009). Personality predicts migration within and between U.S. States. *Journal of Research in Personality, 43,* 79–83.

Jones, R. M., Taylor, D. E., Dick A. J., Singh, A., & Cook, J. L. (2007). Bedroom design and decoration: Gender difference in preference and activity. *Adolescence, 42,* 539–553.

Jung, T., Youn, H., & McClung, S. (2007). Motivations and self-presentation strategies on Korean-based "Cyworld" weblog format personal homepages. *Cyber Psychology and Behavior, 10,* 24–31.

Jussim, L., Cain, T. R., Crawford, J. T., Harber, K., & Cohen, F. (in press). The unbearable accuracy of stereotypes. In T. Nelson (Ed.), *Handbook of prejudice, stereotyping and discrimination.* Hillsdale, NJ: Lawrence Erlbaum Associates.

Kamptner, N. L. (1991). Personal possessions and their meanings: A life-span perspective. *Journal of Social Behavior and Personality, 6,* 209–228.

Kasmar, J. V. (1970). The development of a useable lexicon of environmental descriptors. *Environment and Behavior, 2,* 153–169.

Kramer, N. C., & Winter, S. (2008). Impression management 2.0: The relationship of self-esteem, extraversion, self-efficacy, and self-presentation within social networking sites. *Journal of Media Psychology, 20,* 106–116.

Laumann, E. O., & House, J. (1970). Living room styles and social attributes: The patterning of material artifacts in a modern urban community. *Sociology and Social Research, 54,* 321–342.

Marcus, B., Machilek, F., & Schütz, A. (2006). Personality in cyberspace: Personal web sites as media for personality expressions and impressions. *Journal of Personality and Social Psychology, 90*, 1014–1031.

Maxwell, L. E., & Chmielewski, E. J. (2007). Environmental personalization and elementary school children's self-esteem. *Journal of Environmental Psychology, 28*, 143–153.

McElroy, J. C., Morrow, P. C., & Ackerman, R. J. (1983). Personality and interior office design: Exploring the accuracy of visitor attributions. *Journal of Applied Psychology, 68*, 541–544.

Mehl, M. R., & Pennebaker, J. W. (2003). The sounds of social life: A psychometric analysis of students' daily social environments and natural conversations. *Journal of Personality and Social Psychology, 84*, 857–870.

Mittal, B. (2006). I, me, and mine: How products become consumers' extended selves. *Journal of Consumer Behavior, 5*, 550–562.

Miwa, Y., & Hanyu, K. (2006). The effects of interior design on communication and impressions of a counselor in a counseling room. *Environment and Behavior, 38*, 484–4502.

Naumann, L. P., Vazire, S., Rentfrow, P. J., & Gosling, S. D. (2009). Personality judgments based on physical appearance. *Personality and Social Psychology Bulletin, 35*, 1661–1671.

Orr, E. S., Sisic, M., Ross, C., Simmering, M. G., Arseneault, J. M., & Orr, R. R. (2009). The influence of shyness on the use of Facebook in an undergraduate sample. *Cyber Psychology and Behavior, 12*, 337–340.

Pennebaker, J. W., Mehl, M. R., & Niederhoffer, K. G. (2003). Psychological aspects of natural language use: Our words, our selves. *Annual Review of Psychology, 54*, 547–577.

Prentice, D. A. (1987). Psychological correspondence of possessions, attitudes, and values. *Journal of Personality and Social Psychology, 53*, 993–1003.

Rentfrow, P. J., & Gosling, S. D. (2003). The do re mi's of everyday life: The structure and personality correlates of music preferences. *Journal of Personality and Social Psychology, 84*, 1236–1256.

Rentfrow, P. J., Goldberg, L. R., & Zilca, R. (in press). Listening, watching, and reading: The structure and correlates of entertainment preferences. *Journal of Personality.*

Rentfrow, P. J., Gosling, S. D., & Potter, J. (2008). The geography of personality: A theory of emergence, persistence, and exploration of regional variation in basic traits. *Perspectives in Psychological Science, 3*, 339–369.

Rheingold, H. L., & Cook, K. V. (1975). The content of boys' and girls' rooms as an index of parents' behaviors. *Child Development, 46*, 459–463.

Richins, M. L. (1994). Special possessions and the expression of material values. *The Journal of Consumer Research, 21*, 522–533.

Ross, C., Orr, E. S., Sisic, M., Arsenault, J. M., Simmering, M. G., & Orr, R. R. (2009). Personality and motivation associated with Facebook use. *Computers in Human Behavior, 25*, 578–586.

Sechrest, L. & Olson, A. K., (1971). Graffiti in four types of institutions of higher education. *Journal of Sex Research, 7*, 62–71.

Sloan Devlin, A. (2008). Judging a book by its cover: Medical building facades and judgment of care. *Environment and Behavior, 40*, 307–329.

Swann, W. B., Jr., & Bosson, J. (2008). Identity negotiation: A theory of self and social interaction. In O. John, R. Robins, & L. Pervin (Eds.), *Handbook of personality psychology: Theory and research* (pp. 448–471). New York: Guilford Press.

Tucker, W. T., & Painter, J. J. (1961). Personality and product use. *Journal of Applied Psychology, 45*, 325–329.

Vazire, S., & Gosling, S. D. (2004). e-Perceptions: Personality based on personal websites. *Journal of Personality and Social Psychology, 87*, 123–134.

Vazire, S., Naumann, L., Rentfrow, P., & Gosling, S. (2008). Portrait of a narcissist: Manifestations of narcissism in physical appearance. *Journal of Research in Personality, 42*, 1439–1447.

Vinsel, A., Brown, B. B., Altman, I., & Foss, C. (1980). Privacy regulation, territorial displays and effectiveness of individual functioning. *Journal of Personality and Social Psychology, 39*, 1104–1115.

Webb, E. J., Campbell, D. T., Schwartz, R. D., & Sechrest, L. (1966). *Unobtrusive measures: Nonreactive research in the social sciences.* Chicago: Rand-McNally.

Webb, E. J., Campbell, D. T., Schwartz, R. D., & Sechrest, L. (2000). *Unobtrusive measures: Revised edition.* Thousand Oaks, CA: Sage.

Webb, E. J., Campbell, D. T., Schwartz, R. D., Sechrest, L., & Below Grove, J. (1981). *Unobtrusive measures: Nonreactive research in the social sciences.* Chicago: Rand-McNally.

Wells, M. M. (2000). Office clutter or meaningful personal displays: The role of office personalization in employee and organizational well-being. *Journal of Environmental Psychology, 20*, 239–255.

Wells, M. M., & Thelen, L. (2002). What does your workspace say about you? The influence of personality, status, and workspace on personalization. *Environment and Behavior, 34*, 300–321.

Wells, M. M., Thelen, L., & Ruark, J. (2007). Workspace personalization and organizational culture: Does your workspace reflect you or your company? *Environmental and Behavior, 39*, 616–634.

Westfall, R. (1962). Psychological factors in predicting product choice. *The Journal of Marketing, 26*, 34–40.

Worthing, P. M., Venkatesam, M., & Smith, S. (1973). Personality and product use revisited: An exploration with the personality research form. *Journal of Applied Psychology, 57*, 179–183.

Yarkoni, T. (2010). The abbreviation of personality, or how to measure 200 personality scales with 200 items. *Journal of Research in Personality, 44*, 180–198.

Yarkoni, T. (in press). Personality in 100,000 words: A large-scale analysis of personality and word use among bloggers. *Journal of Research in Personality.* York: Psychological Corp, 1957.

# Index

Page numbers referring to figures are in italics; those referring to tables are in bold.

---

*The Wiley-Blackwell Handbook of Individual Differences*, First Edition.
Edited by Tomas Chamorro-Premuzic, Sophie von Stumm, and Adrian Furnham.
© 2011 Blackwell Publishing Ltd. Published 2011 by Blackwell Publishing Ltd.